Diaries

1939–1972

Dear Judy,

Frances Partridge attains
70 years in this diary and
remains as interested in and
curious about people as ever.

She reminds me of you!

With love and admiration,

Sara x x x

March 2009

Frances Partridge was born in Bedford Square in 1900. Family friends included Henry James, Conan Doyle and various members of the Strachey family. She has translated many books and with her husband Ralph edited the *Greville Memoirs*.

'Mrs Partridge is the last survivor of the inner-core of the Bloomsbury group. Her diaries would be riveting reading even if the story of her personal life had not been so absorbing and dramatic, and even if she were not the gifted writer that she is. A fine translator, a great diarist, a prolific reviewer, who is a national treasure; and to her friends an affectionate companion and great conversationalist – the best company there is.'

Paul Levy, The Times

By the same author

A Pacifist's War
Everything to Lose
Hanging On
Other People
Good Company
Life Regained

Memories
Julia
Friends in Focus

Greville Memoirs
(edited with Ralph Partridge)

Diaries

1939–1972

Frances Partridge

Edited by Rebecca Wilson

PHOENIX
PRESS

5 UPPER SAINT MARTIN'S LANE
LONDON
WC2H 9EA

A PHOENIX PRESS PAPERBACK

First published by
Weidenfeld & Nicolson in 2000

This paperback edition published in 2001
by Phoenix Press,
a division of The Orion Publishing Group Ltd,
Orion House, 5 Upper St Martin's Lane,
London WC2H 9EA

A CIP catalogue record for this book
is available from the British Library.

Typeset by Selwood Systems, Midsomer Norton

Printed and bound in Great Britain by
Clays Ltd, St Ives plc

ISBN 1 84212 062 X

Contents

Dramatis Personae

Brenan, Gerald
Writer and hispanologist. He had been one of Ralph's greatest friends ever since they were together in the First War, despite rows caused by his making love to Ralph's first wife Dora Carrington and to disagreements over the Second War. He was married to Gamel Woolsey, American poetess, and had one daughter. After Gamel's death he lived in Alhaurin el Grande in Spain with Lynda Price.

Campbell, Robin and Susan
Cyril Connolly had introduced us to Robin in 1948, when he was living near us at Stokke with his second wife, Mary (now DUNN). He had lost a leg and won a DSO in the war. After his divorce from Mary he married Susan Benson, writer of cookery and garden books, and himself joined the Arts Council. Robin and Susan had two sons, William and Arthur.

Carrington, Noel and Catharine
Dora Carrington's youngest brother and his wife (née Alexander). Ralph had been at Oxford with Noel, who became a publisher and designer, and died in 1989. They were country neighbours in reach of Ham Spray. Of their three children we saw most of Joanna.

Cecil, Lord David
and his family. We had known David's wife Rachel, daughter of our old friends Desmond and Molly MacCarthy, since she was a schoolgirl, and travelled with her before and after her marriage. Their children were Jonathan (actor), Hugh and Laura. The whole family were very kind to me after Ralph's death and I often stayed with them.

Cochemé, Joan
Painter, especially of children's portraits, and a faithful friend for many years. She hastened to be with me when Burgo died. Her husband was Jacques Cochemé, biologist, native of Mauritius.

Dunn, Lady Mary
Our warm friendship began in 1948 when she was living (and actively farming the land) at Stokke with her second husband Robin Campbell. After their divorce she made an unhappy match with Charlie McCabe, columnist of a San Franciscan newspaper. The situation was complicated by the fact that her first husband, Sir Philip Dunn ('the Tycoon') lived not far away in Wiltshire. Philip and Mary had

two daughters, Serena and Nell, friends and contemporaries of Burgo's. They eventually remarried.

Garnett, David
and family. Only son of Edward and Constance Garnett, the eminent translator from Russian, David was generally known as 'Bunny'. He married my sister Ray in 1921, the year that I was taken on as assistant in his bookshop, Birrell and Garnett. He was thus my boss, brother-in-law, and a great friend for life. When his first book *Lady into Fox*, won the Hawthornden Prize he left the shop to write over twenty more. Ray died of cancer in 1940, and in 1942 Bunny married Angelica, daughter of Duncan Grant and Vanessa Bell. He had two sons by Ray (Richard and William) and four daughters by Angelica; Burgo married the second, Henrietta, in 1962; the others were Amaryllis, and the twins – Fanny and Nerissa.

Gathorne-Hardy, Jonathan (Jonny) and Sabrina
The popular nephew of Lady Anne Hill and Eddie Gathorne-Hardy was married to Sabrina Tennant, daughter of Virginia, Marchioness of Bath, and David Tennant, creator of the Gargoyle Club.

Goodman, Celia
One of the well-known Paget twins, who used as girls to make glamorous appearances at concerts and Glyndebourne. Her sister Mamaine married Arthur Koestler and died at only thirty-seven. Celia's husband was Arthur Goodman, who had spent a gruelling time in a Japanese prison in the war. They had two young children.

Gowing, Lawrence
Painter of the Euston Road Group, had married in 1952 my 'best friend' Julia Strachey. She was eighteen years his senior, a gifted but very unproductive writer, an original, eccentric and at times difficult character.

Henderson, Sir Nicholas (Nicko) and Lady (Mary)
Ralph and I had been friends of Nicko's parents, and he had come to swim in our pool as a boy. After he married Mary they came often to Ham Spray. He joined the Foreign Service when he was refused by the RAF on medical grounds. They had one daugher, Alexandra.

Hill, Heywood and Lady Anne (née Gathorne-Hardy)
Our friendship began in about 1938, when they were both working in the famous bookship in Curzon Street created by Heywood, and which still bears his name. When Heywood joined the army in the war, Anne kept the shop going with the help of Nancy Mitford. In the early Sixties the Hills were living in Richmond with their two grown-up daughters, Harriet and Lucy. Anne had four brothers, of whom the second, Eddie, had long been a friend of ours and a visitor to Ham Spray.

Jebb, Julian
Grandson of Hilaire Belloc, to whose small house in Sussex he sometimes invited his friends. Always interested in opera, theatre and cinema, in 1963 he was a

journalist heading towards television. An excellent mimic and raconteur, and an affectionate friend.

Kee, Robert
Oxford friend of Nicko Henderson, who brought him to Ham Spray soon after his release from prison camp in Germany, where he spent three years after being shot down while a bomber pilot in the RAF. He very quickly became one of our greatest friends, and before long married another – Janetta. They both figure prominently in my earlier diaries, but the marriage became stormy, and by 1963 they had parted and Robert was married to Cynthia Judah. He had one daughter, Georgie, by Janetta, and a son and daughter, Alexander and Sarah, by Cynthia. He is a writer of novels and history – in particular of Irish history – and has also appeared in many television programmes.

Knollys, Eardley
One of the three original owners of Long Crichel House, he was still living there in the Sixties, but had just decided to give up working for the National Trust in favour of his new love – painting.

McCabe, Lady Mary, *see* Dunn, Lady Mary

Mortimer, Raymond
Writer on art and literature, at one time literary editor of the *New Statesman*, then for many years top book reviewer on the *Sunday Times*. Our neighbour when Ralph and I lived in Bloomsbury, he became a close friend of us both, coming often to Ham Spray and travelling with us by car in France. He joined his three friends at Long Crichel House soon after the inauguration. Travel and reading were his greatest pleasures.

Parladé, Jaime
Eldest son of a prominent Andalusian family. Ralph and I met him in the Fifties in Marbella, where he owned an antique shop, which afterwards developed into a decorating and architectural business. He is now married to JANETTA (née Woolley), whom Ralph and I met as a very attractive girl of fourteen, in Spain at the start of the Civil War. Young enough to be our daughter, she became instead one of our closest friends, and figures prominently in all my diaries. Her marriages to Robert Kee and Derek Jackson both ended in divorce. Her three daughters were Nicolette (Nicky) Sinclair-Loutit, Georgiana (Georgie) Kee and Rose Jackson.

Penrose, Lionel and Margaret
and their extremely clever family. Lionel was an FRS and Galton Professor of Genetics; his wife Margaret had been my friend at Bedales School, Newnham College and ever since; Oliver and Roger are distinguished mathematicians; Jonathan was British Chess Champion for ten years; Shirley is a clinical geneticist. All addicted to chess and music.

Phillips, 'Magouche' (now Fielding)

American by birth, her first husband, the famous Armenian painter Arshile Gorky, gave her her unusual name. After his death she married Jack Phillips. Later she came to Europe and lived in France, Italy and London with her four daughters (Maro and Natasha Gorky, Antonia and Susannah Phillips), in all of which places she made a great many friends. I got to know her through Mary Dunn and Janetta.

Phipps, Lady (Frances)

Widow of the diplomat Sir Eric Phipps; she had been ambassadress at Berlin and Paris. She and I made friends late in our lives but had quickly become intimate, agreeing on such subjects as politics, war and peace, sharing many tastes in books, opera, and even for driving Minis. She was a talented amateur painter.

Sackville-West, Edward (Eddy)

had become fifth Baron Sackville at the age of sixty, on the death of his father in 1962. His musical talent had already appeared at Eton, and after Oxford he became a music critic, as well as novelist, biographer, and poet. One of the three original owners of Long Crichel House, he still spent half the year there even after buying Cooleville House, County Tipperary.

Shawe-Taylor, Desmond

One of the three original owners of Long Crichel House. Writer on music and other subjects, in the Sixties, he was music critic for the *Sunday Times*.

Stone, Reynolds, and his family

We first met them as country neighbours during the war, and acquaintance became friendship later when they lived at their romantic rectory at Litton Cheney, Dorset. Reynolds was a brilliant engraver on wood and stone, painter of trees and designer; Janet was a professional portrait photographer. They had four children: Edward, Humphrey, Phillida and Emma.

Strachey, Isobel

First wife of John (Lytton's nephew who had intervened in the Bussy inheritance), but long since divorced. Her only child Charlotte had been a great friend of Burgo's since childhood and was married to Peter Jenkins. Isobel had published several novels and stories and was a dearly loved crony of mine.

Strachey, James and Alix (née Sargant Florence)

James was Lytton's youngest brother. Both were practising psychoanalysts of long standing and James had translated the entire works of Freud in twenty-three volumes, indexed by me. Ralph and I felt towards them as though they were blood relations.

Strachey, Julia

was the elder daughter of Lytton's brother Oliver, was my best friend from child-hood, and remained so until her death in 1979. She was married first to Stephen Tomlin ('Tommy') and then to Lawrence Gowing.

Tennant, Georgia

Daughter of David Tennant, creator of the Gargoyle Club, and Virginia, Marchioness of Bath. I first met her staying with Janetta in Alpbach, Austria, in the summer of 1961, and took a great fancy to her, which built up into a firm friendship.

West, Kitty

The painter Katharine Church. She had married Anthony West, son of Rebecca West and H. G. Wells, who had left her and made a life in America. She lived in a charming little Dorset cottage to which she had added a big studio, and had also opened a gallery and craft shop in Blandford.

Houses

Crichel
(as Long Crichel House, near Wimborne, Dorset, is affectionately known to its intimates). At the end of the Second War three bachelor friends decided to look for a country house where they could gather for weekends and holidays, and invite their friends to stay. There were two music critics, Edward (Eddy) Sackville-West and Desmond Shawe-Taylor, and Eardley Knollys, representative of the National Trust and later painter. They soon found what they wanted – a charming Georgian stone house, formerly a rectory, with three good-sized living-rooms and a plentiful number of bedrooms. Great thought and care were given to the decorations and furnishings; the garden had a well-kept croquet lawn, several statues, and a terrace sheltered from the wind by glass sides and with a floor decorated by the owners with their initials in mosaic. Two sets of what were then called 'radiograms' of the highest quality, quantities of books, a series of resident staff and one or two dogs completed a ménage where conversation, music and croquet thrived. A few years later Raymond joined the original three as a resident 'Crichel boy'. In 1949 Ralph and I spent the first of many greatly enjoyed visits there.

Hilton Hall
near Huntingdon, was acquired by my sister Ray from a legacy and is still inhabited by her elder son Richard and his wife Jane. She and Bunny fell in love with it from a photograph in a newspaper. It is indeed a very beautiful, stately but not large, Queen Anne house, and until Richard's day had been very little modernized. It still has panelled walls, flagged stone floors and a fine staircase of dark carved wood; in the sixties it was one of the coldest houses I ever slept in. All Bunny's children, by Ray and Angelica, were brought up there and loved it dearly.

Stokke
near Great Bedwyn, Wiltshire. Robin and Mary Campbell were living in this rambling, Virginia-creeper covered house when we first got to know them, along with Mary's daughters by her first marriage and Robin's two sons by his. Mary was farming the surrounding land. The large garden was somewhat unkempt, except for Robin's rockery. Indoors the atmosphere was lively and semi-bohemian: youthful feet might be heard echoing along the upstairs passages in a game of cocky-olly, while downstairs in the long L-shaped living-room their elders sat round the big stove talking and laughing with visiting writers and painters or an occasional philosopher or millionaire.

Illustrations

Burgo and Frances Partridge
Clive Bell
Helen Anrep and David ('Bunny') Garnett
Desmond and Molly MacCarthy
Saxon Sydney-Turner
Anthony and Kitty West
Frances Partridge
Richard Chopping and Sebastian Sprott
Robert Kee
Janetta
Ralph and the Hendersons
Burgo at Christ Church
Wynne and Kitty Godley
E M Forster
Desmond Shawe-Taylor and Raymond Mortimer
Ralph with the Brenans
Ralph and Frances Partridge
Alix and James Strachey
David and Rachel Cecil and family
Robert Kee
Julia Strachey
Henrietta and Sophie
Anne and Lucy Hill

Janetta in Corfu
Sophie nearly aged 7
Bunny Garnett
Dadie Rylands and Eardley Knollys

A Pacifist's War

1939–1945

Foreword

It is hardly necessary to say that the following extracts from my diary of 1940–5 were not written with any idea of publication, but as a means of relieving the various emotions aroused by the Second World War, ranging from boredom to horror, fear and disgust. Why publish them? The suggestion that I should do so has come from two directions – firstly from some who want to be reminded of it, even down to the details of our adjustment to the daily grind, secondly from others who want to know (and do not because they are too young) what living through those years was like. As will be seen, few people passed a more sheltered war than we did at Ham Spray, and this may be considered a disqualification, though we were not ostriches: we thought, felt and talked about it endlessly. And I have also been concerned to give some pictures of the life we led there, conversations, thoughts and activities, our values, and the people we saw. Any of our friends' remarks here quoted – and some may possibly find them hard to believe now – were, of course, written down at the time and I can vouch for their accuracy. I have also included various different reactions: those of a young woman whose husband was fighting at Alamein, the relations of an airman killed on his first flight, the baker, the daily help, my old mother and five-year-old son.

But perhaps my chief purpose is to testify to the pacifist beliefs I developed in my teens during the First War, and which I shared with my husband, Ralph Partridge. He is, of course, the central figure in the years covered by the diary, and for that very reason may well remain rather shadowy. We were always together, communicated all our thoughts; he was the focus of my life and I had no need to describe what he was like *to myself*. I will therefore try to fill in the outline a little.

He has, I think, been 'hard done by' in many books on Bloomsbury; the first source of his portrait was his very old friend and rival, Gerald Brenan, whose assessment (inaccurate in my view) was accepted in all innocence by Michael Holroyd in his life of Lytton Strachey, and has 'type-cast' him, as it were, in other subsequent accounts. I am anxious to remove these distortions and substitute as detached a picture as I can.

A brief summary of his record is relevant: having won a Classical scholarship to Oxford from Westminster, where he was head boy, he went up to Christ Church in 1913. Two fellow-undergraduates describe him as 'one of the best brains of his year', 'a man of wide reading who was expected to go far in law or politics', 'noticeably more intelligent, quick-witted and forceful than most of his contemporaries'. He joined up in 1914, when he was nineteen, and served all through the First War as an infantry officer with considerable distinction, gaining the Military Cross and Bar and the Croce de Guerra. By the age of twenty-three he was a Major commanding a brigade, and by the end of the war he had been twice wounded, and buried alive (narrowly escaping death); moreover he had become completely disillusioned with war itself, considered both ethically and practically, and decided that all he could usefully try to do was save the lives of as many of the men under his command as possible. In 1918 he resigned his commission and returned to Oxford, where he was academically idle (though he passed his finals with distinction), and devoted much of his time to rowing with outstanding success. His friend Noel Carrington took him over to Tidmarsh Mill House, where he fell in love with his first wife Carrington and got to know and made a lifelong friend of Lytton Strachey.

As with others of his generation, those ghastly years of trench warfare had knocked nearly all the ambition out of him. His war experiences had moved him deeply; his memory of them was extremely vivid and he often described them to me in detail. When the Second War began he knew what was at issue; what I knew was second-hand, but unforgettable.

To quote others, he was 'a good-looking man of powerful build with the brightest blue eyes I have ever seen and marvellous Rabelaisian high spirits', 'always immensely alive'. He was physically active in fields he enjoyed, such as swimming, walking and tennis; but he certainly made an impression of indolence at times – perhaps because he could happily sit reading a book the livelong day, for he was a passionate reader with a remarkable gift for remembering and synthesizing facts. And he was never bored; thinking, talking and arguing were the breath of life to him. In terms of work his achievement was not very great: after a spell at the Hogarth Press with Leonard and Virginia Woolf he trained and practised as a book-binder, helped Lytton Strachey edit the *Greville Diaries* in eight volumes (acting also as his business secretary and literary agent), spent a number of years reviewing books on history and crime for the *New Statesman*, and published a book on Broadmoor which is still in print. He died in November 1960.

To sum up his character: he was a man of deep and strong emotions; his chief relationships were life-lasting and provided an incalculable sense of support to those at the other end of them. To some he could be formidable. High-spirited and excitable, his eyes would flash and his voice rise in an argument so that the uninitiated thought him angry though he was in fact having the time of his life; laughter-loving and – producing; a great enjoyer and immense fun to be with, having a rogue-elephant streak which could be irresistibly comic. But some people undoubtedly found him aggressive and he was quite aware himself of a tendency to 'lose his wool' or 'blow up' as he described it. To his excellent brain and memory must be added realism with a strong vein of scepticism. He was a dedicated rationalist and almost shockingly truthful. His strong interest in other people was the only feminine thing about him and he was much in demand as a confidant and adviser. Many of the friends who visited us during our thirty years at Ham Spray have told me what a strong influence he had on them.

1939

During the first months of the war – the phony war as it was afterwards called –
Ham Spray House, Wiltshire, was crowded to overflowing with 'refugees' from
London, where air-raids were daily expected. These were mostly the young families
of friends. At the worst we had six children, three nannies, parents at weekends,
and two adults. When week after week passed uneventfully here in England, they
gradually took wing. By the start of 1940 our only permanent winter residents
were a friend with two children; and of course we had 'visitors' – quite a different
thing.

1940

January 1st

As midnight struck, Ralph and I went out into the garden to see if we could hear the bells from the village church. But only total silence met our ears, and 1940 crept its way in, in a dense cold mist. We gathered up the prophecies for the New Year, made that afternoon with Faith and Nicko Henderson,[1] and R. sealed them and put them away in an envelope. How wrong will they be? Then he brought us tiny glasses of neat whiskey to drink to the future.

January 3rd

Cold, cold, cold. An east wind blowing and a hard frost on top of the scattered snow. Across this bleak landscape a horse and cart trundled to and fro all the morning carting manure with a hollow rumbling sound, like a tumbril carrying bodies dead of the Plague. This perishing vision, and also the frightful accounts in the papers of arctic warfare in Finland and of the Turkish earthquake – war, cold, fire and blood – all combine to turn one in upon one's nipped and frozen self, and fasten powers of satisfaction on to small sensual things, pots of cyclamen, the shine on holly berries and cats' fur, the texture of materials. The foreground has in fact become all-important, leaving the vast grim background to fade into chaos.

Rachel and David [Cecil] arrived to spend the night with us. Unceasing talk till bed-time. David is unconscious of his body as he talks but is never still, sometimes flopping on his knees on the carpet to emphasize a point, or with his feet hopping and dancing like two live rabbits in his bedroom slippers. But no one is better company. Talk almost entirely about the war.

Tea nowadays is an extremely snug meal, with hot buttered toast and the shutters drawn, and my beautiful jardinière (which I have painted white and filled with cacti, cyclamen and hyacinths) adding to the greenhouse effect. Three huge pots of arum lilies stand in the corner on a tin tray. After tea today I set to work to wash their leaves, which looked dusty, with an old sock and water in a child's pail. I felt like a zoo keeper washing his elephant's ears. I get intense pleasure from the richness and intensity of my awareness of our circumscribed private world, contrasted with the bleakness and horror of the public one.

War rumours brought us by Paul Cross, who came to lunch: how the Germans have a new kind of bomb no bigger than an orange, which can be stowed in millions in their bombing planes. How the ARP authorities were expecting 70,000 deaths in the first raid on London, and had enough papier mâché coffins ready.

---

[1] Nicko was the son of Faith and Hubert Henderson, Warden of All Souls, Oxford.

January 7th

Mist. Cows meandering in the park like lost souls, while on the lawn a moorhen paced up and down with a donnish gait, slowly lifting its large feet and peering about. Soon after lunch (made cheerful by the remains of yesterday's rosé wine) we drove to visit Gamel and Gerald at Aldbourne. Road crowded with soldiers, lorries and guns. Aldbourne itself looked rather French. A girl pulled an unwilling-looking soldier along by the arm. Girls, girls everywhere, older women and children leaning out of windows. We hear that these troops are leaving for France tomorrow. A young worried-looking officer in high boots directed the manoeuvres of a lorry. We all went for a walk. R. and Gerald shooting ahead, the rest of us slowly climbing a grassy slope towards Upper Upham. Gamel, stooping as she walked, carried her face like the figurehead of a ship. Remarks of Gerald's to R.: 'Gamel is like an iceberg, only one sixth of her shows above water – the rest is submerged and it is best left alone.' 'The truth is, no-one in the world could put up with me but Gamel, and no-one could put up with Gamel but me.' At the moment Gamel is grieving for Llewellyn Powys, who has just died. Gerald 'can't bear Gamel's Powys mood'.

[In 1930 when Gerald Brenan invited us to meet the girl he meant to marry, we went to the encounter full of curiosity. What would she be like? The previous objects of his love had been too various, from Carrington onwards, to give us a clue. We found a young woman whose appearance was arresting; one saw at once that Gamel Woolsey had a beautiful face, though rather pale and sad, noticed next that she held herself badly and with a sort of apathy, an effect enhanced by the 'arty' clothes she was wearing – shapeless purple silk embroidered with bright coloured wools.

Gerald had been Ralph's earliest friend and always confided in him. He soon told us how he had found Gamel in Dorset, staying amongst the Powys family of writers, and actually involved in an intense but difficult love-affair with Llewellyn Powys, whose wife was her best friend. Before that she had lived in the American deep South, suffered several attacks of TB and spent her time lying on a sofa reading poetry and writing it, surrounded by the easy-going civilization of a plantation, and with devoted negro servants hurrying to pick up a dropped hand-kerchief or do her least bidding. Gerald thought an income of £350 a year was enough to marry on, and Gamel agreed, but emotion brought on a haemorrhage and she spent the first months of their joint life in a sanatorium. All in all the start of their 'marriage' (it was legitimized later) was fraught with unreality. But Gamel had plenty of character as well as a good mind with a sharp edge of irony to it; she set herself valiantly to lead the life of a poor man's wife in a small Dorset cottage.

When Gerald returned to Spain and began to achieve success as a writer Gamel blossomed as 'la Sēnora', of whom hardly more was expected than to give a symbolical stir to the marmalade oranges and snip the dead heads off flowers. She developed an individual taste in dress and was the centre of a little salon of admirers; for Gamel was a poetess, who had published one slim volume, who had an air of great distinction, and loved to talk about poetry. As well as her translation from Galdós she wrote an excellent account of the Spanish Civil War from an expatriate's point of view, *Death's Other Kingdom*.]

January 9th

To London by the early train. The Great Western Hotel embraced us, warm and womblike. Left the hairdressers in full blackout lit with minute crosses and balls of light, like a dance in May Week, festive. Avenues of huge trees appeared to loom up and sweep past – a very queer blackout illusion: they are really houses. Then there is the feeling, which one likes to exaggerate, of possible danger – a distinct sharp thrill. I thought, 'Supposing there was a sudden crash and I was smashed-up and dead, how foolish to have spent the last hour of my life having my hair washed and curled.' R. and I had a night out, dancing at the London Casino and watching performances by naked girls who stood about in senseless attitudes but were often young and lovely. Human dramas were evolving around us, among officers on leave with their wives or tarts, débutantes and relentless bony youths.

January 12th

These nights we sleep the sleep of the dead – as if we never wanted to wake up again. Perhaps we don't. Facing the bitter cold last thing at night and first thing in the morning is an ordeal.

R. and I took Burgo for a walk to see the threshing-machine at work on the Inkpen road. It was a very vigorous scene – an academy picture of Energy. Some whacking great cart-horses stood rocking their carts to and fro, dead rats lay about, and all the time the machine was forcing its thick snake of straw relentlessly along; it was like a section of a vast and constipated digestive tract, and the brilliant air was full of whirling chaff. Burgo would have liked to stay for ever, but the freezing cold soon sent us home.

Michael MacCarthy turned up at tea-time with a chicken house. The chickens are coming next week, another step towards making ourselves self-supporting.

January 13th

Skated with Gamel, Kitty West and Noel and Catharine [Carrington] on the pond in the park, to a gramophone playing Viennese waltzes. On we went till the sun disappeared in a pink haze behind the Downs, and a crescent moon rose high above the black trees of the Russian Wood. Gamel crouched by the pondside in shawls and rugs, looking like an Irish samphire-gatherer. She seemed in very low spirits. I told her about Ray[1] but there was no intimacy. The waves between us broke on our separate coasts.

January 18th

Michael MacCarthy came to lunch, bringing us our twelve Rhode Island Red hens. We are rather excited about our new protégés.

In writing a diary all the more important things get left out. Only the decorations get mentioned and the shape of the building is taken for granted. Far the greatest pleasure I have almost every day of my life is simply being with R., or, when I'm not with him, from remembering everything to tell him afterwards. In some ways the outer bleakness created by the war has intensified this very great happiness.

---

[1] My sister, very ill with cancer. Married to Bunny Garnett.

January 21st

A conversation about logic in music. Music, R. said, was a cure for anxiety, because by its formal qualities it solved the problems it set itself, and this symbolized the solution of one's worries reassuringly. I find this logical component of music (propositions, and statements depending inevitably upon them) one of the things I most value in it. I see no counterpart to the marvellous sanity of Bach or Monteverdi in modern composers.

January 28th

'Is it raining?' we asked Edie[1] this morning, when she called us. 'Why no, I don't think so, but the trees are all covered with icicles.' A sharp frost on top of the rain had encased every twig in ice as thick as a man's thumb – a fabulous sight. Each leaf and each blade of grass had its glass envelope and the plants in the rockery were solid coral. The sound of the ghostly glass trees swaying and clanking in the wind was enough to freeze the blood.

Towards evening boughs began to break from the laden trees and fall crashing to the ground. I felt I knew what it was like to be in an air-raid. Crrrash – Crrack – BUMP. And then a terrible sound like a giant's fart; and all the time the wind rose, and whirled those poor icy skeleton trees until they cracked again. It was awful to think of our poor old friends out there, the beech, the aspen, the ilex, and wonder which would be struck next. R. and I sat over the library fire, and while I tried to read he was finishing his review for the *New Statesman*. Then I got out my typewriter and typed what he had written. We were sitting thus, R. writing, I typing, at quarter to twelve when all the lights went out. We groped about in the kitchen, found some candles and took them to bed with us, where we lay for some time listening to that fearful, unceasing, shattering Crrrash, BOOMP, Crrack.

'I believe this is Hitler's secret weapon,' said R. 'If it is, I surrender at once. I can't stand it.'

January 29th

Woke at six. The crashes were still resounding, and as soon as it was light we got up and looked at the damage. A huge piece off the beech, several from the ilex, all the elms along the wall decapitated and the big oak in the field reduced to a joke. It now began to snow. No postman; no newspaper. The scene in front of the house is one of savage desolation. It has a prehistoric look; one expects to see a Megatherium cross the park. During the morning the water gave out and there was no electricity to pump more. The avenue was like a story by Hans Andersen, with the wych elms dangling long fingers covered in glassy ice, and underneath them several little gnomes dressed in black, with faces red with cold, trying to remove fallen branches. In the lane the telephone wires lay tangled and looped in hopeless confusion like wool played with by a monstrous kitten.

January 30th

The last day of this extraordinary month. Very slowly, drip by drip, the thaw began. In the afternoon R. and I with a trowel and a rake hit the branches of some of the trees and shrubs – the cherry, the magnolia – to free them from their ice.

[1] Maid.

They drew themselves up, very slowly, like people stretching themselves. As for the European War, this local war against the elements has practically put it out of everyone's head.

February 6th

Joan Cochemé to stay. I have retired to bed with 'flu. R. and Joan spent yesterday evening, so he tells me, sitting in the library, talking about the last war until far into the night, with the tears running down both their cheeks. I wish that everyone could hear R.'s vivid and detailed description of his war experiences – they are infinitely moving, and pacifism seems the only conclusion to draw from them, as he found himself.

February 10th

My first day up. When I got downstairs the sun was filling the sitting room, whose familiar colours – blue, dull purple and honey – acted as balm to my spirits. I looked at the glowing row of Spanish plates on top of the book-shelf and thought with pleasure and some pride how we had contrived to surround ourselves with a great deal of visual beauty. Clive arrived in time for lunch, staggering in with a huge bundle of washing, like a jovial Father Christmas. James [Strachey] had written to R. suggesting getting Lytton's letters typed with a view to publication. This led to a discussion, Clive throwing up his hands in horror. 'Old Bloomsbury would be dead against it, and if they were published no one would be on speaking terms with their oldest friends.'

Surely it's very odd for the Apostles of Truth to be so queasy about facing it when it concerns themselves?

February 16th

Nicholses to stay.[1] A discussion with Phyllis about martyrs. She said how important it was that there should be people prepared to suffer *anything* for their ideals. This somehow got my stuffy old rationalist goat, and I suggested that the only way to change people's opinions was by persuasion, that unless one changed their opinions one had done no good. It's possible to admire and pity a martyr while being left unconvinced of the truth of his belief. Martyrdom is in fact a form of force on the part of the martyr. All to no purpose, for the light of St Sebastian was in Phyllis's eye. The two Phils embarked on their usual argument with each other about Winning the War: Phil's best remark was: 'This is nothing but a confession of opinion wrung from an idealist who believes we are living in the Jungle.'

February 27th

To Rockbourne to spend a night with Desmond and Molly [MacCarthy]. Desmond came in from having his portrait painted by Henry Lamb, who he said had made him look 'a sly old Yid'. He was dressed, like all Henry's sitters, in a great many waistcoats, one red. He said: 'I must tell you I had a message from ON HIGH the other day. It said "Armistice Day will be on August 16th."' Later he spoke about some 'very fine hogs' there were in the neighbourhood; he took us to see them and although actually sows, they were of enormous size and rootling about in the

---

[1] Phil (Foreign Office), Phyllis and their three children.

richest mud. Desmond delighted in scratching their backs with his walking-stick, making them squawk and grunt. Molly stood aloof, saying she didn't like pigs, she couldn't see any point in them whatever. At dinner she suddenly dropped a bottle of claret on the floor with a bang; it fell over but didn't break. It is, I suppose, the sort of thing that happens daily and Desmond didn't turn a hair. Afterwards, Desmond and Molly sat one on each side of the fire and Desmond read aloud to us while Molly lay back and snored gently. Then she woke up and read us Joad's views on picnic food (which had somehow fascinated and repelled her) with great expression and explosions of laughter. Conversations with these two masters of the art charmed us until bedtime. Stories of Desmond's: 'I was sitting with Logan [Pearsall-Smith] in the garden, in front of a stone path with a bust at the end of it. I said, "Logan, what would you feel if that bust came hoppity hop along the path towards you?" "Disgust."' And 'Once when Molly and I were walking back from Ampthill in the dark, I suddenly said: "Molly, are you sure it's *me*, Desmond, you're walking with and not a spirit from another world?" and Molly *screamed* and *boxed* my ears.'

[Everyone found Desmond MacCarthy irresistible. Even the sharp pen of Virginia Woolf described him as 'my dear old friend Desmond', 'tender and vague', 'sympathetic, humorous, reminiscent and perhaps melancholy in a happy sort of way.' I believe this irresistibility depended less on his Irish charm and wit (great as these were) or his social gifts, than on his extraordinary power of sympathetic understanding. To understand other people one must want to know about them, and Desmond's curiosity and interest were boundless. In many ways a lazy man, certainly one who could never answer letters or despatch his reviews until the very last moment (and to whom posting a parcel would I'm sure have been impossible), where there was a friend in sore grief or a young person in need of a hoist on the literary ladder, he would put himself out to help them with the utmost sensitivity and imagination. At one time he even gave a job in his house to a burglar. I do not know if the plan worked out well.

I called his wit 'Irish', and so it seemed although he was one quarter French and one German. It was not of the lightning-flash sort, however, but expressed itself largely in anecdotes told in a way entirely his own, or in sudden swoops from the particular to the general – such as 'Oh YES, two wrongs DO make a right'.

From photographs of Desmond as a young man it would appear that it was his interested, quizzical, responsive expression that charmed, rather than his good looks. When I first got to know him he was middle-aged, squarely built, with few but telling gestures, careless of his appearance and dress. (Lytton Strachey unkindly described him as looking like a seedy actor.) Could he perhaps have made a distinguished career on the stage? He has many of the necessary gifts – and here there comes to my mind the way he once made us laugh by the rolling sonority with which he read aloud what he described as 'the *snobbish* chapter in the Bible' – the passage about the Dukes in Chapter 36 of Genesis. He enjoyed many things beside conversation – games and swimming for instance – and his great appreciation of the comic, whether in situations or other people's remarks, emerged in chortles of laughter that still had a boyish ring when he was comparatively old. Yet the vein of melancholy noticed by Virginia was certainly there, and I feel sure it came from the realization that many of his early literary projects would never materialize, while at the same time he underestimated the value and influence of his outstanding contribution as a critic. And he never, I think, found it easy to deal with the material world. His wife Molly described how some small ailment or frustration would throw him quite off course. 'Then he flings up his arms and gives up *every*thing, groaning aloud "This life is so *terrible!*" '

Desmond appreciated receiving a knighthood. 'One doesn't enjoy being honoured unless one knows it has also given pleasure to one's friends,' he wrote in answer to our letter of congratulation; but he went on more characteristically: 'I am asthmatical – and my goodness old and dry in heart. I can tell you this; it is not easy or pleasant modulating into old age. And that reminds me of Burgo. Lay your hand on his head and give him my blessing. He has a nice long run in front of him.'

At first sight Molly MacCarthy might strike the unknowing as a conventional and possibly slightly irritable member of the 'Upper Middle Classes', and how very wrong they would be! Fairly generously built, she dressed unnoticeably in good safe suits rather long in the skirt, and shoes with low heels and long pointed toes. Her straight grey fringe came just over her eyebrows and her dark eyes were small and bright. But the first conversation revealed at once that here was an original personality and a fantastic, witty mind.

Her deafness was a dreadful affliction for her and an obstacle to her friends. She tried every device to surmount it, including a box needing batteries that were always running out and a pair of small tortoiseshell horns which gave her a comic appearance that she was the first to appreciate. She spoke in the soft voice of the deaf, but in quick little runs of words, with frequent emphases, spontaneous and unexpected. She was a natural comedian, mimic and raconteuse, and whenever she came to Ham Spray, or we went with her (as we sometimes did) on some outing such as a day on Brighton pier, there was always boundless *fun*. Molly was indeed the arch-priestess of fun; she used to invent it out of other people's remarks and it made the tears run down her cheeks. At Bloomsbury parties she would sometimes perform a turn. Once, for instance, she dressed up as a dwarf fortune-teller, and read the hands of fellow-guests disconcertingly, but acting so well that not a single one recognized her.

Social life was much curtailed for her through deafness and she kept away from the smart dinner-parties at which Desmond was a particular star. To use a favourite word of hers she could be 'censorious', but in the company of old friends she was happy, and warmth itself. Both Ralph and I loved her dearly and I think she was fond of us. She invented a 'little language' full of family phrases which figured often in her brilliant letters, written at speed and with many deep underlinings. They were a joy to get, and bring her to life again unfailingly.]

February 28th

Our morning at Rockbourne flew by in talk. If conversation were always so absorbing and effortless one would never want to do anything else.

Lunched with Pansy and her children – a thin, serene Madonna with her little boy Valentine in her arms. He has a wonderful head with a great forehead and speculative blue eyes. The Lambs' life is uncorrupted by respectability, which I find sympathetic. There were holes in the sofa cover, and books and mess everywhere.

[Some while before I first met Henry Lamb, Ralph had described him to me as the painter who had fallen in love with the beautiful Euphemia Grey, married her and carried her off to join Augustus John's circle in France, where he had later become the lover of Dorelia. His famous painting of Lytton was not greatly approved by Carrington, though she was charmed and attracted by the artist himself; Ralph was inclined to feel that Lytton had been 'made a fool of' by Henry, not just by subjugation to his charms but because the result was his adoption of the bohemian disguise of large black hat, gold earrings et cetera, which was quite foreign to his character. For Ralph, Lytton's great qualities were his intelligence, integrity, affection and wit, but like many Stracheys he had a strong romantic streak and it was to this that Henry appealed. He was exclusively heterosexual.

I first met Henry when he and Dorelia spent a night at Ham Spray in 1925, an occasion referred to by Carrington in a letter: 'He has a most unhappy face but is amusing and charming. Of course he couldn't resist making up to F[rances] M[arshall] a little. She couldn't see a trace of his former dazzling beauty, she confessed afterwards.' Maybe not beauty but attraction yes; he was then forty, slightly built, his sensitivity and habitual tension emphasized by the penetrating gaze of his very pale blue eyes, and with a firm rather too thin mouth that suggested latent cruelty. I got to know him during the following years, and understood why Lytton had called him 'the most delightful companion in the world', though not why he had added, 'and the most unpleasant'. He talked with a quiet intensity as if his life depended on expressing exactly what he wanted to say – and it was generally original and very well worth listening to. I have never met a portrait painter who became so deeply obsessed by the characters of his sitters.

He married Lady Pansy Pakenham in 1928, and they had three children.]

March 2nd

Raymond for a few days and much talk – war, books, people. We drove to a local tea-party reminiscent of the last war. There were two subalterns, one shy, one talkative, a golfing lady, a learned elderly gent, dogs, excellent cakes and innocent jokes. 'Do you read the *Bystander* much?' one subaltern asked Raymond, who said he had 'had a job not to giggle'.

['Can you remember your first meeting with So-and-so?' one is sometimes asked. Yes, for once I can. It was as early as 1924 that Raymond Mortimer and I were both invited to stay the weekend at the Mill House, Tidmarsh, with Lytton, Carrington and Ralph. Our nervousness of a new and strange experience and an alarming host brought us together, and I was grateful to Raymond for taking me off for a walk beside the river, to comment at our ease on the world we found ourselves in. Many years later I remembered this occasion, when he expressed his intolerance of shyness, was even inclined to deny that such a state existed: those who claimed to suffer from it, he said, were merely self-absorbed and shockingly uninterested in others. Certainly the young Raymond of the Twenties (or ever since for that matter) could not have been so described. Lively, quick-witted, interested in every subject, amusing, affectionate and companionable, he became a cherished friend, someone with whom Ralph and I took several happy holidays motoring through France, who visited us often at Ham Spray, and with whom we felt perfectly at ease and able to voice those differences in our views which may have become a little more marked as we grew older. Of course we held others that united us – we

were all three Hedonists, we adored travel, were roughly Liberal in outlook, nour-
ished curiosity and were passionate readers, though Raymond was the most dedicated. (If he ran out of books on a journey he would look round with an expression
of anxious hunger impossible to ignore.) Where we differed was in our attitudes
to War and Wealth. We were pacifists, he was not. We had something of an allergy
to the rich and privileged; Raymond once told us that he found wealth and what
it bought sexually attractive. He had a much higher standard of comfort than we
did, and sometimes lectured us about the lack of ashtrays or the wrong placing of
shaving-mirrors and reading-lights at Ham Spray, yet in the pursuit of some
thrilling and exotic 'sight' he would put up with real discomfort – he had been
known to sleep on bare boards. I cannot forgive Evelyn Waugh for his stupidity in
describing him as a 'wild beast'.

Raymond was not good-looking, but he made up for that by the brightness of
his eyes, his animated expression, and his readiness to smile and laugh. His thick
hair never fell out but turned into handsome grey sculptured curls; his figure was
lithe, he loved clothes and his ties were justly famous. He had many pleasures –
looking at pictures, games like croquet, activities like skating. He claimed to be
unable to sing *God Save the King*, but enjoyed listening to music in moderation
particularly if it was French. Long, shuttlecock conversations about such subjects
as aesthetics, prehistory or psychoanalysis could be enthralling with Raymond. I
think it saddened him to be in disagreement with the young, yet he found it hard
to adapt to new tastes and ways and he was not displeased to hear that his juniors
thought him alarming, nor did he put people at their ease, angelically kind as he
was at heart. I have heard him say that he would have liked to have had a child,
and I can see him as a loving father, but woe betide the child if it didn't turn out
'bookish' (a favourite word of his) and pass its examinations.]

March 10th

The Wests to lunch. Anthony discussed his military service. He finds that CO's
aren't allowed on minesweepers as they carry guns, but has more or less decided
that a minesweeper shall be his fate none the less, and reached calm with the
decision.

While Burgo and I were planting some primroses we had dug up from the woods,
Edie appeared looking surprised and said, 'There's a corporal to see you.' In the
darkness of the hall I saw some big tin-hatted shapes entering the front door. It
could only mean billeting I thought. But one stepped into the light, and it was
Justin Vulliamy and a friend, who had motor-biked from Newbury. Burgo couldn't
understand that they were going to have tea with us. When I said they hadn't
always been soldiers, but friends of ours, he said, 'Are they really *men?*'

March 18th

At Rockbourne, talking to Rachel and David till past twelve. Only last thing did
we talk of the war. Ralph, Rachel and David all in cheerful, hopeful vein; I had to
testify to my gloom. For about the war I am utterly gloomy and hopeless. It amazes
me to hear people talking of reconstruction, Federal union, reforms, as if we were
now at this moment working for them, instead of being engaged in nothing but
disintegration and destruction. If any reconstruction is to come it can only be in
peacetime, and now that we are at war we are much farther from it than we were

last summer. I think I must have wanted to make the others share my depression. David was cheerfully bellicose.

March 19th

We talked of the varying intensities at which people required to live. I said, thinking it was axiomatic, that my great – almost my only – object in life was to be as intensely conscious as possible. To my surprise neither Ralph nor David agreed in the least. What I most dread is that life should slip by unnoticed, like a scene half glimpsed from a railway-carriage window. What I want most is to be always reacting to something in my surroundings, whether a complex of visual sensations, a physical activity like skating or making love, or a concentrated process of thought; but nothing must be passively accepted, everything modified by passing it through my consciousness as a worm does earth. Here too comes in my theory that pleasure can be extracted from experiences which are in themselves neutral or actually unpleasant, with the help of drama and curiosity, and by drama I mean the aesthetic aspect of the shape of events. The exceptions are physical pain and anxiety, the two most stultifying states; I can't hold intensity of experience to be desirable in them.

March 25th

R. and I were in the bathroom when we got a message that Mr Garnett was on the telephone. R. went along to answer it, and it was to say that Ray died last night. R. said, 'I'm afraid I sounded too brisk.' F.: 'What did you say?' R.: 'I said, "That's a very good thing."' F.: 'And then what?' R.: 'Then Bunny said goodbye. He sounded in a terrible state.' I could think of nothing but poor Bunny, faced with the horrible strangeness of death.

Alix [Strachey] hadn't even heard she was ill, though James had known all about it from Noel [Olivier] for two months, showing a remarkable lack of intercommunication. I had a craving to be alone and talk to R. about it, but he hung about with his hens and a bonfire and I felt hurt and abandoned. Later I relieved my feelings by telephoning Bunny and asking him here to meet Richard and William.[1]

March 29th

Bunny and both his boys are with us. Went to meet the boys' train, which was late, so I had time to watch everybody else on the platform. An officer was talking to a sergeant of about the same age, physique, intelligence and apparent value as a human being. This equality made the difference in their demeanour and movements ridiculous somehow – the drawling upper-class voice, casual gestures and slight stoop of one, and the braced attention and fixed eyes of the other. Trivial no doubt, but I have always been fascinated by the language of voice and gesture.

Richard and William arrived at last, Richard self-possessed and talkative, William sunk and hunched in tangible gloom. Bunny and the boys each seemed to be dumbly saying, 'You see we still have each other.'

Bunny and I listened to Winston's broadcast, which he liked and I hated. He said with a distorted face that we ought to broadcast to the Germans that 'we're going to bomb them to blazes'. When the boys had gone to bed, Bunny, who

[1] His sons.

looked quite exhausted, gave us a long account of Ray's death, talking till one, and leaving us flattened by the pathos.

After the Garnett family left R. and I talked it all over. I never stop thanking my stars for the way we completely understand each other's ideas, even when we don't share them.

[When I first got to know David Garnett he was a young man in his thirties – well-built, broad-shouldered, fair-haired and blue-eyed – who seemed ill-suited to the nickname 'Bunny', given him no doubt in childhood by his fond parents. I am glad also to have known that remarkable pair, Edward and Constance, even slightly. Indeed I stayed more than once with Constance in her improbable Kentish cottage, where she led a self-contained life among her pumpkins, giving little away of the brilliant intelligence that had made her one of the earliest Greek scholars at Newnham before she took to translating the Russians. I saw Edward more often, for he used to visit his son's bookshop, Birrell and Garnett, where I worked as an assistant. He was a tall stooping man with a thick crop of yellowish-grey hair crowning his ugly, amiable, pleated face. Both Bunny's parents peered through the thickest spectacles imaginable, with the questioning, but unseeing gaze of fish in an aquarium. Only when he was grown up and ambitious to become a writer, did Bunny get to know his father on equal terms, so he told me, and when he consulted him as to how to prepare for his career the answer he got was: Read, read, read.' The outstanding success of *Lady into Fox*, based on a course of Defoe, caused great jubilation in the bookshop, but quite naturally led him to leave it and devote himself to writing in the beautiful, unbelievably cold Queen Anne House, Hilton Hall, where he lived with his first wife, my sister Ray, and their two sons, and later with Angelica and their four daughters.

In the First World War Bunny and his partner in the bookshop Francis Birrell had been Conscientious Objectors, and worked either on English farms or in reconstructing French villages (as he well describes in one of his best – if least known – novels, *Plough over the Bones*). However, when the Second World War came along he accepted an invitation to work in the Air Ministry with the rank of Flight Lieutenant. There was a side of Bunny that entered enthusiastically into what he was doing, down to the details of dressing up for the part. As owner of a bookshop he for a while wore a bowler hat and carried a rolled-up umbrella. As a countryman he took an innocent delight in his bee-keeping and salmon-fishing outfits: so that it was not surprising to see him happy in his RAF uniform.

When Bunny wanted to look at someone it was characteristic of him to turn his whole head and blue gaze swiftly towards them, until his chin touched his shoulder. This and the purposeful stride with which he would cross the bookshop, take out a book and hand it over to a customer all in one movement, showed the extrovert energy and decisiveness concealed in a temperament that was superficially genial and deliberate. The tempo of his talk was thought by some of his Bloomsbury friends to be very slow and they teased him about it; but though a conversation with him might start at a leisurely pace and be interrupted by long pauses, it usually burgeoned into a lavish growth branching in unexpected directions, for he had an excellent memory for what he had read or experienced. His cornflower-blue eyes might twinkle in silence for several minutes while he hatched his next remark, but then out it came with a rush of sudden fantasy or maybe firmness.

His other activities had the same quality – his letters talked in his own voice. When he learned to fly a light aeroplane with dogged determination rather than aptitude, a visit to Ham Spray from the 'Rabbit in the Air' was a nerve-racking experience. The time to leave had come, but he seemed quite unable to get the machine to start, and paced round and round it, swinging the propeller with a deepening frown. Then a slow smile dawned – he had forgotten to turn on the petrol.

Bunny's absorption in his own affairs was sometimes amusing. When I returned from my first visit to Russia (a country I knew he loved talking about) I was longing to talk myself about peacock-blue churches with gold spires, but he didn't ask me a single question about it: instead I listened to a detailed description of his failing to catch salmon in Wales.

As a friend he was first-rate – staunch, warm and appreciative. He always gave careful and wise advice when it was sought. France was his chosen country, and he spent his last years there in a remote valley lined with box trees, near Cahors. Here he could be seen sitting out of doors under a large straw hat typing out his manuscripts, going to market with his beret pulled well over his eyes, bottling his wine. Here he entertained his family and friends with food he had lovingly cooked himself. The athletic figure of his youth retained considerable dignity even in his eighties, though his movements had become deliberate. He was still ready and eager to dive into a pool of cold water or go looking for wild orchids in the limestone hills. He was a happy, remarkably sane and lovable man.

Ray died of cancer during the Second World War. By 1950 he was married to Angelica Bell and the father of four daughters.]

April 3rd

Bunny writes that 'it was a blessed weekend for me, and how good it was for the boys to feel the world was full of friendly faces. The piano and Burgo's kite ought perhaps to be thanked personally for their existence.'

Gerald rang up to say he could not come over and see Helen [Anrep], as he and Gamel were off to Brighton. Would we apologize to her and ask her to come and visit them there? This gesture is purest Geraldine in style. The formula is that when one of your oldest friends visits your neighbourhood, although you have not seen her for a very long time, you leave for somewhere else *on the very day of her arrival*, and then beg her to follow you there.

Helen arrived this afternoon in an aura of flattery, amiability and vanity, wearing an eccentric hat with her pretty grey hair floating out in wisps from under it.

[Helen Maitland came as a girl from California to study music in Paris, where she became involved with the world of Augustus John, Henry Lamb and the eminent Russian mosaicist Boris Anrep, whom she married. In the mid-Twenties, when over forty, she left him to live as his wife with Roger Fry until he died – thus making a striking move from one aesthetic sphere to another as different from it as possible. Anrep and Fry disliked each other heartily, and the transfer of Helen caused a considerable disruption (if not as great as the Trojan War). At one time it was rumoured that Boris was threatening to tar and feather Roger – an alarming idea to his friends, since he was neither young nor strong. With Roger she led an evidently very happy, domestic life both in Bloomsbury and Suffolk – where Ralph and I often visited them. He was a kind, understanding man, less dominating than Boris; what was more, he adored Helen and credited her with great intelligence and appreciation of art and aesthetics. Some thought he over-encouraged her confidence in the latter sphere. She looked upon herself as the chief patroness of the Euston Road Group of painters, many of whom were her great friends, but I have heard her say that she insisted on respect – they were not allowed to call her 'Helen'.

Her most delightful gifts concerned the art of living – of decorating her house, throwing a shawl over an old chair, arranging flowers, creating a warm atmosphere for guests, cooking them delicious meals with what looked like the minimum of trouble. All these things she appeared to do instinctively, producing a Vuillard-like interior, richly coloured and satisfying to the eye. As a hostess she was charming and outgoing, her manner remained flirtatious and her appearance pretty till she was well on in middle life. I have said she was a flatterer, but this at least showed one of her prime motives – a desire to please. And her sympathetic nature brought her close to people – for instance Vanessa after Roger's death in 1934, and Julian Bell's in the Spanish Civil War. She had quantities of friends and confidants, among whom were Dorelia John, Gerald Brenan and Ralph.]

Shopping in Hungerford. Mr Barnard, the greengrocer, was full of what sounded like wild rumours of Hitler having annexed Denmark and being now in Copenhagen. But it was quite true. We were jerked back into the war like fish that have forgotten for a bit that they are on the end of a hook. We drove home deeply disquieted, and for the rest of the day the wireless was dominant. For the second time the war is coming nearer, looming up large and threatening. Air-raids, invasion, refugees – one's whole body reacts with a taut restlessness, as though one had a lump of lead for a stomach and sensitive wires from it reaching to toes and fingers. The strangely casual voice of the announcer told us that at this very moment large-scale naval engagements were taking place, calling up visions of wallowing ships, shattering explosions, and soldiers sinking like stones because of the heavy equipment they carried. I put on records, Monteverdi and Haydn, hoping that music would have its usual magical effect in restoring belief in the existence of logic and sanity, but tonight it seemed impossible to correlate the two disparate worlds, the musical one of reason and the mad one of events.

April 10th

R. was stirring soon after seven, and at eight he went down to listen to the news. In a naval battle off Narvik, described as 'wholly successful', we lost two destroyers and a third damaged. While these sensational events are happening all other interests are submerged in intense, painful excitement. Gaps between the news are intolerable; human feelings about drowning sailors and terrified civilians flash into my head and out again, leaving only a passionate absorption in the course of events. I can no longer relate them to my beliefs about peace and war – they are insulated. 'Good', one says, hearing of an enemy troopship sunk and thousands of men drowned in the Skagerrak. The Downs tonight looked dry and colourless, with dusty rabbit-scars on their sides. Over them a heavy cloud the colour of a battleship and a crescent moon in a peacock-blue sky. Helen Anrep and I sat by the sitting-room fire talking about the future of Europe, and her belief in progress, which I do not share.

There seem to be two possibilities: an attack on the West through Belgium or Holland, and air-raids on London. Round and round goes my head.

April 16th

English troops have landed in Norway: this news makes most people more cheerful but no less anxious, and I see that even we pacifists may soon become like the Japanese schoolboys, whose photos I shall not forget in a hurry, egging on the perpetrators of an execution with male and bellicose 'give-it-him' attitudes.

The campaign in Norway is our main interest and subject of conversation. This evening I felt, not for the first time, what vast and horrid possibilities lie in the situation. Then, with a sudden click, we return to our quiet and beautiful Ham Spray and its garden. 'I *like* my life,' R. said this evening.

April 20th

Yesterday's rain has produced miracles. I have to keep walking round the garden to see all the new arrivals – two red tulips in the rockery, and the blue anemones in the border. I feel about our garden and view as I do about the face of a crony: everything in it is familiar and charming, even the flaws in its perfection.

Gerald and Gamel came to lunch. Gerald has recovered from his trench mouth but can't get his false teeth in, and as he has exactly every other one missing he presents a peculiar machicolated appearance. About 10.30 at night, after they had gone, we went out into the sweet night air. There was a halo round the moon and a wind blowing the white flowers about in the rockery. The sky was partly covered with an eiderdown of small fleecy clouds. It was very like the sky of the first night of the war, I suddenly remembered, as I walked round the garden staring up and thinking of the contrast between the quiet eternity of the sky and the rumbustious frenzy of human existence.

April 24th

R. said at breakfast: 'I see some curious things dropping from the sky. What can they be? My God, they're wistaria buds!' He rushed out and found them being wantonly picked off and dropped on the ground by villainous sparrows who didn't even want to eat them.

Perhaps the badness of the Norwegian news was too much for us. R. was inclined to feel I was responsible for the nibbled wistaria, his lost knife, and a hen's having laid an egg in the shrubbery which couldn't be found.

I went off for a lonely walk across the plover field, due north from here. Two carthorses were harrowing the field and the plovers screamed over my head as I plodded up the long hill. I wasn't consciously thinking of the war, and only realized after some time that the plovers had been shrieking NAR-vik to my ears. Over the brow I got into that wonderfully strange region R. and I discovered last autumn, with short rabbity turf, deserted barns and groves of thorns growing in a bog. There were masses of the biggest primroses I ever saw, violets, cowslips, celandine and blackthorn. I loved being in this sweet secret place, alone except for the scurrying rabbits and the birds singing in the trees.

Here I escaped from the war for a bit, which isn't so easy while the Germans continue to advance in Norway.

A conversation about the nature of our interest in the conduct of the war. A few weeks ago we thought very little about it, now we are absorbed in the strategic drama of the Norwegian campaign, and are of course delighted when our troops do well. 'If we so much want the Allies to win, shouldn't it logically follow that we ought to help them to?' I asked. R. answered with an analogy: 'It's as if all our money had against our wills been put on a certain horse running in the Derby. We may hate horse-racing, disapprove of it even – yet we still want that horse to win. If we are to remain sane we *must* follow the news with interest, and we *must* mind what we hear.'

May 2nd

After an excess of hope yesterday, this evening's news told of our complete withdrawal from southern Norway. The announcer seemed to dislike his task and sighed deeply as he performed it. The effect on me was crushing and bewildering; I felt even physically sick. What has been painful about the Norwegian campaign has been the struggle to maintain hope, for which at last there seemed some basis. Now it's gone and here is another country to be 'mopped up' by Germany. R. commented on my pinched serious expression. Why did I take it so heavily? There followed a conversation about what subjects one could joke about. I agreed that all subjects could be joked about, but thought not all emotions about those subjects were joke-producing. For instance, jokes arising from acute anxiety over illness would be hollow and false. R. said his ideal was to die joking like Mercutio, and he had seen many people do so. I defended seriousness. This I do with head as well as heart (which is indubitably in a serious mood). What I'm suffering from is the crushing of a hope, built on stronger foundations than I knew, of the war being ended quickly through the Norwegian campaign, and the realization again of the *immense* strength of Germany. Therefore two horrid and inescapable alternatives arise in all their grimness – either a German victory or a very long bitter struggle indeed.

May 8th

Visit to London. So long since we'd been that it was quite like going abroad. Would the crossing be rough and where were our passports? Harrods' sandwich bar was full of spending, cormorant women who were avidly stuffing food into their mouths. To Raymond's flat, where we were joined by Clive and Dora Morris. 'If only there wasn't a war on,' said Clive at one moment.

'Do you still want the war to stop?' asked Raymond. 'I'm not arguing about it. I just want to know.' Clive and I both answered 'Yes'.

[In the Twenties when I was working at Birrell and Garnett's bookshop, Clive Bell was one of the first members of Old Bloomsbury to invite me out. He liked girls, and I knew that it was partly because I was one that I was asked: but he was much too sensitive to press unwanted attentions, and we quickly became very great friends, as we remained for the rest of his life.

Clive led two separate but interlinked lives. In London he owned a comfortable bachelor flat in Gordon Square, and here he liked to entertain his friends to dinner, often dressed in a suit of purple sponge-cloth with black frogs, and surrounded by well-filled bookshelves set between panels painted by Duncan Grant, with pictures by Vlaminck, Picasso and Juan Gris on the walls. He was an excellent host, who had the rare gift of preferring others to shine rather than doing so himself; yet he never seemed to conduct the conversation in an obvious way – it ranged far and wide and usually went on late over brandy and cigars. Among those I met at these dinners were Desmond MacCarthy, Roger Fry, Bertrand Russell, Vita Sackville-West, Lionel Penrose and Rebecca West. Lunch-time guests were invited to the Ivy Restaurant.

In Clive's second life at Charleston there was no central focus, nor even a particular host or hostess, it was more like a collection of people with various absorbing occupations and interests, into which one felt lucky to be admitted. He was more relaxed there: he would get into old tweeds and bedroom slippers, go walking on the downs or sit out in the sun with a book. He was a great enjoyer, whose enjoyment was as infectious as his laughter, and who appreciated the details of country life almost as much as the hours he spent reading and writing every day. He saw the public world through liberal and rational spectacles, and (besides his better-known books on art) defended his views in *On British Freedom* and two pacifist pamphlets: *Peace at Once* (1915), burned by order of the Lord Mayor of London, and *Warmongers* (1938).

Clive often visited us at Ham Spray. He and Ralph were devoted to each other, and Burgo too enjoyed his high spirits and vitality. (I remember overhearing a conversation between Clive and Burgo – aged about five – in which they were describing meals one would *not* like to eat. It ended by Clive saying: 'No, Burgo, ink and spearpoints wouldn't be *at all* nice.') Fond of gossip, in which there was sometimes a strain of mischief or even malice, he endeared even by his comic characteristics, such as larding his talk with French phrases and words, or anxiously rearranging the thick carroty hair which grew on only part of his cranium and had a way of getting out of place. He travelled a lot in Europe, particularly in France, where he had many friends and spoke the language fluently. He had been known to make an after-dinner speech in it full of jokes that brought blushes to the cheeks of the ladies present.]

May 10th

Gerald rang up soon after breakfast. 'I suppose you've heard this morning's news.' 'No – what?' G.: 'They've invaded Holland and I believe Belgium too.'

So the blitzkrieg has begun at last! I felt a grip of fear and excitement mixed, as if a giant's hand had seized me round the waist where I stood by the telephone, picked me up and dropped me again. I called out and told R. At one o'clock an incredible story of waves of bombers swooping over the flat land, and German parachutists dropping out of the sky just before dawn like flocks of starlings. I thought of the jackdaws dropping out of the hole in our great aspen. Then I felt calmer than for a long time. Now it's going to start in real earnest – and it's almost a relief, as if one had lain for ages on the operating table and at last the surgeon was going to begin.

Chamberlain has abdicated, handing over the premiership to Winston Churchill.

May 13th

Everyone makes jokes about the likelihood of German parachutists landing in our Wiltshire fields dressed as nuns or clergymen – a good farcical subject on which to let off steam. This afternoon I was alone in the kitchen when the doorbell rang, and there on the step stood three tall bearded men who addressed me in strong German accents, and wore something between clergyman's and military dress! Aha! I thought, the parachutists already. But when they asked for Mrs Nichols I realised that it was some of the Brüderhof, a community of Christian Pacifists of all nations who live the simple life near Swindon. Curiosity was too much for me, so I asked them to have some tea. Two were very unattractive redheads with scarlet mouths above their beards. It was the maddest of mad hatter tea parties, consisting of me and these three Jesus Christs, all looking at me sweetly and speaking in gentle voices. I told them we were pacifists. 'Are you persecuted much?' they asked, rather taking the wind out of my sails. I felt as if Jesus Christ had mistaken me for John the Baptist.

May 14th

Drove to the station to fetch Julia and M.A.M.[1] Julia and I walked along the grassy terrace under the Downs. I was almost brained by a wounded pheasant. 'Perhaps it's a disguised parachutist,' said Julia. On the wireless we hear ghastly stories of the German advance, calling up a picture of columns of giant machines, a sky black with aeroplanes, and the unceasing crash of bombs and explosives. 'Well, it's fucking awful, that's all I can say,' said Julia. Yet I think a strange calm possesses us all.

May 15th

Returning to bed this morning R. said, 'Well, that's what comes of listening to the early news. Holland has surrendered to Germany.' It has now become a familiar feeling, this dropping of something inside one with a sick thud, an internal bucket into an invisible well of despair. So now the Germans, their armies and aeroplanes, face us across the Channel. In no time – days even – we may all be enduring the same horrors as Holland and Belgium. We talked about suicide. I thought with envy of Ray, and longed to have some safe way of dying within my power. R. said we could easily gas ourselves in the car, all three of us. We were still talking of this as we went along to the bath, and of how happy our lives had been, and so has Burgo's, though there has been so little of it.

My greatest preoccupation is with the question of how to get a supply of lethal pills. I turn it over and over in my mind. I feel it would be the greatest possible help to know that we had death in our power. I look back at our state of a few weeks ago with envy, and hope for no positive happiness but merely for means to keep this acute misery at bay.

May 18th

Like the zooming that under war conditions affects the wireless, the war swings nearer and further, pendulum-wise. This morning it was booming right in our ears. 'Hitler's weather' still blazes away uncomfortably; the world of the lawn is as hot as a furnace.

In the afternoon our attention switched to ordinary things nearer home, meeting Molly's train and shopping. When I got back the Wests had arrived for tea. Molly looked pale and tired, but was in wonderfully eccentric form, producing a

---

[1] My mother.

characteristic stream of remarks and wild gestures. She kept looking out for Julia, having heard she was with us, and mistook Anthony, Kitty and M.A.M. for her in turn. Then when she did appear of course she failed to recognise her.

Everything – sitting on the lawn, Burgo's games of Snakes and Ladders – seemed so like the activity of a normal summer day as to blot out the war. But it was there, like some horrible virus working away under our skins, and in the evening it rose to the surface in the form of deadly fatigue and inertia. Talking to Molly was an effort, and we all yawned our heads off. M.A.M. and Julia went upstairs, but still Molly wouldn't go to bed, until we insisted.

May 19th

Very broken sleep all night. Soon after six I became aware that the rest of the bed was empty. Heard R.'s feet padding round the garden. It has become unnecessary to look out of the window, one knows there will be a cloudless blue sky and glorious sun. The perfection of the weather is getting on all our nerves. It is too phenomenal and everything supernormal is unnerving; also it's impossible not to remember that it is ideal weather for air-raids. The German advance into France goes on. I feel a strong desire to creep away, curl up and become unconscious.

The only happy people today were M.A.M. and Burgo, who spent the morning having a long, intensely dramatic conversation about fire-engines. As they moved from one place to another I heard Burgo say: 'Come along Grannie, and we'll go on talking. I love talking, don't you, Grannie?' And then: 'Oh my stars and stripes!'

The Brenans arrived to tea on bicycles, Gamel wearing a divided skirt and with her arms scratched to pieces from having fallen off into a hawthorn bush. Again the ordinary tenor of life was propped up during most of the day by invisible social supports, but as evening came it collapsed. The nine o'clock news brought no consolation, only a speech by Winston saying we must all prepare to suffer the war in our own country and be proud to share the experiences of our Brave Boys in France.

May 22nd

Rain! Hitler's weather has at last broken. I woke feeling my brain had been cooled by sleep and rain, and began to wonder aloud what we should do if we heard the Germans had landed. I had a job to convince R. that I would trust entirely to his courage and masculine strategy in emergency.

'I don't know what'll happen when the fatal moment comes,' said Julia at breakfast. 'You have such totally different views on the subject, you'll never agree.' (Julia doesn't like married couples to agree.)

But it became evident that we saw eye to eye.

R.: 'Under the influence of fear one does one of two things. Either runs like a hare, or squats like a hare.'

Julia: 'Well what lesson can we draw from the hare?' She went on to say her plan was to make herself look very old and ugly so as not to be raped. R. laughed immoderately at this.

At six o'clock we heard the expected sinister news that there is fighting in and around Belgium. All our eyes meet and have the same expression in them. Went up to bath Burgo, feeling sick, but later unreasoning optimism came over me.

May 24th

Went outside before breakfast to take a breath of the sweet air heavily scented with May. All the May trees have come out at once at the same time as the cow parsley, making a vision of powdered white on fields and trees together. We actually had a conversation about aesthetics at breakfast, quite like old times. The music of Mozart's clarinet quintet, which I played while writing, was like a voice coming from a very long way away indeed. Perhaps one should struggle more to keep in touch with such things, but there is no energy to spare for struggling. I wonder, supposing the war should get back to the eventless, dug-in stage of the old days, would the relief of it make one callous to the bloody horrors, now in progress and the agony of people with husbands, sons and lovers on the battlefield?

At lunch we heard news of the first bombs dropped on English soil, in Yorkshire, East Anglia and Essex. Not many people were hurt and none killed, and I almost felt relief – which I think is because I half expected the first raids to be on a colossal scale – shock tactics. Really dreadful depression settled on me after the news, and I wished I was dead in all earnest.

May 28th

'They're evidently trying to prepare us for something awful,' said R. I went down to hear a promised announcement by M. Reynaud from Paris. In the voice of a worn-out old Comédie Française actor he droned out: *'Je vais vous annoncer une novelle très gra-a-ave.'* It was that (on the order of King Leopold) the Belgian Army had capitulated without warning the French or English. What is to happen to the BEF, already in a terrible position, and now one must suppose cut off?

June 7th

There have been air-raids on the East Coast of England the last two nights, doing little damage. To the Brenans and Bomfords. The Bomfords are giving shelter to a young German pianist; while he was playing Mozart and Schubert for us, two immense police sergeants arrived to see him and paraded past the window, inkpots in hands. Coming home we were stopped by two 'parachute' patrols, who asked to see our identity cards – vague young men, pointing guns at us, as if playing some stupid game.

Raymond arrived by train; we spent most of the day lying under the beech tree, taking refuge from the terrific heat, which goes on and on, parching the earth and withering the flowers and vegetables. Raymond said he felt there was bad news coming this weekend and that Ham Spray would be a good place to hear it. Apart from our Pacifism, he takes much the same view of the war as we do. Sitting in the cool of the evening among the exuberant pink roses and tall valerian on the verandah, we talked to Raymond about suicide. His French doctor friend has been asked by almost all his patients for a safe poison, generally by means of hints.

The wireless room has become a dentist's waiting room and I get at times a superstitious feeling, 'Switch it off quickly and it may never happen'. Well, yes, it was bad news today and it was an effort to struggle back, as into one's saddle after being knocked off a horse by a branch.

June 13th

A black awakening. Germans are closing in on Paris. How *can* we win this war? Oh, if only we could then lose it quickly. I find my personal armour of fatalism getting more and more impregnable as disasters pile one on top of another, but only at the cost of blotting out a vast terrain accessible to thought and imagination, yet which for safety's sake must not be thought of or imagined. I can't help feeling this is a madman's escape, and it produces a very sub-human dead level of consciousness, without elasticity or scope for reflection. We are just pegging along a straight dusty road. Clive arrived to spend the night, very late, as more children are being evacuated from London and the trains are disorganised.

June 14th

Clive's philosophy is unshaken by the war. He has been admirable company. He is determined not to alter his way of life unless he has to, and to go on getting all the enjoyment out of it that he possibly can. And although I'm not sure what he thinks will be the final outcome, he manages to convey an impression of ultimate optimism going beyond the question of who wins. He was just the right person to be with when R., coming back from the one o'clock news, said: 'You were right. Paris has fallen.' Speaking for myself I felt absolutely nothing, almost indifferent. This war deals one so many blows on the head in such rapid succession that it's hardly odd that insensibility results.

Gerald came over on his bicycle, and the four of us sat discussing the news under the ilex tree. He has a horror of the idea of suicide; not so Gamel apparently. Everyone could easily be placed in one of these two compartments. In the first I can only include, with any strong probability, R. and myself, Raymond, Gamel, Leo [Myers],[1] Phyllis [Nichols]. The members of the other group (such as Gerald and Julia) are filled with righteous indignation against the idea. A few days ago a friend of the Brenans living near Swindon tried to get his wife to sign a suicide pact because of the war. She was very tenacious of life, and refused. So next morning he came in and shot her as she sat at her writing-table, and afterwards shot himself.

The Germans in Paris, in the cafés and everywhere! It's very difficult to imagine it. But it's a good deal less painful than to think of Paris and Parisians being burnt and destroyed by bombs. I am certain the French will make peace in a few days. But will we?

June 17th

I got a reply this morning from Margaret Penrose[2] to a letter I wrote her exactly a month ago asking for her advice on suicide drugs. She writes, 'I can't prescribe a poison, but I can produce a cure,' and goes on to suggest our all packing up and going to start a new life in Canada. She also told us that Lionel was thinking of throwing up his career as a geneticist and starting a farm in British Columbia – which seems to me about as sensible as Casals throwing up playing the cello and starting to breed ducks. What would one feel like, I wonder, steaming across the Atlantic? That one was leaving a festering sore behind, very thankfully? R. says

[1] Novelist and one-time Marxist.
[2] A doctor, temporarily living in Canada.

one thing and one only would occupy one's mind – was there a periscope anywhere about?

Well then, at lunchtime Marjorie Strachey[1] rang up. She was hoping to take a party of children to America as soon as possible. Would we like to send Burgo? Mothers might get a passage but no fathers. I said I would think it over, though of course it's out of the question. How could one send poor little Burgo off, entirely away from everyone and everything he knows? And if the Germans beat us, as it looks as though they almost certainly will, we might never be able to join him again.

The French government has fallen and been succeeded by Pétain, Weygand and others. I told R. who was sitting reading by the weeping ash and he looked very shattered. He said he felt quite sick. I can't help thinking, 'Thank goodness the French no longer have to fight.'

June 19th

R. and I to see the Brenans. Gerald, R. and I went for a walk, while Gamel had to attend a Red Cross meeting. Gerald and R. got into a political discussion that threatened to become heated, and I dropped behind and suddenly felt extraordinarily happy, tugging flowers and grasses out of the hedges. Gerald's new line about the war is that we are beaten now, and the thing is to make the best possible terms with Hitler. What a pity, he says, we can't raise a few better Fascists. Mosley is really rather too awful. If we could, he thinks we could get quite good terms – and what does the censorship of the Press matter? R. was fairly flummoxed by this *volte-face*, and tried in vain to drive it home to Gerald that it was one.

The last two nights there have been air-raids of over a hundred planes on various parts of England. Just before midnight I felt R. stiffen and hold his breath. The rumour is that some bombs fell near Swindon.

Phyllis rang up today kindly offering to take Burgo to America. She's going to try and take her children there and return herself, but Phil thinks it's already too late.

June 28th

Brenans to lunch. I told Gerald (and it surprised him) that the police had mentioned him among the local suspects. 'Oh, they have, have they? Well, they'd better not try anything on, that's all.'

To meet Helen, who has come for three weeks' rest. We put her almost at once to bed, for she seems extremely tired, feeble and nervous. No one could possibly have settled into bed in one's house more considerately and tactfully. She talked of the air-raid warnings in Suffolk and I felt her nerve was badly shaken. Talked too of suicide, but altruistically, not with reference to herself. If only she could drop her parade of living entirely for others, and of being an arbiter wearing Roger [Fry]'s mantle.

July 2nd

We left Helen looking like a Goya, lying on the garden bed, with a black lace mantilla over her pretty white hair and went to tea with the Wests.

[1] Youngest sister of Lytton.

I bought some new records in London the other day and this morning I tried them. The Mozart Clarinet Concerto, and a piano sonata played by Schnabel, a Vivaldi concerto. The music was like a balloon whirling us up to a new atmosphere.

The *Arandora Star* has been torpedoed without warning in the Atlantic. It was taking German and Italian waiters, etc., to be interned in Canada, and about a thousand were drowned. That will make parents with American plans for their children quail for a little.

I wish I had kept a collection of the more imbecile letters in *The Times*, all saying in their different ways, 'just see me die, how dashingly I'll do it'. Or the balderdash uttered by politicians. Lord M. says, 'If we must die let's die *gaily*,' and Lord C. that we must do it 'On our toes'. 'Go to it', and 'Keep a high heart', and millions of other parrot cries. While we were shooting French sailors to blazes at Oran, other French sailors were careering round London with their arms round the necks of English soldiers, being fêted and stood drinks. Mad hatterdom.

M.A.M. has come for a short visit. She put Helen to shame with her energy and spirit, describing how she and three octogenarians had arrived for a demonstration of how to deal with incendiary bombs, and were greeted by a surprised-looking man who said, 'Are *you* the fire-fighters?' She is as brave as a lioness and the prospect of raids on London doesn't make her quail in the least.

July 6th

Gerald is now in trouble with the police. It seems he was out with the Home Guard a few nights ago, and used his electric torch to inspect the sandbag defences. A short time later several policemen rode up on motor bikes and shouted, 'You were signalling to the enemy!' Gerald blew up and they became more reasonable, but he was later told, 'We think it only fair to tell you we have reported you to Headquarters as signalling to the enemy.' The head of the Aldbourne Home Guard was sympathetic but thought nothing could be done. He quite agreed with Gerald that these were Gestapo methods – 'Mind you, I think Fascism in one form or another has got to come.' It seems to have come already. Gerald is thinking of resigning from the Home Guard and is very cynical about the hopeless confusion of our home defences.

July 14th

Julia and Lawrence arrived to lunch on bicycles. Helen was lying on her boat-like bed on the verandah, and we sat talking to her as she lay like a queen in a bower of blue agapanthus flowers. I thought she was enjoying the homage, but saw she looked tired and fretful. Julia and I walked together to the foot of the Downs while the others played bowls, and we looked back and saw their figures moving on the lawn, and sweet Ham Spray, pink among its greenery. In these dreary old days Julia's company is as reviving as a shot of strychnine. She told me she couldn't work, and was oppressed by not being in her own house, and by the lorries full of soldiers hurtling along the road.

When I went up to bed I opened the window and looked out. The night was soft and dark, the moon half obscured. Then I saw a finger of light make a delicate stroking movement behind the dark shapes of the trees. I went out on the lawn, feeling suddenly excited, and there over the Downs the searchlights were groping and criss-crossing to and fro, sometimes at feverish speed. Where the cloud was thick they made dense pools of light. For a second or two the reality of the German raids broke through my defences, and I thought of aeroplanes not as bird-like objects, but as machines containing foreign-speaking men whose object was to hurl their lethal weapons on to our dear familiar landscape down here below.

July 20th

We have been told that Hitler has started a Peace Offensive, but no details. It is the first bit of hard news for some weeks. There is a temptation to speculate as to what would happen if we discussed terms, but it's too tantalising, since there's no shadow of doubt we will reject any such suggestion. Now I suppose Churchill will again tell the world that we are going to die on the hills and on the sea, and then we shall proceed to do so.

July 23rd

A letter from Clive with a rather funny description of Margot Asquith asking Virginia to write her obituary for *The Times*. 'Virginia took the opportunity of questioning her about her sex life, which turned out to be exactly what one would suppose – virginity up to marriage and monogamy afterwards – "but I was dreadfully *fast*, my dear".'

July 24th

Raining all day, out of puckered clouds like mackintosh silk. We spent the day with Desmond and Molly at Garrick's Villa – a lovely eighteenth-century house standing in a large garden and looking out over the Thames, a small temple to Shakespeare and a weeping-willow tree. They were living there in space and splendour. Each room had a large bow-window, in which stood a writing-table awaiting literary inspiration, from which could be seen green lawns with an orangery or elegant villa in the distance. Opening what I thought was the door of the lavatory, I found myself face to face with Desmond in a vast study as big and high as a theatre, lined with books and busts. Talked of Boris [Anrep]'s escape from France. Desmond said Boris didn't know what fear was, and when asked to describe the Russian campaign in the first war, he said, 'It was just Ball*et*, just Ball*et*, men running forward and then falling down, just Ball*et*.' Then we paced into the garden in mackintoshes and umbrellas, and along the road to Bushey Park, through fields of haycocks and a wonderful half-domesticated jungle, with tufts of enormous ferns, streams running under bridges, and a bird sanctuary full of water-lilies. 'It's a sanctuary all right, but there are no *birds*,' said Desmond.

August 5th

A German aeroplane was brought down at Heath End, only a few miles away, last night. Two German airmen were taken and three dead. Rumour has it that another escaped and his clothes were found in Pen Wood.

To London for a few nights. The chief pleasure of being there is simply seeing people on buses and in the streets. Then to the Leicester Galleries, an enjoyable spy-film, and to dine with Raymond, who has given up editing the *New Statesman* and joined the Ministry of Information.

Raymond very tired; he says reports from France are extremely contradictory, but give an impression of dazed bewilderment.

The absence of aeroplanes at night made London seem more peaceful than Ham Spray.

August 9th

Lunched with Boris and Maroussa. For over two hours we listened to Boris's account of their escape from Paris in every detail. *It was enthralling.* I can hardly say whether or not it was a pleasure listening to it, for the sensation of sucking in brute reality through one's ears was in fact almost painful. It was as long and exciting as a spy-film, and therefore impossible to write down, though I would like to. I will only say that they would not have got on the train had not their wine-merchant happened to be an official of the Gare du Nord as well, and helped them. Maroussa passed off among some railwaymen's widows, and Boris slipped through while his wine-merchant was embracing the Military Policeman on guard, who most fortunately turned out to be an old school friend.

[Boris von Anrep, as he should properly be called, was a Baltic Baron. He was also a descendant of Catherine the Great and one of her lovers, though he told us that his father grew angry when his children asked about their forbears, believing it to be a purely snobbish interest. Once when we were staying with his great friend Maud Russell at Mottisfont, Ralph and I walked with him into the garden where huge trees stooped to embrace white-painted seats and streams glided under bridges festooned with roses, and stood leaning on the parapet of one of them. The shallow water flowing swiftly beneath must have reminded Boris of the Volga, for he began to tell us about his childhood home on its banks – the large house built of granite below and wood above, the low cliffs and little beaches bordering the river and the paddle-steamers chugging past; he described them all most vividly.

After the 1917 Revolution Boris was in Paris for a while, studying painting and meeting Augustus John, Henry Lamb, Man Ray and Helen Maitland whom he married. When he turned to mosaics I do not know, but before the Second World War he had become a master, perhaps the only master, making floors for the Tate, the National Gallery and the Bank of England, murals in the Russian Church and the Roman Catholic Cathedral, as well as many mosaics for private commissions. He made two fireplaces for Ham Spray, the first commissioned by Lytton, the second as a wedding-present for Ralph and myself. It was characteristic of him that he entered into the tastes and interests of those he worked for. Along the top of Lytton's fireplace was the prostrate naked torso of a young man, looking pro-vocatively over his shoulder. In our dining-room he took his cue for the border 'from the crookedness of the books in our shelves'. For my present London flat he made me a cat warming itself before a blazing fire. I was astonished to find a large wall decorated by him in a church in the middle of Ireland, but not surprised that its prevalent colour was green and its theme St Patrick driving out the snakes.

He occupied in every sense a very large place in our lives and came often to Ham Spray with his delightful 'consort' Maroussa Volkova. Their visits usually began dramatically on the station platform, when Boris used to salute Ralph with a bear's hug and kisses on both cheeks. He was as good a guest as host, and entered with equal originality and energy into cooking or conversation. As good a listener as talker, he would greet other people's remarks with a broad Slavonic smile and a long drawn-out 'No-o-o-O! Ree-ee-ally!'

When, after Ralph's death, I decided to sell Ham Spray in 1961, Boris wrote me a letter which would have made me change my mind if anything could:

I read your letter with the greatest sorrow in my heart. To abandon the house where you lived so long and where happy memories supersede the sad ones is a terrible uprooting.

Whatever unhappiness you feel now it will mellow with time, and happy days of many years will come back in watching your old friends gathering round under the roof which for all of us is a centre of loving hospitality and enlightment and the greatest civilized taste in all things.

Soon afterwards I went to see him putting up the mosaics in the Roman Catholic Cathedral. Boris looked (and was) ill, a splendid crumbling ruin in the midst of what he believed to be his last works.

The last time I saw him was at Mottisfont again, only ten days before his death. At dinner one night he leant across the table and to my astonishment urged me to write about the past and old friends. So strong was my impulse to please him that I said: 'All right, Boris, I will.' Very uncharacteristically, he then repeated twice in a gentle, unemotional voice: 'I love you.'

I never saw him after this weekend, and shall never forget him.]

August 12th

In the afternoon Burgo and I walked across the park and climbed the Downs. Nearly at the top we sat down and watched the reaper in the biscuit-coloured field below. Suddenly we heard terrific air activity, and planes seemed to be dashing about in all directions, though many were invisible behind the clouds. Then a great grey mushroom of smoke rose up from the direction of Newbury. As we crossed the first field, four large bombers swooped over the Downs, making a deafening noise. They flew over our heads fairly low, and on over Ham Spray. The extraordinary thing was that even when I stared up and saw an unfamiliar mark like a cross on their wings, I *still* didn't realise they were German bombers. But I did think how easily they could have machine-gunned our two little figures, I so conspicuous in my red shirt. Wilde, working in the garden, saw the crosses plainly and knew what they were. I never even mentioned the incident to R., so incredulous is he of unfounded rumours, and it was not until Nannie came back from her day out in Newbury that I knew for certain what a good view we had had of German bombers. She had spent most of the day in an air-raid shelter, and the mushroom of smoke had been from bombs dropped near Newbury. There had been something like an air battle over Inkpen. I felt unreasoning excitement for ten minutes or so. Then I thought with surprise of the old days when Lytton and Carrington were alive, and that now bombs fall on Newbury and German bombers go over the house itself.

August 14th

Last night I was making a new blackout curtain when listening to Beethoven. In the middle of the Pastoral Symphony there was a loud but distant CRUMP. I have been unconsciously avoiding imagining the details of air-raids, but this sound brought my unwilling mind a vivid picture of crashing masonry and mangled bodies.

To tea with the Brenans. Gerald is still in a fever about his 'signalling to the enemy' and was talking wildly about 'having it out with them', 'bringing an action for slander' and 'writing to Duff Cooper'.

A noisy day, in one way and another, and we hear that over eighty enemy aeroplanes were brought down.

August 17th

Hot blue day. We bathed, we read, we wrote. In the afternoon the Nicholses arrived. We sat till late drinking sherry on the lawn, as the sky turned pink and the midges came out to bite. Then we gave them a purely home-grown meal – bortsch, roast pigeons, vegetables, figs and peaches. Phyllis, in very fine looks, told us that she was at her mother's house the other day when eleven screaming bombs fell in the grounds. One cottage was knocked to pieces. Then a terrible thing happened: two children whose home it was came back and saw its state, and thought all their family *must* be dead. They rushed off in God knows what dreadful state of mind, and couldn't be found and reassured till next morning.

I imagined that the Nicholses, having got their children safely to America, would feel relieved, and confident that they had done the best thing. Not a bit of it. Even more than parents who have kept their children at home, they worry that they have made the wrong decision, particularly Phil. Phyllis still says she is glad they have gone, though her eyes fill with tears when she speaks of them. 'If the war goes on long it will be a disaster for them,' says Phil. He is the most besotted of fathers, but besides missing the children badly, he feels they will be brought up as he doesn't want, and suffer from lack of parental love. They left after early breakfast. Alone in the sitting-room, I suddenly felt the war close in again round me, signalising its naked presence by three bombers, which crossed the garden with a roar, and veered off, heeling like battleships into the grey streaky sky.

August 22nd

Raymond arrived to stay, waving out of the train window as it came in, and got out curved like a question mark, clutching a pile of books to his chest, sighing and talking. He had been to Charleston and described a heated argument one evening when everyone attacked Clive for saying it would be a good thing to start peace negotiations tomorrow. As he told us this I felt that though he well knew this used to be our own view, he was assuming we must have abandoned such folly, and now toe the line with the rest of them. Anxious not to quarrel, I did not 'take up' the challenge, though vaguely irritated by it.

August 23rd

The *New Statesman*, read in bed, set both R. and me off in a blaze of indignation at the various attitudes it adopts. There is the *Spanish War addiction* to begin with – the view that the Spanish Civil War was the only one worth fighting in. Those who did so criticise the tactics of all other wars, disregarding the fact that they didn't even win it. Then there is the line that *the War isn't so bad*. It's so good for unemployment, it's so democratic, few people have been killed, in fact it's rather a bracing state of affairs. I find this simply maddening. It is intolerable that those who haven't had much to complain of should belittle the agony, for instance, of those who are in constant grinding anxiety about the airman they love. The quiet *natural-history attitude* of Vita Sackville-West ('Our village in an air-raid') is silly, but less violently annoying. All becomes part of the ancient English rural tradition in some mysterious way. Last, but one that I find more and more painful, is the semi-erotic *excitement about the brave young airman in danger*, especially when it is felt by highbrows who take care to avoid all danger themselves, or very old people.

Yesterday there was a short barking match between R. and Raymond at tea. Raymond had continued subtly to goad our pacifist position. R. suddenly almost shouted that it was inconceivable to him that any sensitive person should insist on the importance of the young men of the RAF leading the lives of frightful danger they do when they themselves were *not* risking their lives for the cause they thought so important. The only thing to do if you felt like that was to act like Sir Arnold Wilson and become a rear gunner even if you were over fifty. Raymond took this attack with perfect good nature and hardly tried to defend himself, but I think perhaps he was pleased to have got a rise.

Clive describes Raymond's visit to Charleston (along with Desmond) as 'pure joy till the last evening when we got into a hot and unprofitable wrangle about the desirability of a negotiated peace. Of course if people really believe that after a victorious peace the whole world would live happily ever after, there's no sense in arguing. But *why* they should believe it I can't imagine.'

August 25th

Julia and Lawrence to lunch, at which an old fashioned conversation on art, etc., sprang up. What a relief after war, war, war. Lawrence had been to tea with the local clergyman, who said *à propos* of her portrait, 'Julia Strachey? Any relation of the writer chap who used to live out this way? Fellow looked like a lunatic to me.' He had also been to London and had tea with Vanessa [Bell], Dorelia [John] and Helen [Anrep], and had been much impressed by 'their Norn-like appearance, looking out from the ruins of their past lives.'

Poor Raymond grew very depressed as the time drew near to go back to London and work. He told me how much he had looked forward to his little holiday, and now there was nothing but very hard work, air-raids and uncertainty. The train was late so we left him at the station, and I never saw anything more pathetic and forlorn than his figure sitting on the platform, clutching a packet of food and a bunch of flowers. There is too much of the Prep school atmosphere these days, and most of us wear spiritual grey flannel shorts and snake belts. The station was thronged with returning parents who had been visiting child refugees, and I got home overwhelmed by the sadness rather than the madness of war.

August 26th

The news is now entirely concerned with air-raids. Inside every head in England the same questions are revolving: 'How many killed? How many injured? How is everyone "standing up" to the raids?' Oh, the sordid horror of the news; now it is just one long description of destruction, smashing, mashing and killing. On the way upstairs I saw a monstrous dead blue-bottle lying on its back, and thought it symbolized the world's state. The Germans say we are being unduly optimistic about the mildness of their raids, and that we will change our minds 'in the next few days', since they are revising their technique and bombing by night indiscriminately – the famous 'war of nerves'. Our newspapers tell us how wonderfully unshakeable our morale is.

A long conversation with R. about the French Revolution, Napoleon, Hitler and so forth. I am now in the last volume of Walpole's Letters, and his horror of the violence and savagery across the Channel made me realise what it must have been like having it going on year after year. H.W. was so affected that he felt there must be something radically wrong with the French nation never before suspected, some monster blood in their veins. (Just in fact what people are now saying about the Germans.) But less than a hundred years later they were being taken as the fine flower of an old and dignified civilization.

August 31st

I don't seem to have put down that since they began, air-raids on London have been incessant, day and night, though few have got through to the centre. There is bound to be an exodus.

Saxon [Sydney-Turner] arrived for ten days' holiday, looking very white and old. We were both delighted to see him, changed into his silk summer suit, lying out on the garden bed under the weeping ash with a detective story. We had grouse in his honour and a bottle (the last) of Châteauneuf 1923; globe artichokes, grapes, figs and plums, all homegrown.

[Saxon was the mystery man of Old Bloomsbury and an early intimate of the circle of Vanessa, Virginia and Adrian Stephen. From Cambridge he brought a reputation for brilliant classical scholarship, for having written at least one opera, and even for skill at drawing. However, he spent his whole working career at the Treasury, refusing promotion because it would mean changing to a room with a less sympathetic view, and he was reputed to be the only man beside the Chancellor who could be trusted with knowledge of the contents of the Budget. He certainly had a gift for silence – perverse at times, for he might well remain dumb when talk was required of him and hold forth at length when there was some other urgent call on one's attention, just as he would go pink in the face with the effort of *not* laughing at a joke that amused him. A life-long unreciprocated passion for Barbara Bagenal had turned him into that now nearly extinct species 'a bachelor'. He never forgot one of her or her children's birthdays, and she told me that he wrote her a letter every day, written in his elegant hand with its overtones of Greek script – beginning just 'Barbara'!

He came often to Ham Spray, particularly during the war, a distinguished-looking figure with his finely modelled ivory-white features and hands, and his well-cut suits of great antiquity – white silk in summer, and at other seasons black, with a shirt of royal blue or plum colour maybe and button boots.

In the morning he might be seen advancing down the passage to the bathroom in a silk dressing-gown as shredded by wear and tear as a Hawaiian dancer's skirt, holding a tumbler of water containing his false teeth defiantly in front of him. There was always a volume of Horace or Thucydides in the original by his bedside.

His ability – indeed sometimes his desire – to aggravate could not disguise the fact that beneath this bottled-up eccentric there was a deeply affectionate man, and Ralph and I both loved him and enjoyed his company. Other friends were not exactly expected to do likewise, but received high marks if they did.]

September 5th

R. woke bubbling and simmering like a kettle on the boil, because of the pressure of our inmates. He says one can't talk about the war to M.A.M., gets bored of talking about birds with T., and Saxon won't talk about anything. Nor can he and I ever have a private conversation. Then we talked about intimacy. He said he had never hoped to find such intimacy as he has with me. Nor had I. Nor, let me say here and now, had I expected one fraction of the happiness I find in marriage. Why should intimacy be the secret of married happiness? asked R. Because the enemy of married happiness is irritation. But you can't be irritated by yourself, and when another person is so intimate that they are your other self you can't be irritated by them either.

Burgo and I walked to watch the road being tarred towards Ham. A man with a curly mop of bright yellow hair, looking like a Shakespearean clown, let him use his shovel and then asked me when the war would end. I said I wished I could tell him. He: 'Not so far off neither, it's the food shortage. If we could only starve every soul in the country, that would be the best thing. You have to be cruel to be kind!'

Roused from sleep in the small hours by the vision of Nannie in our bedroom doorway saying, 'There were three quite close. What shall I do?' R. said grumpily: 'Go back to bed.' I got up and went down the passage. Nannie said, 'They *are* busy tonight.' It was the refrigerator down below! Went back to bed but couldn't sleep. Heard three bombs half an hour later. Poor old Nannie, I do feel sorry for her. She would love air-raids to be organized like everything else – we should all get up, take our gas-masks and file into a snug dug-out full of rugs and make tea. I expected to find her sheepish next morning, but she only said: 'Did you hear those three bombs later?'

September 8th

Dead-heading the dahlias, while R. and Burgo collected caterpillars for the ducks and hens off the cabbages. Nothing could have been more peaceful and domestic. Then the one o'clock news brought the news of last night's terrible raids on London, many times worse than anything hitherto. It was still smoking, casualties 400 killed and 1,300 seriously wounded. This ghastly mouthful of reality stuck in one's throat. Lunch was a farce. How could we swallow meat and potatoes as well? We all sat struck dumb, except M.A.M. who tried to look on the bright side and say we could do more damage in our raids than they could. Good God, as if that was a comforting thought! And there's no reason to think they can't go on and on. Nothing to say about the rest of this gloomy day. Didn't want to read, walk or think. What's the point of picking flowers? Is it worth crossing the lawn? Or speaking? What a world to be alive in, if this sub-human existence can be called being alive. After dinner, a loud strange noise in the darkness. The All Clear. Poor Nannie bustled down stairs and fell on her knees with a noise louder than any bomb. I visited M.A.M. in bed. She made me a touching speech saying she was afraid she irritated R. and couldn't bear to do that as she was so fond of him. So is he of her, and she can't possibly go back to London now that the real Blitz has begun.

September 11th

A second raid on London almost as bad as the first. I have been wondering what is happening to St Paul's, and Gerald rang up with the same preoccupation. I suppose it is the Nose of London's familiar face (and everyone knows what noses stand for). It's disgusting to think of that familiar face being destroyed piecemeal. Talked in bed about the awful effects of war on human character – the sinister light of bombs and fires lights up a landscape of isolated hillocks of knobby egotism.

Saxon's departure this afternoon looms up and fills us with despair. He seems utterly unfitted to go back to this horrible life in the front line trenches. He spent most of the day drawing up his Will, and Edie and Wilde were brought in to sign it, looking as if they were in church. M.A.M. still in bed. By way of penance I listened to her optimism for a long time without making a single damping remark.

At tea-time Mrs Hill of Ham rang up to say four frantic people had arrived in a car from London. Could we take them in? They arrived soon after – Mum, Dad, Gran and Sonny from Wandsworth. We made up beds for them all.

September 13th

Our Wandsworth family are moving on to relations today, but they are a foretaste of refugee life. They looked better after a sleep. Lack of sleep was their great trouble, as they had spent every night this week in a stuffy public shelter. Granny, an ex-lady's maid, said she 'felt her nerve going'. The father of the family was still in a highly nervous state, and rolled his eyes like a shying horse as he described how he thought every bomb was going to hit him. The poor things went off early with much hand-shaking, and the sky cleared both literally and figuratively.

Hungerford was full of refugees looking like East-Enders; young girls in shiny black or pink clothes, with faces that ought to be pretty but were somehow stunted-looking, and cigarettes hanging out of their mouths. I felt they thought living in Hungerford would be worse than being bombed. Our Wandsworth family believed that peace *must* come because Londoners couldn't stand this fearful strain and lack of sleep. They were in a way the most pacific people we have lately seen. They had no bitterness against the German people, only sympathy for those we were bombing in Berlin.

September 14th

Mrs Hill on the telephone again! 'I've just heard that twenty refugees are arriving in half an hour. Could you have some more?' R., Burgo and I drove down to the village and waited. Then the bus came lumbering in, and children ran to gape and stare. One very small child thudded along screeching out 'VACU-*EES!* VACU-*EES!*' As soon as they got out it was clear they were neither children nor docksiders, but respectable-looking middle-aged women and a few children, who stood like sheep beside the bus looking infinitely pathetic. 'Who'll take these?' 'How many are you?' 'Oh well, I can have these two but no more,' and the piteous cry, 'But we're *together*.' It was terrible. I felt we were like sharp-nosed housewives haggling over fillets of fish. In the end we swept off two women about my age and a girl of ten, and then fetched the other two members of their party and installed them with Coombs the cowman. Their faces at once began to relax. Far from being terrified Londoners, they had been evacuated against their will from Bexhill, for fear of invasion, leaving snug little houses and 'hubbies'.

September 15th

My thoughts are involved to the exclusion of everything else with the Bexhill problem. Moved furniture to make their two rooms more habitable, talked to them, tried to get the little girl Jean in touch with Burgo. All began to take shape very well, and my impression of their niceness is confirmed, but will they almost die of boredom? Julia and Lawrence to lunch. Julia brought a letter from Beatrix Lehmann who has just taken her Charlotte Street flat, describing her first night in one of these awful raids. How she and her old dog crept down to the basement and lay there wondering if anyone knew they were there. Of the fiendish noises like express trains rushing straight at your stomach, the Giant in seven-league boots stalking all over London, and the comfortingly cockney voice of the ARP men shovelling up incendiary bombs. Julia and L. had spent a night in London before the really bad raids began, and that was quite bad enough. Neither of them slept a wink.

September 16th

Many reports of bombs heard in the night. R. and I heard nothing, but Nannie of course did, M.A.M. also and the Bexhills. Poor Mrs Loker, the mother of the Bexhill family, got out of bed and began to dress in a great state. The London raids are almost the sole subject of thought, conversation and speculation – like a toothache gnawing away at life and spirits. With a sinking heart I feel what remains of me being submerged under the tide of practical arrangements, just as it was last winter, only with infinitely more painful events happening. And apart from the shopping lists, I can brood for hours as how best to fit together the pieces of our Ham Spray jigsaw to make a picture that is most psychologically tolerable.

Lying in my bath this morning, talking to R. and stirring my toes through the rising steam, with the clear watery sun streaming in at the window, I had one of those flashing gleams when the war is annihilated: 'Supposing there wasn't a war!' or '*When* there wasn't a war!'

A resolve: to keep as much lucidity and interest as possible from being submerged by housekeeping, refugees and routine. Not to let the steam from the bath fuzz all the windows till I can see no twigs, trees or sky, but only taps and towels. But as I write it down I fear it will not be kept.

September 21st

I see that in my family R. and I are considered as dreadful pessimists. Every letter from one of them says 'we are all very optimistic here,' conscious I know that we at Ham Spray are not. This optimism in their language – a very strange one to me – means that they think we will win the war. I sometimes think so myself, but even so I couldn't possibly call my state of mind 'optimistic'. It's obviously impossible for them to understand that to us it seems as if in the long run it hardly matters who wins it. That we are pessimistic because the war is horrible in itself, because it is solving no problems and doing no good to anyone, but on the contrary making endless new problems and doing infinite harm to countless people.

A wonderful September morning, rising slowly out of mist; rooks cawing, cobwebs spangled with dewdrops and silky white sheaves of pampas gleaming in the sun. Went blackberrying along the soused hedges.

September 24th

Changes: poor old Nannie has gone, tearing herself away from her adored Burgo. Burgo has started day-school in Hungerford.

Perhaps his first day there stimulated his philosophical comment today on a walk along the Downs: 'Every stick I see is in the world, isn't it?'

R. went to Aldbourne and came back with the news that Gerald has been in trouble with the police *again*. He spent a whole day at the Marlborough Police Station, and R. got to Bell Court just in time this morning to interview a Scotland Yard man and vouch for Gerald's character. Apparently when Sir Oswald Mosley was in danger of being arrested at the beginning of the war he made a bonfire of his papers, but one or two floated over a wall and came into the hands of the police. On one was written among other notes: 'Gerald Brenan, Bell Court, Aldbourne.' The Scotland Yard man told R. that if Gerald hadn't been able to explain this he would quietly have been interned for the duration of the war. The explanation was that he had written a letter to the *Telegraph* urging that Sir Oswald be arrested, and was therefore an enemy of the Fascist Party and his name and address noted as such.

Burgo told me there was to be gas-mask drill at school tomorrow, so I tried his on tonight. It seemed dreadfully tight and he said he 'didn't like it a bit and couldn't breathe in it'. From having longed to put it on he was almost in tears.

M.A.M. came up from the news, her face alight with triumph. One hundred and thirty German planes have been brought down in daylight raids.

September 30th

Taking the washing to Mrs Slater half a mile away we found her still trembling. The lights had been incendiary bombs and a rick had caught fire. The Slater family spent all night in their shelter. 'We don't want them any nearer,' she said with a sort of half-choked shudder.

Visited the Brenans. The cat was looking out of one window of the sunny façade, and Gamel in a turban out of another. Both Gerald and Gamel say they very much want to go to London, but disclaim curiosity as the motive – goodness knows why. It's a very respectable one.

Gerald told us he is writing a novel, which will be a best-seller. And after that he plans a volume of short stories to show the terrible harm caused by the human virtues – kindness, candour, etc.

R. has taken a lot of trouble to clear away the clouds of suspicion hanging over Gerald. For one thing he got Clive to ask his brother 'the Colonel' (who has a lot of influence in Wiltshire) to intercede on his behalf with the authorities. This does seem to have had considerable effect. As the Colonel put it, 'Brenan's name was on Mosley's Death List.'

Late this evening came Humphrey Slater and Janetta from the Osterley Home Guard School, to have a rest from the bombing. They talked most of the evening about the raids, said Londoners talked about nothing else. Janetta with most remarkable candour and realism said that she felt far more terrified than she would have believed possible, and flung herself on the floor trembling all over. H. said she was really remarkably controlled. Her 'tone' about her own fear is the best I've yet struck, though I can't quite analyse why. She longs to get out of London, but is going back in two days' time rather than leave Humphrey alone.

October 2nd

Left Humphrey at Hungerford and went on, with Janetta and Burgo, to lunch at Bell Court off a huge dish of spaghetti. The talk as usual all of London and bombing. In the face of Janetta's candid and sane fear, I found Gerald's endless boastful belittling of the raids in bad taste and rather unlike himself. At last I said I thought he was in no position to judge until he had been in London and seen for himself. He told R. that he thought this was true, and that he wanted to go up.

A conversation about Respect. We drew up a list of people we respected – Darwin, Mill, Hume, Wellington. Janetta said indignantly that she respected no one. I have great respect for her, as it happens, and would have liked to have added her to my list.

Humphrey and Janetta's descriptions of London have been a shock to M.A.M. She had built up, brick by brick, a view that it wasn't so bad, and everyone was bearing up splendidly. She said anyone could see they were both nervous types. It does seem cruel to break her rosy spectacles, but we cannot possibly wear them ourselves.

While I was bathing Burgo he held forth on Hitler's wickedness. 'And Mussolini isn't very nice, is he? And Goering? I wouldn't mind giving Hitler an unripe blackberry.'

October 9th

To meet Raymond. His description of London life was very convincing. He pooh-poohed the Gerald theory that it's quite all right living there at present. His front door and inner door were both blown in, and some windows broken, by a very large bomb which fell round the corner, leaving his flat and all his lovely books, china and pictures accessible to burglars. While he said the raids were terrifying and the lack of sleep and dreariness of everything unutterably wearing, he said the look of things was 'so extraordinary that everyone should try to go to London for a sight of it'.

October 18th

Janetta's brother, Rollo Woolley, now training to be a pilot in the RAF, arrived at tea-time. The effect of his airforce uniform was electric. Burgo was quite flummoxed by it. M.A.M. softened visibly. I think R. and I were also affected; anyway we like Rollo very much. We asked him a lot about the RAF of course, and he answered all our questions, giving us a picture of young men living in the present or the near future, and absorbed in the technique of learning to fly. R. thinks Rollo fully realises the suicidal nature of his career. I don't know. He has no illusions about the war, is inclined to call it an 'Imperialist war with Communists' and 'is not sure whether he is a Communist or pro-Nazi, as there's no difference between them'. Only about fifty per cent of the trainees finish the course. Some fail only at night flying. The best pilots are not Rugby footballers – it's largely a question of sensitive touch and musicians are especially good at it.

Burgo began dancing round Rollo in a state of hero-worship. M.A.M. wants to provide comforts for him, knit him socks – a strange way it seems to me of blinding oneself to the fact that we are asking this young man to lose his life[1] or be maimed, or at best terribly frightened for the sake of what we want.

A conversation with M.A.M. in her room. I said I had no hopes for the future, though many desires. She said, 'I *must* hope or I should blow my brains out.' Well, I can't feel there's reasonable grounds for hope and yet I don't blow my brains out. Of course I hope the war will be won by the USA and Us, though I think ideals will vanish in the final chaos. M.A.M.'s voice was like a drowning man's clutching at a straw, and she buoys herself up with 'things are being done ... people who know tell me ... I firmly believe.'

Poor Saxon wrote very despairingly saying that two of his best friends at the Treasury were killed last night. The Treasury must have been hit, though he doesn't say so.

October 29th

Sitting for my portrait to Lawrence, who had been to London, to order a new suit for one thing. When he got there the Fifty Shilling Tailors in Piccadilly was nowhere to be seen. Then he went to the 'Studio' office, that too had vanished. But what shattered him most was the sight of Vanessa[2] and Duncan's[3] studio, unrecognizable and pulverized. Only a few pieces of Omega pottery and Vanessa's studio table upside-down – and the ruin of that tin Bridge of Sighs we used to clank across, and everyone must have tender memories of.

November 4th

We were sitting round the fire tonight when there was a noise like an old tank or a car passing very slowly overhead, rattling as it went. I thought: 'Yes, it's a bomb; but it's going over – it won't hit us.' Ran up to the nursery, and then came the CRASH. Burgo hadn't stirred (he had been quite seriously ill, but is now better), and I was standing recovering when in came Joan, her hair loose and dishevelled. She looked flustered, and no wonder as she was bicycling up the avenue when she saw and heard the bomb go over. Soon after we had settled by the fire again there was another, and another – CRASH, plop, plop, plop. Good, I thought, I'm getting used to them. R. said, 'Well twice may be a coincidence, but if they do it again it'll look as if they were aiming at something.' And they did. I see that one does, without trying to, learn something of the sounds of raiding planes and their significance. The nastiest moment is when, after a low flight, the engines shut off and there's total silence.

November 5th

Walked out to look at the craters. In the lane at the end of the avenue men were filling in quite a respectable one. They were very jolly. 'Only casualty a skylark,' said one. One of the last of the 'stick' fell in the garden of one of the Ham bungalows, and a little boy, missed by a few feet, was found asleep under the debris. We all enjoyed our sight-seeing expedition but if that little boy had been killed there would have been none of all this joking.

[1] He did.
[2] Bell.
[3] Grant.

R. and I went to see the Brenans. Gerald, back after his two weeks wardenship in London, looking young and lean. All the time he didn't see one person killed. Each night had its 'incidents', houses demolished, people buried or cut by glass, or with all their clothes blown off, shot up into trees, or starred all over with cuts from glass so as to be bright red with blood all over. The amount of blood was the one thing that struck him. Arthur Waley[1] is a stretcher-bearer, and was called in when the YMCA off Tottenham Court Road was hit. He said the whole place was swimming in blood and it was dripping down the stairs, yet hardly a person was killed. All were superficial cuts from glass. He believes that most people cannot resist the temptation to exaggerate. The really terrified people leave London or else go down to the tube, others make themselves as safe as possible somewhere where they can sleep. And he says most people do manage to sleep now, and that many people are enjoying finding themselves braver than they knew.

A gale blew all night – it even blew the duck-house over.

November 20th

R. looked sad all day, and when I asked him why, he said in an extinguished voice, 'I *hate* this war so.' I have been hating it more than usual lately too. It's possible to forget it absolutely for a short time, only to remember it again with a dreary pang, like some awful cancer gnawing one's vitals or a spear stuck in one's side.

Up in our bedroom the usual drone of bombers developed a more menacing note. Then there was a fairly thunderous explosion, only one, but I found myself trembling gently all over. For the droners went on droning for half an hour more. How degrading to lie here afraid, and how degrading to have cause to be afraid.

November 22nd

I wake in profound gloom most mornings, with thoughts of death and suicide. It is so impossible to imagine a tolerable world future, and however much one believes in individualism, it's hard to carry out in practice in present circumstances. At the same time I am ashamed of not producing more spirit; but I am in the grip of a depression that surveys the view and cannot see anything anywhere in the public world to like, admire, or look forward to. It's not altogether rational, but though I know the fog will lift, it doesn't console me.

Managed somehow to write my review of children's books for the *New Statesman* and felt better.

December 5th

The dead-end of the year. I concentrate on the idea of polishing 1940 off, no matter how, hoping that 1941 will bring some new ideas. As for the natural world, there's nothing dead about this December. From the passage window I see every day the swelling buds on the trees outside. Sweet violets are out, the pampas grass white and plumy, and even the hyacinths are poking their noses out of the beds.

The Christmas catalogues appear, much as usual, except for such things as a toby jug, representing Mr Churchill, round which is written 'We will fight on the sea, we will fight in the hills', and for this wonderful historical memento the price is five guineas.

[1] Translator of Chinese poetry.

Yesterday in the House of Commons the admirable Mr Maxton and others brought forward a motion for stating our Peace Terms, with a view to a Conference. In the Peace debate which followed, war-fury raged, and today there are cartoons of bombed men and women with faces like bulldogs threatening to tear Mr Maxton to pieces.

December 10th

Agitating news that our troops have made contact with the Italians on the Libyan front, which R. says means we have begun an offensive. A swoop into the depths and up again at the thought.

December 12th

Good news from Libya every day now. We make a quick adjustment to this new state of things, and the dead level of most people's spirits has been raised from the rock bottom where they were resting. There is indeed wild talk of Italy being 'knocked out of the war already'.

Read more of Voltaire, at first with disappointment, expecting to admire his character as well as his intelligence, so that his trickery and *fourberie* and inordinate vanity were unpleasantly surprising. So were his haverings with the Church. Re-read Lytton on him, and found that (much as Roger does with painters) he made the 'point' of Voltaire clear.

The world was blotted out this morning, cold and silent, in white mist and white frost. Then the sun burst through and floated over the Downs like a large luminous button, while streamers of mist rose and fell in the no-man's-land between us and the Downs. I went for a short walk, with Burgo – a little leaping gnome – hanging on to my hand. Such very great beauty in the physical world renews one's zest for life in spite of oneself.

December 25th

Christmas Day hardly seemed like a real day – everyone in the house has appalling colds, in spite of which an impetus generated by the three children themselves carried all before it. To children this appears to be no trouble at all, and there is an end, thank heavens, of worked-up adult jollity. Lawrence and Julia came to dinner in a very festive and flowery mood, distributing presents, their style perfect. Lawrence made the most of a squealing bun left by his plate. We ate a fine goose and plum-pudding. Then the Christmas tree had to be lit and the Coombs family from the dairy arrived to see it. As usual it looked amazingly pretty. Lawrence got down on the floor and set off fireworks with the children. Julia peered quizzically at everyone and everything, from the tree itself to Nigel Coombs, who was sucking the end of a balloon and making it squeak.

I don't believe the war was mentioned once all day.

December 28th

Everyone has colds still. Burgo awoke in the night with earache but very talkative in bed with us this morning. He asked a lot about Carrington's portrait of Lytton in our room, because as his own first name is Lytton too I think he identified himself with it. I had told him before who Lytton was, and that he was dead. As he is lying down in the picture he thinks he is dead or dying there. He wanted to know when he died and at what time of day, and why, and in what position, and what became of him after he was dead.

December 31st

Poor Burgo again tapped on our door, on the verge of tears. 'Oh my POOR old ear, it does ache!' he said in heart-rending tones. Put him to bed and took his temperature – 102°. Telephoned the doctor. He came at once. 'No cause for penetrating the drum *so far*,' he said. So it was back to a nurse's life, sleeping in the nursery. And so ends 1940 on a note of illness.

1941

January 1st

I start this second year of my war diary stumbling and blundering along, dazed and blindly, hardly noticing, nor much caring about my surroundings.

Raymond's arrival provided the relief of a stimulating adult presence. He perched on the fender, warming himself in his rather woolly brown suit. He says his flat is now uninhabitable; there is a bomb crater which makes it impossible even to get into it except by climbing like a monkey. He lives instead on the seventh floor of a modern block in Piccadilly, with his bed fixed by screws to the floor under a huge plate-glass window – yet he sleeps better than before the war when he could never get off without sleeping-pills.

We made our prophecies for 1941, and opened and read the ones we made last year. Of course no one had guessed the fall of France. And I wonder what we are all missing out among this year's events!

January 3rd

Bitterly cold again. One of the children came in with some huge lumps of ice and said the pond was bearing. Raymond, who was on his way to meet Paul Hyslop at Bath, began plotting to get his skates from London. All else failing, he decided to go by train all the way to London and fetch them. Such a heroic pursuit of pleasure at the age of forty-five fills me with admiration. He said, 'I'm a convinced utilitarian and my entire life is based on the pleasure principle, whereas most of my friends, I notice, seem to conduct theirs on the reverse.' He has been absolutely charming and I wish he were staying longer, which one feels about few people if one's honest.

I got from Clive the most melancholy letter he has ever written me. 'I don't want to live in London again,' he says, 'or in Paris or in Rome – indeed I don't particularly want to go on living at all. But if I do life that honour I make no doubt it will be at Charleston.' He describes London as 'of inconceivable *tristesse*' and says it 'has a moral for those who need it, of whom you are not one – that the war won't end till it has ended everything that makes life worth living; that it is a fire, an earthquake, a pestilence, applied to which the words "win" or "lose" have no meaning whatever'. With every word of which I agree, but it is strange to hear it from Clive of all people, who has always viewed the ideas of suicide and death with horror.

No sun all day, only a dim light reflected from the snow. Burgo helped me burn the Christmas decorations, which we did slowly, enjoying each flare-up and crackle, and the miniature machine-gun fire of the yew branches. After tea we undressed the Christmas tree and packed away all its glitter into the old Spanish tin trunk. It

seems only a few weeks ago, not a year, since we put them away last Christmas –
so short a time in fact that the tin trunk must have been all that time in the porch
outside the front door 'on its way' to the garage.

January 8th

Went to visit the Padels, an Inkpen couple of pacifists (and I think Communists)
to see if they would teach Burgo next term. Mrs Padel is tall, elderly and shy, with
red threads in her cheeks. Mr Padel has a flashing set of false teeth and a beard,
wears knickerbockers and black boyish boots, and looks as if he ought to be skating
English style round an orange on a frozen lake. Their room was full of musical
instruments and books, a bust of Beethoven, and furnished in lodging-house taste.

January 22nd

To see the Brenans. They had staying with them their Italian anarchist friend,
Maria Luisa, wife of the son of King Bomba, the Soho grocer. She is, I think, the
most beautiful girl I ever saw, and with this goes great sweetness, a low husky voice
and apparent intelligence. She had two red marks on her cheeks which I took for
some new style in make-up, but R. was soon wearing them too – they were the
stigmata of Gamel's morning kisses. She often uses her lipstick freely before applying these signs of friendship, gently but firmly like a rubber stamp, to every arrival's
cheek, and the sight of a whole roomful so decorated is comical in a special and
charming way. Gerald and Gamel were in dressing-gowns, bowls of steaming coffee
on the table. It was like Spain again, an atmosphere they will now, I dare say, take
with them wherever they go. Gamel's vagueness and slow movements give one a
delightful feeling that there is no hurry about anything.

  Gerald told us that it is rumoured Tobruk has fallen. But it was not till this
evening that this was confirmed. A flutter of interest is aroused by these victories,
though the apparent brilliance of Wavell's generalship might be expected to do
more. There is no excuse to call this a war diary except that it faithfully reproduces
the apathy of what I take to be some sort of interim period. Much as I suppose a
night-nurse looking after an invalid snatches a quiet moment to fall asleep, I find
one sinks, or hurls oneself, into this apathy, deliberately not thinking about the
future, supposing nothing, wondering nothing, because one assumes it is 'not for
long'. Yet I keep thinking of Thurber's phrase 'then human beings became lower
than the lower animals'. Food is the most important aspect of the war to us at the
moment. But I think most people believe there will be a savage attack on England,
probably invasion, within the next few months, and deliberately *don't think about
it*, any more than they do of scarred London, like an accident on the other side of
the street.

January 31st

Music on the gramophone, Mozart G Minor Symphony, etc., brought sense of life
returning, or of looking up from the bottom of a well to see that there is at least
daylight at the top. During the afternoon there was a moment when I thought the
eternal mist was melting, and there seemed a ghostly lightness above the house.
The birds were aware of it too, and set up a feeble twittering, but it was soon over.

  The nine o'clock news treated us to a touch of last year's grimness. (Like those
unwelcome dollops of cold facts we used to get every night.) An American, back

in USA from Europe, says there is no doubt that in some period 'between thirty and sixty days' England will be subjected to an appalling attack, which will certainly include the use of 'gas on a large scale'. These words and the ideas attached to them sent me rocketing down into the suicide-pit. Gas is something the idea of which I cannot stomach, even if we all have the best gas-masks in the world. R. made light of my agitation, and then reasonably explained why he believed it was impossible to use it 'on a large scale'. In the course of our conversation I found I had quietly bobbed up from my suicide-pit, and the horror of the evening's broadcast had dispersed.

February 1st

Oliver and Lucy[1] arrived about six, Oliver a bulky black shape under a broad-brimmed black hat; I found I had not quite remembered Lucy's extraordinary appearance, and felt terrified she should notice how shocked I was by it. She and Oliver had not met for six months, and I fancy he was a bit flabbergasted too; at any rate as she began to tell us about her war job (looking after a hostel of seventy naval tailors) he sat with his head in his hand, and at one point began to snore gently. Later, when pumped for his views on the war, he surprised us by his pessimism. He pooh-poohed invasion and 'gas attacks on a large scale', but when someone asked the stale old question, 'When is it going to end?' he replied gloomily, 'The only way it can end in the next few years is by the Germans winning it.' Far the most serious aspect, he told us, was the blockade. It is bound to get much worse in the spring, and what we have to look forward to is years of starvation. Gas or starvation? I couldn't help feeling I would choose the latter any day, but perhaps that's because I can't really imagine it, whereas photographs have helped me imagine gas all too vividly.

[My first memory of meeting Oliver Strachey dates back to an evening when he took Julia and me (aged about nine and ten) to a play called *Baby Mine*. It was what used to be known as a 'bedroom farce', and indeed the plot consisted in a great deal of dashing to and fro across a landing, speculating who was inside the various rooms, and – finally – about the parentage of the resulting baby. Or so I remember it. I had never been to such a sophisticated entertainment before, nor been treated so much like a young lady. It was an evening performance and we wore our best frocks.

Oliver was the eldest surviving brother of Lytton, but unlike him in appearance. He had the rough-hewn features characteristic of the Stracheys, but his manner was more genial and relaxed than Lytton's, his laugh louder and his face ruddier; a pipe was usually sticking out of one corner of his mouth, his hands were probably in his pockets, and his silky hair was parted down the middle to form two parallel tunnels. As he grew older it became shining white.

Oliver was gregarious, amusing, amused, highly intelligent, and interested in everything – music (his first love), books, games and puzzles, women (he was something of a pouncer). Food was an exception, and his taste embraced hardly anything but roast meat and potatoes. 'What's THAT? A vegetable? TOMATOES? Take them all away!' I once heard him say to a waiter. Drink was another matter, and

---

[1] Julia's father had an important job in the cypher department of the War Office. Lucy was – or had been – his 'girl friend'.

as he had a very bad head an invitation to dinner entailed scooping him into a taxi in a state of collapse at the end of the evening. Before that, however, one would have been vastly entertained by his funny and lovable company. He was a near genius at solving all problems and puzzles, including the ciphers he cracked for the War Office in both world wars. He was as fond of his friends as they were of him, but on the whole he would be unlikely to put himself out for them. I would call him amoral rather than selfish.

A story he told of serving as a juryman is perhaps revealing. A seasoned burglar was being tried for 'loitering with intent' outside a house with a jemmy down the inside of the trouser-leg. The jury retired and chose Oliver as foreman. 'Well, I think it's a clear case,' they said to each other. 'I don't know what came over me,' Oliver told us, 'sheer devilry probably. But I suddenly thought it would be amusing to see if I could talk them round, by force of logical argument. I did, though it took some time, and we returned a verdict of Not Guilty. The judge's mouth fell open – but he wasn't nearly as surprised as the prisoner!']

February 9th

The fall of Benghazi has excited and surprised everyone; tonight Churchill made the most confident speech he has ever made and in the most confident tone, although there were the usual references to invasion and gas-attacks. I remember how loathsome his early speeches seemed to me, and wonder if it is I who have changed, or Winston? Have we all given in now and become war-minded, where once we stuck our toes in? Or has he slightly changed his note? I'm sorry to say I think it's the former. Now, when he talks about '*wicked* men' and '*filthy* monsters' I only want to laugh, and I can admire some of his concatenations of words, like today's 'Swoop and scoop'. Not that this signifies the smallest degree of alteration in my attitude to the whole situation.

There is also a delusive sense of spring in the air. The birds now sing quite cheerfully in the mornings and catkins in the hedges have suddenly shot out like yellow-green concertinas. As we drove off to Ham with the washing, the sun illuminated every detail of mossy tree-trunks. The fishmonger produced some herrings which he said were specially good and came straight from a Scotch port. At Burgo's school we saw a charming little interior: Mrs Padel reading Rapunzel to the children, the three little girls on the floor by the fire sewing, while Burgo leant lovingly against her chair doing his moss-stitch.

February 13th

A quiet, sweet-smelling morning; a cow moons across the park, followed by a retinue of small black birds. The countryside looks like Peace not War. Went all round the vegetable and flower-beds and the greenhouse, and visited R. in the orchard, which was like an island lapped in fitful sun and balmy air; he spends long hours on end there, muffled in a huge great-coat and scarf, pruning the nut-trees.

Phyllis Nichols to stay. We took her to visit Lawrence and Julia, and we all sat round their fire drinking sherry and eating shortcake. A discussion about what work is consistent with pacifist views – canteens for instance, either for the military or otherwise. Julia objected to my saying that it was no use being an ostrich and pretending the war didn't exist; also that everyone in this country had to eat. How much should one voice one's views was the next question. All shades of opinion here. Phyllis has lost some of her Saint Sebastian complex, and becomes more cynical and realistic. She says she no longer exactly misses her children, though preoccupied with thoughts about them. Her local pacifists, Max Plowman and Middleton Murry, are trying to form a community on the Brüderhof plan. Murry greatly admires a local couple who are so determined to be self-supporting that they eat hardly anything but radishes. He calls this 'an inspiration'!

February 19th

I think I was afraid of the shock of seeing blitzed London, and started the day therefore in a deliberately apathetic mood. I wasn't the only apathetic one, however; our carriage held two rows of dumb jogging creatures, with their heads buried in newspapers. No one bothered to look out of the window, and I was the only one who cleared a little patch on the steamy pane, and peered out as we got to the suburbs. Bomb craters were fairly frequent among the houses by the line. First there were broken windows, some filled in with cardboard, and then a smashed roof or wall, or a whole house demolished. It was somehow or other a neutral unemotion-inspiring sight. At Paddington the glass roof was full of holes, and coming out into the street we at once saw several large gaps where houses had once been, like those left when teeth are pulled out. To the dentist in Langham Place. The BBC and the Langham Hotel were fairly badly damaged, but the effect was not very different from building operations in peace-time – mess, and workmen shovelling earth between hoardings. The BBC has been painted a hideous dung colour, and the church and the Langham Hotel each sported a large Union Jack, with an effect that was both pathetic and ludicrous. On the way to the Ivy to meet Clive we noticed that St Anne's, Soho, had a bomb right through the body, though the spire was still standing.

The Ivy was full of prosperous-looking people as usual, all eating a whacking good meal, meat, plovers and delicious creamy pudding. Raymond told us he had resigned from the Ministry of Information and gone back to the *New Statesman*. He didn't seem at all well and was in his most *distrait* London mood, talking feverishly about new French books as if his life depended upon it.

Boris met us at the Great Western Hotel. (Maroussa had been too nervous to come in to central London.) He told us a bomb had wrecked their Hampstead studio, breaking all the windows and blowing in the doors. When Maroussa shouted 'Are you all right, Boris?' he found he couldn't answer. The studio table was on top of him, pressing his chest. So poor Maroussa started running towards him, but the trap-door in the floor where Boris keeps his cartoons had blown open, and she fell in and cut her legs on broken glass.

In one way this glimpse of bombed London was reassuring, and even more so was the sight of untouched farmland in between peaceful villages. Then the gap made by each bomb is curiously narrow, so that the neighbouring houses may be quite undamaged save for broken glass. A clean slice is often made through a block, leaving perhaps a whole lift-shaft and wall untouched next to a heap of rubble. London certainly doesn't seem reeling from the blows she has received. Then presumably nor is Hamburg, Cologne or Berlin. In fact there may be no limit to what towns and their inhabitants can stand, if they can dig themselves into warrens underground. In a strange way this is far from consoling. It looks as if the war couldn't be won by bombing, and if not by bombing, by what?

Tonight the sky was bright with stars and throbbing with aeroplane engines, and there were fairly frequent sounds of bombs and gunfire very far away, like a giant dog settling down in its basket. R. went out to look, and saw a German plane go over, caught in a searchlight. I often notice with surprise a pin-point desire for a really loud bang, or to hear the church bells ringing – for some sort of *finality* in fact.

February 24th

R., Burgo, Joan and I set off in the car for Devon, where we are taking over R.'s old family home for a short stay. Up came old Hinton, gardener to three generations of Partridges, a splendid old fellow of over eighty, and gave us a warm welcome. The house has a peculiar flavour of Anglo-Indian Victorianism, but the books look inviting – beside Pope, Sterne and Trollope there are a lot of Memoirs and History. R. passed of course into a world of nostalgic memories, where he was partly inaccessible.

February 25th

Though we were woken by a very loud explosion last night, and understand there have been quite a lot of raids, I don't think the war will figure much in conversation here. To the Warren beach – a sandy spit of land half closing the estuary of the Exe. I lay on the sand in a daze, while R. and Burgo were digging castles like fiends in hell at the very edge of the sea. Behind me some soldiers were making some mysterious defences out of barbed wire, and cracking feeble jokes as they trooped sheepishly to and fro: 'Come *on*, Bill, what d'you think you're doing? Playing at sand pies in the garden?' Peace in front of me, war behind, and overhead they were indistinguishable – there seemed so little difference between the Hurricanes and the seagulls swooping in the blue sky. If anything the seagulls seemed poor imitations of the Hurricanes.

These famous defences of our island fortress appeared pitifully unconvincing, and a poor fight we should put up 'on the Beaches' by the look of the few rolls of barbed wire red with rust, which anyone could easily get through with a pair of nail scissors. Where the waves had flattened them they could be stepped over with the greatest of ease.

March 2nd

Walked up the hill to see R.'s land, which is let out to a violet-grower. Hinton says they are 'some of the earliest fields in England'. The gnarled trunks of fruit-trees rose out of the rich red Devon soil, or from fields of daffodils just about to flower; the air was warm and sweet and the sea shone blue beneath us. As for the violets, they were just out and their scent was intoxicating. I ordered a large box to be sent to M.A.M., who is ill in hospital, I'm afraid seriously.

Sirens and All Clear tonight, over and over again *ad nauseam*, as well as the steady zoom of German bombers, a rush of low-flying ones, and the crack-crack of machine-guns. Something that is wholly delightful and even comic is the stealthy passage of the Cornish Riviera Express when an alert is on, as if it were going on tip-toe.

March 3rd

The All Clear was the first sound I heard this morning, later on the voices of the cottagers discussing last night's raids at their front doors. Hinton told us that Teignmouth, a harmless seaside resort, had been bombed, and five people killed.

We agree that we are curiously happy here. Though R. generally refers to his two sisters as Goneril and Regan, I think he is pleased that the old family friends, aunts and cousins have received us all so warmly. One of these, a charming grey-haired woman, asked me 'what R. thought of all this awful business', and later, in front of her warlike little old mother, said boldly: 'I think we ought to get together and make peace *now*. Of course I wouldn't say that in a bus, but one must say what one thinks *sometimes*' – surprising in what is an entirely conventional world.

Took the steam ferry-boat to Exmouth. We had looked at its façade for a long time from a distance, like the back drop on a stage: now it was intimate and close. But how sad an impression it made, once we were on shore. The tall late-Victorian hotels stared blankly out to sea with their plate-glass eyes. Inside one could see white-haired old people, silently lunching off long white tablecloths, with tin dish-covers set before them. R. and I left Joan and Burgo on the beach and walked into the town. Here the inhabitants looked even more venerable, walking painfully with crutches or pushed in bath chairs. When we reached the shopping centre the secret of Exmouth's gloom became plain, like some horrid festering wound. The whole centre of the town had been bombed. Large piles of rubble, twisted iron and debris gave it a terribly sad look, and there were broken windows everywhere. On a shutter someone had written: 'We are still alive in spite of Hitler.' Little Exmouth was a sorrier sight than London, perhaps because it had had no limelight and compensatory glory. Then, out of a pearly grey sky, came a squadron of aeroplanes, flying very high indeed with a menacing hum like a swarm of bees. And an old lady with a long white horse-face waved her stick as she stood on the sea front, and cried: 'There they go! Off to drop bombs in France! We don't want any of the other sort here – we've had enough of them.'

March 13th

Two sirens tonight, quantities of aeroplanes, a rattle of gunfire. And I was horrified to realize that we were sitting over our nice warm fire, listening quite calmly to this sound – which was after all the noise of human beings trying to kill other human beings.

March 16th

Departure day. We piled the car with cockle-shells for our hens, Burgo's favourite stones and shells, gas-masks, provisions and baggage. Hinton came to see us off, bringing a bunch of Devon violets for me; I saw tears in his eyes as he shook hands with R., and they were certainly in mine. We got to Ham Spray by tea-time, and couldn't have had a more glorious day to arrive on. The afternoon stayed golden and mellow until quite late, some daffodils were out, the garden full of vegetables, and quantities of eggs put down in waterglass. But the cats were huffy and refused to forgive us for our absence.

Oh what a pleasure to sleep in the same bed with R., and in spite of the delights of Devon to be back at darling Ham Spray again.

March 18th

Ernest Bevin has announced that he proposes to call up various sections of the population for war work – girls of 20–21, which includes Joan, have to register next month, and men of 41–45, which just doesn't include R. also. So we're back in the war again, and must listen to the wireless and decide whether to be optimistic or gloomy. Most people seem to feel we are beating Hitler because of our successes against the Italians, whereas the enormous German army hasn't even been engaged for the last nine months.

In Hungerford we ran into Julia and Lawrence, and went back with them to Chilton. They told us a bomb fell on Froxfield while we were away. Julia says the crash was deafening and shook the house like a terrier shaking a rat. She bounced out of her chair shouting 'BUGGER!' very loud and very angrily. Lawrence's behaviour was rather odd. He looked at her in amazement and said, 'Julia, what on earth's the matter with you?' She saw from his expression (and he admitted it afterwards) that he was pretending for the moment that nothing had happened.

Burgo and I walked across the fields to the cobbler who lives at the foot of the Downs. While Burgo played around the stump of a hollow tree, I sat absorbing the scene, and thinking my own thoughts about these days which slip so quietly by, as if disregarding the war. How little, except for the much simpler life we lead, it affects us at the moment. Or so I sometimes feel; at others, that it has thrown out couch-grass roots to undermine our peace of mind, invisibly creeping and choking the sources of vitality and enjoyment. We live in the present, as if each day might be our last, and to some degree in the past. The future is so nebulous that one barely thinks about it, and those who die, like Ray and M.A.M.[1] seem to have forfeited nothing we have ourselves. Late tonight I thought again about invasion, not in the abstract but as a solid possibility. Such thoughts come in flashes, lighting up the inside of one's head (where all sorts of fears crouch) with an acetylene flare, and then disappear so completely that it's impossible to remember the feel of them.

March 29th

Hills for the weekend. Poor Heywood looked thin and drawn, his clothes hanging round him. His father has spent a lot of money on buying them a shelter and having it set up in the basement of their London house, so they feel they must sometimes sleep there, to justify the expense.

Heywood and I walked up to the foot of the Downs and sat in the chalkpit. He talked movingly about his horror of the war and dread of raids, his own uncertain position about call-up. He says Anne is much braver than him, and he envies her self-control.

F.: 'Do you manage to sleep when you spend the night in London?'

H.: 'Well no; I simply lie and listen to the aeroplanes all the time.' His misery touched me very much, and it seemed completely rational.

Conversation after dinner about War and Peace. Heywood was almost silent. Anne is an ex-pacifist, who thinks, bad as war is, Fascism is worse. News on the wireless of what really sounds like a naval victory. As we heard the announcement describing the sinking of several Italian ships, all our faces lit up, as with pleasure

[1] She had just died after an operation.

or excitement. Yet what an appalling thought – those huge iron masses disintegrating and exploding, and hurling hundreds of Italians into the sea. It happened so quickly that one ship simply ceased to exist in a single burst of flame, hit by fifteen shells simultaneously. 'Not a pretty sight,' said the Admiral commentator.

A tremendous discussion with R. about what should be the limitations preventing one voicing views one believes to be true – *à propos* of Bertie Russell. R. thinks that Bertie should not (as a pacifist who has recanted after fleeing from the war to the security of the USA) tell all of us who are still 'in' it that he finds war less terrible than he expected, and has therefore decided we must go on with it. We fined down his objection (R.'s) to 'bad form'. I defended both B.R.'s right to change his opinion, and to state it to anyone anywhere, both of which I vehemently believe in.

April 3rd

Opening *The Times* this morning I read with astonishment: 'We regret to announce that the death of Mrs Virginia Woolf, missing since last Friday, must now be presumed.' From the discreet notice that followed it seems that she is presumed to have drowned herself in the river near Rodmell. An attack of her recurring madness I suppose; the thought of self-destruction is terrible, dramatic and pathetic, and yet (because it is the product of the human will) has an Aristotelian inevitability about it, making it very different from all the other sudden deaths we have to contemplate.

April 8th

Sat out on the verandah, trying to write to Clive in answer to his letter about Virginia's death. He says: 'For some days, of course, we hoped against hope that she had wandered crazily away and might be discovered in a barn or a village shop. But by now all hope is abandoned ... It became evident some weeks ago that she was in for another of those long agonizing breakdowns of which she has had several already. The prospect – two years insanity, then to wake up to the sort of world which two years of war will have made, was such that I can't feel sure that she was unwise. Leonard, as you may suppose, is very calm and sensible. Vanessa is, apparently at least, less affected than Duncan, Quentin[1] and I had looked for and feared. I dreaded some such physical collapse as befell her after Julian was killed. For the rest of us the loss is appalling, but like all unhappiness that comes of "missing", I suspect we shall realize it only bit by bit.'

April 12th

Spring began suddenly this morning. R. and Burgo went out to hunt for plovers' eggs, and I wandered out later to join them. The warm air softly embraced me as I walked; this and the trees bursting with purple-brown buds combined together to thaw the frozen corners of my brain.

'Ah, here's the spring!' and then along comes Hitler's spring offensive, and a house built of the flimsiest cards, and not even believed in, comes toppling down. Yet I feel both more detached and more fatalistic than I did last year. Indeed no time has been harder to bear, it seems to me, than the Norwegian campaign. I contrive to live much more within our magic Ham Spray circle, R., Burgo, me, the

---

[1] The son of Clive and Vanessa Bell.

cats, the garden. Yet there lies beneath my pleasure in all that – and it *is* real pleasure – an implicit acceptance of the fact that we probably possess it all only for a little time, that it is a life with no future, that we are sailing along in a boat which has a hole in the bottom.

Wrote letters, sitting on the verandah most of the morning – the sky perfectly blue: peace visible, tangible and audible; the cows lying down in the field; Burgo and R.'s voices by the bonfire under the glossy leaves of the Portuguese laurel, the bees buzzing in the grape hyacinths; far off the hum of a tractor. No aeroplanes. Positive happiness invaded me, and though I know that it is achieved at the cost of ostrichism I cling to it and do not want to lose it. I suppose if I held beliefs of an idealistic sort about the perfectability of man and the innate goodness of the Universe it would be different. As I don't, this actual, momentary, individual happiness is the best I hope for. The processes of nature go on regardless of war and cataclysm; their resources against their own cataclysms of storm and frost seem boundless. Where has that principle got to in the case of human beings, who are, after all, a part of nature?

April 26th

Yesterday Angelica and Clive[1] arrived on a three days' visit. R. and I had both felt anxious about Angelica, whom we barely knew, but she arrived wearing a charming and friendly expression, and struggling with a small Victorian hat, which the wind was trying to blow off her head. Her face is strikingly lovely, with great grey eyes and bistre-coloured skin, and her figure beautiful and distinguished. We are already delighted with our visitors. The weather is fiendishly cold, yet they entertain themselves and us too. In a sunny half-hour I had a talk to Angelica about books and writing, as we sat on the verandah. Then she came in when I was playing the piano, and I got her to sing to my accompaniments. In the evening she brought out a patchwork quilt, which put mine and Billa's to shame: hers was a work of art, she had put so much thought into it and produced such delicate combinations of pattern and colour. What a delightful and gifted creature she is! R. and I agree that she and Clive are our nicest visitors for ages. They have brought a strong whiff of Charleston's civilisation, with its aesthetic projects and ceaseless activity.

April 28th

Early departure of the Bells. Just before four o'clock Janetta rang up to say she was at Hungerford Station. Humphrey is in camp as a private soldier, and 'it is horrible trying to live alone'. Rollo may join her here, as he has leave. We were overjoyed at seeing her again. She told us about the big Wednesday air-raid. She was dining with Ivan Moffat in Fitzroy Square. When the raid began, Eve Kirk, who is an efficient air-raid warden, put on her tin hat and went off, and Ivan Moffat went on the roof to fire-watch. Cecil Beaton stood at the window exclaiming: 'It's *too* fascinating, *too* extraordinary.'

Rollo arrived for dinner in his Pilot Officer's uniform. He looks bigger and stronger, and there's a peculiar sweetness in his expression. Janetta blossomed in

---

[1] Bell. Married to Vanessa, Angelica's mother but her father was Duncan Grant with whom Vanessa subsequently lived at Charleston.

his company and talked about her marriage, which to her 'was an unimportant ceremony and will remain so until I want a divorce'.

Tonight we had a conversation about the war. Rollo believes, in a *simpliste* youthful way, in 'greater organization as a means to greater freedom'. He thinks the Nazi regime comes as near this as anything else. I was just wondering if he would follow this to its logical conclusion by thinking the war not worth fighting, when he said so himself. Indeed his position is an unusual one. He is fascinated by flying and by the glamour of danger, and excited by his own position as a fighter pilot and the world's reaction to it; but he thinks the war a mad one which should never have been begun. Not sure whether he is a Communist or a Nazi, he is unusually clear-headed in seeing their resemblance. Janetta feels the war must be won, to protect the intellectuals for one thing. We all, including Rollo, asked her if she was sure the price was not too much to pay, and she disliked being put between these nutcrackers, and said the war might not – or she hoped it might not – involve great slaughter.

Bunny writes that Angelica was delighted with Ham Spray and its inhabitants. 'Why didn't you tell me what enormous charm Ralph has?' she said. 'I told her it was better to find out such things for oneself,' says Bunny.

May 11th

When Joan brought in the green tea this evening after dinner, she gasped and said, 'Mrs Partridge, I want to leave and do war work, as Tim's being sent abroad.' I went with her into the kitchen, where she told me that he was going in about three weeks' time, and she felt she couldn't bear it unless she was hard at work all day, so she had been to an aeroplane factory in Newbury to see if they would take her on. I didn't know how to show her how sorry I was without upsetting her more, her white face and breathless voice were so pitiful. I came back to the sitting-room so struck by Joan's tragedy that I felt on the verge of tears, and neither R. nor I could read or think of anything else for some time. Here was something absolutely good (Joan's relation with Tim) and it has been struck, and is crumbling away so rapidly that she has to try and drown her misery in the rumble and crash of machinery. And of course it is the happiness of not one but hundreds of Joans and hundreds of Gunner Robinsons, thousands, millions I should say – of all nationalities – that is to be sacrificed in this awful pandemonium. R. went to talk to her. We were both too upset to read.

May 29th

To Raymond's cottage for the weekend, driving through green luscious fields, saturated with rain and thick with buttercups.

Found Raymond alone in the sitting-room, which was overflowing as usual with books, pictures, spectacles, china knick-knacks and medicines. Beyond the tiny green lawn the even darker green river slid silently and rapidly past, and beyond that again was the dense jungle of Magpie Island. This Thames backwater seems further from the war than anywhere we have yet been, with its heavy silence except for the birds singing in the trees, and its moist warm riverside atmosphere. Eardley came back in the evening. Raymond told us he was terribly crushed by the death of Frank Coombs in an air-raid, and this was apparent in his face.

Delicious supper, asparagus, wine, chocolates. Talked till nearly one.

May 30th

Came down to find a log fire burning. At breakfast a refreshingly unwarlike conversation about painting.

The sun came out early, and turned everything dazzling blue, yellow and green. Raymond and Eardley brought out a carpet from a friend's bombed flat; we spread it out at the top of the garden, measured, cut and swept it, in bursts of practicality interspersed with long lazy pauses, when we sat on it in the sun and conversed.

The papers brought the news that clothes are to be rationed from now on. I was impressed by Raymond taking it so philosophically, and setting aside with no sign of a pang his passion for buying ties, shirts and 'woollies'.

We drifted off in the punt round Magpie Island. Again the amazing peace, no sound but the water lapping against the sides and a bird orchestra from the trees. It was such an old-fashioned sensation gliding through the opaque water with tangled weeds trailing from the banks, that I wasn't at all surprised to hear a distant voice singing, 'Oh you beautiful doll – you great big beautiful doll!' Home to a dream of a lunch – lampreys in a marvellous sauce, foie gras and champagne, and then we had to say goodbye and go to fetch Alix and James from Lord's Wood. In spite of the summery heat, James had on two or three waistcoats and Alix a felt hat with ear-flaps to keep out the draught. Ham Spray garden, when we reached it, was bathed in beautiful sunlight, and Burgo had arranged a row of deck-chairs for us facing the Downs.

In our evening conversation Alix reaffirmed her support of the war, 'as I have decided Hitlerism is worse than war'. Yet she is enormously impressed by the formidableness of Hitler, and not entirely in a hostile way, in fact I am inclined to think she holds the most Nazi views I have come across.

[Talking about Alix and James Strachey, of whom he was deeply fond, Ralph told me that Alix had been the active one in the courtship which ended in their marriage, and that the sight of her determined pursuit and ultimate success in face of all obstacles had convinced him that in love all things are possible. I tended for a while to envisage her as *Vénus toute entière, à sa proie attachée*. Certain it was that everyone spoke of 'Alix and James' rather than 'James and Alix' (as is more usual), and yet in a subtle and unobtrusive way James was the dominant member of that extraordinarily devoted couple by the time I got to know them in the twenties. Ralph and I started our joint life under their wing at 41 Gordon Square; it was they who made our elopement possible, and ever since – until their dying days – I felt for them both warm love and the strongest admiration and respect, based on the lucky chance of getting to know them at such close quarters. With their detachment, their integrity, truthfulness, perfect manners and saving streak of eccentricity and hilarious comedy, they seemed to exude a concentrated aroma of Bloomsbury, without occupying a central position in it.

Physically James had something of Lytton's spidery elegance as well as long thin arms and legs. His hair, however, unlike Lytton's, turned early to a beautiful shining silver and his face was small and round. His speaking voice revealed his intense musicality, though at moments of emotion he would turn a vivid pink and be overcome with total inarticulacy. This I saw happen to my dismay when in a reckless moment I made some criticism of Freud's theory of the Id, Ego and

Superego; and in very different circumstances – when Lytton was dying – this speechlessness in emotion became a painful straitjacket, and in a stifled voice he told Ralph how greatly he envied him his ease in expressing what he felt.

Alix, very handsome, lean, big-boned, with level grey eyes and a thick thatch of dark brown hair, appeared often to be trying to solve the problems set her by life as if they were sums in arithmetic. She was the first to see how ludicrous were some of the answers but she stuck to her guns nonetheless. For instance, when the hall porter of the Savoy tried to refuse her admittance on the grounds that the severe black silk Chinese coat she was wearing 'was not evening dress', she set herself to prove to him logically that it was; and won.]

June 3rd

James's charm is irresistible, and I would like to show him the warmth of my feelings towards him in some way, but how to do so is the question, for he appears to live in an enclosed world of his own. Alix grows more absorbed in the eccentric details of her life, her various dodges to protect herself from cold and discomfort, midget efforts towards luxury – like eating lots of mustard because it's very expensive just now. She fills her days with journeys to change her library book, or buy some trifling object, in fact lives much like any old lady ending her days at Torquay. Yet in spite of all, her formidable intellectual character rises like a rock out of the welter of these slightly pathetic activities.

Julia and Lawrence to lunch. The sun came through the mist and we sat and lay on the lawn, bemused by its sudden heat. Julia lay with closed eyes under a green sunshade; Lawrence pulled his chair between R. and James, who were talking about hieroglyphics. The insect world was another topic, and someone said that a wasp, when it sees a fellow wasp is short of food, will bite the tail off and give it to its head to eat. This is supposed to show the superiority of humans, but Alix said she thought it showed quite the reverse – the superior intelligence of insects.

Every evening Alix draws up a stool to the fire and launches some theory or other, crouched there like a witch. James, in his armchair, hardly looks up from studying his hieroglyphics through a magnifying-glass, so it is generally left to R. or me to take the other side. Tonight it was standardization versus individualism. Alix is delighted, highly eccentric individual though she is, at the increase of standardization, and is down on local customs, village shops, and variations in cooking. Her dream is a world of chain stores, where every town in England cooks fish in the way a board of experts has decided to be the best; a world of tins, cafeterias and efficient bus services. She sees no point in variety or change, and holds that there is no sight more debased than a housewife going off to shop with a list and a string bag. Oddly enough the housewife coming back from the lending library or cinema with her head full of fantasies seemed to her a nobler spectacle! Agriculture is a degrading activity, and we should have imported everything we wanted for the war right from the start, tinned it and buried it, thus leaving all available man-power free for the services and munition-making. In spite of our stupidity in *not* doing this she thinks we may well gain a crushing victory. James thought a compromise peace might be better. It was left to us Partridges to stand up for individualism, and say it might even revive after the war. It's strange what pleasure Alix gives by her faithfulness to her own character.

June 6th

Quentin joined our party today. He and Alix had a conversation about colonizing the blacks, Alix maintaining that there was much to be said for the French method of relentless hygiene, hypodermics and drugs, and also relentless interference with their more barbarous religions and customs; I expected to hear her say any minute; 'Of course I think it would *really* be better to exterminate the lot.'

When we listened to the news tonight James said in an agitated voice: 'Yes I think we've invaded Syria.' 'Why,' I said, 'there was no mention of Syria whatever.' 'Yes, that's just why I think so.' (Like Sherlock Holmes's dog in the night-time.)

June 7th

James looked excited at the breakfast table. 'I was quite right, you see. We have gone into Syria.' He spent the afternoon raking the ether for more news, but all he got was Cairo saying, 'Cheerio, BBC.'

Talking to Quentin about the war I told him how I envied him his passionate interest in it. He wouldn't have been born at any other time for anything, he finds it so enthralling. I tried to convey the sense of constant disgust I feel weighing on me whenever I think of it, and he looked at me in surprise and said: 'Oh I see, you are a *real* pacifist.' Why are people so loth to recognise the fact, I wonder. I find no difficulty in recognising their bellicosity.

Yesterday at lunch Quentin and Alix, who have many points of agreement, were saying that it was inconsistent for pacifists to pay their Income Tax, I said, 'Well, I think it's inconsistent of those who support the war in theory not to do so in practice. I don't understand why you, Alix, are not in a factory making submarines.' She turned slightly pink and said, 'Well, my line about that is that I shall be called upon when wanted.'

A few days ago the Japanese policeman arrived and told us that by order of the Government all domestic pigeons were to be executed. He didn't exactly know why, but it was something to do with invasion. So ours were killed and eaten in a pie, but one snow-white one managed to escape and now wheels about against the green landscape. We feel we can hardly bear to condemn it to death also.

June 18th

Somewhere in the middle of the night we were woken by crunching sounds on the gravel, and the engines of motor bicycles and lorries, also heavy steps and male voices. 'It must be the invasion,' was my first thought. Then, realizing it probably wasn't, I still felt that if it had been I should only have sunk back to sleep just as passionately. Later there was knocking on the doors. R. looked out and said, 'The Army is everywhere, lorry-loads of it.' By breakfast-time a sense of drama had possessed the house and its inmates. Our house was, in fact, no longer our own. Processions of soldiers drew water from the tap; others went to the lavatory or to telephone. In the kitchen were pleased, self-conscious faces.

The day became hot, the red poppies so big and bright you couldn't look at them. While I was planting snapdragons along the drive a Scotch army cook came up and said, 'Missus, could you sell me a few spring onions to give a taste to a stew?'

Burgo was mad with excitement. When he got back from school, he and I walked down the avenue; from end to end it was full of armoured cars – huge rhinoceros-like objects, striped and spotted like wild animals – drawn up between the tree trunks. In them and under them and beside them, in bunches and rows and heaps, lay strong, red-faced sweating young soldiers, mostly asleep in the attitudes of statues. I was struck by their look of health and toughness, sometimes of beauty, but their machines, I was just reflecting, were the ugliest things the human mind could conceive, when Burgo gasped out, '*Aren't* they lovely?' As we reached the gate we met Edie just turning into the avenue, flashing a crack at two sentries and walking with swinging skirts and a tossing head and sideways-darting eyes, looking very dashing and splendid, like a Spanish girl.

The Army left with only half the noise they made arriving. The invasion was over.

June 20th

To London for the day. This marvellously hot June weather made it seem like peacetime. The heat somehow dissolves the strained awareness of war, and I even caught myself joining up the gaps left by bombs with my mind's eye. Sometimes I even saw beauty in the sunlit devastation. Bought macaroni and parmesan in Soho, and then to my tailor, who appeared to have been blown up into a higher storey, each floor on his staircase revealing the outer air through yawning holes.

On to the Leicester Galleries to see Vanessa's pictures, and to lunch with Clive off cold salmon, asparagus and zabaglione. Clive said he spent last night at the Shy Bride's[1] house at Ascot, pillow-fighting in the garden with young Americans from the Embassy. H. G. Wells was there, and in a fervour of anti-Catholicism had bored everyone by insisting that we ought to bomb Rome, till at last one exasperated American burst out: 'Very well then, BUMB it!'

On the way to meet Boris and Maroussa for tea at the Café Anglais, I walked through Gerrard Street, moved by a sentimental impulse to look at the old book-shop,[2] but I could hardly recognise it. There must have been several bombs, some taking slices from the great tenement buildings backing onto Charing Cross Road, where the cascades of rubble reached so high it seemed impossible that dozens of people should not still be buried under them. Other bombs had penetrated a theatre, leaving a semicircle of broken seats going right up to the crazy, Chinese-looking roof. This staggering scene boomed through my head and out again, like a funeral bell.

Maroussa's nerve is still gone. She had not been as far as Leicester Square, even in daylight, since the Blitz started, and when I begged them to come to Ham Spray she said: 'What about the Invasion?' for that is her obsession at the moment. I could see she was in a state of permanent dread, her words often faltering in the middle of a sentence. She said: 'I cannot read now, I just sit and sit before the fire till my arm and my thigh is burnt brown by it.'

[There was absolutely nothing synthetic or imitative in Maroussa Volkova's very Russian character. Throwing my mind back to my first sight of her, I remember her at a party given by Boris and Helen when they were still married, in about 1926. Maroussa was quite young then, silent and shy, but beautiful in a very exotic

---

[1] Mary Baker, an American heiress.
[2] Birrell and Garnett, where I had worked for some years.

way. Ralph told me she was a distant relative of Boris's as well as his mistress, and had come over from Russia soon after the 1917 Revolution. She seemed like one of the hangers-on who move silently in the background of a Russian novel. We learned later that Boris almost always had two chief women in his life. Not long after this party Helen eloped with Roger Fry, and Boris and Maroussa set up together, dividing their time between two studios – one in the Boulevard Arago in Paris and the other in Hampstead. Maroussa helped with the mosaics. From the Thirties onwards they came often to Ham Spray, and were among the most welcome of our visitors.

Maroussa's appearance was glamorous and distinctly foreign. Neat in her dress and her movements, she was compact in body and mind, from her small head (with the dark hair drawn smoothly back, the dark eyes that seemed to have no whites and the colourless complexion like cream-laid writing-paper), down to her feet in trim high-heeled shoes. She reminded me of some oriental figurine of polished stone or marble. Her smile was an attractive little snarl, her laugh was husky and low. I am sure she was completely devoted to Boris despite his infidelities; he called her his 'consort', always treated her kindly in company, and was proud of her courage during their terrifying escape from Paris at the beginning of the last war. Afterwards her nerve went, very probably because their Hampstead studio was badly damaged in an air-raid.

The pungency of Maroussa's character came out in her very definite views. '*Noa*! *that* I *do* not like!' she would exclaim. She loved the cinema, and when we asked her what sort of films she preferred I remember her replying without hesitation: '*Sophisticated sintimiental, fascinating.*' And what foods did she prefer? 'Ah! I like such *raice* pudding, such *ryed* meat and such *ryed* wine.' Very occasionally, after some red wine maybe, she would become romantic and starry-eyed as she described pre-Revolution Russia, particularly evenings at the ballet or opera, with officers in gorgeous uniforms, and women in evening-dress and brilliant jewels. One instinctively guessed at an efficient brain behind Maroussa's quiet presence; she had a head for figures and for chess, but never joined in highbrow arguments and was intellectually modest. She had few friends in London – a few White Russians, Faith Henderson ('Faiff'). Ralph and I had the comfortable feeling that she was fond of us and that her fondness implied total acceptance.]

June 22nd

In the middle of another grilling morning, only distinguished from the others by a violent sirocco, Lawrence rang up and said, 'What do you think of the news?' 'What is it? We've not heard.' 'Oh, they've invaded Russia! – a tremendous attack all along the frontier. Poor little *things*!' His voice ended in a high squeak. I rushed to tell the others, feeling I was the bearer of good news. Perhaps I was, as presumably it means that our own turn is to be postponed for a little. R. was cock-a-hoop, as he has long foretold this and even had a bet with me about it. We speculated at intervals all day as to how long it would take the Germans to polish off Russia, and what would be the line of the Government, the *New Statesman* and the Communist Party.

June 23rd

It was some time after waking that I remembered with a start that Russia had been invaded. Last night Winston C. made one of his most brilliant speeches; it will fairly take the wind out of the sails of the *New Statesman* grousers.

These hot balmy transparent days make the time rattle through one's fingers like a fishing-line off a reel. Yet underneath, beating away monotonously, is the pulse with which one is aware of the war, and at this moment, of course, particularly of Russia.

Dora Morris and Eddy Sackville-West arrived to tea, stepping out of their car like two elegant Edwardians. Dora carried a Japanese parasol and wore a turban and pearls, Eddy was in a pale grey suit and floating tie. Tea under the ilex tree. When for some reason I asked Eddy if he ever went to the cinema, he answered with a pained expression: 'No, I never go – it's against my conscience to go to any form of entertainment now-a-days,' and though I would have loved to know how his conscience formulated such a principle I sheered off from embarrassment.

[Eddy Sackville-West, later Lord Sackville, was not exactly a clever man in the sense that his brain was a powerfully functioning organ, nor do I think it would have seemed so if his prejudices had disappeared and given it free rein; moreover he positively disliked argument or even discussion. I often thought that he cherished the illusion that all his friends thought as he did, and that the questions that came up when Wynne Godley was so shocked by his views had been settled once and for all long ago. Rather was he an artist and a scholar, whose special charm and originality lay in his imagination and invention. His humour was a delight, though these are pompous words with which to pin down his exotic butterfly nature. From childhood he had been delicate, suffering from bouts of asthma and being to some degree a 'bleeder'. When I first met him I was surprised to see him take out a little green bottle labelled 'smelling-salts'. Yet though his physical frame was slight he had iron strength in his fragile-looking limbs. Apparently in his youth he was an expert and fearless skier; he drove his car and even played the piano with the same determination and muscular strength.

Before he moved to Long House he lived in a Gothic tower in his family's great house Knole, and here Ralph and I several times visited him. He was surrounded by books, gramophone records and bibelots which he loved to collect. The piano had been his passion at Eton, and I believe he thought of making it his career. He seldom played in the Crichel days, but when he did I have to confess that I found his touch too steely for it to give me much pleasure, although he had such a great understanding of music; and his criticisms were brilliant, amusing and beautifully written, as were those of literature, backed by wide reading in several languages. He also published novels and a biography of de Quincey.

I once saw a photograph of Eddy as a marvellously aristocratic baby in his pram, and it struck me that the face looking out from the huge pleated bonnet had scarcely changed in forty years or more: there was the same fine rounded forehead, slightly tip-tilted nose and large sad eyes wearing a look of pained disapproval.

Later he became a Roman Catholic and bought a second house in Ireland. I do not think his religion solved the problem of his underlying unhappiness, which one could not help being aware of. Perhaps this was partly due to the fact that he tended to fall in love with people he disliked and disapproved of, as he once told me. But I shall close this portrait of him by remembering his gloriously wild shriek of laughter when amused.]

June 25th

R. had a letter from Gerald, describing a visit from his father and new step-mother and then going on to the war: 'Every German woman and child killed is a contribution to the future safety and happiness of Europe, for the worst thing about the Germans is the fact that there are 75 millions of them. When we have won the war the licensed days of taking human life will be over and we shall have to treat them as our friends. Today, death to every German. This will shock you. I see your pained clergyman's expression.' There follows, taking himself I dare say as much by surprise as it did us, a violent attack on us pacifists. 'Those I know seem to me people who for some reason or other are bad at arithmetic. They can't add up even simple sums. Poor creatures, I think, and when I see that they feel sad because they are cut off by their beliefs from other people, that it is often a strain to be natural and at ease, I feel sorrier than ever. And then – this is bound to happen in the end – my curiosity makes me write a letter which is likely to annoy them.' *The old humbug*! What a cheek he has!

June 28th

During the afternoon Isobel arrived from Oxford, also Barbara [Bagenal] and Saxon. Isobel is now a Government servant, translating from Spanish and Portuguese at Blenheim. She is like the *cigale ayant chanté*, she has spent all her dress coupons on frivolous useless things like a white cotton plus-four suit, covered in West Indian emblems. Barbara has brought with her (for health reasons I understand) a Bulgarian fungus, looking like a cauliflower, in a pot; it has to be fed with milk to keep it alive, and she came into the kitchen to ask for its afternoon drink. I looked at it with aversion, and thought I saw waving tentacles. Saxon sits under a tree in his white silk suit, fast asleep, with a volume of Horace on his knee.

[Barbara Hiles was a student at the Slade with Carrington, Dorothy Brett and others, one of those whom Virginia Woolf nicknamed 'the Cropheads'. In her youth she was extremely pretty, with her heart-shaped face, large blue eyes and curly dark-brown hair. Her high spirits and liveliness were much in evidence at Bloomsbury parties of the Twenties and Thirties, where she was often to be seen after most of the rest had gone home, tirelessly leaping up and down to the music like a mayfly. Among her admirers were Maynard Keynes, David Garnett and the man she married, Nicholas Bagenal, but the best known – because his devotion was lifelong though unrequited – was Saxon Sydney-Turner. I think she found his endless letters, even the boxes of chocolate and presents for the children, something of a burden, and at the time we thought her ungrateful, but when she took me to visit him in the old folks' home where he ended his days I remember being struck by her good-nature and patience with him. In middle age her marriage broke down, and she must have been over sixty when to most of their friends' astonishment she took up with Clive. 'An excellent arrangement,' as I have said, because with him her life became much more eventful, including quite a lot of foreign travel and meetings with such of his circle as Graham Sutherland, Kenneth Clark and Picasso. While in her turn she looked after him like a kind nanny.

'Barbara is too nice to mind being left out of the conversation,' he used to say, but I have forgotten who it was who remarked 'the thing is, Barbara *maids* him'.]

July 9th

The heat all day was oppressive and frightening, and we hourly expect it to burst in thunder. Watered the garden again after dinner; the moon, a great circle of sour cream against the grey sky, looked menacing but did not as formerly call up the idea of air-raids – for we have had complete immunity from all night sounds, sirens and evening aeroplanes ever since the Russian campaign began. Nor have there been raids in other parts of the country. Even the food aspect of the war has temporarily faded before the groaning plenty of our kitchen garden, from which beans and strawberries now come in profusion. R. and I have done all the fruit and vegetable bottling ourselves, and thirty bottles make a handsome row on the larder shelf. I wake early, thinking of jam and bottles, and this practical life makes me happy in a new sort of way. We occupy our minds building a solid fortress-like existence to withstand the batterings of war, but I wonder if in doing so we are getting more self-centred and losing our power to be interested in other people.

August 5th

A disrupted and chaotic day. Lawrence came for a last go at my portrait, but I think we are to buy another picture instead. R. was charging about the country to arrange for our beehives to be stripped of their honey.

When I put some jazz on the gramophone for a change, R. said, 'It's very soothing and emollient – probably because it makes nonsense of everything, even the war and the poor old Russians at Smolensk.'

I had written to Clive telling him that three people had told me he was no longer a pacifist, but 'perhaps there was no meaning in the word at present'. He agreed and then makes the following declaration of faith: 'If Hitler proposes peace this autumn I am all for accepting . . . I infinitely preferred the uncomfortable conditions of 1938 to the intolerable conditions of 1941. I would prefer to pay my taxes with a roof over my head and both legs on. I am quite sure, whatever happens, war will never make the world a pleasanter place to live in.'

August 24th

Three days ago we came by train to Haverfordwest, and thence to a farmhouse three miles from Solva.

All responsibility for house and food magically gone; huge meals are set before us, with home-cured bacon, eggs and plenty of butter. There is *no war* here. We have not seen a single newspaper since we came, and all we can hear of the wireless is in snatches through the kitchen door. This evening a familiar sing-song, though wordless, showed that Winston was making a speech. I opened the door and listened for a bit, but was shocked by the futility, hollowness and unreality of the ideas he was expressing, shown up as they were by the amazing beauty of the natural surroundings we have lived among in these last three days, and which I was consciously aware of on the other side of the thin walls boxing in his voice – the fields rolling right to the edge of savage cliffs, promontories covered with heather and tufted plants, white farms among clusters of nearly black trees, streams tinkling between a jungle of wild flowers, buzzards and seagulls overhead instead of aeroplanes. The only sign of war is a cluster of barrage-balloons over Milford Haven – which, as we came home from a picnic, were shining a dazzling silver, like holes in the sky letting light through from behind.

August 26th

Bathed at Solva, and ate our picnic on a stony beach. Fat mothers and evacuee children had spread their towels on the rocks and exposed their dimpled knees and the varicose veins on their legs, while their voices droned monotonously on about knitting and rationing and babies.

This evening we heard a series of soft thuds and aeroplane engines, and peering through the blackout I saw the shafts of searchlights sweeping across the sky; soon afterwards great flashes splashed upwards, which I knew must be falling bombs, but all to the accompaniment of gentle noises like the patting of kitten's paws, and the ever-crossing, weaving pattern of the searchlights. Then streams of giant copper-coloured sparks rose into the night sky, like sparks from a monstrous bonfire. 'They've hit something,' I thought, watching what looked like a firework display.

September 3rd

Three glorious days, sun-bathing and going naked into the cold sea. We have several times seen those extraordinary orange-legged birds, choughs, here. On our last day R. said: 'I have a sort of feeling that I shall see that seal again. It was on a day just like this that I saw him twenty years ago.' And almost as he finished speaking, like a good omen, up there rose a round gleaming head in the middle of the bay – the seal himself!

September 17th

Leningrad has not fallen though every day I go to the wireless I expect to hear the news of it. Neither has Kiev nor Odessa, and the Russian winter is supposed to begin a month from now.

R. said later: 'What animal lives we lead.' F.: 'Yes, perhaps it's time we tried to pull up our mental socks and do a little thinking.' R.: 'That's the worst of war. One doesn't *want* to do any thinking.'

Yesterday on the way to Biddesden[1] we saw Italian prisoners at work on the harvest at the top of Tidcombe Hill. It was a glorious afternoon and from where they were there was a view over half Wiltshire. We caught a glimpse of handsome dark and youthful faces, and extravagant rows of white teeth, as they smiled and waved to us. Each had a crimson disc sewn on his back and an armed soldier was watching them. As we were describing them to the Guinnesses at tea, Michael MacCarthy screwed up his face and said, 'Don't let's be *sentimental* about the Italian prisoners,' which in fact I don't think we were being. They seemed to have no connection with the war, that was one thing that gave our spirits a lift. We talk a good deal about the futility of worry. Well, all I can say is if one can't stop worrying one must just endure it, futile and also exhausting though it is. Anyway, time goes on passing inevitably, and will in the end carry one into the grave where worrying stops.

[1] Bryan Guinness's house.

September 26th

It seems ages since we got back from Wales, and I wrote about worry. Equanimity has returned, even happiness. Ham Spray is a cornucopia from which flow fruit, vegetables and dahlias. Drove round with presents of plums, including thirty pounds to the old Padels. Alas Mrs Padel feels she must give up the 'school' and wants me to teach Burgo myself. That I would gladly do, but I want the company of other children for him. That a mother should teach her own child is one of Mrs Padel's blind beliefs; she is against schools, meat-eating, Mrs Molesworth and water-closets.

The Padels have been trying to persuade me to take up the violin again, and though I could never have dreamed of the possibility without their instigation, I feel very tempted – but sheepish. Mr Padel swears I could play chamber music in six months. What a thought!

September 30th

Another stinker from Gerald to Ralph this morning – the result no doubt of Julia's having told him that we thought he no longer wanted to see us. And I must say he has fairly riled me just as of course he wanted to. He begins by saying condescendingly that of course he is still fond of us. 'It's not pacifism I dislike ... but your particular brand of calling yourself a pacifist and at the same time sympathising with the aggressor rather than with the attacked[1] is very disagreeable to me ... I think your ideas need sorting. We are none of us rational people, but when we fail to give a certain colour of plausibility and reason to our ideas we find we lose contact with other people and isolate ourselves. You would feel better if you had some work to do. And if you served a turn as fireman or ARP warden you would feel better still ... However you can be certain that I am not going to quarrel with you or take against you over your opinions ... indeed I don't regard them as deliberate opinions at all but just as fragments of lava thrown out by your volcano. We all have volcanoes, we are all liable to eruption. This war is a strain on everyone and whilst it lasts life is a perpetual struggle for calm and sanity. Nothing therefore I say here is said *de haut en bas* ... If you have strong feelings about people who resist aggression, remember that I have equally strong opinions about the pacifist-isolationists, who I consider by their short-sightedness and folly have helped to produce this war.'

What right has Gerald to send us, unprovoked, these prosy lectures? Since his first letter we have done our best to ignore it, continued to take them presents of fruit and vegetables, and got my brother Tom to offer him the very job at Oxford he has always wanted (which of course he refused), quite apart from the occasion some time ago when R. went to his rescue with the Marlborough police and Scotland Yard. Well, there's nothing to be done but keep away for the present, and hope – in vain, I fear – that he will somehow regret his behaviour. R. and I cannot help toying with various teasing replies, though we know full well that the only possible answer is silence. The truth is, however, that I for one shall miss their company, and resent being cut off from it. I also find it rather absurd that the only person to pillory us in any way for our pacifist views is Gerald, almost R.'s oldest friend. His reference to doing dangerous work is what amounts to a boast on

[1] Quite untrue.

Gerald's part, because of his celebrated London fortnight in the Blitz – and yet it's not like him to boast. Nor is there a trace of his old characteristic irony and self-depreciation in the whole letter.

October 3rd

Off on my bicycle to the Padels to consider the question of re-starting the violin,[1] for the seeds they sowed have taken root. Mr Padel was waiting for me, and handed me a violin with a sweet and mellow tone. His manner could not have been better designed to cure me of my sheepishness. I took it up and struck a few strange wobbling notes. Before I left we were playing exercises together.

October 8th

A foundation of melancholy underlies these days – Russia, Gerald, the sadness of autumn. In me it takes the form of subhuman apathy, in R. of irritability and saying: 'I don't like my fellow-men', the implication behind which is usually that one doesn't like oneself.

Italian prisoners are now working in the potato fields in Ham; Burgo and I walked to see them and listen to their soaring, trilling voices singing in Italian against a background of English mud and a grey sky. Three soldiers were guarding them. They had nothing against the prisoners except that they got more cigarettes than they did themselves.

Listened to the wireless all evening, well aware that the war is passing through one of the most acute crises it has yet produced. During the News I gradually became aware of a faint voice, speaking in far-off sepulchral tones like Hamlet's ghost: 'Tell us the TRUTH!' Then 'ROT!' it boomed out, and quite a lot more about the Jews and the Americans having 'sold us down the river'. When the news ended, the Voice made quite a long speech beginning rather mysteriously: 'Winston Churchill will never be Duke of Marlborough.' The English announcer then said primly: 'If you have been hearing interruptions, it is the enemy.' The 'enemy' – how fantastic it sounds! But the Voice gave us a great deal of pleasure, so strange a manifestation was it.

October 14th

To combat the anxiety produced by the Russian situation I forced myself to do mechanical tasks, like painting beehives and sweeping the verandah.

In to Hungerford, but there was no food to buy except salted cod, no offal. As we drove home talking about our cupboard of reserve tins, R. said: 'We'd better keep them for the invasion. I firmly believe there will be one,' in such a matter-of fact voice that the Hungerford–Ham road with its familiar ranks of telegraph poles looked all at once menacing and unreal. But I suppose I don't, at this moment anyway, believe in invasion.

Started reading Pepys this evening. Bad news on the wireless – 'A deterioration in the position of the Russian front.' This is the beginning of the end, I thought, and visualized us pathetic human beings like crabs trying to crawl out of the pot of boiling water that is about to finish them off. And then came the Voice again, distantly booming: 'Kick Churchill *out*! We want Revolution! Churchill must go-

---

[1] I had started learning at nine and dropped it at thirteen.

o-o!' And last of all: 'Britain is *doo*med! Britain is DOOMed! God save our King –
from the Jews!' This last word came out in a protracted hiss, and we were quite
cheered up by realizing that the Germans could be so imbecile as to imagine that
such remarks could have any effect.

October 23rd

This morning Burgo hurried in with the news that the rats had eaten a hole in the
passage carpet 'big enough to put your waist through'. True enough. They had
gnawed two very large holes in the floorboards and dragged the carpet through
them, presumably to make nests with.

The Germans have shot fifty Frenchmen in cold blood as a reprisal for the
shooting of two of their own officers. They say they will shoot fifty more unless
the man who killed the officers gives himself up. I was surprised when R. said in a
voice of great emotion: 'There's one thing too horrible to talk about – the shooting
of the fifty French hostages.' In the conversation that followed I understood that,
apart from everything else, he was entering into the state of mind of the German
soldiers who had to shoot these fifty innocent and irrelevant individuals, and that
this action performed completely in cold blood has a horror for the person made
to do it which distinguishes it sharply even from the action of a man who picks
off a sniper with his rifle in the heat of battle. R. has told me everything that
happened to him in the First War, with the greatest detail and vividness; but there
is one he cannot describe without his voice breaking; when he was the Captain
ordered to take a squad of men to shoot one of our deserters, and had to give the
signal to fire. It's for this reason that the last act of *Tosca* is almost unbearable to
him, and by infection to me also.

November 3rd

To lunch with Julia and Lawrence to meet the Pritchetts, only for the second time
and liked them both enormously. V.S.P.[1] has been investigating the arrangements
for dealing with bombed Londoners, interviewing them and visiting the rest-
centres. All these centres are arranged to segregate men and women, but the candid
organizers admitted there was no question of keeping to this when the Blitz was
on. One said, 'I realized it was hopeless ever since a man came rushing in to the
women's part half mad and screaming for his sister. He had just seen his mother
killed before his eyes, and when he found his sister he got into bed with her there
and then and had sexual intercourse with her.' Pritchett said he was very much
struck by the organizers' genuine kindness and understanding, but it often didn't
go with great powers of organization. One woman blitzed her own house to get
compensation, but was detected because she couldn't bear to break her best tea-
set.

November 9th

Bunny and Dermod[2] to stay the weekend. Bunny seems like a man starved of
conversation, having had none for months. He often exclaims that he had forgotten such an existence as ours could continue. We did nothing but talk all day.

[1] Novelist, writer of short stories and literary critic.
[2] Younger of Desmond and Molly MacCarthy's two sons. He was a doctor, a children's specialist.

Richard [Garnett] has gone into the RAF rescue squad, who go out in little boats to save the lives of airmen brought down in the sea. Bunny frankly desires to keep his sons out of danger, yet he is behind the war effort in every other way. R. and I have discussed for hours whether it made it better or worse that, wanting the sons of others to risk their lives, you should try and put your own in safety. We disagreed – he thought it worse. At least I think I disagreed, but cannot quite decide. The primary fact is that wanting other people's sons to be killed to get the sort of life you want and believe desirable is horrible. Given this, I think it's better to be human about your own sons' danger than the reverse.

Julia and Lawrence to lunch. Bunny fixed on Julia the concentrated searchlight of his attention and admiration, and from the moment she came into the room had his head perpetually swivelled in her direction with a look of bursting delight on his face. When she had gone he seized a cushion and hugged it saying: 'Oh Julia, Julia, what a wonderful woman she is! I'd forgotten she existed.' Julia took his admiration very well, and so I must say did Lawrence.

Old Mrs Garnett is failing in health, and when Bunny was there last week she suddenly began talking complete gibberish in the middle of an interesting conversation about relations between Russia and China. He was alarmed and took her up to bed, and at the top of the stairs she suddenly recovered her speech and broke out into indignation, saying that really if she was to lose the faculty of speech as well as sight and strength it was a bit too much. I should think so indeed. Dermod says there's no doubt that the health of the nation has improved if anything since the war began.

Tonight Winston made a most confident speech, offering us no blood or tears whatever, but announcing that we have now achieved at least parity in numbers with the Luftwaffe. This was a great surprise, and it also really looks as if a deadlock was settling in in Russia. He rattled the sword very noisily in the direction of Japan. Should they declare war on the USA, he said, 'England would be in it within the hour.' Thunders of applause from the Mansion House or wherever the speech was made.

November 25th

Dragged myself out of sleep like a boot out of mud, for I was going to London for the day. I felt it a wrench leaving R. and Burgo even for so short a time. Yesterday had been R.'s 47th birthday, and Burgo was in an endearing state of excitement over this event, giving him a gold safety-pin and insisting on crackers and jelly for tea. ('I do want darling old Ralph to enjoy his birthday.')

In the train, three soldiers, all strangers to each other were eagerly discussing the Libyan campaign. A fourth figure, an elderly civil servant, said he had fought there in the last war, and 'The climate was the best I ever knew in my life.' A dark young soldier envisaged the possible taking of Moscow by the Germans. A Scotchman next to me with pale fanatical eyes thought this impossible. 'The B-rrr-eetish would never allow it.' I was much impressed by their friendliness and lack of barriers and desire to communicate.

Lunch with Clive at the Ivy. He was not in a very good mood. He now declared he's indifferent to everything except the loss of the civilized existence he has always enjoyed. He thought war-weariness in England was so great that when Hitler launched his Peace Offensive a large number would be in favour of accepting his terms. I'm afraid he's wrong there. He told me Adrian [Stephen][1] had been staying at Charleston. He has a job after his own heart, namely trying to frighten the shell-shocked heroes of Dunkirk by turning on machines which make the noises of a dive-bomber. If that doesn't work he repeats the process in utter darkness.

December 2nd

Most of the morning in the music-room writing my review of children's books. I felt very virtuous and cheerful when it was finished. Out with Burgo collecting food for the rabbits in a cold, soupy mist. They provide us with quite a lot of solid meat – it's a pity they really taste so disgusting whatever we do to them.

On turning on the news we received a blow. There has been a reverse of some sort in Libya. Then Winston outlined his proposals for getting greater man- and woman-power for the War Effort. Men between 40 and 51 are to register for military service of a modified sort. That includes R. We talked about his position. He has obviously been thinking about it a lot, more than he's let on, and seeing this coming. I got the feeling he found it a difficult subject to talk about, perhaps because his views are not consolidated. He said: 'I rather feel I must testify as a conscientious objector. It's a bore, and one can't guess how it will affect our local life. But I think I must for reasons of self-respect, not that I believe in "sticking my head out for no reason". But I don't think they'll chop it off.'

Burgo very agitated when he went to bed, saying he was 'thinking of horrible things'. Pressed to say what, he said it was about Macbeth and Lady Macbeth and 'all the killings'. A few days ago I told him the story, and read him a little of the play. He didn't seem to mind then, and was delighted by the idea of Birnam Wood coming to Dunsinane. I tried to explain that thoughts were only thoughts and one could think of horrible things and remain intact – but I do not think he believed it. Nor is it greatly true, alas.

December 7th

All the events of today have been blotted out by the evening's news. Japan has opened war on the USA with a bang by an almighty raid on the American naval and air base at Pearl Harbour. No ultimatum, no warning; the damage done has been ghastly and casualties extremely heavy. Nothing could have been more unprovoked and utterly beastly, nor could anything have thrown America more effectively into a condition of war fever. R. and I react differently to the news. He is greatly excited and stimulated, and I think feels it is good news, because it may lead 'to a war of quick decision'. I feel as if I had a load of undigested food on my stomach. The disease is spreading and the possibility of pacifying this vast inflammation must surely become more remote. After we went up to bed, 'What does a Honolulu pacifist do now?' I asked R., feeling that this appalling event would put an almost impossible strain on his principles. Then we argued about whether or not events going on now were more painful than those in the past. R. thought not; I wasn't sure, but I do know that I think of war entirely in terms of individual human feelings – fear, anxiety, pain, and this awful, permanent disgust.

[1] A doctor and psychoanalyst, he was attached to the 'rehabilitation' department of the Army. He was the brother of Vanessa, Thoby and Virginia.

And if these exist *now* and are capable of being resolved or relieved; how not be consumed by impotent desire to do so?

December 8th

A lovely frosty morning, dead still. I biked down to Mrs Slater's to thank her for her plum-pudding, but she wasn't there, only Phyllis bathing an enormous and splendid female baby in a tiny basin. Stopped and talked to her in the hot kitchen while the fat soapy baby sat bolt upright and gazed at us.

In the evening I fetched Burgo from tea at Inkpen. It was exquisitely lovely walking home in the dusk, with the stars incredibly large and bright. Burgo was very excited by the aspect of Venus, and couldn't believe he was looking at a planet such as he had read about. As we walked up the avenue the sky had lost nearly all its rosy colour and the wych-elms stretched their branches in the utter stillness, each making its familiar, amiable gesture. Burgo declared he would 'almost die if anything happened to them'.

Sebastian [Sprott] came to stay. We haven't seem him since the beginning of the war. He looked and seemed ten years younger, twinkling and serene.

[When, at Cambridge, I attended the same lectures as Sebastian Sprott – McTaggart's on Hegel for instance – I was much too frightened of him to address a word to this assured prize-pupil who actually dared to question our lecturer, and little dreamed that he would one day become a dear friend with whom I should feel totally at ease and to whom I would confide my troubles. He had a neat appearance and stiffly erect bearing that reminded me of an old-fashioned wooden soldier. All his movements were precise; he even looked a little demure. If asked a direct question during a discussion of general ideas he would probably answer 'yes *and* no,' but go on to elaborate what was more an attitude than a belief. If this suggests dullness, that was most certainly not his failing. He had been a close friend of several older Bloomsbury characters – particularly Maynard Keynes, Lytton and E. M. Forster. Quite without personal ambition, he spent most of his working life lecturing at Nottingham University, refusing better offers from Cambridge, living in a modest terraced house and making many friends among the miners and their families. Could he be called an egalitarian? In the class sense, yes. He hadn't an ounce of snobbishness in his disposition. Lytton liked going abroad with him – his equableness and wide interests made him a good travelling companion.

After the tragic deaths of Lytton and Carrington I remember him taking me for a walk up the downs and gently and sympathetically eliciting the whole story. It was from this time that my intimacy with him began; I realized his gift for understanding, but he also liked to confide. He was a devoted son and brother, and when his mother died he surprised me by confessing how lost and unprotected he felt without her.

With Ralph he had been on close terms for some time. Thereafter he occupied a special place among our friends and visited us at least once a year, usually in the autumn. He enjoyed picking mushrooms and blackberries, and while we filled our baskets he would unroll for our benefit some drama of Nottingham life, in as much detail as a Trollope novel. Later when I was living alone in London he came regularly to lunch with me.]

December 20th

Took Sebastian over to see Julia and Lawrence, but lovable character as he is, I thought he was a bit rusty in the art of conversation. He likes telling stories, and listens to them with equal concentration. But general ideas? There are a few, like psychoanalysis, he will discuss. He thinks about the war as little as possible, and by this means remains quietly contented with his strangely limited life at Nottingham University. For one of the most endearing things about him is that he is the least ambitious man in the world. His extremely affectionate nature, accepting his friends as he finds them, and (though he sees them rarely) taking up the thread exactly where he left off, is another.

December 23rd

The news, both from Russia and Libya so good that in spite of the Japs I was just thinking to myself the war *might* – who knows – be over in the spring, when the announcer said: 'Since this broadcast began an announcement has been put out from Germany that Hitler has assumed sole command of the Army.' A row between Hitler and the Army? One could hardly have hoped for it so soon.

Holly-picking. This year the trees are thick with berries. As we turned into the avenue with our load, two pairs of cart-horses, each with a man on his back, came lumbering up, silhouetted against the golden afternoon sky. I said how beautiful they looked, and Burgo said, 'Yes! willing, tired, forlorn', which was a perfect description of them.

December 28th

The fag-end of the year. I am very conscious that that's exactly what it is, like a stained, burnt-out cigarette hanging between my lips. R. has been very low spirited – partly because he hates Christmas. He has spent hours sitting in his chair by the fire reading book after book – Bury, Mill, Malthus, all writers bearing on the development of ideas. I envy him, and listen to the ideas they inspire and discuss them with him. Today we had one of those arguments that go right back to the root of things – Ethics in this case. I fished out my old hedonism and found it intact and not moth-eaten from having been stowed away in my mental cupboard. Or so it seemed to me. I was particularly impressed by the fact that it is the only theory which explains, and even makes inevitable, the absolute impossibility human beings find in deciding moral questions – because the hedonistic calculus demands what is impossible: following the results of every action in terms of happiness to a final conclusion. So that the hedonist's behaviour must by definition be founded on guesswork, even when that is informed and inspired.

Well, after a faint flash of hope and excitement over Hitler's taking over the Army, we sink back and contemplate the dreary waste of war: from the Eastern front where the German soldiers freeze and die of wounds which ought not to be fatal (this is supposed to give us exquisite pleasure judging from the voice of the BBC announcer) to the Australians, who shriek that we have let them down in their hour of peril, and who only look to America for help. To Winston who has somehow got across the Atlantic, where he is 'doing his stuff ' and basking in the applause of American journalists and not feeling a pang (I can't help thinking) over all the mistakes, the death and disaster, he is responsible for; and boasting and threatening, and speaking in rolling phrases of what we are going to do to the enemy in 1942, 1943, 1944 and 1945, God help us all!

December 31st

Julia has come on a week's visit. She feels the cold terribly, and huddles in countless jerseys and her coat of false fur, over the fire. It has indeed become piercingly cold, and everything looks dead, drained of colour and life, while the vitality of us human beings is enough, but only *just* enough, to keep us alive.

Opened last year's prophecies, read them out and made new ones. R. alone had scored a success, by foretelling that Japan, Russia and USA would all be in the war. I was surprised to find myself writing down that the war would be over by January 1943. It seems to me it is a logical possibility. Why then don't I feel more cheerful?

1942

January 1st

A letter from Gamel to me today, saying 'couldn't we meet?' I wonder if she knows the nature of Gerald's letters to us. It takes a good deal to make her overcome her aversion to writing. I have written back saying we would love to see her and Miranda,[1] but that there is no question of our visiting them since Gerald says he finds our company intolerable. We will see what happens next.

Julia had temporarily relapsed into complete sluggishness, either sitting over the fire reading detective stories or going up to snooze on her bed. Now she has revived and become her normal fascinating self, all speculation and fantasy. Today she described how Oliver's renderings of opera arias, especially Mozart's and the airy gestures accompanying them, had put her off them for life. Then a talk about male sex-appeal. She defined the exact way a coat should cling to the masculine form. 'It should *mould* the shoulders and back, and then *fall* away from the hips – like a boat leaving harbour,' she ended rather unexpectedly.

January 6th

At breakfast I was amused to find a letter from Gerald to me. I had half-guessed that if I wrote to Gamel he would be the one to answer. It was couched in a mild and reasonable strain. Catharine had told him that R. thought he regarded him as an enemy – but this was not true at all. It was only that after much thought he had decided it was better for them not to meet. Wouldn't *I*, however, come over and see them, if 'I didn't regard him as unmeetable?' I wondered how this would strike R: he smiled somewhat cynically and said, 'Gerald always pulls out the *Vox humana* stop in the end.'

The truth is that Gerald doesn't possess the ordinary affections most people have; his various relationships are seen in purely literary terms. He often speaks of trusty Gamel who has plodded along beside him for so long with a detachment that freezes the blood as if she were some kind of domestic pet. One cannot, or anyway does not, feel friendly to someone one can't bear to meet, and it is absurd to pretend it. R. analyses the situation with his usual detachment thus: 'In our long relationship I have always been fonder of Gerald than Gerald of me; now at last I have had enough of it, and feel all the bitterness of "a woman scorned".' Because of Gerald's affair with Carrington, because of his curiously jealous sense that R. was a better soldier in the First War than he was, perhaps because he identifies him with his father, R. has long been the object of a campaign of rivalry to Gerald, and when campaigning there is no-one like him for laying subtle and

[1] Gerald Brenan's daughter.

elaborate plots to humiliate his enemy and make him look in the wrong in the eyes of the world, as I can testify from experience. In this letter he wants to do several things – forestall all possibility of Gamel visiting us by asking me over instead; get me over, thus scoring a triumph over R. (by condescending to receive me and not him, and so dividing us); and appear well in the eyes of our friends by telling them he has made this conciliatory suggestion. Then he, Gamel and I all look like reasonable people, and R. alone remains outcast, 'the unmeetable'. I have read Gerald's letter over several times, and I believe this interpretation to be perfectly correct. I will not in any case go, and I think probably the best thing will be to ignore his letter. But it is a masterly production.

Lawrence fetched Julia away. We birds are alone again.

January 20th

Looked out to see four or five inches of good soft snow; and no possibility of getting out to shop in Hungerford or take Burgo to school until we had set to, and with tremendous labour dug a passage out for the car. I stood in the fishmonger's shop with a dumb group of patient figures in mackintoshes, with white, pink-trimmed faces. The 'Dutch gentleman' (as he is called for some unknown reason) threw a great fish's head on the grey and white marble slab, and its huge eyes wobbled like jellies.

I have been very energetic these days in physical ways that I can take no interest in, like scrubbing the whole of the nursery floor, and thinking how awful life will be when we have no daily help at all.

January 27th

Now that we are faced with having to do everything ourselves it doesn't seem so bad. Burgo, too, has become sweeter and happier. Last night he said: 'I shall be exceedingly sad when you and Ralph die. I shall come and see you when I'm married.' I asked him what sort of wife he would choose. He said: 'A nice *young* woman, with dark hair and pretty flowered dresses.'

I kept to today's plan of going to London to buy a fiddle from Marjorie Hayward at the Royal College of Music. She was short, with grey frizzed hair. I carried off the violin so quickly that she shouted after me: 'Is the case done up?' I had only carried it a little way when a Jewish-looking gentleman stopped me and asked, 'Do you want to sell your violin, Madam?' I'm fiercely aware of being a violin-owner. Afterwards I looked in on the Hills in their bookshop. Heywood came in just as I was leaving. He may be called up in six weeks' time, and I'm afraid joining the Army may nearly be the death of him.

January 31st

This afternoon there arrived our new 'help', Alice Cooper, Freddie her little boy, and her soldier husband on a week's leave. Alice is a peculiar shape, broad in the beam, with a good-natured flat face and brown stumps for teeth. Having dreaded the invasion beforehand, I didn't mind it when it came. R. says a sob rose in his throat at the thought of this human flotsam and jetsam drifting into our house. He says he's always finding sobs rising, for instance when he heard a pilot describing on the wireless how he got his damaged plane home. This strong human sympathy he has, combined with his sharply ironical and critical side, both delights me and puts me to shame.

February 2nd

I don't know how to describe my state of mind it is so ambivalent – sadness and a sort of content inextricably mixed. The solid background of our days is being restored by splendid Alice, and I now feel stirrings of life, which is not a purely pleasant sensation, but rather more like a leg or arm coming round after it has gone to sleep. It is as if the texture of our existence were a material which had been worked at and shredded by fingers until it became gossamer-thin, but in a patchy way, painfully lacking pattern. It just hangs together, no more; you can see right through it in places.

A visit to Julia and Lawrence 'to give ourselves a tonic', R. said. Getting home cheerful, he then opened the paper and fell into despair. The Libyan situation and the Pacific are both equally catastrophic, the Japs are everywhere. One can well imagine the Germans saying: 'Surely the English can't survive all this. They *must* crack soon.'

'Well, we've got through one month of 1942,' said R. 'One month nearer the end of the war. We've only got to survive.'

February 13th

I have no desire whatever to write anything in this diary, and my only reason for doing so is to show that I am still alive, and not unhappy I might even say. But I have never in my life been less aware of my surroundings, got less pleasure from the visible world, nor felt more completely insulated from thrills of excitement. Our life is all interior. Household things and my relation to R. and B. are the whole focus of my vision; anything outside is a bad photograph – a blur of whitish greys.

Tonight, feeling that my favourite records had been neglected, I put on a whole series and enjoyed them. I don't want to become deaf as well as blind.

February 25th

The greatest pleasure I have these days is watching Burgo grow into an independent being; he is mad about R. at the moment. When I went in to bath him this evening, he looked at me in a dignified way and said: 'What shall we talk about, Horse of Troy?' Now that he is freed from Nannie's bunchy presence and possessions, he expresses his personality even by the queer concatenation of objects in his bedroom – a squeaking bun, his squashed blue velvet slippers and a policeman's black notebook full of strange scrawled memoranda.

At lunchtime Alice came breathlessly into the nursery looking for Freddie. Mr Cooper had just arrived on embarkation leave. We are painfully oppressed by the Cooper drama. The poor man has quite lost his former jauntiness, and instead of briskly polishing up the silver he sits brooding aimlessly over the paper. Who knows what thoughts fill his head? I think of the family like helpless twigs swept along by a torrent. R. said, 'I know what's the matter with Mr Cooper. He's *afraid*. It all comes back to me.' He is to go back to camp, but believes he will be sailing in a short while, and his outfit is tropical.

The news continues as depressing as possible. Men up to forty-six are to be called up, and R. is forty-seven. Women born in 1901 are to register this summer, and I was born in 1900.

March 11th

I wrote a line to Gamel the other day suggesting our lunching together at the Three Swans in Hungerford. She wired back at once, and today I drove through pouring rain to meet her. We sat in the long, dark, upstairs dining-room, our voices ringing out with seemingly bell-like clarity, and at times I wondered if our cynical views of the war might not cause offence. For Gamel really agrees with us. Gerald, so she says, believes that some good will come out of it. 'I wish I could agree with him,' she said, 'but I can't. I think in his case it's a form of compensation for minding it so terribly.' We didn't touch on Gerald's attitude to R. though I half longed to. Now I regret that I didn't, and feel it would have been more human. At the time I didn't want to embarrass her; it needs just the right key to unlock her door and I wasn't sure what it was.

We hear that there is to be no more petrol 'for pleasure'. From June the basic ration is to be abolished completely, and only those with special allowances for special needs may run cars at all. I find the idea rather exciting, I can't imagine why. Masochism, or inverted claustrophobia? Then in a clergyman's voice the announcer told us that Mr Eden had today revealed to the House the hideous atrocities perpetrated by the Japs in Hong-Kong, women raped, civilians bayoneted, etc. The Government had wished to spare the relatives the agony of knowing these things, and so had kept them back until now. Why not spare them that agony a little longer? It is a sinister sign of poor morale, a shot of cocaine to ginger up the dying dog, and serves no other conceivable purpose whatever.

March 13th

R. said sadly that he missed human contacts and relations with friends, which were gradually being strangled by the war, and with them communication which was almost the most important thing in life. I agree most heartily, but was surprised because he often shrinks from the idea of having people to stay, and is never the one to suggest it. In my surprise was an element of shame at my own obtuseness in not seeing that this was what he felt; I hope it doesn't mean a failure of communication between him and me, but there is a terrible lack, alas! of things to communicate.

March 14th

Looking in at the kitchen window with some message, I saw that Alice had a stricken expression. R. told me a telephone message had come saying that her husband was sailing tonight. She had hoped to get a last glimpse of him today, and had been sitting in the kitchen turning over the bus time-tables. Oh, the pathos of it. When I went in to tell her how sorry I was I burst into tears almost before I could get the words out, and she turned with a simple and dignified movement, put her head on my shoulder and wept too.

Michael MacCarthy to lunch bringing us two little pigs, dear little grunters with soulful eyes. We all feel immensely proud to be pig-owners. He also brought us a leg of mutton – an unheard-of piece of generosity which had the most mellowing effect on him. His face always expresses his mood transparently, and today it was genial and alert, with wide-open eyes. I've seen him when the company bored him, with his eyes half closed and a comical look of sour distaste on his face. More rationing – clothes, coal, electricity – and hints of more to come. Perhaps next winter we really shall go short.

March 26th

I am writing now too long after it happened to be able to describe my pleasure in Janetta's visit. The slight veil that swathed her during her subjection to Humphrey has floated away, and I am confirmed in my view that she is one of the most intelligent, beautiful and sensitive young creatures I know.

We sat out in the hot sun most of Janetta's stay, walked to the wood for primroses and picnicked in the bracken. Then we saw her off, waving and hoping she would soon come again, as we have so often done before.

April 6th

Alice's father, a very handsome old gentleman of great charm, came to see her, bringing me a magnificent bunch of Calla lilies (one of the flowers that move me most). He told me he was once a huntsman in the Craven, and described hunting in Savernake Forest, and how the hounds used to mistake young fawns rustling in the bracken for foxes, leap on them and kill them.

Burgo took me to the little copse on the way to Ham. We found it tunnelled into narrow paths opening into miniature clearings carpeted with green – moschatels, bluebell leaves, spotted arums and a few very freshly opened white anemones. As I sat on a log I made a resolve to try and enjoy everything possible for a change – a resolve born out of the sudden unexpected beauty of that midget, almost suburban wood taking me unawares as I sat there on my log.

I feel particularly sorry for R. because his hopes about the war have been constantly frustrated, because he is so magnificently realistic, and also because he has fewer practical tasks to distract him. My conscience is pricked with fear that I don't provide him with enough support. Absorbed in household chores, and basking in his continuous sweetness to me, perhaps I have become lazy towards him in an unpardonable way. And towards myself too. Ever since childhood I have been so terrified of disappointment that I have done as little hoping as possible; and now in a strange way I've given up the war *as a bad job*. I have even lost, with hope, the desire for a crushing victory over the Axis, and returned to the view that a dreary stalemate from which no one profited would be the best possible outcome. Then everyone would be forced to realize the futility and wickedness of war.

This evening another moment of natural beauty made me realize what a cataract I have grown over the surface of my consciousness. The sun came through the clouds just as it was setting, and shot its long yellow rays sideways across the park, making the velvety texture of the Downs and ploughed fields brilliantly clear. The buds on the beeches were copper-coloured, their trunks verdigris green, and one pigeon perched like a bird in a fable on the dead branches of the oak. A rainbow arched over the Downs, and soon the clouds and rain came back and away flew the pigeon.

Burgo in his bath tonight pointing to his balls: 'What are inside them?' F.: 'Nothing at the moment. When you're grown up there'll be seeds for making babies.' B. (giggling wildly): 'I shall sell mine in paper bags at fourpence each. And on one bag I'll write GIRLS and on the other one BOYS.'

April 28th

A letter from Jan [Woolley][1] from Lisbon, where she has just arrived from German-occupied France, after a long, slow, crowded journey 'with no money and no shoes. I'm so thin that I rattle in the bath, and my bones have actually come through my skin in some places.' At the best of times she looked like a Raemaekers cartoon representing Famine, so it's no wonder everyone is anxious to ship her home in the first possible plane. May she come here? she asks. R. has sent off a warm welcome. She might be surprised at the envy her letter excited with its smell of foreign travel, its storks and judas-trees.

When the war enters a new phase it takes some time for us to realize it has done so. The latest is a series of nightly raids on towns of historic or architectural importance. So far Exeter, Bath and Norwich have copped it. The papers describe them as 'Baedeker raids'. Alice asked me: 'Have you seen about these new Baedeker bombers the Germans are using?' Later she said: 'Well, it was Hitler's fifty-third birthday the other day, and I suppose baby Adolf will soon have his first.' F.: 'What *do* you mean, Alice?' A.: 'Oh yes, didn't you know? Unity Mitford. I heard about it from a friend of mine who worked for her. And in the papers too they said, "Miss Unity Mitford is as well as can be expected." '

April 30th

At 10 tonight Alice rocketed along the passage and knocked sharply on the door. 'Mr Partridge, come at once, the dairy's on fire!' R. dashed out to see what he could do, leaving me to ring up the fire brigade. Alice said, 'Mrs Coombs is in a dreadful state. She says there's calves in there.' I could indeed hear a melancholy lowing, and pictured the poor creatures trapped and burning. I walked along to the nursery window and looked out – the whole room was lit up by the leaping red light of the flames as they made their indomitable progress, for the dairy roof was thatched and being rapidly devoured. They made a deep roaring, the wind was blowing them our way and it seemed they must catch our woodshed and piggery and so reach the house. Ham Spray itself was in danger, I thought – my heart beat fast, and I felt a tremendous affection for our threatened house, as though it were a person. When I got close to the fire some little calves were being let out of the big barn, whose great vaulted roof had a bar of fire running along its edge. Inside it a brand new threshing-machine was standing. Somehow or other I found myself, along with the landgirls, one or two youths and Alice, vainly trying to push this iron mammoth out. Above us was smoke and fire, and one landgirl looked up and said, 'Mind the roof doesn't come down.' Soon afterwards the fire brigade clattered up, with R. somehow in control, plunged their pumps into the farm pond and surprisingly soon had a jet of water on the flames. I never for one moment expected them to put out this ferocious fire, but this is just what they did. And a feeling of flatness settled on the villagers who had collected to enjoy the fun and exchange comments: 'We thought it was one of Major Partridge's bonfires.' 'My wife was so worried, she thought it must be Ham Spray.' 'Hope the Jerries don't come over,'

[1] Mother of Janetta and Rollo and wife of a celebrated VC of the First War.

(this had been one of my first thoughts) and, 'Let out the old bull!' Someone did and he capered into a field of cows.

May 1st

Out to look at the scene of the fire. The dairy was nothing but charred beams and black ashes, in the midst of which a black cat was lapping a saucer of milk.

Three churns of milk were practically boiled in the blaze and Mr Coombs gave them to us for our pigs. Wilde ladled some off the top for them, not realising it was pure cream. The poor creatures are now suffering from violent bilious attacks and won't look at food!

May 7th

During the fire Mr Mills told us that Joan was to be married to Gunner Robinson yesterday. R. offered to drive anyone to church, and was busy most of the afternoon, with white ribbons on the car, driving up and down the lane with a beaming face. We were therefore put into quite a flutter when news of another wedding dropped out of the telephone today. It was Bunny, asking us if we would come to London 'for a very special occasion – to be witnesses to my wedding to Angelica'. We were flattered at being asked, even so late in the day. Would Vanessa, Duncan and Clive be there, we wondered.

First we went to Cameo Corner for wedding-presents: a pair of Queen Anne earrings for Angelica and a seal for Bunny. At the Ivy we found only William beside the pair themselves. I think our presents were a success; Angelica was wearing a romantic black hat and veil, and looked lovely in the earrings, which she put on at once. The ceremony took place in a registry office in the city, and we went afterwards to the flat in Clifford's Inn where Bunny and Angelica have been living for some time. 'Now perhaps at last the neighbours will respect me,' Angelica said. We came away with no further clue to Charleston's reaction to, or even knowledge of the event.

May 11th

Raymond and Jan Woolley arrived at tea-time. We pumped Jan about conditions in France. 'Very little indeed to eat: no coffee, no tea, no milk, very little "grease"; only vegetables, a small ration of bread and of meat. There was nothing to drink or smoke in the cafés, but people went there all the same. I used to take a fan and fan myself, so as to have something to do. The French were hostile to all foreigners for eating up their food, and there was no love for the English, though many references to "when you come".'

We sat out under our flowering cherry-tree in idyllic weather eating our tea off a wicker table; Burgo was brown as a nut in nothing but a bathing-suit, and all round us two families of fluffy chicks ran about looking for worms.

Penroses to supper. Alec had been to the Brenans, and told us he had tried to persuade Gerald to 'bury the hatchet'. Gerald: 'The hatchet is none of my making.' 'Oh, *isn't* it?' said Gamel, and Gerald laughed and sent us his love.

May 14th

Raymond writes that he met Clive who told him that Charleston was not warned of Bunny and Angelica's wedding. They say that it is not the wedding itself they object to but the Byronesque pose of secrecy, making it look as though Angelica were being abducted from unwilling parents – which is not very far from the truth.

Janetta rang up asking if she could bring her new friend Kenneth[1] for the weekend. We had Desmond and Molly coming, so beds had to be made up in the nursery.

Desmond and Molly gave a fine display of MacCarthyism – the utmost charm and the utmost lack of consideration. No information about the time of their arrival until Molly rang up after lunch on Saturday and burst out, 'How do you *do*?' She then failed to hear anything I said, and went to fetch a foreign maid, who heard but couldn't understand. She arrived very worried because she had lost her bag, and much telephoning had to be done about it. Whether their rations were in it or not I don't know, but in any case they brought none – not a speck of butter or sugar, which didn't prevent them from taking sugar in every cup they swallowed. Next Molly lost her spectacles, and after Julia and I had spent a long time pacing the garden looking for them Molly was discovered in bed, having found them, but worn out by the struggle. They left by an impossibly early train, and insisted on R. waking up and calling them much earlier than was necessary, so that they shouldn't keep waking up themselves.

So much for the bother they caused. The pleasure is of course boundless, and we had lots of what Desmond calls 'good talk'. I remember there was a discussion about India and that Molly said, 'Queen Victoria was the only person who could manage the Indians. She was a great paper-weight on a heap of fluttering papers.' For Sunday lunch we were a party of nine, with the addition of Lawrence and Julia. It was hard work and I felt physically and mentally exhausted when it was over, but greatly enjoyed it at the time.

I forgot to say that for the last few days the Russian front has once more come horribly to life.

June 6th

I don't know who suggested that R. and I should sleep out, but our tiny bedroom was infernally hot, so we took our blankets on to two garden beds drawn up side by side under a yew tree at the very edge of the water. Slept intermittently, but almost glad to be awake, so delicious was it breathing in the fresh night air and listening to innumerable rustles, twittering and the gentle slip-slop of the river. It was a delicious extension of the day's pleasure, a bonus. Most of this morning I sat out in the punt alone; the fact that I was not on dry land, but only attached to it by a string, made it easier to think with detachment. But separation from the lawn was nothing to the separation from Ham Spray and its perpetual background of swarming, fizzing, buzzing preoccupations and responsibilities. In my punt I read, wrote and above all *thought*, with a rare feeling of enjoyment, while tiny kingfisher-blue dragonflies floated round me or settled on the olive-green water. Lord, how long it is since I attempted to orientate myself. It seems to me I have been blind, deaf and almost inanimate for months.

Raymond gave me a book by an intelligent and candid fighter-pilot to read, and it aroused many speculations, and also talk, about danger, fear, heroism, mutilation, and the reactions of those not actually involved to all these things.

[1] Sinclair-Loutit.

Raymond said: 'I feel passionately that not a single German should be fed by the Red Cross until every Greek, Pole and Czech has been satisfied. Don't you agree?' Of course he was trailing his coat, and of course we stepped on it, saying what really mattered was who needed the food most. Probably the Greeks would come first. Then he testified to his lifelong hatred of the German people, and said he devoutly wished they could all be exterminated. 'Yes,' I said, 'but don't forget they *can't* be.' Both Raymond and Eardley think in terms of revenge, and base their post-war plans on it. I believe all this that the intelligentsia say about the German people will not be credited in a few years' time.

June 13–14th

We were in bed about 11.30 when the telephone rang. R. went down and I heard him say in a serious voice: 'Is he badly hurt?' I sat up in bed, stiff all over with horror. R. came upstairs to say that that delightful old ex-huntsman father of Alice's had been seriously hurt in a motor crash and was in Reading hospital. What was to be done? The hospital wanted to know if Alice could go at once, or if they should ring us up if he died in the night. I lay trembling violently at the thought of this guillotine-blade hanging over poor Alice, and the realization that *we* had to decide when it should fall. I was appalled at my own sense of shock and inefficiency, and the knowledge that I would have been incapable of breaking the news. R. – who always rises to such emergencies – was wonderfully kind, courageous and practical. He decided he must tell her at once, and use our last drop of petrol in driving her to the hospital. I knew he would be as calm and supporting as it was possible for anyone to be. He gave her some neat whiskey and even brought me a glass . . . It was 3 a.m. when he returned to the bedroom with the one word, 'Died'. Then he told me the whole story. The arrival at the hospital had been horrible, Alice was so sure he would be dead, as he was; but even in her misery she was able to think, 'I've been nothing but a trouble to you since I came', and thank him warmly for his kindness. Her world takes death very differently from ours. They rush to see the corpse and kiss it, and in that embrace perhaps they accept the fact of death more completely than someone more sophisticated would. All the way home she discussed her plans for the funeral, forgetting nothing, even that he would have clothes coupons which she might be able to use. It is a perfect form of catharsis.

After talking to her this morning I have no doubt she has been cruelly struck; yet I think of R.'s emotional reaction to Lytton's and Carrington's death, and Vanessa's to Julian's and wonder how and why it is so different.

June 20th

Like a sudden explosion in our stagnant lives, Clive came to stay, and Kitty and Anthony to dinner. After they had gone we sat out with Clive in a bath of warm night air on the verandah, while the light slowly drained away from the panorama of the Downs, and the great white owl in the aspen hissed whenever our voices got too loud. We talked about Bunny and Angelica's marriage. Clive became suddenly unbuttoned, as if released from a vow and for the first time dropped all pretence that Angelica was his daughter. He said Duncan was full of resentment, while his picture of Vanessa was rather tragic. She was bitterly hurt, yet longed to make it up. Bunny had gone down some weeks before the marriage to announce that it would take place, and the meeting was painful in the extreme. Vanessa couldn't really accept it, and when Angelica telephoned later to say it would be next day she complained of the shortness of the notice. R. said she hadn't a leg to stand on, and no more she had, but I see her as painfully caught in the pincer movement of Duncan's resentment and Bunny's victory. Angelica goes down to Charleston for weekends, and the question is, shall Bunny be asked? Vanessa is for trying it. 'I'm devoted to old Bunny,' says Clive, and is secretly enjoying reminding them of the days when both Vanessa and Duncan were always telling him what a fascinating character Bunny was.

June 21st

Very hot still. Sat in the shade of the beech-tree, having endless conversations with Clive. We ranged over the inexhaustible subject of what was of ultimate value. Happiness, said I. Clive said: 'We set too much store by human life *per se*.' The vast majority of lives, according to him, are of practically no value, the criterion – as far as I could make out – was whether or not a person could enjoy contemplating St Paul's. He wouldn't *quite* say it was whether they like what he liked himself, but very nearly.

He says Maynard [Keynes][1] is delighted with his title, and so is Lydia. They came to brave the scorn of Charleston. 'O-ah!' said Lydia. 'We come to be mocked!' And no doubt they were, for Charleston cherishes what seems to me a totally irrational prejudice against titles earned by merit. Any rationalist has a right to object to the other sort. Leonard [Woolf] was far the most scathing apparently. Maynard is very optimistic about the war, sharing this attitude with the Prime Minister, with whom he is very thick. 'Well – we must make the war last another year,' he says however, 'because we haven't got our plans for the peace ready.'

July 11th

Today women born in 1900 had to register for National Service. Took B. with me and went into Hungerford to do so. Other forty-twos seemed to be mountainously large or weakly nervous and uncontrollably talkative. ('Are you married?' 'Married? I should say I am, very much so,' etc., etc.) I was asked the same, any children under fourteen and how many I 'catered' for. I was sent away with a slip of paper, saying that if I was called for an interview I should be legally obliged to take the work I was directed to. People, people. Kitty [West] and her baby have come to stay for a week's rest cure. Roger Fulford over from Oxford to lunch. I know he admires R. but am far from sure he approves of me. He doesn't like 'the sex', as he likes to call women, to be at all free in their conversation. Then I ask myself how he can reconcile his theoretical belief in God and the Royal Family with his practical interest in smut and scallywags. Also I felt he had no right to rub his hands over Burgo's atheistical remarks if he really sets store by Christianity. In *theory* he disapproves of malicious characters like Maurice Bowra,[2] and 'all dons' wives who flirt with the undergraduates and permit loose talk particularly about unnatural vice in the greatest possible physical detail'.

[1] John Maynard Keynes, economist. Married Lydia Lopokova, a Russian ballerina.
[2] Historian at Cambridge.

August 7th

R. points out that I'm trying to take my tempo too fast. Very true, and today I struggled to reform and as a result felt much calmer. Jan [Woolley] left us today after a very successful visit of several days. She went off with her hair belling out under a little round blue cap, looking like a young man in an Italian fresco. As she turned to wave one saw her fine eyes set in a deeply-wrinkled face; they have lost none of their beauty with age and even gain by the contrast. We both liked having her here very much, and feel increasingly at ease with her.

August 17th

Marjorie Strachey for the weekend. Dearly as we both love her and enjoy her rumbustious and eccentric character, I was slightly afraid of a skirmish. We haven't seen her since the war began. She had evidently heard of our views and was I think surprised not to find us more provocative. Much talk about education, but not a lot about the war; then when we were sitting on the sunny lawn on the last day of her visit she suddenly said: 'All conscientious objectors ought to be dropped by parachute in Germany since they wish to be ruled by the Nazis.' R. said, 'Well, thank goodness the Government is more liberal-minded.' Does she ever remember that both Lytton and James and most of their closest friends were COs in the last war, and would she have wanted them to be treated likewise?

There is agitating news of a large-scale raid on Dieppe, by commando and naval forces, with vast losses on both sides. It sounds important – a rehearsal for the second front perhaps? Raymond has come to stay for a week, working all mornings on an essay on Duncan. R. is in low spirits. I have the sense of fumbling, blundering through a long black tunnel. Peaches and grapes ripen almost too fast to eat.

August 20th

Equilibrium restored. Raymond is the best possible company, going to the library every morning and stepping out at lunch-time, a butterfly from its chrysalis.

More and more visitors – what a breathless whirl! – the Hills to stay, both Nicholses to lunch and tea, and then late on Saturday night we heard that someone had sent us an American sergeant called John Yeon. We rushed round rather hysterically, making up a bed in the nursery, pushing debris out of sight, and saying how unlike a proper house he would find Ham Spray, though Raymond indulged in a few fantasies of a different sort, about how much he would enjoy finding himself among 'the intelligentsia and an Earl's daughter'. John Yeon turned out to be tall, dark and handsome, with a tragic, humourless mouth which suddenly flashed into gaiety when he smiled, in fact very attractive in an austere, geometrical way. I don't think he made much of anything, except the view of the Downs – which he convincingly admired, and my saying what a relief it would be if we could shake off the Empire for good and all.

The war news has been unspeakable all week, and there were even a few old-fashioned thuds during dinner. I went out onto the verandah and looked at the dim line of the Downs under a sky of grey felt which seemed to press down on them. It was warm and deathly still, except for the wild raucous shriek of bird or beast from the distant woods, the steady hiss of the owls in the aspen, the wheezing cough of a cow, and a far-off, unsinister 'pom-pom' of anti-aircraft guns I imagine, making up a whole which was mysterious and somehow soothing.

August 31st

All our recent visitors have left – and we remain alone with our reflections. There is, we conclude, very little pleasure in hospitality to those who disapprove of us, and don't want us to have the very things we are trying to share with them. Eating with relish our home-grown honey and fruit, they will with equal relish imply that we shouldn't be allowed to have it. 'Where do you get this petrol? You won't have *that* much longer.' Yet they enjoy being met at the station. Or there's Marjorie's view that pacifists have no right even to live in their native land, eat in its restaurants, travel in its railways, an argument which might as well be applied to Conservatives living under a Labour Government. R. points out with his usual logic that we are English, Ham Spray is our home, and we have a perfect right to live here, although we don't support the official line. On the other hand he does not believe in forcing our views on other people, and again I think he is right; yet I like expressing my opinions and find it tiring not to. As I clean basins, sweep stairs and dust tables, I often find my thoughts congealing into pacifist configurations, and wondering how so many intelligent people fail to accept the supporting arguments. Yet at present that is unmistakably the fact.

Frances Penrose came to a picnic lunch in the garden. There are a lot of American troops stationed near her, and it seems that one of their officers gave a lecture to a collection of local English ladies about how to treat the blacks. They must beware of any friendly impulse towards them, never let them into their houses, and above all never treat them as human beings, because they were not. Frances said the faces of the ladies were a study in delighted horror, as they heard that none of their daughters' virginities were safe and that all the blacks carried knives. 'How are the poor blacks to be entertained?' asked one brave lady. 'Oh you needn't worry about *that*. They are always happy, and make their own entertainment by singing and laughing.'

September 10th

Burgo and I went to a circus at Hungerford, too rare a treat to miss. A green awning cast a livid light as of extreme illness, not to say approaching death, on the faces of the audience and the mainly octogenarian performers, lending them a macabre beauty. We sat on rocking benches above the heaped excreta of horses, which gave off a hot smell. At one end, on seats draped with red plush, sat the children of the upper classes, with their mummies and nannies. The children were clean and brushed, white as worms, and their clothes spotless and well ironed; their little legs hung down limply in clean white socks. When they stood up they looked as though they were almost too weak to stand at all. The mummies and nannies pursed their mouths at the clown's obscene antics. The side benches were filled by the children of the proletariat, strong, active, brown and uproarious. It was the class war in concrete form and I saw it with proletarian eyes. The war has greatly emphasized this war between the classes, while paradoxically enough reducing the difference between them. Whereas the lower orders used to accept, God knows why, the idea that ladies should spend their time ordering meals and jealously preserving their beauty, now (when they flap about inefficiently with dusters) the cry is: Why the hell shouldn't they do more? Of course this only applies to the quiet domestic scene; danger and fear break the barriers instantly.

September 27th

Sebastian has been here for three delightful days. Though we only see him about once a year we take up the threads at once; he is the easiest and most affectionate of friends. One of the oldest too, and I think rather nostalgically of the days when we went to the same philosophy lectures at Cambridge and he was the only one of the class who dared question McTaggart's assertions about Hegel, as he rolled round the room looking like an outsize baby. His position towards the war, slightly uneasy last year, is now frankly escapist. R. says 'he ignores it as much as possible, saying it is an uncivilized and incomprehensible outrage to the intelligence.'

Yet it – the war – has been horribly interesting, with the Germans throwing all they have into the effort to take Stalingrad before winter sets in. It has miraculously *not* fallen, though there is street fighting in part of it.

October 5th

Alice has left us, and under the new regime I do all the cooking. I am managing – no more can be said, and R. has been infinitely kind about my efforts. He says, 'For a woman not to be able to cook is like impotence to a man.'

Saxon is spending a fortnight's holiday here – very sweet, very obstinate and more talkative than usual. He wrote to ask what he should bring in the way of food. I wrote back, 'nothing but your meat coupons'. These are the only thing he has *not* brought. The first sight one catches of him in the morning is a stately figure in a once-good but now indescribably dilapidated dressing-gown over pyjamas to match, parading towards the bathroom with his false teeth in a tumbler of water held somehow rather defiantly in front of him. Unable to greet one in speech, he gives an emphatic nod. He comes down to breakfast in a prehistoric black suit (no doubt made by a first-rate tailor) and a royal blue shirt – or in summer an extremely well-cut white silk Palm Beach one frayed at the edges. Black button boots, a volume of Pindar in the original under his arm, slow but elegant movements and a face beautifully cut out of old ivory, long periods of complete silence broken by moments of sudden animation with a faint rose-petal flush appearing on his pale cheeks – all these are important elements, but nothing can add a final touch to the portrait of this lovable, exasperating, and (I'm convinced) deeply affectionate man.

October 14th

This evening R. opened in Saxon's honour a bottle of Corton Charlemagne 1928. Subdued expectation was on all our faces. Saxon sighed respectfully; then, after a pause: 'A NOBLE wine.' R.: 'If anyone wants to know what Body is – this is it.' It was not only delicious but potent, and gradually I felt infused and vibrating, as a violin string vibrates with a note. The whole world grew rich and mellow. Saxon became reminiscent: 'When did you last have a bottle of this?' R.: 'When you were last here, Saxon.' Saxon: 'Hm. I feel highly flattered.'

The conversation slipped off unexpectedly into cricket, or had got there when I became fully conscious again. 'That was Richardson I believe, but I suppose one would rather be Lockwood ... and do you know who bowled him out? *A. O. Jones* ... They said he finished his stroke before the ball ever reached his bat.' I sat bemused and happy, still vibrating, but not understanding a word.

I have far too little time to talk to R. these days and there's one thing I particularly want to discuss. A day or two ago he received papers saying he was liable to be called-up for the Home Guard or some form of military service. He didn't mention them for at least ten minutes, and then gave no clue as to which way his cat would jump, and even sounded a little embarrassed.

October 21st

Saxon left us. I never felt more truly sorry to see him go.

This was the great day when our pig and Wilde's were to be executed and tension spread through the house like an infection when it was known that Jack Lovelock the butcher had arrived. We were all obsessed by the thought of the imminent death of our pigs. Out of a sort of prudery perhaps I had not been near them for weeks, yet now I caught myself saying 'You and Pig,' to R. when I meant 'You and Wilde.' What a relief when the dull report of the humane killer was heard from the barn. Everyone but me went out to view the bodies and described how vast they looked, suspended from the roof and with blood dripping from them. Burgo said, 'They're as big as barges.' Pailfuls of strange marine-looking objects, pink and frilly, kept being carried into the larder. They seemed clean and not at all disgusting. 'If *that's* all fresh entrails look like,' I found myself thinking, 'things aren't too bad.' Wilde laughed his head off as his pig, draped in sacking, was tied to the carrier of the car and went off looking like a case of murder. Inside the car were my niece Jill dressed as a Wren, Burgo, bunches of dahlias, and the two pig owners. The sides of our pig from which bacon is to be made were laid out full length in the bath in our bathroom which they are now to occupy.

That night we sat up till midnight making the brawn. Head, heart, trotters, et cetera, were all boiled in a cauldron till they became a grey, gelatinous mass, and then seated round the kitchen table with our visitors, like the witches in *Macbeth*, we hand-picked it and chopped it, removing first an eye and then a tooth, or detaching the fat from an ear. After the first horror it was quite fascinating.

October 27th

Raining, raining most lugubriously. Fairly loud bomb explosions during the afternoon.

R. 'rendered down' the lard of our pig – a heroic act, for it made a sickly-sweet, hot, oily smell of such fearfulness that it drove me out of the kitchen. But it invaded every room in the house in time.

This very busy practical existence makes for unanalytic acceptance of what comes along, and not for much thinking about the war, but I believe at this point I would have ceased to do so in any case. I feel about it – the war – as if it were a permanent accompaniment to life, an unpleasant one like rheumatism or the knowledge that death must come, and one that I avoid attending to as much as possible. Fatalism has increased, and so has the desire to put off making decisions as long as possible in case something or other turns up. R.'s call-up is an instance in point. While washing up the other day he directly asked my opinion about it. I had felt certain scruples about giving it, having an instinct that I should in no way try to influence him, but back any decision he made. As I answered his questions I began to see clearly for the first time that I hoped he would refuse, not because I fail to realize that it may well lead to local awkwardness, nor because the matter has much significance; indeed it would be far less trouble to accept. But because it seems somehow not *digne* to act in a way that doesn't correspond to principles that are seriously held. And on a lighter level the Home Guard has always appeared totally useless and ludicrous, with its pikes and hats decorated with leaves. More-over, once R. had handed himself over he would be in the sausage-machine, with no more right to choose his own manner of life than the meat in the mincer.

From his manner I could see that he had been giving a lot of careful and fairly painful thought to the matter, but he finally and with admirable sang-froid filled up his form as a Conscientious Objector and posted it off. Well, this morning another form has come, in which reasons for objection are to be entered, and there is the implication of a tribunal. The net has closed with disconcerting rapidity.

October 31st

We are steadily eating our pig. So much meat is quite upsetting after months of deprivation; we have no appetite for bread and cake, feel overfed much of the time, and dream uneasily at night. But I never tasted better pork.

R. wrote his CO testimony, short, to the point, unprovocative and *admirable*.

November 7th

All else blotted out today by the news that American forces have landed at several points on the North African coast, and do not seem to be meeting great opposition. Rommel still goes back, and fast. It is becoming difficult to resist the sensation that the *tide is turning*. Is it the Second Front? What will the Germans do next? We lay in bed discussing it tonight. 'There's no doubt what they'll do,' R. said. 'They will go into unoccupied France.'

November 11th

He was perfectly right. They have. They've been pretty prompt I must say and my spirits sag at this evidence of their aplomb.

We have had a lovely visit from Janetta, though she was suffering badly from morning-sickness. She dreads 'that catlike inward grin I've so often seen spreading', dreads not doing the best for her child; the one thing she doesn't dread is its birth, and she wants to have it without anaesthetic, which R. thinks unreasonable. Though surrounded by communist-minded young, she still is (and I think always will be) an individualist, and her packed life has made her more tolerant without melting a quite stern critical attitude. Individualism, criticism and tolerance seem to me the most vital human characteristics. She left us this afternoon, and we are very loath to lose her.

Today the church bells were rung all over England to celebrate the victory over Rommel; they will not ring again until peace or invasion. Prospects of peace suddenly loom closer. Next year perhaps? The agitation of the news has brought back the hateful waiting-room atmosphere; so far as mental or intellectual life exists the fire is nearly out, spiritual dust lies on everything and I sit gazing in front of me, wondering 'What next?'

November 27th

Dramatic news. As anyone might have guessed would one day happen, the Germans pounced on Toulon harbour at dawn, where the residue of the French fleet were anchored. As soon as they had dropped mines in the harbour mouth the order was given to scuttle, and every ship is now at the bottom of the sea, the captains going down with their ships, the surviving crews interned by the Nazis.

December 17th

I was at the sink washing up the breakfast things. Enter R., saying: 'There you see how it is. I shan't be here for Professor Frisco' (the Hungerford postman, and conjurer ordered for Burgo's Christmas party). He was holding a summons to attend a tribunal at Bristol on the same day. We only talked a little about it during the day, which was very odd in view of our usual high level of communication. I suppose he will talk about it as much as he wants to. I did ask him if he was worried about it and he replied, 'No. Not consciously.' I do worry, though. Feeling tired after lunch I lay on my bed reading Henry James. Then the story came to an end and at once I began thinking about R.'s tribunal and my heart went thump thump thump. My worry has no very articulate content. I don't even know what to be afraid of, yet I'm still glad he decided to testify.

Dick Rendel[1] came last weekend for his first visit since the war. He is excellent company, tolerant, sensitive and understanding. It has been a delight to him to get into uniform again, red tabs and all, and he is always polishing his buttons. Among other things he told us about the landings from Dunkirk at Dover where he was stationed. His men had to receive the boat-loads and sort out the living from the dead and push them into trains. They were so dazed that if you could get one man into the train the others would follow like sheep. The numbers of dead and badly wounded were appalling – in most of the boats everything was awash with blood. One boat-load of six hundred contained only thirty men who were conscious, and he doubted if any of them survived. In the midst of all this horror (merely to hear about it was like buffets from a boxer's glove), Dick saw men making a cage on the beach. 'What's that for?' he asked. 'The Dogs.' 'What dogs?' 'Why, the dogs from France, the strays the soldiers are bringing back.' 'What will happen to them?' 'They'll all be sent to quarantine, after being carefully marked with their rescuer's name and number.' After the landings Dover lived in constant dread of invasion, for which preparations were negligible. They were shelled and bombed. One day when the alarm went they looked up to see the sky black with German aeroplanes – hundreds of them. 'Well, here it is, now we're done for,' he thought. But to his amazement they all passed over Dover without dropping a bomb. It was the beginning of the Battle of Britain.

Dick also told us about the board he is now on, for testing would-be officers. Adrian Stephen is also on it, as psychoanalytical expert. He is extremely popular as well as eccentric, usually wearing battle-dress over an ordinary suit, which shows through the loops where he has failed to button it, and a forage cap put on back to front. He speaks of the soldiers as 'my patients'.

---

[1] My brother-in-law and Lytton Strachey's nephew. He had been a regular soldier and was now a Colonel.

December 29th

Christmas is over at last. We were over twenty to see Professor Frisco's conjuring display. His personality was most sympathetic, and the things he produced from his hat or tambourines were ravishingly pretty – huge bright handkerchiefs folding to nothing, palm trees of coloured feathers. The tea-table was piled with cakes and jellies and the tree had a proper present for each child. It was much enjoyed, and Burgo thanked me formally: 'I *do* really congratulate you.' But of course the whole occasion was made for me unreal and dreamlike by the fact that R. set off to his tribunal at early dawn and didn't return till the guests had departed. I couldn't get over the queerness of our experiencing such very different days.

As he came up the stairs he said, 'No luck at all.' He told me he had gone there full of belief in British justice, and the conviction that since his pacifism *is* sincere the judges were sure to discover the fact. I was rather surprised that he hadn't anticipated, as I had, the hostile and angry light in which they would view him. We have had ample proof (for instance Gerald's violent reaction) of what emotion is aroused by disagreement on this subject. Anxious not to get angry, he had remained uncharacteristically meek while they lectured him about the Treaty of Versailles, told him as sympathetically as they were able that he was a war-weary veteran of the last war, and made no attempt to question him about his views whatever. The proceedings lasted ten minutes; the Tribunal's findings were 'we are not satisfied that there is a conscientious objection within the meaning of the act in this case,' and 'that the applicant's name be removed from the Register of Conscientious Objectors'. He came away thoroughly frustrated. The facts came out at once, his emotional reaction only gradually, and of course he spent a wretched night thinking of all the things he ought to have said. How I wish we had discussed it more, and rehearsed the statements that he must get out whatever questions the judges asked. We had buried our heads in the sand, like ostriches. He is going to write to Craig Macfarlane[1] to ask if it is possible to appeal, and whether it would be a good thing to get letters testifying to the sincerity of his views.

---

[1] Our solicitor and an old friend.

1943

January 1st

A thorough discussion of R.'s tribunal with Julia and Lawrence. Lawrence pointed out that one trouble is R.'s appearance being so completely healthy and normal, and unlike the judges' cranky picture of a CO. He was full of sound advice, presenting the problem as one of strategy. R.'s beliefs *are* coherent and sound; the difficulty is to present them to the tribunal in such a way that they can put him into one of their preconceived categories, and convince them – not that he is a thinking man – but a believing one. It was a great relief to talk to sympathizers for a change.

January 11th

A postcard from Janetta and a letter from Jan both bring the same news – that Rollo is missing in North Africa, and that Geoff[1] who is also out there evidently believes he has been killed. I felt no surprise; Rollo always seemed to have a doomed air, as if he knew himself not to be long for this earth. Gradually a sense of crushing grief descended on me. We are to go to London tomorrow and had arranged to lunch with Janetta one day and Jan the next. I am a coward about facing human pain, just as I hurry away from street accidents, and the misery they must both be feeling must be near the peak of human suffering.

Death was so much in my mind that I talked to Burgo about it, while I lay on his bed feeling suddenly exhausted. The result: when I ran over to the cowman's cottage with a telephone message, he 'thought I was dead' and burst into tears.

January 13th

Up to London for the night, with suitcases full of eggs for our friends. I really dreaded meeting Jan, but the instant I saw her sitting in the hot lounge of the Rembrandt Hotel with a glass of sherry and Geoff's letters in front of her I realized that her courage was equal to the situation. She began to talk at once about the letters, the possibilities, what could be inferred. There was never a tear and no more tremor than usual in her long thin hands. An old gentleman came up and very indignantly asked us to observe the Silence Rule during the broadcasting of the news. We talked on. Geoff's letters were maddening: instead of definite details about the exact wording of the report, he wrote crazily about feeling Rollo near him, and the stars, and God, and how kind everyone was being to him. So much for his Christianity. Next day we lunched with Janetta at the Ivy; her courage was as remarkable as Jan's, but different.

---

[1] Rollo and Janetta's father.

January 20th

At the present time, when violence reigns supreme, anyone who believes in reason rather than force is bound to feel frustrated and painfully out of tune with their surroundings. As I go through the motions of cleaning baths and peeling potatoes I often think about this subject, and nothing shakes my absolute conviction that progress can never be achieved by force or violence, only by reason and persuasion. Intelligence not dynamite, words not bombs are the only means to convince people, slight as that possibility generally is. And anyway I'm not at all sure I believe in progress.

The two old Padels bicycled up this afternoon to express their sympathy with R.'s tribunal troubles. It has evidently been reported in the local papers, so now at last most of our neighbours know us for what we are, and on the whole it's comforting to be able to appear in our true colours. R. has collected a bunch of testimonials to the sincerity of his pacifism – Clive and Phil Nichols, and promises of others.

January 29th

Julia rang up in great agitation. As a 'mobile woman' she has received a summons to appear at Hungerford tomorrow, with a view to being directed into industry or agriculture.

February 4th

Julia to lunch after her crucial interview, arriving on her bicycle, preoccupied and tousled, her fringe awry and a pensive expression on her face. She had lain awake all the night before, picturing herself in prison as a CO, which she might have spared herself had she mastered the fact that women of her age cannot be actually conscripted. When she said she was writing a book, the interviewer herself suggested six months' postponement. 'What sort of a book?' she asked. 'A novel. But not an *ordinary* novel – it's a novel with a *message*.' She has worked out quite logically that her conscience does not forbid agriculture or civil defence.

A spidery note from Mr Higgs the bacon curer announced that our ham and bacon would 'DV' be ready today. So we drove to Newbury to collect it – the last time we shall have the petrol or the excuse. The frail little old man unlocked the oak doors allowing a glimpse of great smoked pigs hanging in rows, then trundled out our sheeted corpse, and came to thank Burgo with tears in his eyes for having written him a letter of sympathy on hearing that a burglar had broken in, knocked him down and robbed the till. 'I shall keep that letter,' he said. We drove away, Burgo rosily blushing, and R. reciting a litany describing all the rich MEAT we now possessed. A rich, smoky aroma filled the car, and 'DV' we shall eat our first slice of bacon tomorrow.

The last remnants of the German army at Stalingrad have given in to the Russians. When first they were encircled and in danger, this seemed too good a piece of news to hope for. Now it has happened and one begins at once feverishly looking forward to the next phase in this drama, even while clouted on the head by the horrifying details of the capitulation – the enormous casualties, hideous cold, soldiers eating their horses and a posse of generals cornered like rats in a trap, unkempt, unshaven and unnerved.

February 9th

Sounds of a bicycle crunching on the gravel, and in dashed Lawrence, sweat on his forehead and a look of frenzy. A new calamity. Oliver has had a sudden violent heart attack and Julia was this morning summoned to his bedside. She had gone off in such a hurry that she had no time to find out what her own feelings were about the disaster (evidently the worst was expected) much less could Lawrence divine them. He didn't know what to be at, had a desire to munch but nothing to bite on. We feel responsible for him in Julia's absence. When he asked me over to listen to records I went somewhat unwillingly, but I'm very glad I did, for they were Benjamin Britten's *Michelangelo Sonnets*, and I felt I was hearing a work of genius for the first time. We sat listening in Lawrence's tiny sitting-room, with the window open wide and rain falling softly on the tufts of violets outside. We played the records right through twice, but can one trust these certitudes?

February 11th

As I stood bung-eyed at the stove over the breakfast frying-pan, in came Wilde for the chicken pail and burst out, 'Newbury was bombed yesterday.' 'No! Was there much damage? Anyone killed?' 'Yes, quite a few. A school and a church were hit.' It turned out to be exactly true, and some eighteen people were killed. If this had happened earlier in the war people would have stopped sending their children in to school at Newbury. Now it's as if being bombed by the Germans was one of the normal hazards of life, like being run over by a motor car, and there was no use trying to avoid it. Probably it's more realistic than the earlier reaction.

February 13th

A letter from Julia giving a hopeful account of Oliver. He has to lie absolutely still for a fortnight without lifting a finger, literally on pain of death, but it looks as if he would pull through. Julia has a surprisingly strong sense of duty, and though she really rather dislikes Oliver than otherwise, her duty to a sick parent takes precedence over duty to Lawrence, so she has agreed to stay there six weeks and nurse him.

Heywood came over from camp at Aylesbury in his little forage cap. The worst time for him was waiting to be called up, and he seemed more relaxed now, yet he loathes the Army. He described the friendly, hearty young men he lives among, some fresh from school, and how he tries to read in his bunk through the din and horseplay, bangs and bumps. The conversation is on the model of 'this fucker's going to fucking Wales tomorrow'.

Just before tea the telephone rang. It was a telegram saying, 'Jan died this afternoon.' I couldn't really take it in. R. rang Janetta up. She had had a sudden relapse after 'flu, and been sent to hospital. 'When I took her there I suddenly saw she was dying,' Janetta said. 'The hospital couldn't understand why she had died and said she should have had every chance, but seemed to have no resistance at all.' There had been no more news about Rollo, and she had clearly lost the will to survive.

February 19th

Lawrence came over on his bicycle to say that Julia would be home for the night tomorrow. We talked of many things: amongst others, conversation. He described the charm of Old Bloomsbury conversation as lying in its being obsessional in some way, coloured by the speaker's mood or moment of vision. Certainly conversations can take the place of events. Here we've been all winter, cooped up like hens in a hen-run, yet I have the feeling the time has been studded with events (sometimes sad but never dull) because of all the endless conversations with R. which make the daily material of our life.

Raymond, Janetta and Kenneth from Friday to Monday. I was nervous because of the standard of cooking I knew our visitors would require and which my talents aren't equal to, and lay awake on Friday night humiliated by my shortcomings. All through the weekend the stress was on *Food* – what we were going to eat next, or what a good meal we had just eaten, and I couldn't help feeling that sometimes too much attention is paid to this admittedly very important subject. However they went off saying they had never had such delicious *food* – so I hope they enjoyed themselves.

March 5th

After tea a military car drove up and an exceedingly gentlemanly Major in the Guards stepped out and asked if there was anywhere some of his men could sleep for a night or two while on manoeuvres. R. offered them the nursery to sleep in and the music-room for their office and Headquarters. The Major vanished, and it wasn't till the middle of the night that we were aroused by the tramping of boots and the sound of lorries revolving in the drive. R. tumbled out of bed to receive them, while I gave way to feelings of resentment at our darling Ham Spray being thus taken over, but when he came back R. restored me to reason by saying mildly, 'After all, they are human beings, you know. And I always feel terribly sorry for the Army.'

March 6th

The soldiers have taken possession so tactfully and quietly that we begin to feel quite fond of them. An officer or two have gone into Alice's old bedroom; the batman dosses down in the nursery sitting-room, and goodness knows how many others in the nursery itself. In the music-room typewriters tap, and a stream of despatch-riders appear at the door. Burgo is mad with military fervour, and was out early thinking up things to say to the sentries, with his hands in his pockets. If we went anywhere near he would say, 'Don't bother me. I'm having a glorious time with Jack' (or Ted). The guardsmen evidently are 'human beings' and neat and tidy as well as friendly ones, but their activities seem as mad and meaningless as those of ants in an anthill.

March 8th

Sounds of evacuation began early this morning. Feet running, a harsh voice saying, 'Get a jerk on'. When I went in to the kitchen to cook breakfast it was full of soldiers making themselves cups of tea.

They are gone. We went into the music-room; nothing remained – nothing except that peculiar soldierly smell and a few cigarette ends. No, not *quite* nothing. Behind the shutter I found some papers marked SECRET, which R. said gave the exact composition of one of our divisions, and was information of great value to the enemy. Just as we were studying it a motor-cyclist dashed up.

'May I look round, just to make sure they haven't left any documents?'

'Well, yes, they have as a matter of fact,' said R. 'Here it is.'

'GOSH! This is *important!*' and the cyclist, a rosy round-faced boy, shot off. It was strange to find military activity so very like a school game.

Over today hangs a cloud of anticipation of R.'s appeal tribunal tomorrow. He is going through a severe attack of stage fright. Lawrence visited us again, to run over some arguments, and papers with snatches of reasoning on them lie all over the room. At the same time R. breaks off his imaginary dialogues and picks up a book and reads it with a concentration I envy and admire.

March 9th

The dreaded day is over and with complete success. Craig and Raymond met us at the Ivy. R. said he would rather I didn't attend, so I listened passively while the others rehearsed the proceedings over lunch. Craig jotted down the details of R.'s military career and memorized them so quickly and accurately that he reeled them off later without a hitch. Raymond looked huddled and rather unhappy, as I feel sure he was. It showed true friendship to stand up for a pal you entirely disagree with; but he couldn't resist one little dig; 'As a matter of fact, I'm sure if Ralph had a gun in his hand and saw a German aeroplane coming over, he would certainly take a pot shot at it.' Which is the nearest to a silly remark I ever heard him make.

I visited Janetta during the proceedings, and found her finishing a picture propped on a chair, and eating a lettuce. When an air-raid alarm went I was looking out of the window at Regent's Park, and I saw the nannies and children hurry off in various directions, while the soaring wail of the siren shot up again and again over the peaceful scene of green lawns and water, children and swans, reminding me of firework rockets – seeming as they do to leave a tall question mark in the air – or the cries of outlandish birds.

Then R. arrived, having cleared his obstacle with a wide margin. He described the proceedings; Craig's excellent manner, Raymond's nervousness, and his own which at once disappeared when he saw the perfect dignity and politeness the judges applied to everyone. He began, 'I don't know if I made my position clear in my statement ...' 'Yes, I think it was perfectly clear.' They asked a few questions about the date when he became a pacifist, his market gardening activities, and an Oxford don asked. 'I think you take up the Absolutist position?' He even cracked a couple of jokes, which made them all laugh, and then thanked them for their consideration. It was over.

March 10th

The Padels rang up for news and Lawrence came over to hear every detail. It was as if we had had a baby and our friends were kindly sharing in our pleasure. But if one starts to analyze this baby, I wonder what will be found? Relief from anxieties such as being threatened with prison, or unpleasant scenes with the local Home

Guard? Or success in this, as in any other endeavour, especially because it was an intellectual one? I put top the satisfaction of R.'s having acted in accordance with his beliefs, but of course there are a host of minor ones – like wondering what will be the effect on Gerald!

March 16th

The Padels have been deluging me with Communist literature and this evening (after much putting it off) I sat down to read some Lenin. For the theories of Marx and Engels criticising Capitalism I have always had some respect, but Lenin seems almost empty of thought, and I feel he 'argues' from his stomach instead of his brain, mentioning 'violent revolution' as if speaking of a pot of caviare. What I find quite intolerable in Communism is the assumption that it's *better* to achieve a result by violence than by persuasion; and why turning the state upside down and putting the proletariat on top should solve all problems they hardly bother to suggest. I rehearse arguments by which I can convince these kind innocent people that I am not, never have been and to the best of my belief never will be a Communist.

March 21st

An evening speech by Winston was announced. Would it herald some new developments, a Second Front even? After a lengthy and much qualified statement of war aims, the old conjurer suddenly declared that he had received a telegram from Montgomery and the *8th Army is on the move*. So R. was right, and there's an extraordinary feeling of suspense lifting.

April 21st

We tore up our roots from Ham Spray and travelled to East Anglia, to stay with Helen Anrep. How lovely to be in someone else's house; and walking into Helen's sitting-room I was overwhelmed by the beauty of it, lovely china everywhere, chosen with exquisite taste, as are the stuffs draped over worn furniture and the subtle delicate colours of the room itself. All sorts of things from rare Oriental objects to Spanish or Italian peasant pots are combined and unified by Helen's (and I suppose Roger's) individual powers of selection. The room was a perfect background for Helen's smiling rosy face and untidy white hair, as her slight body moved silently and rather elegantly about, unexpectedly clad in a very dusty tweed suit, with fresh feminine white frills at neck and cuffs.

Upstairs were more beautiful things, vases of beautifully-arranged flowers everywhere, and *incredible dirt*. Only the floors of the rooms seem to have been touched for years. Black cobwebs festooned the windows and walls, and dust lay thick on the piles of books piled on every available surface.

Walked with Helen beside the river. When we commented on its being a remarkable indigo colour, she said, 'Oh yes, it's the outflow from some sort of factory – a dye works perhaps,' but with no sign of minding this strange aberration. The Suffolk landscape was both intensely English and somewhat decayed: enormous fallen elms lay in the grass, and we passed the old mills that had become dilapidated and deserted, and overgrown gardens with waves of lilac overflowing their walls. Talk, as usual, about the Euston Road Group, the wickedness of the Royal Academy and the eccentricity of country neighbours. Helen told some very amusing, if scandalous stories about members of the Group. Why they and some of the Bloomsbury painters *worry* so about the Royal Academy beats me.

May 10th

Home again. Janetta has been here for a week, and now she has gone off I regret the things I didn't say. Kenneth came one night, walking unexpectedly into the sitting-room. After a while he handed her a letter in rather an offhand way, saying, 'Oh, here's your father's letter about Rollo.' She read it and was obviously shaken. When she handed it to me I saw that it seemed to give absolute proof that Rollo was dead. His papers had turned up on the dead body of a soldier. Of course while the official verdict is 'Missing', it is impossible to crush hope altogether.

Burgo has been ill and the weather has been appalling; today it pours and blows, drips, patters and oozes. There is no possibility of going out and I have done badly as sick nurse. I came down to supper almost in tears after a prolonged tussle of wills, and found R. supporting and reasonable. I couldn't get on for a week without him.

May 19th

Well – Victory is ours. The Axis is out of Africa. The church bells are to ring.

The blackout comes very late now, so that we don't have to draw the blinds in the passages. I love stumbling and feeling my way along them at night by the mystical light of the full moon which has streamed brilliantly in at the windows lately, and looking out to see the sky full of stars. By day it has been drowsy and still, very quiet except for a chorus of singing birds and the frou-frou of little ducklings running through the grass. The lawn is a hayfield and the garden a wilderness.

July 28–30th

R. and I to the Bothy for the weekend, cool and refreshing as a plunge into water. Raymond was industrious at his typewriter; Eardley, stripped to the waist, digging in the vegetable garden. Raymond gave us a garbled account of Julia's efforts to get exemption from call-up, writing to various friends to ask them to vouch for her work being 'of value to civilization'. He assumed that no one could so perjure themselves. I know for a fact that this was not what she asked them to say, but merely that 'she was a serious writer'. But in any case, even if one doesn't believe this – and I for one do – is it so dreadful to stretch a point to get an old friend out of trouble? It's Morgan [Forster]'s[1] famous issue between country and friend. I went so far as to say I set enormous value on friendship and very little on patriotism, but I saw this horrified them both, and Eardley in particular looked very shocked.

The weekend passed very happily in talking, reading and gliding off in the punt. One evening when we were walking to the pub to telephone, we stood for a moment to watch an endless stream of bombers going over. As men reeled out of the pub on their way to the men's lavatory most of them looked up and laughed or said, 'Somebody's got something coming to them tonight.' Raymond murmured: 'Verona, Florence, Pisa.' Eardley said to R.: 'Wouldn't it be wonderful to be in one of those bombers going over to bomb Germany?' Why isn't he, then? I couldn't

---

[1] The novelist E. M. Forster.

help silently wondering. Raymond and I talked about the curious lack of emotion with which we were watching this gladiatorial spectacle. For this is in effect what it was, and goodness knows how many of those bombers will 'fail to return'. The light had almost gone, and a pale yellow-white searchlight shot its beam upwards against the Thames landscape of rounded trees and luscious meadows, still faintly coloured blue-green and grey.

August 16th

We have had a visit from the Garnetts – Bunny, Angelica and William. Angelica intrigued us by saying that a few days ago Bunny came home from his office swinging his umbrella and carrying a bottle of champagne. 'There's good news,' he said, 'that must be celebrated; but of course I can't tell you what it is. You'll know in course of time, and when it *does* break,' he said, chuckling to himself, 'it'll be pretty striking.'

September 2nd to 9th

A week's visit from Alix and James – and a very eventful one so far as the war was concerned. I have passed over in silence the fall of Mussolini, a huge *bonne bouche* that we digested surprisingly quickly. A few days later James, rather pink in the face, announced that the 8th Army had landed on the Italian mainland, and later still, 'The Italians have surrendered unconditionally!'

It was the nicest visit the Stracheys have ever paid us. We regaled them on home-grown ducklings, plums, figs and melons, and they have never been more benign and friendly.

James on the psychoanalytical front: 'Things have been very bad lately, with so few neurotics, and those there are snapped up by the refugees. However I hope with the approach of peace the situation may brighten up a bit and gradually return to normal.' Alix was very amusing about her endless tussle with her mother, to introduce more heat and sanitation into their house. Mrs Sargant Florence is a remarkable old lady, as handsome in her way as Alix and with the same fine Red Indian features and level blue-grey gaze. She had a considerable reputation as a painter at one time, and has covered the walls of hall and passages with truly appalling frescoes representing a concourse of blind men in a waste place. 'We call them the Willies,' said James with a wild laugh, 'because Alix's Uncle Willy sat as model for them all.' Then she discovered some mysterious equation between music and colour, and published a book about it. She has other strange cranky beliefs, such as that water-closets are 'wicked' and earth-closets 'good'. After endless pleading from Alix, who has delicate health and dreads the cold, her mother agreed to a WC being put in, if Alix would foot the bill and promise to remove it the moment the war was over, and if it was promised that the plug should never be pulled 'except in cases of extreme emergency'. She then must have forgotten all about it. Alix told us: 'Then one day I heard a *fearful* caterwauling in the back yard and saw a stately, gleaming white object standing there, with the plumber and his boy in attendance both looking rather taken aback, while my mother waved her arms and shouted, with her white hair flying like King Lear's: "My whole life's work is destroyed!"' Another story of Alix's: 'I've been having tooth trouble and didn't want to go to London, but I found a sort of defrocked dentist in Marlow, who visited people in their houses with a plug-in drill. It made a horrible noise and worked anything but smoothly, and the tooth he mended soon fell to bits. It must come out, he said, and I had to drive and bring him back to Lord's Wood where he gave me an injection and then found he'd left his forceps behind, so I had to drive him to Marlow again with a frozen gum to get them. When he got to work the gum was rapidly unfreezing, and James and my mother, eating their dinner in the room below were electrified to hear wild yells and the sound of me being dragged round the room in a basket chair.' It turned out he was a drunkard who had lost his practice thereby.

October 4th to 9th

Saxon is spending his fortnight's holiday here. I get more and more devoted to him. His teasing perversity is evaporating with age, and his sweetness of character seems to grow. In the evening R. reads aloud, while I darn and mend, Saxon knits white woollen leggings for Barbara Bagenal's grandchild, and Burgo fetches his knitting too – a dish-cloth.

News from the outside world: Bunny and Angelica have a daughter.

Nicko Henderson, back from Cairo, came to see us, bringing messages from old friends – Bryan Guinness and Michael MacCarthy are both miserable and longing to be home. Eddie Gathorne-Hardy says Ham Spray 'is the only civilized house in England'. Nicko is attached to Lord Moyne in some capacity which involves entertaining visitors from England. He gave an amusing account of Noël Coward, wanting to swim but having no bathing trunks, so he had to accept a long, unbecoming pair of underpants belonging to Lord Moyne. Then he asked Nicko, 'Is there such a thing as a lav about?' Nicko pointed vaguely to some large trees. N.C.: 'No, no, old chap; big stuff, very much so.' So Nicko took him indoors and found a lavatory for him. Soon afterwards Coward came out clutching Lord Moyne's pants, half on and half off, and ran into Nicko with a lady visitor. Nicko rather maliciously introduced them, and N.C. said 'Simply *amazing* meeting you like this. Definitely no sign whatever of toilet paper.'

October 25th

A letter from Julia, which I opened rather anxiously. There has been a renewal of air-raids on London this week, one at least every night, and I wondered how she had been standing them. She writes: 'It is somewhat like having a nightly purge; one is uncomfortable until one's had it – the raid I mean – one grits one's teeth and endeavours to bear up and numb oneself for the short period it's functioning, and then heaves a sigh of relief and happiness when the all clear goes. The noise is comparatively mild. All the same, Germans circling overhead and trying to kill one are Germans circling overhead trying to kill one.' I should think so indeed. 'Very much so.'

I have been a good deal preoccupied by the thought of London raids, and even dream of them by night. The intense quiet here, emphasized by the peaceful autumn stillness, puts them in strong contrast. Julia's letter is full of references to 'little dinner parties', Molyneux coming to buy Lawrence's pictures, visits to his flat at Claridge's, unconsciously I think wanting to make us feel we are missing much of the point of life. I'm not sure whether I do feel it or not. One is alive in one way in the country, in quite another in the jostle of London life. Probably the best thing is to take alternate doses of each.

November 1st

I opened a letter from Bunny at breakfast and out fell a bombshell. 'I am extremely anxious,' he wrote, 'that Angelica and the baby should be out of London during the next few weeks. I am writing to ask if it would be possible for them to come to Ham Spray for the latter part of November. It is almost the only place to which I could persuade her to go without me. I would not write this letter, which I do without her knowledge, if I had not a reason (call it a hunch) which I am not able to tell her or discuss at present. All I can say is that I should be much happier if they were outside London during a few weeks: it may be absolutely unnecessary, but the sight of these soft little creatures makes one timorous.'

This piece of news, and its implications, exploded very slowly into a soft but ever-widening circle of detonations in my brain. A moment's thought made it clear that Bunny was acting on secret information and it might get him into serious trouble if his indiscretion became known. Then came the thought: had he the right to hand on this piece of explosive to me, to load me up with gun-powder and then say: Don't go off. Or not even to say it, but leave me to guess it. For, of course, if he has some inside information that London is destined to suffer some appalling fate during certain fast-approaching weeks, I should *like* to pass it on to everyone living there whom I love and who could possibly get away. Janetta first and foremost. Damn it all, we aren't playing this beastly war game of Bunny's. Why should we be forced to obey its rules, and not put danger and unhappiness to friends first? Yet Bunny is also a friend, and his danger and unhappiness also has to be considered.

Julia and Lawrence were staying the weekend, and I had read Bunny's letter aloud at the breakfast table before I realized its full significance. They reacted violently. Julia at once began to plan to leave London during the danger period, very naturally. Lawrence said that she must certainly go if she wanted, but he wouldn't dream of it. If his friends were in for an unpleasant experience he wanted to share it. All day long the arguments went on, the ripples from Bunny's letter spreading wider and wider. In the afternoon I wrote to him saying we should be delighted to have Angelica and the baby for as long as they liked.

As we sat over our various activities this evening all the lights went out all over the house. Lawrence had been listening to Beethoven's C sharp minor quartet on the gramophone, and the sudden extinction of the music was more startling than the stoppage of light. I fetched candles and put them in pots round the room, and the rest of us went on with our activities in little pools of light – Julia reading a book, R. and Burgo playing draughts.

November 2nd

After leaving Lawrence and Julia at the station, I bought a paper, and the first thing I saw was that a German plane had crashed into Inkpen beacon last night. So that was what fused the lights! It seems odd that just when we had been considering London's peril enemy bombers had been hovering near. Audrey Bonham-Carter saw the crash as she was walking home. There was a huge blaze, and a lot of people from Inkpen hurried to the spot. One of them said he 'found himself falling over a bomb'. The bomb-load was scattered over the Downs, unexploded; the crew were all dead, two – including the pilot – having been shot through the head.

November 3rd

London for the day. I went straight to 41 Gordon Square, where I found Angelica lying in bed cutting up oranges for marmalade. She seemed very pleased at the idea of coming to Ham Spray, but also to realize the awkwardness to us in being let in to the secret of Bunny's 'hunch'. I didn't tell Bunny who arrived later, that Julia and Lawrence were in on it. He took that risk in writing as he did, and I can do no more except beg them to be discreet. He said that subsequent events had made him think the danger more remote: 'Other people didn't take it so seriously and it was that that alarmed me. Now I think they do, and measures are being taken which may stop it altogether.' What IT can be is never hinted at. When Angelica and I were alone together she said she couldn't guess either, but from Bunny's expression when he talked about it she thought it must be something absolutely horrible. The gutter press has been raising a scare about German plans to shell London with huge guns embedded in the cliffs of France.

November 19th

The Garnetts are not coming after all, but going to Charleston, why I don't know. We got an amusing letter from Lawrence on the subject of Bunny's hunch (which has become 'the rabbit hutch'): 'Perhaps tonight it will come clattering or gliding, rocketing, dripping or whatever it is going to do, out of the sky. Meanwhile I am beginning to suspect that the Hutch is everyone's Hutch. The paper has a column about it every day, and today admitted that it was causing widespread comment, which I translate as "universal alarm". I am not at all sure that there isn't a panic on. John Davenport, that well-oiled weathercock, suddenly announced he was going away for three weeks' holiday, and was gone within the hour.'

The whole subject has assumed a grotesque appearance which makes it hard to believe anything will come of it all. If it does, our jokes will look pretty silly.

Clive writes, 'I sympathize with Fredegond Shove,[1] who hasn't spoken to Maynard for years, but – finding herself sitting behind him at the Cambridge Theatre – leant forward and said, "You're the only person who has any power; can't you do something to stop this terrible war?"'

November 25th

Two days running there has been news of huge raids (the 'biggest yet') on Berlin, five times as heavy as the heaviest on London. It's a suffocating thought. We shall go on and on, R. thinks, till nothing is left. Bunny probably knew of these ahead and thought the Germans would retaliate with their famous 'rocket-gun'. I rang up Janetta, who is due on Friday with Kenneth and the baby, suggesting she comes at once in case of possible reprisals for our raids. Thus I have now in effect passed on Bunny's warning without giving him away. Reports continue to come in of the ghastly destruction our two monster raids have caused. The fires are still burning and the cloud of smoke 'has reached the shores of Sweden. The raids won't stop until the heart of Nazi Germany has ceased to beat.'

Frenzy rages in some quarters because the Mosleys have been let out of prison. As neither R. nor I accept the principle that people should ever be shut up for their principles or without trial, the question doesn't arise for us.

---

[1] Poetess; published by the Hogarth Press.

November 27th

Janetta and family are here. A good deal of rocket-bomb talk last night. Kenneth, who is an ARP doctor, was told that none of them was to leave London for the present, cancelling a job in Yorkshire he had been promised, in view of a 'possible secret weapon attack on London'.

How interminable the war seems! Sometimes I feel I'm hardly more tired of the war itself than I am of my own abhorrence of it, ever with me like a bad taste or hole in a tooth.

I am reading Trevelyan's *Garibaldi*, always cracked up as a moving and exciting book, yet I find it chiefly inspires me with amazement at the frivolity of this horrible game of war, with its barbarous rules and disregard for human life, the unmerited respect and blaze of glory accompanying any mention of it. Nor can I feel admiration for Garibaldi himself – a simple-minded, rather stupid, overgrown boy-scout. The ideal of manliness needs refurbishing and bringing up to date. At present it belongs to the caveman era and in spite of all progress in science and education young men can only show they *are* men by hurtling through the air or under the sea to hunt down and kill their fellows. Perhaps that's why there are so many homosexuals nowadays. Sensitive and intelligent males, to whom this idea is secretly repugnant, feel they cannot measure up to it, and decide to be females instead.

R. and I walked down to Inkpen in the dark to fetch Burgo from a tea-party. The stars came out one by one and a Christmas-card moon sailed over the Downs. Then a forest of searchlights sprang up and fingered the sky.

1944

January 20th

This diary has very little chance of existence these days. I thought I was hard-working before, but ever since Boxing Day I've done the entire work of the house, Mrs M. having been ill and run down, and most unlikely to return. Also we all spent the last fortnight having 'flu, one after another. Are we to continue life as it is – possible only so long as we have hardly any visitors – or what? The problem is in the offing, but we don't talk about it much. Barring, in my case, one or two moments when I felt I couldn't bear my days being entirely filled with thoughtless chores any longer, I know perfectly well that I can, and I even manage better than I used; but sometimes I think of our existence in terms of struggling across the Atlantic in an open boat, or lost in the desert in a small car with hardly any food. Don't be ridiculous, I hear a voice say, you have a comfortable house, a productive kitchen garden, and your husband and child with you. Look at what most people have to put up with!

Music is my great solace: quartets every week, and the other day our company was swollen to an octet – an occasion I looked forward to and thought about afterwards much as I used in my youth to think of a ball or party. I found it very exciting to be in a small room with so many instruments at once, and in danger of stumbling over 'cellos and violas if one moved.

February 2nd

We go on as before, but at breakfast the other day there was a near row between R. and me because I read the *New Statesman* at breakfast out of sheer mental weariness. He exploded and said that I was always doing this sort of thing now-adays, and not paying any attention to him. I felt a good deal of sympathy with him, but could only say, 'Well, if you want me to remain a human being you must find me a "help".' He went off at once on his bicycle to look for one, unsuccessfully I fear.[1]

February 10th

Slowly sinking into the bog, down and down. Dog-tired every evening, I doze on the sofa. Up to bed and sleep lightly, toss and turn, and have visions of dirty plates and vegetables waiting to be peeled. Down in the morning bung-eyed, to see the ancient red bricks of the kitchen floor getting blacker and blacker.

---

[1] In extenuation of this collapse, I must note that we had at this time no washing-up machine, clothes-washing machine or vacuum cleaner.

However, yesterday, a miracle, a new figure turned up. Honest brown eyes behind specs, strangely fitting false teeth. What joy, what comfort!

As the pressure eases off, the outer world gradually penetrates my consciousness, as it does when coming round after an anaesthetic. At first I feel greedy for it, drink in the sights and sounds so long crowded out, welcome the few puny thoughts that steal into my mind, and eagerly snatch up books and papers, or listen to the wireless to catch the ideas of others. Then I bang my head on the stone wall of reality – the WAR. All England is on tenterhooks waiting for the Second Front; Japanese atrocities are retailed with relish; the miners are in a perpetual state of strike, colonels are still thundering in *The Times* about 'The cowardly, dastardly and brutal entry of Italy into the War', assuming of course that the entry of all the Allies into the war was courageous, altruistic and noble. There is great agitation about the possible danger to Rome, which is getting ever nearer the battle zone. Are its ancient monuments worth the life of a single soldier? 'Not if it's *my* son,' cries one. 'My son shan't die for any old building.' (Very natural, but you seem to be prepared for him to die in the useless effort to capture a small hill and kill a few Germans.) If only people would realize that their son's dying and killing other people's sons wasn't going to benefit humanity in any way, but almost certainly the reverse. What good did the First World War do?

February 22nd

We have had Angelica for a week, with her baby, Amaryllis. She is a delightful companion and has restored our morale, making life in some magical way more exciting. The cold was appalling throughout her visit, and we went about rubbing blue hands together, and with chattering teeth. Cold and music were the chief features of her stay. She played the violin to my piano and vice versa; we played the Bach Double Concerto, and she sang to my accompaniment. We even had a session at the Padels, Angelica playing the piano in the Schumann quintet. Mr Padel was instantly bowled over by Angelica, and although it was snowing and Mrs Padel ill in bed, he insisted on bicycling over next day in his tweed deer-stalker to hear her sing. Next evening the telephone rang: '*Could* I have a word with Mrs Garnett?' She came back giggling, for he had nothing to say except that he hoped to see her again and 'What did she think of Epstein?' I've never seen such a case of love at first sight.

This last week scattered raids on London have suddenly intensified into something approaching the old Blitz. The other night I was woken by deep subterranean rumblings which shook the house. 'An earthquake', I thought, for it seemed outside all previous experience, but realized it was big guns. It was followed by other 'old-fashioned noises' and then the All Clear. For several days after this the children have been picking up strips of shiny black paper in the fields. It seems they are dropped by German planes to confuse our radio location.

February 26th to 28th

Julia and Lawrence's long-postponed visit. The fiendish cold unluckily continued and put Julia to a severe test. She wore her false leopard-skin jacket and two pairs of woollen gloves even at meal times. When we apologized for Ham Spray being such a difficult house to heat, she replied, 'Well, if it was mine I should have to sell it,' thus offending R. greatly. They were both heroic in the help they gave with bed-making and washing-up, and in Julia's case she hates it so much that it *is* heroism. When I said I didn't want any help with the cooking, indeed would rather do it alone, she said, 'Ah yes, I understand and respect that,' in a voice of great relief. This week of bad air-raids has been a horrible strain on her in ways I recognize: rather glazed expression, lack of interest in other people, letting her appearance get quite extraordinary, while criticizing others for not being 'elegant' enough. Of all the numerous facets of Julia's complex character, her unself-conscious and eccentric side is the one I'm personally fondest of.

March 7th to 10th

Boris and Maroussa. Maroussa thawed, and shook off her irrational fears. She slept well and relaxed, and talked to me with horror of the state she found herself in. She feels mentally tensed up the whole time to ward off the shock of the next raid. Most of their studio has been made unusable by bombing, and she and Boris crouch miserably in one room, listening all day to broadcasts from Moscow. Boris has no job now, and is disgruntled by being treated as an alien who has to get a police permit to come down here for a few days.

From the moment of their arrival on Hungerford Station, when Boris enfolded R. in a bear's hug and kissed him on both cheeks, astonishing the other travellers, their visit was a delight. They are both so appreciative and responsive that one wants to do everything possible for their happiness and comfort. Maroussa had breakfast in bed every day and they went away laden with fruit and vegetables. Leaving them at the station we drove on to visit the Bomfords, where we found Gamel. 'Gerald sends you his love,' she said; and I felt a dart of anger at this *geste arbitraire*, which I suppose in his own eyes transforms his unconquerable hostility to R. into something more compatible with his own view of himself.

April 28th–May 1st

Bunny and Angelica have taken a furnished villa at Oxted, next to old Mrs Garnett, and they invited us all three for the weekend. It was a very ugly yellow brick castellated box, built by two suffragette lady doctors, and gazing out onto what at first sight seems an extremely secluded rustic English scene. A closer look, and one observes other dwellings similarly peering out, discreetly enough, as if anxious not to spoil each other's view. The side of the wooded hill is in fact thickly populated, for in a number of little houses – some homely, some arty-crafty, some mere shacks roofed with black tar – there lives a colony of intensely lively old ladies: widows of Persian professors, Russian revolutionaries, and Constance Garnett herself. They spend their time gardening away besottedly, tottering round to see each other, peering out of beady inquisitive eyes at any stranger, keeping a lot of cats. Bunny's mother is not a very sociable person though full of charm. She lives in a world of her own thoughts, and the pumpkins she grows in her garden are probably as important to her as human beings, but she looks out at stray visitors like ourselves with mild blue eyes, in which intelligence and humour are combined, through the thickest spectacles I ever saw. I suppose she has almost blinded herself with years and years of translating Russian masterpieces for a mere pittance.

May 4th–8th

These few days back at Ham Spray have confirmed my feeling that whatever else it is – ramshackle, not very warm, untidy – it is, at times at least, a centre of life.

Allen Lane has for some unexplained reason asked me to write a book on wild flowers, to be illustrated by an artist called Richard Chopping. He came to do a few days' preparatory work on it, and in an instant a thousand practical questions were buzzing round our heads like a cloud of mosquitoes. We sat up till the small hours going over our plans, and then my head was too full of plant-names to sleep. Richard endeared himself greatly to both R. and me. He is, I think, a very sweet character – affectionate, gentle, kind and inquisitive. Tall and good-looking with rather slavonic features, he is quite remarkably *clean*. We were much impressed by the way he went off and washed his socks every day and hung them on the line. Meanwhile I managed to dash off for an afternoon of quartets, Eardley came for a night, and the Tidcombe boys came over with a pasque-flower to show us for our book.

May 16th

All last night we were kept awake by extraordinary noises – of low-flying aeroplanes followed by loud explosions which shook the house. I suppose they were of enemy origin as the siren had gone. Before going to bed we saw a red flush waxing and waning over the Downs, and a flight of aeroplanes flying north. Other green and red lights were moving everywhere. But by day, too, a new phenomenon has begun – bangs of a shattering loudness burst from time to time on our ears without any warning, making one give a huge jump like a baby when a door is slammed and spill anything one happens to be holding. Audrey Bonham-Carter says that they are so loud at Inkpen that their teeth rattle in their heads, but the local Colonel tells her this will all stop when the Second Front begins. It is degrading to be waiting day in and day out for something so horrific.

Since then our hearts have been warmed to the cockles by a visit from Raymond. How we both enjoy having him here – and in spite of our standard of comfort not measuring up to his I really believe he enjoys being here too. He had just come back from five weeks lecturing in North Africa, travelling out in a military aeroplane, unable to see out or sleep, on a seat made of aluminium scoops. He described enthusiasm for England and cries of '*Vive l'Angleterre*', principally based – he thought – on a reverse feeling towards the Americans: '*Ils sont des barbares.*'

June 2nd to 6th

We have all three been for these last days at dear old Well Farm, the Cornishes in Devon. When I came down to breakfast this morning R. was smiling strangely. 'Mrs Cornish says it's on the wireless that the Invasion has started.' How to describe the effect of this announcement, coming after so long a wait, and so differently from the myriad ways I had imagined it? Something seemed to turn over inside me and then rebalance. There I was, just as before and yet not the same. Something from outside had entered in and become part of me.

We asked if we might listen to the nine o'clock news in the kitchen and found three chairs drawn up in front of the wireless and an atmosphere of church reigning. One half-witted twin was shooed away. Mrs Cornish knitted peacefully.

An elderly woman with bright eyes under a flat hat sat on the sofa. Then in a solemn hush the King stammered forth his banal generalities in which God as usual figured largely. The long-planned invasion had begun early this morning, with gliders, parachutists, 'ducks' and troops streaming across the Channel and landing on the Normandy coast between Cherbourg and Le Havre. Difficulty and losses were far less than expected. So far so good. I could hardly draw a deep breath throughout the broadcast, and looked at the tossing trees outside the window with a sudden stab of realization that our fate now hangs in the balance, as individuals and as a nation. And this, here and now, is what we have expected and waited for with such a horrible mixture of dread and longing, for months.

July 3rd

Of course, as soon as the war came alive again it became impossible to write, and write I have not for three dramatic weeks. While at Well Farm we listened each day to the progress of our armies in France. It was extraordinary how soon the whole position was assimilated into one's being, and ceased producing those 'dentist's pains' and pangs of anxiety and hope of the first day. Now, three weeks later, it is clear that the Invasion has been a success and less costly than expected. Meanwhile the Russians have started a fresh onslaught on the Eastern front, and are hurling the Germans back fast. They are in retreat in Italy. We bomb them incessantly. What prevents them from collapsing utterly? The fact is that I quite soberly feel they may do so at any moment. But there is one thing I haven't mentioned, and that a most unpleasant one – the doodle-bug.

The day after we reached Ham Spray we were rung up by friends to say that they had heard from London that they were being attacked all day by wireless-controlled pilotless aircraft! Could anything be more Wellsian? Since then these pilotless planes, facetiously christened doodle-bugs, have been the chief topic of conversation. Horror falls on some. Others are exempt, for the range of these monsters seems to be strictly limited, and we – thank heavens – are just outside it. But 'evacuees' begin again, and Ham has many new faces in it. The worst of this death-watch beetle is that it goes on day and night; there is no respite from it.

I rang up Janetta, to ask if she would like to bring Nicolette down. 'As a matter of fact I've hardly noticed it; I slept all last night.'

'What's it like?' I asked. 'Very noisy?'

'Well, there certainly are some rather odd noises. But so far I don't mind it much. There was one half an hour ago.'

Soon after this came Julia, our first doodle-bug refugee; also Saxon on ten days' sick leave, arriving covered in dust from a doodle-bug which had landed between Percy Street and Tottenham Court Road just as he was leaving for the station. It blew in some of his windows and filled his rooms with black oily smoke.

'Did it make a tremendous explosion?' we asked.

'No. I didn't hear anything. But then I didn't hear *much* when that land-mine fell in Great James Street.'

People vary greatly in their reactions. Some dislike it more than ordinary bombing 'because it's uncanny', or for such curious reasons as 'because you can't do anything to it' or 'because it's hardly human.' Others less, 'because it isn't looking for me', is 'random and aimless', and even 'helpless to defend itself'. Everyone jokes about it unceasingly, but in a somewhat horrified way. Saxon suddenly burst out, 'I can't think why everyone wants to talk so much about this doodle-bug.' (I can think of several reasons.) An article in the *New Statesman* described English villagers typically referring to it as a 'chap' – 'and then I looked up and there was another chap coming along'.

The object now emerges as a robot plane about twenty-five feet long, projected from a concrete base in France; it flies low and with considerable noise and has a light in its tail. When the light goes out and the noise stops the doodle-bug is about to descend and everyone is advised to take cover instantly. Other doodle-buggiana: a letter from Dorking: 'Have you seen these damn things? I couldn't sleep for curiosity about them, but now I'm satisfied, and have seen several at night and one very close here by day. It flew just over us and crashed into Leith Hill. It was slim and elegant and going with tremendous purpose, like those games where you make a dash for "home" when the "he" is turned the other way. There seem the hell of a lot of them, and they've certainly got a fascination that raiders never had.' Julia on arrival from London: 'I've not heard any good of them so far.' Saxon, in a letter: 'The All Clear went as I was in the taxi from Paddington, an alert as I walked to Dr Gould's, and others most of the day. Barbara [Bagenal] was with me in my flat, marking some clothes, when a "chap" whistled overhead and came down by the Whitfield Memorial Chapel. Some few minutes later we heard another arrive and saw the smoke – apparently it hit the Regent Palace Hotel. Barbara and I went to the National Gallery; the picture "on view" for the time is Goya's portrait of Dr Peral. Against the wall opposite him sits an attendant. When three bells go he takes the Goya downstairs and when one goes he brings it back again. He must have walked quite a long way today.' R. is much struck by this last fact and thinks it ought to be put on record. For more than a week it has rained steadily from heavy grey clouds. If it hadn't been for this there would have been fewer doodle-bugs. As it is our fighters have shot down seventy-five per cent of them.

Old Mrs Garnett's little house at Oxted appears to be on the doodle-bug path to London, and they were so frequent that Bunny has sent Angelica and the baby to Charleston. As for Constance herself, he has bought her a helmet which she keeps beside her while weeding her flower-beds.

There's something obsessional about this new development, which I'm well aware of myself. Anything may happen in this war now, is the feeling, and meanwhile we prepare for the return of refugees. Janetta and Nicolette are expected any day, for six months, while Kenneth is in Cairo.

Last week we took Burgo to do his entrance exam to Newbury Grammar School. We all felt anxious, and Burgo broke into last-minute wails and said he could not, would not go. Then he went to the lavatory and came out having pulled himself together: 'I'm not going to be silly any more. But just tell me this, when you put up your hand do you do it sitting or standing?' When we called for him afterwards he was bouncing and radiant, and had thoroughly enjoyed himself.

August 23rd

Burgo has been accepted by the Newbury Grammar School, and today we took him to see his future headmaster, packing into the car with a lot of baskets of fruit and vegetables. We liked Mr Starr and were cheered up by the interview; for one thing it was clear Burgo had passed easily, and on his merits. Lunched at the

Chequers Inn, and were aware that the news was just starting in the Lounge. Then we heard the Marseillaise. 'Paris must have been retaken!' I said. And so it had. Here is a piece of news that brings nothing but pleasure. An old dog of a Lesbian, dressed as a man, with a stock and cropped grey hair, sat down beside us: 'Glorious news, isn't it,' she said, 'and especially that the Free French did it themselves.'

August 24th

R. and I lay in bed last night thinking and talking of nothing but the fall of Paris and the probability of peace soon. I woke feeling 'I must get up – things are happening.' Janetta said she had been far too excited to sleep, and when I took some eggs to Mrs Mills, the baker's wife, she said, 'I couldn't sleep for thinking peace might come soon.' So we all sit, like people in the waiting-room of a hospital while a life or death operation goes on . . .

In the evening James and Alix arrived, bringing with them as they always do a sense of immutability. Even their eccentricities are continuous. James had been talking to some Russian who said he knew all about the various German secret weapons – V.2, 3 and 4. Also we hear, as we often have before, that the War Office is taking V.2, the famous rocket gun, extremely seriously, and is prepared to evacuate London on a much larger scale should it come into operation as they think it well may. According to James its range is so long that it can be fired from Cologne and still hit London, so that our capturing the north coast of France will make us no safer. In fact nothing will put us out of range except peace. It is a horrible thought and I can't help feeling that Hitler might well let it off in one last mad Guy Fawkes explosion, even though he saw he was beaten. Miles the aircraft designer, told Anthony West that there were some technical problems connected with the rocket that the Germans had apparently not solved yet. He described our reconnaissance aircraft flying over the place where the doodle-bug was tried out, and observing the craters it made. Then one day a crater *eighty yards wide* was seen, and this was made by the rocket. Another rocket story is that the first one was sent off three weeks ago and has not come down yet, which is not quite as mad as it sounds – the theory is that if it goes too high it disintegrates. So – we are a mass of rumour and speculation.

August 26th

The lost summer came back today; the Downs emerged from pearly mists. Burgo and I weeded the front flower-beds, and then, beaten by the heat, I pulled a rug into the shade. But whatever one does just now, whatever one's eyes rest on, more than half one's mind is like a sponge soaked in thoughts of the approaching end of the war. What will peace be like? Alix confessed at lunch that she viewed the letting-up of restrictions with dread: 'Just think of the appalling responsibility of having to choose how one's life is to be led!'

Still feeling hopelessly restless I got Burgo to walk up the Downs. He persisted in talking about death, burial and suicide, asking a lot of questions about all these subjects. How much had R. minded the deaths of Lytton and Carrington? In a trembling voice he said how much he had minded the death of M.A.M. and Rollo. He said, 'It's particularly sad when young people die – as if a hammer got lost before it could hammer in any nails.' As for suicide, he asked about the ways of doing it and I told him, but gave what I hoped were good reasons for not killing oneself. He replied: 'Oh, I feel sure I shall commit suicide somehow.' Then he talked about Alix and James: 'I can't imagine them as parents. It's like Protestants and Catholics – some people are one and some the other.' We were talking so hard that we saw little of our surroundings as we descended the Downs, pale with drought. As we approached Ham Spray garden there were two dark-clad figures drooping across the lawn, like suits of clothes on hangers – the Stracheys themselves.

Julia returned from telephoning Lawrence to say, 'The *on dit* in London is that the rockets will begin on September 1st. I just tell you for your information.'

August 31st

The spectre of GAS has again reared its ugly head. The wireless announced that Hitler was evidently determined to use it on England before he explodes, and that trains full of gas were arriving in Holland and Belgium. One was bombed and gas escaped, causing a panic. R. says he will certainly do it by means of doodle-bugs, which will be very disagreeable and frightening but bound to be a failure. However that may be, the thought of gas always takes the wind out of my sails and the breath from my lungs, though why it should be worse to be suffocated than burst into fragments it's hard to say. This hateful war has gone on five years today.

Tonight came the news that the English have entered Brussels, followed inevitably by the Brabançonne.

September 5th

At breakfast, while reading her post Janetta's face became grey and set. Afterwards she showed me a bleak letter from her father saying that Rollo's body had been found in Tunisia, buried beside his aeroplane, and reburied in the military cemetery, with only a plain wooden cross, but 'later it would be possible', etc., etc. I found it very difficult to know what to say to her or gauge the exact contents of her mind, and was ashamed, for there are few things more important than being able to interpret other people's thoughts.

Bicycled up Ham Hill to look for mushrooms. As always I enjoyed being on what seems like the domed roof of the world. A great wind was blowing but the sky was very blue, and everything looked its loveliest, with the stooked fields in the distance and long ribbons of grass bent by the wind and turquoise blue from the reflection of the sky. Mushrooms were few, and the field was full of swarthy black heifers with coarse faces and stocky bodies; compared to our lovely Guernseys they looked like Australian aborigines.

Julia was back, after a short visit to London for a spell of what she calls 'things *mondaine*'. We do not know for how long, nor does she seem to. She appears rather stupefied, and I think surprised to find fellow-pacifists following the progress of the war so closely. We greeted her with a certain stupefaction also, although there was friendliness on both sides.

During lunch a conversation arose about the menace of Religion in general – Julia seemed to feel especially strongly about Catholicism, though I can't say I make much distinction. Thence to what is called the 'mystical experience' and what it consists in. We decided it was a flash of conviction that the Universe is One and Undivided, and that every part of it has significance when considered as part of the whole. R. described having something like it during the last war when he lay on a wire mattress in a French wood and watched the dawn. I don't think I have ever experienced it, nor do I understand how things like torture and atrocities fit into such a vision of the cosmos. From there we went on, inevitably, to the results of the war. As I talked and thought, the terrible conviction came over me that the only lesson that will be learned from it is that England should be armed and strong. The armament race will, so I believe, begin at once. R. thinks there will be a reaction from this insular jingoism towards internationalism and individualism. I wish I could agree.

Returning from a bicycle ride I found Julia stretched on a rug on the lawn, odalisque style. I joined her, and we both soon became aware of a deep and distant reverberation, like the beating of a giant's pulse, which continued for about an hour and obviously came from a long way off. A *very* long way as it turned out, for this evening the wireless tells us that 'today London and the South of England heard the guns in France'.

September 21st

Our private D-day was three days ago when Burgo, excited but fairly on the spot, dressed himself in full school kit, tie and cap and was whirled off to a new life at Newbury Grammar School, and returned *all right*, as far as we could see, and full of comments. However, it's now clear he is going through a considerable strain and needs a lot of support. It's not the other boys, but the rules and regulations, the terror of doing something wrong that obsesses him. 'My essay was the worst in the whole school,' he almost screamed at me today. I saw his book later and it was marked '17 out of 20. *Good*.' R. is much better with him than I am. Every sight of me prompts a collapse, and 'Please, *please* don't send me to this awful school.' When he left him there this morning R. luckily ran into the headmaster and had a word with him. 'I'm very glad you told me,' said Mr Starr. 'I've been cracking down on him rather – I thought he was being rather superior and needed taking down a peg.' I think he greatly erred in not spotting B.'s intense anxiety and lack of confidence.

He has a delightful distraction at weekends in his new friends, four Italian prisoners working on the farm; he takes them apples and figs, and talks to them in slow pidgin English accompanied by stiff courtly gestures.

October 25th

Going in to the dining-room to lay the table just as it was growing dark, I looked out at our view – which I would exchange for no other in the world, which is always changing and never ceases delighting me. The sky had cleared and was a very pale blue, with half a silver moon hanging over the Downs. A white mist had magically materialized out of the ground, swathing the fields and in it the cows were ambling gently to and fro.

November 8th

As it grows colder and colder, the war gets slower and slower. In fact it seems to have *stuck* – and we must face the fact that it will probably remain so until the spring. Yesterday a few large flakes of snow drifted out of the sky, and in the night a great gale got up and belaboured the house with rain which oozed in at all the tightly-shut windows. Indoors all the mirrors fog up and the walls drip and perspire – liquefaction outside and in, a dreary spectacle.

I'm reading two books at once, one about Milton, one about Beethoven. I went to bed feeling crushed and towered over in the darkness by these two massive figures, the thought of whose thwarted genius (one blind and the other deaf) I somehow found indigestible, like our present daily help's 'turbulent' pastry, as R. calls it.

Or perhaps I was suffering from the knowledge that our pig is to be killed tomorrow.

November 17th

A beautiful autumn day. I sat out on the verandah, where there was everything to please the senses and soothe the eternal inner sense of tragedy and decay. We had told ourselves so eagerly that we shouldn't have to go through another winter of war and now it is evident that we must. Though all arms seem to be raised to strike Germany her death-blow, that blow doesn't fall. In the park in front of me, the light shone white on the backs of wheeling rooks, locked in combat as they clattered out of the ilex with the noise of the opening of a wet umbrella.

December 4th

Burgo has been lately in a state of abnormal mental activity – I suppose the result of the stimulation of school. Or perhaps ideas were put into his head by his coming out top of his form in the IQ tests, with a mental age three years older than his true age. I have been hard put to it to answer all his questions. During his 'rest' he compiled a life of Piers Gaveston from the *DNB*. By bedtime he had taken to *The Tempest*. 'I'm looking up this "blasphemious" in the dictionary.' Then he had developed a passion for the gramophone and one day played it from two o'clock till bedtime without stopping – everything from Fred Astaire to Benjamin Britten.

December 10th

It is the dead season of the year and I have little desire to write in this diary. But we have been through anything but a dead period. In the weeks following our pig-killing numbers of visitors came to help eat it, and this sudden burst of hospitality livened us both up no end. Among others, we have had David and Rachel, Clive, Anthony West, Richard Chopping and Boris and Maroussa.

David and Rachel were charming and animated as ever – David undeterred by suffering from mushroom poisoning, talked entertainingly and without pause between hasty dashes from the room. Boris soused us in his usual richly-spiced soup of Russian flattery. He arrived wearing an elegant suit of lichen-green Irish tweed, the trousers tapered round his massive legs, and black Italian shoes with perfectly square toes, made of the softest leather. Next morning, however, he appeared for breakfast in a cowboy shirt in gorgeous red and green checks, and to remind us of its beauty he several times during the day lifted his pullover from over his stomach to reveal it, while an ineffable smile spread over his broad Slavonic features. He always likes to come into the kitchen and help with whatever is going on, ties an apron round his capacious waist and sits patiently stirring a mayonnaise, enlivening it with some marvellous addition of his own. He has often directed our wine-bottling. Even cutting up parsley needed respectful attention, and he teases me for my sketchiness. He was in his element, therefore, chopping up head, trotters and entrails of our pig to make brawn, carefully seasoning them and adding herbs, and our brawns have never been so delicious. Then he played chess with Burgo as seriously as if he had been an adult; and though I'm sure he would deny being musical, he appeared to be irresistibly drawn to my piano, and sat for hours overflowing the music-stool, picking out with great delicacy of feeling but infinite slowness whatever music happened to be on the desk. He even insisted on accompanying me and my violin, and we crawled like snails through the slow movements of Handel and Corelli sonatas, Boris occasionally laughing softly to himself and refusing to agree that we shouldn't play because we weren't good enough.

His conversation is always a delight, with a brilliant choice of words, surprisingly modulated in tone. Some Borisisms: 'There's no sense in marriage; I prefer *collages* – associations that everyone knows about.' Of Picasso: 'He is a clever crook, who cashed in by *épatant la bourgeoisie* – a *couturier*, a Dior, always thinking up new models.' Asked what a certain lady was like, he thought for a moment and said, 'Coarse.' I remember once a very stupid woman saying at luncheon that she 'simply detested cruelty, especially to animals and children', whereupon Boris smiled up at a corner of the ceiling and said in dulcet tones: 'I rather like such cruelties as these.' The only reference to the war I can remember him making on this visit was, 'So low is our moral disintegration in this sixth year of the war that I hardly can get up from my bed in the morning, and it is only due to Maroussa's cruel determination of not bringing me the breakfast up that I come down moved by pangs of hunger. Somehow I float in idle contemplation of the world, waiting, waiting...'

And so do we all.

1945

January 5th

Ham Spray and its inhabitants forge through this sixth war winter like an ice-breaking ship going through Arctic seas. Partly because we have been subjected to intense cold. First frost and ice, and now light snow, but with it stillness, exquisite pearly skies, and air sharp and intoxicating to the taste as one draws it into unwelcoming lungs. All this sparkle and beauty has helped to keep up our spirits pretty well. This morning we were all out in the snow – Janetta stalking about on Burgo's stilts with her long hair swinging; Nicky trotting purposefully about, a tiny Father Christmas, in her red siren suit frosted with snow; Burgo making snowballs.

A letter from Julia contained the news that a V.2 rocket had fallen horribly close to them, and only a few hundred yards from Alys Russell's house which is wrecked and has all the doors blown out. She writes: 'We were woken by an *almighty* earthquake and thunderclap of thunderclaps, heaving at us out of nowhere; the sky blazed, the house was shaken like a medicine bottle, and splintering glass from windows all round the square (our own included) filled the air. When silence fell one just lay and waited for the walls to crumble and topple slowly over onto one, because it seemed they could not possibly have survived it.'

January 12th

A lot of conversation all day. At lunch about whether the end ever justifies the means. R. believes emphatically that it does not, and this belief is woven into the very roots of his pacifism. 'There are some actions,' he said, 'that one couldn't possibly perform for any end whatsoever – torture for instance.' And it did indeed seem self-evident.[1] As for me, though I think generalizations are the breath of mental life, I'm inclined to mistrust moral ones unless they are treated as averages, like household accounts; the more particular a moral statement is, the more accurate, and the more general, the less so. And I can't subscribe to a summing-up like 'Deliberately killing another human being is always wrong', because I believe in euthanasia for one thing.

January 16th

School begins again today. Not a trace of anxiety or resistance on B.'s part, how wonderful! And he returned in the evening all sweetness and desire to please. The other thing which has sent our morale soaring is that the Russians – whom we had been inclined to forget about – have suddenly launched an offensive on a massive

[1] I wonder what would have been his feelings had he been alive now, to see it (torture) an element in the training of almost every police force and army in the world.

scale, and it seems to be going better than our wildest dreams. Warsaw has fallen, and they are less than two hundred miles from Berlin.

This ice-cold life we lead in the middle of a white, snow-covered landscape, causes what I can only describe as a sort of boisterousness, and there is a feeling of adventure about these arctic conditions. Every morning we get up in pitch darkness, tearing ourselves from our warm bed and rushing along the bathroom passage. Getting up, dressing and bathing, has always been the time of our liveliest conversations.

January 30th

Last night a gale got up, blowing the front door open and filling the hall with snow from end to end. R. and Janetta went to Ham and reported drifts six feet deep. Janetta's eyes were sparkling and her cheeks pink. 'It was wonderful!' she said. The Russians are wonderful too, advancing with such speed that BERLIN is suddenly in the picture.

B. in bed with earache, I was reading him *A Flat Iron for a Farthing*, but today it couldn't be found. With muffled grunts he admitted he had hidden it in a drawer under his shirts 'because it's so sad when the mother dies and I didn't want to have bad dreams'.

The excitement of hearing about the advance into Germany puts us into a frenzy of impatience and I am well aware of wanting to forge along through time as quickly as possible, looking forward each day to evening, and then to the start of a new day, and so on. I said to R. how much I deplored this scrabbling through our lives.

'Yes, I want to get on to the end of the story,' he said. F.: 'What? To old age, decrepitude – the tomb?' R.: 'Yes' (in a serio-comic voice), 'the tomb – that's where I want to get.' 'And separation from me!' I cried. 'Don't you realize that's what it'll be, even if we are lucky enough to die at the same moment – the end of all our happiness together!' '*Don't*,' said R., 'that's something I keep trying to shove out of sight, like Burgo and the *Flat Iron for a Farthing*.' And he rushed from the room, leaving me in tears.

March 13th

There's an incredible sense of spring at the moment. The birds sing; old Tiger capers round the lawn like a kitten; the warm sun comes through the glass roof of the verandah and bathes us gently. Janetta sits out reading; I grub in the rockery to tidy it for the bulbs already bursting out of the earth. It's the beginning of that vegetable *rush* which will carry us breathlessly through spring and summer and dump us, exhausted, in the brown gloom of November. Another month has slipped by and everyone is saying 'It can't be long now.' On the Western front we have advanced to the Rhine and crossed it in one place.

Our daily diet now consists in descriptions of our conquering armies in Germany, and reports about the German reaction to defeat. An ambivalent note is very clear here: on one side 'they are crushed, and do what we tell them, and pretty harmless on the whole', and on the other, 'we mustn't for a moment forget, just because they look like ordinary old people, girls and children, that they are fiends – no less.' Every hour of the day injunctions are broadcast to the American troops not to fraternize – which I take as pretty good proof that they are doing so. Descriptions of the efficient underground life the Germans had organized in these much-bombed Rhineland towns, with thousands of people living together in huge shelters, makes a cold hand grip one's heart. If two such horrible things can co-exist – the bombing and the underground life – why shouldn't they go on for ever?

March 16th

A flying visit from Phil, who is due to leave in a week's time for Czechoslovakia. His ambassadorial life has hardened him into a conventional mould, beneath which he is deeply emotional. He spoke of his brother Robert's[1] death with unconcealed agitation, and I couldn't help remembering how cynically he used to talk about his love affairs, and all the brilliant suggestions for winning the war he used to keep posting off to the War Office. Now it was 'Since Robert died I don't feel I mind about the war or anything.'

We talked about the appalling revelations of German atrocities now coming to light: mass executions of Jews in gas-chambers. 'Why doesn't the man in the street mind them more?' he asked. 'Probably because the world has for several years been one huge atrocity,' I said. It seems to me frightful but true that if people are fed on stories of the mass blowing to pieces of civilians and burning them alive in their houses by bombing they lose some of their sensitivity to further horrors, however ghastly. R. mentioned the gloating way we now talk of burning the Japs in their wooden houses, and are building up a view that the Japs are subhuman just as the Germans believe the Jews to be. The soldier who controls the gas-chamber, like the bomber pilot, may well be just carrying out orders because he dare not do otherwise. But how can either activity fail to have a bad effect on those who perform them?

On to education. R. said that boarding-school violated a child's desire for privacy and hampered its struggle to remain an individual by forcing it to lead a gang-life by day and night. Phil: 'But adult life is a gang-life and children must be prepared and trained for it. How should I have got through the gang-life of the last war if I hadn't been prepared for it by boarding-school?' He was disregarding the vast majority of soldiers in the non-commissioned ranks, who did get through it, perhaps less scarred than he was, though they never went to boarding-school. And any way, even were his premiss true, what an appalling idea that a boy's youth must be devoted to preparing him for the gang horrors of the next war!

Our next subject was promiscuity – in my opinion a natural state of youth, exciting and stimulating without being a great source of happiness. To prolong it often comes from timidity, the fear of risking too much in a more solid relationship. People are laughed at when they have too many shots at marriage, failing and trying again. But they shouldn't be, for they are after the best thing.

March 28th

The speed of our progress towards victory has been headlong this week. Someone suggested the Germans might still have something up their sleeves, and they have certainly been sending over more rockets lately. The other night Nicko Henderson described one falling beside Goodge Street Station when he was just getting off a bus. 'It was only twenty yards off. There was no sound of the impact, just a terrific

---

[1] The poet.

roar that seemed to go on and on and on for hours. All the women in the bus screamed and the men caught hold of them and shouted,'It's all *right!*' We all put our heads down, not knowing what was coming down from above. I asked where it was, and there it was just beside me – not a crater, but a huge pyramid of bricks and rubble. I was the first person on the spot, in evening clothes, and without the faintest idea how to attack this mound of horror. I saw a woman stripped naked by the explosion and with her foot apparently blown off. Ambulances arrived in a very few moments and by the time I had got back again, after going to my rooms and changing, a huge crowd had collected and it was all cordoned off.'

Julia and Lawrence have been anxious to get out of London, and asked me to look for rooms in this neighbourhood. I have taken a good deal of trouble, been to dozens of rooms and rung Julia up every night to talk about the length of the arms of armchairs and suchlike details. R. has been highly sceptical about it all. We asked them for the weekend to look at various possibilities, and Lawrence seemed very keen on several of the rooms. 'I'm sure the Swan will do. We'll stay there two months; it'll be wonderful.' Julia had a cold, far-away look in her eye. 'I dare say it'll be *bearable* for a month,' was all she would commit herself to. After tea they went to see two other sets of rooms, that had seemed to me more possible. When they returned, 'Well?' I asked. 'Both absolutely *appalling*,' Julia said shortly.'It's no good, I should be too bad-tempered. One really can't be happy in the surroundings those cottage women think nice. And the fact is I can't bear to stay in any rooms that aren't Georgian.' So she prefers to remain in London with the rockets, though she admits they frighten her a great deal, to living in a non-Georgian room. It's heroism of her own peculiar sort. On Sunday evening she asked me how I thought Lawrence was looking, and said she was very worried about his health. 'Don't you think perhaps a stay in the country would have done him good?' I asked her maliciously. But I do find it strange that she has to support her happiness on so many material things – fenders and fringes of bobbles – instead of taking it about with her.

April 19th

The weather continuing like midsummer, we determined to treat it as such and set off in thin clothes for a picnic by the splashing mill-pool at Hamstead Marshall. I had bought newspapers in Newbury, and turned the pages as we drove. My horrified eyes fell on a page of photographs from one of the German concentration camps opened up recently by the Americans. A lorry stood stacked with naked corpses; others in the last stages of emaciation lay in ghastly rows, waiting to be buried. Gaunt invalids lay in straw; a man in pyjamas was hanging from a gallows. The text was just as appalling. Then there were photos of plump, quiet bourgeois Germans being taken to see the camp and harangued by the Americans. Many fainted, and others burst into tears, but the photo also showed many smug, placid faces, like those of people waiting for a bus.

Well, R. and Burgo got for a moment into the cold waters of the mill-stream and then we sat eating hard-boiled eggs and watercress beside it. The day was unbelievably beautiful, the grass positively sparkled, heat poured from the blue sky – but none of this could dispel the horror and disgust brought by the newspapers. They haunted me all day. I feel as though the world's sanity had received a fatal blow, and I can't stop thinking of it and all it implies. Reaction in the kitchen: 'Isn't it terrible? Why don't we do it to *their* men, that's what I want to know!

April 28th

The war is shaping to some vast Wagnerian finale. The Russian army has completely encircled Berlin and is pressing through the suburbs towards the heart of it. Hitler is said to be there, personally directing the battle. Mussolini is a prisoner. And Winston has announced that there are no more blackout restrictions. It's quite difficult to leave windows uncurtained and blazing away into the darkness. We have indeed got used to our imprisoned state.

April 30th

A different response from the kitchen this morning: 'How terrible it's been! How glad we shall be when it's all over!' Mrs C.'s feelings had suddenly been touched by a picture of a German mother and the two children she had killed before committing suicide herself. The world tragedy dwindled to a size she could assimilate. Supposing *we* had been invaded. Supposing *she* had been that woman. Mr Mills, bringing our bread, hoped 'it wouldn't be long now. And then I shall be just about glad to get a letter from the boys. The wife's away at Reading for a month; there's more company to take her mind off things, and I reckon I'll be glad if it cracks before she comes back. Mr T. he made me mad the other day. I said I'd be glad when it s over, and he said, "It didn't *ought* to be over. We ought to go and kill every blooming German." I said to him, "You just take a rifle then, and go out there and do it. You know jolly well you can't or you wouldn't say such things. The boys out there don't feel like that." '

R. sits by the wireless all day, with an anxious face, tuning in to stations, like a doctor taking the pulse of a dying man. The patient is already speechless but last night we heard our own broadcaster to Germany saying slowly and weightily: 'Es ist das *Ende*.' And all today anticipation of that end has been like a great undischarged *gasp* filling one's chest.

May 1st

To Hungerford to meet Saxon. The newspapers are again objects of horror to shudder away from, plastered with photos of the heaped corpses of Italian Fascists, or of Mussolini and his mistress strung up like turkeys. It seems incredible to have them handed over the counter by a mild girl in specs, with a front tooth missing.

11 p.m. Have just switched on the late news and heard a portentous voice say: HITLER IS DEAD. I went up to bed before R. and heard his voice and Saxon's from the music-room below. 'What were you talking about?' I asked when he appeared. 'Horses for the Guineas,' he said. 'Trust Saxon never to mention anything of such immediate interest as the end of Hitler.'

May 5th

Waiting, waiting for the end. The last two nights I have started awake after the first dimming of consciousness into sleep, to find myself lying with a wildly pounding heart, as if listening for something. The church bells pealing for victory? Anyway all I heard with unnatural distinctness was the sound of Saxon clearing his throat in his bedroom, forced along the tunnel of the passage.

Before lunchtime we heard that all the German armies in the North had surrendered. Holland and Denmark are free.

May 7th

All day long we were kept on the hop by the wireless telling us that the Germans had signed unconditional surrender but that the announcement had not yet come through – we could expect it any minute. If the war is over then it is over, and I am bewildered to explain this fever of anticipation. The voices of the BBC announcers betray increasing irritation, and everyone is on tenterhooks waiting for the inevitable.

Then at eight this evening the telephone rang, and it was an Inkpen neighbour asking if Burgo was going to school tomorrow or not. (We have been sharing transport.) 'It's just come through – tomorrow will be VE day. Churchill will announce the end of the war in Europe at 3 p.m. It's all very flat,' she went on. 'We've just been drinking a little weak gin.' So here it was at last. Nothing could have been more prosaic than this way of receiving the news, yet on returning to the music-room I found all my restlessness had gone in a moment. Oddly enough, the news of peace actually brought a *sense* of peace, very refreshing like a good drink of water to a thirsty person. R. and I sat through our evening quietly, enjoying the relief from tension. Before we went up to bed we went out onto the verandah and looked up at the sky in which a few stars twinkled mistily, and I thought of the night nearly six years ago when the war began, and how I had done the same, wondering what was in store for us all, and gazed on by those same impersonal eyes.

May 8th

At three o'clock Churchill delivered the promised announcement.

Afterwards we drove to Newbury to fetch the other Inkpen children from school. Every cottage had a few flags hung out, and in most of them a dummy-like figure of an old person could be seen at an upper window, hoisted out of bed probably to see what little fun there was to see. Near Newbury we had a narrow escape from a drunken lorry-driver veering from side to side of the road – he made the V-sign as we passed. Bicyclists were hurrying in to Newbury dressed in their best; little girls wore satin blouses and red, white and blue bows in their hair.

May 10th

I feel happier and more conscious of peace even than I expected. I am very much aware this morning of something that has just gone: a background to our daily existence as solid as one of the scenes in Burgo's toy theatre – a background coloured by the obscenity of violence, and my own disgust at it. The fields, Downs and woods *look* peaceful now, seen with eyes that know the murder and destruction have stopped. If my pleasure in our being at peace is a more or less steady quality, R.'s is growing gradually, as though it was something he hardly dared trust to, and it makes me very happy to see signs on his face that the load is lifting. This morning he was radiating good humour, which was no doubt why the girl cashier in the bank leant over the counter and confided all her marriage plans to him; when he's in a benign mood no one I've ever known attracts more confidences than he does.

I have been reading Flaubert's *Letters*, and have just reached the Franco-Prussian war. How his reactions remind me of ours! First, horror at the bestiality of human beings. As the Germans invade he develops a more conventional desire to defend his country, followed by the most frightful agitation and despair, such as only a literary man can indulge in. *No-one*, he feels sure, can hate the war so much as he does; he resigns from the Home Guard, returns to his views about the beastliness of human beings, is physically sick every day from sheer disgust, and dislikes his fellow-Frenchmen almost as much as the Prussians. As for 'evacuees' they are the worst feature of the whole war.

News of VE Day in London: Janetta writes: 'I've found the crowds very depressing indeed, and the flags and decorations pathetic although often very pretty. Some bonfires were wonderful, bringing back the old ecstasies of staring into a fire, but also having that appalling smell of burning debris, too terrifyingly nostalgic of blitzes. And I so loathe the look of masses of boiling people with scarlet dripping faces, wearing tiny paper hats with "Ike's Babe" or "Victory" written on them.'

Julia: 'We walked to Buckingham Palace, and there found a spectacular scene – all the fountains, balustrades, not to mention trees, were crowded with these little pink penguins in their droves, all facing the Palace, which was brilliantly illuminated with beautiful golden light, and draped with red velvet over the balcony. It was charmingly pretty. Everyone was fainting by the roadside, or rather sitting down holding their stockinged feet in their hands and groaning. A few faint upper-class cries of "Taxi – taxi!" came wailing through the air from voices right down on the pavement; whilst cockney tones, slightly more robust, could be heard saying, "I'm fucking well all in now".' Of her own reaction to peace she goes on: 'It's something to do with the war having gone on just *too* long, one was at last crushed, and personally I no longer feel human any more; I mean the dynamic principle has given way and one feels like a sheet of old newspaper or pressed dried grass.'

At Hungerford Station we ran into Dora Morris who had news of the celebration of peace at Charleston. Quentin made a lifesize image of Hitler to burn on Firle Beacon, Duncan defended Hitler in a comic mock trial, and the 'Baroness' (Lydia Keynes) had 'thudded away in an abandoned Russian drinking song'.

This evening we drove to Shalbourne to give Olive a present of bacon. I remembered how after the First War some pacifists had been turned on by the merry-making crowds, for instance how Cambridge undergraduates had pushed down Harry Norton's garden wall; and wondered if our village neighbours, and 'old retainers' like Olive, might say to themselves, 'Well, *they* did nothing to help. *They*'ve no cause to rejoice.' But the warm way Olive and her family welcomed us and exchanged handshakes and kisses did nothing to confirm my fears.

After all, surely it's only logical that pacifists – of all people – should rejoice in the return to Peace?

Everything to Lose
1945–1960

Foreword

On 8 May 1945 the tiny Wiltshire village of Ham, like every other town and hamlet in the British Isles, celebrated by its VE Day the end of the second Great World War in Europe. An almost audible sigh of relief rose from the whole country. If some of our reactions were strange or inappropriate, we had no need to pinch ourselves mentally, so to speak, to be aware that PEACE was really *here*, even though several months were to pass before VJ Day would strike the gong of finality.

I was living at this time with my husband Ralph and our ten-year-old son Burgo at Ham Spray House, where we had spent the entire war except for a few breaks taken in London, staying with friends or escaping to farmhouse rooms in Wales or Devonshire.

Ham is the first village to be reached as one crosses the Berkshire border going westwards. It lies among fine chalk Downs a thousand feet high, like Walbury Camp, or the Gibbet Hill, where a replica of the old gallows still marks the scene of the execution (and the dramatic murder story behind it) described by W. H. Hudson in *Afoot in England*.

Forty years ago the village consisted merely of a pub, a village shop and post office combined (selling pyjamas and Wellington boots as well as groceries), the small school whose few inmates could be heard monotonously chanting, three middle-sized houses and a handful of thatched cottages, some of which had been prettified and sold to the gentry. One had been the home of a witch, we were seriously told; when she was forced to move to make way for newcomers no one saw her leave, 'but a rabbit ran across the road, and when the door was opened the cottage was empty'. Another belonged to a Mrs Abercrombie, whose name the school-children believed in all good faith to be 'Mrs Apple Crumpet': perhaps this was due to the lively imagination of 'Little Phyllis', who used to come 'up to Spray' to play with Burgo, and who once told me they learned 'Sharpspike' at school.

It was indeed three-quarters of a mile and uphill most of the way before one turned off down an avenue of immensely tall wych-elms leading to Ham Spray itself, huddled among farm buildings. Its charming pink-washed Jane Austen front was on the further side facing the long ridge of the downs and gathering all the sun from the south in its glass-roofed verandah. From here the lawn sloped gently down to a ha-ha, and to reach the world beyond our garden we had to cross a footbridge, elegantly overhung by a drooping ilex tree. Our favourite walk took us across the 'Park' with its formal circles and semi-circles of beech trees planted by a previous owner of the land, to climb the Downs diagonally by a grass track of great antiquity. Here grew a number of orchids among other chalk plants – Bee, Fly, Butterfly, Burnt Stick, and even the rare Musk, whose tiny green spikes I used to search for and count each year for the Wiltshire Botanical Society.

We believed there was no view more beautiful, more inexhaustible in England, and no house more lovable than Ham Spray. Lytton Strachey and Ralph had together bought it in 1924 for the sum of £2,000, which they could then ill afford, and Lytton and Carrington had spent their last seven years and died there. This fact did not fill the house with an atmosphere of gloom, but of course with many memories of them both, and Carrington's pictures and inspired and gay decorations – tiles, painted furniture and papers – continued to beautify the interior for many years to come. We had colour-washed the walls of most of the rooms ourselves. Lytton's old library was completely surrounded with bookshelves made by the village carpenter and both Ralph and I worked there at our separate tables; the dining-room dresser was covered in Spanish plates and English lustre ware; and a large, otherwise featureless room known as the Music Room contained a piano, gramophone and sometimes a ping-pong table. Everywhere were paintings by Duncan Grant, Vanessa Bell and Carrington; drawings by Henry Lamb and Augustus John, mosaics by Boris Anrep. Two four-poster beds and a good deal of Regency and Provençal furniture were not in the best possible condition and often menaced by woodworm. (James Strachey's chair once collapsed in a cloud of dust in the middle of dinner). Upstairs a long corridor that rocked beneath the feet led past visitors' rooms to the old granary that had been converted first into a studio for Carrington, then Burgo's nursery.

During the war we had had all too many practical tasks to do, though Ralph was an expert pruner and I know enjoyed providing us with pears and peaches, figs, nectarines and grapes. As more official 'work' he wrote reviews, mainly for the *New Statesman*, whereas for my part ever since May 1944 I had been under contract to Allen Lane to write a book on English wild flowers in a number of volumes – a sort of modern Sowerby – in co-operation with a young artist called Richard Chopping, who was making delicate and faithful illustrations of each plant. (I mention this project as its fortunes will figure in what follows.)

I first started keeping a diary early in 1940, some of which has been published as *A Pacifist's War*. In it I described many of the friends and refugees who came to Ham Spray; but one of them had by the end of the war qualified as an inmate. This was Janetta, whom we had first met in Spain with her mother, Jan Woolley, at the beginning of the Civil War in 1936. We were staying in the house of our old friend Gerald Brenan in Churriana, and he it was who introduced us to Jan and 'her little daughter, who made everyone's heart beat faster'. The Woolleys had some terrifying experiences in Malaga, which was at that time almost in the front line, and when they returned to England we invited them to stay. At fourteen Janetta was young enough to be our daughter, but she also quickly became one of our dearest friends, and there was always room for her at Ham Spray. Jan died soon after the death of her son in the RAF.

Diary-keeping is a difficult habit to break, and I must confess that I have failed to do so. I take up the thread, therefore, where I left off.

1945

May 19th: Ham Spray

Have we already got used to Peace, and drained the cup to the bottom, of all its savour? I believe it is rather that we have been unconsciously holding back from the pleasure of full realization, just as children often hold back from looking forward to a treat, for fear of the agony of disappointment. Only very gradually are we recovering our old peace-time outlook, and the process is like the pins and needles with which blood rushes back into a crushed limb. It may one day seem absurd to remember what childish delight it gave us today for instance, to take our car out *simply for fun*, with a picnic basket in full view on the seat, and drive up to the top of Walbury Camp, bent on nothing but enjoyment. Even so I was conscious of a faint twinge of guilt, and a feeling that we ought to have been on bicycles. After lunching under the great clump of trees on the highest summit we walked down to Combe village and looked at the little church.

A lot of images have been left in my mind by our outing: Burgo screeching with excitement among the crazy old tombs all scrawled over with ivy and pink and yellow lichens; then peppering me with questions about burials, and with obstetric ones aroused by the graffiti in the air-raid shelters. 'Why I'm interested in dying,' he said, 'is that I simply can't imagine it and long to know what it can be like.' Then, taking a botanical excursion by myself, and finding leopard's bane gleaming under the trees in Combe wood, the starry faces of stitchwort balanced in the long grass and valerian sprouting even from the chimneys of Combe Manor. Coming back to see the two people I love most in the world sitting blown about on the top of the downs – Ralph's bent corduroy knee level with Burgo's rough brown head.

'What a lovely day we've had!' said Ralph.

May 24th

A lot of letters. Bunny writes about his new daughter,[1] and says he 'met at a party an amazingly, an almost embarrassingly beautiful girl, who turned out to be Janetta'. Angelica, recovering from childbed, writes in a serious mood about the Wandering Scholars and the importance of learning Latin and Greek, while Julia[2] ends a wonderful description of VE Day in London: 'Personally I no longer feel human any more; I mean the dynamic principle has given way and one feels like a sheet of old newspaper or pressed dried grass.'

---

[1] Henrietta, who was to become our daughter-in-law by marrying Burgo.

[2] I have described the tragi-comic vicissitudes of Julia's life in considerable detail in my book *Julia, a Portrait* (Phoenix), therefore I do not propose to do more here than say that she was the most original, amusing and eccentric of my friends, and possessed a natural gift for writing which caused her both intense pleasure and agony. All too little of her work was finished, but what little was published won recognition from the critics and many devoted readers.

May 27th

The effects of the Peace are certainly very strange. My feeling is that my 'dynamic', whatever that may be, has run amok somehow and got disassociated from its proper functions. This last week I have often felt as though I were racing to catch a train, and am possessed with a demon of relentless energy which (if I don't stuff its eager maw with housework or botany) will spend itself in futile restlessness. My engine is turning round too fast without properly engaging its gears. The sensation is not altogether unpleasant, in a way rather exciting, but I wish I had not forgotten how to do nothing for an hour or so.

After dinner I began on Koestler's Russian revelations;[1] what an appalling indictment it is, even allowing for his fanatical personality. I sat brooding over the horrors of the world – feeling too hot with the electric fire burning my outer crust, yet a chill numbness within; physical discomfort symbolizing the mental. Without actually believing in progress, I used unconsciously to assume that there was some degree of stability in the stream of human existence which would prevent any great loss of civilization already won. Now it seems as though that very thing had happened, and an almost prehistoric barbarity had spread over the earth. And the *violence* of the present world! Oh how one longs for tolerance, humanity, kindness, and for thought and discussion to come into their own again and drive out black, blind feelings. I wonder if these reflections were the cause of a full-dress argument defending Socialism that I embarked on later with Ralph, and which continued with emotion but not much heat, until after we were in bed. Ralph felt for some reason that my views were an attack upon his liberal ones, but actually I wanted to see if he could put up arguments which I couldn't logically meet. I don't think he did, but I'm not convinced there are none.

June 13th

Before Burgo developed measles we took tickets for Britten's opera *Peter Grimes*. He is now nearly but not quite well, and Ralph has nobly volunteered to take my place as sick-nurse while I go and enjoy myself. So I am taking Janetta, and off I go, with a bag stuffed with eggs and gooseberries for her, and presents for Nicky.

June 14th

Last night Janetta and I went to Sadlers Wells, where a large, excited and mainly youthful audience was collected. Then the opera began and we were all attention, immediately caught by the beauty and startling originality of what we were seeing and above all hearing. I often longed to have some interesting, thrilling passage back to hear it again. In the first act the most arresting scene was the trial and acquittal of Grimes for the murder of his apprentice, when he sings a marvellous aria, expressing the agony of the outcast. The second act included a passage of intense and mounting dramatic excitement which moved both Janetta and me profoundly, where Grimes is pursued and hounded by all the inhabitants of the little town, indignant at his ill-treatment of the boys, and suspicious that he had murdered the last. 'Grimes is at his exercise!' they had chanted earlier – haunting words from Crabbe's poem set to haunting music; and now the ever louder and more terrifying cries of 'Gri-imes! Grimes!' deepen the horror of his plight.

[1] *Darkness at Noon.*

In the interval I went to talk to Henry Lamb, whose pale tonsure I had observed in the front row of the stalls. He is painting Britten's portrait and is, as always, obsessed by his sitter's personality.

'But you know I'm getting old and I like more sweetness in music,' he said, 'and I find this rather too arid.' Then, of the dramatic theme: 'I suppose these buggers have to get their pariah-feelings off their chests.'

Later that evening, when I pondered Henry's comments something that had confused me became clearer. One feels a difficulty in sympathizing with a man whose isolation is caused by his brutality – his ill-treatment, possibly even murder of young boys in his power. Yet that this is what both composer and librettist mean us to do seems clear from the angelic music sung by a beautiful tenor voice. But if for 'ill-treatment' 'love' is substituted, the knot in the emotional thread is untied, and we can feel wholeheartedly for the outcast's position. So what I believe Britten was consciously or unconsciously expressing in *Peter Grimes* was a plea for the freedom from persecution of homosexuals.[1]

In any case left feeling I had had a major experience.

June 20th: Ham Spray

Now that Burgo's measles are over I resolve to get out of the waiting-room and into the train, and start living my life again. (One of his *bons mots* during con-valescence: 'I offer you a penny, Burgo,' said I, 'if you won't mention your sufferings today.' But he lost it in two minutes. 'I'd much rather lose *ten* pennies than not say.')

In summery weather we drove to see the Pritchetts. This was my suggestion, made with some qualms at my audacity, for we scarcely know them but would like to know them more. We settled in the dark shade of a Wellingtonia, to talk to V.S.P. and Dorothy, while the three children went off happily together. Such intelligence and friendliness radiates from V.S.P.'s animated face and gestures that it is a pleasure to watch them. He keeps his eye on reality with a blend of scientific detachment and artistic sensibility, qualities discreetly revealed by his talk, just as letters reveal the writer's originality, whatever they may seem to say. We took our picnic down by the river, fringed with yellow cress and the china blue faces of water forget-me-nots, everything spangled with freshness. I felt suddenly starved of conversation and fell upon it as a hungry man a meal. Pritchett told us about his experiences with the Army in Germany as a newspaper correspondent.

'I was amazed by how much hanging about there was,' he said. 'I thought the Army would either be *advancing*,' – and here he made a sweeping, forward gesture – 'or *retreating*' – pointing behind himself. 'I didn't picture them just *standing perfectly still ironing their trousers!*'

June 23rd

Ralph is not quit of his war-time melancholy and says he wakes each morning to a profound feeling of sadness. I wish I knew how to comfort him. Is it physical, as he sometimes thinks? One thing is certain, the crushing effects of this hideous war on the human spirit will go on for a long time.

---

[1] In Britten's later works there is often a strong moral streak – for instance pacifism in the *War Requiem* and *Owen Wingrave*.

I returned from an afternoon at our old bathing-place in the Kennet with Catharine and our two boys in time to cook supper for Nicko and 'a friend'. I don't know why but I expected a girl. Instead it was a handsome, intelligent and altogether delightful young man, just back from three years in a German prison camp. After dinner he started talking about his life there: it was of fascinating interest. I was struck by the calm and sanity with which he spoke of it, but Ralph noticed that his hand was trembling, especially as he said that in spite of the positive relief it was that there were no small decisions to make in prison, the reverse was also true, and it was torment to feel that you weren't free to take important ones affecting your whole life. He had been released by Russians, who were friendly, full of gaiety and vitality, but barbarians. They raped and looted unchecked by their officers, and the Germans turned with relief to the English and Americans. 'You are *good* soldiers,' they said to him. No complaint about the Germans, who were unfailingly correct. It was typical of them that when they found hacksaws being smuggled into the camp inside gramophone records they didn't destroy the lot as we should have done, but X-rayed each one and passed the innocent ones.

His stories of escape made Ralph laugh until he nearly cried. It was an RAF camp, full of very enterprising young men, who never stopped tunnelling and planning to escape, and many got away, though most were later caught. They undertook the tunnelling chiefly for something to occupy their minds, and reaching daylight was a terrifying moment. The tunnels were inconceivably elaborate. One had a shaft twenty feet deep, with buckets going up and down carrying earth; there was a railway track, with electric lighting and a switchboard worked by a man wearing a green eye-shade. Above them the Germans were constantly probing and listening, but they never found the tunnel. When the outer air was reached the excitement was so tremendous that the first man generally made the hole too small and everyone who followed stuck. Some men made gliders and balloons. Another planned to turn his flying-coat inside out and disguise himself as the Airedale dog of one of the German officers. Some passed out as members of the Swiss Red Cross. Generally the punishment for attempted escape was fourteen days' imprisonment. Suddenly a large number of men were shot as an example – and there were no escapes after that.

Most of the prisoners started some sort of serious study in the camp. Those who didn't went to pieces.

Both Ralph and I took enormously to Nicko's friend, whose name is Robert Kee, and wondered whether he and Janetta would like each other. 'That's the man for her,' Ralph said.

July 18th

Burgo came home from school yesterday evening and told us in agitated tones that the headmaster, Mr Starr, is leaving the Grammar School. Then, with a look of absolute consternation, he burst into tears. Several times he came back and tried to eat his tea only to collapse in tears again. He was obviously surprised at his own reaction.

'I didn't realize I loved him as well as liked him,' he said sadly, gazing out of the window. All the evening he behaved like a man in love, playing Mozart on the gramophone, unable to get to sleep 'because I was so miserable about Mr Starr'.

Today began to the tune of 'Oh, Mr Starr.' The irony of it is that there is probably no other boy in the whole school who has manifested such grief at his headmaster's going, not that Burgo is in any way a favourite. This evening we went to see Mr Starr before taking Burgo home. What a pity he is going – he is an intelligent, sensitive and rather charming man. Burgo is to stay on at the Prep. another year; Starr isn't confident in his ability to pass exams, though he has the highest IQ in the school and 'will go far'.

Janetta and Nicky came back from London. We were delighted to see them. They both look rather dirty: there's still no hot water in their new house. Kenneth is suggesting that they go out to Belgrade, but she doesn't want to, resists thinking about it. She has been seeing Nicko's friend Robert Kee, but I don't know how much.

Election results today. Janetta pinned up the list of candidates and prepared graph paper on the ping-pong table to show the progress of parties. It soon became evident to all our surprise and excitement, that the Labour Party was having a sweeping victory. None of our friends who stood as Liberals got in. True we supported the Liberals ourselves, but they seemed the only party who had a chance against the Tories.

During the long proceedings Janetta asked for 'a little encouraging music on the gramophone'. I put on some Bach and waited expectantly for it to add its colour and triumph to the electoral victory which filled our minds, just as music or the beauty of the garden seen through the window, so often overflow into one's thoughts. But it didn't work – the scene we were contemplating looked squalid and tawdry. Perhaps it was.

[In August we took three weeks' holiday in the Scilly Isles, partly to look for some botanical rarities there. Richard Chopping and his friend Denis Wirth-Miller came with us. All of us were taking the first flight of our lives.]

August 1st

Penzance airport was a grey tin hut. Here we were weighed and signed forms declaring that we didn't hold the Company responsible for our lives. Beside our party of five were two young women going over for the day; they too had never flown before. The tiny aeroplane appeared and we seven souls climbed in, each into our little pocket. It was like fitting oneself into a sponge-bag and seemed hardly more solid. I looked back at Burgo's pale but calm face behind. The engine roared and we were off, gently, then swiftly, bumping a little, making straight for the cliff, over it, and up over the sea as easy as anything. During our preliminary turns, as we curtsied and stooped over the valleys, a most satisfying fatalism possessed me, and I thought, 'I am a part of this machine, if we crash, then we crash.' Now we were travelling smoothly over the sea lying calm and touched with silver light below; it was lovely and exciting. All too soon the islands appeared – fields, bays, lakes, hedges. We're there; it's over – the realization was half-pleasant, half-sad. We were driven to our lodgings – a grey house near the port kept by two mountainous ladies.

August 2nd

Ralph has hired a boat, with a boatman, Mr Nance by name, a statuesque figure with a red carved face. Where to go? Tresco lies ahead and the dromedary humps of Samson to the left. Other distant shapes surround this inland sea. We ask Nance to put us on Tresco. We walk past the orange trumpets of thorn-apples and other brilliant tropical flowers, across the waist of the island to a great sweeping bay, whose snow-white beach is made up of glittering silver spangles, such that rolling one's hands in it they are dressed in sequin gloves. Unspeakably pure and ice-cold turquoise blue water, quantities of pretty shells (purple, white and yellow), strange fleshy plants coiled over the shingle, and no one but ourselves to enjoy these beauties. We bathed naked and ate our picnic on the beach.

August 5th

To St Helen's. The sun is blazing still; all our faces are becoming like riding-boots and beginning to peel.

It has just been announced on the News that a new and terrific bomb has been dropped on Japan, with effects incomparably more horrible than anything yet.

August 7th

No one talks of anything but the atom bomb, and most voices are raised in horror. But the mother of a serving soldier said: 'Surely you'd rather have the atomic bomb and war over than the war going on for ever? Total extinction has much to recommend it and anyway I don't care what happens after I'm dead in the very least.' Her daughter hotly: 'That's one of the things you shouldn't say before the young.'

August 13th

Ralph and I were in bed and nearly asleep when a strange cacophony penetrated our consciousness: the church bells began tolling, and a cracked trumpet hooted out military refrains. Next began the sound of young voices singing, feet marching, cheering and beating on tins.

We woke up completely. Ralph said: 'It can only mean one thing. Peace.'

The contrast between the long tedious frightfulness just ended and the pitiful desire of puny human beings to make *some* sort of noise at all costs was more than I could manage to swallow, and I lay saying bitter things about them, while Ralph rightly laughed at me for not appreciating the greatness of the occasion. The procession clanked off along the pier; then the momentary quiet was shattered by the hooter of the *Scillonian* lying in the harbour, which gave tongue again and again like the last trump. Shouts; more trumpets, rockets and then maroons going off with a deafening whoosh followed by an echo like a whole town collapsing. Silence once more. The sound of a solitary tin being kicked along the street woke Burgo, who came and snuggled into bed with us. 'The whole world is now at PEACE!' we said to each other.

August 15th

VJ Day number 2. We had promised to take Burgo to see the torchlight procession and bonfire, so about ten o'clock, dressed in warm jerseys, we took the road to Penninis. It was very still and no one was about in the velvet darkness. Far off we saw a red blaze tearing along the skyline of St Agnes, where a bonfire must have caught the heather, and the quiet flashing of distant lighthouses, as well as the semi-circular path thrown on near rocks and far horizon alike from Penninis itself, an unmanned lighthouse whose impartiality impressed me as if it belonged to the Solar System. Now human shapes began to gather in the darkness and soon we heard far-off singing and beating of drums as the torchlight procession came winding down the hill under the inky sky like a pagan festival – beating, singing, flaring. In front were children carrying candles in jam jars, and we saw Richard and Denis arm in arm with two girls, all their heads wagging like dervishes. The bonfire was lit, the flames crackled up, and when all was over we three walked back to the beat of drums. I shall always remember this evening with great pleasure; it was a beautiful and moving scene of abandonment to rejoicing.

September 5th: Ham Spray

The Times this morning had a correspondent's account of the effects of the atomic bomb. They are beyond words horrible and sickening to the heart. Now, days and weeks after the explosion, people unhurt at the time are falling ill and dying; even the doctors who came to take care of the wounded are succumbing. The symptoms are terrible – the skin becomes patched with blue, there is bleeding from nose and mouth, and when inoculations are given the flesh rots away from the needle. Death always follows. I thought with despair of poor Burgo, now so full of zest for life and unaware of its horrors. My own instincts lead me to love life, but as I read on, a desire welled up inside me to be dead and out of this hateful, revolting, mad world. Ralph and I talk and talk about it, and the conviction is growing in my mind that this is the *end* of the world and civilization we have known and enjoyed. Either by accident or design, how can it possibly be that someone will not destroy the earth? Any power wishing for world domination can get it in a single night by blotting out all its rivals, without any declaration of war, and Fear, that most potent force, will reign supreme. I see the earth reduced to a few meteorites and moons circling round in empty space. Nobody can deny all this if you put it to them, but human beings are too emotionally drained to react as violently as one might expect. It's as if exhausted humanity had sunk back into inarticulacy.

September 13th

Phil and Phyllis[1] came for the night, arriving to a very late supper. We prepared our warmest welcome for them, Ralph getting out a magnum of delicious wine, whose influence was stimulating rather than soporific, so that an impassioned argument began, mainly between Phil and me, about the Public Schools and the Empire, concerning both of which he takes an ever more ambassadorial view. Thence to the more interesting subject of what was the principal purpose of life. 'Happiness,' said I, 'of course.' Phyllis was looking very fine, and I loved seeing her again, even though it reminded me of the anxious first months of the war, when the whole family were lodged with us here. I grew very fond of her then. I admire her enormous honesty, her perseverance in learning Czech, and in all other ways being unlike one's idea of an ambassadress. They had a lot to tell us about life in Prague. They say the Russians are childlike barbarians, who kill all the milking cows, strip the Czechs of everything (I fleetingly remembered Mrs Chant's brother-in-law), particularly cars and bicycles, and rape all the women. An improbable story they told us was about a Russian who was riding along on a magnificent

[1] Sir Philip Nichols, then British Ambassador at Prague, and his wife.

stolen chromium-plated bicycle, when he met a Czech errand-boy riding a fearful old crock with his arms folded and whistling. 'Give me your bicycle,' said the Russian, 'you can have this one in exchange.' The boy was delighted. The Russian leapt on his old bike, folded his arms and immediately crashed to the ground.

I taxed Ralph with not coming to my aid in my argument with Phil. He says this was because he thought I was getting the best of it.

September 16th

It seems to me that this post-war universe is more fraught with horrifying and combustible dangers even than that of 1938–9. This then, this grey joyless prospect seeded with ghastly explosives, is what the world has torn itself in pieces to produce. But though such reflections haunt my mind I'm also aware of a very strong inclination to turn away from them and merely survey the inner scene – chimney corner, husband and child, friends, plants, cats and crockery. Janetta and Nicky came on the morning train. Sat over the fire all afternoon talking to Janetta, Nicky asleep upstairs. Kenneth has managed to get a permit for them both to join him in Belgrade, and it is now only a matter of waiting for their passage to be arranged. She has written to him very little, while his letters grow anxious and show that he is beginning to realize that 'something is the matter'. Indeed, something – or somebody rather – *is* the matter and that is Robert Kee. Ralph and I are amazed that having decided two young people were made for each other, they too should seem to think so. Yet Janetta feels in duty bound to go out to Belgrade, though gritting her teeth and dreading it; nor does she want to leave her new London house. She described a week's holiday she had taken in the Welsh mountains, never mentioning her companion, nor even if she had one, but we suppose it was Robert. As a returned prisoner of war he may well suffer from indecision and uncertainty; but holding the view I do of Janetta's special attractions I can't help feeling sorry for Kenneth, whose stock I believe to be lower than he knows. We begged her to try and persuade him to come over here rather than plunge herself and Nicky into possible emotional anguish in a background of utter strangeness and the horrors of a Belgrade winter. And then not to be able to get away should she want to! But she sticks to her plan – perhaps from a sort of pride. Or fatalism.

September 26th

All caught the early train to London. Then to Sussex Place to see what Janetta has made of the house.[1] Without signs of tremendous planning, she has made her part of it charmingly alive, fresh, with touches of inspiration in the way she has painted cupboards and windows, and chosen her colours. There is also some of the chaos and higgledy-piggledy of youth. She has the lower floors, opening on to the garden, Cyril Connolly the *piano nobile*. We stole upstairs to look. Oh my lord, what a contrast! I had seen these rooms empty and fallen in love with them. But instead of treating them in any way visually, as a painter his canvas, he has stuffed them with symbols of success and good living – massive dark furniture, sideboards groaning with decanters and silver coffee-pots, Sèvres porcelain, heavy brocade curtains, safe but dim pictures. I think the worse of him after seeing it.

---

[1] Janetta and Cyril Connolly shared a house in Regent's Park.

Janetta found a pathetically anxious letter from Kenneth, realizing something was happening and begging to be told what. She sank down into a chair with a lost tragic expression, and said: 'Oh *dear* – I feel I shall really have to go on with him. I can't face it all.'

September 27th: Ham Spray

Sebastian Sprott is paying us his yearly visit. One always forgets how incorruptibly he remains the same as the years go by, and is slow to fill in the picture of his immense virtues and his few limitations. His angelic good temper, serenity, sympathy for and detached interest in his fellow mortals, also of course his intelligence, are all in the first class. In the second is a curious lack of soaring power in his mental processes. He surprises by the things he has *not* thought or wondered about.

September 29th

Waking early, I saw from my window a sea of white mist spread over the fields, with the cows appearing to swim in it. An exquisite morning, the sky pure and cloudless, the air still, the grass netted with shimmering cobwebs.

Sebastian left after breakfast, and I spent the rest of the morning roasting myself on the verandah and writing. I know I ought to start work on my botany book again, but I put it off till Monday. It is going to be lovely weather for Burgo's weekend and he even admits he likes school better, and is alert, interested and gay. We took him for a picnic to Netherton, where there was a church marked in Gothic type on the map. Perhaps there would be more tombs for him, perhaps it was a ruin? We found the gate all right; inside it we entered what looked like a ballet scene, with shafts of sunlight glancing through huge trees onto yellowish Victorian tombs. One with two broken columns bore an inscription to a young woman drowned from a sailing ship in the nineteenth century; oddest of all, and rather like a Hans Andersen fairy story, the church was not made of brick and mortar, but cut out of yew trees in the *shape* of a church, with nave and spire. This bosky little churchyard had a magic character of its own and I never saw anything like it elsewhere.

October 1st

Existence has suddenly become exciting and interesting though nothing happens in particular. I eagerly anticipate each morning's post; it gives me a thrill to hear Burgo's treble voice say to Ralph: 'Darling! Look, there are the German prisoners going out to work in the field.' It is with rapture that I take my last cup of coffee to the fire. It's as if the beauty of the pattern in an old carpet I had been walking on for years all at once caught my eye and delighted me. I went up to the library resolved to do some work, and the morning flew by studying violets.

A letter from Janetta telling us she had written Kenneth a 'useless, awful letter, saying she wouldn't go to Belgrade and he must come back to London'. Meanwhile Cyril Connolly has been acting the bad angel trying to persuade her she should go. Why? As Janetta has the sense to see, he would like her to be always unattached. She has heard there is a girl living with Kenneth in his flat in Belgrade, which, she says, 'wouldn't help the situation I'm in for'. I rather fear she may be jockeyed into it by material things like the arrival of permits and passports.

To Aldbourne to lunch with the Brenans. It was only our second meeting since the end of the war and Gerald was much more his old self with us today. He amused us very much with his characteristic talk and gestures. I have come to value Gamel's 'goodness' more and more: it is a combination of humanity, kindness and complete lack of aggression. Yet her mind mercifully has a sharp bite. Talking of her great friend Ronald Duncan[1] she said: 'Nearly everyone is mad on the subject of money – sex simply isn't in it.' I said I heard Beryl de Zoëte[2] had become nicer lately. 'Oh?' said Gerald. 'Well, I met her in London the other day and I wanted to hit her on the head with a hammer. It seems she has been convened to Communism, only she will call it "Democracy".'

We were expecting Alix and James to tea, but it wasn't till much later that they arrive in their little beetle car, with pale and exhausted faces looming through the darkness. We had a delightful evening and I thought how wonderfully elegant James was with his distinguished air and long legs and shining silver hair that leaves no print on his pillow at nights. We talked, needless to say, of the atomic bomb. James claimed to know through scientific friends that the Germans were experimenting wildly with it during those last frenzied months before defeat, and those in command were really afraid that in their desperation they might blow up the whole earth.

James and Alix gave us a mocking account of their own life at Gordon Square. They are looked after by a daily woman who was blown up by a bomb and 'is rather queer in the head'. Alix can't cook and refuses to try, so they take their meat ration in corned beef and eat it at a table so close to the sink that they can reach out and hold each dirty plate under the tap while they go on eating bread and marge. And yet James, at least, loves luxury, good food and wine!

October 13th

Busy preparing Helen Anrep's room, shopping and picking flowers. She arrived wearing a hat full of waving bright blue plumes, and carrying a pink sock she had been knitting in the train. Ralph couldn't get over the hat, though he isn't very clothes-conscious. He said: 'I can't *think* what she's up to with it. She must realize no one else wears anything like it. It's really funny – like a hat out of a cracker.'

She amused us with stories about Roger's Quaker sister, with whom she had been staying. With Helen in the house it's very difficult to think of anything else. I wonder if she would have been different if she had never left Boris, and not developed the literary and artistic pretensions got from living with Roger. Yet there is something very warm, mellow and alive in her; also an amazing freshness, taking physical form in her pink cheeks and lips, upright and graceful carriage and springy walk. She makes me feel restless by flattering me too much, and also rather indignant that she appears to think I will take it seriously. Whence does the impulse spring? To want to please others, for instance, by repeating the nice things said about them, is an endearing quality, but the flatterer must take care not to overestimate one's credulity.

---

[1] Poet and dramatist.
[2] Consort of Arthur Waley.

October 18th

Helen leaves us this evening. I was doing housework when she came into Burgo's room and talked to me, while the cold misty air streamed in from the garden. It was mostly about Isobel Fry, in whom she attacks (under very slight cover) all Quakers – even Roger, dearly as I'm sure she loved him. At times I was surprised by the violence with which she trounced the Frys for meanness and puritanism. Of Margery Fry she said: 'If only her connection with Roger didn't make her feel that she must have views about literature and the arts. And she won't let one disagree with her, though she is mostly approving what she thinks she ought to like, rather than having real feelings for painting or music.' And all of it fitted Helen herself to a tee. Then she talked of the pleasure of living and sleeping alone – 'the worst of Men is that they have this curious passion for sharing a bed'. With the introduction of Men with a capital M, I had the distinct impression she was inviting me to complain of Ralph, so that she could sympathize from her feminine heart. But I have nothing to complain of, and share his passion for double beds. Next she turned to cowardice, accusing the Frys of being nervous of the bombing and not trying to conceal it. And yet when she came here in the war I *saw* her fear of raids with my own eyes. Was this an attempt to 'draw' me for my pacifism? When I went off to play quartets this afternoon, Ralph told me she opened direct fire on his views and tried to get him to admit that the war had done good. I think it is because she won't let people 'be themselves' that she is such restless company.

October 19th

A disquieting letter from Richard, who has worked out the time it takes him to draw each flower (a modest estimate, I must say), and affirms that on a basis of 200 working days and 165 non-working ones (not so modest) in each year, our book will take twelve years to complete. Allen Lane has accepted this, so there is nothing to be said, although I am filled with gloom, for when interested in a project it comes naturally to me to go at it full tilt. But from now on I shall make no attempt to hurry Richard, which would be patently absurd, and try and concentrate on the relief of no longer having to nanny him.

October 22nd

Janetta and Nicky arrived at tea-time. She looks pale and tired and it was difficult to keep off the subject burning to be discussed until Nicky and Burgo were in bed. Then, each with a glass of gin and vermouth, 'Now,' we said, 'if you can bear it, will you begin to tell us everything that has happened since we saw you last.' Turning rather pink she did so, and we talked of nothing else till bedtime. In reply to her letter to Kenneth saying she wouldn't come to Belgrade but would like to see him here, he had bombarded her with letters and cables. He doesn't appear to take in the serious threat presented by Robert. Yet she hasn't abandoned all thought of Belgrade, and has even got her passport as asked. *Why* does she still entertain the idea? For it is plain that all trace of love for Kenneth is gone, and that what is left is liking, pity, some respect and a sense of responsibility. Yet she must somehow or other summon up the energy to face him on Saturday and spend a fortnight with him which may well be agonizing. She says she will not marry him, but his energy and powers of persuasion may well get her out to Belgrade. She asks why shouldn't one be happy making a life with a person one likes but doesn't love? And she is twenty-three!

With someone so young and vulnerable we are naturally afraid of being too interfering or dominant. (I more so than Ralph, I think.) Or should I for once say what I really believe, that love is far the most important thing in life, a stronger, potentially more permanent and all-pervading force than the wildest of girlhood dreams suggest. People talk, out of a sort of prudery, as if it vanished entirely after five or six years of marriage, and only an affable, humdrum relation was left, enabling couples to jog along pretty well if they allowed each other plenty of freedom. But it needn't be like that at all. It's a hopeless failure if it is. After twenty years together one can be in a sense just as deeply in love as ever one was. Love doesn't simply fade away like 'old soldiers'; it changes its character, naturally, and matures, but its depth and richness can be as great as ever. And I feel Janetta to be capable, if anyone I know is, of such a relation.

But what of Robert? He is the mystery. Ralph understands his standing back and apparently refusing to try and take her from Kenneth. I'm not sure that I do. The Bloomsbury philosophy of sex, surrounded by which Ralph and I have lived for twenty years, disregards conventions but certainly not human feelings, nor does it sanction causing unnecessary pain. G. E. Moore's *Principia Ethica* set personal relations on a pinnacle for Bloomsbury, yet I think they are less promiscuous than their image in the eyes of the more conventional, whose sexual deviations may be under cover, or – in the case of the very rich – who buy as many mates as they can afford.

The telephone rang: Robert for Janetta. She came back beaming. 'Everything seems to have changed,' she said.

October 25th

Now that Kenneth is coming back, most of Janetta's friends are chary of giving her advice, perhaps because they don't want to be thought of as enemies if she stays with him. Robert has had to dash up to Yorkshire to his RAF Station. This afternoon I drove a pale, sad-faced Janetta to the station.

October 31st

Just before lunch Ralph was summoned to a second session at the BBC, to re-do his broadcast. Now that he knew what he was in for, he was as nervous as a cat and read his script all through lunch.

He left saying he would ring up if he missed the earlier train, but no message came and nor did he. Anxiety and pictures of imagined disasters swamped my mind, and I stood staring into the darkness, sherry glass in hand. Fighting against fuss, I at last gave in and rang up the station. The train had docked three-quarters of an hour ago and Ralph's car was still uncollected. When the time for his arrival by the late train came and went my agitation returned in full force. What *could* have happened? and what *should* I do if he didn't come at all? I remembered Dorothy Pritchett describing her anxiety when V.S.P. was late. 'Oh *yes*! I go through the whole thing – funeral and widow's weeds ...' Then the car lights swept the drive.

It was a repeated pleasure throughout the night to turn and find Ralph's solid presence beside me.

I forgot to say that Burgo and I listened to his French broadcast which came through perfectly, as though he were in the room. I was amazed how good he was, how interesting he made it, and that his French sounded convincing and not at all worried.

November 2nd

We both wrote to Janetta, trying in different ways to give her support, and telling her that of course she could come here whenever she liked, especially if things became too awful.

Meanwhile Burgo's half term holiday began, and plans were made for his enjoyment including a weekend visit from Esme, Pippa and Vicky [Strachey],[1] also fireworks, a bonfire and the burning of a guy. As I whisked round the house making beds I little thought what other events were due to happen that day. For while Ralph and Burgo were meeting the Stracheys the telephone rang, and Janetta's quiet voice told me in tones of absolute exhaustion that everything *was* too awful and she had finally decided against Kenneth and Belgrade, and having done so felt she must leave him at once. Between us we arranged that she and Nicky and Robert should come here this evening, a plan immediately endorsed by Ralph when he arrived back with the Stracheys, who gaped with adolescent amazement at finding themselves in the middle of an elopement.

Ham Spray has been filled all day with a feverish disquiet, punctuated by the ringing of the telephone. Once it was Kenneth for me, merely to say 'Take care of Janetta and Nicky. Robert is a weak immature character and not to be trusted with their happiness.' He went on to say that his relationship with 'the girl in Belgrade' was not important.[2] Ralph and I drove in the dusk to meet the refugees, and there they were looking worn-out and pale, a pathetic group on the dark station platform. Poor Robert, it must have been awful for him arriving among people who were practically strangers, but he put a very good face on it, and possibly it made things easier that he was at once whirled into a scene of eerie festivity, when the old guy was set crazily on a broken chair and burnt in a blazing bonfire under the Portuguese laurel. Unrecognizable figures stood round huddled in coats, and the blaze and the nostalgic smell of burning branches acted as a good solvent to our strange mixed party, blending them together. But Janetta looks quite exhausted, and after two endless telephone calls from Kenneth was almost in tears. All to bed – what a day!

November 4th

I had a long talk with Janetta in the nursery, and Ralph another in the library with Robert, who said afterwards how delighted he was 'that at last he had an ally'. The old house is bursting with all this drama and tension, and as well as everything else there is of course a mountain of work looking after so large a party. But I wouldn't have preferred to be without the Stracheys, who add quite a lot to our curious plum-pudding. Pippa and I drove after lunch to the Padels, and played some Mozart and the Mendelssohn Octet. Pippa loved the whole thing and the

[1] Mother and her daughters, who had spent part of the war with us as refugees. Burgo adored Vicky, who was about four years his senior.
[2] He afterwards married her.

frenzied musical atmosphere, and I love it more and more and gain a little in confidence.

November 5th

Janetta was resolved to go to London to see Kenneth. Ralph tried to dissuade her, or alternatively offered to go with her, and I could hear their voices going on and on in the library; meanwhile beds had to be made and housework done. Robert also offered to go up with Janetta, but she said she felt she must 'do it herself' – which was completely understandable – but would come back on the 4.45 train. Nicky was left in my care, in spite of which Pippa and I managed to squeeze in some more music, while in the afternoon the rest of the party walked up the Downs. Towards teatime a subterraneous crescendo of anxiety could be felt, but as no message came through, the tension relaxed. After tea we had our firework display, Burgo wild with excitement and Nicky sitting on my lap watching them through the sitting-room window, saying 'Oh pretty! Isn't it naïs?' and chuckling softly to herself.

When Ralph and I are alone together we chorus Robert's praises. He's not only unusually attractive, but an intelligent, thoughtful and realistic character. I don't remember Ralph ever before taking such a liking to a younger man. When Ralph and Robert had driven off in the darkness and brought Janetta safely back again, Robert's expansive pleasure was delightful to witness. Janetta herself looked greatly relieved; she said Kenneth had been quiet and matter-of-fact and accepted everything.

November 6th

All the Stracheys left after breakfast. Burgo has been as good as gold with his beloved Vicky; I found a poem he had written to her in his bedroom. It is still his holiday, and the elopers were in the most light-hearted mood they have been in yet, seeming at last to believe there is happiness in store for them. Janetta said Kenneth had been perfectly reasonable yesterday, and had a good deal to say about his girl Angela who is coming to London. He had been 'talking himself blue' to all Janetta's friends, especially Cyril. She and Robert discuss their plans, and at the moment are considering taking refuge in Devon or Cornwall, but it will of course be a honeymoon handicapped by a ready-made child, something full of problems. It has been very moving and disquieting to have these two enacting their drama of All for Love under our roof – as if electricity had been let loose in the house.

Very tired tonight, but just as I was off to bed Robert started talking about his prison life, so enthrallingly that I sat up for many hours more.

November 9th

A letter from a friend saying how distressed she was by Janetta's lack of love for Kenneth. 'She expects too much of husbands, if only for Nicky's sake they should stay together. No one else could be expected to take such an interest in her.' How *can* one expect too much? Or rather, what is the use of husbands if one doesn't expect the highest and the best? And I don't think I'm being romantic, but severely rational. Moreover is there not great cruelty in condemning a girl of twenty-three to spend the rest of her life with a man she doesn't love and who has for some time been living with someone else? Even from Nicky's point of view, would the inevitable disagreements not be disturbing for her too?

The wind blows from the bitter East; we all retract a little into our shells, whether from the chill in the air or sense of anti-climax, and there is a noticeable undercurrent of irritability. Nicky reacts in her own way to the situation, and at breakfast she entered the room at a red-faced tearful gallop, one arm outstretched towards Janetta, her hair flying, a tiny Tintoretto bacchante. Only Robert remains apparently imperturbable, writing and writing away in an exercise book in the midst of every disturbance.[1]

November 12th

Robert left in the school car, intending to look in London for a letter from the RAF and possibly go north that night. Nicky calmer. We all subside into normality.

In the evening a call from Robert. Janetta returned from it smiling. She said he was full of plans, had spent the afternoon with Cyril, did not have to go to his Air Force camp, but would like to come down here tomorrow and then go to Devon.

November 13th

Robert arrived in good spirits, looking very elegant in a grey suit and brown velvet tie. He described his visit to Cyril, who was sympathetic though also worried and concerned. He seemed full of plans, with no sign of 'immaturity'. After lunch I retired to my room and fell deeply asleep. Just before I dropped off, 'How do people live through these things,' I thought, 'when even witnessing them is so exhausting?' I can't think of any three people (for Nicky must be counted) to whom I feel and wish more warmly. Tomorrow they will go, and wearing and distracting though it has been, we shall miss them terribly.

At dinner Robert talked for the first time about his experiences as a bomber pilot before he was shot down. I asked if he would like to fly again in peace-time, and he described the pleasure of 'whisking round up in the air' as being rather like learning to swim. He had always liked flying in England for the pleasure of what he saw. He talked with some cynicism about 'operations' and said that quite a proportion of bombers never went near the target, but dropped their load at the first flak. The crew tended to have a blind belief in their pilot – why? – probably just because he *was* the pilot and they depended on him. But as they came within range of flak there were times when they would lose their nerve and shout at him: 'Oh God! More to the left! They'll get us! Turn back!' Easy enough to believe, but how much can weak imagination really grasp what they all went through?

December 1st

No Mrs Chant. I've had rather too much of this lately and begin to feel that boring duties are endless. Raymond is very sympathetic – too much so. 'Oh dear! the philosopher in the kitchen! I don't like to see that at all,' he exclaimed today.

The alternative horrors of servantlessness and new faces loom before me, and I don't feel in a mood to face either. I was beginning to hope that perhaps now the war is over better times might be coming. But the whole subject is for me fraught with guilt, for I feel deeply ashamed to think that 'our class' should depend on

---

[1] He was at work on his first book *A Crowd is Not Company*.

those less fortunate to hoist us bodily through our physical lives as well as managing this feat for themselves. On Saturday our pig was killed. On Sunday it was cut up and great blood-stained chunks of meat invaded the larder. I attempt, fairly successfully, to think about them as little as possible.

December 11th

Called at the Hungerford labour exchange in search of 'daily help' and found myself all at once in the mangle of the bureaucratic machine. 'Is your husband disabled? Or is there any special hardship?'

'I have a contract to write a book,' I said on the spur of the moment 'but if I'm doing all the work of the house it's impossible to get on with it.' This went down rather well.

'Well I'll have to send up a report on your case.'

A case! So that's what I have become.

1946

January 1st

For Christmas we had Janetta and Nicky, Saxon and no help; but we did have a mass of good things to eat and drink, turkey and plum pudding, extra butter and sugar on the ration, whisky, chocolates and cigars, and a pretty little Christmas tree. Saxon was I think glad to be here again, though he couldn't go further than murmuring that 'he thought it a good thing that his old habit of spending Christmas at Ham Spray was renewed'. He fascinated Nicky by dint of almost invisible nods and gestures in her direction; she and Burgo enjoyed themselves wildly, and it was certainly the happiest Christmas for years.

I gave Burgo his cello, which he was more pleased with than I would have guessed. On Boxing Day he insisted on going to the Padels to have a lesson, but tried to follow everything he was told with such intensity and anxiety that he was quite worn out by the effort. For a day or two he kept running to put records by Casals on the gramophone before breakfast, but already (alas and of course) the spell is loosening its hold, and practising is just another thing I want him to do. He is in rebellion against my desires at present, and though I respect him for it I can't quite think how to deal with it.

January 23rd

Burgo has had flu, but his convalescence moves steadily along; he is sweet and reasonable and anxious to get well. In fact we are both delighted with his frame of mind. He is becoming very much an individual. The chess craze persists, but is being supplanted by a mania for acting Shakespeare on his Pollock model theatre. He and I divide all the parts between us and keep at it so that we are quite hoarse by evening. I enjoy it as much as he does, I believe; it is exactly like one I had as a child, with cardboard scenes of snowy woods and baronial halls, 'wings', and a boxful of characters who slide in and out on metal stands. Burgo thinks and talks of nothing but Shakespeare, takes the greatest trouble over the details of scenery – enhancing it by castle walls built of minibrix, or doll's-house furniture, and reads increasingly well. All this afternoon has been given over to *Macbeth*. This seems so healthy a sign of life that we don't feel anything else matters. The sap is certainly rising.

January 28th

Burgo's new vein of silent stoicism is most unexpected. He never mentioned school last night, so that I feared he might not have realized that term began today. Yet realize it he evidently did, and this morning we witnessed that heroic and pathetic ceremony – the sad pale figure clapping on its head and round its neck the insignia of slavery and suffering. Or so it seems to him at the moment, even though later on fun and excitement will be involved. We both found this spectacle harrowing in the extreme, and many times a term I ask myself whether it is really right and necessary to put children through such torments in order to get them used to the horrors of life.

Burgo's return from school in the evening is a moment when we prick up our ears, or send out feelers to sound the atmosphere. He came back today jovial and full of talk, and after prep returned eagerly to Shakespeare. But at bed-time it was: 'I *hate* school. I know I shan't get a wink of sleep tonight thinking about it.'

January 30th

A letter from Janetta. Everything had been going frightfully well, 'Wonderfully lovely well' until three days ago when Robert was suddenly summoned north by the RAF and threatened with Court Martial for writing some articles in a Sunday paper on life in prison camp in Germany, which the paper had omitted to get censored. So poor Robert is up there plunged in gloom, hanging about the camp with nothing to do, waiting for he knows not what. And Janetta fears for him all sorts of things, the worst of all being a possible prison term, and is trying to get help from various MPs. It's difficult not to get the feeling that 'the Forces' can't really take in the fact that the war is now over – or perhaps don't really want to.

February 2nd

Yesterday at last I was able to dig in at my botany table, and did a good morning's work there, nor did it seem so formidable as I had feared. Burgo has returned each day cheerful from school, and sometimes with good news of top marks or other successes. We act *Hamlet* on the toy theatre, and then Ralph reads *Ivanhoe* aloud.

Drove through streaming rain to Marlborough for a concert by Peter Pears and Benjamin Britten. I had only seen Pears as Peter Grimes, when wig and fancy clothes effectively concealed the fact that he is a large, broad-shouldered man with the profile of a Roman Emperor. He sang most beautifully. Britten, slim, nervous, and with the bright face of a little animal, began each piece looking shyly away as if he couldn't quite face eyeing the music or even the piano keys. But as the music ended he brought his rather pointed nose round sharply towards the audience as if to say 'What do you think of *that*?' The Marlborough boys punctuated the music with gruff and heart-racking coughs, all so alike that they seemed to come from a single ghostly monstrous throat.

February 6th

It has rained and rained from leaden skies. Sudden gusts blot out the Downs in a sheet of whiteness; and to get out of our soaked garden we must wade through moulded ridges of rich coffee-coloured mud. A suitable background for the dismal news dished out to us last night by the Minister of Food that fats and animal fodder are to be cut, and that there is a serious world shortage of wheat, so that it is entirely possible we may have to have bread rationing to save millions from starvation. Well-off and well-fed as we are here I couldn't help a twinge of resentment at being suddenly faced with these facts, when so short a while ago we were being encouraged to think we would soon be enjoying peace-time conditions. But no: the thought of famine in Europe hangs overhead like the dark roof of Paddington station.

At tea Burgo remarked: 'You and Ralph are unkind to me, you know, by being *too* kind. You let me have my own way too much. Now don't go and be brutally unkind because I say that.'

February 28th

A day in London. First to Sussex Place; Janetta let us in. Robert and Nicky descended like a cascade. Beside the horrible business of Robert's Court Martial, they had had a burglary, and dry rot had been discovered under the Connollys' bathroom door. Robert described two days of an Enquiry to see whether a Court Martial is necessary; he thinks he is safe, but had obviously had his nerves rasped by the futility of it all.

[I could never claim to have been more than an acquaintance of Cyril Connolly's – one reason being that my pleasure in friendship is as a two-way concern. Of course he had many close, warm friends, but he had even more admirers and people who were proud to know him. Indeed there was a great deal to admire – he was exceptionally intelligent, clever (not quite the same thing), witty and brilliantly funny, all qualities I greatly enjoy and respect. I still laugh aloud when I remember some of his characteristic witticisms, delivered in his famous 'flat' unmodulated voice preceded by an intensified gleam in his eyes; for instance the description of the traveller returning from abroad to be greeted by an invisible loudspeaker saying: 'Wipe that smile off your face – this is London!' He had great charm when he chose to switch it on, and could look as if he was pleased to see one again. But no one could venture a remark that transgressed his system of values without bringing a hint of the schoolmaster into his manner. What were those values? Obviously literature came in lengths ahead with the other arts following. I doubt if politics interested him much except insofar as they involved the arts. It's rather difficult to relate moral concepts to Cyril. He had a bad reputation about money when he was young and poor; but even when his victims were equally young and poor they bore him little resentment. They enjoyed his company too much for that. Also when he grew more prosperous he was an extremely generous host, and could show supporting and affectionate kindness, as he did to his neighbour Duncan Grant, during the lonely years of his old age at Charleston.

I am sure the same current of warmth flowed towards his children, his loves and his chosen friends; what matter if those outside his inner circle reacted to his company rather as an audience does to a play or concert? On the whole he was unresponsive to other people's sallies, even by the quiver of an eyelid. When he was a guest, Cyril certainly expected best feet to be put forward: we tried to please him and were happy if we succeeded, even if there was a grain of resentment in our happiness.

He probably knew his own failings better than others did – far the most disastrous seems to have been sloth, which so strangely curtailed the output of an original and stimulating talent.]

June 20th: Ham Spray

Richard and I sit waiting in considerable feverishness for the arrival of the 'Tycoons' – in other words Allen Lane of Penguin Books, publisher of our botany book, and the printer Geoffrey Smith. We have a feeling that its whole future is threatened in some way incomprehensible to me by the financial by-products of Peace. This meeting has been arranged by the book's midwife Noel for the whole thing to be discussed. I have some important queries about scope and size, and Richard some others mainly concerned with time and money. As for money, none at all has been offered to me until the first volume comes out, and when oh when will that be? All yesterday I was tidying up the library and my botany table. All this morning I have been trying to straighten out my thoughts and at the same time keep my confidence afloat. I am very much aware of it as a bobbing entity like a ping-pong ball on a jet of water at a fair, perilously kept up by an effort more of auto-suggestion than intelligence. But I must go and make tea ready for them.

June 21st

The Tycoons have come and gone. After an anxious time of trying to prevent all I had to say draining away and leaving complete blankness, I saw the smooth, long-nosed Bentley draw up in the drive. Allen Lane, a stocky figure squeezed into a smart suit of palest grey, was purely and simply the millionaire in an American film. He appeared to be acting a part, an important element of which was manifesting the 'common touch' by revealing a passion for choc-ices. Yet I'm sure he never ceased thinking of himself as the personification of power through money, benevolent but not to be 'had'. This for some reason made him rather pathetic. Geoffrey Smith the printer was a nice solid man, understanding his job and inspiring confidence, while Richard looked very wrought-up and defended his life-work with burning eyes in a pale face. We drank a glass of madeira and then repaired to the library. I found my wits and my tongue once we started talking, but very little comfort or advice was to be got from any of them because they knew absolutely nothing about the subject. Lane is determined to exclude trees from the book, and when I tried to point out that there is no natural line of demarcation between plants, shrubs and trees, he waved me aside with a winning gesture saying, 'Oh, I think of a tree as something whose trunk I can put my arms round.'

So the afternoon spun by, while two incompetent electricians who had come to put in a single plug tore up the floorboards in the corridor with a loud rending noise, or shouted boomingly in the cellarage like Hamlet's father's ghost.

As our visitors were driving off I couldn't resist saying to Allen Lane: 'We've met before, you know – more than twenty years ago when I worked in Birrell and Garnett's bookshop.' His millionaire pomposity crumpled just a fraction at this reminder of his boyish diffident self, travelling the books of his firm and making up to me in the process.

July 12th

Janetta, Robert and Nicky have come for the weekend. We love to have them here, and love all three of them. Also it is going to be gloriously fine and hot. Heat produces a sense of calm and expansiveness, and just as the flowers are bursting out of their buds all over the garden, everything that had become knotted and constricted within oneself loosens and expands and brings delicious relaxation. All day the warm air poured in at open windows, the garden is a bath full of faintly buzzing stillness. All day we lay on rugs spread on the lawn, talked, bathed and picked fruit. The presence of Robert and Janetta, both so beautiful and charming, enhances everything for both Ralph and me, and in exactly the same way.

July 13th

Everyone seems happy, particularly Burgo who is celebrating his eleventh birthday and undoes his presents with frantic delight. A kite, a camera, a tent, books – all are a success, and in each case he rushes round the breakfast table and hugs the giver nearly to death. Drove to the top of the Downs where the kite was flown, while Janetta and I wandered about picking flowers and making miniature gardens and houses of pebbles to amuse Nicky.

A bathe before lunch: the water in the swimming-pool is getting much warmer and our bathes last longer and are pandemonic. Ralph bounces in with a roar and a splash, Janetta knots her hair on top of her head and swims about very fast, breast-stroke but crab-wise, with her head and neck well out of the water, her nose wrinkled with laughter; Robert dives in with a wild gleam in his eye and a wolfish smile and comes up with his black hair all over his face; Burgo squeals and hops without stopping; he carries on like billy-o with Robert, and there is a lot of horseplay and shouts of 'you dirty rotter!' Nicky sits demurely on the edge, naked but refusing to be coaxed into the water. Burgo's birthday tea followed.

It's extraordinary how even in what may seem the smoothest and most felicitous circumstances tiny signs may show that all is not perfectly well between two people, and irritate the inattentive ear like the faint buzzing of a mosquito or the drip of water from a tap. So it was that when Janetta and Robert decided to spend the golden evening walking to the top of the Downs, and indeed set off in that direction only to come to a halt in the field and stand there talking for almost an hour, something in the attitude of their drooping heads struck a chill into my heart. I felt it again when at dinner what sounded like a random remark of Robert's produced a sudden movement in Janetta, making her upset her glass of gin and vermouth and murmur: 'It's the last straw.' 'The last straw to what?' 'Just life.'

July 19th

All left us this morning, by car and bicycle, but how they linger in our minds, attach themselves to tunes and remain with us as the echo of voices or images of beautiful bodies in the pool. It would be strange if several years in prison camp left no tension, and Janetta told Ralph when they were picking fruit and vegetables to take to London that Robert was 'terrifically up and down'. Sometimes everything she did would be wrong. Then he would turn and blame himself. But why, oh why do human beings have to spoil the sweetness of companionship by tossing the burden of guilt and blame between them like some macabre form of football? No lovers can escape quarrels, but these two are too exceptional for one to be aware of them without pain.

[Some combination of circumstances – now partly forgotten – led to my stopping writing my diary for over a year, the only real break there has been in it until today. I had never thought of it as a thing to be kept religiously, and perhaps it would be more relevant to ask why I ever started it again (in January 1948). After all, it had begun life as an uneasy tail tied to the kite of the war, or in other words the war had focused my desire to write, as very likely the Peace could not.

One reason certainly was that in the late summer of 1946, Burgo left Newbury

Grammar School and went as a weekly boarder to a conventional boys' prep school at Kintbury about ten miles from Ham Spray. Surprisingly happy and successful there at first, he wasn't a conventional little boy, and to our dismay he suddenly began quietly taking to the road and walking in the direction of home. 'What was wrong?' we asked, scenting bullying and other horrors. But he had no complaints. There had been a bad thunderstorm, and at length he confessed that he had got it into his head that Ralph and I might have been struck by lightning and be dead. The pattern repeated itself, and there followed many uneasy months for us all, for there is nothing that wrings the entrails more savagely than one's child's inarticulate misery. There were more escapes, and all Burgo could say was that the moment he left the school gates and started 'running away' a feeling of intense happiness invaded him. The trouble was there was no day school within reach and we obviously couldn't leave Ham Spray. We consulted the charming old Scottish psychoanalyst Dr Edward Glover, who talked of 'fugues' and 'fantasies about the death of parents' as common currency, and spoke of the Junior School at Eton (which Burgo had been put down for) as a 'jungle', but the problem remained. Our worry and fear that we were bungling a difficult situation, as well as the fact that it was one about which Ralph and I didn't always see eye to eye, I'm sure made up one reason I stopped writing. Angst is not something one enjoys recording.

Quite a different cause was that the difficulties I had unconsciously foreseen between Robert and Janetta became serious. There was a temporary separation that grieved us deeply, followed by reunion.

But this was by no means an entirely gloomy year. There was a very happy interlude in the summer of 1946 when we all three enjoyed the thrill of going abroad for the first time for six years. We chose Switzerland as a country mercifully untouched by war, and arranged to join James, Alix and Marjorie Strachey at Lugano. What joy it was to feel the prison doors swing open and find ourselves speeding across France again, even though it meant sitting up all night in a full railway carriage. I remember that Burgo had a bad attack of hiccups and that a genial Swiss couple told him of an infallible cure, which I have several times passed on to perfect strangers. And I remember too the amazed delight of arriving at Basle station early in the morning, to find a huge banner of Welcome to us poor sufferers from the austerities of war – a welcome tangibly expressed in bananas (without coupons!), hot coffee and croissants with lashings of butter and black cherry jam. How clean everything was! and how kind the admirable Swiss who treated us with almost embarrassing sympathy – undeserved we felt. Even the Lugano trams were spotless, and conductors in impeccable grey uniforms picked up the used tickets from the floor with a long pair of tongs. We began to identify the Swiss nation with the Red Cross, and admire without qualification all we heard about their impartially humane activities during the war. We swam in the lake, rowed on it and took steamers to picnic on its further shores. Burgo took lessons in diving and the crawl, and the society of our Strachey friends was punctuated by bursts of laughter. Three weeks' bliss in fact. As we left I was struck with pleasurable surprise to realize that a small, non-belligerent nation such as Switzerland, completely surrounded by a terrible war, could yet have survived so well.]

1948

January 6th

All three to London for a few days' holiday treat. Our evening was spent having supper with Julia and Lawrence before going to the Aldwych Farce. A delicious repast of lobster Newburg and a rich cake. Ralph, Julia and I laughed uproariously at Ralph Lynn and Robertson Hare. Burgo often looked serious, but I think he was enjoying it. After the theatre I went on to the second meeting I have ever attended of the Memoir Club. Bunny, Oliver, Clive and Quentin, Dermod and Desmond, Duncan and Vanessa, Morgan Forster were the company. I was wearing a new suit of black watered silk trimmed with gold braid; I had designed it myself and was rather pleased with my appearance. 'Fanny has a new dress,' said Clive. 'Oh no,' said Desmond, 'I remember seeing her in it *years* ago at Birrell and Garnett. It's a pity that braid doesn't make words.' 'Such as what?' I asked. 'Oh, I don't know. Something like "Darling".' Dermod read a good paper about his father; Morgan a very long and slightly boring one about his aunts. He at least appeared to be amused by it, and often laughed at his own jokes, tipping up his curiously-shaped head and exposing a mouthful of neat false teeth to the electric light. My doom is sealed – I am to read a Memoir next time we meet.

[The Memoir Club began as a Novel Club, created by Molly MacCarthy in 1918 with the object of inciting Desmond to write one. This it failed to do and was therefore transformed into a Memoir Club a year later. The idea was that papers should be both confidential and completely frank, and that no one should take offence at anything read. Invitations were sent out by 'Mary MacCarthy, Secretary and drudge of the Club', to the Keyneses, the Woolfs, Roger Fry, Duncan, Vanessa, Clive and E. M. Forster. New members were elected by secret ballot, but as one blackball sufficed to exclude a nominee the Club naturally failed to grow very fast. By the time I was elected it had been augmented by Bunny Garnett, Adrian Stephen, Oliver Strachey, Janie Bussy and Quentin Bell; but it had lost – by death – Roger, Virginia, Lytton and Maynard. Later on, in the teeth of fierce blackballing we co-opted Dermod MacCarthy, Julia Strachey, Olivier Bell, Angelica Garnett, Sebastian Sprott and Denis Proctor.

Dinner was arranged by the secretary, usually in a Soho restaurant, and after it we repaired to the rooms of one of the members, sank into armchairs and sofas and listened while two papers were read aloud. I never knew a more attentive or appreciative audience, and there was usually plenty of laughter. After the papers came questions and general conversation. It was a delightful way to spend the evening, and notes made after several meetings will be found in what follows. The trouble was that it was difficult for the various secretaries (I was the last) to find dates suiting everyone, and also enough new blood to get through the barrage of blackballs. Molly had intended the papers to be kept by the secretary, but as more and more members became writers they all carried them home to act as material for their published works.]

January 9th

A fine crisp morning. Burgo and I went to the HMV gramophone shop where he wanted to spend some record tokens; among other things he chose the music of the Tchaikovsky ballet, which has hooked him. Home on the afternoon train with Robert, Janetta and Nicky, back to beloved Ham Spray, cold, but sweet-smelling, with flowers in pots in every room, black Minnie[1] and a supper of home-made brawn. We meant to go to bed early, but Janetta and I got into a long rambling conversation about Capital Punishment which kept us up for hours.

Robert works hard at a German translation. It wasn't till this evening after a bottle of wine and sitting over a roaring fire that he suddenly said what must have been for hours on the tip of his tongue: 'I hope you are free on the twentieth.' We didn't pretend not to understand that it was an announcement of their marriage, and Ralph said in a very melancholy voice which failed to conceal his emotion: 'I suppose we mustn't say how glad we are.' For however little one may believe in ceremonies, this one will be surely both a symbol and solid evidence of something that has every claim to make one glad. And happy planning for their party filled the rest of the evening.

January 15th

Re-reading Proust is rather like having a fever. So stimulating is the effect of drawing in his subtle, intoxicating complexities that one is left restless, breathing fast and shallow, so that those moments come as a relief when one is carried away by the flood – drowned in it. I cannot decide whether I get more from the translation or the original, and so move from one to the other, at times getting so much interested in the problems of translation itself that I have to have both versions in front of me.

Burgo goes back to school on Monday, and seems only to have realized the fact today, passing as a result into a sort of Laputa, neither in our world nor that of school. We drove in to Newbury for some school shopping and I tried to give my mind to thick grey socks (which must be marked) and speckled sand-shoes. In the afternoon the arrival of Boris and Maroussa made a happy diversion. It takes one all one's time to attend to Boris; he is such a potent force quite apart from his huge size, increased I think since we last saw him. At tea his bulk alarmingly overlapped our fragile Regency chairs. He spreads his legs wide to make room for the giant stomach; and beneath his mouth with its turned down rather bitter expression the double chins hang like those of a monitor lizard. Yet there isn't the least contradiction in saying that he is a pleasure to look at, is full of charm and captivates the eye by his delicate movements with his large hands or the subtle drift of expression over his face, and the ear by the musical play of his voice – even by the long drawn-out '*Eu – eu – eu*' with which he fills in a gap in a sentence. He

[1] Cat.

said one was wrong to put a child's happiness at school first; he must learn, and that involved a certain amount of being unhappy. He described how, when he got a specially bad mark at school, his mother said to him: 'If you get that again, *I'll skin you alive.*'

January 18th

Burgo is becoming as much under Boris's spell as we are – a great blessing as it has distracted him from his uneasy, pre-school state. Today he took Boris up to his room to show him all his treasures, including those in his secret cache under the floor-boards – a signal mark of favour. Boris told us a story about his brother Glyep who is a doctor in Cairo and an ardent stamp-collector. He happened to find a freak sheet without perforations in a small post-office. Soon afterwards King Farouk's Secretary wrote to say that he had heard of Glyep's purchase and would like to buy the stamps from him. 'They have been sent to a friend, a professor in Germany,' was Glyep's reply. Another letter from the King's Secretary asked for the friend's address, but was told the stamps had not arrived. 'Unfortunately lost in the post.' Even this was not the end. When Glyep was out his flat was completely ransacked by the King's agents, but the stamps, hidden in a special poison cupboard, were not found.

January 19th

The fascination that Boris exercises over Burgo has reached such a point that last night at supper he couldn't take his eyes off him, and from time to time put out a hand and – as if magnetized – touched his enormous cheek. We all drove to Hungerford to see our Russian friends off, and then returned to our packing and preparations. If Burgo minded going back (and he said a few days ago that he did) he was wonderfully philosophical and seemed to be trying to make his departure go off as smoothly as possible. At last Ralph drove him away into the darkness with his trunks and his cello, while I sank extenuated on to the sofa. How I hate the whole business! How unnatural it seems! I do believe he was partly excited to be rejoining the world of boys, but for my part I hated seeing the door of his bedroom yawning vacantly, and finding his blue jersey and his sandals lying on the bathroom floor.

[Most parents of my generation had been brought up impersonally by nurses and in the belief that father and mother knew best, so that when the war handed us responsibilities for our own beloved children for which we were ill-prepared, many of us worried too much whether we were doing right – a worry not diminished by knowing something of the theories of Freud.

I hope I have conveyed in the few references to him that Burgo was a happy, funny, original if sensitive little boy before the guillotine fell that took him away from home. I have noticed the same change in many other children. Before the prep school age they are unselfconscious, amusing, and so full of energy and high spirits that they cannot walk along a pavement, but need to let off steam by going hoppity-skip. Then what happens? They are forced into the company of their contemporaries, undiluted except for a few adults of a special species among whom are to be found love of power, paedophilia, and – with luck – one or two born teachers gifted to stimulate budding intelligences. Under the influence of transplantation from the flower-pot of home to an environment fraught with fear and bewilderment, what a sad change takes place! They become fidgety, competitive, suspicious, wanting to be exactly like everyone else, and ready to bang or punch the other boys before they have it done to them. I am of course exaggerating and over-generalizing, but there is some truth in my picture.

I suggest that our English system of packing children off to boarding-school at the age of eight or even six is brutally cruel, as can be seen from watching the departure of any school train at the start of the year. Of course children should learn to mix with their contemporaries, and can have glorious fun and laughter with them – if only they are allowed back to base in the evenings until they are old enough and firm enough not to be battered out of their original shape. I find something very unnatural in herding those of the same age together, and would prefer something approaching the microcosm envisioned in the households described by Tolstoy and Turgenev, where children, adolescents and lovers mix together and the old babushka makes her comments from a corner by the samovar.]

January 20th

We had to catch the early train to be in time for Janetta and Robert's wedding. Fine and frosty weather; a brilliant flame from a hedger's fire, caster sugar covering the fields, and puffs of smoke coming from the mouths of men bicycling to work.

At Sussex Place there were flowers everywhere, champagne bottles on the white-covered table, and the old charwoman's face cracked by a permanent smile. We walked with Janetta and Robert, and Janetta's half-brother Mark to the Registry office nearby. Back at the house again, wonderful food was appearing – oysters, smoked salmon, chicken mayonnaise. Then the guests swarmed in, about sixteen of us in all; someone was filling my plate with food and my glass with champagne, while the heat of the fire brought out and spread abroad the scent of mimosa, so that the whole experience merged into one, and I was borne on the wings of semi-intoxication combined with the sympathetic feelings I had been simmering in all day, through conversations with the other friends – Cyril Connolly, Angela [Culme-Seymour], Julia, Diana Witherby, all of whom seemed as mellow as I felt.

January 27th: Ham Spray

Ralph and I are working in the library – the first real day's work this term. Only during the quiet days between weekends can I seriously plunge into reading or work, and even so it often takes me a day to get into my stride, and I think I read unusually slowly: it seems to me I hear every word resounding through the corridors of my brain, but if one does not, how to appreciate the style – if there is one? Tonight I was reading Virginia's book of essays, some are quite dull, and then comes a brilliant sentence, like this about Proust: 'Suddenly in flash after flash, metaphor after metaphor, the eye lights up that cave of darkness and we are shown the hard tangible material shapes of bodiless thoughts hanging like bats in the primeval darkness where light has never visited before.'

January 30th

Feeling over-sedentary after a hard morning's work in the library I decided to go for a walk, but couldn't persuade Ralph to come too. 'Why do you like going for walks so much?' he asked me. Well, why do I? Because I like the look of the world around me seen from a different position (from that in the car, say); because I like the feel of the wind on my face, the sun also, and the mere pleasure of physical movement.

It wasn't a particularly attractive day. I turned up the grass track that follows Wan's Dyke. At the top, two old chaps, one with a pretty rosy face like a Morland, were digging holes in the bank, and as I passed one shouted to the other. I looked back and saw him hauling up the limp yellowish body of a ferret. Coming back up the lane I suddenly caught several whiffs of purest Spanish village – damp wood smouldering on a bonfire – which brought back a cobbled street odoriferous with hot dust, mules, white walls, everything most different from my surroundings, like a stab from a hatpin.

January 31st

The Brenans to lunch. We hardly mentioned politics, not even the assassination of Gandhi heard about last night. Everyone seems to be sick and tired of them. Instead we talked about people, books and writing. Gerald said to Ralph: 'Your review on Nelson was very good. You always seem to write what you want to say: now I can never do that – I write what my pen wants me to do or something. The man at the points is at fault, it appears to me, and gets onto the wrong line and I can't get off it.' Talked about Bertie Russell and his broadcast discussion the other night with a Jesuit about the existence of God. Bertie put up a bad showing for the agnostics, and the clever Father ran rings round him.

March 1st

Robert rang up yesterday sounding cheerful and eager to come down. He was writing his first review for *The Spectator*, and hoped to get it done before the six o'clock train. What a pleasure to see them both again! Also they seem to be completely in control of their life, no longer buffeted by it, and Robert's book[1] has been having a lot of favourable, some enthusiastic reviews. He is working away industriously at his translation.

Clive arrived at tea-time with a tiny suitcase and a large briefcase containing three bottles of sherry. What would our guests make of each other? we wondered. We warned Robert and Janetta of Clive's comic side. We needn't have worried – they all got on perfectly and conversation never stopped.

March 3rd

We decide to institute the Charleston regime of spending the morning quietly at our various occupations. Otherwise the constant talk would finish us off. But there is great goodwill afloat in the house to make this visit a success. Clive remarks often on Janetta's beauty and sweetness, and obviously likes Robert, saying he is 'very attractive'. Meanwhile Janetta sparkles in the light of Clive's admiration, and has been very funny. Clive was delighted when she produced gestures turning herself into the caryatids which support Cyril's sideboard.

On Cyril's recommendation we had invited two new neighbours, Robin and Mary Campbell, to have drinks with us. They were a pleasant surprise – informal and easy, fairly tough, realistic. In no time we were discussing the reason for the

[1] *A Crowd is Not Company.*

failure of the Ruskin marriage, described in a book we had all been reading.[1] Was it Ruskin's surprise and horror at the first sight of Effie's bush (his experience of the naked female having hitherto come from Art alone)? Mary Campbell is self-confident, rather small, with neat pink and white features. In the evening Clive was captivated by Janetta's description of having her bottom pinched black and blue by Italians. He got rather drunk, and though no one else was more than merry, kept saying: '*Some* of us have had too much brandy.' All of us notice and are amused by his compulsive gestures when talking – the sweeping movements of his hands as though sowing seed, pulling up his trouser legs to reveal a pink leg and then buttoning his coat tightly round him with defiant looks in both directions, as if at imaginary enemies.

March 5th

The last few hours before Clive's departure were spent like most of the rest, talking our heads off. After he had gone I felt I had talked all the breath out of my body and was quite hoarse and deflated. His vitality is tremendous, almost exceeding Robert's. He and Janetta made as if to go, but we asked them to stay on and were delighted when they said they would. Robert was curious to hear more about Clive and Charleston and Old Bloomsbury, and both he and Janetta seemed impressed by Clive – as indeed they might – he is so rosy and lively at sixty-six and keeps the conversation at such an interesting level. An unfortunate misprint in Robert's review for *The Spectator* has made him feel persecuted and as if nothing he did could come right. One glimpsed his potentiality for unhappiness in the fiercest of his repertory of smiles. Janetta took him off for a walk across the fields and he came back marvellously cured but still inclined to panther-like prowling.

March 9th

A summer day in March. The sky was already blue when Ralph pulled the curtains, and immediately after breakfast it was like June on the verandah. Birds sing loudly. Purple crocuses, following on the yellow, are bursting up and bursting out into wide cups in which the bees revel. Minnie appears to be on heat, and wanders round letting out unearthly yells, with an agonized expression and half-shut eyes. Her lover, the farm cat, follows her half-heartedly, while she makes all the running, rolling herself on the ground before him and stretching out her furry arms.

One cannot bear to go indoors, so we take out books, papers and writing-cases, and let them curl up in the heat or float away on a waft of air. I can only give half my mind to anything. I think vaguely about sex (because of Minnie, I suppose) – or *wonder* rather. Is a one-man woman or one-woman man born or made? What is the best technique for a permanent couple to adopt when one of them is attracted elsewhere? And is jazz the music of promiscuous sex only? Spring thoughts! Later I returned to writing my Memoir for the next meeting of the Memoir Club, something which has been causing me a good deal of worry and self-disgust, and then back to Proust and the superb M. de Charlus.

---

[1] *The Order of Release*, by Admiral Sir William James.

March 11th

Most of today we spent with the Brenans, driving to Aldbourne and lunching in their garden. Gerald was very amusing, and ceaselessly fished odd creations out of his mind, like a conjurer producing rabbits. He complained of exhaustion however, caused by seeing a lot of Dylan Thomas who threatens to come and live in their village. At a certain hour of the day, Gerald told us, and a certain degree of drunkenness, his conversation is brilliant, amusing, imaginative and poetical. Then he refuses to go, and gets drunker and drunker, and has to be propped out of the house and away, with his large baby's head wobbling on its stalk. As he left the last time, he started dramatically at the sight of Gerald's row of dustbins, and exclaimed: '*FORty* thieves!'

March 22nd

The news – I can't write about it. Ever since the Communist coup in Czechoslovakia, open war-talk is rising in a steady booming drone. One can't allow the total import to penetrate because of being too horrified and also at the same time *au fond* too apathetic, too weary of the long dismal story, to think about suicide, or any other means of escape. And so, like cornered rabbits we hope for some lucky chance to save us all. But not one voice is raised against this horrible war-talk. Not *one*.

April 30th

We had arranged to meet the Brenans in Hungerford, and all go together to try and find the pasque-flower on the downs above Streatley, where Gerald had seen it thirty years ago. He sat beside Ralph in the front seat giving directions, as the car waddled up a deeply furrowed chalk track marked 'Impracticable for Motors', and on to the highest summit of the Downs. Here we felt very conscious of our altitude; shoulders of pale downland stretched away in all directions, dotted with clumps of trees – it was warm and thundery, with no wind. In front of us we saw the long grass track called the Fair Mile, where the pasque-flower is supposed to grow. Two shepherds were standing there talking, and Gerald got out and pranced ahead to ask if they had seen the flower. I saw their arms waving and pointing; then Gerald came running towards us with a look of boyish excitement on his face. In recent years the plant had apparently moved across a shallow valley, but there we found a large patch of the purple and astonishingly exotic-looking flowers and buds coming up in the homely English grass among their silky grey leaves. A marvellous 'botanical sight'.

September 12th

Campbells and Connollys to tea arriving through the rain in a hired motor; the jeep being too bleak was left for Robin to drive our new hens over in. I was touched by his solicitude for their happiness and comfort.

With his long bobbed hair and smart South of France clothes, what does Cyril look like? A china pug on a mantelpiece perhaps? He doesn't snub Lys, even when she tries to 'produce' him ('Oh, that must have been wonderful, Cyril!' or 'Oh, do you know Cyril was remembered by the waiter at the *Chapon Fin* who hadn't seen him for twenty years?'). Cyril was friendly and often very funny. He wanted to see the upstairs, so I took him up and showed him the library. He has a 'second spouse' complex – he talks to Mary about Philip Dunn[1] as 'your husband', and to me he spoke almost exclusively about Carrington. I didn't get the impression the Campbells and Connollys were very happy together; Mary in particular wasn't quite at ease with him.

November 8th

I have been writing little because we have been through a very anxious time about poor Burgo's unhappiness at school. He is now a boarder at Millfield in Somerset and we feel almost able to bank on his remaining there until the end of this term.

Lunch with Mary Campbell just back from Paris. 'Cyril was there the last few days,' she told us, 'and I had words with him. He asked me why I was antagonistic to him, and under the influence of a high temperature I told him.' She feels he is an enemy to marriage. Did we think it was possible to live completely united to your mate and yet be spiritually and mentally independent? We both said No.

November 24th

A short visit to London, staying with the Kees at Sussex Place. For me there was the Memoir Club, where Leonard read aloud an enthralling, brilliant extract from Virginia's diary, stopping now and then to say tantalizingly that the next paragraph was 'quite impossible'. Several names of suggested new members were mentioned, but Duncan said: 'I shall have great pleasure in blackballing them all.' I find this exclusive and unadventurous attitude of Bloomsbury's deplorable.

A lot was crushed into these days – a party at Karin Stephen's, lunch with Clive, a visit to the library and an evening with Robert and Janetta at the Gargoyle Club, where we ran into Julia and Philip Toynbee. He, poor fellow, is very unhappy because his wife is leaving him, and was making a token gesture of giving up drink for her sake, and resisting the cry of 'Do let's go on to the Coconut Grove or *somewhere*!' – a last resort of the unhappy.

[I never knew Philip Toynbee well, and have no right to do more than try to describe the impression he made on me. The first thing one noticed was his very deep, dark and beautiful speaking voice. In appearance he was tall, dark-haired and loose-limbed, and could have been good-looking but for the ruggedness of his features and complexion. An occasional missing tooth, as he grew older, blotted the attractiveness of his wide crocodile smile – a smile that revealed some of the complexity of his character: warm and ready affection combined with destructiveness and a good deal of the *enfant terrible*. Highly intelligent, well-read, romantic, gregarious, a buffoon capable of outrageous behaviour but who would not hold the recipient's reaction against him and whose friendships tended to be lasting, a sensitive literary critic.

It was during his tenancy of the Campbell's cottage at Stokke that we saw most of him, both there and at Ham Spray, on picnics and bathing parties. He loved arguing, particularly on abstract or political subjects, and so did we. He was good at the game – that's to say he listened to his opponent and returned the ball into his court.

---

[1] Her first husband, before Robin.

A Communist at Oxford, by 1949 he was merely left wing and against most things. Ralph foretold that he would end up as a Christian, and this is exactly what he did, as anyone who read him to the end will know.

Much later I wrote him a fan letter about one of his books and he wrote back:

Thank you for such a very warming letter, it made me nostalgic for the all-too-little that I saw of Ham Spray ... I wish I didn't like money so much. No, not even *like*, which would be something, but *fuss about*. Perhaps I shall take scrip and staff soon and appear bare-footed in Wilts, a wandering friar ready for *instant* corruption at the first gleam of a cocktail-shaker ...]

December 3rd

Walked to the village with a pot of honey for the Christmas draw. A wild, grey afternoon; the children were just coming out of school. They do seem to lead a queer bleak existence. In the desolate square of cement which is the school playground two little girls were holding hands and whirling round and round with sad, abstracted expressions. Is this all the fun they have? I wonder.

1949

January 1st

The New Year arrived with shouts, bells and the voice of Robert Donat on the wireless. The whole hullabaloo was senseless and missed the mark completely. Not so the deep boom of Big Ben, whose voice is the nearest I can imagine to that of God. Impossible not to be moved to some extent by a new year, to listen as if for the sound of a huge body turning over in bed, or the creak of an un-oiled wheel. Ralph and I were standing before the fire, and we clutched each other in a sort of panic, as if the days, weeks and months to come formed a long steep slope tilting downwards, and we were off, rolling down it and couldn't stop.

The morning post brought a pleasant surprise – Burgo's school report, all of it good and the first thing that dropped out of the envelope being a book token marked 'First Prize for Progress and Industry in this group'. Burgo was as amazed by it as anyone.

January 3rd

To the Campbells for a drink before lunch. Robert and Janetta were staying with them; talk was stimulating and lively. The dachshund puppies cantered in and out on short elephant legs, their claws clattering on the polished floor. Mary looks at her most sympathetic when, as today, her hair is unbrushed and she wears corduroy trousers with a hole as large as a potato in the heel of each sock.

Burgo and I have begun acting *Henry VI* Part I on the model theatre. He has become a stickler for detail: dead soldiers (lead) lay before the walls of Orleans, while the plasticine corpse of Henry V was draped in a white shroud. Sometimes I see the miniature world with such infatuated eyes that the delusion takes over and becomes real.

Ralph is up in the library writing something about human credulity, a subject that has always fascinated him – and me too. At dinner we talked of various irrational beliefs: in ghosts, Father Christmas, etc. Burgo thought that when people believed they had seen a ghost, it was really a symbol of fear, and that fear was the worst thing one could be afraid of, so it was really better they should believe in ghosts – rather good, I thought.

January 9th

Arrival of Raymond yesterday evening in specially high spirits has cured us of our slight hump of yesterday. Talk about Charleston and its affairs. Laughing heartily, he told us how Lydia[1] said to him: 'Oh yes, of course Vanessa likes you very much.

---

[1] Lopokova. Wife of Maynard Keynes.

She says you are a "nice old thing".' This morning he has retired into the little front sitting-room to write a review; sighs and groans ring through the door.

The Campbells came over with Philip Toynbee, whom they have kindly asked down to nurse his broken heart. Robin has a quiet subtle style of conversation, but loves an argument. Mary claims not to, but in fact her contributions are usually very much to the point and can bring a generalization out of a wash of general chatter. Philip taps a rich vein of comedy. Starting with homosexuality and whether one would mind one's child becoming 'queer' and if so why, we went on to free speech and Fascism. Philip and Mary held that Fascism was evil incarnate and should be stopped at any price. Robin believed in free speech so passionately that he was prepared to suppress it forcibly in those who were against it. Ralph and I alone cried for tolerance and true freedom of speech, and were gloomily struck by the distance all our three friends had come from the attitude of the Oxford undergraduates who voted against fighting for king and country before the war.

January 14th

Quentin and Julia for the last weekend of the holidays. I asked Quentin, who is secretary, what was the result of the latest election for the Memoir Club. He said: 'I'm afraid there will only be one new member – Angelica. Sebastian and Julia very nearly got in and it's just possible Clive may withdraw his blackball on Julia.' A wave of irritation passed over me at the occasional *stuffiness* of these old Charlestonians! Lovely of course to have Angelica, but we should have had some new blood to mix with this almost exclusively family party. I think Quentin agrees. He also told me about Charleston's indignation at Roy [Harrod]'s biography of Maynard. He had been bold enough to go there for a night to receive their criticisms and told Quentin they were not as bad as he feared, but Quentin admits that the truth is that none of them, particularly Vanessa, can bear to have anything said about themselves at all.

There are, however, several ingredients which make this weekend a failure in my eyes. One is the approach of Burgo's departure for school, and our inability to do special things with him because of Quentin and Julia. Julia has always been a demanding influence in the house, and this time, poor thing, she is sad and wants to take me off on walks and talk about her troubles. In spite of which she has entertained us all amusingly, partly with an attack on Cyril for being what she calls the 'High Priest of Smarty Literature' and a disagreeable character to boot.

January 18th

As I sat sewing a name-tape on Burgo's sponge-bag I tried to pierce his aloofness by telling him something of my own recollections of going to school and how quickly the strangeness wore off. Then he gave me a very delightful smile and said that it was nice to think it was such a short time to half term. At our early lunch he grew livelier – having got so near zero hour he evidently wanted to be up and over the top. To Newbury with school trunk, bike, etc. Several other boys on the platform. The idea that boys are unattractive, misproportioned creatures is quite untrue – these at least were mostly good-looking, well-built, with bright eyes and the bloom of peaches on their cheeks. We said goodbye to Burgo and drove back to Ham Spray feeling like flat bicycle tyres. And very pianissimo did the evening trickle by.

February 6th

This evening after much cogitation I began reading Madame de Sévigné's letters. I am so tired of reading bad books, and books Connolly says I ought to like and I don't. It is heaven to embark on these fourteen stout volumes of reality.

But what, I have been wondering, is the prop which sees the rationalist through acute misery and stress? For Madame de Sévigné it was religion, but for the atheist what? I can only think that he clings to love and friendship; not that these are the only things that make life worth living of course, but that they are the most unifying, coherent influences, unless he has an absorbing ruling passion for work – painting perhaps or scientific research. In personal terms, however, even when I am abjectly miserable I know that I love Ralph and Burgo, and by clinging on to that thread I can probably scrimmage through whatever morass I am in, which is not far from Morgan Forster's religion of personal relations.

February 19th

The Kees for the weekend; the weather delicious; we felt proud to have provided it for them, with sun hot enough to sit out in, snowdrops and dog-tooth violets under the beech tree. A walk to the Netherton Valley: having traversed its smooth green basin we sat down on a bank where flints rose out of the complicated texture made by winter shoots and mosses mixed. Here we were when a grey van drove by, turned and stopped. Out stepped Euphemia,[1] holding a basket containing a huge pat of yellow butter, two pieces of meat and some cream. All 'black' of course. There was something so like a witch in a fairy-tale about this encounter with a beneficent but amoral being that no wonder the Kees thought it a pre-arranged meeting and couldn't believe it was pure chance that made us pick on the Netherton Valley for our walk.

February 26th

For Burgo's half term we had taken rooms at Bath. We got up early and anxiously and were on our way soon after eight, driving through the cold morning, laden with jams and cakes and picnics. As we travelled west we saw some primroses in the hedges, it grew warmer, and our nervous temperature rose a little. But suppose he says, 'I can't bear it, take me away'? This is the first time we have collected him from the Upper School at Millfield, and the first moment of seeing him would probably give the key to his mood. There he was waiting in the drive, case and mac in hand, a little keyed-up but smiling and friendly, not doubting us. He seemed perfectly at ease with us and there was plenty to say. I asked him if he liked the Upper better than the Junior School, and he said 'Oh *miles* better. Edgarly was *awful*, really it was, and it felt like going back to something childish.' So far so good, but it is horrifying to think how much has *not*, at times, been said.

What to say about the future? I feel I have very few securely-based hopes about anything, either Burgo's having a happy life in this dismal war-haunted world or ourselves being free from increasing infirmities of various kinds.

But if one faces these gloomy truths, surely it is possible to be happy by means of taking what comes, expecting nothing, and above all not feeling 'now our troubles are over and we have got into calm water again'. There's no such thing as

---

[1] Married first to Henry Lamb, then Ned Grove.

calm water in life in any sense more permanent than there is in the English Channel. And somehow or other we have now reached an age when people suddenly die for no reason, so that I think we both expect to do it ourselves, or perhaps Burgo's anxieties about our deaths have made us conscious of the possibility, as Ralph remarked when we set off to Somerset, and he resolved to drive carefully.

March 2nd

There was a good chance for turning one's eyes outwards and observing other human beings when we went yesterday evening to a house-warming party given by Philip Toynbee in the cottage he has rented from the Campbells. Beside the Campbells, only Julia Pakenham and her husband Robin Mount were there. Julia has the Pakenham bloom and charm, and the soft husky lisping voice. She is in fact very pretty in spite of having an outward squint, so that one of her eyes seems to be flinging itself skywards in amazement or abandon while the other looks straight at you. The effect is quite fascinating in a curious way, like a permanent gesture. She is very intelligent.

The evening was immensely enjoyable. We talked without stopping, drank just enough to stimulate the mind without fuddling, and that was quite a lot, laughed a great deal and carried on some quite dense arguments. Very shortly after this Philip suddenly melted like a candle in the fire, his features softened, and he gently draped himself round the neck of Julia Mount. When he tried to stand up he nearly fell down again, and when he began a melancholy monologue about his loneliness and how lucky we all were to have mates, we saw it was time to go. He is a touching figure, and he was hospitable and sweet to us all. His new lady doctor friend, Ruth, comes down at weekends, meanwhile there he is alone with an absurd white poodle, shaven all over except for a mushroom of curls on top of its head. This creature somehow symbolizes and externalizes the clown element in Philip, and I feel that by laughing at it and guying it he is able to laugh at that part of himself.

During dinner he told us about his schooldays: how he was expelled from the Dragon School for a start.

'What for?' asked someone.

'Collecting money for Dr Barnardo's and keeping it myself.'

His bewildered parents took him to Dr Crichton Miller, who sent him to work on a farm for nine months, though he was only ten or eleven. The farmer was a slave-driver and worked him desperately hard, and at length he could bear it no longer and persuaded the bailiff's son Jesse to run away with him. They covered some eighty miles, when they were stopped by the police who sent for the farmer.

'Now you've always been a truthful boy,' he said, 'tell me the truth – you and Jesse did something dirty behind a hedge, didn't you?'

Thinking he wouldn't be believed if he said 'No' (which was the truth) Philip said 'Yes, we did,' and of course Jesse said 'No'. All this must have made a deep impression, for he told us he went back to the farm a few weeks ago to look at it.

March 19th

Ralph brought Julia from the station, and on arrival they remained in the car earnestly talking instead of coming indoors. Ralph has a way of launching straight away on to the chief theme in a visitor's agenda, which is tantalizing for me. It was easy to see some important topic had arisen – yes, it was Lawrence. But there was much more talk about books and writing. She was anxious to listen to Robert, who was taking part in a wireless discussion called The Critics, and prepared to be disapproving. 'Why should *Robert* get such a job?' she wanted to know, 'he was much too young anyway.' The truth is, I believe she is jealous because of the enthusiasm Ralph and I show for him. But she has been very much herself on this visit and given us great pleasure thereby. The two Pritchetts came to lunch. V. S. P. was immensely encouraging to Ralph about his writing, saying he is 'by far the best journalist now writing on biographies and history'.

April 13th

Burgo is home for the Easter holidays. We met the Campbells for a picnic lunch at Oare, where Serena and Nell were riding in a children's gymkhana. We ate among the cars in a high wind, surrounded by horsy bun-faced little girls in jodhs, their horsy mothers and dogs – an uncongenial lot. The Dunn children unfortunately failed to get their plump ponies over a single fence and were feeling horribly humiliated. Philip Toynbee really saved the situation by his jokes and clowning, climbing on to the saddles of the ponies, loping off incessantly to the Gents, drinking all the port brought by Philip Dunn and spilling the Campbells' beer – a genial old buffoon. The Campbells have now taken Philip into their hearth and home, unable to stand the pathos of his lonely muddling life; it is an arrangement which does them infinite credit but seems foredoomed to disaster. We stopped there on our way home. Ben Nicolson was staying, and Mary's mother Lady Rosslyn, and above all dogs – three house dachshunds, Philip's comic poodle, and a huge wet spaniel from the village in love with one of the dachshunds. All these creatures quarrelled, copulated, yapped, chased the ducks and dragged their bones over the human beings who sat about on the lawn.

May 16th

Ralph and I converged on Sussex Place, where we found Janetta, Robert and the baby[1] in her pram in the garden. Robert is mad about her, and enters into her feelings so thoroughly that he cannot bear her to cry for an instant. 'Do you think she *knows* how much we like her?' he asked Janetta anxiously. He has a plan to leave *Picture Post* where he has been working for some time and set up as a publisher with James Macgibbon.

My evening was with the Memoir Club. After supper, in Duncan's room in Taviton Street, Vanessa read a short memoir of Virginia as a child, and then Virginia's own account of her early days. Enthralling of course. It aroused in me a desire to know more about their brother Thoby, adoration for whom appeared to have been the great emotion of Virginia's youth – and who was so important to many others also, yet like a large grand mirror his image only emerges as the reflection of all these violent feelings. Though Vanessa read until nearly midnight the paper could not be finished as Desmond was so obviously ill, and had been seized with fearful wheezing while ascending the steps to Duncan's flat. Dermod drove him, Leonard and me home. Desmond sat frozen by breathlessness, with the muscles of his neck standing

---

[1] Georgiana.

out like cords. Dermod was all kindness to him; while he escorted him upstairs Leonard and I sat in the car discussing the relation of Brain to Mind.

July 8th

The post brought a bombshell from Richard containing the news that Lane means to publish our Volume I at *five guineas*, and is doubtful to say the least if he can publish any more volumes after it.

July 9th

I staved off the thoughts which were bound to follow from Richard's letter last night, but of course the moment I opened my eyes they were upon me like a swarm of bees each bringing its sting in the form of a puncturing reflection. After half an hour of this I got up and went out into the unearthly warm morning and took communion in the form of a solitary silent bathe, then padded about on the dewy lawn until it was time to cook breakfast. I can't say my thoughts were very profound, but I was facing the fact that if I have to be divorced from my work and its constant place in the future as well as the past it will be like parting with a piece of myself – a kidney, say. I have the feeling I have anticipated the operation and reconciled myself to it – but am not really sure.

This was the hottest day so far, 88° in the shade. Mary rang up and came to lunch in her jeans-and-jeep mood – candid, sharp, full of good-will and life. We lay panting under the beech tree most of the afternoon talking hard, and every so often one of us, talking as they went, would go off to the pool and dive in. Tassel, the dachshund puppy, was glad to suck some ice. Mary told us about the difficulties of life with Toynbee – much as we supposed: the worst drawback was his abandonment to drink. 'I've taken to watering the gin,' she said.

After tea I forced myself to go up to the library and do some work on my poor book, which will almost certainly never see the light. I am sad but not at the moment agitated. The work I am doing on it has become detached from thoughts of publication.

August 1st

The Campbells gave a dancing-bottle-party two nights ago. Everyone was rather drunk when we arrived, particularly Philip Toynbee (lachrymose) and Robin Mount (comic). Others present were the Pritchetts and Julia (neither of them at their ease), Virginia Tennant, Lord Bath (*'Bath's* the name, not that it matters'), the Kees, Janetta looking lovely in a dress of grey watered silk.

Tonight's cocktail party at Tidcombe Manor[1] was a sort of continuation of the Stokke one which had been going on spasmodically ever since. Julia told me that Philip Toynbee had been drunk and threatening suicide all the weekend. Even the subjects of conversation persisted, for apparently both Philips (D. & T.) returned to the old theme, which under the influence of drink became 'Peasants for bidets' instead of 'Bidets for peasants'.

[I heard much later from Julia that at breakfast that morning one of Robin's little boys said: 'What was that shot this morning?' No explanation was forthcoming,

[1] Home of middle-aged friends, Paul Cross and Angus Wilson.

and it wasn't until she and Philip Toynbee were in the train for London that he told her he had got out his gun and had been 'thinking of committing suicide but not having the courage to, when it went off through the ceiling, bringing down plaster and making a large hole'. It seems incredible that no one heard it except for Robin's boy. Julia gave Philip a piece of her mind. 'I told him, "If you want to commit suicide, commit suicide, but don't make everyone's life a misery as you have this weekend." ' She then advised him to go to a psychoanalyst. He hasn't forgiven her for her unfeeling attitude.]

August 6th

I've been re-reading some of the diaries I kept during the war, and asking myself how different is the frame of mind in which I write now. *Then* the public world and its horrors were constantly in our minds, seen through a sort of dark-room window reddened by our passionate rejection of the things that were happening. We closely followed the thread of the often nightmarish events we read about or listened to on the wireless, and spent hours analysing and arguing about them with each other, or held debates on pacifism with imaginary opponents, whom I can remember trying to convince while I carried out boring practical tasks – spouting a silent speech, for instance, into a washbasin I was cleaning.

Now we have lived through three years of total peace; we still have rationing but don't fear it getting worse (as we did then); there have been political crises and alarms for us to read and talk about *ad lib*. The chief change is that today our minds are much more often full of the books we are reading, the work we are doing, and above all the vicissitudes in the lives of Burgo and many friends whose troubles are very much our concern.

In the early years of our life together Ralph and I used to read aloud a lot to each other, taking turns. Especially was this enjoyable on holidays abroad, and I can remember taking eight volumes of *Clarissa Harlowe* in our rucksacks to read aloud in the bedrooms we stopped in. Now it is more likely that each will tell the other about the book on hand – this has the advantage of being like reading two books at once, and of course often leads to an exchange afterwards. Beside the many books from Lytton's collection kindly left with us for the present by James, to whom he bequeathed them, heavy parcels travel to and from the London Library.

August 11th

To London for the day. I lunched with Richard and then went with him to a meeting at Allen Lane's office. Its huge black leather armchairs (from the German Embassy) were suitable supports in which to receive the news that, in view of the Slump, Lane didn't see his way to publishing our book, the first volume of which is entirely in proof, with Richard's plates looking very charming. I consider we 'took it very well' and I think Lane and his secretary thought so too, but his innocent air of candour covering a businessman's astuteness faintly sickened me. All is not definitely up, since the attractiveness of the first volume might possibly produce a sponsor, but I have decided that if it is really to be the end of our enterprise I should try and squeeze some financial compensation out of them. It hasn't so far occurred to them to offer me a penny.

September 26th: Ham Spray

Ralph is very much set up by the fact that Chatto & Windus have asked him to write a book on Broadmoor and Dr Hopwood is entirely in favour of the idea.

October 1st

Ralph drove over to Broadmoor and spent the whole day there. He came back full of stories, in a state of great excitement and fruitful activity, bringing a lot of papers about the relation of insanity to crime; we spent the evening poring over them. With my flower book in its parlous condition, I naturally feel envious but not, I hope, jealous.

Raymond came for the weekend and Sebastian dropped out of the skies at the last moment. What's more on Saturday we had a great lunch party, with Pritchetts and Campbells added, to eat a Michaelmas goose. I love the way Mary warms one with little blazes of apparently candid affection.

Next day we whisked Raymond over to see Euphemia – a great success; they took to each other at sight. Euphemia put on a magnificent performance as the eccentric ex-courtesan. One of her old lovers, Morty Sands, was staying with her; he contrived to look gentlemanly even in very long shorts and a jacket fringed with old age. Euphemia brought out some of her Inneses and Johns and propped them on a chair one by one, including a very lovely drawing of her head as a girl, by Augustus. She told us it had been drawn for one of her lovers, Turton, who took it to the First War; he was killed and it was picked up on the battlefield. 'Augustus did it the day before Christopher was born,' she said, 'I looked very nice when I was pregnant.' Many of her stories are as improbable as this one.

Followed by a little cortège of bouncing pekinese puppies she now led us into the garden, which was in a state of total Irish neglect, with waddling geese and a long vista of tangled Michaelmas daisies stretching up a slope. Raymond tactfully praised it. Euphemia was delighted.

'Yes isn't it lovely?' she said. 'I never stop admiring it. It's *always* perfect. I never have to say "You should have seen it last week," like Ruth Draper. And would you believe it there used to be beds and flowers and rose-trees, and a gardener – *awful.*'

An evening talk with Raymond about the age at which buggery declares itself. He thought it was decided long before school, and also believed that no buggers can throw balls or whistle. I'm not sure that I agree with him on any of these points.

October 7th

Looking back to the first things I can remember, this still and lovely morning, they seem an *eternity* away (and that is probably no further than babyhood appears to a child of six). However much more of my life is left, I want to extract the most out of it, and feel a useless regret for all those moments spent mechanically, unconsciously – sitting in buses for instance, brushing up crumbs, merely *waiting* – more regret than I do for those instants extended by the elastic of anxiety or physical pain. The fact is I don't know how to reconcile my long-standing hedonism with the value I set on being as conscious as possible, which is not to exclude nebulous, dreamy or atmospheric states of being, but only 'killing time'.

October 11th

To London for several days. In the train we met Gerald with Miranda, whom he was taking up to buy some clothes, so we arrived having already had quite a dose of social life, and went almost at once to the Ivy to meet Clive, the Colonel and the A. P. Herberts. The poor old Colonel has become almost too absurd. He still wuffs like a dog or seal, but all too patently hasn't heard what he is supposed to be wuffing at, and his innocent boasting about the titled people he knows is really rather distressing. I was amused by A.P.H. and very much liked Gwen his wife, who has a charming and original appearance and much character.

Later to a cocktail party given by Macgibbon and Kee[1] – a terrific crush filling the Kees' two large sitting-rooms. I talked for a time to Peter, current wife of Bertie Russell, a Lamia-like woman with an expression of widely distributed hostility. Buttering up was what she appeared to need and I did the best I could but she only thawed at all when talking of her son of twelve who was 'brilliantly clever', 'told her everything' and 'never wanted to go anywhere without her'.

October 13th

Ralph and I went to Cameo Corner this morning to buy me a ring. I had a delightful time there, having out all the cases and selecting those I liked best, making my choice at leisure. And what made this easier was that Ralph angelically insisted on my having not one but *three* rings! All three seemed beautiful in the shop, and yet more beautiful when I got them home, with new previously hidden beauties. I resolve to try and keep my hands worthy of them and wear them constantly.

Before catching our train we went to see Robert and Janetta at Sussex Place. They were just back from a strange wedding-party: Sonia Brownell had that afternoon married George Orwell in hospital where he lies seriously ill with TB. He is said to have a fifty-fifty chance of recovery, and as he is much in love with her everyone hopes the marriage will give him a new interest in life. After the ceremony Robert and Janetta, Sonia and David Astor had a bridal lunch at the Savoy, without the bridegroom of course. The curious halo of emotion which invests weddings still lingered in the room, and the Kees had obviously been much moved by the event.

October 15th: Ham Spray

Saxon is here. His perversity is something to marvel at; it half maddens, half delights me. Ralph took trouble to find a brace of young grouse in London, and these I roasted for our lunch. Nothing could possibly have been more delicious, they melted in the mouth, and neither Ralph nor I could keep from exclaiming how good they were. Not so Saxon; he maintained a rigid silence, and later on in the day mentioned that he had had grouse at the Ivy last week, as if to show it was no treat to him. Yet one can't really feel he means to be ungracious; he likes in many ways to give people pleasure: I think perhaps he feels trapped into inarticulacy, just as children sometimes are, by the mere consciousness that a word of appreciation is expected of him.

---

[1] Publishing firm formed by Robert in partnership with James Macgibbon.

October 16th

Saxon stays in bed for breakfast, so we have it alone together without being interrupted by having to be polite. There is no time nicer in the whole day. Having been half asleep during baths and the cooking of eggs and coffee, the mind now begins to stretch itself and expand into strange shapes like Japanese flowers and slip easily into conversations, usually without a very strong thread which would be alien to the drifting morning mood. Today I think we began with the aesthetic theories held by artists themselves – or sometimes the surprising lack of them. Then on to the attractiveness of characters with something androgynous about them; and finally to the sort of reading we both went in for in our youth. We both remember being rather conscientious hard-working readers, often of books too difficult or boring to us. Now with the wireless and cinema, the young can't be bothered with that. Paradoxically, they read bad books for a good reason – pleasure, while we used to read good books for a bad reason – wanting to show off what we'd read, add them to our personality as it were.

October 18th

Many people regard the Orwell marriage cynically and remind one that Sonia always declared her intention of marrying a Great Man. I see it principally as a neurotic one, for a marriage to a bed-ridden and perhaps dying man is as near no marriage at all as it's possible to get.

October 21st: Long Crichel

We set off today on our first visit to the four tenants of Long Crichel House – Raymond, Desmond Shawe-Taylor, Eddy Sackville-West and Eardley Knollys. Dinner was delicious, and so was the wine. Afterwards we listened to some of Desmond's records. Alas we were put in separate bedrooms, and my mind, teased and stimulated by the new environment and ringing with music, refused to relax into sleep.

[I look back on my first visit to this most hospitable of country-houses with gratitude and affection, nor can I think of any other where I have spent so many happy times both with Ralph and during my later, lonelier life, right up to the present day. And I feel towards that handsome welcoming house, its garden and the surrounding country a warmth such as I hope some of our guests may have felt towards Ham Spray – because though it fell far short of Long Crichel in creature comforts it too had personality and charm. A house can't of course be thought of apart from those who live in it, and over the years the cast of Long Crichel has been altered perforce by two much-lamented deaths and one departure, so that at present the only member of the original quartet still to be found there is Desmond, yet as a household it has still astonishingly and persistently retained its delightful atmosphere. It would be fascinating to analyse (as surely some day someone will) exactly what contribution each of the original four made to the total very special flavour.

Raymond's was certainly not the least dominant. I often remember him in terms of the warmth and the surprising depth of his speaking voice, the softness and beautiful colour of his beloved 'woollies', or a suit of dark-brown homespun tweed, the amusement in his twinkling brown eyes, the despairing sighs that rang through the house when he was at his typewriter. The little daughter of a friend once remarked to her mother: 'Mr Mortimer is a very *cuddly* man.' She was quite right, but woe betide the would-be cuddler who let drop an incorrect date or a fault in pronunciation or grammar! A debatable point would send him in hot haste into the next room, where he would be found down on his knees, consulting one of the stout volumes of the *Oxford English Dictionary*. Long conversations on these themes led to Crichel being nicknamed 'the Prose Factory'.

If Raymond was the cello in the quartet, Eddy was the first violin – at times poetical and mellifluous, at others wailing or strident, always exact and confident. Perhaps it was the effort it had cost him to overcome the many serious illnesses of a delicate youth that had given him in the prime of life the strength of steel wire, the agility of a gibbon. One of my mental images of Eddy sees him elegantly dancing round the drawing-room to pull the curtains or put a log on the fire (he was ever-attentive to his guests' comfort), or – my favourite of all – jack-knifed into a scream of delighted laughter at someone else's witticism. No one could be funnier than Eddy himself and laugh more infectiously. No one could on occasion look more *pained*.

Eardley was the most practically efficient of the four, the one to be relied upon to make decisions about planting trees, or to seize his gun and shoot a pheasant straying on the lawn; while Desmond has always contributed boundless high spirits, optimism, volatility, and interest in everything that comes his way. In one of my photo albums I have a picture of these two which always makes me laugh, by capturing their contrasted characters so perfectly. They are arguing a point in croquet – have indeed been at it for ages – but whereas it's plain that Eardley will hold to his position until kingdom come and nothing will budge him, Desmond is obviously on the verge of desperation.

But to return to our first visit, it struck me at once that what made the company of the four members of the Long Crichel quartet so highly enjoyable was that each played his individual and very different part in delighted awareness of the other three – as of course every good quartet should. And another element in their guests' pleasure was provided, like a sort of counterbase, by an overlapping series of large, soft, affectionate labrador dogs who rushed to give visitors a gratifyingly enthusiastic welcome, filled the hearthrug with their outstretched, golden bodies, or fixed one with doe-like eyes pleading for a walk.

More visits to Long Crichel will crop up again in what follows. I realize that I was rather intimidated by the brilliance of my hosts on this first occasion, but also that the more I got to know it and them, the more I loved and felt at ease with them.]

October 22nd

By the admirable house convention we were left to ourselves during the morning, while the others were at work in their own rooms. I persuaded Ralph to come for a brisk walk along the lanes to Crichel House, now a girls' school. Here we walked beside a wide stream running under stone bridges and bordered by a hedge of tall pampas grass, handsomely outlined against dark green shrubs.

The standard of comfort here puts ours to shame. There is warmth, elegance, the attentions of a stout butler and his wife, not to mention two other maids.

Conversation is lively, easy and flowing, and about almost everything except politics.

I wish I didn't feel absurdly apologetic for my female sex. Looking at the visitors' book I see that almost no women visitors came in earlier days except mothers and sisters. When a marriage is discussed it is generally a marriage of convenience, for some good practical reason like companionship, care of each other's orphaned children, rather than love. I am hopelessly outclassed by Raymond's high standard of feminine 'chic', Eddy's '*nice* women', and the elegance of the bosomy Edwardian beauties in an album lying about. Nor do I think they would agree with Ralph and me in preferring (as I have lately written) a touch of androgyny in both sexes. But really! I am ashamed of such idiotic thoughts! I think they must have arisen as a result of our segregation from each other in single beds in separate rooms. The one allotted to me will eventually be Raymond's – it is grandly furnished with wallpaper of wide khaki-coloured stripes and gorgeous *boule* furniture. I slept beneath an immense old master in a massive gold frame. Our hosts have been unfailingly charming to us and we have enormously enjoyed our stay.

November 1st: Ham Spray

A beautiful crisp day, the edge of its brightness just taken off by a faint autumnal haze, but as fresh as a Cox's orange pippin. The Kees have been replaced by Gerald, who has lately surprised himself by a recrudescence of thoughts about sex. He looks and says he feels years younger all at once, and has gone back in various ways to the moods and thoughts of long ago. Even his voice now ranges between low, poetical and romantic tones and a husky, ironical shriek. A good deal of this mood is due to the vicarious pleasure of seeing his daughter Miranda grow up and become a young woman; but we talked little about her, and rather more about Dr Johnson. Departing, he left behind the last bit of his diary (1927–32), covering several abortive love affairs and the death of Carrington and Lytton, none of which we had seen before. It was a just account, painful and touching. We both read it and it provided food for a long conversation between Ralph and me.

Now Ralph is up in the library writing. I had been happy writing letters when there suddenly came into my head some childhood memories that might make material for a paper at the Memoir Club should such be required of me. I amused myself jotting them down and found – as always – a flotilla of other little memories swimming behind them.

I sit writing with my back to the log fire which crackles softly and flicks tongues of light into the outer fringes of my field of vision. The frost has made Minnie very skittish, but she has tired herself out and lies glossy and extenuated on the sofa, while Ralph is taking notes for a review about Nelson. Happiness.

November 14th

A day in London, partly to do a little Christmas shopping. Hamleys was a seething palace of toys; egotistic children were dragging their elders towards expensive things they coveted, while others just lay back in their push-chairs and bawled. Grandparents lovingly stroked the silky fur of monster Teddy bears. I felt stifled, and hurried away to a very different atmosphere – an exhibition of paintings by Francis Bacon, a friend of Richard and Denis's whom I met briefly last summer. His pictures were impressive, completely original and absolutely terrifying. They reminded me of the thoughts and images aroused by the books Ralph and I read all the time now about the Criminally Mad. They represented nebulous grey curtains fastened here and there by a carefully painted safety-pin through which figures could be dimly glimpsed – faces whose wide-open mouths expressed the ultimate degree of horror and fear. I was very much fascinated by these – less so by some of pink penises tipped by little grinning mouths full of crooked teeth. All seemed to personify the Id, and I took the safety-pins and veils to stand for the inadequate forces of suppression. The artist is said to live alone with his nanny. I couldn't help wondering what she thought of them.

From there to the Hills, where I found Anne and the two little girls having pandemoniac nursery tea. Further excited by the appearance of a stranger perhaps, they stood on their heads, jumped off chairs and brought me their favourite possessions to admire, all in the friendliest way and greatly to my enjoyment. (Adults often do the same less directly and less successfully.) They all walked with me to Paddington through the foggy darkness, to 'have a nice breath of fresh air,' as Anne said. She described a farewell party she and Heywood had given for Eddie. He and Bob started a quarrel with Bryan Howard, which was still going on when she came down from bed hours later for a glass of water. It went something like this:

Bryan to Bob: The trouble with *you* is you're a most fearful old bore.
Eddie to Bryan: Well *your* old friends can't bear to see you any more. Julia says you make her *shudder.*
Bryan to the brothers: Look at *your* friends – Kyrle [Leng] for instance is so middle-class he might as well be a Swiss!
Bob to Bryan: I'm a success, you're a failure. I used not to be able to write, but now I can. *You* could write once, but now you've forgotten how.

And so on.

[The brothers Eddie and Bob Gathorne-Hardy were so alike in some ways that they might have been twins – in others very different. Both had been at Eton and Oxford where they early developed intellectual interests in such subjects as bibliography, botany and archaeology; thereafter they joined the same antiquarian booksellers and became well-known figures in literary London in the Thirties, swiftly going their rounds together, each with a monocle in his eye. Each had an excellent memory and was a natural highbrow. To see them, as one sometimes might, standing side by side at a party, glass in hand, going off into bubbling fountains of talk and rockets of laughter, was a very comical sight.

As for their differences: Eddie, the elder, was something of a rake and idler. He made short work of a legacy he received at Oxford, spending it on silk shirts, good food and wine and first editions of Jeremy Taylor. He was amoral and selfish but disarmingly affectionate and gloriously funny. The words 'My dear' in a confiding tone frequently interrupted his speech ('Do you know, my dear, what the taxi-driver said to me, my dear? He *said*, my dear . . .'). One had only to look at the way he held his hands to see how impractical he was, but he knew how things should be done and could instruct others. Compared to Eddie, Bob was domestic, unselfish, practical and an energetic gardener; unlike him he could sometimes be boring. Anne Hill was their only sister.]

November 16th

Last night the subterranean stream of melancholy which had been flowing beneath my happy secure life broke through its banks and I sat before the fire giving way to it. Lord knows I have little cause – only one in fact, the frustration caused by the collapse of the flower book. I can no longer fork through the subject in the way I loved to, and discuss it with Ralph. The result is my confidence is badly shaken. If this book is to stop I *must* find something else to do. But what? The question haunts me. Feeling relieved by having brought this discontent to the light of day, I put it as it were into a mental rack labelled: Questions to be settled in the near future, and passed the rest of the evening very pleasantly.

November 18th

Interesting conversation about Francis Bacon and his paintings. Denis supplied some biographical details: he loves gambling, luxury, and the company of rich tycoons, and has a project for decorating a luxurious drinking-club in the City for big businessmen to meet in. Sebastian and Richard got talking about mutual Norfolk friends, and seemed to like each other very well. An after-dinner conversation about human credulity, a subject about which Ralph and I think exactly alike. Sebastian charged us with not wanting to believe, and said that he preferred to sit on the fence and keep as many doors as possible wide open. 'Very well,' I said, 'but you can only achieve "knowledge" by shutting some doors and leaving only one open.'

December 2nd

In this last month we have been made aware of the many stresses and strains experienced by friends, money troubles and ill-health also, of older friends like Desmond and Molly slipping gradually into increasing feebleness. Sometimes it's as if everyone was struggling out of a bog or plodding along in some ghastly spiritual retreat from Moscow. Human beings value their power to bestow life – but is it also such a boon? So far, goodness knows I have found my own a thousand times worthwhile. Who knows, though, what is in store? And there are the lonely deserted wives, or those who never found a mate and fear it's now too late – they seem to be playing some horrible children's game like Twos and Threes, each longing to be one of a pair and dreading to be the odd one out. Just as waiting for death – which is bound to get us all in the end – is like that other awful game, where the gym mistress swings a rope with a hard leather pad on the end, round and round, higher and higher, while the children jump till they can jump no more, and the rope twists itself round their legs and catches them.

December 7th

The Wests arrived at tea-time in a large grand car, each in their different way like a bird in fine plumage – glossy and lively. Anthony went off with a typewriter to finish his novel in the music-room, but was always ready to interrupt himself by a sudden flare of animation, becoming all flashing white teeth, snapping black eyes and rumbles of suppressed amusement.

Later we were joined by Boris and Maroussa. With her tinted spectacles and swathed turban, her cigarettes in a long holder, and a foreign accent too good to be true, Maroussa is so much a thriller-writer's picture of a female spy that I wasn't surprised to hear of all their difficulties in getting through the Customs. Boris is monumental, magnificent.

We made it a gala night with smoked salmon, a Virginia ham, pineapple, two bottles of wine and Calvados to follow. I don't know why the subject of religious belief cropped up at dinner, but Maroussa reacted against our tone by bringing out a beautiful little ikon which she carries everywhere in her bag. It was much more surprising to find Anthony on the same side, confirming a suspicion I had got from his book, though I only half understood it.

December 16th

Burgo back this morning, enormous and apparently grown-up and sensible. While we made Christmas cards we had a conversation about life. Burgo: 'Time is whizzing by so fast. And the world is so terrible. But now I realize how terrible it is, I can face it and enjoy myself as a result.'

F: 'What is so particularly terrible?'

Burgo: 'Oh – that it's an uphill struggle all the time. And all the awful things that are going on, like the atom bomb. But I feel that everything will end when I do, because someone will manage to blow us all up. Then human beings are getting more and more like machines; soon their hands will just be pitiful stumps fit for pressing buttons or pulling levers, and they'll even have machines for minds, that can only react to what happens in one way.'

Yet he seems quite cheerful, if rather dreamy, and when I said he seemed to have had quite a lot of fun at school he agreed.

1950

January 24th

As 1949 dragged to its end I got the senseless feeling that it was a bad old year, which had made a faulty start and gone on developing all awry, and that 1950 might well be quite a different affair – its very name had a better ring to it. But now that three weeks of it have flashed past I am not sure that I was right. I don't remember a time when other people's troubles came more closely hailing and snowing around our shoulders, nor when our ears were so deafened by the cracking up of the personal relations of our friends. All these earthquakes have made Ralph and me infinitely thankful for the stability of our own, and rejoice in the harmony of our days and nights together. Burgo too, rapidly enlarging his personality as well as his physical frame, *seems* – thank goodness – to have got over his unhappiness of last year, and went back perfectly serenely to school whence he has written us one sweet and friendly letter. Now, at fourteen and a half, his problem will be to complete his detachment from us, and put down stronger roots outside the seedbed.

March 12th

We were promised sleet and cold this morning, but going out on to the verandah with Minnie I found it cool and sweet, with innumerable birds keeping up a high-pitched whistling chorus like the boys in Britten's Spring Symphony. It has rained in the night and enormous drops were quietly falling from the honeysuckle. Last night we went to have drinks with the Campbells, Ben Nicolson[1] and Freddie Ayer.[2] I was interested in Ayer and wanted to hear him talk, but out of some sort of diffidence I withdrew to a secluded seat on the sofa next to Ben, so that while enjoying talk with him about Lawrence Gowing and Antwerp, I saw and heard a lively spate of words of the sort I most love flashing from Ayer's animated face. Mary scored a general laugh by saying, when asked why she believed in capital punishment: 'Because it's the only way to keep the population down.'

May 16th

Janetta and Robert have been here for a warm spring weekend. We saw the Campbells, had the Pritchetts to dinner and picnicked by the Barge Inn at Honey Street, a very romantic disused canal, where drowned barges lie entangled in a welter of reeds – a sight which in its way symbolized the impression made by certain symptoms shown by the Kees that have revived a buried disquiet. Why

---

[1] Art historian. Son of Harold and Vita.
[2] Sir Alfred Ayer, philosopher.

aren't they happier together, I wonder? Complete satisfaction may be too much to expect at their age, but to hear them talk it seems that a lot is wrong with their life, and Robert has returned to his sad old habit of denigrating Janetta for incompetence, or what she herself calls her 'legarthy'. Her confidence is shaken and she defends herself half-heartedly, as if her chief aim was to avoid annoying Robert. This ghost train running along old railway lines is very disturbing. If Robert goes on writing down her character she will go off with someone who thinks her wonderful and tells her so, and there are plenty who will.

June 5th

Back from half-term weekend in Dorset, finding Burgo well and happy. We saw Abbotsbury in an eerie sea-mist through which the hissing, flapping swans moved like ballerinas; charming little grey cygnets were floating in a kind of nursery pond – and we even saw one break its way out of the egg-shell and lie resting, like a weak, damp snake. To Fleet in honour of *Moonfleet*, which Burgo had been reading. We were shown round the church by a cheerful little negro boy in a scarlet jersey, who must have dated from the American Army's local presence in 1944. We had tea in the Manor House of the book, now a hotel, a plain white building unpretentiously pitched beside the waters of the Fleet, and then walked along the shore through a rough field and a small wood full of 'roast beef' irises. The sun made a poetical moonlike appearance through the clouds, and the Chesil bank was a faint ghost across the water. All Sunday we roasted on Charmouth beach – it was thick with people. Lovers lay entwined behind the shingle bank; children trotted briskly about muttering obsessionally to themselves; balls were thrown, dogs ran and barked, and here and there the mountainous hip of a recumbent housewife reared itself into the air.

June 6th

What an odd lot the members of the Memoir Club looked, gathered together outside Olivelli's restaurant. The day had been a fizzer – 88 in the shade, but in the basement restaurant whose walls are papered with photographs of film stars the air was cooler, and the Italian proprietress, though she gave us a fierce, measuring look, soon brought asparagus and chilled Orvieto. Bunny beamed out upon the rest of the company from within a warm blanket of absorption in his own affairs – his new venture as partner in Rupert Hart-Davis's publishing firm, his cows, Hilton and the boys – the four little girls were mentioned chiefly as nuisances. Across the table Oliver Strachey, dressed in a pale green Palm Beach suit, glared at me rather sourly. 'One of the things about growing older,' he volunteered, 'is that one discovers the true character of one's friends.' Oh dear, yes, I thought guiltily, we didn't do enough for him in his time of illness and trouble.

After dinner we walked in a body through the hot dark night to Duncan's rooms, passing James standing on his doorstep in Gordon Square, a splendid figure in a white silk suit. It was as if all London had shrunk to Bloomsbury and was peopled only by these human portents. The papers read were by Angelica (a beautifully written account of her stay in France as a girl of sixteen), and Dermod, about sex at school. His paper led to a discussion as to whether schoolboys should be beaten.

'Oh YES – of course one must beat boys,' said Desmond, and Oliver joined him. It seemed priggish to attack this fashionable swing of the pendulum, but honesty obliged me to. Only Vanessa took my side. Sitting on an upright chair with her hat on, she pondered for a moment and then said conclusively in her deep voice: 'I see *no* point in punishment myself.'

June 12th

I live for pleasure these days, and find no difficulty in filling my days and nights with it – reading, writing, eating, sleeping, gardening (mildly), looking for flowers and butterflies, listening to the wireless, talking, thinking, playing my violin, being with Ralph – there is no end to the delights. And what do I do for suffering humanity in return? Or for anyone else except Ralph, for that matter? I do believe in some form of Social Contract so no wonder my puritan conscience stirs uneasily in the depths. This state of things cannot last for ever and is too good to miss a moment of, so if my conscience can be stifled I mean to stifle it. All the same I do quite seriously envy people who feel they do some good in the world. Ralph never stops believing that if one is not doing *harm* one can congratulate oneself, and such is the conclusion of many of our ethical conversations. Yet, in my opinion, one of the signs of present-day decadence is that 'do-gooder' has become a term of abuse.

June 21st

Crowds of people at the weekend. To stay: Noel Sandwith, Janie and Olivier Popham[1] (a new visitor whom we like very much). To tea: the Kees, Nicko on leave from Greece, with a friend of his called Donald Maclean. The Pritchetts afterwards for a drink. A strange thing about Maclean – walking on the lawn with Janetta afterwards, I heard from her that he had been a member of the Embassy at Cairo, but had just been sent home because he tried to murder his wife. 'No, *really*?' I said. 'Yes, really – and another friend got his leg broken going to her rescue. It happened because he got fearfully drunk with Philip Toynbee.' He has not been sacked from the Foreign Office, but sent home for psychiatric treatment. He's a tall, very good-looking man, friendly and smiling – charming in fact.

   Noel Sandwith's enthusiasm for plant-hunting made his eyes sparkle so behind his spectacles that I felt my own sparkling too. We all drove with him to a bleak stretch of downland near Bordon Camp to look for *Astragalus danicus* ('a glorious thing with reddish flowers'). After tramping through the long grass like a herd of buffaloes, with many interjections from Noel of '*that* looks a bit funny', we at last found the rarity – an insignificant squalid-looking plant with blue flowers.

July 10th

War has broken out in Korea and for several days loomed larger. Yesterday the first British casualties were announced. It is inevitable (but depressing) to what a degree it has revived feelings from 1939, and nightmare images also, such as being in a small boat slowly but inexorably moving towards Niagara Falls. Yet a sort of excitement seemed to possess our weekend visitors, Judy and Dick [Rendel][2] and Quentin, at the thought of the bravery of soldiers in wartime. Talk is quite openly anti-foreign: all Germans are monsters impossible to shake by the hand, the Italians

[1] Now Mrs Quentin Bell.
[2] My sister and her husband (ex-Colonel in the regular army).

beneath contempt, and the French and Russians as bad as the Germans. Nor is this by any means meant as a joke. Benjamin Britten is a 'bloody man' (and *therefore* a bad composer) because he went to America instead of fighting the Germans.

[A week later we started on a holiday at Deva on the north coast of Spain, with Vicky and her mother Esme as companions.]

September 19th: Ham Spray

Holidays over, we return to find ourselves once more deep in the problems of our friends, far the most agonizing being a new and it seems possibly final breach between Robert and Janetta.

[During our absence in Spain the situation between the Kees had grown intolerable, and finally Janetta took wing to France. To us she wrote saying that she hoped never to return to married life, while a letter from Robert asked us to come to dinner and 'talk, talk, talk'. Such a break between two much-loved friends is as shattering as the sound of splintering glass in a road accident; Ralph and I both felt the tragedy bitterly, and despite our aversion to 'taking sides' in matrimonial troubles, it was natural to try and give support to the person in most pain. While we were away I believe this had been Janetta, but she was now out of reach, abroad with no address, whereas Robert was urgently needing someone sympathetic to talk to, though he admitted that he had even felt a certain relief when she left – until, that is, he got the fatal letter saying she was never coming back. Then he followed her to France and talked to her for hours, but she was still 'adamant'. Turn and turn the facts as we might, Ralph and I couldn't extract a favourable prognosis from them. According to the fiendish law that governs human emotions and makes what is unattainable much more desirable, Robert now desperately wanted Janetta back. Hearing all this, not once but many times on the telephone was, so I wrote, 'unspeakably harrowing. I said what I could, which was little, begged him to come round and see us (but I don't think he will), and went off to chop onions in the kitchen trembling so that I nearly chopped my fingers off in horror at the human capacity for inflicting and enduring pain.' Meanwhile life had to go on.]

September 20th

To London. Met Richard at the Society of Authors, to discuss our position with their cool, kind grey-eyed lady barrister. Richard still hopes to get another publisher, or rather is confident we can. I am not nearly so sanguine, but it seems I may get some financial compensation for my five years' unpaid work. Ralph and I went to Eliot's *Cocktail Party* in the evening – a bad play, badly acted, but thought-provoking. Next day to the National Gallery to see a magnificent late Rembrandt on loan there, and lunch with Clive and Raymond. In the evening the Memoir Club, one of the nicest meetings I remember. After eating the tenderest of ducklings cooked with cherries – a great improvement on our usual fare – we repaired to Duncan's rooms, and listened to two excellent Memoirs: Clive's on losing his virginity and Bunny's on getting to know Indians at school. Just as in near darkness Clive was describing the crucial moment on the sofa with Mrs Raven Hill, and his anxieties and doubts whether he could properly carry out what was expected of him, a feeble knock was heard on Duncan's door, and Marjorie's silver head poked in, saying in a faint, hoarse whisper: 'Duncan are you in bed?' 'No,' replied Duncan, in an equally subdued tone.

'Well, IS there any competent male present?' A roar of laughter greeted this; it came so aptly to Clive's reading.

'The fact is I'm very frightened.' Her expressive face left us in no doubt of the fact. Quentin rose gallantly to his feet, and left the room, to come back in a few moments, saying: 'She was unable to twist the cock.' There is a gas strike at present on in London, by means of which the flow is reduced so low that panicky people think it has gone out altogether. Marjorie must be one of the most alarmist of these, and she had been trying to turn it off at the main.

September 28th

A day of tidying and putting away, and of tactile pleasures: sorting through drawers and handkerchiefs, gloves and beads, for instance, with their different textures – soft, velvety, silken, hard or bright. Then cooking and bottling our home-grown tomatoes. Skinning them I felt like a surgeon, with sleeves rolled up dipping the hot fruit into cold water, seeing the thin skin come off like red rubber gloves. A bird was singing piercingly in the garden and a cloud of gnats danced outside the kitchen window. And all day the telephone went on ringing like a motif in an opera.

In the afternoon came a fat letter from Janetta. She doesn't seem to have resented anything I said in mine, and almost all of hers was about Robert. There is no mention of other people in her life. She talks of perhaps going to Rome, looking at pictures and 'being un-domestic'.

October 5th

The cheerful voice of Mary Campbell came over the telephone at breakfast time. They are just back from France and had been told by the Pritchetts about the Kee tragedy, which she said had upset her terribly and given her nightmares all night. Then she read me part of a letter from Philip Toynbee announcing that he was 'as good as married and tomorrow would be as bad as married'.

Drove to Oxford to fetch Robert, who had been doing some work there. The beauty of the pale green rolling Downs on the way was quite blotted out on our return journey by my intense absorption in conversation with him. We might have been driving through a long tunnel for all I saw. With his violent life-instinct it is impossible for him to sit back and await developments patiently. In this he is very unlike Janetta who, when trouble strikes, folds her head under her wing and sinks to the bottom like a stone. But Robert is already swimming vigorously, and much that he said this afternoon was greatly to the credit of his candour and sense of reality.

October 7th

We have exchanged Robert for Raymond and Janie, the shadowy side of whose genial character is suppressed bitterness, but she is excellent company. I don't think Raymond, amusing and full of ideas as he is, can be called a very good talker (some do think him one as a matter of fact) because his conversation too easily gets on to a well-worn track or even a slightly modish tone supported by such words as 'dazzling', 'rewarding', 'riveting'. The really good talker's response to life is too original and inventive to rely on catch-phrases. V.S.P., Julia and Gerald all have the good talker's gift, and it magnetizes attention. But what a strange thing it is, this ectoplasm spouting endlessly out of mouths, and usually carried off into oblivion.

October 12th

We lunched with Robert in a Swiss restaurant. He seems to be doing very well at his process of reconstruction, and the Life Force is hard at work; but the children are a problem, and Robert is worried about Georgie, who is still in the charge of Mrs Brenan, their daily. Noticing that she was walking oddly he took her to Selfridges to buy new shoes and found that the ones she was wearing were indeed much too small. Robert continued: 'Georgie suddenly made a most fearful mess on the floor. I asked where the lavatory was and when we got there of course it was a Ladies and they wouldn't let me in, "but we'll have the little chap". I said "She *is* a lady," and had to let her go in alone.' This story illustrates in concrete form something that is worrying many of the Kees' friends. It's clear from her letters that Janetta is missing her children badly, but she has made no mention of their missing her. Ralph and I have been discussing the possibility of going to Paris to see her, but only if she seemed to want us to.

October 19th

A little pepper was thrown over the morning by a letter from Allen Lane saying he had been approached by another publisher about the flower book. I felt flustered by this almost certain red herring, and also by the knowledge that I can't really ask Ralph's advice because he has all along been defeatist, and said my contract is worthless and that I shan't get a penny of compensation. I taxed him with this, and he admitted in the most surprising but honest way that he thought he felt jealous of the book, and especially of my cooperation with another man, namely Richard! I asked him if he would have been jealous if Richard had been a woman, and he said he thought so.

October 22nd

A letter from my heroine, the Society of Authors' barrister, telling me that Lane had agreed to pay me £1,500, and we are free to take the book elsewhere! I try to stretch the jaws of imagination to swallow this enormous *bonne bouche*, but find it very difficult. I have begun to consider whether a spring trip to North Africa or Damascus or Italy would be nicest. Ralph is very pleased too.

November 30th

A flying visit from Boris and Maroussa. She is living in a state of constant terror, surprising in view of the courage with which she stood the bombing in the war and the escape from France. Now it is burglars she chiefly dreads: as ill-luck would have it the pub next door to them was broken into and she lay in bed paralysed with fear, hearing them take away cases of drink and terrified lest she should betray her presence to them. She daren't go to the cinema, her greatest pleasure, for fear of being attacked, and when Boris goes out she gets quietly drunk to calm herself.

Boris' doctor brother Glyep has had the most ghastly experience. His wife was bitten by a rabid dog, in Egypt I think it was, but some distance from the nearest Pasteur Institute. She was whisked off and injected, and when the danger period came to an end they went to a ball to celebrate. When they returned that night Glyep looked at the place where she had been bitten and saw to his horror that it had swollen up, showing that she had taken the disease. It meant a certain terrible death, rather than which he took her to hospital and killed her.

December 1st

Soon after the Anreps had left we set off for a visit to Crichel. The air was sharp with frost, and a pale greenish-blue sky lay reflected between black leafless twigs in the still ponds we passed on our way. Not long after our arrival more visitors came to tea – Lady Juliet Duff, Somerset Maugham, and a rather colourless female described as 'a *nice* woman' by Eddy. I sat next to Somerset Maugham at tea and was charmed by him. He belongs in the reptile house, a chameleon by choice, with his pale deeply furrowed face, sunken glittering eyes and the mouth that opens deliberately and sometimes sticks there – as he has a distinct stammer.

A delicious dinner, much jolly talk and Canasta. After Eddy had gone off to bed very tired, Raymond pushed his chair suddenly from the card-table, knocking over and breaking a lamp made of glass. He appeared to be quite unworried, and Eardley said 'Good. That was the only unpleasant object in the room.' However, at breakfast next morning Eddy looked delicately distressed. 'Yes I know,' he said, 'I've got over it now, but I was *terribly* upset. I nearly burst into tears when I heard about it. It was almost my favourite possession.'

It's a great pleasure being at Crichel. Of all our three hosts (Desmond is away) Eddy is the most attentive. His exquisite sensitivity to his own feelings in no way prevents him being aware of those of other people, and I was several times struck by the diverse range of those he talked about with interest and affection. So long as they don't rise above the Plimsoll line of his distaste – by having dirty fingernails for instance – he enjoys his friends to the full. He delights one by the quality of his personality, much as Boris does, but oh so differently; his charm comes out in the rather medieval beauty of his face, his sudden laugh and quick pungent remarks. Eardley has just taken to painting with enormous enthusiasm. He took us to see his pictures in a studio over the garage.

December 8th: Ham Spray

While Ralph was working away steadily in his library I squelched my way through the sodden leaves in the Snowdrop wood, pulling my rubber boots out with difficulty one by one and thinking of what? Burgo and Janetta, and as usual Death – and the contradictory sensations of security and precariousness one gets from its being *there*, round the corner.

The more philosophy I read the more I am amazed by its inexhaustibility. Though the cleverest minds of every age have been considering its problems for centuries there has never been a question of settling any of them once and for all, yet by their very nature they force one to think that they have the truth concealed in them, possible to find. Going on looking into them seems at times to be like trying to apply scientific investigation to the infinite series of reflections in the opposite mirrors of a restaurant.

[Christmas was fast approaching with all its connected problems. We had invited Robert to bring Georgie to Ham Spray, and at first he said he definitely would; later he qualified this by saying that if Janetta wanted to come and see Georgie then, he would absent himself. The reasonable thing would have been for Georgie to stay with us long enough for her to be with both parents in turn. But it was hardly a question of reason by now and events conspired to make this impossible.

On December 13th Robert telephoned to say that Janetta had been seen in London, and from the Campbells came the first news that Derek Jackson was pressing her to marry him. On the same day Burgo came back from school ill; feverish, and depressed because he had had a return of his 'worries' last term. Two days later Janetta rang me up (the sound of her voice, low but calm, was what had been lacking all through these long tortured weeks). She told us she would like to come and see us in January, but there was no grain of comfort for Robert in what she said. On the 21st Sonia Orwell telephoned to say that Janetta had gone back to Paris and Robert to the Campbells at Stokke.

Writing now, some time later, my impression is that the nightmare colouring of the beginning of the holidays (because of Robert's tragedy, Burgo's illness and the piercing cold) persisted through Christmas. To take the place of Robert and Georgie we invited Lawrence and Julia, and they seemed pleased to come.]

1951

January 2nd to 4th

We left Wiltshire under cover of thin snow. It grew thicker and thicker as we travelled east, and by the time we were on our way to the Ivy for lunch with Clive and Isobel Strachey, enormous flakes as big, round and flat as halfpence were lying quite unmelted on the coats, hats and umbrellas of Londoners, as they trudged through the deep slush like absurd Father Christmases.

I had arranged to meet Janetta that afternoon at our hotel, the Great Western, and as I sat waiting for her my heart beat quite fast with agitation. She has been so long the unseen and unheard focus of our thoughts, conversations and conflicting feelings, that it was I suppose inevitable that a certain unresolved sediment remaining from all the pain and anxiety, lay as it were before her door, and she must needs kick it over to come out. She came in looking very charming, and more like the Bohemian of past days than I had expected, unconsciously affected probably by thoughts of Derek Jackson and Claridges. She was wearing nothing but a little short green corduroy jacket over camel's hair trousers, in spite of the bitter weather. We went up to our bedroom and talked and talked until Ralph and Burgo returned. I think she was afraid I would 'take sides' – and not hers. When she had finished her account of the last months she asked 'Do you still hope I will go back to Robert?' It was true that we had hoped; now, seemingly, it was no longer possible. In any case we could only have *wanted* what made her happy. I don't think any harm was done by our talk. She has promised to come to Ham Spray in a few days, and after we had had tea with Ralph and Burgo sitting in the portly green leather hotel chairs, I saw her slip off into the night looking very defenceless against the cold and toughness of life, pale, thin and with a ghastly cough. I was left understanding more, and loving her as much as always.

Charlie's Aunt on our first night, *Traviata* at Covent Garden the next, and on the 4th we returned to Ham Spray with Janetta and her two children. We saw them arrive in the obscurity of Paddington Station, flanked by a supporting figure – Derek Jackson. He greeted us with effusive embarrassment, and the hardly remembered flavour of his personality came wafting across: the over-excited manner, muffled speech, small bright intelligent eyes. He is not without a good deal of charm. Little Georgie was fussed and inclined to break into wails. Janetta looked even more ill than before, and very anxious.

[I first met Derek Jackson when he came to Ham Spray as the fiancé of Poppet John, daughter of Augustus. He was a lively, spontaneous young man of quick speech and winning ways, whose slanting eyes (half-closed when he smiled) gave him a fawnlike appearance. Some time later Ralph and I ran into him lunching with Bryan Guinness, and I wasn't impressed in his favour by hearing him say excitedly, across the huge round dining-table: 'I hate Mozart – I absolutely LOATHE Mozart.' However I don't think this incident had any part in what now seems a somewhat biased impression of him given in these first diary entries. To be honest I believe that jealousy was partly responsible – a jealousy with regard to Janetta that had been completely absent in Robert's case, but then he ranked (they both did) among our most beloved friends. Almost a stranger, Derek carried Janetta off into a world of very different values from our own, and during her years with him she appeared to Ralph and me to be less 'herself' than at any other time.

What then did I leave out? I have not made it clear that he had a brilliant if specialized brain, nor was this obvious during ordinary meetings. It was true that he set what seemed to us a greatly exaggerated value on the possession of wealth, but it is only fair to say that he was much more generous with his own than any other rich man I have known, both by coming to the rescue of friends in trouble and by giving presents of cases of superb claret to those hardly more than acquaintances. His work as a physicist was what occupied the centre of his life, and his chief extravagances were a spectroscopic laboratory in France, race-horses, good wine and French Impressionist paintings, of which he had a fine collection.

After his divorce from Janetta I naturally saw much less of him, until their daughter and his only child Rose began to grow up. During the later years of his life he evidently had a happy relationship with her, he always visited her when he came to England. I met him at her house a number of times and grew to like him more and more and appreciate his geniality and comic style of talk.]

January 5th to 10th: Ham Spray

Child-life was dominant, but talk went on in its intervals. Georgie is a charming little being, whose physical presence (so like both her parents and therefore tangible proof of the unity that is lost) is moving in a special way.

The impression left by these five days is that with that gentle indomitableness that is so characteristic of her, Janetta is pulling herself out of a morass. Derek seems to be the main figure in her life, but I would guess that 'love' is not what she feels for him at present. She and the children went to London one day to do Nicky's school shopping – she is going to boarding school. Next day Burgo went back to Millfield.

January 12th

Back they all came, Nicky – poor little creature – intoxicated by her school clothes and the vista of life that they evoke. What pleases her most is her school tie – a horrid shiny green striped one – and she insisted on putting it on at once. When I was reading aloud to her tonight I couldn't resist adding a school tie here and there to the characters ('the sailors were all dressed in smart blue uniforms *and school ties*') for the pleasure of seeing Nicky double up, turn pink and say 'Not *really*? No, you're *teasing*!'

Janetta has been wonderfully successful in restoring Georgie's sense of security, and I think is very happy to have her with her.

Tonight the Campbells brought Cyril and his new wife Barbara [Skelton] to dinner. Though Mary mistrusts Cyril she was anxious to make the weekend 'go', and she is a great one for rising to occasions. The evening 'went' pretty well I too think, though I feel faint resentment at the way everyone lays out the red carpet for Cyril just because he seems to expect it. Nevertheless I exerted myself to cook a reasonably good meal and please and flatter him, because I knew Mary, Robin and Janetta all wanted him kept happy. I got the impression he disliked me, and was amazed when Mary said afterwards that he had said he liked me very much and 'not had such an enjoyable evening for weeks'. He has become quite humpty-dumpty shaped, his egg head backed by a wild tangle of hair and merging necklessly into the larger egg of his body. Barbara his wife is pretty but aggressively silent; she absolutely refused to be drawn into the conversation.

February 14th

Just before ten p.m. some days ago the telephone rang, shattering our peace. Ralph went to it and I heard him say 'Oh my God,' and immediately guessed who it was. It was Meyer, Millfield's headmaster, to say that Burgo hadn't been seen since tea-time. For half an hour we sat in the dining-room in a state of unnatural calm, drinking whisky and trying to prepare ourselves for a night of no news. Then the telephone rang again. It was Burgo saying, 'I've rung to tell you I'm all right.'

'Where are you?'

'I shan't tell you unless you promise not to take me back.'

Ralph promised he wouldn't do so without Burgo's agreement, and we set out to fetch him from the Bear Hotel, Devizes. The journey there passed in thoughtless relief, the journey home in gloom. Next day I had a talk with Burgo, who was sweet and grateful. I tried to discover what was wrong, but all he could say was that he was in despair, couldn't stand the other boys, they were so 'animal'. In the days that followed a new plan was hatched – by me, because Ralph had been floored by the whole affair and, though managing with a supreme effort to behave reasonably to Burgo, he is filled with what I can only call wounded pride. No one could call him conventional, yet in some way he identifies with Burgo and would like him to be a credit in the eyes of the world. It is I think a typically male attitude – or am I being unfair? The situation would almost be easier if he and Burgo didn't deeply and intensely love each other. I don't know that I can analyse my own feelings clearly yet. I can't of course see the faintest change in my own love for Burgo nor my desire to do the best for him, and there seemed so little choice that I am not gnawed by anxiety as to whether I *have* done that best. I say 'I' all the time, but Ralph has really thrown in his hand for the present.

I must describe what the 'plan' is: he is to have a room at Isobel and Charlotte's[1] in Oakley Street and go to a London tutor to work all day. He has seen Dr Glover, who approves and said that Burgo had come on and grown up no end since he saw him, and was now virtually $17\frac{1}{2}$, two years older than his real age. But having been used to rely so completely on Ralph's support for most things in this life I have found it unbelievably strange to have to take all the decisions and carry them out unaided – go to Millfield and fetch Burgo's clothes, interview tutors and Glover. And although when Clive and the Hills came to stay I don't believe they noticed anything, the fact remains that Ralph and I have been living together for over a

[1] Isobel's daughter, the same age as Burgo and an old friend.

week like strangers for the first time in our lives. Not quarrelling – that might have been easier to bear.

February 15th

Yesterday had the character of convalescence between Ralph and me, quiet, gentle and kindly. Perhaps it was a relief to write down all I did. This morning there came from Burgo a touching little list of accounts, plainly showing the struggle he had had to keep within his allowance. The pathos of it moved Ralph more than anything heretofore, and he is writing to tell him he needn't scrape so. For *of course* as I full well know he loves Burgo most tenderly. (But alas where there is love there is usually jealousy.)

February 19th

Recuperation, convalescence, thaw. I begin to see Ralph's point of view more and he mine. We have seen various friends and their light on our problem is salutary. 'What would you have done?' I asked the Campbells. It is a good way of disarming criticism because no one can think of anything. Nobody so far has suggested ruthlessly returning Burgo to Millfield. The Stones[1] thought it a promising sign of character in him. Gerald took the line that children were a fearful nuisance and the less one saw of them the better. Gamel, meaning to be tactful but not suc-ceeding, told us how some really horrible boy she knew eventually turned out very well! Julia has been far the most consoling:

['I'm quite sure there's nothing to be worried about,' she wrote. 'As regards Burgo himself I feel strongly that his behaviour, though inconvenient, is very healthy and normal, and it shows he has character and spirit and sensibility in my opinion. Of *course* the schoolboys he sees are barbarous animals; I don't doubt it; and if he is upset by this – well, all honour to him say I. I wouldn't have it otherwise. You know Burgo has developed into the most charming, sweet, intelligent fellow, as I observed with my own eyes and ears, and just because he *is* so intelligent and emotional he is very naturally causing trouble in these difficult years. I hear from Isobel that he is turning Communist and is taking her to a Communist meeting!']

February 24th

We spent three days in London this week and they have certainly cast a new light on Burgo's démarche. We had lunch with him on arrival, at a tea-shop near his tutor's; I looked out and saw him crossing the road through the pelting rain and felt sure his morale was good. He strode along in a purposeful manly way – there was none of that cornered, hunched appearance that sometimes greeted us on collecting him from Millfield. Later we saw him at a cocktail party of Isobel's and next day we took him to supper and a Mozart concert. I was glad to learn that he had thanked Julia effusively for asking him out to tea, and taken the trouble to ring up Saxon for giving him dinner at his club. His emotional steam is, oddly enough, provided by Communism, and he buys the *Daily Worker* every day. This produced digs from Ralph but he took them good-humouredly.

We lunched with Robert one day, still sad I fear and rootless. He came back with

---

[1] Reynolds and Janet.

us for a weekend of reading, writing, music and lots of talk. His spell-binding quality never seems to desert him.

February 28th: Ham Spray

I feel rather like a bat hanging upside down in the dark, and even when devoured by fleas putting out small hook-like claws and clutching surrounding objects – such things as a wonderful little group of yellow dwarf irises spotted with black that has sprung up outside the dining-room window in a miraculous fashion. True I planted them there, but I never expect what I plant to grow, nor does it generally. And there is the frenzied early morning singing of the birds.

March 13th

This afternoon I had another go at Hume's *Treatise*. I think of philosophy as a great forbidding house of large rooms, which I hesitate to enter. I walk round, go up the drive, even ring the bell and retreat, before I actually enter the cold interior, where there is the same chill grandeur. Step by step I'm seduced in, and begin studying the pictures and furniture; only my mind wanders off and I wake up as if from a dream and find I am staring at a shut door. That's the *difficulty* of it – as for the pleasure it is much like that of reading music. How amazing that those black inverted match-sticks on the page can be translated into movements which magic-ally produce the very sounds which ran in Haydn or Beethoven's head. But though the printed words bring one in contact with the thoughts of Hume, it's no good just knowing their meaning; an active process of interpretation is needed, requiring a drastic mental effort.

Easter Weekend

Olivier Popham came last night and Quentin this evening. They seem to like each other – what a pity they shouldn't make a match. The Campbells, Julia, Anthony Blunt and Ben Nicolson to dinner. Olivier is the easiest and most companionable of visitors, but I noticed she didn't join any discussion, such as one about vulgarity and another on aesthetics. Burgo was home for the weekend, rather thin but giggly and cheerful, talking of everything including Communism. We had a walk on the Downs flying his kite, the poetry game and quite a lot of fun.

March 29th

Mary rang up to say she had heard from Derek Jackson that Robert seemed to be objecting to a divorce 'under instructions from Ham Spray'. As no one has even mentioned the subject to us we were quite annoyed.

Later, however, Janetta rang up, in a much more confident and happier voice, sounding as though she would like to see us when we came to France. She then wanted to speak to Ralph. Would he ask Robert to divorce her? For legal reasons she couldn't do so herself.

Ralph: 'Does this mean you want to marry Derek?'

Janetta: 'No. I don't want to marry anyone. I never do.'

In the odd way that convictions have of settling on one suddenly like birds perching, I remember that as the car turned into the drive this morning the sense of the pathos of human beings overwhelmed me with a surge of emotion. For the most part *they only want to be liked*. Yet what do they do? Spend all their spare moments rending each other's characters into shreds, or pouncing eagerly on small defects and weaknesses.

May 9th to 19th

A short holiday in France in the company of millionaires.[1] Ralph, Robin Campbell and I took the train to Valence, and thence to the little town of Buis-les-Baronnies, where Janetta's mother Jan had spent the war after she was banned from the coast by the Germans. Janetta was keen to see it and arranged to meet us there, and Mary (who was travelling with Philip Dunn and their two girls, Serena and Nell) was to pick up Robin. A complicated and not at all easy set of combinations.

Buis stands in a charming valley full of fruit-trees, with Mont Ventoux in the background, snow-capped, and yellow tulips, grape hyacinths and narcissus in the foreground. The village centres round a small arcaded *place*, and is full of fine crumbling old houses with beautiful wooden doors.

We stayed in the inn where Jan had taken refuge and helped in the kitchen. The André family had been very fond of her and were longing to see Janetta. She and Derek arrived for two nights in a nine-seater Ford, and soon afterwards came the Dunns in a brand new monster with a wireless spouting *Mrs Dale's Diary*. After they had all gone away Ralph and I talked with amazement and I must confess disapproval of their way of foreign travel. Robin was the only one who wanted to soak in his surroundings, walk about the village and into the fields. The others were perfectly content to sit in cafés all day long drinking endless pernods, talking loudly, seeming to expect local admiration and certainly getting it in the case of their cars. Derek kept up a good deal of buffoonery with imitations in French – sometimes funny, sometimes not. The Andrés welcomed him and Janetta most warmly and brought out old photos and books which Jan had left behind. I think she was much moved by this revival of Jan's ghost. She was looking very pretty in extremely short shorts, but thin and tense; smiling and friendly however. Everyone wanted to make things 'go' and on the whole I think they did.]

Ice-cold, wintry weather, dark grey clouds under which the tender greenery lies like a mockery. I have been suffering rather from world depression, and liable to pitch into the abyss when I read about all nations frantically devoting themselves to making lethal weapons. But I have developed a technique rather like that of the Euston Road painters – 'point to point realism' they used to call it – by which (like a fly) I crawl from one material objective to another, not looking further afield than is necessary.

August and September

We took a second longer holiday, with Burgo, in Ibiza to join Darsie Japp[2] and his family who had rented two little houses there. Flew by unpressurized aeroplane to Palma, and thence by sea to the small pyramidal town of Ibiza, where a crowd stood waving and shouting; and suddenly we saw that we too had our welcoming friend, for there was Darsie Japp, and a weak cry of 'Ralph!' floated up to us. He drove us to our hotel: it was like a set for a Somerset Maugham play about life on a tropical island, and kept by seven German-Jewish refugees, known locally as the

---

[1] Derek Jackson and Philip Dunn.
[2] A painter of the school of Henry Lamb and Augustus John.

Seven Dwarfs. The Japps have made quite a few friends – in particular Eduardo, a painter from Ecuador, and an aristocratic Spanish couple who speak English when alone 'because of the servants'.

The warm pellucid sea, the beauty of the persons and clothes of the natives (long plaited hair, much gold and silver jewellery, silken skirts and shawls), all this was truly marvellous. When they danced, the girls scuttled round with small hither-and-thither steps and head and eyes demurely cast down, while their men approached them in what seemed like an excess of sexual frenzy, and without actually touching them kept up a continuous wild high kicking and leaping. This violently male behaviour applied to the marked modesty of the females had a very erotic effect, as did the monotonous Moorish music on pipe, tom-tom and castanets.

We met the Japps every day to bathe; Darsie entertained us with his stories. One was about the wife of Max Ernst, who was a great hypochondriac. One day she remembered about the cramp got from bathing too soon after a meal, and rushed out of the sea crying *'Max! Max! La congestion, comment ça commence?' 'Avec la mort!'*

December 8th

To London with bad toothache – once in the lee of the G.W. Hotel I had no desire to leave, but we had tickets for *Billy Budd*, 'a queer's heaven' as Robert calls it, and it is true that not a woman appears on the stage (rather as if a composer left out the violins in his symphony) not even a boy's treble, and only homosexual emotions figure. The climax comes when Captain 'Starry' Vere and Billy Budd, condemned to be hanged, are shut together in Vere's stateroom. A spotlight plays on the door (as in *Peter Pan* – 'do you believe in fairies?' Do you indeed?) And thirty-four triads, to which the critics have referred in surprise, punctuate the space of time when the sentence is being conveyed to Budd. The imagination can deal with this as it chooses. But what makes the drama to me so unmoving is that Budd is a tiresome prig, the good boy who sucks up to the headmaster and even when doomed to die is oozing with hero-worship.

After the opera we went to the Hills for red wine and cheese. Here we found the painter John Nash, a charming small birdlike man, with prominent eyes and an unusually high voice. Back to a night made hideous by toothache, and an awakening with my face swollen out like a vulgar postcard. Draw a veil.

December 11th

Face going down steadily – what a relief. Ralph and I lunched with Robert at the Étoile. He has come to terms with his life – or so it seems – and resembles a comet shooting among new skies and strange planets. However, he is still the same charming, funny, fiery Robert. He describes Janetta as having become very firm and decided; this is probably the front she deliberately presents to him.

To Francis Bacon's private view – only six canvases, three being of Popes in purple robes, shouting, declaiming or simply glaring, each from within a shadowy glass box. No one can deny his impressiveness.

December 15th

All to Aldbourne to lunch with the Brenans, who leave tomorrow to fly to America where one of Gamel's brothers is dying. Success has set them both up like a tonic: Gerald's *Face of Spain* has had an excellent reception, and Gamel is delighted by good reviews of her Spanish translation, *The Spendthrifts* by Perez Galdós. What a pretty old lady she will become! Gerald, as at all moments of excitement, was looking positively Chinese, his black eyes reduced to slits by intensity of feeling.

December 31st

What can I say about the last ten days of this old year? Burgo went to London for a party at Charlotte's and returned dead beat having slept not at all but obviously enjoyed himself. The party broke up at five, when it turned out that four other boys and young men were all expecting to sleep on the same sofa as the one he had been promised. 'We spent the night groaning,' he said, 'and everyone got up every few minutes. I had the broadish arm of the sofa, and was lying half on top of the son of the inventor of the jet engine.'

On the 22nd came Robert and Georgie, a dear little girl with a gentle voice and Janetta's lovely grey eyes and long black lashes. When Robert is about she makes a bid for spoiling, so that she ends up most meals on his lap with him feeding her. Anyone else was rejected if they offered assistance, but when left alone with me she was as good as gold, trotting to and fro on her own devices. Robert had brought with him trunks full of toys, and he pondered deeply over her stocking, which was one of my longest stuffed right to the top. No wonder that she burst into tears when all the opening was over and her emotions deflated. Starting manfully as nursemaid, poor Robert found it an exhausting task and to see him wrestling with it wrung my heart, although he got great pleasure I think from her dependence on him. Georgie shows one sign of her background having been disturbed – a tendency to reject all offerings at first blush: 'No-o-o. DOO-O-ONT *want* it.'

I have felt harrowed by having Robert here, and that he is still a deeply unhappy man. He agreed that his philosophy of life is that it is hell, but that one must and could extract one's own happiness from it. According to the Third Programme this is the message of Francis Bacon's painting, and also (according to Robin) the Existentialist's philosophy. Strength through Misery, it might be called.

1952

January 1st

I start the New Year with some courage and a sort of philosophy of life. There is a lot of friendliness circulating in the passages like the warm air from our new radiators. Ralph, too, seems to be manfully turning over *his* new leaf by working steadily in the library.

In the evening all three of us had a talk about financing Burgo in London; Ralph is giving him a bank account and he is delighted. After which we set off for the Campbells where we spent a delightful evening in that warm friendly atmosphere, along with the Pritchetts, drinking some glorious wine – a present from Derek.

January 19th

Burgo's new London lodgings seem to be a great success. Jane [Ainley], his landlady, writes: 'Burgo fits in very well and we all like him immensely. He is most kind and helpful about the sitting-in.[1] We had a small party for the Hinchingbrooke girls who are about his age, and everyone liked each other. Burgo was most amusing at dinner.' Music to our ears!

February 6th to 11th

What a surprise! As I was cooking lunch I heard Mrs Hoare's steps thudding along the passage and down the kitchen stairs. 'Have you heard the news? The King's dead! He died last night in his sleep. Isn't it *awful*?' My first reaction was to think 'Lucky fellow, to die so peacefully.' Then came the implications: a young Queen, new stamps, court mourning – only faintly interesting, but certainly not 'awful'. The wireless has entirely failed to rise to the occasion – first it shut down everything but news. Now all three programmes jointly broadcast the silliest, most nondescript items in their repertory, punctuated by bulletins of thunderous gravity and richly revelled-in emotional unbuttoning. One note they strike is the 'Three Mourning Queens', another is that the late King's devotion to duty is what killed him. Richard Dimbleby made a bold bid to coin a name for him in the history books, by several times calling him 'George the Faithful'. The whole effect is of 'ham' acting; and a lot of nonsense is being talked about 'the relief necessary to our tortured feelings'. What the public is feeling is a sense of great drama, not at all unpleasant; the magnificent sight of a coffin surmounted by a crown and draped with the royal standard carried on the shoulders of enormous guardsmen. (What if they dropped it, muffed it, or let the crown roll on the ground! My word!) Well then of course death is a subject deeply moving to us all, and the King perfectly symbolizes these

---

[1] For her two small children.

feelings, especially with the grandeur of the public obsequies, the black-veiled Queens and so on. But to talk of personal sadness is absurd. When a great actor, artist or writer dies, one feels sad for what one will miss. (Should Max Beerbohm die it would be very sad to know that that charming personality would no longer express itself on the wireless.) But the *King* is after all at once supplanted by a *Queen* who will I'm sure do just as well; and though he was probably a good, hard-working man there are plenty other such.

In fact I feel a craving for a little realism, and a talk with someone like Alix say, who is capable of being interested in this great tide of public feeling without swimming along in it.

This morning at breakfast Ralph suddenly said how feeble and old he had felt this last year, and he didn't want to be 'livened up' and made to 'hop about'. I am seriously worried about his thus giving up and accepting old age before he is sixty. Perhaps he really isn't well I thought as I drove into Hungerford, and – oh dear! – perhaps I do not look after him well enough. I resolved this morning to exert all the energy I possess (and at the moment I have quite a bit) in trying to support and sustain him and making him happier. Looking after someone so dearly and devotedly loved is after all the greatest possible pleasure.

February 14th

Off to London for three days in Barbara Bagenal's flat, two of them on my own. I found Percy Street immersed in an odd perplexity: Barbara's lavatory is out of order, and Sonia Brownell in the flat above dislikes hers being commandeered. The sudden importance of our excrement is a trifle ludicrous. Call on Saxon who was padding round his dusty cluttered room like a melancholy old goat dressed up. Then to see Burgo, in a nice warm cheerful room at Jane Ainley's.

Dined with Janetta at the Ivy: she looked happy, her face ironed out of strain, and was friendly and charming. It is probably true that I miss the girl of sixteen – my goodness how lovely! – who trudged round with her cloak and her stick and her 'disrespect' (a famous remark of hers was 'I disrespect you for what you've just said'); but I know that is senseless. Derek telephoned while we were dining, and asked us to join him and Sonia at their restaurant. This we did, and drank brandy among a smart crowd in funeral black and arm-bands. I still can't help thinking of Derek as a little boy, though a brilliantly clever one. His mind whirls like a mill-race but sometimes on little-boy things, and little-boy jokes amuse him. Sonia was keen to 'go on somewhere', so on we went – first to the Gargoyle and then to Claridges, where the 'Jacksons' were staying *en route* to Khartoum, with a packing-case of scientific instruments, for Derek to do experiments on the total eclipse. At the Gargoyle we ran into Francis Bacon, lit up with drink, reckless, charming, giggling wildly. He joined us at our table, and turning to me asked, 'Don't you think Derek is the most marvellous person you know?' Next we were joined by Lucian Freud, who began a serious conversation with Derek about Art and Science, Derek's contribution to which was eager, amusing and paradoxical. Champagne was ordered and when Sonia, Lucian and I left Claridges it was two o'clock. Outside the front door two handsome, well-educated policemen were standing, to whom Lucian remarked, 'I suppose you're here to prevent all the Kings getting assas-sinated?' (There are seven Kings and Queens here for the funeral.) The policeman looked down his nose and didn't deign to answer. We three took a taxi to Percy

Street, but even at her door Sonia couldn't give up and they left me and drove on 'somewhere else'. When we were at the Gargoyle, Sonia tried to describe to me a little Connemara bay that had charmed her, and something lit up in her eyes, though it was tragically imprisoned by inarticulacy, due not so much to drink as to deep despair.

February 15th

The King's funeral day; the problem was how to get across the path of the procession so as to lunch with Burgo in Kensington. My bus decanted me at Selfridges, and all at once – like a bucket emptying its contents on me – I saw a horde of human beings advancing towards me. The procession must just have passed as their faces distinctly showed traces of a cathartic experience, like blackboards after a teacher had wiped them. I slipped between two files of soldiers and there I was across the frontier, in the milky sunlight of the park. The ponds shone like pale tea, and equally pale was the gold on the Albert Memorial.

February 29th: Ham Spray

A flying visit from Phil and Phyllis Nichols. He told us what it was like to walk in the King's funeral procession – all the preparations beforehand for the gruelling ordeal, like soaping the inside of his shoes. He walked between M. Schumann and M. Stikker of Holland. They were all told to go to the lavatory at Westminster while they had a chance, because at the last King's funeral there was almost a stampede when they reached Paddington, with guardsmen nearly dropping the coffin and rushing off into corners. But this time only one old gentleman failed to stay the course. The word went round that Signor B. was in difficulties and he was ushered to the kerb, where five doctors sprang up and smuggled him away.

The Brenans are back from America; Gerald came to dinner last night. He looked like someone who had just been shot off a machine in a fun-fair, still whirling and dazed and unaware where he was. His eyes were nearly closed with the violence of his emotions and the number of impressions needing to be got off his chest, which spurted forth in an inchoate stream of talk. By the end of the evening he was quite hoarse and we had gleaned: that Americans were much stupider than Europeans; that they were just like Anglo-Saxons; that they were years behind the times; that Gamel's brother was a wonderful man; that he was a pro-Nazi and a monster; that Gamel had cut quite a figure in America; that he, Gerald, had quite eclipsed her; that her family were rich, grand and erudite; that they were of no account whatever. There were also some good Geraldisms – e.g. 'Parents have to learn that they are to their children what a lamp-post is to a dog.'

'Why have them then?' asked Ralph.

'Because in spite of all it is an experience not to be missed, and one gets some sort of animal pleasure in their company.'

Of girls, he said he couldn't resist any who made themselves agreeable to him, in spite of his age. 'I'm just a Sir Walter Raleigh tearing about putting my cloak down in puddles.'

March 23rd

So hot was the sun that Ralph and I lunched on the verandah at my table, vowing that we would often do so again, and were the luckiest people alive to be able to sit here looking out at the beauty of the March view, with its purity of line unfuzzed by any foliage. It was unthinkable to go indoors all afternoon.

I'm reading Veronica Wedgwood's life of her uncle Josiah which starts a train of thought about the change in the intellectual outlook since 1900. *Then* work was paramount. Intellectuals were also idealists, optimists, enthusiasts; they believed in progress, freedom, justice, integrity. Their desire to improve their minds and the lot of the masses was boundless. Against this must be set some lack of irony and proportion, heavy overseriousness; puritanism (or shamefaced suppression). And *now* what? Since the Twenties play has become more important than work, but instead of optimism there is disillusion and pessimism, cynicism, frivolity. Pleasure eagerly pursued, wit and gaiety are all to the good, but less good is addiction to time-killing activities, anything for 'amusement'. Does it add up perhaps to decadence? I believe it does, and that it started in 1918 as a result of that beastly war, and has stamped its pattern more indelibly since the last beastly war.

In spite of the tragic demise of the flower book, my interest in the subject has not declined. Going for walks with Ralph my eyes drift to the hedge-banks, covered as they now are by the intricate mosaic of springing leaves. And each year is different; just as the great Parisian couturiers produce each spring new points in their fashions. This season wild arums are being worn in profusion; dark and glossy, with their wicked-looking blackish spots, they burst in positive cascades down the banks.

[The Campbells had for some time been trying to entice us to go shares with them in renting a house – a battered château rather – in Vaucluse for a fortnight. They told us that Robert and his new friend Oonagh Oranmore were in Paris and might drive down and join us there. In the surprising way such plans consolidate (especially when fired by the positive enthusiasm of someone like Mary), Ralph, Burgo and I duly set off, by sea and road on 5 April, arriving a few days later at the outskirts of a castellated, semi-ruined village of yellow sandstone, perched on a narrow rock. After winding our way up alleys so narrow that the car sometimes scraped both sides between tall houses with vestiges of Renaissance architecture, we finally reached the terrace of an imposing château with windows thrown wide open, and here we found Robin, Mary and Nell sun-bathing.

We soon settled in. Mary held the Common Purse, a visible bulge in her jeans. We shopped in the village, filled up our bottles from the incredibly cheap local wine, and picked asparagus running to seed and greener than the French like it, in the sand by the river. We bathed, read, went on drives and sat in cafés; Nell and Burgo went for milk and bread every morning and breakfast was on the terrace. The evenings were sometimes rollicking with wine, talk and laughter.

A little later Robert and Oonagh arrived in a large hired car. Oonagh looked like some veiled Eastern woman in her enormous black glasses. Her small fragile and elegant body, her tiny hands loaded with huge rings hardly promised co-operation to our housewifery, nor was it wanted, but I found her tragic expression and air of being lost rather worrying. Her rare contributions to the conversation were often strange, for instance, 'I used to carry the Bible about with me *every*where, and read it *all* the time, but people were so horrid to me I had to stop.' And after several days in our company she leaned across the table and asked me 'What *is* your name?' When I told her, 'And what is your husband's?' But her English chauffeur, Teeder, was a constant source of amusement to us with his efforts to carry standards of English upper-class life into this large but uncomfortable house, with its quantities of yellow dust, its shortage of water where wanted and plentiful amount leaking where it was not, and his disapproval of everything French was obvious. All females were addressed as 'Milady'. When he disparaged French food Mary exclaimed 'Shame on you, Teeder!' 'Oh, it doesn't matter, Milady,' he replied, 'I manage quite well somehow.'

After all the others had left for home, Robert stayed on with us Partridges, and a new more adventurous form of life began. Robert, best of companions, excellent with Burgo, steered us up the Gorge du Régalon, a stony cleft between two giant cliffs that almost met overhead, out into a hillside thick with miniature daffodils and irises, and persuaded us to climb the Luberon. By the time we started for England a violent storm had transformed the valleys, lining them with luscious grass and wild narcissi, loveliest and most intoxicatingly scented of flowers.

Arrived back at Ham Spray to bad news. Burgo's tutor had had a stroke poor fellow, and couldn't possibly take him next term.]

May 1st

Burgo and I took the train to London, and while he went off to stay with Jane Ainley in the Isle of Wight I interviewed and engaged a new tutor for him – Alan Tyson, a clever, nervous young man with bright blue eyes, Oxford double-first, training to be a psychoanalyst. Perhaps that will come in useful, as I have just agreed to index the complete works of Freud for James's translation.

May 28th

This morning I fell to clearing my botany table of all its sad and derelict deposits to make way for my Freudian indexing for James. So that is that, and I have now cut the last knot tying me to botany as work, and put it in its place as a hobby.

Mary invited us to dinner to meet Janetta and Derek, adding that Janetta was radiant with happiness; she added that she had mentioned Robert's name to her and saw she had put her foot in it by the lengthening and greenification of Derek's face. She was saying in effect: 'Come to dinner. Janetta wants to see you. But do behave properly to Derek – and leave Robert out of it.'

The expression of happy relaxation was there all right – the only sign of imperfect adjustment was that everyone depended so much on hard liquor. No one was without a glass in their hand all evening. We quite enjoyed ourselves by dint of getting into the same parboiled state, talking freely if somewhat incoherently and swimming along like fish in the alcoholic tide – a dreary state where nothing is exact and where ideas that have come into one's mind with a certain pungency lose their definition before ever they reach one's lips. It isn't our way of life and somehow we felt we were in an alien camp.

June 23rd

David and Rachel to Sunday lunch. We talked of Desmond's death and the question where Molly should live. Someone mentioned the newspaper tributes; 'Oh, I do hate *tributes*,' Molly had said. With her candid eyes wide open and her face full of feeling, Rachel described the funeral ceremony: 'If one had the courage to *force* oneself to look down into the grave and see the coffin lying there I found it looked so peaceful, and that was very consoling.' Janie Bussy, who went to the memorial service, told us that after it was over Desmond's friends gathered outside St Martin-in-the-Fields and stood talking together, and that an impromptu party atmosphere spontaneously generated itself, which seemed entirely appropriate.

July 11th

Social life has kept us on the hop. Darsie and Lucila came for the weekend, driven over by Henry and Pansy Lamb. Hot on their heels came recently widowed Faith for a week. She is so intelligent and interested in other people that a certain lack of vitality is easily forgiven. Conversation was easy and spontaneous between the three of us. Today was the first day of Burgo's exams, and we were half expecting to hear that he hadn't gone to it. But a railway strike gave me the excuse to ring up Juanita with whom he is staying, and she gave us the welcome news that he had gone off perfectly cheerfully, adding that she 'adored him, and loved having him there'.

July 28th

Alix and James have been and gone, leaving me full of admiration for Alix. She is the most intelligent woman I know, the best conversationalist, the most fluent and logical thinker – I don't feel she has received enough recognition for this fact. Then her long serious face from which her grey dispassionate eyes look out, set in a series of flattened triangles, should really be perpetuated by some master painter.[1] Throughout the weekend hearing her talk was pure joy. She listens, what's more, usually calmly, to what others have to say, surveys it with detachment, sets to work spinning from it a threat of ratiocination – and ends in a conclusion that is often fantastic, wild! James too was very entertaining in his laconic, puncturing style. I was interested to see them with Robert; they got on very well, and he and Alix even have something in common – a desire to go swiftly and ruthlessly to the point, say, as well as a streak of the Red Indian, a fierce look under dark thatches of hair. Yet in sheer intelligence Robert was outmatched.

August 6th

Ralph, Burgo and I have just passed a week in Ireland, our first stop being Mullingar where Derek and Janetta have rented for the summer a fine Georgian house in the middle of a spacious park, with mown lawns, clipped Irish yews and formal flower-beds, all very charming. Indoors – every comfort, and the days starting with breakfast brought to us in our soft beds. The country is too flat and featureless for pleasant walking, yet we eat and drink so much that we feel the need of it. Gradually we get the hang of the ideology of the house, which is Derek's, but if he is a dictator he is certainly a genial one. All animals get high marks for being dogs or cows as the case may be. Games are 'not socially OK.' The red rags which turn him temporarily into a bull are the Labour party, God and the Royal family.

'Do you know, Burgo, what are the three most important things in life? Be rich; *be rich*; and BE RICH.' And: 'Don't you agree that the point of making money is not to spend it but to make more money?' Is he teasing? I'm not sure. Burgo loves it

[1] The best portrait of her was by John Banting.

and Ralph is quite good at finding bridgeheads on which they can meet and agree. I am the least at ease with him, but one can't fail to respond to his friendliness; the trouble is that we don't *want* to be as rich as he is. Janetta seems happy and very relaxed.

'You've said several awful things this evening,' she said one night to Derek without a trace of malice, 'and I'm not going to forget them.'

On the way home we were to stay a night with Oonagh Oranmore at her house Luggala in the Wicklow mountains, where a rollicking party for Dublin Horse show week was just ending. There was Robert of course, Francis Wyndham, Lucian Freud and his wife Kitty[1] with her huge dark eyes, perfect teeth and soft cooing voice; Claud Cockburn, tall, dark, ugly and animated. Everyone was eager to tell us the story of Lord Powerscourt's recent ball to which the whole Luggala party had been invited. They turned up in force, no less than three with black eyes; however it was Lucian's tartan trousers that caused the trouble. 'You can't come in here dressed like that,' said the doorman, and this was backed up by his Lordship saying, 'I'm not going to have any drunks here.' And 'If you don't like it you can get out!' Daphne Bath tried to mend matters by saying as she left, with her attractive stammer: 'Thank you for the most b-b-beastly party I've ever b-b-been to in my life.' To which Lord Powerscourt replied, 'I'm so glad you didn't enjoy it.'

We had met our fellow-guests in Dublin and driven to Luggala with them. Incredible beauty lay before us as we climbed the last ridge before dipping into the valley – range upon range of mountains spread around us with their tops still golden in the setting sun, and the deep, green, lost valley below. A big loch of brown peaty water with sheep browsing round a small formal temple, and beneath the domed forehead of a crag the house itself – a fantastically pretty white building in purest Strawberry Hill Gothic style. The front door was opened and we were at once in the hall-dining-room, where a huge fire blazed and an oval table laid for dinner filled nearly all the space. What a magical atmosphere that house had, charmingly furnished and decorated to match its style, dim lights, soft music playing and Irish voices ministering seductively to our needs. In the drawing-room stood Oonagh with her hair down her back, and in her short diaphanous dress looking exactly like the fairy off a Christmas tree.

Ralph and I were borne off to our little bedroom where yet another roaring fire was being lit and our things unpacked. The prettiness of the room itself, the humble bathroom next door where the softest dark brown water smelling of peat awaited us, all made up a work of art whoever was responsible, and a contrast to many of the houses of the rich where one may find a single match sticking out of its box as if one were too weak to take it oneself, and inadequate heating. We were led through another room where Tara, Oonagh's youngest boy, was ensconced in the bath. Garech aged thirteen, with a husky breaking voice and a passion for wild flowers, had appeared during dinner with some friends carrying autograph books in which we were all told to draw or write something *very* funny. When we climbed into bed I for one felt soaked through and through in this pleasant Irish atmosphere.

---

[1] Daughter of Jacob Epstein. Later married to Wynne Godley, economist and professional flautist.

August 16th

Back at Ham Spray we discussed Luggala with Lawrence and Julia. Is it illogical we asked, to be bowled over by the impact of this eighteenth-century life, full of material splendour, recklessness, dash and style, which is of course supported on things none of us approves of – like the assumption that class distinctions are insuperable? What can all those servants feel about the indulgent, selfish display of their masters' goings-on? 'Intense pride mixed with intense pity,' was Lawrence's excellent answer to this question. Julia, more disapproving, suggested that the output of such lives was *nil*. My remembered picture of life at Luggala is mainly attractive, even romantic, and such shadows as it possesses are thrown by child-ishness, insensitivity and competitive drinking. And after sojourning in other civilizations, it is very pleasant to feel alive again in our own.

Ralph on war: It is important, he says, to remember that killing your enemy in war is assassination (it's no use both sides thinking they are acting in self-defence) and that in theory one should prefer being assassinated to assassinating.

September 8th

At breakfast on the last day of a visit from Isobel and Charlotte Strachey the news came that Burgo has passed his exam in all subjects. What a relief! I think I subconsciously believed he had done so, and he admits the same. We are sliding into the assumption that he will now get to Oxford. The next step is a tutorial establishment called MacNalty's where he will work with other boys. Charlotte has become extremely pretty as well as funny and charming.

October 25th

The telephone rang. 'Gerald speaking,' in the low hoarse tone of a sea-monster just arisen from a deep plunge. 'I've stopped smoking,' he began. 'I don't *want* to smoke ever again, but the trouble is it has also stopped my writing. And I can't read either' (this on a higher screech). 'I don't do *any*thing except read thrillers.' I said something to him about his *History of Spanish Literature*, and how absolutely brilliant, lucid, sensitive, perceptive, profound and penetrating it seemed to me. (I have just finished reading *Don Quixote* in Spanish, and I wasn't flattering Gerald – all was truly meant.) He told me he had been asked to lecture to undergraduates, but it was impossible. I said, 'I think it's almost your moral duty to go, as you have such a power of spreading enthusiasm and understanding.' 'Oh no, no, I can't possibly. I can't talk to people; it makes me too aware of my own existence. I love life, but I don't want to remember my *self*. When I'm alone I can be happy and forget I exist. When I talk to people I can't think who and what I am. I say silly things – and then afterwards there's the remorse! I suffer terribly from remorse. Gamel too – we are both full of remorse.'

October 27th

To lunch with the Brenans today. Gerald has begun to smoke and write once more. He is writing his autobiography and has just got to the arrival in his life of Hope Johnstone (who is living in his cottage at present). He fears he may have gone too far, as lately Hope Johnstone, who was titillated at first, has 'fallen strangely silent'.

Gerald's object is to convey to the reader the absurdities in Hope's character without making them apparent to Hope himself.

More talk about remorse. Gamel said in her driest way: 'I'm so eaten up by remorse that I have no energy left over for anything else.' Gerald talked with scarcely disguised satisfaction, of the approaching end of the life of Poffet their cat. 'He has vitamin H deficiency which makes his fur fall out. *Poor* Poffet; we think he will soon have to be put to sleep.'

After lunch the Brenans took us for a walk up the hollow in the Downs below Snap to see a group of hornbeams – very beautiful trees with their sheaves of papery bracts. As we came home in the twilight it struck me that (though I don't altogether like the look beech trees have of being red-headed persons) they were mysteriously moving, standing there with the blood of their fallen leaves below them.

November 12th

To London for the night to go to *Porgy and Bess*, with Craig Macfarlane and Burgo. Burgo had been with us about an hour when I said, 'Well, isn't there any London news? Has nothing been happening?'

Burgo: 'No, I don't think so. I can't think of anything – Oh, well, I *was* nearly arrested for murder last week!' Then the following incredible story came out: (I must preface it by saying that there have been sensational headlines about a young ex-public school boy arrested for pushing both his parents over a cliff). It seems that last Saturday Burgo left his rooms in Tite Street to buy a newspaper. Just as he was opening the front door on his return, five men in mackintoshes appeared from nowhere, and pushed him into the house saying with very fierce expressions, 'We are police officers and we are armed'. 'Then they asked my name,' Burgo went on, 'and they obviously didn't believe it, so I showed them the name-tape at the back of my shirt, and one of them took off his hat to squint down my neck. They asked me if it was my car outside, and I said, 'No. Shall I go and see if it belongs to anyone upstairs?' They said, 'You are not to communicate with anyone in this house.' After a while they let me go for a walk, but one of them followed me at a discreet distance. Nothing more happened, until midnight when a taxi drew up; the police appeared in scores and hustled out the young man inside it – the murderer himself, of course. The car had belonged to his dead parents, and he drove up in it to visit his girl, who lived in Tite Street.' The description, even the photograph of Gifford fitted Burgo to a T: 'A very dark young man, with hair worn long, wearing a green sports coat, greenish trousers and a pullover'.

We were all amazed at Burgo's sangfroid about this episode.

January 3rd

Last night a young people's ball was given by 'the Tycoon' (Philip Dunn), for Serena and Nell, to which we went with Burgo, Isobel and Charlotte Strachey, after an evening spent ironing and dressing up in a fizz of expectation. Burgo looked very fine and what Charlotte described as 'Byronical' in his new dinner jacket, in spite of very long hair and woolly socks. We collected the Campbells and their guests on the way – Paddy Leigh Fermor (high-spirited and friendly) and Joan Rayner (beautiful and shy).[1] I sat in the back of our car with these two, discussing the structure of the human face, and I remember that Paddy declared that he had strong feelings about the runnel down the centre of the upper lip. 'I often think about it,' he said. Wynne Godley and a young sweet-faced Michael Rutherston were also of the party, and tended to form a somewhat bohemian gathering talking animatedly, with Charlotte and Burgo, in a corner of the ball-room.

January 12th

Robert has gone to Geneva on a new job, and the Brenans back to Spain, leaving us with melancholy gaps in the ranks of our friends. The drama of Poffet the Brenans' cat grew more and more Wagnerian towards its close. They insisted on fixing the date of execution as the very eve of their departure, and all the while the atmosphere of wakes, keening and candles grew more intense. Gerald told us that they had been indulging the poor condemned creature with such rich food that he refused to touch anything but chicken or turbot – thus making it quite impossible to change their minds and reprieve him as no one could afford to keep him.

After the dreadful day was over Gerald wrote a horrified letter to Ralph, blaming himself bitterly, saying that they had 'buried Poffet in silk because he had lived in silk', and that one should never keep pets because it was so terrible that one had in the end to destroy them.

Occupational therapy is at the moment my panacea for all ills; I have started working on the index to Freud, and found it such a boon and blessing that I am resolved never to be without work again while I can totter about or wield a pen.

February 9th

Our first visit to London for some time, though its object was not particularly cheerful – to visit the afflicted James and the equally afflicted Bussys. We went straight to Gordon Square, and I received a wave of nostalgia for its dignified

---

[1] They later married.

façades and the tall plane trees with their dangling bobbles of fruit in its spacious garden.[1] Up in the Bussys' flat an overpowering smell of gas nearly stifled us. The whole family has had to fly back from La Souco because Simon has either had a stroke or become suddenly senile. Dorothy at 87, intelligent, charming, sweetly girlish, enjoyed her first flight in an aeroplane; but poor Janie looked worn almost to nothing, her face no bigger than a bead, emerging from Alix's fur coat. The flight had been far from enjoyable for her. She couldn't tell the air hostess that Simon was off his head or they would have refused to take him, and he didn't take kindly to any restraint. All went well for a bit, then he rose to his wobbly little legs and made as if to open the door. Janie managed to subdue him by saying in an impersonal voice 'It is forbidden to leave the aeroplane,' and giving him some chocolate.

If there is a comic side to the Bussy tragedy, there is none whatever about James's. Alix looked pale and haggard, and said she found drink a considerable help. We took her to lunch at the Ivy, and then Ralph and I went by instalments to visit James where he lay flat on his back at the Middlesex Hospital like a wonderfully distinguished marble effigy, waving one long beautiful hand. His eyes are bandaged, so all expression is done by hand movement. Ralph said he anxiously asked how Alix was looking – how poignant that he has to ask! There's no knowing yet what the result of the operation will be, and partial or total blindness cannot be ruled out. Yet so wonderfully calm, serene, even gay did James manage to be – and in her way Alix too – that I begin to see how courage can turn horrible events into inspiring ones.

[The marriage between Lytton's second sister, Dorothy, and Simon was in some ways a strange one; but since at the time of poor Simon's decline it had lasted fifty years it must have been solidly based, even though it had united a highbrow Englishwoman of nearly forty and a penniless French painter, reputed to have sprung from humble origins. True, he was a friend of Matisse, and was steadily gaining a reputation for the originality and accomplishment of his own paintings – many of them of birds, fish and animals, but also including charming landscapes, and portraits of his wife and daughter, of André Gide and Paul Valéry. Dorothy's father, Sir Richard, gave her a fine villa on the Riviera (La Souco, Roquebrune) as a wedding-present, and it was for many years a refuge for members of the family (and friends) in trouble or convalescence. An odd feature of the marriage was that Dorothy (like most Stracheys) was loth to speak French, although reading and understanding it with ease, whereas Simon never learned much English – indeed his conversation consisted largely of grunts to which he contrived to give a rich variety of meaning. Whenever we saw them (and they used to stay with us at Ham Spray, once a year at least) Dorothy spoke English and Simon French. Dorothy must have known French extremely well, however, as she was much admired for her translations from the French – particularly for those of Gide's Diary. I think she was in her seventies when I first got to know her: her grey hair was cut in a neat bob, with a long fringe reaching to the highly intelligent brown eyes that shone through her spectacles.]

---

[1] Ralph and I had begun our life together there in 1926.

February 10th

I am having my first Spanish lesson with Lucila Japp tomorrow. It suddenly occurred to me that if I got good enough, translation was something I could do for the rest of my life; so I have begun working at it quite hard and eagerly. Modern novels so often fail to grip the attention; one comes out from them shaking off clotted humanity with a faint sense of disgust, and feeling that the author has worked like a caddis-worm to make his characters out of conglomerations of material objects – cuff-links, cigarette-cases and fishing-rods for upper-class men for instance. So that it would be a rare pleasure to be able to transfer an old masterpiece into English. All a daydream no doubt.

Last week we drove to Seend to lunch with Clive's brother the Colonel, and bring Clive back to stay. There was a third Bell present – a raw-boned, reddish sister, with Clive's combination of rather coarse skin, clear-cut features and yellowing teeth. We ate in the hall which Violet, the Colonel's recently deceased wife, had tried to make snugger by lining it with stalls and a gate from the stables, and behind these we sat like horses munching hay, waited on by a silver-haired stage butler. Afterwards the Colonel took me round the garden and touched me by the way he spoke of the taste and hard work his wife had bestowed on it, telling me he thought it was lugging heavy water-cans to her plants in a drought that had killed her.

March 2nd

A new visitor this week made a great impression on us both – Freddie Ayer, a clever man as well as a delightful guest, and it was a good idea to have him with Raymond. Each was glad to meet the other and appreciated the other's different kind of brain. From Freddie's opaque and very dark eyes gleams out what seems like an affectionate nature and a certain vulnerability – a desirable ingredient in every human character. I'd expected him to be more metallic and armour-plated – but no: he showed a simple pleasure in the prettiness of our crocuses and a boyish eagerness to be the first to solve the lights of a crossword. We very much liked him in fact.

In the mornings he sat down with paper and pen at the table in the music-room. 'Wouldn't you like to be more private if you're working?' I asked. 'There's another room, you know.'

'Oh no, I can only think with other people about – that is if you don't mind.'

'What is it you're writing?'

'Something I've been working at for some time about our knowledge of other minds. I think I'm almost able to prove that we *do* have knowledge of them. Starting, of course, on the principle of analogy, that because we scream at the pain of our teeth being extracted, when we see and hear other people do likewise it's reasonable to assume that they also feel pain.'

'So, if you can do that, you can definitely disprove the truth of solipsism?'

'Yes.' He walked busily to and fro as he talked and sometimes rearranged the logs in the fire with his foot. He told us about Max Newman's Mechanical Brain and the lengths in problem-solving it had been made to reach.[1]

'Can it play chess?' we asked. 'After a fashion. It's quite good at the end-game,

---

[1] Newman's 'Colossus' was the earliest programmable computer in opposition to the German 'Enigma'.

but there are too many possibilities at the start. Then if it's losing it cheats sometimes; there's a device by which it can flash the words "My turn" and "Your turn", and sometimes when it's getting the worst of the game it flashes "My turn. My turn. My turn".'

Ralph remembered with pleasure how one of the Brain's guardians said that he thought it might soon be induced to appreciate poetry, 'but it would probably have to be poetry written by another Mechanical Brain'.

March 5th

Alix rang up to say that James is sending me another volume of Freud to index, probably just as we start on our motor tour to Spain. Could I take it with me? Under the attack of this gentle voice, so undemanding yet fraught with the importance of the task, I very nearly agreed, but good heavens! An index on a motor tour! So I wrote to suggest working flat out before we go.

Saxon and Burgo for the weekend. On Monday Burgo has to take the Christ Church entrance exam, which produced a certain tension. Saxon is concerned entirely with betting on every day's races. It's strange to see this frail but still elegant and distinguished man, who has spent his life reading Pliny and listening to Mozart and Wagner, giving all his elderly attention to fat brown books on racing form.

To drinks with the Campbells and Ben Nicolson. Mary made the perfect remark about Burgo's exam: 'Oh, I know people who've got into Christ Church who could hardly put a cross against their name.'

In the night the poor fellow was dreadfully sick and came down looking green, having had hardly a wink of sleep. Oh dear!

March 16th

Up early and drove to Oxford. Burgo tense, but able to laugh at jokes and looking a lot better. After leaving him at Christ Church we spent the morning with the Cecils, and Ralph fetched him back to lunch with us there. 'Not too bad', was the verdict on the morning's paper, though it looked atrocious to me. Little Hugh Cecil, coming back from the Dragon School, slipped into the seat opposite me; I watched his small school-bound face.

'How was the Dragon?' asked David.

'Oh, all right. Lambert's decided to stop his feud with Hodge-Brown.' These are two friends of Hugh's. It seems that Lambert is nettled by the thought of Hugh's aristocratic background, and inclined to boast of 'coming of good yeoman stock'. Hugh is going to act as page to his uncle, Lord Salisbury, at the Coronation. When he was told the news all he said was, 'That'll shake Lambert.' David's sister[1] is Mistress of the Robes, and has discovered to her horror that she will have to practically dress and undress the Queen in the middle of the ceremony. She is very short-sighted and dreads being unable to manage the hooks and eyes. Can she wear her spectacles?

---

[1] Dowager Duchess of Devonshire.

March 20th

Good news! Burgo has passed into Christ Church! Both Ralph and I are absolutely delighted and we hope Burgo is too. A success pleases everyone and bounces back like reflected light. His tutor Mr MacNalty is pleased; so even was Wilde when Ralph told him. How nice to go to Spain with this in our pockets.

May 13th

I was dandelioning yesterday afternoon near the empty swimming-pool when I saw a dead hedgehog lying curled up at the bottom. I shouted for Ralph, who came and took it out, but had great difficulty in jumping up from the empty pool; an upsetting conversation followed, one of those that lay a chilly hand on the heart and bring about a discord between the significance of the words spoken and the fresh green of the beech leaves, the narcissi, the pale blue sky. The two refuse to merge and their co-existence is painful. It seems that poor Ralph has been feeling so feeble as to become seriously anxious about his state of health. I blame myself exceedingly for not seeing what I didn't want to see. It shocks me that there should be any watertight doors between two people as intimate as we are. In getting him to come to London tomorrow and see a doctor I hope I am not forcing him to do something he always avoids when possible; but in this case I don't think so. It's my belief he is glad to have made the decision.

May 14th

The doctor was pleased with Ralph's check-up but we await the result of further tests.

Lunched with Clive and Raymond at the Ivy off gulls' eggs and salmon mayonnaise. Last Sunday Raymond reviewed André Maurois' book on Georges Sand, and before setting out to praise the book itself (which I'm now reading and think very good), he devoted a third of his review to saying how wicked and treacherous Maurois had proved himself to be at the time of the fall of France. I tried tentatively to put the general question as to whether this was relevant to a purely literary article on a purely literary subject. Nobody, surely, thinks that the fact that Marlowe was probably a police spy and a disagreeable character has a bearing on the excellence of *Doctor Faustus*; but all Raymond would say was that his conscience wouldn't have allowed him to praise the book without this reservation.

Goodness, London looked drab today: just enough of the Coronation decorations are up to have a fussy and sad, rather than a cheerful effect. Regent Street was particularly disastrous, decked in enormous pink waxy-looking Bedalian roses, through which the grey faces of the houses are anxiously peering.

[On May 16th we received a bombshell from Ralph's doctor. The tests we were awaiting had come and revealed sugar, which meant that he was in some degree a diabetic. To find out what that degree was and how to deal with it he was condemned to spend a week in the London Clinic having further tests, while I stayed with Juanita and spent all my days with him. We went for walks in Regent's Park, admiring the rose garden, and experiencing that strange calm that comes from having no doubt what ought to be done and concentrating on doing it. At least that was what was my prevailing mood and I believe his, too. He was in any case amazingly philosophic and resigned, showing neither irritability nor depression, and remarking among other things that his new diet would give us an excuse to prevent Mrs Hoare putting flour in the gravy. He was given a pocket set to test his own urine by boiling it furiously and watching it turn any colour between navy blue and deep orange (which was bad). How strange that the human body could express its abnormal function in these vivid terms of colour! Preferable to other forms of reaction, such as pain, however.]

May 19th

Dorothy and Janie Bussy for the weekend – Dorothy as fragile-looking as something made of matchsticks, and as alarming to be with as a very young baby. One moment she is completely on the spot, sharp as needles. The next she says 'Indian' when she means 'Chinese' or begins telling us who Beckford was, till Janie (irritated beyond control) tells her '*of course* they know'. There was a conversation about Raymond's article on Maurois. 'Do you disapprove of the book?' I asked.

'*Yes*'.

'Of the book or the man?'

'The man. I haven't read it.'

I thought as much. Yet Maurois turns out to have been quite an old friend, and Janie went so far as to say she 'didn't think he had been so very wicked'. Her case, perhaps the best that can be made, was that a treacherous or false streak in a character must come out in his artistic products. I suspect that to both Bussys, politics are the ultimate touchstone of everything. Dorothy said how shocked she was that Cortot[1] had been invited here to play in a concert and given an enthusiastic welcome. When I said I thought the consideration when inviting a pianist to play was how good he was, she merely smiled and said, 'I would much rather have had a German,' as if this was being very audacious. 'But of course have a German too, if he's good enough,' I said. To Janie intellectual activity that is not founded on politics is worth very little – 'academic thinking is dead, out of touch with what's going on.' And just look, what *is* going on in the world! War after war, violence, bitter building up of hatreds, righteous resentment because old hatreds are dropped. It is morally wrong to do so, the Bussys would have us say. On the same note there has recently been an outburst of indignation because the Crown Prince of Japan is arriving for the Coronation. Could anything be more futile?

June 4th

The Coronation has come roaring towards us like a lorry heard approaching up a steep incline, and now, thank God, has roared away again. There has been an almost maniac note of mass hysteria about it all – culminating in the high-pitched screams of false excitement of the BBC commentators. We walked to the village in the afternoon to see how Ham's Coronation was going. It might have been a hundred years ago. Outside the school some of the children were dancing round a decorated maypole, while opposite them sat the village old folk doubled up on kitchen chairs and perfectly silent. All the ages between had gone off to somewhere livelier, I suppose. The little girls wore pink paper roses in their hair, and when the

---

[1] Alfred Cortot (1877–1962) was the foremost French pianist of his time. During the Second World War he was appointed to an official position under the Nazi régime and after the war was forbidden to play in France for a period.

dance was over they lined up and sang *Land of Hope and Glory*. Ramshackle sports began in a rough field next door, organized by the 'Italian prisoner from Mr Hudson's'. No other representative of the 'gentry' being present, I was appalled to be asked to give away the prizes, and beat a hasty retreat.

The last item of this great day was a firework display at the Romillys's – very pretty as they burst over the water and dropped into it. Here we met Eardley and Eddy from Crichel, the Campbells and Connollys. Dora and Bunny [Romilly] tried on their coronets of red plush, fur and gold balls for our benefit, looking both splendid and absurd.

I suppose it has meant fun for a great many people, though I allowed myself to be momentarily overcome by dislike for the mumbo-jumbo of the service, with its 'holy oil' and the rest, as well as the noisy way the English always pat themselves on the back and say how well the monarchy 'works'. It's just harmless, that's all. Burgo of course is violently against it.

June 12th

To Benjamin Britten's Coronation opera, *Gloriana*, which we enjoyed a good deal more than *Billy Budd*. Apparently the aristocratic but unmusical first night audience were bewildered by the music and took the sight of Joan Cross as Queen Elizabeth I without her wig as a deliberate insult to Queen Elizabeth II. Met Heywood and Anne in the pub opposite where we saw the musical world working away like yeast, and many familiar faces including the interesting Celtic one of Myfanwy Piper framed in its curtains of straight hair. On the way home we stopped at Bob Gathorne-Hardy's to pick up Eddie to stay the weekend. He combined well with Noel Sandwith who came on Saturday. Eddie has become something of a caricature of his old self – in appearance a great fabulous bird, in character a mountain of pretty ruthless egotism, yet lovable and good company nonetheless. Though he never puts himself out for anyone else and is determined to have his own way, he is a genuinely affectionate, wicked, charming old monster. He is one of a good number of characters whose butter of affection is spread wide but thin, who is fond and appreciative of a great number of friends, but very deeply of few. Conversely, we see the narrow and deep type in Vanessa and Pansy Lamb.

Now we are alone again and must think very seriously about Ralph's health. I am impressed and moved by the uncomplaining patience with which he takes it all. A change of diet doesn't – alas – seem to be enough and he will have to take regular insulin, which it was hoped he might avoid. At the weekend there was talk of the Missing Diplomats and whether Donald Maclean was ever a homosexual. 'Oh, yes he was. I've been to bed with him myself,' said Eddie.

July 23rd

Back at Ham Spray after London and the Memoir Club. Somehow or other, but only just, I got my Memoir written in time, the effort leaving me electrically charged and thus ready to enjoy lunch with Clive, Freddie Ayer, Bunny and Angelica. It was enormous fun, and the contrast between Freddie's birdlike quickness and Bunny's soft deliberation was amusing to watch. At first communication between the two seemed impossible, the pace of one having no beat in common with the other. But after some preliminary skirmishing they got going – four semiquavers of Freddie's to one crotchet of Bunny's – and the resulting harmony seemed to satisfy them both, and was principally concerned with the Russian anarchists Bunny had once known. Angelica and Freddie, seated opposite each other, exchanged searching glances but hardly any words. When we left, Freddie and I got on the same bus. 'What did you think of Angelica?' I asked him. 'Striking but not beautiful,' he replied, to my surprise, as I thought she was looking marvellous.

I saw the Garnetts later on at the Memoir Club meeting, which took place in Vanessa and Duncan's new flat in Canonbury. Angelica was in a mood of apparent abandon, tossing back her wine, with flying hair. I talked to Leonard about his selection from Virginia's diaries, *A Writer's Diary*, which he has recently brought out, saying how immensely I admired and enjoyed it. What principles of selection had he followed? 'On the whole I kept to what concerned her work, her writing and reading. Of course there's a very great deal more, and of that a great deal which would cause acute pain to living people.' 'Yes,' I said; 'so I imagined, and was rather surprised you left in that amusing but unkind bit about X.' 'Oh is X still alive?' Leonard said. 'I thought she'd been dead for ages.' I told him how tantalizing it was to know of this hidden gold-mine, asked whether he meant to publish the whole eventually, and if so when? 'Do you think I shall live to read it?' He looked me up and down. 'I *think* you might just about manage to,' was his reply. An argument about the Bloomsbury aversion to accepting honours followed, something I have never understood. What is wrong about such an acknowledgement of their achievements? Why should writers and painters not receive the same ornaments or grace-notes as scientists and surgeons? But I was in a minority, Clive and Duncan being particularly averse to the idea, and seeming to imply that by so doing they would forfeit their independence in some way that I cannot understand.

My Memoir[1] had a surprising, and of course pleasing success; they are I must say an appreciative audience as a general rule, and laugh wherever it is possible to do so. Bunny insisted on carrying it away, saying he 'wanted his sons to know about the Marshall family'.

[One thing I always enjoyed at Memoir Club meetings was a chance to talk to Leonard. Otherwise our paths now seldom crossed. In the days before the War I would see him sometimes in the bookshop where I worked, or dining with Clive, and I was occasionally asked to dine with the Woolfs, or Ralph and I boldly invited them to Gordon Square.

I know from the stories told me by Ralph and other workers at the Hogarth Press that Leonard could at times fly into irrational rages. To me he always seemed as gloriously the same as some well-loved monument: there was the melodious, quavering voice that never altered its timbre nor lost its note of confidence in being right in an argument; the deliberate movements, the slow charming smile, the deeply grooved face, the steadfast gaze from his blue-grey eyes, the hair that still stood up in tufts like a schoolboy's even as it grew greyer. Much of his admirable *Autobiography* was derived from papers read at the Memoir Club – I can still hear his voice saying firmly, 'I was exceedingly intelligent.' I tremble to think that I argued with him more than once about G. E. Moore's *Principia Ethica*. As well attack the Bible to an Archbishop.

---

[1] Foundation of the first chapter of *Memories* (Phoenix).

I remember a pre-war evening when the Woolfs were dining with us, and Virginia was giving an astonishing display of trying to charm the company and make us look ridiculous at the same time by her usual attack on 'the younger generation', and certainly succeeding in the first. In the latter, however, she was worsted by Alix's logic, and Leonard took her by the arm saying 'Come on, Virginia, don't disgrace the older generation'.

It was easy to see what rocklike support he gave to that brilliant, uneasy mind.

Whatever she wore, and sometimes it was very strange, Virginia could not help looking infinitely distinguished, with her thin beautiful face, deep-set eyes, and the accompaniment of a remarkably low-pitched, electrifying voice.

I only once or twice visited the Woolfs at Rodmell, and then it was generally from Charleston. One occasion gave me a chance to see another side of Virginia's character. It took place soon after the deaths of Lytton and Carrington and she showed her sensitive kindness to me in ways I shall not forget. How glad I am I have survived to read the whole of her Diary for I believe most of it to be her masterpiece.]

August 29th

Raymond arrived last night and this morning the three of us are to begin on our drive north for the Edinburgh Festival, leaving Burgo in charge of the house, chickens and Minnie's forthcoming *accouchement*. 'My motoring friend' (a fellow-student from MacNalty's) is coming to stay while we are gone.

[Because it altered the course of Janetta's life entirely, the distressing fact must here be recorded that on the very same day that her baby, Rose, was born, Derek telephoned to say that he had fallen in love with someone else and intended to throw in his lot with her, leaving Janetta still weak from the birth and completely shattered by this cruel desertion. Ralph and I felt very far from clinically objective about this harrowing situation, and it was some time before the seed of relief that the marriage was over could develop into a thriving plant. We had never happily accepted it. Of course we did our best to support and sympathize. Janetta told us that she thought Derek broke the news as he did out of a feeling that if one is going to be beastly one had better be *really* beastly. With amazing fortitude she wrestled with the practical problems confronting her, moved into a furnished house and sent for Nicky and Georgiana from France.]

September 1st

Our drive north was taken gently and well-furnished with 'sights'. Raymond chose Kedleston and Chatsworth – Adam's Kedleston is proud without any hint of a warmer attitude to life, its nose (figuratively speaking) well up in the air; Chatsworth more splendid, with its fantastically beautiful gardens set in a wide valley, great sheets of water, fountains, pollarded avenues and metal trees spouting water from their twigs.

My recollections of the Lake District were so vivid that I feared it might prove a dreadful disappointment. But no, our drive along the shores of Windermere and Ullswater brought back in rich and exact detail all my earliest pleasures in nature. Green and glistening after rain, fresh-smelling, clear as crystal yet with floating scarves of mist, the emerald grass tightly drawn over knobbly limestone, streams rushing downhill between clumps of ferns – leaving this beautiful landscape was like leaving childhood for a second time. We arrived at Heriot Row, Edinburgh, that evening, to be warmly welcomed by Colin and Clodagh [Mackenzie].

[The high-grade musical pleasures of the Festival were well suited by the noble architecture and pure air of the town. We listened to the Virtuosi di Roma, *Idomeneo*, a recital by Irmgard Seefried, and Bruno Walter conducting Brahms. Much social life included a champagne supper party given by the Mackenzies.]

September 12th: Ham Spray

Back by tea-time, finding Burgo smiling and apparently pleased to see us, having put flowers in vases, seen to Minnie's *accouchement* and the execution of superfluous kittens, and enjoyed his visit from 'my friend', who had left two days earlier. Our Scottish stay was an interlude of pure pleasure. After so much spoiling I am reluctant to start scrabbling back among the knobbly pebbles of daily life.

September 13th

Visit from the Cochemés. He has got the job he wanted and they are off to Amman in a few days. I love his vivid phrases and charming French accent. Of Wynne he said, 'I like the albuminous look in his blue eyes, which seems to have lasted over from babyhood.' And of crayfish: 'They go forwards slowly and then much faster backwards – like a very nervous, very clever young man.' Burgo made himself agreeable to the visitors and offered to help me in the garden. Why then did he say suddenly in the middle of a game of croquet: 'I can't enjoy anything'? And how could it fail to give a blow to one's spirits? But Philip Toynbee, at dinner with the Campbells gave him the right foretaste of Oxford in a most amusing style.

October 8th

A new era begins. Today we drove Burgo to Oxford to be installed at Christ Church; some anxiety of course there was, but as the day wore on it seemed that Burgo was welcoming his new life, advancing towards it where he has often shown signs of retreat. We saw with relief that he began to take command of the situation as soon as he found his name in white letters painted over the door, and even more when his scout appeared and said 'Are you Mr Partridge, Sir? I shall be looking after you now,' and went on to produce a lot of useful information. Burgo's rooms (two of them) were large and sympathetic if bleak, their furniture and decoration that of a past age, when a civilized life was more esteemed. I went happily to sleep that night, glad that Burgo was launched on the ideal life for a young man and at a suitable age – seventeen. However Ralph was reminded too vividly perhaps by our glimpse of Oxford of its stresses and strains, and had a restless night worrying on Burgo's behalf.

October 12th

Burgo's first letter from Oxford was an antidote to spectral premonitions: 'I have got to know two other people on the same staircase. Everybody seems extremely friendly and nice. The room is not at all cold once the fire has been lit. There is plenty on my bed, anyway kind Rachel has given me a hot-water bottle. I have repulsed the Rugger and Soccer canvassers fairly easily and ordered *The Times*.'

Driving to tea at Lambourn today Ralph and I got out and spent a few moments in a wood where dark moist ivy made a carpet beneath tall horse-chestnut trees, whose yellow leaves drained of sap hung like the great blunt-fingered hands of workmen. I got back into the car with a chestnut in my hand, so sweetly glossy and giving such a pang of voluptuous pleasure that I wondered whether it is these particles of sensation rather than cerebral activity that makes life worth living. But what would Freddie Ayer say, who thinks the emotions are equivalent to inarticulate screams?

December 4th

Burgo back from Oxford. So now I must see if I can keep up my conversation with these ruled pages through the Vacation – as it now has to be called. Is it a mere habit that makes me do it? Or is there really some salutary effect in the mere expression of thoughts and description of events in words? An entirely selfish one at all events.

[Breaking all past habits, Ralph, Burgo and I spent the Christmas of 1953 in Paris. We had intended to fly (it would have been only the third flight of our lives), but a dense white fog and a strike of security staff at Le Bourget forced us to change to sea and train, and we chugged across the Channel lulled to sleep by the soporific hooting of foghorns. It was the first time we had spent more than one night in the grey spaciousness of the city since the war. Our hotel was the pretty little Beaux Arts where Oscar Wilde died, now kept by a distinguished-looking elderly lady with a stick; its liftless spiral staircase led up and up to an elegant round skylight.

Boris and Maroussa called for us that evening. Instead of imagined burglars, Maroussa has now a real horror to contend with – she has to have an operation for cancer. Strangely enough, this has given her fresh vivacity and she is as brave as a lion. With them we went to the Deux Magots and the restaurant called the Cochon de Lait, where we dined off sucking pig with buckwheat and other indigestible Russian accoutrements. Next day we went to see them in Boris's studio in the Boulevard Arago, the centre where his creations have for many years taken shape. It looked as though it had remained the same, and nothing in it had been moved or dusted, for fifty years at least. On the vast studio table lay a mosaic in progress and some cartoons, while variously coloured little cubes of marble and glass lay all around, spilled on to the floor or were heaped in sacks like Ali-Baba's jewels. The high walls, on which hung pictures by Henry Lamb and Man Ray and more cartoons of Boris's own, led up to a gallery where he and Maroussa slept.

We had a day at Versailles, a morning at the Louvre and a good deal of shopping, Burgo laying out a large sum on ties from Sulka.

Returning to the hotel next morning with *The Times* Ralph told me that dear Molly had died. We feel intense sadness and disbelief that we shall see her no more.

Our last dinner in Paris was at Laperouse, an old-fashioned restaurant of high quality and restrained dignity, recommended to us by Derek. Our menu was *Oeufs Laperouse*, followed by 'the' chicken in 'its' tarragon sauce and a Grand Marnier soufflé, during which we had quite a lively conversation about values. Both Ralph and Burgo appeared to think their place could be entirely taken by cold reason and attacked me for 'highmindedness'. All right, reason is the sausage-machine but whence comes the meat to be passed through it? I defended myself as best I could by saying that it was priggish and puritanical to shun values out of fear of being too priggish and puritanical.]

December 28th: Ham Spray

Arriving home we found the saddest postcard *d'outre-tombe* imaginable awaiting us, written in a quavering hand:

> Darling Ralph and Frances, I am very ill, and sad to be writing that soon I expect it must be my farewell. Perhaps you know it may not be quite at once and so then it will be what is called the beginning of the end. So with all my love to both dearests and all my thanks for the lovely times I have had with you, your most loving Molly.

We shed tears of sorrow, and bitterness too – for before we left for Paris, hearing that she was gravely ill we had ordered a very large bunch of flowers to be delivered at Garrick's villa. It would have been a small comfort to think we might have given her the tiniest last pleasure, but those brutes Harrods, hurrying with the mince-pies and turkeys, deprived us of it by arriving too late.

1954

January 6th

Janetta came to us for the New Year weekend. She is back in trousers, she is back in her original self. An appetite for life is returning to her, but is not much stronger than her appetite for food, which probably symbolizes it. She is very thin, even fragile-looking and seems to have a pleasure in doing without things like sleep or food, which reminds me alarmingly of Jan. One day, awakening from a short nap on the sofa, she began talking about the importance of loyalty to people you were fond of, especially if you were aware of their failings and that not everyone liked them. She applied this to Sonia, who had given her immense support but been accused of battening on disaster by several. She admitted that Sonia had been bent on separating her from Robert. I expect she knows that we like Sonia as little as she likes us; Ralph believes that it is the neurotic side of her character – and the unhappy one too – that damages her friends.

We went over to Stokke one evening, where the Connollys, Freddie and Joan Rayner were staying. Mary was dressed in her new 'Top' covered with pink sequins, a present from Robin. 'Oh, is that your top?' said Ralph gallantly, 'can't I see your ... er ...?' Cyril and Freddie were both vain enough to enjoy the suggestion that they might have been included in the New Year honours. Cyril and Barbara went early to bed and the rest settled round the fire. Visual images were the subject of discussion. I asked Freddie – who rejects them – could he not visualize Mary's face when she wasn't there? 'I know it's round and pink, with blue eyes,' he said, 'but those are concepts.' 'Well, how do you think of blue?' Freddie was now inclined to say that we who believed we had visual images were mistaken, that if we had them they were not coloured, and that the same went for dreams. I find it quite extraordinary that so clever a man can say such things, but perhaps he is colour-blind, as he described Barbara Connolly's coat as green when in fact it was red! As we left he bid us goodbye 'to your coloured dreams'.

When Freddie was at Luggala, Robert – a little piqued at having driven him through acres of wild and beautiful scenery without getting a response – asked him, 'Don't you enjoy looking at all this?' 'Not really,' Freddie answered. 'When I see those sheep grazing on a mountain I at once start wondering what they are thinking about – or whether indeed it's proper to say they *think* at all.'

A return visit by the Campbells and Freddie next day, full of complaints of the Connollys. They had insisted on bringing their coati but it was not allowed to sleep in the nice hutch lined with straw prepared for it and had to share their bedroom, where of course it shat on the coverlet. Barbara sulked in her room and refused to come down to meals. She had asked to be taken to the early train on Monday, which meant getting up at seven.

When Monday came and we drove Janetta to the station, we found the whole Stokke party pacing up and down the platform, their faces lavender with cold. Robin told me in tones of stifled horror that they had got up at seven and called Barbara, only to be told by Cyril that she was sleepy and had decided to take the *next* train. So here they were, but Barbara refused to get into it, saying she had left some kind of basket behind at Stokke. 'She's going on the 1.17 though,' Robin said between clenched teeth.

January 26th

It was a surprise to see the garden covered in snow when we pulled back our curtains. Already it was two inches deep and still falling. While we were in the bath the electricity failed, which always raises a ghost of impotent panic; then comes the positive physical pleasure of making a quick blaze in the dining-room fireplace and seeing a frying-pan with eggs and bacon on it. Round the garden to look at the humped vegetables and prettily outlined trees and bushes. Needing an indoor task I started sorting the great trunk of letters to Carrington that has lain for a long while in the flower-room. They made me dreadfully sad: such feelings of poignant loneliness or ill-usage were set down on the fading pages, and all of it over, and many of the writers dead though their voices go on screaming silently.

January 31st

Last night was the coldest yet. Going to fill my hot-water bottle at midnight, I was horrified to find a 'Moujik's moustache' (Ralph's name for water frozen to a *double* drip when the tap is turned full on), and though I stood beside it for twenty minutes no greater flow appeared. The electric fire burning all through the night cast its friendly glow on our walls, but this morning – total lack of hot water. Wilde went up into the roof. No go. Plumber telephoned for. No go either. My hands ached with cold before breakfast was cooked. Later the cold water joined the hot, so we are without a drop, and worst of all there is none in the lavatories. Over all stretches a sky as cruelly blue as that on a Swiss wintersports postcard; on the verandah icicles two foot long sparkle in the sun. Wicked old Minnie thought fit to lie on my bird-table among the crumbs. The mind freezes like the body, and becomes incapable of any but the most prosaic reflections. Mary telephoned, 'Can we come and have a bath? We've been frozen for several days,' and though we had to disappoint them they gallantly said they would come to supper. It was delightful to have company in our igloo over a makeshift but piping hot meal.

February 4th

The water is 'through'! Long may it be so! The plumber has been, and our pipes are now cased up in wood and sawdust; yesterday evening I revelled and wallowed in a hot bath, emerging soaped, scented and invigorated. This morning I measured the longest icicle on the verandah – it is nearly *five feet* long, strong and ribbed, and tapering to a fine point.

February 8th

The thaw has come, and we set out for London in steady rain, driving through water over sheer ice. How we enjoyed everything! – the warm railway carriage; the intellectual-looking fellow passenger who put in suggestions for the crossword puzzle, and raised his hat with a polite 'Good morning!' on leaving us.

Left our things at Janetta's and went to lunch with Julia and Lawrence. The crisis at the Tate Gallery fills their thoughts. Julia, cooking away in the background, explained that her watch was an hour slow – and lunch indeed appeared about two. Meanwhile Lawrence flapped out of the bedroom wearing a jacket and pyjama legs; he is put to bed by Julia at every moment when the Trustees are not meeting, fed with glasses of milk and carefully ministered to. When we got back to Alexander Square Janetta had just arrived back from Paris. We spent the evening with her *and* Robert oddly enough, as Janetta had asked him to a drink, thinking 'we would like to see him'. Freddie Ayer had been invited to dinner, so it was natural to ask Robert to stay on, as he did, though 'natural' is not the right word. Their manner to each other was friendly, even polite, but controlled, only once sending off a spark on the quite impersonal topic of whether the new magazine *Encounter* was anti-Communist propaganda, run on American money, or not. Robert thought it was, and that it attacked Communism for all the wrong reasons, 'for improving the lot of the lower classes, instead of for *not* improving them'. I do not see the faintest chance of these two coming together again – though neither of them is easily eradicated from the system.

February 20th: Ham Spray

A happy morning, turning into a day that sparkled like a diamond. Saxon was with us, and we sat out until lunch time. Ralph accused Saxon of not eating enough.

'Perhaps I don't eat enough,' he said. 'But you see I don't really want to go on very much – except when I look at something like that view.' It's about the most intimate remark I remember him making to us, and certainly the saddest. However I was thinking very different thoughts – that I was glad to be alive, that life still held much to enjoy.

After lunch we drove to the Gibbet Hill and walked along the Downs. The beauty of the day, the soft clear distance visible so far in every direction, had brought out a mixed bag of fellow mortals – country gentry with their dogs, two Irish priests (bigoted-looking, blind-eyed) and a covey of schoolboys. I left the other two and walked home alone. The dewpond was full to the brim with yesterday's rain, reflecting the blue sky among its golden rushes. When I turned through the gate towards home, I entered a silence so utter that I could hear the voices of the cowman's children in our farmyard. It was four o'clock, the light softened, the trees grew feathery and pigeons wheeled above the corduroy fields. My huge shadow stood like Napoleon on the brink of light and darkness, and then paced downhill ahead of me.

Saxon in very good form this evening, talking about various objects of his love – Plato, Spanish towns, Kubla Khan.

March 8th

Janie has been here talking a lot about two who were (and very likely still are) her heroes: T. S. Eliot and Gide. Of Eliot's strange ménage with John Hayward,[1] she said that she thought he was paying a debt by looking after John – pushing him

---

[1] Writer and biographer, suffering from a degenerative disease.

about in his wheelchair and allowing himself to be silenced in all conversation – as atonement for his deep sense of guilt over putting his late wife in an asylum. Where, Janie says, she certainly belonged. It had been a queer marriage: he picked her up on Brighton pier.

Gide's marriage is a stranger story. He had had no sex of any sort until he was twenty-three, when he went to Egypt and 'almost accidentally' went to bed with a boy. Soon after this he met Wilde and Lord Alfred Douglas and took to buggery with enthusiasm. Meanwhile he declared his love to a beautiful, clever female cousin who adored him. They married, but he decided that she was much too pure to want sex, it would be an insult even to suggest it, and with no previous explanation the marriage began and ended in perfect chastity. He said he was not 'in love' with his boys, only with his wife, but she was horrified by his homosexual affairs, longed for a normal married life and children, and was most deeply hurt of all when he had a brief passage with another woman to whom he gave a child 'as a sort of present'.

March 11th

Eardley described a Crichel visit that went wrong in the excellent phrase 'there was no love in the room'. I thought of this when we returned from Bunny and Angelica's Anniversary party at Hilton, where the reverse was manifestly the case. We had wondered if we were mad to drive right across England and spend the night in an inn in St Ives but how glad I am we did. There were quite a lot of 'good grey heads' and white ones too hinting at the last volume of Proust, but also a large ingredient of youth. Of Bunny's boys, Richard is newly engaged to beautiful and sweet Jane; Angelica's four little girls, wearing their party dresses and highly excited, revolved among us with dishes of caviare and smoked salmon. Looking down one saw an angelic face looking up enquiringly from waist level, munching hard. There was music: William and Angelica played an oboe sonata: Leslie Hotson[1] sang American songs; the little girls played solemnly on recorders. Duncan and Morgan greeted each other like survivors on the same raft.

Now we are back again. Ralph looks well and cheerful, and has had a good report from his doctor.

[When early in their married life Bunny and Ray Garnett were looking for somewhere to settle in the country, they saw and fell in love with a picture of Hilton Hall, near St Ives, Hunts., in the pages of *Country Life*. It was a three-storey, seventeenth-century house, neither large nor pretentious but beautifully proportioned, facing due north through handsome tall iron gates. It was Cromwell country, and the pretty cottages making a distant ring round the large village green seemed hardly to have changed since his day; in fact, when Bunny bought one of them to save it from destruction the men working on the job found frescoes portraying Moll Cutpurse, highway-woman of the period, while on the green itself was an inexplicable old maze. One usually entered the house through the back door into the busy, untidy kitchen where one or two Siamese cats would be prowling and wailing. Many of the rooms had panelled walls; the ground floor was paved with flagstones covered in Kelim rugs, and a staircase of dark wood led

---

[1] American professor of literature.

up to the bedrooms. A collection of bronze and stone heads stared through blank eyes at the visitor from the hall or the garden wall; most were the work of Stephen Tomlin – there were Bunny himself, Duncan, Vanessa and Virginia. The vast beamed fireplaces in drawing-room and dining-room gave out virtually no heat at all from their log fires in winter, even at close range. That was the snag – Hilton was the coldest house I have ever spent a night in, and I used to smuggle an extra eiderdown in the back of the car to help suppress its penetrating chill. There were lovely things – early paintings by Duncan, Bunny's fine library supplemented by his father's and mother's books, Angelica's piano, harp and cello. She was always adding beauty in the form of patchwork curtains and covers, and my two nephews built on a panelled writing-room for Bunny with astonishing proficiency – yet there was no denying that Hilton had at times a sad atmosphere. Was it the dank East Anglian climate, the knowledge that cabbage fields stretched away in all directions over the perfectly flat land? I remember cheerful days in summer, playing bowls or badminton in the back garden, where there was also a big old pigeon-house and a home-made swimming pool and where the four charming little girls and their step-brother, William, were usually enjoying themselves. Ralph and I spent many weekends at Hilton and there wasn't a soul in it we weren't delighted to see; but it was a house of moods, and at times a mute hush could stifle the Garnett family's natural animation.]

March 16th

Robert for the weekend. I lay awake for some hours thinking of his views on bringing up children. He believes that adults should devote themselves entirely to their children's happiness. 'Then,' said I, 'you would have the paradox of each generation focusing on the next and never leading their own lives.' 'Ah, but it's never been done,' he said. 'It would be well worth giving it a try for two or three generations.' He is violently against schools and their stereotyped constriction.

  Next day Burgo came back from Oxford, lively, talkative and seeming interested in his work, friendly to Ralph and me.

March 17th

What do *I* care, I said to myself reading Gibbon, how, when and where the Norman invasion of Sicily began and ended? Why on earth bother to read about it? And went on reading entranced.

  Ralph has been going to the Winchester Assizes to hear the trial of Lord Montagu and others for buggery. It was not a very moving tale that he had to tell. The two little tarts from the RAF made a pitiful showing in the witness-box, saving their skins at the expense of their three victims, Montagu, Pitt-Rivers and Wildeblood, who sat with folded arms in the pillory. Wildeblood is the most to be pitied. Ralph thinks he will get a stiffer sentence than the other two; he has admitted to being 'in love' with one of the cadets. It may ruin his promising journalist's career, hard cheese indeed when no one can conceivably be said to have suffered in the very least. James Macgibbon has suggested Ralph writing a book about homosexuality. I wish he would, but doubt it.

March 23rd

Just lately the atom bomb has refused to be ignored – the hydrogen bomb rather, which the Americans (in the course of letting it off in the Pacific) have found to be about twice as powerful as they expected. Ralph has for some time been calling to me to 'think about the atom bomb', and I have stubbornly plunged my head into the sand. What use to think when there is nothing we can do? What use to think when thinking must perforce reduce one to despair? Better to go on living as best we may on the last feet of mossy turf on the edge of a precipice, enjoying its texture and softness but never looking over the edge. Yet Ralph is right of course. The human spirit revolts at not facing facts, is not content to be shut up in a lunatic asylum happily conscious of being Catherine the Great, any more than it shuns all knowledge of such outrages as the Montagu trial. So yes, we *must* think about the atom bomb.

April 14th

Why, I wonder, did I wake in the small hours of this morning to one of those unexpected and acutely painful 'moments of truth'? In a flash I saw the pre-cariousness of happiness – of mine, of Ralph's and Burgo's, of the world's existence, and saw it very very clearly. Impelled by some strange impulse I got up quietly so as not to disturb Ralph, and crept downstairs to the music room, where I now sit amongst last night's debris, with Minnie still folded in sleep on the back of the armchair. I saw the start of another perfect day through the window but it gave me no pleasure. I thought that to be a practising hedonist was an enormous gamble; happiness to him fulfils the same role as faith plays to the Christian, and loss of happiness is like loss of faith. The Christian says, 'With my body I thee worship' in the marriage service. The hedonist is all the time saying 'With my happiness I worship the world', but when it fails him he is clueless.

I took a life of John Stuart Mill out of the shelf and began reading with growing interest.

May 8th

Janetta came last weekend. She, Ralph and I spent an afternoon of watery sunlight walking in Collingbourne Woods, among huge primroses, bluebells, violets and anemones; following a trail of animal excrement to a badger's lair, and picking up globular flints in the hope that – like a little local boy – we would find one containing a cache of ancient coins. Later at Stokke, I thought how quickly one would be charmed and interested if one saw Janetta for the first time, standing as she now was in front of the fire in her thick white sweater and tartan trousers making her characteristic clawing gestures in the air with her hands.

Next came Robert, and both have been entirely delightful companions. Wherein, one cannot help asking, lies the gap between them? Robert seemed in good spirits, working hard, full of conversation, realistic, entertaining us with his imitations, collapsing into giggles. He was summoned to the War Office last week to be interrogated about his acquaintance with Melinda Maclean, and confronted with a photostat copy of a letter to her from himself. As she has now re-joined Donald in Russia, Robert thought it probable that they were combing her 'contacts' for possible Communist agents, but the idea that they might suspect him of being one evidently doesn't alarm him.

May 29th

To Oxford to see Burgo, and after lunch to watch the Eights-week races among crowds of variously elegant and dandified young men, many wearing beautiful snow-white flannels, straw hats and huge button-holes. There was a great feeling of youth, high-spirits and promiscuous élan; also a lot of pretty girls with peach-like complexions and ugly clothes. Drizzle fell sparsely, the river glittered like tin under a grey sky flaming with sunlight at the horizon; the races created intermittent moments of excitement and roars of 'House! House!' like a cheerful dog barking. Ralph wore his Leander tie, and in the boat-house we saw an oar with his name painted on it. An afternoon of youthful glamour and gaiety.

But soon after we had got home poor Ralph was seized by griping pains, which came and went and came again with such excruciating intensity that I managed to get him to go to bed and telephoned the doctor. He came out armed with morphia and confident of his diagnosis – kidney stone. Next day Ralph was perfectly comfortable, and saying that waking to find himself without pain was the keenest physical pleasure he had ever had in his life. Meanwhile I am still suffering from shock at seeing him convulsed with such fearful agony. There is no threat of the knife, thank God, but he is to have an X-ray to investigate what is happening in his kidney. I dread the dawdling paraphernalia of medical reports. Among our friends Janie has been the most knowledgeably sympathetic, having nursed Gide through an attack when he was over 70. He said, '*C'est pire qu'une accouchement,*' though I wonder how he thought he knew.

Simon Bussy has died in his loony bin.

June 5th

Ralph had his X-ray yesterday, but we shall of course hear nothing for a while and must try not to behave like reasonable animals. Ralph observed that 'the radiographer was a grey-haired lesbian, taking every chance of paying Men out for what they had not done to her, and cooing sweet nothings to the pretty girl assistant.' 'We are told to cut the patient in half,' she said, savagely tightening a strap round his waist so that he couldn't breathe. I sat in the tiny waiting-room watching the patients go in and out – a pregnant woman, a limping elderly man, a whimpering child. At last my particular sausage was ejected from the machine and we ate some belated lunch in the car.

June 14th

Ralph has had no pain for nearly a week and we both faced this morning's X-ray report with some confidence. But standing on the landing while he spoke on the telephone to the doctor I heard him say 'Oh. So you think we had better not go to Sweden.' (We had a tentative plan to go with the Crichel boys to see the eclipse of the sun there.) Ralph is a good deal cast down, and suffering from regret in the form of a craving to put time back physically to a period when an unpleasant fact was *not* a fact. But the position is not it seems to be taken as serious, and for my part I cannot feel really depressed when Ralph says as he did today, that my being so extra kind to him had made his life more than ever worth living.

However, I am jaded today after two late nights and very little sleep. Janetta came here last night with Ralph Jarvis, an easy, pleasant, civilized man whose humorous vein reminds one that he is a relation of the Gathorne-Hardy family. Ralph and I both think he is greatly taken with her. Sat up till one o'clock talking, and got up this morning early to see them off. The night before we were at Stokke when Wynne and Kitty [Godley] came in after dinner with the light of battle in their eyes and fiery cheeks. Leaning back in his chair, Wynne said that they had been quarrelling because Kitty 'refused to hand up her friends' to him: 'If I like them they will also be my friends. If I don't she must give them up. I gave her *all* my friends.'

'Yes – but I like them,' murmured Kitty in a voice that brushed one's ear like swansdown. Wynne invoked his masculinity, and claimed that she must accept his view or do without him. Someone put in a plea for reason. 'I'm sick of reason!' said Wynne. 'I'm not rational man, I'm anthropological man.' I put in a defence of reason and Robin came up with his present craze for 'culture patterns'; Ben Nicolson added quiet and kindly support of women as deserving to be treated as rational beings – but to think it should be necessary! The argument was only about three-quarters serious and it now slid off crab-wise into Aesthetics.

We have had a letter from Alix describing various new physical troubles, and then continuing: 'life does become increasingly hospitalized as one gets on, and yet I like it better every day.' It is a magnificent declaration from someone who has just been through several medical horrors, who is getting old, never sees anyone but James, and whose sensual pleasures are moderate and circumscribed. I find it ringing in my head as I go about each day's menial tasks, and it makes me feel ashamed of myself.

June 16th

Mary rang up to tell us that Janetta had been taken to the London Clinic for an operation last night. A telephone call to the clinic was not very reassuring. 'Oh yes, she's had her operation ... quite satisfactory ... no, she won't be able to speak on the telephone yet ... in a few days perhaps ... Are you a relation? ... The surgeon is with her now.' All this left us much disquieted. Next day, before I could ring up again her own weak, quavering voice came sadly through. She had become suddenly very ill on Friday night with a high temperature and bad pain. 'Peritonitis,' the tiny tearful voice went on. 'They didn't know what it would be when they put me under – probably appendix, but they have taken *most* of my insides out. I thought I was dying and I didn't greatly care, and when I woke and found I had it all to do again I felt faintly disappointed.' Next day she rang again, better and voice stronger.

June 23rd

We've been to London to visit Janetta and spent over an hour with the sweet touching girl, who is mending fast.

Fetched Burgo from Oxford. Tea on the lawn; unable to leave the beauty of the evening, we sat out until the last rays of the sun had left the pampas grass and the long shadows were streaming over the surface of the hay field. I don't think Burgo feels he has failed in his prelims, but he showed me the papers – they look terribly difficult.

July 2nd

Ralph Jarvis motored Janetta down to convalesce with us here. We wanted above all to have everything calm (one of her favourite words) and welcoming; her bedroom looks very fresh in its new wallpaper of red rosebuds on a white ground. How maddening, therefore, that the electricity should suddenly fail. I was the first to fuss, Ralph followed, and then we fussed in unison, preparing to light a fire and cook the dinner on it. But ten minutes after their arrival the electricity came back, Janetta was looking pale but lively, and we are *so* pleased to have her. Put her to bed and after a meal of soup, crab mayonnaise and strawberries we all went and talked to her until midnight.

Ralph J. is more amiable and at home than ever, and has asked to come back and visit her. Goodness knows what he and she are in for. What a relief it is that perfect thought transference doesn't subsist between human beings; it's better far that we have to go on straining our mental antennae to read the signs of those curious clock dials – people's faces, whose hands are sometimes set to show the true time, and at others express deliberate disguises, and where the desire to communicate is often in complete conflict with the desire to conceal.

A telegram from Burgo who is in Oxford for Desmond Guinness's wedding: 'Seen Prelim results. Have passed. Returning six Monday.'

July 8th

Yesterday the Brenans arrived to stay. Gamel has dyed her hair a harsh metallic black, which entirely misinterprets her character; her pretty cream-coloured hands loaded with old rings, however, emphasize the passive elegance of someone who never makes demands but effortlessly arouses other people's desires to take care of her and spare her trouble. While Ralph drove them over to see the Pritchetts, I had a somewhat door-opening conversation about personal relations with Burgo, who returned from a London jaunt yesterday looking very handsome and as if he had had a good time, yet who wanted to know why life was so difficult? I suggested that love and hate tended to get entwined in his nature, and that sometimes he reacted with the inappropriate emotion. 'Well, perhaps, maybe –'

Rather like a clown in a harlequinade, I feel as if I had been juggling with different heavy objects – Burgo's moods, Janetta's health, the Brenans' comforts, and the telephone which never stops ringing. All Janetta's admirers have got on her scent.

Today broke hot and heavy with innumerable flies. Something of a Chekhov atmosphere brooded over our garden with ambulant couples stooping to study a flower. Venturing further, we took Gerald to see the orchids now blooming on Ham Hill – the Fragrant, Pyramid, Burnt stick, and even the Musk, which he had never seen before. Returned to the cool green arbor we have carved out of the weeping ash, where we had tea and discussed hospitality. Gerald said (truthfully) that he preferred receiving it to giving it; Gamel (untruthfully?) that she liked it the other way round; and both produced many reasons why with their five servants in Spain they found it impossible to have anyone to a meal.

Later came the Hills in Janetta's car. Anne has become a splendid old-fashioned bluestocking, and engaged us in a long gossip about Trelawney, Byron, Shelley, the Neapolitan child, et cetera. Burgo is now tapping on his typewriter upstairs; a heavy silence hangs over the fields and trees; even the flies are too sluggish to bother us.

July 12th

Janetta lay on the chaise-longue in the sun turning over her problems and helping us to turn over ours. Hers are the most pressing. Having tried every motor-drivers' examining board in turn to get herself a test, she has so far failed to find one, and after frantic telephoning ran out in tears to Ralph who was picking peas. She needs to have her car for her stay in the house she has rented for herself and the children in Cagnes, and constant jangling of hows and whys in her head have left her looking iller than when she first came to us. I seem to hear the rattle of wooden beads such as children have on play-pens, as we clicked the tangible segments of our problems to and fro, trying out different combinations to reach a solution. Ralph is already envisaging that he will 'have to' drive her down, something I refuse to pity him for.

Meanwhile Janetta has gone off for a night in London to go to a 'grand party decorated in jungle style with about twenty stuffed monkeys', looking much too fragile in her best silk frock; and I have woken feeling stronger after a splendid sleep, and have got out the index box and made a start on the next volume of Freud which arrived two days ago.

July 18th

Burgo has gone off to stay with the Garnetts for the Hinchingbrooke ball. A slight breeze as to whether he should take his dinner-jacket or hire tails was settled by the news that white tie 'and decorations' were to be worn.

The Gowings are here on their way to Stokke. I walked with Julia up the downs. If it weren't such a nuisance her new craze for food faddism would be a matter of high comedy; she is quite obsessed with the vital need for green vegetables – turnip tops for preference. 'Do you think we shall get enough green vegetables at Mary's?' she asked me. 'I'm really very worried about it. Could I ask her if I might just cook myself a cabbage every day? It's so *odd* of Mary,' (I was vividly reminded of Julia's own Mrs Thatcham)[1] 'She ought to see those girls of hers haven't had the right diet by the shape they have become.'

July 22nd

To London for the Memoir Club and to see Janetta's new abode in Montpelier Square, an experience that has the effect of witnessing a rising temperature. By afternoon I was about 103° myself, after driving with her to Maples and spending over an hour helping her choose beds, mattresses and pillows. Back at Alexander Square, the telephone rang, rang, rang. Likewise the door-bell, and I let in Ralph Jarvis dressed as a city man in bowler hat and rolled umbrella. He took Janetta off to *Rosenkavalier*, and when I returned from the Memoir Club I found them munching in the kitchen, Janetta looking exhausted and with a headache but busy cooking eggs. I wasn't sure that Ralph was being as supporting as he might, or realizing that she must leave London as soon as possible – it's killing her. She had miraculously passed her driving test and could go next week, but obviously needs

[1] In *Cheerful Weather for the Wedding.*

a companion to share the driving. Ralph's line was 'driving would simply *kill* you, and what would poor Nannie do then, poor thing?'

July 23rd

Eating breakfast with Janetta, the sun streaming through the window, we discussed the question of who should drive out with her. Robert? He had agreed when the idea was first put to him, but retracted next day, saying he couldn't undertake to go lightly as it were. She felt it would be bad behaviour to try to persuade him, so quickly withdrew. They have been meeting with apparent friendliness; all the same he said no, and work was the reason he gave and is now, I believe, his guiding principle. I was cast down to see this shining chink close.

July 25th: Ham Spray

Incessant drenching rain, beating and soaking. The madonna lilies lie prostrate; it is disgustingly cold. Lord what a summer! A call from Sonia Orwell, saying Janetta's last possible co-driver had fallen through. 'Just as I thought,' said Ralph, 'I always knew I should have to go.' He is inclined to preen himself on travelling with a lovely young woman who will be taken for his wife. 'More likely your daughter,' I say snubbingly. So it is now fixed. I hate his taking flights, going long drives without me, but I know that is absurd; it is the right thing for him to do and it is mainly my doing that he goes.

August 27th

The pace of life this summer hasn't slackened, and like the Red Queen I race along, never quite keeping up with events and certainly never having the time for rumination which I know to be vital. The unspeakable weather goes on – rain, rain, rain, wind, cold. If it clears for an instant – flies! An Oxford doctor says that it has caused depression acute enough for several of his patients to consult him about it. V.S.P. on the telephone: 'Oh yes, I have my revolver always at my elbow.'

The weekend was spent at Lawford Hall arriving in the evening in a peachy glow which bathed the fine old house and its romantic garden in warmth and beauty. Phil and Phyllis are turning it from a melancholy Elizabethan showpiece into a growing organism possessed of beauty and comfort. Ralph and I have a palatial suite, furnished with taste, and our fellow-guest is our dear friend Eddy [Sackville-West]. As for the foundations on which Phil has striven to build it – they are a set of views and values as archaic as those of our grandparents, and Eddy's are just as bad. Phyllis? I don't know; I think she has accepted Phil's standards because it would be too painful to fight against them. Compulsory games was the topic at breakfast one day, and no word raised in opposition to them. 'What, even football?' I asked hopefully. 'Oh *yes*,' said Eddy and Phil in unison, 'boys like it, and anyway even if they don't they must be kept out of mischief. They have no idea what to do with themselves and they must have exercise.' I could hardly believe my ears, but was relieved to remember that Eddy spent most of his spare time at Eton playing the piano and reaching an almost professional standard; also that he must have been excused rough games from delicate health. At tea-time we got on to the importance of class distinctions, the Royal family, the Church and the supremacy of the English over all other nations. ('They are the only people with imagination'!!) Appalled and stifled, while the others trooped off to church on Sunday morning,

Ralph and I walked down to the marshes, and along built-up grassy banks beneath which grey tidal streams crawled away towards the sea, trying to blow away the feeling of stuffiness, and enjoying the serenity of the mud flats coloured mauve with sea-lavender or blue-green with plumy rushes blown by the warm sweet wind.

September 13th

Desmond Shawe-Taylor had invited me to go to the first night of the Vienna State Opera's *Figaro*. Delighted at the prospect of such a treat, I went to London with Saxon and stayed at the Paddington hotel, feeling strange in my room there without Ralph, and afraid of losing my passport to paradise my ticket. With the first notes of the overture the magic began; then the curtain went up to reveal a magnificent plunging view of Seefried's bust as she stood in her low-cut bodice. Jurinac was an enchanting Cherubino, Kunz Figaro, and Lisa della Casa a slightly breathy Countess. What rapture!

September 16th: Ham Spray

Day of Burgo's departure to stay in France with Isobel and Charlotte, and also of the arrival of a postcard saying that one of her sister's children has chicken-pox – a slight shadow on his anticipatory mood. Day also of the Newbury Orchestra's reopening. I have been practising hard and mean to hang onto it like grim death. After a recital I picked up Ralph and Burgo and his luggage and drove him straight to Southampton. We were both strangely moved to see our chick go off to his ship through the darkness. How do parents manage to despatch their sons to war?

September 24th

My visit to *Figaro* has swivelled my attention in the direction of opera, and high time too. We went to Lennox Berkeley's *Nelson* with Juanita and splendid old Count Benckendorff, who did not much approve. He kept commenting to me *sotto voce*: 'It is aMORphous. A pity as the music is good. He understands how to make a certain tension.' Like all Russians he is wonderfully expressive and when words failed him he just threw out his hands and made an explosive sound: 'Pff!' This upset a young man in stiff collar and white tie sitting just in front of us, who kept turning round and looking at us anxiously. Once he even addressed us directly: 'The last act is the best of all. It beats *Peter Grimes* into a cocked hat.' The opera was well received, and it deserved to be. The music was really lovely, and the dramatic content would not have failed had Nelson acted better and looked less like an Aberdeen terrier. The Count drove us home in his small, noisy car, sitting square and bulky beside an empty space provided for the Countess's[1] harp or his double bass.

The next day to lunch with Janetta who is picnicking in her new house with a few sticks of furniture. I get the impression that she is essentially a loner at present, except for her children to whom she is more maternal than ever before. Coming home from Cagnes through Paris she lunched with Derek. He asked her not to divorce him, saying that he would only make a fool of himself – he was good for nothing but work and that was nine-tenths of his life. At some mention of their life together he burst into tears.

[1] Maria Korchinska, professional harpist.

The second opera was *Don Giovanni* with Jurinac singing divinely, and next day we lunched with Clodagh Mackenzie, her charming father [Charles Meade][1] and Ralph and Coney[2] Jarvis. There was the ghost of a plot about this confrontation: a possible desire for us to see Ralph J. in the role of married man, not realizing perhaps that my Ralph and I take a purely passive part in Janetta's emotional relationships, now that her marriage to Robert has foundered. Coney met us with a guarded, rather strained expression, but thawed later. We liked her and found her very attractive as well as handsome – the position was made easier by our children, Burgo and Caroline, being friends.

October 4th

Last week Burgo arrived back from France, looking very brown and well, having 'managed' his travelling successfully, and greatly enjoyed himself. He has been lively and friendly, though inscrutable as ever even in this expansive mood, and I try to keep the rules and in no way force his confidence. He made us laugh a lot with stories and imitations of Isobel at Cannes, has listened endlessly to my new records of *The Magic Flute* and has now gone off to Oxford several days before the beginning of term saying he wanted to do some work.

Our journey to Italy draws very close. I resolve to enjoy it to the top of my bent, and try and be half as nice to Ralph as he is to me.

October 8th

Dark is falling as we desert our Ham Spray ship. At Southampton total silence around the bulk of our solid boat, the harbour lights are reflected in the inky water. Eating our last English meal in the ship's restaurant a sense of liberation spreads like a warm glow from a log fire. The ship now becomes womb-like, and my eyes close over my book. We creep into our tiny cabin and lie like biscuits in a tin.

October 9th

Woken by a loud clattering about four. A faint drizzle, as if through the watering-can's finest rose, sprinkles us as we cross over into the customs' shed and recognize with delight the pernickety voices and ineradicably cross faces of the French officials. The six cars that crossed with us stand yawning their heads off while men peer into their entrails with flash-lamps; in a very few minutes we are off in the grey half-light through the ugly, shattered town of Le Havre. Everything continues hideous and wonderful. Why not start off with a really good breakfast at Tôtes, and my word it is! Perfect coffee and hot flaky dark brown croissants. All day we drive South, to arrive at a small village near Dijon and totter into a bedroom with massive wooden doors, steel-hinged, a floor covered with worn but polished red hexagonal tiles. It's an old house with a huge chimney down which came the pale glare of the moon. To bed, very happy.

October 10th–11th

Through rolling Burgundy, with great trees just tinged with brown standing in the still air as if in aspic, and autumn crocuses. Then we were driving along Lake

---

[1] Alpinist and writer.
[2] Mrs Ralph Jarvis.

Leman, and *suddenly* there was the huge silhouette of the mountain on the far side, smudged in in faint grey, while a single towering snow peak rose out of its wreath of mist like a girl from her chiffon evening-dress. But the Swiss smugness and respectability made this vast natural panorama look like something indoors – a romantic scene painted on the wall of a second-rate hotel for instance. Next day we hastened on to the Simplon. A pass is an exciting thing, to be savoured and thoroughly understood. We breathed in the cold thin air, found some little starved alpine plants, including bright blue gentians among the woven grasses in earth soggy with melting snow, and plunged down – lacet after lacet – into Italy.

October 12th–13th

At Florence we had our first taste of sightseeing. I had forgotten how like zebras north Italian churches are. (I had not been here for thirty years and Ralph never.) What must we see? The Duomo, of course. And the Baptistery and Giotto's tower. The first moments of looking at works of art are tentative and experimental. What exactly am I at? Do I feel anything? What sort of thing should I try to feel? Then it dawns gradually that what I want is to fall in love with these delectable objects – and that cannot be done quickly and at the drop of a match, although occasionally it can so happen. Both of us, for example, fell in love with the less famous of Donatello's Davids in the Bargello – there was something so stylish about his youthful swagger and grace; but it's as if one's hands were full of reins and at first it's hard to know which to choose.

A night and morning and then off through pale, dimpled hills dotted with nearly black trees and creamy oxen with enormous horns. Just as the light was fading the same evening we drove into Rome.

We take at once to the *Inghilterra*, our home for the next week. It stands in a cul-de-sac, is old-fashioned and spacious, with tiled floor and creaking lift. Our room is prettily furnished with antiques and the bed is as big as two. We look in on Henry and Pansy Lamb, also staying here and resting after sightseeing, in a much less nice room than ours; and a note from Robert asks us to have a drink with him, at his 'swish' hotel. All evening the portentous – but as yet untasted – character of this amazing town stood waiting in the wings. What would it be like? Would we ever get the hang of it?

October 15th

I've been all day in a state of electric stimulation but now we've taken our first bite of the vast meal, and have some glimmering of what we are in for. Last night I was a new boy – now I've fastened my snake belt and learned the way to the lab. This morning we went to the Doria Palace with the Lambs. Like us, Henry has never been here before, and is half out of his mind with excitement. I don't think he sleeps at all at nights. He puts on a rather loud check jacket, pulls a peaked cotton cap well down over his eyes and prowls along at a rattling pace, looking to right and left like Groucho Marx. Pansy walks with a rapt and thoughtful face, dressed in good English clothes and 'sensible' shoes. They are a touching pair and we love their company, but this afternoon we went by ourselves to St Peter's and the Pantheon. Dined with Robert in the Piazza Navona. He came here with Oonagh Oranmore in her car, but she has now left, and he works hard most of the day at his nearly finished novel. 'In spite,' he said, looking surprised, 'of a good deal of upheaval in my private life'.

October 18th

The Lambs and Robert have been brought together, and taken a mutual fancy to each other. Having driven the Lambs to the Villa d'Este and Tivoli one day, we persuaded Robert to take a whole day off with us at Ostia. The bathing boxes were all shut, and a single figure – an old lady with only one leg wearing a décolleté bathing-suit – lay on the beach.

October 19th

Now that we have fallen definitely in love with Rome we tried to remember what account friends gave of it – Julia, Raymond, for instance. Perhaps it was impossible for them or anyone to convey its immense distinction, beauty and loveableness. I hadn't guessed that not only the relics of antiquity but the fragments of it (which I have been prone to disparage as stumps of old teeth) are all harmoniously merged with baroque and modern Rome by being made of the same stone, whether silver-grey or honey-colour. Then the fountains everywhere, the display of splendidly gesturing arms, beards and dolphin's tails of stone. And last but not least the personal beauty of the living Romans – their noble carriage, well-shaped heads and fine brows. The modern haircut which covers these small heads with neat but not too curly curls proves that here are still the faces of classical antiquity, as well as of Donatello and Raphael. In sober truth this visit is turning out so intoxicating that all energy is required for absorption, and none left for writing so much as a postcard.

While we were looking at Michelangelo's Moses today a young American said to Ralph 'Excuse me, Sir, but can you tell me why Moses has horns?' Luckily Ralph could, having just read it up in the admirable Baedeker. Called on the Lambs in their new hotel room – much better than the last but Henry has an appalling cold, which we do not want to catch.

October 20th

The buses of Rome are as special as everything else and we now make frequent use of them. You have to become like a piece of digestible food, leap in at the mouth, pass quickly through the teeth (a guichet where a man sits dispensing tickets) and then – taking advantage of all the peristalsis available – work your way through the whole length of the intestines so as to be ready to drop out of the arse at the psychological moment. The buses go so fast that it is a short sharp, profitable agony.

October 24th–November 2nd

For the first days of the homeward journey, we had the Lambs as passengers, ailing both but undaunted and enthusiastic. By Orvieto and Perugia we crossed the Apennines to Urbino in steady rain; there the sky cleared to a Piero della Francesca blue and enabled us to enjoy the splendid town to the full, and not only Urbino but San Sepolcro, Monterchi and Arezzo. The dreadful fact that we may never see these masterpieces again forces us to stare and stare, trying to imprint them on our inner eyes, polishing the memory so as not to lose its brilliance. Two more days in Florence, and at Pisa we parted from the Lambs. The sight of the shattered Campo Santo induced in me a violent sense of shame that our attacking aeroplanes should have so shockingly denuded it of the incomparable frescoes I saw in my early twenties. Then Lerici and Shelley's last dwelling. Leaving the coast we climbed the terraced hills in mellow golden sunlight, through morning-glory, maize, red and yellow vines and turquoise-blue spray – the last mouthful of delight before the plate is snatched away.

November 7th: Ham Spray

This Italian holiday has been our best for years. Every night I go back there in my dreams and Ralph says he does the same.

─────

1955

─────

January 6th: Ham Spray

Twelfth night already, yet not a thought recorded here so far. Not because I have had none – quite the reverse. I have simmered away among a fluctuating wash of them, about life, about death, about old age and where it is all leading? What am I at?

January 10th

Burgo's best Oxford friend, Simon Young, came with Janetta for the weekend. As the time approached he seemed to be silently saying 'do be nice to my friend', though goodness knows there was no need to do that. Even if we hadn't liked Simon I know we would have done our best to seem to, but we *did* like him very much indeed. He is a small clever-looking robin-like young man with a smooth sheet of dark hair falling over one eye, sharp-witted, quick to see and make jokes. He has read a great deal and sinks into a book like a stone. He had a dynamically stimulating effect on Burgo and revealed more of his Oxford life than we had glimpsed before. Simon obviously viewed him as rather wild and anarchical, also a comedian.

Janetta was low with a cold, and voiced sad views of life: 'I don't like it *one bit*. I don't mean that I don't enjoy quite a lot of the things I *do* – I do, very much, but I keep looking up and hating what I see.' We are beginning to hatch a plan to take a house jointly for several months of the summer, in Spain perhaps or Italy.

February 17th

Anne and Heywood are one of the couples we most love having to stay. They have made a great success of their marriage for one thing, and the house swallows them up pleasantly. Also as we do, they like reading and going for walks and Anne loves an argument. She is deep in researches into Trelawney. She brought down some chapters which I read and so did Heywood, who is a severe critic of her. As he read, he said to me 'we neither of us know any grammar unfortunately'. Anne, with a shriek, 'Heywood! Just think if Cecil Woodham-Smith's husband had gone on like that!'

Some time ago when we learned that both the USA and Russia possessed the Hydrogen bomb, and that these two monsters sit staring at each other across land and ocean, each with the means of destroying the globe in their paw, Ralph remarked how ludicrous it was that the generals still went on talking and writing about 'when war comes', in terms of tanks, infantry and air-raid shelters. Now, he explains, that recent tests have shown it to be so far more effective than they ever dreamed, those at the top are forced to accept the stark truth that the next war would in fact end war because it would end the world. There are signs in the papers and wireless that this realization is seeping down into the ranks of the general public.

February 27th: Ham Spray

When we saw Robert in London the electric charge of his despondency was like thunder in the air. Evidently in a state of indecision and loneliness, he was, however – much to our delight – persuaded to come down for the weekend. His proneness to criticize life at Montpelier Square or Nannie, or Georgie's school, points to the source of trouble; but so marvellous are his qualities of realism and interest that once at Ham Spray he became like someone recovering from an illness, however temporarily, and we were pleased to have had a hand in it. With the Campbells, who came to dinner, he was suddenly social but also bristly and truculent. It was strange that after Ralph and I had commented to each other on the three Roberts: drifting and desperate in London, rational here at Ham Spray, and prickly with the Campbells – he should speak of himself next morning in almost identical terms, saying that he knew he 'gave off different emanations' and how hopeless it was to try to conceal an anxious or agitated mood even from Georgie. He had a good phrase about Mary: 'She gets through life jumping from tussock to tussock of treats, and is only at a loss when she can't see another coming.' He came down to breakfast telling of an unhappy dream. He had been trying to pour tea for some people, but nothing like tea would come out of the teapot. Then he looked inside and saw 'nothing but a horrible old osso bucco'. Too plain! He wants to produce love but its source is dry and leathery. Ralph complained of waking every morning feeling his worthlessness. Only I confess to waking in a state of senseless optimism.

March 4th

A letter from Robert, who is – as we thought – fleeing the country on the very day that Janetta returns to it. He writes that as soon as he left us on Monday he was 'caught up and trapped in the thing one is constantly trying to get out of. I really feel I don't want to see anyone but very close old friends these days, with whom there is no need to do that awful acting we talked about. I can't put any conviction into my lines any more.' It is the saddest of stories.

March 5th: Long Crichel

Yesterday evening we drove to Crichel, over the rolling slopes of Salisbury Plain, and under a spectacular crimson sky marbled with purple. We kept exclaiming with amazement as we drove. Yet it was the sight of a sturdy little girl of six reaching up to put a letter in a pillar-box, with her straight hair falling backwards, rather than the incredible beauty of the sky, that brought home to me how interesting life is.

All four 'boys' were at Crichel. The evening began rather badly, with an emotive rather than persuasive argument about horror comics; but ended well with Desmond playing us his new records of Verdi's *Falstaff* all through. Today has been completely serene.

Conversation is one of the things I love to think about, but not while at it –

then I feel excited and absorbed as if skating or dancing, while a retrospective glance afterwards is like looking at the dead embers of a fire from which nearly all the red life has gone. Conversation reaches a high level in this house, although I doubt if any of them except perhaps Desmond really enjoy arguments. (How few people do!) Both Raymond and Eddy admit that they often don't hear what other people say. At breakfast this morning Desmond suddenly burst out in comic desperation, 'Raymond never hears a *single* sentence I say, even if it's only three words long!' Raymond beamed sweetly but didn't deny the charge. What then does this 'good conversation' consist of? Sometimes it's like a lot of people building a sand-castle; one makes the tower, someone else decorates it with shells, another suggests a tunnel. Push it over and start again.

March 6th

Snow was whirling on the lawn when I got up. However Eddy was very keen for us all to drive into Somerset to see a recent portrait of himself by Graham Sutherland, so (wish-fulfilment coming to his aid) 'It's stopped snowing,' he said and no one said him nay. The portrait is a remarkable work and has a considerable likeness to Eddy, but there is something definitely unpleasant about it – whether its tints of mauve and lime green, or that it seems to depict him in the electric chair waiting for his quietus.

April 2nd

We are still cut off from the world's doings by the newspaper strike. To me it matters very little. I listen to the daily abstract given us by the wireless – a little cup of concentrated Bovril – and get the impression that 'news' is not a real thing but an artificial imposition, a sort of false beard on the face of the facts. But poor Ralph is like a man choking for lack of air and light, and has eaten his way through a pile of thrillers which lie in a disconsolate heap round his feet. Shortage of absorbable material led to a long talk about activity-passivity, the difference between equality and sameness. If I don't look out I find myself pushed into an absurdly idealistic position, but this time I was almost disconcerted by the extent to which we agreed. For instance, about education, that though one should obviously aim at the best for all that doesn't mean the *same* for all, but technical education for the practically-minded and the most high-powered teachers for the brightest intelligences.

April 22nd

To London for the Memoir Club. Old Bloomsbury has been in the firing line. John Raymond has just launched a full-scale attack on them all, and Lytton in particular, in the *New Statesman*. He accused them of being 'vulgar', giving no reason for his view and showing his anger too plainly to be effective. So what would they seem like, I asked myself, this wood of old trees under whose shade I came alive myself? I thought there might be some talk of J. Raymond, but not a bit of it. There was the usual, really rather sublime indifference to what the world thinks of them. Then though they are getting old, and have been ill and had operations, they are still admirably adventurous. One and all were planning to take their cars abroad or hop over the Channel in aeroplanes. Bunny pounced on me, making it difficult for me to talk as much as I wanted to to Morgan on my other side. He [Bunny] said he had been writing a story about the 'amazing fact that young girls are always ready to fall in love with men of sixty-five', and would like to send it to me, 'as I value your judgement more than anyone's'.

The papers read were by Morgan and Duncan, and consisted almost wholly of old letters – cheating, really. Afterwards we repaired to Vanessa's, where Julia, who sets great store by manners, sinned against their rules in a manner possibly very wounding to her hostess: after a moment in her sitting-room she gave an exaggerated shudder, went and fetched her heavy winter overcoat and sat in it all evening.

April 30th: Mottisfont

We are spending the weekend in a new milieu – at Mottisfont, with Boris Anrep's friend, Mrs Maud Russell. We take to Maud at once; she exercises her function as hostess with great tact and skill. The party consists of Sir Maurice and Lady Violet Bonham-Carter and Caroline Blakiston (young and attractive actress), and by way of old friends Clive, Ben Nicolson and Paul Hyslop.[1] This business of talking to fellow-guests for hours and hours on end belongs to a house-party technique I am not accustomed to. High marks to Ben for doing it successfully and yet always being himself. Not so high I'm afraid to Clive who got over-excited, boasted really too much about the cleverness of his friends, his Légion d'Honneur and being tutoyé by Picasso. The Bonham-Carters both exuded confident charm – he delightfully beaming, quietly interested in everything from birds to the Crusades. I didn't at first like Lady Violet, who had an off-putting mannerism of smiling at one from very close range with her eyes shut; but she was friendly as well as obviously intelligent. Impossible however to be unaware that beneath her social gifts lay a system of worldly and conventional values which set my teeth on edge, nor was I mollified by hearing her say to Clive that she would rather both her sons had been killed in the war than fail to play their part in it.

Ralph and I had a three-room suite, the softest bed and smoothest sheets. But I felt a stranger in a world where it is assumed that 'we' are innately superior beings to those who minister to us, and deserve to have a better sort of life than they do. I cannot happily lie like a poodle on a fur rug being cosseted by an elderly grey-haired maid who is propping me on cushions and putting everything I could possibly need within my reach, not only because she received a salary for doing so, but because I have temporarily at least become a member of a privileged class. As she put down my breakfast tray one morning she gave me the latest news of the threatened railway strike, adding, 'It's disgusting! It's not British! I'm ashamed of my class, I really am!'

[Mottisfont had been converted from an ancient abbey and still bore many of its characteristics; it blended with its magically charming surroundings like some great rock or tree. The garden might have belonged to a French château. Besides a formal parterre entirely filled with heliotropes purple and mauve, flowers for picking were not much in evidence. Everywhere were smooth lawns intersected by water, and tall trees gesturing with low-slung branches. Crossing the widest stream by a bridge fenced with late roses, one entered woods full of the song of

---

[1] Architect and old friend of Raymond's.

birds and carpeted with wild flowers. The large drawing-room, scarcely used except in the evenings, was a show-piece decorated by Rex Whistler with fanciful and delicate frescoes and *trompe-l'oeils* of white satin quilting, suggesting a set for a ballet or a fairy-tale. It amazed without altogether delighting the eye. Elsewhere one came across a mosaic by Boris.

Ralph and I spent several weekends there, and always enjoyed ourselves, although the ambience was so very different from our own, and in the end the comfort itself and the ministrations of man- and maid-servants had an anaes-thetizing effect. But we both liked Maud very much. Though her way of life was conventional she herself was an original character, with something a little Oriental in her appearance and her movements. She had a great sense of humour and a low gurgling laugh. Also, though she put people at their ease and talked in a relaxed way herself there was a hint of the dark horse about her, a sense of mystery never quite cleared up.]

May 14th: Ham Spray

Ralph and I always enjoy telling each other about the books we happen to be reading. It is perhaps one of our greatest pleasures when alone. At the moment mine is *Education Sentimentale*, and though in some ways it is a failure I am finding it enormously absorbing; Flaubert's every sentence invokes the Frenchness of the French, and how brilliantly, how movingly he writes! Ralph made me laugh by beginning to shout about his author – Rousseau – this morning, although both our heads were actually on the same pillow. He declared this was because he 'didn't feel he had my entire attention'. (Quite untrue.) There are two causes of worry rumbling away in the cellars of my mind; one is that poor Ralph says he often wakes to sadness. This is all the more upsetting because he has hitherto rejoiced in such a marvellous fund of high spirits and power of arousing them in others – me, for instance. And I wonder about his health. The other is that we have heard nothing lately from Burgo.

May 24th

Burgo's silence has broken and on Sunday he brought two friends over from Oxford for the day – a great success and it made Ralph and me very happy. One friend was Simon Young. The other, Harry Graham, a whimsical character, made himself quickly at home and was somewhat teasing to our other guests, the composer Gerald Finzi and his handsome pre-Raphaelite-looking wife, who wanted to consult us about their son's conscientious objection. 'Musicians often seem to me such very *dull* people,' murmured Harry rather outrageously. 'My sister is one and her friends are *terribly* dull.' Dullness is of course anathema to Oxford, though not to Cambridge.

June 1st

The railway strike clamped down on us on Sunday and has assumed a large threatening black shape, not to mention also that the dock strike is now in its second week. One is aware of industries closing down and echoes of war-time stoppages. The slight thrill of drama has all gone – nobody likes it now, as far as I can see. Ralph says he feels shockingly short of vitality. Oh dear, I mustn't lose my new philosophy of 'taking things easy'. I have an index to do, *lots* to do in fact –

and so far as that goes am contented. What I do dread – and hate to contemplate –
is the possibility of advancing through space and time in a perfunctory or semi-
conscious manner; for above all things I cling to the vital necessity of keeping
awareness of one's surroundings sharp and clear, and not blundering along through
a haze created by the frosted spectacles of apathy.

June 29th

I have been carried away on a giant racer of entertaining and other activities.
However I think we got through something almost herculean in the way of a
house-party with fair credit; at least our guests were fed, entertained and looked
after. It was enjoyable while it lasted, and I again had the sensation of the house
resembling a living thing, breathing softly like all the people sleeping under its
spread wings. It began last Thursday, when poor Robin – who had been having
trouble with his artificial leg – came for two days without it. Next came Burgo and
Simon Young, fresh from the Wadham Commem. Ball. This meant inventing
another bedroom, and I swept and scrubbed the little room on whose door
Carrington long ago painted the word SERVANTS. On Friday the Nicholses telephoned and asked if Phil and Anne could come as well as Phyllis! New crisis.
Burgo's room had to be made ready for Anne and he moved into SERVANTS with
Simon. So we had three Nicholses and Craig Macfarlane – eight for dinner. Next
day Martin Nichols and a school-friend were added to the party. The Nicholses
left, but enter the Stones, just when I had gone to have forty winks. Five other
guests invited themselves for the weekend but were perforce rejected. Today I felt
as grey and limp as a fillet of plaice on Wyatt's slab.

July 9th

I have not mentioned the fact that we have rented a holiday house jointly with
Janetta, in Galicia in the north of Spain.

July 14th

Marching towards the deadline of departure. One by one things get folded and
tied in knots, in between bathing and eating strawberries, lying learning Spanish
in the shade: my index is finished, my last violin lesson over, the arrangements
for our August tenants made. Janetta has not yet succeeded in getting a sea passage
for Nannie and the little girls. 'Robert turned up this morning,' she told us, 'looking
very bearish.' 'What about his coming with us?' we asked, and she thought it
might be a 'good idea'. Poor Ralph Jarvis's stock is very low, but he still hopes to
drive out with her.

I am amazed that life seems to get more and more interesting as one gets older –
and also perhaps saner, serener, more tough. It is no doubt the Indian Summer
before the hand of decrepitude strikes and health crumbles.

I don't understand Janetta's attitude to Ralph J. one bit. He has pulled strings
and got passages for the children, so he is to be rewarded by driving out with her,
but she made no bones (when she was here) about not looking forward to the
Spanish adventure. Her presence in the house was like an electric dryer blowing
our hair straight on end. Her desperate restlessness makes one draw short breaths
and fail to sleep at night. From what we gather of life at Montpelier Square it has
been beyond everything, with frantic lovers sobbing down the telephone and

Cyril pacing her room all one night because Barbara has gone off with George Weidenfeld. Robert thinks her children show signs of lacking security, and that she should either centre her life round them or do something quite different. I think he is determined not to get drawn in again himself; he as good as said he would come to Galicia only if she didn't, and her own reason for coming is not very heartening: 'I've nowhere else to be.' Why on earth do I feel so sanguine?

Others who have been here have been the Gowings and Morgan Forster, who is as near to a Good Man as any I can think of, full of kindness and sympathy, understanding and tolerance, yet not at all dull.

[In Morgan Forster's company I have sometimes felt surprised that any personality could make an impression at once so distinct and so muted. For there was no mistaking the flavour of a single sentence of his talk, the voice it was spoken in, or a few words written on a postcard in his delicate, eccentric handwriting; yet these would be presented in a different, apologetic manner, so that the reader or listener might well be surprised to realize what a definite statement had been proffered, and with what resonant implications. Phrases such as 'Only connect' and opinions such as those on the relationship between friendship and patriotism are signs of the width of his influence even during his lifetime.

Yet he always chose to dress in almost aggressively dim grey clothes, woolly cardigans and cloth caps that would have merged easily into a London fog: I think this was because, like his close friend Sebastian Sprott (or Jack as he called him), Morgan felt much more affinity with the lower than the upper classes, and completely lacked ambition, envy and snobbishness. Starting with his mother and his aunts he spent much of his youth among middle-aged and elderly ladies – the prototypes of Mrs Moore of *A Passage to India* – and to such safe backgrounds he often returned after some bold episode in a rajah's palace, where a very different side of his nature was displayed in his obvious pleasure in wearing a turban and Indian dress. One such female confidante was my mother, with whom he lodged at Brunswick Square for several years during the Twenties. They got on well together, but I remember the complete lack of visual taste with which he furnished his rooms, and how he showed me with pride some crimson atrocities called Nell Gwynn candles, remarking 'they have a little womb, you see'. Morgan's conversation was interwoven with subtle humour, and his prevailing expression was one of gentle amusement, but he seldom laughed; when he did the sound was more suggestive of pain than pleasure, or sometimes resembled a sneeze. One often had the impression, when listening to his talk, that he was skating deftly between whimsicality and sentimentality.

Besides seeing him at my mother's house I used to meet him at the Memoir Club, and also in the early days of Ham Spray, where I sometimes played chess with him. He was very fond of Ralph, and continued to visit us after the deaths of Lytton and Carrington, showing particular kindness to Burgo in his adolescent troubles.

A little-known portrait of E. M. Forster by Carrington is in the National Portrait Gallery.]

July 25th

It's the last night at Ham Spray for many a long week, but this fact gives me, I must say, no great pang. I begin clearing and sorting and carrying things from place to place like an ant, to make the house ready for our tenants. Wilde and Mrs Hoare look reproachful – I hardly dare meet Minnie's eye.

Off to Southampton airport in the afternoon, Burgo looking very smart and smiling in a new café-au-lait suit. Among a row of people watching the take-offs I spot Desmond Shawe-Taylor's familiar silhouette. He is fizzing like ginger pop. (At Crichel they say, 'One can't play Canasta with Desmond, he's too excitable,' and it occurs to me he may be too excitable to travel by air also.) Considerable delay, owing to one or two aeroplanes 'proving unserviceable', not a very nice thought. We are off!

August 5th: San Fiz

Woken to a lovely blue morning with a multitude of civilities; we only understand half our three girls say. Breakfast in dressing-gowns in Janetta's room, coffee, an enormous round coarse loaf and honey. We took Dina with us into Coruña to shop; it's a magnificent town, very much alive and with its rows of *miradores* flashing in the sun. Natalia's descents on us are alarmingly frequent, and the trouble is we have many questions to ask her. But in reply to 'What time off do the girls expect, particularly Dina?' she at once tells us how lucky we are to have Dina, how everyone has put themselves out for us, and why has this miracle happened? Because 'everyone is so indebted to My Father'. As Ralph says, he dominates us like the Commendatore in *Don Giovanni*, and as we return to the house from a bathe or outing we half expect to hear his stone voice inviting us to supper. 'My Father' would in some odd theoretical way be 'so pleased' to know we are here, says Natalia.

August 7th

The sea-travellers miraculously arrive soon after two – Nannie pleased with every-thing; no little girl over-exhausted. After a certain amount of explaining and organization between kitchen and nursery we all went down to the beach. Nicky swims quite well, Georgie jumps up and down in a rubber ring made like a fish, Rose paddles hanging on to Nannie. We think the amalgamation of this new chunk into San Fiz has gone well.

August 8th

We begin to wonder whether Natalia realizes she has rented us 'My Father's' house. Today she suddenly came in unannounced with her sixteen-year-old cousin, who asked if we would like him to play us something on the piano? Nothing we would like less, but it was impossible to say so, and we were treated to a loud tasteless performance of tunes from *Tales of Hoffmann*. Not content with that intrusion she walked in later with the cod-faced English wife of a Spanish millionaire from Coruña, whom we could scarcely be polite to. Next, our bathing towels had disappeared from the line where they were drying. When we asked where they were Carmiña brought them, but was followed closely by Natalia saying, 'My Father never liked to see bathing things in the garden.' Ralph and I agree that something must be done – a declaration of independence *must* be issued.

August 11th

And so it was. The first shot was fired when Natalia shouted down to ask had I arranged about the children's tea, and I shouted back, 'Would she please leave that to me.' It is all most regrettable, and as pacifists we dearly wish we could have gained our freedom by simple negotiation, but let's hope that's the end of it.

Very hilarious dinner, with Carmiña and Maruja in tearing spirits and fits of laughter over our difficulty in understanding the difference between a *pollo* [chicken] and *agallina* [fowl] especially when Ralph said, 'Ah – I see – *un pollo es un hombre.'*

The post brought me the typescript of the translation of Carmen Laforet's *Nada*, which I am to revise for publication. Work! but I doubt if I shall be able to concentrate.

Ralph Jarvis leaves today and looked touching and sad in his smart travelling suit. He has been badly on Janetta's nerves at times, but is an endearing character. We are now waiting in something of a San Fiz for Desmond S-T. who is arriving no one knows quite when, on his way from Portugal.

August 13th

Janetta is a different person since Ralph J. left, much more relaxed and easy to communicate with. In any case one-sided love is a heart-rending spectacle. About one o'clock Desmond's car was seen in the drive guided by a village boy in a check shirt. A very lively new breath of air came with him, as well as civilized talk. He enters into everything inquisitively and with enthusiasm.

August 14th

All went to Coruña to meet Kitty West who was arriving by sea and train, but first we spent a delightful hour or so walking through the narrow streets or sitting in bars. Desmond constantly disappeared at speed, but was easily found because of the Portuguese shirt he was wearing, of enormous blue and green checks. Kitty was prepared to enjoy everything.

After dinner we all walked to a tiny fiesta in our nearest village, and Ralph and I whirled round for a little among the tightly-packed dancers. Each of us picked up a strange character – Desmond a knot of boys, Janetta a very young man with a permanent rosy blush, and I a Spanish version of Tom Mix. Dozens of brown, eager, wrinkled monkey faces gazed at us from very close range in amazed curiosity; there was a powerful smell of sweat. Walking home was the best part, with glow-worms lining each side of the road, and – close above the packed dancers – a brilliantly-lit window full of women and children looking down as if from a box at the opera. Above them stood the tall trees in the lamplight under the black sky.

August 16th

This is the week of fiestas. Last night in Betanzos a huge crowd gathered in the Plaza to see the Fire-balloon go up. Suspended by a sort of fishing-rod to the top of the church tower, it inflated very, very slowly as the air inside it was heated, heaven knows how, taking quite half an hour, while the crowd watched enthralled. At last it had swollen to such a vast size that it almost covered the whole Plaza, then up it went, to shrieks and yells, and we saw that it was carrying beneath it a boat full of rockets exploding into the indigo sky – an intoxicating sight. Up and up it still rose, and then a sort of panic broke out in the crowd. I saw a little old woman's face close to my own, agonized and struggling. I was too thrilled to feel alarm, but Ralph thought there was real danger and began issuing military orders in a most impressive way.

Our three girls were dancing all night in shoes too small for them: they are hobbling about today.

August 28th

Unexpected arrival of Caroline Jarvis and Jonny Gathorne-Hardy,[1] excited and exhausted after a three-days' train journey. The Brenans are expected shortly. Jonny is interested in everything, starts general conversation going, has plenty of charm and is nice to the children.

We bathed today on a splendid Atlantic beach where huge rollers come racing in to shore. Only a few natives were encamped at one end, and when she saw us braving the enormous waves one black-clad woman suddenly rose up, very stout and square, stretching her arms as if crucified and shouting above the din of the water. I went up to her and saw that her face was contorted with anguish; she cried to me that there was *mucho peligro*, and that one of her *hijos* had been drowned there. The Galicians are a sturdy primitive race; everything is carried on their heads – earthenware jars, great big parcels, and today we even met a tall woman with a coffin on her head crossing the bridge at Betanzos.

September 6th

Arrival of the Brenans. I think Gerald feels that we are poaching on his preserves. 'Of course it's lovely here,' he says, 'but it's not Spain.' However, I can see he is surprised to find us managing so well. Jonny is a great success with the girls and addresses long remarks to them mainly in English: 'No, Maruja, *grazie*, I don't think I'll have any more tonight.' She laughs flirtatiously and calls him 'Yonnee!'

Gerald, lying on the beach beside Ralph, talked and talked about himself, telling him among other things that he has nothing whatever to say to Gamel, but couldn't possibly do without her. Meanwhile she was sitting on a rock not far away, like a mermaid, gazing at herself in a small mirror, as she often does, not so much from vanity as anxiety.

Janetta, Caroline, Burgo and Jonny have gone off on an excursion to Portugal in their car, leaving us – a much reduced party – with the Brenans and the children. The Brenans have paid Natalia a long visit; they think us idiots to have divorced ourselves from such a fascinating woman, who knows so much about folk-lore (but both Ralph and I detest folk-lore). Encouraged by our visitors, however, Natalia returned into our sala talking to them in Spanish, which sounded beautifully clear and easy to understand after our Galicians.

September 12th

In spite of a certain buried irritation there has not been a single really difficult moment with the Brenans. One feels that Gamel must be treated like a blown bird's egg in cotton wool; she told me she is sad and deeply frustrated to think

---

[1] Nephew of Eddie and Bob and Anne Hill. Biographer of Gerald Brenan.

that she has used so little of such talent as she possesses. Gerald conveyed the same thing more amusingly: 'I feel like a house that is wired all over for electricity, but the current has never been switched on.' They give us no idea how long they are staying. 'Oh, I never make plans,' says Gerald. 'I just do what I feel like on the spur of the moment and get on very well like that.' All too true!

September 15th

Janetta and the three young returned from Portugal, looking brown, handsome, and having had a wonderful time. Jonny is very good for Burgo; he is also, I suspect, mad about Janetta.

The Brenans criticize the way we deal with our servants. 'You allow them to rule you,' says Gerald.

'Well, at least,' says Ralph somewhat mortified, 'we do make them look after quantities of visitors, whereas *yours* won't let you even have someone to tea.'

'Oh no,' answers Gerald obliviously, 'that's *our* doing entirely. The servants love having visitors.'

September 19th

Drove the Brenans to catch their bus. Ralph and I look forward to having some time to ourselves. Our farewell dinner to them was lively and talkative under the starry sky in an outdoor restaurant, eating tender little chickens. One often feels specially warmly to friends who are leaving, and this parting was no exception. Nicky's sharp eyes had noticed Gamel's vagueness and *non sequiturs*: 'If I said, "Janetta wants to know if you'd like to come shopping in the car?" she would answer, "Mmm. *Yes* dear, *wasn't* it?" ' Jonny liked Gerald enormously. Janetta had taken Gerald to Betanzos one day; they drank brandies and Gerald talked incessantly about himself, but his account to Ralph was: 'I got to know Janetta for the first time.' He spends a lot of time with his eyes turned inward, but when he suddenly transfers them to others they brighten like little black coals and his acute mind produces something much to the point or very funny, or both.

September 23rd

As our two months' stay in Spain comes to an end, tapering away as it were to a point, I try to sum it up. I feel it was the very solid creation of many hands. It even developed a sort of Frankenstein life of its own and there are many things we shall remember for a long time. Janetta asked last night how we would feel about doing it again. As Ralph and I walked arm in arm round the garden we talked of our sadness at leaving, how fond we had become of it. Two months? It's nothing.

September 24th

The girls were in tears as we left, Dina with a scarlet nose. Carmiña is the one I am fondest of, she has the Irish quality of always being sweet and kind, whether she feels it or not. All females were warmly kissed, even old Nannie; handshakes for the males. So goodbye San Fiz.

October 1st: Ham Spray

We have been back four days and are only just beginning to come out of the dazed stupor of return. First impressions are that England is very pretty, prettier than

Spain. But what a remarkable difference between our reception at San Fiz and at Ham Spray! Wilde and Mrs Hoare had of course been told when we would arrive, and I half thought Mrs Hoare might be waiting to cook our supper. But no. We fought our way into an utterly cold, bleak house – not a fire burning nor a radiator turned on. No flowers; no pots in the jardinière. In the kitchen *nothing* except a few peeled potatoes in a saucepan of cold water. Goodness, how unimaginative! On the table was a grocer's bill which made me groan: margarine, Bisto, Quix. I groped in the dark garden for a lettuce, cursing. But next morning Mrs Hoare entirely softened me by her friendliness.

October 12th

Of my two jobs *Nada* is done and packed off to the publisher, while tomorrow I start my next Freudian index. My 'life' is relegated to the numerous crannies between, and sweetened by loving companionship with Ralph and the summer warmth and perfect stillness of the weather. Every morning the lawn is pearly with dew and threaded over with spider-webs. A few mushrooms. The leaves have barely started to turn.

All is silence, except for our own voices. This morning we were considering the changing world. Ralph said we mustn't forget it is the next generation, not ourselves, who are making the changes. It is their world, and they have a much less permanent attitude to life than we did. Like gliders, they keep adjusting to new air-currents. One can see their attitude as adventurous, courageous and certainly pragmatic. Ideas are accepted as long as they work; marriages likewise. On the other hand the weeklies are very full these days of cynical abuse of *our* old Gods, the Bloomsbury ones, both of what they stand for and the characters themselves – Virginia, Maynard and Roger. I feel as certain as I am of anything that the journalists are wrong, and that one day it will be seen that they played an important part in the history of civilization. Not probably in my life-time, however.

Last weekend Janetta and Joan Cochemé met here. Joan was 'thunderstruck by Janetta, thought her almost perfect'. I must admit she glowed like the autumn days. I'm glad to say she feels, as we do, that San Fiz was a triumphant success. 'I tell everyone so. I hope you do too.'

October 18th

I wake like a sparrow on my twig, chirruping with trifling anticipations. But we have had two saddening glimpses into the lives of others: one was of Burgo at Oxford, feeling lost and lonely in his town rooms and missing friends who have gone down. The other was of Robert, who exhaled an unwavering air of desperation, as we both agreed, and this was made worse by his attempt to mask it with a large pair of pink-rimmed spectacles – a vizor of concealment and protection or a muzzle to prevent him biting? He left to return to Dublin where he works hard, sees no one and makes his own meals.

November 21st

Another visit to London for Charlotte Strachey's wedding to Anthony Blond,[1] and a party given by Janetta and Joan Rayner. It was so long since I'd been to a party

---

[1] Publisher and friend of Burgo's.

that I wanted to see if the style had changed. Not really. A great deal of champagne and whisky was drunk, yet no one was 'drunk'. In Janetta's long room the noise grew rapidly more deafening until it became merely a matter of guessing at other people's remarks. What's the point of talking under such circumstances, I wondered, even while doing and enjoying it. A lot of very interesting distinguished-looking heads were silhouetted against the dark green walls. Homosexuality was represented by Cecil Beaton, Francis Bacon, Dicky Chopping; old age by Rose Macaulay; old friends by Mary, Heywood and Anne, Paddy Leigh Fermor, Cyril and Sonia. But when it was all done and we were back in bed there was less to ponder about than there is after a good evening's talk: just a noisy rush through a dark tunnel in a train with lights flashing past and quick glimpses of faces in other carriages.

November 30th: Ham Spray

Both of us in bed with flu. I'm reading Wildeblood's book, and find it thoughtful and interesting. Hearing the purple-jowled indignation of Counsel for the Prosecution against homosexuality in his own case and comparing it with the same man's impassioned defence of it in the Croft-Cooke case, Wildeblood realized that barristers were purely actors, and that by the time they had been made judges they could have no feelings about right or wrong or anything else. I think this is true – why do we smugly accept this state of things?

December 15th

Clive and Janetta for the weekend. We were discussing Lawrence Gowing's appointment to be head of an art school. 'He's just a *civil servant!*' said Clive with unutterable scorn. 'Can anyone imagine Renoir giving up any of his painting time to become a civil servant?' This was at the end of dinner and he got up on rather wobbly legs and danced round the table in his purple spongecloth and black tassels saying, 'I'm drunk, I know I am, *all* the same I know that no artist should become a *civil servant.*'

Burgo went off to the Tycoonery for the night, with a lively party consisting of Nell and Jeremy, Caroline Jarvis and John Calmann.

December 24th

Christmas began today – no time to duck or groan. Isobel was driven down by Charlotte and Anthony in time for lunch, bringing a bottle of champagne. Robert came by the evening train; Burgo is back from Stowell so our party is complete.

December 29th

All over now, and Ralph even says it is the nicest Christmas he can remember. Robert and Isobel were a good mixture – it was they who entertained us. It is always a delight to listen to Isobel's drifting voice saying such things as, 'They say that if you keep on *fond*ling rats they grow very very *brave*.' Robert was obviously happier although still lurking behind his preposterous spectacles. He tells us that all London gossip circles round the Connollys' affairs, and that both Cyril and Barbara had been to see Edward Glover, who said he could help Cyril but do nothing for Barbara, who only wanted him to tell her what she wanted to hear. She is to be staying with Bill and Annie Davis at Malaga when the Campbells go there, and Cyril briefed Mary as to what she was to say to Barbara. When she asked him, 'What has she done to deserve such preferential treatment?' he said, 'Nothing, but please do.' However, Barbara has already left for Madrid. According to rumour it was to meet George Weidenfeld, but Cyril didn't know this, rang her up in her Madrid hotel and was told she was out. 'Gone to the Prado,' said Cyril to Robert. 'I told her she must.' Then, as an after-thought he asked the hotel receptionist: 'Is there a Mr Weidenfeld staying there?' 'Oh yes, Sir, just arrived. Do you want to speak to him?' So now Cyril has posted off to Spain.

Ralph says how Stendhal would have enjoyed the Connolly situation, and how Cyril would enjoy thinking of Stendhal enjoying it!

1956

January 2nd: Ham Spray

There can't be said to be much feeling of newness about this New Year. My love for Ralph, which welled up in a sudden fountain last night as I saw how much he was enjoying some gramophone records, is certainly not that. Nor is my frustrated longing to see Burgo more constantly happy.

We have Robert here, a pillar of support, for our other visitor Hester Chapman is quite a formidable steam-roller (though she makes one laugh a lot), or to change the metaphor she has a flavour like pickles, curry and Worcester sauce rolled into one. She was gratuitously unkind about her old friend Julia's last book: 'It was really shockingly bad, I thought.' (snort) 'Well, readable. Barely.' (snort). However she was worsted by little Nell Dunn, who came over one day. Hester took her for 'a silly little thing' and was determined to beat her on the blue-stocking level. Actually Nell was not only looking like a Piero della Francesca angel but in splendid form, speaking lucidly from a clear head and honest heart. From parents and children Hester moved on to how uninteresting the young were, and how much one wanted to be rid of them and 'get on with it'. 'Get on with what?' said Nell in bell-like tones. 'I don't even know what you do.' 'I write, as a matter of fact,' said Hester, closing her eyes with a snort, as who should say: 'Fancy not knowing *that.*'

Next day she asked me, 'Was I sharp with that charming clever girl? I liked her so much and thought her brilliantly intelligent.' For which, I suppose, she must be given due credit.

January 13th

I heard today from the Harvill Press that they are to publish the translation I have been doing of a Spanish story called *Little Andrès* which I have been working at for some time, egged on by Lucila Japp. They write that they are 'quite in love with it', and I like it myself but am positive it will drop like a stone. What with *Nada* coming out with Weidenfeld, it looks as if two of my translations might appear this year.

Two days ago I started reading Saint-Simon.

January 17th

Very sad news came in a letter from Boris today:

65 Boulevard Arago,
Paris XIII

Dear Ralph and Frances

I have the very sorry news to tell you Maroussa died on the 11th January on admission to the hospital. Her cancer developed in her lungs, and although she was with me sitting in the studio till the day before her death sipping rum and smoking till the last moment when the ambulance people carried her away, there in the hospital her heart gave out and she dropped her head and was dead.

You were fond of her and she was very fond of you both.

The void is very great round me. I feel so confused and miserable.

My love, Boris

It wasn't exactly a surprise, indeed we have been expecting it ever since her serious operation of a year or so ago, but her death makes us more melancholy than would that of many people we see more often and more intimately.

January 20th

Mary has dropped out of the sky from Malaga for a few days, and had many stories to tell us about Cyril's doings. He clamours for female company, but abuses his old friends like Janetta and Joan Rayner. He got on splendidly with Gerald one evening, but after the next declared that he was a fearful bore. Mary has been rather like a jolly red sun breaking through the clouds and illuminating a watery grey landscape. This morning we went in to Hungerford to see her off to Spain again, with two letters from us to the Brenans and two diminutive puppies blindly peering from a straw-lined basket.

More stories about Cyril: He had been making up to the pretty and amusing wife of Annie Davis's brother Tom Bakewell at a nightclub in Torremolinos, so much that Tom B. began to grumble. 'Well hang it all, Tom,' said Cyril, 'I haven't had a woman for two months. You really can't complain of my just dancing with Carol.' Next morning Tom Bakewell drove up to the Davis's house and dashed upstairs calling 'Cyril! Cyril!' 'Oh, hullo, Tom, come in.' Tom had been to Malaga and found a nice tart for Cyril, and booked a date for him there and then.

January 31st

Janetta was with us for the weekend when a letter from Robert arrived describing an appalling fire which had almost completely consumed Oonagh's lovely little Gothic house in the Wicklow mountains, Luggala. The fire brigade were delayed by frost and snow, and Robert said the sight of it was so extraordinary that he stood spellbound watching it before he realized that all his belongings and money were inside, and started on rescue work. The letter ended with his saying, 'I was feeling in a very desperate state before this happened and was keeping it chloroformed with work.' Janetta said, 'I wonder *why* he's so desperate.' I deliberately dropped a pebble into the pool by asking if she thought it had anything to do with her, and she said she had been given no reason to think so.

February 6th

Winter has struck, and the cold persisted throughout a short visit to London, mainly to go to Vanessa's private view, where we saw Clive and Duncan, Angelica, Barbara Bagenal and Helen Anrep. It gave me a slight feeling of shock to see this noble-looking woman Vanessa (whose ageing face still has classical beauty) putting herself up for sale to all-comers. Surely it was a better tradition that the painter should not attend his own vernissage?

Afterwards we went on to that of Michael Wishart, whose charming wife Anne is Philip Dunn's sister and has become a millionairess through her father's death. This generally known item of news seemed to spread a wave of worldly excitement through the crowded room, where people stood with their backs to the pictures or actually leaning against them, jabbering their heads off.

Next day I lunched with Janetta and Robert at Montpelier Square, and I realized any idea that my 'pebble' had created a ripple was mere wish-fulfilment. They were perfectly friendly, much in the way that brother and sister are, and with an undercurrent of irritation.

I asked Janetta if her divorce from Derek was through yet.

'Yes, today.'

'And is it rather nice to feel free?'

'Well, yes, it is.'

Robert looked surprised, and said, 'But the trouble is you'll be in it all again in a minute,' and Janetta pulled a face at him. He then began to talk about Sir Roger Casement's Diaries, on which he is now working, and said he was going back to Dublin next week.

February 8th: Ham Spray

Janetta rang up and told us Robert had gone off to Ireland. 'He thinks of nothing but Roger Casement,' she said with a tinge of bitterness. I fear it's true, and I'm also cross with him because he's so pig-headed as to reject the ideas of Casement being a homosexual and that the Diaries are genuine, both of which Ralph and I believe to be as good as proven.

February 17th

Up to London for a night, mainly to have a rest from battling with the cold but also to see a charming, 'sintimiental' René Clair film and go with Ralph Jarvis and Janetta to Rimsky-Korsakoff's *Coq d'Or* at Covent Garden, with splendid singing by Hugues Cuenod and Mattiwilda Dobbs.

This morning we woke in our hotel to find breakfast being wheeled in by a beautiful dark Irish maid, who brought us a paper showing that the Abolitionists had got a handsome majority. Ralph asked her whether she was for hanging murderers or not. 'Well, if it's to be in danger of being murdered I am when I walk the streets I'd rather they were hanged.'

February 29th

Our two Bloomsbury birds put us to shame by being the nicest guests and best company we have had for ages. They can and will talk about anything and everything with unfailing interest and gaiety. I must admit that Vanessa seems physically an old lady as one hears her bumping slowly downstairs, but mentally and spiritually she is ageless; while having Duncan in the house is like having a young irresponsible undergraduate to stay, and I even felt a slight surprise at seeing him reading a solid history book. His hair is quite black still and there is nothing to remind one that he is seventy. Both Ralph and I were charmed by them. The only entertainment we provided was to take them to lunch with the Moynes at Biddesden. Vanessa afterwards compared the rows of faces of children (decreasing in size) around the dining-table to a scene from Mrs Molesworth. Bryan took us upstairs to show us a painting by Duncan, and didn't appear to mind when Duncan peered at it closely and said, 'I have absolutely no recollection of ever seeing it in my life before.'

[I sometimes wonder whether Duncan was the happiest man I have ever known. *Angst* and responsibility played a very small part in his scheme of things, and the rare state of serenity that resulted made him a very refreshing companion. With his remarkable good looks, bewitching Highland colouring of black hair and blue eyes, well-cut mouth curling in secret amusement, and voice as soft as cashmere, he must surely have been aware how pleased everyone was to see him, yet I doubt if he was vain.

Why should he not be happy, after all? Circumstances and his own desires had so arranged his life that he spent many hours of nearly every day doing what he liked best – painting. When I first got to know him, in the Twenties, he was enjoying considerable acclaim. It was very much to his credit that when his popularity gradually seeped away and his name became unknown to art students, he simply went on painting exactly as before, so that at the time of his astonishing come-back to fame he was able to bring up pictures from Charleston when more were clamoured for. The image of Duncan stamped on my memory shows him in the garden at Charleston on a summer day, wearing a broad-brimmed French straw hat, from beneath which his serious gaze keeps up a movement from subject to canvas, up and down. No sign of the vigorous blink that accompanied his talk when he was being fanciful or perverse – a vein that ran through all that I knew of his life. I sat beside him at a banquet given in honour of his ninetieth birthday by the Dufferins, and I'm sure he must have blinked as he murmured: 'I can't think *why*, with all this delicious food, I don't feel hungrier.' Long pause: 'Of course it's true I was taken out to lunch and ate two dozen oysters.' After Vanessa's death I saw him now and again. The straw hat – often with a feather in it – had become a fixture, he sat often with a rug of the Grant tartan over his knees, and a large beard had given him a resemblance to Monet which was noticed by everyone.

Many people said they found Vanessa alarming, but I'm glad to say I never did. From the first I felt great admiration for her, and when I got to know her better and love her the admiration remained. I see her most characteristically, standing bent a little forward from the waist, with a scarf knotted round her head and a crescent-shaped smile like that on a Greek statue of the archaic period curving her lips. Her movements were deliberate; when sitting she would be erect but relaxed, with her hands in her lap or darning a sock. Her voice was quite unusually melodious and deep – a true contralto. She wrote to me about the weekend I have just described that it seemed 'even more perfect and delightful when we returned to find not a drop of water in our pipes and the plumber as usual in a complete state of mystification. I think they ought to be taught that water runs downhill – doesn't it? – and escapes from holes and expands when it freezes. We think of all the delights of Ham Spray, the delicious food, the fireside, and above all sitting at ease and talking to you two.' Her last letter was written in March 1961, a few months after Ralph's death, and begins: 'Dearest Fanny,[1] we have just finished reading *Mansfield Park* aloud and it's really impossible not to think of you. Not that you are in the least degree like that Fanny but you have the same name and perhaps I should think of you even if you hadn't.']

March 7th: Ham Spray

When two people live together for thirty years as Ralph and I have done they must both have a clear mental map of their zones of agreement and disagreement. There are two dangers – not talking about the areas of disagreement because of the heat thereby engendered, and not talking about the overlap because it is thoroughly understood. This morning, however, as if we had been sitting in a boat at the edge of a lake and someone had given it a shove, we were suddenly afloat in the deeps; and a conversation began at breakfast and went on all morning. Ralph started it by describing a feeling of sadness and envy he had felt last night when I was playing the *Eroica* in Marlborough. I teased him about his idleness (which really sometimes worries me). He teased me about my belief in 'creative activity'. I tell him I am not and never have been capable of it, and that it is humble activity without the creation that I seek. His nature is much more 'creative' than mine. Then up came the atom bomb, which Ralph claimed was the cause of his inactivity. I said he couldn't be *quite* sure we were doomed, and that even if we were there were only two logical courses – to commit suicide or go on as before, which is really the same choice to be made when you learn that you have a mortal disease. As we all have. Anyway that there were no grounds for a half-existence, and Ralph has such a capacity for enjoyment and interest, such an excellent brain and power of synthesizing the knowledge it absorbs that there was no excuse for it!

March 10th

Two perfect days, the country glistening under blue skies and a brilliant flood of light; great blue splodges of shadow like marks of a giant's thumb on the flanks of the downs. In thick coat and scarves swathed against the cold wind, I made across to the little pond where we used to skate, which shone like bright metal under the sky. A flock of wild duck whizzed up just as I got there. I lay down on the grass stock still until I saw them very high up in the deepest blue part of the sky, saw the leader tumble downwards and heard the strenuous whirring of their wings as they turned away disgusted by my continued presence. Two tiny birds twittered on a topmost twig. As I lay there doing my bird-watching I felt some obscure internal amusement. When I had set out I hoped to think things out for myself, make some minor resolutions about how to deal with an occasional lost appetite for life, lost confidence in myself, lost heart. It's what Burgo often asks me, and *I do not know* the answer. A session of Any Questions would say: Stop thinking about yourself.

---

[1] Clive gave me this name, which was used by some of his friends – and still is.

This morning we fetched Burgo from Oxford. How was he? All right. Had he enjoyed the term? Not really, but he had survived it.

March 27th

Last weekend we had Simon – who always cheers up Burgo – Robert and Georgie. Georgie is in a state of development combining sensitiveness and courage. When she failed to fold up her Heads, Bodies and Tails paper properly she burst for a moment into tears. I was delighted to see Burgo come to her rescue most understandingly. She adores Robert and he her, but she is made of finer texture than he is. Thought and talked to Ralph a lot about his character. He was awfully funny, charming and clever. But he was bitter and tough when he talked about Janetta. She herself is bewildered. On the telephone she told me that before she went abroad he rang her up several times. Once he said he never wanted to see her again. Another time he begged her to put off her departure until he came and saw her. She did for several days and he neither came nor wrote. He stayed at Montpelier Square all the time she was away, and when she got home she found no sign, no message. Whatever the explanation it's an unhappy one.

April 25th

Robert is staying a week at Stokke and another with us. We paid a happy visit to the Campbells, where his typewriter could be heard clicking from an open window; croquet, Julia and Lawrence at their various activities. Mary's mother, Lady Rosslyn, looking nippy as a girl for all her seventy years, struggled heroically among the brambles with a secateur. A story about Julia's anti-draught fuss. She had asked if she might have *The Times* to sit on to protect her from the cold air that came through the holes in the cane seats of the dining-room chairs!

[From April 25th to May 15th we took our car to France. Robert finally decided not to meet us at Pau with Janetta: during his last few days at Ham Spray I could see him visibly turning against the project and at the same time his tragic expression deepening.

At Granville (a town of tall pale grey houses looking sternly down on a vast expanse of turquoise sea) we awoke to our first thrilling sensation of being abroad, something often forgotten. It's like sucking liquid through a straw. Home life is *in-out*, like the boat-race; abroad it's all *in*. Approaching Pau we first glimpsed the ghostly backcloth of the Pyrenees. There was a telegram from Janetta at the Poste Restante, and she arrived that same evening. 'Robert was torn by the desire to come till the last moment. He came to see me off, and he was quite dark blue in the face with wanting to come,' she told us.

After several days in sight of the challenging Pyrenees we crossed them by the Somport Pass and made for the little Spanish town of Benasque, recommended by Robin Fedden who had used it as a base for mountain-climbing. The Fonda was kept by a family of alpine guides; the dear old father had been up the highest peak, the Aneto, 400 times, and had the soft voice and air of restraint that I have noticed in all those whose livelihood is got from battling with Nature at her fiercest. We had one incomparable, unforgettable day, starting at about 3 a.m. when I looked out of our window and saw the pale light dawning above the pure line of the snow-covered mountains. We asked the dear old hard-working Señora for a picnic and she brought us hard-boiled eggs, raw ham, bananas – and then as a special treat positively *ran* to get us some turrón and rough white wine as well. We walked up into the heart of the mountains as far as we could go, finding narcissi just coming out and very small, sweet-scented white daffodils with narrow trumpets. The promise of flowers to come was almost unbearable; at one point the valley flattened out and was nearly black with the navy-blue buds of gentians. There were leaves of orchids and martagon lilies. 'We leave Benasque with that very special and rare feeling of being *in love* with it, and its extraordinary atmosphere of innocence. We mean to come back when the flowers are all out,' I wrote.

We made a stop on the way home at a village where a château once owned by Colette was reputed to be for let or sale. We asked the way many times – some had never heard of it, others said, '*Ah oui, je le connais, mais c'est pas bon là-bas.*' When we found it at last it was extraordinarily primitive, peopled by Breughel-like rustics speaking patois and the château had been sold; questions about its owner produced an affectionate smile. '*Eh bang, Madame Colette c'était autre chose. Elle n'était pas come tout le mang, vous savez!*' said a large fat bandy-legged woman half hidden by a vast mushroom hat, who might have come out of one of her own books.]

May 28th

Robert has been with us ever since Whitsun, and Janetta joined us for the weekend. Before she came I had a long conversation with Robert, walking up and down the lawn. On the telephone he had said that he must stop floating and make some decisions about his life, but so far as his predicament emerged in speech it consisted in: Should he live in Dublin or London, and how could he earn some money. The question of with *whom* he should live was only skimmed over! He confessed to the ghastly difficulty he had always had in making up his mind. 'When you've bought something – a shirt for instance,' I asked, 'and are walking out of the shop with the parcel under your arm, do you wish you'd bought a different one?' 'Oh, YES, of course. Always!' It was the most revealing thing he said, except that he was quite sure he had been right not to come to the Pyrenees, much as he'd wanted to, because it would have 'begged the question and made the decision for him which he didn't yet feel able to make'. (At which rate, I reflected, you're not going ever to make any decisions at all. Why not a little more courage?) While we were talking, Janetta rang up to say she would like to come down, and asking to speak to Robert. 'Is that all right?' I asked him, 'or will you take to flight?' 'No, I'd like to stay till next week and do my deciding then.' I felt rather as if he were a Victorian young woman being pressed to give his answer to a proposal of marriage.

However, neither Ralph nor I were in the least prepared for what happened when Janetta was actually with us: we agreed afterwards that we had felt we should go away and leave them alone together, so obvious was their obsession with each other. It quite took us aback. Janetta's stream is clear and direct; there are all sorts of baffling currents going on in Robert's. Though he has more to lose and more old wounds to be reopened, it's Janetta at the moment I'm anxious about. On Monday morning Robert came down in his best suit and said that he had decided to go to Dublin at once, dispose of his flat there and move his things to London. But no sooner said than he began casting his eyes back at the shirt he had left in the shop, saying that it was impossible to write his book anywhere but in Dublin. 'If I could find someone to marry me and live with me there – an air-hostess, perhaps.' I said teasingly: 'Perhaps we're being unkind when we open our doors wide and say "Come back here whenever you like." We may be making your decisions harder; we ought to slam the door instead.'

May 29th

This evening has brought our own anxieties to take the place of other people's – poor Burgo rang up in a state of desperate gloom about his coming Finals, he was certain he couldn't pass and was afraid we didn't realize the fact.

May 30th

This is the sort of crisis which Ralph deals with brilliantly while I rely entirely on him. He flew into action on the telephone as soon as we were awake, and arranged among other things to go and lunch with the Cecils and Burgo. We are back from that now. I'm not sure Burgo was glad to see us, perhaps he felt we had betrayed his confidence to the Cecils. He had the tense preoccupation of someone who is about to face an ordeal the thought of which doesn't leave his mind for a moment; but he was pleased because Ralph took him some half bottles of champagne to cheer him up. I only hope that when he begins writing tomorrow it will seem better. Lord knows we neither of us mind how he does, but it will set *him* up if he gets through. Meanwhile these next days have to be lived through by us, helpless in the background.

June 8th

Burgo has weathered his Finals, and no matter if he passes or not it is the greatest victory he's won over himself in his life. We heard nothing after the weekend, and I was like a cat on hot bricks till he rang up on Wednesday saying it was all over and he had had his first sip of champagne. Oh, the relief! And he was so pleased he had stuck it out, though he had a streaming cold and went back to bed at tea-time every day. Ralph and I feel very proud of him, if I may use that corrupt phrase.

June 18th

Janetta put me up for a night to visit the dentist. She told me that after their last visit to Ham Spray Robert had launched one of his great thundering depressing tirades against her way of life, her selfishness and how she brought up her children. She had been crushed and deflated by this wigging, and the worst of it was that he was not cross while delivering it, but seemed to be thoroughly enjoying himself. It reminded her of the old days with him and how desperate it had been trying to make a good, gay life under that withering fire, and I think it has finally convinced her that she could never join forces with him again. The odd thing is that were she Georgie he would see at once that a person can't live on criticism alone.

July 9th

Burgo came back cheerful from a visit to London and a party at the Nicholses'. We all three went to another given by the Garnetts at Hilton. Little Henrietta, most fascinating of the four girls, took a fancy to Burgo, and held his hand with a persistently romantic expression. A week later we celebrated his twenty-first birth-day with a dinner-party at Ham Spray that was lively though put together in somewhat random fashion – the guests being Simon Young, Serena Dunn, Quentin, a great charmer called Christopher Amander, and Rodney Leach (both from Oxford).

August 2nd

Ralph and I are alone for a few days. Burgo has gone to London for a party, and away for the weekend. The news that he had passed his Finals, but with a Fourth, saddened me though I hadn't expected more than a Third. The fact that Ralph took it extremely well did a world of good to Burgo, who showed signs of desperation and defeatism when he saw the notice in *The Times*. Also his own niceness to Burgo has relieved the tension that was building up inside Ralph and might easily have taken a hostile form. Why, exactly, he did so badly is something one can't just dismiss by saying he is 'neurotic', in view of his high IQ and the opinions of some of those who taught him at school. And yet it is as near as we can get to the truth. What above all things I want for him is happiness, and that he should go on developing the power to adapt himself which he showed in his first two years at Oxford but less in his third. He is very much of an individual and he made a lot of friends there. But I know he does not find life easy.

[An invitation to stay with Eddy Sackville-West in County Tipperary was the nucleus of our plan to take the car and explore the south-west, landing at Rosslare and setting off westwards near the coast. People are divided between those who are soothed by Ireland and those who find it maddeningly run-down and depressing. Both Ralph and I belonged to the first class. Irish voices were a joy to us, and we noticed the original way they use words as if they had never heard one before. We loved the rough little fields, needing a hair-cut and containing one donkey or cow, the fuchsia hedges bleeding their flowers on to the ground, the montbretias growing right up to the sea's edge, hydrangeas and tree-mallow vigorously on the march. We stopped at the charming village of Schull, where the streams were as brown as Guinness, and the aloe had run wild, even out on to a hermit's island in the sea itself. There must be something peculiarly rich in a soil that yields such vegetable riot.

Turning northwards, we rounded every promontory by Bantry, Glengariff and Sneem – a little town as pretty as its name, settled snugly among velvety hills; we visited the home of my Irish ancestors on Valencia Island in dazzling weather, and floated on the breathlessly still, gun-metal waters of Killarney. Thus we passed ten days of happy refreshment, rejoicing in our solitude together, before the first note of alarm about Ralph's health came to break the spell. As usually happens with such warnings we did our utmost to reason it away. (He had been on a controlled insulin intake ever since his diabetes declared itself, and looked rosy and well.)]

September 27th

The inn at Clohane, near Brandon, looked so unlike one that I went into the post office and asked: 'Will they have room for us, do you think?' The postmistress clapped me on the back: 'Sure they will – and be *charmed* to have you.' It was very nice, though simple; we ate with our two fellow-guests, an unattractive young Ulsterman with a rucksack and a heavy cold, and an intelligent lady from the Women's Institute, come to teach the villagers dress-making. Apart from upholding the way children are taught to speak Irish, which their parents do not understand, on the irrational basis that 'they ought to have a language of their own', she talked a lot of sense. We learned that Irishmen are loth to marry, confirming that as a nation they are undersexed.

After a windy night the sun came out in glory, and we decided to keep to our plan of climbing far enough up the flank of Brandon mountain to be able to see its celebrated cliffs, Ralph's reason being partly that Gerald had often given them a mysterious connection with Saint Brendan, and so with his own name. As we climbed the wind grew fiercer and the ground boggier. It seemed that a baleful force was shrieking at us, '*No pasarán!*' and I began to feel very anxious about Ralph, who had as usual forgotten to bring his emergency sugar-lump. 'Let's go back!' I said, but he wanted to go on; his face was red, and I knew that it went pale when exertion led to sugar-shortage. Though he is very good on the whole about keeping to the rules, he is admirably determined to lead as normal as possible a life while doing so, and he has a strong dislike of all medical precautions. Oh, how thankful I was when he agreed to give up the battle and return to Clohane.

But on the way to Limerick alas there was another nasty moment, when he hurried across a road to buy a newspaper and returned in a state of near-exhaustion, admitting to a pain in his chest. My problem is that he is fully aware of my tendency to worry intensely about him, and that if I make it too plain that I am doing so he will not tell me exactly what he feels. This horrible dilemma is, I feel sure, one that everybody who loves someone with a physical disability such as diabetes has to contend with.

September 29th: Cooleville House

Here we are at Cooleville House and civilization, with other people's feelings to consider instead of mountain roads, lakes, rivers. But I believe a good soaking in the natural world is a beneficial Turkish bath toughening one against human impacts – whereas (contrariwise) over-indulgence in sociability produces a form of sharp acid that erodes one's vital energies.

This square Georgian house has been painted apricot colour and looks over its lawns at the Knockmealdown mountains. Inside it is as comfortable as care and money can make it. The large drawing-room is papered dark red with stippled white roses at least three feet high all over it – very striking; carpet and covers are another sort of red; four maids wear red uniforms and Eddy put on a red velvet dinner jacket for dinner. The house is in fact a beautifully constructed, smoothly working toy, but the little rich boy who owns it sits with great sad eyes, ringed round with ill-health, as thin as a sparrow and with spots on his poor face. Ralph and I agreed that it made our hearts bleed to see him look so ill and exhausted, yet force himself to be charming, amusing, intelligent and the most attentive of hosts. Elizabeth Bowen came to dinner; we both liked her *very* much. Horse-faced, with big hands and a clumsy body in a short black evening dress and flashing diamond corsage; she has an attractive stammer which makes her start words beginning with 'r' with a whirring sound like a clock about to strike.

October 1st

Eddy tells me he's worn out with being host, and longs to be a guest again at Crichel. I sympathized with him and told him that he entertains one unnecessarily, which is true. A tragic look crossed his face as he said: 'Oh, but I don't feel I can ask people to come all this way just to sit in the *rain*!' Yet it hasn't rained at all since we came and there's never been a dull moment. Though Eddy looks ill he's entrancing to be with, so gay and full of laughter. He rails against the state of things from a purely aristocratic point of view, and often declares his disbelief in, or dislike of equality, but here in Ireland he can live in a way that exists nowhere else, nor has done for about a hundred years. No two sets of values could be more different than ours and Eddy's especially now that he has become a Catholic, yet very warm affection – mutual I believe – exists between us.

Most enjoyable evening dining at Bowenscourt, at a candle-lit table in a vast room full of shadows, servants waiting, and Elizabeth in a white evening dress and emeralds. Afterwards, before a roaring fire in the equally vast drawing-room we played Scrabble. Jim Egan, a friend of Elizabeth's known as the Kerry Bull, was very amusing, inventing outrageous Irish words like AMIDGIN [Imagine]. Our visit to Cooleville, taken all in all, has added its own very distinctive aspect to the view of Irish life we had been gathering on our travels.

October 14th: Ham Spray

We've been back over a week, time enough for the effect of our refreshing long drink to wear off and friends to reappear on the stage. Burgo has taken a room in Tite Street; Robert writes that he is 'in a terrific muddle. How *should* one live?' a question I believe (and hope) we shall go on asking ourselves until we die, and always with the feeling that we've almost got the solution, which remains teasingly round the corner. Robert added, 'How lucky you are down there in the oasis of Ham Spray,' and has been told to come here whenever he likes.

I have had a pleasant surprise in being asked to do a translation for the Harvill Press (French this time).

October 19th

Yesterday Ralph went to London to see his diabetic specialist, Oakley. He is worried by the pains he has been getting now and then in his chest when walking, although our Hungerford doctor believes them to be indigestion. Oakley at once said: 'You've put on too much weight.' He prescribed a strict diet and pills for the pain. 'Fat round the heart' is what he calls it. Ralph had pains on the way to Paddington station, quelled by pills, they came on again while he was sitting quietly in his armchair, and again – waking him up and frightening me into fits – in the night.

October 20th

Another bout of pain in the morning. I kept him in bed and sent for the local doctor (generally spoken of between us as 'Sawbones'), whose attitude alarmed me because it revealed his own alarm. Ralph was determined to get up, and at length was given leave, but with instructions to keep absolutely quiet. Worried to death, I ran like a squirrel from task to task. Sebastian and Raymond came in the evening, by which time Ralph seemed better and more cheerful. They were a welcome distraction to us both.

[Now began a time of nightmare and misery; but as everyone knows who has gone through a similar experience (and millions do), it was by no means continuous, and also we found it possible to live on two levels at the same time – one of anxiety and watchfulness and the other that of the outside world. It was much like walking over a rickety bridge made of broken planks. Every so often one of these gave way and pitched one into the river-bed below. Then up one scrambled again and struggled along as best one could, helped by a strange force which I can only call the life instinct – a fierce determination to exert every ounce of strength and thought to the preservation of our happiness.]

October 22nd

After driving Raymond to the station Ralph admitted to a slight pain. On Janetta's advice we telephoned to tell Oakley of the developments; were they possibly the result of his pills? He sounded alarmed. 'You ought to be in bed. We don't want you running into a thrombosis.' He evidently telephoned Sawbones, who came out later and told Ralph he must remain entirely in his room and do nothing, and that he was arranging for a cardiogram, etc. in Oxford early next week. How bleak these words are as I write them, and yet all the time my head is full of jangling alarm bells and my heart of love for Ralph.

Janetta left us. Robert came 'for refuge. Things are bad here,' he said. *So are they here, God knows.*

October 24th

The day of our journey to Oxford for Ralph's examination. Woke very early, brooding. Sawbones had told me I must do all the driving. 'I don't want to have to come and scrape you off the road,' he said. Oh, the horrible jargon doctors use! I wrote these notes as I sat in the central hall of the Radcliffe, waiting for Ralph to come back.

Living my own life no longer has any meaning, I notice with a certain surprise. My personal greeds are few – music, flowers, whisky, books, and my appetites so *un*-urgent that any strength I possess is available for Ralph's illness, though of course that *is* a personal greed, even without going into philosophical depths. I sit here thinking about fear and the way that a demand on one's courage causes one mentally to twist and brace to take the load. Then I think of Janetta's sensitive and helpful touch on Monday, how she always said the right thing and provided what Sawbones' waffling did not.

Meanwhile my task is to explore every cranny of the situation, however agonizing, and somehow come to terms with it as best I can. It is the combination of doubts about what *is* the best and everything mattering so desperately that is hardest to bear.

They are making poor Ralph run upstairs so as to see how his heart behaves afterwards – this, when he was told to avoid the smallest exertion on pain of death!

Through the heart of the hospital, where I am sitting, people are moving ceaselessly – visitors, stretchers carrying prostrate half-corpses off to be sliced up by one of those stalwart young butchers in white overalls, squat foreign wardmaids wearing absurd little caps like cuffs on their heads. An old man wheels in a barrowful of oxygen cylinders. There's no end to the flowing current, most of it so impersonal, in which one occasionally catches sight of a human face, with anxious eyes brooding over themselves or their nearest and dearest. A faint but definite sour smell pervades everything – the smell of fear, perhaps. So much of medicine seems to be just typing or scrubbing, while I'm aware of not being either a typewriter key or a cake of soap, but just an adventitious bit of grit in an eye. For in these great emporia where the commodity dealt in is human entrails, mind, feelings and thoughts are buried under a mass of tubes and switches.

I turn my mind deliberately to Robert and our conversation last night. The fact to be faced is that he is free from Janetta and from the conflict he was in concerning her, and as a result he is less fierce, calmer. It distresses me that he should reject something so valuable, but there is nothing anyone else can do about it.

Now Ralph came back, having run up several flights of stairs with only very faint discomfort; this was somehow reassuring, but we realized that the Oxford consultant would let us go without telling us *anything*.

October 27th

Sawbones came out to see us. 'I was wrong,' he said, 'it *is* the heart.' The cardiogram had revealed an abnormality of the heart muscle. (We both strove to understand him.) The pain was 'angina of exercise' and being overweight was certainly a part cause. He must take as much exercise as possible short of getting the pain, and go on reducing. There followed a silence, which was worse. This horse-faced man who sweats under the arms and has black fingernails must be the one to stab one to the vitals.

Campbells to dinner. I feel half dead one way or another, and yet all too much alive, thinking and thinking.

October 30th

The nightmare quality of these days is only kept at bay by being constantly busy and as constantly exhausted. Thank God for Robert; I do so hope he'll stay on with us; he has become the perfect companion as before.

I have said nothing about international politics, though there has been plenty of it to think about, and an extraordinary new crisis is blowing up now. Israel has invaded Egypt, as we heard last night on the wireless. Now an unbelievable step has been taken by France and England alone – a twelve hours' ultimatum to both to retreat to so many miles from the Suez Canal. *Or else*. We were at the Campbells' before dinner today listening to the latest news, and I was bewildered and almost shocked by the excitement of the three R's, and annoyed by Mary's tendency to exclaim 'Yippee!' at any bellicose item. Meanwhile Robert has been telephoned by *The Observer* to go to Israel as War Correspondent, and he goes tomorrow. I'm very sorry, I was meaning to ask his advice, and it's been comforting just having him here.

Driving to the Marlborough orchestra last night through the darkness I felt terribly sad and lonely. I cannot forget for a moment my meeting with Sawbones yesterday outside the fishmonger's in Hungerford. I tried to avoid him but couldn't. *God*, how I hate that man, and his grating voice and his coarse red nose. With a grin on his face he told me straight out that he thought I ought to know that Ralph might die at any moment. 'Perhaps I'm being heartless,' he added. Useless to say, 'Yes, my dear chap, you most certainly are.' There flashed into my mind a phrase I had read years ago in a Western novel, and which had always puzzled me: 'When you say that – *smile!*' But this time I turned it round to: 'When you say that – *don't* smile!' I think he must have heard from Dr Oakley (who approves) that we thought of spending the coldest winter weeks in Spain. He – Sawbones – does not approve, and he chose this way of saying so outside the fishmonger's.

[I vividly remember how selfishly I minded Robert's going, just when I had made up my mind to consult him on an important aspect of Ralph's illness: did he think, I would have asked, that Ralph knew the extent of his danger, and if so, should I talk to him about it? For the fact was that I had been so used to confiding all my troubles down to the last grain to Ralph himself that I was finding it practically unbearable not to burden him with my anguish on his behalf. I knew no one who would give advice more truthfully and supportively than Robert.]

November 1st

Ralph listens all day to the news, looking sunk in gloom. Eden must be raving mad. We have started bombing 'Military Objectives' from the air. In fact we are *at war* again, and no one is on our side. America, even our colonies repudiate us. I feel extremely fatalistic about the whole thing – only a sort of contempt for anyone who holds the belief that you can solve problems by killing people. Ralph bought all the papers he could get. Today's had pictures of smug-looking airmen tucking into bacon and eggs after bombing some Egyptians. But nearly all the papers come out against Eden, and corny slogans like 'England and France stand alone' or 'Protecting our life-line' are few and simply *sickening*.

Burgo arrived in the evening, talking and thinking hard about the crisis, or war, or what Eden prefers to call 'Armed Conflict'. He was in Parliament Square last night where a huge crowd, mostly young, were shouting 'Eden must Go!' and being charged by mounted police with batons. Military veterans crawl out of holes and talk about 'pockets of resistance' and 'mopping up'.

November 6th

This evening came the welcome news announced by Eden in the House of Commons that a cease-fire has been ordered in Egypt. Ralph has had a friendly letter from Gerald, and we are seriously wondering whether to go out to Spain after Christmas. Cold is said to have a distinctly bad effect on Ralph's trouble. I have started translating the French book Harvill sent me, and read out my first chapter to Ralph. So quietly and pleasantly can the days pass when we are alone; but at night I often lie awake for hours.

November 20th

A wonderful ripe peach of an autumn day. Ralph and I took a walk along the top of the Downs with no ill effects, which cheered him up a lot. Indeed I'm more than satisfied with his progress. His illness has completely expunged from my conscious mind all those infinitesimal selfish tugs and irritations which arise between two people who live so closely welded together.

Janetta came for a night. When I said I thought most of our friends were anti-Eden, as she is, she said, 'Oh no, I'm afraid we're in a minority,' but named no one except Cyril who takes his stand on snobbish grounds, being proud of the fact that he knows the Edens and dines with them in Downing Street.

This morning the papers announce that Eden is ill and has been ordered to rest.

November 21st

Both of us are feeling low this wintry morning. A breakfast conversation explored the aching area a little, but not to much purpose. Ralph told me he could not guarantee to report on all his physical sensations – life would be unendurable if he did. This of course I perfectly understand and sympathize with; it is one of the unimagined complications of the situation that I must suppress my anxious questions – or even looks – and wear a mask to which I am hopelessly unaccustomed. Secretly therefore I note down that I get the impression that he has felt less good lately. Noel Carrington wanted him to go and see his heart-specialist friend, Geoffrey Konstam, and he agreed to do so 'some time'. I feel at times as if I had been thumping along in the saddle for ages and long for nothing but sound sleep. But at nights I am beset by mosquito thoughts, and toss and turn for hours.

December 3rd

Burgo and Simon are here and have gone off for a walk. Their happiness together and youth are very consoling. Ralph saw Geoff Konstam in London two days ago and was thoroughly overhauled. He said he had definitely had a coronary thrombosis, but it had healed up pretty well and should continue to do so. On the whole the verdict was encouraging but it has left us both a little flat.

December 5th

Ralph has run out of tobacco and has gone in to Hungerford to buy more, raising of course the question of how much attention should be paid to Geoff's dictum that he should cut down on smoking and drink. The truth is I shall have to grit my teeth and watch him doing what is bad for him. He does make efforts but smoking in particular is one of his greatest pleasures. Janetta rather annoyed me by telling him, after our visit to Geoff, that it was monstrous to expect him to cut down on the drink. Perhaps she couldn't herself but many people do it, and I see the two values balanced in imaginary scales – drink and life itself.

December 18th

Christmas is almost upon us. Last week in London we booked places on an aeroplane, thus committing ourselves to whizz through the night to Gibraltar in the middle of January. Is it madness? We both look forward, yet at times I feel sick with panic.

December 19th

A letter from Gerald. They obviously fear and dread our coming to Málaga. 'Here, owing to cold, we just couldn't make you comfortable ... we have been having too many visitors. I, you know, and Gamel too, need a lot of emptiness and calm.' I respect his honest unhospitality, although of course we wouldn't have wanted to stay with them for more than a night or two. And just as chilling as was Gerald's letter, a call from Janetta was warming. Ralph and I say to each other that she is our best friend. I certainly lean on her more than anyone else, young as she is. 'What shall I do with you away all that time?' she said. F.: 'Why don't you come too?' J.: 'I'll come like a shot.' If that's not friendship I don't know what is. I forgot to say that Gerald's letter went tactlessly on to show his readiness to take in Joanna Carrington.[1] 'We should both very much like to have her. She shall have my big room and I will see that she is comfortable.'

---

[1] The lovely young daughter of Noel and Catherine, who had been very ill.

Nonetheless our morale is rather good. Ralph has been very gay and particularly sweet to me. But we admit to pique over Gerald's letter. Ralph said: 'If Gerald were in the Zoo he would have a notice on his cage saying, "This animal is dangerous".'

December 31st

Rain has fallen all day. This horrid old year ends in a flood of tears. I believe that now our greatest pleasure is being alone together. We had Julia and Lawrence and of course Burgo for Christmas; ate a vast succulent turkey and drank champagne. But it was all slightly muffled. On Christmas Day it snowed and the telephone was down. Ralph was agitated by the responsibilities of Wilde's time off, and I made him sit by himself in the little sitting-room, behaving like a bossy hospital nurse when I really felt like a frightened mouse, isolated by lack of telephone. Burgo was angelically helpful, genial and talkative. Lawrence brought us a magnificent present – a picture; Julia made us aware of her criticisms and displeasure. I felt very sorry for her, a woman with nothing tangible to complain of yet so desperately unhappy.

Our only visitors were the Carringtons: they brought Joanna whose beauty filled the room like a glowing lamp.

1957

January 6th: Ham Spray

I started the New Year with a piece of paper on which I wrote: 'Problems to be dealt with' and 'Things to do'. One of the former is 'Cat and Kitten' (what to do with them while we are away?). This flimsy set of scribbles kept me writing cheques and letters all day, but the 'problems' floated in the air like barrage-balloons which I could neither forget nor puncture. Dined last night at the Moynes, where we met Laurie Lee and his wife Kathie. I sat next to Laurie, who is a great charmer, but more than that a very likeable man who wants to give pleasure and is quick and sensitive. Kathie is big and fine looking with a mane of thick tawny hair. After dinner we had some rather eccentric music – Laurie Lee played on Fiona Guinness's Amati, to my piano accompaniment, Bryan singing.

January 7th

Three letters from Spain: one from Gamel saying she had taken a *casita* for us belonging to a Marquesa, but there is alas, no room for Janetta. Another from Gerald was angry and bossy, saying that my letter announcing Janetta's arrival had just come, and it would make things most awkward with the Marquesa. On reading this, Ralph 'over-boiled' (his own expression) steadily for about an hour, which is the sort of thing he is forbidden to do! He says he gets no physical sensations from such irritable feelings, but they make me very anxious. Perhaps we'd better not go to Spain, I thought, if Ralph and Gerald are going to get so worked up with each other. Then we opened the third; it was from Annie Davis, inviting us all to stay a day or two at their house at Churriana, La Cónsula – this is really extremely kind as we have only met them a few times.[1]

January 19th

The date of our departure swoops down on us like a great bird, and whenever I think about it I dissolve into unspeakable panic. The vet came and 'put' poor Minnie 'to sleep'. I kept well away in Hungerford feeling a little sick, partly because it caused me so little emotion. Her sweet black kitten takes up a lot of time, attention and love – rushing from wild antic to wild antic and then hurling itself exhausted and purring loudly on our laps, looking up with round beads of eyes and dropping instantly asleep.

Most of the time I am in a state of depression. I do wish I could find a little courage somewhere.

---

[1] Annie was Cyril's sister-in-law. Both she and Bill were American. They died within a few hours of each other in May, 1985.

[My last entry was of course compounded of fears as to how Ralph would stand our journey. Might the altitude affect him? I had made enquiries about pressurization of aeroplanes and the answers were not altogether reassuring. And was it all a great mistake? Did he really long to be allowed to stay quietly at Ham Spray with no efforts required of him, with his *Times*, his books and his big green armchair? I had to guess, too many questions would only fuss him. Thank God, that obsessional, craven, dank state of mind really came to an end once packing was done, we had left the black kitten in her temporary home and said goodbye to Burgo. A curtain of teeming rain made England a place to get away from, with its scudding angry clouds, soggy earth, and the darkness settling down so early indoors.

On our way through London Ralph declared that he was going to the *New Statesman* to get a cargo of books to review, but it became suddenly obvious he would rather I went. Our night flight to Gibraltar was absolutely carefree; we were only fourteen souls where there were seats for forty-seven. So, after eating the beautiful slices of cold roast beef brought by Janetta, after looking down for a while through 25,000 feet of air as clear as glass to the map of Europe outlined in Christmas Tree lights below, we all stretched out on three seats and fell asleep. Gibraltar was moist, green and *warm*. We picked up our little hired beetle and made off along the coast road in excellent spirits. We had arrived!]

January 24th: La Cónsula

Awoke in our comfortable bedroom at La Cónsula which contains at one end the fiction department of Bill's excellent library. The house is all snowy whitewash and brown wood inside, with square white-covered settees and chairs, fireplaces full of glowing logs. In the dining-room a raised fireplace crackles and spits as handsome Fernanda cooks our *gambas* or grills steaks as big as Aberdeen terriers; wine and whisky gush into glasses, and I see it will be a job to keep Ralph to his regime. But this hospitality is so warm and generous; it is impossible not to be touched by the genuine friendliness of Bill and Annie. 'Thorough' is the word for Bill. All the books, all the music, all the food, wine and comfort a civilized person should require Bill provides.

The Campbells are staying here, and after breakfast Robin took us round the garden, where the trees are palms, mimosas and avocados, and oranges and grapefruit grow in Black Sambo profusion.

January 25th

Springing into action, we have inspected and rented Buena Vista, a solid little house with plenty of beds and a sheltered patio, standing above the road from La Cónsula to Gerald's village, Churriana. There are too few blankets and no sheets or cutlery, but the Brenans have lent us the former and this afternoon we drove in to Malaga to buy the rest: sheets for all the beds – we got the man to cut them with his huge pinking scissors so they will not need hemming. Pillow-slips? A señora of the Casa could make them by tomorrow. *Con botones*? Yes please, *con botones*. So it went on. We were eventually fitted out, and the Brenans' Maria will come and work for us in the mornings.

Returning to the Cónsula we found two new visitors had arrived: Jamie Caffery is an American garden expert, a very friendly, rather comic character with something of the dog in his appearance and even more in his deep barking voice, whose resonance sends the lines grooving his face up and down as he talks. Jaime Parladé is a young, slender Spaniard, with an oval face and long-lashed twinkling eyes. The whole party except us and Robin went off to see the dancer Antonio perform in Malaga.

January 27th: Buena Vista

Yesterday we moved into our new home, dining however with the Brenans. Gamel gave us some more blankets, for the nights are cold, and an electric kettle to boil up our hot-water bottles: However, as soon as we plugged it in all the lights fused! So in utter blackness, lighting tiny wax matches and dropping them all over the place, we fumbled our way to our beds and crept between our new sheets in rooms which have the chill of having been shut up for weeks.

Today we drove along the Coín road to collect wood for our fires and fir-cones to light them with. The almond blossom is just coming out, and when we looked up from our task we saw the mountains beyond Malaga rumpling softly in the evening light and the snowy mountains far beyond. *Not* to live in a country where one soaks all day in such a bath of natural beauty sometimes strikes me as illogical.

January 31st

We all three took our little car further afield today, through villages dazzling with fresh whitewash, past brick-coloured hillsides dotted with olive trees. There were few cars but many more mules, on which their riders sat with that extraordinary style Spaniards show in everything they do, even to the exact angle they wear their hats, with which also they pull out their sturdy wooden chairs and sit in the sun, sewing or preparing vegetables, or tilt them back against the blue-white walls of their houses. As a nation they have remarkable good taste and are not prone to vulgarity, nor do I find, as Robin does, that the way they so often sing at work in the fields or as they walk to the well is sentimental and bogus – on the contrary I believe it is because they are happy or sad and like to express their feelings in their own individual musical idiom.

On and on we went, and up and up, until the sea lay far away below with the shadow of the American battleship which is at present in harbour lying unruffled beneath it. We ate our picnic lunch on the Pass of Leon, which is over 3,000 feet high and had snow below us and some small brown and green orchids around us, while far down in the valley were puffs of grey and pink smoke, which were olive and almond trees. A shout from Janetta who had wandered off (she had found big clumps of sweet-scented white jonquils) and another soon afterwards: 'Irises!'

February 10th

Ralph and I discussed the hard drinking habits of our friends and wondered what they are after? Drowning unhappiness, misting over reality? But none of them seems to be really unhappy, while someone like Julia (who *is*) doesn't appear to hanker after oblivion in drink. In youth, our generation used to take to it spasmodically as an accompaniment to dancing or something that downed the barriers and made people more sexually attractive. It doesn't go so well with middle age and conversation – drunken talk is usually (but not always) a poor affair. Then some drinkers plan their drinking day as seriously as writers do their writing days, which suggests it's a substitute of some sort. Is it a satisfactory one? Or is it more like trying to use spectacles for shoes than loving a pekinese instead of a person. Ralph thought that drinking 'bouts' were in the nature of Dionysian religious practices, and this was confirmed this afternoon when we walked over to the Cónsula and found last night's drinkers lying spent and deflated in the sun.

Gerald has been having flu, but called yesterday to say that Joanna Carrington *is* coming to stay. He sat with us for a couple of hours talking and talking, sometimes looking quite surprised at the words that came out of his own mouth. This interlocking world of expatriates seems to me rather like *South Wind*.

February 19th

Dinner at the Cónsula, and our first meeting with Cyril since his arrival. I was put next to him, and (determined not to be got down by his possible disapproval) I handed him a little butter about his broadcast, but resisted the temptation to lay it on too thick. The result was a conversation enjoyed by us both, I believe. But when we moved to the sitting-room and collected round the fire, Cyril, retired to a far corner of the room, flung himself back in a chair with his face parallel to the ceiling and his eyes closed, and remained thus for the rest of the evening. (Janetta christened this his 'music position'.) She said afterwards that his excuse for this ostentatiously rude behaviour was that he was 'desperately miserable'.

February 21st

We said goodbye to Robin, who leaves tonight, and went with Gerald and Gamel to see the English cemetery in Malaga. It is a very pretty place, and Gerald showed us round with an owner's pride. 'It's the nicest cemetery I know – but it's very difficult to get into now. We're going to the British Consul to book our places. I want to be in this corner here. The only thing that worries me is that I can't think of a good epitaph – it must be in Greek. Don't you think it's charming? It's got a lovely view – that's *very* important.' Feeling he was going rather far, I asked irreverently: 'To the corpses or those that visit them?' Gerald answered huffily: 'I don't think like that at all.' Gerald and I had become separated from the others and as we roamed among the tombs and the charming plants growing among them he let his mind run free about the domain of death, which he clearly found pleasant. I was only half listening.

February 25th

On a morning that was still, hot and clear, we went with Janetta and Jaime Parladé to look at a possible house on the coast near Estepona, attractive but too small; we picnicked on the beach, and afterwards sat under a shady tree watching the beautiful day ripen into a golden evening. Jaime charmed us both by his intelligence and gaiety, and it's as great a pleasure to hear him talk Spanish as English.

February 26th

Though Janetta was subjected last night to a large dose of Cyril's pettishness and a good deal of the 'music position', she returned from dinner at the Cónsula very keen that we should invite him with the Davises to a ceremonial lunch at Martín's fish restaurant on the beach at Malaga. We are entirely agreed, as we shall not in a hurry forget Bill's and Annie's great kindness to us when we first arrived.

It took place today and 'went off' perfectly; Cyril was all amiability. But what an extraordinary object he is becoming! With his great round head passing necklessly into his body; his torso clad in a flashy American beach shirt, ski-ing trousers and fur-lined boots, he looked like some strange species of synthetic man or Golem.

[On 1 March we started on our drive back to Gibraltar by way of Cordoba and Seville. Ralph and I hadn't been to Cordoba for fifteen years and Janetta never; it is one of my two favourite Spanish towns, the other being Salamanca. We went twice to see the Mosque. I received a shock of pleasure, interest and even alarm on entering that jungle of columns, gliding behind each other and continually making new patterns as one moved about; but the emotion it arouses seems to me more suitable to a cave or natural phenomenon than a work of art. Before reaching the strange coastal town of Puerto Santa Maria, with its flat roofs topped with croquet balls and its excellent fish restaurants, we stopped on a ridge with a superb view and an equally remarkable flora – tall orchids, a huge brilliant blue pimpernel, a faded brown scilla and many more, which I eagerly gathered, and contrived to get back to London safely, by putting them each night in our hotel wash-basin. The reason that I hadn't felt sadder when I thought of my stillborn flower book is that it left me a legacy of delight in wild flowers, a certain amount of technical knowledge, and contacts with botanical centres.

We took off in the small hours in a crowded aeroplane full of drunks, and got to London in a tepid drizzle.]

March 29th: Ham Spray

As far as Ralph's health is concerned the Spanish adventure was a great success and I am happier about him than I ever thought to be. Janetta, alas, looks neither well nor happy.

Two days in London yielded quite a lot of pleasure – an afternoon going to *Phèdre* with Julia, a visit to Burgo in his rooms, and another to the Natural History Museum, where I had left my flowers from Spain as soon as we got to London. On my first visit I saw, talked to and fell in love with a wonderful Dr Melderis, a tall, gentle blue-eyed native of I don't know what foreign country, who presides over the European section of the Botanical Department. His domain is reached by a private lift leading up into a library and herbarium – all brown wood shelves and drawers, smelling deliciously of dried plants. On this second visit Dr Melderis was away, to my regret, but two assistants and a passing botanist treated my specimens with respect and even admiration.

But the most stimulating experience was the Racine. Ralph and I had read the play as well as various critiques coming up in the train. Some say that Edwige Feuillière is the best living actress, and her Phèdre sublime; others that it's a gallant failure. I thought neither was true. She's always the actress, you can't forget it, and at best you admire her art and notice it in operation. I never found her deeply moving – no clutch at the throat or starting tear; but is it possible to be moved by the horror of incest, when one doesn't in fact feel it? Ralph thought the love of an older woman for a handsome youth was in itself moving, as was any unrequited love. I agree and regret I didn't find it so. What enthralled and gripped me was the controlled concentrated emotion emanating from the marvellous music of Racine's words, acting exactly as do the libretto and music of an *opera seria* like *Semele* or *Idomeneo*, so I decided half-way through to give way to the poetry and cease to wonder whether the psychology was possible, or try to think Edwige Feuillière was really Phèdre, which did not prevent my feeling so much electric tension through-out that I could scarcely breathe.

April 3rd

My horrid French translation is packed off, the new Freudian index not yet come – though I sometimes wonder if my 'work' is not the frantic leg-movements of a spider just before it hurtles down the run-away hole in the bath.

Ralph's health is still a source of pride and pleasure; he is very good about taking his exercise and not eating too much. Janetta has rented the Campbells' cottage, which is very nice for us. Our house is pretty trim; our black kitten growing into a charming companion, our staff fairly pleased with us, and Spain to look forward to in the winter.

April 28th

Our landscape has been clouded by Ralph's twice feeling some 'uneasiness' or 'constriction' while walking. I feel dreadfully anxious, but must struggle not to show it; I just bow my head in ox-like acceptance of the blows of life, and bitterly regret that I am never, never as nice to him as I want to be and my love for him should make me.

May 2nd

Up early and to London for the day for Duncan's private view. Many old friends were collected under the hot light beating down from the glass roof; very old they seemed, and dusty too, with the flash of false teeth and the glitter of spectacles. Vanessa stood beaming seraphically from under a huge inverted wicker basket. Marjorie Strachey like a swollen spider all in black. I came away feeling saddened. I'm well aware of what in index terms I should call 'withdrawal of libido from the outside world', yet there are moments when something or other, some glue seems still to fasten me firmly to it. For instance, late tonight after our return I stood in the kitchen watching Dinah drink up her bedtime saucer of milk: the old scrubbed red tiles, the kitten's glossy black fur and the white milk, with the electric light pouring over them all from the ceiling and the quiet pattering of the rain outside sent a wave of peace, and acquiescence in the scheme of things, surging over me.

May 17th

A discussion between Ralph and me about Communism at breakfast. We had heard a debating society questioning a leading Communist on the wireless last night. It caused me to wonder whether one doesn't sometimes throw overboard a whole system of ideas just because some of them can be (and are) pushed to mad extremes – whether in fact Capitalism was necessarily right because so many Communist conclusions are wrong. Bound up with this is the dislike I feel at the thought of immense wealth in the hands of undeserving egotistic people, the height of whose altruism is reached by standing their friends large expensive meals of foods out of season, and who attach no responsibility to the power of money. (In contrast to Lord Nuffield and John Christie.) Ralph began to shout at me, and the effort to keep calm, and the failure, gave me an actual feeling of faintness. Later he admitted that he positively enjoyed the battling element in an argument, and when I said how much I loathed it we both became calm and interested again, and branched off into what was the foundation of ethical feelings.

June 3rd

The truth is I am suffering from all-pervading apathy, and though I know its cause all too well I don't know what weapons to fight it with. Some colossal mental effort, like heaving up a mallet and bringing it down on a peg? Where is my courage gone? It's lost, like my spectacles – and just as without my spectacles I can't see to look for them, without my courage I can't make the effort to grab it. If only a living being were like a motor-car and when he or she went wrong one could oil something or adjust the carburettor; but when the psyche is functioning badly, the mind won't get into gear and there's no psychological petrol in the tank there seems nothing to be done, no button to press or handle to swing.

This evening Ralph and I walked across the fields, and he came out of his usual stoical silence and talked freely about his troubles, the difficulty he had in putting up with the sense that his powers are failing or his clumsiness increasing. He made me feel ashamed, and when we got home I realized that something had clicked into place without my pressing any button or heaving mallets. I had found my spectacles.

July 27th

For some reason I can't define I'm counting the hours for the weekend to pass. I feel very tired at a deep level. Robert (here with Georgie) was the life and soul of yesterday evening. Just now, from the music room where he is typing, a melancholy voice rang out, loud and deep: 'When they heard of the death of poor Cock Robin!' Georgie was with me, and she burst out laughing and said, 'It's Daddy!' And who was Cock Robin, I wondered. Burgo, Simon Young and his sister are walking on the downs; Ralph writing a review in the library. Georgie has been writing a story about a King living in a golden castle, being attacked by another King, and returning home to find his Queen had had a baby. (Work that out in Freudian terms!) When the whole Stokke party came over for a drink, Paddy Leigh Fermor read Georgie's story and responded with enthusiasm. 'What shall I put next?' she asked him. Paddy: 'How about a tournament? Yes, I think you'll find that's your best way out – a tournament.'

Robert is now literary editor of *The Spectator*, offering high prices to reviewers to seduce them away from other papers. He walked with us this afternoon through grass sprinkled with harebells, wild carrot and bird's-foot trefoil – the autumn colours, purple, white and yellow, and down below us lay the ripe but still uncut cornfields between the green fur of August hedges. Lovely, I thought, but Robert was contemptuous: 'I've had it all. I simply hate it really. I think we're mad to put up with it.' It's touch and go how long he puts up with *The Spectator* and London life, and I suppose depends on whether he can raise a defence against loneliness.

August 22nd

Ralph wakes up most mornings disgusted with himself and feeling what he calls 'rubbishy' – this makes him very sweet to me, for having to live with such a rubbishy man. I'm more disposed to wake disgusted with the *world* and put the blame on the Creator. Once my eyes are open I tend to see some segment of the immediate future in exact detail, as when lying on a summer lawn one peers into the grass and sees the superhuman struggles of an ant to surmount blade after blade. At other times it's the insoluble problems I carry round – the black bag full of distressful secrets. A sort of thin horny development of the skin seems to have grown up to protect me, but at the first gleam of danger to what is vital to my happiness I become a quivering jelly.

Rosamond [Lehmann] and Burgo arrived together in her car. She was looking quite splendid, not a hair out of place and her bloom as fresh as ever. Last night she warmed up to pleasant old croneydom and we had a good talk about old friends and old times. When Ralph suggested she should write her memoirs, she exclaimed in a voice full of horror: 'But I've had such an *awful* life!' And in view of her beauty, sweet temper and success I suppose she has. I'm puzzled by Burgo. He has I think some schemes for living but doesn't want to talk about them. I can only applaud his independence and hope it is solid and secure. His instinct is right to keep a little aloof from anyone who minds everything that happens to him as much as I do.

August 24th

When we were alone again I pulled up an armchair in front of the fire and read steadily through the grey moist hours. Colette by her husband was my book. Impossible not to love and admire her, and it's one of those books that manure one's flower-bed. I really believe that reading books that don't do this in one way or another is a sort of addiction or mere time-killing. Colette was full of love, not only for flowers and wasps, but for things like food. When she was hungry she was *fiercely* hungry, almost growling with animal longing. She was a sensualist, and if she lacked anything it was – not hate exactly, but negative and critical reactions, something I miss in my friends when they haven't got them.

September 8th

We were bidden to stay with Kitty West to meet Anthony and his new wife Lily, this being the first time they had got together, along with the children. Lily is a tall girl with a fine figure and long limbs – almost a beauty and with a charming and responsive manner. Here were three people trying to do their best under fairly difficult circumstances, and possibly Kitty – who had suffered most in their joint history – tried a little too hard. On Sunday after breakfast on the lawn (delicious smell of coffee and sight of a bowl of figs, bananas and bright red apples) we were joined by Jimmy and Tania Stern. Jimmy is a gifted storyteller, a writer, and an Irishman belonging to the same civilization as Joyce and Beckett, of whom he had many memories. I had just been reading Joyce's Letters and not taken to their personal flavour. 'He seemed so uninterested in other writers, or anything in the outside world,' I volunteered. J.S.: 'So he was, totally uninterested.' F.: 'Was he a good talker?' J.S.: 'He didn't talk much; he only asked questions. When I first met him he asked me questions for a whole hour about my childhood in Ireland. He was only interested in two things: Ireland and his own writing.' F.: 'Forgive my asking, but have you read *Finnegans Wake*?' J.S.: 'Not a word! Wouldn't touch it.' Beckett, he said, was absolutely charming, but a very lazy man; he put off work as long as possible. In excuse for his lack of production he said to Jimmy: 'Ah, but you see I'm inarthiculate.' 'I pleased him by telling him how much I liked the silences in *Waiting for Godot,*' said Jimmy, 'and he said, *"Aren't* they lovely?"'

Anthony's manner was very good, very dignified and restrained, and he was admirable with the children, if perhaps there were less of the satanic gleams and flashes of wit that I remember in the past.

Called at Crichel and on the Cecils on our way home.

October 5th: Ham Spray

The chief piece of grit in our thoughts and discussions at present is Burgo's urgent desire to get a proper job, and his asking us for help in no uncertain terms. Ralph and I have both fired off letters to possible strings, containing SOS's veiled or open. We do not want to go off to Spain with the problem unsolved.

For once the news has produced something purely interesting and pleasant. The Russians launched an artificial 'satellite' about two feet in diameter, which is now hurtling round the earth at a height of 500 miles making a noise between a 'cheep' and a 'bleat', which has even been relayed to us in our drawing-rooms. Nobody seems to know what will become of this man-made object, whether it will disintegrate or fall to earth; but scientists all over the world are having a wonderful time listening to it and recording its path. Last night's wireless suggested a delightful idea: the *next* satellite will carry all sorts of elaborate machines including a camera which will photograph *the other side of the moon*!

October 15th

The divine beauty of these days is like the tolling of a bell summoning me to church to take part in some religious rite I don't believe in. Yesterday we walked on the Downs above Hippenscombe, partly at the request of Mr Grose (who is compiling a *Flora of Wiltshire*) to see if we could find indications that it was the 'Juniper Down mentioned by the angry farmer of Stoke'. The corpses of some dead orchids would also help, and we did find several, only one – the Frog – being recognizable. Such bits of fascinating detective work are an inheritance from the poor dead flower book, but by no means the only ones. As we walked home blue mist was collecting in the hollows between trees which varied in colour from bright spring green to vermilion.

October 17th

As we were driving to London I asked Ralph, 'How would you define your chief beliefs?' 'About values or facts?' he asked. 'Values.' 'I would say, I think, that it was vital to attach oneself to someone or something outside oneself.' Rather a good answer; and since he was too busy negotiating the suburban traffic to ask for mine, I pondered them in silence, and decided that '*Liberté, Egalité and Fraternité*' hadn't been half bad, but needed a lot of qualification.

I telephoned the Natural History Museum and made an appointment with Dr Melderis. He showed me my old specimens all beautifully docketed and pressed and then produced a huge package of pressing materials – the 'flimsies' into which the living plant goes, and the grey blotting-paper sheets that are to go outside and have to be changed like a baby's nappies. It is the most exciting thing that has happened to me for months, and I am as proud of my 'press' and its webbing straps as I was of my violin when I bought it. The good doctor really wants me to collect everything I find in the south of Spain; they are short of material for this time of year. I carried all my equipment away, glowing and purring.

October 21st

We drove Raymond and ourselves across to Essex, to spend a weekend with the Nicholses at Lawford Hall. My opinion of Raymond went up even higher than usual when he told us he still suffers almost constant headaches, which can only be kept at bay by pills. And he was such a good guest, so appreciative and stimulating. There was another person who helped make it a particularly enjoyable weekend – a Dutch lady of immense distinction. Her function was that of Director of the Queen's Cabinet, whatever that means. About sixty and rather heavily built, her smooth black hair hardly tinged with grey was drawn back on either side of an impressively broad white forehead and the features of a benign and amiable goat. Her charming personality seemed to zoom out and fill the room, as she sat quietly knitting on the sofa. 'I only do it because I find it relaxing,' she told me and it was soon clear that her mind was extremely active. She is very musical and possesses all the records of Beethoven's Late Quartets which she loves better than any other music.

Phyllis is becoming more and more like the birds she so loves, who now hop in and out of her bedroom window and inhabit a maze of boughs and twigs inside it. She visited us one morning with a starling perched in her thick curly hair, showing in her bright eyes and rather stiff stance an affinity with her favourite creatures.

Then came Rosamond who descended to dinner in a dress of soft grey pleated stuff, looking so like a Greek statue that everyone gasped. Somehow the Monarchy came up in the conversation. 'I hear you're a Republican,' Phil Nichols said to me. 'You aren't really, are you? You mustn't be – you don't know how important the Monarchy is to the Dominions.' Rosamond declared herself 'a convinced Royalist', and even Raymond accused me of 'wanting to deprive the typist of her daydreams'. 'Surely Marilyn Monroe would do as well?' I said, but the truth is, I am almost totally uninterested in the subject. Pacifism of course came next. 'I don't share your views,' said Phil. 'I believe there are worse things than war.' Maybe, but most of those worse things are fostered and manured by it.

Now we are back at home with Sebastian, the cosiest of fireside cats, and I think perhaps the happiest man I know. He tells us he has never taken a sleeping-pill in his life and didn't know what worry was. I *think* he implied that he had never been in love, but from one of his meaning 'ah's, I guess that he knows no difference between love and sex.

October 31st

In the bathroom today Ralph said that it was a little over a year since his first heart attack, and tried to convey to me what he felt about it. 'It's as if a finger or a hand was laid upon me here,' he said, pressing his chest, 'and came with me everywhere. I'm never alone, always accompanied. But I don't talk to you about it, though not a day passes when I don't think of it.' Nor, good heavens, for me either. I wish I was more certain whether I should encourage him to talk more about it. Oh, what a dunce I sometimes feel!

November 5th

It's tempting to connect the present sudden storms and freak gales with the news that on Sunday the Russians launched a second satellite much bigger than the first, with a live dog inside it! This and its attendant circumstances, such as the frenzy among dog-lovers, deputations clamouring on the steps of the Russian Embassy, or the word 'Satellite' heard from Mrs Hoare's lips, has made everything seem like a novel by H. G. Wells instead of the humdrum world we've been living in so long. As a background to this there is my own sense of feebleness at the approach of our journey to Spain, like two courageous but crazy old people about to walk the plank.

But my morning's post was full of interest: a letter from Kew asking me to collect specimens of *Dianthus* from Spain for them. A cheque for my last Freudian index, and a parcel of children's books to review from Robert. Such things give me a spurious sense of being a 'going concern'.

November 10th

I am writing in the corner of the same room where sit Eddy [Sackville] and the Godleys, our weekend visitors. Eddy has grown a small neat pointed beard, and (what with the bags under his eyes) has become unexpectedly like Edward VII. The first evening of their stay was spent discussing the Angry Young Men and the Establishment, and Eddy put forward extremely retrograde views, which dumbfounded Wynne. 'But I think you're appalling!' he said once. Eddy had been saying, 'I *hate* equality,' and that he didn't believe in education for the masses, the words 'people like me' and 'their proper station' occurring several times. He holds the odd view that the people he employs – cook, gardener, etc. couldn't do without him and that he is being somehow altruistic in looking after them. I ventured to say, 'But I suppose they look after you in a sense?' What, I can't help wondering, would have been Eddy's views if he had *not* been born in the purple? Luckily the argument never got out of the comic stage.

I love the Godleys more and more. Wynne enjoys his own cleverness; Kitty's intelligent sensitivity sometimes seems to worry her. She wears a haunted look at times, and one can't lightly mention the atom bomb in front of her.

November 15th

We shall be off in a week, and I have been tying up a lot of loose ends, one after another. The days are full of bumps and hollows, yet if they weren't time would pass like a gramophone record with no grooves in it and play no tune. I have the horrors of the world on my mind again, though I feebly try not to think about them. Everywhere the same ghastly unsolved *muddles* are spread like slime – Korea, Algeria and the rest. The Americans are deeply humiliated by the Russian success with their rockets; meanwhile the dog in the second one is officially pronounced to be dead. The *Daily Mirror* came out with a wide border of black, and a great deal about soft noses and velvety eyes up there in the stratosphere.

[On 23 November Ralph and I set off for what was to be our longest stay in Spain, in hopes that the mild weather of Andalusia would benefit Ralph's health. Once again we rented Buena Vista, the solid little house in Gerald's village of

Churriana, where also we now had our two more recent friends – Bill and Annie Davis.]

November 24th

As we sped south I realized that Ralph had set his heart on lunching at Bordeaux. And why not? I wholeheartedly agreed – after all, it was his birthday, and the road was straight and fast. Should we go to the Chapon Fin or Dubern? We chose the latter, and also its two specialities: a smooth rich bisque of écrevisses and the filet de sole Dubern, served by waitresses in pleated aprons with priestly seriousness. A witch-like woman at the next table got an appallingly noisy attack of hiccups, and practically stood on her head in a vain attempt to stifle them. I couldn't resist passing on our famous cure (learned in a Swiss train) via the waitress, ending optimistically, '*Ça finira*'. Supposing it didn't! But it did, and there was much nodding and smiling and '*Merci, Madame!*'[1]

November 26th

Reached Madrid today, after a night on the cold plateau of Burgos. Only when I came downstairs in the Hotel Inglés did I realize in an emotional thunderclap that it was the very same hotel where Ralph and I had spent our unofficial honeymoon thirty-two years ago. The pretty blue and white staircase, the lift with its silver-painted trellis, all were startlingly familiar. When I told Ralph, who had been putting the car away, his reaction was quite different from mine. As we sat drinking our third manzanillas in a café he fell into gloom at the difference between then and now, when he felt humiliated by age and illness and that the blaring vitality of Madrid was too much for him. 'Fell' is not the right word – he sent up a shell-burst of gloom with bits of shrapnel in it. I felt a tear or two trickling down my cheek, and didn't much mind if it was noticed by the waiters who stood around with their tragic-monkey masks and long tight-fitting aprons to the ground. Surely, I pleaded with Ralph, we could be content to watch like duennas at the ball, without removing ourselves entirely from its music and excitement. He says he'll tell me more about his thoughts on the subject, and I hope he does.

November 28th

Down the winding road from the Pass of Leon, we dipped into Churriana. In the Brenans' garden a little boy was sweeping up the leaves. Soon out came Gamel, pressed the stamp of her lipstick on our cheeks, and was followed by Gerald and Joanna Carrington. Gerald looks as if he had been through a mangle and every drop of emotion squeezed out, his eyes unfocused. Joanna was pale, thin and composed; Gamel the most welcoming.

December 3rd: Buena Vista

Sitting over our olive-wood fire, sipping Spanish vodka, and feeling steadier and happier now that we are settled in our own domain. We have just been with Gamel to the eighteenth-century aqueduct in the *vega*, to collect specimens of the mandrake that grows there, before it finished flowering – a sinister, almost ugly plant with dirty purple flowers flush with its circular tuft of leaves. I had the time

---

[1] Whose husband had been Lord Chancellor 1945–51.

of my life with it and other specimens trying to press them on the dining-room table, where all my botanical equipment – 'flimsies', drying-papers, trowel, lenses, knives, Spanish Floras, are laid out, giving me a delightful sense of work in progress.

As well as Gerald's Maria we now have a little dark Antonia with a passionate expression and a sweet negroid smile to look after us. She served our dinner tonight on a table by the fire, with great style and an attitude between a matador's and a Flamenco dancer's.

December 4th

Maria had told us that Gerald had a high fever, so we were surprised when he came springing in, saying he felt 'marvellous – perfectly well'. The talk was naturally all about Joanna. He had to unload what had accumulated; no need to turn the tap on, out it all came. He's not in love with her he says but he 'lives through her. There's nothing the three of us can talk about, but every evening Gamel goes off to write her poetry and then Joanna and I talk and talk for hours and hours. I'm a very good listener, you know. Oh, it's wonderful to have her here. Don't you think I seem rejuvenated? I was bored for years before Joanna came.'

December 7th

Gerald came for a walk with us this morning, in a different frame of mind, talking entirely about writing and works of art in general. They should always evolve as they went on, never be seen ahead and entire, above all never be the result of a flash of vision, quickly expressed. Picasso's enormous facility and versatility, and power to do that very thing, had had a fatal influence. 'An artist should always be rather stupid,' he went on, 'like Titian or Cézanne. It's very dangerous to be clever.' Of Spanish painters he said Velázquez was 'vulgar', and he didn't really 'like' El Greco, although of course he knew he was a genius. So, talking as we went, and occasionally stooping to pick or name a wild flower, we returned down the hillside.

In the evening he called on us again. 'I hope Gamel will publish her sonnets,' he said. 'Women always want success. I only want money.'

He hardly mentioned Joanna, but I think he has worn himself out with emotions about her. He's like a piece of patterned stuff that's been washed and washed until hardly any colour remains.

December 13th

The morning hours unroll happily, with sun streaming in and delicious smells. I study my flowers, press them, read, work a little at Spanish. Ralph comes down from the room where he is writing a review, calls my attention to a praying mantis in the garden and goes up again, until he finally descends to drink montilla with me in the sun and talk about Madame de Lieven, the subject of his review. All this time the dappled light in the patio, and the knowledge that this natural beauty spreads around us, up the mountains and down to the sea, soothes and relaxes.

December 25th

Christmas lunch at the Cónsula – on the balcony, cold though it was. Their house guests were Robin and his brother-in-law Hamish Erskine, Xan and Daphne

Fielding, and her son Alexander Weymouth. When we left at about five Burgo and Joanna were still there.

December 26th

Burgo got home in the small hours. They had been to a cocktail party at Torremolinos, dinner at the Cónsula, and back to Torremolinos again. Robin and Burgo had walked some of the way home through the night. The rootless existence led by the expatriates here is not attractive, and I wonder if it is a delusion that ours at Ham Spray is more solidly embedded, with taproot well down in the earth.

December 31st

The Brenans came to us for dinner and to see the New Year in. We had a very jolly evening playing paper games, at which Burgo was most amusing. Gerald's *bon mot* of the evening: 'Wives are like air. You can't breathe without them but when they are there you don't notice them.'

1958

January 1st: Buena Vista

On New Year's Eve we had walked the Brenans home and kissed goodnight in the road. Joanna kissed Ralph and Burgo, but went upstairs without kissing Gerald. This morning he came to see us to vent his resentment: 'I was in a furious rage. I took the presents I had bought for her and threw them out of the window into the street – a pair of earrings and a mantilla.'

'Didn't you go out and pick them up again?'

'Oh no, no. Some gypsy will have taken them.'

I said: 'You can't get kisses at bayonet-point.'

'No, of course not,' but he went on about gratitude, all he had done for her, pride and so on, obsessionally. The fact that she is leaving so soon has put him in a fever. 'Sunday is her last day, and just supposing the Cónsula should invite her that evening! She's fascinated by them; perhaps she would go. I'll never forgive her if she does.' He left us at our door, saying that Joanna (who had gone for a walk with Burgo) had promised to come back early. This was awkward because I knew Burgo proposed to ask her to stay to tea, and indeed there they were by the fire – Joanna's nose had begun to stream and Burgo was lending her handkerchiefs and nose-drops. They seemed rather touching together and I wouldn't for worlds have shooed her home.

January 5th

Yesterday our next guest, Robert, arrived. Today being marvellously fine we took a picnic up the mountainside to Mijas and were joined by Gerald and Joanna. There was a spectacular view of green velvet monticules stretching below us to the sea from where we sat under a group of olive trees, but Gerald sullied the beauty we were gazing at by exploding into Roman candles about the odious world of Torremolinos. 'It's a place where people come to pick up the last crumbs of sex,' was one, and another, 'Sex is distilled there – all the water of love boiled out of it.'

January 8th

We drove with Robert to the Alpujarras in search of rag rugs, eventually found a cottage where they were made and came away with eight of them. The sight of Gerald's old village Yegen, last seen in 1933, moved me deeply. Some things lie hidden in the memory, inaccessible unless they are revived; they can't be called 'forgotten' because they are capable of resuscitation by shock. Such were the dark red shining strings of pimentoes hanging against the outside walls of the houses, the slender poplars standing like ghosts against the distant view, the sound of trickling water everywhere, and the incomparable freshness of the air.

January 13th

Burgo left for home today. We shall miss him sadly. Cyril Connolly entertained us all to a great lunch party at the Gibralfaro, the Parador standing high above Malaga. Robert showed signs of anxiety that the occasion should be a success, and dressed himself in his smart London suit. It *was*, as all agreed, a great success and Cyril was brilliantly amusing as well as a very genial host. We sat at a long table on the balcony; a vase of flowers stood in front of me, and round it bulged the silhouette of the Master, haloed with tendrils of hair and backed by the sparkling sea far below in the harbour. Robert spends a lot of time at the Cónsula, and we enjoy the tidbits he brings back and the news of how the graph of Cyril's moods is doing. 'Better today.'

This evening over our fireside dinner the conversation turned to present-day pessimism, or *cafard*. Where can one look to find enthusiasm for living? I could only think of Paddy Leigh Fermor. Robert thought it existed in technical, non-intellectual circles. As for himself, he kept repeating, he was 'finished, done for' in tones of dreadful conviction. In vain we said that he made a very different impression on other people, how his energy and vitality were the envy of many. If so, what has finished him? Dare one ask him? The war; a failed marriage? His own character is what he hinted at.

January 19th

Cyril's graph not so good today. The poor Davises are getting desperate as to how he shall be entertained, and there is already talk of trips to the Canaries. Today, at a joint picnic inside a Moorish castle, Cyril wasn't grumpy at all. Dressed in a spaceman's outfit, he lay on his back on the grass, relaxed and giggling at his own jokes and even other people's. He was especially amused when Ralph described Gerald's habit of dashing up mountains to impress girls as 'competitive goat-manship'. One of Cyril's witticisms was 'X thinks before he speaks, Gerald speaks before he thinks, and Bill thinks hard before he doesn't speak.'

I've got a request from an unknown publisher to translate Ibañez' *Sangre y Arena*. So after we got home I walked down to the Brenans to see if they had a copy I could borrow, and found a regular *tertulia* going on – Gerald and Gamel, Cyril and John Haycraft, who has a school of English at Ronda and has just written a book about it. The conversation was more of an omelette than a *soufflé*, but entertaining. I was struck by Cyril's proficiency. I took away my copy of Ibañez, and have written to say I would do it. I started my specimen pages this evening.

February 20th

Ralph and I drove to the airport to meet Raymond, and were delighted to see his brown and smiling face, but (asked how he was) he replied 'Not very well, really – rather depressed.' I hope we shall manage to cheer him up! Dinner at the Cónsula, being Cyril's last was rather orgiastic and the drinks very potent. Bill brought out some hashish. I think everyone was more or less drunk by the end of the evening.

February 22nd

Yesterday I awoke with a beating heart and compulsive craving for water. Read for an hour or so, but without properly taking in the words. I resent being made drunk against my will – it's as if someone deliberately passed me on their infectious disease. Raymond, who had a reviving afternoon sleep, was gratifyingly pleased by our olive-wood fire and our dinner (white onion soup, *cigalas* and young peas).

Today is pleasant and sunny; we took him to the Malaga market. Gerald now pops in and out like a jack-in-the-box, and today there was an exchange between him and Ralph in which feelings began to get dangerously high. It was a question of Gerald's portrait of Ralph in *South from Granada*.

Gerald: 'Oh, it wasn't unkind at all. I merely made you out a dashing philistine who slept with actresses – just what everyone would like to be.' (The rather malicious twinkle in his eyes belied his words.) 'Anyway I sent it to you, and you passed it for publication.'

Ralph: 'Yes I did, though my solicitor thought there were grounds for libel. But what I really objected to was your picture of yourself as a selfless angelic character anxious to do everything for us, when really what you were after was seducing my wife.'[1] For some reason this seemed to revive Gerald's jealousy of Lytton.

Gerald: 'I tried to show in my book how much better Lytton's conversation was than his writing. The trouble was that he wrote to make money; or anyway for fame.' (Nothing could possibly be more untrue, and forestalling Ralph who I thought might fly off the handle, I said so.) 'Oh, there's nothing *wrong* in writing to make money. It's a very good thing to do.'

F. (now really angry): 'That's not the point, Gerald. It's a question of fact – whether Lytton actually did write for money or fame. I maintain that neither he nor any other Old Bloomsbury writer did so, and I *challenge* you to prove the contrary.'

After this the heat but not the life went out of the conversation.

February 27th

Our days at Buena Vista are drawing to a close. We have taken Raymond to see the Málaga Cathedral and driven him up the lovely Coín valley. We ended with a dinner for the Davises and Jaime Parladé, when Maria and Antonia worked hard and successfully to make a delicious *pepitoria*. Letters have come from Janetta and Robert. Janetta writes, 'I can't tell you how I am because I simply don't know. I've been desperate, uncertain and muddled.' And Robert, 'An utterly barren and impoverished state of mind. Have never felt so useless and empty.' How sad that 0 + 0 does not make 1!

March 12th: Ham Spray

Warmly welcomed back by Mrs Hoare and Wilde. I mentally list my resolves: To keep calm, count our blessings, look after my chief blessing carefully and lovingly but without interfering a millimetre beyond what his health requires, nor try to persuade him when he's lazy into activities he doesn't feel equal to; to remember that Burgo is a man on his own, leading his own life, even if he does sometimes enjoy the support of parental affection.

---

[1] Carrington.

How little we thought about politics or the world when we were in Spain! Now – a new feature of life – American bombers cruise overhead *all the time*, carrying the Bomb. The people of Newbury are made deeply anxious by this activity, as we see from the local paper, and also by some alarming accident that occurred at the airfield only a week ago. Nor were they reassured by the frantic haste with which the personnel scrambled over eight-foot walls for safety, before doing anything to warn the neighbourhood. There is, it seems, quite a movement of a pacifist sort afoot. Ralph, who always rushes to the papers and wireless, has been wanting to talk about the problem ever since we got back, but I was too busy with unpacking and proofs until last night, when I settled down to read them. My feeling when I did was that I was staring into a lunatic asylum full of raving maniacs. How can people ask 'Ought we to renounce nuclear war?' *Of course* we ought to. Apart from the direct moral issue, it isn't a question of 'death rather than slavery' but of killing millions of innocent people, destroying the globe rather than slavery. Nor do I think our risk would be increased should we refuse the Bomb: those are more likely to be bombed who present a threat to others. Ralph remarked that by taking a stand against the Bomb one would find oneself in the company of cranks, emotionalists and Communists – considerations which don't affect me in the least. Later this evening he said that he really completely agreed with me. Even if the pacifist movement does gain ground, however, I don't see that it can possibly be effective. No, we shall go on building launching sites; the Bomb will go off, and whether it was by accident or design will make no difference.

March 18th

Janetta came down for a night in spite of the arctic weather and having just had flu. When I asked for news of Robert her face broke up like water into which a stone has fallen. The cause of the 'unhappy muddle' of which she had written was that the question of their joining forces had again come to the fore. Though she obviously wanted to make the position clear to us she spoke in a sort of palimpsest through which I glimpsed a very sad position – for as one of them advanced the other retreated, and the only clear fact that emerges is that each is terrified of the pain the other can cause them. Also in practical terms that Janetta is going to France with the Godleys and X, while Robert remains 'desperate' in London.

March 20th

A night in London. Ralph lunched with Robert. When he mentioned Janetta's departure for France next day 'Robert's eyes flashed fire'. She had never told him; and this although – apart from any other reason – he likes to be about for Georgie's sake when Janetta goes away. When Ralph taxed Janetta with this her answer was characteristic. With the most innocent expression she said: 'But I thought he knew. I didn't *not* tell him.' The four travellers to France were at dinner at Montpelier Square, full of excitement and plans, which I envied them, as I also did their youthful spirits. Kitty Godley looked touching but rather absurd, dressed in the newest and most unbecoming fashion – a grey tweed 'sack'. A great deal was drunk.

March 22nd: Ham Spray

Ralph and I started on our quiet working life this morning. He retired to his library and began on a review. I set out my paraphernalia – dictionaries, Roget's *Thesaurus* –

in the music-room and began translating *Blood and Sand*. All this is satisfying in its way; but I wish the *cold* didn't get worse and worse, and am horrified to have brought Ralph back into it. Next time we should surely stay away until the end of March.

April 1st

After a frigid fortnight, belated spring has come to England bringing serenity with it. Ralph is unfailingly sweet to me; Burgo appears (at the moment anyway) to enjoy and be interested in his life and the book he is writing for Anthony Blond; Ralph's health has been better. It rests – this happiness – precariously on dozens of tiny legs. We were able to sit out for the first time since we got back; the lawn lies in satin stripes where Wilde has mown it; Dinah sits alert and glossy by my side and the sky is blue. We had Robert and Georgie for the weekend and Burgo for one night with two friends, Francis Nichols and Michael Shone, at the start of a walking-tour.

Deep in *Blood and Sand*, I am beginning to take an obsessional and vicarious interest in bull-fighting, and spend a good deal of time reading about it.

April 12th

The Gowings to stay, great trenchermen both and their curves getting slightly out of hand. Julia expressed herself perfectly satisfied with Newcastle and what she called the 'inner life'. She is still working on the play she began in about 1940, and enjoying it I think, although it's pretty clear it will never be finished. She asked me how much I got paid for translating, and I told her about £200 for three months – not too bad. 'Ah, but for how many thousand words?' she wanted to know. 'A hundred thousand.' 'Well, of course I only write *three* words in that time,' she said, a trifle proudly I thought. After lunch both Gowings bolted upstairs like shot rabbits, and slept solidly until five, when they came down and ate a hearty tea. Ralph, Julia and I had a lovely walk through primrose-spangled woods, but she notices very little visually and not much that is said. The 'inner life' is indeed what she leads.

Coming home we were talking about the appalling difficulties of young mothers in the modern world, who wanted to remain civilized while looking after their children properly. Julia suggested that everyone should bear their children from the age of fifteen onwards. 'How could one possibly force them to?' asked Ralph. 'Oh, some "world convention" or "climate of opinion",' she replied airily, and when we both broke into hoots, she took it amiss. 'Oh well, you're so sure you're right, I shan't tell you my reasons.' There were no difficult moments during the weekend, however, and Lawrence was always appreciative. But Julia *is* a difficult guest, and reflecting in bed why this was I decided that it is because she really hates being one, and would rather have her material surroundings under her own control.

April 21st

A letter from Gerald this morning refers to the conversation at Churriana last February, which had touched on sore areas of the past and embarrassed Raymond. 'Your remarks out here were unjust,' he writes. '... If there are moral rules in these things it was you and not Carrington or myself who broke them.' This naturally brought Ralph's hackles and prickles up until he resembled a porcupine. But when he had calmed down an interesting conversation developed. How fascinatingly human situations that one has been contemplating for years just as we have our view of the Downs and the ilex tree (have the hedges grown? Has that tree got beech disease?) – how fascinatingly they emerge like negatives in developing-solution, to reveal some new picture covering the same system of facts and feelings. We all knew even before Joanna went out to Spain that Gerald would identify her with Carrington. Her own parents do it, Ralph sometimes does; I always feel it's rather hard on this charming and beautiful young girl to be saddled with the very unusual and potent personality of an aunt whom she never even knew. Now, as we talked the subject over at breakfast it came out clearly that the brief burst of hostility between Ralph and Gerald in Spain this last winter was due to the fact that Gerald was involved with *Carrington's ghost*, and that when Gerald came up to tell us how wonderfully he and Joanna were getting on, Ralph felt that the message was, 'You see, I've got Carrington after all.' As he developed this bit of the roll of film he said that he believed this was in Gerald's mind also. What an excellent plot for a novel!

April 30th

Tranquillity, solitude, *happiness* alone with Ralph. Perfect weather, midsummer temperatures and a soft blue-green bloom covering all.

In the evening we listened to an argument on the Third Programme between four Oxford philosophers – or rather three and (rather absurdly) Philip Toynbee, who wasn't up to their subject, the Philosophy of Politics. It was a dazzlingly brilliant performance, arousing both admiration and envy – for surely nothing can be more enjoyable than the ability to think so clearly, and to emit streams of quick, exact and lively sentences, weaving and interweaving, with which they dealt each other tough boxer blows. Not that they got anywhere in particular though stimulating things were said all the time. Stuart Hampshire wanted to limit the scope of philosophy, confining it to the exploration of abstract and general aspects and excluding what men actually *do* want, while poor old Philip, a sheep that had wandered into the wrong pen, bleated away in his deep rich voice about philosophy meaning love of knowledge, adding that the philosopher 'used to be thought of as a Wise Man who would teach us all how to live'.

May 23rd

There has been a crisis in Algeria, including a near *coup d'état* on the part of the generals, and a declaration by de Gaulle relayed over the wireless, that he was prepared to take over the Government. Robert is flying out there tonight as correspondent for *The Observer*. We therefore must do without his company.

June 16th

I have finally killed off my matador, and posted him off to be typed. Robert is back, much impressed by de Gaulle's intelligence and dignity in the 'hysterical and thoroughly nasty atmosphere of Algiers'. Robert, or his Arab driver, had been shot at once, the bullet shattering the windscreen. He said: 'They have a way of rushing up and slashing your jugular artery, so I kept mine covered with a newspaper.'

Another letter from Gerald, who has a new girlfriend called Hetty, though he declares there is still room in his life for Joanna. 'Raise your glass and say "He died of happiness!"' he ended in a thoroughly embarrassing letter, the result of which was that Ralph discharged his feelings against Gerald by getting quite cross with *me*. 'Well, what *am* I to do with them?' (his feelings) he said comically. He is the reverse of William James's dog, which wagged its tail and therefore felt pleased – his voice gets angry and indignant, therefore he starts to *feel* indignant with the nearest person – in this case me, the ostensible reason being that I had asked Gamel to stay, feeling that she had been having a very thin time of it.

June 20th

Much talk with Ralph on the way to Marlow to see Alix and James. One gets so used to being inside one's own head that it's tempting to assume that other people's have similar wallpaper and furniture. Mine keeps a fairly steady pattern and I don't often move the things I bought when I first set up house, except when I rather unsuccessfully let in a little light here and there, or put in new curtains or flowers. Ralph said today that he had no such basic set-up, nor fixed 'philosophy of life': but that from time to time he got hold of what seemed an all-illuminating idea, plugged it in and flashed it round – which seems to me a brilliant analysis of his manner of thinking.

The outposts of Old Bloomsbury in the Marlow woods were as ever true to themselves. The household gods stood firm and tall – Freud, Lytton, Mozart, Fritz Busch, Stanislavsky. The Strachey family, one might add. Though admitting that Bloomsbury was now in the trough they were convinced they would rise again. Will they or not? Their figures have become very small, like those of people rapidly disappearing down a road, but whether this is perspective or their actual size I can't be sure. At lunch (off corned beef and tinned carrots) James remained quite silent while Alix proclaimed her belief that class distinctions must be brought to an end. I heartily agree, but not – as she went on to say – that public schools should be forbidden by law. She added that if the lower classes had more material blessings and free time they would become civilized in spite of themselves, yet she was too honest *not* to reveal that her housekeeper dislikes having almost nothing to do. 'She is rather bored and lonely. There's the telly of course, and now she's bought a dog.'

Delightful visit from Robert when we got home. His star is rising, his ambitions being realized, success, money and jobs just round the corner.

June 30th

At the weekend a lively argument sprang up between Janetta and me. It began in the kitchen as I was cooking *truites aux amandes* (without really knowing how) and I criticized a very rich friend for selling his house merely to make a profit. Janetta said I was being monstrously unfair, and that it was just as reasonable for a millionaire to make money as for a poor man – something I couldn't accept. His profit may be vital to the poor man, but unless the rich man wants to do something splendid or very generous with it his profit is futile. I admitted that I didn't like rich men on the whole, and thought them with some exceptions corrupted by power. 'You are being moral,' said Janetta, and 'Yes, certainly, why not?' said I. At this stage we moved into the dining-room and started eating our trout and continuing the discussion with Ralph and Jonny Gathorne-Hardy: Why shouldn't a rational being think about values? I wanted to know; Janetta said she hated the idea of them and could only think of them in terms of religion. People were unique and should never be generalized about or subjected to praise and blame, but merely 'apprehended'. Interesting, though not wholly tenable if one believes generalization to be the essence of intelligent thinking. 'Can we change the subject?' she said suddenly. Jonny: 'Oh no, I want to go on talking about it.' But we didn't.

In bed that night Ralph and I pondered the question: Why do the modern 'young' dread ethical concepts – good, bad, or even true and beautiful? Ralph thought money had taken their place as something you can't do without, and the more the better. Their hopes of 'happiness' are low-pitched. Or perhaps in their eyes good, bad, et cetera seem like outworn myths believed in by their parents but not by them, just as God or the supernatural did to us.

July 6th

All our visitors left us, including Gamel, who has I think enjoyed all her English visits, and both Ralph and I really enjoyed having her here. Ronnie Duncan had liked her sonnets and made her feel she was 'an old poet of promise' she told us with her 'dove's laugh' as we call it. She spent some hours on her knees in front of a trunk from the Aldbourne cottage, as a result of which she proposed giving some of her letters from great men (such as Bertie Russell and the Powyses) to a library.

Robert told Ralph that there was 'someone new' in his life; she was 'very nice', but he wasn't in love with her. What did Ralph think of a sort of companionate marriage? Ralph has another hectic letter from Gerald saying many incompatible things about Hetty: there has been 'gaiety, gaiety', jealous scenes, she has danced wildly to jazz records, gone into a 'genuine spiritualistic trance', 'spoken with tongues', and 'got too fat'. Most of it complete *rubbish*. Then he breaks into authentic Brenanismo which I always find irresistible: 'Heigh-ho said froggy, who I dare say was the same advanced age as myself.'

Weekend at Crichel, delightful as usual, though after days of preoccupation with the crises in the Middle East and the American landings, it was strange to find them all quite uninterested, and fully occupied with their own activities. Raymond has developed such an obsession with grammar, spelling and punctuation that I caught him in the act of saying that these three ingredients alone made a good writer. It is comical to hear their fury over 'Oh really! *Folie de grandeur!*' while they remain indifferent to the fate of the world now hanging by a spider's thread.

Ralph and I sometimes feel as though we were wearing snake belts and grey flannel shorts, sitting at our desks eager for a chance to put up our hands, and dreading a quick rap on the knuckles with a ruler. Our meals were quite delicious and mostly eaten out of doors, the weather being so splendid; there was plenty of lovely music, croquet and several animated discussions, one about Free Will, and another about the monkeys and the typewriters, Raymond looking like a very alert and mischievous monkey himself.

July 23rd

Ralph lost his ancient but adored Parker pen, the only thing he can write with, that symbolic and valued treasure which has weathered about thirty years' constant use. We have been frantically searching for it for two days all over the garden wherever he had been pruning or fruit-picking, with loud comments to each other, while Wilde was digging the weeds under the music-room window. At last Ralph asked him if he had seen it. Wilde: 'I didn't know what you was looking for. Yes, I picked it up first thing this morning under the strawberry net.' I found myself humming a tune, and quite a bit later remembered the words: '*Mon Dieu quel homme!*' Ralph told Mary about it at lunch. She said: 'After having twice had the front gate shut in my face by Wilde I can't understand why you're so keen on that man.' Well I'm not, for one.

July 27th

Burgo and Simon Young arrived last night in full Moss Bros wedding togs, looking very charming and gay. Burgo is back again, and firmly declares that he will finish his book before he goes abroad with the Blonds; we are amazed and delighted.

We took some of our gooseberries and raspberries over to Stokke, where Robert is having a go as paterfamilias with Georgie and Rose, as Janetta has postponed her return from abroad. Later he brought them over to tea. Apparently he and Ralph were discussing the solution for Janetta's life when I was out of the room, and Ralph audaciously told him that it lay with him, Robert. 'I haven't ruled it out,' he replied. He is wonderfully good with the children. They lapped up bowls of raspberries and cream, got into the cold pool and put their big, black smelly dog in the rubber boat.

On Saturday night he brought 'my television friend', Cynthia Judah, over to dinner.

August 14th

Yesterday Ralph and I drove over to lunch with Janetta and the three little girls, who have rented a house just over the downs at Combe for a few weeks. The children played happily on two swings under the old apple-tree growing in the middle of the rough sloping lawn, while we lay in the hot sun and blustery wind talking to Janetta. Asked about her plans for the future, she said she was dreaming of leaving England, and getting away somewhere warm.

Ralph talked afterwards about her restlessness with more criticism than I feel. He thinks her desire to get away frequently from family responsibility (though the most sensitive and kind mother when with her children) is something innate and compulsive, and will probably never leave her. But I remembered her lying talking on the lawn in her check cotton blouse and with her hair tied back from her serious delicately cut profile and was touched by the image. She is as she is – someone exceptional, unique. Why try and alter her, even were it possible? Certainly she is restless at present, but I see this as the product of her native independence coupled with unhappiness.

I finished reading Ibañez' *La Maja Desnuda* yesterday, and don't think much of it. I have been busy typing out my report on his earlier books for Elek[1] and they are a very different matter. Ralph has been married to Chateaubriand, not me, for the past week. He is reluctant to put down his *Mémoires* even at mealtimes, and certainly to come for a walk.

---

[1] A London publisher.

August 27th

Yesterday I got a letter from Burgo which gave me a shock in the solar plexus from which I've not yet recovered. He and the Blonds have had a horrible motor accident in Yugoslavia. Their car, driven too fast by Anthony, skidded on a wet road and collided violently with a telegraph post. Both Anthony and Charlotte were taken to hospital, not seriously hurt, I gather; Burgo escaped with bruises. The car was a complete wreck, and the windscreen 'turned to horrible bath-salts'. I imagine it all too vividly. Burgo had to deal with the Yugoslav police, who made him stand by the wreck for an hour to warn other drivers. He then had great difficulty in finding himself a room for the night, but was at length put up in a private house, sharing a room with two workmen. Robert said comfortingly that to survive such an experience is fortifying, and I believe that this is true. They have now gone on to end their holiday, peacefully I hope, in Venice.

September 9th

Hearing a while ago that poor Rosamond was shattered by the ghastly news of the death of her daughter Sally of poliomyelitis in Jakarta, we wrote and asked her to stay. She wrote back that she would like to come, if we were ready to accept the fact that 'Sally's life still went on'. We replied that we would listen with the greatest interest to anything she felt like telling us. She has just left us after two days in which we thought of nothing but her and her grief, trying to guess at what she found difficulty in saying. She was looking very splendid, but it was only necessary to talk to her for a few minutes to realize that she was shaken to the core, and we both felt profoundly moved and sorry for her. When the three of us were alone together, we embarked on the whole terrible story, and her response to it. The fact that it involved beliefs that neither of us holds made what she had to say no less tragic and interesting, and we went on talking far into the night. She described her state of mind as one of '*blinding* certainty'. She conveyed the agony she had suffered very vividly, and said more than once that she didn't want to go on living and didn't know how she could.

September 21st

The blue of the sky matches the morning glories on the verandah, and Burgo's scarlet shirt (he has come down with Simon) adds to the cheerfulness of a weekend when everyone is in a good mood. Except Robert, who rang up in great agitation last night to say that his father was dying. When he arrived (with Cynthia) and we asked how he was, he replied characteristically, 'Oh, he packed it in last night,' which was not, needless to say, the last we heard about this event.

The weekend was in its odd way rather hilarious, except for Robert's news. Simon and Burgo were full of jokes and chatter, while Robert made us laugh with descriptions of his lightning visit to Venezuela and Brazil for the telly. There was chess, bowls and music; visits from Mary with Eduardo Paolozzi,[1] also Janetta and the children. Robert looked quite exhausted, and obviously wanted to talk about his father in particular and death in general, but there was no chance in this cheerful house-party atmosphere. On Monday, the rest having left, Janetta reappeared with Georgie and Rose; but as the little pitchers' ears were never far away

[1] Sculptor.

nothing at all personal could be said, though there was one mysterious interchange between Ralph and Janetta.

Ralph: 'You're not thinking of doing anything frightful?'

Janetta: 'No, not at the moment – I can't really, as I didn't last week.'

And what either of them meant I really don't know.

September 27th

A visit to Alix and James, such as we made today, gives us a glimpse of our own futures. They are just so much older and crazier than Ralph and me; like hens they have been chivvied a little closer to the execution shed, and are cackling louder and losing more feathers though they aren't yet inside. It's true there was something almost comic in their competition over their symptoms (James has been frightened by the local doctor about his blood pressure, and Alix wanted to have blood pressure, too); but the terrible plight of the old as they are herded towards death is no laughing matter at all, and there are many implications branching from the central situation, none of them pleasant. For instance, should Ralph and I ever conceivably find it too disheartening to go and see this fascinating pair of eccentrics, which I doubt, just because they have sunk a little further into the bog, what will our young friends feel about coming to see *us*?

One of the few consolations of age, I agreed with Bunny the other day, is its irresponsibility. 'This world is no longer any of my making, or much to do with me. Take it away and do what you like with it. I don't even greatly care if you drop it and break it. I'm interested in a detached way by your antics, that's all.' No, I'm afraid that won't do. Nobody wants to end up as a selfish old person insisting on having the railway carriage window up (or down, as the case may be), besides which it's physically impossible to be so disengaged.

October 27th

Robert is with us on a working visit. Except for the extra tingle from his vitality we lead our normal life. Each of us works in a separate room and we meet for meals, walks, and talks and reading in the evening.

He took himself off at short notice on Friday just before Janetta came down. I'm not sure how deliberate that was; Janetta told us it wasn't. To us he was definite, reasonable and articulate about it. The net result was that past feelings couldn't be cancelled out, and that she could work her own problems out better without him.

November 4th

Two days completely alone with Ralph and Dinah, working at my translation, talking to Ralph, walking with Ralph through the damp yellow-green and black lanes, listening to the wireless with Ralph, spending the nights coiled up beside Ralph in our warm bed. I can even discuss with Ralph the nature of the pleasure it is living with him – perfect relaxation without dullness. Being with anyone else, even my dearest friends, imposes the faintest possible strain, gives a tiny twist to the key in the mechanical mouse's entrails. With Ralph there is absolutely *none*. We are like two mutually supporting creepers, each propping the other up and at the same time drawing sustenance and stimulation from the other's sap. But if I were to start writing down all the inestimable advantages I gain from living with Ralph I should never stop. One is being able to say *immediately* everything that comes into my mind to someone who likes to hear it. Another is the pleasure of leading two lives instead of one, and one of them male. I can't think, I can't bear to, how people manage to live without a mate. Ralph is unendingly kind and loving to me, appreciative, nicer far than I deserve. The two halves of the world's greatest pleasure are loving and being loved, and I never stop thanking my lucky stars that I have them both.

November 9th

Before dinner Burgo heaped up the fire in the music-room to such an extent that the chimney caught fire. I remembered a scene of my youth when I did the very same thing, and how guilty I felt when the episode ended in the fire brigade roaring up the drive. Not so Burgo. I noticed a sort of triumph in his manner as he made me go out of doors and look at the tall red flames pouring from the chimney into the night sky. Large lumps of molten soot fell into the grate, the house filled with an acrid smell like cabbage cooking. I felt infuriated with him, and Robert too, as they lounged on the sofa discussing whether it would be a good or bad thing if the house burned down, and leaving Ralph to take practical steps, with a calm and good humour which I confess amazed me. He knew he mustn't get agitated, and so he didn't, although this is just the sort of disaster he finds very hard to take. However, the blaze mercifully subsided peacefully.

November 28th

Ralph made a snap decision not to come to London for the day, cancelling his doctor's appointment from a motive about which I am uncertain. I therefore got alone into my train like a fairly resigned sheep going to the slaughter of a luncheon date I didn't look forward to, with my fur jacket and *Dr Zhivago* for company. I read the latter all the way to London, with great interest and pleasure. Here for once was a new book that demanded all one's attention, that was unskippable, by which simple pragmatical test I judge it to be a good book. I finished it on the way home. I wonder how much Ralph will like it. For my part I admire it for a good many reasons; but it's a book you must take as it is, not complaining at the occasional thinness of its shimmering weblike texture, enjoying the brilliant passages of description, scenes made vivid by a poet's eye. At Harrods, with the strangest feelings, I came upon a pile of Burgo's book, published today, and bought a copy.

December 8th

I feel flat and tired, I don't know why, after a most *un*-taxing weekend. Heywood and Anne are always relaxing and companionable. Burgo, though dignified, grown-up and enormously more socially equipped, seemed to be a thousand miles away behind arctic ice-floes. On Saturday we drove to Savernake forest. Burgo and Heywood strode off down the avenues, while Ralph, Anne and I meandered gently through groves of young pines carpeted by their damp and scented needles, until we reached the Grand Avenue, with its noble colonnade of beech-trunks bathed in silver-gold light. Anne was as usual spoiling for arguments – themes I remember were drink, the Royal family and money. Talk too about Janetta, and how she hates being pinned down to *plans,* a trait that is inconvenient but also part of her charm. She clearly feels they are destructive to freedom, and would like to invent everything anew for herself, nor will she ever use a current phrase, even in the ironical way that Julia and Robert sometimes do.

Everyone has now departed; there's a wintry silence, except for the crackling of logs in the grate. Paralysis of thoughts deliberately strangled at the root for fear of what they might lead to leaves my mind a blank.

[I realize that I wrote the last entry, and others that included mere hints, under the stress of sharpened misery about Ralph's health – probably due to his having had tired spells, discomfort or pain on our walks, or that change of facial expression I had learned to watch for and dread. I have always thought of myself as being more or less rational and unsuperstitious. Yet I see when I re-read these tense pages that I did *not* completely face up to the future in either of these respects. There is usually an element of uncertainty in illness, I told myself: doctors aren't always right. For instance Sawbones had tried to put us against our winter journeys to Spain, yet Ralph had visibly profited from them. At the time he was taken ill the treatment of heart patients was a great deal vaguer than it is now, when he would presumably have been given surgery; even the idea that vegetable oils produced less cholesterol than animal fats was new and unproven. 'Try it if you like,' they said, and we made it a part of his regime that he didn't resent, as he would have being forced to stop smoking.

I have suggested that I became superstitious because I remember a strong irrational feeling that if I exerted my every thought and all my energies to keeping him alive I might be able to do so, and I look back to those last years of Ralph's life as a strenuous, unabating campaign. I have no idea whether this had any effect on him – presumably not. It was merely that I was obsessed with the need to wage it. And I was unrealistic in that I do not remember ever giving my mind to the problem of how I should live without him. No, my wakeful nights were devoted to ways and means of keeping him with me. He and I never discussed the possibility of his death although there were times when I wondered if he would like to and I should have encouraged it, especially in view of our otherwise complete intimacy. I shall never be sure of the answer to that question. At the time it seemed a physical impossibility. That some loving couples do manage to talk to each other about the inevitable death of one of them I know from experience, and I greatly admire them for it.

Looking back it seems to me that I forged along my chosen path in a state of semi-numbness, and that just as one's tongue avoids a tooth with a tender hollow in it, so I tried to avoid the aching chasm in my mind.]

December 10th

Awoke feeling hardly capable of pulling myself out of the matrix of our warm bed. Ralph said afterwards that I never spoke to him once during our bathroom session. One of the worst things about my being depressed is that it sinks poor Ralph like a stone. He looks at me with the sweetest possible expression and says: 'I can't make you happy.' Whereas of course he does everything to that end. The fact is I've been unbearable company the last few days, and he has done very well to put up with me.

December 29th

Christmas is over, and Burgo and I are both in bed with flu. He arrived in very high spirits though, bringing us a magnificent pot of caviare, and next day came Isobel, whose company is always a pleasure. She told a story of how when walking through the Park she saw a man waving wildly to her out of a car. 'I *thought* it was *Leo*nard Bing' (a friend of hers), she said, 'so I ran up and *got* in beside him. And then of course I saw it wasn't Leonard at all but a man from the Turkish Embassy.' 'What was he like?' '*Very small* and *dark*.'

After Christmas came Robert, who spent the best part of two days in the library with Ralph in earnest conversation. Serious though the subject was – for Robert is trembling on the verge of a vitally important decision – a good many bursts of laughter reached me in my bed of sickness, as well as the sound of much pacing up and down. Taken over by the eerie fungoid spread of fever and discomfort, I let my mind wander vaguely off to Robert, to Burgo, to Isobel, and then turned it off by main force to Saint-Simon and the death of the Duc de Berri. At least nothing can be done about *him* now; he has the great merit of being out of range of worry.

1959

[In the course of time some of the gilt had been wearing off the gingerbread of our winter trips to Churriana, and yet – and yet the climate was the best in Europe, and we would find Janetta there with Georgie and Rose. We decided this year on a compromise: we would spend five weeks at Buena Vista and four more in Southern Portugal as an experiment.

A few days after crossing the Pyrenees we stopped at the Parador at Benicarlo. In bed next morning Ralph told me that he had had a short attack of angina in the night, but didn't get up and swallow an emergency pill because he thought it would worry me and *I* wouldn't sleep! Such sensations were to be expected when taking exercise; it was his having it when in repose that had alarmed the doctors, and it had not occurred since the first time. I realized that I might at any moment have to make a decision, try to dominate his much stronger will, halt our advance, call a doctor and put him to bed. Of course I betrayed my preoccupation, and he insisted that he was now all right and that we should go ahead.

We reached Almería without further mishap, checked in at our hotel and went out under a pinkish lavender sky with a silver thumbnail moon, to a café which was the meeting-place for the men of Almería. Many of them had nothing but a glass of water and a newspaper in front of them. There were old men sunk in their own carnality and the weight of their ponderous stomachs, with faces a yard long, three chins, loose Hapsburg lips and gloomy eyes stewing away in dark sauce. Next to one of these sat a distinguished-looking man with silver hair, and one hand on the top of his cane, while the other held a small book of poetry, which he was reading attentively. We were in Spain all right.

'As we drove up the road to Buena Vista, "Here's Gerald," said Ralph. He was just turning off towards his house, and his companion must of course be Hetty – a stocky young woman, staring at us out of bold brown eyes, with long hair hanging loose and orange trousers. Gerald said rather uneasily: "Oh, we're not coming to call on you. You're tired – you've only just arrived." And the next moment we were being welcomed by Janetta, Georgie and Rose. Janetta had lit an olive-wood fire in our bedroom, and we felt delightfully looked after.'

We were soon encompassed by, though not really involved in, the life of the 'coast', where gossip was the daily currency, and items of human news were picked up and tossed about like crusts of bread by pigeons, and frequent excursions were made into the 'hippy' life of Torremolinos by *voyeurs flambés* in alcohol. Gerald and Hetty, Janetta and the Davises all took part in these sorties, but they had no charm for Ralph or me. In fact there were days when I wished we had never come. But of course there was much to enjoy – for instance a refreshing visit with Janetta and Georgie to Jaime Parladé in his father's house looking out over the sea to the frowning brow of Africa. Jaime was a charming host, and we got to know him better and delight in his company. Then another day we went with the two Brenans and Janetta to dine with Mina Curtiss (née Kirstein) at her grand hotel. (We had known Mina since the Twenties, when she and her friend Henrietta Bingham arrived in London from America and took fringe Bloomsbury by storm. Mina had been the more beautiful and far the more intelligent of the two, while Henrietta had a fatal glamour for both sexes. Mina had kept in touch with her English friends and become a distinguished writer and authority on Proust. Now in middle age she was a sparkling talker and a 'character'.) The dinner she gave us was crushingly huge, the *pièce de résistance* being a battleship made of crayfish decorated with lemons, eggs and carrots all cut to look like something else, reclining on a bed of mashed potato grey with careful moulding to make it represent the sea.

Another night we went to see the famous dancer Antonio dance *The Three-Cornered Hat*. I thought as I watched him about the difference between male and female movements in the Spanish dance: the male conveys intense lust and at the same time restraint – the result being a sort of *anguish*, expressed in face and gesture. His hands appear ready to tear his partner apart, while never actually laying a finger on her. She, on the other hand, combines frenzied enticement with complete submission. One talented girl left the stage leaning so far back that she was practically prostrate, with her arms twirling round her head like wild snakes.

Of course we saw a good deal of the Brenans. They too enjoyed our mountain picnics. Sometimes the movement of the car had the effect on Gerald of an analyst's couch, and loosened an uninhibited stream of memories or thoughts about age and youth, through which one could see Hetty's face. We preferred these outings to our visits to the Casa Brenan, where Gerald would put on his Cool Cat clothes, there was jazz on the gramophone and the unattractive Hetty – a well-filled bolster topped with a shiny yellow face – reigned as Queen. It was as if the dear familiar picture of Brenan life, the house decorated with Gerald's exquisite taste, his own fascinating and funny talk and Gamel's old-world eccentricities, had all been crudely bedaubed with paint. Still, after he had got the latest news about Hetty off his chest, or even said that if Gamel 'were not there' he could live happily with Hetty, he would launch out in his most harmonious and friendly style about writing, or the effect of war on young men, or every sort of subject.

Just before we left Spain we dined at the Cónsula, and Annie took me up to see Cyril, who was ill in bed. He motioned me to a chair with a royal gesture, lay with his large face on the pillow 'in music position' and began talking about Robert and Janetta. The last news he had heard was that they were going to set up house together, he said. I didn't want to be pumped and found the conversation painful. Perhaps the acutest thing he said was, 'At least Janetta has made a life for herself, even though it may be precarious and unsatisfactory, but Robert – apart from his work – has made no life at all.' Next day, February 21st, we left for Portugal.

We arrived at the small seaside town of Praia da Rocha – visited by us with Julia twenty-five years ago – and found the same yellow hotel perched above the wide sea, with its fantastic cliffs and hard sand beaches; the same horse-drawn *tartanas* for hire, jogging uphill to it, painted smartly in black and yellow with white linen curtains. We found also comfort and warmth and plenty of glassed-in verandahs. Our breakfast was brought by an elderly nanny in a starched cap, murmuring what sounded like 'Poosh-cat, poosh-cat' or 'zzzz' as she set down the tray. Both people and landscape were gentler, softer if less exciting than those of Spain, and the prune-like eyes of the Portuguese seem to express nothing but anxiety that we should be happy. We are. A splendid letter from Janetta in London, saying she has begun to hate the rat-race but both Robert and Robin tell her she mustn't, 'it's what life's about'. She's evidently seeing a lot of Robert, yet we are both now convinced of the hopelessness of our daydreams for them, and wonder why we clung to them so tenaciously. I see it as a matter of Geometry: The angle formed by Ralph and me on one side and Robert on the other = the angle formed between Ralph and me and Janetta. If two angles are both equal to the same angle they must be equal to each other. QED.

At Praia da Rocha we had found exactly what we wanted at the moment, and could carry on the sort of existence we liked, as we couldn't at Churriana with its warring stresses and strains. It hadn't been just captiousness that made us think so.

After three peaceful weeks had slid past, we set off home, by Lisbon, Coimbra and the *Chapon Fin* at Bordeaux. On March 22nd we were back at Ham Spray.]

March 23rd: Ham Spray

So here we are, having slipped imperceptibly back into our old slot. It's raining softly, but warm. Various things aren't working and require visits from 'the Men': one of these is the telephone, which gives out a gnat's voice through Atlantic rollers. Last night I said to Ralph that I thought Robert would soon tire of his wild dashes for *Panorama* (America last week, the Congo next), and that he was too critical to go on 'encapsulating' them for the public. So I was amused when this morning he burst out on the telephone: 'Really, it's absurd the way I dash about on these television journeys; it's just like taking a *pill*. The other day I looked at a map of Brazil and thought "I'd like to go there," and then I realized I'd just BEEN.' However, most of his talk was about his 'problem' which is just as acute as ever, yet the thought of a final decision makes him feel trapped and desperate.

Mary arrived to see us, spreading a glow of good humour. The gist of what she had to tell us was that Derek Jackson has been pressing her to marry him, but she was not proposing to at present. She was not in love with him, 'nor am I altogether happy about him,' she added. (Her divorce from Robin is through.)

March 26th

Easter weekend is bearing down on us, and it looks as if we shall have Burgo, Robert, and Janetta and the little girls. I can't understand why certain of life's responsibilities – those concerned with keeping our Ark afloat and with other people's troubles – put such a much greater strain on the organism than those to do with work, which positively buoy one up like cork floats. Ralph and I have been discussing the possibility of reconstructing Ham Spray to suit a recluse life for 'two elderly people'. The effort and expense would be stupendous, but it might leave us afloat, instead of being dragged under the sea.

March 30th

Our long, delicious solitude was broken on Good Friday, when the Blonds dropped Burgo with us, Robert arrived looking pale and exhausted but able to be very funny and stimulating, and soon after came Janetta with the children. None of them seem in very good shape, and ever since they began to arrive I seem to hear the steady mounting whine of a siren inside my head. Why can't human beings congregate without this fever and fret?

The ground was, as it were, well ploughed by the discovery of the happiness Ralph and I had alone in Portugal. Into it fell the seeds produced by social life and other people; and from those seeds plants have grown, which are now staring me in the face – mostly taking the form of conclusions about what I want and don't want:

I *don't want* competitive social life, or occasions when large gatherings are shouting and drinking together, but only to be with people I am fond of, old friends or stimulating new ones. I *don't want* variety and excitement for their own sake. I *do want* peace, including quite a lot of privacy, to live with my darling Ralph. I *do want* some sort of work, and opportunity to pursue my other activities like music and botany. I *do want* health, comfort, and ability to go on enjoying getting sensual pleasure from my surroundings.

A wonderfully simple charter for living! Or perhaps just 'cutting one's cloth, et cetera'? Or a Freudian flight from reality? Or acceptance of reality?

Easter weekend wasn't altogether easy, I don't know why. Burgo was helpful and friendly, telling us of his project for a new book. Janetta was kind, sweet and sympathetic, dealing with the children in a stoical, rather noble way. Delightful Rose is a little Leibniz monad, reflecting the universe *in toto* with dewdrop clarity. Georgie is temporarily fenced off and shut away. My normal manner of talking to her produced 'I don't know' and a violent shake of the head. Janetta then told me I was intimidating her, which I took greatly to heart. I think the situation between her parents has made her creep into her shell.

April 9th

As a result of indexing Freud, I awoke this morning saying to myself 'It's a case of Mournful Prementia,' an imaginary ailment that (with its suggestion of melancholy and prediction) somewhat conveyed my mood.

After dinner at the Gowings' last night the conversation broke up two by two. Lawrence and I talked about different people's views of the universe. When I suggested that it was hard to get along with people who thought it wholly marvellous Lawrence claimed to be one of them – as an artist at any rate. When he painted a portrait, however ugly the sitter, he felt 'that every hair of their head was significant and wonderful, an integral part of the universe as a whole,' or if it was a landscape that not a leaf must be altered. As he held forth eloquently along these lines my own fundamental but buried optimism caught fire. Yet I still couldn't get beyond an ambivalent attitude – a feeling that the universe was both wonderful *and* terrible. 'The hairs may be exactly right,' I said to Lawrence, 'but what about the desperation, anxiety and loneliness inside the skull?' And he agreed. But even therein, I sometimes think, what I call 'interest' (and is perhaps the same thing as Lawrence's 'significance') is to be found. I differed from Lawrence in that what I find marvellous is consciousness itself, the sentient mind's response to its environment, rather than the shape and colour of that environment. The physical world is patently full of horror and ugliness as well as beauty and happiness, but the power of the human psyche to respond with interest to so much of both kinds is a constant marvel, like the heart's power to go on beating.

'What then,' said Ralph as we drove home, 'what then if the individual loses his power to respond?' Ah, what indeed?

April 14th

The wind is giving half-hearted banshee wails through the bright sunlit garden. Dinah and I sit together in the little front room; we have left Ralph in the music-room because I feel my presence doing jobs when he doesn't want to do anything is fidgeting to him – for, alas, he is not feeling well. I first knew this when he got out of bed at seven this morning and took a pill, after which he lay sighing and restless in bed. I had to exercise the utmost tact to find out exactly what he was feeling. I'm certain he won't want to go to London tomorrow, nor should he; but he wants me to go without him and I *won't*. Ever since our last journey to Spain I have had an uneasy conviction that he's less well than before. It's dreadfully depressing for him but so it is for me, and he can't expect me to go on as if he were quite well when he's not. In that sense there are no frontiers where he ends and I begin.

April 15th

Well, in the end, fortified by a talk to Janetta on the telephone and with Ralph's unwilling consent, I sent for Sawbones, and he arrived promptly, first treading fairly heavily on my feelings by telephone, which I was prepared for. He wasn't too bad. Ralph's present state must be taken as a 'warning', and he must rest absolutely for four or five days. He took all appropriate tests and left stronger sleeping-pills, which were useful.

April 16th

Two telephone calls from Janetta – *angelic*, and the best friend in the world. She's actually driving down for the night and I look forward to seeing her more than I can say. Meanwhile I'm trying not to rush blindly about like a hen with its head cut off, which is dreadfully disturbing to Ralph. He got up for a few hours today but was glad to get back to bed, doesn't want to smoke but *says* he feels better.

April 17th

I have lived through the last two days on a somehow supernormal plane, and am left rather broken but still upright, waiting for whatever comes next. I *don't* want to set down great wails of self-pity of all things, nor make lists of the symptoms which Janetta, with her unfailing sensitivity, elicited from me. Before she arrived I had suggested that Sawbones communicate with Geoff Konstam, but all through dinner and after Janetta kept up a forceful offensive for us to get him or some other specialist *at once*. She was perfectly right, and I can never be grateful enough. My difficulty is, as always, Ralph's absolute hatred of calling any doctors in. Janetta's company was enlivening to us both, but had some results not so good, in that it induced him to drink more than I now know was good for him, and eat too much of the delicious smoked salmon she brought. The night was appalling and virtually sleepless for us both. However, Geoff Konstam came as promised next day, and Janetta volunteered to stay long enough to drive him back again. So today has been the day of doctors, and had I had the energy I would have been amused at Sawbones' fantastically deferential treatment of the headmaster. Janetta and I sat talking in the music-room like husbands whose wives are having babies up aloft. After she and Geoff had left, leaving behind the news that anti-coagulants are to be tried, Ralph has become quiet, resigned and philosophical beyond belief.

April 20th

Robert and Burgo both came for the weekend. Janetta had warned us that 'Robert was in a very bad, desperate way'. But he saw Ralph several times, and had obviously not felt as shocked as Janetta at how ill he was, which was reassuring. He does in fact seem better, there is even a sign of pepperiness, on which he commented himself with a mischievous expression. In the sweetest and most touching way Burgo suggested staying on to keep me company. He has been extremely helpful and does everything I ask him.

May 3rd

Ralph is doing fine, and Geoff Konstam seems now not to want him to take anti-coagulants, which delights him. I don't know how much it is worth recording the nadir of gloomiest days, but it *is*, I believe the extraordinary power of human resilience, arguing as it does some basic kind of optimism. This evening I drove through the spring night to Marlborough for an orchestra practice, thoroughly enjoyed it, and came back purged and purified. It's as if the prevailing blackness of the craggy landscape I had been traversing, haunted by miserable worry about Ralph, threw into relief the peculiar joys that were to be had from practising a boring bit of Elgar with a heterogeneous collection of Marlborough masters and their wives.

May 6th

Again I have carried my solitary breakfast tray to the verandah. I am determined to savour this day of calm and sedation by natural beauty to the full. A warm breeze is fluttering my letters. The garden is full of swooping bird-shapes – the martins arrived yesterday; Dinah is intoxicated by them as she gazes from under my chair, and also by the quivering grasses, the general buzzing and twittering to the steady accompaniment of the cuckoo. The tulips are all out now, stiffly balanced on top of their tall stalks.

Yesterday I took my first day off since Ralph was ill, to go to Duncan's private view at the Tate. I talked to many friends – Morgan Forster, Freddie Ayer, Roger Senhouse, Bunny and Angelica. Raymond described a visit of Cyril and Janetta to Crichel together. 'She doesn't keep him in order, does she?' was his comment. Poor Janetta!

May 18th

I'm *delighted* with Ralph. Two days ago Sawbones came out, tested his blood-pressure and said he needn't come any more, and that Ralph might do what he liked within reason. He came down to breakfast next morning, and went with Isobel and me to have drinks at Stokke. He talks with all his old animation and doesn't get tired by people. His face has a quite different expression; it's as if he had been restored to the world, and was overjoyed to find himself in it. He is angelic to me, and anxious to get back to helping with household tasks. At Stokke we sat out in the sun talking to Freddie Ayer and Eduardo about Bertie Russell's philosophy, Madame de Staël and Duncan's pictures.

In the evening I started reading Bertie Russell's new book, as usual tougher and stiffer than one thinks it's going to be. Why try? Is any juice coming out of this mouthful, or are my teeth just going automatically up and down to no effect? Then a little squirt of something tasty goes down my throat, and it at once seems worthwhile. Faced with a fence, I often take a gallop or two round the field before my mind gets over it. And it's disheartening to find an avenue of thought blocked by 'pain of infinite regress', even though it's just what is to be expected in this mad universe.

May 28th

We have Clive and Barbara Bagenal here for two nights; they seem quite a married couple, and I think it is an excellent – if unexpected – arrangement.[1] Vanessa is said to be much relieved by it. There's no malice in Barbara: set her off on a subject like marmalade or pot-plants and she will prattle happily for hours. Clive may seem a little older, but his appetite for life is undimmed. He has brought me instructions from Vanessa that I must keep up my duties as secretary of the Memoir Club, and that Denis Proctor is to be admitted as a member.[2] This morning our happy couple are positively spoony together, and Clive's clear voice was heard resounding through the passages: 'LITTLE Barbara, how have you slept?'

June 5th

I was lying with my volume of Saint-Simon on the grass bank below the verandah this afternoon, when I noticed a lot of bees hovering over it like small furry aeroplanes surveying the terrain. Very unusual bees, wearing full Elizabethan breeches (yellow with black spots). They seemed to be looking for places to bore holes, and I became so fascinated by their activities that I quite forgot the Regent and his debaucheries, and tried to help them by clearing two little bare spaces. One splendid arch-bee actually disappeared into one. I called Ralph, who said the yellow plus-fours were pollen-bags, which showed they must have nests and young in the bank. Probably I was lying on some. I moved, and sure enough the adventurous bee emerged from its hole looking exhausted, with thin brown legs where its smart bloomers had been.

June 15th

It wasn't only the ravishing weather that made this a specially good Crichel weekend. Everyone was relaxed; the talk was as good as the meals; there was croquet, walks, sitting in the sun. We were alone with Raymond on Friday night, and heard about his weekend visit to the Winston Churchills: how much he liked and admired Lady Churchill, how impossible it was to talk to Winston, who was now quite gaga. Desmond and Eardley arrived next day from Glyndebourne. Of the three Desmond is the most ready to launch general ideas, springing from a liberal and above all optimistic outlook. We talked about the hippy generation and

[1] They were inseparable until Clive died in 1964.
[2] Civil servant and Chairman of the Tate Gallery.

their philosophy (Eardley seemed not to have heard about them, and was indignant because they had been 'kept from him'). He was affectionately teased by Desmond. Did we feel differently towards the universe because of its sinister developments of the last twenty-five years, someone asked. Desmond was inclined to believe in progress; the rest spoke of the universe somewhat as if it was an old friend who had shown a new side of his character by treachery.

This is the first outing we have taken since Ralph's last bad spell, and the great thing for me was that he never seemed in the least uneasy, nor I about him.

July 13th

Ralph came with me to London for the night, Burgo driving up with Robert. Ralph was reading Burgo's translation in the train, I Robert's new novel.[1]

Visiting Robert's flat we admired his new carpet, chair, and moving Irish gramophone records. Then came the television set, but ah! there we were unable to follow him. He showed us *Tonight*, said to be one of the best programmes. It certainly riveted one's attention in a horrid, compulsive sort of way, yet I was bored and rather disgusted, and longed to be able to unhook my gaze from this little fussy square of confusion and noise on the other side of the room. It's so old-fashioned and amateurish! 'Ah here's one of the great television personalities – the best-known face in England!' said Robert, and a charmless countenance with the manner of a Hoover-salesman dominated the screen. It's contemptible, it has nowhere near caught up with any of the other modes of expression; it's the LCM of the common man, one's mind has to shrink to get inside it. It's as light-weight as a feather duster, yet vast numbers of people are daily and hourly beaten on the head with it.

July 23rd

Writing in the train, on the way to London and the dentist. I *hated* leaving Ralph alone. In spite of all my efforts to think ahead and arrange for his wants, I fancy he is happier when I'm there looking after him. This business of 'managing' woke me early this morning and tossing in the heat. Sometimes I feel I *can* manage quite well, when even swinging along the passage on two legs seems an amazing achievement; at others I see a pattern of success and failure more realistically. But in the basement of my mind lurks a feeling of being some awful sort of sham or fraud. Self-confidence is like the horizontal boom in the school gym. Sometimes one can walk blithely along the top – but at others it is a question of travelling along uneasily below, hand over hand, and even then only to drop off.

July 24th: Montpelier Square

London in the heat – what an unbuttoning! What a Bacchanalian rout crowds the pavements, wearing brilliant beach shirts, bare legs, sandals, crinolines, jeans. Normally many people wear their clothes rather for the unwritten things they say than because they suit them: whether it is their background (families in the Highlands, social and political values) or to declare their readiness for sex and adventure. But when it's as hot as now they strip off this print, these flags they've been waving, with one idea alone – to be cool and comfortable.

[1] *Broadstrop in Season.*

No sign of anyone at Montpelier. Then Janetta came out of her room, looking unhappy, with no voice, saying she had flu. Burgo came up from the basement shiny with sweat, about to have a bath before going to a Hinchingbrooke party, which Jonny and Janetta were also invited to. Prettily dressed in pink shantung as she was, she decided not to go after all, and soon afterwards in came Robert. Their manner to each other couldn't have been more friendly, with a distinct touch of flirtatiousness on both sides. 'Oh yes,' she said later, 'he's been perfectly all right for some time.'

Evening alone with Janetta, eating avocado pears and fried eggs. She told me that Robin Campbell is to marry Susan Benson, which was no surprise.

July 24th

Life begins early at Montpelier, and swells to a crescendo with the voices of the children and the Italian *au pair* girl. Janetta lay in bed looking iller than before, with her hand on the white telephone. Georgie's swimming sports and Nicky's return to school loom large. Nicky's huge trunk stood waiting to be packed, and Georgie's bathing-cap had disappeared. When I returned from my session at the dentist, the confusion was wilder than ever. Yet in spite of the mess and moments of near-collapse, the life of the house saves itself by the skin of its teeth, and perhaps gains in vitality by performing this feat. I made my way slowly up to my room on the top floor, past Janetta's bedroom, where she had retired to bed, and the nursery floor, where Robert was playing trains with Georgie and Nicky.

Then out I went to my first Memoir Club meeting as secretary, which of course made me anxious. But dinner for fifteen went well. I sat next to Dermod and opposite Vanessa and Duncan. The reading, in Leonard's rooms, began with Julia's *Animalia*, and went on to Leonard on religious belief, both extremely typical of their writers.

August 7th: Ham Spray

After a night of *bonsoir tristesse*, slow to sleep, I wake early and lie groping among the spectres. The tent-pegs of my anxieties fasten me firmly to the old, brown, much-trampled earth. Human beings spend the first half of their lives looking forward, and trying to improve and believing in the possibility. The habit dies hard, and there's no fixed point when one can say: 'The *dégringolade* has now begun.' And long ago though I crossed this rubicon, if indeed it exists, I am still aware of stubborn stirrings within.

Have been reading Plato's *Symposium* and reflecting on the effect it and most of the rest of Greek literature must have had in fostering homosexuality in public schools, for it is subtly presented as noble and idealistic; and linked with Truth and Beauty (while heterosexuality is treated merely as a practical arrangement). And what with the knock-out personality of Socrates, how could they possibly resist?

August 21st

A letter from Gerald, who now longs to detach himself from Hetty, and get away to Italy with Gamel – though the prospect bores him as Gamel 'is no company, just a ghost' and 'dissatisfaction is in her blood'. I doubt if this mood will last; the next letter will be full of praise of Hetty. Anyway she is the obvious alternative to what he calls *'la présence Gamellienne'*. He also had some amusing stories to tell about Ernest Hemingway and Ken Tynan, who are out there at present, getting very drunk and quarrelling about bull-fights. Was three inches from the heart too far for the final stroke? asked Hemingway. 'If you were in bed with your wife,' said Tynan, 'such a distance could make quite a difference.' Extraordinary to hear of the endless Torremolinos round going on.

Our weekend party consisted of Boris and the Hendersons, Burgo and Jane M. Boris was as ever quite magnificent, his thoughts rolling out clothed in his inimitable language and even more inimitable accent, accompanied by a stream of expressions changing from deep sadness to a great mischievous moujik's smile, revealing squat brown teeth. He and Nicko played a lot of chess, often in the garden. On one side of the table sat Boris, huge and motionless, wearing a look of deep scorn. On the other side Nicko, nervously frowning and muttering under his breath. The Hendersons' company was a great asset, and Mary one of the most tactfully helpful visitors we have ever had. But the greatest good of all was Burgo's having a girlfriend. It seems a more important event than his getting a degree, and may well be more use to him. Jane is very attractive, oncoming and friendly, with a saving grace of nervousness. She hasn't got that appalling confidence of most pretty girls.

September 21st

I have spent the morning, clock in front of me, doing my Spanish article, which is now in hand. Much enjoyed the weekend with Robert, the Godleys, and Burgo. To begin at the end, he is in some way loosened up, with curly instead of straight lines on his face, still restless and explosive but liberated. What he wants to be at now is a rampaging bit of sex, I believe. It now comes often into his conversation, and he has his own style about it – destructive, violent and funny. Robert was with us for an afternoon before the Godleys came. We strolled across the fields, discussing his problems, and he at once came out with the fact that he has an appointment with a 'head-shrinker'. He talked of his desire to 'settle down', without mentioning names, but only 'people', 'one' and 'other people', though this anonymity brought him to the edge and over into giggles.

September 28th

We were glad to see Anthony West and Lily after two years' absence. However, Anthony was in a rather provocative mood. Some of the characters he attacked may have been stand-ins for Rebecca – Madame de Staël and George Eliot, for instance. Seeing me at work on an index of Freud's *Jokes*, he carried it off to the verandah, and came back with burning eyes saying: 'I was checking up to see whether Freud had a sense of humour. He hasn't, *has he*? These jokes aren't funny at all, *are they*?' It seemed pointless to tell him that he was talking through his hat – the jokes weren't Freud's, but *famous* jokes, many by Heine or various philosophers, which had been thought funny by a lot of people, and that Freud was taking a scientific interest in the reason why.

On our getting up to our bedroom on Sunday night Ralph fell silent, then made the familiar gesture down his breastbone and admitted to 'discomfort'. I must not show the gloom this casts me into or he will keep such things from me.

October 17th

Janetta and I drove over to Stokke cottage, which has been rented from Mary by Robert. There we found Robert and Georgie, the house half-painted, and Cynthia upstairs interviewing an upholstress. Robert described the colour schemes: the kitchen was to be black, white and red. Janetta: 'Good heavens! Like a luxury flat of the Thirties!'

November 2nd

The Toynbees are staying at Robert's cottage; they came over to us for a drink, Sally pregnant, Philip booming away in his irresistible velvety *basso profundo*. Afterwards I asked Robert about the marriage, adding that I found it hard to believe Philip capable of love. 'No, I doubt if he is,' Robert said, 'and I don't believe I am either. Though of course I recognize there is such a thing.' The relationship between Robert and Philip is like that of two businessmen, advancing and punching each other semi-comically in the chest. In an argument as to why the Labour party lost the Election they got so heated that they yelled (and boomed) at each other, both saying true and sensible things which shot past the other like missiles going wide of their target. Philip thought that if one believed one's principles were right one shouldn't scrap them just because of failure, but consider how to persuade one's adversary more forcefully; Robert that we must beat the Conservatives, and use any means to that end. Philip has a good arguer's mind, and listens to what one says as very few people do, a pleasant change from those who merely hold their breath, let their eyes glaze over and wait till one has finished.

November 6th

Winter has begun. A brilliant frosty morning, with all the dahlias and zinnias suddenly blackened and dead. Janetta arrived at lunch-time, and immediately afterwards she and I drove up on to the downs and took a walk in the already opalescent light which would soon be a fog. She talked about Cynthia entirely without malice, said that she was very kind to the children, but that she felt sorry for her as Robert was often so fierce to her.

I am insisting on a few perfectly quiet days for Ralph, but wish there could be more. A plague of visitors lies ahead, curse it! Trudge on!

November 19th

Our heaviest weekend – with the Pritchetts and the Hills – was a great success, enjoyed I believe by all including me, in spite of grey, grim weather. It ended in a long discussion about tragedy in general and *Othello* in particular. Was it one of the best tragic plots in the world or not? V.S.P. thought not, because it hinged too much on tricks and devices, and not on Fate as Aristotle thought it should. I thought that what made it so tremendous was that the violent emotions involved were common to everyone – love, jealousy, lust for power; and that whether trickery or Fate set them off didn't greatly matter.

So much for the weekend, which left Ralph and me so fresh that we took on a visit to Dora Romilly (piteously ill, poor creature), drinks at Stokke, and visits from Kitty West and Burgo.

I have just finished the nineteenth and last volume of Saint-Simon. Approaching the end of the tunnel I couldn't bear to come out, and braked hard; but now I'm through, and this vast, densely populated stretch of history lies behind me. Not until reaching the very end do I feel that in a sort of way I am conscious of it as a whole, yet I am afraid of losing or dropping that vision. Another thing I'm aware of is a warm affection for Saint-Simon himself, in spite of his vanity and snobbery. I remember his passion for truth, his curiosity, his intelligence. I shall move on to something that links with him if possible – the Letters of Madame, the Princesse des Ursins, or even the Big Miss, as Lytton used to call her.[1] Saint-Simon is I suppose the longest book I ever read in my life.

December 6th: Crichel

In bed at Crichel, whither we came on Friday afternoon under a luminous peacock blue sky with a crescent moon. Here we are with Eddy, elegant in a letter-box red sweater, Eardley and Raymond, and all around us this marquetry box of coloured, complicated, patterned comforts. I noticed last night how the differing styles of talk of Eardley on one side, and Raymond and Eddy on the other, show that he is an artist and they are critics. Where Eardley is responding and reflecting in a way that is entirely his own, the other two are busily amassing and assessing facts. The result is that I often find what Eardley has to say the more alive and interesting. Between several walks, meals and much lovely gramophone music we got happily to the evening, when Michael and Sonia Pitt-Rivers came to dinner. Rather to our surprise the *Crichelois* treat this marriage between a lifelong homosexual and a neurotic forty-year-old woman as if it was perfectly normal, and they would be happy ever after and why not? They certainly bounced in laughing and talking. At dinner I sat between Raymond and Michael, who is a great talker. There's hardly a subject he doesn't fall upon with the avidity of a starving man pouncing on a juicy steak, though in fact we talked mostly about trees or his travels in the Far East. Lots of funny stories and excellent imitations followed one another without pause, and his memories seem to be arranged on a bookshelf in front of him, so that he finds one in a moment and takes it down. It's not so much a conversation as a very brilliant turn.

December 28th

Janetta and her children took over Stokke for Christmas, which was as usual a gruelling endurance test for almost everyone – except the children, who moved like ecstatic ghosts among mountains of parcels, toys, books, television sets and Balmain fur coats. Robert was a heroic figure, working manfully to live up to his standards, and backed by the devoted Cynthia. Janetta was the most worrying casualty. She looked grey with pallor and admitted to feeling 'whacked'; as she had about seventeen people to every meal it was hardly surprising, but she said that wasn't what had exhausted her, it was 'seeing people she didn't like'.

On Boxing Day Robert brought over his guests at the cottage – Woodrow Wyatt and his wife Lady Moorea. He combines socialism with snobbishness, is clever in a quick rather than in a deep way, gregarious, confident and greedy. He ate a colossal dinner, fell asleep in his chair before the music-room fire, and snored.

As for me, I am in the grip of anxiety now that our departure day approaches,

[1] La Grande Demoiselle, cousin of Louis XIV.

especially in view of Ralph's obvious fear of being hurried or harried. I dread lest any small mishaps common to journeys might affect him and can think of no magic talisman to quell my fears except the one word COURAGE, which I have written on every page of my pocket diary.

December 29th

We had Robert to ourselves for supper last night, a perfect companion. After going over Christmas with a fine comb and deciding how everyone 'did', we got on to psychoanalysis, both in theory and practice. It was fascinating to hear about it from someone as realistic and averse to mumbo-jumbo as he is. One thing he came up with was that the infant's pleasure in suckling was fully sexual. But if so, wouldn't there be extreme differences in the psychological patterns of the breast- and bottle-fed? Robert also finds it convincing that some states of adult rage are speechless – because they refer back to the pre-speech period of infancy. I was rather struck by that. And here is a fragment of the psychoanalysis of everyday life, which has only just occurred to me: on Christmas day at Stokke I saw a pretty jewelled object lying on a table and asked what it was. Cynthia's present to Janetta, a key-ring. Something clicked at the time, but only now do I see the significance of the present of a Kee-ring.

December 31st

Last day of 1959 and last day here. Six men arrived this morning and carried off some of our furniture to prepare for re-decoration in our absence. The cushions are left on a heap on the floor, as a sign that we must *must* go.

Janetta came down to encourage us on our way, and Robert – alone now at his cottage – made a fourth at tea. We have had a cheerful, very adult postcard from Burgo in Athens. But the wind wails, and my *angst* wails with it.

1960

[A new variation had been decided on for this year's winter in the South: we would make for Alicante, an attractive town with an even better climate than Málaga, and find a comfortable hotel there with none of the burden of housekeeping and social life. If we were lucky Janetta might visit us there and we would be away for three months.

By way of Bordeaux and the *Chapon Fin* we reached the Savoy Hotel at Madrid. From the window of our comfortable bedroom I was watching the life and movement in an arcade below, when Ralph asked if I'd like to go out for a moment and I said I would. We strolled up and down admiring the coloured lights decorating the kerbside trees in readiness for tomorrow's *Los Reyes* (the Children's Christmas), when 'after five minutes, to my indescribable horror and remorse, Ralph was seized by one of his sudden bouts of exhaustion. We went back at once and he sank into an armchair. After a pause he said, "I'm all right now. I'm as right as rain." Then, *sotto voce*, "No, not right as rain. I shall never be right as rain again. That's the worst of it." Once in bed he fell asleep immediately, but I was much too anxious, and lay penetrated and saturated by grief. For it must be faced that he finds this journey much more testing than last year's.'

We were fortunate in reaching Alicante before the blizzard that a few days later brought unaccustomed cold winds and even snow, isolating a busload of people all night not far from the route we had taken. Oh, what a relief to be there, installed in our old-fashioned, very warm hotel. Ralph was soon feeling much better, and eager to walk along the esplanade with its paving of mosaics in wave pattern, set between two rows of tall palm-trees. 'The air was warm and sweet, the blue water of the harbour was full of boats, and hundreds of white doves were settling down for the night in the branches. We talked and laughed as we walked.' So it had not been all misery. 'Our fellow-guests in the hotel are mostly ancient Spanish couples,' I wrote, 'who have come South from a colder clime and are waiting for Godot. The old men glide with shuffling steps into the dining-room preceded by their wives. One such, seen from a distance is a tragic-eyed Goya, sallow-faced and with dyed black hair; looking closer one sees a fragile, bent, white-haired old woman. They are all treated gently and with respect by the staff. To Spaniards "*la vieillesse est une dignité*" (Chateaubriand, whom I've just begun to read).'

I brought no pressure to bear on Ralph to take walks or short excursions, but did my best to fall in with his desires, read his expression or tone of voice. However, 'I long for a sweet Janetta to discuss things with, and help me keep them in proportion. As I haven't got her I must swing from branch to branch through my private jungle, improvising as I go.'

So the weeks passed, and for some time the fierce cold refused to loosen its grip.

Perhaps to keep his morale alive, Ralph sometimes insisted on coming out, to the Poste Restante say, when I *knew* he shouldn't, when he felt the worse for it before we got home, but stubbornly refused to take a rest in a warm cafe. In a rational conversation next day he admitted to having suffered from 'trouser-panic' as he called it, namely fear that I was getting too bossy. If only he could have perceived the quivering mass of uncertainty within me!

Then a telegram came from Janetta that she would join us at Almería. We were delighted, but almost scared at the thought of company, for we have been a long time alone, even if all our friends and Burgo have been splendid correspondents.

The drive to Almería went well, Ralph saying he felt 'very strong', and what joy to find Janetta there, already having moved her furniture to humanize her room. As I guessed she would, she had an invigorating effect on Ralph, and I know he felt her a support. So in a different way were the Brenans who arrived a week later, Gerald with flu, so he said. When I was alone pressing my flowers in my bedroom he came to see me. 'In the very nicest, most friendly way he asked me in detail about Ralph's health, listened attentively, and said that if at any moment we were in difficulties or needed a doctor a telegram would bring him to wherever we were. I was moved and grateful for his understanding. Gerald really isn't feeling well himself, and his friendliness in coming is a thing I shan't forget – Janetta too has been angelic.'

Janetta left with the Brenans to stay with them and with Jaime, but came back to us again for a hotter spell, of excursions and flower-hunting. Before we started on our journey home she told us she now loved the idea of leading her own life – independent except for the children.

By the monastery of Poblet and Tarragona to Paris.]

March 16th: Ham Spray

The transition from Paris to Wiltshire was almost too quick to take in, but our shock-absorbers worked so well that we have slid back with hardly a creak or squeak and already feel that we've not been away. The 'pig's bathroom'[1] looks very smart with its new marbled black, yellow and white décor. There are some pretty new curtains in the library and Mr Wells has done a lot of touching up and repainting. In fact our house doesn't look too bad at all, and a round trip of the garden showed us dogtooth violets under the beech tree and tarragon and cineraria in the greenhouse.

I am trying not to press too hard on the accelerator, but coast, as we did in Spain. It is fiendishly difficult.

March 20th

Of all the people we saw at the weekend I feel we did well by everyone except Robert and Cynthia. Janetta was particularly and unjustifiably appreciative of – heavens knows! 'what we do for her'. We do nothing. We merely love her and are eternally grateful to her. But we also love Robert, and being with the three of them – Janetta, Robert and Cynthia – all together makes us uneasy in spite of ourselves. Robert was not at his most equable, and various mutual friends had got

---

[1] So-called ever since it was used to salt and 'pet' our pig in the War.

into his dog-house. Poor Cynthia may well be having a difficult time with him; I really felt sorry for her.

March 28th

A few minutes ago the telephone rang, and as I went to answer it I said to myself, 'It must be Burgo.' And so it was, just arrived from Paris. Asked how he was, he replied, 'Much as usual'.

I have just been listening with deep emotion to Mozart's *Requiem*. When a composer with the hand of death already on his shoulder expresses his response to his coming end in his own peculiar language, he must surely reach the summit of intense personal feeling, comparable perhaps to Shakespeare's when he writes of love and jealousy in the *Sonnets*. The *Requiem* seems to me to convey the splendour and tragedy of man's life faced with death, and bathe it in a light of *acceptability* in a way that no impurer art than music can. By thus revealing the major drama of approaching death – the whiteness to be cancelled out by dense blackness – through a mesh of logic and lucidity, the *Requiem* arouses an extra-ordinary sense of ecstasy that is both musical and philosophical, like the pleasure got from Beethoven's late quartets. Has it no more significance than a cold bath which sets the circulation going? I can't believe it.

April 12th

Returning from a day in London, I met Robert arriving for dinner in the darkness of the drive. Towards the end of our pleasant evening he broke the news to us that he and Cynthia were to get married. She was going to have a child; and his only fear was that Janetta and Georgie might be upset. The terms we are on with Robert made it impossible to act an enthusiasm we didn't feel. In fact we both felt as if someone had died; but I did say truly that I was very glad to think how happy this would make Cynthia.

Janetta, who came down next day, had heard the news and took it staunchly, saying that Robert would be glad to have the child and Georgie wouldn't be upset at all. Robert is bequeathing Burgo his flat in Percy Street, a great bit of good luck for him.

April 19th

The visitors for our 'small Easter party' have just gone – Isobel, Burgo, Simon Raven and Richard Chopping, increased by extra people every day. From the social point of view it was easier having so many, as they mixed, sparkled and fizzed together, and also went off on their own. Richard was a great support, spreading his golden-hearted amiability round him. Even so I began fraying at the edges, and Ralph said he felt 'weak' and looked it. When Annie Davis (staying at Stokke) begged us 'to come over and organize potato races for Téo's birthday party', it was not exactly music in my ears, but Richard and I went, and found Annie struggling manfully; Téo pale with the desire always to win; Robert sulking in his tent like Achilles; rows in progress between Georgie and Téo. Janetta had taken time off to visit the Gowings, but told us that 'Easter had been ghastly'.

Robert came alone later, in a calmer mood, and able to laugh over his con-versation with Cyril about marriage: 'You must just look at it as if it were a three-year contract,' he had said. He was delighted that Robert was 'joining him in the trap. There are two things that happen – either you have half your face torn away, or you just turn into a marker-buoy – *Wreck here!*'

May 23rd

The Kee wedding has taken place, and Burgo has moved into the Percy Street flat with Poppet John and her husband. Robert tells us he gets on very well with them, is having his photograph taken for an article, and is working six hours a day. When Robert asked him if he was coming down here for the weekend, he replied, 'Good heavens, no!'

[From June 1st to 9th, Ralph, Janetta and I took a short holiday in Ireland, part of whose purpose was to collect botanical records for the forthcoming *Atlas of the British Flora*. Luckily for me both my companions entered into my search with apparent enthusiasm. I read not a single book except Irish Floras and Guides, yet the time was crammed to bursting with rich sensations, mossy smells, constantly varying light, and the freshness of a satisfying draught of spring water faintly tinged with earth and growing plants. We had made no plans, but never wrangled about 'where to go'. At Kilkee we found an Irish San Sebastian, with the beaming faces of small Victorian houses ranged round its *concha*. One huge purple-faced old lady sat in the glassed-in verandah of our hotel, silently watching the world go by. There was very strong Irish whiskey, home-made brown bread, a bowl of butter, peat fires and hot bottles in our beds. Turning north next day we reached the famous and immensely tall cliffs of Moher. Janetta, suddenly panic-stricken, took one look and exclaimed, 'They're *beastly*. I hate them.' However, her VC blood forced her to lie down on her stomach and look over at the sheerest point.[1] At Ennistymon 'we first reached the limestone, and shrieked in unison as we came upon a great patch of the purple flowers of bloody cranesbill, and everywhere saxifrages and orchids. Best of all were the fantastic ash-coloured rocks of the region called the Burren, in whose crevices a mass of rare plants were growing.'

We had booked rooms at Leenane for the Whitsun weekend and from here we took a day on Achill, 'a hazy hot and still day, which suited this foreign region, where huge plantations of rhododendrons grow wild on the slopes of tall round-browed mountains rising abruptly from the plain. Their Moorish purple-pink was the dominant colour except for fuchsia red. Janetta felt a tug to the West, although it is inhabited by her ghosts, and bravely booked herself on a boat to the Aran Islands. As Ralph and I (too craven to go with her) were walking by a river a man rushed up to Ralph shouting, "Have ye got yer fishing-tackle with ye? There's three lovely throut just over there!" It was inconceivable to him that any man shouldn't own a rod.'

June 17th

We have been back here exactly a week though it seems more. Last weekend we decided to bottle our barrel of Tarragona wine. Burgo and Simon came down for a bare twenty-four hours to help, and all Sunday we had Robert, Cynthia, and Debo (the Duchess of Devonshire) helping too until about seven, giving me the restless feeling of being hostess at a weird sort of cocktail party. Were the guests getting

[1] Her father won the VC in the First World War.

bored and their backs beginning to ache sitting in that dusty box-room, which smelled every moment more like a bar-parlour, what with the drops soaking into the wooden floor? However, everyone emerged well from the ordeal. Burgo organized the operations very efficiently, and Robert and Simon stuck to them good-humouredly. I took the Duchess and Cynthia out for breathers into the garden and greenhouse: the former is a real charmer, very pretty, gay, quick-witted and alert to everything. I don't know much about Burgo's present life, but he seems much more grown-up and self-confident, and Simon must be given some of the credit as he's more of a friend than Burgo has had before. They have fantastically grand ideas about food and wine. I don't know the source of a (presumably apocryphal) story about Simon and his ex-wife. After he had broken with her she telegraphed: 'Wife and baby starving'. Simon is supposed to have wired back: 'Eat baby'.

June 21st

On Saturday we drove to Crichel for a weekend of continuing heatwave, all day and every day spent in the garden and all meals eaten there. A menace of thunder faded leaving a cloudless forget-me-not blue sky and a light breeze ruffling the swags of roses that covered the house. Our three hosts all looked in excellent trim, agile, thin and young for their ages. Desmond, wearing nothing but bathing pants and a thimble-shaped straw hat, slowly turned a ripe terracotta. In the evening came Kitty West and Maud Russell, both in different ways gamely fighting with their backs to the wall. Kitty is selling her house and moving to London. Maud is retreating with dignity and style before the encroaching tide of old age.

Conversation at dinner as to whether the curiosity felt about the private lives of great men was justified. Eardley firmly declared it was disgusting, even in the case of Shakespeare's Sonnets or Byron's letters. After dinner a stray remark of mine about Aaron Copland made Desmond leap spontaneously to his feet and carry some of us next door to hear his clarinet concerto not once but twice, thrusting the score into my hand. I find this elastic and excitable responsiveness of his simply charming.

On Sunday evening Cecil Beaton came to dinner and wore everyone down by staying rather too long. Dressed in a pink shirt and Palm Beach suit, his smooth pink face is rather like that of a sly moose or gnu, slit by a narrow little grin. I'm not sure how much I like him. I would guess him to be selfish and vain, malicious at times, but also affectionate in a limited way. Desmond dozed off on the sofa, Maud and I had a pleasant female talk about our sons, and Raymond and Cecil did some name-swapping.

June 22nd

To London for a mediocre performance of Verdi's *Otello*, and to visit poor little Joan Cochemé in hospital. She was lying in a small white cubicle off the TB ward, with her pale face propped between pillows and her eyes closed. When she opened them and saw me she burst into tears. She has been having an appalling time, with operations on her lung under local anaesthetic. The pain was 'horrible'; I felt I was talking to someone on the rack. As I walked away down corridors as long and thickly populated as Oxford Street I was both impressed and horrified by this juggernaut of medicine on which we all depend. The sight of poor afflicted Joan lying in the middle of it, like a fly in a spider's web left a bruise on my consciousness.

June 28th: Ham Spray

Very hot and lovely weekend with Janetta and Professor Dick Sanders of Duke University, who is writing about Lytton and all the Stracheys. I wasn't sure how they would get on, but she soon saw the intensely human, emotional being that lies underneath the donnish exterior and American pursuit of culture. After lunch he said with satisfying firmness that he wanted to 'have a snooze and then go for a walk'. We found him later wandering in cornfields still sopping from a thunderstorm; so Ralph gently started him down the avenue in the direction of one of Cobbett's Rural Rides, and he was off like a shot, returning later with 'a rock' as he called it – a round black stone – as a souvenir.

We had the Kees and the Godleys to drinks on the lawn. It was quite clear which were the Professor's favourites. He took a huge fancy to Robert, and said to Ralph about Janetta, 'She's *very* attractive. Doesn't Frances ever worry about your falling for her?'

Ralph and I planned how to share Dick Sanders. I was to take him walking on the Downs next day, and in the afternoon Ralph would drive him over to Alix and James. I enjoyed both the walk (it was a radiant morning) and our talk – it was largely about immortality. 'I only believe in total extinction,' he announced, 'but if I were to be offered the chance of existing for ever, in a bodily as well as spiritual form, *I should jump at it*. I love life.' This pleased me, but I confessed that personally I clung to the thought of total oblivion, whereas eternal life without ageing or maturing was an idea that filled me with dread and honour, adding that as animals in a vegetable kingdom our nature seemed to me rooted in the concept of change and decay. 'Yes,' said the Professor, 'Shakespeare really said the last word on that in *King Lear* "ripeness is all".' So then we got on to Shakespeare, and were in complete agreement that *Othello* was the best play that he or probably anyone else ever wrote. I took him down to Combe, to peer into the little church and over the wall of the Manor, and told him the local legends about Nell Gwynne and also the gallows. He gobbles up these crumbs so eagerly that it's a pleasure to throw them to him. Indeed he's a most likeable man.

On Monday we had a letter from poor Joan, who now has a clot on her lung and is to be moved to another hospital and operated on today. I spent some time telephoning to get news of her, and then paced the lawn with Janetta, talking sadly, she of her feelings of depression, I trying to explain how I expect nothing of life and think only a week ahead. She left us, as ever sad to see her go.

July 11th

Janetta came to see us, bringing Paddy Leigh Fermor – whom we both like unreservedly. He is as ebullient and enthusiastic, as life-loving as Desmond; intoxicated with words, foreign languages and verbal jokes. We passed a hilarious afternoon, doubled up by his stories and excellent mimicry, and charmed by the way he looked lovingly at his own bleached corduroy trousers and navy-blue socks and said they reminded him of Piero della Francesca. I saw exactly what he meant.

July 29th

Last night, at about half past eleven, Ralph laid the *Interpretation of Dreams* down on his knee and began to enlarge on the thoughts it aroused in him. They concerned the 'Day's residues' – those minute incidents which in Freud's view act as setters-in-motion of dreams. Ralph thought that this was because the response to some sensory stimulus had been interrupted, thus producing 'steam' which emerged in the repressed material expressed by the dream. The discussion that followed brought out in a fascinating way certain differences in our two characters and ways of thought that we must have known about for years, namely that Ralph's mind favours induction – seizes an essential particular and moves from it to a universal, in the way common to innovators; while mine is deductive and goes in the opposite direction. His is the sort of mind that makes discoveries, while mine carries out the donkey-work of criticism and analysis.

'And what about memory?' I asked him at one point. 'Oh perfectly simple, it's just running over a tape-recorder of past stimuli,' he replied, gazing dreamily into space and obviously in a state of mind when everything was 'perfectly simple'. Of course I tried to show that it was not, but though he gave a polite appearance of listening he was really waiting until he could carry on with the thread of his own thoughts. I tried all the same to explain to him how I thought of the sensory stimuli as a swarm of bees simultaneously assaulting my five senses. He was amazed, and said he had no such feeling. How I envy his powers of concentration, his exclusion of the irrelevant, the simplicity in fact of his approach, which is something to do with the way he fell at once to sleep when we went upstairs, while I lay tossing and turning and thinking about my swarm of bees.

August 8th

Joan has been with us for several days, recuperating from her operation. We took her to dinner at Kee Cottage, and a somewhat ill-matched argument arose between her and Robert about Apartheid. Joan doesn't believe she thinks the blacks are inferior, only different, and Robert – with the blazing eyes of the skilled television interviewer – was sharp enough to spot the truth though she hadn't revealed it. I was a little uneasy about my convalescent, and took Robert up for no-balling once or twice. For instance when Joan said her black cook 'was sweet and she loved him', Robert would say, 'Ah! You see? You're assuming it's *odd* for him to be sweet. Why shouldn't he be?' Or if she criticized any black person, naturally he pounced at once, so having it both ways.

September 6th

A new consignment of Spanish articles to translate has made my work-table into a battlefield. I managed, however, to get the first two off before the weekend, and there's no doubt I feel happier and droop less when I have slightly too much to do. Our weather gave us patches of brilliant blue between solid islands of cloud, and our visitors (the Godleys and Isobel) appeared to enjoy the lazy days – all they were offered – mostly spent in the garden, now luxuriant with dahlias, zinnias and groaning pear-trees. Kitty maintained that there was nothing self-indulgent about having children – it was pure altruism, an opinion which was fairly sternly contested. She went on to say that 'as they hadn't asked to be born, the least parents could do was to leave them all their money'. None was to go to spouse, friends or causes.

September 10th: Mottisfont

Boris and Violet Bonham-Carter were here when we arrived, to be joined by Violet's son Raymond. Boris is a little muted in this house, or perhaps just by age. Some of the air has gone out of him, leaving him deflated and with dark bags under his eyes. Conversation, conversation, conversation – it goes on like a marathon: at meal-times all in the form of tête-à-têtes often without switching direction for an immense time. One snatches a breather from one's own (and a little food must be swallowed also) and sees the other pairs hard at it, looking into each other's faces with the deepest interest. What a strange go it is! Yet I am enjoying it, and so is Ralph. Yesterday after breakfast I walked out and found Boris's large shape bent meditatively over some patches of tiny cyclamens under the cedar tree. We walked off towards the river with the little woolly dog of the house bouncing beside us. Boris talked all the way about his work, obsessionally. He lives for it alone, and has no relaxation except chess problems. I was about to offer myself as a sacrifice for a game when he said it made his heart beat uncomfortably and he had given up playing. He gets up at 5.30 every morning and is at work at Barnet by eight. He goes to bed at eight.

Tea was like a scene in Henry James – spread under a huge tree, with cucumber sandwiches and home-made coffee cake. After it we played crazy croquet in the sideways light from the setting sun, which all at once turned into a huge red ball and disappeared, leaving us chilled. Boris's croquet style is magnificent. In his capacious trousers, cut to fit an earlier stage of corpulence, he curves his body into a vast croquet hoop, seizes his mallet low down by the head, gives his objective one searching glance, and aims – often with deadly effect.

At dinner that night he dismissed Picasso, calling him 'a clever crook' who 'cashes in by *épatant la bourgeoisie*, a couturier, a Dior always thinking up new models'. With Noel Blakiston on my other side I was discussing the importance, or otherwise, of the Classics. Thence – the transition was his I think – to belief in God. I said: 'Well, I shall ask you straight out: Do you believe in him?' He said, '*I don't know* whether I do or not.' It seemed to worry him.

The arrival of reviews of Leonard's *Autobiography* in the papers gave Violet a text to pour scorn on poor erring Bloomsbury. The gist was that they were fighting battles that had been won long ago, stating obvious conclusions that 'one' had long ago reached with no difficulty, or – in Leonard's case – being 'downright naïf'. Then came her bigger guns. '*Such* a pity that Keynes was led away, for a while, into pacifism. *So* stupid not to realize that Desmond MacCarthy was the most distinguished of the group.' Raymond and Harold Nicolson's reviews of the book she took as a form of ridicule.

Was all this leading up to her full-scale assault on pacifism to Ralph during dinner, which induced him to declare his own position openly, and particularly his horror of women who so gladly and proudly sacrificed their men? Whereupon, for the second time in our presence, she made her famous declaration: 'I would rather see both my sons DEAD AT MY FEET than under German domination!' I only heard of this interchange from Ralph later in our bedroom, but I saw from his red cheek and angry sparkling eye that feelings were high.

The Bonham-Carters left after dinner. It was like seeing a whole army disappear with flags flying, and the rest of us settled to a peaceful game of Scrabble.

September 15th: Ham Spray

Rang the Kees for news. How were they? 'Pretty bad, really,' said Robert, and went on to say he'd been having a tough time with his analyst. When I answered his question about ourselves by saying, 'Rather boringly calm at the moment,' he exclaimed, 'But that's just the trouble – *my un*calm is so boring.'

Ralph has been quite exceptionally angelic to me all this summer. It is not nonsense to say I have never felt more loved. What can be the reason for it? It almost makes me anxious.

September 22nd

We were expecting Clive and Little Barbara for the weekend, both somewhat invalidish. So the very strong voice of Janetta on the telephone, just back from Spain and proposing to come down too, put courage in us both. 'I shall be quite ready to carry up trays. Shall I *bring* some trays?' She added, 'There's lots to say about Gerald and Hetty. My gosh!'

Ralph has just driven off to Marlborough in response to a summons to serve on a jury. I am green with envy.

September 28th

Janetta arrived looking fine; brown and strong in her white jersey and skirt; calm also, tolerant of Barbara and very nice to Clive and us. When Clive heard that we had asked the grieving widower, Bunny Romilly, to dinner he was quite indignant: 'NOT OLD BUNNY! Really, Fanny! Even the Crichel Boys don't ask me to meet him, and once when it was suggested Eddy said: "You don't think we'd insult any of our friends by asking them to meet *Bunny*, do you?"' Later he was heard calling from his bedroom: 'Since there's a *peer* coming to dinner I shall put on a white shirt, and perhaps Ralph could lend me a tie.' Bunny arrived a little tight from a cocktail party and couldn't get a single sentence finished, but Clive's natural good manners rose to the occasion.

Robert and Cynthia came for a drink on Sunday, and there was a splendid display of snake-charming by Robert. His technique is quite brilliant. Clive was in fits of laughter, blinking wildly and pulling his trouser-legs so far up his legs that he looked as if he was going paddling. But Robert goes one better than making people think him charming – he makes *them* be their most charming.

October 6th

Thoughts about the Bomb have come to the fore because of the vote for Uni-lateralism at the Labour Conference last week. Robert has been reporting all the political conferences. He told me on the telephone that he is now a Unilateralist, in spite of the fact that the speeches in favour were rotten, and Gaitskell's (on the other side) excellent, because he thought it showed new life and genuine feeling in the Labour Party, something also that was gaining strength. A letter from Acland in *The Times*, saying that as we were set now atomic war was inevitable and that there was literally nothing to lose by altering our present outlook, weighed with Ralph more than Robert's or my arguments. But how unreal such huge possibilities as atomic war and occupation by Russia seem as I write them down!

Henry Lamb's death was announced in *The Times* yesterday. His face looking out of the page is so vital, his gaze so piercing, that it brings the sound of his voice instantly to one's ears and makes his non-existence incredible.

November 7th

Last weekend came Bunny, Angelica and Amaryllis Garnett. My heart-cockles warmed to dear Bunny, rosy under his white thatch and overflowing with geniality. Angelica worried me, however. She radiated a feeling of desperation, and I'm ashamed that I have no idea what it's about.

But the lack of manners of Bloomsbury struck me not for the first time. When Cynthia, enormously pregnant and without Robert, came to dinner, they made no attempt to take the smallest interest in her, look at her or talk to her. Nor, my goodness, do they pass one anything – one could starve for all they care.

November 14th

At the very end of a jolly evening entertaining the Gowings, Julia brought out her 'she's made her bed and she must lie on it' attitude to Angelica. Why did she seem so desperate? I had asked. Was it hard work, cooking for seven? 'Serves her right for marrying old Bunny and having so many children,' Julia said tartly. 'Why didn't she arrange her life better? One shouldn't have children recklessly. *I* didn't. There's such a thing as family planning.' Yet in her own case, no one makes heavier weather than Julia over household chores, and the way they interfere with her peace to write in. I wonder why she is such a severe judge of her fellow men – and women – and doesn't see that conflict between strong incompatible desires is the great human predicament.

November 21st

Robert and Cynthia spent their last weekend at the cottage before the baby's arrival was due. Georgie and Rose, both touched but giggling, took me to see the baby's room – a red nest with the receptacle for the little creature itself standing lonely and expectant in the middle. I was struck to the heart by the pathos of human procreation. Robert, looking very handsome even for him, was back from America and full of his adventures. He had returned by Air India, and I liked his description of the jubilant cry of the Indian pilot on making an excellent landing: 'Oh boy! Oh boy! How is that for smooth? What you say?'

November 28th

I have just driven Eddie Gathorne-Hardy, Simon and Burgo to the station. Burgo was delightfully freed from any melancholic tinge, and his mind was revolving like the efficient organ it is.

Last night before dinner I missed Ralph for a while. For the thousandth time I wondered, 'Is he all right? Could he perhaps be feeling ill?' Usually after the first panic and wild wobblings on my base, my equilibrium has been restored. This time, however, I felt it was odd that he should be in the library at this cold evening hour. I ran upstairs and found him lying down. No, he was *not* all right. Going through the kitchen to look at the stove he had suddenly felt a constriction in the chest, like two bars. He took a pill and then another, but remained limp and drowsy, wanting no food and unable to face the company. I am in a spurious way so armoured against these set-backs that a dreadful unearthly calm settled down on me, partly to make me able to face his dread of my 'fussing'. But along with this grey *tristesse* was the awareness of a huge crater opening, black and menacing. Paralysed in mind and hardly able to talk, I went downstairs and cooked dinner and somehow sketched a part in the conversation until the meal was over, when I was able to go up and lie beside Ralph.

This morning he swears he is better, but is in no great hurry to get up. We must 'greet the unknown' with all possible common-sense, but I am full of doubts which I cannot voice to him.

November 29th

Throughout yesterday I sank slowly into the pit, as it became gradually clear to me that 'something or other' did happen in the stove-room on Sunday night. Ralph was comatose and fighting a desperate rearguard action against admitting himself ill. He becomes furious (frighteningly so, because bad for him) if I treat him as such, and I identify myself so completely with him that the difficulty of overriding the line he has decided to take is almost insuperable. Is this another heart attack such as the second, of last spring, which was followed by three weeks in bed, or only one of the many alarming but transient 'incidents' that left no trace? During yesterday's battles my anxiety for Ralph, my agonizing dread, gradually wrenched itself away from the part of me that is identified with him, leaving a ghastly bleeding wound but at least the satisfaction of doing what I believe is right and indeed urgently necessary. I told him therefore that I had rung up the Hungerford Surgery, and arranged that Sawbones' locum should come out to see him (Sawbones himself being away). This made Ralph really indignant: 'I can never tell you about my sensations if you behave so foolishly.' I couldn't tell him that it was impossible to face another night of desperation and fear, lying with beating heart listening to his short difficult breathing. 'What would Janetta advise?' I asked myself, and I knew the answer. I rang up Geoff Konstam this morning and gave him a detailed account of Ralph's state. Oh God! He, too, is just going off on holiday. Geoff does not think it sounds serious, but he was in favour of the locum coming and has given me the name and telephone number of the heart specialist at Reading Hospital. It was a great relief to discuss things with him, and after a brief flare-up Ralph has accepted the inevitable. Words are quite useless to express my tortured state, the swords of mental pain that stab me through and through. A good nurse should keep all signs of anxiety from her patient, but how can I achieve this with Ralph, who knows me all too well, and can read everything that is written on my all-too expressive, furrowed face?

5 p.m. A tiny doctor with a serious face fringed with red hair came out this morning and will come again tomorrow. Absolute stillness in bed is his prescription, and it is no easy job to enforce it. He thinks there has been another slight 'infarct', and rang up Geoff to discuss the position. Meanwhile I remain in the rack, gripping as best I can on to sanity by means of practical things. Deathly silence, the clock ticks loudly in the hall. It has been a sorrowful business for poor Ralph to accept that he *is* once more ill. I dread the evenings when my thoughts get the upper hand, and above all the nights.

November 30th

But last night was much worse than my fears. I dropped into exhausted sleep, but soon awoke and listened to Ralph's struggling breathing for four hours, while the clock snailed round its course. But why describe such agony? We are both alive this morning – that's all I can say.

Morning calls to Red-beard and Geoff, visits from Red-beard – but I have antagonized him, I see. There is something so futile about him, and I couldn't bear the snobbish reluctance he showed to get into touch with the Reading specialist who unfortunately happens to be a Lord. Yet to some extent we depend on him, and I try to choke back my horror that this little mannikin should be relevant to the health and safety of my darling Ralph. I pressed on, screaming silently from every cranny of my brain, until I got him to arrange for the lordly cardiologist to come tomorrow. Geoff seemed to take things more seriously when I described Ralph's breathing. It seems that he took two sleeping-pills while I dozed last night, one seeming insufficient, and Geoff thought this might have affected his breathing. He has recommended a new sort for tonight. I dashed in to Hungerford to get them. Not available, I have ordered them to be brought out by taxi from Newbury, and we have got them now.

Ralph does seem a little better this evening and with more appetite for his supper. He has even read more. I went downstairs while he was eating, and listened to Berlioz's *Symphonie Fantastique* on the wireless without much pleasure. I left Ralph a walking-stick to bang on the floor if he wanted me – but I never expected to hear, nor shall I ever forget that dreadful 'thump, thump, thump'...

December 1st

Now I am *absolutely alone and for ever.*

Hanging On

1960–1963

Foreword

The last published volume of my diary – *Everything to Lose* – ended with the death from a heart attack of my husband Ralph Partridge on 1 December 1960, and its final words were: 'Now I am absolutely alone and for ever.' Though I had lived under the ever-present shadow of this possibility for the previous four years, I had been sustained by bouts of irrational hope, and the blow was a crushingly final one – something in a completely different dimension from any anguish I had ever had to face before. Suicide has never seemed to me a wicked action but I am certain it is an extremely selfish one, causing pain and bitterness to those who are trying to prevent it. I was very much aware of this; also I think my life-instinct was naturally strong, and it emerged in a desire to try to 'hang on', and even to tell my closest friends that I meant to do so. What follows is the story of that struggle. But when suddenly bereft of the person I loved best, the companion with whom I had for more than thirty years kept up a river of communication which I believe was unusually wide and deep, how could I possibly choke that impulse into silence? Looking back, I feel that I only survived because I kept an outlet for my emotions, memories and speculations, instead of stifling them at birth. Why publish something so unbearably sad? I may be asked. Because virtually all adults learn sooner or later that there is a great deal of sorrow in life, that it is interrupted by disasters and crushed by stresses; that death and bereavement come to everyone and have to be faced. But most also know that it is not *all* sad, that in its very essence lies something glorious and splendid, that the stuff it is made of arouses constant wonder and interest, that even when one cannot stop crying one must suddenly laugh. So that though this volume may be full of tragedy it has a happy ending, in that it describes a sort of victory and return of courage.

I make no apology for my atheism. It is a position I reached at a very early age, and I consider it is better founded and less destructive than most religious faiths; but I do hold to my ethical values very strongly.

Ralph died at Ham Spray House. I began to write this diary a few weeks later in a small hotel on the French Riviera, where I had come with my great friends Julia (née Strachey) and Lawrence Gowing, who very kindly suggested my going with them on a visit to La Souco, Roquebrune to value Simon Bussy's[1] paintings.

---

[1] Lytton Strachey's brother-in-law. His death and his wife's – intestate – had left problems by French law.

1960

December 17th: Hotel Mas des Héliotropes, Roquebrune, Alpes Maritimes, France

I cannot write about these last seventeen days – not *now*, anyway. Nor can I see that I shall ever want to remember them. It's been all I could do to live them.

What has surprised me is that just because the blow has been so mortal, as if roughly, savagely cutting me in half and leaving me with one leg and one arm only, I am with what seems to me total illogicality under this menace struggling frantically to survive. Kitty West wrote to me that Ralph had once said that if I died 'he would not go on' and I know that's true. How much more rational and logical that seems. What earthly sense in this pitiful frantic struggle? The life-instinct must be much stronger than I knew.

My instant awareness of loss was total, final and complete. He was gone, and nothing that remained had any significance for me. Yet I feel it's impossible that I can be really aware of what lies ahead and still want to live. Ergo, I'm *not* really aware of it; I have buried and suffocated some part of it, and one day I shall wake and find I've been falsely bearing the unbearable, and either kill myself or go mad.

Another discovery I have made: compared to the torture of being on the rack, the deadly fear of losing everything – *having* lost it, utter desolation is a state of calm. I have nothing to lose, I care about nothing. I may be stumbling on, blindly pushed by some extraordinary incomprehensible instinct, but I *don't care* at all. *There's nothing now that matters.*

It would be ungrateful, though, not to mention the fabulous kindness of friends, which alters my whole view of human nature – the Carringtons, the Gowings, Burgo, Robert, each and all coming forward radiating strong beams of kindness, thoughtfulness and imaginative support.

Yet I'm painfully aware that I am a street accident exuding blood on the pavement, and it's a ghastly strain for each of them personally to be with me. They do want to help (and God knows they do) but if they could know my wounds were tied up and the flow of blood stopped, they would naturally be happier away from me. Yet with the greatest gratitude I have to accept their heroic kindness. And oh, *Janetta!* – what a debt I now have to her; flying back from Greece, taking me in and making a real refuge for me at Montpelier Square with all her rare and exquisite sensitiveness, gentleness and strength. But I said I'd write no more and I won't. I'll draw another line and begin with the start of our journey yesterday. All the same, I do think the impulse to write here is perhaps salutary, a first attempt to let up the terrifying, iron clamp which I have fastened on my thoughts.

The Gowings and I left England by the Blue Train yesterday morning *en route* for the South of France. Janetta drove me to the station. I could hardly bear to leave her and felt my eyes filling with helpless tears. Like a child going to school, however, I felt better once we had started.

Julia in a deep black extinguisher of a straw hat hissed in my ear as we got into the Golden Arrow: 'I *must* fight against my terrible desire to be taken for a millionaire duchess. Too shaming!' As a traveller she is surprisingly dominant and speaks confident French.

First impact with the cruel Frogs was appalling. *No* porters rushed on board at Calais and we only by the skin of our teeth, and after countless misdirections yelled in cross voices, found our *wagons-lit* at last. After which came a sort of oblivion, followed by the usual speechless drained exhaustion about nine in the evening, not improved by the infernal racket of the dining-car. I saw that this worried poor Julia, who tried to get me to talk about flower-collecting. Lawrence is anxious for her to stop being anxious, and the thing she's most likely to be anxious about during these three weeks is me. I'm already beginning to feel anxious about making her anxious. There's also, of course, the permanent undercurrent of her anxiety for Lawrence.

This morning, December 17th, I woke from drugged sleep to hear rain lashing the carriage window; looked out and saw water bucketing from the pale sky onto the vines which stood as it were in rivers. So it has gone on all day. When I walked up the hill to the village, I noticed the weather with detachment, but the smells, crannied plants and lights beginning to twinkle in Monte Carlo over the grey and purple sea brought a kind of balm.

December 18th

Writing letters sitting up in bed before my breakfast tray arrived, an agonizing process, drawing tears and blood. I can only do a few at a time.

December 22nd

I notice no one ever mentions Ralph's name to me, though I often do to them. I find this horribly unearthly. Julia and Lawrence are endlessly kind to me, and I do hope Julia's worry for me is not exhausting her. This morning she came into my room to say she would stay on till Clive and Barbara arrived, letting Lawrence go home alone. I tried to protest, but she waved my protests away and tears welled up to contradict my words.

Letters 'of sympathy' still arrive and I toil painfully through the answers. I long to hear from friends like Janetta, Joan Cochemé, Robert or Mary; but naturally no one wants to think about me, though they wish me well. Only my own efforts can make me otherwise than a black spot to be avoided, and I have no strength to make efforts.

December 28th

So the days pass. A sort of routine takes shape and I'm getting better at dealing with the surface of things. Rather to my surprise I find I want to be alone quite a lot in my room. When my thoughts grow unbearable I either translate[1] (in the day-time) or take to dope at night.

I bitterly regret that last night I upset Julia by talking cynically about vitamins!

---

[1] I had the job of translating a book on alcoholism from the French.

They belong to her scientific credo, and I resolve never to do such a thing again. Relations with Burgo are curiously normal, as if the parental element had been wiped out; but I think he's restless at not hearing from either Simon Raven or Anthony Blond.

December 31st

I see it is vital to keep a tight grip on my reins; any loosening of them, any momentary wondering what to do next, is fatal. I simply *must* make the decision, however arbitrary, to do *something* – it hardly matters what. At moments I feel I am best alone. At others a dreadful panic of this endless colloquy with myself arises in me, making my heart gallop.

Natural history of the Gowings: so long as Lawrence can arrange his day to allow of writing, painting and plenty of sleep he is the happiest man alive. He has no desire whatever for expeditions, discoveries, change or social stimulation.

Julia is of course in a perpetual state of dissatisfaction with her environment, for all the intense pleasure she may get in watching cats, or in the ambience of this place. Yet even in that she's very capricious. This has always been a key place to her ever since her childhood's visits to the Bussys at La Souco or her writing *Cheerful Weather*[1] here; she thinks of it as the one place where life was run on oiled wheels and she could sail ahead without obstacles into her 'creative writing', as she always calls it. The first few days here she was day-dreaming with Lawrence about buying or renting a villa here. 'Julia has "twigs in her beak",' he said. We even went and looked at one – she and I – a couple of tiny cell-like rooms with no amenities. Soon afterwards she announced that she had no desire whatever to live here.

Last night I was talking to Lawrence about the obstacles one felt to setting to work. How I justified not sitting down to translate by saying, 'In this mood I know I'll do it badly'. He thought one *should* sit down and try, because by overcoming the obstacle, one sometimes did one's best work. (This in fact I had done earlier in the evening, but without this happy result.) Julia resented this because it didn't consort with her view that the 'creative writer' – but none of us except her is that – must wait until 'the spirit calls', or 'the unconscious takes over'. I forget exactly how she worded it. In fact it was hardly ever possible for him or her to operate. I'm struck by the amount she *excludes* from life – the whole political word (so does Lawrence almost as much, neither of them wants to read the paper), a large part of literature, all music.

[1] Her first book, *Cheerful Weather for the Wedding*, published by Chatto & Windus in 1932.

1961

January 2nd

Dick and Simonette[1] came over from Nice to lunch on Saturday. Julia, Burgo and I went down to La Souco to meet them on their way up from the bus. When they appeared outside the French windows I almost laughed aloud. Dick looked as if he'd come to a funeral, in a deep black, long undertaker's overcoat and black hat, moving at a snail's pace, his eyes bulging in his white apprehensive face. Simonette's looks are still very fine. She wore a black 'busby' pulled over her eyes, tight London suit, black stockings and pin-heels. (Julia afterwards defended her 'heroism' in tackling the cobbled steps in these heels. 'But for what?' I asked. 'Aesthetic effect,' said Julia.) Simonette certainly came full of suspicion on behalf of the Bussy *héritiers*, of whom Dick is one, and made several remarks like 'It's all quite different', 'Where's everything *gone*?', 'But where have things been tidied *to*?' and so on. They say John[2] is doing his level best to bugger everything up, has consulted agents and solicitors on his own and is convinced that Pippa, Marjorie[3] and probably everyone else want to deprive him of his rights. By the end of lunch we had, I think, convinced Dick and Simonette that if John went on in that way no one would get a penny. But Dick's line is that he is a Quietist – translated into common English he's so lazy that he don't do a thing, even in his own interests.

I felt quite ashamed of our funereal guests when I led them onto the hotel terrace and they ungraciously made no greeting or acknowledgement to Monsieur Pons.

This is all pretty dull, but it has been the only intrusion from the outside world, so it was a relief to have to think of it. The first day of 1961 was dripping and foggy, cold, dank and pitch dark. Feeling as I do, on the rack all the time, these outward misfortunes make no difference. I'm in a Japanese concentration camp anyway and expect nothing more than survival. But for what? Heaven knows.

A lot of letters on Saturday including one from Janetta, lovely and long.

January 3rd

I'm worried about Julia and her arrangement to stay on with me here. She doesn't write her book, and never will. Yesterday there was a great parade of shutting herself in her room with it – but she dozed and read a detective story all afternoon. Contacts and general conversation are reduced to meal-times and seldom get anywhere. My heart bleeds for Burgo, who is doing very well in suppressing his youthful impatience, to make it fit in with Julia's strict boarding-house rules. One of these is that after our dinner is finished we sit in creaking chairs round a basket

[1] Richard Strachey, nephew of Lytton, and his wife.
[2] Dick's younger brother, another *héritier*.
[3] Lytton's unmarried sisters.

table and *no one speaks,* for fear of distracting anyone who is reading. I find this strangely inhuman. Last night Burgo was in a lively mood, wanting to talk about *The Journal to Stella* which he was reading, and being quite interesting about it. Pinched disapproval from Julia, whose eyes were bent unseeingly on the *New Statesman.* She and I have not made much contact lately. I would have liked to discuss the problems that face me in the future – but feel she doesn't want to; and she has still never *once* mentioned Ralph's name. What a relief it was to get a long, moving, excellent letter from Gerald yesterday, almost all about him. Yet Julia is heroic in her intentions and it's ungrateful to find fault with the result, especially as I feel her anxiety for me is spoiling what ought to have been a holiday for her. I would really rather she returned to England with Lawrence than leave me feeling responsible for her unease.

I somehow do manage to work and I clutch at it like a drowning man. I have to – I'd sink otherwise, not that I do it effectively or well.

January 5th

When Julia came into my room I tried to say that I didn't want her to make sacrifices for me, that – much as I should enjoy her company – I would be quite all right alone, but I have only to speak of such things and the silly helpless tears well up and brim over. She was kind, sweet and good, and while I was in the bath left a little note in my room which touched me deeply, begging me to say no more about it. 'When something happens to you it *literally* happens to all your friends.'

Burgo is my chief anxiety now. Anthony Blond doesn't send him his *laisser-passer* to Monte Carlo, nor does Simon communicate his plans.[1] The poor boy is therefore literally in the air and getting increasingly, and I think justifiably, angry with Simon. What of that apparently benign and genial, but arrestedly juvenile figure? Burgo also told me that when they met last in London and he wanted to talk to Simon about his childhood feelings about Ralph, Simon merely said: 'You never liked him, did you?' which was very obtuse.

It looks anyway as if Julia and I have another week here. I think of it as 'doing time' and try to avoid remembering that nothing lies beyond but more time. What Burgo will do if he still hears nothing from Simon (to whom he wired yesterday) I don't know. Lawrence leaves us the day after tomorrow.

January 8th

Yesterday morning brought a letter from Simon for Burgo and at least some definite news to relieve the waiting-room atmosphere. He 'can't possibly get to Tunis before February 17th, if then' – no reason given – 'but will be going off skiing in Austria for a fortnight' instead of meeting Burgo in Tunis. He describes his own behaviour as 'treacherous' and says he will 'crawl' to Burgo when he sees him. Burgo seems relieved at least to have certainty where there was chaos and confusion. There were tranquil episodes today (a lovely day). In the afternoon Burgo and I had an adventurous walk ending in a wilderness of brambles and huge stones covered in herbage, and my all but losing my trowel and my botany spectacles, thrown out of my basket by the impact. Burgo was patient and angelic, spending twenty minutes looking for them with me, and at last we found them. In the evening we

---

[1] To meet Burgo abroad.

lost dear Lawrence – a great sadness to see him go off in the darkness.

January 9th, afternoon

Burgo's troubles seem endless. Today he heard from Poppet that her step-daughter is already in 'his' flat, so he has nowhere to go if he does go back to London. This excruciating business of trying to share his burdens is finishing what sanity I had left, and I cannot be in his presence and not share them. Today great wafts of loneliness have found cracks and crevices and come washing in. Tears, blood and sweat.

January 12th

It's almost a surprise to find myself still alive, still here. Burgo has done very well, pulling himself together with an effort, and has booked himself a flight back to England on Sunday.

This evening he and I move to join Clive at Menton (Burgo for three nights only) and Julia returns to England. My tremulous fear of change is under hatches. I'm braced, and almost longing to get out of the dense smell of cats and the coughs here. A full stop of a sort, some fixed plans, and on I go, *somehow* or other.

January 17th: Hotel des Ambassadeurs, Menton

I've been quite ill the last three days, with enough of a fever to make me consent to see the doctor who came to see the *patron's* wife on Sunday – a little dynamic Groucho Marx, who rushed in, shot questions at me, sounded me, took my blood-pressure and prescribed antibiotics and stuff to rub into my back. As my temperature rose, and as during the night I choked and sweated, I wondered of course how ill I was going to be and thought hopefully of death! Here was a threat to my precarious life-instinct ... What did I feel? I asked myself in one of the endless colloquies that take the place of my conversations with Ralph. That I longed to be dead but couldn't bear the thought of dying (pictured as lying in a French hospital with tubes up my nose, squalid, lonely and frightened). I suppose millions of people feel both these things, and the ones who act logically and take overdoses are just braver, or madder – or what? In some strange way, the worst thing that has ever happened to me in my life has made me feel saner than before.

Barbara and Clive were in this hotel on Thursday night and until I went to bed on Saturday afternoon I thought both of them were going to drive me mad – Clive by his frantic fussing about everything (particularly being late – he dashes in to meals at 12.30 and 7.00 if he can) and Barbara by her repetitive chatter. But since I've been in bed she has been so kind and helpful that I feel quite conscience-stricken to think what I wrote to Janetta about her. Burgo left on Sunday; since coming here he was as sweet, kind and thoughtful as possible and I shed tears to see him go. None the less, I hope he will soon make himself a life apart from me, chiefly for his sake.

This illness (I'm nearly well, thanks to dynamic Groucho) has put my power to stand solitude to the test, and it's not come out too badly. I can not only fill long hours with reading and writing but think to myself for quite long periods, although it's thinking of a wretchedly poor quality, dismally needing the stimulus that Ralph's more creative mind gave it. There is a vast area that I still can't force my mind to enter – or only by making little tentative dashes. Though in theory I know that everything ought to be explored and faced, the instinct of self-preservation prevents me. There's also the fact that it's as if a piece – half – of me had gone. What is left is not exactly bereaved, it's *incomplete*.

January 18th

Better. I'm somehow fortified by having got through this ordeal by isolation, although there was a moment of panic yesterday when I thought I shouldn't. Groucho visited me last night and has allowed me up in my room today and tomorrow, and down on Friday. In his magnetic mesmeric way he convinced me I must do as he said. Raymond arrived last night, sent up a huge gorgeous bunch of carnations from Nice market which glorify my room, telephoned me, and came to see me this morning. He has been a great tonic to me, setting going some degree of that communicable fluid which does not flow in chats with Little Barbara. I am rather saddened by Clive, who seems to have stepped quite a long way out of this world into the next, but perhaps there's still some recuperative bounce in him.

It has been something to be allowed to bath and dress and eat my disgusting lunch at my table, and also a good post has come, letters from Heywood, Julia and Janetta.

January 22nd

The breakfast waiter has a very strange way of intoning, singing almost, as he comes in with my tray: 'Bon *JOUR*!!! Ca*FÉ*!! La *NEIGE*!! La *PLUIE*!!' he intones pessimistically. I do in fact look out and see a sky of dirty grey cotton-wool fitting down close over my mountain's round forehead. Yesterday I went out, however, to lunch with Raymond in a fish restaurant in the port and felt much the better for it, until Groucho (who had come to look at Clive's leg, swollen after slipping on some steps) depressed me unutterably by saying accusingly: 'You are *not well* yet. You are *cheerful* because your temperature is down, but you still have a spot on your lung and it might all begin again.' Result: hardly any sleep last night and cough worse today. I couldn't help fancying it was with delight that he found from the X-ray that poor Clive has cracked his tibia. It's all for the worst in the worst of all possible worlds. Clive sat dejected like a small boy disappointed of a treat and said that if he was confined to his room he would throw himself out of the window. Raymond strode round the room arguing with Groucho. Clive has to be put in plaster today, and will stay up for a day or so, so the sickroom atmosphere continues. Poor Raymond!

January 23rd

Bad to worse. Barbara and Raymond took Clive to the clinique where his leg was put in plaster but the surgeon told Barbara he was not to use it for *five weeks*. She seemed on the brink of tears and collapse (I can't blame her) and said Clive must not be told. Oh, the sadness of old age! If two days in his room made him want to *se jeter par la fenêtre*, what now?

Terrific undertakings, moving all Clive and Barbara's things to a suite with a bathroom at the end of the passage. Raymond and I scurried to and fro carrying Clive's pathetic possessions. Staff, usually so friendly, in a rage at this. Ambulance men carrying Clive upstairs, who even in this predicament was able to catch sight of himself in a looking-glass and pat at his wig. The tragi-comic effect of this masquerade of clowns! I do *not* include Raymond, who has remained dignified, elegant and sweet-tempered throughout. After Clive had been installed in bed, Raymond, Barbara and I drove off up the Gorbio valley to a smart, expensive restaurant got up in peasant style, with gigots of lamb revolving and blackening on a spit over a roaring fire and a terrible tenor caterwauling to a guitar. This meal was rather a nightmare to me as my voice vanished completely. By evening, Clive was in tears, Barbara also, and Raymond beginning to panic on his own account. Slept well but am still voiceless, damn it.

January 24th

Yesterday was pretty desperate. By evening suicide thoughts were in the ascendant. Also other thoughts of flying back to England at once. *What am I doing here?* Heaven knows. Appeals to me from Barbara to help keep Clive's spirits up; and I gladly would but how can I with not an ounce of spirits of my own and no shred of voice to simulate them with? This last hampers me dreadfully – I can do some sort of perfunctory flapping with words, but without them I sink into patent glumness. What use going out with Raymond to a noisy restaurant when I can't utter? I said I would stay in, therefore, in the glassed-in verandah and try and get rid of the great toad which sits on my chest and paralyses my vocal chords and – I must admit – fills me with terror of being sent back to solitary confinement. All day I was hiding from Groucho, scared stiff of his accusing 'You are NOT well yet.'

January 27th

Yesterday Raymond left, angelic to the last. I had had a severe panic the night before, lying awake dreading the close quarters, the married life as it were that lay ahead with Clive and Barbara in their flat at Garavan, as they have kindly asked me. This flat, large and spacious with a nice garden, has two big and lovely bedrooms but really no place for a third person – except a slit containing a bed like a *wagon-lit* bunk, with no wardrobe, nothing. Barbara has a nannie's desire to involve us all in each other's physical functioning, and this I most emphatically don't share. Just as to Nannie the sight of a baby sitting on his pot is sweet and funny and the be-all and end-all of her life, she would like all the barriers and reticences to go down between adults. So I now diagnose her setting her false teeth beside me on the table as a symbol of the same attitude that makes her trot to bring Clive his yellow box of false teeth ('Buttercup'), when he wants to eat. (Campaigning by Raymond and me made him put them in more often, but now Raymond's gone he's given that up and is toothless all day.) And yesterday *pour comble*, Barbara wanted me to stay in the room while Clive *fit pipi* as they will both call it. That settled it. A glorious day yesterday – and I walked off by myself around the bay of Garavan to try and find somewhere where I could live *en demi-pension* and lunch in their flat each day. The grand Hotel des Anglais offered me a small room at the back. I was rather nervous how Barbara would take this, as she had begged for 'support' with a little clutching claw on my arm the night before. And she took it very well. I was able to put it as a form of consideration for them. Immense relief.

January 28th

My bid for independence has set me up quite a little. I must now contrive to *take* that independence.

January 31st

The last two days I've taken long walks by myself up the hills, clutching at the rope-ladder of my visual impressions, rejecting with some success the pointless imaginary conversations liable to invade my head. The two cemeteries on their twin hills were the objects of my first walk. A madwoman in a fur stole, talking aloud and waving her arms like King Lear. Italian-looking children speaking French. A solid little girl carrying a black cat uphill in loving embracing arms. At the upper cemetery a widow in deep black dabbing her eyes with a handkerchief and confiding in her taxi-driver.

Last night the doctor rushed in to see Clive and he is to come down in his chair to lunch today but mustn't walk for a fortnight. Little Barbara has just been in for sympathy this morning – Clive is fussing because she has a hairdresser's appointment (an inch of grey hair has appeared each side of her parting). Will I dress him? Oh, God, is there no way of avoiding her dragging me in as second nurse? I've suggested she change her appointment to this afternoon, and she says she'll try.

She did, and a good job too, seeing the frenzy of nerves Clive got into over being dressed, even by Barbara. What would it have been like if I had tried? We've had 'potty' and 'eidy' today; what next?

It's been a marvellous day, warm, soft, still and fine, the mountains' edge sharp against the blue sky but a few hanging wreaths of cloud. Again I've walked myself to a standstill, this time to Cap Martin, but come back almost in tears. Along the front one meets so many couples of all ages affectionately walking arm-in-arm with their mates, and I feel nothing but *brute envy* of them. Rather panicked about being unable to steer my thoughts, until by dint of walking I stupefied myself into one big eye. There are always strange sights to see. On Cap Martin sat a white-haired lady listening to Bach on a very good portable wireless, and what seemed to be a poet was staring at the waves coming in over the shingle and adding a line from moment to moment.

Perhaps these solitary walks are going to be too much. Between the Scylla of solitude and the Charybdis of Barbara's conversation I don't know what to do . . .

February 1st

These pitiful scribblings are like scratches on the vast monolith of my desolation, and I only go on having recourse to them because they are in some way an outlet. Alas, I can't tell Ralph what a desert my life is without him, describe the extraordinary wooden unreality of it. Nor can I tell Barbara and Clive. They are Arthur Prince dummies to practise the sound of my voice with. Yet I *can't* get down to the deeper areas of my misery – because it's a region so painful that the scalpel (being held in my own hand) recoils instinctively from the exposed nerve.

We got Clive downstairs to lunch and dinner in his wheel-chair in the lift. It cheered him up enormously and he sat up till his usual bed-time, 9.15.

February 4th

I moved to the Hotel des Anglais yesterday afternoon. Though my bedroom is smaller and scruffier, the plaster crumbles, the handle of the wardrobe comes off at a touch, the basin refuses to hold water – the rest of the hotel is grander than the Ambassadeurs. The dining-room is immense and stately with parquet floor (over which many waiters shoot about like comets, pushing vast sluggards' delights); there are several enormous lounges and a useful 'writing-room'. In this I sat down stubbornly to work at about four, and from then till now I've not seen a soul to speak to. It seems to me instead of a recuperative treatment, I'm subjecting myself to some hideous test or punishment here. Can't think what I'm at. Again the desire to fly home has appeared. Why, why, why have I returned to the life of a scribbling schoolgirl in this solitude? Yet there is the blue sky stretched above the mimosa-clad hill.

February 5th

An awful night, but morning is always better, and the pure intense blue sky still stretches up over the hill. During the night I felt it was madness to stay on here, subjecting myself to this unutterable isolation – I longed to be back at Ham Spray with Dinah.[1] But the trouble is I don't want to be *anywhere* – I want to be away from wherever I am. When I'm in this grizzly hotel I want to be with Clive and Barbara. When I'm with them I want to get away as fast as possible. I want to be nowhere. I want desperately to be dead, but can't face, or can't think how to achieve that happy state.

So this morning I'm undecided, and have no one to thrash out my problems with. I must in any case stay here a week or so, because of letters. Then I will try to alter my technique. New plan for living – work late, to get over the *ghastly* evenings? More blue pills. More sun and exercise.

February 6th

I really rather 'enjoyed myself' yesterday afternoon, perversely enough, walking into Italy along the Blackpool-like main road, and back home under the great prehistoric cliff and the Grotte des Enfants.

Clive is low and depressed again, leaves out his teeth and says he wishes he was dead. Rosetta, the Italian maid, kept repeating '*Povera Rosetta, molte tribulazioni*' as she served lunch: Barbara went on and on about her collar-bone, broken many years ago. Her power to irritate me seems to have been raised to burning-point by proximity under difficult circumstances. And I too have my *tribulazioni*, which I sometimes think they forget. I've got through today without sinking too far into the pit and with only a few tears. I'll say no more. This hotel is really maddening – it deliberately sets itself to produce *cuisine Anglaise* – roast meat and boiled potatoes *every single day*!

February 7th

Sitting up in bed, trying to sort out the fragments of my life and make a little sense of it. If I worked hard at my translation I could finish it in about three weeks. Should I do that and then go home? Or join Anne and Heywood in Paris? Move

[1] My black cat.

to Clive and Barbara's flat? I'm terrified of trying yet another change only to find I can't stand it – for the real fact is I can't bear living without Ralph. But I must stop saying that. I've *got* to bear it and a lot more, too. Or get out.

February 16th

After my last entry I took a great haul at invisible boot-straps and somehow managed to brace up and pull myself together. The spectacle of the self-pity over at the Villa is really a moral lesson. Also, I see from my friends' letters that my extra gloom lately has been conveyed to them in mine, and they are worrying about me. This won't do; I can't just become a public nuisance. After letting the picture of being on Janetta's snowy mountain soak in my mind for a bit I fished it out and found almost nothing but fear and horror at the thought of drawing iced air into my lungs instead of this, which is balmy, carnation-laden. Of clanking funiculars and that maniac, ruthlessly competitive, obsessional winter-sports world. On the other side, the real delight of being with Janetta every evening and the gratification of my desire *to escape* which I know for what it is. So I've written to say no.

Well, this great effort to pull myself together worked, much to my surprise, and again produced that sense of being strengthened by the mere fact of overcoming horrors. (Robin Campbell, who has a talent for saying encouraging things, says in a letter I had yesterday, 'Your life does not sound all mimosa, but in some strange way I slightly envy the lonely and up to a point fortifying life of the hotel in winter. I'm sure it does recharge mental batteries, but then one needs something to use the accumulated power on. I have no doubt at all that you will manage this too.')

Clive has passed another stage and now puts feet to ground. He sometimes gets irritated with Barbara and says quite tartly, 'I'm never allowed to get a WORD in edgewise.' Nor is he, nor am I, and yesterday her delaying by chattering when Clive was waiting to be helped onto the sunny balcony made him angrier than I ever saw him in his life.

A letter from Bunny with a weird compliment: 'You are infinitely refreshing – like the advertisement of some detergent or soap that takes the film of dirt and despair away from one'!

Well, when I come up to my lonely little bedroom I find nothing at all refreshing there (the chambermaid will shut the window at night): it seems to be full of the sour aroma of sorrow, and I recognize it as mine.

February 17th

I watched the total eclipse two mornings ago and I never expect to see a better one. It was due to be total at eight-thirty, my breakfast time. My bedroom piece of sky turned an unearthly lavender colour very gradually about eight, and tucking in my nightgown and putting on a skirt and my fur coat I went down to the hall. Looks of complicity and faint embarrassment on the faces of porters, *valets de chambre*, etc. We were all engaged on something a little queer. Outside was deathly stillness, each palm tree leaf transfixed, and the pure sky over the milky calm sea was a huge Covent Garden stage for the prima donna, the sun. One or two watchers leaning on the balustrade the other side of the road – the dress-circle. I ordered my breakfast tray in the glassed-in porch full of potted plants, and while I ate it saw with a thrill that the obvious bite out of the sun's side was gradually increasing.

The climax was astonishingly swift. Darkness rushed over the earth, yet it was never very intense. The encroaching shape seemed to make a sudden move and step right in front of the sun and then it was bang in the middle, with an unequal fringe of light all round and some glowing red carbuncles here and there on the very edge. Horrors! One carbuncle was swelling, expanding, blowing out like a great balloon. And I saw that it was the sun beginning to come out the other side – why did it look so different going in and coming out? The act was over; it seemed to have been staged for me alone. It was beautiful, strange and exciting – but no unexpected wave of emotion surged through me, no mystical thoughts about the nature of the universe, no sense of evil nor primeval fear. But I'm very, very glad to have seen it, and went up to my room in a state of catharsis. It's the first thing I can say I've enjoyed for itself.

February 18th

Sometimes I imagine I have been undergoing a long, long surgical operation or series of operations. 'Yes, I'm afraid we must remove one arm, one leg, part of your side. Yes, the whole amputation will be done at one go but there will be a long subsequent stage of minor operations sealing off nerves and arteries, grafting new skin, cauterizations. Painful? Yes, very, I'm afraid, but nothing can be done about it; you must just hold tight to this bar when the pain gets unbearable, bite on the bullet. Prognosis? Well, your life will be limited, of course, but it will be life of a sort.'

A feeble attempt at 'fighting back' last night was not a great success. Had dinner earlier and walked off into the town, to cinema or casino I wasn't sure. One thing I did enjoy was the beauty of Old Menton by night – long golden-brown streaks like fine corduroy lying on the inky gelatinous water: the palm trees lit from below were a vivid acid green colour like painted tin ones in a child's tropical set: the beautiful church floodlit. But the film was so bad that I came away before the long programme was over, as for the casino it seems quite dead, except that during the interval the audience dashed out and staked a few francs. The croupiers weren't really paying attention, and gave people whatever they asked; there was no excitement.

February 20th

I'm inordinately surprised that I seem to see my situation so clearly and in such detail, like a view seen through a very clean windowpane. Ever since Ralph died that has been so, and it's never different, even in dreams. It's as if 'total eclipse' had brought 'total awareness' going right down through all my submerged layers. Unaccountably though, yesterday was definitely better, and I don't quite understand why 'total awareness' doesn't bring a little more control. Anyway, I pegged through yesterday looking neither to right nor left, and as I write this date today I tell myself my deliverance from this special hell isn't far off. Only to move into another, of course; but I hope the discipline of this solitude has made for some strengthening-up of invisible weak joints.

February 23rd

'Discipline' is the answer, I believe, to the question that foggily arises often in my mind: What in God's name am I doing here? I'm trying by means of disciplinary mental gymnastics and rest combined to learn a technique for leading my new life. I faintly hope that practice and exercise will strengthen unused muscles, and teach me a few of the sort of 'tips' my alcoholics get by with.

February 25th

Suddenly this French episode, like the last phase of the eclipse, is rushing to its conclusion. My hands are already tightening a little (as I foretold) around my prison bars. The shadow of the world to come was thrown on my page by two letters from Craig in answer to a vague one asking him how much money he thought I would have and whether he agreed I must sell Ham Spray. His conclusion is £1,300 a year, after deduction of tax. However, as he calculates £3,000 as Ham Spray's selling price, i.e. probate valuation, which is *insane*, I'm wondering if he isn't going to be quite a hindrance rather than a help. I awoke in the small hours indignant and sat up in bed doing sums, and also wondering whether really money trouble wouldn't finally and absolutely destroy any desire to persist.

March 1st

I think of England like a chess-board and want to know the position of the various pieces. Mary's absence from Stokke for so long is a loss for me. What of Robert? Last night at the Belle Escale restaurant Clive had 'a pain', turned white, panicked, got a frightened little boy expression and 'thought he felt sick'. Having safely got out of his plaster yesterday and been told his leg is completely healed, he now clings to his 'pain'. Barbara has only to leave him for five minutes and he begins muttering to himself, 'I don't know where BARbara's got to, I'm sure.' Soon afterwards he's calling 'BARBARA!' in exactly the same voice as a child calling 'NANNIE!'

March 4th

The day after Barbara and I had gone to Castellar, which I fell so in love with, we took Clive there to lunch – a great success, excellent lunch (*poulet chasseur*), eaten in hot sun. The *patron*'s jokes at the expense of Clive, whom he described as an 'old carcass', trying to live up to his two wives (Barbara and me) seemed a touch macabre, but Clive didn't appear to mind, presumably because they were in French. I decided to walk down, lost my way and plunged over a rough hillside which soon became a precipice down which I slid and scrambled – worth it because there suddenly flashed on my dazzled eyes a field of brilliant red anemones (*fulgens*) waving in the sage-green shadow of the olives. A deeply moving sight. This I put together with the pleasure I got from a bus-drive twenty miles inland next day to Sospel, a mountainy village standing on a river in a wide basin. Here all was far behind Menton – coconut-matting grass, only the earliest signs of spring, but going for a walk by a stream I found many banks covered with primroses and violets, great clumps of blue hepatica and spring squill. If I get (as I here undoubtedly do) my greatest solace from the visual aspect of nature, isn't it madness to try and live in London? Such places as Castellar and Sospel with their limpid air and clear light bringing out every roughness of wall surface, dent my mind profoundly and give me the support and sustenance that religion gives some people.

March 5th

What permanent effect do the surroundings in which one experiences violent or deep emotion have on one's mind? This place has bitten deeply into mine, leaving me with impressions that are superficially beautiful and soothing, like the great wide black grin of the bay edged with shining teeth, the gently-heaving water dimly seen by moonlight, yet have a sort of mocking irony about them. I don't think I shall ever want to come here again. There are other sounds and sights, like the comic, slow, gentle grunting rise or fall of the lift in this hotel, which makes me even now want to laugh and cry together.

The Graham Sutherlands came to see Clive and Barbara a few days ago, and yesterday invited Barbara and me to have a drink in their villa on the Castellar road. Here were human beings at last – who made the magistrates, bishops and retired businessmen in my hotel seem like zebras and camels. Graham Sutherland is an interesting, inscrutable man with curiously penetrating eyes, a good forehead, and the face of a writer or don rather than a painter. I guessed at his lower-class origins but found myself stumped for other clues. Kathy his wife is a handsome Irish Japanese-doll, friendly, funny, and very likeable.

Only four days left here and they look like being full, which is a jolly good thing.

March 7th

I have existed – somehow – now for three months without Ralph. Bob Gathorne-Hardy said, 'Think in terms of one day only; you *can* always manage a day more.' It is exactly the instructions given in my translation (*Alcoholics Anonymous*) for curing oneself of drink.

The Nicholses were very nice and friendly, Phyllis looking handsome and no older. Phil attacked me with questions about the future of Ham Spray, with a directness I liked. The Lairdess was in the lounge when I got back, along with five friends all now staying at this hotel. They are oh so jolly and friendly, Admirals, Generals and Honourables, and oh so dull. I have devised ways of *not* going through the lounge (it's full of English now, and *how* they shout and drawl both at once): instead I take the lift up one floor, then crab it along sidewise and down again to my little womb, the *salle d'écrire*. The smug, exhibitionist English voices reached me all the same, quacking on with their unimaginative implications that everyone is so civilized and can never be taken by surprise, that there are no such things as death, cancer, atom bombs, unhappy love or madness.

March 8th

Tomorrow I go! leave hold of my bars, throw myself off the cliff. Yesterday I had a visit from Eddie Gathorne-Hardy wearing a bright mustard-coloured shirt. He sat in the hotel garden astonishing the English by remarking loudly: 'It's my FUCKING brother,[1] my dear.' When going on to speak of his financial troubles he suddenly gulped and was silent. Could he be crying? I didn't dare trust my senses and pat his hand. It seemed incredible, but of course he was, and a few minutes later he took off his spectacles, brought out a large white handkerchief and mopped away the tears. Not having really absorbed the facts, and anyway not sympathizing with his attitude that the world is beastly unkind in not supporting him financially for

---

[1] Lord Cranbrook ('Jock'), who had refused his request for more money.

doing nothing, my heart remained cold, my mind wandering and a small wave of
emotional distaste rose momentarily up like heartburn within me. The lovable old
scholar and lover of literature and the arts was still there however, and I enjoyed
his company in a way. It *was* company. He hopes to touch Mrs Howard, mother
of Brian, for a large sum before going to Greece, in spite of busting her car to the
tune of £180 last time he visited her. Did he hope to touch me? I don't think so.

Meanwhile John Banting,[1] genial slow old duck that he is, was visiting Barbara
and Clive at the villa.

Coming out of the restaurant after dinner into the black sparkling night I was
struck with pleasure-pain, a cool-warmth of emotion. This great beauty, which
because of the psychological state it impinges on in me, seems always like a crust,
has lain all round me for weeks and weeks. It has been in a way my best friend
here. Yet I can do nothing with it; it washes over me like a very small wave, leaving
me as I was before, a changeless unabreacted lump. Walked very slowly back to
the hotel (dreading the *five* friends of the Lairdess likely to be in the lounge), alone,
alone, ALONE. My independence, such as it is, gives me a meagre feeling of pride,
and rears up like a thin unpleasant cobra. I am aware of the usual mixture of
confidence and lack of it. Given propitious circumstances and a limited space of
time I know I can get on with people like the Lairdess and the Sutherlands. I found
a note from Kathy Sutherland begging me to stay a night longer as 'Kenneth Clark
was longing to meet me'. Thank heavens I can't; this is only the result of Raymond's
kind advocacy, and he would certainly have found me a disappointment.

March 9th

The last morning here. Yesterday I walked uphill between the two graveyards to
lunch with Madeline Stewart-Mackenzie. Attractive little meal set on a table out
of doors under a sweet-scented white buddleia, just freshly out and covered with
butterflies. As I walked down again and looked at the steep terraces above the
town, silent and still in the everlasting sunshine and a motionless haze, they
reminded me of the illustrations to *Paradise Lost* in the copy I knew as a child,
with the different levels of heaven, hell and purgatory, delicately detailed but
bathed in mist. Purgatory is what they represent to me; and I feel when I think of
the future like someone who's been holding their breath under water for a long,
long time and now – about to draw a fresh one – isn't quite sure what will come
pouring into their lungs.

I set to and started sorting letters, packing, and now I must embark on the next
terrace of my purgatory.

March 14th

D-Day, I must cross to England; though of course it's Ham Spray that is the great,
terrible, unknown shock I must now face. Will it have been softened by all these
intermediate stages – Menton, Paris, London? The Hills and I had two nights here
alone and then last night they both left. I've not 'done' much in Paris. Went to
the Berthe Morisots and the Musée Jaquemart-André in which the Exhibition
stands. On Sunday – a lovely day – went with the Hills and three *jeune filles en fleur*

---

[1] Surrealist painter.

(Harriet[1] and two friends from her finishing-school) to a park on the outskirts and lunched there. The girls were very charming; they varied from worldly sophistication to infinite childishness, buying balloons and saying, '*God*, how exciting!'

March 16th: England, Lambourn

Fidelio last night with Janetta was almost unbearably moving. The music poured over the frozen substitute for a human being that I now am, and violently thawed it – a painful process, because some feelings deliberately crushed under tombstones turned in their graves, and the blood painfully ran into them as pins and needles do into limbs.

I had too many people to confront in London, too many stockbrokers and lawyers in particular. A long session with Craig, which at the time seemed satisfactorily lucid and practical but has left behind a deathly sense of unreality. Then I took refuge with the Gowings in the country.

Lawrence came into my room yesterday and made me a speech of extraordinary kindness, which brought tears of gratitude to my eyes, saying that I was the only person who didn't 'interfere with their spiritual life' and they wanted me to come as much as I liked. He then lent me his car to drive to Ham Spray, and Julia came too.

Well – Ham Spray – there it was, extraordinarily the same as it has stood and looked through all sort of tragedies, moods, personal dramas, and the successive deaths of Lytton, Carrington and Ralph. Houses are impassive things, more like great rocks in the middle of a waterfall than made-made creations. It didn't look or feel to me haunted, nor did I expect to see Ralph at every moment – as Janetta did when she returned there. It merely seemed dead. And though it's as near being my home as anywhere at the moment, it didn't magnetize me; it wasn't a living organism at all – just walls, books going mouldy, and a piano whose keys stuck when I touched them. Craig wants me to set about selling it at once; there was pressure from Noel[2] too, and I suppose they are right – but I feel hustled. I saw Mrs Hoare,[3] and Wilde[4] – who had just two things he wanted to say, both egocentric: that he would like to have the first refusal of buying his cottage, and that the agricultural wages had gone up since January 1st.

March 29th

I have passed my first night here. 'Our' bed has become 'my' bed and I have faced the great shock of return, which in fact produced an overwhelming gush of affection for the dear place, '*this* is my home', 'I belong here', and this in spite of my firm determination to leave it.

I spent my first nights here with Janetta and Burgo for company. After that, alone with Maria and Rose[5] tucked away upstairs, my heart thumped, panic seized me and I took to whiskey, watching the clock tick past till I could decently go to bed. I have a feeling that the longer I stayed here, the more the friendliness of the house would become a comforting support to be leant on rather than adding to

[1] Elder daughter of the Hills.
[2] Carrington, one of Ralph's executors, and his brother-in-law.
[3] Our village daily.
[4] The gardener.
[5] Janetta's Spanish maid, and youngest daughter Rose Jackson.

my sense of deprivation. So I now hope the whirring wheels set going by house-agents and buyers may allow me to stay here on and off throughout the summer. They ring me up, squabble about 'sole rights' like dogs over a bone, and one, a pale schoolmistress from Thake and Paginton has already been to see it, and didn't bat an eyelid at £9,500.

'Fill every moment' is still my motto, and there's been no difficulty so far. Typescript of *Alcoholics Anonymous* to correct and send off. Sample of *Zoubeida* to translate. Endless house organization, food ordering. Rose likes to spend some time with me, and Maria sinks into her detective stories.

March 31st, Good Friday

Translating most of the day in an empty, lonely house, Rose and Maria having left on the early train. Thake and Paginton's clients are to come and see the house on Monday and with the possibility they might buy it I'm faced with the future – NOWHERE, or tied to poor Janetta's tail, such a kind sensitive tail, too. But I know my solution must include peace, privacy and above all, *independence*. I cannot substitute any other dependence for what I've lost, and feel I must take that, with all the horrors of loneliness involved. I explained this to Lawrence and he understood me more than Julia did, who read me a lecture as vivid as she could make it on the horrors of loneliness. As if I didn't know them!

A fever possesses me at times when I think of moving out and constructing my life elsewhere, and look round at all the millions and millions of 'things' clutching at me with their dense cloud of associations and asking me to decide: keep or destroy.

April 1st

The house is now rather full – Janetta, both children and Maria, Burgo, and comings and goings from Kees, Hendersons, Gowings. But this very approximation of the life of the past makes its essential differences startlingly plain, and I remember the glorious uproarious laughter of the past. Have just had an interesting, human and sympathetic conversation with Burgo, but which has given me a sight of his own drifting state. Very adult, very acute, very intelligent but full of undischarged love and therefore not happy.

Sometimes I think of a *complete* upheaval – to live abroad.

April 2nd, Easter Day

Nicko came to dinner last night. We talked of religion, and an argument developed from my saying that we who believe in good and beauty are ultimately accepting something on faith alone, just as the religious do. Nicko wanted to deny this but didn't have his reasons ready though seemingly enjoying the argument. Janetta brought up, more reasonably, the fact that there were numerically *more* acts of faith in religion. With a pink patch on her cheek, she said she could never possibly marry someone who was a believer, and hinted that it was morally *wrong* to do so. Also that she didn't believe in marriage. I didn't enquire whether she meant the religious ceremony or lifelong companionship.

April 4th

Potential buyers of Ham Spray came yesterday afternoon, a day of soaking drizzle, the Downs invisible. I liked the man – an honest, ex-RAF type; also two friendly and musical little girls. They spent a long time here and I think were 'interested', only time will show how much. When the time of their expected visit arrived, my heart beat so painfully I felt I should die of it. As usual, calm came with the start of the ordeal.

Today the skies still weep in utter silence. I have been rung up by various friends, Rachel asking me to stay – nice that – and just now Bunny Garnett. They have heard I'm here and their motive is entirely friendly. Burgo left for three nights this morning. He has been kind, sweet and helpful to me, but I'm not happy about him ... I am now alone in the house. I feel as though I were surrounded by grey ash and that the less I look about me, the better.

April 11th

Yesterday three lots of viewers came to see the house in pouring rain and plugged round in macintoshes and gumboots. Burgo supported me gallantly. An offer at £8,000 'take it or leave it' was telephoned through by Craig in the afternoon. Not yet, I said – for £9,500 is the price I had asked. After nine the telephone rang. It was the agent who had sent all the viewers: 'I've got good news for you. I've sold your house, and at the full price.' Murmuring approval, I felt my heart drop like a stone, and from then on the agony swelled and swelled, and Burgo was even more upset than I, and retired to the music-room to play *When I am laid in earth* on the gramophone. I went up to bed feeling I was a murderer and had killed Ham Spray with my own hands. Struggles to keep equilibrium and rational thoughts going were defeated by emotional sounds from Burgo below who was drowning his feelings in whiskey, bangs, 'Fuck!' shouted aloud, and other remarks into the void; tramping feet to and fro in the music-room. Somehow the night was got through, though not improved by Mrs Edginton, the buyer, ringing up and asking if she might 'come and see *our* house again tomorrow. Just poke about a bit, you know?'

Oh, God! Vanessa has died and Morgan has had a heart attack.

p.m. They, the harmless viewers, are back. My house isn't my own. That is, I don't feel I can go up and sprawl full length on my bed as I should like. I sit alone in the music-room, tense and pretty near the end of my tether. How endurable is it going to be, living here these months ahead? Will it be like living with a husband who has told one he is going to leave and set up with someone else?

They are prodding holes in the rotten floors, and no doubt finding all sorts of horrors. If they won't have the house after I shall have the struggle to do all again. Meanwhile I sit here on red-hot nails of restlessness, finding it impossible to concentrate on anything. I wonder if there's any book in existence which would hold my attention.

April 12th

Righting my position gradually. One thing that helped was the arrival of two more buyers called Elwes, who appreciated the house for what it is and therefore endeared themselves to me sufficiently for me to ask them in and offer them sherry. They seemed dead keen, and determined to oust Colonel Edginton if they could.[1] As the Colonel and his lady had gone off very markedly *not* looking me in the eye, I felt (as now transpires) that might be easy.

April 18th: Cranborne

Slept as I have not done since returning to Ham Spray in the Cecils' spare bed. A letter from Boris imploring me not to leave Ham Spray upset me greatly: 'I read your letter with the greatest sorrow in my heart. To abandon the house where you lived so long and where happy memories supersede the sad ones is a terrible uprooting of your life. Is it wise? The unhappiness you feel now will mellow with time and happy days of many years will come back in watching Burgo and his friends, and your old friends, gathering round under the roof which for all of us is a centre of loving hospitality and enlightenment and the greatest English civilized taste in all things. To ruin all this will be a disaster for all of us and primarily for you and Burgo ...' and there was lots more in this vein. David was reassuringly firm on the other side. Now I have eased up for a space and sailed into an inland sea of relaxation and half-wittedness, shot with currents of *angst* so disconnected that they seem like lunacy. But I loved the delightfully communicative and articulate family atmosphere last night, with Jonathan (aged twenty-one) in his red velvet jacket and Laura in pyjamas and dressing-gown. Jonathan talks lovingly and freely to both his parents, and is a visibly sweet character, with very long sensitive fingers.

April 20th

Today I leave this kind sheltering roof. I strolled with David yesterday through the gardens of the other two Cecilian houses in the village – the beautiful Manor House belonging to Lord Cranborne, and Lord Salisbury's red-brick Georgian one. Spots of rain fell between the flowering cherries (dazzlingly pretty in spite of their tasteless combination of flower and leaf colour). A Shakespearian clown with a thick black wig was cutting logs with a tearing dental sound. The comfortable secure class-conscious civilization of the past lay around us as we discussed the tendency to 'depression' of the young today. Both Jonathan and Hugh (who arrived today from Lismore, very cheerful and amusing in MacCarthy style), say that their friends suffer from this depression. David likes to ignore the black side of things and wanted to belittle it; last night Jonathan again repeated it. He put it down to dread of war and so many having done military service – which gave me a momentary pleasure as at seeing a sum done correctly. It is so very logical. Much argument about capital and corporal punishment last night, wherein I found myself in complete agreement with Jonathan and so was naturally impressed by his intelligence. Rachel wavered, and it was David who with considerable emotion defended the diehard view, while constantly saying with a smile: 'I don't know what I'm arguing about – I really agree with you. I used not to but I do now.' He has an emotional dislike of the new 'rational' or 'moral' approach to punishment – surely it's odd to use such words as terms of reproach? – and stoutly maintained that nine out of ten boys would prefer being beaten to having to 'build a wall' –

---

[1] The Elweses signed the contract shortly after this, and it is symptomatic that I didn't record the fact in my diary.

the most boring task he could think of. Everyone brought up their guns against him. Jonathan, to whom it was closer, vividly described the morbid and terrifying atmosphere before a beating at Eton, when all the younger boys were confined to their rooms and the prefects stalked through the corridors swishing their canes. David was surrounded and cut off and ultimately defeated by us all, and he didn't take it altogether smoothly.

April 24th

Amazed and horrified at the relentless passage of time, the long white empty lengthening stretch of life without Ralph in it. That's why friends tell the bereaved to *hang on* and the time will pass. It does, all too fast, carrying one further and further away from the only real happiness, before one has the strength even to clasp the painful memory of that happiness close and be sure it never hazes over. I see Ralph shooting off, away, back, through an infinity of empty space like a star on its orbit, and must submit to his flight. I am astonished by this long blank bit of my solitary life and dread it should be prolonged so that my thirty-five years with him might seem not the whole of my life but a part, in shocking falsity of emphasis.

April 27th: Montpelier Square

Supper last night with Julia and Lawrence in their Percy Street flat, eating a frozen Woolworth meal out of foil dishes (no washing-up, my choice of three sorts); much laughter, altogether delightful.

My red and grey room at the top of the house is a haven, but has become full of my own sadness so that the air seems opaque with it.

Last night here; packing up. This evening I talked to Nicky[1] and ate a schoolgirl's supper with her in the kitchen. Much enjoyed this: why didn't I do it before?

These London days of looking at houses and flats have brought me very little but dislike of the ugliness and noise and hectic confusion of this town. Walking along Victoria Street, among worried pale jostling faces, seeing nothing that wasn't hideous, I longed to get away and hide, turn my face to the wall. (Yet, most of the time I see that my only hope is to be here.) I was on my way from the Roman Catholic Cathedral to see Boris putting up his mosaics. Plunged into the great dark place with its high walls and domes of brick sooty as Euston Station, and after wandering past a few devout kneelers or candle-lighters I heard unmistakable voices softly speaking Russian behind a boarded-off chapel marked No Admittance. Boris looked ill and sad, a magnificent crumbling ruin among what he believes to be his last works. I was staggered by their size: huge saints and apostles go right to the ceiling and their large Jewish faces and enormous black eyes stared at me as I climbed ladder after dusty wobbling ladder right to the barrel roof, where Italian workmen were putting up a round motif. Impressive, huge, yet I didn't altogether like it. It seemed to lack some of Boris' subtlety and poetry, the colossal hands and feet were clumsy. Then a brilliantly-conceived lamb about to be sacrificed, or a snake or a bowl of fruit caught my eye and charmed me.

I was painfully moved by talking to Boris, by the recollection of his letter begging me not to leave Ham Spray and by anxiety about his mosaics there.

[1] Janetta's oldest daughter.

A social evening with Cyril, Diana Witherby, Julian Jebb and Magouche,[1] who is like Janetta in a lower, warmer key. Together they remind me of the duet for soprano and mezzo in Verdi's *Requiem* – the 'black-edged paper' as Desmond Shawe-Taylor describes it. She's the only person I ever met who seems at all like Janetta. I like her thick dark hair, low rich voice, warm smile and large eyes. In fact, she's very attractive indeed.

In the train back to poor dear Ham Spray. My own shipwreck has filled me with terror and amazement at the mortal danger run so serenely day after day by anyone who loves anyone else. Yet they calmly buy toothpaste and plan for weeks and months ahead, just as I did, with heaven knows less justification than most. It's the only way to live, yet it seems patently insane.

May 10th: Ham Spray

Here I have been now two nights. Burgo arrived to keep me company, his own idea. He is pleased (and so am I) because he's been given the job of film critic to *Time and Tide*.

Today suddenly spring (summer almost) burst over us. My present task, which I've been hurling myself into since I got back, is sorting out James's books from mine – the first step in the pulling-down of the construction that is Ham Spray. Looking for more Lyttonian papers in the little closet next to the library, I came across some Carrington documents – the huge list of presents she left as an unsigned postscript to her Will, and a letter to Ralph left with it. Of course I've read them several times before, but this time in a new light. The letter, deeply moving and touching, yet had a strain of masterfulness – of wanting still to have control from *outre tombe* which I remember Ralph resented at the time. She wanted him to '*promise* always to live at Ham Spray'. Well, he did live there – but I remember that I was surprised how almost cynical he was, in spite of his shattered state after both their deaths – because she still wanted to hold the reins, even while planning to renounce life. Her request that Tommy should be commissioned to make a tombstone over her ashes in the shrubbery was the one he resented most violently.

He was, I realize now, being characteristically realistic. He felt very strongly that by choosing death regardless of other people's feelings, she had abnegated her right to control the lives of those friends – in particular himself and me. We were going to live in Ham Spray because it was his and we wanted to. We had decided to make our life there and we did so for nearly thirty happy years, but it would have been a different matter for us to live with a *memento mori* in the shape of a tombstone within the confines of our small garden. In his own Will, Ralph made no stipulation or request for me to live at Ham Spray. He was too rational not to see that this was *my* choice – and I have made it.

May 25th

In glorious summer weather I dismantle my life and my past, accompanied in turn by Joan Cochemé, and now Isobel Strachey and with much active help from Burgo. The business of taking these companions into a sort of ersatz married life is not as difficult as I had feared, just because it is in no way a simulacrum.

---

[1] Phillips, later Fielding.

What is to be done about Boris's mosaic fireplaces when I leave? I had hoped to take away the one Boris made as a wedding-present for Ralph and me; but the tesserae of both had been hammered into the cement before it hardened, and the job would be difficult. I wrote to Boris about it but he is still hard at work in the Roman Catholic Cathedral, has been quite ill and must be over seventy. He begged me not to let any unqualified person attempt to do it. I talked to Mrs Elwes on one of their very tactful visits to their future home. She is a nice, civilized woman; she knew all about Boris's art but 'happened not to like it' and felt it wouldn't 'go' with her Chinese and other antiques. She has agreed to cover the fireplaces carefully and see that they are undamaged.

June 21st:

In the train to Windermere, the unfamiliar landscape chug-chugging past. Six weeks of dismantling, destroying and coal-heaver exertion have left the inside of my head a watery white blank, anaesthetized and disintegrated into hundreds of pieces as small as those of a mosaic. Iris Murdoch's new book has at least one good sentence in it: 'How are you?' 'Dead, otherwise fine.' But such deadness is a mockery of the black velvet oblivion I dream about.

June 26th: Skelwith Fold, Cumbria

Tom[1] and Nadine's solid house, freshly whitewashed and with slate slab floors, stairs and fireplaces of an intense blue-green-grey, looks out onto two gardens rampant with roses, foxgloves and ferns, and on one side through the bare stems of two firs to a small green mountain snugly fitted into its velvet turf, but with grey rocks coming through here and there. All my energies are geared to adaptation to my different hospitable environments. The effort is great and the prospect of change makes me quiver. I prune my own desires right back to the root, which results in an unreal subhuman state, with sudden geyserlike outbursts. Tom and Nadine are both very kind. I slept my drugged sleep in my little ground-floor bedroom or sat doing my translation on the window-ledge. Long walks, picnics every day, all beautiful and quite physically tiring. On the hottest day we toiled up to Stickle Tarn under Langdale Pikes and sat by the high steely sheet of water watching climbers roped with nylon tackle the last rock face. The waterfalls between rocks covered in deep green moss, the astonishing cleanness, lack of anything hideous or vulgar; the quiet, sweet soft vegetable peace; the particular beauty of deciduous trees growing at the water's edge single or in groups – feasting on all this greenness and beauty has cast a temporary veil over my sharpest pangs.

July 3rd: Kyle House, Skye[2]

Absorbed by the business of adapting, I have written nothing, thought nothing, and now my stay in Skye is nearly over. Last night Colin took me and the weekend visitors (Smythes) a long drive along the coast after dinner, in a light that was neither day nor night, but such as you'd expect on the moon, cool and mysterious. Sea like pale watered silk, rippling in; the mountains towering up with magnificent suddenness yet insubstantial and grey-blue. They challenge, impose on one, cry

[1] Marshall (my brother) and his wife.
[2] The Mackenzies' house.

out, 'Look at us', drag one's attention. The track growing ever rougher and smaller, and fields yellow-white (like the white hair of ex-blondes) with ox-eye daisies, ended in a low farm and a grassy slope covered with orchids going gradually to the sea. Oh, what peace! Mr Smythe (he calls it Smith) is a little bent seventy-year-old solicitor, with sharp humorous eyes like a Skye terrier. His trousers are braced up to almost under his chin and it's a pleasure to see a thought which amuses him dawning on his face. His wife balances her huge body on table-legs swelling out at the ankles. She's a 'good' woman, worthy, broad-minded, musical and with an almost morbid interest in the troubles of others. She took me for a drive, ostensibly to show off her car, but I suddenly felt she had scented sorrow in me and wanted to draw it out like a vacuum-cleaner. I resisted.

This morning it rains – yet it's beautiful here beyond dreams, and soothing (though I'm not soothed, but palpitating with dread of the future). As we drove back after our night-drive the car wireless announced Hemingway's death 'accidentally' cleaning his gun. Lucky chap – or perhaps just brave, rational chap? – or selfish chap? How can one tell?

I dreamt very vividly that my dear silver bracelet (a present from Ralph) snapped ruggedly in half and I was staring in horror at the jagged break when a voice took me to task for being so selfish. Hadn't I noticed that the other half had flown through the air and cut the arm of a stranger, a harmless plump girl? A clear warning to keep in mind that my bereft state can cause pain indirectly to others too? A tip to be less self-absorbed?

July 11th

Back here with Janetta (very comforting and strong) and Burgo (in-turned and pacing). Now I'm near the end of two hard-working days almost alone (I'm sleeping at Stokke), I suppose I've never been quite so alone, and I've not really minded it. All today sticking red and white tabs on furniture, telephoning, arranging, feverish.

With Janetta's encouragement I've decided to be off next Saturday week to join her in Austria, shortening this nightmarish uprooting process by a week; crack! – one by one the roots come out of the soil.

July 24th: Alpbach, Austria

Ham Spray is a closed book. I am here surrounded by nursing-home peace, and relieved of the ghastly pressure like a huge iron weight descending on me during these last weeks, surrounded also by a landscape which is curiously hideous and yet enjoyable, and with the delightful company of Janetta, Georgia Tennant and Rose. More I shall fill in later. At present just one thing: it's over. I'm here – away.

July 26th

Being here went bad on me for the first time, and the intensity of my loneliness rose up like a great iceberg. All yesterday Janetta and Georgia were away fetching Georgie[1] and Julian Jebb from Innsbruck. Rose and I played games, sitting in bathing suits on the hot balcony, walked to the village and swam, came back and cooked our lunch.

We are living in a regular Tyrolean chalet of solid wood. At first sight I thought

---

[1] Kee, Janetta's second daughter.

of them all as hideous, as the landscape is fundamentally; I've come round to the style in a *sort* of way – see its point, though it's not a point I like: the smell of the wood, the solid tables and cupboards and benches built into the walls, the fact that everything is so well-made. We look out on intersecting valleys, with too-close mountainy hills far too densely covered in crawling mats of pines. Little green plump alps appear here and there among these pines and on each is a chalet gazing out under its wide roof like a poke-bonnet or an ark. The village is nothing but hotels and tourist shops, full of hideously ugly German tourists: men like bloated beetles in shorts on skinny legs, fantastically fat women, all walking with an ungainly straddling waddle, propped on long sticks. The ambience is innocent, naïve and goody-goody, *stupid*, jolly and wholesome. Very holy, too – one can't walk a yard without coming on Jesus on his cross.

Georgia Tennant at twenty is remarkably mature and a delightful, intelligent, high-spirited girl. Tall and strong, with fine long plump limbs and a shock of darkish golden hair half veiling her round pussy-cat face. I like her enormously and she has been very nice to me. She's a passionate reader, enjoyer of jazz, avid for life, one of Lawrence's students. She's highly responsive to her company. When Julian came, 'queer' though he obviously is, her face softened and broadened and caved in like a yielding sponge. Not so with Derek, here the first night, too old I suppose, though 'normal'.

Julian – what to say? He is euphoric, friendly, very articulate; he launches into imitations, crows with delight; everything seems to be *SIMply* delightful, his world full of *BRILLiantly* clever people and *MARvellous* books. But I like him very much.

No letters have come for me, I don't know why, and I have written none. Craving the amputation to be complete, so as to profit from perfect detachment from all the obsessional problems and commitments of the past, I resolve to concentrate on a few things such as books, flowers, translation, sleep.

Last night the usual thoughts of flight or withdrawal came crowding in: to a hotel in the village, home to England and heaven knows what. I know I must stick it out, but when the Campbells come I think I should have to go anyway, and I dread Janetta trying, out of kindness, to take on too many of us here. No one seems to have any notion of going, so I shall.

July 28th

Arthur Koestler and his 'secretary' Cynthia, known to him as Angel, live in a chalet like this one, a quarter of a mile away. They came in for a drink two nights ago, swaggering after climbing a mountain, Koestler dressed in the beetle-like Austrian uniform – shorts and long socks – yet speaking scornfully in what to us sounds a German accent of 'Krauts'. Conversation about this last night – Julian was shocked by it because he thought of Koestler as virtually a Kraut himself; I because I hate all those contemptuous national nicknames. Koestler has adopted Austrian civilization under his wing, and is galled that Janetta (one of the few people he respects) shouldn't appreciate it and the landscape. 'The peasants vould not like that. I thinks it so vise of them,' he says, lecturing us about their way of life. Little Arthur's Austria may or may not be true to fact, but it doesn't attract me. He mentioned that the Wayland Youngs were coming here soon. 'I don't agree with his politics, but I like him,' he said. 'What are his politics?' I asked. 'Never mind that,' – running on quickly – (he doesn't listen to other people). I thought this

unnecessarily snubbing and couldn't help saying: 'It would have been more interesting to know.'

August 1st

Janetta and all the others went off on a jaunt to the Bromovksys yesterday morning.
Last night Rose, with whom I was alone, was sick and she has gone on being sick
if she ate or drank anything all today. She has been almost unbearably stoical, and
when a few suppressed tears began to gush silently this evening I was on the point
of joining in with a gush of mine. All day I've been bungling everything, translating
badly, reading, reading, reading to Rose, feeling heartbreakingly responsible for
her, mopping up sick. Janetta is supposed to come home tomorrow – I hope to
God she does.

August 2nd

In bed. I've been reading a book about the North face of the Eiger, often in the
middle of the night. It's strangely gripping and horrifying, this superhuman and
pointless struggle which the climbers keep trying to justify. So is my struggle
superhuman and pointless, and all that is at the top of my Eiger (if in the end I
devise ways of going from handhold to handhold, tying myself into bivouacs,
putting in crampons and pitons) is death. I've been trying to think back to
moments of objective pleasure – like the eclipse; to moments when I was able to
drag myself along the rope by hauling on my courage – as at Braham. What is so
awful here is the sense of disintegration and *dégringolade*, of having no centre or
base at all (Ham Spray). This is even symbolized oddly in having left my dear
leather writing-case behind – deliberately – for it seemed to hold together the
threads of my life. It's *vital* I should set myself to find a new base – it's my only
hope, though a slim one.

August 3rd

Yesterday morning I telephoned Janetta for instructions about Rose and most of
the day the battle to keep anything, even a drop of water inside her, went on. Sent
Lisl our maid for the doctor, and his prescription of milkless tea and rusks seemed
to work – from then on, 5 p.m., the tide was turned or stemmed.

   Janetta did come back, all of them did last night, about ten. The return of
humanity at the end of my third day of isolation.

August 6th: Alpbacherhof Hotel

The most brilliantly fine day we've had, very hot, and with the mountains so clear
against the flawless sky that they seem to bend towards one and be within reach.
It's better being here, in a way; I have privacy and peace and no sense of guilt at
occupying Janetta's best room. I'm getting on better with Julian, thanks to *him* –
he's the one who makes the efforts.

   All morning a religious procession shuffled staidly and gloomily round the
village. I was interested at first and liked some of the fancy dresses but by no means
all. (The older ladies wore small top hats with gold tassels tilted forwards and long
black bands down to the ground; some of the young men had guyed their own
masculinity by putting on hats with huge feathers and roses. This local silliness is
what it's hard to swallow.) Janetta and Julian drove off to Innsbruck to meet the

Campbells; meanwhile Georgia and I hung about watching the procession slowly coil and twist round the streets of the town to the accompaniment of muttered prayers, and simple-minded tootling on trumpets and drumbeats. I got increasingly depressed by the stodgy stupidity of it all, the peasant mentality Arthur Koestler seems to admire – which has not the smallest similarity to the wild, obsessional, and exciting drama of popular religious manifestations in Spain. Koestler and Cynthia stood in front as the procession passed – he in his best town suit, head bent, a benign all-embracing, patronizing smile on his face, nodding to the grocer or whoever he knew. On my way to the Alpbacherhof, toiling through the heat before lunch, of course I met him and he pulled up. 'Vell, how did you like it?' 'Very interesting. I am delighted to have seen it,' I said, and asked some questions to give him a chance for one of his favourite lecturettes. 'But I thought it rather sad.' Koestler: 'Oh, no, they are *absolutely* sincere.' F.: 'I'm sure of that, but they seem uninspired. However, religion always fills me with gloom.' K.: 'Ah, it fills me with *envy*.' F.: 'Yes, I suppose it makes them happy. But at that rate one should envy lunatics in their asylum with their delusions.'

All afternoon I sat on my private balcony looking at the best of the view and worked steadily, with a break for a bathe, iced coffee with Julian and Georgia, a visit from Janetta and Robin. Supper at Janetta's house. Seeing the restlessness (not an unhappy one) resulting from seven people living in one large railway carriage, the mingled irritation and pleasure caused by the kittens and their little rolls of shit and big half-eaten mice everywhere, and the impossibility of real privacy, I was glad I had even this rather austere retreat to come to.

August 7th

Very hot yesterday; I plunged into work. Julian came to lunch alone with me, and we had it in the grilling heat of the balcony, ill-protected by an umbrella. Discussion of the effect of Janetta on people – interesting to see it from the viewpoint of the young. He and Georgia are coming out of a period of almost agonizing obsession with her and her values, and it was fascinating for me to open a window and peer back through time into that lost world of desperate fixation, swinging wildly on the swell of favour or disapproval. Having always thought of her as remarkable and adorable, this is nonetheless a new projection of her shadow as dominant, and holding the key to everything in her hands.

August 13th

This afternoon I at last broached the inviolable mountains, and have come back intoxicated and delighted, with a large bunch of alpine flowers – yellow saxifrage, the wild rhododendron and others I've not yet identified. What a strange thing it is, the challenge of the mountains! All these three weeks I've been looking at their woolly sides askance, hating them, and feeling oppressed and dominated by them. This morning, wintry cold, there were horrible glimpses of snowy summits through the clouds – miniature Eigers hostile to man. When, after solid Sunday lunch the sky began to clear, on the spur of the moment I set up off the most available Wanderweg marked on the map, and picked out with red dots and arrows on walls and trees. Immediate peace, as I very slowly rose, sending the village down a rung or two of the ladder, and reaching up to the snowy heights with each step. That's the great charm: the ever-changing view of things. Great peaks suddenly rise up and peer at one over the shoulders of mild green hills. And then there's something magical about the change of status from fly crawling on the wainscot to eagle up among the clouds. It wasn't much of a climb, but I kept a very slow steady pace. Yesterday's rain had brimmed the streams tearing downhill, and sometimes which was path, which stream, I didn't know. But the banks of flowers led me on as much as the Hansel and Gretel attraction of following the red blobs through the woods, across luscious fields and then up the higher reaches of the valley, to the pass I was heading for. I came to a small mountain tarn; pale velvety cows pressed by me, jingling their bells, and driven by a small tow-haired boy. Through the pass and up into the woods, where were masses of shining-leaved bushes of wild rhododendron, and other flowers I'd not yet seen. This was a corniche path slung halfway up the back of the grim peak of the Gratzlspitz. But it was getting late and I turned back, scrambling beside the gushing stream; more flowers, helleborine, a monocotyledon with delicate white flowers balanced on hair-thin stalks. I returned triumphantly sated with these visual and sensual pleasures and pleased to have stretched out and grasped them for myself, and slept like a log for nine long hours.

August 17th

The grip of the mountains has made itself hard to ignore. Georgia and Julian aren't tempted by them; Janetta mainly hates, fears and dreads them; I love and fear them; Susan loves them as a baby might love a coal fire – not knowing what power they possess, and bravely (because they give her vertigo). It's always been the same with me: as soon as I catch sight of them I'm impressed by their challenge, 'Come and battle with me'. Then if I do tackle them, the respect and fear are conquered and love gets the upper hand. Now, with increasing age the desire to stand on their very summits gives way to the desire to get at and ravish the secret charms of their higher reaches.

I woke this morning at four after a nightmare – Ralph had died 'again', and I knew that he hadn't been *really* dead before but now he was; I stood in my bedroom at Ham Spray, half empty of furniture, feeling a creeping paralysis of loneliness and cold. Woke to deluging rain and fearful cold which has gone on all day, the clouds hanging low in the hair of the woods, so low that one can hardly see the snowy peaks through them, the melancholy sound (on top of the steady fall of rain) of the spout from the roof shooting its contents into the valley. Oh, for a fire or radiator! Oh, what a beastly climate! I'm really glad to be heading home. Yet here people go about in their cotton dirndls with puff sleeves, aprons and just an umbrella, and the maids 'dry' the bedding by shaking it out of the window in the rain.

August 24th: London, Hamilton Terrace[1]

I lunched with Burgo two days ago and went with him to a preview of the last film Gary Cooper made before his death. There was a moment when the clutch of Gary and whoever the heroine was, like two monkeys keeping together for warmth, pierced my armour. The shrinkage in my present life comes from the loss of that monkey-warmth; but four days in this racketing Dickensian town haven't quite shattered me yet. It's very nice being alone with Craig in the evenings; such a

---

[1] Staying with Craig Macfarlane to look for a flat.

delightful, kind and understanding companion. Two Spanish servants and a daily keep our bachelor life supported. We sit down to delicious little three-course dinners by candlelight and with half a bottle of claret each evening. Last night we listened to Glück's *Iphigenia* from Edinburgh. And I consulted him about my day's house-hunting, which is what I am here for.

Each day it has rained from a leaden sky and I've rattled round in buses to agents or flats. When I was coming back this afternoon a very old lady appeared on the bus' step: 'Oh, I'm so POOR and ILL! And I've been so worried,' she addressed us all, and willing hands helped her to a seat, encouraged her, told her where she must get off and that the doctor she was going to see was very good. She was reeling into her seat in one direction, while next to me a very old man reeking of drink was falling over backwards in his effort to get off. I couldn't help a stifled snort of laughter and felt I had let down the bus side by such inhumanity. I'm not really discouraged yet in my search, though there seem very few flats going and those very expensive. I may break out, I think, and spend more than Craig thinks I should. I've been able to project myself into two of them, and an unearthly calm prevents my panicking yet – even though the future is so inscrutable.

I've contacted some friends and see there should be no shortage of them here in London. In an odd way I can picture myself here, if only I had a big, light room looking on to trees.

August 28th

I seem to be moving rapidly towards the decision to take a flat in West Halkin Street, Belgravia – that is if it's not already gone. And am amazed that I can look at this constricted possible nest, now hideously furnished with fur rugs and leather chairs, without horror. London, too, seems like a foreign country – yet I think I was right to choose to live here. It's at the opposite pole from Ham Spray, and life in a country cottage would have been a hopelessly pale imitation. I don't think I would have guessed at one result of Ralph's death, which is that I find myself more interested in other people and more able to be at ease with them than I was when the whole body of my libido flowed into the proper channel. It's nine months since Ralph died.

August 31st

The decision to take the West Halkin Street flat is made, the deposit is paid and I'm only terrified lest Craig with his cautious exploration of leases, etc. might let it slip through his fingers, which I would now feel as a serious frustration.

Yesterday Janetta arrived on her dash home from Alpbach and came to see it. She seems to approve greatly and fermented my anxiety to get it. I've been through days when my basic optimism has risen from the marble tomb it has been lying in, days of great heat when London looked exotic and foreign and exciting, so that my antipathy to the idea of living in it suddenly collapsed like a pack of cards; the usual elation too, accompanying a sense of *managing*. I've been absorbed in getting to learn this new town, map in hand, mastering the bus routes and the ways of dealing with special London problems.

September 2nd: Lambourn

I left London behind yesterday in a state of unimpeached radiance and heat, after a morning spent shopping with Janetta, and lunching off smoked salmon and champagne. She was *piano* with toothache and drugs to ease pain, but everything she does and one can share with her has her own distinct flavour. Arrived here at Gordon House, I went with delight to sit in the coolness of the Gowings' garden. Kees to supper, very nice; the main subject which extended itself at all was concerned with people's attitude to war, and how different was that of a fighting man (Robert) towards the bombing or drowning of enemy babies or sailors to one's own.

This morning my new little car arrived, dumpy, virginal, comic, engaging. I drove it over to Tidcombe to see the Hendersons. I think I shall love it. I do realize how thankful I must be that this new vein of constructiveness has (it does seem) improved my morale out of all recognition, as has the unexpected impression London has made on me.

September 5th

Grey and surly day yesterday, so – there being too little light for Lawrence to paint – he sat in the arbour thinking about his painting. As he sat looking into the woods with his easel in front of him he discovered that what he saw, with the closer edge of his visual field and the greatest depth in the middle, was much like the hollow half of a sphere. He sat as it were inside a globe, and as he's at present trying to think of the world in abstract terms he became preoccupied all day by trying to work out how various mathematical shapes could be fitted into this hemisphere. (Hexagons for instance, composed as they were of six isosceles triangles.) Seized with the desire to demonstrate it practically, he rushed to the village toy shop and bought a large child's ball *on approval* (I saw it in the hall in a plastic bag, as large as a melon), then sat trying to fit hexagons onto its surface with a ballpoint pen. *They wouldn't go.* This great discovery delighted him, tho' I can't remember what he deduced from it. But it delights me too as being so characteristic of his original and eccentric nature. Then he had a job to rub off the ink marks, but finally it was done, the ball returned to the shop and at dinner he told us how he had spent the afternoon, Julia staring at him as if she'd never seen him before in her life.

September 8th: Long Crichel House

On I move once more to shelter again under the kind wing of friends – Eardley and Raymond at Crichel. I buzzed there in stately fashion in the little white egg of my car. It's very, very nice to be here. I do think I've made headway since the last time with its crushing moment of panic, grief and lostness. I am a bit more stabilized now. Relaxed, communicative evening last night talking to Raymond and Eardley and listening to Haydn quartets. Raymond greeted me most warmly, started 'You look ...' and then, seeing there was nothing to be said about my looks, fell silent! This sort of tiny incident delights me. I know I look appalling, worn and hagridden and even older than I am, though Julia was kind enough to say she'd noticed a change for the better. Why then find it delightful? Just because actions, tones of voices and expressions have proved again that they are an easy language to read, which can be deciphered in a flash.

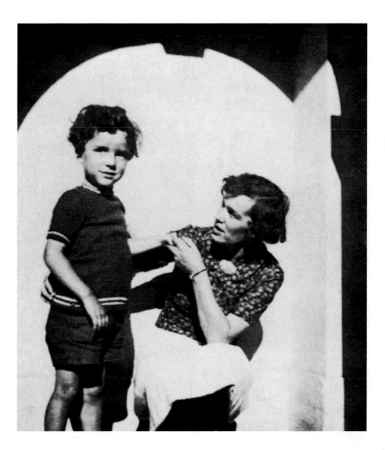

Burgo and Frances
Partridge

Clive Bell

Helen Anrep and David ('Bunny') Garnett

Desmond and Molly MacCarthy

Saxon Sydney-
Turner

Anthony and
Kitty West

Frances Partridge

Richard
Chopping
and
Sebastian
Sprott at
Ham Spray

Robert Kee

Janetta

Ralph and the Hendersons having breakfast at Ham Spray

Burgo in his rooms at Christ Church

Wynne and Kitty
Godley at Ham Spray

E. M. Forster
at Ham Spray

Desmond Shawe-
Taylor and
Raymond Mortimer
at Crichel

Ralph with the
Brenans in Spain

Ralph and Frances Partridge

Alix and James Strachey on one of their annual visits to Ham Spray

David and Rachel Cecil at Cranborne, a family party: Lady Emma
Cavendish, Hugh, David, Rachel, Jonathan and Laura Cecil

Robert Kee
thoroughly awake
at breakfast-time,
Ham Spray

Julia Strachey
drinks sherry on
our verandah

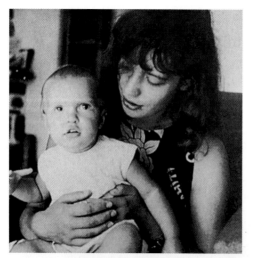

Henrietta with her baby
daughter, Sophie Vanessa

Anne and Lucy Hill at Cadgwith

Janetta in Corfu, making ink drawings of olives

Sophie, nearly 7, in West Halkin Street

Bunny Garnett writing in his garden at Le Verger de Charry in the Lot

Dadie Rylands and Eardley Knollys in Alderney

September 10th

Duncan came the night before last. I can't help wondering what the inner equation is by which he deals with a situation more or less like mine[1] – the withdrawal of half the interest, vital flow of his life – and realizing that as little as he betrays it, so probably do I. In his stained ill-fitting suit he looks rather like a Jewish pawnbroker, standing a little apologetically and as if about to shuffle off or rub his hands together; rather hunched, looking up and blinking anxiously at us from his still forget-me-not-blue eyes in a crumpled rose-petal face. Yet his air of apology, seeming to say, 'I don't really know how to behave. I'm not concerned with the world and its values.' This childlike innocence wouldn't take in anyone, nor does it take in Duncan himself. He has an excellent opinion of himself and quite right too, is probably well aware of his terrific power to charm, and certainly confident that his values are the right ones, and that what he excludes and doesn't know about isn't worth knowing. I think this self-confidence and lack of self-criticism (which could also be called unselfconsciousness) is the salient thing about his character, and derives from the fact that so many people have loved him and been in love with him, and Bloomsbury always spoiled him and laughed delightedly at his half-unconscious wit. Buoyed up by which, he's been able to dedicate himself simply and directly to what he wanted to do. He must be ranked, along with Bunny, among the happiest men alive.

I'd been saying to Eardley on a walk that I wished one could talk to him directly about his grand-daughters, or Angelica as his daughter. Eardley thought it impossible. We wondered if Vanessa's death might make a difference. And then David Cecil came to dinner and did it – referred quite gaily and unconsciously to 'your grand-daughter'. No sign of surprise from Duncan, yet I can't help feeling it *was* a slight shock to him because he *had* overlooked the fact that everyone in the world knows.

September 17th

Just as I was consoling myself that I was beginning to come to terms with my existence, yesterday's change of scene brought a pitiful sag and wavering. As when trying to go through a hoop in croquet, very much depends on keeping confidence flying, mainly it would seem by auto-suggestion. Courage, courage ... You *can* do it all right if you try. Leaving Crichel was like going back to school, and yesterday had the blank, washed-out quality, neither here nor there, of the last day of the holidays.

Then came a flood of longing for the only companion whose company was also relaxation. Now I can only relax in solitude, and to do that I risk futile restlessness.

September 18th: Stokke

Moved on here yesterday, driving Mini with more confidence through blazing heat. Stokke always reminds me painfully of Ham Spray. I walked with Mary over her fields, and helped her weed a bed.

I've not said that while I was at the Cecils' the chief Nuclear Disarmament supporters, including eighty-nine-year-old Bertie Russell, were put in jail because they refused to be bound over not to meet and 'sit down' in Trafalgar Square on

---

[1] Vanessa's death.

Battle of Britain day, which was several days ago. In spite of this, hundreds did meet and sit down, and one and all who were still there at midnight were taken to jail, including Nicky, Harriet Hill and Henrietta Garnett. Slowly, painfully but eagerly they described their grim experience to an audience of Janetta, Anne Hill and me. Harriet was rather tragic about it, Nicky came out at her best. I got her to tell me about it all in more detail yesterday – how rough the police had been, hauling them along the ground by their arms, throwing a young man on top of them when they lay there; how an inspector had kicked her; how the police had called them 'stupid cows' and asked each other, 'What shall we do? Shit on them?' About their bewilderment and uncertainty and the grimness then and flatness now; how it had been almost a relief to get in the Black Maria, but the journey rattling along in cells had horrified them; how no one had given them anything to eat until they were brought up at Clerkenwell Court and fined £1 each at lunch-time next day; how they were crowded into an airless cell with a lavatory in it which everyone had to use; how some were wet and shivering from being thrown into the fountains; how sixty of them slept on a huge 'mattress' or 'sheet' but the police woke them up by raking the different wireless stations every hour like the Gestapo; how Nicky had testified to her beliefs when asked if she had anything to say; how anxious she felt now about what had happened to her friends, and whether she had done what she should.

This situation has aroused indignation even among some Conservatives and started lots of arguments, whereas among my friends were some who spoke intolerantly about them all '*wanting* to be roughly handled, longing for it'. In the afternoon I ventured to set my own position to Nicky: 'Why don't you "sit down" since you're a pacifist and against the bomb?' she asked me. 'We need some grey heads.' I said because I didn't think 'sitting down' convinced anyone, only arguments could do that. (*She* wouldn't be convinced that the bomb was right just because people who believed it was 'sat down'), that I wasn't, however, against any form of demonstration so long as they didn't adopt the very means they were against – some form of violence, and that blocking roads or railways was that. Useless to say: 'Yes, but the alternative is so much worse – the bomb.' That was the warmongers' own argument. She got excited momentarily, but then was prepared to consider my points; there's no doubt she feels violently about it – and Lord knows she's entitled to, young as she is and enjoying her life and wanting to go on doing so.

September 22nd: Montpelier Square

I hesitated whether or not to go with Janetta to an evening reunion with Joan Rayner's[1] group of intellectuals – Cyril, Quennell, Bowra, and so on. Decided my vitality wasn't equal to it, and I'm glad I did, for the description given by Magouche and Janetta next morning was uninviting. Cyril had snubbed Janetta. Social life here in London, rolling, clattering and thundering all day long, is a very different affair from the country variety: and there is so much to stimulate conversation that it's less of an effort. I'm not sure if less thought goes to make it, or whether the swift onrush of more and more talk effaces what has gone before even more completely. I cannot help probing my wounds and speculating as to what effect

[1] Now Leigh Fermor.

being unable to communicate with an alter ego has on my mental process – do I now cease to have those thoughts I used to love to exchange with Ralph?

Lunch with Bunny yesterday. Talked of Angelica's bastardy. He showed that he was unaware that it was universally known, and said that they had not told his four daughters but realized that Amaryllis had somehow heard, 'told by her school friends'. The reason he gave for discretion was consideration for Clive's feelings.

October 2nd

Shuttled back to Montpelier after another venture into the country – Hilton Hall this time, ramshackle, bohemian, improvised, beautiful house full of beautiful things neglected, tattered and thick with cobwebs. Music in confusion and disarray, rolls of dust under the bed, bathroom like a junk-shop, the basin leaning out of the wall, furniture propped on books, stains, cracks everywhere, no bulbs in the lights, a smeared single coat of paint on the walls of my room, not enough blankets on the bed. But delicious meals, plenty to drink, and every object chosen with taste. I do react somewhat against the do-it-yourself philosophy, by which everything home-made is by definition held to be better than everything that's not – for that simply isn't so. But it is a very warm, lively civilization, lit up by the presence of Bunny and Angelica's four blooming daughters. Two were making their first ventures away from home – Amaryllis came down on Saturday after her first days in a theatrical school, displaying a budding actressy manner under which one can read intelligence, sweetness and enthusiasm for life. Poor Henrietta, the most dazzlingly attractive of the four and the most interesting, is being sacrificed (so it seems to me) to some strange principle, by having to spend a term in a frightful Do-the-boys-Hall of a coaching establishment, with a regime of old-fashioned austerity. She came to lunch on Sunday, and was funny about the bleakness, stinginess and horrible food, and about being turned out-of-doors to walk for two hours in the rain in the flat East Anglian landscape. I felt indignant that she should be subjected to this and perhaps for ever associate work and learning with everything repressive and uncivilized.

With Bunny I had many conversations on all topics, and discussions of the new volume of his memoirs he's writing – very mixed, a curious mawkishness comes in occasionally while other very tricky situations like Ray's illness and death brought tears to his eyes. Angelica has thrown up her violin and hardly ever plays the piano, but spends every odd moment thrumming very old, pure music on a guitar; and when she sits with her family in the evening talking isn't enough; she feverishly knits. I wondered about the effect of Vanessa's death in bringing her closer to Duncan.

My flat is now *really mine*. Today I received the keys, ordered a fireplace and arranged about the electricity.

October 3rd

Janetta had friends in yesterday evening. Talked of suicide with her and Raymond, who held it was always an insane action. In this as in other things he said I found him very different from his country self: a stay with millionaires in Venice had brought out all that is most un-serious and worldly in him. We talked of 'human butterflies': again Raymond defended them but no one could think of any except Raymond himself, and an Italian lady he had recently met. Paddy Leigh Fermor bounded round the room thundering: 'But they're appalling! The Italian upper classes are FRIGHTFUL! – weak, philistine, *vain*, *DULL*!' Next it was whether we were being fogies or not in failing to appreciate modern painting and drama. Was this a period of decline? Raymond and Paddy thought so – Patrick Kinross[1] said every fogey had said this of every period of civilization. I said it worried me to miss so much possible pleasure and to think we might be like the people who cackled with laughter at the Impressionists. Janetta said in her gentlest voice that it didn't worry her *at all* – there were so many other things she greatly enjoyed. The clock ticked on to one, and the mixture of personalities in the room was violently stirred, bubbling and subsiding by turns. This whirling restlessness and public expense of spirit is perhaps typical of London life, and I don't altogether care for it. Upstairs, gratefully snatching at oblivion. London is an iron lung, which grips one and forces one to go through the motions of a living being almost against one's will. I shall miss Janetta terribly when she goes abroad in two days' time. Her kindness and generosity have been deeply touching to me; I think or hope I've managed to fit in with the way of life (not-planning ahead) and it will be an effort to wean myself so as to carry on my life here without her. My flat is now infested with decorators and I 'hope' to move into it at the end of the month. I long above all for some regular work.

November 11th: West Halkin Street

Here I am alone, on my desert island, amazed to realize that I've been here and slept here in my solitude for over a week. Each night I hear thumping footsteps and platitudinous voices overhead and in an odd way I find them comforting. Now, a Saturday, I'm testing myself out by staying in London for the weekend, and it pours with rain from a grey sky. Yesterday for the first time my flat seemed to come alive and now I look round at what I've planned and constructed and wonder what it's really like. The hall with its rich, dark Indian pattern wallpaper is still heaped with books and without a rug. The bedroom, soft peaceful grey and white, bow-window, countrified pictures (landscapes, cats, owls), and the sitting-room warm pink, mustard, green and purple, have emerged just as I meant, and now the books, china and piano complete it. I asked Eardley what sort of a room it seemed. 'Very scholarly,' he replied.

November 12th

There was a special meeting of the Memoir Club at Charleston last weekend, gathered to hear Roy Harrod read aloud fifty-year-old letters between Lytton and Maynard. It was a fascinating correspondence, strikingly modern in language; communicating closest friendship and a desire to share feelings and thoughts, but with values in some respects different from those of today. Love seemed less exclusively a matter of sex. Though tossed by jealousy, despair, hope and ecstasy, it was total love; what's more, for intellectual equals instead of bell-hops and sailors. Lytton at first confided his love for Duncan. Maynard was full of sympathy, declared himself 'in love with the fact of Lytton and Duncan's mutual love'. The drama came to a crisis when Duncan suddenly began an affair with Maynard himself, and Lytton was told and wrote a touching, rather noble letter about it.

[1] Writer.

But his friendship for Maynard never really recovered. Lytton's earlier letters were brilliantly good and I thought perhaps this blow had produced the sense of emotional mummification he developed later.

Before the reading began, Duncan had met me in the darkness at Lewes station and while driving me erratically to Charleston explained that Roy was anxious lest he should find these letters embarrassing. 'I suppose I ought to, but I don't, and I'm only worried whether other people may be embarrassed on my account.' I found Clive looking older and rather thin. Roy arrived after dinner, spry, confident and talkative. The extraordinary house, so lovingly decorated with paint every-where, was ice-cold and uncomfortable but provided us with good food, abundant wine and lively talk. The potent Bloomsbury atmosphere encircled us. I was given Vanessa's bedroom, looking out on the frozen garden trimmed with a neat edging of grey shrubs; there was a bath behind a screen in one corner and faceless portraits on the walls. The reading went on nearly all Saturday and Sunday in the studio, Roy reading well but very fast while we sat round in a circle now augmented by Sebastian, Angus[1] and Leonard. Between lunch and tea some of us put on coats and walked on the slopes of the downs. Leonard, now eighty, with his noble face hanging in string-like folds, walked up the steep hill with me, easily outpacing Angus.

November 15th

I hate doing my life sentence and would gladly abandon it for ever – would like to lay down my life as one drops a handkerchief. Death is always in my thoughts now, and tears make a high-water mark in the inside of my head. Why live unloved, unwarmed (who cares if I do or not?) with no one to laugh with and share my preoccupations? Why haul and heave to pull my courage up from the bottom of the well it has dropped into? Since one must fix on some landmark ahead, I'm going to try to think of going to Spain in just over a month's time, as a prisoner thinks of the next visit he's allowed. Misery is a dreadful acid which dissolves the mental processes, obliterates the memory and slows up the responses – an attempt to commit suicide on the part of the brain.

November 16th

I have been navigating a bad patch of my London life, and yesterday was one of my worst days. I couldn't stop crying and my skeleton life stood naked with bare bones projecting before my eyes. My lack of interest in living made dozens of trifling things go wrong. With relief I sank into bed, to be woken by a wrong number at four. Talking just now to Janetta on the telephone I was so aware of the dire acuteness of my crisis that I felt surprised it didn't communicate itself to her. But after almost a year of bereavement, in which everyone has been infinitely kind and I have probably seemed to be well on the way to recovery, how can anyone possibly realize that it's *worse* now than ever, or if they do, how can they fail to be bored by the fact? *Better*, a little, today. The sun shines. I realize why this access of despair has come: all this last year I have been preparing to live my new life, by demolishing the old. Now I've got to begin doing it and it's a ghastly mockery and I hate it.

[1] Davidson, translator from Italian.

November 20th

I'm back in my flat after a weekend at Stokke, with Mary and John Julius Norwich. He's a nice, clever, interested young man, apparently almost aggressively normal and well-adjusted. I walked out, each of the two cold autumn days, under hedges of faded papery leaves, drained of all colour. Then turning past the foresters' cottages quietly smoking into the still air I began to climb the path which leads back to Stokke. It seemed to me I saw someone standing at the top near the gate and for a moment I vividly, passionately imagined it was my darling Ralph, standing there with his loving welcoming face, and my longing for him was something concrete and solid hanging in the chilly air.

I have begun on work in the shape of trying to edit Desmond MacCarthy's letters, at the request of his family. I have begun to return hospitality: Cochemés, Lawrence, Japps have all been here. Discussing suicide with the Cochemés, Joan looked at me with her round eyes and said: 'We're all afraid of *you* committing suicide.' Life and death seem at times so trifingly different from each other (a squiggle here, a line there), that it doesn't seem odd at all to talk lightly of suicide. But I've done nearly a year of my life-sentence and where have I got to?

December 1st

Yesterday's anniversary is over. I thought I was immune to such considerations, but realized I didn't want to be alone in the evening and was glad to go with Isobel to the film of *The Turn of the Screw*. A year of my sentence is *done*: impossible thought. I have had a nice musical evening with Ralph Jarvis and Laurie Lee, been anxiously stirred and touched by Burgo in his new flat, and gone to a private view of Henry Lamb's pictures (where Pansy did the honours). And so on, so on, so on. I work intermittently at Desmond's letters, changing my view every few moments as to how good they are.

December 2nd: Chatsworth

I embarked for Chatsworth yesterday afternoon with Janetta, Andrew Devonshire, Adrian Daintrey[1] and Patrick Kinross. It was already dark and wet when Janetta called for me in a comfortable limousine and we sped across London to St Pancras. Beneath the great straddling station arch were trucks and trucks of Christmas parcels and a large, patient crowd. Among men with guitars and coated greyhounds we found our party. The loudspeaker repeatedly announced delays to our train and we relapsed into our First Class carriage an hour late. Standing in the train bar drinking whiskey, Adrian Daintrey, a delightful and amusing character, told me at length and in detail about Edna, a prostitute with whom he has had some sort of relationship for the last ten years. How I envy such communicativeness! As if in a dream I abandoned myself to the journey, including the silken smoothness of our drive through the darkness to the great house, waiting for us floodlit. Beautiful, sumptuous, splendid objects loomed up, and – still in a dream – I walked into my palatial bedroom lined and curtained with dark red velvet, with its fine gilt and white four-poster, and a quiet maid waiting.

Now it's morning and I lie in bed, a huge breakfast greedily eaten, looking at the exquisite proportion of pale blue sky to pale green landscape seen through the

[1] Painter.

enormous windows. I slept badly and feel hardly equal to facing the day. To do so, I try forcibly to turn my thoughts outwards. Daintrey, for instance. Is he lonely? I like him.

December 3rd

Dazzled by the great beauty of this place (the park, waterfalls, fountains, statues and marvellous contents of the house – Rembrandts, Tintorettos), draught upon draught of it. In cold bright sun we walked across the vast sheet of greensward, past the tall plume of the fountain blowing sideways, to see some remarkable crocuses flowering out of doors; through the orchid houses, and rows of cyclamens in pots.

This beautiful house, and it really *is* beautiful in an unforgettable way, nonetheless is a *thing*, a great *object* reared up indestructibly in the middle of vulnerable human relationships. What can anyone do against it? It is the master, the strongest force. I'm constantly reminded of Henry James: it is what might happen in one of his plots (perhaps does) that a house should be the most important character. Snow began to fall quietly outside, lying like a cloth on the stone table on the terrace, and the sky grew dark. Andrew took us to see more and more remote treasures – gold and silver stood gleaming in glass-fronted cupboards, looking far more alive than the small man whose whole life consisted in polishing and handling it. Much longer here and one would be defeated and routed by this formidable house and its cargo of rare objects. Adrian and I spent several hours turning over marvellously lovely drawings by Rembrandt or Inigo Jones. He manages to keep his original and comic personality intact; for my part I grew steadily more consciously expressionless.

When I reached home at tea-time, I found a letter from Eardley saying he proposed we set forth to drive to Spain in little more than a fortnight, and also a touching one from Gerald, written on November 30th: 'This is the saddest of anniversaries and I thought I'd just write you a letter to say – but what is there to say? Only that I haven't forgotten it.'

December 7th

Why, WHY did I ever struggle on? Was it some faint stirring of the life-instinct, lack of courage – or even the reverse, a perverted desire to be brave? I have spent now two days in *passionately* longing to be dead – floundering through the barest necessities of life. Janetta and I lunched with Boris yesterday, after clambering the dusty ladders to admire his mosaics in the Roman Catholic Cathedral. As we praised them, he laughed softly. Afterwards I went with Janetta to buy Christmas toys at the Army and Navy Stores, and watched her stroking teddy bears while the tears rolled uncontrollably down my face. Poor Janetta – I felt appalled to rest weight on her already overburdened and fragile boat.

December 14th

Better again, and resolving, for a while at least, not to harp so much on my own misery.

Dinner with the Kees last night, to meet the present literary editor of the *New Statesman*, Karl Miller, and his very pregnant, jolly wife. Arrived at eight-thirty to find the wife waiting (as I was) for the others who returned from a cocktail party, wound-up, with their wheels still whirring. Karl Miller is an intelligent auto-intoxicated, young and ambitious Scot; doesn't want to hear anything from anyone else, but just to do his own turn ad lib, which happens to be skilful and often funny. But few people want to spend the whole evening laughing heartily at someone else's capers; it was like a night out with stockbrokers. There was quickfire, showing-off talk about the situation in the Congo, which I can't understand anyway; also some sex-badinage. I liked Terry Kilmartin, literary editor of the *Observer*, but I didn't enjoy the evening much, especially when Robert said to me: 'How are you getting along? Are you enjoying London? Cynthia thinks you really *love* the rat-race!' I tried to put my mood of rejecting life into a semi-comical frame, but Robert wouldn't have it and swept it aside – 'Oh no, I'm *sure* you're enjoying yourself.' What can he possibly have meant?

December 21st

Eardley and I set off for Spain two days ago and they have gone well, in marvellous weather, crisp and cloudless, frosty, with a clear pale blue sky. Our first night was spent at Granville, the Normandy *plage* Ralph and I visited a few years ago and vowed to come back to. Yesterday to Madame de Sevigné's Les Rochers; I was moved to see the allées – 'les charmes' – she planted, and imagined her showing them to her son. They are small and stunted still.

December 24th

Lying on my cell bed at Palencia. Eardley and I are getting along very well. No *gêne*, and I think no irritation.

There is so much to talk about – after five days we have not run out, nor been reduced to compulsively observing our fellow-guests. And the constant movement, the steady stream of visual and other impressions has worked well. Bordeaux is quite spoilt – the *Chapon Fin* modernized and its restaurant temporarily shut; the lovely old market being pulled down; tiny new trees in the allées. 'I expect they'll have cut down the quincunxes,' said Eardley, and they practically had. In Spain the best has been a nice old-fashioned hotel full of clocks at San Sebastian and that glorious town Salamanca where we lunched today. After still, sunny and frosty weather across France, Spain has lashed us with rain and cold winds, indigo clouds scudding over the plateau of Castile and a strange apricot light on the horizon.

December 29th: Churriana[1]

Journey's end, and I sit up in bed in my long cold room at Churriana. Am I going to be able to stand the discomforts (but if they – the Brenans – do, why can't I?): the lack not only of bath but any hot water *at all*, save what is boiled up in kettles; the plugless lavatory, smelly and dripped-over, the *cold*, compared to my warm London flat? Yet everything is beautiful and spacious, and I'm ashamed to be so materialistic. But I'm going to master the technique of living here I *think*, that's to say enjoy the immense bounties offered me by the Brenans and avoid Julia-esque carping at the discomforts. Against the latter I put up small stubborn rearguard actions. I've been given a tiny electric kettle in my bedroom and this I plug in at night for my hot-water bottle and at mornings for an all-over wash – about a pint

---

[1] The Brenans' village.

of boiling water does it, and I feel it would be death to give it up and lapse into squalor. The smell in the lavatory I combat by flinging the window wide open when I go there. The outside air today is sweet and warm, but I don't think anyone notices, any more than they do the smell. At the top of the house, a sort of roof room, formerly open on all sides, is now glassed-in, and here I have my work table. It is perfectly beautiful, each window framing a different view, Malaga on one side, the nearer mountains on another, tall bamboos and the garden on the third and fourth. The sun pours in on me now and I feel fortunate to be here and allowed to exist in this sweet peace. A soft sound of gobbling turkeys comes up from below. Gerald has given me his autobiography to read.

1962

January 1st: Churriana

As I approached the end of Gerald's autobiography[1] (about the War) I found myself recoiling from going on – not that it wasn't interesting. But because his picture of Ralph in the War, accurate as far as it goes I dare say, but infused with all his own (Gerald's) feelings of envy, hero-worship and mockery mixed, is in any case not 'my' Ralph, I realized from Gerald's letters some time ago that he felt a deep subconscious need to discharge on me everything he had felt and thought about Ralph all his life long. Last night, since I'd reached that part of his book, he began to do so; a torrent of words, and of thoughts and impressions tumbled from his mouth, many of which I didn't want to hear; they fell like heavy stones on a raw bleeding wound. Gerald is an extraordinary man. He responds in such an original way to books and the visual world, and yet is blind as a bat to other people's feelings. Or am I being impossibly fastidious? It was in fact extremely painful to me to sit in the battering fusillade of his impression of Ralph, as he talked on and on egotistically, with glazed eyes, *relieving* himself as it were, and the effort to respond with temperate, balanced remarks exhausted me. There was much, too, about Carrington, justifying himself as he always does. 'Nothing had happened,' he said when Valentine's disclosures made Ralph so furiously jealous. Except, as it turned out, that Gerald and Carrington had fallen violently in love and had been secretly meeting and kissing! Because he had 'no thought of going further', Gerald exonerates himself utterly, and thinks Ralph unreasonable to have minded the treachery and deception as he did. I dread having more of these long-dormant bombs exploded round me. I work at Desmond's letters nearly all the mornings in the roof room.

January 9th

Our life here is one of cold grey austerity with little or no sensual pleasure, and the sun after two brief peeps at us, has disappeared again. This morning at breakfast, I had a discussion with Gerald about asceticism. It's a surprise to me to find how deeply ingrained in him it is, deriving he says from reading at school that Hannibal's army was defeated by giving way to luxury! At times I feel nipped and deadened by this bleakness; by the dust and dirt everywhere – the fluff lying inches deep all over my bedroom floor, mixed with feathers and bits of paper; by the total disregard of comfort; the cold, kept at bay with such a constant struggle; the war against the cats, messing in the passages and rooms (the passage stinks of them), licking the butter and being sick on the beds; ('they can't help it,' Gamel murmurs

---

[1] *A Life of One's Own* was published later in 1962.

fondly); by the smelly unwashed lavatory; by the unloved, uncared-for meals (baked apples twice a day every day and uneatably tough steak); by the fact that it's been impossible to get any clothes washed since I arrived except what I can do myself in my borrowed baths. Yet all this seems shamefully base ingratitude. Mary Campbell has arrived at the Cónsula and my heart leaps up at the thought of seeing her today and being warmed by her sunlike radiance.

January 19th

Gerald, Gamel and I walked to Torremolinos yesterday afternoon, Gerald springing along in front (his head set woodenly looking neither right nor left, with the expression of a bulldog on a trail, his eyes unseeing except for a sudden dart towards some wayside plant); Gamel creeping behind; I uneasily shifting from one to the other. We talked of what we thought about when alone, and whether we were most preoccupied with present, past or future. Gerald declared he 'never thought about the past'. Gamel countered quite crossly that she'd never known anyone who talked so endlessly about their schooldays and childhood. She liked thinking about her earlier life, not recent years because they were too dull – nothing had happened. She also said revealingly that when she thought of the past in terms of visual imagery *she saw herself* among the other figures.

Back to a quiet evening. Gerald and Gamel both snored in armchairs round the fire while I read about the stars. Hetty's little boy Jason is with us during her absence in Morocco and comes for reassurance, poor worried little creature, that he is really the centre of the universe.[1]

January 21st

As Gerald and I went into Málaga yesterday afternoon he monologuized all the way down the road to the bus, and continued as we wandered round the town on various errands, picking up after each stop, and going on where he had left off. It was more about Gamel than Hetty – about the strangeness of their marriage and the ways in which he found it unsatisfactory; chiefly the lack of warmth and affection. 'I must have warmth and love. I'm very good-humoured really,' he said. 'I never know whether Gamel's fond of me or not. I'm very fond of her, of course – I like her voice, her way of dressing, I like to see her about the garden and in the house, but . . .' The complaints were familiar: that she *did* nothing, boasted endlessly of having taught the servants to cook mashed potato but that was *all* she had taught them; that she didn't 'run the house' but left everything to him and Rosario; lived in the past – and not even the real past, but one she had invented – that she was so reserved that they could talk of nothing but their cats. I tried to make him agree how well she had taken Joanna and Hetty, with what restraint and dignity, and I think he realizes this, though he likes to think that he has given up all sorts of delights for Gamel's sake, such as going to Morocco with Hetty yet again. I pointed out that he'd had a wonderful time when he *did* go (I didn't add that it had nearly killed him) and that he'd had a tremendous lot of fun all round and Gamel hadn't interfered with his obsessions at all. Possibly he resents her passenger attitude to their joint life from a financial point of view – what does he get in

[1] Gerald's latest hippy girl-friend and her little boy. A number of hippies had drifted to southern Spain. Besides giving shelter to Hetty and her little boy, Gerald had rather comically adopted some of their manners and language himself.

return? Neither housekeeping, nor companionship, nor demonstrated affection. Yet he readily admits she rises to an emergency extremely well.

January 24th

Gamel remained in bed all yesterday, feverish and coughing. Conversation between Gerald and me is easier in her absence. He started talking about Carrington again, and produced three fat packets of her letters which I read far into the night and finished reading this morning. I'm glad I did: I found them enthralling and extraordinarily good as letters. I became fascinated afresh by her personality – something close to genius – which poured itself out so freely in these long, original, poetical and amusing letters that there was not much left to go into her painting, or even her conversation. And whence came the violence of her dislike of children (and marriage too) and resolution never to have any? Was that Lytton's influence? I'm sure this dread of losing Lytton was the operative factor in most of the major actions of her life – marrying Ralph, for example. Lytton wanted her to. Might she even have gone off with Gerald had it not been for him? That she was the active one in their affair was very plain. But when the chain of circumstances and human behaviour is spread out before one it is impossible to guess how important each link is in the chain, how easily things might have gone differently.

The excellence of Carrington's letters has made me rather discontented with Desmond's, and I'm growing to be doubtful whether they'll really make a book.

January 26th

Two marvellously lovely days and Carrington's letters to Gerald have swept me along, with no time (mercifully) to look right, left or in front. They have interested me enormously, perhaps especially since I got to the period when my love-affair with Ralph began. She seems to have been marvellously unresentful and unjealous, marvellously able to fall a little in love with innumerable people as well as cats, birds, and what she called 'visions' or 'images' of the outside world. And a letter I read last night gives one clue. She hated being a woman; her sexual feelings were really very unimportant. What she loved was the mingling of personalities, she loved people too for their appearance of 'literary' value, couldn't forgive them for being ugly. And she always became resentful when one of her lovers made sex of prime importance in their relation. She explains this to Gerald – in 1925 I think it was – when she felt unable to respond to him physically because he set such store by it, and said that this was what had made her relation with Mark Gertler and Ralph so difficult. 'Since Ralph had ceased treating her as a woman they'd got on much better.' This, I think, explains her lack of resentment at my carrying him off. Also this *un*womanliness explains her horror of children and maternity, and the intense pain and gloom (always referred to at length) heralding her monthly periods and accompanying them, something now thought often to be psychological.

Janetta will soon be here, but I think very little about the future, my flat, London, Burgo, for it is still an unscripted area.

January 27th

Curious effect of reading, as an appendix to the Carrington letters, some drafts of letters from Gerald to her – her own letters left me feeling her a golden character, remarkable, a near genius. From these agonized scrawls of Gerald's one detected the other side of the picture – that she would never quite let him go, yet couldn't help tormenting him. Taken any way it was a moving tragedy. Yet had they, for instance, gone off together after Watendlath,[1] what would have come of it I wonder? Very little in terms of duration, I believe. For the fact was she was most loving when the object was unattainable – Gerald when banished to Spain, and (all her life) Lytton. I felt much moved when I came to the packet marked 'Last Letters', and read two she had written after Lytton's death, and then my own telegram: 'Carrington died today. Can you come. Will meet you anywhere.'

January 28th

I thought that the Carrington letters were all read and that this chest full of the past (whose lid I had lifted, peering into what it contained) was now shut down. But last night Gerald found fourteen consecutive missing letters of hers and one of Ralph's, which, had they been discovered by a biographer writing about the Byrons or the Carlyles, would have been thought 'very important indeed'. They revealed that the crucial moment in the quadrangular situation (Gerald – Carrington – Ralph – me) was in January 1924 when I spent a week in Paris with Carrington and Ralph, who were on their way back from their second Yegen visit. Ralph's letter to Gerald mentions the possibility of 'going off with F.'

At the same time Carrington had been writing from Paris her most loving, promising, encouraging letters to Gerald, letters which might have induced him to hope for anything he wanted when he came to England later that year. 'Ralph will be happy with Frances,' she seems to say. 'Why shouldn't you and I . . .?' Then came the letter from Ralph I have just mentioned, and Carrington opened it. She told Gerald she 'read' it, and it's clear he hadn't meant her to, also the envelope has plainly been torn and clumsily stuck down. So the researcher into the past can follow that her subsequent behaviour followed directly from her having read there Ralph's suggestion that he might leave her for me. There is a *complete* withdrawal of promises to Gerald, a retraction into herself, and a pathetic panic, filling pages on end with fears lest he should write something that Ralph might resent. As Ralph said, 'No one will ever know' what part he, or Ham Spray, or Lytton took in the whole conglomerate of the life she feared to lose, but did fear desperately. Well, she did gradually, I think in the years between 1925 and 1932 when Ralph and I were living in London, realize that she *wasn't* going to be utterly bereft, and I think she gained confidence thereby. Looking back, I think the solution we found was a civilized one.

By giving me Carrington's letters to read, Gerald has done me a great service: he has made me think more freely and realistically, and this has come about by means of starting with a period which was prehistoric – before my time, and gradually developing through the drama we all shared to the more or less settled compromise life right up to Carrington's death. My historical interest in seeing things I lived through from the other side has carried me along and the result has been not only that I am the wiser about certain things in the past but a certain catharsis has spread its benign force and warmth, invading areas of more recent pain. I am again really grateful to Gerald; I don't know how much of this was deliberate, or *why*

---

[1] The hamlet near Keswick in the Lake District where Gerald and Carrington had first fallen in love.

exactly he wanted me to read the letters, but he has done me a service, yes.

February 7th: London, West Halkin Street

So here I am, have been for two nights in my so-called nest, and thank heaven it even has a slightly home-like feeling. Certainly I felt none of the repulsion for it I did before I left. I think Spain was a relief – there was company without a taxing strangeness, there was the curious catharsis from returning to the past, there was the effect simply of side-stepping out of my groove. And I suppose it should be comfort of a sort to find that it happens so, and presumably would again. I have been busy all of these two days settling myself in in various ways. I think I've engaged an admirable Scotch body as weekly help. I trust my impressions, and I swear she's what I want.

Last night Burgo came round for a drink. He was perfectly inscrutable, not unduly cast down I'd say, but I don't even know that – and I found myself wondering what on earth he feels for me. I know no one who succeeds so totally in veiling his persona from view, and heaven knows what goes on in his head. His most forthcoming remarks, which led to a 'real' discussion, were about criticism being a low form of activity, like advertising.

February 21st

I am making strenuous loops as with a giant crochet-hook to fasten myself to the outside world. One loop is a series of violin lessons with a friend of Kitty West's,[1] a Hungarian once a child prodigy and now a self-possessed and enthusiastic teacher. I'm also attacking the *technique* of being alone. I force myself to spend quiet evenings by myself, as I have just done now – working till dinnertime, then listening to the wireless and reading. My violin teacher tries to make me think of my left hand as if it were moulding a lump of clay; I feel that in a more violent and effortful way that is what I'm trying to do to my daily life. It doesn't give me satisfaction exactly, but helps me stave off pain.

March 9th

One day last week I drove to Golders Green to dine with Lionel and Margaret Penrose. Jonathan, the English chess-champion, was rather silent and morose. He's trying for his PhD with a thesis on thinking. Lionel, given the smallest opportunity, talked about chromosomes and showed them to me through a very light elegant microscope. Stained a pretty lavender-pink, there they were in double hanks tied round the waist, chromosomes from the blood or tissue of a child, before my very eyes. I could have listened to his exposition of normal and abnormal chromosomes for ever, and under his tutorship soon began to see which patterns were abnormal. He says there is no cure for Mongolism in spite of what the newspapers say.

April 16th: Stokke

Reading D. H. Lawrence's *Letters* – what a phenomenon! Before he became a puff-adder or poisonous toadstool ejecting hate, there was (at twenty-one) something quite extraordinarily mature, original and even well-meaning in him. What exactly

[1] Kato Havas.

went wrong and made him so full of venom? During the First War he seems to have been *literally* mad. His personality obsesses me – I relate it to everything I see and hear, and too many theories which seem to explain it occur to me. His Messiah-complex and fury because the world didn't respond as if he was Jesus Christ. But the sad thing is that he should have become warped and stunted (even though so productive) after such an early and dazzling maturity.

We are an all-female household here at Stokke – Mary, Magouche and Janetta with their little girls. On Sunday Mary came with me to call on the Elweses at Ham Spray – came staunchly, dressed in black leather and prepared, I could see, to support me through all sorts of reactions I didn't in fact have. Why didn't I? I've had more of a pang catching sight of the Downs and Bull's Tail[1] from afar; it's often the little unexpected thing which strikes to the heart like a fine stiletto. I was thinking mostly about the Elweses when I arrived, hoping they were happy and didn't regret, feeling responsible even for the icy weather. Did I put some pad of anaesthetic to my heart, so that I felt detachment and interest?

April 18th

To *Tristan* with Mary last night – a VAST experience, more like being subjected to a natural upheaval than a work of art; like being a rock over which break (one after another) small wave, small wave and then *huge* wave – working up to rhythmical crises. Like the copulation of elephants these crises take an eternity to come to climax. I did feel, though, 'I am enjoying this', especially in the second act; and hardly ever – but sometimes – 'Oh, we've had enough of this. Do get along to something else.' Woke in the night with a migraine and its dull echo still lingers. It's dark and gloomy and raining and I'm sunk pretty low in depression of a negative sort. I shall miss Janetta and our almost daily telephone talks, *very* much indeed.

April 26th

A lot of sense has 'happened' but I'm doubtful how much I have extracted from it. I don't give myself time, but hurry on compulsively to the next thing. I went to the Gowings for Easter and another week is almost past since then. On Easter Day there came a sudden stunning explosion into spring. I have a confused memory of two long and beautiful walks with Julia over the rolling hill-fields just bloomed to velvet with a soft green, a pale sky of misty blue above us, a little negress with woolly hair, and her black hands eagerly thrust among white violets on a bank.

I drove the Coldstreams down, Bill[2] and his pregnant Monica. She is an Irish redhead, an ex-Slade-model. Her pregnancy made her adopt an Epstein-like attitude with her head thrust forward and her hands clasped protectively over her stomach. Bill is a very charming, intelligent fellow, active-minded, articulate, curious about everything, and with strange hankerings after Establishment values. One morning at breakfast he and I argued along Eardley lines about the privacy of the famous. Bill was for preserving it. 'What business of theirs is Stanley Spencer's private life?' he asked. I said the question surprised me, from anyone so very much interested

[1] A beech hanger on the Downs.
[2] Later Sir William, head of the Slade.

in other people as he was. 'Oh of course I'm neurotic about it. I dread people invading my privacy – so much so that I never write letters for fear of committing myself.' He and Lawrence talked excitedly about art, administrative and otherwise, and Bill kept bursting into infectious giggles.

Julia has taken the physicists' universe under her wing. One must not say a word against it. It is a miracle. She found fault with Leonard for writing about the 'sinister futility' he felt it to have. 'Didn't he realize,' she declaimed, 'that all his pleasures in life, sunlight, nature and so forth depended on it being just as it was?' 'May one not criticize it *at all*?' I cried. 'Must it be perfect in every detail? It's like saying that because your life depended on your mother you mustn't say a word against her.' But Julia very quickly takes offence if one disagrees and Lawrence becomes restive. Yet truth to tell, I find something both endearing and comic in her adoption of the starry spheres, entropy, the Brownian movement, as her special protégés; and she is always ready to start a lecture on them much in the style of her aunts and reminding me somehow of a dog walking on hind legs with a lump of sugar on its nose.

April 27th

I look back on last night with unsorted feelings. The arrival of the Master[1]: at first a crossish baby expecting to find me alone and have a literary talk, but finding Jonny and Julian in occupation. I led him to my bookcase and shamelessly offered him baits to ingratiate him. He was soon on the floor, happy, with his fat legs splayed out and hair flying wildly; then his own jokes and embroidered fantasies brought twinkling geniality and he was busy signing my copy of the *Unquiet Grave*. My own tongue was tied – apart from the effort of materially seeing to my visitors' 'wants' I could *never* feel at ease with Cyril. Robin and the Godleys came; Burgo brought Henrietta Garnett and rather unexpectedly they had the demeanour of a pair of lovers. I admire his good taste. 'None of my business' is my feeling but I'm not sure if Bunny and Angelica would agree.

April 30th

Writing in the train after Crichel, Morgan lay at his manifest ease in Raymond's 'pram' letting the delicate skin of one cheek scorch to a clownlike scarlet in the sun, while his rolling head directed his kind pale eyes like the beams of a lighthouse on person after person, charged with sympathetic interest. He does make the impression of *enormous* humanity and tolerance. Eardley's new friend Mattei Radev was there, an enigmatic but handsome Bulgarian with thick cream-coloured skin and a black shock of hair over the trapezium of his forehead. Raymond was applying himself almost too assiduously to the great man's comfort, irritating Eardley, shouting (too loud for Morgan's very slight deafness) the terribly over-simplified remarks the deaf have to put up with. We were bathed in sun the whole weekend; we sat in it; I walked and picked cowslips, primroses and bluebells in it; we played croquet on a lawn of the tenderest green. On Sunday night after Morgan had left us, the other four of us went to dinner with Cecil Beaton, embowered in red plush, rose-covered chintzes and silver-framed photographs. I liked all but the last and was amused by Cecil's slow but pungent remarks. ('He's always been

[1] Cyril Connolly.

unlucky – had his lovers *shot* under him' and so on.) I gallop round like a fairly tired horse bracing myself to take jump after jump: the five-barred gate, then the water-jump: and more lie behind.

May 7th

To Charleston for the weekend. Alas, it rained and rained quietly and wettingly all Saturday and Sunday, and I was cooped up with Clive, Duncan and Barbara in a very stuffy room. Through the window the greenish veil of rain turned the garden rapidly greener and merged the drooping willow branches with the green water. Through the green gauze of this driving mist the strange female statue they have set up on the further bank of the pond leaned forward, gazing at us and looking curiously like Vanessa herself or the spectral governess in the *Turn of the Screw*.

I spent my time searching more slowly than I need have through Clive and Vanessa's boxes of letters[1] and coming away with quite a good haul – some twenty-five. Clive was wonderful at answering questions and I think enjoyed doing so. We had delightful conversation. I'm not sure if Desmond would have allowed it to be the 'good talk' he loved to record. Lindy Guinness, the twenty-year-old rich girl who is a pupil and friend of Duncan's, came to tea. She's very pretty, friendly and confident.

May 12th: Stowell[2] (The Tycoonery)

Magouche and I came down by train. Things one does with her are never dull, have lots of flavour. We talked and laughed all the way, and ran into Lord Jellicoe who was amusing and lively too. At the end they produced a Rookery Nook situation by each taking the other's identical suitcases away with them. I was looking forward to exceptional comfort and a lot of peace and quiet. 'We'll have breakfast in bed,' Magouche and I said to one another. But when we went up to bed, we were asked to come down in dressing-gowns about nine. All these servants, and an elderly lady can't breakfast in bed? I've got up and dressed – but I envy Magouche who has had the sense to lie low, breakfastless. Now I must get a walk by myself *coûte que coûte*. I shall plunge myself whenever possible in work.

Later (quarter to seven); the day so far hasn't gone badly. A picnic was forestalled by the dank uncertain weather. I went off for a walk along the canal by myself, a necessary freshener and stabilizer; we've just had another communal one in a bluebell wood. Last night we had Jeremy Fry and his wife Camilla to dinner – both had a good deal of charm. Later in the evening Philip came and sat amiably beside me on the sofa, but in answer – or rather, *not* in answer – to a question of Magouche's about new places for travel being 'opened up', he burst out that he didn't want more places opened up, the desirable thing was to close them down – make them accessible to the lucky few, and return to a civilization of 'individuals' not masses, etc., etc. I said I thought it true that at present the masses didn't much enjoy exotic places, but in time education would make them more able to. Philip: 'Education doesn't do any good, only standards handed down from parents to

---

[1] I was still editing Desmond MacCarthy's letters.
[2] House of Philip Dunn, generally known as 'The Tycoon', who had been Mary's first husband. There was a question of their re-marriage, which later took place.

children.' F.: 'That *is* education – and when the present young are educated and
have been to universities they'll be better qualified to educate their own children.'
Philip: 'There are no universities now, only technical colleges.' F.: 'Oh, come now,
there are several new ones being built – Brighton, for instance.' Philip: 'They're
not real universities: they don't *discuss* in them.'

I remained very mild during this interchange (I say this on Magouche's evidence
who was amazed that I did – for there was more that was provocative which I've
forgotten). My theory is that he deeply disapproves of both Magouche and me,
but as we've both been too polite to try and aggravate him by putting forward
views he wouldn't like, he's been reduced to attacking the views he knows we
hold. That's been quite annoying enough for him. Poor fellow, he's ghastly bored,
restless, doesn't know what to do with himself. His one idea is (like all millionaires)
to fill in his time with toys and games (cards, croquet, ping-pong) and with trying
desperately to keep his body as trim as possible. He has heated up his swimming-
pool and in spite of the cold of the day insists on swimming in it; he goes riding
every morning. And what's it all for?

June 6th

In the evening a dinner-party at Maud Russell's – Peter Quennell, the Connollys,
the Lennox Berkeleys, Boris, Patrick Kinross, the Baroness Budberg. Lennox Berkeley and I talked about abstract art. With Boris it was suicide; he wore his most
corrupt, endearing, tobacco-stained Moujik smile. 'Where is the difficulty?' he
said. 'One dies every night when one goes to sleep. It is only necessary to see one
doesn't wake up; take more pills than usual – if that doesn't work, take a few more.
But one must die quietly and pleasantly – not like the Nazis, gasping and choking
and writhing with prussic acid.' The self-consciously 'good talkers' at the table
were Peter Quennell and Cyril. Peter soon turned his back on Deirdre Connolly,
by-passed the Budberg, and shouted across to Cyril at the opposite corner of the
table. An answering sparkle and smile came back from Cyril – indeed, they talked
to each other most of the evening and the wonder is that two such egotistical
talkers will hear each other out enough to stimulate each other. Towards the end
of the evening these two literary pundits came and sat each side of me – the poor
slice of ham in their sandwich – on the sofa. The subject was literary of course
(Desmond) and I felt their benevolence flooding down on me as from twin bedside
lamps. Indeed, both were markedly genial, though for some reason I find this as
embarrassing as the opposite would be.

The suicide talk arose from something which happened in the morning.When
good Mrs Ringe let herself in at my door there was a man's voice with her. She
came to me later and told me she'd 'had to bring her husband'. He was terribly
upset because the man who lived opposite had hanged himself last night; he was
a great friend, they saw him every day, and his wife had come to them for help
when she couldn't unfasten the door. They were there when a policeman had
broken it in and told them they'd better keep away. Mrs Ringe's face as she told
me expressed all the humanity, the good taste, the kindness that's in her character.
She's a wonderful woman, and I love her dearly.

Bunny came to lunch with me the other day. From his talk he showed that he
knew there was an attachment between Burgo and Henrietta, and doesn't mind it.

In fact he seems glad, and rejoiced my heart by saying that Henrietta said 'Burgo was *the kindest man in the world*'.

June 19th

All day I had been tidying-up the Desmond position, I wrote to Michael[1] suggesting that three days' or so hard work 'on the spot' was necessary but it wasn't too late if he wanted to back out. I haven't an idea what he'll say, but I half hope he will want to drop it, for I feel discouraged about it. Meanwhile Gollancz has asked me to revise a Spanish translation – and this I've said I'll do next month, whatever Michael's answer. They have also offered me another Spanish book to translate afterwards; I'm half tempted, half afraid. My confidence is only up to my ankles – in every department, work, violin, driving my Mini. I drove it to the Tate to see the Francis Bacons this afternoon. *Well* – they are very impressive of course.

June 24th: Aldeburgh

Aldeburgh – or rather, a pleasant little inn in the village of Westleton, eight miles away. Janetta and I have been for two days engulfed in the mild salt Suffolk air; vast sky, huge elms, churches too large and fierce for their villages but softened by thatched roofs, grey sea washing in over steep shingle densely matted with purple sea-pea and yellow stone-crop, heathy commons smelling of broom and gorse. The Aldeburgh festival itself is dominated by hero-worship for 'Ben', who has only to appear waving a Prince Charming hand for the audience to be convulsed by applause. Janetta and I were to some degree in rebellion against the no-criticism decree, and perhaps went in for too much of it.

Sociological aspects of the Festival centre round the Gathorne Hardys and their Queen Bee.[2] When we went to dinner there, Janetta completely won the old lady round in the most magical way. There is a charming humanity and intelligence, and responsiveness also, coming from Lady Cranbrook's grey eyes. Bob was there rattling away like a machine-gun. I was asked several times by him or his mother, 'Have you ever seen *Tillaea muscosa*?'[3] and told the story of how it had been found close to Snape church. It became a sort of absurd refrain, and (as I remembered the same had happened on both my previous visits) I was glad to stop on the way home and find the little thing.

Night thoughts were about Art and Beauty. The second of these seemed irrelevant at the Bacons. 'How ever did we come to value Art?' I asked myself, beginning to unpick and go right back to the start, then taking up the threads again when I woke in the small hours. 'Biological bait' were the words that came into my mind, or they may have been there before, certainly the notions they represent have: that we call 'beauty' what attracts us to get our biological ends – the ripe red of a strawberry, the bloom of a young skin – but that art consists in cultivating these attractions for their own sake, just as skating may have begun as a means of crossing a river, but from the pleasure in their skill people worked out a means of artfully cutting figures on the ice. But where, in all this, does such impressive ugliness as that of the Bacons come in?

[1] Desmond's eldest son had carried off most of his father's literary and personal letters.
[2] Dorothy, Lady Cranbrook.
[3] A very small and rare wild plant.

July 26th: London

Gerald's book – the first volume of his memoirs, came out yesterday. Looking at what he says about Ralph, I *still* feel that there is a certain maliciousness in the picture. Some element of hero-worship, as he says, but more desire to make fun of him than he's aware of and I find this hard to tolerate. He emphasizes the contrast between his attitude to pacifism in the two wars, without making it clear that it's far more respectable to think fighting justifiable when you yourself are of an age to do it and change your mind later than the reverse. The Hills at dinner last night had been reading it and I felt they were pregnant with reactions. It took very little to coax out of them that they had felt exactly as I do about the portrait of Ralph, and think it gives no notion whatever of his mental calibre.

My head's in a whirl after lunching with Rupert Hart-Davis and Richard Garnett to discuss Desmond's letters. After reading his edition of Wilde's letters I greatly respect Hart-Davis' scholarship. He's also a natural all-rounder, a Bonham-Carter almost, but does he deliberately set out to charm? He opened fire on me by telling me that he'd known and been fond of Ray. 'I hold the private theory that she had been Bunny's inspiration and that he'd written nothing really good since her death.' He launched therefrom into the account of the row between them when they were publishing partners and (taking the bull by the horns) went on: 'The trouble was, of course, that it wasn't about what it was supposed to be about – which was money. He thought he was angry with me because I'd been financially a rogue, but really it was because of the unreliability of his literary judgements.'

August 12th: West Halkin Street

Cyril came to have a drink with me two nights ago, and I'm glad that I decided to take him undiluted. I grow to like tête-à-tête conversations more and more; nearly everyone is at their best when not schizophrenically divided between various listeners on whom they want to make different impressions. Guards were lowered, a sort of rapport established, and Cyril seemed at his ease with me as never before. I have always admired his intelligence and imagination and he's almost the only person to whom I would apply the word 'wit'. But this time I also liked him. There was a free and easy moment when he was seized with a cramp in his side and hurled himself back into a chair and undid his trouser buttons. Having read some letters from him to Desmond I had realized that he had, as a very young man, been in love with Racie Buxton.[1] Tentatively I remarked that I had gathered that he had been fond of Racie. '*Fond* of her? I was *madly* in love with her!' He told me he had been until then exclusively homosexual and this was a shattering and new experience. Patrick Kinross had at the same time got attached to Racie's sister Ros. Desmond had been very understanding, Rachel kind and helpful, but Molly adamantly obstructive. As a result of which Racie's parents were told that their daughters' young men were both 'upside down', or homosexual in MacCarthy language, and they were forbidden to meet. Cyril resents to this day (and I think with justification) not that they were forbidden to marry, but that the relationship was thus forcibly nipped and broken, instead of being allowed to flower and develop. So that he always felt deprived, and even though he fell in love with Jean[2]

---

[1] Horatia, niece of Molly MacCarthy.
[2] His first wife.

soon after, she felt that it was on the rebound – she was a substitute Racie.

August 21st: Alhaurin, Spain

The shock of change, and the confusion of some of the last two days has been great. On Sunday I was lunching peaceably with Isobel and sitting in her London garden listening to the Sunday English chatter over the wall. That same evening at nine-thirty I left the ground on my way to Spain, and nearly all the way, if I cared to look out from my window in the tail of the aeroplane, I saw towns and villages spangled below – sometimes in evil shapes like sinister sprawling insects. Only now, aloft in this mysterious transition, did I begin seriously to project myself into the next few weeks. Bump and swerve – poor landing – we were down, and as I walked across the field, I could see haloed against the footlights figures waving, whether at me or not I couldn't tell. Yes – there were Georgie's marvellous long brown legs in shorts, Rose, Janetta's neat head, Jaime, Joanna Carrington (just off back to England) and Gerald.

By the time we reached Janetta's house at Alhaurin it must have been 3 a.m. and all the way in the car my intoxicated nose drew in strange musky smells, maquis-like, indefinable smells of heat, while in the headlights I saw the brittle brownness of the Spanish grass. The shock of arrival was stupendous – the breathless moonlit walls, mountains still magically clear and sharp with a starry sky behind, the balmy odoriferous warmth.

Janetta and I sat by the swimming-pool talking for an hour and still I couldn't believe I was really here and hadn't the smallest desire for sleep or feeling of fatigue.

All ordinary rules of life are in abeyance here. It will be a pleasure to discover the new ones. The heat by day is intense, and the *only* way to keep cool is to get into the swimming-pool at least every hour or so. Georgie and Rose are there all the while. Last night I couldn't sleep till I had stolen out in the darkness and submerged myself in the tepid water. One is alert, rather stimulated all the time; the heat is so violent it's nearly an enemy.

I have the Southbys' very grand bedroom with a vast triple bed. Janetta prefers the book-room; there are two fine bathrooms, very civilized. This is the stage on which who knows what *dramatis personae* may shortly appear. As for me, I am relaxed and content, in the physical delight this place engenders.

August 24th

Janetta went to Torremolinos to fetch Jaime. Later we were joined by Georgia Tennant and Nicky, Julian and a friend, so the house is now quite full, but with no sense of permanency about it. I am aware that plans are being rapidly and hectically developed, but can only guess what they are.

Janetta and Jaime have vanished again, and I find myself vaguely in charge of the two boys and the four girls. We have two lovely and efficient maids but as they too have not been kept informed, Paca greeted my explanations with agitation. She couldn't understand the comings and goings, the mattresses on the floor, and there had been 'mucho trabajo' ever since the Señora had arrived. This is partly because it is their pride to rise to the level of events, and they generally do.

August 28th

Janetta returned in the evening. How lovely to hear her voice, as she sat in the darkness with Jaime outside the front door. Julian and I went to call on the Brenans and got a much happier glimpse of them; without snapping and sparring. Gerald sat like a figure carved out of polished bone or an oriental sage, letting drop his original and surprising remarks. Julian's conversation is usually very lively and varied, and he's exceptionally responsive to whoever he's talking to. I must say that during the three and a bit days of Janetta's absence there had been great solidarity and co-operation in the captainless ship, Julian in particular always ready to inject his own high spirits into anybody who happened to be depressed. With Janetta's return he suddenly went to pieces. Perhaps he had felt wounded by her going as soon as he arrived and before he could get whatever he had on his chest off it. Did I write 'high spirits'? He began to give her a long account of what we had done in their absence, and burst into tears when he thought she wasn't listening. 'I was obviously boring you!' he wailed.

August 30th

5.30. I was about to have a bathe before going to lunch at the Cónsula when I was bitten by a scorpion. My bathing-suit, hung from the window to dry, had fallen on the terrace, and I picked it up and prepared to put it on. A stab of fiery pain pierced my little finger, and as I dropped my bathing-suit on the floor a horrible pinkish creature like a gamba ran out. The pain quickly burned up my arm to my armpit. What had I heard of scorpion-bites? You lose a limb? Die? Go mad? In a rather shaky voice I called to Janetta, who quickly and kindly came to my assistance. The maids, consulted, said it was best to go to the doctor for an injection, so off we went, with my finger in a tumbler of Dettol. By now I was aware I wasn't going to die at once, but the pain was bad. The doctor was fetched, and with a large crowd looking in at the windows he gave me two injections – one for the pain and another in the vein for antitoxin. I have lain on my bed and the pain has steadily diminished till it now hardly bothers me; the good doctor returned on his motor-bike and pronounced me well.

August 31st

I have had a sad letter from Gerald, who had himself weighed and found he had lost a stone since April; from this his mind was drawn irresistibly to the notions of cancer and death. Of Gamel he wrote: 'Her malady is in the mind, she disagrees with everything I say. She doesn't realize that if she had had a little more honesty with herself and with life and didn't shut herself up with her illusions she might have made more use of her talent. If I have, as I naturally suspect, a fatal disease, what I regret is that I shall not be able to look after her and Hetty.' I must try and get some conversation with him alone, but the dreaded Hetty is – alas – there now.

September 6th: Alcudia[1]

The beauty of this place and the fact that it has one of the best views I ever saw came as a surprise. A long low solid two-storey farmhouse, five minutes above the sea over which it gazes from a vast terrace – a farmlike terrace, uneven and

---

[1] Philip Dunn's house in Mallorca.

patterned with pebbles in the shape of a star; in the centre a solid prehistoric-looking stone table. Philip has made a rush roof in one corner to give shade, and there we eat. The main sitting-room also has a farmhouse character – very tall with stairs going up in the middle and painted white and royal blue. There are lots of trees, algarrobas, figs, olives, and across a narrow channel lies an island with a lighthouse. Beyond the bay the ever-changing mountains turn from bleakest grey rock to velvet. Mary met me at the airport, beaming and welcoming, accompanied by Philip's comical queer majordomo – an Englishman known as Don Carlos. She and I were alone that night, dining deliciously under the rush roof. The Tycoon arrived later with his German girlfriend Hildegarde; he says she bores him stiff, but she seems now to have him more securely hooked, and as marriage to a millionaire is what she wants she may well get it.

It's nearly as hot as Málaga – too hot to sleep. Otherwise I'm happier than I expected – because of the beauty and Philip's unusual geniality. We have quantities of slaves; everything is always being tidied, and water sprinkled on the terrace to cool us. We are pampered poodles who can't possibly do a thing for ourselves, but must have any toy we want brought to us instantly. Our first day passed quietly; at night Henry and Virginia Bath arrived, with their fairylike little girl Sylvy and Derek Jackson. Yesterday we took the motor launch, loaded up with drinks and books and sun-oil, to a little bay where we bathed in crystal clear water, varying in colour from pale aquamarine to ink. The Baths seem to be a charming and united little family. Virginia is like her daughter Georgia, but where Georgia is alert, critical and ironical, Virginia is soft and yielding. Henry can be very funny in his own curious style. That mysterious fluid which after a while flows like water between any group of people has begun to circulate. I'll not be able to see it all in perspective until I'm back on my own territory. But I know I shan't forget the beauty here.

September 13th

At lunch Philip violently attacked those intellectuals who showed how 'yellow' they were by leaving the country when war began. Derek is allowed to have his special knowledge, the arts are given their proper place, otherwise it's down with the intellectuals and up with the millionaires. Everyone is drinking more now, and Derek also had one of his epileptic outbursts about the War having been caused by the Labour Party wanting to get 'our' money away from us. The next moment he will be saying he prefers Khrushchev to Kennedy and that he's practically a socialist.

I almost think it is my unvoiced protest against the values all round me that is keeping me awake at night. Virginia was inspired to say that she hated the way everyone was 'sniggering at things which are terribly sad and important', and I felt she was an ally. Yet it is so useless to argue that I don't begin.

September 11th

I was called to act as interpreter between Philip and a local carpenter-house-agent this morning from which it seemed that for more money, at a price, he is willing to sell a large part of his land for exploitation, or even – at a price again – the whole place. Much good millions do anybody! The Mallorcan suggested that he should even take over the dear little lighthouse island which lies in the centre of the marvellous view and build a bar, with dancing, '*de lujo muy caro*'. 'You're not meaning to sell this lovely place?' I asked, when the man had left. 'Well, if I'm offered enough money I MUST,' was his reply, encapsulating the philosophy of the rich.

Now I'm gloriously *alone*. All the others have gone off to Formentor in the boat to lunch with other millionaires – Whitney Straights. I'm thankful to have been allowed to stay at home.

September 19th: Lambourn

Back, morally shaken, though feeling physically strong and well. Yesterday I drove Julia down to Lambourn. The landscape inside my head is as glum and grey as what I see outside the window, or penetrated on a short icy cold walk up the road, round, back, trying unavailingly to alter my mood. I'm anxious not to disturb Julia's 'working' day, but she worries about me and I'm afraid may have realized my deep despondency. How can anyone who hasn't experienced it imagine this state of gritting one's teeth, and *enduring*, day after day, week after week? It is delightful being here though sadder than when Lawrence's optimism pervades the house. Julia talked to me about her work and I find it as usual fascinating, but she seems to be entangled in a cat's-cradle of her own fantasies.

September 21st: West Halkin Street

The quiet, rather sad little interim at Julia's has resigned me to London. I've seen quite a lot of people in these two days, and the spectre of solitude doesn't stalk so grim.

A letter from Hart-Davis was waiting for me saying he does not think Desmond's letters good enough to publish: 'A charming person with very little to say and no great gift for letter-writing. Of course, if all his love-letters had not been destroyed the general picture might be very different.' At the same time Michael writes airily saying he has found a 'host' more letters he 'wouldn't like to tell me where'. My chief feeling is one of relief, and that it serves Michael right for trying to suppress what human interest there was. I have two jobs ahead – a Freudian index and a Spanish translation and to these I propose to devote myself.

Last night, at Janetta's. I'd rather hoped to see her alone but we had Magouche and Julian, Robert and Cynthia, Johnny Craxton in afterwards or before. A very great deal was drunk. Janetta's room was embowered in flowers: huge white lilies, freesias, gentians and small pink cyclamens. Robert gave amusing imitations of his new Independent Television venture, and when I asked him how it felt cutting his navel-string to the BBC, he replied, '*Bad*. Bleeding all over the place.'

September 24th

I think I've reached a new stage; or perhaps only realized that I ought now to embark on a new stage: and that is to lie *in* my solitary London environment, to allow myself to draw a deep breath *here* in West Halkin Street, to let my foot down through the water till it rests flat, to face what my life is, and try to lead it. For with all my pride in accepting the reality-principle I have not done that hitherto. I have restlessly, feverishly, exhaustedly done anything that offered, snatched up any temporary solace which would get through an hour and prevent my thinking. Why has it taken me so long to realize it?

October 7th

Weekending at the Hendersons' cottage at Coombe. A wonderful gentle sunny autumn day – two, in fact. The intense pleasure I get from all my eye lights on here may be connected with the feeling that here is the country I love and belong to. The subtle curve of the valley between the downs reminds me of the one on the way to Lower Green that Ralph so loved and often commented on; the softly parting marbled roof of clouds, infinite quiet, smell of sweet decay, rusty berries in the hedges. I feel at home and at ease with Nicko and Mary.

Lying in bed, my breakfast eaten, I dreamily look at my own mental processes in aquatic terms: starting from the surface where a sheet of un-coordinated sensations lie like duckweed, one can penetrate into the depths among partly congealed ideas connected into little groups like frog spawn. Deeper still are the fundamental assumptions about values, which have sunk by sheer weight and settled on the submerged floor, sending up a stream of bubbles from to time. I've thought a lot about individual values and how much they differ. I particularly like Bertrand Russell's 'All my life I've been convinced of the value of two things – kindness and clear thinking', to which I would add love, friendship, desire for knowledge (or curiosity, which is the same thing), peace, natural and man-made beauty, and probably many others.

While here at Coombe I've enjoyed talking to people who know a lot about public affairs and are deeply interested in them, such as Nicko and two other diplomats, Michael Stewart and a distinguished-looking silver-haired Frenchman called Walper. It's hard for me to keep even dimly afloat without Ralph's tuition, and I'm ashamed of my fearful blanks. The division between the arts and public affairs seems to be growing wider, and there are art-lovers who are proud of knowing and caring nothing about politics.

October 12th

I'm reading a serious historical account of 1914. It occurs to me that the ghastly waste of human courage and expense of spirit in shell-holes and mud of that time is comparable to the dreary plod of friends through their present woes, ending in the final awful stretch that so many (poor Clive, perhaps) are embarking on, and I soon shall, perhaps very soon. Two letters from Julia crashed into my consciousness this morning. She asked me to come to dinner next Monday, and thank heaven I threw up my extra night at Crichel and said I would. What has happened is perhaps worse than Julia realizes, and I can't forgive myself for critical thoughts of her. After ten years of what seemed such a happy if unusual marriage (Lawrence eighteen years her junior) which everyone has pointed to as proof that *anything* can work wonderfully well, Lawrence has burst out to Julia with the emotional admission that he has suddenly fallen in love with a girl, teacher at his school, and she with him. His proposition is that they should have a *ménage à trois* – a shattering blow and shock for poor Julia. She wrote two letters, one in utter desolation, the second pulling herself heroically together and saying that what makes Lawrence happy will make her also. She has met and likes the girl.

October 24th

I've just been rung up by Burgo and went over to see him and Henrietta. What delight to see him so happy with that lovely girl and she with him; it's the best thing that ever happened to him. They've been quite alone at Bunny's cottage in Swaledale for three weeks and are as much in love as ever. More, I'd say.

October 28th: in bed at the Cecils' at Oxford

Shades of 1939 loom at times – in various ways – very large. At my orchestra on Wednesday I saw Margaret Penrose and when I crossed over to talk to her about the Cuban Crisis her intelligent round eyes grew rounder still and full of dismay. She told me Shirley[1] and all her schoolfriends were in every state from hysteria to angry tears. I thought of poor Henrietta's face yesterday and the look of real anguish that crossed it and the tears that welled into her eyes as she spoke about the stupidity of it all. I can't forget the difference between the attitudes of the young to their unique and precious lives and ours to our old done-for, worn-out ones. What's more, I feel it's to their credit they mind so much and that there's something wrong with the young who don't. They lack feeling, thoughtfulness, imagination.

The *only* good that could come out of this situation is for it never to happen again. The last thing we should say is, 'If they could, so can we.' In that case it really was totally useless. Over and over in my head I recapitulate: one OUGHT TO MIND. OUGHT TO BE AFRAID. To be indifferent to nuclear war is nothing at all to be proud of – it is like standing unmoved in front of Goya's *Dos de Mayo*.

I met Auden for the first time at Janetta's on Friday. A delightful man, half shapeless schoolboy, half genial tortoise. He thinks Kennedy was perfectly right and when I said, 'Then shouldn't he have gone to the UN?' he said, 'Oh no, there was no time' – the invariable argument for making war without notice.

My fellow-guest here is called Julian Fane – author of a good little book called *Morning*. I drove him down and back in Mini, started with a very good impression of him (sensitive, intelligent, enquiring, gentle) and still hold this, yet am aware too of a conformist nature matching a tall, fine-boned, delicate-looking appearance and clothes that spoke a language of caution. David said enthusiastically, 'You're the best-dressed man I know!' from within his own dashing, spivvish clothes to this safely-dressed friend in a dark blue mac, narrow tie and black shoes. This, the language clothes speak, is what always interests me about them rather than whether they are fashionable or not.

Walking round the beautiful and extraordinarily unchanged colleges, their old grey bones draped in yellow leaves, Fane talked of Somerset Maugham, saying suddenly: 'He's an atheist and doesn't believe in a future life. Have you ever noticed how disagreeable such people are?' Obviously I didn't say I was both.

November 1st

On Monday morning the Crisis abated, with the news that Russia was prepared to withdraw the Cuban bases. Straight from the unconscious rises my death-wish, left without immediate hope of fulfilment. I see that I'm really disappointed at *not* being atomized although deeply relieved that Burgo, Henrietta, Shirley Penrose,

[1] Her daughter.

Georgie and Rose are not. No need for logic in the Id – the most inconsistent bedfellows in the way of emotion can be found tucked in side by side.

A sharp rise of spirits last night came when Boris put in my mosaic fireplace – a glorious blazing fire and cat, so gay, so comforting, providing as it does just the elements that my flat needed that I laughed aloud and alone when I looked at it, and got so over-excited that I went to my orchestra a whole hour early.

November 6th

I spent yesterday morning in close company sitting cheek-by-jowl with a young, wholesome and pretty Oxford graduate (female) going over the proof of my last Spanish translation.

In the course of this long gruelling morning's work a shattering telephone call came through from Little Barbara saying that Clive's operation this morning had been 'frightful'. It was cancer and they had removed a great deal, including bone, and he was still unconscious. And poor old Saxon died yesterday – that at least is nothing but a mercy. The release of the sick and old is a thing one must welcome and if poor Clive is to have no more tenable life than seems likely, I wish it for him too. They way out! Oh, where is it, for the old and decrepit? Could hardly face my evening's dinner-party (Eddy Sackville and the Godleys with Dicky in afterwards) but somehow screwed myself up to it. Though it was rather as if I too were some ancient matador putting on his 'suit of lights' and creeping to meet the bull. Well, I've asked Barbara to lunch today. I'm struck by the difference between having to go through one's own hour of doom and feeling pain on behalf of others. The force of the first calls on all one's powers of resistance, whereas the second produces no outlet but quavering unhappiness.

November 7th

I've just been to see Clive and read *The Times* to him for nearly an hour. His courage and self-control and on-the-spotness, in spite of a tube in his nose and another in his arm were beyond everything, and I suppose surprised me only because he is an anxious character by nature, inclined to fuss about unnecessary details beforehand – but this, as I should have realized, is very common in intelligent and sensitive people. Slightly tense and apprehensive when I arrived, I felt only waves of affection and admiration for dear Clive, as soon as I was in his presence. His consideration and tact is wonderful and he made perfectly acute comments on everything I read him.

I seem to be having a sort of cocktail party next Tuesday, which I rather dread, but it's my way of paying Boris for his glorious mosaic, and like everything else it will come and go.

November 14th

I spent the afternoon of my cocktail party in perfect calm, partly organizing it, partly typing a Freudian index. I felt not the smallest anxiety about it; it went roaring along, and indeed I quite enjoyed it. And here I sit next day, feeling full of energy, and really quite puffed-up because of having got through my party 'on my head' as it seems to me. Cooking dinner for four is far more of a business. Burgo and Henrietta's mutual devotion gave me intensest pleasure. Janetta sweetly asked Boris and me back to dinner, along with Magouche, Paddy and Joan, Eddie

Gathorne-Hardy. When they all charged off to yet another party at the Harrods' at midnight, I marvelled, and felt thankful I had no temptation to go. At my party everyone behaved in character: Raymond talked to me seriously about the mosaic, said he adored it – as I believe he did – but wanted me to alter the surrounding colours and the rug in front. Rosamond murmured: 'Oh – darling! What a lovely party! How brave of you and how clever!' Julia spent hours in front of my looking-glass like a deb at a ball and then delighted everyone with her conversation. Julian was most kind and helpful with pouring drinks. And so on.

November 19th

What remains in my mind most vividly from the rich stew of last weekend at Stokke is the journey back by train with Eduardo Paolozzi sitting opposite, and the glare of a bright wintry sun shining in our eyes and lying on the surrounding fields like lacquer. My first response to him when he stumped into the living-room with his impassive face and slow husky 'Hullos' all round, was a sort of amazement. Surely no one of intelligence could have such a *changeless* expression? And at dinner that night I was cross because he accused Raymond of being 'bitchy' as a critic – the evidence being that he didn't like Peggy Ashcroft in *The Cherry Orchard*. But he's very thoughtful in his deliberate way, and our long talk in the train was interesting – largely given over to his account of what 'occupied his mind at the moment', how he liked to run his life, his attitude to wife and children, and getting away from them, and work.

December 5th

The thing I must write about and which has loomed far biggest for nearly a week in my mind, to be thought about lovingly and anxiously at all hours of the day, is that Burgo came to tell me last Friday that he was going to marry Henrietta. I felt instant joy. But the possibility of such happiness for him of course makes me tremble for him. Henrietta isn't quite eighteen, and I know I shan't be able to help looking nervously after their little boat as it pushes out to sea, but in any case this is something entirely good and *plus* for Burgo. The wedding is to be just before Christmas – and I shall come up from Julia's for it.[1] I now have a stake in the world, and the only steadying thing I felt before was that I hadn't. Perhaps I might be some use to them both, and that is a troubling and moving thought.

I have been reading through some of my old diaries and am staggered by the screams of pain that come from the pages, because I feel and know – surely I can't be wrong? – that I have had an extraordinarily happy life for the most part. Is it just that unhappiness needs to find an outlet whereas happiness enfolds one like a warm rug into silence?

December 7th

The fog closed down more densely than ever last night into a thick, almost black mud-pack pressing in on us. Through it Burgo and Henrietta and the Kees came to dinner. The happiness of the two young delighted me. I feel as if an exotic flower, an orchid perhaps, had suddenly bloomed in the London fog and I shake with terror at what might happen to it. But it is a happy agitation.

[1] I had promised to stay with her at Lambourn while Lawrence and Jenny were together.

Yesterday I lunched with Eardley (we have met each foggy day like explorers in the desert). Conversation about violence; it aroused my amazement that everyone shouldn't view it with the horror I feel for it. It started from the fact that Joan had been unable to stand the film of *Billy Budd*, and had to come out, and I attacked the story for violence, sentimentality and priggishness mixed. To my amazement Eardley asked on what grounds 'one could justify being against violence'. I replied with what seemed to me at the time a conclusive argument – that violence is nearly always at the expense of other people's happiness and that the appetite grows on what it feeds on. To enjoy looking at violent films and plays or promote them was to manure a plant that was bound to bear sinister fruit. But how, how can it be necesary to say anything so obvious.

December 19th

Like a piece of meat soaking in a marinade, I have for three days been lying soaking in Julia's country peace, leaving far behind the gas-ring of London life on which I have been a simmering bubbling pot. What a difference! So far the change has been purely restorative and I feel myself developing into a cow from chewing the quiet cud of this luscious pasture. It is, I realize, my first longish spell of country life since I left Ham Spray and everything is, I believe, going very well. At any rate I'm getting great enjoyment from Julia's company; she has arranged the house so that almost nothing has to be done in the way of cooking and shopping, and helping to do that little gives me a modicum of self-respect. We are looked after by dear little Mrs Rose, piping like a blackbird in the kitchen (what the Gowings call her 'tuneless whistle' but it has a charming flutelike quality), and the evening meal is usually all got ready in advance and therefore tends to be warmed-up meat, say, with warmed-up brussels sprouts and warmed-up mashed potatoes, followed by warmed-up mince pies! It suits me fine, though I'm not sure how Julia fits it into her own food faddism. We both do long hours of work (though my progress with my Spanish translation is shockingly slow) and take many brisk walks on brilliant cold mornings with blue sky, perhaps a wind and the sensational English winter gloss on leaves, red berries and twigs. Mrs Rose is to be told over Christmas that Lawrence's old aunt is desperately ill and that's why he's not coming down. She has, in fact, just most conveniently died.

The Charley's Aunt element which has always beset the Gowings' lives is here, mercifully relieving gloom. It is even more present in Julia's new 'Goblin Tea-Made', which might be something out of one of her stories. She staggered to my flat last week with three large parcels done up in Christmas wrappings, and I brought them down in my Mini. When undone they revealed a device combining alarm-clock with a kettle and hideous square teapot with the spout at one corner. Julia spent hours putting it together and brooding over the instructions anxiously and lovingly: ' "Depress platform". Now, what on earth can that mean? Oh I suppose this is it, but it seems to be permanently depressed on one side already. I can see it's going to be me that's depressed, not the platform.' We then went round to someone in the village called Maureen who had a similar machine, for enlightenment. Julia plans to be woken at six-thirty or so and do several hours' 'work' before breakfast. 'But the worst of it is, I simply *hate* tea,' she ended up surprisingly (after saying it had 'cost the earth'), 'so I plan to put Nescafé in instead.' The machine has worked and so far she is delighted with it. What goes on in her working hours, either here in her bedroom or in the London Library, is a mystery. Quite a lot of it is reading books of popular science, highbrow weeklies or articles on electronic music, from which she makes notes and derives stimulation.

December 20th

There is only one danger I have to keep a wary eye open for in conversation with Julia, and that is to avoid anything like a rational argument.This sounds more cramping than it is: there's a whole world of fascinating talk left, exploring our way through regions of cobweblike delicacy concerned with human behaviour, books, aesthetics and lots of other things. I've long known that if some matter of general principle arises about which she feels deeply but has not the equipment to argue logically, and if I get into my arguing boots (which boots I see to *her* seem more aggressive and combative than they feel to me, their wearer – who loves arguing more than almost anything) a sharp note of fear comes into her voice and she begs for the subject to be changed.

December 21st

It's probably impossible in this life of seclusion with two prime egotists sitting in the middle of a carefully-constructed nest, for tiny incidents not to bulk large. Amused as I am by them, I become irritated at times as a result of Julia's obsessional pernicketyness. Everything must be done just so and not another way, no room for improvisation – the opposite (directly) of Janetta, say. Yet though I'm sure Julia is convinced her methods are the best, just look at the difference in the meals which result! I do hope I shan't be offered 'warmed-up Spam' again. I can hardly swallow it, and was staggered when offered some in my sandwich lunch for today: 'A Spam sandwich might be rather nice?' Might it, indeed! The exact ritual also has to be preserved concerning the coffee-pot, the stove, the amount of air let into rooms, the turning-off of electricity. The water in the coffee-pot must go to within half an inch of the top *exactly*! The coffee must be ground 105 revolutions *exactly*! When I started to pour myself some coffee before it had all dripped through, Julia rushed in to say I mustn't do it because it would alter the *exact* proportions she had arranged. But this morning came an Aunty-Loo[1]-like cry from the ash-bucket outside the garden door: 'AH! now I'm afraid it's not a very good idea to put paper in the bucket – only ashes – in case it catches alight.' ... Needless to say, I hadn't been near the bucket; these were the residues left by the 'men' who had been putting anti-burglar screws on the windows. This house is full of precautions against every contingency. Having said all the above, I really must add that stifled but hilarious amusement makes up for the bulk of my response to it, and irritation is a minute seed and has all been exorcized by setting it down.

December 23rd

Burgo is a married man. Everything about the wedding was to me deeply touching and charming and it has left me in a state close to anguish. I hadn't expected that I would hardly get to sleep last night for the passionate longing I felt for Burgo and Henrietta's happiness. Burgo's confidence and assurance over the wedding arrangements amazed me. Everything was splendidly organized and they had done

---

[1] Alys Russell, first wife of Bertrand Russell, brought Julia up.

it all themselves – lobster mayonnaise, and fruit flan made by Henrietta herself as she hung her head bluebell-wise with modesty to admit. I think they both enjoyed the whole thing to the full and so did we all – Bunny, Duncan, Angelica, Amaryllis and David Gillies, the best man.

Notes on the wedding: the absolute charm of Duncan, arriving with a button-hole in a white paper bag, beaming at everyone. The geniality of Bunny, who suddenly began talking about the necessity of leaving one's body to the doctors with a look of great jollity on his face (more suitable to the occasion than the subject). His father's mistress, old Nellie someone-or-other, has just died and when Bunny went to arrange the funeral he found to his relief that the body-snatchers had already been, and all trouble and expense were spared him. 'You just ring up the Ministry of Offal, Sackville Street,' is what I remember him saying but I suppose he can't have.

December 26th

I am living in a dungeon whose walls are made out of the intense cold, within which Julia's and my dark and secluded existence is enclosed. Here I sit all day in this dark sunless house – the room in which I spend my day is like a Spanish 'interior' room looking on to the frozen courtyard where sparrows and starlings noisily quarrel over scraps of bread. I feel as if Julia and I were serving a prison sentence. For what crime? Or to what end? She, I suppose, gets the satisfaction of believing she's toiling towards an artistic achievement, but I can't feel anything like that about my translation – merely that it's an activity I enjoy, and which will bring me in some money – for what? To *live*. In brief, I hardly feel human here, though I greatly enjoy Julia's company, and am like a schoolchild counting the days to my return to West Halkin Street.

December 27th

Claustrophobic, soft and white, the snow is falling steadily, and lies already inches deep in the garden where the birds quarrel noisily over their crusts. Julia and I have been out for a walk along the slippery road, dressed more or less like scare-crows, Julia holding an umbrella only part of which would go up, and wearing an immense mac over quantities of jerseys and coats. Twice she fell suddenly full length, noiselessly into the snow. Cars slither and slide around corners, stable-boys go by on spindly bow-legs or greet one from bicycles. Last night we had a delightful visit from Janetta and Jaime. What excuse for Lawrence's absence did Julia give to Janetta? She certainly told the Carringtons that Lawrence's Aunt Edith was gravely ill. But some people have been told he's abroad on Gulbenkian business. Some, I fancy, have had a story combining both elements and, between the two, poor Julia is completely bewildered. I heard her muttering to herself: 'That's it, I think Aunt Edith had better die today.'

December 28th

The pall of snow still shrouds us, so the prison sentence goes on, and contacts with the outside world have been barred by the snow. A very slight thaw but the snow is still thick, and walking up the road towards the Carringtons I was dazzled by the virginal beauty of the Pollock theatre[1] trees, smooth fields, and in back gardens the lovely sight of wheels, tubs and farm tools each with its thick white coat. The sky had turned a pale apricot and the furthest slope of the hill was an iced wedding-cake faintly blushed with palest rose against the baby-blue sky.

I've thought a lot lately, with more detachment and even pleasure than I've been able to before, about my life with Ralph. It would be terrible if, in the process of growing scar tissue, I should lose the completely focused sharpness of remembering the details of our happiness together, of our tremendous jokes and laughter and of the life-bringing current of his love.

December 29th

C'est le dernier pas qui coûte. Some cross remark shouted up at me by Julia about the sitting-room cosy stove suddenly let loose all my indignation at being spoken to twenty times a day as if I were a half-witted kitchen-maid whom she was hoping to train but despairing of, instead of an elderly highbrow. I lay therefore in bed, fulminating against this pressure of her bourgeois, cautious life-style and every fibre in me that believes in spontaneity and freedom and bohemian improvisation was in revolt. The irony of it is that she is the only one who has seriously mismanaged the stove and jolly nearly burnt the whole thing out one night.

Oh, well, there's nothing to be done but stick it out somehow. I toyed with ideas of saying I couldn't bear it and must go back to London, but it would be too cruel, situated as she is. To add to the general horror, yesterday a bitter wind arose and howled round the house and much more snow has fallen and looks like falling. The Kees were due to come to dinner tonight but it will obviously be impossible, and I would have welcomed a diversion.

---

[1] A toy theatre of traditional design.

1963

January 1st: Lambourn

But how is it possible to believe that we have crossed into a new year when the same deep eiderdown of whiteness lies feet deep over everything and more, *more* snow is falling from the sky. I lay awake last night listening to the Lambourn church bells dismally tolling for a full hour the death and birth of the years. Afterwards the blessed silence was broken by the wild yells of Lambourn stable-lads.

January 2nd

Telephone call from the Carringtons, who are worried about Joanna, snowed up at Buttermere. Julia was struck because they said, 'We thought you'd like to know we were all right.' 'I see we ought to have been *worrying* about them!' Julia said to me in surprise and this led to a lunch conversation wherein I'm afraid I trod badly on her spiritual corns. I said something about the importance of friends being brought home to one by the snow, and that it was odd to find ourselves so nipped by the fight against the cold that we almost lost the desire for communication with them. Then Julia said that she 'hadn't time for friends in her life' and I (voicing a long buried secretion of irritation) replied that if I didn't value friendships I should shoot myself. Julia turned rather pink and declared that a creative writer with no servant had no time for anything else. I said that it seemed to me she *had* a splendid servant and also that I thought most creative artists and writers did have something to spare for friendship. The highest names were used as examples – Henry James, Flaubert, Turgenev, Charlie Chaplin – but oh! what a mistake it all was, and I was much to blame for driving her thus into a corner with some of her own assumptions, which are pretty neurotic. The fire catches the wisps of dry hay before one can stop it. Afterwards Julia generously came and apologized for 'having lost her wool', saying that she could only put it down to 'having some of Oliver and Marjorie's genes in her'.[1] After this all was smooth and serene.

January 3rd

Yesterday's snow seemed to amplify the sounds of the squabbling birds, of the cold winds rattling the frozen bushes, of Julia clearing her throat upstairs, and Mrs Rose's 'tuneless whistle' in the kitchen. Meanwhile the approach of a new blizzard was reported at intervals all day in sinister tones by BBC announcers. At lunch yesterday Julia suddenly suggested that we should cut and run before it struck; and as soon as lunch was over I went to make enquiries of the garage about the

---

[1] Julia's father and aunt.

state of the Newbury road (thirteen miles), the running of buses and possibility of hiring a car. 'You'd be safest in a bus *if* you can get one,' was the reply. 'Otherwise we never know, and with this blizzard we can't never know if the men'll get through with them.' So, crestfallen, I reported all this to Julia, who is panicky beyond anyone I've ever met.

January 6th: West Halkin Street

We're out. I got to London yesterday and am on the whole immensely glad to be here.

The 'great blizzard' turned out rather a flop, though it did lay down another three inches of snow and some drifts. Then, two days ago, a slight thaw began and sun came out, and hearing that people were 'getting through' to Newbury I began to hanker to go in my Mini if it were humanly possible, and to say to myself: 'If other people can get through, why shouldn't I?' So I took a spade and hacked out a path through the somewhat softened three-foot-deep drift outside the garage door, behind which Mini had been so long imprisoned, having done which I felt triumphant and a great load of claustrophobia lifted. I asked Julia if she wouldn't come with me. After only a moment's pause she said she would be so nervous that perhaps it was better to go by jeep from the garage, and train. From this decision flowed calm and amiability, though there wasn't a moment from then till midnight when she wasn't making preparations for every emergency in minutest detail. She says she's always done this, even when young.

I really enjoyed the freedom and adventure for Mini and me in getting out. The road to Newbury was slushy and narrow between high banks of beaten snow: after that it was plain sailing, and I got to Halkin Street (with what a sensation of escape!) just in time to buy whiskey and bacon before the shops shut.

January 21st

Eardley, the Cochemés and the Penroses all dined here last night and we had (I thought) a delightful evening with interesting and lively talk, ranging part of the time into scientific territory – sympathetic ground for both Cochemé and Lionel; and Lionel in his diffident offhand way delighted us all by describing experiments now being made to enclose a fertilized human ovum in a rabbit's uterus – 'or perhaps a cow's', he added – 'to produce two tiny people'. There was talk also of giants. He told us about a woman he'd been to see in Ireland who had given birth to five children each weighting from thirteen to fifteen pounds at birth, and finally one of eighteen pounds. At three they were like children of ten. When adult they were of normal size and splendid healthy specimens. Eardley told the extraordinary story of the canaries which apparently sing elaborate tunes dating from the eighteenth century, and having been handed down from canary to canary.

February 9th

I think a lot about marriage, and the astonishing effect of clamping together two personalities, who however deeply loving and mutually appreciative, have each a separate core – not perhaps incommunicable but almost unalterable. Ralph was a very strong character and the disappearance of that constant source of interest, vitality, amusement and sometimes irritation has left me a thin grey husk. I particularly miss the rogue elephant side of his character which gave me so much delight and made me laugh so often.

February 24th

A visit from Julia yesterday, wrapped to the eyes in furs, scarves and flannel petticoats. Returning Gerald's last book which I had lent her, she launched an attack on Gerald and Ralph (I think now it was chiefly Ralph she was aiming at): 'I was deeply shocked to find they actually *enjoyed* the War.' I was amazed by the naïveté of her thinking that young men of nineteen could have been pacifists while they were actually engaged in a war. For she looked back with the innocence of her curiously unfurnished sixty-year-old mind at this other world of young tough men, and (as usual) judged. She also talked a lot about her own neurotic character, and said several times, 'I can't live alone.' What is my responsibility towards her, as her oldest friend? I am selfishly wondering, and so far my answer is: I'll do everything I possibly can, short of giving up my independent solitary life. She asked me about myself and how I found living alone and I was able to answer quite truthfully that I found it the only possible alternative to living with Ralph.

A delightful evening, going with Desmond, Eardley and Pansy Lamb (after dining here) to a concert at the Italian Institute in Belgrave Square, given by some madrigal singers. We were in the front row looking at these six intensely Italian figures sitting round a dining-room table. At one end the chief soprano sat with her vast plump bosom and arms rising from her evening dress, rolling her beautifully socketed Italianate eyes with an infinitely comic, charming and coy expression towards the plump baritone at the other end, who with curvilinear gestures of hands covered in gold rings and gold bracelets was conducting the proceedings. An oval-faced counter-tenor looking like the young Marcel Proust delighted us all with the way he threw up his head and contributed his *miaow miaow*'s to that famous chorus, and the bass was a handsome Roman-looking brunetto with sculptured hair. The music was lovely, and gay too except for the heavenly but sad Monteverdi *Lasciate mi morire*. It made me 'climb up two rungs of the ladder' of well-being. The whole atmosphere of the concert, including the Italian faces amongst the audience has switched my mind towards the beckoning charms of Italy.

March 1st

Musically speaking, I have been hovering between two stools. Vaguely discontented with my Hampstead orchestra, I eagerly hurried off yesterday to try another, a Medical one heard of from the Penroses. The first two sessions were alarming, a *much* higher standard, a conductor with a difficult beat, a programme they had already been practising for some weeks. Then, at the third go last night, the authentic magic caught on. What had seemed almost out of reach was suddenly attainable with an effort, and the excitement of becoming integrated into this huge mass of combined sound set a match to the sticks that had been waiting unlit, or at most giving out a little greasy smoke. It is a much bigger, more professional affair, very much alive, and composed of intelligent interesting faces, old and young, white and black, including a lot of German and Austrian Jews. Our concert has Hephzibah Menuhin for a soloist. The excitement, the lift and intoxication with which I flew home down the Edgware Road last night has proved to me this is what I want, and though it's difficult for me, I now *think* (with hard work) I can perhaps make the grade.

Ever since Burgo's wedding, Bunny's remark about the convenience and simplicity of leaving one's body to a hospital has been rumbling in my mind and finally I took action on it. Two days ago I found myself staring in bewilderment at an envelope with 'INSPECTOR OF ANATOMY' written on it in large black letters. I thought for a moment I'd gone mad. But no, this is the gentleman who arranges for the hospitals' corpse-supply. I must admit it gave me a slight *frisson* as I saw myself laid out cold and stiff and pale, or kept on ice for two years, which seems possible. I shoved it away with a little burst of escapism. Then yesterday, 'This won't do,' I thought, and fished it out and dealt with it. I rang up HM Inspector. A delightful humorous Scotch voice answered, recommending me to leave myself to 'the nearest medical school' – because 'ye might die up in the north country or somewhere'. So it's done now and I feel another cupboard has been tidied.

March 3rd

Yesterday, for the first time for some while, my direct pleasure in my surroundings produced the conviction that the 'stuff' of which the visible world was made was both beautiful and exciting. It was like the return of the sense of taste after influenza. Pale but distinct, there it was, the pure but hazy blue of the sky, the cream stucco of Belgravia house-fronts, the faint brownness at the end of twigs, the sharp fresh smell of earth, wood, spring perhaps in the air, the sound of gentle hopeful twittering. It's as if a helpful person had given me an arm and hoisted me up a step, just as my contact with my new orchestra did on Wednesday.

March 7th

Last night I dined in a new world, with Nicko and Mary Henderson. Arthur Koestler was there; I'd not seen him since Alpbach, and his first remark to me was, 'Are you still against religion?' 'Oh yes,' I said. He looked inclined to take this up and pursue it, and at some point I said I was a hardened rationalist or something to that effect. He looked cross: 'It is out of fashion now.' I laughed – provokingly, I dare say – and said, 'I don't care a pin for fashion.' 'No. Nor do I,' he said quickly, but more crossly still, and then with a lecturing expression: 'There is no longer a basis for rejecting religion.' There's no means of discussing ideas with Koestler, as Ralph long ago found out. You can either listen to him haranguing or not. He won't listen to you. I don't think the better of him for that, clever man though he undoubtedly is.

March 14th: London

Spirits low yesterday. Julia was disapproving and snubbing on the telephone as only she can be, telling me I led a 'whirl' of a life, 'telephone ringing all day', 'arrangements squeezed in with difficulty'. When I said this had no resemblance to the truth she said with finality: 'Oh, yes: Lawrence noticed it too.' She went on to say that she wasn't feeling well enough to go out or see people, only to work. And thus I was put securely in my place. I feel a little hurt, I suppose. She has herself experienced the difficulties of living alone and found them so crushing that she told me she would do anything in the world rather than face them again.

My solution is different from hers. I couldn't possibly live *except* alone, but I deal with my problem in my own way by seeing people every day, and throwing myself as much as possible into their lives.

March 15th

Today is my 63rd birthday, so I've just remembered, and perhaps that's why such an all-pervading, soggy but also fluttery and fevered gloom settled on me from the moment of waking. I take my surgeon's scalpel and plunge it into the living tissue in the hopes either of finding the tumour or letting out some of the poison.

Loneliness has been accentuated by Julia's 'writing me off' (so it seemed to me) the other day, as a futile member of the rat-race unworthy to mix with serious people like her and Lawrence. Of course I'm exaggerating this quite deliberately, just as one feels a sore place to see how much it hurts. I've thought a lot about our lifelong friendship and wondered how much rivalry there is in it – on either side – and how much I am over-critical of her. Why isn't it easier just to appreciate people for what they are – as dear old Bunny does for instance – rather than dissect them so remorselessly? I am in a mood at the moment to take the guilt for most things on myself and perhaps I can turn such a whipping-bout to good account and resolve to be better.

My work is one source of anxiety. *The President*[1] is finished and now being typed. I'm very dissatisfied with it indeed. The publishers think it's an 'important book'. I have been so embedded for months past in the appalling difficulties of the task that I have hardly any notion how it will read. Ralph thought I was a good translator, and I had confidence in myself – now suddenly I've lost it all and am full of anxieties. And this translating has been such a source of security and happiness to me in the past; I hate to think of giving it up. Part of this uneasiness comes from my dread of stepping out into the unknown with no banister to lean upon in the shape of a daily task. How to meet the emergency, what reserves to call on? It's always the same: courage, courage, courage, a realistic and rational attitude to the problem.

March 23rd

Last night I went with Eardley to hear Dadie[2] speak on Shakespeare and Troy at the Royal Institution – very, very fascinating. The lecture room is a steep circular bank of seats – so steep as to be very uncomfortable – and these were filled with distinguished-looking, highly intelligent and elderly faces. At the centre and bottom of the amphitheatre stood the lecturer's desk under a strong light, and exactly as the clock struck nine Dadie rushed impetuously in, bent over the desk, leaning both hands on it and launched forth without an instant's pause into a lively torrent of words, the beginning of his discourse. It was really admirable. He read his quotations in a voice of intense vitality and emotion, leaving me convinced that Elizabethan literature was a dazzlingly exciting, tremendously inspiring affair. Nothing of the don, nothing arid about him – just this splendid, infectious enthusiasm.

---

[1] A translation of the major work of Miguel Asturias, Guatemalan Nobel Prize winner.
[2] George Rylands, doctor of English literature at Cambridge.

April 2nd

A page has been turned and fallen back with a loud flap – I have handed *The President* in to Gollancz and no more can be done to it. The last week before its final launching into Henrietta Street was quite fantastically hectic, my 'emotional little' typist having let me down at the last moment. I got an agency to take it on but my luck was out: the last parcel of typescript disappeared in the post and I began to feel the physical universe was against me. However, a delightful postman telephoned me to say he had just opened a bag and found it, so I dashed off in trusty Mini and picked it up somewhere near Clapham Junction! Arriving at West Halkin Street after the weekend I found a telephone message to say that Mr Hilary Rubinstein would especially like to see me when I brought in the last chapters.

My heart sank. So this was it: I had been summoned to the headmaster's study. 'No, Partridge minor,' he would say, 'this work simply isn't good enough. You must do it all again.' Or, 'We'll have to scrap it,' or something. Off I went to face my Waterloo. Then my astonished ears heard a jolly Mr Rubinstein say that Mr Gollancz had read all the first part and thought it splendid and was delighted with my translation. Shortly afterwards the great man himself blew in, haloed by his fluffy grey hair, hand outstretched and said: 'I *congratulate* you. Your translation is really excellent!'

The shock was almost too great. What must a condemned prisoner feel when they bring a last-minute reprieve? Flatness I suspect, and so did I. I still do, though I know that somewhere beneath it lies an immense relief.

April 25th

Here I am back in my grey bedroom,[1] making an effort to get to grips with the restless, competitive, jealous, unsatisfied life of this town.

It is the usual problem: I try to straighten my knife and fork and make a neat rectangle in which the meal of my existence is to be swallowed. All yesterday I was busy nibbling at the fringes. I must have a few flowers. Various items of food must be bought. Stamps, the bank. But these are only preparations, painless – or nearly painless – ways of preparing to prepare to face my life. Work: that is the first problem. I must now get down to Desmond's letters, but I would so very much rather have a translation to do.

April 26th

On Wednesday, the day of my return, I watched Princess Alexandra's wedding on Eardley's television, and dined at Magouche's in the evening with the Campbells and Tom Matthews. The Campbells described their Easter at Lambourn with Julia, and how obviously amazed she was with the goings-on of William.[2] From Julia herself yesterday I wasn't surprised to hear that William had been a good deal too much for her: she had never, she declared, been at such close quarters with a small child for so long. We went on to talk about Carrington and her suicide. Last time Julia and I met, Michael Holroyd (who is writing Lytton's life) had just been to see her and she had 'tried to give him some idea of what a remarkable character Carrington was'. I'm not sure how much her present crisis had made her think of

---

[1] I had been to Skye to stay with Colin and Clodagh Mackenzie.
[2] Campbell, their son.

the past, nor how much it will be egocentricity on my part to believe she equates Lawrence – Julia – Jenny, with Ralph – Carrington – me. I feel a distaste for putting a special case (and this my own) into the general framework, since each of these cases has its own extraordinary peculiarities. In our 1924–31 situation there was the all-important figure of Lytton, Carrington's devotion to him, the shattering of Ralph's trust in Carrington by the affair with Gerald. Yet I see that *my* view of our joint pasts is not everyone's. As I saw it, when in 1925 the question of Ralph and me going off together arose, Carrington's panic was chiefly lest she should thus lose Lytton. Julia now tells me that Carrington told her that Ralph's withdrawal with me made her fall as it were in love with him again. I believe this may to some extent have been true, though during the four years in which he and I lived in Gordon Square Carrington and Lytton gradually got more and more used to living virtually as a married couple. In her discussion of Carrington's character I sensed in Julia (as I often have before) a very strong ambivalence, references to her genius and remarkable personality being coupled with others to her 'tortured sense of guilt which must have come from deep hostility to others, to her self-confessed masochism, and the strange duplicity and dishonesty of her character. I always thought there was something villainous as well as tragic, something coarse and cruel too, in her face.' Thus she unexpectedly ended her analysis.

May 14th

Dinner last night with Burgo and Henrietta. Henrietta cooked a delicious meal; Burgo looked bloomingly contented. But having till now shown little signs of her pregnancy, Henrietta suddenly looks weighted and burdened by her child, and my heart goes out to her rather anxiously. The thought of this new being – only a few months off now – kept me restless and wakeful on and off all last night. Today it has rained and rained and I have slid almost unconsciously through the day. A small translation job for Weidenfeld occupies me at the moment.

May 15th

Arthur Waley has just been to lunch with me. Seventy-four, but I must say one wouldn't guess it from the smooth graven oriental mask he presents to the world, and the head well-covered with only partly grey hair. He goes to the British Museum on a bicycle every day and seems wiry and athletic – though rather like Charlie Chaplin seen from the back, with his legs in their baggy trousers under a short tight jacket. It's not this, though, that gives one a hilarious desire to laugh in his august presence – but rather the elaborate air of superiority, the desperately flawless face he presents to the world. Not once did he by word or glance betray the smallest interest in my flat, my pictures, my books, or ask *one single* question about my life. What I was working at, whom I saw. This puts me in a quandary. I must either press on with questions, enquiring into every detail of *his* life and habits, while seeming stingy and ungenerous with information about my own, or volunteer what is obviously not required, and plank down an occasional gobbet – there! take it or leave it. (I havered between the two.) More than once he showed how he values status, prestige, recognition. He talked a lot of Beryl's important role in the dance world, the letters she had had from famous people, the lectures she had given, the articles he was collecting for publication. I suppose he loved her in his way, but it seems as if he loved her reputation even more. He talked

about various famous people, or literary friends like Gerald, in a slightly condescending way. He admitted having 'adored' Rupert Brooke at Cambridge, but
was eager to tell me how they had both taken their translations of Propertius to
their tutor, who said Arthur's was much the best, and how this had made Rupert
turn scarlet with rage. What a thing to treasure in your memory!

May 28th

My Papacy translation is packed away in its coffin. The proofs of *The President* have
come – dare I look at them? When they are finished a little lagoon of calm should
stretch ahead.

I had a delightful, peaceful, relaxed weekend alone with Raymond at Crichel –
easy and pleasant to the same degree that the last time I was alone with him gave
me the feeling *he* at least was not at ease. This augurs well for our Italian trip in
September. Talk flowed between us, we picked up our books when we wanted,
worked, played croquet and while he took an afternoon nap I walked in summery
heat through the quiet woods.

June 1st and 2nd: Stokke

Whitsun weekend looks like being blazingly fine. After Sunday lunch on the lawn
in a warm breeze, a talk with Magouche, a walk by myself in the forest and an
hour or so correcting my proofs, things and people began to pile up; more and
more people telephoned wanting to know if they could come and by evening we
were a *horde*, and I was succumbing to my anti-frothblowers' feeling. No, that's
not true, I was stimulated by the company and at dinner hooked myself into various
nooses of topics with Robin Fedden, Julian, Tristram Powell and an occasional
Magouche. Then there is an uncertain adolescent belt represented by two Fedden
girls, Natasha Gorky and a confident blonde friend, and (yet younger) Janetta and
Magouche's four little girls. Even this isn't the end – Georgia is expected today and
one of Tom Matthews' sons. Heaven knows where they'll all sleep or be, especially
if the weather doesn't hold up. It makes fifteen staying in the house, God help us,
and the Jellicoes have been asked to lunch. I like to concentrate on my surroundings
in detail and depth, not just to let the whirlpool of sound, thoughts and colours
rise up and swirl, and then subside leaving pointless lack of recollection. I'd *like* to
pay attention to these adolescent girls and discover a little about them – as it is no
one has time for them, they're left to sink or swim. It's as if one were trying to
throw up too many juggler's balls. But nearly always a Stokke weekend begins this
way. And why even try to pull shutters down over one's awareness of other people?
I can't: they interest me too deeply and agitate me too much. Last night Natasha
and Chloe her friend refused to come in to dinner, but sat looking at television.
Magouche was furious, and Robin said they 'bloody well ought to be made to'. I
felt for their adolescent escapism from the standpoint of my sexagenarian brand
of it.

Janetta asked to come to our Medical Orchestra concert on Friday; I felt she was
for once playing the part of my mother or aunt. It was in the great greenish black
cavern of the Central Hall, Westminster. But I have enjoyed remembering the
whole thing – the curious, rather pathetic excitement and *angst* in the performers'
rooms, with the ramifications of responsibility between conductor and orchestra,
and the special tension of Hephzibah Menuhin (only Adrian Boult looked and was

supremely lackadaisical), the friendliness engendered by this tension, the fact that it 'went' a good deal better than expected from the rehearsals and that our conductor was obviously pleased with us.

The detectable note of an over-loaded plate, and the assault of too great a swarm of bee-sensations has fuzzed the brilliantly fine Whitsun weekend, like a negative taken into the eye of the sun. Nearly all that left its mark on the negative was good in itself, there was just too much of it for me, the oldest by some ten years of a party which went down through every age-group to Susannah[1] and Rose. I did in the end make touch with the adolescents – the Fedden girls in particular – who responded at once to an invitation to talk about themselves, while Julian and Tristram always have their noses up like fox-terriers to catch any remark that may set off a conversation.

People came and went, there were seventeen to lunch on the lawn on Monday off turkey decorated with buttercups and cowparsley, ham mousse, cold rice salad, aubergines. Lord Shackleton, a Labour peer, turned up to stay the night, as did Tom Matthews' very American son. It was a masterpiece of organization by Magouche (with great support from Janetta) never showing effort, always providing delicious food, and drink; with conversation unflagging and at a high level, with rough croquet and ping-pong and the records of Britten's *War Requiem* (twice played right through and listened to attentively).

Verdict on Britten's Requiem after a fourth hearing: It is a great and moving work and perhaps the most valuable piece of peace propaganda there has been. How much is this due to Owen's marvellous poetry? As I followed the words more closely I saw that Britten had built up the work to a climax where the intense bitterness and sadness (the 'titanic tears' of the earth) stands side by side with the greatest glorification of God. Does he think the two compatible and somehow equatable through the beauty of words and music? But having soaked in the tragic violence of Owen's sonnets, how can one turn to the glory of God, in any sense of 'God'? It's not ironical, that's clear. And if THAT, then how can one accept THIS in the same breath? I suppose it's the same reconciliation that must take place in every true Christian between his worship of the universe and his sense of sin and evil, and how that takes place is something I've not begun to understand.

June 6th: London

Continuing heat-wave. Have just had a picnic lunch with Heywood in Belgrave Square, sitting on a rug in the shadow of an immense black-trunked tree, sipping white wine and eating cold delicacies. It gave me pleasure to profit from the great heat in this way.

But the day began badly. I woke at 4.30, listened for a little to the unearthly hush and then lay for three hours or more staring miserably and anxiously into the blank that is my future. While I am busy I manage to keep the awareness of this dreadful blank in some sense thrust to one side. Though I think of Ralph times without number and in various ways every day (sometimes almost with the same pleased amusement and vividness as if he were alive) I contrive *not to face* his absence fairly and squarely. But as soon as the pressure of work or people eases off, back rushes the tidal wave of longing and loneliness and pain, almost unchanged

[1] Phillips, Magouche's youngest daughter.

since the very first. I stand like a sombre black rock while it washes and swirls over me, unable to do anything but just endure and wait. This is what happened this morning, and I was full of wonder at the self-deception which had made me seem (as I suppose) to others to be making a go of my life. This morning I felt myself drowning in envy for everyone who had someone to be responsible for, to be responsible for them, to discuss their worries and minute daily experiences with; to go and lean on in moments of weakness, huddle up to for blessed animal warmth, to love and be loved by. Oh, what endless courage one has to keep stoking up to walk one's cold frightening path alone!

The President went off only yesterday – but the day before Dermod came to dinner and instead of this being an encouragement to me to go back to Desmond's letters, it's done just the opposite – made me decide they must definitely be abandoned. He has veered right round as a result of a visit from Michael, and now shares his view that it is 'too soon'. When I said that I was convinced we'd better give it all up he protested, but I'm sure he was relieved. He talks of wanting to avoid the 'sensational' as if any of Desmond's letters were *that*! Obviously even those to Cynthia Asquith would have been censored by the family. No; it's impossible – and I have few regrets. If I had another book to translate I should have none. He asked me if I thought Desmond 'would have minded' publication, and I searched the inside of my head and said truthfully that I thought he would have liked the idea of being faithfully presented to posterity.

June 11th

Last night I dined with Magouche, her two Gorky daughters, Eduardo Paolozzi and a successful painter called Kitaj. Magouche has a stained-glass glow about her which heartens one, and looked really beautiful in a clotted-cream wool dress with thick bright blue beads. We sat out on her terrace then indoors talking – talk borne along on two rival streams: one was Eduardo's curious, very personal brand of naïve thoughtfulness. His censor lets everything through, opening the door with a wide respectful gesture to the simplest, most well-worn of notions, which are ushered in as if they were exotic and original inspirations – such was that 'really the Conservative Party are behind the times'. The other was Kitaj's compulsive and fanatical Marxism. He was expecting to find a defence of class distinctions in Magouche and me, and clearly disconcerted somewhat by the ground being hacked away under his feet when I quickly handed him the monarchy, religion, the House of Lords and the public schools. Did he believe in reality of progress? Magouche asked. 'Yes, *absolutely*,' and his closely furred face, so reminiscent of Van Gogh, crunched up with badger-like rebarbativeness and aggression. He is not at all a stupid man, however, and interesting though not entirely likeable.

I've had a letter from Dermod taking it all back. What's to be made of that?

June 12th

Unreal effect of living in this permanent Mediterranean radiance. A fillip given by my being offered a job yesterday by Weidenfeld, to translate a short art book from the French – and also by being with people I greatly like or love. Janetta suddenly was at my door, looking fresh as a daisy in a pink suit and carrying a bunch of rosebuds.

A series of early-morning telephone calls from Julia. Yes, she and Lawrence would come to dinner; she wanted to know at what time. 'About this dinner party ...' F.: (exasperated) 'It's *not* a dinner-party, Julia, just old friends eating together. I've not asked another soul and won't if you like.' Then as it so happened, Robin Campbell rang up, full of friendliness and having left his family in Wales. I therefore had to telephone Julia and persuade her that this didn't make it a dinner-party – it was difficult, because I already heard her drawing herself up into her 'social occasion' position. Lastly, about five-thirty she rang up with 'bad news'; her temperature was 'just over 99 and she thought she shouldn't go out'. Well, at the end of this series of calls I was luckily able to get the Godleys to come and eat the delicious piece of salmon I'd already cooked for dinner and we had a very nice evening.

Today I lunched with Frances Phipps, who was rejoicing because Kennedy has made a speech *in favour of peace*. How astonishing that this should seem a surprising event. Yet it does, and is the most politically encouraging thing that has happened for years. He's actually tried to sell peace to the Americans, and spoken well and feelingly, without clichés – 'I speak of peace, as the necessary, rational end of rational men. Too many of us think it impossible. We need not accept that view. Our problems are man-made – therefore they can be solved by man.'

June 30th: Charleston

A wet but happy weekend. Now the sun has come out (on Sunday afternoon) and shines down heavily from between the clouds onto the wet sweet-smelling garden, bringing a lot of flies buzzing everywhere. The steamy air smells of manure and roses. I'm sitting alone on a long bench which looks like something for carrying coffins to the grave, in the clumsy but charming paved garden made by Quentin. A little basin of duckweed-covered water edged with his home-made tiles, columbines sprouting from between the mosaics in the pavement that the frosts have left intact. This time I'm entirely captivated by the Charleston ambience and feel its civilization rather than its ramshackleness. At every turn Barbara tugs the conversation back to herself, or her children or the eminent Bloomsburies she likes to feel she was so very close to. I have heard many stories for the fifth or sixth time – the one about the Musk orchid for about the tenth – but I was asking for this when I brought back Butterfly orchids from the wood at the end of the drive. Yesterday I climbed in a strong wind and sprinkling rain to the top of the Downs, collecting any flowers I liked the look of, like shells on a beach, and on the lowest slope came to a great plantation of Fragrant and Spotted orchids. I've really been happy here; Clive and Duncan both in splendid form. A very interesting conversation on ambiguity prompted by listening to *Pelléas and Mélisande*, which scoured the edges of a fascinating subject without clearing the middle. What is the pleasure one gets from ambiguity, or lack of definition, such as that opera arouses? Duncan thought it thrilling, in a way that nothing completely defined and exact can be. I feel a reservation, doubts. For a thing to have two – or even several – meanings may give a complicated and interesting result. But for it to end in a fog of uncertainty which is never resolved, somehow leaves me frustrated and feeling swindled. Do I miss something? *Why* should imprecision as such be thrilling? Something to go on pondering about.

Clive asked me at tea whether I thought my character had changed much in the last twenty years – because, he went on, he thought I had become more 'active'.

July 5th: London

I have been immersed in old letters and found it disturbing. I swing between over-
and under-estimation, in the course of which a lot goes into the waste-paper
basket. Ralph had the theory that 'everything must be kept'. I know that simply
leads in the end to total destruction, and there's something melancholy in the
thought of all these tin boxes, full of tied-up letters, such as I saw at Charleston.

Last night I sat for about three hours reading my own letters to Ralph and
throwing away quite a lot. I woke at five this morning and went on with it,
although finding deep sadness in this stale dry dust emanating from the rich and
living years. As our lives became bound together and the time came when we were
virtually never apart there was hardly ever an occasion for writing, and I have the
feeling that pen and paper was an unsuitable vehicle for intimacy and love that
expressed itself so completely and so easily in conversation and caresses.

July 11th

I feel sometimes like a waiter compelled to go round a room crowded with people,
holding out a tray on which they put their empty cups and glasses of ideas. The
Cecil family are delightfully free with theirs, and slap them down without waiting
to be asked, but sometimes I look in surprise at what my tray has collected and
can't make head or tail of it. Some of Hugh's contributions, freely given though
they were, seemed to startle even himself. Laura will come to a sweeping conclusion
about human nature beginning, 'I've always noticed', and is amazed because
nobody else has.

Yesterday I had a delightful evening with Eardley, dining and talking hard. (Did
I talk most or hold the tray? The tray, I think.) And afterwards we went to a party
at the Tate for a retrospective show of Ivon Hitchens' paintings – a huge concourse
of art lovers in evening dress, moving dreamily about among candles. Not a face I
knew, save Cressida Ridley's. The paintings were perhaps too much alike, but if
only the best had been on show one would have admired their soft richness, their
gentle and persuasive quality. One sank into them like well-upholstered chairs.

Whenever dire need of support comes over me my mind flies to Janetta. Who
else, young though she is, and also so leant upon and weighed down by everyone?
I know that her great kindness and responsibility would make her always come in
answer to a direct and urgent appeal, but that's the one thing I don't want to add
to her difficulties by making if I can help it, and I'm very far from that situation
at the moment. Yesterday we arranged to spend the evening together tonight, but
from this morning's conversation I rather think she's forgotten it. Robin is dining
with her, and I dread so much to press in when not wanted that I didn't say to
her, 'We were going to have this evening, do you remember?'

July 18th

Took Julian and the Jenkinses to *Oh, What a Lovely War!* They were enthusiastic; I
couldn't feel the same. Was it because it seemed to do no more than twang on an
old tired nerve? Or was it that the play is trying to shock people into a view that
I've held so long that I had no further response to make to it? Or that its thesis –
that war is unspeakably ghastly and the 1914–18 war was far the worst of all – is
something I feel more deeply and painfully than anything else, so that this rather

slick, deft, vulgar trifle didn't seem to go far enough for me? I was groping about for the reason of my lack of reaction (not a tear, not a genuine irresistible laugh) as we strolled through Leicester Square, when Julian mentioned Owen's poems as if they were comparable with the diaries and songs (genuine material though these were) quoted in this revue. This gave me a sharp, quite violent shock, for Owen's poems hit the nail right on the head, and never make the slightest error of taste. To mention them in the same breath as this cheap, well-meaning, trumpery affair seemed strange.

July 19th

I lunched alone with Janetta and Robert, which brought a great wave of nostalgia for the impossible back again. Yes, even now. It delighted me to find Janetta in total agreement with me about *Oh, What a Lovely War!*, but better at analysing the reason for her reaction than I, or possibly not having such cause to suspect personal reasons. Robert stuck up for it but not aggressively and put his case well. He thought it of particular importance that it was the work of the young who had experienced nothing and probably read little about the 1914–18 war, so that their reaction of horror was genuine and fresh and peculiarly their own, and he found it deeply moving.

August 1st

How I wish this baby would arrive! These last days have been coloured by sympathetic feelings for Burgo and Henrietta, full of anxious empathy, a sense of responsibility, and self-questioning how to support without interfering or fussing.

I heard with considerable agitation that Angelica, Bunny and the twins had all gone off to France with no prospect of returning for weeks. What is to be made of this seeming desertion which leaves me especially anxious not to do likewise? I was reassured by a telephone conversation with Henrietta's doctor last night an hour after he'd seen her. She was 'fine', everything was absolutely normal, and if the baby is not here by next Wednesday they will 'induce' it, and put a term to their waiting. I think of them and their child and its future endlessly, and feel as restless as a cat.

Bank Holiday Monday

Arrived at Halkin Street after a Stokke weekend with mixed feelings. It is my own. I can do absolutely what I like in it – but that means that I must develop a desire, an impulse at least and force myself to carry it out. Otherwise disintegration. I rang Burgo and Henrietta, who seemed pleased at the idea of coming to have a picnic supper with me, and the evening passed pleasantly away. I drove them home soon after ten-thirty, and about an hour later when I was settling into bed the telephone rang. It was Burgo, saying that Henrietta's hands and ankles had swollen and she had an irritating rash. Now was my chance to be some use. I went round to their flat and my first impression was that nothing much was wrong. Poor Henrietta lay on the tumbled bed, managing to look very pretty though so heavily laden, in her simple white nightgown. The swelling was not acute; she had a definite sort of nettle-rash though, and she was afraid, from a book she'd read, she had toxaemia. I sat talking to them until at last a little sandy locum tenens arrived and examined her thoroughly. All other doctors connected with her were away on this mad festive beano. Talked to Burgo in the sitting-room where I saw the touching sight of a tiny half-knitted pink garment lying on the collapsing sofa. The doctor announced that she *had* toxaemia, and sent for the ambulance. In a surprisingly short time a dark-blue-clad officer had arrived and she had gone down in her nightie and a thin dressing-gown, and Burgo too, to face her fate. What courage it needs – yet almost every female faces it. Burgo didn't return, so I realized he'd gone in the ambulance and took myself off.

It is six o'clock on Tuesday and I've heard nothing except a call from Burgo this morning to say the doctors at the hospital said it was not toxaemia but some sort of allergy. However they are keeping her and I hope it will be 'induced' today or tomorrow.

August 7th

Nine o'clock in the morning – the sky has again become a sheet of purest blue, and the pigeons sit in a row on the roof looking in at me. Yesterday passed in unnatural calm. The fact that Henrietta is in professional and skilled hands is a great relief. Knowing that the 'inducing' might not start until today I restrained myself from ringing up and heard nothing till Burgo came in the evening, having been to see her. I've just rung up the hospital and heard Henrietta's voice saying quite jubilantly, 'I've started to have it.' Thank heavens for that! It shouldn't be too long now.

August 8th

Very perturbed by calling the hospital and being told 'no change'. Last night Burgo thought the child should have been there already. He had been with Henrietta during the afternoon when 'contractions were coming every five minutes', but I feel he has no real conception of how much more tremendous the whole process had to become. I spent most of yesterday, and am today, in the middle of a familiar frantic attempt to wait calmly.

3 p.m. I'm seriously worried. Rang Henrietta's doctor at lunchtime and he broached the possibility of a Caesarean if nothing has happened by tomorrow morning. 'I don't understand it,' he said, 'she's so young, everything's normal, and she does everything she's told.' Yet she is having contractions, but no more. My heart bleeds for her, and I don't know how to get through the time.

August 14th

The gap is the measure of how long it took me to recover from catapulting so hopelessly into agitation. Henrietta and Burgo's dear little baby, Sophie Vanessa, is now five days old and Henrietta is recovering from the operation. Their delight in their child is marvellous to see and they express it with refreshing abandon. I have been twice to see Henrietta and had Burgo here a good many times – hoping not to seem interfering or fussing, but now sure that attentions and interest are appreciated. I have been much moved – obsessed is really the word – by the whole thing. Each night as I close my eyes to the darkness this obsession returns, even if it has been quiescent all day. The baby looks very like Henrietta, with a wide mouth and perfect little hands.

August 16th

I've been all day on the run – to see Craig in the morning – to visit Henrietta in the afternoon – a drink with Isobel in the evening. I feel like one of the silver balls in machines in fairs, which gets shot up by the insertion of a penny, bounces wildly from metal peg to metal peg, rattles here, slides along there, jingles and jolts until it drops into the last hole of all from which there is no return. Henrietta comes out of hospital on Friday, and after buying her a pram with Burgo and driving her home – what then? It's difficult to strike a happy balance between doing all one can, and longs to do for those one loves, and backing gracefully off the stage. I see clearly the warning Ralph would have been the first to give me: don't interfere in their lives. But I'm aware of one thing at least: here at last, in flesh and blood, is a motive for going on far stronger than any I have encountered during nearly three years of struggle.

Other People

1963–1966

Foreword

The last volume of my published diaries, *Hanging On*, covered a period of about three years starting from the death of my husband Ralph on November 30th, 1960 – a time during which I was making desperate attempts to establish some sort of *modus vivendi* out of the ashes of an extremely close and warm married life. It was a question, too, (by my own choice) of leaving Ham Spray House in Wiltshire, where I had been surrounded by the country and surroundings I loved, for the stark loneliness of a London flat. By the end of the book in the middle of August less than three years later I had to some extent come to terms with my new life, largely thanks to the incredible kindness and support of my friends. Our only son Burgo had settled happily – also in London – with a young, beautiful and charming wife Henriette Garnett, and the birth of their child Sophie on August 9th, 1963 made a *coda* to the book and seemed to give me a fresh interest in the future. I believed that a spell of reasonably calm and contented life lay before me. I was wrong. On September 7th out of the sky came death and disaster. Without any warning Burgo was struck dead by a heart attack while telephoning his friend Peter Jenkins.[1] His condition had not been suspected and Henrietta and I were told that nothing could have been done even if it had. I was too stunned and shattered to write anything in my diary except a bleak statement of the facts, adding 'I have utterly lost heart: I want no more of this cruel life.'

A few weeks later Henrietta (who had been incredibly brave) took two-months-old Sophie, and was whisked away to stay with her parents David ('Bunny') and Angelica Garnett in their house in France, while I went on dumbly preparing to carry out a previously made plan to go with Raymond Mortimer to Apulia. I don't think I was even capable of realizing at the time what a heroic act of friendship he showed me in going ahead with it. I made a deliberate but unsuccessful decision to live in the present.

[1] The political journalist.

1963

September 21st: Rome

Among many devastating emotions and events of my last days in London, first came my increasing love and admiration for Henrietta, and the bitter-sweet taste of all she told me of the happiness she and Burgo had had together; next Bunny's arrival, rosy and amiable, but not saying *one* word of regret for Burgo, only talking about settlements and arrangements; the tremendous kindness and solid support of Robert Kee, Julian Jebb, Joan Cochemé and many others; my visit from Rosamond Lehmann, and her hopeless woolly attempt to interest me in the spirit world.

Yesterday morning Raymond and I left London and flew here smoothly. The struggle to make my tired muscles of courage and composure respond to my will resulted in great physical fatigue, like the useless effort to use one's legs after running down a mountain.

That same afternoon Raymond and I travelled in a train lined with red plush to Bari, and after being first rejected – '*completo*' – were taken in by a comfortable hotel on the edge of the sea.

September 22nd: Bari

The old town of Bari is charmingly pretty; a network of alleys and tunnels, brightly painted, with birds and flowers hanging outside, old women sitting on kitchen chairs knitting, and countless scrimmaging children. The two churches were noble Byzantine-style buildings with shallow rounded apses – their silvery stone in strange contrast to the white, pink and blue of the streets. Our sightseeing however has almost immediately got confused in my mind – Mola, Monopoli ... What did we see in which? Where was a doorway with two columns supported by wistful cows? Where a font carried by putti? Where a bishop's chair weighing down the crushed heads of two lions? Mixed in with all this sightseeing came the business of getting our hired car from the garage (an eggshell-green Fiat) and the awful angst of trying to remember how to start it and then drive it. I had not bargained with the novelty of a lefthand drive and almost at once scraped very slightly against another car, but towards the end of our journey I began to relax. Raymond can't drive, so I'm glad to be able to repay him for all he has done for me, all the paying of bills as well as planning of sightseeing, for his sweetness too and benignity to everyone.

We had decided to make for the extraordinary region of the Selva which is covered with small beehive shaped houses called *trulli*, the domes generally grey, the rest freshly whitewashed, and the domes smartly finished with a little cup and ball of white. Rising everywhere among groves of olives and vines, they looked quite fantastic and often very pretty; sometimes like collections of tents.

In our little car we clambered up and up through the *trulli* and the olives, high above the plain, and here at last stood our destination, the Villa Paradiso. It was obviously a summer haunt and lunch place, not a soul there but us. Very soon its queerness began to emerge. The rooms *looked* fine – but when Raymond put his attaché-case on a table it collapsed at once. The light above my bed would only stay on if you held the switch up in the air. As I was looking forward to an evening read I asked for it to be mended. Two youths took the switch apart and put it together again over and over, giving themselves electric shocks, for three quarters of an hour. Then *'sarebbe meglio'*, I contrived to say, *'di darmi una altra camera'*. They went to fetch the *padrone* who was simply furious. 'Change your room?' he yelled at me. 'Why?' *'Perche sono "cansada" e vorrei riposarmi?'* I said relapsing into part-Spanish. *'Zanzara??'* they all cried in astonishment. (It means 'mosquito'.) I bethought myself of *'stanca'* at last, and grudgingly a new room (there were obviously dozens) was provided. I was lying quietly on the double-bed when half of it collapsed! I slept that night on the other half.

Our dinner was niggardly and bad, and the only red wine available had a label with 'Happy Drink' on it. We dared not try it.

Tuesday was a longer driving day, about 120 kilometres, and at the end of it getting into Lecce (which proved to be a large, populous animated town crowded with cars and jay-walkers and one-way streets) about finished me off. But I think perhaps it more effectively numbed the aching nerve of the source of my pain than any other day hitherto has done. We have got so far away that the navel-string attaching us to normal life is stretched as thin as silk.

September 26th

Our last day at Lecce. Last night, over a plate of inedibly tough meat in a restaurant, Raymond and I tried to hack out our plans. As I rather feared, he may want me to drive longer distances than I like. I said four hours in any one day would be too much, that I was feeling feebler than I'd thought. (This is true. I've had several migraines.) He was angelic and said of course I mustn't, but it means cutting out a good many of the desirable sights and this distresses me as well as him.

September 27th: Gallipoli, 6 p.m.

Lying on my bed in the first of these disgusting Jolly hotels I have yet sampled. It is a monk's cell, smelling strongly of stale tobacco. Apparently no one who is not part of a married couple is allowed to have a bath in these marvellous modern hotels: they have no private shower even and public bathrooms do not exist. Worst of all it is miles outside the town and on a noisy crossroads. We arrived here early on a golden afternoon and I would have loved to walk round the town after a brief rest but felt too nervously exhausted to set out again at once. The driving *is* exacting: and poor Raymond is hopelessly bad at map-reading, inclined to ask me (in a mild voice while other drivers hoot) which I think is the way, and not realizing that the one thing the driver needs is to be firmly directed. However he is angelically good-tempered and never minds asking the way of strangers. Because we went astray more than once and tried to take a road which stopped suddenly with the cheerful notice *Pericolo di morte*, it turned into quite a long day's drive. I feel discouraged this evening. Can I do it? That's the question that at present occupies my mind to the exclusion of anything else. I have my dear glass of whisky beside me this evening and hope with its help to get sufficient strength to drive us into the unknown streets of the town for our dinner.

But I mustn't forget the great visual pleasure and beauty that today has provided: Ótranto's splendid church with a vast twelfth-century mosaic (an enormous tree and hundreds of grotesque animals and figures) stretching all over its floor. The sea in the harbour in stripes of turquoise and navy flecked with white. Our lovely drive along the Adriatic coast towards the southernmost point, by a fine road bordered with trees and rocks, looking down through olives to the blue sea and little havens full of blue and green fishing boats.

Raymond has been incredibly kind. He went out reconnoitring while I lay fuming and unrelaxed on my bed, and when dinner-time came we drove in to a little fish restaurant floating like an ark in the port, ate red mullet and drank a lot of mild rosé wine, then walked slowly through the pretty little old town, illu-minated and *en fête*, with strings of girls and dashing young men, old women sitting beaming, while small children reeled along intoxicated with their gala toys.

September 29th: Taranto, 7 a.m.

From my quiet little bedroom I see and hear nothing but sea and sky and the chug of fishing-boat engines. None the less I woke about five this morning, to the usual doubts – can I do it? etc. Must try and glean an afternoon rest. Yesterday was very hot. Found my first batch of letters, fifteen or so – the most human being two from Joan. They twanged on the painful strings of reality.

7 p.m. (same day), Altamura, in a much less quiet bedroom, with a glass of whisky by my side and feeling pretty desperate. There is a fortnight more of this 'holiday' and I'm wondering if I can survive it. What a hollow mockery it is! True there is constant visual beauty, a flicker of interest here and there, amusement even, but it all lies like scum on the surface of a stagnant pool of heartbreak. And if I don't let myself plumb those dark depths, I'm haunted by the fear of shock – the dreadful moments of realization: that huge white face pressed so suddenly and menacingly into one's own. I should get out of this world, this life. It's the only rational thing – I know it. Yet either cowardice or some obstinate clinging to life may well prevent me. I've no confidence in anything any more, when such savage backhanders may come at one any moment. I'm pretty nearly in a state of persecution-mania. Well, what use is it anatomizing my melancholy?

October 1st: Andria

At Castel del Monte (a pink octagonal castle) I felt too weak to visit it. Instead I let Raymond go alone; went to have a drink in a café and rushed to be sick. We'd hoped to stay in that strange place (there were a few rooms) but none were left, so on to this rather meaningless town of Andria we came. Alas, I had all afternoon been aware of a flu-like ache in my legs. I now began to feel boiling hot. I swallowed some aspirins, but when dear Raymond poked his solicitous face in about six-thirty I had no doubt I'd 'got something'. Raymond's thermometer showed a temperature of 102° and he insisted on getting a doctor, a nice young Italian who gave me some pills which strangely enough seem to have worked, and today I feel almost normal but am still quite happy to stay in bed. I'm terribly upset at bringing this distress on Raymond, and don't know how to make it up to him and become a more lively travelling companion. To tell the truth the driving had quite tired me out and I'm glad to take a total rest in bed.

At Castel del Monte I found a mass of the only pretty autumn flower I've seen – the yellow crocus-like Sternbergia.

October 4th: Manfredonia

Two peaceful days of eating, sleeping and reading have been almost serene, and brought a feeling of intimacy and affection between Raymond and me – not that it wasn't there already. I think we understand each other better and for my part I love him more warmly than ever.

A few letters from England met us here: Bunny's is the one I wake in the night and think about. Henrietta and Sophie have returned to England already and he says their visit was a great success. Henrietta 'came more alive' – as if she had not been frantically and frighteningly alive in London – and this was partly because he had left the parcel containing her pills behind. Then comes a cheerful description of their life, visitors and the meals they cook.

I feel somehow in spite of all that is endearing in Bunny a certain ruthless selfishness and lack of sensitivity. He simply can't begin to imagine the nature of the shock Henrietta experienced if he thinks she could have got through it without pills.

Also there is something irksome to me in the way he cheerfully throws the responsibility on me for helping this poor eighteen-year-old girl deal with lawyers, flats, clearing-up, finding somewhere to live and all the rest of it, and gets back to collecting and purging his snails and cooking them with lots of butter and garlic.

October 5th: Hotel Jolly, Caserta

Well of course in the end I wrote to Bunny letting out something of what his letter had made me feel. As for the Garnett lack of responsibility towards Henrietta, I put in rather a sly dig, saying that I was very sorry they couldn't persuade her to stay longer in France but that I supposed they 'couldn't be very worried about her or one of them would have gone back with her to help'. It's really rather monstrous of me, because I'm trading on Bunny's affection and good opinion of me – but I did somehow want to give a clue to the fact that I personally was done for, in need of support myself, and that I felt it was their turn to take a hand. Why in heaven's name don't they *want* to?

October 6th: Caserta

Raymond and I got our excursion to Monte Sant' Angelo. A strange and rewarding expedition. We foolishly took the 'old road' up the three thousand feet to the town, and it soon lost all pretence at a surface and tossed us between pot-holes, slabs of living rock and dusty white runnels worked by the rain. I am glad we took it, as our approach to the town along the very summit of the ridge was dramatic in the extreme, while below (whenever I could snatch a glance) the wide sweep of the bay dropped quickly down and away, the sea became aquamarine and only faintly rippled and Manfredonia a white blur. Triumph – there we were at the top and it was suddenly cold. A fierce town, full of barbarous little boys pretending to throw stones at the car, attaching themselves to us and badgering us: the rapacious cynical atmosphere of all pilgrimage places. The pilgrimage church was extraordinary too. One descended about eighty steps to find it hollowed out inside a prehistoric cave. This morning, brilliant once more, we took the train to this place and after lunch went to see the Royal Palace – Italy's Versailles. The palace was the most pompous and splendiferous building – surely the wretched little Bourbon kings must have felt dwarfed rather than aggrandized by these vast wide staircases, enormously tall rooms decorated with gilt, and huge statues and complicated inter-arching corridors.

October 8th: Naples

We have been in Naples two days in a comfortable, expensive, sympathetic hotel on the port. I like it, but it is almost too vast, and the streets are congested with hooting streams of crawling cars. Its liveliness is almost crushing. There are organ-grinding musicians touring the restaurants round the port, swooning tenors bellowing into one's ears, and the inevitable brides in faintly bluish muslin are everywhere, attended by slightly hysterical wedding parties lasting for hours.

Yesterday we went to look at the huge and magnificent gallery at Capodimonte: superb Masaccios and Bellinis and Botticellis; a whole room full of Titians; Greco and Goya.

October 10th

I'm counting the days till we get home. I wish we could go tomorrow. I'm conscious of the character of the town, but I never want to see it again as long as I live. See Naples, yes, and then die.

October 11th: Ravello

However today has been a better day. We got up early and took a bus to Amalfi and Ravello. It was without exception the most sensational road I've ever travelled on and I would rather have been in a small private car than in this immensely long monster driven full lick and with bravura by our young and dashing chauffeur. We swirled round corners, lingered by overhanging cliffs, leaned over narrow parapets, and far below was the blue sea and a series of fantastically picturesque villages with their ports full of fishing-boats. Amalfi was hot and summery and people were bathing; I would have quite liked to stay there but on and up we came to this windy but charming village. The hotel is comfortable, has sunny terraces and (I do really believe) eatable food.

October 14th

This evening, DV, will see us back in London. With all its commitments, sources of worry, faces of friends, piles of letters. On the whole I am anxious to get back, though the last three days have provided the dazzling, hot, balmy weather we have missed for so long. We took a taxi all the way back from Ravello, stopping at Pompeii for over two hours and no extravagance was more worthwhile; we saw the best, and compared to Herculaneum which is a livid mummy, Pompeii is pretty and has weeds springing everywhere, its paved streets intact, much more like a living town. The casts of people and dogs caught by the lava left me unmoved. The obscene paintings were shut away behind hatches, only shown to men – '*non va bene per le donne'*. Far the most striking thing was the painted room in the Villa dei Misteri with beautifully preserved strange, emotionally charged figures, large and boldly painted on a shining crimson ground.

So here we are back at Naples, not knowing quite what to do with our remaining time, for we have picked its bones pretty thoroughly. I must say that Raymond's natural sweetness makes him accept eagerly any suggestion I make, rather than at once seeing its drawbacks as some would. Slept badly thinking of how to get astride once more that infinitely intractable horse my LIFE, of all the 'things to do today' in London, wondering about Henrietta and Sophie, and what I'll find, and whether anything has happened in my absence (births, deaths) and about Janetta and Joan.

And I do hope the gush of London swirling round me will restore me a little to life and thought. It's really not fair to inflict poor kind Raymond with my dazed stupidity.

October 16th

I'm back. Infinite kindness and thoughtfulness of friends – Joan and Janetta especially. Henrietta and Sophie to lunch yesterday – Sophie's eyes are becoming black as night and she has a distinct look of Burgo. My friends' anxious faces looking to see whether love for the two of them is going to pin me to life.

October 18th

I am lying on my bed at 4 p.m. trying to fight off despair. I'm not sure that I *can* stand much more of this. I have no libido to put into anything. It suddenly seems to me an act of insane folly to try to go on; it strikes me as illogical, irrational, even uncharacteristic behaviour, which I'm unable to justify and feel positively apologetic for. I am like a trailer that has broken loose and is rattling down hill out of control.

October 20th: Cooleville House, Ireland

Every word that I wrote last was true, but of course it is not logic nor rational processes that hold one to life, but only blind instinct. Talked a little to Janetta on these lines.

If anything could bring peace, relaxation, anodyne, it is this sweet and soft green country, whose flavour is on one's lips from the first moment of getting to the Aer Lingus station. Enjoyed my solitary flight. We were in clouds most of the way, but approaching Cork I saw a pale lake of blue opening ahead and on landing found myself in the middle of gentle all-pervading afternoon sunlight. A beautiful drive through this mellow evening glow, lying dazzling bright on the unexpectedly broad rivers, and lighting up the mixed colours of the already 'turning' trees. Recognition with pleasure – of the little fields tufted with rough grass and thistles, the groups of children on the empty roads, the lack of hurry, the absence of angst. It is like settling into a soft and especially comfortable armchair.

Found Julian and Eddy Sackville snugged in over the fire in the fine red room. It's a great comfort to find Julian here – three's company, two's none, or rather I want a rest from pseudo-marriage, and I am always afraid of 'paining' Eddy. It is enormously comfortable here in an old-fashioned way, food delicious. A horsefaced breezy middle-aged spinster came to dinner and I toppled into bed exhausted and slept soundly.

October 21st: Wexford

After lunch we drove to Wexford for two nights of the Opera festival, and I am lying in bed after the first of them – *Don Pasquale*. Lord, I find it cold though, and everyone else says how warm it is. I put the eiderdown from the second bed on top of me and slept in my dressing gown. The efforts of the Irish to please are most touching – there is a bowl of fruit in my bedroom. When I came in last night a complimentary packet containing two chocolates to bring 'sweet dreams' lay on each pillow – that which was assumed to be male flavoured with rum, the female one with orange. In a further attempt to make two people out of me they had wrapped my dressing gown round a hot-water bottle in one bed and my nightgown in the other. I was very glad of both, and plan to go out and buy woolly vests or a very thick Irish sweater.

This is a friendly little festival – the weather so very unfestive (blowing and raining), the theatre a good way short of full, but the performance professional and lively.

I said I shouldn't see my Italian journey in perspective till I got home and it was true. Now I see that it was not a 'failure', that it was a salvage operation carried out more or less successfully and entirely thanks to Raymond's kindness and patience. My God, the electric fire has gone out! Time to get up.

October 23rd

Back at Cooleville. Julian and I spent a morning reading in Eddy's new plant- and window-lined conservatory, oval in shape, both of us lying on long garden chairs. Julian was supposed to be reading a book for review, but I looked up and saw his eyes fixed, wide open and sad, over the top of his book. He is too vulnerable ever to be really happy. Back, oh back in rat-race London: speeding up of heartbeats and breathing, restlessness, times of near insanity.

I find it less and less reasonable or practicable to make the effort not to seem sunk in gloom, yet I would be prepared to guess that I do on the whole succeed in creating a false impression except to near and dear friends like Janetta; I'm constantly and painfully aware of being monstrously deformed by affliction, someone to be avoided by all: this makes me long to creep away into my hole and hide my head, and attain oblivion – the temporary one of sleep if I can't have the final one of death.

Ireland was a poultice on my pain, a sweet draught of illusion, thankfully lapped up – but one of the things I find hardest to deal with is that I cannot leave any empty space in my waking day, for fear of the desperate thoughts and feelings that crowd in. They can force the barrier of some delightful passive occupation like driving or walking in beautiful country which makes me prefer to it some footling activity like playing Scrabble. Scrabbling through my life somehow is what I seem to be doing, but God only knows what is the point of it.

Last night I dined with Janetta, Julian and Georgia Tennant and felt I was a grim skeleton at the board. Julian got fussed and over-talked himself; Georgia was inscrutable, and I wondered what had passed between her and Janetta since I last saw Janetta who looked rather sad and exhausted.

November 1st

I padded out in pouring rain and lunched with Heywood Hill, and in the evening Richard Garnett came for a drink and I went to my Medical Orchestra. The feeling of deformity by affliction still oppresses me. It is as if I was a pilot whose face had been horrifyingly mashed about in the war. Is one to force people to accept me, when they would much rather forget I exist.

Doctor Dicks[1] came beaming up to say he saw Burgo was a father. Oh dear – how to spare people and myself embarrassment? I wince and shrivel for hours ahead over such possibilities. And I have nothing funny or interesting to contribute to the general pool – just dark thoughts, or fierce rebarbative conclusions summing up my dislike of the Universe. I am very clearly aware of my slow subsidence into the bog.

I lay on my bed most of the afternoon reading Ottoline Morrell's Memoirs and finding her uncongenial; she was fundamentally a silly woman, who thought with her heart not her head; her enthusiasms were fuzzy and sentimental – 'I love heaths and wide open country, Milton, loveliness and Mozart' is the sort of thing she says. Her editor Bob Gathorne-Hardy treats her respectfully like royalty, and quotes her feeble remarks just as those of the Queen are set down. I must say she and her husband Philip did back some writers and painters, but the only thing I really respect her for is her pacifism.

November 8th

Pearly beauty of a November morning, especially crossing the Thames, from a train to Dorset and the Stones.

I've had some pretty bad dips into the suicide well lately, though I usually emerge more or less sane after a night's sleep. Deep loneliness, a pitch-black night of it, invades me at times. Sometimes my mask seems to be effective, but I almost despise myself for it. I despise myself also for the *sheer cowardice* that prevents my killing myself. If there was a foolproof easy way, I believe I'd take it at once.

But I'll try and think of other people now.

November 15th: Crichel

I feel a need to stocktake. What has been on the credit side? The great beauty of that South Dorset landscape, kindness of the Stones and thoughtful cosseting provided by Janet, interesting conversation with Reynolds, walks in steep little valleys, smaller than they looked so that sheep on the far side seemed like cows, the pleasure of seeing Kitty West happy with her new shop at Blandford, and driving to London with her. Then in a quiet week I would single out going to *Don Carlos* with Duncan Grant and dining afterwards with Eardley Knollys and Edward Le Bas[2] at the Ivy; calling on poor old Clive Bell, ill again and looking thin and pale; going to my orchestra.

Eardley and I came here last night and found Desmond Shawe-Taylor, Eddy, Raymond and Cressida Ridley.[3]

Still stocktaking when I woke this morning about exactly what my position in

---

[1] A member of the Medical Orchestra I belonged to. I played the second violin, and our weekly rehearsals were one of my greatest joys.
[2] The painter.
[3] Daughter of Lady Violet Bonham-Carter.

the world was. I now have no one who belongs to me, who loves me and cares what happens to me for some instinctive reason – as Ralph and Burgo and I suppose M.A.M.[1] long ago did. I must face the fact therefore that I shall only receive affection according to my deserts and if I contribute to other people's happiness. I can do this a bit I think by taking an interest in their lives which is entirely genuine. But I easily lose any confidence I ever had in my ability to be good company or a social asset.

This morning's light on the situation was to face me with a fork in the road and a signpost pointing each way. *Make up your mind*, a voice said in my brain: If you decide to die, go to the London Library and study forensic medicine, do everything to ensure success and a neat get-away.

But if you decide to live, you must realize that no one is backing you instinctively any more. You are, and ever will be alone, to fight toothache, illness, worry, the approach of death and every other problem *entirely alone*. This may sound ungrateful for the vast and bottomless kindness of Janetta, Joan, Raymond and others. But I don't think it is – it's only realism.

November 29th

Yesterday, after lunch with the Japps, Henrietta and Sophie, I drove the last two to the clinic for poor Sophie to be jabbed with various plagues. For quite a half hour I sat in the womb-heated hall where mothers bent over babies of all sizes and toddlers roamed about, crooning over large public teddy bears, tugged at each other's hair with poker-faced hatred and made other more friendly contacts. Some were quite hideous, though dressed with spotless, loving care. I felt proud of Sophie's noble round head, thoughtful intelligent eyes and general look of distinction. But I am half-terrified of getting too fond of her.

December 8th

At David and Rachel Cecil's, Oxford, in their new little doll's house – an improvement on the last, though every word can be heard through its thin walls. Walked with David and Rachel in the Parks yesterday afternoon – very cold, quite still. Coming home we saw a colossal orange sun sinking into the blue haze. The night was bitter and I'm not surprised to see the trees closely coated in frost this morning.

There were three young men at dinner last night – Hugh Cecil and his friend David Tweedie drove down from London and are still here; Simon Whistler spent the evening. He is the son of Lawrence Whistler[2] and his first wife Jill Furze, a very beautiful woman who died giving birth to the second child. Lawrence took her sister Teresa to live with him and look after the two children and later married her. She too, according to David and Rachel, is beautiful, intelligent and remarkable. There were two more children. This boy Simon was charming and good-looking, but more than that. He stood out from the three as being an interesting character, with a certain unusual, quite unpompous intensity. He's a professional musician and plays the viola in an orchestra at Amsterdam; age twenty-three. He took David aside to his study after dinner and asked him about a book his father has written (not published yet) about the dead wife, his mother; did he think Teresa – his

---

[1] My mother.
[2] Glass-engraver and artist.

stepmother and aunt – would mind? The book is deeply emotional, 'sentimental', Rachel hinted, and intimate. Simon too had read it, and been moved to tears, though he was only four when his mother died and he could hardly remember her.

David and Rachel's interest and sympathy with everyone are remarkable – it's not true that absorption in your own family leads to shutters being drawn over the rest of the world, if anything the reverse is.

December 9th

Something of a talking marathon, but enjoyable. Thinking to find the house deserted at churchtime, I descended to the drawing-room and was at once involved with David, at home because of a cold. 'Do I talk too much? Rachel says I do – nicely of course – and that I shout people down.' The boys left in the morning and David went out to lunch. Left alone with Rachel I asked her about her religion and the subject came up again after dinner. Quite interesting, though there were areas which seemed almost indecent to probe. Rachel may have thought for a moment that my adversities had made me feel the need of religion and that David might convert me. I don't think it even flashed into my head that I could unconvert them. How could an omnipotent and beneficent God allow the world to be so cruel and beastly? was my chief question. Rachel would have liked to deny the evil but couldn't, and obviously hadn't thought much about it – her faith was incredibly simple, a hot-water bottle tightly clutched against her person. When I put my question to David later, he surprised me a little by his genuine fervour – I'd thought his answer might be more conventional. Also by his admission that God must be personal. (Murmurs of dissent from Rachel here. Hadn't they discussed it, or did she know from her experience of Desmond[1] how ludicrous this seemed to the irreligious?) David said: 'Not that he has a nose and all the rest of it of course – but since *I* know *him*, he (being greater) *must* be able to know me, mustn't he?' Unlike Rachel he at once admitted the evil and suffering in the world, and was even prepared to say it outweighed the good. So far as I could make out, his explanation was that 'men now suffer as Christ suffered.' Their consolation must be that they are like him returning good (in the form of courage, or – even more – acceptance) for evil. I had said that I saw no good coming out of concentration camps – only more hatred and bitterness and wars. Because of this prevalence of evil in the world, David seemed to be informed by his faith of a necessary 'transcendent and eternal world of good'. I thought I detected that he felt this must exist because it would be so awful if it didn't. His faith first came to him in a religious experience lasting several hours in a hotel in Naples when he had been ill, but he had had others since. He sets great value on the rituals of religion and particularly on taking the sacrament. Of their children Jonathan mildly accepts religion, Hugh had a painful crisis in his belief at eighteen and, though David thinks him the most naturally religious of the three, does not go to church. David suggested that he might go on going, and see what happened, but Hugh said the ritual made him supremely uncomfortable. Rachel dreamily 'hoped he would return to the fold'. Laura discussed belief with her agnostic friends.

I'm glad to have explored this shut-away region and am interested in what I

[1] MacCarthy, her father.

discovered there. I don't think it was resented and no fur flew.

December 17th: West Halkin Street

I float so low in the water that the weight of a dead leaf submerges me. Janetta was coming to lunch today – the last chance of seeing her before she goes to Spain? but she rang up to say she'd forgotten she was lunching with Rose MacLaren. Well and good. As I am frankly killing time at the moment I went by myself to the twelve-thirty showing of Garbo in *Ninotchka*. Perhaps that wasn't lowering but coming out into the so-called daylight was, and brushing past figures with drab pinched faces, and having a sandwich and a Bovril in an awful café where everyone looked as though they were just going to drown themselves and the waitresses worse – expressionless, gone under. Now I'm back at my flat, feeling almost unequal to going to see Janetta at six as she asked me.

December 23rd

I spent a large part of today with Henrietta and Sophie, and now at quarter to five I am in charge and Sophie is beginning to cry fretfully and suck her thumb. I have found this contact with my 'family' delightful, exhausting and harassing. A very good no-barrier feeling between me and Henrietta. The day was completely filled – there was only just time to hoist the innumerable baby appurtenances up to her flat before I dashed off for a drink with the Japps and supper with Isobel Strachey.

Boxing Day

Gordon House, Lambourn with the Gowings for Christmas, as I was last, but the circumstances are very different. Lawrence and Jenny[1] are here. Christmas Day was totally ignored. In the afternoon Julia and I had a long and delicious walk, with the rolling spaces all round us disappearing in faint iridescent colours to the horizon, the winter trees standing with squiggly black twigs against the pale sky. The to-do about yesterday's turkey was terrific. It must be cooked *à la Gaylord Hauser* exactly twenty-three minutes to the pound, not a minute more or less. Therefore it must go on soon after eight. I was surprised to come down at nine and find the oven not yet turned on nor breakfast preparations begun. A mistake had been made in the sum and it had to go in an hour later. There followed a complicated scheme by which the egg-boiler was to go off every quarter of an hour and shifts were to be allocated for basting the bird. After much discussion Mrs Rose turned up and took over the entire lunch. The preparations for last night's dinner – two veg and cold ham occupied Jenny and Julia at full pitch for several hours. I have said I'll do lunch by myself today as this seems the easiest way of helping. Otherwise one runs into Julia's rules. Again no one was down by nine this morning, so I began to make breakfast, and had put the eggs in the saucepan, when Julia came and took them out, dropped one and broke it. It was against the house rules to put eggs in before water!

While she was getting the tea this afternoon Julia dashed into the television room and said: 'This is very egotistic but I must say what's in my mind. If only I had been able never to cook a meal since I wrote *Cheerful Weather for the Wedding*, I should have written any number of books. I had heaps of ideas. Young writers

---

[1] Wallis, later Gowing.

ought to have a grant so that they don't have to cook.' 'Well that would need a full-time servant to look after each one of them,' I said, thinking how little help the presence of Mrs Rose every day from ten till two seemed to Julia.

December 27th

So one more Christmas has blown past our ears almost unnoticed by mine. The good manners preserved by the triangle in this house are immaculate – yet there are storms beneath the surface.

1964

January 1st: 16 West Halkin Street

A nice evening here last night, with Clive, Little Barbara Bagenal and Kitty. It was a good idea to have Kitty, she was lively and friendly to both and stayed on after they'd gone, leaving just before the death of old 1963. I was in bed reading when the eerie sound of the jangling bells struck my ear – more like the distant baying of hounds or yelling of a crowd at a football match than any sound of rejoicing. Why rejoice indeed at the passage of time? I can only hope that 1964 won't be as bad as last year, it could hardly be worse. I dreamt of both Ralph and Burgo together last night, back in the anxieties of Burgo's adolescence, and awoke to stare into the deep black hole of their joint absence.

January 14th

The Gowings' crisis has intensified. Julia came here in a state of tremulous agitation which drove her eventually to see Craig and ask about a divorce. I feel great reluctance to leave her without my feeble support at this juncture.

January 20th

I suppose my most important event last week was lunching with Victor Gollancz and Victoria Ocampo (literary queen of Latin America) at the Savoy. I liked her – a full-blooded, intelligent, blue-haired, warm-hearted Spaniard. I *may* translate her autobiography, and we sat until four-thirty on a sofa in the Savoy, discussing the problems of translation and the inadequacies of Bunny's translation of her last book from the French. Our table near the great window overlooking the river had an amazing view. After soup, and roast beef and Yorkshire pudding, Señora Ocampo declared she'd heard about something called semolina pudding and would like to try it. A row of waiters with real looks of perturbation on their faces hovered before her. There was none. Then I saw on the trolley a bread-and-butter pudding and asked her if she had ever tried that very English confection? She tried it, we had coffee and were thinking of departing, when the Greek chorus of waiters reappeared like birds on a twig and still with anxious expressions, bearing a small specially made semolina pudding. It's much to her credit that she tried that too.

It has set me up to feel I have gone a peg upwards in the translation world and I do believe Victoria Ocampo might help me to work. I've long wanted to get in touch with her.

January 22nd

I have rounded a bend of sorts, but the state of apathy in which at times I trudge on horrifies me – the way I deliberately force myself not to think (in a certain positive way at least) about Ralph and Burgo. Rather than be reduced to unutterable selfishness, I sink myself in the lives of other people, Mary, Julia in particular, and listen to their problems with obsessional concentration. At the same time I continue to notice with surprise the complete egotism of suffering. Julia always makes a heroic effort to ask me about my life, work, state of mind; they don't exist for Mary. As I lay in bed before dropping off last night I pondered over the inordinate difference between Mary's way of thinking and mine – but it doesn't impair our mutual affection.

February 14th

Janetta is back. That is the most important event on my human level. After *Aida*, Julian and I went to Montpelier Square – where were Eddy, Jonny Gathorne-Hardy and Sabrina, Magouche, Mary, Diana Cooper and Lord Norwich, Patrick Kinross and a few others. Oh yes, Billa Harrod to whom I talked for some time. It's not 'my world' but I was fairly at home there, and then the door opened and in came the dear brown face of Janetta. Very nice to see her. On the telephone this morning, she said how 'everyone she'd wanted to see' was in that room and I realized the lack of overlap between her and me. They were smoking hashish apparently, though I noticed no difference in those who'd had some (Julian for instance). On the telephone also she'd said that Robert and I 'were the only people who were cross with her for not coming back earlier' – this according to Georgie, whom I've not once seen.

March 4th

Baby-sitting for Henrietta, listening to the crooning and sleepy mooing of Sophie in her crib next door, and feeling shamefully unsuited to carry the weight of her existence even for so short a time. The gestures with which she idly slapped her bottle or pointed her well-developed ballet dancer's toes while drinking from it delight me. Next week Henrietta goes off to Spain for a couple of weeks leaving Sophie with Angelica.

I've not written for a week and feel I must plot the graph of these days. I realized with quite a shock that I have grown to love London, almost to be 'in love' with it as though it were a person, to feel proud to belong to it (be a 'member of the wedding'), and I appreciate its various moods. Yet it's a short cry from the feeling of loneliness, crushing impersonality, restlessness and noise to this other – almost new – delight in the tall, pale houses and taller, black trees, the sparkling lights, the new clarity I seem to see in the air, and the signs of spring – twittering, green shoots, earthen smells.

Just after I wrote last I had a desperate call from Julia, summoned her round and spent long hours talking over her situation. Since then they have decided to tell the world about the divorce, and I got her in her desperation to say she'd come to Italy with me, perhaps even at once. Later the date was fixed – April 9th, and I wrote to ask Joan Cochemé to take rooms in a *pensione* in Rome she had found. Yesterday there were signs of wavering on Julia's part and I shan't be surprised if she doesn't come, indeed I pressed her not to feel tied as I would go anyway. I'm going to pay her ticket and if possible her *pensione* also. What worries me a little is that while patting herself on the back for 'facing up to reality' she contrives to be miles from it – or at least one leg is up in the air if the other rests on *terra firma*.

March 5th

I broached to Isobel last night the possibility of coming with me should Julia fail. She charmingly said she'd be delighted to come, had never been to Rome, and was prepared to do so at the last minute.

Henrietta left for Spain yesterday. She and darling little Sophie were here last week for lunch and who should turn up but Denis Wirth Miller also. He had had yet another scene with Francis Bacon, who fired some home truths at him ('tactless, insensitive, lazy'). Of Bacon's new boyfriend, a burglar, he said: 'He's very good at cracking safes and that's a *creative activity*.' I didn't take this up at the moment but it has been rolling unpalatably round my head like a marble.

March 17th

Last night Julia announced in somewhat regal style that Rome was 'on', and she came to dinner to talk about it. But the cloud of fuss she put up has I fear somewhat taken the heart out of the whole project. J.: 'I couldn't go by jet aeroplane'. F.: 'Why ever not?' J.: 'Not sure why. Is it because it's too dangerous?' Catching an aeroplane at nine-thirty was impossible – she must defrost her fridge and then 'my make-up takes me two hours'. It's gloriously funny in a way, but it has given me a foretaste of what the smallest arrangements will be like.

April 9th: Rome

Here we are. Six p.m. – a delightful *pensione* found for us by kind Joan Cochemé, and I lie on my bed relaxed, preparing to take a swig of my aeroplane whisky, and *thinking of Julia*. I should really have kept a record of all the fantastic fuss that has exercised her these last weeks. When we were discussing aeroplanes I forgot to say that I mentioned the Alitalia line by which we have come. 'What's that?' she asked suspiciously. 'Not one of these charter planes?' I assured her it was the regular Italian line. Over the Easter weekend an Alitalia plane crashed and I fully thought that would finish her, but I rather doubt if she ever heard of it, for she never reads the papers. But two days ago she rang up to ask whether we could find out the exact measurement under the seat for her hand baggage. To catch the five-to-one plane she got up at six-thirty, and I must say that the journey went without a hitch, although there's not a moment when she isn't dreading the next contingency and planning how to deal with it. At present it is the fact that there certainly won't be enough coffee for breakfast. Joan looked at me in consternation when we were alone briefly. I feel strong and able to face anything at the moment but I know there are great hulking reefs ahead. Also I do want time to myself, or alone with Joan sometimes. My resolves are three: to remember Julia is desperately unhappy, to treat her fuss merely as exaggerated farce and even enjoy it as such, and to be as adaptable as possible.

The limpid, pure blue sky of Rome greeted us in full glory and so did the magnificent regal personality of this noble town. I'm sure I shan't feel short of things to do while I'm here. My room has a tiled floor, ugly modern furniture, a table, a desk, and a window looking out onto Judas trees. I've been working very hard, was typing an index for James until seven-thirty last night, so I shall be glad to rest for a little while. If only I don't run short of material.

April 11th

Sitting up in bed, seven-twenty a.m. The Aventino, where our *pensione* is, charms me with its beauty, tranquillity, Judas trees in flower, drifting clerics. One could have no more delightful eyrie from which to try and become a member of the Roman wedding – but it's going to be difficult with my poor panic-stricken, half-crazed companion by my side.

She does think it beautiful, appreciates the architecture but fear makes it only possible for her to enjoy it briefly. What can I do for her? In her situation of being hedged round by multiple terrors her only 'defence mechanism' is fuss, fuss, FUSSISSIMO. 'Are you sure this is the way?' she asks me of a road already known by heart, 'don't you think we came in the other way last time? How do you *know*? How can you tell it isn't the other bridge? Are you sure this is the Corso? But *how* do you know?' And she will ask a policeman, or not one but three. What must it be like to be encompassed by such dreads? Her hair rinse might fade, they might not give her enough coffee for breakfast, we might be poisoned by the water, forget the number of the bus, and so forth. She is terrified of crossing the road (almost refused like a horse) and won't go up in Joan's lift – preferring to walk up five floors. Being late, forgetting the name of the street we are going to: everything scares her. As for 'taking a chance' ever, it's out of the question.

I'm trying to think of her as an invalid. I sometimes really think she is going off her head. Her memory is so weak, either from drugs or other things, that she asks me the same question ten times over, and I answer hollowly, knowing it will be dished up again in five minutes' time. She has brought a ready reckoner given her by the bank to convert lire to sterling, yet she asks me over and over and over what 1000 lire is worth, and when changing money the other day she again asked the clerk the value of every separate note. I'm filled with embarrassment often, and ashamed of my embarrassment of course.

I made a little headway I think yesterday by getting her to recognize that her fears were not rational, that they were in fact phobias, and suggested treating them by the method of thinking 'What shall I do if the worst comes to the worst?' told me by an agoraphobic friend. I found that one of her chief fears about buses is that she can't remember the name of where she wants to go. Nor can she in fact. Getting into a bus in front of me, she panicked totally – the word Aventino is too much to remember.

6.20 p.m. I don't know how I could have written so heartlessly about trying to enjoy Julia's farcical eccentricities. They are a great deal more than a joke – a desperate tragedy which bids fair to sink me too. This morning, however, went smoothly. We walked gently along to the Villa Farnesina (Julia's idea) never losing the way once. I led her straight to the door; there wasn't another soul in the place. Later we sat on a wall of huge, pale stones looking down at the grey, sliding Tiber talking about Adrian Daintrey, and then explored the island. 'Was I sure this was the *right* island?' she asked. I assured her there *was* only one. We went on to a trattoria recommended by Daintrey, and there over a good and cheap meal Julia spoke almost in tears of her feeling that she might have to go home. The impact of Rome was too much for her, she was terrified all the time. I told her she must of course go if she wanted to, *at once*, and I think talking relieved her. I'm really afraid of a complete breakdown, a crisis. How too can I conduct my own life I wonder? I only like to leave her for a short time, and she takes no joy in her surroundings whatever.

April 12th

A gulp of the true pleasure of being abroad. Wandering out this mid-morning along the Via di Sabina, which contains three churches, I found a wedding going on in one and became one of the congregation, watching the solemn little pair as they knelt before the altar banked with white flowers. All up the aisle were bunches of white roses connected by tulle swags. Sightseers prowled, as I did, unheeded. An elderly and very plain spinster – German? – in thick lisle stockings peered avidly at the symbolic representation of what she herself had never experienced – union with a man. I watched just as eagerly, following all the ritual; the priest took a swig of something, bride and groom did likewise, photographers flashed away unashamedly, and with deadly solemn and dreary expressions the couple advanced down the aisle. Outside – beams, and formal pecks from all friends, male and female.

Last night Joan telephoned and came to see me, we had an hour or so's talk and then saw each other home through the public gardens. It was a relief to share my worries a little with her. This morning I found Julia in a mood of valiant realism. A nightmare had brought her phobias psychoanalytically to the surface. She now feels that Rome was the best place for her to come, even though it has been hard for her. All at once she was her fascinating original self again, not confused and groping but trying to explain that the mythical figures on the Villa Farnesina, Raphael's Galatea and the rest, had acted violently on her emotions as symbols of what lay beneath the surface of her life. My line will be to convince her that she is someone who has just suffered a drastic surgical operation when in a very weak physical state. She said she would like to stay in her room and write about her mythical experiences.

April 13th

Ay de mi, I cannot sleep for thinking of poor Julia, and woke this morning – not to sleep again – before five. Such an in-turned uninterested, apathetic travelling companion is quite outside my experience. I think with amazement of Eardley, Raymond, Janetta, and my darling Ralph. Yesterday we passed a soothing day which I hoped would be more to her taste. The sky had cleared to a palish blue and kind Joan asked us to lunch on her terrace. 'Oh, on the terrace?' 'Yes, she thought you might like to bring a hat.' 'Oh I don't think I want to sit in the *sun*. Well I must think what clothes to put on for the smuts – must keep something for best.'

Lunch was prettily laid out and delicious, and nothing could have been nicer than to look down from so high up at the town, the crawling cars reduced to gently buzzing insects. After lunch Julia said she would 'read her Conrad', was established in a *chaise-longue* and lay there with eyes closed apparently asleep for about two hours, while the rest of us washed up and chattered. About four o'clock

Joan and I set out for the Janiculum – would Julia or Elizabeth[1] like to come too? Elizabeth (a handsome girl now, and sane – at the moment almost my favourite quality) said she wanted to finish making a dress. Julia said 'she was too weary' and indeed she looked it. So Joan and I went off by bus to a pretty public garden at the top of the hill where we walked among the Sunday crowds, enlaced lovers, tiny boys dressed as men in peaked caps, and bouncing children. Then to the church of San Pietro in Montorio with its dear little Bramante *tempietto*. Joan would have liked to walk further, but I felt we should return to Julia and sure enough she said to me rather accusingly later that she had had another bad patch after tea – a wave, of exactly what I don't know. We dined in the hotel, and I felt I should almost die of sitting opposite this shut, obsessional face and knowing that she was suffering my presence and all her surroundings as best she could.

At the moment, I can't help it, I hope she will go home, and I think she should have a course of treatment in a nursing home. Selfish feelings well up in me to the effect that I too need some sort of holiday and that to look after someone in her state is nothing like one.

I try to get her to say what she'd like to do because I know anything I suggest will be found fault with. But when the moment comes to study the guidebooks and decide, she can't face it. So desperately I lay Rome's wares before her and try to interest her in one or another.

April 14th

Triumph! Julia has by some form of conjuring trick pulled herself suddenly together. What an extraordinary character! It happened on Monday night – apparently she lay 'thinking out her problems until one o'clock'.

Now there is the miracle. After facing her facts she began yesterday as a new woman. Luckily it was a marvellous day. She said firmly that she wanted to go sightseeing, and as it was Monday and the museums were all shut we set off for St Peter's. Twice on the way she asked me '*Where* is it we're going?' When writing a postcard on St Peter's roof she wanted to know what our *pensione* was called. But the change in her all yesterday was heroic and stupendous – in the late afternoon she even ventured out in a bus to the Capitol by herself. I'm simply delighted at these signs of recovery, and also full of admiration for the effort she made. In a way she really enjoyed her visit to St Peter's, thrust her tentacles into the rich sensorial stuff surrounding us, and had comments to make thereon. Phew! – I breathe again, or so it seems. We dined with Joan and Elizabeth, and this morning there has been no decline at all: we spent long hours walking across the Borghese Gardens and looking at the pictures in the Gallery. Late home to lunch.

April 16th

Julia's new look has been magnificently sustained and I am filled with admiration for her courage and determination. What's more her effort has, I'm sure, had a therapeutic effect, she does for a time forget her troubles and focus on the things that surround her. In her epic wrestling match with her devil in the watches of the night she did achieve a real victory. On Tuesday night we made our way through the darkened streets to the Piazza Navona and dined in a restaurant there.

[1] Joan's step-daughter.

The Piazza Navona was looking marvellously beautiful, dignified and far from crowded. The fountains were bathed in light and the turquoise water spouted forth. Julia was at her best – inspecting Bernini's creation from every angle and commenting on it all. It's particularly the animals she likes – 'Do look at that dear old lion – he's got such a *scholarly* expression,' she'll say. She has got herself, wrenched herself, back into her normal position of being a fascinating companion.

Our expedition to Tivoli and the Villa d'Este was a great success with us all; we moved slowly down through the painted rooms and terraced fountains and ate our picnic lunch at Hadrian's Villa, lying in the lush grass. Picked wild flowers – a blue anchusa, a vetch with black velvet wings – and wandered peacefully through the ruins. Dinner at the Cochemés. Cochemé (back from Cairo with another scientist from the Food and Agriculture Organization) was there. It was delightful to hear the scientists talking about their subject – locusts – and how I envied them their rapturous, flashing-eyed absorption. Cochemé described watching a baby locust hatch out in the warm sand, force its way to the surface, take a vigorous but tentative HOP, fall on its nose and start again. One of their objects, he said, was to 'induce sexual maturity earlier in locusts'; I can't imagine why, as they are trying to exterminate them.

April 17th

Coming back from this morning's sightseeing (the Gesù and the Doria palace), I told Julia how much I admired the way she had dealt with her phobias, and heard from her how at twenty-five she had been faced with a really awful attack of panic, dread of the universe, inability to understand the relationship of mind to matter or anything else – 'I think it has a name, something like "panic fear".' It had taken her months, but she'd gone down to the roots of it and taken it apart leaf by leaf. Her passage through life is a triumph of equilibrium, for I think she's well aware of the dark streaks in her character.

April 19th

This evening's sightseeing was a great success. We went to two sights Julia had seen before and liked, I never – churches by Borromini and Bernini near the Quirinale (I also took her to Sant' Andrea). Everything went well and all sights were enjoyed. Santa Maria della Vittória, much disapproved by Baedeker, is the sexiest little church I ever was in. Incredibly richly encrusted within with gilt and various coloured marbles, it leads up to an altar which is simply an illuminated vagina surrounded by radiating gilt beams. On the left is a very finished gleaming white statue by Bernini of Santa Teresa swooning backwards on the brink of an orgasm, while a pretty angel with a charming teasing smile raises an arrow to penetrate her. All the commentators, whether favourable or unfavourable, have hardly been able to overlook the obvious sexual symbolism.

Perhaps the clue to Julia is that she can't get over people not being exactly like her. What's more she thinks they oughtn't to be different.

April 22nd

One is always right when one senses a crack in the human crust, through which passions will soon shoot volcanically upwards. They did, yesterday evening, but no harm I believe has been done – even perhaps the air is cleared. We had, after the usual siesta, a successful excursion to Santa Maria della Pace yesterday afternoon. I know that the number of things I have to repeat twenty times in answer to the same question does exacerbate me ('the cloister is by Bramante. No, not Pietro da Cortona – Bramante'); also, the problems she expected me to give the answer to from my head, which she doesn't in the least want to know and won't remember for more than one second. ('What would the date of the Etruscan statue be, do you happen to know?' 'I suppose you don't happen to remember where the 95 bus stops, do you?') She has also a way of putting the most naïve posers like, who is Auden and what is the Légion d'honneur. The last amazed Cochemé.

April 25th

How can I make Julia enjoy her last few days, and not feel the whole thing was a big mistake? Her mind is at present preoccupied with the journey home and I think she's looking forward to going. Will she think of the whole thing with horror? I resolve to exert my utmost from now through these five days to sympathize and support her, for she's probably got a tough situation to face on her return. Today we tackled the Vatican museum rooms, meaning to look at the Pinacoteca, but after the immense walk outside the huge sloping walls and then inside the building itself the crush in the Raphael rooms was unbearable – just a dense sea of bobbing heads, a sort of human brawn, and a voice shouting 'Keep to the right!' We backed hastily away and went to see the Pinturicchios and the splendid primitives in the Pinacoteca.

Dined with the Cochemés and had a livelier evening than usual owing to an argument about Free Will and Determinism. Joan declared that she was a determinist and Julia that she couldn't conceive of anyone not intuitively being aware of free will – both of which was like a Conservative saying he simply couldn't conceive of anyone being a Socialist and expecting you to take that for an argument. I produced my traditional defence of determinism, and Julia challenged me rather aggressively to say what determinism was and so I jolly well did tell her. Julia put up some fascinating skirmish movements with remarks like 'Well, that famous scientist (whose name I forget) whose book I gave you to read and you said you liked, seemed to have a sort of hunch that there was free will.' Everything was, however, perfectly friendly, and Julia came away saying 'Well, we put up a fine Punch and Judy show for them, didn't we?'

But *now* – careful, gentle, sympathetic: I must be endlessly patient with her, and that is no easy task, for I realize that Julia has not these last weeks given me as a person a single thought, other than conceiving me as a banister to hold on to. I wish I'd been a better one. In my own defence I must record that it's these moments of irritation that I set down, but that I have really striven and struggled to contain my exasperation with her and a good deal of the time with considerable success. Alas I am not a serene and placid character. This morning I said to her that I felt perhaps it would have been better for her if we'd gone to some quiet sunny spot like Ravello. So I now think it would – but not for me, nor do I know how she would have passed the time though it takes her very little to do that. Almost her sole indoor activity while here, other than reading a few pages of Conrad, has been 'writing her notes'. This consists in trying to jot down the names of the sights seen each day.

However, today has passed in perfect serenity and amity, and Julia has made obvious efforts to remember that I too am a human being. Santa Prasséde and Santa Maria Maggiore this morning; my pocket (or rather my basket) was picked in a crowded bus.

For all my preoccupation with Julia I've not ceased to be sharply, disturbingly, excitingly aware of Rome's character and grandeur. It keeps me bubbling and simmering – could being married to a marvellously beautiful woman be in the same way a perpetual agitation? But it could be one who wears hideous clothes, as Rome wears cars. Last night returning quite late, it was a pleasure to see the angles between the narrow cobbled floor of the Via Lata, which leads past the Doria palace, and its stupendous walls, clear of any obstacle – so that the street had the design and proportion its architects intended.

April 29th

9.30. Obsessional fuss has returned to swamp Julia. To see her scuffling in her bag over the dinner table to find her bill with her newly done ('hopeless my dear') hair-do like a Skye terrier hanging over clawing front paws, was really tragic. What heavy weather she makes for herself! Once again she began to retrace the network of circumstances in which she enchains herself. 'Well you see I couldn't bring a note-case because the one I have is stuffed with things like cleaner's tickets.' F.: 'Couldn't you empty them into a drawer and bring the note-case away with you?' J.: 'You don't suppose I've got a drawer in my flat, what with all Lawrence's dirty clothes and paint rags and huge boots?' It transpires that she's carried all her English money about everywhere as well as her Italian – an envelope of notes, a purse of coins. 'Well what do *you* do?' she asked. F.: 'Put all my English money, passport, traveller's cheques, and air ticket into my small suitcase and lock it.' 'What, all the English money loose?' F.: 'Why yes.' J.: 'Oh I couldn't possibly bear that. I like everything neat and in its right place.' F.: 'Well, you could put it in an envelope inside the case if you wanted to.' And so on *ad infinitum.*

She complains of the cold – no one else does. The trees are out in full spring greenery, roses bloom and scent the air in the corner of our square, the ground is becoming dotted with the fallen flowers of the acacias and the Judas trees.

May 2nd

After seeing Julia off to her aeroplane, I returned to the hotel, packed my things, and Cochemé kindly came to transport me to my temporary nest in Elizabeth's room – a little ocean-going cabin in their flat.

Sudden arrival of Raymond in Rome two days ago, and I came here with him last night, after a complicated but successful day seeing Tarquinia. This was after several days' soothing spoiling by Joan in the river-side flat, looking out after dark from the terrace at the Tiber glittering along in one direction in the light of the street-lamps while the stream of red rear lights of cars flowed down the other. Above stood the peaceful block of the Aventino with its dark trees and churches, looking like home. Above again, the intensely rich deep indigo sky. One would never be tired of looking at it, any more than the downs at Ham Spray, but grow to love it more.

Tarquinia was extraordinary, both beautiful and interesting. We descended the stairs into about eight little funeral compartments, along with a serious Italian couple and the guide, and found ourselves surrounded with lively brilliant paintings of leopards, dancing girls, musicians, horses, all drawn in with a sure, fine, bold line and then brightly coloured. No sense of individual artists, though they covered several centuries in time. Small not very interesting obscenities. Why this lack of individuality? Is it that one can't read it, any more than the expressions on a Chinaman's face? How much do we miss by this?

May 7th

A lovely day yesterday, soaking in the Sienese richness of the Pinacoteca, in the afternoon to the Duomo. In the evening almost exactly the same flavour of pure, ecstatic, devout richness was produced by a concert we went to in an extraordinary room in the Palazzo Chigi. Four unlikely looking men – they might have been dentists or criminals – got into a close knot together and sang motets by Palestrina most beautifully.

Raymond is serene, and benign, delightful company. We get on very well. I must have been pretty difficult on our last sad journey I now realize.

May 13th: Assisi

I can't believe that the day after tomorrow I'll be surrounded by cream stucco, grey pavements, the telephone, all my 'things' and a pile of bills. It has grown really hot the last day or two so that one fears it a little and plans to creep into the shade. This is our last day here and we have taken the train to a dear little town called Spello, with Roman remains and Pinturicchio frescoes, and back again here.

Walking into the huge church, you are overwhelmed by all the frescoes brilliantly decorating its walls – the Giottos in the upper church, Simone Martinis and Lorenzettis in the lower. I've been driven frantic by the fact that the Franciscan friars refuse to put any lighting in the lower church but a glowworm glint here and there, so that one strains one's eyes almost in vain into the obscurity. When I asked one of them if it was possible to have more light he angrily said no it wasn't. They don't *want* us to see these masterpieces (Lorenzetti's *The Descent from the Cross*, Martini's *St Martin*), they don't *want* anyone to have such voluptuous pleasure, they don't *want* it themselves. The odour of sanctity is dense, stubborn and stifling. A nun stood in a rattling bus, reading her missal, a friar in the crypt where St Francis is buried obviously liked being in glum near-darkness; another tourist came up and protested because Raymond and I were discussing the frescoes in spite of the *silenzio* notice.

I can't think of any place where religion has expressed itself in the past with more brilliant, creative gaiety and now exudes such suffocating inhibitory negativism.

But Nature reflects or echoes the brilliance and gaiety of Giotto and Lorenzetti. The weather seems set fair, the gardens at Spello were full of huge roses. I dream of sightseeing.

May 20th: West Halkin Street

Arriving with Raymond by air on Whit Friday I walked into the dead cube of air contained by my sitting-room. One piece of ivy and two twigs stood in my Spanish jug; my heart sank like a stone. The weather radiant, as hot as Rome. Janetta in Majorca, everyone I rang up was 'away for Whitsun', except Margaret Penrose who was just going. 'Why don't you come too?' she kindly asked and I did. The feeling of dreadful unreality and loneliness, which hit me like a blast of hot air when I opened the door of my flat was dissipated by finding myself at the steering wheel of my friendly Mini spinning off into the blue-and-green, Bank-holiday-jolly countryside on Saturday.

The Penroses' National Trust show house has a cardboard appearance but is immensely livable in, like a stage set which has had a lot of use. Margaret is rapidly becoming as round as a football; she rolls about the house with a 'cheerful bumpy sound'. There was a bearded anthropologist and his wife, a mental nurse, on Saturday night and next night a medical student girl friend of Shirley's. These very intelligent girls giggled like any others about young men and parties when left together. Lots of fascinating talk, much of it scientific; ramshackle croquet, a walk with Margaret. Lionel has found that one in every hundred babies born to a mother over forty is a Mongolian imbecile and one in every forty-five if she's over forty-five. Surely this should be widely publicized?

May 21st

I've been driving about London in a daze, landing beyond my destinations in unknown surroundings – all because of thinking of Julia. Thinking of her kept me awake till four last night in spite of a lot of pills (which I'd been trying to wean myself from). Oh dear, oh dear, oh dear, oh *dear*. I fear she's beyond my aid. After two warm letters thanking me cordially for the Roman holiday she asked me to dinner (a 'quiet bite') last night, and I went round feeling eager to know how things were going.

I rang the downstairs bell and started up the stairs. Before I got to Julia's door she had emerged and stood poised like a fashion model at the top. It was as if she had been bewitched by some extraordinary spell and she gave me a quite unexpectedly frosty reception. Instead of the usual Hallo, and welcoming smile, this time there she stood, every gesture studied, in a neat black dress, with a bright pink scarf carefully arranged round her neck. 'I say, my dear, you're looking very elegant,' I said. 'Is it a dinner party?' 'Oh no, very much not so,' said Julia. But the grizzly thing, the wounding, chilling thing was that I felt her dislike and dis-approval hitting me like a wave, implicit in her cold eyes and her mask-like face. There followed a grand display of her social manner. 'Do sit down.' Head tilted back, a scornful *grande dame* expression. A great many 'Oh reelly?s' and the symbolical sniff. I made a bid to get a note of relaxation and intimacy into the conversation, but it was so futile that I literally felt like bursting into tears. My saying I'd seen Bunny who had been to the Bussy sale, and preparing to tell her about it, met with: 'Oh well, I'm really not in the least interested.' We drank our whisky, I feeling more and more desperate, and she then insisted on taking me out to eat an expensive meal at Lyons' Grill and refusing to let me pay my share. Throughout her manner was artificial in the extreme, like someone going through a part in a play, and we left at nine-thirty. Ten minutes later I saw as we stood on her doorway that she expected me to go home and not come in. A little later I was tossing and turning in bed, thinking how much she must have hated the Roman holiday, looked back on it as a nightmare and borne a strong grudge against me for taking her. I'm left quite uncertain what was the explanation. But I'm very sure that she feels no affection at all for me at present and a great deal of dislike, also that I can't bear this remote withering formality from someone I've known since she was eight. The result of my nightly tossing is that I've decided to keep silent and apart until such time as she makes a move in my direction.

This has been extraordinarily upsetting; I don't know how it will end.

May 29th: Hilton

I live on two levels at the moment. Underneath is the sad grey lumbering tide, my longing for the end of it all. On top (I can say with truth) I am enjoying being here at Hilton during a hot beautiful weekend; and there's no inconsistency. Also I believe that the subterranean flood is unguessed at by my companions. Yet it's there all the time, the first thing I wake to when I become conscious in the morning.

Have enjoyed things I've done with both Bunny and Angelica separately but am saddened by the sudden new feeling of their being two quite disconnected people. Bunny told me something of this and it's evidently true – not on his side but on hers: those grey eyes look at him very coolly now; I would be frightened if I were him. I drove her down and have talked a lot to her about all sorts of things, theories of art, writing, people. I find her fascinating to talk to, extremely intelligent and stimulating. Bunny showed me a lecture he's written about Galsworthy and Morgan Forster. I read there a quotation from Forster – 'Kindness, more kindness, and even after that, more kindness; I assure you it's the only hope' – and was glad I'd not given way to my rancour against Julia. I nearly did, then I saw the folly and futility and dishonest reasoning, and merely sent a postcard asking her to lunch next week. If she comes, and I'm by no means certain she will, I shall bite back and swallow anything she could possibly take as critical. I think that remark of Forster's is profoundly true as a matter of fact, and I shall try hard to bear it in mind.

May 30th

'Kindness, more kindness, and even after that more kindness; I assure you it's the only hope,' and in spite of despair I walked out of the garden into the hall, heard a Siamese cat yowling, smelt lunch cooking, felt the warmth of the lawn underfoot and thought, 'I love the stuff life's made of.' Yet it is so beastly and cruel, like a hideous dress made of the finest velvet. In my despair I do, I must, hurl myself head first into the lives of others, attending only to the superficial sense-perceptions of my own. One suffers though for others. I notice poor Bunny's slightly bewildered loneliness because of Angelica's withdrawal, and his kindness and sweetness to his children touches me also. I feel Angelica hates this house or at least takes not the smallest interest in it. The meals have been fairly perfunctory, I was put to sleep in dirty sheets (a thing I don't relish); the bath towels are frayed rags. No love for poor old Hilton from her now.

June 8th

Julia's rejection is like a painful thorn; I can't forget it. It's the first thing I remember every morning. I dread its turning bad and festering. Why is it that it rankles so?

In the middle of my unhappy restlessness the telephone rang and it was her. Her call couldn't have come at a worse time, with my hurt feelings lying so close to the surface; and to hear her saying, 'I hope you weren't offended by my hermit letter,' or words to this effect, was too much for me; then, as I hesitated, she added: 'You sound as if you were.' I said something about the feeling of being 'totally rejected' not being pleasant, and that I hoped she would let me know when her 'hermitage' was over. I should be delighted. She did just say, 'You're not totally rejected', before I rang off, and I felt indignant at being thus officially honoured with readmission. My feelings distressed me by being so out of hand; I was shaken by heartbeats for hours after. Oh *hell take it all*. A lot of things have combined to make me feel all on the wrong leg somehow.

June 9th

As I almost expected, a letter from Julia in the post. What it would say I hadn't really pondered, yet having read it I feel I might have guessed. It is still 'My dear'. 'For a long time now', she writes, 'underneath all your *intense kindness* I have felt, palpably and unmistakeably, a hostility there in you towards me. Whether you are aware of it yourself or not I don't know. But at any rate you were so tart and unfriendly, again, when we last met at Percy St that I just feel too crushed to face it all for the time ... If you are not aware of the feeling yourself no amount of going over our words and conversation would avail for in my view it is not in the words so much as in your whole face and manner. For of course such feelings are catching, one reacts defensively and gets hostile also, so by this time I too have got prickly to say the least of it. I think the fact is our feelings for each other are ambivalent...'

June 10th

After all this I realize I now should simply dread a meeting, and that I believe she is suffering from persecution-mania or something very near it, and I remember how every *woman* we saw in Rome was described as 'looking at her oddly, having such an unfriendly manner' – Alvilde and Joan, for instance, but *not* Jim Lees-Milne nor Cochemé.

Last night Nicky had a twenty-first birthday party, and I went for a while, and presented her with a silver necklace which she put on and it looked fine on her. The glamorous young (art student friends) thudded and pranced in the crowded room and I would have been happy to watch them for ever.

June 25th

Shocked by the terrible news of the death of Arthur Goodman in a shooting accident, while Celia was at Aldeburgh. What will this delicate and sensitive creature, with two children to support, do without the husband on whom she seemed to lean for everything? I can't forget it. A nightmare feeling hangs in the hot air. I have felt tense all day, hurrying from one thing to another.

June 26th

Vague and fruitless longings: for the energy and concentration to read something tough and stimulating. For such books to appear, crying out to be read. For a less literal mind. For the power of getting off the earth more frequently into the less stodgy atmosphere of imagery and analogy – I do so enjoy it when I rarely do. For calm, to be turned on like a hot-water tap.

I went to Wimbledon last week, with Nicko Henderson, Janetta and Georgie – the first time for over thirty years I reckon. Sat in the best position in the centre court and was ticked off for talking too much by a fanatical pipe-smoking addict in front. It was an absorbing, but not really exciting nor beautiful spectacle. Long ago I seem to remember agile, athletic white-clad figures leaping like gibbons against the smooth green background – but not a bit of it now. The modern male singles player is not a beautiful specimen. Often round-shouldered (occupational disease I'm told) even bandy-legged, awkward and ungainly, he plods rather slowly, head bent, back to the service line, goes through a ritual childish bouncing of the ball on the ground, has a painful epileptic fit and (if lucky) sends his first service so hard that his opponent doesn't even move towards it. If unlucky it's a double fault and the plodding starts again. There are of course rare moments of emotional tension, match point etc, and one does become strangely involved, but modern tennis reminds me of those rams one reads about, whose horns grew so long and curly that they pierced their own brains and killed them.

July 1st

Bunny to dinner to cheer my last evening. Quite unnecessarily – he arrived in a self-confident, ebullient mood from his publishers' cocktail party where he got off with a young female writer. Just before leaving, his voice churning almost to a standstill, he told me this strange story: a fortnight ago he had fallen asleep after lunch in his boat on the embankment (whose Yonghy Bonghy Bo discomfort I'd quite needlessly grieved over). He woke and saw in front of him 'the extraordinarily beautiful colour and texture of naked human flesh'. A woman he had always loved and been attracted by – and been to bed with a long time ago – had come to see him, found the door of the boat open and him asleep, and got into bed beside him. A few months ago, he told me, he had felt there was no point in life. Now he was better.

Devoted to Bunny as I am, his mood of sensual self-satisfaction has always faintly embarrassed me, yet I wouldn't have missed that curious boat story. We talked a bit of the past – of how Molly MacCarthy had long ago (in the First War) refused to believe some sexual adventure he was describing – he was making a mistake, it didn't happen, she implied. I visualized suddenly and very clearly her knitted brows and pursed mouth, shaking her head, tampering relentlessly with reality. Of Vanessa and Clive as man and wife, he said that Clive's 'enormous vitality, noisiness and vulgarity' had been just what Vanessa needed to release her from the bondage of Sir Leslie Stephen. She had been very beautiful, very gay, with a streak of *enfant terrible*. When on a trip to Greece she got dangerously ill with typhoid, Clive wouldn't go near her – he had even then a morbid horror of illness, and she was nursed by Roger Fry; he fell in love with her and they had an affair. Clive's with Molly started about this time and (Bunny thought) was a major circumstance in the drifting apart of Clive and Vanessa. The sequence of these emotions and relations has become confused even in the memory of those closely involved. The Clive–Molly affair was long and serious. Desmond and Clive were close friends throughout. How was this managed? Had Desmond already begun to be unfaithful?

Marriage – infidelity – divorce. How can the equation be solved? Talked about this to Robert and Cynthia the evening before. Robert, doing a telly programme on divorce, had some amazing stories: of the wife whose husband hadn't spoken to her for years but wouldn't 'give her cause' for divorce, nor did she dare leave him because she would lose her means of subsistence – the six pounds he handed her 'in a fan' every week. And of another woman who had lived as the wife of (and had children by) a married man. His wife wouldn't divorce him, but pestered him for maintenance money until he committed suicide. His insurance and pension goes to his legal wife. The mistress, Robert said, was obviously an awful character, but the tears flowed down her face as she talked, and she showed Robert the suicide notes to her and her children which were deeply moving. Her old father had had a seizure and died from the shock of the news.

Very good description by Robert of the state of being at one and the same time deeply moved and completely detached and cold while he listened to the weeping woman. A different attitude to suffering was described by Bunny about Nerissa who had been attending the murder trail at Leeds of a man who had strangled (or shot) his mistress. 'Could anything be more boring?' she asked, but luckily the visual aspect of a trial had fascinated her.

I spent last weekend at the house of Julian's parents: I'd not realized it had been his grandfather, Hilaire Belloc's house, bought sixty years ago, fitted up and left unaltered, not a thing done since, hardly a cobweb removed, no electricity or telephone, ceiling so black with lampsmoke that Tristram Powell said 'how nice to have black velvet ceilings!' Hundreds of books of sixty years past, pedigrees of family cats with details of their lives, crucifixes, holy virgins, presentation objects covered with inscriptions, rooms pitch-dark, and painted dark brown or red. It is a civilization of a sort as original and odd as Charleston but how different. I saw that Julian loved it and I found it lovable through his attachment to it. The country round is exceptionally rural without being wild: fine oaks; grassy lanes; fields of plumy grasses taller than Rose with the evening light shining pink through them; a wild garden in which a comfortable vegetable plot had been cleared, and a small lawn enclosed by fruit trees, shrubs and purple lilies made an outdoor 'room' where we ate our meals and read. Julian was thoughtful, and neat in a sailory way, an efficient housewife. I drove Georgie and Rose down on Friday night – Janetta having been kept in London by her brother Mark's having been desperately ill. She came for the day on Sunday. As always I enjoyed talking to Julian enormously, and gave no thought to the passage of time.

July 15th

At the Cecils' I again met Iris Murdoch and John Bayley. I have not taken so much to a pair for a long time. He, with his dryness, great humour and effervescent vitality, provides the right seasoning to her charmingly unselfconscious solidity, good head and warm heart. They are deeply devoted to each other.

Yesterday to hear *Curlew River* in Southwark Cathedral – Britten's latest exploitation of cruelty to boys. It didn't stir me, musically or dramatically – I didn't know what he was after. Very different were two Handel operas last week, especially glorious *Semele*, put on with unspeakable visual vulgarity (Woolworth gold, a decor like the Follies in about 1900, a large gilt crescent moon beneath which Semele lay among shot silk pouffes, women's dresses of the same period with heavy head-dresses, prim and respectable).

July 29th

Last days before departure to Spain[1] overcast with thundery sense of doom and

---

[1] To stay with the Hendersons, but above all to see if Henrietta and Sophie were 'all right'.

restlessness. Last night I spent at Jonny and Sabrina's with an all-young company –
his brother Sammy, Harriet and Tim Behrens. I drank rather a lot and hope I didn't
talk too much in an effort to remember that the young are bored by one stressing
the difference of age (so I've often been told).

August 3rd: Alhaurin de la Torre[1]

The plunge into all this dreamy heat and scented beauty was more effortless than
I had expected, but (hot as England has been lately) it has had the combined effect
of a huge injection of some over-agitating drug.

On Saturday I handed in my trusty little Mini, friend and companion for nearly
three years, in exchange for a new one I have ordered. Then, having said goodbye
to Mrs Ringe I made my slow preparations to go over the top. Mary, Alexandra
and Nicko picked me up at four a.m. Having gone to bed at ten I felt I'd had a
night's sleep. Calmly and effortlessly we were off. It was already almost light, but
the cabin lights were put out so that we could snooze and I slipped into a
strange no man's land, until at seven a tray of breakfast sausages, coffee, toast and
marmalade was set before me.

Now it was Sunday. Hazy, hot and fine at Gibraltar. We crammed somehow,
luggage and all, into a small, new, blue car and sped off. Stopped and bathed on a
nondescript beach, in a fairly warm sea. Soon after eleven we drove up to El
Rascacio where Henrietta, Sophie and Nerissa were supposed to be. It is a charming
white farmhouse set back from the road in a bower of trees and geraniums. I asked
a maid for Henrietta. '*No está. Está a Málaga.*' Was Sophie there I asked (explaining
that I was her *abuela*), or the *hermana* perhaps? Yes, Sophie was here and awake,
the *hermana* '*está durmiendo*'. We walked out on the terrace where waiters were
clearing the tables and there under the shade of a tree was a pen in which were a
couchant, brown dog and Sophie, sitting erect and solemn and rather pale, almost
unchanged from when I last saw her except for paler hair. I was too dazed to make
much sense of anything, so that when the maid called me to say that Henrietta
was on the telephone, and I ran up and found a sleepy Nerissa with her hair
cascading round the receiver softly murmuring into it, my wits were loose and
jangling as she handed it to me. A faint far-off voice said: 'I'm in Malaga ... Have
you heard all the awful things that have been happening?' 'No, what?' (bracing,
as now I always do, for the worst, and more than the worst). 'A friend of mine
from Dartington was horribly beaten up by her boyfriend, a Puerto Rican, at the
Rascacio; he hit her with a bottle and she had a miscarriage and had to come to
hospital. It was awful. I couldn't leave her.' 'Is she going to be all right?' 'Yes, but
I can't leave her.' 'Where could I get hold of you?' She only said in this faint, far-
off voice: 'At the Hospital.' And then I returned to try and take in Sophie and ask
Nerissa what had happened and if she was all right there, and see that the
Hendersons weren't kept waiting too long. Impressions of Sophie: she was calm
but a little less dynamic than she used to be – the heat? – a few insect bites on her
delicate cheek – a lovely curly smile, much interest and affection from all the
maids and men, the gardener included.

[1] The house had previously taken by Janetta, and now by the Hendersons.

August 4th

My mood of angst could not survive this fabulous all-drugging heat. However one may scream at the horrifying new sky-scrapers sprouting along the Costa del Sol, there are still a few places that have kept all their vivid attractiveness unaltered. For instance our *pueblo* here – Alhaurin de la Torre. Less squalid perhaps than it once was, the main street is a succession of snow-white one-storey houses each with a flowerpot hanging and a figure, male or female, precariously tilted against the wall on a strong straight-backed chair. The inhabitants greeted us with relentless Spanish stares and warm Spanish humanity when we applied to them for help or information, and let us into their shops although it was Sunday and they were really shut. This house, pool and garden is far more delightful than I remembered, the two servants more ravishingly pretty and amiable. In Alhaurin two men on horseback were caracoling about the streets in happy, unbridled exhibitionism on pretty, excitable horses with small, pointed heads, red-tasselled saddle-cloths, no stirrups.

I took the Hendersons to visit the Brenans last night and this was a great success. The garden was bursting with huge yellow canes striped with green, rare plants and creepers. Gerald went swiftly away and picked a 'moonflower' for us – which had just that minute taken five minutes to open its snowy five-inch saucer on a long slender tube.

Back to our dark patio for a marvellous meal of gazpacho, chanquetes[1] and salmonetes.

August 7th

Henrietta is here. Two days ago she telephoned in the afternoon and we arranged that I should borrow the car and fetch her from the hospital for a day or even a night. Yesterday I went off alone into the sultry heat of Málaga (95° in the shade most of the day). The sweat was pouring off me when I arrived (after two boss shots) at the right hospital in the Limonàr district, walked upstairs and found myself in a large, light room with bed and sofa, terrace and washing room. Henrietta was with a fair, pretty girl whose face was contorted with pain as she sat on a chair while her bed was being made, and the Puerto Rican lover, a lizard-like, smooth young man in blue jeans and sandals was treating his victim with tender care. There was coffee, and brandy being poured into it. My urgent desire was rescue – to get Henrietta away as quickly as possible, and I did so. She filled in the details as we drove. She had invited the girl out to stay at the Rascacio and she had brought Andrès (who is disapproved of by Sarah's parents and had already beaten her up before). At the end of the evening session Henrietta was clearing away when she heard a terrible noise like a dog howling – it was the wretched Sarah, and she was covered all over in blood. He had cut her face and lip with a bottle, and beaten her about the head. The nightmare was that Henrietta had to go with her and her now distracted lover to search for Jaime Parladé and doctors in Marbella, who couldn't be found for some time. I can't really bear to think of any of it, and when I saw with what relief Henrietta slipped into the pool here and fell asleep on the grass, and responded to the kindness of the Hendersons, my own idea was to prevent her going back to the hospital at all, where she had led a

---

[1] Tiny little fish, special to Malaga.

ghastly few days, not going out, or hardly, devoured by mosquitoes, and with no bathing to refresh herself. Seeing her relief at the idea, I urged my attack more forcibly and now I'm afraid I may have overdone it. She must of course do what she wants. I think I can perhaps deal with the money aspect, as Andrès hasn't a penny; Sarah's mother is 'very rich but mean'. Another complication was that Sarah was pregnant and had a miscarriage after this battering. She then seemed much better, but when Henrietta rang up the hospital yesterday, she had had a high fever. I want more than anything else to extract Henrietta from this sordid imbroglio, but I see the danger of pressing her until she behaves below her standard of what a friend should do. For she has some, if not very strong, affection for Sarah who to me is nothing at all but a pathetic piece of flotsam, and though her drama makes me feel sick, it is sickness coupled with detachment.

I'm writing in bed before breakfast. The zz of a mosquito woke me very early and when I had my light on hunting for it Nicko called me out to look at a passing Sputnik. The garden was deliciously cool and the morning star shone brilliantly in the pale sky. The Sputnik moved along at a pedestrian pace and was an unromantic spectacle.

August 8th

The fierce heat continues. Yesterday it was nearly 100° in the shade. Mary and Nicko drove off to Ronda for the day leaving Henrietta, Alexandra and me – for my part only too thankful to relax – on the brink of boredom, sweating in the shade or on the bed. Alexandra is a sensitive, intelligent little girl, very responsive to any move towards her. After the long, hot afternoon the three of us walked down the road to the *pueblo* and braving the intensity of Spanish stares and an attack from a child with a water pistol, bought a little rocking chair for Sophie. Nicko and Mary returned after dinner fairly exhausted.

This morning Jaime has arrived, like a good fairy, bringing the £100 it is thought Sarah will need for the expenses of her lover's savagery. This is the payment for some pictures Henrietta is painting for a house he's doing. Meanwhile, Henrietta has gone off with him to Málaga to hand it over and get back her clothes, and the future seems to be taking shape. But OH, the heat! It is too much. I've sat since breakfast listening to the fresh, cold water filling the swimming-pool, and I'm sweating into my clothes. There's a sort of voluptuousness in it, but it drains all one's energies.

August 9th: El Rascacio, Sophie's first birthday

102° in the shade yesterday. But though the wolf's bite was so ferocious, it was heat of a less crushing abnormal sort. Lunch at the Cónsula[1] under the trees. Henrietta was there looking ravishing with a blue band round her head, Jaime, Mrs Rupert Belleville, and two American members of Café Society – Ethel de Croisset who has considerable elegance, and a white-faced creature who has none.

Henrietta went off to the Málaga bullfight with Jaime and then to the Rascacio, where I too am, having been driven over before lunch by Nicko and Alexandra. Will I be able to stick it here? I'm by no means certain. A nice young man called Martin (friend of Henrietta's) is here, still pale-skinned from England (he is

[1] Where Bill and Annie Davis lived in Churriana. Both Americans, Annie was Cyril's sister-in-law.

supposed to be playing his guitar at nights); Nerissa too, fierce and purposeful. We all got lunch, with great difficulty, for the vagueness and incompetence of the organization is great; Sophie sat gurgling her little Spanish gurgles, on various people's knees and when asked to '*baile*' she will curl her wrists in a very authentic way over her head. She is much more 'all right' than I thought at first, but the girl who is engaged to look after her is a rat-faced little creature, horrible and untrustworthy, and Nerissa is determined she should get the sack, saying she stole, wore Henrietta's clothes and dropped Sophie in the pool while she was away. Now I have retired to my room for a so-called siesta. It is one of a row of old cow-sheds converted into rooms by curtains and when the door is shut there is practically no ventilation. What to do therefore, when I leave it?

I am virtually living in a night-club. It comes to life about nine p.m., when the red-sashed waiters hurry round laying the table, the grill is lit and lamps set burning under the trees. Last night Nerissa took me in hand; she's a splendid girl – intelligent, realistic, burning with purposeful desire to find out about life. Talking to her was like talking to a contemporary; she was the making of my evening. My trouble is that I'm used to spending my evenings in talk or reading or music, and if those fail I go to bed. Whereas almost everyone who frequents this place expects to drink and bray steadily from about nine until three.

This morning my breakfast came like lightning. A new and unpleasant thing is a raging wind, tossing the eucalyptus trees and making my door and the yellow striped curtain that hangs over it flap frenziedly. I hear strident voices from the children by the swimming-pool. No other sign of life at twenty to eleven.

Last night Henrietta was rather seriously gliding about among the guests, taking orders for dinner. Enid, the English lesbian proprietress, stood hump-backed and soft-voiced in front of the grill in the garden.

Janetta, Jaime and Julian arrived last night, all in the last stages of fatigue. Julian seemed near tears and said he was sorry but he was half mad with exhaustion and must really go to bed. The golden-brown image at the other end of the table looked at him but made no sign. The poor fellow sat down again and I remembered what it was to be involved with Janetta's strong will, and resolved always, somehow, to keep my liberty of action. I felt too sorry for Julian to stay, and it being about twenty to two I said goodnight and went to bed.

What is wrong with the life of the expatriates out here is that they are entirely cut off from the stream of civilized life, threats of war, new books, or ideas, but lie drowned in heat and coaxing themselves into oblivion with drink, sunbathing and swimming, and living mainly in the dark when sensibilities are anyway lulled.

August 14th

Isobel Strachey's arrival and mode of 'taking' Spain has been marvellous. Fresh as a flower she stepped from a taxi just before lunch-time, wearing a charming striped cotton dress, and was at once (and has remained) delighted with everything. She complains of nothing, even if the light in her bathroom won't work, and appreciates everything, doesn't fuss. What a difference from Julia! Everyone likes her and she speaks slow but fluent Spanish in exactly the same linguid drawl as she speaks English. Her pleasure has increased mine no end.

Martin the guitarist has been disgruntled and unhappy and then rather ill. He is now better and happier-looking, and has started to play the guitar in the evenings. He does this beautifully and with great sensitivity. To hear him thrumming gently in the half-darkened garden, even though it is to an audience of chattering French tourists with potbellies or dyed yellow beehives and silk pyjama suits in peach or turquoise, is something I've greatly enjoyed, and so do they. Last night a large party got him to sit at the end of their table and looked really appreciative of his delightful playing. I like also to watch his pale, dedicated face, turned sideways into the darkness. I have now realized that he was the young admirer of Henrietta's I heard about in pre-Burgo days. He is gentle and intelligent and sweet to Sophie. I like him, though he might be weak and too dependent to give Henrietta the support she needs.

We dined with Jaime in his delightful new Marbella house two nights ago. Isobel and Nerissa came, and Ed and Julian were there. Jaime told us it was his first dinner party and we sat at a white table in the darkened patio.

August 17th

Jaime has managed to pull a new nurse for Sophie out of his hat and the change in her has been amazing: she has come to life, developed adventurousness and energy – this I think the rat-nurse had contrived in one way or another to quash, principally by putting her to sleep half the day.

Nerissa appears unable to understand why she shouldn't continue to stay here free, nor does she show any desire to do anything in the way of work. I spent a lot of time writing to Bunny, and then tearing up my letter and starting all over again. In the final form I told him they were leaving here but made the least possible of the reason for it. I said nothing about the beating-up.

Last night Henrietta, Isobel and I sat under the trees playing Scrabble while ants crawled along the branches and dropped into our hair.

August 21st

On my last evening at Marbella Henrietta arranged to rent an ugly but well-equipped, little house, bought a new cot and a push-chair and ordered a mattress. I told her I'd contribute towards all these expenses. I left them all gaily packing up and even sweeping up the unspeakable filth and mess of their quarters to go to the new house. I hope they will be all right, poor impractical dears.

Tomorrow I leave here, driving with Jaime and Julian to Portugal, where we are all due to stay in a house rented by Janetta for herself and her children.

August 23rd: Portugal, the Algarve

Here we are blessed with a much purer air and sea, great beauty, a beach of fine, soft sand, kept somehow or other scrupulously clean and enhanced by the very pretty striped tents and awnings under which sit monumental middle-aged women looking out to sea. Janetta's house is modern, airy and spacious, furnished with local things – rugs, stuffs and plain furniture. It is all much much nicer than I expected, and waking each morning (this was the second) to peaceful cluckings of fowls, and voices of maids, one looks out through the long-skirted fig-trees to a bluer, calmer sea. The sun seems more burning, the air more translucent, a greater sanity and serenity prevails.

August 24th

Last night as we dined by the light of candles and a great harvest moon, Julian launched an attack on bohemianism. 'At the other pole you get conventionality' I suggested, but he wouldn't have that and substituted 'a dashing upper-class life'. Jaime said that Henrietta and Nerissa were the only true bohemians he had ever met and he found them 'absolutely glorious', pleasing me with his appreciation of the two dear girls in spite of the muddle that went with their vitality and spontaneity.

September 16th: West Halkin Street

Back two nights ago, and though London has drenched us with rain and blasted us with wind, I returned to find it loveable and even welcoming this time. Indeed if only I had a piece of interesting work I believe I could settle down and face what comes next. I would like to dig in here for a good six months, and an excited letter from Eardley about a project to take a house on the lake of Orta together next spring leaves me rather apathetic.

The bad news that one always expects to hit one in the face like a slap is here all right – poor old Clive is dying according to Barbara. Angelica had prepared me for this; on my return I found letters from Barbara and when I rang her she dissolved into tears and said he had pneumonia and cancer of throat and lungs, so the doctors believe, had no voice and couldn't swallow. How can one do anything but wish him to die quickly, dear and affectionate old friend. Half an hour later she rang up to say he was 'much better' and wanted to see me very much. Round I went, with an immense hitch at my moral courage I must admit. I suppose one gets a little more able to take these harrowing scenes – the shock at least is less, and I was fully prepared. He's terribly thin and has no voice beyond a croak or whisper. I kept up a monologue for about half an hour, dreading chiefly that I should miss one of his attempts at saying or asking something. Then I read to him out of *The Times*. Barbara says the doctor has faithfully promised he shan't suffer at all, so it's to be hoped he'll let him die as quickly as possible. How much he knows he's dying I can't tell. Barbara thinks not, as he wondered why the masseur hadn't been to treat his neck, and the reason was it was quite hopeless. He told her he had dreamed he was dead, 'and then I woke – and I wasn't'. I found myself wondering if it would be possible to talk rationally to a dying person with his death as an accepted fact – say in effect, 'Well, it's a loathsome world and you'll be well out of it.'

September 17th

Clive died last night, thank heaven. I went round to Barbara's earlier, with wine, grapes and a pie. She flung herself into my arms saying, 'Clive is dying.' I didn't know whether to believe it or not, gave her whisky, got her to tell me how the day had passed. She had noticed a decline when she went round that afternoon: his colour was very bad, his breathing difficult and he couldn't swallow at all. She wasn't very coherent, poor thing, and I gathered that she was alarmed by his difficulty in breathing and that matron had come up and told her she had better go home, she'd had enough. The doctor had been telephoned to and said that Quentin must be sent for. She heard matron tell the nurse she didn't think he'd last long. Yet he was thinking clearly and making his pathetic croaked remarks till she left and when she told him she must go as she was having supper with me, he said 'Give my love to Fanny.'

September 22nd

Lunch today at the French Club with Philip Toynbee, Terry Kilmartin, and a pretty but slightly spotty Jewess, all of the *Observer*. I was touched by Philip's inviting me (the result of the letter I wrote him praising his book, which he'd sent me a copy of). He was very charming, wonderfully articulate, and surprised me by sudden human and outgoing remarks showing awareness of others. Why surprise? Because there's enough of the rebellious clown about him to rouse an expectation of his being somehow not always quite human. In fact, I like him very much, and do greatly admire his originality and vitality as a writer. Almost at once we got on to the subject of God – and *goodness* how I wish Ralph could have heard his extraordinarily accurate prescience justified! He always declared with absolute conviction that Philip would end up a mystic and probably a believer in God, and he admitted both these today. It was enjoyable to argue with such an intelligent and voluble supporter of religion. Oddly enough, his chief justification is the necessity for a first cause. When I brought up the problem of evil, he drew a picture of a well-meaning but *bungling* God, who simply hadn't succeeded in making the universe as good as he would have liked! 'And when I've finally proved he does exist, I promise you shall have the scoop for the *Observer*, Terry! "*GOD EXISTS*". You'll be able to splash it across the headlines.' (He failed to see that making God the first cause only gave a name to the enigma and pushed it one stage further back. What caused God?)

September 30th

A letter from Julia yesterday as friendly and affectionate as if no cloud had ever passed between us, and oh with what relief I shall shovel earth over that grave! But glad as I am, I can't help thinking that her behaviour taken in sequence has been rather mad.

A curious shifting within the foundations of my life has been making itself felt lately. My roots have loosened a little in the soil as if preparing to leave it, as if realizing anyway how slight is my hold and function on this earth. To adapt has become more and more my aim, though I dare say my friends would be surprised to hear it in view of the way I sometimes blurt out my views. None the less, from my vantage point within my ego I know this is true. I know I am 'an outsider' in everyone's 'life story' and that my own is virtually over. I begin to see too that some of the things I thought I valued – London, friends, work in particular – are just techniques for getting through the rest of my life.

October 3rd

Last night I went round to Angelica's studio and saw Sophie and Henrietta just back from Spain. Sophie is adorable; her hair shone fine and golden in the electric light. She studied me thoughtfully for quite a few minutes and then became extremely friendly and high-spirited. She walks quite well, a few steps at a time, lifting her feet like real walking – not toddling. I watched her bath and melted with love for her.

October 5th

I spent most of yesterday with Henrietta and Sophie, taking them to Kew for lunch and to spend the afternoon with the Kees. Alexander[1] and his little friends were charming with Sophie, who staggered happily among them in a pair of green corduroy dungarees I'd given her, eating ice-cream cornets and playing with Alexander's mass of toys. She even went on a child's roundabout tenderly protected by two boys. Then we took her out for a walk in Kew Gardens in the Kees' pram. The gardens were deep in a dreamy, still haze, and crowded with Sunday visitors. On the whole the figures, whether romping children, old folk humped with age, or enlaced lovers, improved the landscape. As in a dream we mooned into the various glass houses, all lit with a pale glimmer from the autumn sun, and wandered in tropical dampness round pools with blue and pink water-lilies floating on them.

October 8th: Cooleville House, Co. Tipperary

I'm here, in Irish peace, though I spent a far from peaceful, distracted morning preparing to come.

    Arriving not much before seven, I was soon drinking whisky with Julian and Eddy and conversation went on all evening, ending in quite a lively argument about 'second-rateness'. It started by Julian's defending and my attacking Torremolinos, and the manner of his defence was to bring up Tim Willoughby[2] as an example of someone who 'liked the second-rate'. What is one to make of such a line? Of course I rose to the bait and Eddy also entered in on my side, but listening to my supporter I realized he was using the word 'second-rate' solely in a class sense, and thought that Tim, as an aristocrat, was letting down the side. So there was I being priggish as usual about 'standards', Eddy defending class distinctions and Julian – ? well, I'm not sure. Nor did our discussion illumine my search for the germ that causes the prevailing diseases of modern life.

October 10th

As so often on a visit, even in the happy old days when it was less vital to be able to swim in alien waters, I sometimes feel my engine stalling and resenting being driven, a heavy effortful sensation which I shall hardly be here long enough to outgrow. Both my companions have been charming, and more than that I have felt warm affection and respect for them both. Is Julian unhappy? I don't think so, but he probably knows he will return to that state on Monday; he may, however, have achieved detachment from Ed. I suppose his chief trouble to be that he longs for mutual love, rather than more sex.

    Last night a grizzled spinster with a red-lined nose like a rocking-horse came to play Scrabble and have dinner. I didn't like her.

October 26th: The Noel Carringtons' cottage

Woken by a dream of bungling. At a nameless station in East Anglia I left my purse in the wrong train and saw it steam out. Here I was, without ticket, money or spectacles – helpless. Then, I suddenly came across Ralph who marvellously reassured me and told me what I should do; he was both in the same world as me

---

[1] Their son.
[2] An aristocratic young hippy, who later drowned when sailing in the Mediterranean.

and outside it. The dream was obviously a cry to Ralph: 'See how badly I'm doing without you!'

Noel has given me the typescript of Mark Gertler's letters to Carrington to read. A few days ago I was reading Gerald's to her. Gerald wants me to sell these to the Americans for him, and I feel copies should be made first of these very remarkable documents into which for some years he poured the major part of his writer's response to life. Gertler's letters are not really good, but from both rises the image of the fateful character to whom they were written.

October 30th: West Halkin Street

Henrietta and Sophie here to lunch yesterday; I had Sophie alone with me all afternoon, leading an intense unflagging mental and physical, exploratory life. I never tire of watching the expressions on her mobile face. How utterly impossible to look at its satin smooth, delicate curves and imagine old age, even maturity. She struggled to solve every problem the physical world presented her with, and when one – a zip fastener – defeated her she laid down her head and broke into a silent wail of frustration.

November 12th: London

Last night I had a successful dinner party – I really think it was, and two lots of guests have rung up to say so. Eardley, Angelica, the Kees and Campbells came and we had a bottle of Colin Mackenzie's Moselle, two bottles of Derek Jackson's superb claret, smoked salmon and leg of lamb. I enjoyed it and did not feel exhausted, though owing to a bungle on my part it was preceded by playing quartets with Angelica and Margaret from tea-time onwards so that I had to baste the joint between movements. I am pleased that I felt equal to it all, and it signifies a little elevation from the recent trough.

November 18th

Janetta gave a cocktail party for Sonia last night. I only spent a short while there, but long enough to pick up a number of impressions. Sonia looked buxom and handsome, with eyelids painted bright forget-me-not blue. But almost her first remark to me was one of fantastic pretentiousness and condescension, to the effect that she liked funny old London more than she'd expected to – everyone here was so slow-witted compared to the quick, intelligent French. 'Oh you mean all of *us*, do you?' I asked. The third person in this conversation was the poetess Kathleen Raine who stood before me like an unsmiling schoolmistress, and at one moment stared at me so hard I felt her gaze scrape my cheek. I realize now that my reluctance to go to the party came from knowledge that Sonia and I are incompatible. I dislike her pretentiousness, and am pretty sure she dislikes me. So let's give it all up.

November 22nd: Charleston

Yesterday I drove Henrietta and Sophie to stay with Duncan and here we all are. As we approached the smooth couchant, enormously high shapes of the Downs a pervasive calm and contentment enveloped us – Henrietta and me at any rate, for Sophie was by now asleep. It has been with me ever since. Plunged in this Old Bloomsbury civilization (for all we may have laughed at its 'croquet hoops', and the paint peeling here and there) I am overpowered with pleasure and emotion at the sense that all round me *real* values have been aimed at and achieved, and that the house, garden and all it contains is a unique work of art, something lovingly created and kept alive. Even now when nearly all of them are dead, it is the same, and I have been struck by the fact that the feeling I have for it is partly gratitude, such as a very good performance on an instrument produces. One thing I am absolutely convinced of is that the lasting value of what Old Bloomsbury stood for and did will go on being recognized – indeed it *is* being recognized. Duncan says that it is people between thirty-five and fifty who find his pictures too old-fashioned, and the young are beginning to like them again. A troop of young people came yesterday afternoon and sat in the studio and looked at them. Sonia (who is at the Connollys') said of course she didn't like them – they aren't nearly avant-garde enough for her. Her mind works in such a boring, intensely conventional way. You must always like the latest thing, support the latest writers. She's added several toads during a visit here and a visit by Henrietta and me to the Connollys, such as when we were talking about Arthur Waley, and Duncan said, 'I believe he's living with a very intelligent lady in north London.' 'Oh yes,' said Sonia noisily, 'I did hear all about her and it's fascinating, and she does something very remarkable but I'm afraid I've quite forgotten what it is' – wanting to show that she was in the know but quite unable to make the smallest contribution. After she'd left here on Saturday evening Henrietta said, 'I think she's a huge *fraud*. I liked her voice and her looks rather, and her laugh and her strong neck, but she never says anything.' I tried, probably overdoing it, to be amiable to her, but another toad dropped out when we were talking about Charlie McCabe and I was giving a fairly unflattering picture. Was there nothing to be said for him? 'Yes, that he had quite a good head and used it to think for himself,' I said. Sonia (impatiently): 'Oh that's so silly – why not let other people do it for you?' (As she does, with fraudulent results.) Another time, after she'd admitted that she didn't like Duncan's painting and the Connollys said they liked it enormously, I asked her who would be her first choice to buy a painting by if money was no object? 'Well I think I'd buy a Francis Bacon,' (absolutely safe, well-established, avant-garde choice), 'but of course I'd be much happier buying books.' 'What books would you buy?' 'Oh standard library editions of all the great writers.' She's perfectly dull and conventional, and a first-rate man like Duncan shows her up for what she is. But I for one have never never caught a tinsel gleam of what takes people in.

But why spend so much time uncharitably analysing Sonia's defects when I have been so emotionally stirred all the time I was here by the first-rateness of this Bloomsbury world, the charm of Duncan, the calm and peace which gently lapped us round from the beautiful Downs which have been all weekend swathed in tepid mist, with a total result of great reassurance – it's like the repeated reassertion of something one believes to be true and is glad is true. Last night, very gay, delightful talk, and some television-watching in the studio for the three of us, Duncan, Henrietta and me. Sophie has all day padded happily about crooning in a sweet, high voice, with bright eyes and blazing red cheeks, interested in everything and occasionally pointing at the pictures with a little cry. She, Henrietta and I called on Lydia Keynes and the Connollys on Sunday morning. I had never been inside Tilton. Lydia's face is weathered like a nut so as hardly to be recognizable; she wore a handkerchief on her head and a small string cap on top of that, and was muffled in a fluffy dressing gown. She skipped agilely round us, greeting us with cries of welcome and ceaseless talk. She had to begin her 'pyottering' quite soon, that was why she had asked us to come early. 'I always do my pyottering – then I can talk to no one.' Her voice-production is marvellous, her choice of words very original – no Sonia she. She told Henrietta she was looking beautiful, snatched up Sophie and held her clasped on her lap for a while, and to me she said as I left, touching me greatly: 'It is such a long time since we met but I heard of you often, my dyear, and have thought of you with great tyenderness!'

Cyril and Deirdre were at their nicest. Cyril so adored showing off his bibliophile treasures that it was a great pleasure to flatter him about them. They both, and their little girl,[1] were exceptionally friendly and contributed quite a lot to the great cockle-warmingness of this weekend. I am full to brimming with it, but now the time has come to face London and grey solitude. I felt it was essential first to try and shred apart the texture of my surroundings here and discover what is so valuable in it.

I took Celia Goodman and Julian to *Il Trovatore* the other night. Celia liked Julian, who was, of course, all the time angelically attentive and kind. I myself was bowled over by the opera itself, and loved watching the elegant and dedicated movements of Giulini, as he conducted without a score, with difficulty glimpsed through the forest of heads. Before Julian came I talked to Celia for a little about her problem of where to live. She is more fixed on central Cambridge than ever, but no nearer finding a house. What on earth can one do to help her?

November 29th

I've been at Crichel since Thursday, all four present. Desmond arrived breathlessly for lunch on Friday looking like a black-beetle in a leather coat and turtle-neck sweater. This produced an audible groan from Raymond and a very strict po-faced speech of disapproval later on from Eardley. Why do they mind so much something that is purely superficial and unimportant, and to my eyes rather endearing? I suppose it's the unavoidable grating together of essentially different individualities. As with old married couples, this stridulation increases with the passage of time, but is often less painful to the participants than the observer might assume; the converse pleasure in each other's quirks remains constant. Eddy and Raymond were rather fiercely critical of the fuss Eardley and Desmond made over social occasions, after a quite easy, pleasant lunch party (Reine and Jemima Pitman, Mary Potter.) 'Desmond isn't much good at making conversation,' Eddy said accusingly. They neither of them seem to think it rational to find it a boring way of spending the time. As referee on the sidelines, I tend to be recipient of these criticisms of each other.

Another bit of inter-Crichel criticism: 'Raymond is extraordinary,' Eardley said to me, 'he's just like a little boy. He came into the drawing-room yesterday and said: "I've had a sleep and done an hour's work and now I'm going to have a bath." Or else he says: "I've been reading for two hours and now I'm going to bed." ' I do notice, now he mentions it, this slightly eccentric habit of Raymond's. Old age? Eddy shows this in snoozing off for quite long periods, a look of sad boredom on his tilted face, and perhaps an occasional tiny snore.

---

[1] Cressida.

One can't help, in this headquarters of homosexuality, being slightly aware of one's sex, though I believe I think of it less than most females even of my age. Eddy and Raymond have an old-fashioned view of the female character, including silliness and illogicality – the opinion of a 'cracker-motto' in fact. If he feels likewise Desmond is too good-tempered to let it show. With Eardley I really feel most at ease with my unfortunate disqualification, for I believe he thinks it a good and civilizing influence to have a female about. On a walk yesterday Eddy, Eardley and I passed close to a bull which was in the act of hoisting itself onto the back of a young ruffled-looking heifer, with its long sad-looking penis preparing for action. 'No sight for a lady,' said Eardley.

December 16th

I finished a very difficult translation sample yesterday but was left too wound up by it to stop jigging about like a monkey on a string. Last night I dined with Adrian Daintrey in his new studio beside the Regent's canal, which glittered between the trees and festoons of freezing mist. Other guests were Edward Le Bas and a sophisticated grey haired lady, thin as a lath and with a beak like a bird, the living spit of Osbert Lancaster's Maudie Littlehampton and this was almost her name – she had plenty of sense, a deep voice and quantities of jangling bangles. We sat on a backless bench and there was no hard liquor – only thin white wine. I drove them all home and then slept like anything, to wake this morning in a curious state of euphoria.

Julia rang up this morning to say she had been badly let down by Sonia who for ages has been suggesting they join forces in a house. When Sonia was in England a house was found and bought for her by Michael Pitt-Rivers.[1] She told Julia there would be a ground floor for her, Janetta took Julia to look at it, and both she and I tried to infuse Julia with enthusiasm for this new project. Now Sonia writes from Paris to say that Michael has been 'so sweet' about the house that she can't ask him to pay the extra to convert the ground floor to Julia's use. 'Never mind Julia, we'll find you a nice flat quite close.' Poor Julia – it is good for her persecution-mania. I had been so moved by this helping hand Sonia was offering Julia that I nearly wrote to say how all Julia's friends felt grateful to her. The only thing I was prepared to credit her with – good-heartedness to her female friends – now seems to have to be discounted.

December 23rd

I dined with Julia last night – she showed me Sonia's letter: a discreditable maundering of egotism laced with protestations of friendship and 'I mean's'. Was distressed by the sharp note of fear in Julia's voice – she can 'only just get along with the help of her Purple Hearts', 'fears she's heading for a mental home sometimes', 'feels quite suicidal especially since this blow of Sonia's, 'simply HATES and is TERRIFIED by living alone'. We drank a good deal together, and got on very well, thank heavens. With pencil and paper we tried to work out what her finances are, they're not bad at present, but she feels, and very likely rightly, that she is going to be gradually cut down.

Before this I called on Henrietta and Sophie and gave Sophie my Christmas

[1] To whom she was briefly married.

present, a woolly push-along dog, large and I hoped comforting. She seemed to like it, pushed it about a lot and screamed passionately when an exceptionally sweet young man who was there took it away to oil the wheels for her. Their gallant life touched me to the quick. Henrietta has made the flat look much more human, even gay, and is altering the Ham Spray library curtains which I gave her, which should humanize her sitting-room.

December 24th: Christmas Eve

I'm here at Sandwich Bay in the huge Edwardian monstrosity of a house lent to Magouche and Janetta by Michael Astor. Just been down (10 a.m.) for breakfast. Franca[1] gave me a warm croissant, and some coffee, not a cat stirring. Met Janetta in the passage and she said, 'Oh yes, they're all lie-abeds.' I'm grateful for a Christmas refuge. But it's like living in a golf club. Perhaps that's what makes me uneasy. Magouche's mother, Essie, is here too and is just the sort of lady you'd expect to find in a golf club. Erect, grey-haired, brisk and friendly but basically conventional. I see now that I'm designed as her opposite number. The children make up slightly uneasy pairs and have not quite shaken in with their mates yet.

A thick sea mist encloses us, the sun – briefly visible – has now vanished. It's absolutely still and absolutely silent. This is no more stifling in effect than our totally tasteless millionaire surroundings. Out of the window, so far as I can see, *three* perfectly flat golf-courses lap up to our very walls and reach away in every direction until the hulk of another millionaire's house rises out of the mist, a dim shape. My bed is soft and warm, there is mock Tudor furniture and a dressing table with skirts, prints of ships on the wall. The house belonged to Lady Astor I find, and it is her personality I suppose which stamps it. What a neutral one! Oh POUF! Give me air! I have been deeply disconcerted to find myself so put out by a house's atmosphere. The natural antidotes would be work, if I can do some, or going out walking, but the thick white mist is not inviting.

Strange that the civilization hanging in a house like smoke remains so potent, even when the owner is away, even when she's dead, that one can hardly breathe at all and certainly not sleep in it if one finds it uncongenial.

Christmas Day

The sight of stockings stuffed with really valuable things as well as all the immense riches under the tree, but chiefly the background of what this house represents makes one willy-nilly feel that a redistribution of wealth would be a very good thing, and I hope that Mr Callaghan will succeed in extracting some of it from the pockets of such as Lady Astor. For just as Mary finds 'the smell of money' attractive, I always find it repulsive.

December 27th

Things going from bad to worse, and I feel sunk by my own inability to compete with my surroundings. Like an unco-operative sulky adolescent I have withdrawn a good deal into the privacy of my room. I find no driving force – what should it be? social sense – to impel me to go out and make an effort with Mr and Mrs Edward Rice at lunch, nor yet to face an intrusion of young Rices and Byngs here.

[1] Magouche's Italian servant.

A cruel plan, the latter seems to me, for it will plunge all the young here into embarrassment. Making conversation, as against talking – what a miserable thing it is. We had a big dose of it last night: first the arrival at seven – much too early for the late dinners of this house – of Edward Rice, an attractive, extremely rich sixty-year-old and his younger, smart, knicker-bockered, self-confident French wife. Leonard Byng, Isobel's friend (and I suspect ex-lover), also had a French wife, a governessy, pretty, little smug thing. The ethos all these people brought with them was 'Money is Power'. 'Democracy is dead,' they cried, but also 'George Brown is one of my best friends,' and 'Wilson is too much of a conservative for me.' A veneer of culture thinly disguising jungle behaviour in the department of sex and fascist beliefs. The whole lot made my hackles rise, very likely without due reason. Achilles is not the best judge as he sits sulking in his tent.

Magouche came into my room this morning to say we were invited to lunch with the Rices. Would I like to come? Prepared by Janetta, I begged to be let off. Then she said that that would be quite all right as Maro[1] was longing to go. And I could keep an eye on the young here. It turns out that the twenty-year-old French nephew of the Rices and three of the young Byngs had been asked back to lunch here. This would seem to be head-losing at its worst. The four youngest never spoke to the visiting adolescents when they came last night but withdrew onto the stairs by themselves. Natasha[2] is in bed and refuses to come down; this leaves poor Georgie to be responsible for the visitors. She caught Janetta in the passage just now and almost screamed for mercy.

December 28th

London again, and it gave Janetta and me a beautiful, pale, frosty welcome as we drove over Westminster Bridge. Since getting in at lunch-time I've not seen anyone except shop assistants, yet I've been in a way less lonely than I was at Sandwich. My God, in what a dismal dejection I went to bed last night, in spite of the great kindness of Magouche and Janetta, the charm, grace and sweetness of the six girls. As one visitor, French Mrs Edward Rice, said, the house was like a Turgenev novel, with the children playing cards on the floor, Natasha and Maro bending over their embroidery frames and at the same time chattering and laughing – the cap fitted and I fitted only too well into the role of ancient great-aunt or governess, sitting in the corner with the samovar, to whom everyone is kind but who serves no function. It's this I've felt – useless, desperately lacking the fertilizing warmth of being loved and having someone with whom I can laugh and who is interested in anything at all that I've done or thought, and vice versa. So a draining away of confidence, a shrivelling dislike of my own character – all this dreadfully overloaded my boat yesterday until the great grey-green waters of despondency nearly came over the gunwale.

How much are other people aware of such inner struggles I don't know. Probably hardly at all – they have their own problems and preoccupations. So I hope that my anti-socialness didn't get through.

Actually the evening passed gaily and with relaxation, playing racing demon and watching the girls twist to the gramophone. Susu is a marvellous little dancer

---

[1] Gorky, Magouche's eldest daughter.
[2] Gorky, Magouche's second daughter.

and it was a joy to watch her, but she stops at once if she sees your eye on her. She's a very attractive little being. I tried to express some of my gratitude as Janetta and I set off up the lightly powdered road to London.

1965

January 2nd

The New Year has made an aquamarine-coloured, chill, transparent, scentless entry. It is like a 'new page' covered with austere pale blue squares in an arithmetic book, and its aseptic flavour, perfectly tolerable by day, gives way at nights to a rather dreadful bleakness, while I fetch about – look everywhere, think of anything – rather than accept its presence. I've had some bad moments, sounding the depths and scraping the edges of the bucket of my loneliness, being assailed at odd moments by vivid memories of Ralph and Burgo and finding myself defenceless and unprepared.

I drove down to Lord's Wood to see Alix and James yesterday morning – no change in the way of life here, with all its eccentricities and endearing inconsistencies. A walk with Alix, dressed in Canadian-looking long fur coat and top boots, through the winding paths she has cut through the bracken and brambles on the common.

'From here, you see,' she says, 'one can either take this wide path where we can walk two abreast or go single file under this natural arch covered in ivy, but I don't like going too far in that direction because that's where the dog-fanciers live.'

Much talk about the Labour party, which they both staunchly support, and prison reform, education and so on – but never stodgy or dull. They both remain intensely interested in the way the house is run; there is a revolving electric grill and spit in the kitchen. Otherwise the same stuffy heat, windows draped with crackling plastic curtains to keep out the draughts, the same getting up and washing the plate you've just used in the middle of the meal. They live mentally speaking entirely in the psychoanalytical, Strachey and political world. Michael Holroyd has produced the first volume of his life of Lytton for James to read and James was appalled and said it 'simply wouldn't do'. Lytton had been made a 'disagreeable, weak, silly and laughable character' – none of the force of his personality has come out, nor his wit. Holroyd mocks at G. E. Moore and 'the Society'[1], which James still holds in religious respect (when I asked if he could tell me if it still went on he replied, 'No, I can't: I daresay you can guess the answer from that'), but is totally unaware that he has presented an unflattering picture. The question is whether any picture could have satisfied James. To what lengths does his hero-worship obscure his judgement? Also, what will happen? James thinks he has the power to suppress the book entirely *at a pinch*, but obviously doesn't intend to. He has insisted on Holroyd making a lot of changes, and also that the first volume shouldn't be published until the second (which takes over at

---

[1] The 'in-term' for the Cambridge Apostles.

the moment of Lytton's literary success) is finished. Alix's view was that there was something 'frog-like and unfeeling' about the book and that Michael Holroyd had no real interest in Lytton or Bloomsbury.

I'm delighted by Alix's occasional sallies into fantasy. Last night we had a fine leg of mutton cooked on the electric spit. After we'd cleared away our plates she said thoughtfully: 'There's something *disgusting* about mutton, which I don't feel about beef – a sort of heavy, cloying breathiness. You notice the same thing if you meet a shepherd in a lane. It's the sheep, I suppose.'

January 3rd

Every strange environment takes a little getting into, but this – and it's certainly strange enough – takes less than most. I've walked out into the woods several times with Alix, enjoyed the pure piercing smell of the earth, moss, frost and rotting bracken, the delicate compositions made by trunks of trees that are too slender because of competition from other trunks. Indoors – physical stuffiness and a smell of old clothes and covers that need cleaning; *anything* but mental stuffiness; idealism about the United Nations and the need to improve the lot of the poor, inconsistently blended with *folie de grandeur* about all Stracheys and anyone connected with them ('My cousin – what's her name? – Peggy Ashcroft'), and Eton and various other nuclei round which snobbishness may gather. Admirably well informed about international affairs, they reel off the names of the presidents of small black or brown states in a way which makes me ashamed of my ignorance. Naïve interest in television's most humdrum and soppy programmes about the Wild West, policemen or lawyers. These I enjoy, but I couldn't if they weren't a rarity.

January 14th: London

Janetta came to lunch and told me that she had been reading *The Waste Land* obsessionally and with an almost total incomprehension that had reduced her to tears. I spent yesterday morning doing the same and I can understand her attitude. Is it a great take-in studded with flashes of true poetry from the author of the *Four Quartets*? Incomprehensibility, and especially obscure and erudite allusions that take the reader by the lapel and draw him into the same college common room, are as much of a bait as shockingness. People so love to think they are among a few initiates. I don't think, and never have, that it's a *great* poem. The relief when one strikes a line of Marvel, Webster or Spenser shows it up. Exactly why it had such an enormous success I'm not sure – but believe it was partly chance.

Rain fell out of the sky in pailfuls after Janetta and I had pleasantly eaten our boiled eggs and grapefruit together, when Cyril arrived to pick up some shirts she had bought him from the sales. He was genial, even benign, brought out a bag of lychees and sat eating them, leaning back with a napkin spread over his broad front, peeling them voluptuously with stubby fingers. Janetta had said: 'Don't ask Cyril about *The Waste Land*.' 'I think I *will*,' I said, and did. What's more, it was a good thing because he loves instructing and did it extremely well.

Janetta is off to Spain, Magouche with her. She won't tell me when, yet I've asked her several times. Does she know with her acute sensitivity how dreadfully I miss her?

Julia? – alas, alack. A bad evening. Was I off my guard because the last went so well? One can never afford to be that. But today she savaged everyone and got under my skin in the end: Dicky and Denis, of course, had been 'too babyish for words' with their 'birthday boy' attitude to the publication of *The Fly* and Denis's childish jealousy. Of Julian – 'Well, since you ask, I *can't respect him*, but let's not say any more about him.' Then there is her attitude that everyone else has all they want in life and no right to complain. The Campells, for instance, had 'no right to complain' of the interference their children were in their lives, yet she would hardly accept my view that they both adored their little boys. In fact, I don't believe she sympathizes with other people's troubles or joys *at all*.

January 18th

Last night I dined with Bunny, just back from America, and Angelica in her bohemian studio. It was freezing cold – the studio stove just warmed the side of the body toasting in front of it. Angelica was wild-haired, beautiful and grubby, and had an outsize baking 'potato' in her stocking. Bunny was magnificent – brave as a lion, full of interesting news of America and Mexico and his lectures. At seventy – or more? – he's planning a trip to Mexico again next Spring, and meanwhile to drive with Angelica all the way to Greece, Yugoslavia, Macedonia, Bulgaria perhaps this year. I think this is the most sensible thing to do – wear out one's remaining years with exciting and exhausting travel rather than carefully preserve them for the sake of tame and prolonged existence.

Isobel and I went to 'that RUS-sian film they say is so good. It's called HAMlet.' She was in her scattiest mood, regretting her wasted youth in the Argentine playing tennis and golf, not being properly educated nor active enough in the pursuit of young men. (Ralph and I always thought Isobel *too* active, and that she frightened them off by her determined pursuit, so incongruous with her flower-like femininity.)

Bunny and Angelica seem to have re-entered an area of mutual warmth and affection most delightful to witness.

January 19th

A dinner party here last night, the company – Johnny Craxton, Godleys, Georgia. Conversation streaked along without flagging till they left.

Winston Churchill has been dying for the last three days. My theory that the crowds waiting for this event are re-enacting the scenes at Tyburn was not accepted by anyone, yet it seems to me self-evident. They are trying to get a 'kick' – in this case from the drama of the grand old man's slow demise. If they were to go away for a cup of tea just at the moment that the notice of his death was posted on the door or given to the press they would feel cheated, like someone who left a football match just when a crucial goal was scored. Wynne accused me, burning-eyed, of being averse to all irrational behaviour. In the course of the evening we talked also of T. S. Eliot and incomprehensibility in poetry, of hedonism, and finally of drug-taking, *à propos* of *The Naked Lunch*. Georgia spent a long time trying to tell us, with obvious sincerity but uncharacteristic inarticulacy, how the attraction of 'junkies' made other people take to drugs out of admiration and emulation. This was partly their being against the police and the Establishment – the bad boys of the school; their recklessness gave them an extraordinary glamour in her youthful eyes. I asked if it became legal, would people still want to take drugs. 'Oh, NO!', yet when I said the problem seemed simple, then: make it legal and it would stop, that wasn't acceptable to her.

Then we got to the mainsprings of art and Bunny's theory that its purpose was to enlarge one's experience; because one can, for instance, only be either male *or* female, and has in other respects limited opportunities for knowing about the world and people and life. Wynne and Kitty, orientated psychoanalytically, wanted to define it (art) in terms of 'resolution'. 'Fortinbras,' said Wynne, 'resolved the tragedy of Hamlet and made everything all right, so that one wasn't left in despair.' Kitty said books she greatly admired – Henry James for instance – left her in deep sadness, and quite 'unresolved'. To my hedonistic eyes, Fortinbras is totally unimportant, and I believe it to be mainly the aesthetic qualities – the poetry, the satisfaction one gets from the formal relationships, shape and development – that make *Hamlet* so magnificent a play. I suggested that literature is always impure, and depends on being connected with reality at as many points as possible, not abstracted from it. Abstract art has pushed the emphasis on formality to its logical conclusion and that has proved absurd. It is if a couturier were to lay such emphasis on the style of a dress that he ignored the female inside it.

January 30th

Listening to Winston Churchill's funeral, now in progress, I wonder exactly what causes other people to feel so much while I remain totally blank. The paraphernalia of mourning, honour, exaltation and grief have been heaped so high and into such a cumbrous pyramid that it was bound to topple and collapse into the near-grotesque. Yet people have shuffled for four hours in biting cold to look at the catafalque. The symbolism and the universal and endlessly moving drama of death itself must, of course, have something to do with it. But I think millions of people really do believe what is constantly being said, that he was 'the greatest Englishman' – Shakespeare even included! The whole of London therefore seems to be awash in this deep black soup of emotion, though any individual (like Mrs Ringe)[1] I talk to is 'sick and tired of it all'. And I don't doubt those who have stood all night to see the procession go by will experience some devastating but satisfying catharsis. Even I find it hard to turn off my transistor which is blaring out funeral music, the occasional ludicrously fierce bark of sentries and the agonized voice of a female announcer 'carrying on' bravely in spite of her voice being almost annihilated by tonsillitis (as it sounds). The Archbishop's voice, rather groggy, offers up 'a hearty vote of thanks to God' for delivering this our brother out of the miseries of this sinful world and begs that we may all be speedily so delivered! The choir bursts into a sing-song used by soldiers in the war: 'John Brown's body lies a-mouldering in the grave.'

January 31st: 5.30 p.m. Sunday

And I've been alone all day though I've heard a few voices on the telephone and walked out once to post a letter and look at the state of Belgrave Square Garden. I have been grovelling in the past making dubious extracts from letters and diaries for Michael Holroyd and his biography of Lytton. It is a pretty lowering business and has left me trembling.

---

[1] My 'daily'.

February 2nd

My 'grovellings' went on yesterday and have raked up a substratum of confused feelings. Do I want this young man to have access to any of it? Should people in no way concerned with feelings that were private, tender or painful have access to them? I'm aware of such conflicting motives in myself that I don't trust my own judgement and am seized at moments with a desire to burn all the papers I have. Yet the obstinacy of Noel Oliver in refusing to show Rupert Brooke's letters to his biographer has always seemed to me irrational and selfish. Last night Leonard Woolf talked on the wireless with dignity and perfect taste about Virginia. What would Ralph have said I should do? I feel desperately the lack of his judgement to consult. The whole surface of my mind feels tender so that the notes of a Beethoven cello sonata seem to bruise it as they fall from my transistor. Shall I ring up James and ask his advice? But I know that it is on my own assessment that I must ultimately rely.

I'm collecting reactions to the Churchillian frenzy. Julian, whose response appeared to me 'sound', said that some of his friends had been in a state of tense emotion and glorification of Churchill. Dicky took it for granted that the past week had been one of agitation and excitability (and therefore of drunken outbursts at Wivenhoe) and when I asked him why? – 'because it stirred up feelings about the war'. If this is true, if Churchill's death and the panoply decorating it, has glorified, idealized and romanticized war and disguised its sordid beastliness then it has been disastrous indeed. And I rather fear it is so. What surely is certain is that the mass emotion we have just witnessed is not really, as some describe it, a 'sense of loss', for the old man has been dead and gone these last ten years.

February 3rd

Yesterday I made a great effort, pulled myself together, and decided off my own bat and without recourse to James, what to give Holroyd this evening. Possibly my interview with him will raise further echoes, but at the moment my feeling is all for the truth and nothing but the truth.

February 4th

I was right – my evening with Holroyd did raise echoes – and they kept me awake until about three last night. But I liked him. I was pleasantly surprised by his friendliness, quickness in the uptake, accessibility and (so it seemed to me) good judgement. At one moment he started to talk compulsively about himself, and I feel a little compunction at not having led him on further. Anyway, we passed three hours talking without *gêne* about the past and looking at photographs and I had no difficulty in deciding which, or what to say, nor do I think I ever saw reason to suppress the truth.

February 6th

The best has been said for the Funeral by V. S. Pritchett in a remarkable article in the *New Statesman*, which I prophesy will be quoted in all history books for the period. Even he doesn't answer the question he himself asks: What were the feelings that touched personally every man, woman or child who saw it? His real answer seems to be a response to the perfection, imagination, and admirable timing and taste with which the performance was carried out, though he seems to *think* he's saying it was the nation's recognition of greatness. Tristram Powell, who had been a moved spectator of everything, contributed to this same effect and also thought that it was as a symbol of mortality that it was particularly moving. He added descriptive touches that made it vivid – like that of a little man in a Russian fur hat suddenly seen walking in the middle of the processional route, bowed forward with his eyes on the ground, who then suddenly indicated a patch of the road that wasn't adequately sanded, and minions hurried forward and did it. He was the Chief Gritter!

February 9th

I'm very glad indeed I got Julia to come to dinner last night. She is, after all, the person with whom I am most at ease, the oldest of my friends. I'm glad too that I decided to behave as if our last meeting had been perfectly normal and easy. It's possible she even thought it was – she says now she was feeling very strange under the influence of some new drug now abandoned. Last night there wasn't a breath of difficulty between us.

February 21st: Crichel

I was intrigued enough by what Raymond told me last night about Mycenae, Pylos and Knossos to spend the whole bitter cold afternoon reading the book he is reviewing. I've for so long pushed the phrase 'Linear B' to the back of my mind. Now it turns out to be perfectly simple, something one can grasp in five minutes.

The arrival of Desmond brought a rush of friendly warmth and tail-wagging about tea-time. There's always a certain amount of friction between him and Raymond who becomes a trifle governessy and disapproving with him. When Raymond had left the room Desmond said to me that he was getting rather fussy, there was surely no need to be 'cross all yesterday' just because of missing his train.

February 22nd

Raymond's Mycenae-Crete obsession became almost comic in the end – he could talk of nothing else at all, and as he had been mugging up his facts from several solid tomes Desmond and I were at a disadvantage. As we drove yesterday to lunch with Lady Juliet Duff I knew that Desmond was longing for the lecture to stop, as I was, especially as there was so much to look at in the way of pale beautiful sweeps of hillside, all the colour drained away by a sudden onset of cold, except for the faint brown of twigs and their buds. At lunch we had Beverley Nichols, Lilian Braithwaite's daughter, Joyce Carey, and, of course, Simon Fleet – with whom I think I got on quite well. The tall handsome rooms were full of lovely things including a table covered with pots of flowers – large pitcher orchids, jasmine, aconites and snowdrops – and looked out on the beautiful frozen garden. Roaring fires, voluptuous cats; talk about cats, 'the young' and Alcoholics Anonymous. But oh, poor Raymond – he looks awfully thin and worried, and takes life so hard. His seventieth birthday is approaching and two parties in his honour are being held – one by the *Sunday Times*, one by Hamish Hamilton – to both of which I've been asked. I don't think he's happy and I feel sad when I think how little human contact we made this weekend. He took no interest in my life, but heaven help us, what is there to be interested in?

February 26th

I must really put an end to my inward-looking temperature-taking; forget myself utterly for a while and sink into the concerns of other people. This I have in fact been doing the last few days, caught up without effort or by design in the affairs of Mary in particular. We were to go to a matinée on Wednesday afternoon, lunching here first, so when she rang up on Tuesday and asked if I had a few moments during the day I sensed an emergency under her calm tones and was not at all surprised to hear her say as she sat down on my sofa, 'I'm wondering whether to get a divorce.'

March 3rd

I have two books to translate if I want. I am doing a French life of Conan Doyle first. I feel breathless. Calm, calm is my objective but I doubt if I shall achieve it. I'm lying in bed looking at thin snowfall on the already covered roofs. Total silence. A feeling of boundless strangeness. Who am I, and what am I doing on my island mattress?

Yesterday I went to lunch with Faith to meet Boris Anrep who looks a really beautiful object now in his reduced but dignified old age. He turned to me at lunch and said, 'You know Helen died two days ago?' It so happened that I had been looking nostalgically at old photos of her at her most charming, pacing the Ham Spray verandah with Bunny, only yesterday, and reading bits of my earliest diaries, which give a cynical but affectionate picture. It was a shock, though I have for the last years thought of her with guilt, because I didn't go and see her and I knew I ought to, but couldn't face the uneasiness of her welcome. It wasn't possible to think my last visit gave any pleasure to speak of to Helen. Ralph and I both expressed our affection for her in the old days – he particularly: it's lately that I've been remiss. I think perhaps she was a little, too. What a very strange character, compounded of vanity and charm. The vanity may well have been based on a sense of inferiority to Boris, as one is tired of being told, but what struck me most was that she underestimated her *real* qualities – talent for life, gaiety, good taste – and overestimated those that didn't exist, such as being a pundit about the arts and the mentor of the young, infallible. She was erratic, wayward, graceful, amusing and charming; and a lot of that charm was bound up in her appearance – her marvellously fresh complexion, untidy silky white hair, elegant movements, and eccentric, dilapidated style of dress.

March 11th

Margaret Penrose on the telephone spoke about existence very much as if it were a makeshift, a coat bought off the peg, not made to fit. What *IS* it like? I never stop thinking about it and in the course of my long life my views undoubtedly change. Although one loses the youthful sense of its malleability and its splendid possibilities, its loveableness goes on, and this seems to me strange considering the fearful battering it gives one. 'It' is an always felt, even dominating presence, a bicycle to be ridden, a horse to be mastered, an adversary to be wrestled with, sometimes a purring cat lying on one's lap or a draught of heady wine gulped quickly down. Now – at sixty-five – I do think of it as a makeshift but still with a certain glow about it; a threadbare carpet with a worn but glorious pattern.

Margaret seemed to feel that most normal people could have taken unto themselves a large number of different mates, and this I suppose must be true – because it would be purely superstitious to believe in the gravitating together of kindred souls – yet I find it impossible to accept in my own case.

March 23rd

One of Gerald Brenan's 'spiky' letters, chiefly to tell me that Henrietta was not happy and Sophie running wild, ending, 'I thought you'd like this budget of news.' After his well-known 'desire to cause pain' what a relief to lunch today with Anne [Hill] who loves passing on good news and had a good and cheerful letter from Henrietta to Harriet to report on.

April 3rd

Yesterday began a 'great' weekend at Stokke, lovingly planned by Mary for some weeks – me, Julia, Jonny and Sabrina, Ben Nicolson. Ben is evidently moved to find himself here after ten years; shades of the past envelop him, his long Spanish face falls into deep melancholy and then lights up into hectic mirth. Julia is the one we are all anxious should enjoy herself and I wasn't sure she was doing so at dinner last night, seated between Charlie McCabe and Ben. She has backcombed her hair into an enormous frenzied haystack, otherwise she seems on the spot and her original and amusing best. I say 'otherwise' because it is, I think, a form of concealment or fending off the world. Jonny and Sabrina delightfully loving to one another. Sabrina is pregnant and I was touched by Jonny's look of real consternation when I said I thought the farmers were watering the milk. 'Good heavens! What shall I do? I must get cream or something for Sabrina.' I like her thoughtful search for the words she wants to express her ideas, often very successfully. Talking at dinner of religion or mystical experience, she described very well how once after being 'terribly afraid' she got an almost mystical experience from the sense that she was *accurately* able to orientate herself again – as if that accuracy came from outside. An uneasy moment when Charlie, feeling perhaps that he wasn't registering, began to shout a story down the whole table to me, and Mary thoughtlessly tried to 'take it away' as a footballer does the ball.

I do feel glad I don't any longer have to be responsible for large house parties – what a sweat and anxiety!

April 4th

The weekend is now going along merrily, and I take off my hat to Mary for her excellent compounding and arranging of it – seeming effortless, though of course it is not. Balmy, heavenly day yesterday. At lunch I told Sabrina about Jonny's remark about the cream – her face softened into a smile; then after a brief pause she said: 'Did he really say that?' 'Yes.' 'Tell me again.' Work and croquet in the morning; after lunch a walk in the forest with Julia. She was appreciative of Mary (who has been in and out of her famous 'doghouse' more than once) and even of Charlie to some extent.

April 11th

At the Cecils' at Cranborne. It's Sunday morning and I'm lying in bed, having woken fairly early and started reading Lady Cynthia Asquith's diary, one volume of which is here in TS. David, Rachel and Julian Fane[1] (who is my fellow guest) rave about it and her. I think one can detect a lively character full of charm but the diary is not really good. Why, I ask myself? I think she's fallen for the fatal temptation of feeling she must write something every day, and recording movements and facts rather than responses to them: 'Beb[2] and I took the motor to lunch at Downing Street, Winston, A.J.B., etc., etc. Sat between X and Y, interesting conversation.' Disconcerting references to 'lack of whimsicality' as if it were a defect; pure gush like 'she was so darling'. Here was this poor woman with her husband at the front, many of her friends being killed, her eldest little son turning out to be mad, and she writes lists of social engagements or 'shopping at Harrods'. One almost feels she is cold-hearted, certainly vain, and I note the absence of anything visual. The best things are remembered remarks – like Margot's of Katharine Asquith, who lacked vitality: 'Death could take nothing from Katharine.' I'm anxious lest too much of my critical feelings should come out to these hero-worshippers, who obviously loved her and treat her like a rare blown egg in cotton wool.

As usual it is a very comforting house to stay in. Many enthralling conversations, about *Hamlet* one night, violence the next, a walk yesterday afternoon through a sparkling wood carpeted densely with fresh green garlic leaves, anemones and tufted primroses. Hugh and Laura[3] are here – Hugh the more inarticulate, yet one is aware he has plenty of thoughts. I admire David's fatherly patience while he struggles to express them. I like Julian Fane: he is like a blond pale Leo Myers, but without Leo's formidable cynicism and intelligence. I have the feeling Julian Fane finds me too unfeminine, but can't be bothered to try and seem less so. At lunch I did of course make certain criticisms of Cynthia Asquith's diary. Did toads leap out? Or did I successfully gulp them down again? I'm not sure.

Laura is now reading the diaries and takes a position closer to mine than any – she sees the funny side at least of the way Cynthia is always 'going shopping': 'to Harrods to buy a white suit' immediately after seeing her husband off to the front or hearing the ghastly news of a wounded friend. Julian Fane with rather anxious blue eyes tries to get me to admit they are 'brilliant'. I hedge – hoping to confuse the fox-trail of my fairly strong dislike of them, and not only for them but the whole civilization they stand for. Or at least feeling that it lacks something of the more integrated realistic ironical civilization I most admire. But what, exactly? After Julian Fane had gone, David brought down from an attic two thick tomes, privately printed – one to the memory of the Grenfells, another to the Charterises killed in the First World War. Such books are always horribly painful with their mixture of the steel of genuine agony with the golden haze of idolatrous love. I pored over the Grenfells, from curly-headed angelic boys to a really terrifyingly tough-looking Julian, who wrote *Into Battle*, that paean to destruction. All the time David paced the room, making no bones about being emotionally stirred by the unwrapping of these coffins. Of course he was: this was his world and these were his values; he has the same conviction as they did of belonging to 'the chosen few'. Yet with the best will in the world, I could smell nothing but dust.

---

[1] Writer, charming aristocrat, at that time a bachelor.
[2] Herbert Asquith, her husband.
[3] Younger Cecil children.

April 15th: Thorington Hall

With Lionel and Margaret: 'Are you SURE you don't mind sleeping in the panelled room?' This is because it's supposed to be haunted and many people would die rather than sleep there. 'Not in the very least,' I say, forgetting that perhaps because unloved it has its disadvantages. Rather large and square, it has only one picture on its panelled oak walls, an eighteenth-century portrait of a man 'who is always looking at you'. A small bone-hard child's bed crouches against one wall, and there is virtually no other furniture. Having no heating or fire of any description the chill of all the past winter hangs in it, but going to bed in vest, cardigan and dressing gown and clutching my hot-water bottle, I managed to sleep.

Staying here is a nice mild American medical scientist, working on a book with Lionel, whom he clearly adores. His face is oval, dusky and unformed like the pictures of Nabokov but less tinged with emotion. Last night Jonathan, with his quite pretty wife Maggie, arrived too. I'm very grateful for the chance of getting out of London, shall enjoy Lionel and Margaret's company greatly and hope to get on with my work.

Last night a story of Lionel's delighted me – it was about W. H. Rivers, expert on shell-shock (indeed, the man who discovered there was such a thing). He was lecturing on the subject and had an intermittent stammer; suddenly he got absolutely stuck and after wrestling with the word for ten minutes he seized a piece of chalk and angrily scrawled on the blackboard the word: TERROR.

April 16th: Easter Day

I've been given the 'telly' room to work in: here I spent all yesterday morning, and propose to spend this, with my work spread out on an oceanic dining-room table – happiness. I have pulled up an electric heater and am doing my best to warm up after the rigours of the night in my quite exceptionally cold, dark room. The weather has turned bitter cold and an intermittent gale battered my windows; now and again a yew tree just outside struck them with a loud bang and at 5 a.m. the door of the priest's hole creaked and then crashed open – this lies behind the idea of the haunting, I dare say. Yesterday an art master from Lawrence's school – Francis Hoyland – came to lunch to see about renting Lionel's barn as a studio. Talked to him about his methods of teaching art. He suddenly became enthusiastic and said that as works of art all started from the body of the perceiver – here he seized a bottle of HP sauce, a tomato and a loaf and arranged them roughly – he taught his students to go back to their own bodily sensations. When I suggested that perception was not purely bodily but also mental and that the knowledge of what HP sauce was, for good or ill, played a part in the act of perception, he got almost angry.

After lunch Margaret, Jonathan and Maggie, George Smith (the nice American) and I got onto five bicycles and went spinning round the lanes. Uncertain at first, I was delighted to find I could still do it, after at *least* a twenty-year gap.

April 20th

The intense cold tightened its pincers and three nights in the glacial dankness of the haunted room were quite enough. All the same, I loved being with Lionel and Margaret, and liked the gentle American also. As for Jonathan, he was almost completely silent, though he doesn't seem unhappy. I pleased the Penroses by saying their house had the atmosphere of a 'reading party' and though I've never been to one I regard this as high praise. Lionel and George worked at their book on imbeciles; I at my translation; Maggie at something to do with maths papers and Jonathan at chess. I think Margaret, in spite of having to cater for us all, felt a little short of somewhere to discharge her warm and boundless energy, her considerable intelligence.

A conversation with Lionel about scientists comes back to my mind – he said how maddening the French ones were, insisting on being so logical, as if no one else was: how peevishly they quarrelled over some minute piece of knowledge, and who was to have the honour of first discovering it. 'One scientist I shall always remember because he said, "Knowledge is extremely important, but who discovered it is of no importance *at all*." I thought he deserved a great deal of honour for saying such a thing but the worst of it is, I can't remember what his name was.'

April 24th: London

I met a new and very likeable character last night – David Sylvester, the art critic. A large, plump man with big, sad, dark eyes and a jet-black beard crawling all over his cheeks and surrounding very red lips. Clearly extremely intelligent, not very happy, emotional, both gentle and violent (the two at war with each other) and anxious about himself. The conversation was interesting and moderately excitable – centring round religion (we're both anti-Christian), teaching children to read (we didn't agree there) and violence. I said that it could be statistically proved from criminal records that men were more violent than women. He took this up rather hotly, as if I'd said they were *wickeder* (which of course I hadn't) and declared that if men were violent it was because women so wickedly refused to breast-feed them – this was *always* possible if they really wanted to, he said – and also wickedly 'castrated' their sons and husbands. I looked at him rather sharply and said, 'Have you been psychoanalysed?' whereupon everyone laughed and it seems he's still at it. More than once he charged me with being 'sophisticated' – 'a person as sophisticated as you are'. That's not a word I've ever applied to myself.

April 26th

I've already noted Eardley's suggestion that I join him in renting a house in Orta, north Italy, but without enthusiasm. However, the 'yes-person' in me has taken over, and we are setting off in a few days' time. I shall stay a month, Eardley longer. The house belongs to Nigel Dennis, author of *Cards of Identity*.

April 29th: Paris

The first night of my journey to Italy with Eardley. Here after all I am, lying on my comfortable rough-sheeted platform bed waiting for *petit déjeuner*. The walls and curtains are covered all over with *coquet* bunches of flowers on an egg-yellow background. I look out onto the quiet courtyard.

The days before departure saw the overcoming of various obstacles. I gave a dinner party to Heywood, Julian, Henrietta, Mark Palmer and Georgia – the young stayed late. I felt Heywood to be an elderly ally and he amused everyone with stories about Harriet's six-year-old twin stepdaughters. He had just taken one to the Zoo. 'How can you tell a man-bear from a woman-bear?' 'Well, you look underneath.' 'And what do you see there?' 'You see some balls and in front of them a penis.' Slight pause. 'Now you've embarrassed me, Heywood – you see, I call them something different.'

On my penultimate day, I went to the lunch in honour of Raymond's seventieth birthday at the *Sunday Times* – I suppose about thirty of us in a long boardroom with printed menus with our names on them. I sat between Morgan Forster and Leonard Russell (one of the *Sunday Times* staff and husband of Dilys Powell). She, Lady Clark, Lady Churchill and Janet Adam-Smith were the only other females. Leonard, Duncan, Dadie, V.S.P., and Roger Senhouse were there, and the room was full of affection and good feeling. Lunch disgusting, and not much to drink; afterwards, Raymond rose to his feet and spoke uneasily from a fluttering piece of paper. I gave him a little Georgian silver pillbox, which I think he really liked. Though a purely formal occasion there was a sort of glow left behind by it and I travelled home on a bus with Duncan.

Now D-day – yesterday. Eardley had to go back for his spectacles, didn't allow enough time to get to Southend, and left most of the maps behind. We got on fine, though, yesterday and I only hope it may continue. It's always a surprise what rough, wrinkled, noisy, bumpy aeroplanes car travellers are expected to go by – but pleasant being one of a half a dozen, and soon with no effort we were spinning off over the pale sprig-green plains of northern France, under fierce showers and long periods of sun.

April 30th: Nancy

Divinely beautiful town. We have spent the night in the large sumptuous hotel that overlooks the Place Stanislas. A festival of university actors (amateurs) from all over the world is going on in the theatre here, a magnificent building lined with cherry-coloured velvet and the twin to our hotel. One of the very nice things about Eardley as a travelling companion is his eagerness to go to anything of this sort, and go we did, coming out afterwards into the splendid square, discreetly floodlit so that the stone ornaments along the roofs stood out almost meltingly against the night sky, and the fountains and gilt gates at the corners blazed brilliantly against the equally brilliant green of the trees behind them.

The performance consisted of three troupes: Americans from Indiana, Turks, and French. The Americans were deplorable in their complete lack of talent, and clumsiness; the house booed loudly. The Turks, though – what an experience! They were really first-rate, and the audience applauded them wildly. (These were mostly charming young people from the university here, or the visiting teams.) Stylized rocking, springing from foot to foot was the basis of all their gesture and movement – as if to show themselves alive, or as a child will pick up and thump on the table the doll or creature that he is making perform in his play. At one side sat a man beating out a rhythm with his hand on some sort of drum, or occasionally picking up a trumpet and blowing it. Within this extreme formalization the characters were brilliantly differentiated by the exact way they bounced to and fro. It was like ballet, so that the fact that one understood nothing hardly mattered, even when the comic character recited a very serious poem in a funny way.

May 1st: Luzern

We are supposed to arrive at Orta today – what angsts, surprises or disappointments may that bring? From beautiful Nancy we drove yesterday morning to Colmar and spent some time looking at the Grünewald *Altarpiece*. Both agreed, as we got back into the car, that we felt shattered and disturbed. I think I 'liked' it less than Eardley did – the great thing about it is the extraordinary intensity of emotion it contains; I can't think of any other picture that arouses it so violently, unless perhaps the Piero *Resurrection* at Borgo San Sepolcro or the *Lamb* at Ghent – but both are much better pictures than this. What is more, though there are these disturbing, violently emotional passages in the Grünewald, there are others of real falseness and sentimentality. Nor am I greatly impressed by what many modern painters have apparently been struck by – the grim reality of the crucifixion. But should a great work of art leave one disturbed, agitated and confused? Surely not – however deep it goes, the Piero, *The Burial of Count Orgaz*, *Othello* ought to leave the problems resolved and smoothed out. Why the Grünewald doesn't do this, for all its mastery is a problem to which I see several solutions. First: the very intensity of the emotion like an overpowering smell pours from the picture and prevents one reacting to its beauty, colour, design as much as one otherwise would. Second: it taps the unconscious, as Bosch does, by means of horrifying creatures, and suggestions of unspeakable desires and deformation – and leaves these substrata in unresolved chaos. And third: the passages of sickly, vulgar unreality and sentimentality – vulgarity of a specially German sort – making a clanging and unpleasant discord with the sombre grim realism of the rest. So, though I came away feeling I'd had a sensational experience, I do most definitely not bow down to Grünewald in deepest awe and respect; in fact I resent not having been left with that golden sunset glow a really great picture leaves in one's mind.

The Swiss – that's the other subject I've thought about. To cross from depopulated beautiful unspoiled France (though Nancy it is true, is hardly to be taken as typical of any country) into this small over-populated, stodgy, methodical, prosaic land, is a portentous experience. At once the houses began closely edging the roads in interrupted villages, the cars crawled in an endless queue. What can have made people propagate so much faster one side of the boundary than the other? Then every material thing is ugly, or rather made without consideration for beauty or taste. The rich damp green fields with their kingcups and cuckoo flowers, the tearing streams were some relief as we drove up into the hills, but everywhere, everywhere man was vile – or rather, *deadly dull*. A glorious natural vision before we plunged down into Luzern was provided by the pale, huge, pinkly-lit transparent-looking Alps hanging high and ethereal far above us in the sky, and seeming grand and pure compared to the crawling grubby cars, people and concrete or wooden houses below. Our hotel is all that's most Swiss. Everyone speaks excellent English, but treats us in a slightly governessy inhuman way, without the real humanity of Italians or Spaniards, or the intelligent crossness of the French.

May 2nd: Orta

Well, here I am in my bleak un-windowed bedroom at 7.30 a.m., with the rain falling heavily outside. We arrived yesterday, mid-afternoon, May Day and a weekend, to find the pretty little town jam-packed with humanity, and cars forcing

their way slowly along the narrow streets. We broke our way into the garden of
'our' house – a strip of rough grass, very narrow like a London back garden. It goes
down to the lake's edge where a pretty willow tree droops over it and makes a tiny
region where one might eat out. The house itself is very narrow and tall. When we
had collected the keys and made our way in, the dankness of having been shut up
all winter hung everywhere. At the moment it doesn't seem extraordinarily feasible,
but yesterday our immense desire to make a go of it was augmented by the
astonishing arrival of Bunny and Angelica almost before we had looked round. All
the floors are made of rather dusty brick-coloured tiles. Nothing works, including
an electric fire in the top room (where Bunny and Angelica are sleeping in their
sleeping-bags). The room I'm now in has no window or heating, and I had to lug
upstairs a mattress from Eardley's room so as to have something to tuck in; but we
drank whisky, made up the beds, went out to eat in a restaurant and were very
jolly.

This morning my mind is full of problems. How long will the Garnetts stay? I
feel responsible for their being here, though not perhaps for their forgetting our
dates and coming so early. After they've gone Eardley and I will each take one floor
and arrange accordingly – I don't think I mind which. Hope of a glimpse of the
douceur de vivre has temporarily gone with the sound of rain, through which for
some hours I've heard the Italian birds chirping stridently, on a very different note
from the twittering French ones. Then I feel responsible – why? – for keeping
Eardley's spirits up. I was tremendously aware as we arrived yesterday of *his* feeling
responsibility for the place, and desire for me to like it, so with the ludicrous
inversion human beings go in for I strained every nerve to reassure him. Both of
us are worrying hard.

How I long for some physical satisfaction to hang on to! – warmth of a fire, sun,
coffee. We have none of these.

May 3rd

Now all is well – very well, I think I can say. The Garnetts with their bravura and
appreciation saw us through our teething problems. The rain stopped soon after
Bunny and I had stepped out together along the narrow streets (whose roofs almost
meet overhead and so keep off the rain) to buy bread, milk, coffee and butter.
There's an extraordinary satisfaction about acquiring these prime necessities, and
by the time the table was spread and hot coffee being poured into cups, the sun
had almost come out and we felt much warmer. A splendid honest *donna* of
seventy-seven called Herminia came and cleaned the bath (left strikingly dirty by
the Garnetts, who have evidently been roughing it); we found deck chairs and
dragged them out into the garden, bought eggs and salad and fruit and cheese and
bunches of herbs. Halfway through the afternoon we walked along the shore of
the lake by the narrow marge left between the softly lapping water and sloping
luscious fields full of fruit trees, small, intoxicatingly sweet narcissi, and large white
violets. Everything was pretty.

May 4th

Today has been a full and important one. The morning was radiant and balmy.
While the Garnetts went off to telephone, Eardley and I set about like two ants,
rearranging our quarters. He is to have the Garnetts' bedroom: the black hole

behind it where I slept the last two nights is to be a dressing room with clothes-hanging space for both. I have the *sala* to work in, and sleep in the bedroom behind it. This is dark, but not so bad as my recent hide-out and I have moved the bed to give a magnificent reading-light. I dragged beds, pushed and shoved, unpacked everything down to the last pill bottle and spread out my dictionaries. I have even done a good day's stint at my translation, and changed £10 of traveller's cheques. We are in fact afloat. We have even called on the next-door neighbours, the Cappellis and taken a drink with them. Middle-aged both, with rather quizzical faces, they hint at many mysteries connected with our house and the Nigel Dennis family.

I feel *peace* descending and that I shall be quite content here with Eardley and that we have made the Casa Forbes into *our* house. *We* now *live* here.

May 5th

First breakfast *à deux* cooked and eaten. Herminia is crashing about in the kitchen. The top lavatory is not working, nor are the electric fire and sitting-room main light. The Dennises either have strikingly little love for their house, no taste or sensuality, or no money. There's not a single carpet or picture in the whole house. In the afternoon we drove up the hill behind the village to its summit, finding a place where great quantities of big blue gentians were growing, and on and up, to small elegant pure white crocuses and dogtooth-violets. Though there are not many flowers, what exquisite ones! We ate indoors by the heat of our god-given butagaz fire, for though it is warmer already, it's pretty freezing in bedroom or kitchen. Yet how marvellous to look out and see a clear dark sky, stars and a crescent moon.

Herminia treats us as though we belonged to a superior order of beings, both delighting and embarrassing us. When we got back from the mountains we found her hurrying excitedly along the street with a bundle wrapped in newspaper. She had brought us some lettuce thinnings, radishes, and a huge bunch of buttercups, daisies and dandelions!

May 7th

A pearl-grey day. Sounds come clearly across the silver lake. The peace is incomparable, and one cannot believe in the invasion of weekend tourists which will begin presumably tomorrow. Yesterday the sun came out. Sitting out in it and reading the newspaper was so delicious that translating my verbose French professor[1] (who has just compared the Sherlock Holmes stories to *Paradise Lost!*) was set aside; this was too good to miss. A visit from the Cappellis, bearing a huge and splendid gift of azaleas. Fearing that Herminia might feel her buttercups outclassed, I was solicitous to give them fresh water in their jam jar, but the vase shortage is so great that I had to rush upstairs and fetch the lavatory brush container for the azaleas.

Full days, scented evenings, really hot sun all afternoon. Each morning Herminia brings more and more bunches of flowers; when she has something worthy of her – lilac or may – she really arranges them very prettily. We try and keep her fed with short snatches of such conversation as we can manage. Yesterday, admiring

---

[1] Pierre Nordon, author of the *Life of Conan Doyle* I was translating.

my sheets, she said how extraordinary the Forbes were to have such a fine house and no nice things at all. 'What about the Signora?' I asked. 'Does she do anything in the house?' An owl's hoot went up. '*Hoo! Dolce far niente, tutt'il giorno!*' She illustrated this by resting her cheek on her hand. Then she told us how the *Arandora Star* (the ship that was sunk full of Italian waiters) included her son-in-law and two other relatives. And a pacifist chorus followed from us both.

An expedition by car up an endless series of *lacets* to a mountain village where the old people still wear the clothes you see in Victorian prints – gold earrings, headscarves, small shawls and very full skirts.

The regular life in sweet surroundings with a companion who likes much the same things as I do should be and is very soothing. Indeed, I've felt relaxed and contented. Up on the hillside yesterday I got a waft of mountain magic: every sound carried, crickets and cuckoos and a dog barking in each farm, and the extraordinary clarity and distinctness of female Italian voices. One farm had some baby rabbits lolloping round it, loose. The path wound into pretty woods and out again. I longed for Ralph to admire it with. I think of him and Burgo a great deal here, and dream of them a lot.

The nights are the least pleasant part. Facing my cold dark room is a slight ordeal, lying under the thin blankets patched with Nigel Dennis's underpants, waiting to get warm.

May 14th

As the weather grows more summery, our petals gradually unfurl. People have begun to bathe in the lake. The nights are perfectly clear unless for a slight haze, and the beauty of the twinkling lights across the water seen between the tall shapes of the cypress trees is almost too obvious to react to. Eardley and I have talked of all sorts of subjects, general ones like art and war, and personal like our pasts or homosexuality; and last night he talked a lot about life at Winchester and his feeling for his brother – these I believe to lie deep in a guarded region of his ego, and I am flattered that they came out spontaneously.

The day before yesterday there was a major event – the kind Cappellis from next door arranged to get us seats for *Simon Boccanegra* at the Scala. I felt an intense thrill at finding myself here in this famous opera house about to see the opera that was almost first on my list of desiderata. When the lights dimmed, they for a while left all the boxes faintly lit – the prettiest sight in the world, like a honeycomb of cherry-coloured silk hung with occasional clusters of moon-like lamps, and we heard beautifully from our seats in the galleria.

We flew home swiftly through the night.

May 18th

The other day Eardley took me to call on two aristocratic elderly Italian ladies, Bianca Negra and her sister, who live at the village above us in a magnificent house (a 'national monument') painted all over the outside in dull purple, ochre and blue, but mostly shut up now as they can get no servants. They were a delightful pair, intelligent, civilized and amusing, speaking excellent English. A little puzzled – as the Cappellis were – as to what terms Eardley and I were on, they quickly thawed and showed us one small charmingly painted room. I mentioned wild flowers. Their eyes lit up. The younger sister said, 'Some people have a normal love for flowers, some an abnormal one. Mine is *ab*normal.' They began to tell us where to go, and above all to the Val Formazza above Domodossola. The very next day, though it was Sunday and looked unsettled, we were off like a shot.

We drove up the long deep valley from Domodossola towards the Swiss border, winding gradually between its steep granite sides and clambering by *lacets* among enormous grey blocks fallen chaotically from the mountains. We ate our picnic leaning against the noble slope of one of these, which had cherry-coloured primulas growing from its cracks. Then on again up and up, past a vertical waterfall and *then* we entered a new world which I hope I shall never forget the look of in all my life. A high valley, a basin of short turf, with the snow mountains all round and melted snow from them running in a stream down the middle. The smooth slopes were thickly sprinkled with marvellously clear-coloured alpine flowers, a beautiful mixture of purple and white crocuses, very blue forget-me-nots, yellow pansies, gentians big and small, primula farinosa, orchids yellow and red, a glorious pale yellow pasque-flower and two other anemones. My reaction was certainly 'abnormal', worshipping and intoxicated. We shan't find any other flowers here to equal them. We drove on till the road was blocked with snow and then turned home. After this really immense thrill, it was almost a relief to find it raining when we surfaced yesterday and it kept quietly on all morning.

June 3rd: West Halkin Street

I have re-entered my life at full gallop with rather unearthly energy and am already almost 'straight'. To my orchestra the night I got back and also to see Janetta. Yesterday Mary came to lunch and Julia to dinner. I have spoken on the telephone to nearly all my friends. Mary sounded cheerful about Charlie's new job – which makes them far better off and improves his morale, 'But he's jolly disagreeable, all the same, much of the time.' She'd just had a flaming row with him about Magouche – he had practically said she must choose between him and Magouche, that she was 'bad news', a 'nasty piece of work' and other equally revolting phrases.

Julia and I discussed the Colmar Grünewald. She praised it for giving a lifelike and convincing picture of Christ's sufferings on the cross 'instead of just a young man with flu'. What perhaps worries me about Julia is that she avows that she wants to find a new life-companion – this, at sixty-three, and regardless of her extreme fastidiousness.

June 5th: Lawford Hall, Essex

I thought as I got into my soft bed last night how uneasy I had for many long years felt in this house and that now I don't – not in the least, here or anywhere else. I've been broken in, exactly like a horse, made to go round and round under whip and bearing rein until I simply can do it without minding. Will this state of things last? Or will it crumble? It is a comfort, that's the best that can be said about it and what I've learned I've learned in the school of utter loneliness.

Talking to Janetta two nights ago, I mentioned Julia's desperate craving to find a new mate at the eleventh hour, which I can barely even understand. 'Oh, but almost everyone I *know* is trying and longing to do that,' said Janetta with a furrowed face. 'They may be miserable in their marriages and want to get away, but it's the one thing they think of – to find someone else to share their lives.'

Thank heavens then for this one small mercy that I've never, never for a second envisaged or hoped for a second best.

June 18th

I notice somewhat ruefully but without surprise, that I often spend long hours with people without their asking me a single question about myself. Kitty, for instance; not a word asked about my five weeks in Italy. Bunny came to dinner last night and was a delightful companion; we talked of all his daughters and their problems in turn, about his work, about William, the question of where to live, and finally – in a voice that trembled a little – about his relations with Angelica. So happy they had seemed at Orta, but (as Henrietta suggested) they have floated apart since their return. Angelica has talked of 'coming back to live at Hilton'. But now she has found a 'little rather slummy house near the Angel' and is all agog for that. As I heard his sad and quavering voice saying how he hated the idea of living in London, that it tired him dashing up and down and he got melancholy and lonely at Hilton with no one but William, my heart contracted with sympathy and affection. But not one word about *my* life. I have none, and everyone knows it. Perhaps that's the answer.

Yesterday I lunched with Magouche who, not being trained in Bloomsbury's school, did ask politely about myself.

June 24th

Listening to Callas in *Tosca* as I stirred a mayonnaise. Last night and tonight were devoted to Handel operas at Sadler's Wells.

Magouche seemed horrified when we got there ten minutes before the curtain went up, and suggested our fighting our way through the milling crowds to get whisky. As we'd each swallowed two quite stiff ones in my flat, I counter-suggested that we shouldn't. 'But what shall we *do* for ten minutes?' she said very spontaneously. I didn't say 'talk', or look about us – in point of fact we hardly had time to read the plot of the first act. But I was interested at this idea that if they weren't drinking there's nothing two people have to say or do after a certain hour. Another phrase in common currency: 'I need a drink' or 'I don't need a drink but I'd like one.' How many whiskys a night are *needed* by whom? I certainly need one. What would happen if we were wrecked on a desert island?

After the opera last night, Magouche and I went to the Campbells where Susan had provided a really magnificent spread of curries for us and we fell on them greedily. Little Arthur as usual woke twice and came down and sat on Susan's lap, surveying us out of his enormous blue, wide-set eyes.

Janetta came with me to Handel's *Rinaldo*. She described the party at Chatsworth for the coming-of-age of the heir last week. The special train with people in evening dress (including Princess Margaret) was watched by spectators as they trooped sheepishly up the platform. Then the great house, where everything was perfect – beauty everywhere, banks of flowers, delicious food, baths full of champagne, but Janetta was dealt a blow at the start by hearing from the conversation of two strangers that Andrew Devonshire was ill in bed with a high fever. He appeared for a very short while looking hectic and strange, and was then sent back to bed and visited by a doctor with a hypodermic. The great barrier of the house and all it stood for, the conventions and the Establishment, prevented Janetta going in the most natural and friendly way to visit him in his room. This is one of the things I loathe about conventions – that there are places where they sharply cut into warm, good, human feelings at their tenderest points. The party had been fixed for June in hopes of the pleasures of a summer night, but the rain lashed the great windows mercilessly. As all the Rembrandts, etc., are of priceless value every corridor had a 'watcher' in it. There was nowhere for the young to go and spoon, away from the eyes of the hordes of elderly female relations, great-aunts and grandmothers who were ranged round the walls, watching more keenly than the official watchers. The young generation were kept in awe by the elders of their own kin.

July 3rd

Living alone resembles living with someone else, in that one can have strange and different reactions to one's partner – one's Self. It can get on one's nerves; of course one can criticize it sharply. At the moment I'm doing all of these things. A loving mate sympathizes and encourages and tells one it's not too bad (and one is not too bad) really. Alone, I castigate myself unmercifully – for an impatient, arrogant, inconsiderate, bungling brute. And what good resolutions can be pulled out of the bog? Never to speak one's mind sharply, always to be patient, think before one speaks, put up with things. How dull...

I want today to be a parenthesis – a long leisurely ———. I wonder if I shall achieve it. Literally having posted off the last dollops of Conan Doyle yesterday, I realize that it requires an enormous effort to be still, to relax; so at eleven-thirty here I am still in bed with the Sunday papers spread over the alps of my knees. Last night I was at Glyndebourne with Isobel, Anthony Blond and his very pretty and quite intelligent friend Andrew. Anthony is an extraordinary mixture of tough crudity and good sense. You never know which side will be uppermost. Last night the good sense was. He really admires and appreciates Isobel (and how she blossomed under both their appreciation) yet I know he has sometimes been unkind to her over work. Black and white, a chequered man, whose saving grace is that he wants to be liked. Not to want which makes one appallingly uncivilized, but it's a rare thing, luckily.

The wound-up, never-say-die part of me is trying to read an article on President Johnson's attitude to the spread of nuclear arms and read it critically. Something else, the hedonist perhaps, wants to slip away and not attend. But on the whole I enjoy the thought of a quiet recouping day, with a human contact in the afternoon to stave off possible loneliness.

The satisfaction in trying to face some small bit of reality comes I suppose from the need to armour oneself against the horrors of life (knowledge is safety – the only real weapon of defence). Indeed the desire for knowledge may have its biological source in this same instinct for self-preservation, but seems to have become a craving on its own, with its own special gratification. And there is the converse anguish about the corners of dark reality that have not been faced. These I feel link up with childhood fears, peopling the corners of 28 Bedford Square with imagined monsters, which must surely have been the horrors one knew were waiting to spring out from the very stuff of life, as much a part of it as the thorns on a bramble. I'm sure that this facing and acceptance of reality and exploration of it in detail is an intense pleasure. Other people's feelings are a large part of reality, so that it leads to making contact and trying to sympathize and understand. It is, I suppose, Freud's 'reality principle' I'm groping after. I keep being reminded of my school-days. I see myself at the blackboard trying to construe a piece of Virgil or something, and Mr Badley tapping his impatient sand-shoed foot and saying in a soft irritable voice, 'Get it right, Man! Get it right, Man!' I've been *trying* to 'get it right' ever since, but with long gaps of inertia and idleness.

I wonder what's happening to Julia. Would like to 'get her right'.

July 6th

Two mornings ago Julian rang up to tell me he had heard a rumour that Eddy Sackville had suddenly died. There had been a crackling on the line, and, unable to hear anything but the voice of bad news, my heart stood still for Janetta who had been flying to Gibraltar. So that when the truth got through and was confirmed, it was almost a relief. I have ever since felt increasing sadness – waste – loss – a hole in the world. This grizzly snatching by the hand of death of someone who (though always delicate) everybody believed would live till ninety like his father, someone of my generation, does bring it home how our ranks are thinning. Very grimly, one does ask who will be the next – it might well have been Boris, Leonard, Craig Macfarlane, even Raymond. Life suddenly seems a mere antechamber to the tomb, and I really feel at the moment I should live as if it were, though I know that isn't sensible. And the inescapable fact that the ranks will go on thinning steadily, hole after hole, till I leave them myself stares me bleakly in the face.

When Julian told me the news I could only clutch at the consolation that there would be no one total wreck of a person left behind. A great many people do mind dreadfully, though. I spoke to Desmond on the telephone – 'I shall miss him *terribly*,' he said in a broken voice. So will Raymond. Last night a woman who said she had met me in Ireland and whom I couldn't remember at all rang up and talked to me about him for ages; after first asking 'could I tell her anything about it?' she kept saying: 'He was *so* fond of *you*,' and I felt I should say the same to her but was deterred by not knowing the face I was speaking to. People have a curious desire to get together round the memory of a person who has died, and to insert themselves as far forward as possible in the ranks of the bereaved. How do people who believe in foreknowledge make it work out? Would they have translated their last meeting with Eddy in some peculiar way? I'm trying to remember when mine was and I think it was when he dined here and we went to a play about three months ago and we talked particularly happily and easily for hours after. And as Desmond said, 'What will happen to Crichel?' – that delightful anachronism.

I rang up Frances Phipps just now. She's going to Eddy's funeral, most gallantly because otherwise she'd feel 'that she hadn't said goodbye to him'. 'Eddy's form of Catholicism made him believe in heaven – so I hope he's in it!' she said with her delightful laugh.

July 16th

Frances Phipps to lunch. We had rather a mortuary conversation about Eddy's funeral, to which she had been. For some time I have had a sneaking feeling that she was trying to make me see the religious light. She is a born proselytizer, and I suppose that it was foolish of me to think I could sometimes question her about her faith because we are such great friends and because she seems to hold it in such unorthodox form. I have made no bones whatever about my own disbelief, nor have I been in the least tempted to be aggressive about it. She is lavish in her protestations of friendship and often says that I'm 'the only person who understands' her feelings about peace and war, left-wing politics, etc. But then – in the way thought and feeling are translated into physical signs – I've learned to recognize the occasional proselytizing mood in her lowering her head, fixing me with melancholy and mesmeric blue eyes; her voice subdued to a chanting drone. She described the suitableness of Eddy's last resting place, the green village church-yard, the reactions of various people, Paul Hyslop's unbridled tears and other friends' disapproval of him, the earth thudding on the coffin, the genuine sorrow of some of the people who worked for Eddy. Well and good, and I was moved and interested. Then she told me details of the actual seizure that killed him, how he had come gasping into the bedroom of a priest who was staying with him, then shut himself in the lavatory, locked the door and was found there dead. There followed a gossipy anecdote about the friends in Ireland deciding it 'was better to say he died listening to music'.

All this interest in the manner of death and the disposal of the remains I find utterly antipathetic, and I became inarticulate in my attempts to express to her that I felt the moment of death final, and that any attempt to extend one's love to the corpse and its trappings was worse than a mockery. That should be reserved for memories of the person – the only things that endure. At the end of our conversation the real kernel of her discourse was laid on the table – Raymond, she felt, '*should* have come to the funeral', he should have turned back and 'seen the last of Eddy'. I at once realized I too was being condemned. I defended Raymond of course (including myself mentally in the defence); but she is I think incapable of understanding the rationalist's attitude. No one expects her to share it, but I hoped she accepted my irreligion just as I accept her religion. When I tried to close the subject of immortality by saying that I had no desire for it whatever and the thought was quite appalling to me, she attempted to convince me that it could be both desirable and thinkable. She again said how frustrated she was by the fact that she couldn't get on more intimate terms with Raymond – but alas, I know he finds her irrationality upsetting.

The injustice of her attitude to Raymond and Eddy's funeral was underlined by a call from him, now back in England, sounding terribly broken-hearted. He said my letter had 'reduced him to tears' and he comes to dinner on Monday. I was much moved by the desolation in his voice and his wanting to come and see me. Whatever I wrote him was from a better motive (sympathy) than my letter to Frances – self-justification inspired that, and I already regret it.

July 18th: Doddington Hall, Lincolnshire, Sunday morning, 8.15 a.m.

Rather glad to have woken a little early and be able to compose myself to my surroundings. We arrived on the evening train on Friday – Ralph Jarvis,[1] and Caroline[2] and I and the chief guest, Steven Runciman, whom everyone is anxious to please and propitiate. I took to him very much, and enjoyed his anecdotes and his way of pulling down his upper lip like a stage Irishman and staring fixedly at one with a 'What do you think of *that?*' expression after making a *bon mot*. Other guests – who should they be but 'delightful Peter Hesketh' whom Julia marked

[1] Owner of the house, a music-loving banker.
[2] His daughter, afterwards Lady Cranbrook.

down years and years ago as a possible husband, now matched with an elderly-looking wife. I wonder what Julia would think of 'delightful Peter' now. He's an architectural expert and for many long hours yesterday – six about – we all racketed around looking at houses all over the flat plate of the Lincolnshire countryside. I enjoyed visiting Grimsthorpe, built by Vanbrugh and inhabited by the Ancasters, parents of Jane Willoughby. Lady Ancaster showed us round – there was something raffish and feline about her which appealed to me; slight form, darting movements; precious emeralds and pearls round her neck and an emerald brooch clasped on the top of her straight, brown hair. The only son and heir disappeared off the Costa del Sol about a year ago, was presumed drowned, and obviously was. He seems to have been a charming bad lot, drug-taker and heavy drinker. His parents and Jane are still heart-broken, and I was touched by Lady Ancaster's method of distracting her mind – 'occupational therapy' as she called it – painting in the sow thistle and other weeds in her Bentham and Hooker. Then 'delightful Peter' insisted on taking us to look at one of his old homes now an open prison, gloomy, derelict and charmless, and kept up a running commentary of 'There used to be a wood here. My father planted this avenue. There used to be five gates on this road.' Steven Runciman looked round and muttered to me, 'I'm not impressed.' The general conversation in the car was all about properties, inheritances and ancestry. The extraordinary smugness of tone – 'Who was *she*?' 'Oh yes, that belonged to old Lord Liverpool.' 'Oh, was *he* the one with the wooden leg?' 'Yes, did you know him?' 'Why, very WELL INDEED!' 'Oh, really?' The snobbishness, the slow self-confident drawl in which all these exchanges were made – and they were pursued to incredible lengths – gradually sickened me.

July 20th

I'm horrified by the way the loss of a loved and lovable human being is quickly translated and degraded into material terms, and I can't help connecting this with this preoccupation with tombs, services, and all the rest. Wills inevitably come next. I cling to the recollection of Eddy as a unique and lovable person, and hate to see his figure disintegrating, as a tower crumbles when blown-up by dynamite on the cinema, and turning into *things*, properties, material obligations.

Yesterday Eardley came to see me and we walked round and round Belgrave Square. Afterwards Raymond came to dinner. Eardley gave a very different account from Frances's of the funeral – not an unfeeling one, though I don't think he greatly loved nor misses Eddy. The rigmarole and mumbo-jumbo had appalled him, and seemed a dreadful mockery. He described vividly the one moment that had been 'touching and beautiful' – when two strong men with long shining spades had started shovelling earth on the coffin with heavy thuds. But both he and Raymond were preoccupied with bequests and lawyers. Eddy left all his pictures (worth thousands of pounds) to Eardley, all his books to Raymond, and his records to Desmond (neither of whom want any more), his house in Ireland to his heir's eldest daughter. Raymond is obviously 'cut up' as the saying goes, and mentioned Eddy's death almost with tears, describing himself as 'numbed', as feeling as if 'half his brain had been shot away'; 'Eddy had a much better memory than I have,' he said, 'and he knew far more about my past than I do myself.' Eddy had been much his oldest friend. He looked shrunken, pitiful, crushed. 'I was so sure he would outlive me. I don't feel I shall live much longer.'

Eardley had told me he didn't want to go on with Crichel and couldn't possibly afford it. I thought probably Raymond might hope that it could be prolonged in some new form. But no. No question of their being able to afford it. Yet he hates the thought of the sorting, moving, selling, and doesn't relish the idea of living in Canonbury altogether. And then – in plaintive tones – he said that Eddy had promised 'to look after him in his old age if he got too tired and ill to work', but he has made no provision for this. Poor Raymond, he feels bereft and just when he most needs security, insecure. And yet, and yet – the material considerations did seem to me to oust the human and psychological and emotional ones a shade too quickly, and I feel the closing of the happy, brilliant, charming Crichel episode sorely.

August 3rd

I drove Henrietta and Sophie to Hilton for the weekend. All four glorious girls[1] were there. Fanny has as much character and intelligence as Nerissa, though in a slightly different way. She has taken to music like a duck to water, or like Nerissa to painting, and plays with fiery zeal on flute or horn. We had a lot of music. There were fascinating arguments – one about killing animals. 'The desire to kill *waxes* or *wanes*,' said Nerissa leaning forward with blazing eyes, 'but it's absolutely *basic*.' Amaryllis is in a way the least original of the four, though sweet and charming; the faint affectation all professional actresses develop veils her. Henrietta is the warmest and the most full of human instincts. All four girls slept and slept as if they could never have enough sleep and make up their arrears, which I'm sure was true. Angelica cooked marvellous puddings and pies and looked exhausted and anxious, and no wonder. Sophie trotted or staggered about with cries of 'Hal-LO!' or 'Funny!' or 'Oh dear, *dear*!' or more often streams of gibberish. Dear little girl, I find her almost more touching than I can bear. She adores Henrietta and if unable to obtain her entire attention flings herself on the ground in a passion of abandoned despair. Henrietta runs up to her with warm and all-enveloping gestures – I think she's very good with her. But of course someone is needed to take the burden off her. Duncan came on Saturday, so we were an enormous party.

August 8th: Cranborne

The first taste of real summer arrived unexpectedly yesterday. I sat out sweltering away deliciously on the lawn trying to do exercises in Russian, and later walked with David Cecil to the Manor to get a potted cyclamen. Welcome stillness and deep shadow enveloped the beautiful house and garden, with draperies of clematis and late roses covering the old walls.

Francis Wyndham came yesterday – a little piano on arrival, he has now revived and shows all his excellent judgement, and talks delightfully in his curious faintly cockney voice. Laura and Hugh are here also. There are two new Portuguese servants to whom Rachel is heard shouting loudly in pidgin English in the kitchen.

After lunch I took a rug on the lawn and lay in the sun with my head under the speckled shade of a small tree, reading Françoise Gilot on Picasso. Oh, blessed horizontality! I heard a loud hammering noise, transmitted by telegraphy along the flat surface of the lawn, and saw a distant bird tapping its beak and listening.

---

[1] Daughters of Bunny and Angelica – Amaryllis, Henrietta and the twins: Fanny and Nerissa.

It whisked me back, as did the soothing position I was lying in, to the old days at Ham Spray.

Dickie Buckle, writer on the ballet, came for a drink, a fresh-faced, sailorly man, with a healthy interest in everything. He told us about a visit from Nureyev, 'a very spoilt young man'. He arrived by car at Buckle's cottage, said first, 'It's a *very* long way,' and then (looking round), 'I thought you would have big estates.' Buckle told him he was taking him to see an old lady 'who used to know Diaghilev and Nijinsky'. 'OH, I'm so tired of people who knew Diaghilev and Nijinsky!' But Juliet Duff talked to Nureyev in fluent Russian and completely won him over.

The weekend talk has touched often and stimulatingly on ideas and generalities; but has kept away – by pure chance I think – from moral or political issues. Last night the subject of aesthetes and dilettantes came up. Why were these now terms of abuse? Would one rather be called one of these or 'an intellectual'? Francis Wyndham preferred 'an intellectual' as 'more honourable'. David said he would hate that, envisaging pipe-smoking, hairy, humourless dons at red-brick universities (rather conventionally, I thought), and liked to be thought of as a dilettante. I don't think he *is* one. 'A roomful of dilettantes' Francis thought was 'not the sort of room one would like to be in'.

August 11th: London

Given a long stretch of time virtually to myself, the possible area of things to think about is boundless, a vast gromboolian plain where (in theory) it is possible to take any direction one fancies. The result of course is that one is lucky to have a single thought. Here I am in the Euston–Windermere train on my way to stay with Tom and Nadine: solitude in a crowd, for every seat is taken. A strong smell of boy comes from a carriage full of campers. It is hot. I've already eaten some stodgy sandwiches in the 'Buffy' car, and done an exercise in Russian. Just now a railway official, gorgeous in gold braid, draped himself round the door of our carriage and asked each of us in turn, 'Where you for, love?' in the most stylish way imaginable. In contrast, the passengers refer to each other as 'the gentleman in that seat'. Like the realms of possible thought, the world of visual sensation is laid out through the carriage window, far and wide, as if specially for my possessing, and I have really felt that I stretched out and took for instance a small secret green pond, quite round and encircled by elms, or a huge bright pink sow lying in a field with her piglets round her.

August 21st

Gerald and Gamel suddenly arrived in London yesterday morning and I got them to come to dinner. Neither of them at first sight seemed in the slightest degree ruffled by having travelled all night and having taken rooms in a noisy, unsympathetic hotel. Gerald rang me up in the morning. 'HULLO, Gerald,' I cried. 'Welcome to London!' There was as usual a very long pause and then: 'Gerald speaking,' slow and weighty. How pleased I was to see them! Having been deep in Gerald's forty-year-old letters it was extraordinary to be made aware of the continuance of his essential characteristics. Imagination but no judgement; or rather, those judgements he makes are rooted in emotion. During dinner he began saying how *boring* Shakespeare was. His plays were completely undramatic, no one could sit through *Hamlet*, he preferred Pinter or *Who's afraid of Virginia Woolf?* –

they at least were 'contemporary'. I found myself aflame with anger all at once, and attacking him just as he wanted me to, and as I know Ralph would have done, though throughout the previous two hours of being with him (as indeed all the evening) I had felt the warmest affection and delight in his company. Gamel was her usual self. The more she drank the more she tossed off remarks like, 'Don't be funny, Gerald!' and 'You know it's nothing of the kind,' and references to 'I happened to be re-reading Montaigne the other day,' and I was amused when she (the idlest of women) said she couldn't imagine how anyone could get along without work. Georgia came in briefly after dinner, filling my room with a radiant glow, as had Henrietta earlier in the day. What pleasure both these girls gave me. Henrietta looked perfectly lovely in a very pale pink linen blouse and less heavy make-up than usual, bringing out her delicate skin and lovely dark grey eyes. Georgia had been down to stay with her and Duncan at Charleston and I could feel in them both how the influence of that extraordinary and ever-fresh civilization had pulled against the superficial glamour of the dashing young people who live for their own beauty, sex-appeal and clothes and keep themselves in a state of hectic stimulation with drinks and drugs. I mean of course the young men laden with jewels, the long-haired, lace-shirted dandies of the Ormsby-Gore party, whom Francis Wyndham defended so hotly at Cranborne. I found myself doing the same at Maud Russell's dinner. Yet, yet, yet – I can't go all the way with their empty thoughtlessness, and the prig in my nature resents their lack of seriousness. The curious thing was that contact with Charleston and the country should have produced a rather similar reaction in both Georgia and Henrietta.

Jonny and Sabrina have had a daughter. Henrietta describes Jonny's wild excitement, and told me that when she was making him some supper in his flat and Sabrina rang up he went down on one knee to the telephone. I sent her a large bunch of flowers, and was flattered (seeing that I hardly knew her) to hear that Sabrina had said to Jonny, 'I don't want to see anyone beside you and the baby – not even darling Frances.'

August 27th

Grey, horrible, cold weather, wet roofs. I have been working all out, unable to stop, much too wound-up and tense, alone a good deal of every day but far from empty-plated. Yesterday Noel came to lunch and we went through various Gertler difficulties. I realize that while I felt I have 'given him' all the letters to Carrington, *he* thought they were legally his 'as next of kin'. The main complication here is that if I was wrong in thinking that all her possessions went to Ralph and thence to me, I had no right to give Gerald *his* letters, which have gone off to America to be sold. The copyright in Carrington's own letters is also in question. It's rather an interesting Trollopian situation. When I sorted all those trunks at Ham Spray it never entered my head that everything in the house was not mine. Noel has been equally assuming that both letters and copyright are his. Over lunch we agreed this should be straightened out by an expert and this is going to be done. After Noel had gone I went on working steadily till 8 p.m. – perfectly mad. Listened to Stephen Bishop playing the Emperor Concerto and went to bed early with my head buzzing with words, tunes and more words.

I've finished reading Gerald's letters to Carrington. His astonishing lack of judgement comes out over and again. Meeting Lionel at Alec's house he says he seems 'Nice but very stupid. Though science seems to be his business he knows much less than I do.' The truth on its head and several times multiplied.

Yesterday morning I suddenly began to fret and fume over the lack of news about Russia. Rang up the Wayfarers' Travel; I should of course have done it long ago. All is now settled, Kitty and I fly at early dawn on September 8th with the rest of the party who are not going by sea, and do our extra four days at the end of the visit. Everyone is pleased. I've rung up Kitty and it's a great relief to have it settled.

As far as the MacCabes are concerned[1] I'm still convinced Charlie won't come and doubtful about Mary. I got a mysterious message from Stokke to say there had been a slight mishap – Mary had lost her passport. And her Russian visa of course! I guess that she's getting out of coming.

August 30th

Neither Charlie nor Mary come to Russia. The passport loss was genuine and strange, but it's not the whole explanation. Charlie says they 'can't afford it and after all, she's now had her fun pipe-dreaming about Russia'.

It is Bank Holiday Monday and I have come back to London after one night and day of chewing the cud of rusticity with Noel and Catharine. On Saturday night Gerald came to dinner with me; we were alone together for four hours and at the end of it I felt thoroughly battered by his egocentricity. 'I've been talking about myself all the time, as usual,' he said rather ruefully. It's not exactly selfishness; it's merely that he isn't in the least interested in any other subject. I occasionally tried to say something – not about myself, heaven knows, but about some other topic. At once his eyes glazed over with boredom. The most *dis*interested emotion he voiced was appreciation of Georgia. We talked a lot about the past – Carrington, Watendlath, the 'Great Row'.[2] Of *course* I believe what Ralph told me absolutely, rather than anything that Gerald says, but my memory is alas unreliable, and the most inscrutable part is the Valentine Dobrée episode. I found a letter from her to Ralph, inchoate and emotional, utterly uncontrolled. I wanted to read it aloud, but Gerald wasn't interested – it was too remote from himself. He is quite indifferent to Hetty[3] now – she was a masturbatory object to him, indeed I think all his sexual activity has been in the nature of masturbation, and it's that that shocks me about it. His latest adventure is with little Teresita, the mere child who works in the house. He thinks she may be sixteen now but isn't sure. He sat on my sofa under the light which shone mercilessly down on his bald head – where a curious long lump like a prehistoric barrow has appeared – describing how he kissed her and put his hand down the front of her dress and gave her presents and she came to say goodnight to him when he was in bed, and one day he hoped to get her into bed with him – of course he wouldn't '*do anything*' to her. He tells everyone this and I wonder what feelings it arouses in others – whether, as in me, a sort of disgust at the thought of an old man of seventy lecherously pawing a young girl. And there's 'nothing physical' in it, of course!

I do enjoy Gerald's company, but my God, it's exhausting.

---

[1] Charlie and Mary had suggested coming to Russia too.
[2] This was the name given at Ham Spray to the highly charged explosion between Ralph and Gerald as a result of the revelation of a secret relation between Carrington and Gerald.
[3] His latest girlfriend.

August 31st

I have just been to Russell Square to collect tickets and vouchers for the Russian tour. So it seems I am a registered item in this strange parcel. Looking up from my seat in the bus at the grey clouds driving through the blue sky, I thought what a long way away Moscow seemed. Well, calm, calm, I said to myself. And nothing to lose.

My work has more or less closed down. The last obsequies of Conan Doyle are done up in a parcel for John Murray. My brain seethes ineffectively with the Russian I have been struggling to stuff into it. I quail and thrill alternately at the thought of the rapidly approaching unknown. I spent most of yesterday going to Kew with Gerald. His love for plants is one of his most endearing qualities and he was a perfect companion able to enjoy the signs of race in some exotic face (a tropical shrub bearing unmistakeable affinity to a milkwort) as well as their purely visual aspects. As usual the water-lily houses were the most stunning – water-lilies blue, pink and white rose from the steaming water, while all around them were spires of red and blue, or hanging swags of coppery green, strange cucumber-like fruit and purple trumpets. In another house we saw the great waxen leaves of the Victoria Regina with its stiffly curled-up edges veined with red, and a flower like an untidy pink hearth brush, and noticed the taste shown in letting a different small green water-plant fill in every available cranny of the water's surface between the monster leaves. Climbing a white metal spiral stair, we looked from a height on the palms trying to break their way out of the crystal-palace roof; dangling waxy fuchsias; sprays of delicate spotted orchids; grey and crimson leaves; epiphytes sprouting in myriads from mossy stems.

September 8th

'Your seven o'clock alarm call' hauled me from the lowest depths of sleep. Of course I got to the air terminal half an hour too early. At the check-in I was given a sharp look: 'You're going on to Moscow?' 'Yes,' I said proudly. 'Well, I'll label it right through.' (Kitty West and I were going for some reason via Paris.) Moscow, magic word! Beautiful in itself and glittering and spiky with associations. Descending to the 'toilets' I thought with a pang of amazement that this mythical entity, in existence for centuries but for me hitherto only the scene of Russian novels, was now suddenly to become real. It was pouring in London, grey at Le Bourget. Kitty and I bought whisky and chocolate. We looked about for other green Wayfarers' labels and spotted two: a large, smooth, solid American male and small, middle-aged female like a guinea-pig, an Italian Baroness from Venice. She was inconspicuously dressed and wore a navy-blue bathing cap, yet contrived to suggest wealth; her expression never changed all day, whereas the American (Zerbe his curious name) flashed his teeth at us, patted us, name-dropped hectically, and was occasionally dynamically useful. Through the Moscow door at Le Bourget we stepped at once into Russia – a smallish grey aeroplane bearing the magic letters АЗРОФЛОТ. We had two plain but kind and informal hostesses who brought us vodka and a delicious lunch – caviare, steak, peaches and a glass of wine. Half mine fell on the floor, the trays were so ramshackle. One air hostess opened our bottles of mineral water sharply with her teeth, remarking that it wasn't pleasant to do. Now real happiness began, as, rising from among the other toads squatting on the tarmac we soared swiftly and were up and away eastwards towards a totally new country. 'Oh yes, this is happiness,' I thought, swamped by excited anticipation and sense of adventure. 'I am off to Russia.' Then a doze. Then Moscow and the first taste of Russian ways of doing things, of something that isn't unfriendly so much as stubbornly inflexible. Our passports were whisked away at the very door of the aeroplane. In the airport, bewilderment. No one told us anything; we saw people filling in forms and did likewise; we queued with others for our passports. A new 'Irish Georgian' appeared, a nice soft-voiced elderly man called Hughes, dressed in comfortable tweeds and clutching a crumpled ball of mackintosh to his stomach. He spoke of wanting to come to Russia because of 'having very little more time', as if he had some fatal disease. We were shepherded to a bus, making off for the 'domestic' airport for Leningrad, through a dead flat plain covered with trees (mainly birches with slender white trunks) and small, gaily painted but rather dilapidated one-storey wooden houses like toys. Darkness fell. At the 'domestic' airport there was something of a frenzy while an intelligent, worried girl had to turn our vouchers into air tickets in two seconds; then we tore across the airfield to where several colossal aeroplanes were crouching, only just in time. I shall never forget the strangeness of being suddenly inside this huge, dimly lit and poorly ventilated crocodile, which seemed to be full of large, power-fully built Russians, with serious faces, returning perhaps after the day's work in Moscow. Less than an hour's flight ended in a stifling fug before the doors opened, and Kitty began wailing a little. We were taken to a room with an elaborate cut-glass decanter and a glass on the table and I took a fortifying swig of my whisky. I am enjoying trying to use my few words and read the alphabet. At last we set off in another bus and drove for miles and miles through the outskirts of Leningrad. 'Here is the Europa Hotel,' said the Intourist guide. The rest of our party were there, having only just that moment arrived by sea, and were swarming like bees round the Intourist desk in the hotel; this they continued doing for some hours. In the middle of the swarm were the bowed heads of our leader Mariga Guinness[1] with her floating dark curls, and a Russian who turned out to be our chief guide, Valentín. Slowly we were sorted out and rooms ascribed to us, passports collected. Tired now, disorientated by the change of time, and hungry, Kitty, Mr Hughes and I went in search of food. It was late but we got a plate of cold meats and salad in a large vulgar dining-room with a band playing old-fashioned jazz very loudly, and couples revolving in the style of a village dance of twenty years ago. We had of course no money, for one can take no roubles into Russia, and not yet any coupons for meals, but in the end they agreed to let us pay next day and we went upstairs to see our rooms. They are magnificent. I have a hall with lots of pegs and a large bathroom leading off it and a big, old-fashioned sitting-room with sofa, armchairs, writing-desk, plenty of lamps and my bed in a curtained alcove. Hurrah!

September 9th

I woke feeling expectant about six (which is four by yesterday's time), nor could I sleep again, but lay reading in my delightful bed alcove with its rough linen sheets buttoned round the blankets so that they won't tuck in. Breakfast of fruit juice,

[1] First wife of Desmond Guinness, née Princess Marie-Gabrielle of Württemburg. Between them they ran the Irish Georgian Society.

water, sweet buns, toast, strawberry jam, and excellent tea without milk.

The morning was spent on a bus drive round the town 'to orientate ourselves', with many pauses to get out and stroll round and take photos. Immense spaciousness is the first impression – huge squares, broad streets without much traffic, gardens and parks everywhere, buildings on a noble scale, eighteenth-century palaces lining the river banks, all painted yellow, green, blue, terracotta, and picked out broadly in white and surmounted here and there by a golden dome or spire. The centre of the town is intersected by canals, rather like Amsterdam. A gently sunlit day without wind with these gilded pinnacles gleaming palely through it. What a ravishing town! But somehow I had expected it to be grey and all this prettiness of colour astonishes me. One is well aware that the Neva is flowing out between flat islands to the Baltic and that the Arctic is not so far away. People of Leningrad strong and square, women with huge busts; a fair race on the whole with good complexions; all are adequately dressed – not poorly, but no one is smart. Children warmly clad in caps and leggings of bright colours filled the gardens and playgrounds. Little flocks of tots moved along the pavements in tiny crocodiles holding onto strings. The most exciting buildings this morning were Smolny Church and Convent – a cluster of bright blue buildings with gold onion domes. They were being repainted and the oldest paint was of an extraordinarily beautiful and intense peacock blue.

After lunch exhaustion began to set in – at least among the air passengers. But off we drove in our bus to St Isaac's Cathedral. The official state religion being Atheism (a stimulating thought) most of the churches are treated as museums. But religion is tolerated and some churches are described by the guides as 'active'. St Isaac's is very magnificent with pink and grey marble and stupendous malachite columns, but as a whole vulgar and ugly. A spoilt rich woman in our party called Lady Dashwood, known to Kitty, tried to get us to go home with her by taxi, but I had a map and longed to walk home and so peg out a claim on the city. Crowds were hurrying along the pavements and drawing fruit juice from scarlet slot machines. I thought they looked a good deal jollier, less hag-ridden and apathetic than London crowds, and I could all at once see what the regime is trying to do, by throwing open their glorious buildings to everyone and turning what were once private parks of the rich into public gardens available to all. Our fellow Irish Georgians are inclined to condescend and murmur, 'They have no luxuries of course,' disregarding the public possession of all these works of art, good music, theatre and films. I've certainly had no more sumptuous hotel bedroom in any other country.

Early to bed but far too stimulated to sleep.

September 10th

I'm a little worried about poor Kitty who droops and turns pale very quickly. She tends to lose everything and get into a near panic. I feel quite tough by comparison, though I live in a disturbingly spangled electrical state of overexcitement.

This morning was dedicated to the Hermitage. Kitty and I endeavoured to make straight for the paintings but officials tried to whisk us to the cloakroom to remove our coats. At last I said, 'Ya nyeh kashoo' ('I don't want to') which produced friendly roars of laughter. Discovered afterwards that this is obligatory – as Valentín told us, Russians would think it 'disgusting' to bring dust from the street into houses or museums. They also preserve the beautiful inlaid wooden floors of the palaces by making everyone put on felt overshoes, and to the same category of appreciation of their own treasures belongs the scrupulous throwing of paper and cigarette-ends into special urns provided for the purpose. We saved the Impressionists for later and devoted the morning to superb Rembrandts, Titians, Chardins, etc. In the afternoon taken by bus to the Fortress of Peter and Paul across the Neva. The church is richly and delicately gilt inside and contains the tombs of most of the Tsars; we sat for a while in the sun on the landing-stage looking across the river at the pale gold domes on the home shore. On the way back we stopped for a moment to look at a baroque belfry and its separate church, both painted deep peacock blue. Unlike most of the churches it was 'active', and this may have attracted our Catholic Irish companions. By the canal outside a lot of old folk were sitting, wearing chauffeurs' hats and headscarves of traditional design, others were drifting into the church, crossing themselves again and again, saluting, waving, bending almost to the ground in an ecstasy of devotion. We were all at once in old Russia. The inside of the church glowed with dark ikons, candles and gilt; the bell began to toll, and more and more gesturing, murmuring figures came pouring in. Some men suddenly rushed in at the door carrying what I suppose was a coffin. I felt a scrabbling at the back of my knees and turned to see an old crone in black down on all fours kissing the floor. Our two devoted professors, who come with us everywhere, led us to the 'winter' church on an upper floor. This is a museum, but there were beautiful ikons everywhere. I liked this church, St Nikolai, as much as anything I've yet seen.

September 11th

'Russia – I'm in Russia,' I say to myself every night as I get into bed and the thought intoxicates me. Sleep is the difficulty, surrounded by so much to think about and try to remember. A radiant morning. We drove in our bus to a landing-stage on the river where we got into a sort of spaceship called a hydrofoil, which shot us with great speed and smoothness out into the Gulf of Finland towards Petrodvorets. The sea stretched limitless on our right. A fine Saturday had brought large crowds to the Peterhof, an immense palace dominating fountains and statues in terraces down to the sea, all the statues brilliantly gilded and gleaming in the sun. Just when I was off to look at the lake and the other pavilions, I was caught by Mr Hughes, who takes everywhere with him a book written by himself on the work of the Goldsmiths' Guild, which he touchingly but rather boringly shows anyone who will bother to look. We sat in the sun eating our packed lunches, and afterwards went on to the ravishing Chinese pavilion of Oranienbaum, once the palace of Menchikov, with its painted ceilings, rooms lined in crimson lacquer, beads and pearls, and inlaid woods. It was surrounded by real country. We wandered through damp grass between slender birches and little duckweed-covered ponds. Yet another palace nearby, Catherine the Great's Montagne Russe, was an astonishing bright blue and white birthday cake standing on an artificial hill; she used to have herself pulled down this snow-covered hill by a carriage in the shape of a swan.

Three palaces made a tiring day ending with quite a long drive home. At dinner the Baroness pitched into the regime and commented on the poverty of the things in the shops. I'd noticed that every pretty little wooden house had a television aerial. 'A sign of poverty', she said, 'just like Sicily. They all have them there.' F.: 'But surely they won't buy them if they actually lack food and fuel?' 'Oh, yes, they buy them on hire-purchase. And look how shabby this hotel is. Nothing is *first rate.*' I wanted to say how much I preferred the decayed palatial splendour of my enormous room to the wretched Jollys of her own native land.

September 12th

To Novgorod today – but first we visited two more enormous palaces – how can one possibly keep them all apart? By bus to Pavlovsk – built for Paul, son of Catherine the Great – a beautifully proportioned, yellow, late eighteenth-century building (by the Scottish architect Cameron), with wings almost meeting in a circle.

And on to Tsarkoye Seloe to see Catherine the Great's colossal blue rococo palace with bronze ornaments. Raymond's French friend, Philippe Julien,[1] muttered: 'Épatant! Some want to see one thing properly, others as much as possible. I belong to the second category.' And he marched purposefully off, as he always does, sketchbook under arm, hunched, spectacled and mackintoshed, and then sat or stood to make quick sketches of whatever he wanted to remember. Catherine's Palace is indeed a *stunning* building, vast and ornate with its golden domes, more the equivalent of Versailles than anything we've yet seen.

Our guides find us distressingly individualistic. We are all in the impossible quandary of trying to store our impressions. Kitty, I and a pleasant couple called Lord and Lady Dunleath walked round the shores of the huge lake and looked at various pavilions. Mr Zerbe is photographing them for another book in collaboration with Cyril.

It took us about three hours to get to Novgorod along a perfectly straight road across the plain, lined with small wooden houses painted different colours, and, oh joy! I have a monk's cell to myself with its own fairly squalid bathroom, a wireless and television set also. Sunk into stuporous sleep after an exceptionally good dinner.

Lady Dashwood has left her suitcase behind in Leningrad, and is furious; she always expects privileged treatment. She carries a small folding chair about with her everywhere, as she is suffering from the result of a motor accident in which someone was killed. 'That *awful* Valentín,' she drawled to me. 'He's a toad. SO rude.' I'm rather fascinated by him as it happens; he makes an impression of forceful intelligence and considerable specialized knowledge. I thought, but didn't say, 'It's you, Lady Dashwood, who is the toad.'

September 13th

Our morning's sightseeing at Novgorod provided new sensations and a rustic interlude. Valentín was in a specially genial mood and announced that he had arranged a trip on the great Volkov lake by steamer for us. It soon became clear that he had an intense love for and interest in the characteristic architecture and art of the Novgorod churches, which have indeed a startling simplicity and beauty. This formerly extremely ancient and beautiful town, and its lovely churches, was almost completely wrecked in the war. One church contained part of a striking

[1] Well-known illustrator and water-colourist.

fresco by Rublev, painted in reddish brown, of a row of bearded prophets sitting in huge vases and waving elegant hands. Valentín became really eloquent and interesting when he described the special qualities of this dramatic painting. Now we took the boat from a landing-stage painted green and pale blue, to see another church. I began picking what wild flowers I could see and our fellow travellers brought me new specimens – there were blue patches of wild delphinium. We climbed the hill above the marshy plain, whence we looked over the vast lake to Novgorod with its domes.

The hotel gave us a good lunch including a magnificent bortsch with bacon, herbs, bay leaves and plenty of cream. Then came the long drive back to Leningrad airport, and into the huge dimly lit otherwordly aeroplane which would take us this time from Leningrad to Moscow. Russian flying is tough; there were many aching ears and one young man had a nosebleed. There followed a drive through the darkness into the heart of Moscow and arrival at our hotel quite close to the Kremlin, whose domes, topped with crimson stars, shone through the darkness.

September 14th

I felt pretty strong this morning as we set out to the Kremlin – first to the museum called the Armoury, which in spite of its name was full of marvellous things, jewellery as rich and beautiful as any I've seen except at Constantinople, sumptuous horse-trappings, and saddles studded with diamonds and turquoises: royal crowns based on a band of fur, jewelled ikons. And then the Kremlin churches. It was late afternoon now, and the plum-coloured sky behind the clustered golden domes was an incredible sight. The insides of the churches were painted to their full height with dark rich ikon-like frescoes and hung with ikons also. The paintings and ikons have the dramatic and emotional intensity of the Siennese, and express the same deep devoutness as we saw in the gesturing old people pouring into St Nikolai's Church. I long for more time to think and digest than we ever get – it is different from anything I expected. We came away stuffed with visual sensations and a good day ended with a night at the opera, *Boris Godunov* at the Bolshoi, a sumptuous production which closely reproduced the ikons and frescoes we had just been seeing, the gorgeous robes and fur-trimmed crowns.

I am full of admiration and respect for Valentín but he has his tough side. When Kitty said rather shrilly, 'I don't like this sort of thing,' in one of the palaces, he snapped, 'Not so loud, please.' He has been heard to refer acidly in the bus to 'some people who are dropping bombs on Vietnam at this moment'. When I showed curiosity about the insides of the little wooden houses he shut up suddenly.

Lady Dashwood always feels she has a right to be squired by some young man, the younger the better. 'Come and sit by me, darling!' she says as she gets into the bus. Today she had to make do with Mr Zerbe, whose florid appearance and loud laughter at his own jokes has made him rather unpopular. Philippe Julien I think has both enemies and supporters. With his independence and high croaking voice he's quite an oddity among us, but his manners are good.

September 16th

Our bus took us to the Pushkin Museum and Kitty and I spent the whole morning there. The Russians were eagerly queueing to see the pictures on loan from the

Louvre, and one everywhere saw serious furrowed faces studying the paintings with deep interest.

Went later with the Baroness in a taxi to see Tolstoy's house. It stands in an old part of the town among old wooden houses, like the little village ones but bigger, and as Philippe Julien said it is 'very touching'. The trees in its large garden made it dark and there were no lights. We shuffled round in felt slippers looking into Tolstoy's study, the Countess's boudoir, the children's rooms with their white beds and rocking horses. There was no entrance fee and the sturdy old women who let us in and kept watch that we damaged nothing shook our hands warmly on leaving.

Some of our party went to look at Lenin lying embalmed, and were full of their reactions – Lady Dunleath told me he was 'disgusting' with a look of horror on her face, 'so small and shrunken, with his hair dyed red, and it was somehow shocking that he was wearing a lounge suit'. Zerbe 'wouldn't have missed it for anything' and 'found it both beautiful and moving', but since the Americans embalm all their dead I don't know why he was so impressed. He is bursting with rather terrible vitality and even writes an occasional column for the *San Francisco Chronicle*.

September 17th

I have been suffering from dysentery and in two minds whether I dare face the long bus ride to Zagorsk. I'm thankful I did – it was one of our most striking outings. First we took our leave of nice old Mr Hughes who was flying home today. He had asked me about my family, and hearing of Sophie's existence gave me, most touchingly, a little doll for her. He is an old dear as well as an old bore, but is very modest about his musical gifts – I heard from someone else that he had learnt from Henschel, almost become a professional and sung the part of Christ in the *St Matthew Passion*.

Valentín told us that, having discovered we were 'a very heavy drinking party' he was taking us for a drink at the restaurant in Zagorsk before we went into the monastery, seeing over which was one of the most enjoyable leisurely things we have done. A tiny church enclosed a holy spring and a bearded Archimandrite was rattling among his bottles, dishing out water like a barman. In the sunny sheltered space between these buildings a lot of old people were sitting on benches, munching apples and bread and feeding flocks of pigeons. The air was mild and still, immense peace reigned. We entered the oldest church, one of the most highly revered in all Russia, called after St Sergei, founder of the abbey. It contained the shining silver coffin-like tomb of the saint. Old women with headscarves stood and sang with raucous passion, crossing themselves, bowing and saluting, went up to kiss the tomb or give candles to a handsome old priest with bushy grizzled beard and eyebrows, and a tall black hat shrouded in drapery, who took them and fitted them into a high candlestick. Another priestly figure, hatless and with long black hair parted in the middle, was leading the singing in a fine baritone. Near me a waxen-faced woman was taking bites from an apple and screeching out a hymn at the same time. We wandered out and sat in the sun again, watching the priests crossing themselves as they hurried through the courtyard.

The restaurant gave us a superb lunch and Valentín came round with a bottle of old vodka, a deep golden colour and mellow and delicious. We were all given some; and as a result in the bus back to Moscow nearly everyone slept.

Bung-eyed with fatigue as I was, I couldn't resist fitting in an Oistrakh concert before we caught the night train from Moscow back to Leningrad. We are all being worked too hard; the constant impact of the other members of the group is tiring – one often has to 'make conversation' as if at a dinner party. Our taxi took us to the wrong hall and we tore into the concert hall just as bells were ringing and everyone streaming in. We panted into our seats more dead than alive and abandoned ourselves to the logical, beneficent language of music. The two Oistrakhs played the Bach Double Concerto, then the son played the Brahms Violin Concerto, his father conducting. We found our party at dinner and had time to be for a short while on our beds until the appointed hour when we had to go to the station. Tired to the bone, but chewing the cud of the marvellous sources of my tiredness, I went with the others to the station where a long red train stood quietly steaming. There were two berths in each compartment and Kitty and I soon got settled in one. The Baroness stood on the platform saying she couldn't possibly share with anyone she knew, she must have a stranger. Lady Dashwood stood in the doorway of hers with her hair round her shoulders looking as if she would have a good try at keeping it to herself. Zerbe was in the corridor in an open-necked white shirt, sweating vodka at every pore, and shouting, 'Nobody wants to sleep with me!' Nor did they, it seems. There were roars of laughter from further up the train. We pulled out at midnight, noisily but smoothly, and soon afterwards I knew no more.

September 19th

Many of our party are fervent Catholics and wanted to attend services of two of the 'active' churches. We set off first to the beautiful blue St Nikolai. The upper church was packed with prosperous-looking devotees standing in rows listening to Gregorian chants – well sung in fine voices, but I always find them boring. Kitty and I went down to the lower floor where as before an elderly and plebeian crowd were swarming, gesturing, murmuring, babies squawked and a handsome young priest held up a cross to be kissed. I saw a young woman come up to him with starry eyes of love, and pour out what seemed to be a brief confidence to which he briefly replied. We moved further into the heart of the church. 'What's that?' said Kitty. 'It looks like a buffet.' It was a table covered in flowers among the crowd of worshippers (many of them munching out of paper bags). Then I saw that among the flowers lay the corpse of an old bald-headed man with a bandage over his eyes, while his poor old wife leaned over him in a statuesque attitude of grief. 'I've never seen a laid-out corpse before,' Kitty murmured with an expression of horror. We went out into the sunny garden outside the church and sat on a bench. A nice Russian woman opened a conversation with me. I told her that I didn't understand, but this only produced a flood of more Russian. How I wished I *could* understand! The humiliation of not doing so! I brought out one or two of my few words and just took in that she was referring to the old religion revived, to the Hermitage, even to Tsarism. All I could do was shake her warmly by the hand and say goodbye on parting.

The hour for our Irish friends to depart approaches, and Kitty and I begin to plan our four remaining days. We already feel more relaxed and unhurried, knowing that we shall be able to return to the Hermitage at our own tempo.

Tonight many of us walked through heavy rain to the circus which has a great reputation and a famous clown, Popov. He was indeed very brilliant and I liked some acrobats with a happily bouncing little boy among them. Our architectural professor was sitting in front of Kitty and me – he was anxiously waiting for '*les ours*' to appear. They did, but it was an agonizing sight. A huge troop of them came pouring in on their hind legs, big and small, but all with thick glossy coats so that at first we felt they must have been trained by kindness. They ambled round in a comic and engaging way, but when they began to do their more difficult tricks – climb ladders, swing from trapezes, or whirl a blazing torch between their front paws – it became clear that only extreme cruelty could have made them do such unnatural things and I began to hate the false smile of their hard-faced trainer as he gave them lumps of sugar. Then bicycles were brought in of all sizes, and finally a motor bicycle, and when some of the poor bears fell off with their furry paws enmeshed in the handlebars attendants hurried forward and hit and shoved them so savagely that I heard myself booing faintly.

September 23rd

Kitty and I have now had two days of independent life in Leningrad and I'm sitting up in bed on the morning of the last. Instead of floating on the surface of Russian life and being whirled effortlessly about in Intourist buses, we have mixed in it, and sunk into it deeply. We have walked the crowded streets, shopped, travelled in trams. How has my first impression changed, if at all? I don't get any sense of glumness or drabness. Uniformity yes – I suppose it's the price that must be paid for fair shares for all. So far we have met with nothing but friendliness and helpfulness. In the great Dom Kneegi, an immense bookshop full of books in many languages, a friendly man came and asked if he could help us. We were stopped in the street by a girl who wanted to air her English. It was excellent, but when we complimented her on it and asked if she was an interpreter or Intourist guide, she said no, she worked in the theatre, had never been to England, but didn't want to be a guide because 'you had to say what you were told instead of what you wanted to say'. If she hadn't been rather tiresome we could have taken her to a café and she would have told us anything. As for the shops, they are stuffed full of second-rate and rather ugly goods and Russians eagerly buying them. The cold weather had produced a queue for fur hats, which are cheap even on the exchange foreigners get. I bought one for Sophie.

We have enjoyed being on our own and mastering trolley-bus routes, the coupon system and so on. I bought a Russian-produced guide to Leningrad and read the bit about Lenin at the beginning with horror – the insane jargon about 'class struggle' and 'dictatorship of the proletariat', the maniacal persecution-feelings about the Mensheviks or other wicked deviators from the strict line of Leninism. All this is very mad, silly and worse, and one can't as a tourist possibly gauge how serious it is. Mariga says the atmosphere has changed enormously in one year. Everyone seems to be at work, and very hard too. I think they are enjoying having more things to buy. Certainly the regime does not appear to live up to the view that material values are the sole or even the most important ones. Theory and practice have diverged. Perhaps a little while ago it would have been rash for me to note down these reflections.

Tomorrow England and West Halkin Street.

5.40 p.m. We have been lucky to have a brilliant blue day for our planned walk this morning. We made our way through noble Arts Square to the Summer Garden, everywhere passing or crossing little canals on the way. It is a flat shady park bordered by the wide Fontanka canal on one side and filled with eighteenth-century statues and groups of organized but happy-looking children in bright-coloured suits, caps and leggings. There were a good many fathers pushing prams. So this is what they do! I'd noticed all the street-cleaning and even ploughing was done by women. Out to the Neva, where many-coloured buildings line both banks. Crossed the bridge to the green Stock Exchange and its two red columns, past the ravishing forget-me-not-blue Naval School, the long disappearing vista of red University buildings; white, green, yellow and again red palaces, all the way to the next bridge, when we crossed back onto the Neva's left bank. We walked for three hours, sitting on a seat in the sun now and again to nibble chocolate, and we couldn't have had a nicer morning.

After a late slow lunch the sun was still shining. I have been taking photos all day.

September 24th

'The last morning' I wrote yesterday. But was it? Last night before dinner we went to collect our Leningrad–Moscow air tickets from the Intourist bureau in the hall. A crowd of Finns who had missed their aeroplane were booking telephone calls to Helsinki. The young women at the desk are amazingly efficient, multilingual and kind. (It was not so at Moscow.) They produced our tickets and asked to see our passports, which Valentín had returned to us when the Irish Georgians left. One girl with a round dutch-doll's face began to giggle over them, and the others crowded round. They asked us a few questions. Then, 'Your visas expired on the 20th,' they said. 'They'd never let you go out with these.' Kitty wailed: 'Oh, what are we to do? We must tomorrow. We've got our air tickets to London.' My heart sank like a stone. I knew there wasn't a London flight every day. Perhaps new visas must be got and new photos? The whole country had suddenly turned into a prison. I envisaged hours of waiting before we should know whether we were going or not. 'Don't worry,' they said kindly. 'I think it'll be all right. Leave them with us and we'll see what we can do. The visa office opens at nine o'clock and you needn't start till after eleven.' Kitty and I went to drink reviving whisky in the foreign currency bar. We were both suffering from shock. But I feel more philosophical this morning. I don't see how much worse could happen than our having to stay an extra day or two in this lovely town. The weather has – thank heaven – become beautifully clear and fine again.

I'm dressed and half packed and in a moment I shall go up and see how Kitty is doing.

September 25th

Kitty was serene and calm, though she made the very foolish suggestion that we should 'risk it and try to get through on our extinct visas'. We looked in at the Intourist desk and were told to come back after breakfast. When we did so, they handed us our passports all correct. Everything from then on went smoothly. We were well looked after; a car drove us to the airport, where we made contact with a nice couple from Edinburgh. We had several hours at Moscow airport and lunched with them and did a little more shopping – for caviare and toys.

So we left Russia on a smooth and 'taken care of' note. English aeroplanes are certainly better pressurized. Reached my flat at ten-thirty London time (and after one by Moscow time) and to my horror my key wouldn't open the mortice lock. I called on my neighbour, Sir Cecil Trevor, who kindly gave me a whisky and telephoned the police for me. An all-night locksmith came and let me in.

To bed, but still too excited to take easily to sleep.

October 1st: London

I have passed five hyperaesthesic days since I last wrote, trying to master the unholy state of agitation Russia has left me in, and going back there every night when I close my eyes, with onion domes flitting across my field of vision and a sense that the map of Russia lies all round me.

I have been deeply touched by my kind welcome; it was wonderful to find Janetta already back, and having filled my flat with glorious flowers. Mary too has sent me a bunch, and I have seen them both, and Robin and Susan, and Julian and Henrietta and Sophie, Raymond, Eardley and spoken to many others on the telephone.

October 17th

Last weekend, dreading it, I went to Little Barbara's at Rye. I have never got on better with her; we were both on our best behaviour. It seemed to me that I was going chiefly out of affection for Clive – but this makes doubtful sense. Just before I left on Sunday night she took all the wind out of my sails by saying, 'I have enjoyed your coming and I know you only came out of kindness.' I was appalled, and overdid myself in protestations. That one should condescend towards another human being is bad enough, but that they should know it and tell you so is fifty times worse. I got real pleasure from Barbara's 'dinky' little house with its picture windows collecting all the sun and looking over the Marsh, Rye Harbour and the river winding out to sea, from sitting in the sun, weeding the bricks, driving onto the Marsh to look at a solitary little church, and (perhaps most of all) visiting Roger Senhouse's house in Rye. He was away and had left Barbara the key. We walked straight into total confusion – every piece of furniture and almost every part of the floor was heaped high with dusty books mixed with old newspapers and dirty pyjamas. We went on, picking our way with difficulty, up to the top of the house, and it was the same everywhere; books and more books, letters, newspapers, loaded ashtrays, priceless china, pictures, catalogues – not a square inch anywhere where he could lay a plate and cup or write a letter. Barbara says he sometimes invites her to a meal, when he clears a space somewhere with his arm and lays down some delicatessen from the shop next door. In the chief sitting-room the walls were lined with book-filled shelves with pretty plates on top, but it was almost impossible to see them through the chaotic stacks of other books, filling the room, weighing down sofas and chairs. The kitchen stank and the stove had a thick coating of black treacly substance. Good pictures hung on the walls every-where, but many, many more were stacked face downwards. In the bedroom an unmade bed and a great many crumpled suits on chairs and the floor. The garden, about which he talks as if it were Sissinghurst, is a small rough patch of grass with a few nasturtiums, towered over by a tall wall of corrugated iron on one side. He must lead a complete fantasy life here. No one could possibly accept it as it is, and none of his willing female friends are able to face embarking on it. Seven maids with seven mops would take at least seven weeks to tackle it.

Now here at Kitty's – once again marvellous peace, distilling all that is pure, soothing and satisfying about country life.

October 31st

Wet Sunday in London. I have Sophie here for the afternoon. She has been quite amazingly jolly and good, and has now after a little touching mooing to herself, gone off to sleep on my bed, at which I feel inordinately proud.

Last night to a splendid performance of *Trovatore* with Julian and Janetta, Giulini conducting with such vigour and enthusiasm that Janetta (who was sitting exactly behind him) was bounced up and down in her seat. From the first bars the supply of excitement was so dense and rich that I expected it might soon exhaust my ability to respond, but the performance was kept at such a high level that it was impossible not to.

Supper afterwards at Boulestin's. Janetta and Julian's relationship develops and strengthens with time. I can't fit it into any known category; the nearest perhaps being devoted brother and sister. Julian told Magouche his feeling for Janetta was as near being 'in love' as he'd known with a woman. He depends on her as well as appreciating and loving her, and desperately wants the other people he likes, like Desmond, to appreciate her too. What exactly Julian represents to Janetta I don't know. She takes him with her everywhere – he is even going out on her week's dash to Marbella. They must meet or telephone at least once a day.

On Saturday I lunched at Montpelier with the two of them plus Sonia. I don't quite know what to do about Sonia – I had almost written her off because of the irritation produced in me by her intellectual pretensions, drunkenness and catty remarks about Janetta. But she had been so kind and constructive to Julia, and I so hate Julia's own style of 'writing people off' that I've resolved to make another effort to like her – also because I know Janetta would be pleased if I did and she has come to live in this part of the world. Julian and Janetta both said afterwards she had been 'rather too noisy' and aggressive.

November 1st

Janetta has just been here briefly and has left me asking myself various questions. No one in the world supports her friends with a stronger and more sensitive hand and she will think imaginatively of tiny details (worrying for instance whether I was getting on all right with Sophie yesterday). Yet when Sonia arrived very drunk to see her last night (with Francis Bacon also drunk and his friend George sober and helpful) Janetta felt she couldn't do anything to stop her or show disapproval, and went on plying her with drinks until at last Sonia rose to go and fell flat on the floor. After she and Julian left me the other evening (after *Trovatore*) they went to a gambling club and spent all night there. I asked about Julian going to Spain with her and she 'wondered why' or 'how' perhaps he was going. She is very fond of him and has boundless influence over him, he adores her, she doesn't hesitate to say her mind to him and yet – I think this perhaps is the crux of it – she won't say anything with *moral* implications.

How far should responsibility for friends go? Is it as important not to use your influence to draw them into habitual extravagances they can't afford (though *you* may be able to) or conversely to speak up for your scale of values however priggish it may seem, as it is to come to the rescue when disaster has struck.

November 10th

Can I keep my London life going at the reduced tempo it is gradually adopting? Well, it's worth trying, for the competitive racket is beyond me; I can't tear along with the speed and noise of Mary's Mini, nor do I have the least desire to. I have a new slow, gentle way of getting through my days. Work slows up as a result; I no longer attack it in a frenzy; Spanish Armada finished yesterday – I ought to begin James's index today – but shall I?

Henrietta has a new boyfriend, a member of Amaryllis's theatrical company, called Ocky. He has been there the last two times I went to Clarendon Gardens and come here with her. I like him very much and hope the attachment may become serious – he is very good-looking, gentle, musical. I hope there is a firm link forming. The trouble is that the whole company is going to America in about a week for six months – and Janetta said that Henrietta wants to go too and they to take her. What happens to Sophie then? Is this going to be a moment when I should step in and take over?

When Bunny rang up yesterday and asked to come and see me I thought he wanted to talk about this project but underestimated his egotism. He hadn't even heard of it and quickly dismissed it, saying Henrietta couldn't afford it, the fare alone was £170. He had met Ocky and liked him, but I was struck not for the first time by the easy way Bunny takes fatherhood, loving its pleasures and not concerning himself greatly with the responsibilities. He wanted to talk about himself, tell me the plot of his new book at length, expatiate on his hatred of London and distaste for Angelica's 'squalid little Islington House. I spent a night there, but I never shall again. There's nothing to put your clothes down on except the floor, which is inches deep in dust.' Just like the last time, he talked and talked about himself and asked me no questions. What indeed could he ask? My role is to be 'a good listener'.

December 4th: West Halkin Street

An evening here dedicated to listening to the records of *Simon Boccanegra* with Julian and Janetta.

We had a rather delicious little dinner and bottle of Derek's claret half-way through the opera, and Janetta told us the sad story of Sonia's birthday dinner party for Deirdre Connolly. Raymond was one of the guests (a slightly unwilling one as I happened to know). As he left he thanked Sonia warmly for the delicious dinner and then said, 'Aren't you a lucky girl to have this lovely house?' She was drunk as usual and blazed out with: '*Lucky*? – *a house*! You don't think *that* makes any difference when all the time … etc. etc.' I don't exactly know what the words were, but they were delivered with a shriek and she banged the door angrily on him. It seems that Sonia was not really upset at what she'd done, but only said: 'After all, I've never liked Raymond.'

December 16th

I've just had an entirely young lunch party – Henrietta, Sophie, Nicky, Nerissa, Julian. Nerissa spoke bitterly of Angelica waking her up in her basement flat by coming (as arranged) to see her, and looking at her pictures and liking all the wrong ones. Nicky said what a nuisance it was for a French young man she knew, who had been given a marvellous car and not insured it and driven slap into another, smashing both, and then run away, that he was now in trouble with the police, 'poor fellow'. We were supposed to sympathize. Henrietta talked the other day about various kinds of dope she had taken.

December 22nd

Henrietta rang up, full of all the sweetness and generosity she can surprise one with, accepting what I said in a recent letter about values and going so far as to say she thought I was right. I almost burst into tears. I have seen her twice since then – yesterday in her own warm, rich-coloured sitting-room, with the handsome badly made curtains, a broken, unmade bed, Sophie padding round in bare feet and Nerissa lounging on the bed. Today she has been to see me here, and oddly enough I once again feel she is using me as moral litmus paper in spite of the dusty answer I gave her last time.

This time she asked what I thought about drug-taking. It is much in the news; it is the fashion among the dashing, picturesque young, who search for new sensations because they are deadly bored and their lives as well as their heads are empty. I didn't know how to answer her question. I was dismayed. I can't always be saying, 'Don't' but I can't to this say, 'Do'. She pressed it rather urgently – perhaps there were wonderful sensations one ought to try? I think I wedged in some antibodies of a sort – saying that it was of course exciting to experiment in the world of new sensations but it was a mad world, a world of the bored and futile, and of the lunatic asylum.

December 25th, Christmas morning: Litton Cheney

Here I am again slung aloft in the tiny spare room, between two solid walls and two that are almost all window through which I look out on a faint blue sky criss-crossed with bare boughs and fine twigs and can just glimpse the pale green tilted fields below.

After an evening with Cressida, talking for hours on end non-stop and really covering the range – religion, ethics, politics, human relations – I drove down to Stokke on Thursday morning. Oh, poor Mary and oh, the sadness of that house – it's *not* imagination, it's a thick exudation, felt and smelt as soon as one enters the front door. The fact that the 'girls' (Charlie's daughter Nini and another, a Russo-American called Masha) had decorated up the hall with holly and quantities of red satin bows and covered the hall table with carefully 'wrapped' parcels and more satin bows, and that a Christmas tree stood mournfully in the corner (only a few of its electric lights working) all increased the deep gloom pervading the house. Mary tried to jolly everything along, the girls mooned and loafed and went off to make Christmas puddings. Masha was a great lump of a girl, wearing a white Irish sweater grey with grime, and splitting tweed trousers on her shapeless legs; she smoked endless cigarettes, held in fingernails sharpened to a pink point, and her dark brown hair was streaked with yellow dye. Charlie was like a time bomb whose charge was very near explosion point. He would rush in at the door like a bull and ask who had left the bathroom tap running, or merely fulminate against the Christmas preparations, shouting ironically and rather comically of the tree, 'ISN'T it delicious? I could eat it – and I *shall*!'

Then yesterday, Christmas Eve, I took a slow cross-country course by by-roads across wild and remote regions and beautiful, deserted country. Yet my few short stretches on main roads told a different story. I really loved picking my way from Collingbourne to Everleigh to Fittleton and Amesbury, Gillingham and Cerne Abbas over great rolling khaki-coloured downs decorated with sepia or indigo hangers and copses; a slight rain falling, warm. I arrived in the moist dusk to find this house beaming at me from rows of candles in every window and similarly glowing within. In sharp contrast to the dismal festal apparatus of Stokke, this is genuine and heartfelt if childish and innocent. Last night after dinner Reynolds read aloud *The Tailor of Gloucester*, with fourteen-year-old Emma sitting beside him smiling with shining eyes. He read very well, and it was easy to swim along with the current.

Now I've just been brought my breakfast tray, and an enormous striped football stocking stuffed with bath essence, quince jam, matches and so on! Soon afterwards came Emma and Phillida with the contents of their stockings on trays – a profusion of things, precious and otherwise. Now they have all gone off to church and the bells have stopped their loud pealing only a few feet away from my eyrie, and I feel delightfully alone.

December 26th

The Christmas spirit was sustained to an almost fanatical degree all yesterday. I longed for it to blow its fuse and let us all flop, but the major parcel-giving was reserved till after tea and Winnie the cook and a splendid daily (Mrs Olive Myrtle by name) joined in the Christmas dinner. It's lucky that the weather is fine, and yesterday Reynolds and I took a long walk by lanes edged with cascades of glossy hart's-tongue ferns, across the shallow valley to the hills beyond and back again. Janet makes one anxious by her tension and the trouble she takes. She's just been in to say how she hardly slept at all last night. Reynolds is charming, serene and unselfconscious. There is also staying here Janet's sister Gabrielle, head of the WVS of all England, and her husband George, a pre-school headmaster.

Now today, when I see a beautiful day and frost-sprinkled fields, we have all gone to drive to Budleigh Salterton to visit Reynolds' sister. I would much rather not go, but I detect from careful sounding that I'm expected to. So I must now get up and buckle on – such as it is – my armour.

December 27th

The day was of such crystal loveliness that I enjoyed the drive and most of all our stop at Lyme Regis to walk along the Cobb in warm soft sunshine, look about and remember. Every place we passed through had recollections of the past – Bridport where Ralph and I spent a week deciding to throw in our lot together; Budleigh Salterton itself reminded me of our visit to Devon during the war, and there was even a Mrs Partridge living next door to Reynolds' sister who may well have been Aunt Amy.

Sylvia Townsend Warner and her lesbian companion came to tea, and afterwards a tall dark clever-looking admirer of Phillida's for the night. I've had a long talk with Janet's WVS sister and her husband severally, and now they have gone off and so should I. Tomorrow I shall be back on my own rusty old rails.

1966

January 1st

Isobel and I went to *Boris Godunov* last night at Covent Garden and enjoyed ourselves greatly. The performance was long and at about eleven-thirty she and I were returning through Trafalgar Square in my Mini. Massed crowds of youthful figures were all around the fountains and streaming across the roads – the intense blackness of their leather coats making them look slightly sinister, but more so were the watchful figures of large policemen and, under Admiralty Arch, a police ambulance and two police cars drawn up as if to charge, or as if a war, not jollity, was about to begin.

Coming back from Oakley Street I was curiously tempted to return and see what happened in the heart of London when midnight struck, but laziness won, and I met several cars with drunk drivers wandering over the road. 'Poor things,' said Isobel, 'they have so little fun, no outlet – so little *room*.' This morning I read in my *Times* that thirty-two people had been charged for drunkenness or assaulting the police, and in Trafalgar Square there was a 'clash between bathers and others with beer tins and rolls of lavatory paper'.

January 9th: Iden

Poor old Dick Rendel[1] has died after an operation for cancer and a week of hideous anxiety for all concerned. Jill[2] rang me up early on Thursday morning and told me that Judy[3] had asked for me to go down, and if I might perhaps take her abroad somewhere. I have been here at their cottage for two nights with Judy, and Jim[4] (who flew over from Australia but is going back in about a week), and it's sheer agony. Judy is very good and brave, and I think only takes in the half of it so far, but last night, after a numbed patch, realization began to dawn on her. I talked to her in her bedroom for some time and then crept through to sleep in Dick's old room – a tiny cubicle, without so much as chair, table or electric fire, just beyond. I hear every sound in her bedroom and I can't get to my room without disturbing her. Last night I felt completely desperate, what with sympathetic pain for her, and puzzling over the problems of the future – is she to go to the village funeral tomorrow? How is she to go on existing alone here? The family have cast me for the role of support, thankfully and as if they were calling in an expert on bereavement as they would a plumber. I may be one, but this only makes me know only too acutely what she is suffering.

[1] My brother-in-law and nephew of Lytton Strachey.
[2] His daughter.
[3] His wife, my eldest sister.
[4] His son, Professor of Genetics at Sydney.

Then my new translation came yesterday: I made a very slight start and it is interesting, but also fairly tough philosophical sociology. I need reference books; I need privacy for about four hours a day. Here in this gnome's cottage there is only the dining-room, a sort of passage through which everyone comes. With my torturing thoughts for Judy, how can I concentrate on work? I feel I ought to take everything over, including the shopping and housekeeping, or always be prepared to do so. But there are questions, questions. I can't stay here for ever – each day is torment. But what happens to her when I go? My present plan is to go to London and get more books and clothes and then return for another full week which I hope I can endure. Judy has left her Librium pills at Hastings and won't fortify herself with whisky. I think my line is too realistic for her. The funeral, even if she doesn't go, is going to be a horrible strain and relations will flock here expecting meals. Could I take her right away – and where? Who will take over if I do stay until Monday week? Jim takes the line that she will decide what to do in her own good time; that Jill fusses her. This is true, but Judy needs help and who is to provide it? I don't want to desert her – I wish to God I was not just starting a new book, always an anxious time for me. And there is another complication which I shy away from: Janetta has had a letter from her doctor saying she must come home and have a hysterectomy – she will be arriving next weekend. Julian is back from Spain and told me two days ago. I want to be at hand when this happens.

January 11th

I see the encephalograph of my mood has been following its usual 'spike and wave' pattern.[1] As is my habit, I plumb the depths, find them intolerable and stagger up to the surface. (Interesting that I first put 'deaths' instead of 'depths'.) The day after I wrote with such despondency I somehow pulled myself together, forced myself to get going with my new book, talked to the family about my inability to stay here for ever, and managed to take over the cooking from Judy without much effort. Jim is a constant solace to me – in his way extremely clever, loving argument and talking about general ideas, he provides a constant challenge, which I enjoy meeting, and can meet on the whole. Of course I couldn't on his special subject of genetics, but there I don't try, I just ask questions. I like him very much – he is gentle and considerate with Judy and a stimulating element in the house. Perhaps there's a trace of the Rendel-Strachey vanity, but his interest in reality neutralizes it.

Then yesterday was the funeral. Tom and Nadine came down for it and lunched here, the house filled up at tea-time. Judy touchingly put a black velvet ribbon in her snow-white hair but made no bid to go to the ceremony. She and I sat by the fire and talked. I hope I'm doing the best I can for her and not being too bossy. I found, as I always have, the congealed family atmosphere after the funeral intolerably suffocating, and the Kentish cold has now set in with acute severity.

I slept very badly last night and I feel pretty *triste* and *morne* personally, and dread Jim's departure on Thursday or Friday.

[1] Sign of schizophrenia.

January 12th

God grant we don't get snowed-up. After bitter winds and iced ground, it is now beginning to fall. I'm in a little train rattling to London 'for the day'. I thought with longing of a night in my own bed and returning tomorrow, but it seems that Jim has to be in London by one o'clock tomorrow to catch his aeroplane to Sydney.

Yesterday came the letter from Janetta which Julian had told me was on the way. She and Georgie will be back on Monday probably, and I've told Judy I must return then. I thought it best to say quite plainly that Janetta was the person I was fondest of in the world and who had done most for me and utterly propped me in my times of trouble. I think Judy accepts this fully, and there seems to be an idea that her friend Dorothy Carter will move in when I leave Iden. Yesterday morning Jim went to London and Judy and I had several long conversations. She said that she felt physically ill and weak, and I said I thought that absolutely natural, and that after Burgo died I felt my legs were giving under me all the time. She burst out, 'Oh, that was so *awful* – and I feel we did nothing for you.' No, they didn't, but nor I suppose did I want them to.

January 22nd: At Celia Goodman's new house, Cambridge

Silently compressed in the grey-whiteness of windless thaw. Last night the Provost of King's, Noel Annan and his wife, also Tom and Nadine came to dinner. Celia says Noel Annan is a great friend, one of those she came to Cambridge for, yet she hasn't seen them more than once since she arrived in August. And now he is moving to London to be Provost there. Gabriele Annan is an attractive and intelligent German: when I praised her, Celia bridled rather. What of Annan? Very Cambridge, relaxed, smooth, urbane, with a loud free laugh and frequent 'don't misunderstand me's'.

He said nice things to me, such as that Michael Holroyd had said 'how sweet I'd been to him': made himself very agreeable, had taken the trouble to know who my 'daughter-in-law' is, and so on.

This morning Celia and I went for a drink at the Provost's Lodge, where everything was sumptuous but safe. What a breath of fresh air Maynard must have introduced in his day. I looked at a rather vulgar portrait of him, which however revealed the sparkling intelligence of his eyes, and thought how he shot ahead behind the high-powered engine of his mind, cutting a swathe through the conformist waters and caring not at all for public opinion or the trammels of success.

Noel Annan spoke about the Lytton–Maynard correspondence, which is at King's under some decree that it shan't be read. I almost blurted out that I'd heard it read that icy weekend at Charleston some while ago – and then realized in time that this is a deadly secret. Holroyd dined with me two nights ago and went through the Ham Spray albums; I'm pretty sure he told me then that *he* also had read the above letters, but the Provost of King's had not. I did ask Annan if Holroyd saw them when he came to King's and he said, 'Oh, no. I've not seen them myself.' The trouble about such secrets is that they appear to me so needlessly treated as such that I forget that that's what they are supposed to be. Holroyd asked me some questions about Carrington's affair with Beakus Penrose[1] and her pregnancy by

---

[1] Youngest of the four brothers.

him and her unhappiness, and I realized that I can't ever see any good reason not to answer such questions truthfully.

January 27th

Oh dear, oh dear, oh dear, Julia and I have quarrelled again, no other word for it; and the truth is that when she said, 'Then we'd better not meet,' I felt nothing but relief. I don't know how I shall feel about this crisis later, but I have woken this morning still feeling calm.

How did it happen? Did she arrive with a sediment of hostility? The first thing she talked about was the shamefulness of Roland Penrose's[1] allowing himself to receive a knighthood. I said – what I think – that this is to set too much store by titles; they are unimportant frills and furbelows added to life, or rather like clapping when a singer has done well in the opera. 'Well, you and I never agree over anything,' she said rather tartly, and so I steered quickly away from this dangerous corner and all was amiable for several hours.

I mentioned Janetta's coming operation. She never asked a single question about it – nor said a word, not even 'Oh!', yet she took it in, as I saw later. She asked me not one word about myself.

Disaster was brought on when she began to say she was 'bored by' or 'didn't care to take part in' any conversations with people who were not experts, i.e. knew all about technique, history, etc., in any of the Arts, – books, pictures, music, the cinema, television. At one moment she said that she was too sure of her opinion to want to hear other people's. She implied that such people as Magouche and Janetta had nothing worth saying about art, and of course I felt she was implying the same about me.

I remembered how much I had enjoyed long and delightful conversations of this very sort with her – one about Proust on a walk at Lambourn, another about the Grünewald crucifix came to mind. I felt hurt and also amazed by her condescension and arrogance. I should have let the subject drop, but I couldn't think how, and I suggested that art could lead into other spheres of ideas, anyway that ideas were the best thing to talk about, and to cut off art was to lop off a whopping great hunk. She merely replied, 'I'm only saying what *I* enjoy.' When I started describing the sort of conversations I liked, and how much (for there's nothing in the world I like more), she answered crossly and at cross-purposes, thinking I was still discussing *her* likes and dislikes. I felt there was nothing left to talk about – we had talked for hours about *her* life; was this the only thing she wanted to talk about? I literally dried up, chatterbox though I am by nature. Nothing seemed worth projecting in the direction of this dry stone wall.

Then when she was going I said something more about Janetta's operation. When I thought of Janetta's enormous kindness and sympathy to Julia, the way Julia had quickly brushed both aside seemed to me quite insufferable. Egotism, arrogance and condescension are a heavy price to pay for stimulating company and originality, and they dominate her at present – even if this is ascribable to temporary insanity – to a degree that positively floors me. I still feel them thundering in my ears like the clatter of passing express trains.

When I told her about Janetta, 'Is she worried?' Julia asked. 'Well, what do you

[1] Second of the four brothers.

think?' And my fatal final shot was, 'You're really TOO unsympathetic about other people's troubles. And it's not for lack of sympathy yourself.'

February 5th: Crichel

Drove down here with Eardley yesterday. Dreadfully tired, I longed to go to sleep and suggested to him I might. Desmond was amazed at my temerity and thought I might well have been told to get out of the car. Apparently Eardley *hates* people to go to sleep in his car. Anyway I didn't, and we had delightful talk of the exploratory kind we always do (more really than is possible here when everyone is present), though I don't suppose Julia would have approved of it. At the moment, having recovered from her dictim, I feel subjects for talk are boundless and that it's an exhilarating activity. Last Thursday night, having invited the Pritchetts and Lennox Berkeleys who didn't know each other well, I did wonder a little anxiously 'what we should talk about'. There was no difficulty whatever, and the evening was a success, I think. Julian came in after dinner and stayed for a while after they'd gone. He started on rather a strange, obsessional, 'darning' tack about Jonny's visit to Janetta which I had interrupted. (It was my first visit to her and I remember saying more than once, 'Oh, don't go, Jonny, I don't want to drive you away,' and he said he simply *must* go, and left.) It seems that as soon as I was seen at the door Janetta quickly said to Jonny: 'You will leave me alone with Frances, won't you?' and he was deeply wounded. Julian laboured this over and over, and wouldn't hear of it being simply that she was tired and dreaded two people at once. She is now doing very well and comes out next week.

February 10th

I seem to have been too long in a constant state of tension, physical and mental. How shall I get out of it? At nights I'm aware of my mind racing like a feverish squirrel into various corners, taking a quick anxious look, and on to the next thing. I feel tempted to disappear to a country inn for a week but of course I should be dismally lonely. Last night I had another dinner party (I plan no more for *weeks*), with Robin Fedden, Magouche, Boris and Maude. This morning both Maude and Magouche rang me up and talked at length, largely about the other.

It seems extraordinary that I have found no time to record a visit from Bunny, during which he told me with considerable emotion that his estrangement from Angelica had reached such a point that she had written saying she wanted a divorce. He showed me her letter; it was affectionate but firm. I suppose he has been ruthless to others in his day, still I don't like the idea of this blow so late in his life. He was extremely spirited on the whole, declaring that he refused to be self-pitying or deterred from getting the most he could out of his few remaining years. Happiness and unhappiness are the liquids, the distilled water in people's batteries. Joan Cochemé came yesterday and we spent a pleasant quiet evening together. I greatly respect her Scotch sense of responsibility for the people she loves.

February 12th

Went to the House of Commons for the first time in my long life yesterday, with Dicky Chopping, to hear the debate about homosexuality. We would never have got into the Strangers' Gallery but that Dicky sent a note in to John Smith, our new Member for Westminster, and he came out and let us in. There we sat in the gallery of this Gothic brown interior looking down on the green benches where a scanty, frightfully bored-looking crowd sprawled among their order papers. At the end, like an idol, or a very elegant porter in the sort of chairs they used to sit in in smart halls, was the dapper bewigged figure of the Speaker, one black silk leg cocked over the other. I have long wanted to go to the House and was delighted to be there, but it was an unremarkable and unstimulating sight, more like a board-meeting than the centre of our government. Nobody said anything of the smallest interest, but there was much talk about the 'brilliance of the speech' of the honourable Member for Hartlepool, also of these 'unfortunate people' (buggers) as of creatures horribly deformed but perhaps needing pity. Roy Jenkins spoke in fine ringing tones, clearly and to the point. Another Labour Member was disastrously slow and woolly – one hadn't the ghost of an idea what he was trying to say; most of them mouthed, put their fingers in their waistcoat pockets, spoke of the 'other place' and showed every sign of enjoying themselves and never wanting to stop, just as their hearers showed every sign of intense boredom and usually flocked out noisily whenever a speech began. There were a number of shocks of long, greying hair; the square pale clever face of a Foot (I think) stared up at us women, Queers and Indians in the gallery. Among a row of peers in the front of the gallery sat Patrick Kinross and a small restless white-haired man, whom Dicky pointed out as 'Boofie' Arran who had brought in the Bill to the Lords. I think I owed my deliverance before boredom had really set in to a schoolboy and very characteristic impulse of Dicky's. Lord Arran left. In a trice, 'Shall we go?' said Dicky, and pelted after him. He caught him up on the stairs and panted out: 'I'd like to thank you for bringing in this Bill!' (I thought he would say something more personal and he told me he'd meant to add: 'As a lifelong, married homosexual'.) Lord A. looked a little surprised but not displeased. 'So you think I did right? I've LOATHED every minute of it.' Now appeared a figure in knee-breeches and a white finely pleated shirt without a collar, black jacket – heaven knows what he was (Black Rod?). Standing with one well-turned knee bent across the other he began a stagey, almost shouted conversation with Arran, largely for the benefit of Rich and me or any other audience. 'I used to be in the Navy, and in my view there were three things you should never have on your ship – rats, buggery and thieves – I couldn't make up my mind in what order ... But now if you and I wanted to go upstairs and misbehave ourselves, I can't see any harm in it.' The logic was far from plain. Dicky's revealing features were riveted excitedly on this pair of show-offs, while I lurked slightly uneasily behind. Then we got into my Mini and drove through the gathering darkness to Wivenhoe.

We heard later that the ayes for buggery had got it. Modified jubilation. I wonder very much whether quite a few who get a kick from being outsiders and rebels won't feel a sort of disappointment, and perhaps have to try some new eccentricity.

I tried this theory out on Denis at breakfast next day. He agreed. Is it just an age difference that so distinguishes Raymond, Eardley and Desmond, who don't talk all the time about homosexuality, any more than heterosexuals do about their sex life, from Dicky and Denis and some of their friends who can never let the subject drop?

February 25th

Yesterday I met Raymond at the Bonnard exhibition, and pushed him round in the wheelchair he had reserved for the purpose.[1] It was a pleasure to find how much we agreed as to the pictures we liked or disliked, and I enjoyed this my third visit, though Raymond was rather a heavy baby and the wheelchair not altogether tractable. The figure of Lawrence looking much older, stooping and grey-haired came towards us. With visible excitement he said how incredible he found it that Bonnard had never painted while looking at the object. He goes to America for a month tomorrow with the Turner exhibition. Resentment has definitely got the upper hand in my feelings towards Julia, most un-pacifically. I think of her as a bully, and still have no desire for her company. I feel exhausted by adjusting to her and always anxiously considering her feelings and reactions. When Sonia was going to the cinema to see a Fellini film with Julia the other night and expressed doubts about it, I said without thinking: 'Oh, Julia's mad about Fellini. She's sure to enjoy it.' 'Oh, I'm not worried about *Julia*,' Sonia said, 'It's me I'm thinking about.' And I realized how Julia has for so long automatically inhibited my 'thinking about me' when I'm with her, and how at last the worm has turned.

Bunny has just been to lunch. He tells me Angelica rang up this morning and said that she had been persuaded by Rosemary Peto and another friend to put aside any idea of divorce for the present. With rain streaming like the saddest of tears from the pitch-dark sky he talked on and on, and I gradually put together the grounds of difficulty between them. They are as I supposed physical. I tried to suggest that their relationship might be well worth preserving even without the sexual element, although he himself had said that the necessity to communicate his feelings and experiences was something he greatly missed. But he seems to feel his physical rejection too bitterly still – and doesn't want to see her for the present. We talked of Henrietta also – she rang me up yesterday under the influence of hashish which had made her feel so mad that she hoped never to take it again. If she really doesn't it will have been well worth it.

March 4th

A delightful visit from Henrietta and Sophie yesterday has greatly reassured me. Sophie was ebulliently gay, tore about, went to sleep when asked, and referred to me as 'the Frances'. I had a long talk with Henrietta in which all her occasional nonsense dropped off and nothing but sweetness and sense remained, as well as a great deal of honesty. We talked about Bunny and Angelica – she doesn't think Angelica has any other person in her life, but that she does very much want to shake off Bunny, William and Hilton. She blamed them both to some extent – Bunny for teasing Angelica, Angelica for rebuffing Bunny, but I think she was more on Bunny's 'side'.

I went a few days ago to a party to celebrate the Spenders'[2] silver wedding and Matthew's[3] twenty-first birthday. The ICI galleries in Dover Street were crammed to bursting with a lively crowd of all ages – from the glamorous young to Diana

---

[1] He was recovering from an operation.
[2] Stephen and Natasha.
[3] Their son.

Cooper and Iris Tree. At one end in the obscurity jazz music was thrumming, and dancers were pounding obsessionally up and down. This and the vast horde of guests made it only possible to talk if one put one's mouth to an ear and bellowed into it – none the less I had several quite intimate conversations, enjoyed myself very much, feeling like a corpuscle in the blood stream of some huge animal organism and stayed till about one o'clock when the old were fast thinning out. It seemed very much an 'occasion' and a memorable one, faces were alight with friendliness and intelligence. Having wondered if I would 'know anyone' of course there they all were – Robert and Cynthia, David and Rachel, Rosamond Lehmann, Mary and Charlie, Koestler, V. S. Pritchett, the Ayers, the [James] Sterns, Julian, Tristram, Georgie. As Robert said, 'The people we know are very nice.' I caught sight of Julia among the throng and at one moment I went to talk to Cynthia not noticing that Julia was on the other side of her. She moved very quickly away.

March 28th

I have been weltering in the gore of my own life, a very odd experience. Last week Michael Holroyd brought me the second volume of his life of Lytton, asking me to read and correct any factual inaccuracies. Of course I plunged in at once, deeply interested, at first with a sort of horror, then with amazed admiration. For I think the impression he made on me of being a realist is accurate and that he has to an astonishing degree kept close to the facts. Perhaps he has probed too unmercifully, even the bedrooms and beds are explored for data; but he has relied enormously on written materials. The story of Lytton's last illness and death and Carrington's suicide made moving reading. I liked very much Lytton's comment on dying, when near his end: 'Well, if this is death – I don't think much of it.' Also how when incredibly weak he still talked philosophy and wrote poetry. When he complained that poetry was becoming difficult the fat plain nurse said, 'Any poetry that's written round here will be written by me.' Lytton in a very faint voice: 'My hat!' I also liked the remark of one of the eminent doctors who attended him: 'I should quite dote on that chap if I saw much more of him.' The portrait of Ralph is, as I'd expected, rather unsympathetic. But the only really inaccurate portrait of a *situation* is of the Gerald–Carrington–Ralph row, Watendlath and after. I shall try and put him right on that.

But – what astonishes me is this young man's power to make me see Bloomsbury with slightly fresh eyes. The impression of life, originality, working out their own standards, intellectual integrity, and fearlessness is still there. But – in Lytton at times, though he was not a good letter-writer and therefore shows in them his least serious side – a certain silliness emerges, a tendency to dismiss everyone and everything, however slightly outside the inner circle, as 'odious' and 'horrid' or 'infinitely dim'. Dogs, and children too of course – but not the rich upper class, to whom to some extent he capitulated.

April 3rd: Crichel

Besides the three present inmates we have here Pat Trevor-Roper[1] and a young man who is intelligent, beautiful and well informed, called Andrew Murray-Thripland. Raymond is enchanted by him, Desmond also, Eardley a little growly.

---

[1] Eye surgeon. About to take Eardley's place in the house.

I had quite a long talk with him alone yesterday, discovering that he had been to Eton and then read philosophy at Dublin, then became a press correspondent in the Middle East and is now a stockbroker, but he means to give in his notice tomorrow. I like Pat Trevor-Roper very much. He's a quick, eager, clever man with a perfect passion for facts and information. Raymond is in his element, always coming up with some odd piece of knowledge; someone runs next door for the OED or the Encyclopedia every few minutes, there are comic arguments, as when Pat declared that up to a certain date no doge died a natural death and Raymond challenged him. Andrew is absolutely up to the level of it all, well-versed in Gibbon and knowing at once what Roman Emperor had an aunt called Livia, as well as a lot of unrelated facts. It is lively and amusing, but I miss more general ideas as usual, though at the moment – rather weary-minded – I'm hardly able to produce any.

But I love being here and it doesn't discontent me at all being odd man out. Yesterday afternoon Eardley, Moses and I went a very long walk, cold and beautiful, all round Crichel lake. The trees are only just coming out here and there, large ash buds bursting from mainly bare twigs, whereas the fields are fresh green and we walked between great tufts of enormous primroses. It was bitterly cold and the lake quite rough, dry straw-coloured rushes rattling and creaking in the wind.

We had a general election last week and, as everyone knew they would, Labour got in with a large majority. Bunny dined with me and he and I went to look at the results on telly at Montpelier Square with Julian, Georgie, and Georgia, Jonny and Sabrina, Tim Behrens and Ed Gilbert. Except for Julian and me, *everyone* had voted Conservative (including Bunny) and some for trivial reasons. I was pleased that Bunny took to Julian.

At dinner Bunny told me Angelica is now wavering about the divorce but he is hesitant. 'I love her and I want to express my love.' Does this mean that he simply won't have her except on his own terms?

April 15th

Last night Michael Holroyd came to dinner to collect his life of Lytton volume 2 and my corrections and some Gerald–Carrington letters. I had spent the afternoon re-reading part of his book in the light of my feeling that he may have under-estimated the 'nobility' of Old Bloomsburians. It is a question of stress – they were also of course a little absurd. But what I decided from a second reading was that the most damning impressions came from their own mouths. Lytton in particular went all lengths to depreciate and make fun of the members of his own circle (unbridled cruelty about Clive, E. M. Forster 'a mediocre man who will come to no good', 'dullness exudes from Desmond in a concentrated stream'. Lionel Penrose has 'entire absence of brain', Julian Bell 'half-witted', Logan Pearsall-Smith is 'senile'). This is made worse by his own great susceptibility to flattery and appre-ciation especially from rich duchesses. Indeed, success mellowed him as it usually does. Michael was aware of this and thought it should not be concealed. Our evening left me still liking him and respecting his judgement. I think he also respects mine, and he came nearer talking about himself than usual – he is going on holiday to Spain next month with a rather hysterical girl in her car. (He can't drive.) His girlfriends 'are inclined to be neurotic or schizoid'. He is obviously heterosexual and gravely hampered by lack of cash. I do hope he makes some money out of this book.

I gave Michael a few letters between me and Carrington to show that our relationship was more complex than he had realized and far from purely hostile.

April 19th

My evening with Robert was so delightful that I remember nothing of our conversation, having been too deeply engaged in it. We talked of psychoanalysis though; he now goes only once a week. Like me, he believes in the theory but is doubtful about the therapy – though he described how after one session he suddenly felt detached from his own tormented unconscious, and looking at it as if from an astral plane without being agonizedly involved. He said also how usually the awareness of the infantile source of his states of mind failed to clear a path in that subterranean turmoil, and this I can very easily imagine.

Dined last night with Raymond and the Pritchetts at the Travellers' Club ostensibly to talk Turkey, but in fact we talked mainly about books and other things. Dorothy wheezy and unwell, complaining of insomnia. V. S. P. has a curious coldness, possibly of an over-sensitive man who doesn't want to be upset by other people's horrors. He talked of 'sympathy' as something to be regretted and weak. I don't really feel sure that if one were sinking in a slimy river he would pull one out. But who would? Robert of course, Janetta, and Julian; Mary would have a try.

April 20th

With Mary to a party at Murray's for Paddy Leigh Fermor's book – enjoyable. A roomful of interesting literary faces, and such a very handsome room, too – Robert, V. S. P., Raymond, the Berkeleys, Patrick Kinross. Normally I shrink before such things, but if I get there I am glad I've gone: it's entirely a matter of confidence. Poor Mary is low and looking worn. I fear gnawed by unhappiness about Charlie and uncertainty for the future.

This morning on the spur of the moment I rang Angelica because there's been no news from Henrietta. She was expansively friendly and forthcoming – and after quite a long talk raised the question about the 'Dy-vorce' as she calls it, between her and Bunny. I said my say, as to not liking the mechanical interference of the law in tender human relations. She told me she was now definitely against it, but it was Bunny – perversely – who was insisting. What a mess! She explicitly said it 'had been going on for some months', which looks as though their trouble was recent, and also that 'she didn't want to marry anyone' – or perhaps 'there was no one she wanted to marry,' not quite the same thing.

Though preparations for Turkey have advanced, Raymond told me on the telephone that his back was hurting him again and I suddenly feel the trip will not come off.

April 21st

Another odd experience last night – a dinner with the 'Anti-Shakespeare Society', invited by Lionel and Margaret Penrose. A large gathering of solid, intelligent-looking middle-aged and elderly people in evening dress, including the Duke of St Albans and Lord Wakehurst, both directly descended from Lord Oxford who is the favoured candidate of the society. When I told Sir John Russell, a hatchet-faced legal light, that I too was descended from Lord Oxford (which is true), he looked at me in ludicrous amazement.

There was a strong element of *snobbery* about the supporters of Oxford, though I don't know if they thought Shakespeare's two noble descendants – both of whom made speeches – were worthy offshoots. The Duke, a pink-faced youngish man with an unbridled smile, excused himself for not bringing up a portrait of Oxford from his country seat, but gave no reason. The 'man Shack-speer' or 'the man of Stratford' was mentioned several times with smug and pitying smiles. I asked Lionel what on earth all the eminent scholars who thought Shakespeare wrote Shakespeare had to gain by their beliefs if they weren't true? And he muttered something about vested interests, Establishment and scholars always being heated. I forgot to bring up Ben Jonson to Marjorie Sisson who is an Oxford addict and was sitting next to me. Indeed, not a single argument was produced except for Sir John Russell declaring that *The Tempest* was obviously not by 'Shakespeare' (it was written after Oxford's death), one reason being that the 'cloud-capped towers' speech plainly showed that he didn't believe in an afterlife, while the author of *Hamlet* did. One speaker alluded to Shakespeare's ambivalent sexual tastes, and Mr Christmas Humphreys briskly waved aside any idea of his being 'cissy'. In fact everyone was completely woolly-minded.

April 26th

During most of my drive to Lambourn and the Carringtons last weekend I was wondering whether to take my courage in both hands, ring up Julia and ask her to have a walk, so putting an end to the indigestible and undigested lump of our disagreement. When it poured all Saturday afternoon I admit I felt a certain relief that no decision need be come to. On Sunday, however, blue sky and warm wind put another face on things and I had sufficiently rehearsed what I would say – that I wondered if she would care for a short walk; she could think about it and ring me back. It was Lawrence to whom I gave the message, as Julia was in the bath, but she soon rang up and said she would like it very much.

I am very glad the deed is done. It has cleared a patch of guilt on my theoretical 'pacifism in private relations as in public affairs'. I knew it was right to make a move, yet wounded pride and other ignoble feelings, perhaps just dread of p and q-minding, held me back. There was quite enough to say about people and events without going into dangerous territory or making any allusion to our last meeting, and we both with one accord avoided red lights. The nearest was when I asked if she had seen Sonia since she came back from staying in Spain with Janetta, and if she'd enjoyed herself. Julia said hurriedly that Oh yes, she'd seen her, and she said she'd felt very sorry for Janetta. She never realized before how unhappy she was. Obviously Sonia's visit wasn't a great success, and her hostility to Janetta is pretty plain in this comment. I dropped the subject quickly.

May 6th

For some time I've felt great reluctance to write a word in this book and the mere thought of it produces a dull wooden thud like a croquet mallet striking a peg. I'm not sure why – I've been 'getting along' quite all right but in a curiously unreflective way that I don't at all relish. Again I think of mallets and pegs – the apparatus of some fairground game, in which I bounce uncontrollably from obstacle to obstacle, not mistress of my face, unthinking, and slightly unfeelingly.

Since I finished my last translation I have been going through the Desmond letters with a red pencil and I'm simply not sure what sort of a book they would make – whether perhaps something a little insipid emerges. Prolonged contact with anyone through their letters, diaries or memoirs is a stringent test, almost like marriage. But I do like his unmalicious sympathy and understanding. I've had no shortage at all of things to do and people to see, and the trip to Turkey now hurtles towards me and absorbs all plan-making instincts.

I've just remembered an interesting story told me by Professor Postan at Cambridge.[1] I asked if he had known John Cornford, killed in the Spanish Civil War. 'Yes, he was a pupil of mine and a most remarkable, brilliant and formidable young man. An odd thing happened not long ago. I was correcting some history papers for a colleague who was ill. I didn't look at the names in case I knew some of the students, but I suddenly had an extraordinary sense of *déjà vu* – the turn of phrase, the ideas were familiar. Could the student have cribbed from something I knew? I looked at the name – Cornford; the paper had been written by the *posthumous* son of John.'

May 9th

Back in my nest after a short ice-cold weekend at Thorington with the Penroses. That paper-thin old house let in the shrieking wind which hurled rain against it all Sunday, and I felt anxious for the thinly-dressed wife of an American paediatrician who spent the day with us, and heaped more logs and coal on the fire whenever Lionel wasn't looking. As always I loved being with the Penroses though, in spite of material discomforts – apart from stimulating talk, their geniality, appreciativeness and tolerance are at the moment what I particularly like. How though can so clever a man as Lionel think Shakespeare's plays were written by a syndicate?

Bunny had tackled Lionel on the Shakespeare question at a Cranium dinner[2] and he rather accusingly suggested this was my fault. 'Why, of course I told him about the Anti-Shakespeare dinner,' I said. 'I didn't think there was any secret about your views.'

Side-stepping among the values of the Penrose family I inevitably check them against those of other friends – Janetta, Magouche, Julian, Henrietta; and the Penroses get top marks for constructive kindness, music, intelligent thinking. Shirley and a nice plump girlfriend were swotting for exams with unheard-of-persistence and enthusiasm (medicine and Greek philosophy respectively). Lionel would look up from a sheet on which he was writing mathematical formulae to join in the general conversation. He seems to have discovered something new about Mongols[3] which excites him greatly – there are, he now thinks, two sorts; and another discovery concerned miscarriages, which have never been properly investigated. But analysis of two hundred showed that fifty were abnormal as to chromosomes.

Barely keeping warm by sitting on top of the log fire and wearing two jerseys and a flannel shirt, I never stirred out all yesterday but on Saturday I walked off

[1] Munia Postan. Professor of Economics at Cambridge.
[2] A dining-club dating from the late twenties.
[3] Now always referred to as Down's syndrome.

along the green lanes alone, beside the stream and up the hill to a bluebell-carpeted wood. A magnificent swan sailed silently along the narrow strip of water and hissed menacingly when I stooped to pick some *cardamine amara* by the water's edge. Further on his wife proudly arched her neck over her nest. I enjoyed my bath of greenery.

May 12th

Raymond has just rung up to say he has German measles! I feel incredulous, yet that 'it had to be'. He told me he had it as a child and the present diagnosis was made by a 'very young locum'. Anyway, it is such a trifling complaint that one would be prone to ignore it. But the sound of his deep voice, anxiety-soaked, ringing up with reiterated alarms has begun to unnerve me, and I feel if some other less anxious person would take his bookings over I should be almost relieved. But who? Bunny? Anyway I suppose he will want to postpone, not cancel our journey. All my present activities – my Turkish lessons and so on – have had the stuffing knocked out of them. I had begun reading the history of Asia Minor, and in every sort of way letting myself gradually down the steps into the swimming-bath of next week's journey. Thank heaven frustrations and disappointments seem to matter less than they once did.

May 14th: Crichel

Oh dear – not out of the wood yet by a long way. Shall we, shan't we go to Turkey? I don't know, but at the moment it looks very doubtful and Raymond seems a most unlikely and (it must be said) rather undesirable travelling companion.

Yesterday afternoon I drove down here, heard tapping in the drawing-room, and found him at his typewriter. He at once said he felt far from well, was still covered with the rash, and showed all the symptoms of abandonment to a literary man's dejection. In the course of the evening things got worse. Eardley arrived starry-eyed from having bought a little country house with Mattei Radev. (This was a fresh blow, as I think Raymond had always believed he might stay on here.) After hearing about it Raymond went up to his bath, but returned to dinner in a much worse, a really deplorable state – preoccupied, self-centred, impatient. There's no question, I now see, of his being pressed to go unless his rash is *quite* gone in the next two days – and this I begin to doubt. At dinner he was pitiful, had forgotten to brush his hair, interrupted Eardley's and my remarks with impatient strings of 'Yes, Yes, Yes', burst into thunderous blimpish disapproval of the Labour Party, of Harold Nicolson's bad spelling and all 'young reviewers who didn't read three or four books round each book they reviewed' (as he did for his dull piece about the Zulus last week), and was inclined to contradict everything anyone said in a very dictatorial fashion. I encouraged him to go to bed, sat talking to Eardley for a while and then went up early myself – and brooded.

Well, I've reached several conclusions. I must at once make clear to him that of course there's no question of our going till he feels perfectly well, and perhaps give him the chance to back out altogether. How I wish my companion was to be Eardley or Desmond. I don't want to nanny Raymond through Turkey and I'm reminded of how Ruth Lowinsky complained of being made to wash his under-pants! I'm ashamed of my fickleness, for of course he is now one of my oldest friends and one whom I see from old diaries used in the past never to fall from grace. But in the last ten years or so we have grown in different directions. I do feel sorry for him, and I'm not as heartless towards him as this outburst may seem to show – and I realize very vividly that it would be much too cruel to try and persuade him to come to Turkey if he is not feeling well. That's absolutely final and I shall hang on to it for all it's worth.

Mrs Spicer has just brought in my breakfast tray. I gather Raymond is no better and is not dining out at Michael Pitt-Rivers's this week. 'It *is* a shame. He does *try* so hard. He *tries so hard in the world*, Mr Mortimer does. You know, he's a sweet person.' And so he is, of course, and does.

May 15th

Raymond followed hard on Mrs Spicer, and as a result of a bad night and no diminution of the rash and my determination not to raise obstacles, an hour was spent postponing our departure for one week. I think it highly likely he'll be perfectly well by Tuesday, but what does it matter? Now I've changed gear and don't care a bit, and he is enormously relieved, so it's well worth it. Pat Trevor-Roper and his friend Andrew arrived for lunch and confirmed the genesis of the famous rash – he was also much impressed by it. Poor Raymond – I've been hard on him. How could he feel 'himself' if his body is in such a state of protest?

May 16th

I drove back to London this morning, and now lie with my swollen and aching leg up, cursing smallpox inoculation in general. I left Raymond as spotty as ever and not (I feel) tremendously sanguine, though the presence of charming Andrew made him put as good a face on his troubles as possible and even look better. I asked Pat if he thought it would certainly be gone in a week, and he said, 'Oh, yes,' but I thought I glimpsed a reservation in his eye, and he said rashes were always slow to go. Yesterday was brilliant and beautiful, today also; we played croquet and lay on long chairs in the sun. I went a long walk with Eardley and Moses (too long, I fear, for my leg). The feeling that Eardley is a real friend gives me great pleasure. When we are alone I don't 'think what I'm going to say to him' at all – nor I believe does he. I'm interested in his thoughts, we pursue anything that comes up (like associations in pictures), we drop a subject and come back to it. I can't help contrasting him with Raymond, who is a good man, and who 'tries hard in the world' but has less resilience or power to shift his angle of vision. I'd better go on while I'm about it and criticize Raymond's way of stating categorically something which he's quite unable to support in any way. A tiny example – we were talking about Falstaff whose 'nose was as sharp as a pen and 'a babbled of green fields'. The latest interpretation, Raymond said, was 'a table of Grenville (or Grenfell)' meaning a picture of the Admiral. But 'How? Why?' I asked; 'it doesn't appear to make sense.' 'I can't remember, but it seemed very convincing and is now generally accepted.' Then at dinner he declared that pragmatism amounted to much the same as Christian Science. Again I asked how in the world he made that out? All he will say is, 'Well, isn't it?'

May 17th

My leg is just as painful and turning somewhat blue, so I'm quite glad not to be going today. Meanwhile I loll on my bed, surrounded by books and papers and have long talks on the telephone – an immense one with Frances Phipps who is dining at Buckingham Palace tonight. She goes with an admirably detached curiosity about it all, and I shall ring her up tomorrow and see if she's engaged Harold Wilson in talk about Vietnam.

May 18th

Paul Hyslop telephoned. Raymond was better, but had 'sounded cross' because Paul hadn't sent our air tickets back to the agents – I should think so! We can't get the new ones till he does. Then he said flatly and so far as I can remember in these very words: 'If Raymond *dies* while you're in Turkey you don't need to bring him back or do anything special. I thought you'd better know; he wouldn't want it.' Oh, what a cheerful holiday this promises to be! I wonder if the message originated with Raymond?

May 20th

Dined last night with Magouche and Robin Fedden, and was taken on afterwards to Joan Rayner's, where were Connollys, Betjemans, Patrick Kinross, Johnny Craxton and so forth. I was sitting between Cyril and Deirdre and put several feet wrong with Cyril. One sees at once when one has done that, as he delights in showing disapproval. On the other hand if one is lucky enough to amuse him (I did once though I can't remember how) he wrestles desperately to control his smile.

I'm wondering a little what I'm in for in the way of Turkish muddle. The only arrangement Raymond has had to make – getting our tickets to Izmir – has been bungled: first they went to the *Sunday Times*, then Paul failed to send them back to the agents. Now mine has still not come, though they say they posted it yesterday, and Raymond's has gone again to the *Sunday Times*.

May 22nd

So off Raymond and I seem to be going, though I feel as if I had been cast somewhat for the role of Dr Moran, whose detailed medical account of Winston Churchill's last years has been appearing in the Sunday papers and exciting a lot of interest.

Raymond rang up and added to the funeral note by saying he had been to Craig Macfarlane to make a new will also, he had 'felt awfully queer after lunch – it quite worried me'. 'What sort of queer?' 'Oh, just dizzy and strange.' Then belatedly, 'But I'm quite all right now. I'm sure I shall be in *top form* tomorrow.'

May 24th: Athens

Thank heavens that with the passing of the years I seem to have lost all sense that there's anything odd or frightening about flying – although I know it would take very little indeed to resuscitate it. Eardley drove Raymond and me to the airport and left us there in what Raymond said he felt to be 'a specially horrifying form of Dante's Inferno', while to me it looked rather more as the central Post Office must to a parcel. I felt confident I should be dispatched and arrive at the right destination but all the alarms that have preceded our departure, and my awareness of Raymond's anxious forebodings, resulted in my 'not greatly caring' whether I did or no. We were passed through the sorting compartments effortlessly, except for occasional, convulsive checking-up of vital organs (spectacles? passport? ticket?)

and soon we were sailing along with uneventful smoothness through the layer of haze which seemed to be hanging over all Europe. A sideways somewhat horrific glance at Mont Blanc; the Gulf of Corinth sprinkled with islands like a paperchase – and Athens. How strange that a place only once briefly visited, and that exactly thirty years ago, should immediately present a familiar face. I find it as I did then for the most part unattractive, too white, too monotonously spread over the plain, except for its astonishing focus. I'm trying not to wave my antennae too obviously towards Raymond. He very sweetly bought me a bottle of lovely Dior scent at the airport as if in apology for his *faiblesse*. In the aeroplane there was a good deal of whisky-and-pill-swallowing; but I think he's relieved to be here. He has a surprising and touching way of talking ('making himself agreeable') to all and sundry includ-ing unlikely housewives from the Midlands, whom I can't help feeling he mistakes for 'cultivated people'.

It was six by Greek time when we got to the hotel, and he went at once to rest, arranging to meet at seven-thirty. I couldn't for a moment consider staying in my room all that time but set out walking through the small streets between the Olympic Palace and the Acropolis – a very nice part of the town, full of tavernas and shops where carpets were being cleaned and picture frames made, wine and vegetables sold. Soon I found myself on the lower slopes of the backside of the great object itself and began climbing by twisting lanes of small white-washed houses, with old black-clad women immobile on kitchen chairs, cats and pots of flowers at every corner. Except for the fear of keeping Raymond waiting I would have gone on to the top, for the light was fading and the town was slowly melting in a pink misty glow below me. I returned, feeling I'd visually (but not at all historically) nipped and possessed a minute fragment of Athens without wasting a moment. Had a swig of whisky and felt ready for anything. When Raymond appeared we more or less retraced the path I'd followed, passing a mysterious sign reading BOTTOM in different coloured lights (one of Eddie Gathorne-Hardy's night haunts?), and sat down in a restaurant with a garden under the deepening sky looking up at a delicate crescent moon and the silhouette of the Acropolis. Kind and handsome waiters looked after us. We ordered moussaka. Was there any fish? 'Only screams', they said diffidently (shrimps – or rather prawns). This made a delicious meal with some warm, white unresinated wine. Raymond was aghast when three young men stood up before three microphones holding very shiny electric guitars. 'They're preparing to *torture* us,' he said in his profoundest basso – but they sang traditional Greek songs in soft voices and a restrained style, and I for one enjoyed it. Raymond was anxious to be back in the hotel by ten (nine o'clock English time).

May 25th

Hazy hot-looking morning. We took a taxi up to the Acropolis. It was crowded with holiday-makers, many white-headed, picking their way with stiff legs over the rough platform of stone. The complete image, both visual and auditory, including the loud American voices and groups of lively, very black-haired Greeks, was suddenly *there*, as something I had never forgotten; the nobility, purity of line and Godlike arrogance, the very pale curdled cream of the stones. Perhaps the Erechtheion gave me less of a thrill at second sight, and what I'd remembered as rows of Vanessas,[1] smiling enigmatically and tilted slightly forward in the museum didn't turn out to be quite that, but were beautiful none the less, and remote, and smoothly polished as if they'd lain under the sea. Out again into the powerful but not crushing heat. The silvery stones we walked over were sprinkled with red poppies and yellow crucifers.

After lunch a small nearly empty Turkish aeroplane chugged us at what seemed a snail's pace over the dusty brown coastline, the Aegean, and then the identical dusty brown coastline of Turkey to Izmir Airport. Raymond picked up a plump and pretty American girl who turned out to be a member of the Peace Corps – a voluntary do-gooder, all honour to her. I heard him telling the passport man clearly, slowly and amiably: 'I am delighted to be here. I am sure I shall enjoy myself very much. But I am OLD.' This went down extremely well and he got a lot of 'patting and holding' as he calls it. Intense scrutiny of passports. But life very Turkish – it bounced and rattled, though the road was good, and the driver kept half leaping to his feet to try and close a trap door which had mysteriously opened in the roof. The country we drove through might have been southern Spain except for less attractive cottages. Olives made pools of shadow for sheep and cows to lie in; gentle hills – a *kind* landscape. Izmir was at once more oriental, with its minarets, bazaar-like shops, piles of amphorae, and vine-covered alleys crowded with people carrying baskets.

But my first walk in the town hasn't greatly charmed me. There are quantities of huge-winged American cars, some belonging to the American Army and often driven by negroes, others surprisingly converted into Turkish taxis. The extent of the American occupation begins to arouse Yankophobia in me – one hears the twang on every side, particularly from horrid little shaven-headed juniors. Then a peasant woman swathed in a black veil comes by leading by the hand a little girl of about six wearing the prettiest Turkish trousers under a tunic.

Is Doctor Moran taking enough care of his patient? I do hope so. Raymond retired for two hours while I took my walk and was in bed again before ten, from which I conclude he is very tired indeed. I question him often about his back, feet and sleeping, and he answers in great detail; so he must be very preoccupied with them. I really see rather little of him – but he was cheerful during dinner, eaten in our hotel restaurant: a huge plate of kebab and yoghurt. Afterwards we walked through the warm night to the sea. This very comfortable hotel can only have us for three nights and we want to stay four. We shall have to think again.

May 26th

My room looks out on a waste land of trees and logs – part of the Park of Culture that has run to seed. This morning there is a peasant woman there with her head and shoulders swathed in a bath towel and a sheep browsing on the end of a lead.

I was wakened by the telephone saying 'Günaydin' to me, and managed to ask for breakfast in my swotted-at Turkish. Raymond had made an appointment with the Consul, and we set out thither along the sea front – it turned out to be a long way, and taxing to poor Raymond, who sighed but pegged on valiantly. The Consul, Mr Wilkinson, a rather charmless man with false teeth and a dark brown wart on his nose, addressed me several times as Mrs Mortimer and was friendly

---

[1] Bell.

and helpful. A visit to the tourist agency to get Raymond's press card and a tiny cup of dark mud in a café took up the rest of the morning. Plan-making over lunch. Raymond remarked that 'we were not likely to differ much'. I hope not. The fresh, warm, salt-laden air and the benignity of the sun dissolves and relaxes my anxieties and I see that in this kindly indolent land one could soon give up doing much except sit on a divan eating sweetmeats. There are extraordinary dishes on the menu, translated as 'Bülbül Bird's nest', 'Lady's navel', and 'The Imam has fainted'.

After my 'Bülbül bird' I lay on my bed and began to read my Penguin Herodotus with pleasure. Afternoon drive to the Agora, our first glimpse of I suppose many columns and fragments of antiquity. My response was mildly pleased; I was more delighted by our subsequent walk through the crowded streets of the bazaar. Tomorrow is Turkish Independence Day and a national holiday, so the town is already hung with crimson flags with crescent and star, while each little booth displays shiny shoes, coconut-covered cakes or artificial flowers, and barrows are loaded with juicy cucumbers and black cherries.

May 27th: Pergamum day

The Consul warned us of Turkish unpunctuality and sure enough both breakfast and the bus that was to take us to Pergamum were late. The latter was a small battered *dolmüs*, full to bursting with very fat red-faced Germans, to Raymond's horror and almost equally to mine. He and I were on the back seat – the worst, and there were anyway no springs to speak of. Bouncing out over the appalling *pavé* roads of the suburbs was a gruelling start to our excursion and I felt very anxious for Raymond's powers of endurance. But we are now safely home and he says it was 'much less exhausting than he expected', and he has been in splendid spirits all day. Once out into the country the road improved and I gazed eagerly about at this first sight of rustic Turkey. Camels – several strings of them – slowly moving along with expressions of vast disdain, another group including young ones collapsed into heaps for a rest; buffaloes, storks; workers in the fields using implements with such short handles that they were bent with their bottoms higher than their heads under the noonday sun – the women wearing full trousers and a scarf or tablecloth over their heads, men with heads swathed in turbans, or Colonel Lawrence fashion. The Turks do seem rather a melancholy and defeatist race, as Patrick Kinross said, and though this was a national holiday there was very little gaiety. It was two hours' drive from Izmir to the Acropolis itself, astoundingly poised on the summit of a conical hill out-topping its neighbours and with the theatre plastered against the steep topmost slope, looking as if the audience must topple from their seats into the plain. The prevailing colour of the stone was a curious dull bronze, like the dancing-shoes of my childhood, and exceedingly dark red poppies grew among the stones. Our guide's yells in deafening German, followed by hastily epitomized English were not inspiring, and for some reason the ruins left me rather unmoved in spite of their splendid situation. But I enjoyed the whole day, perhaps most of all the drive through the wide valleys and gently sloping hills.

Back in Izmir, we found Independence Day being celebrated in a jolly but stodgy and family way; Ataturk's statue was piled with wreaths and the streets were full of people carrying or dragging their children. Meanwhile the sky turned a lurid purplish red with black tadpole clouds, all reflected in the quiet sea, and a few piratical-looking ships became silhouettes of innumerable lights. Raymond and I sat down at one of the restaurants on the sea front. I was delighted with the valiant way he had stood our long day's outing and didn't want to discourage him from going to bed soon after nine, which seemed to be what he wanted. So I walked back to the hotel with him and went out again not long after, curious to see what was going on. The crowds were thicker now and I felt a little sheepish about my solitude and glad when some Turkish girls sat down beside me. Soon everyone began to crane forward and stare down the esplanade, and the insistent, ferocious sound of drums beating a slow, ponderous rhythm grew gradually louder and nearer, until up came a procession of soldiers or sailors all dressed in white; short, square and strong, with shiny white crash helmets fastened by broad bands under their chins. The most extraordinary thing about this frightening display was the way they lifted their short, snow-white legs in time to the shattering drumbeat, not in a goose step but with *'knees high'* (like Strauss's Electra) and then stamping masterfully on the ground. I felt these strong, square men were longing to go and kill someone, and that the roaring and clapping of the crowd was purely warlike.

May 28th

Today we had to move for our last Smyrnian night to a lower-grade hotel. In the morning to the archaeological museum – but I have to confess that these headless deities and fragments of groups don't greatly thrill me. Peered dutifully at tiny objects of metal, clay or gold, wondering what they were used for, and walked out into the flat and flowerless Culture Park with its hideous modernistic buildings, feeling unstimulated. Thence with relief into the life of the town; bought postcards and sat drinking limonata in a café. Was reproved by Raymond for being so unhygienic as to lick my stamps. After Raymond's nap we set off in a taxi to Teos, a fishing village picturesquely embraced by the ruins of a Genoese castle, from the walls of which hung a beautiful prickly plant with large pale flowers and cascades of purple stamens – the caper. Women in brilliant trousers stood staring at us from under an ancient gateway and some children burst into rockets of laughter at our comic appearance. How odd, I thought, we've hardly heard any Turkish laughter till now. Yet they break easily into gentle and friendly smiles tinged with melancholy. They seem well disposed to the English, preferring us to Germans and Americans, but fatalistic and without much energy or enthusiasm. Our little mustachioed taxi-driver brought out a tiny Turkish guidebook in order to enlighten us quite incorrectly about what we were looking at, and thumbed it over hopefully, muttering about Dionysus and Anacreon.

The classical site of Teos, a mile or so further on, was rural and enchanting. We drew up at the edge of a field, and there through the old olives and a forest of flowers (mullein, anchusa, umbellifers and these very dark red poppies) we saw a few stout incomplete grey columns. A bronzed man appeared with a little boy and soon afterwards, stepping proudly in her trousers and bare feet and carrying a short-handled hoe came a handsome little girl of about ten. 'Mehraba!' they said, and 'Mehraba' I replied, and then explained that I was English. 'Ingiliz-im, anlimiyorum' (I don't understand) and 'Vah Vah' (my favourite phrase = What a pity!) ... The ruins were a total jumble, but made really beautiful by the wild flowers springing up all round them and enveloping them. When I started to pick them the children brought me more and more, and then leaves, berries, sticks, wheat, anything, till my arms were full. There wasn't another soul in sight except this charming little family, until a youth rode up on a donkey, to whose 'Mehraba!' Raymond replied, 'How are *you*?' in his best cocktail-party voice. A white pony was browsing among the stones. Lovely drive home in the golden afternoon light – the quadruped-like workers were still hacking away with picturesque but terrible industry at their fertile fields.

May 29th: Villa Park Otel, Antalya

I see I shall have to go on about Raymond a bit – the usual obsession with one's fellow traveller. It is not yet ten, and he has gone off to bed, leaving me high and dry, though the town is *en fête* in a purely Turkish fashion (hardly any tourists here) and tinned music is blaring from several loudspeakers so as to make sleep, one would have thought, impossible for hours. He told me he takes a sleeping-pill about ten, even after having an hour or two's sleep in the afternoon. Can anyone need so much? Then in the small dining-room he eagerly turned from me to talk to two quite nice Swedes and a pretty ghastly American, and of course it is the usual thing – travellers' tales of things seen or about to be seen. He does it I think consciously and almost perhaps on principle. He's mentioned it being a habit: 'I talk to everyone.' But I must remember he's an invalid and not strong at all, and I must look after him in his fragility. He dutifully writes dozens of postcards, sighing and groaning, and denying that he enjoys it.

This morning our nice little taxi-driver called to take us to the air terminal. The aeroplane was almost empty and we sped pleasantly and briefly over quite high mountains streaked with snow. Our hotel here consists of two villas on the edge of the park which ends in cliffs overhanging the sea and looking at the most sensational mountains across the bay, tier upon tier of them, with dromedary humps.

The town is exciting and beautiful and while Raymond dedicated himself to the ritual siesta I went out in the full heat of the afternoon to have a look at it. The mountains were rising out of swathes of mist like a beauty in a Victorian photograph. Leaving the park I turned to the small deep harbour full of pretty fishing boats and with a tiny mosque on the quay built over a spring of fresh water from the Taurus. Streams from these mountains flow through the town (one down the main street between two rows of palms) and fling themselves over the cliff into the sea. Steeply sloping up from the harbour is the oldest part of the town with crumbling brown walls, some tall trees with enormous leaves and the fine big houses of the Seljuk quarter, their gardens overflowing with roses, stocks, bougainvillias; they have enormously wide eaves and projecting upper stories – sometimes bellying out like giant wash-basins with their curved undersides painted with delicate patterns. There were wooden lattices so that the women could look out without being seen, and at the height of the afternoon when every café and lane was full of pleasure-seekers I several times looked up and saw a female face. An old woman smiled and waved at me; a young beauty with her hair bound in a silk scarf leaned her gold-braceleted arm on the sill and looked out wistfully. The festive crowds are all Turks yet the mixture of clothes is surprising. I saw veiled women swathed from head to foot in black, or others in Turkish trousers walking arm in arm with friends in short skirts and high heels. An old bearded man was carefully carrying a bright green chameleon on a stick, and snake-charmer music poured from loudspeakers.

May 30th

It took me half an hour's telephoning to get my breakfast this morning; when it came it consisted of quite good tea with lots of hot water, a piece of goat's cheese, olives, toast and some sort of preserved fruit in syrup. I read my Herodotus with it and reflected about the ancient world and the way people feel about it. He is a very lovable writer, realistic and practical and infinitely inquisitive. I'm sure he wouldn't have been in sympathy with the religious awe and humourless intoxication with which people like Freya Stark respond to the classics. Yet in spite of amazement at the learning and civilization of the ancients, I'm appalled by their brutality – nothing but impalements, hostile expeditions and executions, mingled with the boring utterances of the Oracle of Delphi. I like Herodotus best when he is describing the habits and customs of some foreign race like the Scythians, often hilariously, and one can't believe a word of it. The semen of the Ethiopians, according to him, is black!

The tourist agent arrived as he had promised, but his amiability began to sour under Raymond's criticisms. He's obviously used to a diet of flattery and satisfaction, and Raymond told him our rooms were much too dear for their simplicity, that one needed skill to be a hotelier, and that Turkish hoteliers had no idea of the needs of western Europeans. I'm horrified by this attempt to impose our English standards on a strange, still unspoiled country whose charm partly lies in its primitiveness. I neither want it to be quickly corrupted, nor to view it from the safe distance of an international hotel, like a hunter watching lions and tigers from his platform in the jungle. I said this, hoping to start a conversation, but he only said, 'Yes, perhaps'. And so it always is. The town has few taxis, but a lot of very pretty crimson victorias drawn by two horses. This morning we took one of these to the 'best' beach, a long stretch of shingle, overlooked by the glorious mountains and with a bar, restaurant and bathing boxes. We both had a delicious bathe in warm clean sea, and lay in the sun for a while drinking Turkish vermouth.

After Raymond had gone to bed I couldn't face being imprisoned in my room to the melancholy accompaniment of hours of fair music from the park, so I walked out into the night and took a ticket for the variety show in the marquee there. After three Turkish Beatles singing into microphones in a variety of languages, a wonderfully beautiful girl came in and did orgiastic oriental dances, ending by working herself to a climax with her private parts presented to the audience and her body leaning backwards parallel with the stage. 'Miss Strip-Tease' followed: a slip of a nymphet dressed in gauzy Victorian clothes, who minced immaturely about the stage taking them off one by one, stretching a gawky arm towards some man in the audience and piping 'Yes?' This seemed to me totally unsexy, but the audience loved it and roared out 'Yes!' Then a large chubby negro sang some songs with traditionally flapping arms, and a conjuror dressed as a matador flew round the audience abstracting their wrist-watches; but by now I'd had enough.

May 31st

I wonder what Raymond is writing in his diary? I'm afraid there are no remarks about me as tart as mine about him – I almost wish there were. He's too kind and nice, and anyway I'm quite sure is only noting down '*ra*vishing temples' and good or bad 'little 'otels' and restaurants. I can't stop thinking about his character, and more especially about the way his mind works. I remember Eardley once saying to me: 'I don't like going about with Raymond – he will *tell* me things all the time, and I don't *want* to be told.' And it's quite true: the suppressed schoolmaster is all-powerful in him. On the whole, unlike Eardley, I rather enjoy being 'told' but I can't bear it when he 'tells' the Turks what's wrong with Turkey, for their own good as I think he believes. Then I'm amazed by his idea of what conversation is – purely the interchange of information, hardly ever a delightful dovetailing and communication of impressions. He will be kindness itself if I say I have indigestion or a blister on my heel, but I would so much rather he was interested in my thoughts and prepared to reveal his to me. He seems to have almost given up thinking, though he loves using his eyes and imparting information. When this palls he picks up a book and acquires some more. Travel is a great revealer – it revealed terrible things about me to Julia, as I must never forget. I think with gratitude that Eardley and I have been better friends since Orta than before.

We started off this morning in our minibus, with our amiable pair of Swedes, two Turks and an intelligent charming boy as guide who was going to be an archaeologist, spoke French and had pretty teeth. It was a glorious outing enjoyed by us all. Our guide neither roared at us nor hurried us, and as the day was to include a long pause for lunch and bathing at a little beach near the innocent village of Side, he stopped the bus for me to buy a bathing suit at a large village shop on the way, and helped me to wave aside two or three expensive ones in garish artificial silk with false breasts and buy quite a nice striped cotton one. To lighten the load, I leave my bag at home and put camera, money, etc., in my Spanish basket. Raymond comes free-handed and is inclined to add Guide Bleu, his bathing trunks and cigarettes to it. I'm guardian of the Common Purse also, which is quite a responsibility, but I hand it over for him to make the manly gesture of paying.

We lunched after our bathe at a restaurant on a platform over the sea, off stuffed peppers (called '*dolma*' after the stuffed buses) and fish. I talked to a grey-haired Turkish ex-airman who had quite a lot of English and found him a really nice human being – interested, intelligent, humorous and friendly. So I was dismayed later on to hear Raymond lecturing him about how badly the hotels were run and how good modern ones catering for Western needs and tourism in general were what Turkey needed, how the pillows were too hard and there was TAR on the beaches. (He has mentioned this often in tones of catastrophic doom.)

Into the town for dinner this evening at a quite good restaurant, bleakly fluorescent and full of Turks. The English translations of the Turkish dishes on the menu sent Raymond into wild giggles. Instead of 'Houri's navel' we had 'Woman's thing' and there was 'Cauldron Ox bottom', 'System to Holland' and finally 'Krasky' and 'Krisky'.

June 1st

We decided to take today easy. The hotel has a very small terrace with about half a dozen quite comfortable chairs and some tables. I found Raymond finishing his breakfast there when I got up after mine (in bed as usual). The day was fine and the air delicious, but he disappeared soon afterwards to his dark back bedroom and spent till noon groaning over four postcards. As if playing a sort of game, I've set myself to get him to discuss some general subject or talk in some other way than just purveying information. Last night in the restaurant he followed this thread for so long and with such animation, poor fellow, that I'd finished my first course before he'd begun. For there was nothing for me to say. Then I wrenched him away to Crichel and its future, which 'took' for a while. He's anxious, probably with reason, about Eardley's departure. We talked of Mattei and he said he liked him and thought him intelligent. 'But there's one thing that worries me. He's got very little general knowledge, about history and literature.' F.: 'But do you really think that matters? Someone like Julia who has practically none is a delightful companion because she's so original and responsive.' R.: 'Yes, but you know, I mean, I mean, one's little jokes about Bloody Mary may not be understood.'

In the afternoon I started what I thought a good subject – respectability, *à propos* of Henry James's *Siege of London* which I've been reading. He beamed kindly and even looked interested, but wouldn't say a thing. Yet with all this there's something so touching, so angelically kind about the dear fellow that of course I feel very guilty at thinking or writing such things.

June 5th: Otel Imbat, Kuşadası

I've just had breakfast on my private balcony at this much grander new hotel, sitting in the shadow but looking out on the milky blue sea with a few clouds making pearly reflections and the distant hills of Samos behind. It is a brand-new, hideous but comfortable affair in a superb position among olive groves, with cornfields sloping to the sea. When we asked where one bathed they said, 'The beach will be finished in a day or two.' We looked and saw men putting down sand on the shore, which soon turns into a sort of mud. But our rooms are large and sunny, with shower and lavatory; and you have only to walk out of the front door to be in the country. Walked with Raymond to the nearest headland, picking flowers and feeling a welling-up sense of peace and happiness.

The Pitt-Riverses had asked us to dinner and we were received by the charming William. Soon Anthony and Tanya Hobson[1] bobbed up through the hatchway, then Michael from the hammam in the town, and his aquiline-nosed actress mother. We all sat on deck drinking whisky for some time. The Hobsons brought an exciting message – Jock Jardine of the British Council at Ankara had been there during the day. He was driving to meet Eddie Gathorne-Hardy at Izmir, and they will be at our hotel tomorrow night. He offered to drive us to Miletus and Didyma on the following day and said they were going on to Bodrum and had booked rooms there. Why didn't we do so too? Hopes aroused, but as it may well turn out to be impossible, I don't want to get too involved.

We all dined in a restaurant on the Quay. I sat between Michael and William, but as Michael directed all his conversation to me I couldn't talk to William as

---

[1] My second meeting with a couple with whom I later became great friends.

much as I'd have liked. Michael was amusing about the Hilton Hotel at Athens, where he said you could live an entirely self-contained life. 'You want to post a letter?' he told his mother. 'There's a post office. Buy films? Cash a traveller's cheque? All here. You needn't go out *at all.*' Whereupon an American fellow traveller chipped in to say he'd been staying there a fortnight and had not gone out once. 'Well, why not stay at the Hilton in London and turn on the television?' I asked. 'Oh, the Athens one is best. If anyone feels they are going to be ill they should fly immediately to Athens.' Then we got on to religion, the problem of choice, Free Will and determinism, Buddhism. As I know nothing about it I can't tell if he's right in saying that Buddhism is founded on determinism – or rather fatalism which is quite different. You must accept what destiny hands out, and so intervention is always bad, even to stop a father cruelly beating his child. This hypothetical cruel father occupied us enjoyably for some time. Now it was nearly eleven – late for Raymond – and a heavy shower was heard pattering on the roof, so we took a taxi home to bed.

June 6th

We were sitting in the hotel lounge this evening when Jock Jardine appeared – a lean, hatchet-faced, obviously queer man in shorts. Eddie was 'resting' he told us, and it was some time later that he toddled in with his distinguished performing-bear-like gait. They are on their way to Antalya in J. J.'s car, and it soon became disconcertingly clear (over rakis) that it was far from certain we should get even to Miletus and Didyma with them, much less to Bodrum, which is about 300 kilo-metres and we should have to hire a car back. Eddie *seemed* to be delighted to see us, but I very soon realized that it was he who was obstructing Jardine's friendly offer, out of sheer selfishness. He's afraid of being squashed in the car, or of my expecting to have the front seat. He even said to me as we were fencing round the subject of Bodrum, 'There wouldn't be room for your luggage in the boot, my dear.' I think he'd told Jardine not to take us anywhere, but as we had practically accepted his lift to Miletus and Didyma it was almost impossible for him to refuse.

At dinner Eddie consolidated the outline of his grotesque selfishness by com-plaining because Anne and Heywood have come to live in his mother's house in Suffolk, which Heywood has now bought and made comfortable with central heating. 'I can't see why they don't go on living in the Lodge, my dear; it was agreed they shouldn't come into the house until Mamma dies. They say they can't afford it, my dear, but I simply don't believe it, my dear.' The Lodge is a tiny labourer's cottage for which they have to pay quite a large rent.

Jock Jardine has found us a taxi to fetch us from Miletus and take us to Priene. I abandoned Bodrum as soon as I saw Eddie *didn't want us*, but it is pretty disagreeable not being wanted on tomorrow's excursion, though he tried to put a good face on it. I couldn't resist a slight tease about the 'famous Gathorne-Hardy selfishness' and got a crocodile smile in return.

June 7th

After all, we had a wonderful day yesterday seeing such incredible beauties that I feel tantalized by my desire to capture them in the only way open to me – with my camera. I had a colour film in it, but doubt if I've caught the soft glowing greens and blues of the Meander valley – or plain rather, for it is very wide between

Miletus and Priene; or the hundreds of storks' nests, some with baby storks in them (sometimes three or four nests quite covering a small roof); or the pair of storks copulating with clashing bills on top of one of Didyma's tallest columns; or the groups of camels by the roadside; or the little parties of children with brown faces and tawny hair (the little girls look ravishing in their trousers); or the great caravanserais of exotically dressed toilers coming back from the fields (the women with check tablecloths over their heads, and trousers made of beautiful faded and often patterned materials with a preference for magenta, dull green and peacock blue); or the sheer loveliness of the poplars turning silkily in the breeze. The fear that all these magical impressions (now clear in my mind) will instantly begin to fade, torments me.

We set off at nine (of course I saw that Eddie had the front seat) and followed a beautiful winding road across the plain, and along a dusty track to Didyma. Here there is just one 'sight', the colossal temple to Apollo. The few standing columns are fabulously tall and the walls and foundations on a stupendous scale. The flights of steps for the priests to go up are vastly wide as well as high; the walls made of massive stones (white, or blackened as if by fire) so beautifully fitted together that letting one's eyes slide along the surface is an excitement in itself. There were tunnelled passages with the builders' initials engraved on them, and bits of sculpture or ornament pristinely sharp and clear. This must be one of the noblest Greek temples after the Acropolis at Athens. As we were leaving we met the whole Pitt-Rivers party arriving.

June 9th: Samos

Getting here – it is in Greece – proved unexpectedly difficult. Our taxi was slow to come; with what now seems incredible nonchalance we wandered to the tourist office to get our tickets a few minutes before sailing time, only to find that we couldn't pay with Turkish money, but only with Greek and we hadn't nearly enough. Meanwhile time was passing and our taxi-driver was adding to the hysteria by hooting steadily on the horn. We screamed, and were at last handed our tickets; then we charged off to the boat, with bags, with whisky bottle and basket of wet bathing things, and Raymond with his heavy leather case of medicines. At last we panted on board our little vessel – the 'Afroditi' bound for Samos.

There were only three other passengers, all German. The boat was run by three Greeks – the Captain, the engineer and a boy with blue eyes, a beautiful profile and a charming smile, who looked after us solicitously, brought us blankets and cardboard receptacles if he thought anyone looked like vomiting. One of the Germans retired to a cabin and did so. The sea was beastly rough and we rolled and pitched like mad for nearly two hours before reaching calm water in the lee of the island. I felt theoretically 'all right' in so far as that is consistent with loathing every moment. Raymond, on the other hand, was in his element, happily dashing up and down the tiny heaving decks and stairs in a way which terrified the cabin boy. We had been sitting on plastic chairs with our feet braced against the rail, talking intermittently to a doctor from Stuttgart, I with my eyes fixed on Samos, counting the moments until we should get into sheltered waters, when the Captain in voluble Greek ordered us below into a minute stuffy cabin (the upper one was occupied by the sufferers). Not knowing what to expect and fearing the worst, down we went. But soon afterwards the sea grew calmer and we ascended again and watched the sun setting behind the silhouette of Samos. At last the twinkling lights of Pythagorion came into view. All round us the machine-gun rattle of Greek pounded our ears; we clambered into a taxi and drove across the island to the further port of Vathi.

Here I am now sitting on the balcony of my room in the Hotel Xenia, continuous and cataclysmic noise having woken me at five-thirty.

June 10th: Samos

Raymond has taken a new lease of life because he finds himself in Europe, whereas I am homesick for Asia and (ludicrously enough) for a country where I can *just* make myself understood. Not that this island isn't beautiful – it certainly is; but I miss the potently Oriental strangeness. In spite of the lack of water and general ramshackleness of our quite expensive hotel (the grandest in the island) Raymond feels he is in 'civilization' again, and I see he must have been more afraid of Turkish outlandishness than I realized.

Well, here we are on the return voyage to Kuşadasi, and the sea is fairly calm and blue, the sky serene.

June 11th: Back at Kuşadasi

We had been invited to have a drink with a certain Rosie Rodd (briefly met at the port restaurant when the Pitt-Rivers boat was in) and she called for us here in a little car. A tall handsome woman of about fifty, a friend of Mary's and sister-in-law of Nancy Mitford, she is now living in the openest sin I ever saw with an American soldier about half her age. Raymond had been alarmed by her dominating voice on the telephone, but we found her lively, warm, enthusiastic and quite without malice. She drove us along a narrow stony lane and stopped beside a tall Aleppo pine at the door of a tiny love nest bowered in English garden flowers and looking through the olives at the blue sea. It consisted in one not very large room crammed with a confusion of Victoriana, Wedgwood teapots and *trouvailles* from classical sites. Rosie Rodd opened a door revealing a mere cupboard with a double bed in it, and another (pitch dark) which was the bathroom. We sat outside and drank whisky, with a pug puppy gambolling round our legs. Rosie addressed the American lovingly as 'sweetheart' or 'darling' and was anxious to bring him into the conversation. He remained fairly silent however, though he never said anything stupid, and looked at us with dignified pale blue eyes. She has the untouched confidence, overflowing chatter, and scattiness of an ex-deb, but I liked her courage, enterprise and vitality. From among the splash of her talk, we learned that 'Ken' had been stationed in Turkey, 'sold someone a tape recorder illegally' and as a result been tried several times and condemned to ten months in a prison on the Black Sea, and then 'banishment' (she tossed off the word as if it was a normal one) here at Kuşadasi. But he was loved in the village, and adored the Turks in spite of all and spoke good Turkish. She obviously expects to be 'loved in the village' too and implies that she is. They call her 'Lady Rodd' and when her lover had to go away for a while the milk boy asked if he could sleep outside her door to protect her. She's an amateur botanist and bird-watcher and told me about places I long to go to and even suggested that she might drive us to Lake Bafa. I should *love* this, but after the disappointments of Termessus and Bodrum I don't want to hope for it too much.

June 12th

Our voiceless taxi-driver called in the afternoon to take us to Ephesus. It is indeed very splendid, suggesting, more than any other ruin we've visited, a city of vast size (as it must have been with a quarter of a million inhabitants), yet the imagination falters before the effort to fill in the gaps. It's easy to approach these classical sites in a schizophrenic mood, torn between the purely visual – accepting them as beautiful chunks, or fragments of stone garlanded with flowers – and a hesitant attempt to envisage the past. On the whole I stick to the first, partly out of laziness, yet I am interested in their history.

7 p.m. I'm lying on my bed looking out at the fading sky and pink tops of the mountains, hearing the jaunty Frenchified hoots of the taxis and the confused hubbub of conversation rising from the street far below, and thinking that I know now I've lost my heart to Turkey. As much as to Russia? Not quite. But it has lived up to the impression I glimpsed when Ralph and I went to Troy thirty years ago.

June 14th

Arrived in Athens, Raymond set aside his Asian angst and became spirited and lively. We found letters and messages at our hotel, and the unexpected and lovely surprise that Janetta was arriving tonight to meet Paddy and Joan, and all would be staying at the Olympic Palace too. I had left a note in Janetta's pigeon-hole and until she opened it she had no idea we were to be in Athens. We went up to her room and sat having the most *human* conversation for weeks.

It was arranged for us all to dine with Paddy and Joan, and Peter Mayne, a novelist. Raymond was made desperate by the familiar, inevitable delays. Out of his 'delightful rut' and not in control of times and arrangements he could no longer keep up his manners, and hardly talked to Janetta at all at dinner. Paddy took us to a garden restaurant some way from the heart of the town and the conversation was lively and much concerned with words. 'Ribcage' and 'foolish' were tossed about by Paddy and Peter Mayne – an odd, not uninteresting man much given to 'patting and holding'. I asked him about the sex life of the Turks. 'Do you really want me to tell you? Well, they're extremely *tender* and affectionate. Also – and I should know – they've got the smallest cocks in the world.' I said to Paddy that I didn't feel I could believe a word Herodotus said after reading that the Ethiopians had black semen. He almost choked, turned pink and then went off like a rocket: 'Black semen – yes – black semen. I'd forgotten about that. Rather like those advertisements of STEPHEN'S BLUE BLACK INK – do you remember? – they used to be in railway stations. A *great black splodge*.' (Nudge, nudge.) 'Or perhaps it would be just a black dribble.' And went on for ages – ridiculous, fantastic, and endearing. I felt pleasurably intoxicated by the company, talk and animation. A discussion began as to whether we should all go and watch a rehearsal by Nureyev and Margot Fonteyn (who is a friend of Joan's) who are performing in Athens. But it was obviously long over. Or 'go on somewhere', and if so, where. I was touched by Paddy's eager, obstreperous devotedness, leaving all decisions to Joan, only wanting her to decide and looking at her expectantly like a curly wet dog that has just fished a stick out of a lake and bounces about as if to say, 'Only tell me, mistress, where to put it and I'll do it at once with joy.'

June 15th: West Halkin Street

The solitude of my flat, my life, struck me like a slap in the face. No flowers, no papers, no Mrs Ringe, nor has she come this morning. My post provided nothing consoling. I was glad to hear Mary's friendly voice from Stokke, and Bunny saying he would bring my Mini up today. The empty space of my flat in which I was floundering drove me to pick up Freya Stark's *Ionia* (which had seemed unreadable before I went to Turkey) and go back over my travel-tracks. The photographs of some of the ruined cities had been taken before archaeologists had reared a column or two on end, so that there was merely a jumble of grooved cheese-like segments. Ephesus was such a one, I think. And what a difference those few up-ended columns made, merely by suggesting the portentousness of the whole. All the difference so important to human sanity between jargon and sense. A jumbled ruin is like a visit to a lunatic asylum. Exactly what sets a site alive depends on a lot of variables though – the broad Arcadian avenue with its massive paving slabs leading down to the silted-up harbour made sense for me, and so did reading in the guidebook that (unlike most ancient streets) it had lighting. I know there's a lot I want to think about, which (had Raymond been someone else) we should have talked about in Turkey.

June 17th

Two days have taken a little of the ache out of the bruise of my return and I've seen several friends – Bunny, Julia and Mary. Bunny brought the news that Henrietta and Sophie were back and I went to see them yesterday. I was let in to the pandemonious, sluttish, charming flat by Nerissa and little Sophie, and Henrietta ran up the stairs soon afterwards looking brown and excited in a pink frilly blouse and short evzone's skirt. My mingled pleasure and anxiety for them both, the desire to ask questions and yet not probe too much, and to attend to both of them at once, led to a confused state of mind that got me (I fear) nowhere. Sophie is taller, very *rubia* from the Spanish sun, pale, with a guarded anxious expression in her dark eyes – all right though I think. Henrietta looked tremendously blooming. Why then do I worry so about her? I expect I shall continue to do so unless or until she marries some delightful person who will be kind to Sophie. Bunny came yesterday with my car, rosy and beaming, and talked to me exclusively about Wales and the fish he'd caught (or not caught) there last weekend. I could hardly believe he wouldn't ask *one* question about Turkey but he didn't, and I volunteered nothing, waiting to see if he would. He still didn't. Perhaps no one is really interested, but most ask out of politeness.

June 24th

Yesterday Duncan came to see me to discuss the agitation he felt over what Holroyd has said about him in his life of Lytton. He left it for me to read, and I devoted last night to it – after dashing round to see Janetta, just back from Greece.

June 30th

Angelica wholeheartedly supported Duncan, saying, with an adamant, disapproving expression on her face, that one couldn't publish such things about living people. I pressed her a little further – was she in favour of suppressing all

Lytton's feelings about Duncan and indeed about the other people in the book, like Roger Senhouse? Had she read the preface starting with James's announcement that Lytton was a homosexual? Did she think one could possibly write a life of him without revealing that fact? But I suggested rather tentatively that the parts about Duncan could be cut, removing anything he found objectionable or too physical, or about his own feelings. It didn't seem to have occurred to her that it was hard on Holroyd that everyone had handed him all the letters and material, and after he has toiled at it for years on end, they scream and say, 'He can't publish THAT!' What surprised me about Angelica's response was that instead of saying 'Duncan finds it too painful,' which would be hard to answer, her first remark was, 'Duncan has a lot of conventional friends who'll be horribly shocked.'

I can't sympathize with pandering to conventions – but the subject is complicated and difficult. I don't see any sense in biographies that suppress or distort the facts, and I should have thought the days of Lytton and Duncan's love were· long enough past to be harmless. Also this attitude of Angelica's reminded me of the absurd pretence of Charleston that Angelica was Clive's daughter – kept up long after everyone knew about it, just as of course practically everyone knows Duncan is predominantly homosexual. There was always that foot fumblingly advanced by Bloomsbury towards the conventional or aristocratic enclave, their Victorian childhoods perhaps coming to the surface in a way totally inconsistent with their defiance of *idées reçues* – God, patriotism, and monogamy. As I'm wholeheartedly in sympathy with their setting up their own standards, I hate their not having the courage to uphold them publicly. To me anyway it's an important discrepancy. Perhaps this very thing makes me disagreeably aggressive sometimes, as when Jack Donaldson said at lunch that he 'was completely behind the American action in Vietnam' and I couldn't let it pass without expressing my strong disagreement, and saying that it seemed to me the most squalid war there'd ever been. But even though I'm ashamed of getting overexcited and losing my calm, I think one must stand up for what one believes. This, along with the futility of war, is perhaps the central belief in my credo. I admire people who stand up for homosexuals being free to carry on their love-affairs, and it seems to me it's now very old-fashioned and ostrich-like to pretend that no one knows that they do, and always have done so.

July 14th

The Holroyd business has been a continuous obsession. He came to bring me back some photographs one evening and I felt uneasy at the thought of the chopper ready to fall on his head, so when he mentioned Duncan I thought I'd better say, 'I did gather he was rather agitated.' Holroyd was obviously surprised, hadn't thought he'd mind, but was expecting possible trouble from Roger Senhouse. And will get it it seems, for, from what Raymond and Angus Davidson have told me, Roger too is upset. His affair with Lytton has been gone into in great detail by Holroyd, including their complicated life of sexual fantasy. Holroyd said to me that he was prepared to refer to Roger anonymously, and perhaps this would have been better. I lay awake till two one night thinking about it – I'm enormously interested in the different reactions, particularly among the homosexuals. Having known and been friends with so many for so long, I'm more than faintly surprised at their secretiveness just when their position seems about to be legally ratified.

For in conversation they are usually confident and jolly about their 'persuasions'. Yet they evidently cherish the belief that half their acquaintances don't know about them, and I've often thought they enjoyed play-acting at being 'normal'. Yet it's hardly possible to remain a bachelor these days and pass off as such. Angus was very old-maidish and prissy. '*I* certainly shouldn't like anyone to read some of Duncan's letters to me,' he said with his eyebrows going up into his hair.

James, having talked so hysterically about the book on the telephone ('Had I seen the bit about Ralph and me?' he asked among other things. And what am I supposed to mind?), has now calmed down to a state of reasonable fatalism. I spent a night at Lord's Wood with him and Alix and was made to read some of Holroyd's literary criticisms of Lytton's books, which I found pretty unreadable. James now says no one will read the book so it doesn't matter. He seemed to be in complete agreement with me about anti-Bowdler principles, and this was a relief to me for I feel quite strongly about them; but he thought the people in question (Duncan or Roger) must have the last word. The person who emerges most strangely from all this is Bunny, who has violently entered into the lists in favour of wholesale suppression. He and I had a fairly heated conversation on the telephone about it. I said of course that no one wanted Duncan to suffer a moment's pain on account of the book – but from there we got to discussing what should be the basis for suppression. 'Well, a lot of people would be very shocked,' said Bunny. 'For instance, you should just have seen the people Angelica and I lunched with on Sunday! They would have been horrified.' F.: 'What sort of people were they?' B.: 'Colonels and conventional old ladies'. F.: 'I really don't think one should set one's standards by those of Colonels and old ladies! And I'm particularly surprised because if I may say so, in your autobiographical books you haven't been at all reserved.' B.: 'No. I know; but I've made it a rule not to make revelations about people who are still alive, or have relatives alive who would mind, like Lydia about Maynard.'

Since then I've wished I'd told him how many people have said to me that they were appalled at his publishing Ray's anguished, intensely private and personal letters when she was dying of cancer, and (what's more) that, though I was amazed at his wanting to do so and found them very painful reading, I defended him *on principle*. Alix agreed with me that this was the most disgraceful revelation she'd ever read in any book, and I suppose that I and the rest of my family might be thought to mind as much as Lydia about Maynard. Knowing myself as unable to keep anything to myself for long, I expect I shall come out with this to Bunny sooner or later. He had gone down to Lord's Wood two days before I did and amazed Alix by his red-faced truculence, and talk about libel actions.

August 6th

I dined a few nights ago with Eardley, Jim Lees-Milne, Mattei and his French friend Roger on the top of the Post Office Tower. It was the most exciting thing I've done for ages. Luckily it was a brilliant evening, pure clean skies, washed of all but a few dramatic clouds. Before ascending we looked up at the great glistening object in awe. I've always admired it, but said to myself, 'I'll never go up *that* thing,' and I half-expected to feel afraid, and almost queasy should it sway slightly in the wind. But nothing of the sort. Favoured beings with our dinner tickets, we jumped the long queue waiting to go up for a four-shillings look at the view, and were swept swiftly up thirty and more floors and decanted at the top. The restaurant is just beneath the windblown observation terrace and gets just as good a view; it revolves slowly, sometimes one gets the feeling that it has stopped, then it seems to go quite fast. A waiter warned me away from standing on a place where one of my feet was being carried in the opposite direction from the other. We looked all the time at London spread beneath – St Paul's and Big Ben were tiny pimples, Tower Bridge a little toy with the river winding away beyond, Regent's Park a huge domain of noble trees and velvet lawns with long slanting evening shadows. There was no sense of vertigo even I think for Jim who had dreaded it. As the daylight faded, twinkling lights of all colours came out and I felt I *adored* London.

August 10th

I was well-prepared for Sonia: calm, with the soft pedal down and my tempo deliberately slowed. And my word, a good job too! She's really a monster. She arrived looking blooming and tidy and braced, noisy but fairly level. I was in a mood of cool observation by this time, my 'wool' absolutely glued to my head, and so it was with surprise but almost no emotion that I noted that she launched at once on an attack on Janetta's way of life – her passion for Spain, the pointless life she led there, the futility of her friends (Jaime and the Davises), the gloom of La Cónsula, the beastliness of Spanish food, even the site of her new house was all wrong and was sure to be eventually ruined. Then over dinner the subject of Julia began, and now I was suddenly being addressed as if I were a public meeting, in a loud continuous roar, with the gaps filled with prolonged fortissimo 'ERs' so that I shouldn't get a word in edgeways. She kept repeating, 'Well now, let's see. ER. We must get this straight ... ER. We agree something must be done about getting Julia out of Percy Street?' I had of course quite a lot to say on the subject but I really had no desire to impart it to her, so my problem was easy. I did, I think, attempt to say that I didn't consider Lawrence had really behaved badly although he had caused Julia such pain. ('Oh, I've no patience with Lawrence. Anyway, I don't know him. So that's that.') Nor was it the least use saying that I firmly believe that it is the greatest mistake to deal with these painful and delicate human imbroglios in terms of praise and blame; one should rather look at them as impersonal cataclysms. Or that with Julia of all people it's a lifelong delusion that some material change will make her happy ('If I had a servant for four hours a day' or 'If I could do up my flat'). They are mere assuagements and alleviations. No need to set them aside on that account, but it's useless to expect too much of them. Or that I didn't hold with relentless interference in other people's lives. I literally never got a sentence finished before she began shouting at the full pitch of her lungs. I began to suggest that I might talk to Craig, since Julia was consulting him. 'Oh, CRAIG's absolutely useless. He was so *cruel* over my divorce. He had no conception how painful it was.' When I said I thought he was too gentlemanly for a divorce lawyer she said, 'Gentleman my foot! He's no gentleman. Julia likes him because he thinks he's an intellectual.' Craig! The most modest and unassuming of men. And so it went on. I've never been so browbeaten, bossed and bullyragged in my life. I suppose Lady Reading marshalling her assistants for some local government campaign *might* go on so – but an acquaintance whom I'd asked to dinner! I can only think she hadn't a clue about what I feel about her, that I really despise her pretentiousness, and now had added to my picture of her a full awareness of her crude, raw, arrogant, insensitive bossyness. I was pretty well given instructions to ask James for money (which I eeled out of), go and see Christopher (which I declined), and talk to Lawrence, which I said I was prepared to do, and so I've long been. But I refuse to carry out her 'instructions' and *tell* Lawrence that he has to cough up £750 a year for Julia at least. I said I was anxious to contribute financially myself, but I'm blessed if I'll consent to be on Sonia's committee.

I then plied her with more drink and deliberately switched the conversation. When I said something or other seemed rather illogical she burst out about this 'awful Bloomsbury logic'. There were several aggressive attacks on Bloomsbury, and she returned to 'her best friend Janetta' to tell me that she had 'deeply offended Mary MacCarthy[1] by making a pass at her husband' and that she 'ought to have her head examined'. I've heard Janetta's account of this episode, which is anyway ancient history to be so treasured and brought out now.

It was really far worse than I'd expected, but *so* awful as to be almost funny. I shall never have any more to do with Sonia than I can possibly help. And I shall conduct my relations with Julia, who has been my friend since she was eight, according to my lights, not Sonia's.

August 12th

I had Sophie to myself yesterday for longer than I have for some time. Angelica brought her to Henrietta's flat, from there she came with me to lunch at Magouche's and thence back here till evening. The result has been something like falling in love. She has tugged so violently at my heart-strings that when I sat alone last night thinking about her I was aware with amazement that the tears were running down my cheeks. She is a touchingly responsive little creature and her delight in a small suitcase I gave her full of tiny wrapped objects gave me delight also. She wouldn't let go of it all day and when I said it was her 'suitcase' to take in the train she wanted to go in the train at once. Such an effusion of love for her arose in me that I couldn't resist giving her an enormous hug and saying, 'I *love* you, Sophie' and she looked at me with a little smiling face which I thought showed she didn't dislike the idea. Indeed, when I left her at Angelica's house there was an almost embarrassing moment of not wanting to go in. 'No. I don't *want*.' And even inside the house she raised her arms and face to me imploringly. What made me cry? Her vulnerability, my longing to make her happy, and my impotence. To love someone in a protective way is agonizing.

September 6th: Ireland

Oh, the magic, how quickly it takes effect. Arrived at Cork, I crossed the great grey river and went into a pub for a drink. An orange-haired barwoman was cracking jokes with a talkative regular, who at once included me in the conversation. It was at this moment I knew I was glad I'd come. Then the long bus ride, over two hours, wrapped in a kindly lethargic co-consciousness presided over by the conductor, with schoolchildren getting in and out and sitting touchingly grasping their tickets with satchels strapped to their backs, smelly schoolboys talking Gaelic. Outside green, green, green under a low canopy of soft grey clouds, often raining, sometimes grey like a grey pearl. Surprised again by the brilliant colour-sense of the Irish who are adding new colours to the old blood-red, egg, and darkish green of their

[1] The American writer.

houses – forget-me-not and strawberry ice, and striking combinations that made me think of Leningrad. Bantry in the rain and Robert, who drove me in his little battered car about five miles towards Glengariff and down a long tree-lined drive to the 'Irish Tudor' house they've rented.

September 10th: King's Land[1]

Perfect, ripe summer weather and the delightful company of Julian and Magouche. But I must return to Ireland. It was only when I was describing my stay to Julian and Magouche last night that I fully realized how I loved that green country. The bromidic soothingness of the climate; its variety. Stormy and wet when I arrived, the wind dropped, all nature stood still and the sea in the inlets turned to glass. From the terrace of the grey stone house the lawn sloped down through huge clumps of hydrangea, red-hot pokers and montbretia to the rocky shore. Indoors there were enormously long baths full of brown water, the smell of peat fires in the evening and an 1890 decor – heads of animals shot in Africa, an elephant's foot mounted as a stool, assegais and old faded military groups on the walls. The General to whom it belonged, now eighty-eight but elegant, debonair and completely on the spot, lived next door, in sin or ex-sin with his handsome sister-in-law. A charming bespectacled Sheilah Murphy came to help most days. There was even supposed to be a cook but the very first day she went with Cynthia to Bantry to 'show her the shops', she borrowed a pound, bought half a bottle of Paddy and got completely plastered. She then started on the Kees' stout and took to the floor of the kitchen lavatory where she spent the whole afternoon redfaced and happy except for cooking two disgusting meals, and went home taking all the coffee, most of the tomatoes and a good many other things bought that morning. It was too like Somerville and Ross to produce anything but hilarity, and next day Cynthia sacked her.

I shan't forget Robert's kindness to the children and me, his fascinating talk about Irish history, philosophy and ideas.

September 14th: Churriana, Spain

There was Gerald at Málaga airport, and off we went to Churriana. An almost painful familiarity of sights and smells, but a huge new block of flats has reared itself at the corner of the Coín road. The substitute for Teresita, Little Mari, ran forward and kissed me on both cheeks. Antonio,[2] slightly more toothless, shook me by the hand and we sat down in wicker chairs in the patio by the familiar sound of the trickling fountain. Gamel is terribly bent from the waist upwards and feels her way along on tottering legs. Gerald says, 'Gamel's very well, really.' I don't think she is. But their life is calm; there is only one resident cat and the house smells less than it did, and looks lovely.

September 16th: The Beach House, Marbella[3]

The night I spent with the Brenans a colossal thunderstorm exploded, rain streamed into the patio and grand pianos fell out of the sky. Everyone is delighted; it was

[1] Formerly the home of Hilaire Belloc, Julian's grandfather, in Sussex.
[2] The gardener.
[3] A small house rented by Jaime during the bathing season.

badly needed and has laid the dust, but left a grey morning swathed in damp veils. Gerald didn't speak of his novel and though I gave him a letter from Julian about it, no word was said. When we walked up the hillside (without Gamel, 'she walks so slowly'), he told me about his visit from a girl who arrived out of the blue and went to bed with him. 'She was madly exciting. I've never known such a girl. The trouble is that as one gets older an orgasm is a very mild affair. When one was young it was like reading *Paradise Lost* for the first time, now it's as dry as *Paradise Regained*.'

Soon after six o'clock Janetta arrived having just seen someone off at the airport. Gerald had told me she was looking marvellously well and young, but the golden brown of her sunburnt skin doesn't conceal the fact that she's too thin and strained, and when I asked her how she was she said, 'Desperate'. (These two days have been for me packed full with impressions, but they lie jumbled like drawers of ransacked underclothes and I don't know when I shall be able to sort them out.)

Not till yesterday therefore did I begin to take stock of this lotus-land in which so many questions arise and there is never 'time', concentration or application to answer them. There's something frighteningly dreamlike about being surrounded by what Julia calls the playboy life. I don't mean Janetta and Jaime of course. Jaime goes off with his briefcase to work every morning on his new hotel La Fonda, and I've not seen Janetta so domestic for years. They both seem happy. Yet the surrounding waters that wash around them are full of lost souls – people who under a smiling guise live under the sway of the death instinct – who kill time, let their minds rot, chatter, have another drink and wait for something to happen.

September 18th

Mark Culme-Seymour has just driven up and asked if he could have 'one quick drink to give him courage before going off to the Windsors to lunch'. Otherwise the morning has begun much like others. It is one o'clock and we have breakfasted and Jaime has driven off in his car. Lunch will be somewhere about four, dinner between eleven and twelve; sleeping hours from two or three until eleven or twelve. I have tried to adjust to these times but it's a physical effort, such as crossing the Atlantic causes (so I imagine) and I can only begin to do it by pinning myself down to sleeping on late which I dislike. Last night I went to bed to the loud thumping of Beatles on the gramophone and voices next door, feeling, like Janetta, 'desperate'.

Two days ago, one golden evening, when the crested mountain was softened to velvet by the fading light, Janetta, Rose and I drove up the valley to the land she has bought at Tramores. We forded a river and at the last turn of the track where her property began a horseman was drawn up in a dramatic attitude. Her land is a rich and fertile triangle of orange trees, olives, persimmons, grapes, bananas, in a deep basin of mountains whose edges cut cleanly against the pale evening sky. It is a beautiful place, a very peaceful and secluded one; the ruined Moorish tower is very grand and beside it stands the original farmhouse, now empty and waiting to be rebuilt for Janetta. Beneath, in a sort of cleft, is the new little house where her tenant farmer Miguel, his wife and three children live. They hurried out to meet her, and out also came a young man who is making baskets from palmettos – they were lying out drying on the threshing-floor. An old crone, younger than me no doubt but bent over more sharply even than Gamel, looked at me out of bright brown eyes, snatched my hand and kissed it. Some turkeys were gobbling in a shed and almost at once Maria, Miguel's wife, with little Salvador her youngest child in her arms, began to gobble too, partly with hospitable invitations to visit her *casita*, partly with complaints of stopped drains and things that didn't work, all in thick Andaluz. I couldn't understand half of it and was amazed by Janetta's courage in embarking on this new adventure and taking the responsibility for so many souls.

October 3rd: West Halkin Street

London life closes around me and drags me along with it. My mind is beset with grumbling boring questions, consonant with the pelting, pouring rain that never stops.

I've been remembering my extraordinary dinner party (along with the Hendersons and Anthony and Tanya Hobson) at the house of a very rich young Spanish banker and his wife out in the country a good many miles from Madrid. It was like a scene in a Russian novel. We arrived through uninhabited hills dotted with holm oaks, up a rough track and were suddenly confronted by a huge luxurious house. About four men-servants ran to open our car doors; every sort of drink and delicacy was spread to receive us; our young pregnant hostess was expensively dressed and completely assured, the soft music of Vivaldi and Mozart was swooning from an inner room. Mary told me afterwards I'd 'done extremely well' with our young host Jaime at dinner. He certainly wasn't easy to talk to, though his English was perfect with a slight north country accent, for I felt he wasn't really interested in anything but money – what an astonishingly all-absorbing topic that can be! We talked though somehow or other, and then I suddenly felt my blood simmering at the obsequiousness with which one of his servants was handing him cigars, cutters and lighters on a tray, and the fact that he took them with a gesture implying that the man did not belong to the same order of human being as he did at all. I spoke of it to Nicko and Mary afterwards and they said, 'Oh, all rich Spaniards are like that. They're hundreds of years behind the times. They never thank servants for anything, like we do. Jaime and Pirou are exceptionally enlightened.'

October 4th

At first on returning from abroad there is solitude and silence all round, a vacuum in which one has no place. Now all sorts of mosquitoes buzz in my ears. I awoke at six this morning and finished reading, for a report to Gollancz, an extraordinarily gloomy but powerful French novel which has affected me a good deal as *Cañas y Barro*[1] did long ago. Julia came to dinner, and I can't say I feel easier in my mind about her. She had 'touched bottom' soon after I went to Spain, couldn't go to the London Library, couldn't eat, and lay on her bed feeling frightfully ill. She realized it was the purple hearts (now up to four or five a day) and by sheer will-power she has reduced them now to one or even none. 'The thing is, I was really frightened.' Her present *modus vivendi* is the wildly impractical one of drawing on her small capital to employ a typist to whom she dictates her current work. 'I can't write any more. I must get it straightened out. As I lay on my bed I felt this was the one thing I must do, the one thing of importance, before I die.' She admitted the task

---

[1] By Blasco Ibañez.

would be endless, for it would only be a first draft and all to do again. So at present she is spending £1,200 a year out of an income that is much less, *only* on getting this story finished – and how good is it? Of course that's not the way to think of it. It's her lifeline at the moment. Oh, the struggle of it all! I can't get over the fact that such misery can be produced by love alone if it assumes unlucky combinations. No hate at all, no 'desire to cause pain' is necessary.

October 6th

Henrietta and Sophie have come to lunch with me and Henrietta has gone out to shop for a grand ball tonight, while Sophie sleeps contentedly in my bed – that is, she went off to rest most happily.

Last night I dined with Raymond to meet Lord and Lady Snow (Pamela Hansford-Johnson). It was a dull evening. Once people have become public figures they seem to be pretty well doomed. All they want to do on social occasions is to show off, and secure to themselves admiration, which is hardly necessary in view of their own tremendous opinion of themselves. Lady Snow is a solid, noisy, avid little woman, her plump form balanced on spindle heels. She held the floor continuously and confidently, far from stupidly but expressing herself tritely in such phrases as 'and the lot'. Another give-away expression is, when speaking of a third person, not 'so and-so is nice, clever or charming,' but 'I SIMPLY adore', or 'am terribly fond of so-and-so', subtly turning the limelight once again on the desired spot. She said she had been a correspondent in the Moors case[1], as a result of which she had come round to the view that such books as de Sade's should not be available to the young, and was writing a book to this effect. There would be 'terrible screams from intellectual quarters about free speech and so on'. 'It's not that I mind sex,' she said rather oddly, 'but I can't stand sex combined with cruelty and violence.' I said I was against cruelty and violence as such, regardless of what it was combined with, but she had no interest in anything an unknown elderly female had to say, and I only bothered to speak to either Snow throughout the evening 'to keep my end up' and because I knew Raymond wouldn't like it if I didn't. I can do it after a fashion, but I consider such contacts completely pointless. One is a mere claque, and I soon got tired of compulsive clapping. Lord Snow does look very like a snowman and as he drank steadily all through the evening, helping himself liberally to slugs of Raymond's whisky after dinner, he began to dissolve slowly in its golden rays. His wife kept a sharp eye on him and I drove them home, but he was virtually asleep and I expected his large head to subside any moment on my shoulder.

What incredible conceit it is for such people to think they are conferring a favour – as I felt they did – on Raymond by coming to dinner and drinking half a bottle or more of his whisky, and boasting. Raymond rang me up this morning to apologize.

October 8th

A very different evening last night, with James and Alix in their hotel next to the BBC. It is brand new, with an express lift that swirls you upwards to a restaurant providing tasteless synthetic food and drink. I think they are being treated to their

[1] Child-murders by Myra Hindley and her boyfriend.

stay as part of the celebrations of the completion of James's translation of Freud's *Complete Works*, which ends with a banquet tonight to which I am going in my capacity as indexer. I found them in the cocktail lounge – Alix looked splendidly distinguished, so did James but also rather disquietingly aged, pink and tottery. They were touchingly enjoying their splendour. We discussed what 'cocktails' we should have. It's a long time since anyone has offered me such a thing, and we ended with three 'bronxes' made of orange juice very dimly laced with something. James was naturally agitated at the thought of the dinner and the speech he must make at it, yet enjoying the idea of being the hero of the evening. During dinner there was some talk of Holroyd's book. Not a good word for it. Holroyd told Raymond that James could not bear the faintest criticism of Lytton to be made. James has written an immense letter of complaints to Holroyd which he says he took surprisingly mildly. Then Alix and I got going on the Labour Party. I see that, as with James in the case of Lytton or Freud, she has her heroes who can do no wrong and must not be criticized. She admitted she was getting persecution mania over the attacks on Mr Wilson and his policy. I wish I'd asked her if she didn't think criticism should always be allowed of any party. The trouble is she reads only the left-wing *Sun* which is far more critical than *The Times*. She wouldn't agree that even the Conservative press was quite enthusiastic about Mr Wilson when he first came to power. (However, this morning a large red self-satisfied man came into the greengrocer's where I was buying a cabbage and said in answer to the question, 'What would you like, Sir?' 'There's only one thing I want – for Mr Wilson to drop dead tomorrow.') I said I deplored unemployment being an even temporary aim of the Labour Government and also their setting more stress on things than services. Alix said this was the only means to an end which was in itself good and right. We also talked of crime and whether Lady Snow's notion of suppressing the pornography of sadism had any sense in it. I was fascinated to note that Alix so strongly holds the Freudian belief that human beings have a given content of aggressive violence, and that if you stop up one exit you will only find another being used, that she clearly didn't feel anything could alter the amount of violent crime and was indeed amazed to hear that it had increased threefold.

October 12th

Woken at about one o'clock last night by a cramp-like pain in my chest. I looked for a while into an abyss of fear, and then into a bleak stony avenue of 'curtailed activities', 'going gently', having to give up my precious nippyness, and for a moment sympathized with Munia Postan for 'wanting to die on a mountain'. For of course, in any case, activities must be dropped as one ages. Poor Ralph, during those long years of restriction, of finding people walked too fast for him, and of wanting but not being allowed to carry suitcases! Did I ever show him enough sympathy and consideration? Or did my own fearful anxiety on his behalf make me nag him too much? Well, no use thinking along these lines.

Detachment is the most difficult of all positions to take up. When love-affairs and marriages explode, other people quickly line up as if for prisoner's base, and wave the flags of those they've decided to champion. How or why should one blame either party, is my commonest reaction. Yet I see my attempts at remaining uncommitted sometimes strike a chill on those partially inclined. Today I went to have a cardiogram and Dr Hensman has just rung up to say that it showed certain warning symptoms – a sign that I must be careful. I hear this at present with apathetic resignation. 'I must take things very quietly for the next fortnight' and will 'for the rest of my life have an excuse for not doing anything I don't want to do'. Heigh ho. I have the feeling that one can get used to *anything*.

October 15th: Stokke

Mary drove me down here yesterday. We talked all the way. On arrival at Stokke we found Mary's half-crazed mother Lady Rosslyn, and a pile of letters for Mary including a long one from Charlie.

Lady R.: (greeting me) I *am* so sorry about your husband.
F.: It's me that's supposed to be ill. I'm afraid my husband has been dead for some years. You do recognize me? Frances Partridge?
Lady R.: Oh yes, of course. How stupid of me. How lovely for him! I shouldn't say that but you know it's so awful being old, one's in everybody's way. No one wants one.

She is in her odd way rather delightful, quite a character, fumbles for her thoughts and words, and comes out with something at an odd and original angle from what she wanted to say. But she *cannot* stop talking for a single minute. Even when Mary was busy telephoning an order for animal food her mother kept going up to her, with a sort of jealousy, waving a clock at her and asking questions. It is farcical but also tragic. We were alone for quite a long time and I couldn't read – even the newspaper, or even do a crossword, she kept breaking in on me with a slow quiet ceaseless stream of prattle, in which an occasional wrong name would cause me to rack my brains furiously.

Last night Julia arrived and was brilliant with Mary's mother. 'I remember so well your telling me about welcoming some large wild animal – a tiger or a lion perhaps? – on some rain-swept quay or other,' she began. 'I don't know where it was.' Lady Rosslyn looked totally blank and incredulous but Mary coming in said, 'Oh yes, it was a leopard, and in Caracas.' She whispered to Julia and me that her mother had been drunk as a lord at the time and gone on caressing the leopard though it clawed her dreadfully. She was once an alcoholic, then became a fervent Catholic (or perhaps always was) and was cured. She has just recently at eighty or more started tippling again, and who shall blame her? She's to go into a new convent next week and is as afraid as if she had to embark on a new school. Poor old thing. And she talks of having been in 'the mental home' with a look of pale distress. Indeed, she wrings my heart and I like her; but my God, she's exhausting.

November 2nd

Janetta is back. The sun has come out. I feel a renewal of vigour. She came to have a bacon-and-egg supper with me on her first evening in England and we had a good long talk about very many things, but 'there are a lot more' she says. I think she'll stay about a month, pacify her children and dependants, convince them they're 'all right' and then be off again. I did say what I could in praise of the splendid way Julian has held the fort of Montpelier Square during her absence, cooked fish pies and worn an apron.

November 6th

I try to savour what is enjoyable about a weekend in London: waking to silence more profound than that of a Sunday morning in the country, there being no one for me to bother about just as there is no one to bother about me, hence indulgence in selfishness. Out of my window a pale blue uncertain sky, the Sunday papers all over my bed. Yesterday I lunched at Montpelier Square and go again I think today. Janetta was looking tired, and when after lunch Julian and Andrew Murray-Thripland arrived flushed with wine and talk, her face suddenly became pink and crumpled and she retired to sleep on her bed. Nothing is more exhausting than being endlessly at the mercy of people squatting like toads, drinking and talking. I felt she had a lot on her mind, and she told me briefly that she 'had wanted to get back to Spain by the end of the month, but was wondering whether she could leave them all'. Her present note is very different from her arrival one (of universal 'all-rightness'). Nicky and Georgie having vanished as well, I felt bound to stay and talk to Julian and Andrew – but not only that, I enjoyed it. We talked of the desire for power in human beings, especially as it appeared in 'making a pile'. They were both apparently dazzled by it, to me it is an entirely worthless passion. Julian repeated that it was anyhow 'interesting'. 'Only clinically, as case history', I said. Does one say what one really thinks in these arguments? Andrew is thoughtful but rather inarticulate. I think Julian has fallen for him, because the whole shape of his face has altered. We talked and talked till four-thirty, when we all three plus Georgie got into Andrew's sports car and shot off through the streets. His lack of knowledge of where he was going, and Julian's protests and attempts to hush me when I said the best way to Halkin Street from Montpelier was not via Hyde Park Corner, and then our running out of petrol in Wilton Crescent, built up the composition of youthful wildness and afternoon abandon in whose bowl I was a pretty odd goldfish. (Later) Back from another excursion to Montpelier Square. What is to be done about the erosion and dissipation of Janetta's vital spark by so many people, of whom I'm one? Arrived to find the girls helping handsomely in the kitchen with lunch preparations, and a large crowd in the back room. Some went off, but we were at once refuelled by the arrival of Harriet [Behrens] and her two children. Human currents between these individuals were all friendly and appreciative and there is, I suppose, a warming effect of sheer company, like a hot bath, or a brisk walk, though I felt more enlivened by a prisoner's tramp round Belgrave Square gardens, where I was the only person but a sort of physical *bien-être* was engendered by the exercise, the suddenly gentler air on my face.

A desire for privacy came over me, and here in my flat, silent except for the ticking clock, I have it.

November 10th

Yesterday was the sort of day I enjoy. Julian came to lunch and we had rich conversation for several hours, finally going into the important question of Love. He says he has been afraid of falling in love with Andrew and is putting on the brakes hard. He himself has nothing but painful scars from his one experience of love; nor was being loved by someone whom he didn't love an experience he's eager to repeat. So poor dear fellow, he tries to keep the whole emotion at bay. Rather to my own surprise I began defending love as an irradiator of the whole of life, and also saying that he hadn't yet known mutual love which was the most marvellous thing in the world, and mustn't try to escape it. And also, something that I've always felt about Julian, that he has so many qualifications for a long-term relationship that it would be sad if he refused to let himself have one. Asked him about his feeling for girls, as he seems to like them so much; he said he did, but not in the least sexually, and laid claim to low-powered sexuality. Earlier, ranging hither and thither, we had laughed over Raymond and Desmond's anxiety for him to 'wear frills' at Michael Pitt-Rivers' dinner party tomorrow.

The saddest news I've had lately is that poor little Charlotte[1] is seriously ill with some as yet undiagnosed blood trouble in Bart's hospital.

November 19th

On the foot of my bed lies a packet of close-typed stodge – a French book about Charlemagne which is my latest job to translate. Why am I doing it? I don't need the money. I should like to know something of the period – but I suppose the real reason is I want to 'keep going' as a translator.

Julia came last night in such a broken, tremulous state that it was a fearful strain being with her. Things get no better for her, and I do fear they may get worse. When I asked her if she would almost rather not see Lawrence if she had other engagements she said, 'Yes'.

Janetta asked her to lunch the other day and told me how charming she had been to her children. When I asked Julia about them, she hadn't a good word for them. The Campbells have asked her for Christmas, at which I was relieved. But there's no gratitude really, it's just 'I couldn't think how to get out of it.' It's all part of her turning her face to the wall. I feel very much shaken by her. She hardly seemed 'there' much of the time last night, but was saying, 'No!', 'Really?' or 'Is that so?' in total unawareness of what I – or Eardley, who came for a drink – had said. It is torture being with her, poor creature, at the moment.

November 21st

Winter is here, and in an attempt not to fug and fossilize, especially now I'm on a steady 'job' again, I tend to walk about a mile round Belgrave Square gardens in the afternoon. As usual today not a soul was there (sometimes there's a dear little talkative boy) except the grouchy old gardener moving like a Niebelung through the blue fog of his bonfire of leaves. The trees are nearly bare; I looked up and saw a single motionless grey pigeon perched high aloft. The pale sun lit the top storeys of the stuccoed embassies and flashed brilliant signals from the attic windows. I barely got warm in my brisk encirclement, but felt a glow of blood in my limbs and cheeks.

This morning I drove back from the Cecils at Oxford with Clare Sheppard. Sydney[2] was also staying at the Cecils' for one ghostly night, spreading an effluvium of endearing melancholy. Rachel gets kinder and more understanding and outgoing; she is a 'good' character, where David is rather amoral, and has few ethical responses, though many affectionate and aesthetic ones. People came in and out; Hugh, with whom I had a long interesting talk. (Research into the First World War

---

[1] Jenkins, née Strachey, later diagnosed as having leukaemia.
[2] Clare was Rachel's first cousin. Both she and Sydney were sculptors.

and the League of Nations has made him almost a pacifist.) I didn't take to a friend of his called Bertie Bell – Irish, pinkish, ebullient, though David says he's 'romantic and dashing': the romance has made him marry a spoilt Persian beauty; the dash caused him to drive round Belgrave Square three times at 70 m.p.h. showing off to a girl, for which I'm glad to say he was fined £200 and his licence taken away for three years (he boasted of this). Then the delightful Bayleys and Laura, pale and mini-skirted, in her first term of St Hugh's. I went to lunch with Frances Phipps in her extraordinary hotel just up the road. She's in the seventh heaven, and has entirely altered the course of her life, from being an anxious mother and grandmother to an eternal student. She is now in some way a registered under-graduate and goes regularly to read her essays to a tutor. After lunch in the fumed oak dining-hall, she took me up to her room, upholstered in throat-pastille and sage greens, and read me one of her essays – a vivid account of the Battle of Sedan. Very good and lively. She would I'm sure have liked to go on and read me them all, but happy as I was to see her so obsessed, and dearly as I love her, I had found two hours of listening to her non-stop lecture on Foch, Clemenceau, the League of Nations, and the Fourteen Points as much as I could take. She barely ate any lunch for talking. I tried sometimes to ask an appropriate question, but she galloped at least four times round the entire landscape before I ever got an answer. How strange it was to be sitting in this unsympathetic hotel room with a person I love, counting the minutes and taking sly glances at my watch to see when I could decently go. Yet a lot that she had to say was fascinating – it was the inchoate nature of it, the inability to divert her on to *any* other theme, or even aspect of her own subject, that made my visit to her – yes, alas, boring. But I respect what she's doing and am touched by the way it has all gone to her head. She means to get rid of her London flat, and is quite content to go on living in this hotel – 'So nice to have no housekeeping'. If only Julia could live in some such way!

Frances spoke enthusiastically of Rachel, less so of David. She feels he's 'cold', and that he doesn't care about ideas! Had we talked about them? A lot about books and writers (Ruskin we'd both been reading about) and people; but he wasn't in a mood this weekend to descend into the depths of first principles and value judgements.

The subject of Desmond's letters wasn't once mentioned, so last night I brought it up myself – the result confirming me that I at least will have nothing more to do with it. I couldn't get much out of David; he showed no signs of wanting to use them as the basis for a life of Desmond, and has quite different ideas from mine as to what makes a good book of letters. Again they said, 'It would be so nice to combine some of Molly's letters.' Again I said what a lot of work this would involve as she never dated them, again they exclaimed, 'Oh, yes, I see!' Here and now I rule a line under that episode, and shall try to devote no more thought to it.

Talk and company as delightful as ever, discomfort as great. Wine and biscuits ran out yesterday. 'Well, I'm afraid there's no wine left,' David said cheerfully. 'It just can't be helped.' But it could have been, and other people, everyone else I know down to those with only a fraction of their income, always do help it, I couldn't refrain from reflecting.

December 1st

Dinner last night for Iris Murdoch, the Kees, Janetta and Julian. It went off very well; everyone liked Iris – how could they help it? Her magnificent realism, her Joan-of-Arc-like quality, her way of attending to what everyone said, weighing it (to the accompaniment of a very Oxford 'Yes, yes, yes') and then bringing out her response, her evident enjoyment and sense of fun. She arrived in a splendid antique military coat made of the finest black face cloth with gilt buttons; she tucked in and drank plentifully (how she must suffer at the Cecils'!), she talked. Everyone was at their best, particularly Janetta, who gave a wonderful description of sobbing real tears over a book in Harrods' book department, and was also very amusing about how she viewed the universe in terms of 'me, them and IT'. Apart from the constant tugging at one's watchfulness involved in hospitality I enjoyed the evening very much. Talk was general, right round the dinner table, and also individual; they stayed till nearly one o'clock.

As Janetta was leaving she said that she was tempted to postpone her flight to Spain next Tuesday, and stay and go out with Rose ten days later. 'Oh, do,' I said. 'It would be so nice for all of us.' 'Well, I think I might. Of course Rose is quite all right. She doesn't worry. But I do.' And then, suddenly veering like a sailing ship tacking she said, 'The only thing is I do want to help him,' (Jaime, though she didn't say so) 'with the preparations for opening his hotel.[1] It would be real work, and I'd like to do it, and I think he wants me to.'

A story of Janetta's about returning from Paris in a crowded uncomfortable train with Diana Cooper, after all flights had been stopped for fog. Janetta fell asleep and then woke to see Diana's blue eyes staring fixedly at her. She gave a slight smile. No response, and she realized the face had been so often lifted that her eyelids wouldn't close over her eyes, and she was asleep.

Mary's news is quite extraordinary. Charlie arrived suddenly at Stokke, changed the locks on all the doors and wouldn't let anyone in, not even Ron the farm worker to collect the milk-check books and the milk itself from the fridge. He has a detective with him, so is sparing no expense to be aggressive. He has got all his things back from store. Ron comes over to the Tycoonery to report to Mary and tells her that Charlie sits at her desk, which she hates. Who washes up, I wonder? Ron also reported that the detective came and said, 'Couldn't you let me have a drop of milk? I'm sick of eating my cornflakes dry.' What can Charlie hope to achieve? He must be quite mad.

December 9th

Dinner alone with Janetta last night. Why has it left me a little sad? When we sat down to a most delicious meal of watercress soup and roast pheasant she commented that I was sitting on the very edge of my chair and that it was characteristic of me. F.: 'I suppose I feel I must be ready to dash off at a moment's notice.' J.: 'Yes, and I think it's that lack of calm that produces your physical troubles.' F.: 'I'm sure it does – except that I'm not quite sure which is cause and which effect. Do you find it hard to be calm?' J.: 'No, not in the very least, but then I've got the opposite physical temperament.'

I woke this morning very early and thought that all this was true, but is calm

[1] La Fonda, at Marbella.

what I want from life? I don't feel it's my chief aim, which still is (I think) intensity of consciousness and realism. But one must relax so as to defeat anxiety and wipe the slate for awareness. Yet there's something to me a little dull in calmness as an aim.

December 17th: Crichel

'It's extraordinary that a professional literary critic should have no idea of writing at all. I mean he writes like a computer, without any pulse of life, any sense of the rhythm or flow of language.' Thus Raymond at breakfast this morning about some book he's reviewing, and oh, alas, every word is applicable to his own productions. However, I must admit that I have not for ages found him such a delightful, easy yet stimulating person to be with as he was this weekend. One day last week he rang me up in a voice grey and shaking with despair, and told me that Simon Fleet had died. (He pitched down a steep staircase after drinking too much brandy and broke his skull. He was not, it seems, a heavy drinker but had no other cure for the despair which he's been suffering from.) Could I, would I, come down to Crichel and keep him company, Raymond asked. He was alone with a servant problem to tackle and feeling depressed. I'd promised myself a quiet, industrious weekend in London and made several dates and arrangements. But after first saying I was afraid I couldn't, I thought better of it and rang back and said I would. At first I didn't take in how much he minded about Simon Fleet – I thought he was a mere acquaintance. But I'm very glad I did go. I couldn't think what to take to cheer him up and then on an impulse took my Turkish diary, edited it most carefully in the train and read it aloud to him. Wild success! I felt a little guilty about the bits I was *not* reading.

December 19th

Getting on so well with Raymond gave me enormous pleasure. Why should one carp at and criticize one's friends, as I fear I sometimes did in Turkey? Yet I do believe he gets obfuscated by some curious cloud when he's on his travels. We had delightful conversations about the way a literary critic should approach a poem. I do hope Crichel may, somehow or other, be kept afloat, and it almost seemed as if the will and vitality to do so does exist. Raymond and I didn't see a lot of each other – breakfast, lunch and the evenings only – work for us both in the mornings, snooze for him while I walked after lunch, and once I found him in bed again (blankets to chin) not long before dinner. Much sighing of course, groaning it might also be called, over the typewriter, and sometimes as we both sat reading, his heavy breathing would fill the drawing-room, seeming to declare with each loud and laboured inhalation: 'Continuing to live is a burden, and I do it under protest.'

Then Shakespeare's sonnets, an endlessly profitable subject. Two were quoted in the book Raymond was reviewing, along with some critics' comments. These missed the point to a degree which astounded me. One took great trouble to prove that Shakespeare was not a Metaphysical poet – but whoever said he was? Yet he was 'speculative' in the sense of soaring from the particular to the general even if his soarings are never built into a coherent system; another critic said that his 'imagery had no tension'. Heaven help us – why do such insensitive brutes bother to read him? Both the quoted sonnets were on the theme that I find so moving –

starting from the sadness of age, 'parallel lines' in the brows, and ending with a sudden magnificent leap to his superb confidence in the immortality of his own verse. How I hate these dry niggling modern critics who tease away factually at poetry, wondering which month robins nest in, or whether Wordsworth and the 'Solitary Reaper' were really alone in their field.

December 21st

More than a week ago I went to a lunch party at Adrian Daintrey's, where were Joe Ackerley,[1] Diana Cooper and three others I didn't place. I never had a good look at Diana Cooper before and thought her still quite beautiful, rather to my surprise. The great blind blue eyes gazed out under the becoming shadow of a busby, the line of her chin and neck were (even if as a result of surgery) pure and clean, her figure trim. 'A triumph for face-lifting', I said to Mary on the telephone. 'Perhaps we all ought to do it?' she giggled. Then two nights ago she confided in me that she thought of having it done, and has booked her bed for soon after Christmas.

December 28th

Christmas is over and soon the year will be done also. I look back on its disappearing surface like a featureless road rolling away from the back of a car, and don't know what I can set on the credit and debit sides. Turkey was a credit, certainly. On Christmas Eve in the middle of the day I drove quietly down to Eardley's new house, the Slade near Alton, and yesterday back again into London's intense holiday silence. Never have more people been killed on the road than this Christmas and I saw driving that was savage and horrible.

When I reached the Slade at three of a mild winter's afternoon, I wondered if this could really be it. A square box facing north and built of dark red brick, with a steep slate roof. But Eardley and Mattei are so touchingly excited and happy with their new toy that I soon began to see it with their eyes. No difficulty with their famous view, which composes itself beautifully – a line of elms (one fallen, improving the design) running down a wide waterless valley with a copse beyond. Inside, the house is warm and cheerful, excellent central heating, pretty paint and papers. We spent a quiet time, hanging curtains, cooking and washing-up, going for walks, and I sat at a table in front of a sunny window translating. Drinks one evening with John Fowler[2] in a house full of fantastically pretty things and from what I saw of its architecture fantastically pretty itself. Fowler is like a fruit that has gone soft and squelchy ('*sweet* of you' etc.) but has a hard go-getting core. Mattei says he's very kind. We sat in a tiny room in which everything was elegant and tasteful, drinking whiskies, and I talked to a charming young man about Gibraltar. There was an American with one of the silliest faces I ever saw (but handsome), who kept making noises like a cow or sheep with some little gadget and then tilting back his face and going into a peal of foolish laughter.

The local farmer and his family, all radiant with goodwill, came up to the Slade for a drink and a look at their old home in new hands. I can't imagine what they made of our strange trio. I think Eardley, Mattei and I were all at ease together. Mattei is becoming a splendid cook and liked to tackle it alone. I wonder why

[1] Literary editor of the *Listener*, and writer.
[2] Well-known interior decorator.

Eardley has such strange reserves about Crichel? When I told him Raymond was anxious that he and Mattei should go down as visitors he said, 'I don't think I want to go to Crichel any more,' looking indignant and red-faced. But surely it's unkind of him, and unfriendly to Raymond and Desmond not to go ever? Has he some grudge against them or merely guilt?

December 31st

Today, the last day of the year has inevitably a dreglike quality. I'm spending it without human contact, and in London. Now, at 6 p.m., I confess I've not felt lonely at all, and have been busy all day, reading late in bed, shopping, and all this afternoon at the London Library, checking up on Charlemagne. As its familiar smell engulfed me pleasurably I looked round at the large number of other inhabitants – some old, some industrious, some sleeping, some reading *Punch*, John Julius Norwich hard at work on his book; and saw this scholarly activity as a form of rather crazy self-indulgence, an escape from the anguish of the world into this womb of paper and dust. Several queerish figures, talking to themselves, hobbling or 'toddling', a large handsome almost young man who made a disturbing impression of not being all there. He arrived when I did, walking with very long legs but tiny steps, I saw him later gazing blankly at some photographs of ancient boats.

So ends 1966, a year – I think – of some degree of moral convalescence.

Good Company

1967–1970

Foreword

A human life easily translates itself into geographical terms: at times a long road seems to wind up a valley and climb a pleasant wooded hill, followed perhaps by a sudden plunge into an unexpected ravine, streams have to be crossed without bridges, tall rocks cast shadows. My readers have had to follow me through some patches of black country, but I hope that by the end of *Other People* they felt the atmosphere was lightening somewhat, while by a series of shallow steps a wider viewpoint had been reached. I have said that calm was never the main thing I wanted from life, but I began to feel settled in my London flat – it was my home, and the need to take off for foreign countries was not so urgent, although travel remained one of my greatest delights.

The title of this volume celebrates those who shared my journeys or the firelit warmth of their interiors. It also brings back to my mind a song which I was fond of as a child, when I was told that it had possibly been written – both words and music – by Henry VIII. How amazing, I thought, for a king to be so clever! The song begins:

Pastime with good company
I love, and shall until I die ...

I only hope I shall.

January 1st

On the morning of New Year's Day I walked into Hyde Park. The sun was dazzling and the blood was beaten into everyone's cheeks by the cold but windless air. Every relationship was displayed there, woman and dog, young man and mum, parenthood in all its forms, contented marriage, solitude. On the whole the aspect was encouraging, making life seem a boon and people welded together by affection, and over it all the clatter of light, rippling water, oars on rowlocks, boys' falsetto laughter. A little boy pedalled by on a bicycle with brown hair glistening like a peeled chestnut; a highbrow father was trying to inveigle his little girl into an interest in mathematics ('But you see it doesn't make any difference whether they're cats or rats, they'll take just as long to get there.' Little girl: 'But how can you tell if some cats or rats won't be much slower than others?' Father looks at watch). All the pairs of men I passed had their spectacled eyes fixed on the ground, saw nothing at all of the surrounding beauty and were mumbling of super-tax and profits.

January 14th: Alderly Grange, Gloucestershire

Arrived last night and was met by Alvilde Lees-Milne and driven through the starry night, a thumbnail moon about to sink behind the horizon. Also on my train was my fellow guest, James Pope-Hennessy,[1] whom I had spotted in the bar talking with animation to a handsome guardsman. First impression of him – too much name-dropping, and he used that offhand drawl which seems to imply that nothing really matters. After dinner I changed my views about him a good deal. He has a type of face I rather like – Russian, feline, with curious, wide, slightly prominent eyes coming round the corner of his head. There was some talk about travel to Russia, and then James Pope-Hennessy suddenly came into the open in favour of what the Russians were trying to do – put an end to class; he said it was the root of all evil and no country was more class-ridden and snobbish than England; of course what we must do was get rid of the Royal family – it was 'no good to man or beast'. I was amazed and rather pleased to hear my own views supported but Jim said, 'I couldn't disagree with you more.' James is a talkative, articulate fellow and quite a lively argument went on until Jim seemed unable to say any more in defence of his views, and suddenly got up and left the room saying, 'This is so boring – let's go to bed.' Consternation was expressed by James in 'Shall I go after him? He's really cross, isn't he?' None the less we all went upstairs. 'Ought I to go by the morning train?' said Pope-Hennessy to me with a

---

[1] Writer, biographer of Queen Mary.

feline grin. Alvilde: 'Jim minds so terribly about all sorts of traditions being kept up.' What happens today I wonder? At breakfast Alvilde told me that Pope-Hennessy had been to see Jim to 'make it up, with absolutely no success whatever'. James Pope-Hennessy came down, pretty indignant. I left him and Alvilde alone together; she was pitching into middle-aged men who wore their hair long and greasy. (He does.) He said, 'It needn't be greasy.' She: 'It always is.' But he stayed on till yesterday evening, presumably forgiven.

January 16th

Down to breakfast, feeling very glad to be here but that it is more comfortable without James. I took a long walk with Jim and the two whippets yesterday afternoon, and he told me more about 'Jamesy' as they call him. 'He's a *fiend*!' he said with feeling, 'he always has been,' and now 'the worm has turned.' How to sum James up? Clever, very. I've been looking at a book of his and it's well written. I was also charmed by the photo in it of his meltingly beautiful Eurasian grandmother. He's genuinely an iconoclast but out of bad motives not good, I suspect; the 'desire to cause pain', and the rather better one to 'be a rebel'. No love, I should imagine. Malicious, snobbish? irresponsible. Jim says his anti-royal feelings partly came from disappointment at not being knighted or received into royal circles because of his book about Queen Mary. I should have thought 'Jamesy' was too intelligent for that; last night he said, 'If I tell some people I've danced with the Queen they almost have an orgasm.' Jim says he has broken up marriages ruthlessly, brought a handsome Malay boy back to England and cast him off, and is always sponging though he made a fortune with his *Queen Mary*. He has been much spoiled by Harold Nicolson and many old ladies, and his arrogance is the result. When he left last night the atmosphere lightened. An octogenarian Lord Methuen came to lunch today, a delightful man, speaking in the quiet voice of the deaf, ironical, charming and full of interests. He had gone to Russia with the Lees-Milnes, and had been digging hard in his garden, about which he spoke as ardently as about his three kittens. He had a noble profile like a long-nosed Roman emperor, plenty of hair, pensive blue eyes and great gentleness.

January 23rd: London

I heard Fischer-Dieskau in *Arabella* two nights ago, and it was the most moving thing that has happened to me for weeks. I was bowled over, so were the whole audience, from the moment he advanced – tall, intense and burning-eyed, bear-like in his fur-collared coat, till the last gesture when he flung his arms towards Arabella on the balcony.

January 24th

Janetta is due back – perhaps has already come – for a week. I don't know why she is making such a short stay. Heywood and Anne have been for the last week at Montpelier Square, spreading their genial familiar warmth which Georgie and Rose have certainly enjoyed. Georgie meanwhile has suddenly stepped ahead into maturity. I took her to *Rigoletto* a week ago and thoroughly enjoyed her company. I had been afraid she would be bored, but I was aware of her beside me, leaning forward attentively with Janetta's absorption and seriousness. Slightly shy with me at first, she relaxed and became a delightful evening's companion. Anne was much struck by her responsibility for Rose, and for washing-up and tidying. Also she's fast becoming a very beautiful girl – I feel sure now she'll be 'all right', and the genes will triumph.

Last night I drove Julia to Quentin's lecture on Bloomsbury at University College. There was a good deal of talk about various wrangles, or occasions when Blooms-bury was misjudged – by Johnny Rothenstein, Wyndham Lewis, D. H. Lawrence – mainly confirming the view, it seemed to me, of Bloomsbury's touchiness, and revealing too little of their other good qualities of reasonableness, courage, realism and high spirits. Lionel and Margaret, Julia and Lawrence all dined here last night. Lawrence was extremely amusing, in fact really brilliant, holding forth in a slightly tipsy, fantastic way about the artist's vision when enclosed within the globe of his extended arm (paintbrush on end), and about the 'circle subtending the move-ments of the painting arm'. Lionel responded and the conversation moved 'like spiders in the moon', to quote *The Voyage Out*, taking long silent steps balanced precariously above the real world, and able to dart off into unexpected corners at a startling rate.

February 3rd

Today Janetta takes off for Spain; I saw her briefly yesterday. Her two extra days have given her the chance to carry out a triumph of generalship. What will happen when she goes I don't quite know but she told me she thought Julian wanted to come to Montpelier Square, and that she would be back in another six weeks to see how they all were. Perhaps it will be quite all right. I'm just as influenced by her powers of persuasion as anyone else is, and of course feel just as much personal sadness at the loss of her incomparable company. As I left she begged me to ring up Georgie and I will. I took my *Othello* records for her to play (after her response to *Rigoletto*) and Janetta was anxious I should know that she often heard Georgie playing them. I said they were probably worn with use and she told me she had dreamed of them, and that when she looked at them 'they were pitted and scratched and grooved like the outside of the moon. Then I put them on and the most marvellous music came out.' How should this dream be interpreted?

I am full to overflowing of Turgenev at the moment – because of reading a life of Pauline Viardot, which has enthralled, moved and stimulated me. A remarkable and in some ways admirable woman, but did she deserve the lifelong devotion of this lovable genius? She obviously had a streak of austerity, or it may have been relentlessly putting Art first and uprooting her feelings for Turgenev, not letting go till they were both about fifty. And the irony of it was that both he and she seem to have assumed that she was the genius, whereas, as the book concludes, 'It was through Turgenev, who had always been prepared to sacrifice everything to her, that her name would ultimately be remembered.' What a somehow touching remark of poor Turgenev's when dying of agonizing cancer of the spine – 'Goodbye my dear ones, my whitish ones.'

March 6th

Last week Bunny and Raymond fetched up to dinner with me almost accidentally. They responded delightfully to each other; and I've never known Raymond listen so attentively to someone with a tempo so different from his own. It was worth the effort – Bunny's description of Mexico and America was seeded with unexpected and original images and phrases. (Angelica too has been greatly inspired by the journey and spoke of New York with her magnificent eyes blazing from a brown face, looking as beautiful as an Inca. That was when I went for music to Islington.) I sat back and listened to the two literary gentlemen, happy for once not to obtrude my own views. Towards the end of the evening they got onto the subject of class – and agreed that the 'best came to the top', and the upper classes were cleverer and more beautiful and therefore deserved their privileges, just as if they were two Wilcoxes from *Howards End* which I'm now reading. Why have the intellectuals of today returned to the views derided by those of 1909? It is extraordinarily baffling. Forster's philosophy of love and human relationships, 'connecting' and all the rest may be a cake that is soggy in parts but it stands up very well to what has been put forth since in the sphere of Moral Philosophy. And Bertie Russell, in the Sunday papers, described the moment of almost mystical revelation when as a young man he realized the value of love and understanding and became a pacifist, which he has always remained. This side of what Bloomsbury stood for has been to some extent forgotten – and they are thought of chiefly as back-biting cynics (which some of them of course were).

This weekend with Julia to Stokke – Mary's first weekend back there after the bust-up with Charlie McCabe. Supremely perfect spring weather. I had two long walks with Julia in Savernake Forest; as we returned yesterday afternoon towards a Greek temple of grey beech trunks lit by sunlight, she amazed me by saying she couldn't possibly have walked there alone – it would have seemed too terribly sad and lonely. She wondered how Mary could bear it. Yet Stokke welcomed me and Mary with such peaceful warmth; and I believe very little, if any, sadness.

But Julia has suddenly stopped contemplating her own inner landscape and in the most marked way started to take an interest in the outside world, to read the papers and serious books, and talk about such subjects as Vietnam, which has been right outside the range of her vision for months or years. Her vitality and originality are enhanced: she seems to have shaken off a grey dressing-gown of obsessional brooding, but oddly enough the same wand that has opened her eyes to reality has also made her look older and more like the one-time 'owl in an ivy bush' instead of an ageless sleeping princess. I welcome the change and wonder if there can be a connection.

March 14th

Last week saw the 'balloon go up' once again, and perhaps finally, for the Gowings. Lawrence suddenly rang up, came to see me and told me he had decided to get Julia to divorce him and marry Jenny. My role was easy: he only wanted me to listen. I told him of course no one could fail to imagine the strain this had all been to him. He showed more understanding of Julia's nature than she would, I think, credit him with; felt it appalling that this should happen to her of all people, with her childhood fear of desertion; deplored the purple heart habit, instituted (he said) by a foolish doctor; and said how unlucky it was that so many things she really liked – such as music – had to be ruled out because they were 'melancholy'. The bad fairy had cursed her with the inability to enjoy what was available.

Since my talk with Lawrence, he wrote to her to break the news, and I have had long telephone talks and an evening alone here with her. With the help of purple hearts she seemed to face the new crisis bravely and resentfully. Anger is a vital form of energy for getting over humiliation. She doesn't want for the present however to see Lawrence sometimes for dinner as he'd hoped. So now Julia's friends must rally round for all they're worth – the Kees, the Campbells. Our evening together went very well until the end when she began dismissing various friends of mine who are also fond of her and full of kindness and goodwill. Mary is really 'too silly'; Janetta 'couldn't possibly be intelligent' if she liked a certain French film Julia and I didn't care for. F.: 'But surely you don't feel no one can be intelligent who doesn't agree with you?' Pause. J.: 'I know *you* think I do.' Yes, alas, I do.

At Kitty West's last weekend I met John and Myfanwy Piper and liked them very much; I admired her solid, sculptured body, very intelligent face and low musical voice. The talk that evening was very much alive. At Crichel we found the Berkeleys with a charming prep. school son. Everyone in the room was nice, yet the bicycle tyre of conversation went flat several times and had to be pumped up again. One afternoon Kitty and I sloshed along the muddy paths of her woods and gathered huge bunches of wild daffodils in tight buds. I read with pleasure Keith Vaughan's diary. Julia said to me: 'What a pity we know so few people who ever *think*.' But he certainly does: he gives a moving account of being a CO in the army on non-combatant duties; and particularly of the arrivals of German prisoners. The English expected monsters, so did the Germans. A moment of embarrassment followed by infinite relief on both sides. Oh, why couldn't this moment of truth have been made more use of?

March 17th

Francis Bacon has a new show on in Bond Street but there isn't much 'newness' about it except his increased popularity. In the narrow gut of the gallery, turds were slowly circulating. I stepped close and hoped I was 'appreciating the quality of the paint', but it gave me no pang, thrill or lift. Nor did I get the electric shock his first shows produced. I detected a feeling of depression, and revulsion caused by the carefully and thickly laid on backgrounds in unpleasant colours, the patterned carpets, and the horrid raised boot so many of his solitary characters project at one. There they sit, mashed and mangled within the prison walls of their rooms, relieved only by a bell-rope or electric light. What is this extremely clever man trying to say? Julian last night gave an illuminating reply, which like the best criticism made me want to go and have another look. He says he is proclaiming again and again and again the dreadful loneliness of the human animal. But what worries me is the lack of *visual* element in this presentation – it seems too cerebral. The eye is not stimulated or pleased – quite the reverse – and I came away blank of feeling, either positive or negative. I feel teased by the problem he raises, and want to read his own account of what he's after – but I mistrust the high value he sets on accidents.

March 31st

The weeks to come are parcelled out into a series of visits and journeys to and fro. I am trying not to feel hectic – to take it calmly. Two foreign trips loom ahead. I'm amazed to find myself pledged to go next month with Rosamond to Sicily and looking forward to it; sitting beside her in her flat discussing plans, I peered into that over-lifesize, smooth, handsome face, like that of a vast primitive goddess, the enormous soft, deer's eyes, the pearly opalescent skin, and felt a certain wondering affection. Next week, I go for a week to Cornwall with the Hills. Where does work come into all this? I refused to take on a book for Weidenfeld this morning, for I am still in theory pledged to John Murray, with Lawrence's Cézanne hovering in the background. Of course it pleases me to have these possibilities.

I have an evening to myself – oh selfish delight! Anxiety about Julia made me ring up and ask if she were free, but I was intensely relieved to hear that she had friends coming to supper. How she is going to stand the total separation from Lawrence demanded by divorce depends very much on support of her friends. And they give it; but she runs through them rather fast. The Campbells asked her for Easter, but there was not any joy in her account of her stay. 'Are *all* parents and their children so *inharmonious*? Do they all look so *cross* all the time? ... Of course they were entirely wrapped up in their own concerns, so they had no time or energy to spare for me ... No conversation, no ... Well, there was all this washing-up ... I was thankful to have it, as it prevented my brooding ... And then I rested twice a day, so there wasn't time for any more.' Ben Nicolson has asked her for August to a large Italian house he has taken, with the Toynbees and Kees. 'I shall go, and stick it out as long as I can, but I dread it really. I simply hate Italy in August. Then there's all this sun-bathing and lying about in bikinis – I can't do that, and I shall feel so out of it all. And I loathe pines and sand, which I know it is all down that coast. Well, and Philip Toynbee may well be an awful nuisance, so I'm not looking forward to it a *bit*, still I shall go.' I think only to me does the full flood of her critical depreciation come pouring out. What worries me most is the feeling that she does at times simply sink slowly into the bog of her own despair. It is pretty bad just now. I hardly like to go away and leave her, and noticed that she wanted to know the dates of my disappearance. I must help her somehow to get through this grim stretch.

April 25th: Palermo

Rosamond and I left London blue, blossomy and warm, and travelled smoothly to Rome, where squirts of rain were being discharged from a leaden sky and icy gusts blew our skirts up as we walked down the gangway. Ros seemed equable, ready to giggle, and above all sane, an important quality in a fellow traveller. She told me she had never driven abroad, even in an English car; so small wonder that she wanted me to drive at first. We were anxious to get away from the unhelpful Avis official and he from us, and I asked few questions and hoped I would remember how to drive a Fiat. On the whole I did. Without too great trouble we reached the hotel I had rashly booked on the recommendation of Gerald, forgetting his passion for austerity. It looked distinctly bleak and dingy, with under-blanketed beds and no hot water. Rosamond took this with great good humour, but oh dear no!, it won't do at all.

April 27th

Our new womb is a great improvement but a cold wind still rattles the palm trees. We wear everything we have, including woollen vests. Gradually Rosamond relaxes with me and her personality unfolds. In spite of having been left by at least four men (Leslie Runciman, Wogan, Goronwy Rees and Cecil Day-Lewis) she clearly nourishes in her heart a conviction of being universally beloved and desirable, and

I think these defections appear to her like astonishing mistakes or just incomprehensible folly. She thinks Wogan 'would really like to be back with her' and makes no bones about wishing they had never parted. (She is innocently proud of being an Honourable, and – another curious tiny vanity – has taken a year off her age though her passport reveals it for all to see.) Julia once said she lived entirely by wish-fulfilment and I think this is true; but she's boundlessly interested in people, and likes to talk in biographical or autobiographical terms. In this, as in much else, she is the eternal feminine. Her size and her innocence together give me a somewhat odd feeling of having unfair advantage over this large iridescent fish I am playing – iridescent in fact because she covers her face with some pearly opalescent substance, and this looks striking under her thick mop of white hair tinted a pinkish colour.

This morning began agonizingly, because Rosamond wanted me to drive her into the *centro* to see the various sights there. The traffic was appalling and there was absolutely nowhere to park, so on her suggestion we gave up and headed for Monreale, whose great Norman apse is lined with mosaics and features a huge and magnificent Christ. Ros was much concerned with the expression on the face of this Christ – was it 'wise', 'sad' or 'powerful but gentle'? I have the impression that she thinks of all these images as portraits – even though several hundred years in arrears – of an actual man. Back at our Jolly, I couldn't resist taking a walk while she rested, and found my way between old golden palaces crumbling into tenements and crawling with children to one which has become the National Art Gallery and contains a very extraordinary Antonello da Messina virgin. Coming home, I gazed down dark side alleys hung with washing as if with bunting, where squalid and poverty-stricken families were living, surrounded by paper and debris that swirled round their legs in the cold gusts of wind.

April 29th: Éricé

Ros went to the hairdressers before we left Palermo. She has brought her mauve rinse with her and I think the assistant put in too much of it. Her head is now covered with bright Parma violet floss. With a pink scarf round her neck, crimson lips and a bright blue suit, the effect is striking the say the least.

Éricé is perched on a pinnacle rising a sheer two thousand feet from the plain, and Rosamond bravely drove us to the top, though she now confesses she is given horrible vertigo by heights and cannot bear to look over steep places. In thick mist or cloud we found another Jolly, and were each given a monk's cell with a big window. The wind hurled itself screaming against mine all night, and before darkness fell I looked down through the drifting clouds to occasional gleams of sunlight on the sea crawling far below. On the way up, near the top we were stopped by two men who looked to me like the police who check lorries for contraband. 'Dove vanno le signore?' they asked. When we said, 'To the Jolly Hotel,' they smiled and let us go on. I thought nothing of this, but Ros was convinced they were members of the Mafia, and has been ever since haunted by their 'evil looks and sinister smiles'. I began to realize that her mystical views imbue events with esoteric, half-good, half-bad significance. She seems to be a sort of Manichean.

April 30th

Ros had asked me to drive down the mountain as she would have to close her eyes not to see the precipices. Éricé was still shrouded in cold dense mist, and after a brief look at the village down we came, out of it, into glorious sunshine, with the sea sparkling and blue below us. The man at the Jolly had recommended a cross-country route; it turned out to be a slow and appalling road, at times nearly impassable, but ran through the most beautiful country, so that I'm glad we took it. Sheets of flowers now unrolled under a blue sky – either formalized in squares of dark red clover and pale blue flax, or in a wild profusion of yellow, purple and white, while convolvulus (blue and purple) sprawled everywhere. All at once I saw an extraordinary white, lily-like flower growing in a bank (I still don't know what it was). I stopped the car with a yell and came back in triumph – only to the dread awareness that we had a puncture. What now? Here we were on a small deserted road in the wildest Mafia country. Then a young farmer appeared on a motor-bicycle and we begged him to help, Rosamond actually clasping her hands in a pleading gesture. He was our saviour, changed our wheel and we set off again and by way of Selinunte finally reached Agrigento.

But my God, could this really be it? This forest of skyscrapers standing on a hill? It was indeed, and we climbed up to the town in a queue of cars, through traffic lights, hated the look of the place and didn't much like the monks' cells in the new Jolly (I see it will be Jollies, Jollies all the way, for Ros feels safer in them, with their stuffy smell of commercial travellers' cigarettes). To bed plugging my ears against the almighty racket in the road outside.

May 1st

I've come up to bed, early as usual, after our first real talk at dinner about Rosamond's mystical beliefs. As if suddenly uncorked, out they all poured – her 'absolute certainty' of survival, the continued existence of minds 'in finer bodies', her belief in 'saints and sages' (of whom Jesus is one and her crazy old colonel with whom she wrote *A Man Seen from Afar* is another), reincarnation, the mystical experience. I can't remember exactly how it began, but I felt it was bound to some time, and was mainly concerned to affirm and maintain my own position without being aggressive. Indeed I *am* very much interested, though not exactly in the way she supposes. I asked her if she still had frequent contact with Sally? She was evasive. Not so much. She didn't need it, since she now had the certainty of survival. This part of her mind is all softness like a huge marshmallow – anything could be absorbed by it.

I have never travelled in so ladylike a fashion. Like characters in an E. M. Forster novel, we seem to be gliding through Sicily in an invisible barouche, gloved and veiled, provided with a primus to make cups of tea at any moment. We haven't once sat in a café. I suggested it this morning, but met with reluctance; I think she felt it looked 'grubby' or 'squalid'. Her appearance often creates a sensation and I'm sure this delights her. The guide in the cathedral here asked if it was the English fashion to wear hair of such a colour. In Palermo a woman also asked politely about it. She sometimes half-complains, half-boasts of being pursued by men, that the waiter puts his head into her room and wishes her goodnight, for instance. 'It's so maddening and silly.' This morning among the temples of Agrigento two quite young and handsome Sicilians offered to accompany us to Pirandello's house, and while we were watching a pretty little bride being photographed clasped in her husband's arms against the sunburned pillars of the Temple of Concord, the photographer asked if he might take our photo too 'as a memento'. What in the world does it mean? Was it just the possibilities of a striking colour photo offered by mauve hair, orange dress and blue cardigan? I'm faintly embarrassed by such incidents but not much, and this evening I feel rather hilarious, perhaps because the supernatural has popped out like a Jack-in-the-box. I would like it to go back and remain there, however.

May 2nd: Piazza Armerina

The barouche rolls on. The queenly figure bends her head like a swan and smiles sweetly from under her sunshade; the little companion looks beadily and inquisitively about her. A brilliantly fine morning and May Day crowds welling up and oozing slowly everywhere led to something of a *dies non*. Driving east along the coast we found them coagulating and streaming along the road. Gerald had told us to 'spend half an hour at Palma', where the ancestors of the Leopard[1] came from. We drew up and walked up a flight of broad steps sprouting with grass and weeds to a handsome baroque church, but a crowd of little boys so nagged, hustled and pestered us, and I was so disgusted when one spat into the car at me at close range, that we soon left.

May 28th: Syracuse

The Roman villa at Piazza Armerina was a splendid sight. Set in a luscious green valley full of singing birds and the sound of water, it is very well arranged, so that one can walk round an unobtrusive plastic roof and gaze down from a height on these extraordinary mosaic floors, where elephants and other African animals are to be seen being embarked on a ship, where cupids catch enormous innocent Edward Lear fish, and female athletes wear bikinis.

I did most of the driving to Syracuse today. We had tried to reserve rooms by telephone at the Grand Hotel, the only one in the old town, but when we got there we found that by some 'mystical' (?) error we had actually been booked at the Jolly instead. It stands on a large main road halfway between the classical sites and the old town. While Ros rested I went to the post office on the port, where I found a letter from Alix – and when I saw how short it was I instinctively knew what news it contained: the unimaginable fact that James had died of a heart attack. Why had the possibility never occurred to me? Why did he seem immortal? Simply I suppose because it was useless and painful to contemplate his death.

Ros had a letter from her 'boyfriend', the old precognitive, Jesus-conscious colonel. He warned her of the evil influence of the Mafia who 'definitely practise black magic' and this has reinforced her impression of the sinister viciousness of the faces of the two men on the hill at Éricé. When we were talking and joking about the number of earthquakes and eruptions of Etna that Sicily is subject to, she said, 'I think he would have told me if we were in danger. When I went to Egypt he told me I should be in need of special protection.' Well, I'm treated to a good deal of bunkum daily!

[1] The Prince of Lampedusa, author of the book of that name.

May 4th

Last night I had another dose of spiritualism, mysticism and reincarnation, and I am getting a bit bothered by the suspicion that Ros has hopes of me; for my isolation with her here, natural curiosity and even politeness make me not only refrain from saying, 'Shut up; you're talking utter rubbish!' but actually draw her out. Each evening we repair to one or other of our rooms and drink whisky from tooth-glasses before dinner. I did seduce her to sit briefly in a café for a cappuccino yesterday. In the afternoon we visited the catacombs and the quarries where the Athenian prisoners once worked. Bus-loads of schoolboys and girls followed us screaming like starlings wherever we went, carrying their vitality and noise right into the strange depths of the cavern called the Ear of Dionysus. They were convulsed by the sight of Ros's hair, and several girls came up and asked what nationality she was, and (with broad grins) whether English people always had 'pink hair'.

She told me as a great confidence how when she was in Egypt she noticed that an Egyptian guide who was showing her round a museum suddenly began to tremble and shake as he stood beside her, until at last he said: 'Forgive me, but I've known you before. This is terribly agitating. I can't go on being your guide. Perhaps you were formerly some Egyptian queen.' I told her I thought her long eyes going round the corner of her face did give her rather an Egyptian appearance, and she at once agreed. But how much of this episode and the guide's remarks have been fished up from her unconscious? I must try and keep her to more mundane subjects.

NB. I mustn't forget to chalk up in Rosamond's favour a fit of really abandoned, uncontrollable, infectious giggles over the expression and manner with which one of the waiters described the various available ices to us.

May 5th

Heading towards the end of our holiday, I feel a growing anxiety to get our trusty little white eggshell of a car safely to Catania. We had decided to devote yesterday to Noto, and as we were missing out the other baroque towns (Ragusa, Modica, etc.) it was perhaps a relief to find it very slightly disappointing. But we saw and admired the cathedral and several other golden baroque churches. Their strikingly *lay* appearance, more like town halls or ballrooms than churches, offended Rosamond. Then to eat tough rubber tubes of macaroni in a small restaurant whither we were directed by a policeman. While we were there in came a couple of South Africans. Ros instantly fell for the bronzed, blue-eyed, virile-looking husband, who spoke good Italian and obviously knew Sicily well. She'd met him before, seen his photograph, known him in a previous existence perhaps, thought he might have been a general in the last war (too young by far) and found him 'extremely attractive'. This *déjà vu* impression has taken her by surprise several times; she had it about a man in the Syracuse Museum. It is part and parcel of the esoteric quality she likes to attach to ordinary circumstances.

May 6th: Catania

Last night for the first time I began to feel wound-up and exhausted, after a day when I had done all the driving as Rosamond has strained her wrist. In bed I read about the earthquakes, and eruptions of Etna, the lava's slow crawl down the mountain, repeatedly destroying Catania. What a queasy uncertain part of the earth's crust we are on, I was thinking, when suddenly my reading light went out. Going to the window, I saw that the whole town was in darkness, and I was seized by the impotence of being unable to strike a light. Suppose it *was* an earthquake, suppose the Jolly hotel began to crumble, what a horror to be able to see nothing! I stared at the cheerful lights of passing cars and thought how spirits and even sanity absolutely depend on light, and wondered how medieval prisoners ever kept going in pitch darkness. But after half an hour it magically returned and I read and slept.

May 7th

Episodes from Rosamond's past come out in the course of conversation and I am gradually joining them together. The impression I got of her being an unconfident blushing girl when she was at Girton and I at Newnham was only partly correct. She must already have been a spoiled beauty and her father's darling. Some innocent but unhappy love-affair was the basis for *Dusty Answer*; then came marriage with Leslie Runciman, about which she says little or nothing. Wogan and Day-Lewis were the great passions of her life; Goronwy Rees, another Welsher, was also passed over in silence (not *once* mentioned) though I remember how she confided in Ralph and me at the time of his defection that it had been an appalling and 'incomprehensible' blow to her, she felt 'he still loved her though he didn't seem to realize it'. Her family and Wogan's both tried to stop their marriage, and she was sent to America to forget him. Then she spoke of Tommy. Wogan adored him, and she had fallen completely under the spell of his charm; he often stayed with them at Ipsden. Once, while she was dancing with Tommy at a party, she 'told him how much she loved him'. 'Oh, you do, do you?' he said, looking coldly at her. 'Well, you'd better not, because I'm doing all I can to break up your marriage.' Cecil Day-Lewis's desertion was a complete surprise and shock and she still cannot get over it, or recognize it as genuine. It's a measure of her innocent vanity that she still thinks of it as 'wrong and mistaken'.

Rosamond has a deep horror of heights and had to steel herself to climb to the theatre at Taormina which has only a very slightly plunging view. She told me she was worried about this – it seemed to be getting worse. As we started home, another unfortunate experience: following a sign saying 'To the autostrada' we wound up a twisting road behind the town, only half-noticed that a passing car shouted 'Attention!' and came round a corner, Ros driving, to find ourselves at the edge of an unprotected cliff. She jammed on the brakes (the handbrake is very feeble) and got hastily out. I went round the corner to investigate and found that the road more or less petered out between a new building and the cliff. We retraced our course, me driving, and she said, 'I couldn't have done it. I should have passed out.'

Yes, I not only feel I know her better but am fonder of her. Almost all barriers have been crossed, our different attitudes to the unknown have been plotted and left as they are. Among other things we talked of today was the unfortunate meeting between Hester Chapman and Elizabeth Bowen at Crichel. Elizabeth was so appalled, and no wonder, by Hester's attitude of prurient interest in and exposure to the world of her stepdaughter's sex-life that she suddenly burst out violently,

'Shut your bloody trap.' Hester returned to London and told Rosamond about it in floods of tears. I can't quite make out the relationship between Ros and Hester; some rivalry certainly comes into it. She told me Hester had been indignant because she flirted with the guide of their Egyptian tour, allowed him to hold her hand, and call her 'darling'. Hester thought she was 'making a fool of herself' as she doubtless was, but what did it matter? She also snorted with indignation whenever mysticism or the supernatural was mentioned.

May 14th: Stokke

I came here last night after spending the day with Alix at Lord's Wood. I arrived here soon after twelve and we talked without stopping until after five. It seems to me astonishing now that I could have wondered if she would want to talk of James's death and her feelings. (Perhaps because I think I'm right in saying that when I went to see them after Burgo's death they never mentioned his name *once*, and I marvelled at such ignorance of human emotion and its workings on the part of professional psychologists.) There was no question this time – Alix started at once with simplicity, directness and moments of breaking down, on the story of James's last days. We talked of other things also of course – politics, Sicily, Julia – but far the most about James, the past and how she was to deal with the future. Now and then she struck with a sharp metallic clang on some painful truth recognized by me years since, as when she said with almost a sob: 'I'm so terrified of forgetting him.' I tried to reassure her, 'You *won't*,' but of course in a sense she will – only so very, very slowly, and by losing first the unbearable sharpness. It's in a way a drawback that I know so much about the state of bereavement. She didn't ask, 'How soon does it get better?' or I would probably have answered with unpalatable truthfulness, 'It gets worse for at least a year.' As I knew she would be, she was absolutely realistic, dignified and courageous in spite of total grief and loss. My awareness of it was agony. I drove through the matchless beauty of green woods and fields from Henley to Streatley and Newbury, aware that I was sitting bound up and tense in my seat, spent the evening talking to Mary, and then (after getting into bed early) the delayed effect of my pain for Alix zoomed out of the darkness like a huge crow and clutched me with its claws and beat its great black wings at me. I couldn't sleep but lay tormented and doubting. Had I done all I could for her? Was she all right? Two things moved me greatly and in a particular way: when I was leaving, the voice of genuine feeling in which she said, 'Goodbye, dearest Frances, I'm fearfully glad to have seen you,' and the fact that when I asked if there had been no one she could summon to her side, she said, 'Well, I had thought perhaps you might come.' It took me a long time to take this in. All the time I was with her I was reacting and counteracting so furiously to her sorrow and mine that there was no time for weighing or sifting. Hence my tortured thoughts last night. Should I not have firmly announced that I was coming down to stay till her brother Philip comes back from America in a fortnight? Or would this be an invasion of her privacy and the desire to 'collapse' at times? Would it be taking too much on myself? Her remarks had surprised me because I'd never thought of her as setting me high among her friends, but rather that she and James were two of the people I most loved and admired and was delighted and amused by, and whom I thought of as a mythical, indissoluble pair. And as I'm cursed with hypersensitivity to other people's feelings, which sets my heart racing as it raced last night, I doubt whether I'm fitted to support and sustain someone in the extremity of grief.

May 15th

I have written to Alix, suggesting coming again next week for a night on my way to the Carringtons and perhaps another on the way back. I thought a lot about how I should word it, making it easy for her to say no or yes, or allow me to go for one night or more. Discussing this with Mary led to a talk about sense of guilt. She claimed not to know what it was – if you've done your best then there's nothing to be gained by self-castigation. But even so un-neurotic and kind a person as Mary must surely have factual doubts sometimes where the material in question is the subtly vulnerable and complex stuff of human feelings. How can anyone be sure they have done the best they could? Yet Edward Glover[1] would perhaps have agreed. For I seem to remember he thinks both sense of guilt and anxiety are neurotic, whereas to me there are many cases when it would be irrational not to feel them.

One thing Alix and I talked about was aggression. If James had been there I don't feel she would have dared put forth the very interesting suggestion that Freud was mistaken in taking the death instinct as basic and aggression as a form of it turned outwards. And that, on the contrary, aggressive instincts have an obvious part to play in biological terms of self-preservation, and it is more correct to say that the death instinct and suicidal impulses are a turning inwards of the primary instinct of aggression.

I have loved being alone with Mary. All yesterday the birds kept up their mellifluous, surprisingly loud, sweet and complex music. They still do today, though it is as wet and dismal as yesterday was sunny and cheerful. A morning such as this makes one remember how lonely one can be in the country, how the mercury in one's thermometer can sink like a plummet. During green, sweet, musical, scented yesterday, everything we did was a pleasure. Mary and I spent an hour or so planting out begonias, asters and marigolds in a well-dug flower-bed and watering them in.

May 16th

I'm oppressed not by what Julia calls the eeriness of the universe, but by its tragic grimness; by the swoops made by death and the horrible necessity of wondering where it will strike next; by fear of my own; by U Thant declaring that we are seeing the preparation of a third world war; by reading that one in every ten people is now doomed to be killed or seriously injured in a motor accident; by the prevalence of futility, drug-taking and boredom; by finding myself so quickly able to subside into the morass when I believe that I have found stability; by effervescence and restlessness and noise. And, constantly, by the absence of Janetta.

May 20th: Lord's Wood

I drove down here yesterday, and am spending one night with Alix on each side of a weekend at the Carringtons'. Although I had the greatest difficulty in sleeping last night, the actual topics we spoke of for so many hours yesterday were not

[1] Freudian psychoanalyst.

actually so harrowing as before. James's name of course came up a great deal, and I noticed the pathetic change from the 'James likes' or 'James always does this' of last time to 'James used to' this time. Alix has taken on a superhuman task in contriving to be here alone since he died; I believe she has seen very few people. I'm full of admiration for her, and as I looked at her distinguished profile in the lamplight last night I thought she was still really beautiful. She says the 'evenings are rather fearful'; she does what she touchingly thinks of as 'taking to the bottle' – that is to say she drinks one not very large glass of South African sherry! She was anxious to 'break the habit' of being unable to look at television because of the sadness of the empty chair in the darkness. It was my task last night to fill that empty chair. She can't bear to listen to music. She confesses to 'panic fears' in the night, yet doesn't like to wake up the Johnstons above. I think after the first shock, she is just able to envisage the bleak future, and she confesses that from her point of view the atom bomb going off (which seems highly likely at the moment) would be a relief. I think her powers of adjustment are pretty good – and her brother Philip, I'm glad to hear, arrives on Wednesday, the day after I go back to London.

May 27th: Hilton

Drove Bunny down here yesterday through greenery pale and viridian but always strikingly luminous under towering storm clouds, with heavy showers beating up and departing. Angelica and Amaryllis arrived soon after us, William was here, the fiery Nerissa arrived for dinner. I have the room with the smudged grey walls on the top floor and am happy there, in spite of the sheets on my bed being dirty and crumpled, dead flowers in a vase, and the bathroom next door an inconceivable chaos of stained and battered objects, forests of dirty tumblers, old bottle tops and decayed toothbrushes. The personality of the house is still unique and original. I spread my work over a rickety table in my room – feeling the necessity for a private bolthole, away from Angelica's endless violin-playing and William on the oboe, probably later to be joined by Fanny on the horn. Much talk to Bunny on the way down; later some to Amaryllis. Being an actress has set its indelible mark on her, so that I feel she can never be anything else. I do hope she will be a success. Her large soft eyes, low voice and cloud of soft hair make her look vulnerable, and the compulsive need for dollops of indulgence (cigarettes – the act of lighting gives a necessary hoist to the ego – drinks) is not a symptom of happiness. Nerissa and Henrietta also need these things, but clutch at them fiercely and positively. I'm fascinated by these girls and their ethos and habits. Their hands are covered with rings old and new, one on each finger. Last night Nerissa asked me to play chess, her present enthusiasm, and beat me soundly. Then talk to Bunny about why the young hurl themselves into this dangerous, expensive and self-destructive habit of smoking. Richard and William never did, apparently. I suppose smoking is a sign of weakness of character – a need to shore oneself up by the signs of maturity and ritual movements, a crutch, a walking-stick. Natural therefore to adolescents, but a rational person ought to be able to shake it off afterwards.

May 30th

My days are packed much too tight. I deplore this congestion and the fact that conversations, scenes, faces flash by without my being able to take stock of them. Argument was pretty lively at Hilton, ranging from subjects like the difference between sarcasm and irony, to violence, and the 'new philosophy of the young' which seems to be tinged with Zen Buddhism, and voiced by the Beatles. A new record by the Beatles was played; I see little talent, or originality, no power to excite in them, and of course said so. 'Yes,' the cry went up, 'that's true, but then they don't aim at that. What they give off is a sort of serene acceptance. You feel *happy* when you listen to them.' Hitching this on to a later conversation with Georgia (who arrived later with Henrietta and Sophie), it seems to me this current philosophy of youth is above all passive. Acceptance is good, so far as it goes, but I cling to my belief in activity being better than passivity. The younger generation seem like opium-smokers, lying about soaking up sensations, pouring cigarettes, drink, cinema, television and marijuana in at the portals of their senses until near-satiation is reached. Yet Georgia said, 'Surely youth is the time you're supposed to feel excited.' Her face wore its puzzled look. An eerie impression of a lot of people endlessly sucking on hookahs comes to my mind.

Sophie ran about excitedly from person to person till at last she became over-stimulated and fretful. Angelica and Bunny toiled for our benefit and I fear tired themselves out. Nerissa helped valiantly, Henrietta looked rather wan, Amaryllis went off to visit Leonard at Rodwell, Fanny came with her lover, a professional conductor. Their love was more exhibitionist than any I ever saw; they were constantly entwined in its tense throes, exchanging loud kisses. She has grown up with a bang, like Alice after eating the mushroom. There was music one evening, and she stood in the doorway playing softly (and then suddenly very loud) on her horn, looking like a Piero della Francesca angel.

June 4th

At the Dolphin Hotel, Thorpeness – a village of 'refined', select, mock-Tudor seaside dwellings, two imitation Tudor gateways in red brick and a bogus Norman church (Leslie Hartley thought it genuine, the old ass) lined up in front of a long shingle beach stretching all the way to Aldeburgh. Our party has settled into four little rooms side by side and found a workable, mutual wavelength fairly easily. But there is some spring that has to be wound up to maintain it. Last night we went to see the two new operas, Walton's *Bear* and Lennox Berkeley's *Castaway*. Packed in to the uncomfortable seats of the Jubilee Hall, we found Anne and Heywood and Alvilde Lees-Milne beside us, Celia [Goodman] behind, and when we drifted out in the entr'acte innumerable familiar faces – Desmond, Pat Trevor-Roper, Freda Berkeley, John Julius Norwich. There was a charm in floating about in the still, twilit, pearly space between the hall and the shingle bank, a disembodied feeling of being wafted rather than supported on legs. A certain rivalry, as I had foreseen, between the two operas. Greatly hoping that Lennox Berkeley's would be good, I thought it only moderately so, while Walton's was an uproarious success.

June 6th

On Sunday we lunched with Lord and Lady Gladwyn, a cold spread with delicious wine after drinks – of which I took too many – in the garden. At lunch I was pleasantly situated between Desmond and Jock Cranbrook.[1] On then to hear some choirboys in sailor suits from Vienna singing in Blythburgh church. On the whole

---

[1] Anne Hill's eldest brother.

I remain stony to these disembodied voices, their famous 'purity' seeming a purely negative quality – amounting to a lack, in fact, of various things like maturity, emotion, expressiveness. I was pleased therefore, as well as amused, to hear Desmond say with feeling (and only partial truth): 'I *loathe* boys!' Another splendid concert in the new hall at the Maltings, Snape, whose acoustics are magnificently warm, rich and alive without being in the faintest degree fuzzy. And yesterday I left the others behind in what was obviously burgeoning into a hot summer's day, and returned home to be greeted in London by headlines two inches high: IT'S WAR. The Middle Eastern crisis between the Arab States and Israel has developed, as how should it not when both sides were longing to fight each other. So here we are. My own feelings are leaden, but a dreadfully soulless lead, throwing off no reflections. How quickly they could blaze up, of course, I know. On the wireless last night various brave young voices declared their intention of setting off at once to fight or work for what they believed right, though their vagueness as to why they thought it right or even what it was was quite amazing. In the streets everyone was buying papers, and words like 'call-up', 'they're horrible people anyway' floated round, while a sympathetic girl gave an exaggerated shudder – 'Brrrr!' – after glancing at her paper. So here, I suppose, we go, at the very least into total dishonesty, corruption and mass hysteria. Frances Phipps has sent me a heart-broken wail. Such a situation almost literally 'breaks her heart'.

June 10th

Janetta's talents for organizing have as usual begun to make sense of her difficult problems. Arriving full of strength from Spain, sun, love and hard work, it is in a way sad to see her courageous barque nearly sunk by the weight thrown onto it. She sits up to Spanish late hours and gets up with English earliness, brooding over her problems. She has already planned to let Montpelier Square, find a flat or independent lodging for Georgie and carry Rose off to Tramores, where a tutor will be found for her for the next two terms. Altogether she has the reins of her life pretty firmly in hand.

June 28th

An urgent need to pick this book up and stand it opposite me; to hold a con-versation with it, since I have no other vis-à-vis. If only it would answer! How impossible it is to manage without a 'best friend', if one cannot have a 'best beloved'. Janetta's disappearance has, I suppose, emphasized the fact that though I have many friends, none is 'best' in that he or she can be summoned to my aid when, as now, I suddenly feel myself uncertain and foundering, after years (literally) of apparently 'getting along'. Last night after my orchestra I went round to Montpelier Square, and found a curious scene. In the back room was a rather subdued party – Robin and Susan Campbell, Sonia Orwell, and Julian dressed in brightest pink and seeming rather overexcited and probably drunk. I had no private talk with Janetta, and am not sure if she really wants me to go to Spain in the autumn. All I have to go on is that when I said the Hendersons had asked me to Mijas, she said she 'would be furious if I didn't come to her too'. To be honest I feel a curious antipathy to that whole coast and its life – not, of course, to lovely Tramores, and if I do go there I would like to bury myself up there among the mountains and hardly approach the horrible coast. Then I must take some work.

Oh, I don't know, I don't know. I'm floating on a mounting tide, a very unaccustomed wave of uncertainty mixed with a feeling of not belonging anywhere. I'm distressed at my own prickly inability to fit into the lives of other people. Julia has asked me to go to Lambourn, and I've said I will next Monday, but shall I be able to stick it out? I think she would like me to go for more than a week, and in theory perhaps I could, but I so dread my own irritability, though I never stop trying to gulp it down.

Tonight Julian comes to dinner, something I look forward to very much. At his best he is almost the truest sounding-board and metronome I know. I have an idea why he vanished completely into another room when I was there last night. Perhaps I shall discover whether I was right.

June 29th

Yes, partly, and also as he candidly avowed, he was in a state of upset and sorrow about the occasion for our being gathered together: Janetta's departure, with her three nymphs, all looking particularly nymphlike, attractive, graceful and in a state of excitement about taking wing – Rose to Greece, Nicky to Paris, Georgie with Janetta to Spain. This was the reason why Julian had dressed in such brilliant pink clothes and wore a hectic pink expression. He honestly admitted what I see I was not up to admitting – being painfully saddened by Janetta's departure. His pink clothes were a touching attempt to hide the deep sadness which later exploded into tears in her bedroom. She is so important to us, we all miss her so, and worry rather broodily over her.

July 25th

Like a powerful red express train the heat wave drives its way steadily along its track. The stations are crowded with crimson-faced travellers, great or small, white and black, turning up their tortured faces towards the announcement board, then dragging their suitcases and paper bags and fretful children towards the grille where they stand sweating for hours like prisoners in a concentration camp. Around the Slade, where I spent last weekend, the trees have bulked out their dark green, full, summer silhouettes and the cornfields begin to turn yellow. The sun was almost too hot, yet how delicious was the air and free from flies. Eardley and Mattei were radiant with happiness, feathering their nest – and it has begun to bloom and flower, even though I'm surprised at their apparent vagueness about colour combinations. We were all happy I think, cooking, weeding, digging, translating. Yet there were moments when Eardley chilled me with his relentlessness about Crichel. So anxious is he to take away from them everything that is legally his that the Slade overflows with sofas and more and more pictures. 'And I'm going down to *swipe the lot*,' he ended up saying. He also asked how I thought Crichel was getting along, and said he 'thought it was running to seed terribly'. I'm afraid he wants it to fail, and I don't quite know why, now that he's quit of it. Ungenerous, surely?

July 27th: West Halkin Street

Dinner last night here, with Julia, Julian and Robert – three of my favourite companions, yet in a way I would have preferred being with any one of them alone. However, it seemed vital to support Julia through the remaining evenings before she leaves for Italy, and so the party evolved.

Julian arrived first, wearing the pink jacket that now seems to me rather like a hurricane cone. As a comforter and distracter of Julia he was perfect, and she was enthusiastic about him afterwards, but he brought a small tornado into my flat with its four inhabitants. Yet he was extremely amusing, and entertained us with brilliant imitations of Cyril Connolly and television life.

Robert started several of the general themes I so love. One of them arose from watching a would-be suicide trying to throw himself into the Haymarket for several hours on end yesterday afternoon. Robert's own inclination had been to turn away and escape as fast as possible. He dreaded seeing the man jump. But most people behaved quite differently. A youthful crowd was making a gala of it, thrumming guitars and watching with detached interest. Not ghoulishly, Robert thought, though a girl in his office said she 'longed to be there, it would be so exciting and interesting'. Perhaps their indifference was much healthier than his fear? Robert wondered. I said it didn't sound like indifference, which never keeps anyone waiting about anywhere for hours. Thence we got on to the difference between pity and sympathy – sympathy is surely far more desirable than pity – and to the fear of death and how it affected one's beliefs, with Malcolm Muggeridge as an example.

August 4th

Worry, when it takes over and fills the available space in consciousness, is like a sound starting small and faint and gradually swelling, and when you think it can get no louder, doing just that – swelling, blaring like an air-raid siren spelling danger, yet not having the saving grace of sirens – that they eventually descend again from their summits. Worry merely goes on shouting in one's ears until total exhaustion or restlessness takes its place; and it is always waiting in the wings to return.

Bunny came to dinner last night. He says he lies awake worrying; he is worried about Angelica, who has had what seems to be a small cancer removed from her breast. Yet in spite of all he gives a rather unearthly impression of being immune, detached. I do wish that the passing years would bring me such detachment and immunity. Instead I find myself increasingly involved and vulnerable, sometimes absurdly so. For instance, I have been re-reading Turgenev, beginning with my favourites, *Smoke* and *Torrents of Spring*, but when Ganin (in *Torrents of Spring*) deserts his sweet Gemma for the predatory vamp, I could not bear to read it. Quite literally I leapt ahead to the tragic conclusion and after swallowing it at a gulp (which seemed somehow easier than slowly advancing into doom) I went back over the ground again more slowly. It was a relief to talk to Robert yesterday – there is almost no one with whom I feel more in agreement about nearly everything. He at once put his finger on the flaw in the drug-takers' philosophy: its scorn for the reality principle. If one is to live in this world one must want to understand it as it is, be fully conscious and appreciate it with both mind and emotions as it is. To do otherwise is to be with Rosamond in her spirit world.

August 24th: At Nicko and Mary Henderson's rented villa, Mijas, Spain

The change is so easily effected and all my surroundings are so violently familiar that only last night when sleep was almost entirely unattainable did I realize what a shock of adaptation there always is. Fingers of consciousness kept going out into the night, and I couldn't stop being exquisitely aware of what I couldn't see – the land sloping down from this villa across humped hills towards Fuengirola, the nearer folds of hillside and their houses, the olives, the road winding off to Torremolinos, the mountain summit seen year after year from varying distances and always with a futile craving to be on it. All these imagined sights were the more vividly imprinted because this basin-like fold of the hills acts as a sounding-board and echoes every noise clearly and faithfully (dogs barking, cocks crowing, a stray motorbike, babies squalling), with acoustics as good as Snape Maltinghouse. Last night as we sat eating on our balcony, voices came very clearly from the restaurant in a pretty little old house opposite.

Mary very kindly met me at Málaga airport in the full heat of 3 p.m. and whisked me up into the hills. Almost like last year, there is a heavy, crushing heat hanging over everything – the sky partly veiled – and I should think there will any minute be an enormous storm. The sound of crickets all the time is deafening. The dry aromatic smell and the dusty brown landscape are old friends, and as we drove at once off the hideous main road we left the horrors behind.

Nicko is away, returning tomorrow. Staying here with Alexandra[1] are Rosamond's granddaughter, Anna Philipps, and an old-fashioned-looking, solid, blonde cousin of Alexandra's. Anna is attractive, bespectacled, dark, with a sensitive interesting face. They all seem very young for their age, and squeal and coo and make a fuss over the dogs.

Today the two girl visitors go.

I've eaten my breakfast – the heat is *tremendous*, the sky deep blue over the mountains, hazy over the sea. I'm wondering a very little how I shall pass my time – reading, I suppose, and writing letters. In the evening a visit from Janetta, Julian and Rose. We all sat on the balcony – the soft evening light had by now slipped away over the monticules between us and Fuengirola, over the sea, over the far horizon. Down below us Rose and Alexandra swam like slim, elegant crayfish in the pool, and were joined by Julian. All three visitors combined very sweetly to give me a sense of being welcome and its being worthwhile to have come out to see them. My room at La Fonda[2] awaits me – I begin to get a notion of what it is like there. Janetta looks smooth and happy.

August 26th

The ferocious heat changes moment by moment to a sky overcast with long tresses of pale grey seaweed and hot wind. Nicko due back from Madrid; the whole house – wife, daughter, three servants and above all the dogs – were visibly awaiting their lord and master. The large elegant dalmatian stared out anxiously at the landscape, started at every sound, and last night in the moonlight suddenly left the house and dashed across the valley looking for Nicko. Now and then he flops down with an impatient sigh, flinging out one leg sideways like a ballerina dancing *Le Cygne*.

[1] The Hendersons' only child, now Countess of Drogheda.
[2] Hotel beautifully decorated and run by Jaime, with Janetta as chef.

August 31st: Marbella

Yesterday I moved to La Fonda, and now at nearly ten, I am sitting up in the Greta Garbo suite waiting for my breakfast. My rooms are *extraordinarily* pretty – they couldn't possibly have been done up with greater taste. I have a large bedroom and sitting-room looking onto a jasmine-covered terrace and a huge old Victorian bed draped in lace. Its chief drawback is that it is directly above the bar, where chatter, tinned music and long, inane conversation goes on until two o'clock. Janetta had chosen me a quiet one on the top floor, but the occupant flew into a rage and threw my suitcase downstairs.

Janetta, Rose and I drove to Tramores. It simply is a masterpiece, looking as if it had always been there, and surrounded by matchless freshness and greenery and the circle of the lovely mountains. Even the fact that an absurd collection of film people were trying to shoot a scene under the Moorish castle couldn't rattle it. It stood firm and didn't yield a particle of its personality. Below the house, down to the huge swimming-pool of very warm water, everything that has been planted has sprung up and flourished. There are *huge* thorn-apple bushes, dangling their great cream-coloured flowers, morning glories, marvel of Peru, stocks, zinnias and a thousand other plants, while below the pool came fields of sweetcorn, laden fig trees, greengage and walnut trees. This then, is my first impression of Tramores – total subjection and admiration – not a single word of criticism. It is as if I had been confronted with a work of art and I bow down, most humbly and gratefully. I must get up, so will write no more now.

(Later) A man from the *Sunday Times* has come to interview Mark Culme-Seymour and Janetta about Donald Maclean. Hearing I had been at Nicko's he pricked up his ears. He too was on his list. Items of gossip momentarily aroused interest among the few sluggish occupants at the Fonda – 'Melinda Maclean has gone off with Philby.' 'No! Really?' 'And have you heard the very latest from Churriana? Bayard Osborne[1] has gone off with a mother of three.'

This morning I asked for my breakfast on my terrace, and am now lying on the lace cover of the big garden bed, protected from the faint morning sun by the roof of jasmine. It keeps dropping large, white, scented aeroplane propellers on me and they blow across the tiled floor in light drifts; I enjoy the isolation and peace, and have a mind to spend today very quietly and much alone, writing letters and not being at anyone's beck and call. Also I think it is Janetta's last day with Jaime before he goes on holiday and I very much don't want her to feel responsible for me. I have seen her a lot each day, and she has been sweetly solicitous for my comfort. But we have not had a lot of deep-going conversation. When she gets up to Tramores – we went again yesterday – she is a bewitched princess, and moves slowly round looking lovingly at each fruit tree or datura, considering the placing of a tile or the colour of a door. Her tempo becomes slower, and she must need this relaxation after several hours working in the Fonda kitchen each night.

September 4th

Jaime gone, Georgie gone, and soon I shall be gone too. I took a taxi to the Beach House yesterday, equipped with papers and book and a determination to do nothing contentedly all day, and in this I succeeded. No thinking goes on on this

[1] American painter.

coast; conversation is fragmented and the most *suivi* I had was with darling little Rose at dinner. There is something almost frightening in her rare sensitivity, the highly-tempered, delicate but strong material of which her character is made. I feel often as if a valuable, fragile and irreplaceable vase was within range of my fumbling hasty movements. I asked her if she could imagine living at Tramores and her face suddenly shone as if a candle had been lit inside it. It's clear she is in love with the place, almost as Janetta is, and she was pleased when I praised it wholeheartedly.

September 10th

Back to West Halkin Street and the Brenan crisis. A last visit from Gerald, and this time he didn't attack me. I was relieved when Julian said today that he had noticed how aggressive Gerald always was to me, though he believed he was as fond of me as of anyone, because I had begun to ask myself if I somehow provoked him. But on yesterday's visit he was all kindness and dulcet sweetness. Gamel has had two goes of her treatment. I can't help thinking she knows, and perhaps would rather 'play it' Gerald's way. This I felt when I said goodbye to her. 'I may never see her again' was the thought that echoed inside the tin can of my head. My brain is full of 'hundreds and thousands' and I cannot make much of the prospects lying ahead.

September 14th

Yesterday morning Julia rang me from Sonia's house, where she had taken refuge, and asked if she could come 'and rest on my bed that afternoon'. I gathered that things were not perfectly smooth between her and Sonia, who was just off to Paris. Julia arrived at two sharp and lay on my bed with the curtains drawn, neither reading nor sleeping for a good three hours. This, she says, just gives her strength to face the evening; she rests, but 'has never in her life fallen asleep'. I remember she used to do it in Rome. I am amazed by such a disrespect for the valuable waking hours. Before disappearing she amusingly described how impossible Sonia had been – bossy, hectoring, downright rude, finally saying that she 'was quite exhausted, and part of the reason was having to have Julia to stay'. Julia: 'Do take some sleeping-pills, won't you, and get a good night's rest.' S.: 'Sleeping-pills? Do you want me to kill myself?' With teeth set: '*Do you?*' She then bustled Julia off to bed, where she was going anyhow, and came back saying: 'Now into bed with you. I'm Nannie and I'm going to see you undress.' Julia has taken a great fancy to the young librarian who has been helping Sonia with the collected works of Orwell and she thinks Sonia is jealous. It's quite possible. Her other fixed belief is that Robert is a homosexual. In spite of acknowledging his great kindness to her in Italy, she criticized him because in company 'he never once addressed a single remark to her, but always either to Ben Nicolson or Philip Toynbee.'

September 19th

I have been toiling steadily at revising Napoleon,[1] and am anxious to burrow through to the end. Meanwhile I have seen dozens of friends, and read the first volume of Holroyd's life of Lytton, which Raymond kindly lent me in proof.

---

[1] I translated four books on him by the French consul on St Helena.

What will the world say of it? I wonder. It is a monument of hard work and conscientiousness, yet I don't think it will fail to rouse shrieks about who these arrogant Bloomsberries thought they were, and why they were so beastly about each other. Nearly a dangerous corner with Julia about the book the other night. I don't quite know what emotion was the source.

September 21st

A disconcerting letter from Gerald. Half is written by a disconsolate husband ('We sit round watching her slowly die'), yet the emphasis has subtly shifted and he is now anxious *not* to prolong her suffering.[1] 'It's like the case for capital punishment, twenty years' imprisonment is infinitely more cruel ... When Gamel ceases to enjoy life I shall hope for a quick end ... She has been a little despondent ... [The cobalt treatment] *might* prolong her life by a few months but of what use will that be if it is to make her feel depressed?' Then with almost shocking suddenness he reverts to his new girlfriend Lynda. He has asked her 'to come and live with him when the time comes'... and she has 'gladly accepted'. Then – really, really! – 'the very fact of my loving Gamel as I do makes me require someone on whom I can turn my affection when she is no longer here. *I feel Heaven has sent Lynda!*' (My italics).

September 22nd

When Michael Holroyd comes to spend the evening with me I describe the same graph each time. A surprised feeling of sympathy and easy communication to begin with: then (as he gradually becomes more at his ease) I begin to wonder: *is* he too confident of his literary judgements and criticisms? How much can one plot a human shape by what it likes? He loves Chekhov (good start) and also Turgenev, whom he read when quite young. But doesn't like Henry James or Proust – and his newest enthusiasm is for Sylvia Townsend Warner.

I talked about the account he has given of Carrington's suicide, and how I had not had the faintest recollection of Bryan Moyne's gun being borrowed by Carrington; moreover felt completely sure that Ralph, Carrington, Bunny and I had *not* driven back from Biddesden with the gun in the car. Possibly she asked Bryan on this occasion and went to fetch it later. All this because he wrote as if this had happened under Ralph's nose. I had talked to Bunny, Gerald and Julia about it, and all from various sources confirmed my view. But last night Holroyd told me that it was from *Gerald* that the story had in fact come! F.: 'But didn't you realize how uninterested Gerald is in the truth?' M.: 'Perhaps, but I admire him so enormously as a writer?' What makes someone into a 'great friend'? This I feel Gerald to be, and yet, and yet, on two of my last four meetings with him he attacked me violently. I am aware that he has done all he can to depreciate Ralph in print, and may well do more.

September 26th

I took Sophie out from school and brought her back here last Thursday. She is such a darling little girl, so full of rare qualities, sweetness, sense and fun, that I find it unbearable to contemplate any possible unhappiness for her. This is, and always

[1] Gamel had been diagnosed as having inoperable cancer.

was (perhaps disastrously for Burgo) my besetting failing, leading to self-torment and guilt, but perhaps not to the beloved creature's happiness. Sophie has grown up enormously through her holiday with Quentin and his family and her mind has leapt ahead, stimulated no doubt by his older children. There is nothing she seems unable to take in – except perhaps death, of which she is frightened. When someone was mentioned (not Burgo) who was dead, she gave a noisy shudder and said, '*I* shan't get dead, shall I?' And I loved the way she sat at the piano, not vaguely banging, but picking out notes in a really musical way with curled fingers like hammers, singing as well, often trying to and succeeding in singing the note she was striking, or if she failed, saying 'No, that's not right.' Always perfectly in tune, and often to fanciful, imaginary words.

October 18th

No one writes to me, I was just thinking, and then suddenly a huge fat envelope from Gerald came through my letter-box – thirty-eight pages, covered in small, close writing. Fascinating, of course, yet sometimes terrifyingly inhuman: here (jumbled together) were Gamel's character, her relation to him, the torturing conflict between wanting her to die quickly (so that he shan't miss the chance of his Lynda[1]) and genuine pity, his views on all Lytton's books, Freud, Wittgenstein, death, life, love, determinism. The only subject he cannot see clearly at all is himself, as is much and comically in evidence. He is the innocent, unworldly 'poet'; so far as I know he has never convicted himself of the slightest malice even. I laughed aloud when I read that *Gamel* was responsible for his peering at girls over cliffs, 'there is nothing of the voyeur in me'(!!) He has been peering over cliffs ever since I knew him and long before Gamel ever came to England. He also says, 'Of course I couldn't tell anyone about Gamel's drinking,' implying that he nobly suffered in silence, while the truth is that I've never met anyone he *didn't* tell. But his letter is extraordinary, enthralling; it's strange but true that I count myself as fortunate in having *such* a friend. The letter took me quite an hour to read and I was shaking with agitation, indignation and amusement when I finished reading it.

November 9th

Bunny came last night to talk about his present situation.[2] I have never known him nicer, more realistic, without pride, complaining that he didn't enjoy feeling self-pity but was in no way indulging it. All that I like most in his character came to the fore. He talked of Angelica without any bitterness but with great sadness. He himself was after all twenty-four years older. 'When I married her I didn't expect she would stay with me so long.' Then he made some very accurate comments on Angelica's character. He said he had stronger paternal feelings than she had maternal ones. I asked if she went in for self-analysis? 'Not usually. But a year ago she tried hard to analyse herself, and after a long time she reached the conclusion that it was *my* fault she wanted to leave me. I told her I didn't hold myself responsible in the least, and that quite shook her and she said I was probably right and we'd better try again.' I asked why he thought she really had wanted to

[1] Price, his new friend.
[2] Angelica wanted to leave him.

leave him? 'The need to express herself; she's full of talents and has never given enough time to them, or else gone off on some side issue like mosaics.'

November 23rd

My horror over Gerald's last two letters kept me in a fever all yesterday, and went on even after I had tried to discharge it in a fairly strongly-worded letter. I told him his letter had 'greatly upset me' though I didn't say how, and then went on that I felt a violent need to say one or two things. First, *Money*: Here I told him what I was trying, with Janetta's help, to do; and suggested that the bills could be met later or by selling some object and I begged him not to worry Gamel in any way about money. His cruel insensitiveness about this appals me. My second point was that he must get in a nurse at once; the moment has come. It is too awful for Gamel to be in the hands of two jealous squabbling people. Of course I didn't put it like that, but I did write less sympathetically to him than I ever have before. Janetta completely shares my blood-curdled horror. Julian was disposed to be more sympathetic and understanding towards Gerald, and to interpret his behaviour classically as showing a sense of guilt. But *does* it? I'm not aware that Gerald has ever shown any signs of such a thing in his dealings towards anyone, and of course I think of Ralph and Carrington and the events of the past. What sense is there in saying someone is 'suffering from a suppressed sense of guilt' if they show no trace of it except violent egotism and unawareness of others?

November 27th

There was the pleasure last weekend at Hilton of seeing Bunny cheerfully providing delicious roast pheasants (plucked and cooked by himself) for three of his girls and Sophie and William and me. And the counterbalancing feeling of shock when I heard the three girls and William planning to go north to their cottage in Swaledale and leave him quite alone for Christmas. And Sophie is to be sent off for a whole fortnight, to stay with one of Lucian Freud's mistresses called Bernardine and her two little girls.[1] Postponed a day or two because she wasn't well, she seems to be going today, and Henrietta says one of the little girls is her best friend and that Sophie wants very much to go. I expect she will have great fun with the other children – and it seems that the Swaledale plan may be off, so perhaps Bunny will have company for Hilton. So I can set aside my fanciful plan of taking rooms at Brighton for Julia, Sophie, Bunny and me! None the less I go on moving around these chess-pieces endlessly in my head, particularly when I wake in the night and their movements are informed with the weak-mindedness of my post-flu mood. I long to drag myself into a more profitable orbit. But if I glance further away – to Spain, say – there is Gamel dying and Gerald probably angry with me for my interfering letter; or there is Janetta who writes to no one.

December 23rd: The Slade

Yesterday morning I drove quietly down through silent mist, and here I am away from everything. Julia came to dinner the night before I left, looking fantastically young and pretty, dressed for a cocktail party which she had failed for some reason to get to; she was interesting but peppery. At last having 'done her budget' – a fatal

[1] Esther and Bella.

move – she had decided that 'after the essential expenses she had only seven pounds a week for everything, so couldn't possibly afford whisky'. She had therefore tried something called 'Dry Fly sherry' and not found it to her taste. There was about twenty minutes' fulmination against 'the cosmos'. My shameless canvassing had got her a second kind Christmas invitation, to go to Golders Green with the Penroses. But the other evening she was furious because Margaret had 'rung up to ask when I wanted to come' in a practical rather than a welcoming way.

December 24th: Christmas Eve

Sweet and blessed peace is what one gently inhales here like the incomparable air. Yesterday was a day of method. I translated all morning at the table in 'Mattei's little French sitting-room', warm, silent, a few logs speaking quietly from the hearth, and (outside) the rural scene lit by mild sun. Lunch of cold things – salad, the ham I brought, cheese and fruit. After lunch I walked for a while up the lanes by myself, while the others toiled planting fruit trees. How I did *not* envy them, and how intense was my pleasure as I looked up at the fast but quietly moving clouds (moonstony, pigeon's breast-feathers, pearly pinks and blues); or into the hedges where there were such surprising signs of life – ferns fully decorated with orange spores, catkins and buds; and collected a bunch of these springlike twigs and ferns as well as ghostly skeleton grasses and umbels, to add to the pale pink chrysanthemums in the drawing-room. My lane was new to me and provided sudden dips and climbs and sideways glances along field-paths and hedgerows bloomed over with Old Man's Beard. I had to return, but hardly wanted to. The immense sun, almost as pale as the moon, had nearly vanished behind the hill.

A little more work; gramophone records, reading and bed. My room is very snug with a comfortable bed; I like the fact that no one goes into it, and it is all my own.

December 26th

Raining and blustering with a soft and distant roar most of yesterday; we didn't go out at all. Turkey for lunch, work, reading Van Gogh's letters, at first unattracted by their constricted, religious, adolescent quality and the feeling of his charm-lessness. Then comes the extraordinary explosion into articulacy and feeling as well as writing – page after page of it, when other careers are abandoned and he takes to painting. And again when he falls in love. Before one's very eyes a genius bursts into flower from what was a nondescript, cramped bud.

Meanwhile Eardley and Mattei play Canasta as they do every night, revealing their characters and the nature of their relationship. Squared up face to face across a table set in front of the fire, it is a flirtatious battle, in which Eardley becomes more masculine and Mattei rather feminine.

December 28th

I rang up the Penroses, unable to resist asking how Christmas went off with Julia.

Margaret: 'It was *marvellous*. Frightfully nice. We enjoyed it enormously and I really think Julia did too. I hope so, anyway.'

This morning I rang Julia: 'A bloody awful Christmas. Oh, they were very kind of course, all of them, but I simply felt like a stray cat.'

Why does the stray cat feel no gratitude for being taken in, I wonder, as a stray cat of many years' standing. I didn't hear much more about the horror of staying at the Penroses'. Lionel and Shirley had passed with honours; Margaret failed. Julia three times said she was 'inharmonious' whatever that meant, her food was appalling and her housekeeping ditto. She added: 'Some of it was quite funny really, but I should feel *disloyal* telling you over the telephone.'

1968

January 1st: Stowell (the Tycoonery)

Sunday lunch with the Barings and Annabel Lindsay at Shalbourne. A large Victorian gathering with delicious food and wine. Quite a lot of talk to the Tycoon in the morning. He has read a lot, with interest and care; he tells me he rehearses the book he is reading if he wakes in the night. He's not a clever man nor a stupid one, but he's fierce to anyone who gets in his light. Even this has exceptions – he is an adoring grandfather and loving father. I think I got on with him rather well, by dint of talking a lot about books and letting his outrageous expressions of opinion fly by, like cricket balls you don't attempt to field.

Now I'm speeding back to London in a warm buffet car, frosted with human breath, through which I see the country covered in thin snow. I feel as if I were abroad, especially as three women are talking French. At dinner last night the Tycoon was positively jolly. I talked a lot to Jacob. Everyone spoils and humours the Tycoon like mad, whether because he's a millionaire or just an ill-tempered man I don't know, but I have to admit there's something likeable about him.

January 13th

There has been trouble at the Kees' – fairly bad. Robert came to lunch yesterday. My fear that he wouldn't talk, that I should see that shut – more than shut, locked – expression was not fulfilled. But my heart was wrung by the pallor and anxious sadness of the face waiting outside my door; though it melted quickly in conversation, it is of course the understratum. Certainly our conversation did no harm; I don't know that it could have done much good. I did get him to talk quite freely though, curbing my own natural volubility. Nor did he reject my suggestion of a London working room, with weekends of family life – but I doubt if he could face a more definite breach. I said my dread was that he'd let things just slide till they got as bad again, and he seemed to accept this possibility. We talked on such subjects as why he had to ill-treat his wives and be angelic to other people, without really clearing them up. He knows it's true, refers it back to early childhood. Some talk, too, about mind and brain, and of a suggestion he had heard or read (not new, surely?) that there is only one entity, not two – that all mental processes can be put in terms of brain, and that what we call 'mind' occurs only when the brain reaches a certain degree of complexity. Computers will achieve it in time. Yes, I can take that – easier perhaps than their having feelings (in what terms can the affective side of life be expressed on this new view?): a computer is to give a concert of its own work at the Festival Hall. Would it feel stage fright, its proprietor (owner, husband, what the hell must one call it?) was asked. 'Oh yes, very probably.'

To go back to Robert: he obviously wants to try and make a go of the marriage, but does Cynthia? Or rather, can she face going on trying? When I think back to her quiet voice saying she must leave, and that perhaps she should just have done it without saying so, I feel doubtful. It was because of this that I tried very tentatively to see how much the marriage meant to him. He said that 'he was very fond of her,' that she was 'a good companion', that he 'admired her'; but it's clear he knows that their minds work on very different planes.

January 18th

The Kee crisis has left me in a hyperaesthesic state. I wonder continually how they are 'getting on', but have not dared ring up. Also Julia; and then there are Gerald's letters describing Gamel's approach to death with increasing vividness, obviously moved by it to his maximum degree of sensibility. He has great power to convey what he feels, and I feel it with him – particularly that sense of the loneliness of dying. In trying to avoid Gamel's feeling too much alone as she goes into the dreadful arena, he spends hours and hours holding her poor hand or stroking her forehead. I am deeply touched by this, and I believe in some way he has come nearer to fully loving her, now that she is dying, than ever before. And this is something to do with his being in no way a realist, but appreciating things acutely through his imagination.

Yesterday I saw no one bar Mrs Murphy, and quite looked forward to it. But when evening came and I sat down to read for the second time an essay by Lionel on Consciousness lent me by Margaret, and when I tried to marshal my wits and read it critically, thinking what the implications were, and whether he made out his case – or indeed what it was – I began to quiver all over with the effort and agitation, and after I got into bed lay awake for hours of sparkling but futile consciousness, almost hating this stuff I generally rate so high in my scale of values, or wishing I could at least temporarily be quit of it. I'm interested in the difference between the scientific and the philosophical approach. Lionel writes entirely as a scientist; he sets before one strange patterns of facts (that can only be mutely accepted), and then leaps forward to throw out a number of 'hunches' – for instance, can people 'share' the 'same state of consciousness'? He worryingly, and rather unphilosophically however, doesn't say whether by 'same' he means 'identical' or 'similar'. Of course great discoveries are made by hunches and Lionel *is* the man to have them, but unless they are supported by some evidence – just a little – they strike almost as hollowly as Rosamond's about the spirit kingdom.

I have rung Cynthia; they are going on much as before, except that Robert seems calmer. I have also rung Julia, who has been looking after a girl living in her flat who has 'flu. It has taken her out of herself.

Julia was condescending about Lionel's Consciousness paper – to *me*, not him, needless to say. 'When one's reading these scientific papers week by week, one begins to realize that all scientists work by hunches. *You* won't like that. Mystical, eh? I don't suppose you liked his saying inanimate matter possessed consciousness.' F.: 'But he didn't say that.' Julia: 'Well, he thinks so anyway; he told me so. And I was pleased that my hunch was the same as his.'

Later Margaret rang up, asking my opinion of this paper, and said, 'I can't think why Julia imagines he supposes inorganic matter to have consciousness. He doesn't believe any such thing.' It delighted me when Margaret said at the end of our conversation, 'You've cheered me up, no end,' and I realize (and wished that I'd been the first to say it) that *she* had cheered *me* up.

January 19th

Bunny to dinner last night, and lots of what Desmond called 'good talk', among other things about communication. He said, what I have always believed, that losing the loved one through death is in a way easier to bear than their simply taking themselves off. (He has after all experienced both.) There is inevitable resentment and bitterness against the once loving person whose other life has bereft you. Bunny said he felt he didn't know what to do with his desire to communicate – to make a present to Angelica of everything he did. This is immensely understandable, and I so very well remember that awful sense of amputation.

What happens when in the long rung one does adjust? A sort of parleying with oneself is set up and goes on almost continuously. You could call it thinking, but sometimes it doesn't deserve the name. When I wake in the night words are nearly always running through my head. Real thinking is harder work alone than when one has a shadow-boxing partner, as I did always with Ralph. Last night too with Bunny I noticed how much easier it was to think when there was his wall to bounce my tennis ball against. Thinking all by oneself is a fearful effort.

Oh, God – another twenty pages of feverish rambling from Gerald – poor Gamel is not dead yet and the doctor won't give her morphia 'as it would certainly kill her'. The barbarity of the religious!

January 23rd

Gamel died last Thursday, thank God. I had reached a point of wondering if I should telephone Janetta to ask her to get a doctor from Málaga or Gibraltar to overpower the local monster and give morphia. Yesterday I found a short, calm, *relieved* note from Gerald.

January 26th

I came home from the first night of *Aïda* to find a letter from Janetta, crossing mine. She described – what I had been aware of – Gerald's gentleness and calm during the last terrible weeks of Gamel's life. Also the briskness with which he was dealing with what was left of her – burning bedding, stacking and giving away clothes. A very good thing, and I remember doing it myself, but it brings home how very dead the dead are. Memory is all there is of immortality. I think his mainspring may recoil quickly and we may soon hear of Lynda again.

February 5th

I've returned from a visit to Anne and Heywood, with (in the background) Eddie and the poor old lady, who has taken a big stride towards the tomb. Her life seemed to me unbearably sad to contemplate, and anyone who loves her must surely long for it to end; but Anne said firmly that she was positive she enjoyed many things and didn't want to die. I wondered if this was that old brute guilt in Anne trying to cancel out her natural longing for her mother to die. Last night, with a full gale blowing, lashing rain and pitch darkness, I was appalled to see a mop of white hair waving outside the window of Anne and Heywood's 'bicycle-shed'. Heywood, gently and tenderly as ever, helped her in, and she sat down panting in a chair, and began to talk confusedly about the nurse who is fetched from the village to spend every night with her. Lady Cranbrook can never remember why or when she comes, resents and complains of her coming, but would be frightened without her. This evening, hours before it was time for her to be fetched, she must have suddenly begun to fuss about Heywood having to drive and get her. She evidently suggested that Eddie should go instead of Heywood. 'He refused. He said he was sixty-six,' she said with a sudden flash of amusement in her dead blue eyes. 'Was he cross?' said Heywood. 'Not cross. *Firm*,' she said, still smiling. Then she burst into tears. Why should she have this nurse? She didn't want her in the least, and she was quite unnecessary. 'No, you know you really *love* having her, Mamma,' said Anne in a brisk but comforting voice. 'She's just like a sort of *lady's maid* – she does all sorts of things like filling your hot-water bottle in the middle of the night.' When she had gone, Anne and Heywood dismissed the tears as unimportant. It was always happening. But I felt that what she was crying about was her hateful plight – not just a brush with Eddie – and that she does not want to go on living, even though she may be frightened to die.

The *Sunday Times* has a wide spread from Holroyd's next volume – my Carrington portrait of Lytton is very large across the top, with Carrington and Gertler on either side. Next week I suppose it may be Ralph or Gerald. Heywood has read the book and feels it quite astonishingly outspoken and that I, and other living people involved, 'must' – or should? – 'mind'. Roy Harrod also feels, so I hear, that I shall be very upset. But then he is a conventional man who thinks that homosexuality and illicit love should be hinted at but not described. I am at a loss to analyse my own feelings, past and present, and certainly to prognosticate the future.

February 10th

A dinner party two nights ago, and not having had one for ages I took an enormous amount of trouble. Delicate cucumber soup, *boeuf créole* (with rum, black olives and pimentoes) and even a *crème brûlée* which I have never made before. Duncan had been the focus of the party, and he was ill with a cold and couldn't come, but Boris made as good a substitute as anyone could, looking like a monumental Buddha in his elegantly cut, wide suit. Georgia at once noticed the 'yards and yards of stuff' that had gone into the trousers. Someone else noticed the special chic of his square-toed shoes. No one could fail to be struck by his splendid presence.

Bunny was bowled over by Magouche, and I was rather surprised by her on-coming response, which made Bunny's face radiant with pleasure.

Now next day I feel rather flat. Am going to peg on and finish my task. Then wing off to Spain.

February 13th

I asked Julia to dinner, to eat the remains of my dinner party. Was she perhaps annoyed at not being asked to it? She arrived in a rather dictatorial mood; asked for – or ordered – a pot of tea at 6.15 – '*Strong, please,*' and then settled down to go on reading one of Gerald's letters written when Gamel was dying. I could tell from her comments that she had been planning to pull him to pieces as she came along the street, and I don't like these blood-sports. She soon began saying that he seemed to her 'frog-like', 'inhuman' and 'boring'. Didn't I agree? Then came the sinister remark, 'I can detect it in his voice and face.' Ever since this traumatic phrase was applied in her stinker to me, I cannot help feeling it is really aimed at me when I hear it. However, nothing could have gone more smoothly than the whole evening. She got on to the 'stray cat' theme, and I said the world was full of stray cats and we were all stray cats, and listed a few others. They were all disqualified in one way or another. She hugs her misery to her and desires no competition. My claim to be a stray cat was waved aside – 'Oh no, you've got your boyfriend Eardley.'

Sunday brought another dollop of Holroyd – really very vulgarized by the Sunday paper. 'Trouble at the Mill House', and a huge portrait of Ralph and Carrington. It shocked me, and the next lot may do so even more. I mentioned it on the telephone to Julia. She brushed it aside – she won't hear of any criticism of Holroyd, yet she has only by her own admission 'pecked about' in his first volume.

Duncan came to see me yesterday. How magnetically delightful he is! He says Angelica writes ecstatically that she is wildly in love with George Bergen[1] though she admits he is difficult.

February 17th

Saturday morning in London. I am already ducking in anticipation of the next instalment of Holroyd tomorrow in which I suppose I shall probably figure, and already my friends have been commiserating with me, one and all (except Julia) appalled by the vulgarity of newspaper popularization, but it is rather feeble only to object to this treatment by the papers when one is the victim oneself. Everyone (except Eardley) to whom I have talked about Holroyd's book thinks it 'very badly written'. Julian had a very good phrase: he is a 'literary buccaneer', and in this case has cashed in on the Bloomsbury belief that the truth must be told. I'm going to see Alix today – I wonder what her attitude will be.

February 22nd

What is the source of my horrid agitation? The end of my translation and the explosion of Holroyd's book and violent anti-Bloomsbury feelings, as well as finding that I *do* mind the appalling vulgarization of my own and Ralph's and dear friends' lives in the Sunday papers. Roy was right then to some extent. I don't mind the book, but I suppose none of us would have produced the information we did had we known it was to be distorted by the Sunday papers into the likeness of a *News of the World* account of the lives of film stars.

Last Sunday there was a picture of sweet Ham Spray's face (a photo taken by me, as it happened) with a screaming headline about the 'Abode of Love'. I was overcome by a wave of indignation, but what on earth is the use?

Everyone else I have spoken to about it thinks the Sunday extracts appalling. I was delighted by a postcard from Desmond saying; 'Would my prosaic and unfanciful old friend (my hat!) consider coming with me to the *Queen of Spades*?' These adjectives were Holroyd's estimation of Lytton's view of me.

Meanwhile some of the reviewers acclaim the book *as* a book and others like Muggeridge and Grigson take it merely as a text for an anti-Bloomsbury and anti-

---

[1] American painter, had been a lover of Duncan many years before.

Lytton screech. Muggeridge, going particularly far, says that Holroyd's *Carrington* is a 'marvellous *comic* portrait', that she was a 'nymphomaniac weirdy' and 'the poor lady took her own life.' Squelch! – it is all rather disgusting and I wish now the book had never been written. I'm glad James did not live to read these frenzied hymns of hate. I am now starting to read Volume 2 carefully and with as much detachment as possible, and I do find it absorbing.

I must remember some very nice things to counterbalance these murky agitations: going to *Mastersingers* with Julian, on the very night of Heinemann's party for Holroyd. Six hours of rich all-enveloping experience, and the music having such powers of penetration that it is with me still, all the time circulating in my head. Poor Julian was quite exhausted by many nights of too little sleep, but he sat attentive and wide-eyed beside me like a touching child. He is the perfect companion for such things.

Again and again and more and more and more do I feel that loving people is the one great pleasure in life. Sophie, darling little girl, provided more of that pleasure when I took her to lunch at the Kees' at Kew. Paralysed by shyness at first, she suddenly unfroze and when the children of Caroline Citkovitz[1] joined us, all six had a wonderful time running in the park. It was a great joy to see Sophie running with scarlet cheeks, clambering on trees, turning somersaults. I had to run too, she wanted me to turn somersaults. 'I'm much too weak,' I said. 'You're *not!*' She asked me if I had a grandmother. As I drove her home she fell fast asleep, and I looked at her ravishing little profile beside me, knowing I should remember this moment.

February 26th

The last instalment of Holroyd has appeared in the Sunday papers, and, perhaps because of the genuinely moving nature of the material, it was not vulgarized. I'm glad it's all over, however. I wonder what Ralph would have felt about it. I'm unable to guess when I meet people I don't know well which camp they will be in. I've finished Volume 2 and think it on the whole extremely good and (to me at least) enthralling. Nor do I charge my agitation over the last weeks to Michael Holroyd, but to the vulgarity of the papers. How good Lytton was as a writer I now propose to reassess for myself, and leave the critical chapters till after doing that.

I stayed with Kitty last weekend: iced beauty, pale blue skies, blue tits doing acrobatics just outside the window, only one brisk solitary walk, a lot of talk and reading. Frank Tait and Billy Henderson,[2] who came to dinner one day, questioned me closely about Carrington. So did the Sterns[3] with whom we lunched yesterday. I try hard to get her right, but even allowing for all intrusive emotions it's not easy. Also I'm bewildered by the nature of the antipathy aroused in Muggeridge and Grigson. I don't see how any reader of the book can be unmoved by such touching and constant devotion.

[1] Née Blackwood. Married to Lucian Freud and Robert Lavell.
[2] Doctor and painter.
[3] James, writer, and Tanya.

February 29th

Am I perfectly mad to persist in my plan of going to Spain next week, in face of such slight encouragement? Gerald writes short, sad, distracted letters, showing plainly that he is desperately keyed-up at the thought of Lynda's arrival, but not revealing whether it would be a relief or the reverse not to be quite alone with her. Nor if he can face having me for a week until Janetta returns from Morocco, which seems to be her plan. Both he and Janetta write of a fortnight's incessant rain, the road to Tramores being cut off. When Gerald's last letter came I nearly cancelled my whole trip, he seemed to show so little enthusiasm for my visit and the ghosts of his lack of welcome in the past rose up suddenly to haunt me. I wonder, too, if his aggressive mood of last September may be revived, and though I feel I can stand it at the moment, and want to try to help and comfort him I may well fail to do either.

March 5th

Weekend at the Carringtons', and *endless* discussion of 'the book'. No, my agitation over the whole subject has not died down, and I am really somewhat dreading the re-turning of the soil that will be started off by Gerald. Julia this morning suddenly spoke with warmth and kindness of Ralph, saying how fond she and Lawrence had both been of him and that she had looked up Holroyd's description of him and found it 'totally inadequate'. I was moved to sudden speechlessness. This image is of course Gerald's creation and had it not been for interpolations of mine it would have been further still from the truth.

I went to London to find a further letter from Janetta still mentioning no dates, but saying they would be 'going to Morocco almost at once', and I pictured myself marooned with a hostile Gerald, waiting, waiting for Godot. A slow bruise emerged as a result – but Janetta has applied Ellerman's embrocation by a touching cablegram today saying she is putting off Morocco and will collect me on the eleventh. *Infinite* relief, but I do feel guilty lest she has put off Morocco for me, though I telegraphed her not to. She ends: 'Secretly fear Gerald's house rather cold.'

The best comment on Holroyd's Lytton is Frances Phipps': 'Oh, that *book*! When I die I'm going to have SHUT UP put on my tombstone.'

March 7th

Airborne at last. Flying almost bores me now; I never even bothered to look out, but munched my way through re-heated meat and tinned peaches. I had expected sweet warm air to enfold me at Málaga airport, but it was cold and grey as London. At Gerald's I found Rosario and the little girl Mari. Soon Gerald appeared, looking years younger. How totally unexpected! Lynda had arrived the day before but gone to ground with a bilious attack. Gerald: 'She's a *very* nice girl, very intelligent, quite different from what I remembered. I wouldn't have recognized her. I've done very well for myself. I think she'll be happy here. She wanted to be quiet and read, but she's very attractive and if she wants to have her boyfriends to stay she can, I shan't mind. We sat up till two or three last night talking.' F.: 'What does Rosario make of it?' G.: 'Well I don't know, but she said to me, "Don Geraldo, you must get yourself a girl." I've been terribly lonely, especially in the evenings. I can't live alone. I never think of Gamel. I don't think of her *at all*. Sometimes I dream of her, but I don't think of her.'

The house is extremely cold and smells of tom-cat. I am evidently to sleep in Gamel's room, in the bed where those ghastly scenes Gerald's letters described took place, and where she died. Do I mind? I don't think so, but I feel a lack of sensitivity in putting me there. Also I've had to ask for another blanket.

After tea in the *mirador* Gerald and I strolled up the familiar hillside path while he talked with unseeing eyes, mainly about Holroyd. He half-identifies himself with him, feels *he* has written the book or at least contributed most of the material, is delighted with his own portrait in it. He is making Holroyd his literary executor, and has asked him to stay. (I wonder if Julian and Jonny know they have been ousted.) He was very friendly and warm to me, without prickles or raised hackles. Lynda appeared before dinner, wrapped in a warm, blue dressing gown. She has a wide, pale, oval face with truthful brown eyes and a friendly catlike smile, a soft voice. I liked her.

I have told Gerald I don't want to be entertained, and will fend for myself. Of Gamel he said, 'We were very remote these last years; perhaps I was to blame, but we had hardly anything to say to each other. I have no desire whatever to talk about her illness. Most of what I felt for her was intense pity.' It's extraordinary, come to think of it, that so voluble a man should ever have been short of things to say. He never is with anyone else. His lack of desire to talk of Gamel and her death is unique in my experience of bereaved people – but a huge relief.

It *poured* with rain, drumming on the garden lilies, this evening.

March 8th

A night of shallow sleep, seeming very long and strange. Each time I woke I thought, 'I'm lying on Gamel's deathbed.' This made me want to open the window and it was terribly cold. 'It's the coldest day we've had,' said Gerald calling me. But the sun is shining and I'm sitting in it now against the far garden wall on a small hard iron chair. There's a border of freesias in front of me, clumps of violets beside me. I shall hope to spend every morning here till the sun goes off. Gerald told me Lynda would 'be reading in the *mirador*'. Actually she was talking hard to him in his bed-sitting-room as I went out. I don't think he'll waste much time before he starts making up to her after his fashion. He says he has been feeling ill, and the *practicante* comes every day to inject him, but he looks very well, and I now think much of the scattiness of his recent letters was due to anxiety about Lynda. I think he is really quite pleased for me to be here, but there is nothing I can do for him, none of those services most of my friends seemed to think I could provide. He is *perfectly all right*. What an extraordinary being!

March 9th

Oh yes, Gerald is an astonishing character. It is all to the good, no doubt, that he does not miss or think of Gamel at all; yet surely this means total lack of love for her, in the ordinary sense of the word, all these years they've lived together? He makes an impression of being happy as a sandboy now. I went to my room to lie down after lunch but it was much too cold. He came in and asked me eagerly, 'Do you like Lynda?' I said truthfully that I did, very much. '*Isn't* she a nice girl? *Aren't* I lucky? *Lucky Brenan*!' She appears to me sweet-natured, serious, a reader, reserved, attractive rather than actually pretty, thoughtful, but does not give herself completely away. Gerald is in an excitable state, shows off a good deal ('I never show off'), and is beginning to reveal that he feels like a boy again by running when other people would walk, even hopping and jumping, and saying *what* a pity it is he never learned to dance almost as if he still might. I can't really imagine what there is in this situation for Lynda, and wonder whether her poetry means much to her and how good it is.

In the late afternoon Gerald took us both on an enormous three-hour walk on the hillside (in itself a show-off), nearly to Torremolinos and back, among olives and carobs, orchids and iris. Lynda was amazed and exhausted by this performance.

Much Holroyd-Lytton talk. I refused to agree that Lytton's *Landmarks* was taken in chunks from textbooks or a pot-boiler, or that he had read none of the originals. Again I was struck by Gerald's seeming to feel that Holroyd's was *his* book. 'I wonder why he speaks of Valentine Dobrée as being deformed,' I said vaguely, 'I don't remember that she was.' He looked slightly cornered. 'Oh yes, I told him that. I think one of her legs was longer than the other, or something. I'm not sure what.' F.: 'And then was she ever in an asylum?' G.: 'Oh, that was what *you* told me, I think.' (!!) I traced the source of this – a long letter – destroyed by me unfortunately as too prosy – from Bonamy to Ralph saying that he (Ralph) was upsetting his wife or words to that effect, but I don't think anything about asylums or even nervous breakdowns was mentioned. There has been little talk about Honor except that she slept under eight blankets and with this I now sympathize deeply. I go to bed in my underclothes under three blankets and with a hot-water bottle and wake in the night, frozen.

March 10th

I've begun reading Gerald's autobiography and find it of course fascinating, though he stands over me talking and talking as I read, so that it is hard to concentrate. He's like the fountain in the patio, gushing night and day without pause. Yesterday I took the autobiography out into the last pale rays of the sun to read in peace. When I came back the torrent was still pouring over Lynda.

This morning the cold was worse than ever. The starry sky under which we walked to the Cónsula gave way to rain and icy wind, grey sky and fresh snow on the mountains. I ran through the patio, where the huge leaves were being drummed on with a melancholy sound by the rain, and into the little dark bathroom, to revolve frantically for a few moments under the shower turned as near scalding as possible. No matter how hot the water or how long I stay under it, I am freezing when I come out and blot myself with a curiously unabsorbent towel. Impossible to spend the whole day crouched over the butagaz heater in the *mirador* so I put on coat, fur cap (thank heaven I brought it) and walked alone up the steeper slope of the mountain.

At nights the long hollow corridors of this house echo with the sound of Gerald clearing his throat. By day he champs ceaselessly on his false teeth. No laughing matter, look at it any way you like, and an indication that though Gamel has only recently died, he has been fundamentally a solitary for many years.

March 12th: Tramores

I'm quite knocked out by the astonishing change in ambience. I was right to trust Janetta – she even came earlier yesterday than I expected. I was therefore only at Churriana for four nights. Janetta is more sensible of the gloom, discomfort and cold of that house even than I am, and attributes a deep sadness to it. But to me it also trails an aura of seigneurial grandeur and romantic beauty.

Yesterday morning, Lynda asked me to walk into the village with her and we were just setting out when we ran slap into Janetta. Did Lynda want to ask my advice as an old friend of the strange septuagenarian she has settled in with? I shall never know. Gerald has repeatedly said to me, 'Of course there will be no love-making. I shall just make a companion of her and grow fond of her,' in his obsessional muffled monotone; but he has already started exploding into scabrous remarks and reminiscences (boastful on the whole) about his youth, and bringing out naked photographs of girls he once went to bed with. I feel touched by Lynda, who seems to be sensitive and reserved, and might react against his prurient voyeur characteristics.

Janetta drove me, talking all the way, along the familiar coast road to Jaime's house in Marbella. Sitting in his little patio under a blue sky, I felt I had crossed into a new continent. I had self-inoculated myself against the inevitable delays and didn't therefore mind them in the least. We finally set off to Benahavis where we waited for Jaime in his Land Rover. Weeks of rain and flood have nearly destroyed the road beyond and we shook and bounced up it and through the swollen river to Tramores. Met by Serge and pregnant married Nicky, beaming with happiness. Janetta bought her some blue and white wool and she at once started knitting a tiny vest, calling constantly for help and advice. Serge was rather silent as we sat round the fire last night. Janetta and Jaime both feel that he is 'against the world', and to some extent out to get from people what he feels the world has denied him. He and Nicky have lingered on and on here, and their departure has been several times postponed. How they will live when they get to London no one can imagine, as he has no money and no work. I grope for the key to his character, and it interests me. I asked Janetta what Georgie thought of him. 'She's very impressed by him.' Janetta and Jaime seem extremely close and happy, and Jaime said he adored Tramores and could hardly bear to tear himself away. Janetta is absorbed in the things growing in her garden, almost to the exclusion of everything else. Each bud is lovingly inspected every day. The house is a marvel of taste and beauty, and basic furniture has sprouted as it were from its walls. The silence and peace are wonderful. There is as yet no electricity; that is the only real deprivation, for our tiled bathrooms are useless, and beaked jugs of hot water arrive every day. But I love the soft light of candles and lamps, and a log fire burns in my room.

March 13th

Voltaire was fortunately absorbing, for Janetta returned very late, bringing a carpenter with her, and we lunched about four. Dinner nearer eleven than ten. After lunch I started to walk up the bed of the stream behind the house; but as I advanced into the huge circle of wooded mountains they rose up menacingly as if to swallow me, so that I was suddenly submerged in a nightmare feeling of loneliness. There was also an almost complete absence of flowers into which to project my libido. I turned home sadly and helped Janetta weed her terrace, which I enjoyed. How much does she think about the future? Hardly at all I believe. She has a letter from Derek saying he has married a French widow and that it 'might be better for financial reasons that she and Rose shouldn't return to England for a year'. I asked if she had thought of doing so, and if so, when. J.: 'I don't think I *need* go back, do you?' She warned me to keep off Vietnam with Serge as he felt so violently about it. But he came back from Marbella, drank more whisky than usual, and started the subject himself. I can't resist an argument, but I was on my guard. I think he was surprised to find my sympathies totally anti-American (I'm told this is the litmus-paper he tests everyone with. I thought he had taken a dislike to me, but since this talk he has been very friendly.) He said he thought we should give military support to the Vietcong. I declared my pacifism – and pessimism. I asked Nicky if she was still a pacifist; she looked thoughtful and torn. Serge launched an attack on pacifism as being unrealistic, saying one ought to compromise. I said my deepest belief was in correspondence without compromise between beliefs and actions (including speech).

March 16th

I have been surprised by Janetta's complete absorption in her life here, and lack of any thread of desire leading back to London, Georgie, Julian, Magouche, all that is happening there. When Nicky and Serge have left, and after Rose goes to live with Derek, what will take place on these cleared decks? I'm not at all sure how much she plots the future, nor how. But her pride in this magic creation of Tramores, and love for it, is of course completely understandable. I question myself: what do I feel for Tramores? If I were Janetta, should I love it as I loved Ham Spray? Yes for its beauty and atmosphere and the fact that it is a growing organism, but with its appalling road and the village quite a trudge away, and without light, hot water or telephone, I feel we are putting back the clock to the eighteenth century.

This morning I woke about eight, opened my shutters and lay looking out at the serene morning; only part of the mountains were as yet lit by the sun, but it gradually crept up and picked out the branches of the fig tree outside my door. I lay happily reading Voltaire for about an hour and then went to the kitchen and asked for breakfast. Luisa came back late to say, 'Señora, no hay pan.' I said I'd have a boiled egg. By ten o'clock Nicky, Rose and Serge were all champing and prowling. Serge at last set off in the now mended Citroën to the village. At eleven I saw him returning, and at the same time Janetta came out of her room holding some tiny biscuits and smiling her most cajoling smile: 'I brought these *for you*. How *stupid* of Luisa not to see them!'

March 24th

Woke to find the Tagus muffled in thick white mist. We kept waiting for over an hour the chauffeur of an English queer and Lisbon tycoon, Dicky Wyatt, who was to drive us to his country house in an idyllic homosexual setting, with blue and green parakeets flying loose in the trees, wild orchids in the grass, *soigné* lunch on the verandah. Wyatt was very put out by our tardiness, as he had meant to take us to see a beautiful house nearby before lunch, and had instead to sacrifice his siesta and do so afterwards. (Janetta pointed out that his conversation was a jigsaw of clichés.) The house was extraordinarily beautiful. Bacaloa Villa-fresca was its name, and I hope to remember at least the large tiled balconies and formal garden, the great ornamental water with its lake-house also lined with old tiles.

Drove on through lovely country to Tamar, stopping to pick hoop-petticoat daffodils and angel's tears. Janetta and Jaime want to dig up almost everything they see, even some plants that already grow wild but unnoticed at Tramores. Failed to get into the Pousada, but had an enjoyable night in a luxury hotel.

March 25th: Tamar

Raining dismally as we went up to see the famous sight, and it went on doing so without pause, all day. Cold also. Our spirits weren't really damped, only our clothes and hair as we got out, obsessively drawn to further sheets and sheets of hoop-petticoats and angel's tears. Got to Cáceres for the night and walked in an icy wind and occasional rain through its splendid streets of brown houses decorated with armorial bearings.

March 27th

To the Alcázar, the cathedral, and the Convent of La Caridad where I read there were two pictures of corpses by Valdes Leal that 'made you hold your nose'. An ancient nun showed me round, babbling and sinking to her old knees and getting up again, telling me with apparent joy that '*Polvo somos y a polvo volveremos.*'[1] Here Janetta and I parted from Jaime and set off in her car via Ronda to Tramores, where Nicky came out to meet us: 'There is some bad news, I'm afraid.' The *tia* had left in a dudgeon and Luisa said she wouldn't stay either. They felt they were being suspected of stealing fruit or eating too much; they find it lonely and dull, and hate the old-fashioned way of life. Poor Janetta drove off rather crestfallen to cook dinner for the Fonda, Jaime's hotel. On the way from Seville she talked a good deal about her plans. She has cast in her lot very definitely with Tramores, Jaime and Spain. Georgie must make the best of Montpelier Square and plan her own life, as Janetta did at her age. I found a letter from Gerald, writing about Lynda like a happy bridegroom on his honeymoon, but one who is not allowed all the favours he longs for.

April 8th: London

I arrived back in a miniature heat-wave; blue sky, temperature in the 70s; I tore off my Spanish clothes and for the first time for nights had no fire or hot-water bottle. A week later it was snowing, I have to admit. However, on the whole I find my old addiction to Spain slightly dwindled – as a place to *live* in, that is to say, and London more civilized, comfortable and stimulating. When I was in Dorset last weekend I compared that magical and flowery landscape with Spain's. Huge clumps of enormous primroses crowded every bank, mixed with tufts of violets, purple and white, celandine and hart's-tongue ferns.

April 17th

Mary said to me after finishing Holroyd's book, in rather an odd voice: 'By the way, I was always told that Carrington committed suicide because she had no money and no Ham Spray.' 'Nothing of the sort,' I answered. 'Lytton left her almost all his money, £10,000, and though Ham Spray was legally Ralph's he was only too eager to persuade her to live there.' I said no more, nor did she, and it was only later that I began to wonder who had 'told' her this, and thought 'Julia, of course'. For she has over and over again brought up to me a remark of Car-

---

[1] 'Dust we are and to dust we shall return.'

rington's that she couldn't face life in a bed-sitter in Notting Hill Gate, and I have felt the latent hostility in this. No one who has been involved in trying to prevent someone from committing suicide and failed can help feeling it a sore place, and resent it being deliberately scraped. Then over dinner with Jonny and Sabrina, Julia and her 'nephew' Ian Angus,[1] I rashly or perhaps mischievously mentioned Mary's remark, but of course without saying I had any idea whence it derived. 'Oh, I think *I* may have been responsible for that,' said Julia. 'You see . . .' and she told the Notting Hill Gate story all over again. I rather hotly said this was a libel on Lytton and Ralph, and indeed Carrington herself, and then immediately changed the subject. I really did instantly forget the whole thing, for I caught the quick look of surprise on Jonny's face. The evening continued very jolly for several hours. Julia must have brooded, however, for she wrote a muddled little note, saying that she felt I thought she was accusing Ralph of meanness in not 'dishing out more of Lytton's bequest to Carrington' and she really always thought him very generous; and that she never knew what Lytton's will was and still didn't.

I wrote a fairly long and detailed reply, saying I was amazed at her last remark, because she had asked me a good many times what were the terms of Lytton's will and I had always told her. (They are also set out in full in Holroyd on page 629.) Then I repeated them all over again and explained that there was no question of Ralph's 'dishing out' Lytton's money, because all of it except Ralph's £1,000 was left direct to Carrington.

Is it absurd to have such feelings over things so long past? Yes, I dare say. Bunny, because he had been involved to some extent at the time, got my point at once and shared my indignation at the libel on all three – Lytton (for not providing Carrington with money), Ralph (for not handing over Ham Spray), Carrington for being moved by such materialistic motives. 'And it's *not true*,' he said. Afterwards he told me had been pondering the question and thought Julia must identify herself with Carrington and have felt in some subconscious way that Lytton should have provided for her, Julia. I returned to London from Easter expecting a reply from Julia, and finding none I have rung her up. She was friendly and very apologetic, 'for letting things go in at one ear and out at the other'. So, thank goodness, another dangerous corner has been rounded.

Hilton for Easter – bitterly cold though sunny. I was very content to be with them all. The garden was ranged through by Richard's boys, three little cousins and Sophie, running around like a fairy on tiptoe, with her splendid little bullet head erect on its stalk, rosy-cheeked, excited by the company, bright as a button. She is fast learning to read and understands everything you say to her; she has a loving sweet character and adores Henrietta, though they sometimes swear at each other and even come to blows, like cat and kitten.

Henrietta was being very domestic, helping Bunny and making clothes for herself and Sophie. I do rather worry about Bunny, poor fellow. He showed me friendly but perhaps unimaginative letters from Angelica. There is a possibility she might come over in the summer, with Bergen, to sell her little Islington house and find somewhere else 'grand enough for him'. Bunny really dreads seeing her, as he told me in a voice that broke with suppressed feeling. His way of combating despair is to fall in love with Magouche and her younger daughters collectively, and to work

---

[1] A librarian of University College, and a friend of Sonia's.

in the house with a frantic energy that betrays his restlessness. The girls helped a lot but he insists on doing the shopping and most of the cooking, all at the double, writing, entertaining his friends, tidying up.

On Monday evening he admitted to feeling 'dead tired' and I begged him to go and lie down. He fell fast asleep, but woke up with a start when it was time to have a drink with two old friends in the village. He looked so stricken and ill and anxious when he came downstairs, that I suddenly panicked on his behalf, wondering how to get him to take it easier without pointing that unpalatable moral: you aren't as young as you used to be?

What is left of Bloomsbury tends to treat the practical side of life in two ways – Bunny, Angelica, probably Duncan, Gerald, all have a curious liking for dirt and cold coupled with rich, home-produced satisfaction of other sensuous appetites (excellent food, drink, conversation, books, music); whereas the homosexual element – Crichel in particular – insist on their comforts and convenience but cannot lift a finger for themselves. Their food is therefore good only contingently on supply of good servants. The first group travels widely but in ramshackle style and never spends money on taxis or good hotels, nor do they worry so much about manners and grammar (the formal details of life) as the second, to whom both are of paramount importance. They also travel enormously but generally comfortably.

April 19th

Julia arrived to dinner last night, unbuttoned a thick, black mackintosh and laid down an umbrella. (The day had been perfectly fine and rather hot but she told me she dials the weather every single morning before she goes out, to find out if there's a possibility of rain.) Sniffing the cooking smell, of veal and vegetables, she said, 'I'm glad it's meat as I had nothing but a chocolate bar for lunch. I *can't* eat by myself. I simply *won't* cook for myself, and I'm getting so *thin* [a rising note of hysteria] that my bones are literally sticking out of my body.' Then, as I began my usual exhortations and encouragements, she switched off with noticeable success.

At dinner she began telling me about a correspondence she had been having (by letter and in person) with Lawrence about Ingres and neo-classicism. Afterwards she read the letter, and a long fascinating conversation ensued, in which I most luckily saw the point of most of what she said. Ingres and the neo-classicists were to her mind shallow, and their defect was that there was no reference in them to what lay outside the picture space – the unresolved mysteries of the universe. She therefore found them smug, static and dead, instead of life-giving. Lawrence's letter was characteristically imaginative and interesting: he described a picture as being an entity in its own right, erected like a 'flag' or 'building', and having a 'sharp pride' in its own existence. He liked this phrase and repeated it as a sort of litany. The drawback is that only in theory can a work of art stand alone. The threads of association are made of unbreakable material.

April 27th

Came down to Thorington with the Penroses last night, in preparation for our sad outing tomorrow. Janetta paid me a long midday visit yesterday, interrupted briefly by Amaryllis, Henrietta and Sophie. Janetta was charming to Sophie, the model of how an adult should behave to a child of four, drawn into her brick constructions as if she couldn't resist it, and inventing original pagodas made of teapots, bricks and cups – so that Sophie quickly sensed that she was as much involved as she was herself.

Alone, we talked long, forking the ground deeply, about all her three daughters, and her plans for letting Montpelier Square. She is 'worried about Nicky and Georgie', and Serge came in for a lot of criticism. Now that she works very hard herself, Janetta has become intolerant of those who don't, and Serge is one. She told me how, when she'd been criticizing the young to Julian for their desire to get what they could out of people while making as little personal effort as possible themselves, he had defended them, saying it was because they felt the world so awful. Yet she told me he had resented her attack on 'the awfulness of all the Piccadilly crowds, the hideousness and pointlessness of everything'. I ventured to say that the same process of vulgarization was happening everywhere – in Marbella for instance; also that London had life and a power to stimulate unequalled anywhere. London minds revolved and responded, and this made it an exciting place to live in, which is the reason why I don't even envy Janetta living in her beautiful valley.

April 29th

The dreaded visit to poor Frances was not so bad after all. The picture drawn by Roland Penrose, and the fact of her telling Margaret on the telephone, 'Of course you know I'm dying,' may both have been exaggerated by evening drunkenness. A friendly lady received us (about seventy and immensely carefully dished up like a trifle, with dyed yellow hair, a thick mask of pink and blue maquillage and her elegant figure encased in bright pink slacks and jazz-pattern jumper). It was some time before Frances appeared, looking fatter and older, walking with a tottery step, her head shaking as she spoke, her utterance intercepted by long pauses. But what she said throughout our visit was to the point and sensible. If she is dying and knows it she is remarkably brave, and that is what I would expect of her. I have promised to go again, but I think for one night only. How can one possibly refuse? Roy and Billa Harrod also came to lunch, which was really quite jolly. Thinking of Frances and the possibility of death, I feel human beings as a whole *are* extraordinarily brave. Apart from the way they accept their various shocks and bereavements I can think of no one who has gone screaming out of life, as they have every right to do.

Another back-wash of Holroyd. Roy, tight-lipped, was saying that James had behaved in a dishonourable way, because after being allowed to take microfilms of Maynard's letters to Lytton on the strict understanding that they should not be published, he had let Holroyd do so. I flew to James's defence, but was I right? Or if I was, have I incriminated Holroyd, Noel Annan, or the librarian of King's College, Cambridge? The only thing I cling to is that the truth is always best.

May 1st

The prig and the hedonist battle away inside me, but I don't see why they shouldn't co-operate. The prig responds to certain things in Bertrand Russell's scrapbook of an autobiography, particularly his feelings about the insane horror of war (1914–18 in his case). I admire him too for being able to analyse this with such detachment, singling out the strands of his great love for England and his desire that the

Germans shouldn't win from his utter rejection of the war-frenzy and desire for instant peace. What's more he never stopped acting on his beliefs, however futile these efforts may have been. He went to prison for them, and made the best of it uncomplainingly, continuing to read and write philosophy there, though it can have been no joke. E. D. Morel, who did likewise, came out a shattered man with snow-white hair. Another thing to give one pause is that both Russell and Wittgenstein, two of the most brilliantly clever men of their day, gave away large inherited fortunes because they felt they had no right to them.

May 2nd

Lunch with Janetta, Julian, Cyril and Jennifer Ross. Cyril came in beaming, and seating himself in an armchair like an egg in an eggcup, began at once: 'I have three things to say. I moved to Eastbourne yesterday. I adore it. I'm flying to Tanzania tomorrow.' He then entertained us with an amusing fantasia – a conversation in which he tried to wheedle letters and books out of Hemingway's son who lives in Africa. Very funny, and we all showed our amusement and made an excellent audience. But why *want* Hemingwayana? It really seems very odd.

May 6th: The Rectory, Ham[1]

I drove Ben Nicolson down here for the weekend. The journey was made interesting by his giving me a dramatic account of the discovery of a remarkably outspoken diary of his mother Vita's, and the discussion between him and his brother Nigel as to what was to be done with it.

Robin has been genial and not uninteresting to talk to; Ginette is rather too flattering but attractive and pretty. Pat Trevor-Roper didn't arrive until Saturday, along with Joy and Den Craig.[2]

My first night I felt and knew where I was by means of thousands of nerves that penetrated the surrounding green fields and little woods in every direction making an invisible network in my brain, so that I couldn't sleep. Next morning Robin dropped me on top of Ham Hill; I walked there for a bit and then back. On Sunday, hearing that poor Mrs Elwes was in hospital, I walked up to Ham Spray and explored the garden. What *did* I feel? I think I had deliberately put a mute on my strings, so that everything was muffled. I saw with sadness how the dear face of the house had been ruined, as with a false moustache, by that hideous porch and the removal of the verandah; I noticed the loneliness of the ilex tree, and the melancholy jungle round the swimming-pool, and that the dogtooth-violets I had planted under the beech tree had flowered recently. Then I walked back, feeling a little bruised.

I shouldn't have gone to Ham at all. I forgot that when one is a guest one has to try and be pleasant.

Julia has formed a project of writing something about Carrington, based on C.'s letters to her. I encouraged it, as I do all her plans. She rang up yesterday to say that on reading the letters she had been dismayed and amazed to find how 'flirtatious' and 'sexy' they were, and that she thought them 'too personal and private'. She felt Carrington must really have been 'in love with her'. So I'm sure

---

[1] Staying with Robin and Ginette Darwin, a stone's throw from Ham Spray.
[2] She had been married to Beakus Penrose, beloved by Carrington.

she was in a way, though perhaps it was partly fantasy. And she had a special way of talking to Julia as if she was a princess which I think Julia enjoyed at the time.

Today she rang again. Did I know what other women Carrington wrote to in this style – with 'real lust and love'? I mentioned Henrietta Bingham, Catharine Carrington, Poppet and Vivien John.

May 15th

I was invited by Sonia to a farewell dinner for Janetta and Jaime, and it has quite knocked me out. All today I have felt limp and apathetic. What was it? Sonia's overexcitement and fuss (not nearly as bad as sometimes), or simply the feeling of *too much* of everything? Certainly too much drink – champagne before dinner (and choosing whisky I was given a stiff tumbler-full), hock, claret and Château d'Yquem. Quantities and quantities of excellent food. Conversation rather stimulating and good. The sympathetic pear-shaped face of Francis Bacon was crumpled into general geniality. The white and black cubistically-designed head of Lucian Freud was very much less sympathetic, and Julia was indignant because he talked to her about the responsibilities of marriage, as if he had ever shown the faintest awareness of them. Poor Julia looked frail and tottery, as if she hardly knew how to bear any of it, and indeed told me on the telephone next day that she had 'hated every moment of it'. I sat between Jaime, who turned his sparkling gaze often towards Julia, and Sonia. Towards the end of the meal her gasps and unfinished sentences and overemphasis began filling the room with invisible steam.

Immediately after dinner Lucian and Francis went off to meet Princess Margaret at Anne Fleming's, so they said, and Julia set off home. Janetta, Jaime and I prepared to settle for a gossip with Sonia, but she showed us in no uncertain terms that she wanted us to go. So go we did.

May 23rd

Janetta's departure day. I am glad for her sake; she is longing to get back, and says she has hated London.

Julia came last night bringing Carrington's letters. Oh, the muddle she's in! Her attempt to sort them had not even reached the stage of putting pieces of the same letter together, much less getting them in order. The drawings chiefly of cats and Carrington herself in varying moods and attitudes are simply delightful. I tried to encourage her, but felt all the time she would never do it.

June 6th

Yesterday evening Julian, Georgia and Henrietta came to dinner. I give the prize to Georgia, whose appearance and talk were simply splendid. Julian, perhaps tired by the end of the evening, struck me as more irrational than usual, and when he said that parents '*must* love *all* their children', all three females pounced on him and said this couldn't be done to order. Julian: 'Then why did they have them?' Henrietta: 'To give tangible expression to their love for their mate.' All this arose out of Tolstoy. I'm left by Troyat's book about him feeling that he was a volcano ceaselessly erupting torrents of lava, which might take the form of masterpieces or of absurdity. But I do not feel that the tragedy of his marriage was all his fault.

Talk of violence followed naturally on the horrific news of the shooting of Robert Kennedy. Serge had been talking to Julian in praise of violence, and amalgamating it in his philosophy of life. A friend of Julian's saw Hartley's letter attacking Leonard in the *Listener* office and said, 'You *can't* print that – it's the letter of a madman!' Leonard has written an admirably restrained reply. Georgia had stuck up for Bloomsbury standards against the aristocracy in a house full of them (including Diana Cooper). I felt too disintegrated by departure to take a strong line in the conversation, and sat back enjoying the enviable vitality of youth.

(Airborne) I met Margaret and Lionel in the inferno of the airport. They only just got there in time and Margaret described to me how Lionel had had a worrying symptom – 'an artery in his leg partly blocked'. He is going to meet his Polish girl before he joins us in Vienna, but at the last moment blamed Margaret 'for not refusing to let him'. Robert Kennedy has died – a good thing, as he was terribly damaged, poor fellow. We have put down at Munich – very hot – but remained on the tarmac, and are now off again through dense cloud to Klagenfurt, where I suppose I shall suddenly awake to reality, whatever that may be.

June 7th

Our Vanguard banked steeply into the green valley of Klagenfurt. Then we were down and it was a warm, faintly sunny afternoon, with no wind and signs of recent heavy rain. A young man in a car (the hotel chef it seemed) met us and drove us thirty-five kilometres to our destination. Coasting along the opposite shore of Ossiachersee, he pointed out our pension peeping coyly from between two curtains of conifers. These enemies are everywhere, dense, stifling, with tall straight trunks. The moderate-sized mountains are blanketed and woolly with them, and with villages like the toy sets you buy at the Christian Aid shop in Sloane Street dotted below, made up a tame, smugly domestic landscape. Where is the wild and beautiful Carinthian country spoken of by visitors to the Bromovskys? It's not at all what I like, but I feel friendly towards its soothing, unfrightening peace and even its slight absurdity. The lady of the hotel speaks excellent English, and my dread of not having a room to myself was unnecessary. We have two single rooms. Mine is a tiny cupboard, reached by a rustic ladder at the back of the house; it has no window at all, so one must either keep the door open, or shut it and breathe through the slits in it, as I do at night. Except for a Canadian in the adjoining cupboard, all our fellow guests are youngish, jolly, Austrian married couples with good cars. Margaret came back from wandering among the pines, saying she had found an orchid, and the bathing place just below the hotel (whose lawn slopes rapidly to the lake).

After the rain the pines give off a wonderful smell. Aeroplane whisky, a good dinner and early to bed in a state of placid relaxation, as I thought, but not a bit of it. Electric antennae seemed to be radiating from my brain, piercing the woods and going right across Europe to Munich and London. Cars came noisily home and parked under my 'window'. After that the nightingales got going and I remained tortured with wakefulness for many, many long hours.

June 8th

When we arrived we felt the water of the lake and it was so warm we thought of bathing. I wish now we had, for next morning low clouds were straggling in the wool of the mountain, and though breakfast was laid on the terrace, big drops began to fall. A hideous, dark, damp Alpbach day. We set off to walk to the village of St André. At times Margaret talks compulsively about her matrimonial situation: Lionel rang her up last night. Dunyusha[1] is taking him to some mountain place, a sort of Polish St André. No mention of her husband. At dinner poor Margaret asked me: 'Would you call what I'm feeling jealousy?' After lunch we struck up a *wanderweg* among the pines in intermittent rain. The red spots on their trunks looked like fresh grazes on a child's knee, and the pleasure in following them is very childish too. The vegetation was exciting and I brought back a harvest of flowers. Our walk took us to one of the landing stages further up the lake, whence we chugged delightfully back in the little lake steamer.

As usual after only a couple of days I can't help trying to sum up this Austrian ambience and I do not really like or anyway greatly respect it. There's something too smug, simple-minded and childish in their attitude to life, their wooden houses, their uncritical jollity, their stupid way of going about in low-necked, cotton peasant dresses with puffed sleeves when it's cold enough for thick sweaters. Reading about Vienna in Ilse Barea, I learn for the first time about 'Biedermeier' and recognize it. Yet this sweetness must all be too good to be true, for nearly every famous Austrian in her book seems to have committed suicide; so there is obviously some desperate non-facing of the black side of life. I'm sure they are sensual, but in a healthy Bedalian sort of way. As it is cold, a roaring fire was lit last night under the hunting-horn in the dining-room. Afterwards tables drew together and there was noisy talk, loud laughter and card-playing. Margaret and I retired to her room. She told me this morning that she sat up until after four last night writing a not-to-be-posted letter to Lionel in an attempt to discharge her feelings. 'Were they feelings of anxiety, indignation or just pain?' I asked, and I think she said, 'All three.' She returns to Lionel's rankling remark as they parted: 'Why didn't you prevent my going?' I told her it was just a magic ritual – like throwing salt over one's shoulder – to get away from guilt by throwing it on to her.

June 12th

Today we go to Vienna. Margaret is worrying desperately about Lionel, who has been in Poland five days now, and regulations don't allow more than ten – 'half-time' as she says. But she's a prey to gloomy forebodings, and veers from the belief that Dunyusha is madly in love with Lionel to the idea that it is all some fantastic political plot. 'What does he *see* in her, I want to know?' Her outpourings are repetitive but also truly pitiful, and I listen and listen and listen, and try to think of something comforting to say, such as reminding her that he has telephoned once and sent a telegram since he went. She thought the telegram 'might have been sent by Dunyusha'. I've been wondering whether I ought to say that Lionel is behaving monstrously, but though I am deeply sorry for her sufferings – and they are worse than I expected – I don't really think he is. She says I'm more 'detached' than any of her friends. Given the opportunity, I would, I think, be prepared to tell him how very much she minds, but she is in a state not far from persecution-mania.

---

[1] The Polish young woman with whom Lionel was having an affair. He was to visit her while I kept Margaret company in Carinthia.

June 13th: Vienna

It's much warmer here, clear blue sky. But when we arrived, there were no letters or messages from Lionel. Margaret exploded. I'm by now too bewildered to know whether her fuss and outcry is justified; but one might as well say: 'Is a person justified in screaming when his leg is broken?' She's in agony. 'How can he do it? I can't understand it! He must be a *fiend*.' Or 'What's she up to, I want to know? I think she's a bitch. Yes, that's what she is I believe, a *bitch*!' Her irrationality at those moments is rather a surprise and leaves me at a loss how to respond. To a Mozart concert in the courtyard of one of the houses where he had lived. A sunny fresh morning – *great* pleasure.

June 14th

Got home from the concert to find Frau Professor Weiniger, an elderly female anthropologist, deafer even than Margaret, with a level, pale blue gaze that reminded me of Alix. She had come to settle about Lionel's lecture, and came with us to one of the old-style Viennese cafés, where most people were reading the papers or drinking small cups of coffee. One can get all sorts – I like *Mocca braun* which is strong with a little cream. Margaret characteristically plumps for wishy-washy *mélange*. As she says, 'Our tastes in food are different.' She is violently attracted by the tinned soups and plastic plates of egg or tunny salad soused in vinegar to be got in the self-service establishments. I can hardly swallow them and am longing for a meal of hot meat and two veg.

On to look at the Karlskirke, and on our return home found news – hurrah – from Lionel that he will return on the Sunday aeroplane, or 'by the night train if there is fog'. Margaret snoozed out of sheer relief until it was time for our evening's outing. A great deal of walking through the old town and past the university to the Maria Treu church for another concert. I find that my plastic meal can be humanized by a *viertel* of red wine, always quite good. I sat gazing into the high domed roof painted with swirling figures among clouds shaped like diving hippopotami and upside-down cupids, while the organ filled the vast space beneath with booming Bach, Telemann and Frank Martin, supported by a flautist. I have never liked those liquefying, overlapping reverberations of sound made by an organ, specially in so large and resonant a building, and I wasn't greatly moved by the music. We walked home past the floodlit buildings of the Ringstrasse – the two museums and the House of Parliament. The delightful feeling of getting to know Vienna is now well under way.

What will it be like when Lionel joins us? When I said to Margaret that I was longing for a 'hot meat meal', she replied, 'We'd better have it before Lionel arrives; he doesn't like meat.' F.: with some indignation, 'Well, *he* needn't eat it!' I'm keeping an entirely open mind as to whether or not I go on with them to Prague, according to how our triangular stay works. If I don't go with them I think I'll stay here bravely alone over the weekend as an experiment and then fly home.

June 16th

Yesterday began badly. Poor Margaret came into my room waving a telegram and saying in a quavering voice that Lionel was *not* coming by air on Sunday after all (he had his ticket) but on the night train, thus missing Haydn's *Creation* on Sunday evening, which he loved and had been particularly keen to hear. She had wired to him that we had a ticket for him. She was hysterical and distraught. 'Shall I wire again?' F.: 'But what could you say?' 'Simply "You bloody old fool"?' she said with a laugh, but then fired off all the explosive charges she had in her locker. 'What does he *see* in her? He's just a silly old *man*. He's *seventy*!' The mention of fog in his previous telegram aroused Margaret's suspicion at the time, and I do now see it must have been some sort of preparation for this delay, for the weather maps indicate that there's as brilliant June weather in Poland as here. Vienna is having a heat wave, brilliantly sunny with a light breeze. It has really been awful to witness poor Margaret's agony. She laughed as she told me that she once before, in the middle of the night, sent him a telegram saying, 'Silly old man'. I tried to persuade her it was useless to send off any more telegrams, for it would be too late to alter his plans. He should now be back at crack of dawn on Monday (tomorrow).

All day yesterday she was a prey to sudden glooms and hysterias, rushed to the whisky bottle, finished it off, bought more, rang Frau Professor Weiniger to see if she would come to the *Creation* on Lionel's ticket and failed to get her. There have also been letters and telephone calls from the Czechs who want him to lecture in Brno and Prague. I suggested she left Lionel to sort this out himself, and perhaps reap the reward of his delay, for his professional life is very important to him. I try all the time to reassure her, but persecution-mania is very infectious and I begin to feel doubtful of my power to judge the true situation and am secretly terrified of something going wrong when I should have a serious case on my hands. Still, I do really believe he will turn up safe and sound tomorrow morning.

Later to another church concert – Haydn's *Nelson Mass*. As we sat in physical agony in the torturously uncomfortable pews, with our backs to the source of the music in the organ loft, we seemed like a bed of reeds through which a tide was flowing. It gave me a fellow-feeling for the man sitting beside me to see that he was gently swaying or shifting in that tide. (I'm not really drawn to those who take up an austerely motionless position when listening to music, nor yet who sit as if cogitating a problem.) Then he made a silent but pretty bad fart, and at once took off his spectacles, as if with an impulse to disguise himself, which I could easily understand. If Lionel doesn't arrive tomorrow, what then? Margaret is getting up to meet his train at 7.40 a.m. at the station. All her obsessions on the subject have been repeated so often today that I could think of nothing new to say in reply.

June 17th

8.15 a.m. I heard Margaret's voice shouting loudly to the girl receptionist. With my breakfast came a note she had left for me that has left me simply gasping. She wrote: 'I'm so afraid Lionel may not be on this train. Perhaps someone used his passport on the plane yesterday. One of us should go to the embassy. Just *supposing* I am prevented from coming back here from the station . . .' and she went on to give dates and numbers of passports and visas, addresses of friends in Warsaw, etc., and ends, 'Here are the two phoney telegrams.' Why phoney?

9.15. Lionel has just arrived looking bronzed, happy and not a day over forty-five. He was delayed by a slight collision on the Polish railway. Goodness, it might easily have been worse.

June 18th

Not only did Lionel's arrival give the lie to Margaret's different fantastic theories – I see her wild letter was written at 5.30 a.m. – but he is entirely in command of everything, and has rung up institutions and fixed lectures and seminars with complete efficiency. (Margaret had told me she always had to do this, and that he was entirely dependent on her. She also said that she had to do all the German talking, but Lionel speaks quite well and Margaret is almost worse than I am, with only two sentences: 'Bitte, wo ist ...' or 'Bitte, haben Sie ...'.) Lionel has obviously been rejuvenated by having a wonderful time with his girl, whereas poor Margaret is exhausted by jealousy and persecution-mania and looks quite done for; she almost dropped asleep over lunch in the Café Mozart, and briefly did drop off in the opera last night. I commented on Lionel's efficiency. 'Oh yes, he always gets what he wants.' But he has of course been lively interesting company, and is full of stories about Vienna in the 20s, when he was here with Frank Ramsey,[1] Adrian Bishop and others, and wants to do what they all did then – eat *eierspeize* and drink beer in cafés and go to the gallery of the opera house.

I thought I'd leave Lionel and Margaret to settle down together, and went off alone, bought a nice pair of yellow sandals, and booked my ticket home today week. I've definitely decided not to go with them into Czecho for those few days.

June 19th

It gets hotter and hotter. I can go stockingless in my new sandals and wear a thin cotton frock. Penroses still deep in plans. This morning I told Margaret I was going to the art gallery and she met me there. Among the superb collection of Titians, Velázquez and Rembrandts, I was moved to see Ralph's 'favourite picture in the whole world' – Tintoretto's *Susanna*. I lunched alone out of doors in the park, having the almost invariable meal of omelette and salad, with *apfelsaft*. Omelettes are specially good here, *baveuse* within and crisp without, stuffed with pieces of bacon.

Afterwards I walked and walked in the heat – how one walks in this town! I wandered through the Hofburg and its library, and into a church where I found myself gazing at the row of pewter mugs containing the hearts of the Hapsburgs – the Duke of Reichstadt's is a very small one. I am trying to get a seat to see Jurinac as Mimi in *Bohème* on Sunday night.

In the evening with Margaret to hear Lionel lecture to a learned and deeply interested gathering about chromosomes. Enthralling. It seems that a man who has two or more, instead of only one X chromosome, is definitely more prone to violence and aggression than normal men, while a woman with two or more X chromosomes is merely stupider than usual. So masculinity = aggression, femininity = stupidity. He showed us slides of abnormal ridge-formations on the hands and soles of the feet, associated with genetic aberrations like Mongolism. The lecture hall was electric with attention and with loud creaks from the wooden benches, when anyone shifted their bottom. A Japanese (or Chinese?) sat in the front row taking notes assiduously. Vienna is full of them. Afterwards questions were asked. When all was over people crowded round Lionel.

Margaret touchingly said today that she wanted to pay for the seats she had

[1] The Cambridge philosopher.

ordered from England 'because I'd been so kind'. Of course I won't let her, but it makes me regret my criticisms of her. This morning in the art gallery she explained her delusions – as they now seem – about Polish plots, by saying: 'You see, it's such a relief to me if I can think Dunyusha is plotting and scheming. I'm sure you can understand that.' And of course I could.

After the lecture we went to look in vain for Freud's house in the Berggasse. Later, an enormous walk in the dark to places connected with Lionel's early life in Vienna,[1] all round the old town, through streets of portentously tall houses, under bridges, up steps. Lionel was being psychoanalysed at that time for bed-wetting, so Margaret told me later. Having heard this I naturally saw the course on which he led us in symbolical terms. Down a deep sunken street called Tief Graben (Deep Trench) under a bridge and towards the Hohe Market. 'I'm always dreaming about Vienna,' he said as we walked along, 'and in my dream there's always somewhere I'm trying to get to. Now I realize that it's here.' When we found a large fountain in full operation in the middle of the marketplace, it seemed too good to be true. Lionel is very much in the saddle, and, far from expecting Margaret to make all the arrangements, a little inclined to criticize hers.

June 20th

The Penroses bicker a good deal. I dare say it is the mere easing of surface tensions, and better ignored. This morning's plan (Lionel's) was to go by tram to the little space of Baden, where there were associations with Beethoven and Mozart and pleasant woods to walk in. We were to meet at the hotel at eleven. Lionel appeared but no Margaret. Later she too turned up and all day long they were both referring to the monstrous way the other had gone off and got lost without a word at the Mozart museum. Margaret said to me: 'You see how he goes on as if I didn't exist? Just as he only got one ticket to Cornwall when we were both going.' Yet on the other side I've suffered more than once from Margaret's habit of vanishing suddenly and without a word at lightning speed, like a billiard ball rolling across the cloth and disappearing into a pocket. Apparently Lionel accuses her in the middle of the night of wanting him to die, so that she can be a merry widow. I hesitate to take the conventional Freudian interpretation of this – but whatever Dunyusha is like, she certainly makes him happy. He looks much older as well as more harassed and unkempt since he got here. It's true that he often treats Margaret as if she were an imbecile; I think her deafness is partly to blame and this is one reason why I urge her to wear her hearing-aid. She is loth, but makes valiant efforts.

At last we got off to the Baden tram and trundled pleasantly out of the suburbs. It is a charming, unspoilt spa, with a lot of pretty Biedermeier houses, innocently encrusted with curlicues, caryatids and lion's heads. We ate under a sun-umbrella outside one of the sulphur springs.

After lunch we walked up a wooded hill to a café with a view. When we descended it was music time, and in a bandstand where Johann Strauss was once conductor, a string orchestra was playing delightfully in their shirt-sleeves because of the heat. The elderly cure-takers were sitting with programmes, clapping the music under the trees. For once I thought I saw serenity and peace in this picture of old age.

---

[1] Where he had come to be psychoanalysed – by Freud, I believe.

June 23rd

I have been alone here in Vienna since lunch-time yesterday, when the Penroses took their bus to Brno. I wondered if I should start swooping into that dreadful spiral of loneliness. But no, thank heavens, nothing of the sort. Yesterday morning Margaret and I went to the Spanish Riding School, where a training session of the white horses was going on. All the horses that draw Viennese cabs are white or grey, so I imagine they move on when too old for this highly-skilled performance. I took the opportunity to tell Margaret that I thought she needn't really worry; that Lionel was deeply devoted to her *au fond*, and quite incapable of dastardly behaviour. Also that I thought the well-meaning friends who tried to alarm her about Dunyusha's schemes were not doing her a service. I saw them go with sadness and great affection. Then off to my room to plan the rest of my time. A sort of intoxication came over me at being on my own in this capital city. I can manage the language sufficiently well to get by, and feel I now know Vienna rather better than London. The fine weather has returned. To Prince Eugen's two splendid baroque palaces – the Upper and Lower Belvedere, joined by a sloping garden of fountains and statues. Both house collections of paintings and statues in their magnificently ornate rooms.

June 24th

In the morning I walked for hours, right up to the Danube canal, back to the old university, and several churches and Prince Eugen's winter palace.

My seat for *Bohème* was in the front row of the gallery rather at the side. I laid my head on the red plush rim and saw pretty well and shed tears at the end. Next to me was a young man helping repair his girl's make-up, as I walked off to Sachers for supper and a slice of their famous *torte*.

July 8th: London

The months ahead stand like a lump of clay waiting to be moulded into something tractable. I think I shall go to Cyprus with the Hills, but not to Majorca with Mary and the Tycoon nor to the South of France with the Jarvises. This evening Tom rang up to ask me to the Lakes: of course I am gratified by these extremely kind offers. There being no valid reason why I shouldn't accept them all makes it more difficult to decide. Yet I don't want to rattle to and fro like a ping-pong ball.

Henrietta and Sophie have been twice to see me. They were in London to visit Angelica. Sophie looks tall, a little thin, composed. The first time she came she was very good and absorbed herself in various activities. The second time I was harassed by work and a migraine, took them out to the café next door, and she was fractious and whiney. But on the whole I think the extraordinary life they have been leading is fairly all right for her, and certainly it makes Henrietta happier. She talked a lot about their caravanserai[1] and the principles they live by – four young men and Henrietta and Sophie in a big tent, with five horses and a cart. They move about, dressed in romantic clothes, cooking on wood fires, looking after their horses, a goat and a dog. They believe in non-violence, 'being good and kind' (hurrah, I said), are *almost* vegetarians. Things began to acquire pluses and minuses as I talked to her: animals and nature plus; cars minus; spirits minus 'but

---

[1] Of hippies, headed by Mark Palmer.

I've introduced them to wine'. What about marijuana? I expect so. Thank heavens flying saucers and attendant mumbo-jumbo is out for Henrietta at least. She wanted to talk about Mark Palmer's extraordinarily gentle and sweet character, 'he's as near a saint as anyone I've met.'

Last weekend I went to see Alix and collected Carrington's last diary from her. She had just read it and thought Noel should do as he liked with it, 'because it reflected nothing but credit on her and on Lytton'. I would have loved to have stayed longer at Lord's Wood – there's always so much to talk about with Alix. Then on to the Carringtons', where Noel, Catharine and I all read it. I found I remembered it pretty well. Catharine was so upset by it that she had a sleepless night twenty-four hours after reading it. I wondered if it was partly the shock of finding herself coldly described, as 'dim'. But of course the finale is desperately moving. There can be few descriptions so lucid and so harrowing of committing suicide, yet she wrote it all faithfully down; then came the horrible return to life to see Lytton die, and then the no man's land shadowed by her obvious determination to do it again. Noel came down to breakfast on Sunday with the plan that a collected edition of her letters should be published. Would I do it, he went on to say? I made a number of excuses, and then said I couldn't face plunging into the past for several years. He understood this and accepted it, saying he felt the same. He suggested Bunny, and perhaps that's a probability.

Reading about Beakus Penrose and the pain he had caused poor Carrington by his wooden insensitivity, telling her for instance, 'You see, I don't find you sexually attractive,' when she was in despair because of being older than him, I remembered him as he was, 'just a Figuerhead [sic] after all' as she wrote, not the intelligent and charming character Lionel and Margaret like to make him out.

July 10th

Under a pitch-black sky to the private view of a huge Matisse show at the new gallery on the South Bank. Their confidence, simplicity, and concentration gave my spirits an enormous lift. They intoxicate and overwhelm, yet so completely focus his view of the world that painting seems to be something entirely for the painter and not the looker. After talking to Cyril, Robin and Susan, I came face to face with Angelica looking radiant and beautiful, and she has promised to come and have dinner with me.

July 15th

My work is packed off. I've bought my ticket to Cyprus. I feel too idle to think or write. Last night Angelica came and we had a delightful and most interesting evening. Would she mind, I wondered, that I'd asked no one else? Would she think I was trying to 'pump' her? I took the bull by the horns therefore and said I found one never talked to anyone if there were a lot of people and I had very much wanted to see her. Then we started off on various impartial subjects, Matisse, etc., thence to Henrietta's plans and only over dinner did we come round to Bergen. (Bunny barely mentioned, as it were *en passant*.) She talked most freely and humanly, and I was much touched, as one always is by that generosity that opens and reveals a person's inner feelings. And I take back everything about ice-maidens. I even think she has lost some of that disturbing quality in the furnace of her affair with Bergen. The training given by a pure Bloomsbury background – a training I would say that ultimately conduces to honesty, directness and of course utter disregard of *idées reçues* – has stood her in good stead, even if it sent her blinkered into the sort of annexe to Bloomsbury that Hilton was. I was again astonished by her courage in going off to Bergen. She seemed to be amazed by it herself. Said she hadn't known him at all; he was a perfect stranger. I tried to detect some antibodies to his influence produced by return to England – I don't think there are any. She says she will stay till October, 'perhaps longer'. She wants to go back to New York, loves it, and yet, and yet, she talks of getting a separate studio from Bergen so that they shan't live on top of each other. She is clearly still under his spell, thinks him an 'extremely remarkable person, who has in some way been torn apart by his mixed blood' (he is part Russian, part Spanish). 'Unhappy?' I asked. She weighed it. 'Yes, certainly unhappy.' I have strongly the feeling that being a realistic and intelligent person, she has not in the least been warped by this disturbing experience. It has merely had the effect of causing her to go through a delayed process of maturing. Although she is fifty, her hereditary and acquired characteristics have enabled her to weather it without getting embittered.

July 22nd: Thorington Hall

Whence I came on Friday evening with Julia, Lionel and Margaret. All appeared to be going as smoothly as silk, and then, suddenly on Saturday night Julia rounded on me with a swift venom that (temporarily I believe) dissipated my goodwill. She made me aware that I must have been appallingly on her nerves *without knowing it* – that is perhaps what is so humiliating. The circumstances are almost too absurd to write down: Julia had spent about three hours of Saturday afternoon behind drawn curtains, lying on her bed, and I took her a cup of tea. She came down about seven with her face very carefully made up, but I think under the influence of her pills, so that her remarks were wider of the mark than usual. Watching the telly she was very irritable with the Penroses for not understanding their own set properly or being sure which network they were on, and I could see that she could hardly sit still, her exacerbation was so great. A tiny thing occurs to me – Margaret and I sat side by side with legs outstretched on the sofa to watch a programme recommended by Julia and enjoyed by us all. Twice Julia got up from her armchair and said, 'Do sit here, Margaret; I like a stiff-backed chair.' And twice Margaret said good-humouredly, 'No thanks, I like having my legs up.' Then she drew our attention to an odd face in the background of the telly screen and I said, 'Oh yes, I see; he has got a very low forehead.' Whereupon Julia shot out of her chair and with a really viperish glance almost shouted at me: 'Frances, you're *always* talking about low foreheads.' I said feebly, 'I haven't mentioned them once this weekend.' 'No, not this weekend, but you *always are*.' After a pause, 'That was meant for a joke.' This totally unexpected repetition of an attack she's made on me before (saying that I repeat myself, i.e. am a crashing bore) had a traumatic effect on me, I don't know why. I went to bed but couldn't sleep for love or money. I tossed and turned in more senses than one. That is, I felt like a worm that was at last turning, that could take no more. In the course of my tossing I detached myself from my sense of responsibility for her to such an extent that when morning came my chief idea was to keep out of the way of someone who found me so maddening. I therefore left her and Margaret to go for a walk alone together. And on Monday morning I was forewarned and able to deal with her momentary hostility without the smallest pain. In a second incident, over the breakfast table, Julia asked me a question when my mouth was full. When I answered she said, looking at me sharply: 'I can't hear what you're saying.' 'Perhaps you're getting a little deaf?' I said, having noticed that she was, and heard her say so. 'Oh no, I think it's that you're not talking distinctly.' 'Well, I'm famous you know, for my loud penetrating voice,' I said, and was backed up by Margaret from the larder with 'Frances is the only person I can always hear.' What interests me is that as I had been so hurt by her Saturday night onslaught I had assumed she must have noticed it. If so she presumably felt I needed a little more correction. I realize that I was absurdly sensitive on the first occasion, but I made up for it by not minding the second in the least.

July 27th: In the aeroplane to Cyprus

Met at the airport with the dreaded words, 'Two hours' delay', and the crowds were appalling. I queued to send a telegram, then among desperate women and children for one of only *five* smelly apertures to pee in, and this only just gave time to queue at the bar for a whisky one minute before it shut. The queueing, excreting, ingurgitating hordes, of which I was one, seemed like souls in hell, yet without any looks of torment on their faces, oddly enough.

Now, aloft in the sky, I am in heaven. The aeroplane is less than half full; little boys are prattling behind me and a baby bouncing in its cot affixed to the luggage rack. The great thing is to realize the complete passivity of flying, and thank God for this inactivity. The voice of our captain keeps hoping we are enjoying ourselves and will have a pleasant holiday.

July 28th: Kyrenia, Cyprus

Writing next morning I look back on the flight itself as pleasant, easy and dreamlike, with moments of near rapture. Then we were down at Nicosia, among voices jabbering, in Greek? or Turkish? and there was Anne looking about her from within an unusually long mop of white hair, and Heywood bronzed and beaming, leaning back slightly as he advanced. There was a post office strike, so of course they hadn't got my telegram. Also two of their three servants had left, which sounds like an unmitigated blessing. We drove through the darkness; stopped by a polite Turkish patrol, and soon afterwards we were turning into the gate of Kasaphani House. Anne wanted to postpone every subject so that we could go into it *properly*, a good reason and one I appreciate, but I began to fear they would all be shelved for ever.

July 30th

Our servant Paraskevi is a nice middle-aged woman, swinging a colossal bottom as she walks and carrying a small, neat head proudly erect. I admire the way that without even knowing the Greek alphabet, Anne plunges manfully in, with the aid of notebooks and phrasebooks. Paraskevi only has a few words of English. This interest in the language had infected me, and is part of the absorbed curiosity I feel in a new place. The history – yes, I want to find out about that too, and also something of the Graeco-Turkish situation. On Sunday evening we walked up the lower slopes of the range of tall hills behind us, as far as the first village. One woman replied with a rather reproving 'Gùnayden' (Turkish) to our 'Kalymera' (Greek). I feel despairing of botany as everything is paper-dry and brown, and literally nothing in flower except quantities of the tall, blue, round-headed thistles we used to grow at Ham Spray.

Yesterday, Monday, we went shopping in Kyrenia, a very attractive little port with a huge, pale golden castle sprawling beside it like a Trafalgar Square lion. No Greek–English dictionary to be bought in any of the bookshops! 'We have never been asked for one.' Most of the shop-assistants talk good English, but Cypriots look as if they didn't do much thinking. Looking into the bright grey-green eyes shining startlingly from the faces of George (the travel agent) and his brother (who sells postcards next door) however, I couldn't help feeling they could if they wanted to. There are a good many United Nations soldiers in pale blue caps, blond Canadians or Scandinavians, handsome on the whole but with the consciously virtuous air of school prefects. What must the Cypriots feel about them?

After lunch I sprawl naked and face down on my bed, turn on the electric fan and generally sleep for a short while. Life begins again about four, and the indoor thermometer seems to remain steadily between 80°F and 90°F day and night. Heywood has hired a car from George, the travel agent, and yesterday we drove up to the village of Bellapais and went over its noble abbey. The vast refectory rises sheer from the mountain side and all its windows open onto the plain and sea. Strolled through the charming upper alleys of the village till we got onto the tufted aromatic slopes above it. Women seemed to have clustered up here in their gardens (leaving men as usual in the cafés lower down) and were embroidering and chattering. Children all call out 'Hullo' or 'Bye-bye'. A very handsome Cypriot woman took us onto her roof to admire the view and we longed to know how to say 'How beautiful! How marvellous!', both of which we looked up as soon as we got home. One is impotent without such phrases.

I'm re-reading Durrell's *Bitter Lemons*, between scurries into Greek phrasebooks, English newspapers, guidebooks and postcard-writing.

August 1st

Here we are launched into the month of perhaps most terrific heat. Impossible not to think of it as an enemy, and there was a moment yesterday when I began to dissolve and weaken in it. At the least effort one's body streams with fortunately scentless sweat, and if the car is left in the sun it becomes a red-hot furnace. Our routine is to bathe before breakfast, staggering from bed and returning hardly less dazed to eat bread and black cherry jam and drink Nescafé. If I wake late and bathe during the morning there are other people inhabiting our little beach, and patches of the sea have become actually hot. This absorbs the morning, just as yesterday morning was absorbed by my going with Anne to shop in Kyrenia. The market is cool with fans and far from crowded. Only the English seem to shop there. Where do the peasants buy their food, I wonder?

Paraskevi is delightful, and quite obviously charmed by Anne's friendliness and loud rumbustious laugh. One hears them in the kitchen slowly enunciating words in each other's languages fortissimo as to a deaf person and then suddenly breaking into a gabbled duet in their own. When Anne says 'ξψχαριστώ' ['Thank you'] Paraskevi lays her hand on her bosom and says with feeling, 'Me ξψχαριστώ' ['I thank *you*']. Then there is our comic dog, called 'Pooch' after Mr Behrens[1] although

---

[1] The owner of the house.

it is female. She is a ludicrous animal, with eyes hidden by fountains of black hair and a crooked smile of apparently false teeth. After making water she points her leg backwards like a ballet dancer.

The thunder-shower has freshened the garden and I went out in the afternoon to pick roses, geraniums and jasmine, but the mere effort of cutting off the dead leaves and arranging them in a vase produced waterfalls of sweat. Later we drove off westwards through Kyrenia and along the coast to the monastery of Lambousa standing alone on the rocky shore. The Byzantine church had an innocently cheerful iconostasis and rickety pulpit.

August 5th

A gentle day yesterday, ending with supper in a roadside café, off-white Aphrodite wine and a splendid selection of *mezès* (hors d'oeuvres).

On the way home, reeling through the dense thrumming darkness between the headlights of cars, we talked about the sadness of always seeing strong young men in the cafés, in their clean white shirts, tapping their feet to the insidiously sexy music, and no girls. Then Anne, shouting slightly as she endearingly does when drunk: 'But really I think there's something to be said for the system, my dear. The girls are protected and secure, and suitable husbands found for them. I really think Lucy would have preferred it, my dear.' Heywood and I teased her, but not very seriously. Yesterday evening we drove up to St Hilarion castle perched on the highest peak of the range. I wasn't prepared for the state of frozen warfare subsisting up here. The castle and a large part of the range is 'held' – whatever that means – by the Turkish Cypriots, and no Greek is allowed through except if escorted in a convoy by Land Rovers full of UN troops. These tall, handsome, bronzed athletes from Canada, Denmark or Sweden are to be seen everywhere in great numbers, walking or driving about in their pale blue caps. As we climbed to the pass a notice said, 'Welcome to the Free Turkish Zone', and a new sort of face and figure let us through the barrier to the castle. Instead of the very square, strong, black-haired Greeks, these were tall, lazy figures with gentle, amorphous features. Such a one showed us over the sensational Andrew Lang-Gothic castle straggling over the crests. Up steps and steep slopes we panted behind his strong, booted legs, and looked down through light, drifting cloud to Kyrenia far below. On the way home we tried to take a side road to Bellapais, but two talkative UN sentries stopped us, both telling us there was a Greek post there and they wouldn't let us through. They encouraged us to try; tourists could help break down the barriers, and we did, but two very young Greek boys, waving rifles inexpertly and sheepishly, turned us back. I felt outraged by the sheer silliness, and the friendliness of the Turks makes me prefer them to the Greeks.

August 9th

Back last night from a much-enjoyed two days' tour, dusty and tired, streaming with sweat and longing for a bath and hair wash, we found a telegram from Sheelah Hill asking Heywood to ring her up that night. Their Aunt Dorothy has been very ill, is over eighty, and we all supposed she had died. Anne and I tried to persuade him not to agree to go home, feeling this was all too likely; but as a result of his angelic kindness and anxiety for Sheelah he returned from the telegraph office in Kyrenia having got through quickly and saying it couldn't be helped: Aunt Dorothy was dying and had asked for him, and John and Sheelah wanted him to fly back at once. He has booked a flight for 1 a.m. tomorrow, only hoping that in the intervening time (today) news of Aunt Dorothy's death might make it unnecessary. While he went to telephone, Anne talked to me about her mother's death in a jerky and deeply felt way. She told me how when she was sitting beside the semi-conscious and slightly restless old lady, she had suddenly sat bolt upright in bed and cried aloud, 'My life! My life!' conveying an anguish at losing it that was acutely painful to Anne. She clasped her mother in her arms and kissed her continuously, saying urgently, but she felt unconvincingly, 'It will be quite all right!' 'But do you *know*?' her mother kept asking. This shattering episode broke poor Anne down completely, but luckily the doctor arrived and took command. Anne retired in floods of tears to sit with Anthony and Eddie and though she heard 'shouts' from her mother's room this was nothing out of the way – she always gave tongue at the least thing. The relief of the whole family on hearing she was dead was very great. All this came out with a characteristic expression of groping among her feelings and memories with a desperate honesty I found extremely touching.

August 10th

No telegram announcing Aunt Dorothy's death. As the day drew on, Heywood's expression grew more miserable and resigned, and I began to feel guilty for not having bullied him sufficiently to stay. But what right had I to do so? Yet I'm sure that though doomed by his own kindness and responsibility, and the offers of help he had sent to Sheelah (in the confident belief that she would reject them) he would have loved to be kept back by his coat-tails. I said something of the sort as we sat on the loggia in the darkness and he said, 'No, my dear; thank you, but I really must go.' Like Janetta, Heywood cannot speak loudly or forcefully. But this doesn't mean – any more than with Janetta – weakness of character. When the time came we all drove through the moonlit night to Nicosia airport where a vociferous Levantine crowd were milling around, and off went poor Heywood through the door of no return.

August 12th

So we sit here, awaiting telegrams from both Lucy and Heywood, and this evening we shall go to Kyrenia and send several more. The wind has completely dropped, making the heat seem more tremendous than ever. It was frightening yesterday: the plain round Nicosia is a blinding white desert under merciless and constant attack from the cloudless sky and the fiery ball of the sun. We had to get there in the full heat of noon, so as to see the museum. It was relatively cool and full of lovely things, but after five minutes there I began to stream with sweat and feel so weak I thought I would faint. Then I recovered and we spent nearly an hour happily absorbed. Snack lunch in the air-conditioned airport and the long wait and watch for the arrivals from Turkey, who didn't include Lucy. Coming out of the airport was like braving the hot breath from a furnace-room.

August 18th

Drove to Nicosia in time to see what was once the meeting-place of the Whirling Dervishes, and walk thence through the Turkish quarter to the chief mosque, Santa Sophia, through which we were led barefoot by a Turk in a Delacroix turban. Back to the airport to meet Heywood. Anne is so terrified of flying that she now refuses to do it, and in order to get here she and Heywood spent five stifling hot days and nights on the Orient Express and as many more in a stuffy cabin at sea. I asked her if she felt nervous when her nearest and dearest were flying. 'Not in the least, my dear,' she replied with complete honesty. 'It's just that I find the particular *sort* of fear I have when flying unbearable.'

Heywood was the first to stride out from the aeroplane ('He always does, my dear!'). Aunt Dorothy is not dead yet.

Now I'm in the airport at Nicosia myself on my way home, and a rumour of one hour's delay is going round. A feverishly keyed-up young man beside me keeps leaping up and striding to and fro. The tune of the soprano solo in Fauré's *Requiem*, which both Heywood and I had been frantically and unsuccessfully trying to remember since last night, has just swum effortlessly into my head, perfect in wind and limb, and now repeats itself there *ad nauseam*. Strange are the workings of memory. So here Fauré and I sit together and shall sit for another forty minutes, inextricably amalgamated. I shall now relax and recapitulate the last two days.

I had made a provisional plan for a day's outing for Friday, but feared that Heywood might be too tired for it. In the morning he swore that he was not, and had 'slept like a dog'. So we set off, and had one of our best days. Not too hot either, with a freshing breeze. Skirting Nicosia we made west across the middle of the island, stopping to look at another Byzantine church. I grow fonder of the landscape, and today we drove through lush and varied land, with red soil, plantations of citrus fruit, bananas and palms. I could wish for some camels. Then turning off our fine tarred road we bumped up into the lower slopes of the Troodos mountains to see the famous little church of Asinou. We had to pick up the priest in the last village and at first he couldn't be found, in spite of a helpful Cypriot with very little English talking about the 'Pub' or 'Papa', or was he saying 'Papa was in the pub'? Hard to say, especially as he answered 'Yes' to all our questions out of desire to please. At last a noble figure with a tiny bun appeared and got in beside us. He also spoke no English. The church was extremely small, but inside was entirely covered with paintings in brilliant colour, in the strongly outlined, stiff but lively Cypriot Byzantine style. St Mamas rode on a grinning tiger, the naked damned bled or were coiled in snakes in hell. When we dropped our priest he raised a hand in blessing, and Heywood forgot himself and did the same to him. Onwards towards the classical site of Vouni, an astonishing place, chiefly because of its staggeringly beautiful position on the top of a conical hill whence one looked in both directions along the coast and over the royal blue sea, from low walls, all pale cream-coloured; the guide told us with his brown face wrinkled in delight and his strong white teeth showing in a grin how he had himself dug up various objects we had seen in the museum at Nicosia. He pointed along the coast to a Turkish village, where they had shot at him, 'pip-pip-pip', when he tried to dig up some remains on an islet. We were tempted to go further west, by the beauty of the coast, but a UN checkpoint stopped us, and a man speaking with an Ulster accent asked, 'Do you know the rules?' 'No, what are they?' 'No stopping for the next two miles.' 'But we wanted to go to that village along the shore and bathe.' 'Well, I'm afraid you can't.' 'Why not?' 'It's against the rules.' We hesitated. 'It's a Turkish village, isn't it?' 'Yes.' 'Well, we've always found the Turks extremely amiable to us.' The UN man went off again, returning to say, 'The sergeant says you can go on, at your own risk.' Heywood and I were keen to go on. Anne said that the man was only doing his duty, and the UN were a splendid and highly valuable force. So they should be, indeed, but I now realize what extraordinary tact as well as other qualities they need. Perhaps they sometimes help keep the bristles erect on the backs of the two hostile packs of dogs; perhaps they maintain the very situation they are supposed to be calming down by emphasizing the barrier between the two races. We *did* go on, at any rate, feeling rather dashing and wondering exactly what 'our own risk' meant. We reached the shore and bathed from a row of ramshackle huts mostly without doors, returning intact from our dangerous incursion among the Cypriot Turks, and feeling very much in their favour.

August 20th

Can I really have been back only two days? My arrival was misleadingly quiet and easy. A telegram from Janetta saying she was arriving tonight; could I dine with her? Before that I saw Julia looking better than I had expected. She ate nearly all her meal and was amusing about her weekend at Crichel. 'They are sweet fellows, but terribly far away somehow. I couldn't help feeling a lot closer to Moses. What a delightful dog! Then the worst torture of all befell me. You know how I loathe Benjamin Britten's music? Well, out of sheer politeness I had to listen to the whole of *Billy Budd* played with deafening loudness.' At the end she admitted she had hated it, and the logical-minded Desmond couldn't understand why she had let herself in for it. Nor could I.

Today I've had Bunny to lunch, and hope for Janetta tonight.

August 21st

And got her, none the less welcome for being delayed, and oh the pleasure of making contact so swiftly and completely. We ate salmon trout and mayonnaise and drank Bunny's white Burgundy. She has left Henrietta and Sophie at Tramores, though this didn't come out at once, curiously enough. She gave me a careful report on Sophie, partly very good – Henrietta is sweet and loving to her, Sophie looks well; Rose and Jaime had had long talks to her and reported that she was 'very bright'. But the bad is that the life of being trailed around in a cart behind Henrietta and Mark Palmer has obviously given her an uncertain feeling.

But how for a moment can I set aside the horrifying morning news that Russia has invaded Czechoslovakia? Robert rang up this morning to say he was flying out there at once for television, and his voice was electric with the half-excited sense of emergency. Though my heart has plummeted to my boots and beyond, and the familiar thoughts of 'it's quite enough; time to go' return, I notice with alarm that the very muscles of panic are tired.

August 28th: Cranborne, with the David Cecils

I love my fellow guests, Iris and John Bayley. On Sunday night, I remember among many conversations that took light and dashed away like forest fires rather an odd one about executions. If one had (like so many historical characters) to have one's head chopped off, would one prefer it to happen in public or in private? David and John said in public, we three females no – but David's enthusiasm for a public execution was what astounded me. With phrases like 'make a good end' and 'I would feel I owed it to myself', he pranced proudly about the room like some sort of heraldic animal, eyes aflame. Stranger still, he had no doubt at all that he *would* make a good end. I suggested that like other intensely emotional moments in life – having a baby, or making love – one would rather be in private, and that with the end of one's life so near, all paraphernalia would seem futile, and an efficient quietus would be one's sole concern. I think Iris and Rachel, after hesitation, joined me – Iris with the qualification that if one were dying for a cause one believed in, one might make an effective last speech. And so she would, of all people. One of the things I like about Iris is that she's not afraid of saying 'high-minded' things.

Almost Cypriot heat, sun, lovely walks, and this stimulating company. In the background the moving, agitating drama of Czechoslovakia, not over yet. It has been a near thing that passive resistance and high moral courage have not triumphed. As it is they seem to have saved awful bloodshed and resulted in a painful compromise. Russian Communism has been seriously discredited with other Communist parties and I am at times haunted by the dread that it is the beginning of some huge and grizzly campaign, or even of nuclear war. There's a horrible feeling of *déjà vu* about it, a reminiscence of Munich, and perhaps the noble Czechs have merely gained themselves and the world a few months' grace.

September 8th

Robert invited himself to lunch yesterday. What a pleasure to indulge in two good hours of concentrated conversation, both on the personal level, and of course Czechoslovakia on the non-personal one. I was infected – though I had the disease already – by his great enthusiasm for the Czechs' achievement, and felt real excitement over the fact that the lesson they have taught the world is primarily a moral and a pacifist one. That he felt it to be this (as he obviously did, saying, 'You would have been tremendously excited') from his first-hand experience was a great encouragement to my native optimism. He described the state of Prague as being wildly exhilarating, even though some friends he has there were of course wondering whether they should leave the country. The first Russians who arrived were very young and inexperienced and completely in the dark as to what they were doing or even where they were. Some really thought they were in Belgium or Germany. They became demoralized so quickly that they were removed after four days and new, tougher troops sent in. The Czechs eagerly gave help to people like Robert who were smuggling out television films.

September 10th

Gerald to dinner again last night. He's much better alone, and we talked for a long while without friction. He says he's so much excited by company that he always loses his head and is bitterly ashamed of himself afterwards. 'If more than two or three people are present I can't think, I just talk.' That's his difficulty – he goes on talking without thinking. I took it as a sort of apology, as I believe it was meant.

September 22nd: Hilton

My pleasure in seeing Henrietta and Sophie again wasn't quite unmixed with worry. Dearly as Henrietta loves Sophie, she has naturally not recovered from the trauma of so short a while ago and now she is finding life hard, and unable to cope with. Meanwhile Sophie has become a fascinating little being with dark eyes and gold-tendrilled hair, affectionate, lively-witted and thoughtful. My heart is almost unbearably touched by her, and I also feel desperately sorry for Henrietta and that somehow we must find some way of giving her a rest.

There is also the sadness which fills Hilton itself, crumbling around Bunny, who struggles on with such extraordinary gallantry. Nine to dinner on Sunday – I don't know how he does it. I said to Henrietta I wondered what would happen to Hilton if William were to marry his girlfriend. She evidently hadn't considered for a moment that Bunny might not go on much longer wanting to live there alone and cook for his girls and their hosts of friends whenever they chose to descend on him. After a silence she said she supposed it was 'unimaginative of her'.

October 12th: The Slade

Henrietta seems to be moving towards a possible solution. She is trying to arrange for Sophie to go to the same state school as little Frances Behrens[1]; what's more, Jane Garnett[2] has been angelic and very helpful, and may be able to put her up in term-time in their Islington house.

Dadie is here, and his company is always exhilarating. His mind moves much at the same speed as mine does and we often take the same point of view. Pouring all yesterday afternoon, with squelching grass and dripping rose-bushes, a howling wizard wind crashing against the windows. Raining softly all this morning. Only at lunch-time did that grey lid start sliding back showing a pale blue sky, and about four this afternoon Dadie, Eardley and I set out for a brisk walk. Incomparably lovely views in all directions, trees still fat with grey-green leaves, very rich blue shadows and the distance clear and remote.

October 13th

To dine at John Fowler's last night in his very pretty house near Odiham. He seems a nice, sad, kind man. The evening was awkward – the other guests were Michael and Rachel Redgrave.[3] Dadie made much of the honour it was to meet such distinguished people, but did not warn us that Michael Redgrave was as heavy on hand as could be imagined and generally drunk. He was in fact both and had just fallen into a muddy ditch on his way to dinner. I sat next to him and at once realized what I was in for when I looked at his lost, impassive face, like a stuffed fish behind glass. I did my best; Eardley, on his other side, never addressed him once, and Dadie was laughing and shouting with Rachel Redgrave (very nice she seemed to be). My task was hopeless. I had to repeat everything to Michael Redgrave, who was totally uninterested in all of it, except when I admired his spectacles. After dinner there was a long walk in the dark to the 'studio', and I couldn't see a step and fell down and barked my shin, bleeding like a stuck pig – mainly after returning home and taking off my stocking. I was greatly touched by Mattei's extraordinary gentleness and consideration in bringing TCP and Elastoplast while I spattered the bathroom with my blood. Dadie cheered us on from the sidelines and Eardley vanished altogether. Hating the sight of blood, perhaps?

[1] Child of Harriet and Tim. She and Sophie are great friends still.
[2] Wife of Bunny's eldest son (by Ray) Richard.
[3] The actors.

November 4th

Dined with Magouche. After dinner a troupe of young came in – Georgie, Antonia and Jean-Pierre's[1] sister, and a boy who had just been sent away from school for smoking cannabis.

Someone mentioned the words 'good', 'moral', 'ethical' – it might have been me, fresh from talking about G. E. Moore with Paul Levy[2]. A visible shudder of horror went through them all. I asked the expelled boy why he disliked the words? F.: 'There's nothing wrong with "good" or "moral", is there? What do *you* think "valuable" then?' 'Oh well, you know, it's rather difficult. I'd have to think about that. I suppose nowadays it's mostly – you know – material things like television sets.'

But what of Paul Levy? He is a young Jewish American from Harvard who has come over with a grant to write about G. E. Moore, and I met him at Oxford and the Cecils' at Cranborne, and talked to him a bit about Moore's theories. He declared he would like to find a Bloomsburyite who wasn't a Moorite – I put up a tentative hand. 'Why?' he asked. 'Because he didn't *really* refute hedonism,' I said, 'and used "desirable" as if it meant "ought to be desired" instead of simply "is – or can be – desired", so introducing his own naturalist fallacy.' I scored a hit with this random shot. 'Oh, well, that's exactly what our modern American philosophers say.' I was loth to risk any further less successful plunges, and though I tried to draw him on his own views he wouldn't be drawn. He immediately won me by talking of Alix (with whom he spent two days) with enormous admiration. He's quick, intelligent, sympathetic, interested, amusing. He has given me Lytton's Apostles papers to read – they are well written, thoughtful, and mature compared to the yardsticks of some of today's young. But I must beware the danger of intolerance, and sticking up for the friends of my own youth, who were intolerant themselves and perhaps vain. As Alix said when I visited her yesterday, Paul Levy might be a very clever confidence trickster, but I'm prepared to bet he isn't. I took to him very much.

From Alix I went to the Carringtons' where I was given to read a lot of correspondence from Carrington to Alix and (both ways) with Lytton, and also Lytton–James. An interesting letter of Carrington's to Alix described the Watendlath situation exactly as Ralph did, and twice referred to Gerald's 'Larrau plot' for Valentine to divert Ralph's attention. During the weekend Julian Vinogradoff[3] rang up to say that there was a paragraph in the *Daily Telegraph* announcing that someone called Ken Russell was going to make a film based on Holroyd's book. She is frantic – Noel too was very upset. I loathe the idea, but haven't yet sorted out my feelings about it.

November 25th

The Ken Russell film has occupied my mind nearly as much as the question of Sophie's school did, and my thoughts about it came somewhat to a head this morning. I flew into action, partly because Rosamond suggested my ringing up the Society of Authors and consulting their legal expert. She says – and I have had various opinions on the subject, some disagreeing with this – that as Alix has the copyright for all Lytton's letters and I for all Carrington's and her diaries, she and

[1] Georgie's boyfriend and later husband.
[2] Biographer of G. E. Moore and later writer on food and music.
[3] Only child of Lady Ottoline Morrell.

I could make the film more awkward for the producers by refusing the copyright of any extracts to the film-makers. I am going however to see Holroyd this evening and find out what they do propose to do. According to the paper there will be some 'sensational casting'. Who in the world will play Lytton and Carrington – and is Ralph to be in? He must be, of course, and I mind this much more than the possibility (suggested by some of my friends) that I might be in it myself. I mind the idea of the false Ralph they will create very much indeed, whether rationally or no.

I rang Alix, who had received the news passively the day before, appearing to think it was nice of Holroyd to write to her about the project. She believed what he wrote: that he hoped the film would increase the sale of Lytton's books.

I have been supported in my bellicose attitude by Noel (who writes frequent agitated letters) and very much so by friends like Faith Henderson, Rosamond, the Penroses.

November 28th

Michael Holroyd was very friendly and I'm glad I asked him to come. He even said he was glad to know what we all felt about it. Perhaps nothing is gained; it may be out of his hands and in the tougher ones of the BBC and Ken Russell. But he has admitted to obtuseness in not realizing what pain would be caused, and said he is sorry, and will do his best to prevent it. This morning he rang again to say that he had made his protest.

Last night to Eliot's *Cocktail Party* with Wynne and Kitty. In its way it was riveting, though apart from Alec Guinness and the heroine the actors weren't good. There is also great sadism to my mind, in the play itself. Wynne was in a strangely keyed-up state perhaps because of his intense feelings about the myth of the Crucifixion, and he sees Eliot's Celia not as a 'saint' as I did, but as Christ himself. He frantically resisted any attempt to discuss the play in the intervals, but wanted to do so at length and in detail afterwards – and we did so over a bottle of wine in my flat. Wynne said he had been deeply moved by the play, which I had already guessed from his stifled sobs at one point. He was suspicious at first of me as an anti-Christian; he sometimes accuses me of teasing him for being a believer, but I'm most careful not to do this now I know he is such a serious one and the boot is really on the other leg. He attacks me – lightly, usually – for being a rationalist. Well, I hope I am one. It was an interesting evening, because of Wynne's first-rate intelligence. This afternoon he rang up to apologize for being irritable 'mostly to my wife'. I certainly didn't think he had been to me, except when Kitty and I were told we mustn't discuss the play in the interval, which I thought uncalled-for.

December 1st

I give up. I shall become a recluse. I've had a letter from the BBC, speaking of the proposed Lytton films as a certainty – there's no sign of Michael having affected them in any way – and they hope for my 'approval and support'. What to do next? I beat against a stone wall, supported only by Noel. I still propose to battle on, though with very little hope. But I must not get megalomanic, and think that my futile flappings can make any difference.

December 15th

I'm very anxious lest taking in Sophie should be too much for Richard and Jane. I have been to Alwyne Villas several times to see her, when she was away from school with a cold and earache, and I found her being devotedly looked after and quite gay, and she was sweetly affectionate to me. When I called her 'sweetheart' and asked 'if she minded', she pondered a long time and then said, 'You can call me anything you like – because I *love* you.' I think about her a great deal of the time, and at others brood over this somehow defiling and disgusting Ken Russell film.

December 20th: The Slade

I have dived into still waters, like the little tarn above Ullswater where I bathed among water-lilies a few years ago. Peace – *yes*, unutterably soothing, and of course I keep asking: why do I stay in the clangour and frenzy of London, wound up like a clockwork mouse, inner mechanism whirring even when picked off the ground, palpitating senselessly, restless without purpose, flying to the telephone and then deliberately calming my voice? Why, why, why? I was not a little doubtful what it would be like here alone with Eardley in the total isolation of the Slade, without telephone or newspapers. But *at once* it applied a gently soothing poultice and I really do believe it is exactly what I needed.

December 23rd

The settled peace and calm here has exceeded my expectations. Only the weather is wild, and for the last two nights flurries of rain and hail have hurled themselves against my bedroom windows with such a deafening noise that I've had to sandwich my head between two pillows. We listen on the wireless to the news of the three astronauts who are attempting to encircle the moon, I with fascinated horror as if forced to witness a gladiatorial show, while to Eardley it is 'romantic and glamorous'. Yet he is a timid, rather than brave man, afraid of blood and pain, who, though by no means a pacifist, avoided risking his life in the war I'm not sure how and daren't ask.

I go walks by myself every day and prefer it that way. I keep up a tin-whistle piping of trifling and repetitive thoughts, and do a lot of looking. This afternoon up the hill opposite by a sunken lane with ivy everywhere – climbing up the trunks of all the trees, trailing down again and carpeting the ground, thus doubly binding the trees to the earth, tall dark evergreens are decorated with old man's beard like the spangled cotton wool on a Christmas tree.

December 29th

My stay is nearing its end. I have very deliberately slowed my tempo, and taken things at a very steady pace. It has been a nursing-home cure, with very few moments when I have had to screw myself up to do anything. Last night we went for a drink with neighbours, meeting there two appalling figures straight out of the Ark. Brigadier Antrobus was voted 'all right', for he scarcely opened his mouth. Mrs Antrobus sitting next to me, was a ghastly female. The subject of Bedales came up as usual, and everyone looked at me as some sort of freak. I asked Mrs Antrobus if she would recommend a child to go there. 'Why no – you see they have no religious instruction. And then I'm a *square*,' proudly. We prattled of possible snow, nice walks, and cars. 'We have two. You see we have to fetch our daily, and we don't want to do *that* in the Daimler, so we keep a Mini.' Eardley was impressed because the Brigadier had been at College in Winchester, 'the highest possible intellectual standard'. Well, much good does it seem to have done him.

My thoughts are turning homewards and nestwards, and with that of course comes anxiety about the various people for whom I feel responsible. Snow covers much of England.

1969

January 3rd: London

Now that I have – only this morning – handed in Carpentier to be typed, the chief thing I have on my agenda is my battle with the BBC. It is not yet over. Robert nobly came to my assistance and wrote a letter to a high-up person (David Attenborough, no less), sending me by telegram the news that this great man had 'promised they would not go ahead without my consent'. He warned me they might go on trying to obtain it, and so they have. I found a letter from Swallow of the BBC, asking me in very polite terms if I would meet and discuss the matter with him and Ken Russell himself. I hardly dared say no, but Robert advised me that I must. It would be fatal to make them put themselves out to persuade me. So – greatly daring – I wrote to say 'it would only waste their valuable time, as I had Attenborough's written undertaking not to go ahead'.

Standing up to this incomprehensible and now rather dreaded juggernaut makes me tremble. What am I protecting so tigerishly, obstinately from the BBC? Ralph, I believe.

January 10th

The BBC situation ended with a loud bang. My polite letter to Swallow was met by an almost grovelling one from Julian's Central European boss. It came by return of post and when I saw the red letters 'BBC' lying on my hall floor, I trembled. I felt persecuted, harassed, badgered, 'why can't they leave me alone?' Hearst, as he's called, hadn't really read my letter and thought I was complaining of wasting 'my' time, not that of the great Russell and Swallow. He began all over again about Russell's eminence and outstanding skill. Would I come and see one of his films? Next morning I woke early, writing letters in my head. Robert and Cynthia, and Julian were coming to dinner, so I rang Robert to ask him to bring Attenborough's letter – my pass to freedom, without which I do see that the project would certainly go through. Robert at once urged me to write my mental letter *at once*, and post it *at once*. Why, I wonder? Was it because he feels engaged in this particular battle or likes battles in general. Anyway I did, and am sorry. I wrote in violent indignation, saying I had Attenborough's written assurance they would not go on without my consent and I would *never* consent. That I hoped Russell would find another subject and leave us in peace and that this correspondence might now end. In fact I said: *shut up*.

When Julian came, he was appalled; so much so that I really felt very ashamed of myself. I should have kept my original coolness throughout; it's never a good plan – or very seldom – to fly off the handle. Anyhow I have, and it's given me a certain relief. I was becoming obsessed by my battle with this huge Megatherium, the BBC. They are now 'the enemy' to me, but of course I'm deeply sorry to have upset Julian by my bad behaviour to his boss.

January 22nd

Penroses, Georgia, Bunny and Pat Trevor-Roper came to dinner. Bursts of Roman candles from different quarters until nearly one. Everyone unselfconsciously but vigorously themselves (except perhaps poor Lionel, who is not at all well): Bunny saying, 'Sex begins at fifty,' Pat explosively appreciative and bubbling, Georgia quite splendid. Two nights ago there was a 'grand' party at the Dufferins for Duncan's birthday. Eardley and I got there at nearly eleven and hardly dared enter, the house looked so pompous and dead. But we at once saw countless familiar faces – Bunny, Amaryllis, Henrietta, Raymond, the Connollys, Quentin and Olivier, Holroyd, Mary Hutchinson, and some glamorous hippy young. Georgia (coming late) was caught by Bryan Guinness and I almost laughed, her face went so rapidly dead under the withering fire of his amiably booming conversation. Raymond 'thought Eardley seemed chilly' and wondered what's happened about the studio.

The Ken Russell film crisis is not yet over. Robert rang up to tell me he had had a letter of protest from Attenborough because I took his undertaking as a pass to peace and freedom, and wouldn't see Swallow and Russell. He still firmly says I mustn't, but that they are sure to try again. From Julian too I get the no doubt false impression that the whole telly world is a-buzz with this crisis, and I feel amazed at the extraordinary way I am venturing to try to stop their plans – also sick sometimes when I think of it; it's so very unlike the sort of thing I generally get involved in, so public and immolative.

January 24th

Well, I've had a sight of the enemy – the great civilizing force of television at close range, and I must say it was not impressive. They occupied my flat from two to five yesterday afternoon in order to photograph Bunny in a 'congenial setting' speaking about George Moore. The net result of at least fifteen people's work, or what passed as such, will be (so a female friend of Julian's told me) about two minutes on the screen. In they poured, technicians with huge, black, helmet-shaped lamps on legs, camera men (at least five of these I should say), two near-gentlemen, one in public school clothes, another with long hair, Chinese moustache and a thick Irish sweater, neither of whom appeared to have anything at all to do; the director, with a massive head, who didn't know what a violin-stand was; the interviewer who retired into my bedroom 'to change his shirt and put on a wig'; a little girl detailed to assist in this operation; a big, blowsy make-up girl who did no making-up and sighed for a set of Scrabble; two other females, one – Julian's friend – whose only task during these three hours was to give me a cheque for five guineas for the use of my flat. Fascinated and inquisitive at first, I soon became dead bored, and sat in my bedroom reading *The Tenant of Wildfell Hall* (equally boring in another way). I took an occasional peep at Bunny sitting in the glare of the lights, with his beret pulled over his poor eyes to protect them, like a man under torture. Most of this host of people had nothing, or almost nothing to do, yet contrived to look as if they thought they had. None had brought a book, but total silence was called for when shooting was going on. I couldn't help commiserating with them; they looked surprised. They smoked a quarter of an inch of innumerable cigarettes and piled them up on any likely or unlikely object; they trooped into the lavatory and peed remorselessly and loudly, like horses. Julian's friend told me they were trying to make this documentary for three different sorts of people – the educated who had read George Moore, the literate who might want to, the illiterate, who wouldn't (I paraphrase her). *'But you can't do that,'* I said. And their activities seemed, though polite and well-meaning, futile, unimportant, sterile, anti-life. I felt that if they were not bored they ought to be.

January 26th

Perhaps I was too hard on them, for in fact they 'meant well', as I was aware. And looking round the world this seems to be true of rather few – not true for instance of the disgustingly cretinous football fans, busily destroying the trains and buses that take them to their pleasure, or of the murderously vicious speeders, or those who are so avid for their material gain as to lose sight of everything else (a lot of strikers probably). I don't know quite where in the dismal picture to put people of near-criminal stupidity like the delegates at the Vietnam Conference who have wrangled on and on about the *shape* of their conference table while people go on dying and fighting; the perpetrators of violent films, feeding the sadism of the public, including children, so as to earn a little more money; psychologists who tell everyone they must be aggressive because aggression equals activity and creation; and everyone who contributes to the materialism of the present day, and in order to make money sinks all standards to the lowest common denominator. It's impossible to look at the *Radio Times*, it's so vulgarly hideous and aimed at those to whom past beauty is non-existent and present beauty is sex only.

What has psychoanalysis done for the world, when so much violence has still to be released both in fantasy and action? And can people have been even sexually liberated if they need so many strip-tease joints, which one would imagine could only gratify the bottled-up or immature? Why can dress designers not consider the shape of the female form, and why must they so painstakingly deglamourize it? Why must the young either drown reality in drugs or yell slogans of destruction like children in a nursery?

I have just (Sunday morning) passed a little group of black-haired men standing opposite the Spanish Embassy, shouting at intervals: *'Asesino! Asesino!'* They are to demonstrate this afternoon against Franco's declaring a state of emergency in Spain.

January 28th

Margaret rang up and asked to come and see me yesterday. Her troubles are really grim – Lionel with leukaemia and the torturous situation about Dunyusha. I know Margaret tends to fantasize a good deal so have to have my grain of salt in readiness when she tells me that Dunyusha's one object is to come to England, supplant her as Lionel's wife and have several children. The letter I was shown from her did not support this view, but actually thanked Margaret for being nice about her abortion and sending her flowers. I'm sure she wants to come to England but can she want to found a family and settle down with a seventy-year-old professor with leukaemia?

February 16th: Hilton

Henrietta and I drove down here yesterday morning. The cold is deathly. Yesterday in the drawing-room, with electric fire, radiator and smouldering logs, I was so paralysed by it that my fingers refused to write. In bed I wore a vest, flannel night-gown, bed-jacket and winter dressing gown, and over all that an eiderdown which I'd smuggled in in the boot of my Mini – yet I was no more than comfortably warm. But none of this mattered beside the ghostly melancholy that drips from these walls, apparently unnoticed by its inmates Bunny and William. Bunny in a handsome suit of blue check, steps about as briskly as a young man. William retreats into his room with huddled shoulders and tootles on his oboe. Henrietta and I sit in the dank, cold, lightless drawing-room.

It was nobody's fault that Sophie was babyish and endlessly demanding, and on the whole Henrietta was patient and sweet to her, until (unable to bear any more) she spoke to her in a rather remote voice, whereupon Sophie lay on the ground and sobbed as if her heart would break. I took her away almost by force, and read to her in my room, feeling heart-broken myself.

February 18th

Henrietta, Sophie and I drove back, through falling snow at first. I'm only too aware of Henrietta's desperate unhappiness. She left Sophie with me in the after-noon; after one rush to hurl herself into her mother's arms as she was leaving, she became almost at once far more grown up and lively. She read brilliantly from two little books I'd bought her, sat picking out tunes with real pattern and rhythm on the piano for some time and sang several songs perfectly in tune. There was nothing but jollity too when we got back to Alwyne Villas, where Richard was awaiting us like a benign father figure. In fact she seemed a very 'all right' little girl, and undoubtedly bright in her wits.

March 5th

Shaking with sobs, convulsed with doubt, neurotic pains and other symptoms, changing his mind five times daily, poor Lionel – a pitiable prey to love, at seventy – has at last posted off to visit his girl in Warsaw. Margaret has stood up to the stress of it all most heroically, her worst moment being when he implored her to ring up Dunyusha and say he wouldn't come – *he* couldn't, as her voice melted him. But Margaret couldn't, because she knew she'd be blamed by them both afterwards. She merely said Lionel wasn't well, and Dunyusha got him to the telephone and persuaded him to come. One of Margaret's treats during Lionel's absence was to be a weekend in Amsterdam with me, but this has been 'on' and 'off' so frequently that I stopped thinking about it. Now it seems we are going, and the day after tomorrow! My prayers are directed to Margaret's not getting involved in the hectic world of fantasy as she did last summer in Austria – but I'm afraid she has given Lionel her telephone number.

March 6th

Julia for a long talk on the telephone this morning. She told me Bunny went to see her about her Carrington letters last night, worked his charm and has carried them off in triumph. We talked about Julian's forthcoming radio programme on

Virginia, to which he has asked her to contribute. 'But I don't think, with her relations alive, I could say what I want to.' 'What would that be?' 'Well, Leonard used to say that he wondered why people stared after her in the street, but I could tell him it's because she wasn't *at home in her body*, wore such awful, cheap clothes and moved so ungainlily. But of course I can't say that. If it's just going to be another outpouring of adulation, what's the point of that? Then I don't happen to admire her writing very much – all this harping on beauty and describing life in terms of flowers and frills. It's girlish gush like Rosamond's. And I should want to say that too.' I wonder whence comes Julia's terror of people getting too much or too unqualified praise – that is except in the case of Chekhov and Saul Bellow.

Also there's a certain arrogance in her assumption that her criticisms might damage Virginia's reputation. But she ended on a sad wail: 'Nothing gets any better, and I start drinking whisky after breakfast now and can't eat.' She pays two cooks to cook one meal each a week at three guineas a go.

March 23rd

I saw Janetta twice, and the ease and pleasure in our communication has changed my outlook. The pleasure of loving so unique a person whose affection I'm profoundly grateful for, can't be exhausted. When I say she's 'lost' and 'gone' I'm lying. What's more, in spite of arriving in this inclement, grey ice-box I think it has given her great pleasure, and perhaps some of the mental stimuli lacking on the 'coast', to see her friends and realize how very much they want to see her. Her life with Jaime sounds fine. There's no major source of worry in any of the three girls, only the flooding of poor Tramores (swollen windows and doors, bulgy, soaked books, wet-marks on walls) is a great grief – I admire the realistic almost self-mocking way she talks of it. This – since realism has always been the quality I most value – is brought home to me by finding myself in the presence of nervous collapse here at Litton Cheney, on which I'm afraid I've failed to make any impression. Reynolds is in a state of grief, self-laceration and mourning, and has been so for ten days, because he ordered two large trees that menaced the house to be cut down. It is as if they were murdered corpses lying there, and the gap in a hedge left by their fall is an agony to him. Janet found him yesterday looking at it with tears pouring down his cheeks and his hands over his face. On our first evening he referred to 'the knot of his utter misery and guilt'. Then and next morning I tried all I could think of by way of reassurance. I went to look at the trees; he had covered their stumps with ivy-fronds like flowers at a funeral, but I moved them aside and declared with conviction that the proportion between phloem and bast was wrong, that the rot had clearly set in, and they must have been dangerous. I told him that where the gap looked like a raw operational wound it would close up and nature take over, and very quickly too with spring at hand. I told him the extra light and sun (shining yesterday luckily) were an asset, and that there was something as a landscape gardener, artist and tree-lover he could treat as raw material and mould to his design. I went round and looked at all his other splendid trees, and said he was anyhow not suffering from tree-starvation. I said that man had always grown trees and then cut them down and burned them, and that logs and fallen trees were handsome, healthy objects. I tried sympathy pure and simple, saying how deeply I had suffered from a fallen tree at Ham Spray, which was quite true. I tried a slightly tougher line, saying that what was done was done, and that however much one loved trees they were not people. I got a little tougher still and said that irrational emotion could only be dealt with ultimately by one's own courageous effort. If one *wants* to starve or grieve to death, no one can stop one.

I think he believed me when I said the trees had begun to decay, and for a moment pure sympathy had some effect. But by yesterday the black cloud of mourning was there as before. I hadn't had the least effect.

Both nights he has read aloud to us from *Middlemarch* in a low voice, with evident pleasure and well, but so very softly that he seemed to deny our presence as listeners. He is an intensely charming man but at the present moment one wrapped up in his own neurosis – and I admire Janet's patience and kindness to him.

April 9th: Crichel for Easter

The divine weather stayed with us all the while and turned on the heat as well. We sat out between the glass shelters; there was croquet; Moses panted in the shade. I did *not* however preserve the silence of an Indian Brave as I had meant, but am ashamed to say I discharged some of my melancholy (for it didn't quite clear up) on to Julian. Why the poor fellow should be treated so just because he's sympathetic I can't think. I look to see how the heroes and heroines of the memoirs and biographies I read deal with their last lap, and it is always (at best) a feat of endurance. I remember poor Edward Lear, and also Princess Matilde Bonaparte, a delightfully warm, good-humoured, enjoying character.

Raymond's face, just as yellowed and crinkled as mine, emerged distressingly from a harsh, cherry-red turtle-neck pullover patterned with peacocks' tails. Etymological problems filled the air between him and Desmond with fine dust, although Julian and I put up mild pleas for tolerance, variety and change. Then, over and again, Raymond gave proofs of his sweetness and affection, and returned from a ruler-wielding schoolmaster to a 'very cuddly man'.[1] Desmond ran about in his youthful and attentive way, worrying me in view of his recent eye operation and of the fact that he was clearly anxious about certain renewed sensations in the operated eye. Pat returned straight from Nigeria on Saturday and showed seemingly casual indifference to these very natural fears.

Raymond suddenly, *à propos de rien*: 'I know I've not got a first-class nor a second-class brain, but I'm cleverer than most people.'

April 22nd: Arras

Arras is the end of our first day's journey. Almost as soon as we reached Southend airport 'Mr Garnett' was called for on the loudspeaker. He at once thought Angelica (who is ill) must be dying, but it was merely that our hour of departure was earlier than he had reckoned with. We were carried over the sea at a stately pace. Looking down I could see its sandy floor through shallow water, and very soon, we were across and near Calais. Threading tiny 'white' roads we passed on to Arras and arrived with no map of the town, at rush hour, and in drenching rain. Bunny had a vague recollection of a big place where he had once stayed with Angelica. We asked in cafés and circled the suburbs and at last found a rather grand one. Dinner

---

[1] As he was called by Caroline West when about three.

in a cheap restaurant while young men sat singly with newspapers, or in pairs talking their clever, delicate language.

April 23rd: Aisey-sur-Seine

In a charming little village inn, cheap, clean, with window-boxes of egg-yellow pansies and the lovely combination of cream-coloured stone and grey paint. A few yards away, the 'infant Seine', as Bunny calls it, glides and then tumbles under an ancient bridge, and cows like Alderneys, a soft mouse-grey, are driven along the village street. Weather still wretchedly cold and wet but neither of us is wretched. Bunny's stamina is amazing. We drove from nine till seven yesterday with a fairly long break at Meaux – a detour made simply in order to buy its special mustard, but I enjoyed seeing the noble cathedral after lunch in a restaurant humming with noise. 'What famous man was its bishop?' I asked Bunny, who couldn't remember any more than I could, and then inside we saw it was Bossuet. Beautiful country from Meaux to the Seine, trees only just coming out but grass brilliantly green, cowslips, fat white cows looking as if they gave excellent milk and butter. Bun is very good-humoured, but I feel I must be the only female he has travelled with in separate rooms, and only hope he doesn't feel humiliated before the hotelier. His deafness is greater than I realized and in the car almost total. I lean towards him and project my remarks loudly towards his ear, but am nearly always greeted by a cheerful 'what?' A very good dinner: leek soup, trout, and goat cheese, before a wood fire, with an excellent bottle of wine. Bunny thaws out in the evening; at lunch, either from deafness or fatigue he appeared to me curiously shy. He talks affectionately of Magouche. Of Henrietta he says he asks and knows nothing.

April 25th: Piacenza

Well, what a place! 'Pleasance' says the map ironically, in brackets. There's a holiday in the town, with flags and pleasure-seeking crowds. Unable to find the most modest of hotels, I stopped a promising-looking passer-by, who turned out to have a disastrously cleft palate and made ghastly noises, though obviously wanting to be helpful. Fired by his astonishing energy, Bunny insisted on leaving behind Pavia, which looked much nicer, and it's my rule for happy travelling to give in on such points. Anyway, we are in for the night in a modern hotel on the outskirts, whose staff are hissing with exhaustion after serving holiday meals all day. There's no question in Bunny's mind of slackening our pace, and what he said about dawdling along for five to seven days is rubbish. No time to buy a postcard, look at a single sight, take a stroll, yet in my foolish credulity I thought this was what we should see eye to eye about. Each morning he's eager to be off, and off we go. I feel like Alice and the Red Queen. This morning we headed towards the Mont Blanc tunnel, slightly dreaded beforehand but quite unalarming. Bunny expected forty kilometres of it, I twenty, and there turned out to be only twelve.

Out into soggy snow and sun; we coasted down the Val d'Aosta and had our first picnic by a stream. Last night at Bonneville I lay awake for three hours wondering if I could suggest a little less haste, but of course I didn't and again we drove all day, often at about seventy miles an hour, at which speed the little car is bumpy and erratic. I can't but admire this stupendous feat of endurance in a man of seventy-seven, but by evening his hand shakes and his face is red, so my pity is often aroused. And I regret the places whizzed by unseen, and wonder what I would do if he had a stroke driving at seventy miles per hour.

Interesting conversation, *en route* about homosexuals. They are 'frightened of sex', says Bunny, and their life is 'lacking in richness'. Stopped for a drink in the Piazza Cavour of a nice town called Vercelli and had an argument about Garibaldi. I asked the boy who brought our drinks what holiday it was. '*Di fascismo*', he said sheepishly and incorrectly.

April 26th: San Sano

We have arrived and I have come to my senses and see the past four and a half days in a new light. Magouche was not expecting us before Monday at earliest, and our thundering advance now plainly shows as a valiant and obstinate attempt on Bunny's part to beat the band, and prove that he's not a dead dog yet, but a *man*. I can't help retrospectively resenting not having spent at least one more night on the way, looking at Italian towns, searching for flowers or lying in the grass after picnics. I may be hypersensitive about outstaying, and in this case anticipating, my welcome. In any case Magouche was, of course, much too polite not to greet us warmly, though she has a couple of Italian visitors and their little boy already staying in the house, and hasty bed-making had to be done. And I could so well imagine her muttering 'Good God, it's not them already!' as she ran downstairs to meet us.

Her house stands bold, solid and dominant on the rounded summit of a hill, looking out over other softly rolling hills and valleys thick with oaks and olives, towards Siena. Its central tower has two rather low openings onto a loggia, which give it a somewhat grumpy expression. Matthew and Maro[1] are nest-making vigorously, planting trees, gardening, planning swimming-pools and garages. The furniture is solid to match the house, simple, a little austere, and there's nothing for prettyness alone and no pictures on the walls, windows rather small according to Tuscan farmhouse tradition, central heating. Almost the best room in the house is an enormous bathroom, with a vast bath that can never be completely emptied. Moved by the same sort of impulse as Janetta with Tramores, Magouche, Maro and Matthew have created something very different. I don't know who is responsible for what.

April 27th

Breakfast-time announces itself without a watch by the sound and delicious smell of coffee being ground and toasting bread. We sat outside under a mulberry tree which is only just starting to unwrap its buds. Hot sun. On this southern side of the house there are preparations for a lawn to be made. Sat in the sun reading and writing till it was time to start on a picnic which was to speed the Italian family to Rome. We ate beside an artificial lake. After lunch Magouche and Maro flung themselves shrieking into the water; Bunny took Matthew off to fish; I went looking for flowers, fell down and returned with bleeding legs as usual, and the dear little boy, Albertino, made love to frogs. Suddenly Matthew burst into applause as Bunny was seen at the far end of the lake capped with his white hair, preparing to dive off a long board, which he actually did twice, with great heroism, for the water was icy. The Italians left for Rome.

[1] Magouche's eldest daughter and her husband, son of Stephen and Natasha Spender.

April 28th

Getting into the San Sano way of life. My bedroom is severely simple, with a hard monk's bed which I find very sympathetic. I'm impressed by Matthew and Maro's unfashionably energetic lives. Matthew digs and waters and chops wood all day long, comes in with red cheeks and eats huge meals. Maro, smooth but pallid, looks as if consciously trying to produce a child, but doesn't. Two women from the village come in and help. Bunny strides off to the porch of an old barn and sits at a stone table writing. We drink a lot of the local Chianti and eat minestrones, pasta and home-made brawn. Everyone becomes jolly over dinner; Bunny tending to hold forth.

April 30th

Fine blue morning. 'Let's take a picnic and go to Volterra,' said Magouche at breakfast, and no one expected the skies to open and deluge us with rain. It's tantalizing to be in such lovely country with extraordinary things to see all round, and find such disappointing weather. I think of Orta and Sicily, scenes of two other dubious Italian springs. Matthew and Maro stayed at home controlling their mounds of earth and lorries. Bunny, Magouche and I picnicked by a sweet little Romanesque church on the way to Volterra, and Bunny put away a quite alarming quantity of red wine and a good deal of food too, which, however, had no effect on him until we were nearly home, when he looked as though he might collapse. 'Are you all right, Bunny? Have you got a migraine?' 'No, not a *migraine*.' He is ashamed of every sort of weakness, so that it's difficult to know how seriously to take it. As he grows older and tends to feel tired, he turns to wine to help him out, rather than give in, and presents a tragic spectacle, reminding me for some reason of the dramatic news that de Gaulle was rejected by his compatriots two days ago, with a last dreadful '*non*'.

As we approached Volterra we saw it across the valley preparing to wrap itself in a dense sheet of rain, and then down it came in floods streaming over the huge, many-coloured paving-stones of the noble streets till they looked as brilliant and variegated as pebbles under water, olive green, purple and burnt sienna. We ran into the Duomo, Baptistery, the small but interesting Pinacoteca and the extraordinary Etruscan museum. Arrived home, we put the exhausted Bunny to bed and our soaked clothes to dry, and Magouche, Maro and I sat over a wood fire drinking whisky and talking female pacifist talk, and saying how we disliked those intellectuals who pride themselves on our having 'kept the peace' by means of the bomb race. And at a very jolly dinner in the village restaurant, I said what I thought of people who 'dismiss' all Germans – namely that they were racists as much to be condemned as anti-Semites and anti-blacks, and that we must remember what a huge contribution to civilization the Germans had made.

May 1st

Tears – an unexpected development. At lunch-time it was still cool and cloudy and we lunched indoors. Bunny was talking, as he loves to, about figures of the past – Rupert Brooke in this case. How James [Strachey] had been in love with him and then carried off Rupert's girl, Noel Olivier. Maro said: 'You mean he couldn't get one, so he thought he'd have the other.' Bunny did a full, glaring half-turn and burst out in a pressurized voice: '*No*, it wasn't like that *at all*. Don't always assume the worst of people; just *for once* try thinking well of them.' She carried it off well, though daunted, and said she supposed it came from belonging to the persecuted Armenian race. It seemed to have blown over, but later when I was at my table looking up my flowers Magouche whirled through like a ship under full sail saying, 'Now everyone's in tears – Maro *and* Bunny!' I could indeed hear Maro's sobs and hysterical voice, then Bunny walked quickly through with a red, folded, gloom-stricken expression.

I'm on Maro's side. Bunny was quite unnecessarily fierce; he can't both insist on talking about his old friends and also jealously guard them from the comments of those who didn't know them. But this is just what he does want to do, and last year there was an explosion over Tommy. The first premises of Maro's character have to be accepted, and she sometimes talks without thinking, but I like her energy and directness, and her devotion to Matthew all these long years is very touching.

Peace was confirmed by a long walk for all of us except Matthew, who keeps to his dedicated life of physical activity. The favourite of the two cats came too – a tabby tom with apricot underfur, who trotted down the woods with his tail in the air, displaying his furry balls, and then got lost. Flower-hunting; Maro dug up everything. Bunny tried to leap into the air to get down a strange form of mistletoe from an oak. We crossed the river, traversed the other side and waded back through icy water and so home. I'm slightly alarmed lest Bunny's exhibitionism gets him into serious trouble.

May 2nd

Better weather at last and steadily improving. Magouche and I drove to Siena together. The beauty of that truly glorious town knocked me backwards just as it had on my two previous visits, though possibly the Duccios in their dark, velvet-hung gallery crowded with Italian schoolboys and girls, seemed to ask for admiration so insistently that they got less. With lunch in the piazza, pictures, duomo, cafés and postcards, we passed six hours very happily.

Dinner of globe artichokes and chicken; anecdotes from Bunny, intercepted by long pauses. Laughter, drink and bed.

May 3rd

Perhaps too much drink, as everyone admitted to sleeping badly, and acid home-brewed Chianti may have been to blame. Sunny morning. Yesterday's post brought a batch of letters; one from Janetta asking me to join her and Jaime in Minorca – so very soon that I quailed at first. Much as I love being with friends and staying in their houses, there's an effort in trying to fit in, understand, not grate on other people's nerves, which gives me a desire for the only form of true relaxation that now remains – being alone. And this, when it happens, is often a bitter disappointment. But after this first shrinking response I thought how much I loved being with Janetta and Jaime and wrote to say, 'Yes – next month I would love to.'

May 4th

Magouche, Bunny and I spent the day in Florence. I don't like it nearly as much as Siena – its character has dwindled under the invasion of commerce and tourism, till it's just a large, noisy, bustling town in which are beautiful things. I sat alone in a café on the Piazza della Signoria, while the hideous voices of three Americans quacked on beside me about things and money, should they have ices or not, and whether there should be a discount on the bill. I only tried to see a few things, but enjoyed them. Magouche put me down outside the barrack-like church of the Carmine – walking alone inside I saw in one corner a band of upward-gazing worshippers and knew this was where the Masolinos and Masaccios were. They talked in hushed whispers only, in the awful presence of art. In the Bargello I ran into Bunny, his colour scheme of bright pink and snow-white startlingly at odds with the Donatellos and Verocchios. Somehow I don't feel his reaction to art is so much visual as literary, but it's strong, and he likes to look at what he looked at before. For lunch we drove out into the country to a smart restaurant in the stables of a Medici hunting-box. Depressed, unwelcoming waiters, but the best meal we'd had in Italy.

May 5th

Magouche's great outgoing warmth is much in evidence here, and to Bunny she is extraordinarily sweet, but perhaps there is an element of destruction in the way she eggs him on to prove his strength and youth, takes him on immense walks through rivers, or – above all – asks him to roll the new lawn. He came in so redfaced and done for after this that I exclaimed in horror and said he shouldn't do it. Magouche: 'I know it. But one must ask him to do things sometimes or it's so depressing for him.' Reminding me of Janetta long ago, pressing Ralph to eat and drink more than he should, 'to cheer him up'.

May 6th

Magouche likes a generous way of life and to go shopping with her is an eye-opener in lavish spending. Later in the afternoon she and I walked to the village dressmaker and ascended for a fitting to her dark shuttered room, entirely filled by a bed for three. Below three Norn-like females sat stitching, giving me the sort of glimpse into other lives I love. Afterwards we walked on through lovely woods and the cold inclement afternoon. I tried to turn the conversation from Magouche's girls to her own life, but she gently and politely resisted and said at present she had none. Yet later on, when we had lost our way and let ourselves in for a long, long walk she began talking of Gorky,[1] and I feel that he is now more real than Jack Phillips[2] or even Robin Fedden. She compared Gorky with Othello for jealousy. He was beside himself, if she talked to anyone else. She had 'given him everything' and believed everything he told her, much of which turned out to be lies. Her honesty and recklessness and destructiveness all appeared in the last act, 'when he became paranoic' and violent and threatened suicide. Did she think he would kill himself? Yes, on the whole. She could see no other end. She took the children and went to her mother; he telephoned to one of his friends saying he was going to hang himself and then he did. Did none of his friends hurry to his side? I asked. Yes, but he was too late. She was young and the demands made on her by the violence and urgency of the catastrophe carried her through. It had become more painful later, and still obviously does obsess her. Yet she hasn't a morbid sense of

[1] Her first husband, Arshile Gorky, the famous Armenian painter.
[2] Her second husband.

guilt and looks at it honesty. He had been violent as well as jealous and his doctor thought she should take the children away. I suggested that she couldn't still have loved him. 'Oh yes, I loved him *tenderly*, but I couldn't stay with him. And, of course, the poor fellow had a series of ghastly calamities – serious cancer and a colostomy, his neck broken in a car accident, a fire consuming many of his pictures.' Magouche gave me oddly little sense of his personality, probably because I've known no one in the least like him; but she sets very real value on his 'marvellous work', and there was something deeply moving in this tragic, honest and terrible story. On our walk we reached a deserted farmhouse, solid and towered like Avane, with a steep green field running down to the river bed, a vine trained across the space between house and stables, a marvellous view. We picked stems of quince in flower and very pale mauve irises. Our devious return down endless valleys and steep hills nearly finished me off and I felt I was in the hands of the death-instinct. Does she remember I'm nearly seventy? On my return I lay prostrate on the sofa and drank rather too much whisky. Spenders in Siena today. Bunny in bed curing his cold.

May 8th

Got up early hoping to warm myself in a hot bath, but for once the water was merely tepid. I've got into more than a full quota of English clothes. Magouche decided that we must defeat the cosmos by driving off somewhere regardless, and we had a most delightful excursion. At San Gargano we saw a ruined abbey and (far more exciting) a round church decorated with zebra stripes, unrestored and lined with perfect Lorenzetti frescoes. On the way to Massa Maritima we picked orchids and other flowers, and the sky became royal blue in patches. Arriving home we saw a car outside the house. 'Who *is* it?' cried Magouche in alarm. It was Miranda Rothschild,[1] her present husband Ian Watson and a solid little girl, called Da'ad, child of her first husband – an Arab – who ill-treated her and died a violent death.

May 9th

In bed this evening, rather drunk and in a flux of contradictory emotions. My first reaction to Ian Watson was physical repulsion from his too red lips sunk in a black beard. Then came a certain sympathy because of shared views on various subjects. Also awareness of the kindness and intelligence behind his high, well-shaped forehead (Julia is quite right – I do value foreheads and hate their absence). Miranda has a neatly pretty face and very short hair and drops her ceaseless chit-chat like water on a stone in a flat 'silly little me' voice. She is at once irritating and rather charming.

This morning in spite of the continuing horror of the weather we set off in the Watsons' car, leaving behind Da'ad and the Spenders. Lunch in a small town restaurant, Sienese pictures at Asciano and then to Pienza where the serious rain began. Huddling from the weather we saw the sights of this lovely little town better than when I visited it a few years ago with Raymond and the Cochemés. Miranda – sitting at the back of the car with Magouche and me – never stopped her prattle for a moment and I began to be maddened by it. She doesn't understand

---

[1] Daughter of Lord Rothschild (Victor) and his first wife Barbara.

stillness and quiet, or how to soak in impressions, she is self-absorbed to an alarming degree – everything comes back to herself. They are supposed to be looking for a house to buy here, but whenever we see one she sets up her dismissive monkey-chatter: 'Oh no, no. There isn't enough bareness, not the right sort of trees. I don't like it, do you Ian? It's too *bushy* – too *pubic* if you know what I mean. No, I really want a sort of *castle*.' She's obviously a spoilt, little rich girl, but scratch her and you find a bohemian eccentric, and perhaps a 'bitch'. 'Bitchily' is one of her favourite words and it was applicable to what she said to Magouche about Matthew – she was 'worried about him. There seems to be no *joy* in his painting.' She's quite a good mimic – favourite targets Paddy and Joan. She spars openly with Maro, who gives as good as she gets. Maro is fond of talking disparagingly about 'awful old hags of nearly fifty' or 'horribly ugly girls', with an arrogance that would be un-charming even if she were younger and more beautiful than she is. 'Just as a matter of interest, do you never want to have anything to do with ugly girls?' I asked her. 'No, I'm a fan of beautiful girls.' At dinner I had quite an interesting conversation with Ian from which I gather he's deadly serious, works at research into Byzantine art, can't really laugh at himself, had a stormy childhood rejected by his parents ('I was *extremely* violent'), and now loathes violence, has undergone periods of depression and insomnia, is very neurotic in fact. At Oxford he was often intensely unhappy, was befriended by Maurice Bowra, and 'five out of ten of his friends committed suicide'. He found his best friend dead, a brilliantly successful young man. How true it all is I don't know, but it tumbles out with adolescent excitement, many 'you know's' and 'sort of's'.

May 10th

The beauty of the day! That's been the great thing. All that we've longed for and expected since that first picnic. This gentle landscape engendered an idyllic *Month in the Country* atmosphere, and nearly everyone worked hard on the lawn, rolling and raking and removing wheelbarrows full of stones. I walked alone down into the riverbed and back, picking flowers. Some pretty awful visitors to dinner. An Irish poet, thin-lipped and egotistic, his stupid, attractive, sexy wife. A little boy of four who romped and talked unflaggingly and without quarrelling with Da'ad till 2 a.m. Ian had rather typically brought a spit and started too late roasting a side of lamb on a much too weak fire. It seemed as if it would never cook and the visitors were longing for more drinks and sitting with empty glasses. They brought also a bearded au pair boy on his way to Balliol, a lower-class Communist, quite clever probably, but with his back to some invisible wall or other, and almost speechless. At last we decided to tear the half-done meat with our teeth and say how marvellous it tasted. The guests now showed an immense capacity for putting away the drink and stayed and stayed disastrously. The benches we were sitting on grew very hard, yet it would be fatal – we felt – to move upstairs. A conversation flared up (and led a brief crazy life) as to whether you would save a Cézanne or a spastic child in a fire. Maro threw herself rather hectically into defence of art, the poet and au pair boy were passionately pro-human being (the child somehow became a 'plastic child'). I threw in Shakespeare and Mozart's works with the Cézanne in an endeavour to make a *reductio ad absurdum*. Then the poet began a very long, boastful story with carefully studied gestures, about how he got out of the RAF in spite of being, as he repeated several times 'an athlete, their champion runner'. Maro and Matthew said afterwards they had heard this story several times before and his wife always laughed at the right place. Magouche, Maro and I held a council of despair in the kitchen: how to get them to leave? We tried yawning and letting the conversation drop – no go. I went upstairs to bed, and the poet's wife (who was Frieda Lawrence's granddaughter) seems to have said to Magouche, 'Do go to bed. I'm afraid I can't possibly get them to come away.' What a desperate state of things! Miranda had gone to bed before they came, suffering from 'cramp in the stomach'. Ian said almost proudly that they both had terrible migraines and when I started to discuss cures as a fellow sufferer, he said, 'Oh I'm just absolutely *out* and delirious for five days. Nothing's any good.' Lawks.

May 11th

The weather is now quite perfect and we've had I think the best day of our stay. The Watsons went off house-hunting in the Volterra area. The rest of us and Da'ad took a picnic to the valley below the deserted farmhouse Magouche and I discovered last week. Wading through long grass, past a spring of purest water surrounded by a little wall and tufts of mint and fern, we came to the shallow river, took off our clothes and rolled in the cold water. After our picnic some lay and read, I looked for flowers and then we walked up the hill to the farm. The view it looks out on is now clad in much denser but still fresh greenery: oaks, chestnuts and cypress, and behind is a sort of tableland with vines, quince in bloom, white iris and apples. A poetical, Virgilian day, ending in a serene afternoon.

Our breach with England has been complete because of an Italian postal strike. I speculate about them all from time to time – Sophie, the Kees.

May 14th

Bunny and I got off at last, at about noon. Both Magouche and I have been worrying about his journey to the frontier along the hateful and perplexing autostrada or the dangerous and terrifying coastal road. We picnicked in a sea of poppies and long grass, stopped at San Gimigniano when all was shut, and reached Pisa at four-thirty. I heaved a sigh of relief at being still alive after the last lap of my journey with Bunny, though I don't usually consider him a dangerous driver. I liked the look of the Hotel Nettuno on the Lungarno, old-fashioned and its long past days of grandeur commemorated by a photo in the hall of the unmistakeable bulk of Queen Mary getting into a limousine in 1925. That was shortly after my first visit to Pisa, when the Campo Santo and its frescoes in all their brilliant perfection gave me a major aesthetic experience, like seeing the Parthenon for the first time – it may have been partly its quality of 'firstness', but so it was. I wanted now to see what the effect of American bombing had been – but oh my God, I nearly burst into tears when I did. It was like looking at the face of a great beauty mashed up in an accident, or Avane's hills covered with skyscrapers, but much much worse; for instead of that dazzling and complete freshness I so well remember, only a shattered wreck remains, a ghostly spider's web in parts, with huge white patches and much gone altogether. It's enough to make one a pacifist simply to know that it was destroyed by our allies' bombs. Bunny now decided to stay the night in Pisa instead of pressing on, and took a room in my hotel. So after a rest, we walked out into the town dominated by the university students at this hour, and little cars tearing about with squealing brakes. We sat in the tiny animated

Piazza Garibaldi watching the students drinking what looked like water, but may have been vodka. A jet-black Othello was pouring his passion into the ears of a blonde, long-haired Desdemona.

May 15th

I've seen Bunny off, and hope he'll be all right. A hot day is opening its jaws to gobble us all, and I sit at breakfast listening to the members of an American bus tour jawing away about money and possessions. Now I'm on my own until take-off this afternoon.

June 14th: Crichel

Boris is dead. Desmond told me on Friday night and it shook me horribly. Could he have had a feeling that he was near his end that last weekend at Mottisfont? I got the impression that he had moved as it were into a different key, and now it is as though his declarations of affection were a sort of valediction. Oh the sadness of losing one old friend after another! And the hole he leaves in the universe seems very large and black. He must have died only five days after I left Mottisfont, and of course I wonder if his fall had something to do with it.

Tomorrow back to stern reality and life on my own, after being pillowed as I've been for quite a while on other people. Desmond and I have got on very well as solitary inhabitants here. We had the whole of *Idomeneo* from Aldeburgh on Friday night – glorious. Last night part of a Bellini opera – *La Straniera*, poor stuff. Kitty's party came to drinks and croquet: Caroline West brought over her Ghanaian lover, bearded, *shiny* with blackness, white teeth flashing and a high giggle. I thought him an intelligent and kind, friendly man, and admired the way he didn't turn a hair when Kitty said her plumber had 'worked like a black'.

July 1st

Janetta and I spent a lovely, warm, English summery weekend, all 'blooming, buzzing confusion' with Anne and Heywood, going on Sunday to the *Fairy Queen* in Blythburgh Church. But she came down at least one morning with her face small and pinched from a sleepless, worried night, remembering how her children so often said to her after they had made some awful mistake, such as refusing to take their exams, 'Why did you *let* me do it?' Yesterday she obviously still doubted whether she and Robert should have given the necessary consent.[1] But of course any other behaviour was impossible. Even the ghostly adumbration of heavy parent behaviour would be more suitable to a quite different civilization.

In the warm summery haze, and gentle vegetable beauty, I picked my way happily around fields of clean, strong corn where grew 'weeds' (or flowers) in very clean, strong colours (red of poppies, blue of bugloss, yellow of charlock, chalk-white of campions). I had a feeling of having 'stepped sideways out of life', due partly to pain-killer drowning slight toothache which has left a dreamy impression of the weekend in my mind. And all those East Anglian figures floated in and out too – Jonny, John and Sheelah Hill, Lucy. I loved being with Janetta, noticed her anxiety over Georgie with sympathy, and was amused by her longing to travel first class. I said (about this last) of course I would if it was crowded and she wanted to,

---

[1] Georgie (who is under age) wanted to marry Jean-Pierre Martel.

but that I had an egalitarian feeling that there should be no such thing. 'Oh I don't,' said Janetta (gratuitously for well I knew it), 'I think it's so nice that someone who is old or not feeling well can pay extra.' I pointed out that these weren't necessarily the people who could afford it.

July 7th

Dinner with Patrick Kinross, Janetta, Paddy, Julian and Coote Lygon. After dinner Magouche, Miranda and Ian Watson. Very enjoyable. Relations between children and 'Mum and Dad' being on my mind, I brought them up to Julian at dinner. Violent resistance. *Yes*, of course they were responsible for everything that befell their families. Much later, drink taken, he returned to the subject and the true reason for this forcefulness was revealed – a recent crisis in his own Mum and Dad's life: their decision to leave Kingsland, his desire to keep it for himself. He said a great deal, much that was very interesting, touching on his deepest feelings. But my position is not shaken in that I do think it futile to go on blaming them, and blaming their Mum and Dad, and so on, back and back in an infinite series. One should, except in a few grizzly cases, be able to enjoy being one's own man at seventeen or eighteen, shouldn't one? Two struts awkwardly supported my argument at the moment, that's to say the feeling that the old should remember their youth and not behave like old colonels, and that the young should shoulder their own lives and not sit back and blame their parents all the time.

Janetta looked tired and ravishing in a pale yellow Moorish trouser suit. How little is distilled from hours of talk.

July 12th

The tempo got faster and faster, culminating in a *prestissimo* that whirled through Georgie's wedding day, a French-style wedding day beginning with lunch at the Ritz for twelve or thirteen encircling a big, round table. *Luxe, calme et volupté*. Walking the long and spacious corridor, to see with pleasure Jaime advancing towards me, and soon afterwards, Rose, looking very much herself; Nicky, brown, strong and *décolleté*; the amusing, provocative face of Serge. Robert arrived last, and blew Cynthia up for 'doing the placements all wrong'. I sat between Julian and Jean-Pierre (very fine in white linen suit and black shirt). Georgie wore a black trouser suit; in the evening, in a white one she looked really lovely. Moving in three cars through one of London's 'worst traffic congestions', we at last reached the Register Office at East Sheen, watched the ceremony performed in a Nissen hut surrounded by hideous bunches of flowers, and returned to our bases to gasp for a while before setting out for the evening party at Kew. That was exceedingly pretty and well arranged.

July 15th

A flawless, pale blue sky spreads overhead. Heat tremendous, tropical. I spent last evening by myself, reading and listening to the wireless, in a cotton dressing gown, mopping myself with a damp sponge. Yesterday Joan and I lunched in the square garden, lying in the shade on an eiderdown, drinking iced orangeade. The heat somehow intensifies impressions, such as of the delicate strong beauty of Ben Nicholson's paintings seen afterwards. He is a great painter I believe; just as at this moment (still in bed) I am questioning whether Conrad is, after all, a great writer.

Yet I approached *Victory*, which I'm now reading, full of expectation and backed by several enthusiastic commendations, one from Frances Phipps. At once I was struck by a strong, male smell reminding me of Kipling; he is horribly at ease and relaxed in his own masculinity (like Kipling), rolling about in it as in a club armchair. And I don't like this boy's book-adventure-*Huckleberry Finn* flavour, nor its glorification of violence. Not at all. I rather think a novelist *must* have some femininity in him even if he's a man, like Henry James and Proust.

July 22nd

In the last twenty-four hours men have landed on the moon, and for once I wish I had a machine with which to view this extraordinary event. Yet I confess I have very ambivalent feelings about it. At dinner with Tristram and Virginia Powell last night it was the chief topic of our talk, and Jonny said he had sat up virtually all night: he was a keen moon advocate. How the young talk about the television, the wireless! I am positively alarmed by the obsessional nature of their interest, much as I am when I see a too large child in a pushchair, with its mouth stoppered with a 'comforter' or 'dummy'. It's not so much the passivity as the lack of choice, the uniformity of this sucking-in process that I see as baleful. By discharging an identical dose of soporific liquid – and it does often send people to sleep – into the mouth of every child and adult in the country, it must surely standardize them, even if the diet were good – and of course most of it is bad.

But I've left out William and Linda's wedding, which was a very jolly affair, though it now seems like a faded dream. The evening was fine enough for plates and glasses to be taken out into the garden where the midges devoured us. The first person I recognized was Sophie looking very charming in a pretty, white muslin frock, excitedly running about with her cousin Edward Garnett and other smaller and larger children. Late in the evening came Tim Behrens, grinning endearingly out of his ruined face, Serge and Nicky (very handsome in a long, white dress, with Bekalelis[1] firmly plastered on one hip), and the narcissistic Mark Palmer in golden velvet trousers. Some moved off to the pool, and I saw the naked shapes of Tim and Fanny Garnett fling themselves in. Serge was telling everyone the egocentric news that now that his film was going to be produced he had lost all desire to do it. A groaning board of food, cold dishes, Stilton cheeses; the drink supply began to run short later and had to be supplemented from Bunny's cellar. William and Linda seemed very happy; Linda had invited a large, vital cohort of her friends and relations; a difference in lifestyle between them and the rest of us had been invisible until they'd had a good deal to drink when they suddenly exploded into noise and laughter, kicked up their legs, filled the drawing-room, thumped out 'For Me and My Gal' on Angelica's piano, danced wildly about and fell down. Angelica did I think join in – but I shamefully couldn't imagine how to amalgamate with their boisterousness and soon after left, to return to the hotel at St Ives where Angelica, Duncan and I were staying.

August 4th

I'm suddenly committed to go to Portugal with the Kees a week tomorrow. I don't know whether I'm looking forward to it or not, and hope it isn't just the fruit of

---

[1] Their son, now an artist.

some dreadful restlessness. Meanwhile I have been 'managing' fairly well. *Linguistics* (translated from Spanish) is just on finished – thank God. It really has been a corker.

August 14th: Portugal

I enjoyed the journey in a muted sort of way. Cynthia's mother[1] came and sat beside me in the aeroplane; we looked down at the mouths of Garonne, Douro and Tagus spread glisteningly below in turn. Robert met us at Faro airport and as he drove ran down everything, unconvincingly, and as a sort of insurance against disappointment. I can see he likes it really, and so do I, what with the limpid sky, carts with dogs running under them, women wearing scarves over men's felt hats, the pure and scented air, decently built houses, some brilliantly coloured, or white, or outlined in royal blue. Ours seems to be solidly built with plenty of wood, tiles and whitewash and a very nice shady eating-terrace. The children are brown, naked seals already.

I'm greatly struck by Robert's practical geniality. He wants to be – and so far has been – supporting to everyone, including Cynthia, and quite exceptionally so to her Mum – 'Sylvia' now to me – who obviously dotes on him; he wants things to be all right.

August 18th

I'm now thoroughly embedded in the life of the others and trying to get on with them all. I mustn't forget Sylvia is there, nor show when delicious little Sarah is too much of a good thing. I'm particularly anxious to be 'all right' with Cynthia, and not let my delight in Robert's company and mental processes lead to ganging up with him. And I do admire her tackling spirit and have never found her more attractive looking. But Robert's endless benignity and *patience* (yes!) give her no cause for complaint.

Full-scale Sunday excursion yesterday, very successful. In hot, still weather we drove to the cathedral and Moorish castle at Silves (densely planted with cannas, hibiscus and bougainvillaea) and on up to the Caldas de Monchique. Found it all just the same as in 1934, only there was this time a Sunday concourse of peasant picnickers happily spreading their bottles and food on stone tables in the shade of huge trees. If only they wouldn't spit so. Hearing the dreadful preparations as they come down the path one longs to shout: 'Oh *do* just wait till I've gone past!' But of course they don't. They needs must void themselves of their beastly gobbets anywhere and everywhere. We had our picnic on a hill-top under some fine cork oaks: these and many other things – for instance that the Portuguese radio should play Schumann – fill Sylvia with innocent amazement. Everything smelled delicious under the speckled shade and we ate tender little roast chickens, bread, fruit, cheese and wine. In sweltering heat we piled into the car and drove on to Marmalete and Monchique, and then – craving a bathe – made for the nearest sea at Praia de Rocha. It was a sorry sight, rapidly turning into Torremolinos, with monster blocks of flats, night-clubs and battalions of cars. The tiny tartanas still play to and fro, looking rickety and absurd. Drove to the furthest beach and bathed in a beautifully calm evening sea. Sylvia showed childish disappointment at having no bathing-

[1] Sylvia Judah.

suit, and Cynthia gallantly lent her her own white one, in which her mother stalked into the sea looking like a Raemakers cartoon of famine. Sarah hurled herself into the movements of swimming with enormous spirit and vitality, her little wet head sinking again and again. Cynthia has a very nice figure in her swimming rig.

August 20th

About four we all drove along the coast eastwards and I was overjoyed to find the little chapel of Nossa Senhora da Rocha where I went with Ralph. My memory of his pleasure in it, so exactly in tune with my own, was strong enough to produce a haunting strangeness in the fact that he wasn't still there beside me, but I loved its white simplicity, blue tiles and little many-sided spire; but though everyone seemed to like it, nobody did so quite enough to please me. Below were two beaches linked by a tunnel, on one of which we stationed ourselves, slowly withdrawing from the large rollers till we were right up among the brilliantly painted, obviously functioning fishing-boats. Sylvia gallantly sat in a hole dug by the children above the water-line until the sea rushed in and made her look like the sages in the *Just So Stories*. Then the Kees vanished leaving her surrounded by interested Portuguese children. She has a sort of dignified humour in such situations which warms me to her. Robert's black head vanished out to sea among enormous waves. Sarah's courageous little figure looked fascinating in minute shorts and a wide-brimmed Portuguese hat.

11.15 p.m. I always thought kindness was Cynthia's quality, yet she is sometimes quite fierce to her poor old Mum. The first time was when she arrived very late from the beach and we had been unable to persuade Barbara the maid even to start preparations for lunch until two-fifteen. Sylvia said harmlessly enough, 'We're all starving.' Whereupon Cynthia exploded in a burst of indignation.

But tonight has been *much* worse and I'm at my wits end what to do. Poor 'Grandma' knocked one of her already swollen legs (insensitive too from diabetes) on a rock on her way up from the beach. She made light of it, but when Robert and I returned from Portimão we found her sitting on the sofa with her leg up and a horrible great purplish-black swelling as big as a tennis-ball on it. I had never seen anything like it, and was appalled. She was supposed to be going with Robert and Cynthia to have a drink with the landlord, but Robert and I suggested she stayed with her leg up. When Sylvia went out to say so to Cynthia, who was making a mayonnaise on the terrace, she answered her mother's 'Robert doesn't think I ought to go out,' with 'Oh Mum, I'm *sure* he couldn't have said that! Why ever *not?*' implying that she was making a fuss over a mere trifle which should be ignored. So Sylvia went, but returned early and put her leg up again. I was reading to Alexander, but whenever I looked up and my eye caught this terrible blackberry-coloured object, I was so horrified that I lost my place in the book. I brought her her supper and tried to spoil her a little. She said: 'You'll make me burst into tears if you're so sympathetic.' Alexander was worried too, and kind and helpful, escorting her to the lavatory. I was in two minds whether to go over and beg Cynthia and Robert to telephone for a doctor (there is a telephone at the landlord's), and I really thought they'd have had the sense to do it. Not a bit of it. When she had gone to bed with painkillers and sleeping-pills I asked if they didn't think they should now do so. 'But what could it *be?*' said Cynthia and Robert: 'If it's not better in the morning, we will,' but I felt they both thought I was fussing.

12.15 a.m. We're in for a bad night – and what *else* I wonder. Cynthia went to see her mother and administer belated sympathy after settling another of Sarah's outbursts. Poor Sylvia has begun to groan. 'Oh *God*!', and if I were her I should indeed be frightened. I hardly feel it's worth trying to go to sleep, what with the agonized sounds coming from next door, the incessant barking of a dog and the probability of more yells from Sarah. So I'm trying to read Beckford, but my lamp gives a dim light and his personality depresses me.

August 22nd

My prognosis was alarmingly correct. Sylvia's moans and groans were so distressing that I went into her room some time after 1 o'clock. She tried heroically to be polite, but was obviously in agony. So I went down and knocked Robert and Cynthia up, saying that something must really be done. Cynthia was still sceptical. Robert, following on her heels, came in to say that the swelling on the leg had got very much worse and he was going to telephone for the doctor. All his enormous reliability in an emergency now came to the fore, and (unable to get into the landlord's house) he drove off to the village night-club and somehow got the address of a Lagoa doctor. All this took some time, while Cynthia stayed with her mother, and I went down for a slug of whisky which I felt sorely in need of. What a relief, when Robert returned with a stalwart, black-clad figure behind him – an English-speaking Portuguese doctor. I listened to the proceedings from my room, heard him say Sylvia had ruptured a vein, and that she must either have an operation next morning or keep the leg quite still, until the blood was re-absorbed. Robert said afterwards he made Johnsonian jokes, smoked the whole time and fished out his implements from his pockets or a grubby old bag, remarking that the danger was infection. While he applied an ointment to 'disperse the thrombosis', I could hear from exclamations that the whole great swelling had burst and blood gushed out. Cynthia hurried for a basin, and apparently the pain was instantly relieved. The doctor bound the leg up tightly and soon after went away, while I was swallowed up in oblivion. But my God, supposing this had happened without the doctor being present!

When I came down this morning Cynthia was obviously feeling remorse and shame, and mollified me with an apology and a kiss.

August 26th

A perfect day to visit that best of all Land's Ends, Cape St Vincent; then on to Sagres, and down a rough cart track, until the car had to be abandoned and we walked on down a magically wild valley to a vast deserted bay, with tilted stratified cliffs and the rollers breaking in a mist of shining spray on miles and miles of hard sand. The sides of the valley were covered with tufts of sea-lavender and horned poppy and peopled with little birds. I hung back to botanize and saw the four silhouettes of the others walking into the glimmer of this incredible beach, like the figures at the end of a film about the shape of things to come. Cynthia walked off along the beach and vanished in the mist, in a desire to be alone, perhaps, which is something I can always sympathize with.

But there were unaccountable delays on the way home – a drink at Lagoa was very pleasant, but by the time we got home it was very late, the doctor had been,

Sylvia had had to hobble round lighting the lamps (or sit in the dark), both children were exhausted and had screaming fits, and Cynthia herself was dead beat and went early to bed.

One evening in the course of conversation I said I thought it was important for children to accept the fact that adults too had their rights. Dead silence from both Robert and Cynthia. Then the young wife of Dr Wolfson, who is studying for a PhD, told me on the beach how difficult it was to work with the children in the room. I asked if she had no small room where they weren't allowed, and she seemed amazed at the idea. 'But children can and do accept rules,' I said, 'and they can also have a place where adults sometimes aren't admitted.' 'Children first always' is now the almost universal practice and I think it's disastrous.

This morning all is serene. Incredibly hot; England tomorrow.

August 27th

Packing begins. Sylvia seems no worse; Cynthia complains of a very sore throat. Barbara the maid arrived with a look of self-pity gleaming through her spectacles and said that '*tudo roda*' – everything was spinning. We all worry about Sylvia's journey.

I've just told Sarah to stop squirting her grandmother's bandaged leg with her water-pistol or 'I would spank her'. She rushed off bawling to her mother.

September 2nd: London

Whirling days. Immediately after Portugal, off I went to Crichel for Bank Holiday – Dadie was there, a great life-enhancer and stimulator, laying the dust of etymology and raising that of general conversation. He has an excellent effect on Raymond of whom he takes devoted care. One sometimes hears him accused of heartlessness, but in practice one can't fault him.

And now I must begin ordinary working life and a new translation. Julian came yesterday, and told me among other things that he has been 'cohabiting' for the last fortnight with a girl called Tammy. 'No love-making though.' Amazement, gratification, speculation. I have always hoped for something like this and thought it possible – but if it doesn't develop into a proper love affair I suppose it may not last. He very naturally 'doesn't want to analyse it' and is 'suffering from shock'.

September 12th

Dinner with Julia last night. In order to meet on common ground it seems we can only talk critically of people, plays and books. She spent the first hours talking about Carrington, mainly in order to prove that she was a unique person and a genius, yet she couldn't resist an occasional backhander at her. The Kees had been to dinner the night before, quarrelling on the way and arriving separately. But Cynthia told Julia that there 'had been no trouble at all in Portugal'. Her 'tough line' with Robert, noticed by me, is deliberate according to Julia, who also declares that Cynthia is 'utterly fed up with Robert' and only stays with him for the sake of the children.

Latest Julia story – when staying at Thorington, she sat down on the lavatory and 'did what she had come to do', but when she tried to get up found she couldn't! 'I was caught in a vice, my dear, an agonizing pain! And when I did get away I was bleeding. I looked and saw the seat was badly cracked. So as I'm always so rude these days, I went straight in to Margaret and Lionel and complained about it. Margaret said she knew about it; someone else had complained three weeks ago. I said, 'Well I do think you ought to have put up a warning notice.' Margaret said a new one was on order. Lionel looked very cross indeed and went off to look for a file, muttering, 'The princess and the pea!' Or pee?

Yesterday to a party given by Jane Garnett for Sophie's sixth birthday – about nine little girls and one shy little boy. She has never in her life had such a party, with such a spread of jellies and cakes, balloons and crackers, such games and prizes, combining to produce radiantly appreciative faces and rewarding the hard work Jane must have devoted to it. Sophie was a delicious little figure at the head of the table, intoxicated with excitement and showing a good deal of social talent.

November 21st

I'm surprised by finding so many things still intensely enjoyable. At a Handel concert, I remember especially my pleasure in watching the movements of the string players coiled round their instruments.

Then I enjoyed giving a dinner party last night and four of the guests have rung up to say how much they too enjoyed it – it was to Christopher and Joanna Mason,[1] Eardley, Bunny, Magouche. Afterwards Duncan arrived and was made much of.

A visit at lunch from Julian, whom I've not seen for some time. Poor Tam has been very ill with pleurisy – he suggested it was of neurotic origin and confessed having 'behaved badly to her'. A taxing situation, in which he must have longed for bachelor freedom, irritated by her incessant cough and incessant smoking.

Desmond, back from Africa, invited me to the BBC to see this second moon landing on a colour set there. 'Or are you anti-moon?' I was moving toward the decision that I was, but this was a chance to find out, so I accepted rather to his surprise, and after a buzz of frantic planning over the telephone off we went and were ushered into a tiny special viewing studio. 'You must lock the door,' they said, 'or you'll get a crowd in.' We both felt that would be uncivilized, so we left it open, and it was soon a black hole of Calcutta, with large men trampling on our coats and hats. Beside some exaggeratedly lifelike portraits of announcers and the technical experts of Houston, we saw in a dim blur – we would not have known had we not been told – Conrad descending the ladder on the moon. It was a humdrum, ordinary sight, he might have been putting his feet down on Paddington platform; nothing could have seemed less magical, and they kept up a dreary murmur of figures and letters; peppered with 'Attaboy's' and 'OK's', or at most 'it's fantastic'. I regretted the once inviolate, white-faced moon of yesteryear. But our experience was short-lived, as the telly-camera went wrong, and we soon after went away.

My foreground is richly invested with the figures and faces of charming, loveable friends – but the background is dark and louring. There have been horrifying revelations of a deliberate massacre by the Americans in Vietnam of literally hundreds of civilian natives. And after a shocked response from most quarters, George Brown burst out shouting: 'Why don't the Americans stop weeping and *get on and finish the job*.'

[1] Painters; Joanna is Carrington's niece.

November 27th

The Julia situation has gone very very far beyond a joke. She came to dinner here alone, her eyes half-closed with 'sedation', her poor legs tottering under her, her hatred of life hanging in my sitting-room like the mushroom cloud from an atom bomb. She began at once on her weekend with the Hills (she went the weekend before I did). I swear I didn't encourage her. And there was nothing but criticism: 'Really these country weekends! One hopes for a breath of fresh air, but not a bit of it. Nothing but driving round in a closed car to heavy lunches in hotels.' Heywood had already amusingly but not unaffectionately described her visit to Snape. She lay in bed, receiving the breakfast tray brought up by Anne but not touching it till nearly lunch-time, and after lunch retired again. One day he'd driven her to the sea in hopes of decoying her for a walk, but she wouldn't get out of the car. To me she said perfunctorily, 'I always like seeing Heywood – and Anne too, of course' – whereas Anne had been enthusiastic about the fascination of Julia's conversation, and said 'it ought to be recorded on tape.' Then came the horrors of her present life, poured out with all the symptoms of persecution-mania. 'I really do feel there's a jinx against me. Things happen to me that no one else suffers from. I told you about how I couldn't open the windows because a cat came dashing in, and about all the knobs coming off the doors? Well, then these shrimps started coming out of the taps with the water, and believe it or not they got bigger and bigger. Then – just to show you what it's like – you may have heard a thunderclap the other night. Well, it evidently struck my house and all the electricity went. Of course the landlord pays no attention to anything. And I get so many wrong numbers, and people can't get me when they want, yet if I ring the engineers they don't answer. And of course there are these mice still.' All this is viewed, not as the stuff of life, but as something keeping her away from her true life – her mythical writing. The most dismal symptom of all is that she says she hasn't brushed her teeth for months, it's too much trouble. 'Don't you find they feel rather horrid?' 'Oh yes, but washing them would be worse.' Indeed, letting go with me as she did, and I hope it did her some good, she suddenly looked her age and ill into the bargain. I'm desperately worried about her. It's pitiful. I can't forget the tone in which she said, 'I hate my life. I hate every *moment* of it. Sometimes I throw things about and break them.' Is she going mad? I almost fear it. Her purple heart intake has gone up to six a day and her doctor now says she must reduce them. But what can she hope for? And when she has run through her Arts Council grant, what will become of her? Unable to sleep for brooding over her plight, I wrote her a letter to tell her how much her unhappiness upset me, and to suggest a change of scene, with which I would gladly help her financially.

December 2nd

Julia rang up again today. I think my letter really pleased her, and it opened a possible door (which of course she will quickly slam like all others) that in itself may be a minute alleviation. She wanted to tell me of fresh disasters: all her cleaners and cooks had given up. (I dare say they find her too difficult.) The electric fire in her bedroom had gone wrong, and she had backache. Looking at her back in the glass – a thing she hadn't done for years – she 'thought it had become a very queer shape'! She's going to consult her doctor. Meanwhile she won't go away at present because she 'can't leave her doctor or her hairdresser'.

Margaret is anxious to get her to go to a wonderful analyst she has been consulting herself.

The pages of my life are filled with the graphs of other people's dramas. Whether to record them or not, I hardly know; but my own life is otherwise a blank.

The Penrose drama has speeded up and got so complex that I have left it far behind. Lionel has been in hospital for observation and treatment of his heart condition, and this, with the imminent threat of Dunyusha's arrival, set Margaret dashing about like a whirling dervish, consulting his cardiologist, and a solicitor and psychoanalyst on her own account. How much of what she says can one give credence to? They all, including the psychoanalyst, Doctor Schoenberg, sympathized with her and – according to her accounts – said something must and should be done to stave off Dunyusha's arrival. The head of the Medical Council, the Home Office, the Immigration Authorities, all were to be invoked. In fact, absolutely nothing was done by any of them, and Dunyusha is now here. Yesterday Margaret was 'very glad she hadn't stopped Dunyusha coming', and said that 'she had done Lionel a world of good'. When she comes this afternoon I may hear a different story.

December 20th

At Rodborough Road I at last saw the mythical Dunyusha – and she's no fiend in human shape, no schemer or even vulgar flirt I would say, but a slight, pale, attractive and gentle-looking girl, with a high, well-modelled forehead. The only disadvantage: a compulsive giggle. What was I to say to Margaret who took me into another room after dinner to hear what I thought of her? In fact I said almost nothing. It is pain for Margaret, pain undiluted not to be told you hate Dunyusha on sight. Lionel had a touchingly apologetic air.

A very, very good evening with Julia, the best for years. She said of Lawrence, 'I want to ask you if you think he treated me cruelly?' 'Well, of course I think he caused you the worst possible unhappiness; more than you've ever had in your life.' 'Yes, that's not what I'm asking. Was he *cruel*? I'm not objecting to his wanting his sex life with Jenny but his throwing me off as a friend.' I negotiated this awkward corner by saying I thought him an extremely self-centred, egotistical man, though not deliberately unkind, and that in pursuit of his own ends he had perhaps been rather ruthless. She talked then of her writing, which is now entirely autobiographical but in novel form – the shape given by her own life: loneliness and desertion as a child, misery with Aunty Loo, and in her marriage to the heartless neurotic Tommy, and then peace and happiness (tremendously idealized of course by loss) with Lawrence, ending in the dark night of loneliness and desertion closing in again. 'A very good theme,' I told her. 'Yes but the trouble is it can't be published in my lifetime.' 'Nor in Lawrence's?' 'Oh, I don't mind *what* happens after I'm dead.' I urged her to go on with it none the less and enjoy her dedication to the writing itself, to the struggle rather than the final fruition, for the struggle was life. It had occurred to me that there could be a Henry Jamesian plot in which the novelist finished her book and then killed herself so that it could be published – a sort of *Revenger's Tragedy*.

Next morning she rang up to say 'the very moment you left me I found I had 'flu.' But in her new mood even this doesn't make her bitterly complain – 'flu *and* a cracked spine! 'I so enjoyed last night,' she said (and goodness so had I, and goodness there's no one like her at her best) 'and especially what you said about life being a struggle.'

The last note struck during the week before Christmas concerns the American philosopher Chomsky. Paul Levy came for a drink and we talked a lot about him. How grateful I am for being seduced into taking a hard bite now and again on such a philosophical crust. Also Paul was interesting, illuminating for me what had not been apparent in the pamphlet *Syntactical Structures* which I read before. I think I see where Chomsky is tending – back to Kant and *a priori* ideas. He is searching for the basic structure of the mind by means of patient excavation of the dry deposit of linguistics. Just as the eye can only see as it is built to see, the mind can only apprehend according to its structure. Well, I've long believed that in a way – I'm not quite sure what way. And I definitely sense a whiff of mysticism if not religion emanating from Chomsky's way. Paul made great play, as Chomsky does, with the creative element in language, and the way children and simple people soon learn to use language grammatically, and sentences they've never heard before. But they *don't*, I kept thinking; half the world repeats others parrotwise, and at the lowest level it's not much more communicative than the barking of dogs. Chomsky (and Paul) believe in some basic deep structure common to all languages – and don't we get back to God that way? I see language as only one among many means of expression – voice, dress, gesture, facial expression being others – learned with varying skill. So that from the child Mozart to an unmusical dustman is a very long leap.

December 21st: Crichel

Off from London two days ago, laden with books and work and tins of Coca-Cola for Tam, for peace and escape in the country for over a week.

I drove to Crichel through a dank white landscape; at times white bees were flying at the windscreen. Got there before Raymond, Desmond, Julian and Tam. Raymond, seeing the Coca-Cola tins, looked and sounded disapproving. 'Oh, doesn't she *drink*? Well, I hope she's not a veget*a*rian.' Later, hearing the reason, and having taken to her, as everyone does, he respected her for it; and is in an amusing, lively mood, and at his sweetest to me. I was surprised by the thought, 'Does he *want* to frighten the young?' Tam and Julian seem happy together and in an altogether natural and unembarrassed way for which I give them (specially Julian) high marks. I like Tam more and more, and her being seemingly quite un-shy is a comfort.

She gets on very well with Desmond, who obviously likes her, but all is not perfect between him and Julian.

December 22nd

This reached a climax last night when Desmond – having deferred writing an article all afternoon in order to listen to records with Tam – retired after dinner to finish it, like a naughty schoolboy with its homework. The rest of us started playing paper games amid fountains of giggles and shrieks of laughter. Desmond came in, jealous, pathetic – 'What fun you're all having!' – and stood there in his bright pink corduroy suit, his face equally pink and his mouth turned down with disappointment. But alas! at this moment he caught sight of the libretto of a record lying on a table, forgotten where Julian had left it. There was a quick, short, verbal scuffle, and Julian's face was left with an X sign of irritation stamped across it. They ruffle each other, in spite of real affection and appreciation on both sides.

Now, Thursday, I'm alone with Des, all the others having gone off. I drove Julian to the Cecils at Cranborne and talked for a while with Rachel who was unwell in bed.

December 26th

Desmond has great power to touch – he makes one feel that he craves affection and yet it never quite comes up to his hopes. He is aware of how his fussing upsets people and is sorry. He talked again of longing to retire and live entirely at Crichel. I was surprised, for his urge to hear music and be in the swim of it seems so strong.

Life Regained

1970–1972

Foreword

Among the motives for keeping a diary, one generally finds love of the truth and a desire to record it. Writers who enjoy powers of invention or fantasy will take to another medium and probably become novelists. I have often envied Emily Brontë, Anthony Trollope and Lewis Carroll (for instance) their ability to create an imaginary world and set it in motion. In the published notebooks of the great inventor Henry James, he reveals how his most elaborate plots were often fed by a stray remark at a dinner party, rising like a spring to create a river of words. While I remain chained to the truth, I have often regretted that I didn't start diarising earlier when life was full of excitement and thrills, instead of filling so much space with sadness and longing. Perhaps a little in *Good Company* and more now in *Life Regained*, I am aware that I am sending down roots and spreading stems of my *own*, though I miss Ralph and Burgo and the warm life of Ham Spray not a whit less and never shall. In this volume I go to three new countries – Poland, the Channel Islands and Corfu, and four old ones – Russia, Spain, France and Italy.

1970

January 4th

In bed, a dark morning and cold. Penetrating this new year has been very queer. London is a plague-stricken and deserted city. Voice after voice rings up, choked, to say they 'have flu, can't come'. Indeed, Mrs Murphy hasn't been since Monday (the day after I got back), increasing my solitude. The cold has been intense, and I am well aware that this year I shall reach the portentous age of seventy. What satisfaction I get out of my present life lies in making a sort of Chomskian 'synthetical structure' of it, stuffing it fairly full, and sometimes oddly. Work of course, the fag-end of Napoleon,[1] mopping up my flat sketchily but systematically, reading. At first I avoided public places – the flu epidemic is quite serious – then I gave up and went in one day to the coughing, sneezing hotbed of the London Library Reading Room, and also to *The Magic Flute* by myself. (The way other people impinge when one is alone! Ingratiating snarl of highbrow civil servant; Angelica, Fanny, Amaryllis and Quentin's girls eating ices in the bar.)

I feel I have been unconscious for a week, a zombie stamping round but getting some pleasure from my own staunch stamping.

Georgie has had a baby girl; I went to see her and was wrung and harrowed by the perilous mystery. Yesterday I drove down to see Alix for lunch, and spent the evening playing records of *Walkyrie* with the score, which kind Desmond lent me.

Julia is literally the only soul in London. I rang her up as soon as I got back. A loud wail of despair. 'Shall I come and cook you some lunch?' 'Oh, yes, DO.' I asked what she would eat. 'Nothing, really. Perhaps a little scrambled egg and spinach.' She did in fact eat *nothing*. And, my word, the business of being a bullied kitchen maid – memories of Lambourn – very quickly fills me with irritated indignation. 'Oh, no, no, not *that* saucepan, that's for eggs.' 'For heaven's sake, don't put water in *that* jug, it's full of germs.' A pretty girl came to clean the flat, and got the same treatment. I fled, I'm afraid – the fuss, fuss, fuss too much for me. Yet I do see, though she does not, that having someone to find fault with is her great pleasure in life. On the telephone she nearly admitted it, and said unprompted: 'I HATE everyone!' 'Well, that can be a pleasure,' I said and she gave her new, diabolical chuckle and said, 'I think it can.'

I went to lunch a few days ago with the Penroses and stayed to play trios. A short talk to Margaret afterwards. Dunyusha had come to take Lionel for a walk. She comes every day, and Margaret admits she is 'a good nurse' and Lionel does what she tells him. But, 'She turns him against me.' Poor Margaret, standing shapelessly

---

[1] Translation from the French writer Gilbert Martineau, about Napoleon.

with a pregnant-looking stomach (the result of her compensatory stuffing with food), told me how Dunyusha had said to her, 'Please forgive me for *being young.*' And also that 'Lionel was very seriously ill, might die at any time, and must be allowed therefore what he wants.'

What amazes me, in a house of doctors, is Margaret's apparent uncertainty as to how ill Lionel is. She doesn't even know whether he's had a coronary or not, merely repeating that the 'cardiogram wasn't very good'. I don't understand this attitude. How can she possibly control his regime unless she knows the facts? Why not get in touch with his specialist, as the local doctor is said to be 'no good'? Why not get one who *is* some good? Perhaps she doesn't want to know.

January 8th

I have got involved in a strange 'intrigue' – I feel it as that, though it may not be. Michael Holroyd, Paul Levy, and the busybody Lucy Norton are trying to collect Bloomsbury material, letters, etc. for the library at King's. After telling Alix that hers might be worth £200,000, they now want her to donate them – virtually speaking – to King's. I felt worried, not knowing how comfortably off she was and whether she might not need funds suddenly for illness. Now I have been approached too by John Carter of Sotheby's, who previously wanted to sell my Lytton–Ralph correspondence.

Tomorrow I am summoned to meet Carter, Holroyd, Paul, Lucy, the librarian of King's and a solicitor from Lord Goodman's office at an hotel in Bond Street. It's really very odd indeed, and I have mixed feelings – principally that I have said my say to Alix on my last visit, and that as for my own fence I shall probably sit on it.

January 9th

I have just been to this extraordinary gathering to consider the possibility of Alix forming some sort of Strachey Trust with her collected papers, and handing them over to King's College, Cambridge. I got a distinct impression of a sort of conspiracy being afoot – the protagonists Michael Holroyd, Paul Levy and arch-spider Lucy Norton. What Lucy is after I don't know, but I suspect it is some instinctual gratification. Michael has a hare-brained scheme to use the 'Trust funds', whatever they may be, to found a Union Catalogue (in computer form) of all manuscript material in private collections in England and the USA. I exonerate him from everything except perhaps hyper-idealism. Paul has this also in view, but I'm not sure what else. There were also present John Carter of Sotheby's, a bright little solicitor and the excellent Dr Munby of King's Library, who talked good sense and didn't even seem mad keen to get Alix's papers; there wouldn't be room at King's but he would sound out the University Library. Lucy viewed me with suspicion, knowing that I'd seen Alix lately and talked about the Trust scheme; she stated several times what were Alix's feelings and views (incorrectly, I thought, but I let it pass) and made one totally false statement – that if she were to sell her papers she would have to pay both capital gains and income tax in one year. I asked the solicitor if he could confirm this and he said, 'No.' 'I'm sorry,' said Lucy.

I hear the music of the three 'conspirators' straight from *Ballo in Maschera.* My main contribution to the meeting was to say, towards the end, 'I do feel we're talking as if we were all being very kind to Alix, and almost saving her money, whereas the truth is that *she* is making an extremely generous gift.' This was

warmly seconded by Dr Munby. There was later some question as to who should
go and explain to Alix what had been settled. Lucy, it was suggested, along with
the solicitor. Michael said, 'I think it would be a good thing for Frances to go.' F.:
'No, I don't really think so. I have absolutely no qualification except being devoted
to Alix.' Lucy: 'We rather overlap, perhaps.' I was careful not to compete or
contradict Lucy in any way, but I don't think that I took her in. I don't like her,
nor greatly trust her.

The meeting had a curious sequel. Paul rang up at lunch-time and insisted on
coming and wasting most of my afternoon, sitting staring at me from blue eyes
out of his halo of orange curls with a worried and confused look. I was unable to
find out what he was after except that I think my detached – or pro-Alix – remarks
had suddenly made him see that the three of them hardly seem to be acting in
Alix's interests. He appeared concerned as to what John Carter was 'up to'. I said I
didn't understand what Lucy was 'up to'. P.: 'I think she's a sort of Universal Aunt.
She's always trying to protect Michael and me from people.' How can they bear to
be deluged in the thwarted maternal feelings gushing from that vast, cushiony
bosom?

January 18th

Janetta and I have hurled ourselves into the net of preparations for Warsaw and
Russia. I feel mezzo-terrified and mezzo-excited at the prospect. Will she love it as
much as I did? We go first for a week to Nicko at Warsaw. But what about the
COLD??

Two evenings with her, the first at Chapel Street (with Rose, Jonny and Julian)
would have been simply delightful had it not been for the incursion of Sonia,
desperate, deplorable and drunk. None of us could stand her shouting for long,
and first Julian, then I, then Jonny fled from the dining-room. I felt ashamed
afterwards and tried to atone by allowing her to 'bumble on', but it was thunderous
bumbling, interspersed with deafening 'ER's about her new friend Decca Treuhaft
(née Mitford), replacement for Mary MacCarthy, saying alas simply nothing, and
losing sentence after sentence in midstream. Finally (guilt again) I let her talk for
a full twenty minutes about Flaubert's 'use of three tenses'.

Much more shattering, though both events were collisions with a desperate
human being, was a telephone call I made to Julia yesterday to ask how she was.
After two words she started to blow me up savagely for not having found her an
electrician. 'When you *knew* how cold I was and that my electric fires weren't
working!!' Words literally failed me; uneasy guilt overwhelmed me. In the long
and almost comic list of things, mostly mechanical, that she told me had gone
wrong, and which she daily settled by telephone, I had detected persecution-mania
and doubted many of the facts. How pick out the electric fire? I had advised her
to call in the GEC itself, rather than some little man round the corner, as she
admitted when I reminded her.

After attacking me thus in trembling tones, holding me responsible (someone
must be) for her sufferings, she said, 'I'm getting angry and rude. I'd better ring
off.' That was impossible, so I told her I really did expect her to call on me for
services. What else did she need? Well, her pension hadn't been collected for
weeks. F.: 'All right, I'll come round and do it.' J.: 'You can't do that. It needs a

witness to my signature and then someone to witness that you've witnessed it.' F.: 'I'll manage, don't worry.' Then I asked if she wanted any food bought for her. She said a new French servant was coming in and had cooked her a huge stew, but of course bought the wrong sort of oranges. 'Just what I told her *not* to get. I'll tell you what I'd really like, but you must promise to let me pay for it. I've got money – some *pâté de foie gras*. Also some dressed crab and a little smoked salmon would be nice. And some thin-skinned oranges.'

Well, I've said I'll go on Tuesday morning, collect her pension and take some things. (I offered to go yesterday, but she murmured something about her typewriter.) 'For heaven's sake don't come too early, not before eleven. You've no idea what I look like before I've got my make-up on.'

I continue to think about Julia. Her request for sumptuous delicacies is of course a pathetic 'love test' and by getting me to bring them and then throwing them away (as she did the food I cooked her before) she will probably satisfy some part of her libido.

January 20th

Prophetic words. This morning Julia rang up to say she thought perhaps she didn't want the dressed crab, smoked salmon and *foie gras* she'd asked me for. I told her I'd only bought the two latter, and the *foie gras* was in a tin. We then had an insane discussion about oranges. I explained that the very thin-skinned ones were not in season now, but I'd bought some Spanish ones whose skins were thinner than the Jaffas. J.: 'The thing is, I've had so many of these oranges that they paint and then varnish over, and they're quite green and sour inside and have none of this carotin you know that oranges ought to contain.' 'Well, perhaps you'd rather I didn't bring them.' 'Yes, better not I think, and then the smoked salmon really doesn't agree with me, and I've got this big casserole of cooked food.' (Why did she ask for smoked salmon, then?) 'I'll keep that too, then.'

Could anything more exactly have followed my prognostications? She tried rather feebly to put off my going to get her pension for her, until a less wet day, but truth to tell I wanted to get it over, and destroy one of her grievances against me. But OOF, what a morning! She really is most horribly disagreeable to me. I tried to swallow my indignation when she contradicted me flat about what I had or had not said on the telephone, but not very successfully.

Had she got her pension book ready? Dear, no! 'I think it's in my bag ... (scuffle, scuffle). Doesn't seem to be here. Do you know what it looks like?' F.: 'No, I don't have one.' J.: 'Well, I'd better look in my other bag ... (more scuffle, scuffle). Not here either.' Finally three immense bags stuffed with papers and pills were brought and the contents emptied in a heap on the floor with a gesture of protest. J.: 'Not here either.' She then looked in her first, current bag and found it. There followed a fantastic business over each of the five coupons. Though she had to put the same thing on each one it was necessary to start from scratch each time. 'Let's see now, what do I put here?' What she had taken to be the necessity for 'a witness to the witness' was designed for those able only to make a mark! Done at last after a full three quarters of an hour of frenzied impatience on my part, and several disagreeable remarks administered with a viperish look on hers, I left in the rain for the post office. 'You'll find this awful queue of course, and do be careful crossing Oxford Street, it's very dangerous.' No queue, no questions asked – but Julia had forgotten to sign on the front of three of the five coupons! I said to the assistant was this really necessary, as she was quite confused. 'Oh, yes! she ought to know. She must have done it dozens of times.' So back I trudged, raining hard now, and up her stairs again. She was apologetic this time, but I was determined to get the job done, and back I went, and back to her with the money. Then the long trek home through Oxford Street, shiny, congested and hideous, to the welcome comparative sanity of my own flat.

This pattern of my relations with Julia must not be repeated – it is too squalid. I shall keep out of range of her banderillas for a while. She made no ghost of an attempt to detain me or talk of other things. When she has got one in the role of servant, only that aspect is allowed to exist, and I cannot and will not occupy it again if I can help it.

January 28th

At Crichel last weekend, news of a terrible drama. Pat told us that Andrew Murray-Thripland's youngest brother was slowly dying of leukaemia, and that it was only a question of how long the process would take. If not too long, Pat hoped to carry Andrew off to Mexico. His mother sat by the boy's bed all day and said that when he died she would kill herself. On Sunday evening the telephone rang and Pat (returning from answering it) poured himself a large whisky. 'The boy has died,' he turned and told us, 'and his mother took a train to Brighton, cut her wrists and is dead too.'

February 18th

Andrew Murray-Thripland rang up and asked to come and see me. He was here over an hour talking about his ghastly experience. Might he commit suicide? Of course I wondered, but I don't think so. I heard the whole story – how his mother had shut herself away from life when his father had died ten years ago. 'She really committed suicide *then*,' I said. But, an intelligent woman, she had been responsible for her four boys, though wanting to shove them out into the world, *not* be a spider mother in fact. When the youngest, Patrick, aged sixteen, got this deadly and horrible disease she had decided what she would do. I think she might well have killed herself anyway when he was grown up. 'Any friends or lovers?' None, he said. She still carried on her archaeology.

Patrick died suddenly when she and Andrew were lunching near the hospital. They came back and were told. She thrust some papers at the nurse from her bag, and while Andrew went to telephone his brothers he told the nurse to look after her. When he came back he found she had dashed into her car, locked herself in and made off.

My attempted consolation was that with such determination he couldn't have stopped her. He might have that time, but she would have done it again. I instanced Carrington and the cruelty of bringing her round. *Not* being sorry for the dead in their peace. She had, in a sense, a right over her life. She had died ten years ago and been unable to come to terms with life. *Not* blaming himself, he displayed a classical reaction. He said he felt rejection, guilt, deep sorrow and fury on his mother's account, less on his brother's.

February 19th, British Embassy, Warsaw

My relief was great at finding myself human and calm on the morning of departure.

Only seven souls in our aeroplane and the flight was perfect. A pale blue day after yesterday's dark bluster. Looking out as we prepared to land, I saw a boundless snow-covered plain, with some patches like spilt tea that were really forests. Then we crunched down, buckled on our clothes (not the full quota reserved for Russia, but fur coats, caps, gloves and boots) and took a first breath of Polish air. Yes, it *is* certainly very cold, but crisp, dry and bearable. It doesn't seem to whip tears from the eyes, nor is it a knife at the throat. Nicko and Mary stood beaming there to meet us and we rolled smoothly off in their large Daimler behind a fluttering Union Jack, to this extremely ugly building, badly designed by the architect of the Post Office Tower. It is very warm and comfortable; there is a sweet young butler always bowing from the waist, called Casimir; the most inhabited room is sympathetically untidy with books and papers, hyacinths and daffodils in pots. Janetta and I each have a typewritten programme of our days' events. Mary looks exhausted, with black circles under her eyes, yet after we'd had coffee she insisted on driving us out in her Mini to the Old Town – so-called, for it is entirely rebuilt, a macabre ghost of what the Germans deliberately destroyed.

All eyes as we drove, I saw strong, handsome people tramping purposefully along in leather coats, high boots and fur hats, and making Breughel-like groups against the rather dirty snow heaped at the sides of the road; houses painted dull yellow or sage green, an art and craft shop selling amber, striped rugs and wooden objects decorated with poker-work. There is a lot of space, wide streets and squares, and of course that universal deadness given by the funereal pall of snow. I think I shall soon tire of that, but feel intense excitement at being in a new country.

February 20th

Those speculative ideas which are often launched by the first days abroad, where are they? There is too much still to discover about this Communist world. I feel shocked when Nicko said his junior staff and their wives were not allowed to mix with any Poles, for 'security reasons'. This is just what we used to complain of the Communists doing surely? There is a half-hearted appendix that it 'wouldn't be fair to the Poles'. But what is the use of having an embassy here at all? We aren't, after all, at war with these individually friendly and apparently admirable people. Surely every sort of intellectual and cultural contact should be kept going, and the embassy staff should be harbingers of peace and friendly relations, rather than gymnasts gyrating on the stiff climbing frame of diplomacy, while trying not to drop their secret information.

Almost opposite the embassy is a large and beautiful park in which is one of the few royal palaces still standing – Łazienki (Polish letter ł pronounced W). A visit there was our morning programme and we walked through the still, refrigerated air along paths of beaten snow. It lay quite thick on each side between the slender black tree trunks, and very tame and hungry red squirrels came hopping through the white silence asking for food. We were accompanied by two ghastly bores from the Ministry of Works, here to consider improvements to the embassy; one is staying in the house; both are square, bottled, unresponsive, navy-blue clad, and no one would guess to look at them that they spend their lives swooshing from

Moscow to Ascension Island. The curator of the palace had a sensitive, intelligent face with the fine bone structure and good forehead that seem to be Polish, and lit from within (as a turnip by a candle) by the flame of his great creative passion to combat the damage the Germans had done to his palace, and faithfully, meticulously put it back just as it was. Just, in fact, as the Russians do. There's astonishingly much, even words, in common between the two countries. Yet the Russians have always been their dreaded enemies. I can't think about Russia yet.

I am handing over our travel arrangements to Janetta to an unprecedented degree and, with the utmost relief but feeling guilty too, lay on my bed reading about Poland's history while she went off to the Orbis Agency.

To *Tosca* in the evening, accompanied by our two plainclothes policemen – the Ministry of Works men – who sat woodenly showing no sign of either pleasure or pain. The large audience coughed and talked maddeningly throughout. The performance was moderate.

February 21st: Cracow

Yesterday morning the long black car swept us in warmth and comfort to the National Museum, where we were handed over to two experts – a deathly pale girl with an appalling cold, and an intelligent and humorous bearded man. Both spoke English brilliantly.

Poor Mary looks more tired than ever after a three-hour session with the private detectives. In the afternoon, Nicko, Janetta and I took the train to Cracow.

Instant relaxation. We were alone in our carriage except for an ancient ancient man, during the five-hour run. After gazing out on the snowy wastes I began to long for green; then darkness fell, and we took to our equipment of hot soup, whisky and every other thing thoughtfully put up by Mary. Cracow station was crowded with short, strong, vital people, hurrying home in their fur hats, warm coats and boots. We found our rooms in a nice, old-fashioned hotel and walked out into the town – the silhouette of its massive sloping walls, towers and arcades looked very splendid. We descended into a drinking-place in a cellar frequented by university students, and drank a hot, delicious spicy wine made from honey, a sort of mead. Supper of Mary's collations in Nicko's room, whisky, wine, cold chicken, high spirits.

In the train I ploughed on through the horrifying nightmare of Polish history. It is appalling; worse far than Ireland.

February 22nd

For the first time today I got a sharp twinge from the oppressive nature of the regime. On the whole I'm not greatly impressed by complaints of the 'poor quality of things in the shops' made by Nicko in the style of Michael Pitt-Rivers. If they prefer to spend money in doing up their palaces and castles, all honour to them.

This morning a strong thaw had set in, but light snow was falling and gradually the snow turned to ugly slush and pools of blackish water. By daylight the ancient buildings reveal dingy, peeling walls and there is an all-pervading air of grimness. In the shops, faces are wooden and unsmiling. The answer is 'No' or 'No more' to everything asked for. In spite of the thaw, or because of it, it's bitterly cold. I'm longing for spring warmth, flowers, freedom, *green*.

My breakfast, got with some difficulty, was a glass of tea with a 'Pickwick tea bag' swinging in it, a leathery roll, bread, excellent butter and jam. We present coupons given us as tourists, and Janetta and I hope that hers and mine will pay the whole bill for the three of us.

The Daimler has arrived here mysteriously, and in it, with our Union Jack gazed at inscrutably by the dark figures in the streets, we rolled off to the Czartosyski Gallery, a collection of pictures and furniture made by a cultured Polish nobleman, including a superb Rembrandt and da Vinci's portrait of a girl with a ferret. Another charming and scholarly curator took us round. His English was pretty good, but he was stumped by one artist: 'It is by the Master of the Half Woman – no, that's not quite right.' F.: 'Oh, you mean the Hermaphrodite?' He laughed heartily at this and when I saw the picture, which was of a well-developed bosom encased in red velvet, I felt rather sheepish. Good pictures too by Gozzoli, Lorenzo Monaco; splendid tents captured in Turkish wars; one of Shakespeare's chairs carefully encased. Janetta and I went on to Wawel Castle and saw more tents, tiled stoves – very tall and handsome – frescoes, rooms hung with Spanish leather. Our tiny, schoolmistressy guide clutched her shawl round her shoulders, lifted her square head backwards and spouted scholarly information like a dictaphone.

Lunch in our hotel, with a young Oxford undergraduate of Polish extraction doing a year's course here. The head of the English faculty came for a drink and Nicko was asked to visit him later, but, 'Please do not come in the embassy car if you don't mind.' They clearly must be living in fear, though it sounded extraordinary to hear Nicko ask the undergraduate, 'Are you *under much pressure*?' When asked if Polish girls tried to get him to marry them so as to get English nationality, he replied modestly that they did. Poor Nicko, who had spent the latter part of the morning at the university, suddenly looked quite exhausted, and Janetta and I begged him to have a rest and leave us to prowl in the town. After reading of the appalling horrors done by the Germans, it was strange to hear the sacristan of the Cathedral describing its famous altarpiece of brilliantly coloured, gilt and (it must be said) Germanic figures, to a group of tourists in the German language. In fact this town might be an Austrian one, and I'm not really bowled over by it, as one is supposed to be.

A longish rest and read, then conversation with Janetta in her rooms about faraway English things – Rose, Alexandra's relations with her parents. All these three sets of parents, Janetta, Magouche and the Hendersons, are sharply critical of the others' bringing-up of their daughters. But we agree that Nicko does his job as ambassador perfectly. Trouble-taking and kind, he conveys the impression that he represents a civilized country and is personally charming and totally unpompous. Very high marks indeed. We dined in a small, simple and good restaurant, where the portions were mountainous.

February 23rd: Warsaw again

Cracow looked more attractive on Sunday morning with snow falling on the people slowly oozing out of the church opposite my bedroom window. They are a religious race (RC) and in this the Russians have been unable to interfere. The large square had a new coat of snow over the slush, and old women were selling tulips and roses at ten shillings each for young men to give their girlfriends, as well as wreaths of immortelles of a drastic violet colour, prettily powdered with snow. Bought some grain for the hungry pigeons and at once had four or five pairs of fierce pink feet clutching my hand.

Started driving homewards in the Daimler. Of course I enjoy this regal comfort, being tucked under a fur rug by the chauffeur, this temporary assumption of luxe. The white landscape seemed more varied than from the train; we even crossed a low range of hills where the road became icy and slippery. I enjoyed the 'human interest': wrapped-up children, boys skating on a pond, skiers and tobogganers, a few horse-driven sledges – one with two ladies holding up an umbrella to the snow, another packed tight with nuns like a medieval painting – geese, a solid black dog sitting in the snow. We drew off the road up a farm track to eat our lunch and the chauffeur (returning from a pee) grinningly said that the military police had just shot by in their car, so presumably Nicko must have been tailed all the way from Warsaw. It is hard to take in this extraordinary and sinister mystery-game that is being played, and almost impossible for anyone used to rational behaviour to believe in it. We talked at length about Lionel and Dunyusha. Nicko, not knowing them, treated it rather as farce, but obviously thinks Margaret is probably right about Dunyusha's intentions, and that she is after British nation-ality. Also Lionel's money, for though Margaret never seems to realise it, I believe he is a rich man. Then talk of general ideas, theory of punishment, retribution, deterrent. The others both snoozed; I gazed. We passed through a large, hideous, rebuilt town, called Kielie I think, and Janetta suggested a stop in a café. N.: 'Oh, you *can't*; it'll be appalling! Ghastly!' However, the chauffeur was given orders and with difficulty found one, full to the brim with cheerful people. Nicko and I drank fruit syrup, Janetta had a symbolic cognac. We had lots of drink with us in the car. When she again suggested a stop in a sordid-looking café attached to the petrol station where we filled up in the outskirts of Warsaw, Nicko opposed his will to her formidable one, saying we were nearly home, and this time he won.

Back in the warmth and comfort of the 'Residence' as it is called, welcomed by Mary and dogs.

February 24th

Ah! Out it came, the sun, and with it the sky turned pale blue over the sparkling, refreshed snow. There has fortunately been no wind.

Janetta has been so invariably sweet and considerate to the Hendersons (as well as to me) that I taxed Nicko yesterday, having once said how 'cross' she was. Perhaps she had changed, he admitted, but she could sometimes be really rude. I believe that this is quite unconscious, and comes from the concentrated pursuit of her own ends which temporarily blinkers her.

For lunch we had several English Poles from the university, a young Spaniard, the ex-Polish Ambassador to Paris, a dynamically attractive middle-aged man who seemed to be talking extremely freely at the other end of the lunch table, and afterwards absorbedly to Janetta in one corner of the huge and hideous reception room, leaving her stimulated and agitated. He told her that many things are much better now than they were. Where there was poverty, starvation even, shoelessness and illiteracy, people now have enough to eat, keep warm and dress well. Having got these things, the young have naturally begun thinking and talking about freedom. He had been a good deal in Russia and even there found young people whose flats were full of secretly printed literature, who knew that liberty throughout the Iron Curtain countries must come from them, from within Russia, but also that they had to bide their time. An Anglo-Polish student next to me said the standard of education here is now extremely high. But he was deeply depressed because, although his mother was Polish, the Polish students would not be friends, only acquaintances, and the very fact that he spoke perfect Polish made them suspicious. The poor Poles cannot for a moment risk a Czechoslovak disaster.

Today Janetta and I were taken peacefully and alone to another palace in the outskirts, baroque, charming, light and airy, with beautiful flock wallpapers; and after the lunch guests had gone, she and I and Mary walked in the Łasienki Park, our fingers and noses isolated into tingling blobs by the cold. But the air is crisp and invigorating and one's nose mercifully doesn't run.

Another student to supper. Ping-pong – I can still beat Janetta.

February 25th

Day of the plunge. It could hardly have begun worse. Magouche, expected at ten-thirty last night, has still not arrived this morning. Telephoning the airport, Nicko was told that she had put down at Poznan, several hours away by train or car, because of fog. Janetta was strained and nervous, while Nicko and I rather heart-lessly enjoyed *The Times* crossword puzzle. After further calls it seems she has probably stayed the night there. Apparently flights are often delayed or cancelled for fog or snow.

Yesterday was a packed day. Janetta and I were taken to see the film of the destruction of Warsaw, sitting alone in a cinema in the square of the old town. Twenty restrained minutes of horror. Is it right to foster the necessarily furious resentment such things produce? Or rather, is it useful? Janetta and I argued it in the square. The sun had come mildly out, setting off the Poles' superhuman achievement of reconstruction.

But far the most striking tribute to their energy and intelligence was the College of Music, which we were shown around by an English student who had been at the Royal College of Music in London, and told us Warsaw completely outclassed it. The modern building was beautiful; the equipment incredibly good. Hundreds of practising rooms, all perfectly soundproof, the pianos all Steinways and Bechsteins, rehearsal rooms, libraries, elaborate recording and playing-back devices, by which a student can telephone to the basement for any recording to be switched to his practising room. They work there all day till nine at night; the course is five years. I was much moved by such a successful effort directed towards one of the great civilizing influences in the world.

Lunch with Wapler, the French Ambassador here, another middle-aged charmer; an elderly female Bibesco and a delightful Polish composer (friend of the Berkeleys). All sophisticated, amusing and civilised. Wapler depreciates everything. Going to Russia? 'Mais c'est *idiot!*' The composer told Janetta that the Berkeleys tried to persuade him to leave Poland, but he wouldn't. Someone must stay. All his friends were here. But he has lost his job and become poor because he spoke up against the invasion of Czechoslovakia. He came with us to the Madame Curie Museum, cracking ironical jokes and smiling with steel-trimmed teeth.

Some time this morning Magouche turned up in a taxi while Janetta was going the rounds of the stations in the Daimler. She had come on by train after a few hours in bed at Poznan.

February 26th

Here I am in our long-thought-about, half-dreaded train to Moscow. I have got up from my sleeper and struggled along to the breakfast car to use my first coupon, brought me by the Intourist man in the middle of the night. A beautiful morning, with hot sun and a clear blue sky over virgin snow; but the night must have been cold as there was frost *inside* my window, and getting from one carriage to the next I stepped through rocking infernos of whirling snow blown up from the track. Breakfast was pale sausages, greyish mashed potato, a glass of tea, and bread and cheese.

Our fears of having to get out and change carriages or even trains at the frontier in the middle of the freezing night were groundless, though both Russian and Polish travel agencies misinformed us, and might well have driven us to do so out of mutual hostility. We started the night in a grubby, second-class Polish sleeper, but moved to a first-class one going right through to Moscow. We didn't cross the frontier till about 1 a.m., after a frightening invasion of military officials in fur hats with impassive faces. All money and traveller's cheques were examined, gold objects listed, and then a young man with blazing blue eyes flashed his torch under my bed. And a strong, cross Customs woman pointed fiercely at the Polish apples in my basket and said proudly, 'No fruit allowed into the Soviet Union'. Huge arc lamps fixed at a great height made it seem even more as though we were going into a concentration camp.

February 27th: Moscow

It is a disappointing fact that it is less of a thrill being here just because it is the second time. Moscow is actually *familiar* – a place I know. 'Being in Russia' is no longer a miracle; nor does such snow as there is make much difference – it is dirty, urban snow. 'I suddenly see,' Magouche said, as we walked to the Kremlin. 'Everyone *is* the same. They're all equals.' I'm not sure if she meant it as criticism – a little, I think. The universal winter rig is much like that of the Poles: fur hats, good warm coats with fur collars, boots. In this they look more attractively and suitably dressed than in summer. Though I respond with admiration to this equality, I wish they could be more eccentric without losing it. For equality needn't be identity.

After breakfast in the train yesterday I fell peacefully asleep on my berth. Woke and joined the others for lunch, and it didn't seem long before we arrived at Moscow station, an hour late at five o'clock. We were met by an Intourist man with the ears of his fur hat flapping. Like children being greeted by a master at school, we were on this list, our names known. We were to go to the National Hotel, where Kitty and I were last time. Our taxi driver thought otherwise, and firmly took us to a scruffy-looking one called the Berlin, but he was obliged to toe the line. Everyone addresses us in German, and there are many of them about. Janetta's tactics for communication are to speak slowly and softly in English and if they don't understand '*one word*', as they generally don't, she seems to find them stupid, like a conventional Englishwoman.

Our rooms were well warmed, bathroomed, unattractive slits with no outlook. Both Janetta and Magouche have an instantaneous desire to get things bettered, set people running about on their behalf, put up with nothing. They at once tried to change rooms. Impossible – in this country they have probably met their match. They are both extremely kind to me and for the most part make allowances for my seniority, but last night they insisted on walking for miles in the cold night looking for the Georgian restaurant which, when we at last got there, slammed its door in our faces. Back, therefore, to the restaurant of our hotel, huge and unattractive with a thumping band, four couples revolving in an old-fashioned clinch, and food taking hours to come.

February 28th

Janetta finds the bridle of regulations extremely irksome. She likes to ignore them, and would rather eat in a special restaurant where you pay in dollars than use our coupons. This we did last night after an intensely enjoyed performance of *The Three Sisters* at the Moscow Art Theatre, beautifully staged and acted so that there was complete realism, perfect illusion. They all seemed to be living through these events before our eyes for the first time. Afterwards we drank vodka and ate caviare.

The morning had been gloriously beautiful with a bright blue sky, and we spent it in the Kremlin. The museum and one of the churches were shut; a new little church, very beautiful indeed, had been opened, and we explored at our leisure. Slow but quite good lunch afterwards in an old-fashioned and un-touristy restaurant. Then, I left my two more energetic companions and walked home, buying stamps and postcards.

March 1st

I realise I am to some extent irritated by Janetta's claims to special treatment, just as she probably is by my submissiveness. Our food arrangements all today were significant. Breakfast can now be had on trays in our rooms, but we overslept and barely had time to snatch a biscuit and a glass of home-made tea before the private car and guide we had ordered came to take us to Zagorsk. We ended our sightseeing at about one-thirty, but it was a holiday, and our expectation of eating in the good restaurants I remembered there was frustrated. There were huge crowds of people. Outside the tall white wall of the monastery were a lot of booths where healthy, good-humoured females in peasant dress were selling food of various kinds. 'Oh, look!' said Magouche. 'Cold chicken, hard-boiled eggs!' So I bought enough for us three, and our guide and driver. Meanwhile Janetta was eating a small portion of coleslaw out of a cardboard plate and offering it to us on a spoon. 'It's delicious! Oh, *do* have some! Wouldn't you like it?' The fact that our guide and driver had gone back to the car and obviously wanted to be off affected her and me in opposite ways. And not only did Janetta refuse to touch either chicken or eggs, but the force of her personality made Magouche refuse to touch them too, though it had been her idea to buy them. Our guide nibbled a bun, and the remaining store hung about, to be pecked at by me at odd moments during the next two days. Janetta refused to eat any of it, even when we came in so late one night that we could get no food anywhere else. I was reminded of Ralph's account of how she had to invent skiing for herself and would not take advice even from the instructor they had hired. Here, she is inventing Russia for herself. No sooner had we got back to our hotel about three-thirty than Janetta and Magouche went off to the dollar restaurant and came back saying triumphantly that they had got 'delicious food and paid in *roubles*'. I rather unkindly pointed out that the food was exactly the same in all the hotel's several restaurants, and that it wasn't so very clever to buy in roubles what we had already paid for in London in coupons.

The day ended, and the opera over, Magouche suddenly and firmly said she was going straight to bed and Janetta and I were left to eat our delicious caviare and drink our delicious vodka in exactly the same restaurant where they had paid in roubles – but paying in coupons this time. What she eats must be *special*, must be eaten *late* and must be her own deliberate choice. She has already said this morning, 'Let's have lunch *late*, like we did today.' But if you aim at three your food comes at four, by which time my appetite has gone.

Zagorsk: Well, there it was, just as I distinctly remembered it. The thrilling view of the onion domes and tall blue baroque tower seen over the great white wall. New this time was the nipping cold that pierced boots and gloves and made it impossible to stand still for a moment out of doors. And the crowds! Mothers' Day had brought a horde of old women swathed in greyish scarves and booted in felt. 'You'll find all Communist countries smell of hippos,' Nicko had told us – and here we were in the thick of that smell, unable to get into churches without squeezing past these squat, rank-smelling figures, all in putty-coloured clothes, creeping along, propped on sticks, kissing the walls and floors.

Last night's opera, *Don Carlos*, was in the huge new glass theatre inside the Kremlin. The size of the auditorium and of the stage itself meant that the singers could only make themselves heard by throbbing and straining away in front of a long row of microphones. Better draw a veil on this despondingly vulgar and unmusical production. It was turned into a pageant for the masses and the score and even the plot cut about to suit. The audience ate, made love and chattered as if at such a pageant, and when they rushed out in their hordes to the inevitable 'garderobes' it was like being in some frightening public uprising, and ropes had to be thrown across the foyer to keep back the oncoming waves of assault. I noticed that the audience knew enough to applaud the most famous arias, but not to be critical of the atrocious screams of the Italian 'prima donna from La Scala'. We cannot face this vulgar place for the ballet tonight and go to *Uncle Vanya* instead. Snowing as we came out.

March 2nd

Uncle Vanya was almost, if not quite, as enjoyable as *The Three Sisters*. What a magnificent play! It went on snowing most of yesterday with a cold, searching wind. The coughing in the theatre was dreadful and we hear that there is a lot of flu about. To the Pushkin Museum in the morning. Magouche and Janetta came out discussing whether it was right for the 'masses' to see these masterpieces, and what they got out of it. Janetta thought it was for them just a place to keep warm. She seemed upset, almost speechless and near tears, while Magouche appeared to think, as I do, that many of the young people who go there are studying the pictures with care and intelligently – not holding hands or giggling at all. It is an education, even if they have not got very far with it. You might as well say children should give up arithmetic because they can't understand long division at first sight. Janetta is evidently appalled by what she calls, characteristically, 'IT'. There have been many IT's in her life, and the Russian classless society fills the part perfectly.

Lunch at the Georgian restaurant pleased everyone; there was a huge and varied selection of hors d'oeuvres, on which we stuffed ourselves.

I find walking about, head down, Angora scarf wound round my face, no joke in this bitter, snow-laden wind, so I left my friends to visit St Basil and went back for a sleep.

When I woke this morning it suddenly became clear to me that I never in my heart of hearts wanted to come to Russia this time. I've never cared for snow, nor the shrivelling effect of cold. And I think I knew some of the excitement would wear off on a second visit. Why didn't I hand over to Magouche? Partly because by then I had accepted the challenge never to say NO to an experience, and was deeply involved with tickets, etc. Before that I didn't want to disappoint Janetta, who was so excited by the idea, and Magouche only made up her mind at the very last moment. I saw (rightly) what a splendid bolster-banister she would be. For some curious reason it's a fortifying relief to realise this – that I never wanted to come, I mean.

Of course I am enjoying many things enormously – our morning in the Kremlin, the Pushkin, the two Chekhov plays, Zagorsk.

March 3rd: Leningrad

Yesterday was another cold morning, snowing. I packed my bags and set off in a taxi with Janetta and Magouche to the Novadevichi Monastery. This was an item on my own special list, but alas, the church was shut. The taxi man was amiable and agreed to come back for us in an hour and actually did. No *nyet*-man he. Janetta and Magouche wanted him to wait for us, a typical form of extravagance, but he said he couldn't do this. A bus-load of German tourists were also plodding round. We penetrated the long hall of the monastery where two bodies laid out for burial were more sweet-scented than the old hippo ladies and priests crowding the passage outside. Then we walked through the snow, down towards the river Moskva lying invisible under the general whiteness. Crocodiles of healthy children, rosy and well-wrapped little bears, a sleeping swathed baby being pulled on a sledge, boys doing flat skiing. We seemed suddenly to be in the country. Rather a good lunch at the Metropole; it is grander than the Europa. Afterwards we pounded about through the endless halls of GUM, where the proletariat were avidly buying things, and sparrows chirped stridently in the glass roof. Magouche and Janetta shopped enthusiastically, chiefly for children's felt boots. I found nothing to buy.

The blessed white witch vodka turned our departure in a flurry of snow into an adventure. Fur-hatted figures paced the platform under the high vault of the station and soon the big red train steamed in. A woman knocked off the icicles hanging from the letters ЛЕНИГРАД on its side, and they jangled to the platform. There were two berths reserved for us in one carriage, one in the next, where I was quickly joined by a small Russian female tub. Janetta and Magouche most sweetly offered to change, but I felt a moral obligation not to be too fussy, and stayed with my tub.

March 4th

How greatly I prefer Leningrad and its inhabitants to Moscow and the Muscovites. They smile at us, they show desire to help rather than stubborn non-response.

We are at the old Europa and all have identical suites of the sort that Kitty and

I had in '65 – hall, large bathroom, bedroom and alcove. My companions, however, cannot be satisfied with anything; nothing is quite good enough for them. I think their creative impulses must be starved! Magouche had to move her bed out from the wall to get more light, not noticing that the light swivelled; she turned round her writing-desk, and sent for 'Bolshoi' light bulbs. (A large friendly woman has just brought my tea and lemon, toast, delicious blackcurrant jam and butter.)

At first sight, under a pale blue sky, Leningrad looked warmer than Moscow in the snow. But our walk up the Nevsky Prospekt soon showed us that it was not. Not only is the *fond de l'air* extremely cold, but an icy wind sweeps round corners and grips one's throat. My Angora scarf is a godsend. My hottest outfit is thermal underwear, jersey and quilted jacket, thick tights, woollen trousers, fur coat, boots, gloves and hat. A lot of this has to come off and be put on again at every visit to a museum or restaurant. It is splendidly warm indoors. Near the Hermitage, groups of charming little 'bears' were happily playing in the snow.

It was a delight to take the Hermitage slowly – today the Poussins, Chardins, Watteaus – and this time I noticed the rooms and furniture more.

Magouche and Janetta have been shopping and returned with jams, tea, tisanes and Nescafé. They have two little boiling outfits and spent hours brewing various hot drinks, their eyes blazing with obsessional pleasure. I hear the bubbling and hissing whenever I go into their rooms. I stick to whisky, which I prefer. We have taken to Scrabble in Janetta's room. They have just told me that in Moscow a boy asked them to change money to send to his relations in England. He said he liked England, that the police were 'bad here'. They told him they couldn't, and he said with deep feeling, 'For GOD's sake do it.' It must have been harrowing, but they didn't give in; I don't quite know why.

March 5th

Almost imperceptible snow falling yesterday morning, when we set off rather late to the statue of Peter the Great and St Isaac's (shut). To the Hermitage with Janetta, where we lost each other in the lavatory. Glorious Rembrandts, sordid cafeteria snack, Rembrandts again. One can now get *The Times* here, from under the counter and at a cost of six shillings. Dropping with exhaustion, I staggered back, lay on my bed and read it.

In the evening to Mussorgsky's *Khovanshchina* at the Kirov Theatre, reopening after its redecoration. A special gala occasion, and it was wonderfully pretty in its new dress of gold and baby blue. The opera superbly put on and well sung. Though enjoying it enormously, we were quite unable to follow the complicated plot and came away before the end to avoid the rush for transport or a cold, long walk home. Russian basses are splendid. At eleven-twenty, with one and a half acts still to go (and not a bite or sup since lunch) we squeezed into a crowded bus smelling strongly of drink; fur hats were nodding round us and I saw hardly anyone insert their 'honour' payment into the automatic machine. It was indeed almost a physical impossibility to reach it. (This was the only occasion when I induced my companions to use public transport.) The fur hats woke up and got out at their stop, to my amazement.

March 6th

A blue sky appeared early; by lunch-time there was brilliant sunshine and it was thawing fast. Now and again the ice in huge pipes broke up suddenly and disgorged an excremental sausage onto the pavement with a crash. Men shovelled snow from the roofs and we walked in danger, but on the shady side of the Fontanka the roofs were still white and fringed with long, glittering icicles. A feeling of spring cheerfulness infected the crowds in the streets and many were buying flowers and fruit (expensive apples and oranges). We took a taxi to Peter and Paul's Fortress. Thence Janetta guided us deftly to Peter the Great's wooden house. To the Astoria for quite a good, dilatory lunch, and walked home along the Fontanka.

Janetta, who was feeling unwell, cried off the evening's entertainment – a concert of folk music. I enjoyed its high spirits, the talented balalaika player and singers, cheerful colours, and very genuine if humble audience. All round us were the barrel shapes and stout legs of women who looked as though they had been shovelling snow all day. They loved the traditional music and the high, clear voices singing comic songs; there was no chattering and moving about, only utter absorption. I would have liked to stay to the end, but deferred to Magouche's obvious feeling that half was enough. We had been driven there by a sweet young taxi man with a rosy face and dimples who absolutely refused to take a single kopek for his fare. What can have inspired him? Desire to be friendly to foreigners? When Janetta and I were in the main bookshop trying to get translations of Chekhov, a young man with a sensitive, intelligent face asked in excellent English if he could help us. He told us he read a lot in English. What did he like? Oh, Dickens and Shakespeare of course, but 'many, many – Hemingway, Kingsley Amis'. We would have liked to offer to send him English books but didn't dare.

March 7th

My realisation that a second visit is less exciting than the first obscures the question: has IT deteriorated or improved? 'Things in the shops' are no better; 'they' perhaps look more prosperous and well-dressed; one can get *The Times*. Janetta is very much disgruntled and depressed by IT – I sometimes fear she is disappointed and emotionally upset by the whole adventure. I have woken this morning embarrassed by realising this and feeling that it was partly my enthusiasm that fired her to come, and that though I truly came chiefly for her sake, it is she who is now unhappy. I spoke to Magouche about this; I'm not quite clear what she feels, as she is so anxious to please. I don't think Janetta will regret having come, however.

We used our half-day trip coupons on an afternoon guided expedition to Tsarskoe Selo in a bus with a young English couple. Our little female guide was intelligent, and answered all our questions about wages, living conditions, with apparent frankness. As we drove through the hideous blocks of flats (she lives in one), she said that before the Revolution this region had been covered with peasant shacks, where they lived without water, light, sanitation and transport. Now they have all these, and two bedrooms, sitting-room, bath and kitchen per family.

The great palace looked wonderful, standing in bright blue state in the snow. As we walked in the park, the guide and I talked about books. She told me how she adored Dickens (their favourite English writer, it seems) and I told her how I loved Turgenev. So did she, but her daughters found him too old-fashioned. Members of her 'groups' had given her a book on Nicholas and Alexandra to read. Her criticisms were sharp, but we all thought fair. It was 'sentimental', and she 'almost laughed when she read about the *poor* Tsar dancing with tears in his eyes after his coronation, because owing to an error a few hundred peasants had been shot by his soldiers'. She thought him the 'most irresponsible of all the Tsars'. I would have thought 'incapable' was nearer the mark.

March 8th

After various tussles with Intourist we left for the Hermitage, with an introduction from a Russian botanist Magouche knows who has telephoned the director or his secretary, to let us see the Scythian gold. We were shown into the office of a gentle, scholarly, washed-out elderly woman, who treated us with unmixed kindness, talked to us in French – though her English was quite good – and promised to take us into the basement after lunch. Saw the Cézannes and other modern French pictures; some of the Matisses have been sent to Czechoslovakia. A girl student, an American, approached Magouche and told her she had been here nine months. What was it like? Hard. The work? Yes, that, and the life too. They slept in dormitories. But she loved it here. Did they manage to have some fun? Oh yes, *lots*; but it was all in private houses and apartments.

The Scythian gold was both extraordinary and beautiful. Along with it was a collection of precious objects, jewels and jewelled boxes from Tsarist times. Having exhausted our admirable guide and ourselves, we crept home and I fell on my bed feeling I would never rise again. But I did, and washed my hair, and then at Magouche's bidding rushed across the road to a Beethoven concert in their chief concert hall. We were in the front row, under the grand piano, looking at the unlikely lower half and 'pig's-trotter shoes'[1] of the female soloist pressing the pedals. The orchestra sat up very straight and stiff, holding out their violins as if they didn't belong to them, the pudgy unathletic hands of the second violins hardly ever leaving the first position. They played the 'Pastoral' Symphony in an academically correct and unemotional style.

March 13th

Woken at six (soon to become four by western time) and driven to the airport, arriving far too early, for a short, tranquil and empty flight. Coming over the Kentish coast with my thoughts focused on grass and green (*Verde que te quiero verde*) I looked down and saw it as white with snow as Poland or Russia. Round and round we went above London (no snow here) with the sun first on this side then on that, till at last we swooped down through the opaque clouds with that strange feeling of not altogether unpleasant finality.

March 14th

On the eve of becoming seventy, I have been feeling it something obscene and to be ashamed of; then came the determination to be more realistic. In the event I have been deeply touched by the kindness of friends. Janetta has just given a delicious lunch for me at Wheeler's, with Jaime, Robert and Cynthia. I have had flowers from the Campbells, a treat at the theatre from Margaret tonight (*Uncle*

[1] A phrase of Molly MacCarthy's.

Vanya) and a most unexpected telegram from Lennox and Freda Berkeley. So the dread occasion has been gently eased past as it needs to be, and this great and friendly kindness has made it tolerable. But I have thought a lot about death recently, even more than usual, and my awareness that there isn't so much further to go is not sad at all.

March 17th

Good Lord, I've said nothing about Julia, yet now she is in the foreground of my thoughts. The first news I had on my return was that she had finally sent an SOS to Margaret to say she was too weak from lack of food to go on any longer. Kind Margaret hurried round, was shocked by her white, thin, ill appearance and asked if she would like to go into hospital. Unqualified YES. So she is now in the psychiatric ward of St Pancras Hospital, resting in bed, eating better (so they say) and all completely free. I've seen her twice, the first time very briefly, but my second visit yesterday preys on me. Not that she seems unhappy; in an extraordinary way it appears to have been an immense relief to her to give up, not to pretend to be all right, and leave all the business of life to others. She isn't mad, though she gets a little muddled and looks dreadfully ill; but the others in her ward are. They mostly get up during the day and go to the 'badminton and television room', but Julia very wisely refuses. So she has the light, quite pleasant ward mainly to herself. But a crazy little sprite haunted it yesterday, sitting on her bed sobbing and rocking herself, talking to imaginary people, sometimes on an imaginary telephone. And suddenly while I was talking to Julia a prostrate figure was carried through to an inner room by fierce black nurses. An attempted suicide? I could see her being laid out on the bed and hear the nurses saying crossly, 'Now then, Ada, what have you been up to, eh?' Julia's face expressed only a mild surprise. Indeed it expressed very little on the whole – not the ghost of a smile, merely a gaunt despair which I found dreadfully tragic. She told me how she had fallen and hurt her chest while trying to get to the lavatory in the night. She talked almost in a whisper, and said her chest hurt, and in every way behaved like someone whose least movement was agony and effort. I fetched her water, propped her pillows, but her sad, dead expression didn't change. Yet she *didn't* (wonderfully enough) *complain*. I drove off to dinner with the Campbells feeling shaken and rather crazy myself. It is always necessary to her to blame someone for her sufferings, and if Lawrence is the First Villain, I believe she has cast me for the Second.

March 26th

Another visit to Julia in her psychiatric home yesterday. Finding her bed empty, I was looking about when a tall, good-looking, youngish man asked if he could help. He turned out to be her doctor, Alan Gardner. When I asked, he said, in some ways she was better, but they were worried about her physically, and taking all sorts of tests. I found her in a sitting-room upstairs reading the paper, her eyes curiously suffused with pink, as I now remember – perhaps she's using them more than before. It was a largish, impersonal room with a circle of chairs in which one or two stout dummies were sitting in absolute silence. A young, rather attractive girl came in briefly and addressed Julia by her christian name. Julia said, 'He always does that.' 'It's a she,' said the dummy next to us. 'I must remember that,' said Julia. I can't get over the feeling that she's *extremely* ill – indeed it increases. She spoke quietly and indistinctly. I did my best to guess at what she meant, but sometimes it was impossible. At other moments, mind and voice cleared together, and she would answer some question about Chekhov quite sensibly. But the impression is as of someone who has had a stroke. There are signs of intolerance of her surroundings – the food is appalling, quite uneatable, cabbage with all the vitamins boiled away, etc. I was surprised she had expected anything else. The tea is undrinkable and she can't bear the canteen. Her companions are all terribly depressed and she has nothing in common with any of them. 'None of our class,' she said in a whisper, 'not a single one, and many of them awfully disagreeable.' All of this is too true. Perhaps it's only to her completely sane visitors that the insanity of the other patients would seem the worst feature. Our dummies were quite enough, but there were occasional wild yells from down the passage. When I left she said she would go back to her ward. 'I'll come with you,' I said; but she wouldn't take my arm, only leant heavily on the banisters and climbed the stairs like a child, a foot at a time. She insisted on going *up*stairs, and said, 'Yes, this is my bed,' but the alarmingly black face of a nurse said, 'This isn't yours – it's the men's ward,' and down we had to go again. 'But I mustn't forget your chocolates,' she said, scrabbling under the chairs. I had taken her none, only some glossy magazines.

April 2nd

I'm shaking like a leaf and have taken to the whisky bottle. Peter Jenkins has just rung up. It has been clear for some days that poor Charlotte is near her end, and now it seems as though she might not last out the night – how I hope she does not. Peter wanted me to get in touch with Isobel, and find out how much she realises. I said I'd try and get her here tonight, and at once – but she won't come. So I've had to be content with saying I'll go round to her at any moment and be ready – to do what? Once again there is this agonising desire to help, and lack of certainty how.

   Later: Peter rang almost as I was writing this. 'Charlotte has just died.' Terrible, pregnant words. Death is truly as Chekhov said, 'a cruel thing, a disgusting punishment'. I told him I would go to Isobel at once, and as I drove off in my Mini of course I felt the echo of a journey over six years ago. It is unsafe to assume that people react to grief in the same way; this is what puts a peculiar strain on the comforter. She has to intensify her sensitiveness and stretch her powers of apprehension to the uttermost to see what the other person wants or needs. I have on occasion failed in the past to realise that they wanted to talk and weep out their horror and dismay. With Isobel I'm sure I was right in taking the cue that, while not shirking the facts, she didn't want to give way to emotion. She took to a punt, not a boat with a keel. And I got on board with her, sparing myself the depths of sadness when possible, but I noticed as so often before that sad grammatical sign of using the present tense: 'Charlotte has...'

April 24th

A moral struggle to force myself to go and see Julia. I said I would like to present her with two weeks in a luxury nursing home pending arrangements. Julia, firmly: 'I don't want to go.' What about the private room at the end of the public sitting-room, I asked. No one had told her about it, said Julia, and obviously envisaged a comfortably furnished, tastefully decorated flatlet, for when we peered in and saw a bright little square room with large window looking onto the daffodils, she said, 'It's rather bleak and hygienic, isn't it? Not quite the sort of furnishing one would like.' When I suggested a table to type or write at might make it habitable, she brightened a little. But there were signs of the old pernickety, tart Julia – complaining of 'terrible draughts round one's legs'; not having any of her clothes washed; of her distress because of Dr Gardner mentioning her 'confusion', 'when he was talking to *you*'. 'But I've never talked to him!' I cried. I think she confuses me with Margaret. Of visitors arriving without notice 'interrupting her work'. (Her 'work' was reading an illustrated magazine)...

Last night came Peter Jenkins, a very balanced and stable bereaved husband. I respect and admire his rational approach to the problem of Amy,[1] his obvious deep grief for Charlotte, admiration of her 'extraordinary bravery and elegance', and yet the realism with which he talked of his 'girlfriend'. I hear she is Polly Toynbee, daughter of Philip.

May 4th

Back now from my breathless week in Alderney, and have stepped into full summer. Yes, Eardley, Dadie and I *did* get to know our island; from the moment we saw it spread like a soft green map beneath our tiny, slim, yellow eight-seater aeroplane on Monday to the similar view on Saturday, by which time it was thoroughly known, understood and absorbed into my being and I saw it left behind with a pang.

We were out all and every day, three of them magnificently sunny; we lunched twice on grassy ledges on the cliffs; we walked round every bit of the coast and down every lane. It was a great success for all three. We all loved it in the same way and wanted to do the same sort of thing. Dadie was tremendous fun and constantly enjoyable as a companion even when being the complete scoutmaster. 'Wholesome' is his favourite word, used half ironically. He walked me off my legs, going at a spanking rate, and often six yards ahead of Eardley and me, his comically purposeful figure, head poking forward on his rather sloping shoulders in a floppy windcheater, striding and striding. On our hot days he was happy to lie and read, and I searched for flowers; when the mists closed in he managed to make me walk much faster than I wanted to, for all my determination not to. What would he have said if I'd asked, 'Why so fast?' We all liked whisky, buying postcards, discussion, jokes, Scrabble. Dadie made his own rules for this, and was wildly competitive; however I beat him, in spite of his firmly squashing any word he hadn't heard of, like 'almug', all colloquialisms and words of foreign origin, etc. There was hardly time for me to list and look up my flowers, or read, and none at all for this book.

May 15th

Julia is back at Percy Street. She came to dinner last night with Bunny and Eardley. She told me she had 'learned her lesson', which is, I hope, to drop purple hearts and keep on eating. With her return to sanity comes a good deal of her old tartness. I asked if she liked her new maid. 'No, not much.' And when I said I'd been to see

[1] Daughter of Peter and Charlotte Jenkins.

Pansy, she said, 'Oh, bad luck.' About her sister Barbara she is ambivalent; half piqued that she won't have her to live with her for ever, half desirous to prove that it would be awful to live with her for three months.

May 17th: Litton Cheney, abed Sunday morning

How the Stones pamper one and treat one as 'special' – impossibly so – resulting in guilt feelings. My fellow-guest is that gross object Leslie Hartley, who has become so repellently fat, and such a dedicated full-time hypochondriac and insomniac that it is surprising to hear him say something perceptive or funny, as he often does. His fat can hardly be thought of as such, but is more like liquid in a silken container. Can he be unaware of the impression he makes, and is it in spite of or because of it that he tries to ingratiate himself by pawing, patting and nuzzling up? I had just pounded quickly through his last book, a hopeless affair, when he rang the front doorbell (the Stones had gone out) and stood there, mottled and perplexed, in front of one of the bearded thugs he employs to drive him, and whom (he told me later) he had just quarrelled with and sacked. Since then he has slept and talked about not sleeping so much that I have retired with relief to the third eleven of insomniacs. He has thrice said to me in a meaning, confidential tone, 'I think my insomnia comes from *below the belt*', my eye naturally gliding to what is there – a great smooth rounded protuberance which must have caused his tailor much difficulty.

We were a large party for dinner – the delightful Hubbards, both of whom I find immensely attractive, and Sylvia Townsend Warner with her white pointed face like the Queen of Diamonds and absurd diction. I sat next to John Hubbard at dinner and talked about Chomsky whom I had been reading in the train. He (J.H.) has a delightfully quick darting mind and his eyes blink as he leaps from stepping-stone to stepping-stone. Sylvia Townsend Warner was unexpectedly forthcoming and talked to me intimately on the sofa about the death of her female mate.

May 22nd

To Christopher Mason's film about Charleston and Duncan. A gathering of the Bloomsbury relics – Bunny, Angelica, Angus Davidson, Little Barbara, Quentin and Olivier, Raymond, Desmond, Carringtons, Penroses. Everyone was enthusiastic and indeed it is a great thing to have done. He has very sensitively caught the atmosphere of activity, peace, tremendous fun, beauty, and comical ram-shackleness; he has suggested through their portraits the personalities of the dead – Roger, Maynard, Vanessa. Not enough about Clive. After the film a bar was opened and a jolly party developed. Bunny, Magouche and I dined along with a beautiful American called Jane Gunther, who talked to me with love and admiration about Anthony and Lily West. She says Lily is absolutely 'brilliant' but I didn't gather in what way.

June 21st

Yet again – failure, *total*, with Julia. Yet again she flounced out of my flat banging the door and saying that we are constitutionally unfitted to get on with each other. I must accept this, and failure too, which is always disagreeable.

I think her mental state is by no means all right. She told me she wanted to ring up Margaret at Thorington, and I discovered that the reason was to find out the address of the hospital she had been in. When I said I could give it her, she admitted that she hadn't the least idea where it was, not even that it was in London. All she wanted to do in my flat, which could not be done in hers, was tie up a parcel of some clothes she had borrowed and put the letters (substituting a milder one to matron) in envelopes. She had no idea how many stamps went on a letter.

June 24th: Spain

Janetta was waving from Málaga Airport terrace, and in no time we were purring along the familiar yet ever-deteriorating coast road in her magnificent white Mercedes. It is incredibly luxurious, privileged and comfortable. I capitulated to its grandeur at once and delighted in her delight in it. At Marbella we drew in beside Jaime's little old house, now doomed to be pulled down, and looking forlorn and dwarfed by a huge skeleton block of flats going up next door. Enter suddenly Jaime in a red check shirt disgruntled by a business lunch. We didn't linger but set off for Benahavis. The country isn't nearly so parched and papery as in August – there's a lovely lot of green and some flowers. Very smoothly and tenderly Janetta took her superb car through the ford and there we were met by Georgie, Jean-Pierre and their sweet little Chloe, laughing and with forget-me-not-blue eyes.

Janetta has a huge staff. There are a married couple, dark, beaky-nosed Temi (who has a wry intelligent expression and rattling talk); there is the washerwoman, 'Auntie'. We live therefore in old-fashioned luxury, and as Janetta shops and cooks, it's hard to know what the servants do. 'Almost nothing', she says. But they are a happy community, and this is invaluable to her, even though they eat mountains of food.

The house has not changed, but blossomed and burgeoned, putting out new embellishments everywhere – plates, jugs, pictures. Every time Jaime comes he brings it a 'present'. (Last night he had a glass picture of the Virgin under his arm.)

I had merely nibbled my one o'clock aeroplane lunch so hunger began to gnaw before our ten-thirty dinner. I slaked it on a few ripe strawberries while picking them; then whisky. A first swim in the pool. I mean to do this every day, also to be as accommodating as I possibly can to Janetta's way of life and other people's feelings and desires – probably to quiet my conscience for my recent failure with Julia, and prove to myself that I'm not an entirely selfish irritable old brute. Luckily adaptation seems so far effortless. Everything here is so perfectly designed to soothe, comfort, rest and content the spirit that I can't envisage getting bouts of prickliness or doing anything but revel in my surroundings. All to bed soon after dinner: it's not, oddly enough, very hot.

June 25th

Woke to the sound of rain. Or was it the fountain? Behind my four-poster bed with its lace curtains there is actually a BELL, and when I press it Temi appears within three minutes with a tray of coffee, bread and home-made marmalade. Was it rain, I asked? Oh no, nothing but a little mist. It is, however, raining quite hard. My room is darkened by a dense screen of creepers to keep the terrace cool.

Jaime disappeared early and I settled to correct the proofs of Robert's book[1] on the terrace.

[1] *The Green Flag.*

A first dip into the beach life and the sea itself – pellucid and warm. Janetta, Jaime and myself – the young were expected to join us but didn't – bathed and lunched off *pez de espada* and *chanquetes* at a quite attractive beach restaurant, where only the human beings were vulgar and garish, exposing the glistening meat of their bodies.

Very much hotter, crushingly so. Arrived home, I got at once into the pool and then sat solidly at Robert's book, which needs an unexpected amount of correction.

In the cool of evening I walked alone up the stream and climbed uphill through dry maquis plants and pines. The three young dressed up considerably in preparation for a descent on the town. Georgie is loving and compliant towards Jean-Pierre, who seems to be champing for something to do. Left alone, with darkness falling, Janetta and I naturally discussed them all. Later we sat out at a candlelit table beside the gurgling fountain under an infinitely remote black velvet sky sprinkled with tiny stars.

July 4th

Janetta, Jaime, Ed [Gilbert] and I went on a projected weekend trip to the National Park at Cazorla. It was late already and night fell as we wound up the endless lacets of the Ronda road, entering the town at its last moment of *animación*. Crowds in impeccably clean summer clothes filled the streets, and the air with the harsh sound of their voices. The façade of the old bull-ring gleamed white in the lamplight. As we sat eating in a small café, I felt tired. But afterwards we drove on through the darkness, reaching the parador at Antequera in the small hours.

July 5th

The night was appallingly hot and the Antequera dogs indefatigable. Oh, those dogs of Antequera! All night long, bass, tenor, treble and counter-tenor dogs performed tirelessly in every possible combination – solo, duet, trio, quartet or full chorus. I half stifled myself with my head under my sausage pillow and contrived to sleep a little. We started early next morning and drove through such beauty that it was impossible to feel tired; rolling plains of pinkish-white earth, sown with olives, large and small, in varying patterns, and finally up through pinewoods to the new parador at Cazorla, a National Park where people come to shoot deer and wild boar. Janetta and Jaime have a large room overlooking the famous view and commiserated with Ed and me for our two monks' cells overlooking the garage. Actually I don't like the 'view', which consists of smooth English lawns edged by a precipice and beyond it scratchy grey mountains, mostly pine-covered. We stopped on the way up to look at some tall orchids, irises and thalictrum growing in a damp armpit.

July 6th

This parador stands at four thousand feet, but in the full heat of morning we climbed another two thousand feet in search of a 'rare violet' which the porter said might still be in flower, but only just. We found some bunches of violet leaves and I rushed into a thicket in search of flowers, found none and tore my legs to ribbons. I grew stronger as we climbed, perhaps from the excitement of seeing so many strange new plants – pink with grey leaves, clear blue, yellow or white, scrambling over the rocks like lichen or coral, all bathed in brilliant light and brooded over by the scent of pines and maquis. No sooner had we got down and I had crammed my flowers in water than we were off again, winding through the network of roads. Lunch at a *venta* under its flowery trellis, off fried eggs, salad and wine. Our table was set among pots of geraniums and two red-legged partridges in tiny cages. Afterwards, drowsy beyond everything, we all wanted to go home and subside on our beds.

At about seven, we set off by another route to the 'nacimiento del Guadalquivir', which Jaime was anxious to see. Following a wild damp valley beside the infant river (Ed and I got out and rushed whooping after some giant orchids) we came to the source itself – a still pool of dark water enclosed in a smooth barrel of rock. Mysterious and awe-inspiring, and all round was freshness and greenery, a surfeit of plants, including a lovely red-brown foxglove. 'There's a wolf!' cried Jaime, and only he and I saw it – a greyish creature slinking along, with a rather bushy tail. Uncertain of the way home, dusk falling, we took a rough track that bore us aloft through sensational Gustave Doré peaks, to the charming little town of Cazorla terraced on the lower slopes of the mountains. It was full of Sunday evening gaiety; even adolescent boys wore spotless shirts and trousers, and the little girls had been lovingly arrayed in freshly ironed frocks, bows in their hair and white sandals. We sat in the square, making our dinner off whisky tapas while we watched this lively pageant: grandparents with the littlest children on their knees, bigger ones racing each other with prams full of sleeping babies, abandoned moenads flying round the square or circling in ritual and obsessional isolation, or running with their arms round each other's waists. Hardly any were quarrelling. Behind in the darkness stood magnolias and oleanders in flower, the handsome tall façades of the houses and the indigo sky with a thumbnail moon. It seemed a perfectly happy existence. Really, I reflected, perhaps it wasn't so bad being a human being here. I thought of Oxford Street and people futilely struggling for enjoyment from telly, cinema, etc. In the mountains we had asked the way of a forester's wife, whose contented face seemed to show that she missed none of those so-called civilised things, but was busy and happy with her isolated lot. Home through the darkness smelling of pines.

July 13th: Alhaurin el Grande

It's always an effort to adjust to a new life that is not one's own, though I do it so often that I'm becoming almost an adept. We breakfast, dine and go to bed much earlier here than at Tramores. The heat is if anything greater, lacking the breezes from the sea. Lynda is smiling, beautiful and serene, but there's an undercurrent of nervous tension about her, repression, monkishness; she has even become more flat-chested. If we are alone for a moment Gerald tells me of his love for her and boasts of his good fortune. He doesn't fail, either, to emphasise that it is wonderful for her to have a house, a car, freedom to 'work' (but what *is* this work?). And can this attractive girl continue to abjure sex? The heat drives everyone to their beds in the afternoon. In the cool of the evening we drove into the vega and had a walk. Literally only when the sun is sinking is it possible to do so. At dinner, it needs only two glasses of wine to make Gerald argumentative and coat-trailing. Perhaps I irritate him; perhaps I remind him of the agitating past; perhaps I have slipped into the skin of their last visitor. At any rate there was an abrasive note in his conversation last night. I tried to brake for all I was worth – but perhaps not sufficiently.

July 14th

I sit outside under the shade of the large balcony and listen to the deafening noise of the crickets. In the bank opposite my bedroom some beautiful blue birds called bee-eaters have their nests. Their swooping erratic flight is as exotic as their kingfisher colour and they utter whooping cries. I have just walked with Gerald to see a rare and very poisonous wild delphinium; not far but the sweat rolled down my face. Today I shall be back at Halkers, impossible thought.

Yesterday passed as before. After tea a drive up the hillside to Coín. All the images I connect with Spain were there – the mountains, velvet-folded in the evening light, men riding loaded mules, a smell of burning aromatic wood; the hour of the *paseo* with the girls in crisp clean frocks and the whitewashed houses greenish under a sky shading from pink to lavender, piercing purity of sounds which find no obstruction in the clear air. Nostalgic smell of rue on fingers that have picked it. Lynda is a little hypochondriacal and neurotic or just easily tired. Gerald is loving and supporting and admiring, but it must be like living with a hedgehog and I wonder that she puts up with him so well. She always speaks quietly to him, never a cross word, but I do feel there's something nun-like and unhealthy about her very restraint.

We dined out of doors by candlelight and he boasted about women who had been in love with him – Helen Anrep, Angela Culme-Seymour – and then returned to the perennial analysis of Carrington's character and behaviour. It's very peaceful here, very beautiful, but I'm glad not to be staying longer. I haven't Lynda's dedication, nor motive for it.

July 16th: West Halkin Street

Back two days, but my toes have hardly touched bottom yet. I have seen Eardley and Joan and Cochemé, and talked to many others on the telephone.

Julia has been staying at the Savernake Hotel. At first the food was 'delicious'; after a week it was 'quite impossible'. She is too isolated and thinks of going to the Three Swans at Hungerford. Mary asked her to lunch, but when she said would she come over again when I was there for a weekend she replied, 'I wouldn't dream of it. Frances and I have fallen out.' M.: 'Whatever about?' J.: 'I'd rather not discuss it. I know you think she's marvellous, but I don't.' M.: 'So you mean you really don't want to be asked while she's here?' J.: 'Most certainly not.'

What is my reaction? A sigh of relief principally. But sadness too, and a sense of waste.

July 22nd

Back from two days at Glyndebourne, staying on my own in an Alfriston Hotel, full of noisy children and middle-aged parents who had not a single thing to say to each other at breakfast but splashed boisterously in the swimming pool after dark. Solitude in a crowd is always rather an eerie experience, though I was not much alone, going to Maw's new opera with Desmond on Sunday night and visiting Quentin and family and Duncan next day before *Eugene Onegin*. No sooner back than the telephone begins ringing and I have someone coming to every meal until next weekend. Yesterday Nicko for a drink and Joan for supper. Nicko and I talked of Robert's book – agreeing mainly – and he also told me that about eighteen months ago Janetta had consulted him about the legal aspects of her marrying Jaime, saying that 'they might as well', for 'conventional reasons', etc. This surprised me as I suppose conventionality in those I love and respect always does, yet I have a ghostly feeling I've heard it from Nicko before. When we were in Warsaw he asked her about the marriage project and she said, 'Oh, no, Jaime doesn't want to.' This must have been when I left them alone in the hotel at Cracow.

August 4th

Not exactly thoughts, but confused emotions, were aroused by being given the proofs of the Carrington letters to read by Noel at the weekend. They are amazingly evocative of her personality and that included an element which was near-genius, or so it seems to me, original, inventive particularly when combining melancholy moods with high comedy.

Far the best were written at Tidmarsh, when all her feelings were concentrated on Lytton and painting. This was also the best period of her painting. By the time I knew her a certain disintegration had begun, partly from her different love affairs, with Ralph, Gerald, Henrietta Bingham, Beakus, and her social life. There was also her strange guilt about what she often refers to as her 'inside' – her more intimate feelings, her painting, being a female – and this made her secretive about her work and produced the tendency to lie which so maddened anyone who was in love with her. But the result is still a very fascinating book.

August 18th

Back in London after a very nice visit to Eardley with Dadie (whom I drove there and back in my Mini). We all got on extremely well, without so much as stepping back to see if and how we were doing so. I really love Dadie's company. The mesh of his enjoyment has become, it seems to me, much wider – Julia would disapprove, but I like it. On the way home he told me that Roger Senhouse is dying. And full of life, energy and enjoyment as he is, he declares that he 'looks forward to dying himself'.

I returned to find two boosts to my ego in my post – a nice letter and cheque from John Murray for my last translation, and the offer of a new one for Knopf, via Hilary Rubinstein. These two items people a silent and lonely day, with hardly a tinkle on the telephone, but lots to do. Wrote to Bunny, read *Julius Caesar*.

Last week I had two delightful meetings with Duncan. He came to *Carmen* with me at the Coliseum, arriving with wild hair and somewhat tremuloso, having walked all the way in haste from the Embankment underground. (He belongs to the generation that almost never takes a taxi.) He was thereafter absolutely alert and interested, and remained the best possible companion, eating cold supper in my flat until midnight. Next day I went to have a drink with him in the basement of Pat Trevor-Roper's house where he is now lodged. He has made it very attractive, with lovely pictures, painted screens and books. Beside Pat, we only had the unprepossessing 'Don' (poet Paul Roche) and 'my new friend, David Pape', a young Canadian. I asked Eardley what was supposed to be the point of Don? 'He has the most beautiful figure in the world.'

Georgia took me to Ken Tynan's pornographic revue *Oh, Calcutta!* at the Round House. I got there early and stood watching the mixed crowds coming in – self-conscious, demure, hearty and 'beat'. The show presented no surprise except perhaps that beautiful naked bodies are more beautiful when fully displayed, and the bush is an adornment. There were some lovely girls, particularly a negress; two muscular Michael-Angelesque young men and two others that were flabby and unattractive. There was something inevitably phoney in the assumed lustfulness of their movement and dancing, when no male had the ghost of an erection. And the little sketches were despicably feeble, their prep-school humour sprinkled with defiantly uttered four-letter words. Could anything have been made of such a performance? Yes, if it had been (a) really funny and (b) really pornographic.

I got a fearful tickle in my throat and nearly expired of trying to stop coughing. Georgia thought I was upset by the performance, and said she was, and 'had no idea it would be all about SEX'. I'm not sure if I managed to convince her that I was not in the faintest degree embarrassed, but I've had a brute of a summer cold for a fortnight and can't get rid of it.

August 20th

Julian's voice on the telephone made me realise how much I have missed him and worried about him. 'Not without reason', he replied, and came later in the afternoon to tell me the pathetic story of Tam in Italy. As I suspected, he took time off and went with her to Richard King's Tuscan house, taking in a couple of operas and a motor drive from Verona on the way. Though far from well, Tam was set on this part of the holiday. But she couldn't unwind.

Julian is the last person who can stand such a strain, and he was worried by her inability to keep a face up to the rest of the world, and only reveal her tremendous anxiety to him. With her earlier symptoms of paralysis, the picture looks like hysteria, as described by Freud.[1] Julian is going to report on her state to the Hospital for Nervous Diseases, where she was before. But Margaret tells me there is a complete schism between the doctors there and the psychiatrists. The nerve doctors refuse to bow to the Unconscious. It is as if all the wind instruments in an orchestra refused to pay attention to the conductor.

The load on Julian's back at present is piteous to contemplate. Tam has no money and no job; there's no one else to take responsibility. I urged him not to try living together as soon as she comes back, on the grounds that two drowning people are worse than one. He always says she has lots of friends and I hope he can find one to shelter her for a while; meanwhile she clearly needs psychiatric treatment.

September 24th

Yesterday afternoon I went to a preview of Tristram's telly film of David Cecil talking about his friends. Walking among the macaws and other exotic plumed and feathered birds of Wardour Street, I suddenly met three birds of more sober appearance, but distinction and confidence, peering and stalking slowly; visitors from another world. 'Cecils', I thought at once, and so they turned out to be – the

---

[1] November 1994. Poor Tam, now the wife of Andrew Murray-Thripland, the mother of two children and a qualified lawyer, is in a wheelchair with multiple sclerosis.

Duchess of Devonshire and Lady Harlech ('Mina' and 'Mowcher'). We herded into a tiny theatre. Rachel, in a really comically hideous hat, suddenly said urgently to Tristram: 'Would we let you down if we *ate a sandwich*?' (It was five o'clock.) She took one out of her case and began munching avidly, reminding me of Molly (MacCarthy) in her sudden abandon to the physical. David was much at home on the screen, easy, witty, and sometimes plumbing depths beneath the relaxed talk; confidently presenting his values – his hedonism, Christianity, enjoyment, and worldliness. Yes, that last I suppose on reflection was the sediment that was antipathetic to me. The famous people he had known included Lytton, but he spoke of him with a certain condescension.

September 30th

Weekend at the Cecils with the glorious Bayleys, Hugh and Laura. No more congenial company could be found, and conversation raged like a forest fire. Beautiful Indian summer weather.

Sebastian has just paid me a long lunch-time visit. He wrote that his 'dear friend Charles, who looked after me for forty years has died. I am in a distressed condition.' Well, so he was I'm sure, though he looked pink, plump and well. The garrulity of mourning. I've long since learned my lesson, and I at once began asking about Charles. I have only to open my ears and listen, and out poured a stream of symptoms, nurses, decline, funeral arrangements, wills. After which he moved to Morgan and began all over again. I think he thoroughly enjoyed telling me it all, and so did I hearing it, not being emotionally engaged. Morgan's 'policeman' Bob and his wife May told Sebastian that only after he had become ill did Morgan confess his homosexuality, and they were amazed and appalled. What puzzles Sebastian is that Morgan met Bob years ago through another policeman who was a 'roaring Queer', and as Bob's only charm was his looks he simply doesn't believe that the relation was platonic. Also he (Sebastian) has been left all Morgan's 'chattels'. These include books and diaries which he has been reading, in which (though there was much about lust – it figured largely in Morgan's life) the only likely reference to Bob was 'Bob and I ~'[1]. Conclusive, I should say. I didn't realise how important a figure Sebastian was to Morgan, perhaps the most important in his life. He has left him also a life interest in all his royalties, capital, etc., so he has done pretty well. Talking – or rather listening to it – about Morgan, it struck me he had been something of a leprechaun in the MacCarthy sense, and I asked Sebastian whether he thought he had warmth of character, deep affections. From his rather uncertain reply I deduced that he didn't. Response to the warmth of others, preoccupied with lust, but not a man of outgoing feelings. The thing that struck Sebastian most had been the *misery* expressed in the diary. All diaries got that balance wrong, I said. One rushes to them in moments of gloom, not to confide triumph or optimism. But what was he unhappy about? About himself, his idleness and ineffectiveness. Simon Raven's picture was not far off the mark, Sebastian thought. Beside the homosexual novel there are a number of pornographic stories and the diaries, and all will some day probably see the light.

---

[1] Presumably a code sign that sex had taken place.

October 23rd

Bunny has just been to see me fresh from America. To my utter amazement he said his publisher there had talked admiringly of my translations, saying that I wrote such excellent prose.

Last night Raymond came here to talk about the Carrington Letters which he is reviewing. I gave him as good a tutorial on her character and life as I possibly could, interesting myself a good deal in my task. I feel I know her emotional construction through and through – but had to think hard when trying to analyse some of her mental processes. I was relieved because Raymond had been moved by the exchange of letters between Carrington and me over my going to live with Ralph, for it cost me quite an inner wrench to agree to Bunny's publishing them. Raymond thinks the book as a whole fascinating, the end profoundly moving, and likes least the whimsical letters, as I do.

He and I went on to a party at Jock Murray's in honour of Iris Origo's new book. The company was dwindling, but we dined afterwards with those two and Mrs Murray. It mystified me that Iris, whom I've met but a few times and briefly, once again singled me out, insisted on sitting opposite me at dinner and carried on a high-powered, rather intimate, electrically charged conversation with me. But I was flattered, and still more so when she said to me, 'You've always been a life-giver.'

At the party I was introduced to Jack Lambert, Literary Editor of the *Sunday Times*, and little Kelly Clark, Kenneth Clark's pretty and intelligent daughter. Lambert at once greeted me with an exaggerated deference in which I smelt a rat. He had 'long heard about me', etc., etc., etc. Then, with hardly a pause, he launched an attack on Bloomsbury. 'I'm proud to say I'm Raymond's BOSS,' he said aggressively. 'And Cyril's and Desmond's. Of course I've always found Bloomsbury infuriating. They were so supercilious, they *despised* everyone; I simply hate it.' Kelly Clark intervened and said Raymond was the kindest of men, not supercilious at all. And look what a charming man Duncan was. J.L.: 'Oh yes, Raymond *is* supercilious. They all were and are. What I feel about them' (warming to his work and talking louder, shouting almost) 'is that they're just *dolls*.' (He repeated this more than once.) 'There's nothing to them at all. No one cares now about anything they did.' F.: (mildly, I hope) 'You mean Maynard and Virginia's achievements are worthless?' He brushed this aside with a hasty 'Yes', and returned to his dolls. I can't remember responding except that Kelly and I looked at each other with exaggerated gestures of dismay and I said, I think: 'Well, you *are* going it.' And then, 'You know, I think a lot of people a good deal *younger* than you don't agree with you,' which was, I daresay, below the belt. I felt appalled that Raymond and Desmond should work for such a master, who was evidently seething with violent hatred and frustration, and seemed to me a thoroughly nasty man.

November 2nd

This week sees the combined explosion of the exhibition of Carrington's pictures and the publication of her Letters edited by Bunny – they are sure to arouse in some that hostile anti-Bloomsburyism that appeared after Holroyd. I have read the book and returned to it, and the past has been ruffled up and revived with all its conflicting and violent feelings. How strange that the sex life of a living person – Gerald – should be so openly revealed to the world. Discussing what the dead 'would have felt' has never seemed to me what Freddie Ayer calls 'meaningful', but had Carrington known when alive that her letters and diaries would be published, she 'would have been' amazed and horrified, I imagine. But the activation of this emotional area makes me feel tense and as it were pregnant and that I shall be quite glad when Thursday is over.

Julian rang me and talked in considerable distress, for almost an hour. How I wish I could console him! He comes to dinner tonight and I do hope I can get him to unwind and unload a little of his sorrows, which seem chiefly to be *desperate* anxiety for Tam and guilt because he feels he can't bear the burden for her without cracking himself.

November 4th

Julian kept up a bold front, particularly about his work, which has presented some worrying developments. But when at dinner I asked him about Tam he couldn't restrain his tears, to which I added mine. It was heartbreaking to hear him say, 'One *mustn't* abandon people,' and he repeated how much he loved her, yet on the evening that she came to London and he told her that living together was impossible, I was amazed to hear him say that he had told her she 'was a bad wife, not to ask him about his work', surely unnecessarily cruel when he was sacking her? Small wonder she quietly departed, taking most of her things, before he was awake. Oh, the pathos of it all. If good, kind, sensitive people can torture each other so, what must it be like to be mixed up with real brutes?

The Carrington pregnancy ends tomorrow; the 'waters break' with a review by Holroyd in *The Times*, I believe.

November 6th

Holroyd's review was immensely long and very favourable to the Letters. Now I sit up in bed pondering over the opening ceremony to the show at the Upper Grosvenor. The crush was inconceivable – quite a large room was continuously wedged with young and old, for hours on end. No fear of being face-to-face with Julia, whom I glimpsed in the distance, but every soul I knew seemed to be there. The pictures were invisible and not many people looked at them; those who did, commented appreciatively.

Among disquieting encounters – I had one with a bearded man who turned out to be Raisley Moorsom.[1] Having exchanged a few words with him I thought I had finished – but no, he returned later and, fixing me with a gimlet gaze, insisted on talking about the remote past in the very centre of the throng where our words were drowned in the surrounding hubbub. Finally he shouted softly, 'You made me more unhappy than I've ever been in my life.' What could I reply?

The show was to be opened by Lord Eccles, and Bunny brought him to introduce him to me. His face was familiar. I dimly remember hearing that long ago, when I was a young bookseller's assistant, he had taken a sort of distant shine to me. His speech in fact began in the most ludicrous and insignificant way by saying that he had opened a book out of which fell a piece of paper saying 'Bought from Frances Marshall'. Uncomprehending amazement from the vast majority present who had never heard of the creature. Next day, he went on, he was asked to open the

---

[1] He had been in love with me in my twenties.

Carrington show, so 'of course he agreed'. He then proceeded to make my blood boil by saying that Carrington was not a professional painter and only painted to assert herself and because she didn't want to have a child. He ended on a note similar to Jack Lambert's – about what a rotten lot the Bloomsburies were.

November 9th

The re-turning of the field of my deeply ploughed emotions by the publishing of Carrington's Letters has been more agitating than perhaps I expected.

On Waterloo Station, on my way to stay with Kitty, I met the jet-black Osé and Caroline West.[1] Osé politely and with snowy smiles offered to carry my suitcase and I felt apologetic for having got myself a first-class ticket for fear of the crowds on this late Friday train. In my comfortable carriage I was suddenly accosted by a nicely dressed old lady about the 'blacks' and how everyone hated them. (I'm sure she hadn't seen me with Osé, but I rather hoped she would on our arrival at Salisbury.) 'In Australia,' she said proudly, 'where I've lived for a long time, we manage things better; they travel in trains like other people, but *they go back to their reserves at night.*' The gap between us was too big to begin to bridge, so I hummed and hawed and waited for her to shut up.

Osé is indeed very, very black, a shiny black lined with pink, with little eyes and very thick lips. When I had got over the slight shock of his appearance head-on, as it were, I saw that he was rather beautiful, and admired his domed forehead and delicate gesturing hands. He is also intelligent and thoughtful, though his obsessional Marxism leads him to take every problem back rather boringly to that first principle so that what might be an interesting conversation subsides in muffled sand.

Before leaving London I wrote a short, sharp letter to Lord Eccles, encouraged by Janetta.

The Sunday papers produced their right and left about the Carrington Letters – Raymond so tenderly flattering and consoling that I feel he has almost overdone it.

Little Joan rang up this morning to say with characteristic deflation that she had been to the Carrington exhibition and there was no one there but Quentin and she thought she 'had a slight, decorative gift, not really good'. She has told me at least three times that Virginia Powell has 'a *tiny* gift, of which she has made the most'. Eardley, of course, has none. Ralph used to tease her and tell her to her face the fact that she couldn't bear to hear any other painter praised; and got her to laugh and admit that it was torture to her.

Margaret spent the evening after Carrington's show with Julia, who apparently pitched in to me, hot and strong, and has worked up a lot of things I never said into never-to-be-forgiven insults.

November 10th

In my letter to Lord Eccles I said that it was quite untrue to say Carrington wasn't a professional and that if he felt so antagonistic to her and her circle I couldn't think why he consented to open the show. He replied that it had been 'silly to ask

---

[1] Kitty's daughter and her African husband.

him, and sillier to accept' and 'he only did it for the frivolous reason you know' –
i.e. my name in the book.

I went to see the Carrington pictures this morning, viewed them at leisure and
pondered over her gifts, her character and my feelings about her. In championing
her cause, as I did to Lord Eccles for instance, I have to some extent suppressed
my own criticisms, such as they are. Looking dispassionately at the pictures (which
are shockingly hung), I thought they showed an immense natural talent, which
perhaps never fully matured. Looking round, I felt the colour glowed, but there
was something static, rather than productive of that heart-leap of excitement. The
public response has led to what was saleable – her drawings – being very quickly
snapped up, but I think her letters have aroused even more interest.

November 20th

Last night I togged up in my best and went to a party for Pat Trevor-Roper far away
in Highgate. A large, noisy, smartish crowd gathered and drank and shouted at
each other till hearing became impossible. After bellowing at John Hill, Sebastian
Walker, Adrian Daintrey, and Cynthia Gladwyn, I found myself trying to guess
from the rat-trap opening and shutting of Bob Gathorne-Hardy's mouth what he
was saying – something about Julian Vinogradoff having gone quite mad on the
subject of her mother whom she didn't care for when alive, and refusing to let
him, Bob (Ottoline's only surviving literary executor), publish the second volume
of her memoirs. Whether Bertie Russell was or was not her lover somehow came
into it. I joined Raymond with plates of food, felt an immense wave of fondness
for him, and as I have now quite decided not to go on a Hellenic cruise with
Eardley, Mattei and Dadie, I suggested that he might meet me in north Italy after
I had (perhaps) spent a short while with Jaime and Janetta in Corfu next spring, a
plan very much more to my taste.

December 7th

The load of other people's unhappiness that landed on me yesterday sank my ship.
It reduced me to loathed palpitations and a feeling of desperation because I can
never be sure of getting time for work, dull slog though it may sometimes be.

The drive home from Lambourn ended stickily, as most of the traffic lights
weren't working (the Government and the electricians' union standing up to each
other like two bristling dogs). Nor was my wireless. It seems likely I shall have no
heat, light and nothing to cook on. Must buy some candles and a torch.

I rang Janetta and she came to lunch and I loved seeing her. Then Bunny rang
up and gave a huge sigh over the telephone. 'What does that mean, Bunny?' 'Oh,
I'm LOW!' – in a shaking voice. 'Not physically – emotionally.' I have asked him
to dinner.

Bunny arrived in a great state about his current love. Did she really love him as
she seemed to when they had an evening together, or not at all, he asked, and I
tried my best to console him without falsifying the facts as I believed them to be –
which always seems to me too disrespectful of the confiding friend. It's difficult,
though, and not always successful. I said I thought she certainly loved him, but
probably not as much as he did her. That her life was very full of lovers of various
sorts, concerns, pure sociality, restlessness, and that the *only* thing he could do was
make the most of what he'd got. To try and 'clear the air by a row, so that she

would realise how insensitive she'd been' was quite fatal. One couldn't enforce love, and a sense of guilt didn't increase it, quite the reverse.

He took me out to dinner, and I hope I cheered him up a little. Did I reconcile him to his position *at all*? I doubt it. Once or twice he said, 'I'm perfectly crazy.' Or, 'Why won't she come away from it all and live with me and be my love?' He was at times very close to tears.

4.30 p.m. Today was supposed to be the great day of 'political strikes', but blackouts held off here until the coffee stage, when the electricity suddenly went completely. I sat down then to my work table, but darkness is beginning to fall and my flat has got gradually colder. No fires, of course, and no possibility of cooking anything or boiling a kettle. Well, I thought, I'll sit near the radiator. And found to my dismay that that, too, was going cold. So, no hot water either! If it doesn't come on before evening and there are no street and traffic lights I don't intend going to the orchestra; it will be too frightening, and probably cold when there. All I can do, and I've done it, is get into bed and light two long orange candles fixed in bottles. Really, what a go! I wonder how Julia is managing?

All I have for company is my little transistor wireless. Doorbells don't ring, lifts don't work, and I'm doubtful even about the telephone.

December 9th

We are in CRISIS. Yesterday, as I lay in bed at 5 p.m., Magouche rang up and suggested my going round. She 'had a fire'. I did, most gladly, and found Rose, Mary and later Janetta and Tristram Powell. Mary is treating it like the war, and frankly adoring it. I find it hard not to bristle at this a little, although I know it is partly that she enjoys helping people in distress. Perhaps, also, a background of boredom. This morning we have wintry sun, and so far no absolute cuts, merely great reductions. The shops operate on few lights, 'patriotically', people compare their sufferings, ladies whisper over the counter, 'Any candles?' as if asking for dildoes. There are none anywhere. What happens if and when my five, long, peach-coloured ones expire?

December 16th

Electricity cuts over, Christmas bearing down on us, people vanish. Magouche is off in a day or two; the thread of life dwindles. For that reason perhaps I've put more concentration into my relations with those few people I have seen. Margaret and I went to the theatre last night, and I longed to cheer her up by some special attentions for the bleak time she's been having (Lionel off with Dunyusha all the time, evasive, untruthful, and – when he is there – saying everything is 'her fault').

Lord Snow booms away on the wireless that we're 'all done for'. A sympathetic Russo-Germanic growl from Professor Karl Popper says that there's no such thing as certainty, only degrees of belief. This is something I've long had a high degree of belief for. 'What is truth?' he was asked. 'Correspondence with facts,' he rapped back. 'We know what that *means* even if we are unable to be sure what it *is*.' I find this sympathetic and reassuring. He reckons induction is out as a valid means of acquiring scientific information – it only reduces the field of error.

December 21st

A Sunday in London yesterday. Strange, and in its way eventful. Got up slowly after a good go with the Sunday papers in bed then, after an early lunch, I went off to see a show of Morandi at the Royal Academy; not one of those pictures had I ever seen before, but a postcard Lawrence used to keep on the dining-room mantelpiece at Lambourn quite bowled me over and had remained in my mind. Rightly so. He is a superb artist, splendidly sure and subtle. A long time since I looked at pictures by a comparative modern so satisfying, and I would have adored to possess one.

Back at my work table I suddenly heard far-off but unmistakable sounds of revolution; organised shouts, pulsating to a regular beat like a dog's bark, gradually getting nearer. I put on my fur coat, went out on the balcony and saw a procession coming up West Halkin Street, carrying banners, shouting and walking sluggishly. A police car headed the long cavalcade (nearly as long as the street), two police buses followed and there were lines of policemen hedging it in on each side. They were shouting 'FRANCO OUT!' and other things in favour of freeing the Basque prisoners; of course they were heading towards the Spanish Embassy. But though to me a crowd is always frightening, and crowd emotion more so, I felt more pathos than menace in this one. They seemed to be wearily and hopelessly performing a ritual act of drudgery. They seemed like a faecal mass relentlessly and slowly pursuing its way down an intestine. And I wasn't interested enough to follow them into the anus of Belgrave Square.

Next came the arrival of Robert to fetch me to see a live television performance by Noel Annan in the series 'An Evening With'. Perhaps because I didn't try to make him confide, he suddenly and apparently effortlessly began. Sitting on my sofa, looking rather desperate but not embarrassed, his hair very long and now sprinkled with silver, his face deeply grooved, he began suddenly: 'Things have been very bad in the home lately.' And went on with what seemed like detachment to say that he thought both he and Cynthia would be glad to end their marriage tomorrow, except for the children. We discussed how much their bad relations upset the children. He said: 'The normal thing in such cases is for one to find someone else, and neither of us has.' That he did 'look around, but couldn't seem to find anyone attractive'. At the time I was relieved because he was so detached and realistic; now I'm rather worried, as one must be when someone is so low, and then I suggested, as I have before, his finding a temporary place separately 'for working in', to see what it was like. 'But I don't know if you much like being on your own?' 'No, the trouble is I hate it.'

The telly performance was amusing for me, as I'd not seen one before – the religious formalities, staring light, silently revolving cameras in the back of which I could just see a tiny picture of what they were looking at. Noel Annan was amusing and lively, we all thought, but the producer irritatingly commented that we were a 'dead audience'. Drinks afterwards and dinner with the Kees, who gave a convincing performance as a secure and happy couple.

Christmas morning, Cranborne

I've woken in peaceful comfort in David and Rachel's spare room, a crisp, still morning, very faint sunshine and snow lying (and also falling) thinly. My room has big windows on each side, and pale light streams in, revealing this understated vision. On the mantelpiece an elegant clock ticks away and gives a silvery chime, harmonising with the rest of my surroundings, but rather disturbing in the small hours.

David and Rachel have hurried off to early church. David's Christianity, I deduce from various signs, gains on him, though this doesn't alter the lively, debonair front he presents. I wonder how it affects his attitude to the inevitably increasing pre-occupation with death, and what and how precise a fairytale his intelligent mind envisages. I really would like to know, but this sort of thing can't be asked, bother it.

Hugh and I arrived in time for lunch yesterday; Laura is in bed with a cold. Rachel is solicitous for everyone's comfort, as aware of one's material needs (and others too) as David is of the drift of one's thought. Perfectly delightful, easy conversation. Hugh's style of talk makes him odd man out from the rest of the family – somewhat ponderously pursuing a subject in a way that is enthralling when one has him alone, as I did over Scientology and the Process. A little walk with Rachel, looking like a robin in a dear little brown knitted cap ending in a scarf. Perfunctory references to Christmas decorations – with wild, uncoordinated gestures David tore the most unsuitable greenery, such as privet, from the hedges and then left his gatherings in a basket in the hall.

I have a delicious sense of there being *heaps of time* – I don't worry about getting up, but lie snug in bed where (breakfast over, with its coffee mysteriously full of large black grounds) I've been trying to bring my mind to bear on an article about Wittgenstein. The desire to keep philosophical muscles active that are long since, I fear, atrophied, is probably futile, like the desire to keep physically nippy or able to read the notes of music. But I wouldn't, I think, try if the trying didn't produce a few exciting gleams among such murky darkness.

Boxing Day

More snow, inclement, and a whirling wind. I was traumatised by Warsaw and Russia last February, and now really fear wintry weather. Yesterday David and I walked through the deserted precincts of the Manor, looking tragically beautiful in its thin white carpet, and picked up a little pile of discarded holly with berries on it. Today looks far less tempting.

The chiming clock on my mantelpiece has mercifully stopped; in fact I believe I made it do so by turning it round. So now there is peace, and that extra silence given by the snow and lack of posts and newspapers. And very welcome isolation, though I know I shall be quite ready when the time comes to re-enter my own life.

Presents were exchanged in Laura's room, bottles of bath essence hastily smuggled to Hugh by Rachel for him to give to me; exclamations of 'Just what I wanted! Telepathy!' My Indian silk scarves seemed to go down well with all.

I spend a good deal of time in my bedroom, reading. Galloped through *Vile Bodies* – pretty good rubbish, really. I was hardly amused at all. Laura is still mainly absent, a pity because her astringency is a valuable ingredient. She came down to dinner last night, and we were discussing some young people having displeased their parents by refusing to get married with a huge fuss. David suddenly got emotional and excited, and said they might at least do this one thing to please their parents. Everyone at the dinner table was against him, and thought that their form of marriage was their own affair. 'Yes, of course,' said David, pink and angry, 'but I should think *less well* of them, if they were so selfish as not to consider their parents' feelings.' Someone said wasn't it equally selfish of the parents not to consider their children's feelings? And David actually replied, 'After all they'd done for their child!' A few minutes later, when we were talking on quite another theme, about paying or not to go into museums (and here we *all* agreed), David took Laura up sharply and she showed, by look and word, that she had become aloof. David said, in a rather insensitive way I've heard him use before with Jonathan, and a little condescendingly: 'Oh, I don't want to be *snubbing*.' Whereas it was plain to me that, for a moment, Laura was acutely critical of David. I think he overestimates the influence he has over his children, and of course the steam from the marriage question came from his uneasiness over Laura's possible marriage to Angelo.[1] But he was admirable in one thing – that after consideration he withdrew what he had said about the need to marry as your parents like, a very hard thing to do gracefully, when his feelings were engaged. For of course he has a very sharp and tender awareness of other people, especially his children, underneath the smooth, even smug enamel surface that came out in his telly interview for Tristram.

He and I had a discussion in the passage, moving from foot to foot on the stairs, about Hamlet's religious beliefs. He thought his excuse for not killing Claudius when praying (that in that case he would send him to heaven) was genuine and didn't see that if so, it was much beastlier, or even less Christian I would say, than one can conceive of Hamlet ever being. Nor would he hear of Hamlet having been tormented by speculative doubt. So he seemed to me to miss the whole point of his character, turning him into a bigoted fanatic and doing so with a somewhat fanatical gleam in his own eye.

Reynolds, Janet and Emma Stone to tea. How Janet suffers to be beautiful! She wore a puff-sleeved crimson blouse and a long tight pink skirt with an agonisingly wide tight belt, pink stockings and purple suede boots. (Someone told me she was at a Royal Command concert the other day in a long white dress with a white bandeau round her head, and a white rose sticking straight out in front 'like a miner's lamp'.) It's all rather gallant, but what happens next? Emma has bloomed suddenly, as girls do, and softened, and was all in sage-green velvet, carefully copied from Kate Greenaway. Reynolds crooning compulsively, and a little too gushingly. They do overdo it a bit. Both were enthusiastic about the Carrington Letters, which they're reading, but when Janet said to me, 'Your sister seems to come alive to me for the first time,' and I remembered that all that is said is that she was 'remarkably ugly' and what savage things in other letters (not printed and I believe suppressed by Noel) about the death of poor Ray's malformed baby, I unthinkingly blurted out, 'But Carrington didn't like Ray at all.' This, of course, put Janet in an awkward spot, caught her out gushing to no purpose, but I tried to retrieve the situation by saying how she did emerge from the White–Garnett letters, and assuming she had confused the two.

I must get up, from my soft warm boat between two windows filled with falling snow. It's nearly eleven.

---

[1] Hornak.

December 27th

Probably I wasn't fair to David, he's an exceptionally loving and sensitive father with very few lapses, and I noticed that he slipped off after dinner to Laura's room after his tiny brush with her and talked to her for a long time. Family communication is at its usual high standard. Last night Hugh was following a train of thought aloud to David, and as it came out, almost painfully, in jerks between 'sort of 's', 'you know's', 'I mean's', I was most deeply impressed by the kind and ingenious way David acted as midwife, anticipating what he wanted to say but not too actively, and reining in his own impatient thoughts in the interests of Hugh's safe delivery of his. It was such a moving display that I couldn't read my book for listening. After we had all gone up there was the usual burst of happy excited talk from Laura's bedroom; I could distinctly make out that all four were talking at once, and '*on dirait*' a cocktail party.

How the time spins away! It began snowing big, claustrophobic flakes at lunchtime, and we walked out masochistically wrapped up as in Russia, Rachel and I together, David and Hugh striding on ahead. Doubts about going to Cecil Beaton's cocktail party, but we crawled off in the dark along slippery white roads. Cecil Beaton very white-haired now, and looking rather ill; his room densely packed with a hopeless hubbub in which surely I saw no faces I knew? But, oh yes, Lettice Ashley-Cooper, Billy Henderson and Frank Tait, Vivien John, Reine Pitman and her daughter Jemima, the Baths and Georgia. Jemima had shrunk from a once-handsome, blooming young woman to a plain schoolgirl. When I asked her if she still ran concerts, a fixed mad stare suddenly came into her eyes and she said, 'Have you heard of the Maharishi? Well, I work for HIM.' Reine told me she had seen Julia last week; she'd told Reine she thought of going to the country again, and looked ill and thin and unhappy. But as usual what is said, or shouted, on these occasions, is very small beer indeed.

I read *Hamlet* all yesterday afternoon and talked to David again, finding a meeting-point about Claudius. Now I've gone on to *Othello*. Woke in the night and read more. It seems insane to read anything else, when there is always inexhaustible Shakespeare.

December 28th

Snow and Shakespeare combine to freeze and preserve my existence here in a way that is marvellously soothing. Last night David read us the prologue to his next book on the Cecil family in the fiery heat of the drawing-room. His writing has become quite illegible, like shorthand – he has therefore to dictate his books. It was a description of Hatfield, patient and loving, vivid and skilful, and he took any small criticisms we made very well, much better than I thought he would. I looked across the room at Hugh and Laura and wondered what they were thinking. Hugh has burgeoned and become his own man, and only needs a little more articulacy; he admires and loves David.

1971

Here we go *again* – it's a weary thought. On 1 January I had a bad go of New Year melancholia, with its dreaded undercurrent of near-madness, tottering reason. But Julian came to dinner and the pleasure of his company and conversation restored me, or set me up at a higher elevation anyway than where he had found it. This London Sunday has swathed itself in freezing butter-muslin, and the futile pleasure of reading the Sunday papers turned to pain. *Horrible* things – with their tales of squashed bodies at football matches, and gradual self-strangulation of each other by cigarette smoke, poison in fish, noise, marijuana. I pushed them aside and hurried to get up and drive off through the pale mist to buy some bread and meat to give Faith, invited for supper tonight.

Yesterday, piano quartets with Margaret, Shirley and Anne Ottaway. We all played badly, as if thinking of other things. I lingered and talked a little to Margaret, who had rung up, desperate, a morning or two ago when I couldn't talk to her. She had been lectured through the night by Lionel telling her they had nothing in common whatever and never had had throughout the forty years of their marriage. It is too cruel. The two swaying trees making up a marriage, unless they intertwine and prop each other up, do seem to set up a grizzly form of mutual abrasion. And I feel Margaret has little love left now for Lionel – yet she is obsessed by him; meanwhile she gets fatter and fatter week by week, stuffing herself to compensate for lack of love. Oh, how sad!

January 13th

Skimming along, as if on roller-skates, I have lately had several sources of quiet happiness. Two outings with Sophie at the weekend. She has become such a dear little girl, and so thoughtful you can talk to her about anything; every moment I had with her was a delight. At the play she wished that 'books had a button you could press and all the people come alive and move about'. At the film of *The Railway Children*, which was very soppy and had caused me several spurious lumps in my throat, she told me 'Sometimes when I'm happy I cry.' She has suddenly grown up, and showed me some excellently written, spelt and expressed holiday work she'd done for her school. That, then, was all golden good, though the thought of her advancing into the frightful world agitates me deeply.

Today, going to a bookshop off the King's Road to buy Iris Murdoch's lectures on Ethics, I looked in and saw David inside with a wave of affection. I wish I had masses more book space; buying books is so enjoyable.

I grow more and more intolerant of the rich and their passionate clinging to their privileges, even including Mary, when she tells me with delight how the friend who took her to the cinema bribed the commissionaire to get them seats ahead of the queue. 'I love that sort of thing,' she said with her cream-licking expression.

January 18th

Weekend at Crichel – all three denizens and Dadie – was immensely enjoyable, though the dust of etymology grows thicker at times. One hardly dare open one's mouth, and the conversation is disrupted while Raymond, burning-eyed, takes a ferret run to the OED next door. 'Never mind – it's the only exercise the dear fellow gets,' says Dadie with his sweetest smile, behind which (enhancing it) remote savagery lurks. Raymond returns triumphantly: 'It's not "de-suétude" but "dé-suetude",' and a coda follows: 'I like to get things right.' He is a little febrile, but says he feels well, and this is borne out (on past observations of mine) by this schoolmaster's mood being in the ascendant. When Raymond is at his sweetest it's a sign he's not feeling well. He does look extremely thin, especially in his touching new pair of 'off the peg' bell-bottoms which reveal that his own bottom is quite unpadded, the usual folds and pockets not being there to conceal this fact. Desmond is suffering from toothache, poor fellow. Pat, just off to Borneo, suddenly looks older. But it has all been delightful in spite of the breath of powdered chalk and blackboards. A lot of my pleasure came from Dadie's immensely life-enhancing presence, and – on the whole – good nature. He did 'rib' Raymond once rather fiercely and I don't think Raymond enjoyed it, though he 'asked for it' by saying, 'I always *nod* to our postman when he brings the letters in the morning.' Dadie: 'Oh, REALLY, Ray? How *extremely* kind and condescending of you! You mean you *actually* say "Good morning" or something of the sort?'

Dadie read a lot from Wordsworth's *Prelude* to us – and other things – and very greatly did we enjoy it. I wish poetry could be more often read aloud, and so well. It doubles the pleasure.

On a walk, Dadie and I talked of nothing but Shakespeare.

January 21st

To Duncan's eighty-sixth birthday party last night – eighteen people to dinner in his basement, and a lavish meal of soup, garlic bread, cold meats and salad, lots of wine. I crawled home at midnight with fearful indigestion, not the least of the things I couldn't digest being close contact with Julia, whom I hadn't expected to see. Close only in the sense of proximity; we greeted each other – no more. I had a momentary brave urge to talk to her, but the occasion didn't offer and I don't think she wanted me to. Butting in when not wanted is not what I like. Otherwise there were many old friends – some had become impressively large: Ros, Olivier Bell appear to be draped monuments. Quentin looked much older than Duncan. He's let his beard grow wild, long and grey and seems to have come straight out of a book of Mrs Cameron's photos. Angus Davidson wailed distressfully about his tiny personal worries and said rather smugly, with his eyebrows going up to his hair, that it was wonderful the way Duncan never worried, but *he* did 'and if one's the worrying sort there's *nothing* one can do about it', with a grimace that was somehow ladylike. I talked to Freda Berkeley about anorexia; her son has a girlfriend who's got it.

As Duncan's party wore on and people left, the survivors grew slightly tipsy, inclined together, threw their arms around each other. Freda and Pat were openly making the most of their last time together (emphasised by a drunken squeeze, him to me) before he goes to Borneo tomorrow. Amaryllis and Nerissa were both peering out of clouds of hair. Fanny has returned to being a male impersonator. A cloistered world, but very lively.

I've just finished reading Iris Murdoch on the Good. She illuminates, but never really gets to grips with the philosophical concept. In other words, she states her credo but hardly tries to justify it, and this I miss.

January 26th

To *Hamlet* with Magouche – an extraordinary evening. I expected to be dismayed but was not; in fact Alan Bates perhaps came nearer to my view of Hamlet's character than anyone else has; he also said the poetry well and showed that he understood every word. With a good King and Polonius, and not bad Gertrude and Ophelia, the fact that the performance took place inside a large shining biscuit-tin didn't worry me at all (it was meant to concentrate attention on the miraculous words, and in a way it did). One was left to enjoy the amazing text. Was it moving enough? Perhaps not, though I was totally gripped.

January 30th

At the Slade, alone with Eardley and Mattei. On Friday night, Eardley and I had an immense discussion about values, right and wrong. I fear I may have talked too much, or too egotistically. Cold, sopping weather, unattractive. Walking alone along the lanes I thought what a good thing I hadn't tried to make a go of living alone in the country.

We've also talked about politics, which obsess me unusually at present. I'm a little surprised at Eardley's lack of interest. I'd thought he would be able to answer the sort of questions Ralph always so splendidly did. And he went so far as to say £16 a week was 'about right for a postman with a wife and two children to live on'. Really, if he thinks for one second what he spends on himself, how *can* he? But I'm astonished that anyone who assumes, as one must, that the present inflation must be stopped, should be quite happy to make the lowest-paid workers suffer for it. Perhaps they have to, but so should the highest. I'm awash with rather priggish indignation and it's liable at any moment to overflow.

February 4th

I got back to find my flat full of a fierce and penetrating cold. All the central heating was off. When I asked little Mr Sultana [a sort of caretaker, Maltese], mad marmoset that he is, he replied with a crazy chuckle that he'd been able to get no fuel for five weeks and after next Monday there would be no hot water. Gloom and hysteria mixed. I turned on all the electric fires and left them on all night.

The state of the world has not depressed and obsessed me so much since the war. And I find hardly anyone agrees with me that under Pigling Bland[1] and his catastrophically stupid henchmen we're heading for total disruption – strikes, strikes, strikes, and he does nothing to stop them but grow a few more double

[1] Ted Heath, Frances Phipps' name for him.

chins, go swimming and boating and burble about the 'British people'. Does he really suppose you can or ought to put back the social inequalities of a hundred and fifty years ago?

February 20th

Once more at Cranborne with the Cecils, in my same large soft bed, the clock ticking and the electric fire giving off pistol shots. I couldn't get to sleep last night, tired though I was. Perhaps because the evening's conversation had taken a restless turn. At dinner I decided to do all I could to get into rapport with the thoughtful, mysterious Hugh, who sat beside me. I think I succeeded, and our talk went on and much later in the drawing-room it drew in the rest. There's always something going on in his mind, and one has only to take the end of it gently in one's fingers like a piece of wool – the 'end', that is, that he casually lets fall – and it will unwind. I had exactly the feeling of someone moving their hands from side to side during wool-winding. He was talking about his own subjects, his attitude to the work he is doing, and to work in general, and how much it should interfere with living his life. His desire to start again *at once* when his present task is over rather surprised me. Should it be the story of a German general in the jungle in the First War, or the history of certain thinkers who interested him?

E.: What did they think about? The nature of the universe?

H.: Yes. *Near*-religion, but not quite.

Later we moved on to boys and schools, why prep-school boys could have real friendships, but when you got to Eton the business of keeping afloat in this impressive institution left no room for friendship. Ramifications between forms of school culture, the way a small, ungifted, unathletic boy can employ a group of loutish myrmidons, all this enthrals him, and his face grew animated as he followed the drift of his thoughts. Of course I was horrified to hear of the suffocation and stultification of small boys' friendly feelings to each other. Hugh emphasised how natural *protectiveness* was among schoolboys – which of course became suspect later as homosexuality.

This is a subject that brings out the worst in David, who began his heraldic prancing, turning pink and repeated again and again: 'I don't see how *I* could disapprove of Eton, since *I* was happy there.' We had all been describing people who were wretchedly unhappy at school, and of course it came to my lips and Julian's, and nearly overflowed: 'Yes, you could disapprove of it if you considered the feelings of others.' Well, of course, that's unfair – he often does, but there is a layer of relentless egotism, evidenced in his famous failure ever to pass the biscuits. Again and again he returned to the charge if any of us suggested that schools could be improved, and any criticism of the Eton system made him irritable and on the verge of reminding us 'what he had sacrificed to give Hugh the best education in the world'.

It's lovely having Julian here, but he slightly tends to make everyone's contribution into a performance – perhaps by his very appreciation; I feel tired and want to relax and 'be myself' such as that is. Julian and David were preparing a telly programme, Rachel and I drove over to have a drink with David's cousin Anne Tree. Julian Fane was staying there, and David casually implied that Rachel was 'in love' with the gentle, introverted fellow, and would drive any distance to see him. She certainly talked to him exclusively while two exquisitely pretty little female sprites, one very dark, one fair, dressed up as oriental princesses behind the sofa with shrill cries of 'Don't look! Don't look!' They were our hosts' adopted children.

On the drive I talked to Rachel about Carrington. She has just finished reading the letters. People often ask me what she was like and I try to give an accurate picture. On the whole she's credited with more cruelty and less deviousness than she really possessed. A sort of reserve prevents my reminding people of my own intensely happy thirty years with Ralph, yet in a sense I feel I've betrayed him by not doing so, and long to tell the forgetful and oblivious world about it, and about my daily, ceaseless missing of him.

February 28th

Today, a cold, still London Sunday, but a lot has happened. I met Janetta in Belgrave Square Garden and we walked round looking at the fine, huge trees with their roots in London's underground, and the pathetic plots of crocuses and miniature daffodils mashed up by scampering dogs. Then I followed her to Chapel Street, finding there Nicky, Georgie and Jean-Pierre, and the Macgibbons' left-wing doctor son Robert, who talked interestingly and at a terrific rate about education, noise, industry, medicine and boredom.

News that Henrietta is in London and may visit me later. Janetta pressed me to stay to lunch but I felt drawn to my blessed privacy, and am now listening to the broadcast of *The Makropolos Case*, which I saw last week.

Yesterday, at Golders Green, Margaret told me Lionel had hit her hard that morning and she had hit him back. She fulminated against Dunyusha, longing for me to throw fuel on the fire of her hatred. This I won't do, after seeing the use that's always made of it; nor have I seen Dunyusha lately, or had reason to review my view of her. Julia has begun ringing Margaret up again, and Margaret says she 'can hear she is again in a bad way'. My feelings are horribly mixed – anxiety and affection warring with sheer *relief* that I can no longer be called on to haul her out.

March 6th: Snape

Thin snow was being shovelled into corners by a Russian wind as I arrived here last night. This morning there's a white carpet and, often blowing parallel to the ground, big light flakes with a hole in the middle of each. 'Like corn plasters,' I said, and Heywood muttered, 'God shedding his corn plasters.' I love being at Snape, and would gladly go through three times the physical struggle to get here. As I sat for expensive hours in my taxi to Liverpool Street, I thought about all the *paper* in my life, the respect I treat it with and always have – it's the only thing I'm tidy and organised about. It struck me as sad, and that perhaps it had taken the place of flesh and blood, becomes too important, and that may be why I've minded the postal strike so much. Has my life become too much 'on paper'?

In my room is a bowl of primroses, deep purple violets and sugar-tong snowdrops. I finished reading Lytton's 'autobiographical pieces', started in the train. What a dear little boy, appreciative and eager for life and impressions. Sex as usual disrupted the perfection of his early balance. The best are an excellent description of Lancaster Gate, the detailed account of a day with the Bells. In the diary of his last journey to France quite alone a few weeks before his death, a certain selfishness emerged. Even when thinking of those he loved or was attracted to, Roger, or Le Mooncalf, he was entirely egocentric, not trying to interpret *their* thoughts and desires.

March 7th

With Heywood in his jaunty little cap to Aldeburgh to shop. The bitter weather brought everyone out in frisky defiant gear, wool caps with pompoms, and sailing clothes. We called on Ruth Gathorne-Hardy (wife of Anthony and mother of Jonny) in her suburban villa, its drawing-room newly papered in really hideous orange check. I like her, her broad swarthy face, her self-deprecation. She asked about Carrington and I gave my stock (but I believe accurate) account.

I've felt frivolous, reckless and inconsequential – a nice change from what I fear may be my sometimes tedious solemnity. It might be quite enjoyable to throw my cap over the windmill and become a wholly farcical old lady – but no good, my seriousness is, I think, deep rooted. I remember Julian telling me that Gerald had said the great thing about me was I was *gay*. Good heavens!

Resisted Heywood's suggestion of a walk in the afternoon and happily read by the fire.

March 10th: London

Went with Margaret to a lunch-time showing of Visconti's *Death in Venice* – a marvellously beautiful, but shapelessly overflowing and sometimes crude affair. Margaret has been in an intensified stew about Lionel. She is now afraid Dunyusha may leave England by the end of the month, and dreads what it may do to Lionel's health; thinks he may actually die of her departure; thinks also that this is what he thinks. So that, ironically, she now almost wants Dunyusha to stay. She gets through two bottles of whisky a week, but says sturdily that she can 'manage'.

She and Cynthia both give bad accounts of Julia, who sounds as if she is going to pieces as she did a year ago. She told Cynthia she was 'disintegrating completely' and she dined with them last night, getting lost on the way and arriving at nine-fifteen. The story of her muddled sadness has wrung my heart once more and given me an important craving to do something to help her. But what *can* I now do?

March 16th

This morning two calls from Cynthia about Julia, after one evening when she was confused and drunk or doped, fell asleep in the theatre and dropped her knickers on the floor. She's hurt her leg by a fall in her flat. I pass messages between Margaret and Cynthia, and Margaret is going to see her tomorrow.

March 19th

Janetta has just rung up and said characteristically: 'Jaime and I are going to do that *marrying thing* tomorrow.'

My reaction was a warm glow. I don't feel there's anything else to say about it. As I was striding up Sloane Street this afternoon, I ran into Jaime, who looked brown, happy and young. I'm dining with them and Magouche tonight. Is my pleasure rational or not? For *very* great pleasure it undoubtedly is, not perhaps quite unmixed with fear, but the fear that's involved whenever happiness launches its boat.

March 20th

I slept soundly but woke in a frenzy of agitation difficult to analyse. At the thought of the fast impending marriage: *deep* emotion, in which happiness and anxiety were mixed. There's something to my mind especially touching about people who have been lovers for so long, suddenly making this outward and symbolical gesture. Last night I met Janetta, Jaime and Magouche at Pruniers after their film, full of welcoming things to say to Jaime (I had already conveyed my pleasure to Janetta on the telephone). We talked about the coming wedding. 'I do wish I could come and be bridesmaid,' I said, and was told Magouche and Julian were doing this. I couldn't make out how they wanted the news of their marriage taken. I still don't know; but woke this morning into one of my full *bungling*-neuroses, a sense of having done the wrong thing, been clumsy, failed.

I dashed round packing, distractedly wondering what to do, and thank heaven had the idea (and was able by some freak at eight-thirty to carry it out) of ordering a very large bunch of flowers from Pulbrook's to greet them after the ceremony.

My fluster remained though I'm well aware of the insignificance that 'what I said or did or didn't do' has in their landscape. The thing is that I'm so deeply moved by anything nearly concerned with Janetta's happiness. I reflected that when Magouche asked me to dine with them, yesterday on the telephone, she didn't 'tell' me they were getting married. If *only* she had – I could have adjusted and responded better to them. But what use are 'if only's'?

April 5th

Now the giant's elbow has given another horrid nudge. Just back from a weekend at Crichel, the telephone rang. 'Italy wants you.' I hadn't time to wonder who or why, when Joan's voice came through, saying she had something 'very sad' to say. Cochemé had had an appalling heart attack and died in her arms. Elizabeth and Brian[1] are with her. I asked if she would like me to go out at once. She said no, but she would let me know if she would later. I could sense the realistic, brave, wound-up way she was taking it, and even as we were talking I heard her say: 'Oh, here are the undertakers,' and to someone else, 'They'll want to measure the body.' That enormously vital, clever, seemingly indestructible little man suddenly reduced to 'the body' – it's amazing, horrifying and dreadfully sad. Shaken and shaking, I passed on the news to those friends she mentioned.

April 13th

The afternoon was interrupted by the unexpected arrival of Nicky, whom I was enormously pleased to see. I gave her tea, access to a bath, and a drink, and she told me with a look of beaming jubilation that she had a new 'friend', that it was simply marvellous, the 'best thing that had ever happened to her', she 'had never dreamed you could be so close to anyone. I mean, it's not just an affair.' She had just been to Wales with the 'friend' and his friend, and vividly described her amazement at the beauty of the country (never seen before), the 'little black-faced cottage' they had been lent, with currant bushes just coming into flower. I listened in delight.

Now today I get an enthusiastic letter from Knopf, who seem delighted with my

[1] Cochemé's adopted daughter and her husband.

translation. This is a good send-off for my little holiday in France, which starts tomorrow. And after a wobbly beginning to the day I quite begin to look forward to it.

April 15th: Le Verger de Charry, chez Bunny[1]

France seemed an enormous country, as my stopping train crawled across its dull central plain. Then suddenly I was looking out at Souillac, and thinking back to my visits with Ralph and Raymond, then with Ralph, Burgo and Vicky Strachey, and finding its image deeply imprinted (though full of holes) on my mind. Very hot in the train, my all-male companions sprawled in shirt sleeves. I saw blackthorn in flower, cowslips under the fruit trees and a faint powdering of green on branches, solid farms and châteaux, grey shutters and brown roofs.

Cahors at last, and Bunny flapping penguin arms. After shopping he had driven his car into a field to read the newspaper, and it wouldn't start again. A passer-by came to his help, and he'd finally got a taxi which drove us out to this sweet little stone house on the hillside in the dusk. 'Ah *mais*, vous êtes bien dans la campagne!' said the driver. We passed the splendid château where Angela Penrose[2] lives, and see its round pointed towers from our windows.

The cottage looks out over the valley through the mossy trunks of several elms and an oak. Bunny sleeps in the sitting-room, where there's a huge open fireplace, a long table. The furniture is all solid, old, walnut, French. My room leads off on one side, on the other a nice kitchen and bathroom. Bunny looks quite a lot thinner, younger and less red in the face: it suits him here.

Now (10.30 a.m.) after breakfast of coffee, croissants and honey, he has gone off to see about his car and will return the Lord knows when. I'm savouring the all-pervading peace – a velvety, solid peace of muted colours. Outside my window is a quite large rough grass plot edged with box and backed by a grey cliff. I slept long and deep and feel soused in calm, as if I had been suddenly steeped in it, and it was streaming through me.

Last night we supped off soup and omelette and Bunny read me a letter from Angelica. He says Henrietta had a narrow escape from death in the Sahara, as they were without petrol, water or food for two days and had no compass.

The pearly mist shrouding the valley is beginning to lift.

April 16th

The sun came through and the valley emerged in full beauty, fruit blossom and luscious spring grass. I am enchanted by my surroundings. A tunnel-like path between the trees drew me down to a tiny hamlet and a church below. Bunny returned for lunch out of doors at a round table under a tree. Outbreaks of surprisingly interesting talk about truth and whether ethical and aesthetic values were absolute or relative to culture. He reminded me that we had had a fierce argument long ago, because he wouldn't accept that Shakespeare *was* less good during the seventeenth century just because he was less appreciated – but seemed prepared now to agree that if beauty and good are relations between beholder and object, that question doesn't even arise. Then he went on to say how much more

---

[1] David Garnett (after separating from Angelica) had taken a cottage in a village near Montcuq.
[2] Daughter of Alec, married to a Frenchman.

important individuals were than communities, with an analogy of trees that are planted too closely being unable to develop as individual trees. More conversation in the evening, after supper of avocado pear, porridge, cheese and red wine.

April 18th

Our days are full of gentle, peaceful activity. I hear every sound from Bunny's room, and the first in the morning are deep sighs as he forces himself to get up and start the day, surprising in such a euphoric person. He makes our breakfast of coffee and warms up the croissants, while I have my bath.

Then, for me, walks and flower-hunting, letter-writing and reading, a little reluctant work, while Bunny writes his novel. The limestone hill behind us is covered in junipers, grape hyacinths, potentillas and two kinds of orchids.

Bunny has given me a chunk of his book to read. It's so extraordinarily unlike anything else that I can't judge it, and describes the Caucasus in 1840. The horrifying central incident in which a terrible old father kills his little son in order to smuggle a treasured ikon inside his dead body, appears to be true and happened to an ancestor of Frankie Birrell's friend Basil Koutchichachvili. Talk of books led to W. H. Hudson and the block that prevents my reading him. I took *The Purple Land* to bed and was surprised by the quality of the writing and at the effortless ear (which few writers now possess). But found it too romantic and picaresque, with its flawlessly beautiful Pre-Raphaelite heroines. I'm giving up the attempt and trying *Far Away and Long Ago.*

Yesterday morning we drove to Cahors in Angela's car, and I drove Bunny's now mended one home after shopping. A crowded market day, with stalls selling monster cauliflowers, little cream cheeses wrapped in chestnut leaves, espadrilles, écrevisses and trays of live chicks.

Thundery rain in the night has turned everything greener and brought the wheat up by inches and more fruit trees into flower. Star of Bethlehem on the hill. We lunched off fresh sardines, with roast chicken and spinach in the evening. Conversation largely about Magouche – her fierceness in the past and recent 'adorable sweetness'. He described an incident in Corfu some time ago, which she had told me about. B.: 'I was enjoying myself playing about in a rough sea, with waves probably twice as high as this room. You know? Magouche seems to have told me to come out, but I couldn't hear what she said and anyway refused to take orders.' This septuagenarian boasting of manly toughness was not to my taste and I remembered that she described him as being almost in a state of collapse. I told him my sympathy was entirely with Magouche – one shouldn't be so inconsiderate as to show off by courting danger. Going too far? He didn't seem to mind.

April 21st

On the limestone hill I found two more orchids yesterday, *purpurea* and *lutes*. The ground was purple with *morio* and further on the 'spider' was common as buttercups. A white rockrose just opening. Sun very hot. I tried to fix my handkerchief into my botanising spectacles as a veil. Picked branches of cherry blossom to decorate our sitting-room. Bunny looks on at my floral activities with kindly amusement.

Evening conversation largely about Shakespeare. Bunny surprises me by liking the comedies best, I the tragedies and histories, and I suppose most of all the sonnets.

April 23rd

Wild wind and a threat of rain yesterday, so we put off our trip to Moissac, and shopped in Montcuq instead. I settled to solider work, from which my rapture in our natural surroundings has distracted me but the rain beating against this solid little house made it seem a mere walnut-shell. Bunny said he was feeling gloomy, and loud sighs and later loud snores came from his room.

About four it cleared a little and I set out in a mac and thick shoes, walking briskly in the cooler air down to the valley and along beneath the château. Then I climbed the next hill and found several fine deserted-looking farmhouses and sheets of orchids, including a new one, *Burnt Stick*, and lilac trees in flower. Deviously home by the château to find Bunny still depressed. Whisky, followed by porridge and the usual talk in two armchairs.

April 25th

Yesterday, amazingly, it cleared, and though sopping wet underfoot the sky turned blue with some cauliflower clouds. We set off for Moissac, following tiny roads that wound through villages and past desirable old farms bowered in lilac. But while we were marketing in Moissac, inky black clouds gathered and disgorged a cold deluge on us. Lunched in a simple restaurant frequented by people who had come to market, and then went to look at the superb church doorway, cloisters and the musée. Bunny talked at lunch about various episodes of his past. I'm sure his successes with women aren't just boasting – Minna, Indian Sushila, Italian Giovanna, Magouche, and he handed me a letter from Diana Gunn (the mother of Henrietta's Nicholas) to decipher a word, and I caught the concluding words 'my darling love'.

We talked of loneliness, partly. Bunny doesn't often ask personal questions but he did enquire if I felt it. 'Often,' I said. I asked if he thought he'd ever return to Hilton, and in a tremulous voice he said: 'The truth is I don't want to. I love the house, but it's too full of ghosts.' I stated my belief in the arch-importance of friendship, and he rather characteristically dived at once into an account of his own lifelong friendship with Harold Hobson.

April 29th: London

No sooner home on Monday night than I rang Chapel Street and was asked round to supper. I found there Magouche, Julian, and Janetta and Rose (both off to Corfu next day). I like to think of them there.

Now, Thursday, I've had three days to sort myself out, and suppose I have more or less done so. But there are outstanding confusions which I can't make sense of. My future for one: (1) more work has come. (2) Raymond expects me to go abroad with him, and I don't know quite when but fear sooner than suits me. (3) I'm half expected in Corfu. (4) Joan will return in May or June and definitely expect me here, where I must be. I'm unkeen about the Raymond trip and have decided to use (4) as an excuse. But I dare say I shall end up at a loose end.

Borges and his translator are to be in London next week. I'm putting the last touches to my translation of his interview, and have been at the Hispanic Institute trying to clear up some points. Nearly every morning as I set forth into the streets I feel that I'm one of two things – a fake, someone pretending to be a translator and almost pretending to be a human being, and, secondly, a ball of paper rolling down a moving staircase in the underground...

Two letters from reviewers of the Carrington Letters in America awaited me here. Gerald writes that he's doing it for the *New York Review of Books*; 'I have written it very impersonally, without mentioning the fact that I knew her'! Anthony West is doing it for the *New Yorker*: 'I hadn't realised what a devil she was ... unconscious devilry, but it's amazing how lethal her proceedings were ... a terrifying picture of somebody hell-bent on the way ... The combination of egotism and insensitivity which Gerald brought to his collaboration with Carrington in her Ralph-wrecking operation seems to me almost to justify the use of the word *wicked*.'

May 5th

Magouche has struck an icicle into my heart by telling me in strictest confidence that Robert had had some attack of depression during Easter when staying with friends in Holland. I've not seen him, but during a long talk on the telephone he said that the Dutch holiday 'had been quite a success'. If only one could break down this deadly reserve of his. I may hear more from Magouche; she has sent me an article by him in the *Listener*, on death, in which he says that 'the fact that we are all going to die is the most important single one in our lives'. But is it? It's like saying a full stop is the most important thing in a sentence. Or talking of memorial services, etc., as 'secret ways of dismissing the dead. And this is the last thing one wants to do ... I still find it an insufferable affront to them personally and to humanity in general.'

Death. I write about it to Joan, and await her arrival and her desire to talk about it with a slight inner quaking. I think often about it. We all do, after sixty or so. I believe a lot of one's activities are some form of reaction to it – pretending it's not there or playing at eternal youth, which one doesn't even in a ghostly way believe in.

May 11th

Last night I went to one of the 'Evenings with Borges' at the Central Hall, Westminster. Di Giovanni read his translations of the poems and Borges commented – but, alas, the poet only read one himself in Spanish, a sonnet about Spinoza. His appearance and personality seemed extremely familiar and also quite delightful. His blind face stared out over the audience with a look of vulnerable sensitivity, of desire to pick up with his ears what he couldn't with his eyes, that I found deeply moving. The eyes themselves, destroyed though not entirely lifeless; the long Spanish upper lip and the mouth moving silently in time with the English translations which he obviously knew as well as the originals, the very quick, and ironical crescent moon of a smile that crossed his face and disappeared in a flash as soon as it had come, the occasional appearance of being moved to tears by his own words. 'That is a very *in*timate poem,' he would say. He is an impressive and charming man, his English fluent and idiosyncratic; his knowledge of all literatures – particularly English – was dazzling. And he has been unable to read for the last sixteen years.

I gave di Giovanni my translation. He was a friendly, clever, Italian-looking fellow, and he at once said with what he called 'brutal frankness' that in Borges' case it would be necessary to read him my transcript and alter anything that was not as he (Borges) *would say it in English*. 'Of course,' I said.

In the poems there were several references to his not believing in immortality – not *wanting* to – which I found sympathetic. To old age, to his blindness, and to being 'rejected by a woman'. I gather from di Giovanni that his wife has done this recently. He married her at seventy, a year ago, and spoke in his interview about 'belated happiness'. It's seldom that one is confronted by a personality so entirely charming and admirable: impossible in a sense not to fall in love with that little grey man, moving along slowly with his stick.

Another such was Duncan, my fellow guest at Crichel last weekend, a gloriously summery one. He began badly by stumbling on the stairs at Waterloo and falling full length. I didn't see it, mercifully. He looked a little white, and more than usually windblown, but made light of it. 'I'm quite all right. It's nothing. I'm quite used to it. You see, I do it the whole time – and I've learnt that the great thing is not to put out your hand to save yourself.' How he touches one merely by being so splendidly himself, and also so funny, courageous and eager for experience. He was pleased, I think, by Desmond's sensitive and affectionate consideration. He sat drawing us as we played croquet, enjoyed records of *The Magic Flute* in its entirety and visiting the Cecils. (Pat whirled us there and back in an open car at quite terrifying speed, but Duncan didn't quail.)

May 12th

I'm back from dining with the Kees. There were Brian Inglis and his wife, and Terry Kilmartin. It was 'in-talk' about 'in-groups' – in-telly, in-journalism, and somehow as pointless and gossipy, uninspired and unprovocative as conversations about whether you believe in ghosts, or 'Where have you been?' or 'Have you seen so-and-so lately?' My fault very likely, but all of a sudden it became ashy for me. Cynthia was looking pretty and friendly, Robert handsome but haggard, and when he came out to see me off he said something about 'all human relationships being meaningless', and the street lamps shone on his face with its dreadfully sad expression. What can one do about it? What could *I*, one of those 'meaningless relationships', do? Yet I can't bear to do nothing, and lay wondering what.

May 14th

Irritability – how to keep it under? I fear it when I go to the Penroses as I do tonight. Yesterday we were playing quartets, and Margaret took my precious bound volume of Mozart quartets and violently broke its back *twice*, though I'd screamed the first time.

It's quite a problem though, when one feels fond of someone who tramples so on one's nerves. And what shall I find the position between Lionel and her is like, now that Dunyusha has returned to Poland? Margaret says Lionel is in a very bad temper all the time. I believe quite a lot of it is due to her simply not hearing (because she's so deaf) the noises she makes. But as she's highly intelligent one is tempted to try and persuade her – to wear her deaf aid, to lose some weight, and so on.

I liked a phrase from Henry James's notebooks: 'the immense mild summer rustle, the softened hum of London'. It's not applicable any more, alas, and I'm almost shocked to find myself able to tolerate the increased noise in West Halkin Street.

May 21st

Margaret has just told me on the telephone that, having strained her back, she was forced to let Lionel drive her Mini back to London, which he did 'appallingly, and hitting me all the way'. Also that Julia had rung up from her Sussex hotel-nursing-home to say it was 'hell down here' and Margaret mustn't come till she was back in London – quite soon now. Poor Phyllis Nichols, I suddenly hear, has had two awful operations for cancer. No wonder we all feel hemmed in.

Oh, poor human beings, how they are put through hoops!

I listened to a broadcast record of G. E. Moore and another philosopher talking about memory. Fascinating, like watching a masterly game of chess. Moore advanced a bishop; memory was (or could be, I forget which) *direct perception*, not as Russell so wrongly said a deduction. Longish pause. Then another piece was moved by a very gentle voice: 'Then would you say, etc. . . .?' Pause. Quietly but weightily, Moore brought up yet another: 'a perception, but of course one that was subject to possible error'. It was an impressive and amusing display.

May 29th

Joan here for another evening. I am full of admiration for the courage by which she has – all alone – lived with her grief, accepted it, hugged it to her bosom one might almost say. She has deliberately thought about nothing but Cochemé, death, her life with Cochemé and now wants to 'get back to life'. Listening to her, I feel she is braver than I ever was, leaving no corner of the agony unexplored – as a bad tooth with the tongue whereas I know I poured drugged sleep and books in on mine to stifle it. Her recovery will be all the more effective for this, and there's always the ironic fact that one is in a way strengthened, unified by the sheer horrifying *simplicity* of the situation that has to be met in terrible grief.

She arrived last night, gasping out that Elspeth (with whom she is staying) 'won't leave me alone – follows me into my bedroom, lies on my bed, follows me into the lavatory, even'. I was indignant when I heard that she had told Joan she should never have told Elizabeth she was Cochemé's bastard. What falsity, and how criminal to deprive Elizabeth of an important feeling of a human link with the man in whose house she was living, and who was someone as remarkable, as intelligent, and as Joan said (with one of her occasional flashes of brilliance) as 'oaken' as Cochemé. Anyhow, it has been proved that adopted children brood and brood as to how their real parents could have been so cruel as to abandon them. So this at least she was spared. My relations with Joan have been particularly easy.

But whatever the cause – probably the revival of past feelings, some of them undischarged – she leaves me restless, tense and unable to sleep.

June 3rd

Magouche and Arshile's daughter Natasha Gorky held a party last night for her wedding to her Chinaman Ed. It was the most visually glamorous affair (mainly young people blended together by Magouche's great warmth – she's the best 'hostess' I know). There was a certain punctilious grave ritualism ('ancestor-worship') on the part of the married pair. Natasha looked ravishing – for once the word is no exaggeration – in a long off-white dress, low-cut, of some cottony texture, pleated, and of most distinguished cut, her beautiful oval face set off by her smooth raven hair, which was drawn back and fastened with a red peony behind. There were lots and lots of glamorous girls and young men, and among their legs little Saskia Spender romped recklessly to and fro, obviously intoxicated by the fumes of other people's champagne. I met and talked to Nicky's Patrick, and liked him; Georgie and Jean-Pierre looked elegant and happy; I talked to Jonny, Nell, Tom Matthews, Ian Watson, and Antonia's Trevor. Mary seemed oddly out of place, and badly dressed. But in the course of a long reel of coloured impressions, the strangest and most disagreeable was that made by the Connollys.

Cyril was to me as he always is: an amiable kiss, a perfectly meaningless invitation to visit them at Eastbourne, a proud father's production of an equally meaningless snap of his little son in a pushchair. He had come with one purpose alone – to get an invitation for Stephen and Natasha's daughter Liz Spender's coming-out ball tonight, and he brought it off. Apparently he and Natasha Spender have not met since an occasion when Cyril wheedled some precious first edition out of Stephen, and Natasha begged him to return it (as it had been a special present to her from Stephen) and he declined absolutely. Hearing of the ball, and determined to go, he stood Stephen a good lunch at his club, but got no invitation. Magouche says he was wild with rage over this, and towards the end of the party he cornered Liz Spender, sat down beside her, and after ten minutes' intensive talk came away carrying a huge invitation card like the rabbit in *Alice*, a perfectly shut smug expression on his face. Then made for the door, without a word to Magouche (whom I was talking to) except, 'Goodbye. Come on, Deirdre, if you're coming, unless you want to catch the next train,' in a voice as flat as a tin tray. And out he marched. Magouche says there will be hell to pay. Natasha will be furious, and poor Liz get into trouble.

But how extraordinary to want to go where you don't wonder but *know* you're not wanted.

June 4th

Feeling a little like over-stretched elastic as a result of social life and work, both speeded up, and the tug of the unhappy world near and far, from little Joan's personal misery (she has just rung me up and cried like a child down the telephone: 'I don't *want* to go on. I hate my *tiny* life!').

I had hoped to keep most of today free for work, but Margaret proposes to come to lunch and I can't say no.

June 12th

And I don't really want to write anything down – any of these complete trivia that make up my day, different elements in the stream rising to the surface by turns, mainly work and rain. I have been hard at it finishing off number 4 of my Latin American interviews,[1] and on the whole liked working hard a good part of each day. This last fellow, Cabrera Infante, is an exile from Castro's Cuba now living in London, and yesterday I went to see him, to check a few points. One of the Natural History episodes I enjoy – zoology in this case. Already knowing quite a lot about him from his interview – such as that he was married to an actress and liked

---

[1] A book I had translated from Spanish.

making love to her, and that he owned a Siamese cat, I was not surprised to see a large, almost empty room with elegant cat and trousered wife (shrouded in a mane of dark hair) crouched on a mattress in one corner. The writer was a swarthy, stocky man in his forties, his rather negroid appearance relieved by a sweet and intelligent smile, and very delicate small hands. We despatched our business, I think with mutual respect and understanding.

Julia is back in London, finding everything marvellous, especially because Lawrence was in the flat to greet her and has made friendly moves. Margaret took her to Suffolk for the weekend. Though tortured by pain from her own 'bad back' she carried up Julia's tray each morning and Julia didn't appear till lunch-time except one day when she came down in a furious rage, saying the milk was cold. (Very likely; it usually is.) Margaret confined herself to saying, 'Don't shout at me!' and later on Julia apologised, saying she 'was too ill to go on visits'. Sequel: a telephone call from Julia, wanting to continue the quarrel, always a difficult thing to do with Margaret, by suggesting that she should be psychoanalysed as she was 'evidently totally unaware of her surroundings'. Margaret said she had been visiting an analyst. J. (surprised): 'Did it do any good?' M.: 'Well, anyway I enjoyed seeing you, and you were very useful as a buffer between me and Lionel.' J.: 'Lionel? He never addressed a word to me!' Not a word then or at any other time, of thanks. Margaret said she crouched over the fire the whole time and never went out at all.

June 14th: Snape

I've been here two nights. It is the Aldeburgh Festival and rain deluges steadily from a grey sky, except that Heywood and I snatched a brief walk yesterday morning, through warm, still air with a hint of sun and the cat-smell of flowering broom. The immense sociability of the festival means that people walk in and out at all hours – meals and drinks are nobly provided, and the kitchen is a wilderness of used saucepans, bottles, etc. The way that both Anne and Heywood deal with these incursions, kindly, ironically, unfussed, compels my admiration. Also here is the little bird-gnome John Nash,[1] limping, rather older, his eyes no longer starting out of his head with brightness, but alert and interested in everything, and quick to come out with his opinions. Yesterday afternoon Anne, he and I sat 'listening' to the Maltings concert – deep snores from them both, and he is a great music lover so that it seemed somehow sad to see his little knob of a head polished and brown like the handle of a walking stick, forlornly thrown back on his chair and his mouth wide open. Jock and Fidelity fresh from lunching with the Queen Mum (everyone here is interested, respectful and a little proud of her coming to the festival in her red helicopter), Celia Goodman, and a whole gang of Humphrey Brooke's all came after the concert. I like talking to John Nash and think we get on rather well. But I've not mentioned the little family – Lucy, Scotch soft-spoken Geordie and baby Justin, who is usually somewhere in the room in his pram. Next to John Nash, I've of course enjoyed talking to Heywood and then Geordie, whom I've taken a liking to. A tall, very dark, handsome man with several days' bristle of beard, marvellous teeth and almost black eyes. He is gentle, helpful, loving and attentive to his little son. I'm more surprised that he's intelligent and ready to talk – about India for instance. He answered my questions about the Pakistan

[1] A painter at the Slade with Carrington who he was in love with.

horror (cholera epidemic, ejection of refugees, starvation), and how it came about, in a thoughtful, well-informed way.

June 15th

Rain all day, appalling nightmare rain. I didn't go out until the evening concert – Janet Baker singing marvellously – and ended with a migraine. Worked fairly hard at tidying up my manuscript, while little John Nash groaned over his arthritis in a chair, was ready for talk, at one time nostalgically romantic and *almost* boring (he's never quite that) about being an army artist in the war. Odd that someone who has become distinguished as an artist, eminent even, should be proud to tell you stories about what amounts to prep school life, being hauled over the coals by commanding officers. But he's delightful. His wife Christine came to pick him up; an old Slade friend of Carrington's (John told Heywood that when he asked Carrington to marry him she said, 'No, I can't. You'd much better marry Christine.') She has a round face like a stuffed pincushion, uncritically enthusiastic, friendly and dull.

June 16th

The tiny thread was almost snapped yesterday when Anne, Heywood, Rose Gathorne-Hardy and I were eating dressed crab after the Purcell opera. A terrified call came from Lucy next door: 'Mummy! Come quickly!' My mind instantly rushed to the truth – the poor little creature had choked on his own sick. How do they ever get reared? The crisis was past before Anne got there, but Lucy sat shaken to the core, and most vividly described what she felt – 'everything seems quite unreal'. I could hardly bear it for her – nor the touching sight of Heywood sitting over the fire later with the homunculus cuddled on his lap – Justin's dark eyes gazing reflectively and contentedly into the flames. Whether it was the agitation of this near-catastrophe, or what, I couldn't sleep, and am now whirling back to London dazed and done for.

I brought Anne and Heywood Gerald's review of the Carrington Letters and Anthony West's letter about them to read. They were enormously interested and Anne came out in fiery indignation against Gerald, exploding about his treachery, hypocrisy, monstrous behaviour to Ralph and constant denigration of him since his death. No one can take up the cudgels more vigorously than Anne, and she was on the point of writing to Gerald, arranging in some way for Ralph to be rehabilitated and the world told what a remarkable, impressive, lovable person he was. 'Well do, go ahead,' I said. It's not much good my saying so, though I think it.

The skies cleared yesterday morning, enough for Heywood and me to drive to a botanical site John Nash had told us about and walk through long damp grass beside a narrow 'cut' reflecting the blue sky for miles in both directions, set off by a number of swans and yellow waterlilies – and growing right in the stream, hurray, a never-before-seen and pretty plant, *Hottonia palustris*.

June 22nd

An enormous pink poppy, brought back in a tight bud from Snape, has just dropped its petals with a plop in the ashtray like the weeks of this curious summer.

I drove down to Eardley's on Friday afternoon in rain so thunderous and cataclysmic that I felt the world was ending. It collected in rivers at the edges of the roads, rose in dense mists to cloud the air, and was sent by other cars in great waves against my windscreen. A hell of wetness. Yet with surprising fortitude, the fields, the roses in Eardley's garden, the birds, all perked up next day in a warm, blustery, drying wind, as though nothing had happened. Joan was there – just the three of us. Mattei didn't come, perhaps finding the atmosphere too feminine. For in spite of the trousers she wears, Joan does spread an intensely feminine radiation around her. She and I went two walks; she needs to be talked to incessantly (and I remember finding this tiring when she was a guest at Ham Spray). I left her and Eardley to it, and did some translating in 'Mattei's little French sitting-room'. I hope she doesn't demand too much of Eardley. I don't *think* she will. If she doesn't, he could be a very great support and comfort to her. Her desire to talk about Cochemé all the time, and now and again emotionally and tearfully, is salutary for her, but sometimes embarrassing for others.

Very nice evening with Julian at the new Pinter play *Old Times*, which we both found gripping and stimulating. He is the perfect companion to analyse such impressions with, but though we spent some time on it, some clots were left undissolved. Georgia appeared after dinner and gave a marvellous account of her new job at the College of Heralds. She went to the annual Garter ceremony in pouring rain and was moved to tears by 'the star quality' of the whole Royal family, who drove past her at close quarters. 'Film stars are simply *nowhere* with them.' It was 'something to do with the way they carried their heads on their necks', 'were so beautifully groomed': she 'got a terrific buzz from them all, *even Princess Anne, perhaps most of all Princess Anne*'. I listened in surprised delight, quite positive that none of them had as much 'star quality' as she, Georgia, has.

July 6th

Early and somewhat anxious awakening. I'm getting tired of my own company – tired of being *married to myself* for so long, and that's what a solitary life is after happy marriage, apart from the longing for support, the warmth of ever-present love.

I got, however, a certain feeling of warmth from a beautifully fine weekend at Crichel. That is I went to bed supported by the sense that those dear fellows had affectionate feelings for me as I for them. I hope it's not a delusion. When entirely surrounded by homosexual males it's impossible not to be conscious of being odd woman out. But this left me very soon and a feeling of perfect ease and comfort followed.

One painful situation developed, though. Desmond approached me with the suggestion that he should join Raymond, Dadie and me in Italy in September. Would I suggest it to Raymond? I felt very dubious how Raymond would react and he did with immediate and violent shakings of the head. 'Dadie would chuck, and I couldn't face it.' What was I to do? Desmond had, in my view, broken an unwritten law by his suggestion, but I hated the thought of his feeling rejected and unwanted. It's plain he has no conception that his violent excitability makes him an 'impossible' (so everyone says) travelling companion. Insensitiveness? I suppose, in a way. I was left in the awkward position of dreading being alone with either Raymond or Desmond because of the inevitable clarifications. At breakfast on Sunday I found Raymond alone and said, 'We must have a word about this painful matter.' He then took a quiet but masterful line, said he'd thought it over and decided it was quite impossible and would tell Desmond so, as unbrutally as possible. He did so after breakfast, and of course poor Desmond *was* hurt and spoke to me later about it. I tried to pour unguents on the wound as far as possible, including a suggestion that he and I took a trip some time, to show that by me at least he wasn't unwanted.

Margaret on the telephone this morning in great distress. I found it rather shocking that this wasn't so much because 'Lionel is in a poor way. I don't think he'll live long,' as that she had to 'take that tart's (or 'bitch's' alternately) letters to him every day in hospital, and then he reads them'. Also that Barry, the doctor who seems to be a rival – or so Margaret thinks – for Dunyusha's affections is 'trying to get her over here, and it'll be simply *awful*. I don't know what to do about it.'

The threat of Lionel's death, to me such a preponderantly terrible fact, hardly seemed so to her. But I may malign her. She was more or less in tears, saying, 'I don't see why I should be supposed to be the only person not to have feelings.'

July 17th

After a patch of scratched chicken-pen life, dry, aimless and shapeless, I suddenly today came alive to some experiences describable as *joy*. Playing trios with Margaret and her friend Anne – for some reason we all played better than usual, exploring unfamiliar works and not entirely at sea. Then talking to Lionel, convalescent after his spell in hospital and sitting in his large garden with a rug over his knees. At tea, I questioned him about a telly programme he's just done with Eysenck (on race and IQ). Listening to the definitively explicit expertise of his answers, and being aware of the power and accuracy of his mind was joy, and I felt a wave of real love for him which was joy too, although there is the dread that he won't be with us for long. Now, listening to Caballé singing *Traviata*, alone in my flat and not at all minding being alone – that too is joy. Not only excitement, but joy.

July 27th

With Raymond I penetrated the world of the Lees-Milnes. Neither of us felt entirely at ease. Raymond, hunched and miserable in the queues at Paddington, said he would have turned tail had it not been for me. As we ate breakfast together on the Monday morning train home he asked touchingly, 'Did I disgrace myself? I really dislike staying with people who hate me ...' 'But they don't!!' I protested in all honesty. 'Oh, yes, Alvilde does. You see, we committed the unforgivable sin and invited Jim to Crichel with his boyfriend, and Alvilde got in her car and drove across country and made a scene. She wouldn't come in.' She is a bristly Aberdeen terrier, someone *hors la loi*, one is never at ease with her ... and yet and yet, I feel a sneaking sympathy for this poor little rich girl. She and Jim are outwardly loving, 'darlings' fly back and forth, yet according to Raymond the affair with the boyfriend is still paramount. So Alvilde buries her spiky heart in the garden, which is a glorious success, proliferating up walls, cascading, abundant, making blue pools round the feet of trees. Surely some sort of feeling emerges in all this beauty? Yet any other gardener would have given me some flowers to take to London and I would have asked any other hostess to let me pick some.

We were given delicious food, driven round to look at churches, and introduced to several strangers. One family interested me greatly. Charles Tomlinson, a poet, an original and accomplished artist, a don in English literature. A tall man, whose thin, sensitive, ascetic features corresponded with his sensitive, delicate and exact poems and designs. Sitting next him at dinner, I learned that he was a great friend of Octavio Paz (whose interview I'm now translating – and I've since come across references to Tomlinson in it). It's odd. He's not a charming man, but the delicacy and precision of what he does moves me quite a lot. His plump pigeon of a wife and two brilliantly clever, musical little girls, who never look at the telly but read George Eliot and play Schubert, might have been too good to be true, living in their pretty cottage at the end of a deep valley, taking no newspaper, having no wireless – yet they interest me. I mean not to lose sight of them altogether if I can help it.

Truth to tell my spirits are low, and I don't feel very well. Last night I lay in my nightgown on the sofa in the box of my sitting-room, lights out, tall oblongs of white-painted stucco opposite, listening to Christoff singing *Boris Godunov*. This box, I thought, has contained me for over ten years, like a solitary sardine in its tin. When the opera was over I tumbled sadly into bed.

July 30th

The husbands of absent friends left alone during the hols came to dinner. Robin last night, Robert next week. Robin, who came half an hour before he was expected, stayed till twenty to one, quite a long stretch of tête-à-tête, easy enough, though I began to long for my bed towards the end of it. The chief impression he left was of a tired horse longing to sink down between the shafts, not enjoying its daily trot with a burden. I think his relations with Susan are particularly good – he rang her up long and lovingly. But he longs for retirement and is bewildered by feeling so tired. No doctor seems to be keeping an eye on him, and he said he felt in some sort of decline. I said we all were, and he surprised me by saying, 'You're the only person who doesn't change. You haven't changed *at all* ever since I first knew you.' This must be rated a compliment (I knew of course he meant mentally and characterologically) and one shouldn't record it. But naturally I was pleased.

August 2nd

My jaunt to King's Lynn Festival with Desmond is successfully over, though I feel flat as a pancake today after a non-stop drive of about four hours from Blickling Hall (near Cromer) to London. Desmond drives much better than people say, but he had set himself a time to arrive and was straining every nerve to do so. While going posthaste ahead he asked me at times to help him out of the sleeves of his shirt, because the sun was shining, or in again because it wasn't, or to fix a funny little peaked cotton cap on top of his bald head. I enjoyed myself very much and he didn't once 'go off with a bang' and was delightful company. All the same, there was the slight strain of anxious adjustment to another person, anticipating their desires, with the added knowledge that Desmond doesn't like too much compliance.

Our hotel at King's Lynn was comfortable and gave us delicious food. First night of performance of a new 'Dialogue for Cello and Orchestra' by Lennox Berkeley, and another work by Elizabeth Maconchy. Enter the Queen Mum, tittupping along on pig's-trotter shoes with, I must say, a very gracious and pleasing expression, radiating charm – even if consciously – and even if it struck me her face was a little like Harold Wilson's. Being in a church, our seats were incredibly hard, and I find it a distraction being in the house of God, my mind going off onto the subject of religion.

Next day, Saturday, we pelted round Lynn, looking at exhibitions and fine houses and down onto the great grey-green estuary of the Great Ouse. Then drove out to lunch with Lady Cholmondeley at Houghton Hall, where we found the Stones and Berkeleys all staying. Everyone had told me it was 'the most splendid house in England', so perhaps it disappointed me a little. *Too* splendid, too pompous, too lacking in grace and charm or lightness of touch. The same for its furnishings and, apart from a fine Holbein and some Gainsboroughs, the pictures weren't 'all that delightful'. Lady Cholmondeley (out when we arrived) returned with a coarse-looking MP whose nose sprouted black hair and who was once Billa Harrod's lover, perhaps still is; I disliked him. Lady Cholmondeley was extremely chummy, and seemed to single me out, heaven knows why, for her attentions; she sat me next to her at lunch, 'Otherwise I shan't see you and I've heard so much about you from mutual friends.' I trust she will drop me after this. It's not a world I like, and too much of a strain pretending it is.

Desmond and I drove off to another concert, of baroque music, after lunch and the evening ended with a firework display across the Ouse.

August 4th

A splendid conversation with Robert last night, the best sort. We went first to *Claire's Knee*, a film recommended by Julian, and agreed in our estimation of it as on the whole pretentious and failing to tap the emotions of any real profundities.

Both these our conversation *did*; as for the first, I felt a tear trickling down my cheek. Robert did that infinitely flattering thing of talking with apparent openness about himself and his feelings, his life, his relations with Cynthia, and assuaged my undercurrent of anxiety about his suicidal tendencies. He is taking a new form of treatment by pills, not psychoanalysis, from a Jewish doctor who has 'the attitude of a mechanic' and describes his trouble as 'variable depression'. Whether as a result of the pills or from relief at his family being away for about ten days, he seemed more 'all right' than usual. This doctor asked him point blank if he and Cynthia would have parted except for the children. It's clear they would, and that Robert thinks they still will when the children are older. 'It's been so really *ghastly* for such a long time. The trouble is we're neither of us able to get along on our own. We prop each other up, at least I suppose we do.' He said he thought it was worse for Cynthia than him, that she was permanently scarred and embittered, her not eating is 'aimed at him'. The doctor had them both to a joint session and said to Cynthia, 'You're afraid of this man, aren't you?' Well, no doubt with reason, and I noticed that Robert betrayed no shame over this fact. Also that he was pleased that, though Cynthia had told the doctor that 'it was getting worse all the time', she had 'given herself away' and 'been caught out' saying something else which proved it wasn't. I begged him to hang on like mad to his marvellous, unequalled sense of reality, also to all the pleasures he's so good at extracting – from music, places, books, and above all his interest in everything that happens to him, including misery.

There was lots more on another level, about the cinema and Mr Wilson, the

Labour politician whom he has seen a lot of lately and got to like better. 'He's a little man, a cheekie chappie, who happens to have an excellent brain which almost overbalances him.' He said he was fundamentally simple, adored the whole business of politics, and sincerely felt the most important thing was that the Labour Party should be back in power. Otherwise, *principles* or real sympathy for the Clydesiders thrown out of work – none. Nor did he have bad principles, he hastened to add. Merely none at all.

August 6th: Cranborne

I don't like the feeling of being witlessly, mindlessly pushed along, 'like a bagatelle ball' as Julian said, so that I find myself out in West Halkin Street with a basket on my arm, unaware where I'm off to. Also of the skein of the past and its sensations rushing by and *back* through my fingers, of the helpless struggle to fish out some small minnow from it. In the end I do often catch it, but after such an effort it seems worthless. Also in a cowardly way I take less chances, lead a more cautious life, submitting my antennae to less stimuli at once, to save dwindling energies.

Last week was a series of nose-to-nose contacts. Robert far the most stimulating. Then Joan, Faith, Margaret. My fears that Joan and I wouldn't make a go of it were I think unjustified. In the world of nose-to-nose one must be aware of, and face up to, the regions of non-overlap and extract what's possible from the overlap. But it's quite possible to enjoy in a different, detached, even amused way the areas of non-coincidence, and not get frantic with desire to alter them, or irritated as Julia does. There's quite a large, wide contact-bond between Joan and me – her liking for the truth for one thing. Outside it is a certain amount of conventionality, not taking moral judgements back to source, and I mind the way she suddenly switches off and doesn't listen. But we sat talking very easily in her bedroom on the top floor, and then looking out saw the now wonderfully clear sky of London had turned translucent peacock blue, and through the tossing tree tops, the sparkling lights of a skyscraper looked really pretty, with one silently moving aeroplane light seeming to have become detached from them. With Faith I talked politics; she is very clever and on the spot, but becoming what to me seems passionately reactionary like most of my generation, and we disagreed with near-heat.

How glad I felt to see Julian coming up the Waterloo platform. We talked intermittently in our full carriage, and of course ceaselessly since arrival here. I love the way David becomes immobilised by talk in the middle of some practical activity like carrying a suitcase into the house. So much so that when he's driving the car, I feel he might come to a halt suddenly in a stream of traffic. Then Rachel clatters downstairs with a wild, tragicomic gesture of welcome reminding me of Molly.

August 8th

Great excitement because Hugh was bringing down a girlfriend, with the bizarre name of Mirabel [Walker]. They arrived at teatime. She turned out to be a voluptuous near-beauty, with a generous curly mouth, dimples, low warm voice, a friendly and outgoing nature. In the Mini, driving to have a drink with Cecil Beaton, I pinned Julian down to sit behind with me and discuss two crucial films and their implications, through which I could hear Rachel and David exchanging their impressions of Mirabel in excited *sotto voce*. At Beaton's were Frank Tait and a plain, goggle-glassed daughter of Osbert Lancaster ('an aggressively unmarried mother', so Rachel told me).

This morning, reams and reams of conversation – about selfishness with Rachel and David; when it was fatal and uncurable, when not. The former when it came from the lack of the sort of imagination that wants to enter the minds and feelings of others, the latter when it comes merely from being habitually spoilt, and contact with a tough and more selfish loved one (for one thing) can sometimes cure that. Julian laid himself out on the new 'relaxator' bed, asked me to psychoanalyse him, but answered 'Censored!' to all my questions. Since lunch there emerged from him a hatred of 'being preached at', of 'the eternal schoolmaster' so prevalent in the English character, and a strong resistance to Morgan Forster because of his 'disguised morality'. I was interested, feeling (perhaps wrongly) this to be a temporary obsession. For how, I asked, could one have novels, which deal with human relations, that don't involve moral issues? I should have said *values* – for the word 'moral' made him wince as it does so many. And of course I felt guiltily aware of the 'schoolteacher' within me. But he has one himself!

David's *bête noire* was the 'novelist with the divided mind', e.g. Graham Greene. What was wrong with Aldous Huxley as a novelist? None of us could now read them. And I said I was shocked by the credulity of a man as eager for facts as Raymond yet who fell for palmistry, mescalin, probably flying saucers, which didn't seem to me admirable as it did to Julian. Open-mindedness – I feel minds can be *too* open, the doors can get positively flabby from being allowed to flap about too freely. I felt, as I often feel when in company with people I'm very fond of and in the habit of communicating with freely, that Julian was taking part in a sort of shadow-argument with something he thought I was thinking and very likely wasn't. Or was *I* doing that? But I'm amazed by shrinking from the voicing of values of any sort; they are the breath of life to me. Lack of imagination? Selfishness? *Not* to realise how others feel about them? In this house there is so much repercussion, doubling back, unpicking, restitching, that one runs aground suddenly on a hidden sandbank, forgetting the side-streams one had been about to follow.

August 13th

Julian gave a charming party to which I went with Georgia who dined with me first. Julian's 'nest' has been redone and glows with prettiness and probably the love of the friend who redid it. Tam and Andrew Murray-Thripland were there, Joan Leigh Fermor (a nice surprise), Betjeman and his 'Feeble',[1] Diana Cooper, Judy Montague (*very* plain). I most enjoyed talking to another Andrew from the BBC, a colleague of Julian's, and was entranced and magnetised by his wide gaze and slow charming smile and what seemed to flow out from his face and voice – utter integrity, the best sort of curiosity, someone of rare sweetness and loveability. I left about one, still feeling fresh and untired but, as always, determined to go before either sensation stopped.

[1] His nickname for Lady Elizabeth Cavendish.

August 14th: Thorington, rain falling

My six weeks as a wandering Jewess began yesterday, when Mrs Murphy went off on holiday. I began very quickly to feel lost without her. I miss her. She supports me.

I meant to drive down here early in the day but Margaret asked me to bring Lionel who was in London for the day. The 'arrangements' had that professorial and ramshackle uncertainty typical of Lionel. I had wanted to avoid Friday's grizzly rush-hour, which is a degradation and futility that I try to cut out. Impossible, of course – Lionel when cornered with some difficulty by me, said he'd be ready between six and six-thirty. The traffic was '*er*palling';[1] it took over an hour's slow grind, among furious, vicious, hooting cars to get to Rodborough Road at all. Lionel was on the telephone; enter three charming young Spaniards who are living there at present, jabber jabber in two tongues. Lionel appears, coated and hatted, holding his drooping paws up in front in a gesture of professorial helplessness reminiscent of Sir Frederick Pollock[2] and perhaps characteristic of learned men. We start to get in the car and he remembers a hundred and one things he ought to do. At seven-fifteen at last – departure.

Well, of course Lionel is a delightful companion and he talked happily and entertainingly about his own subject. Told me a story of a sex change he had been called in to adjudicate on – a registered male becoming female and marrying a man. Chromosome tests were not – as they usually are – conclusively male or female, I couldn't quite grasp why or how, and he believes it is a case of a genuine hermaphrodite with rather rudimentary womb and testes, who has a legitimate right to choose which to be. The traffic congestion was frightful and by the time we reached a faster road it was dark and I was tired. I really *hate* hurtling along between sky and earth as it seems, amid a wilderness of moving lights. Largely guesswork; and with great relief we turned off into narrower lanes, for the last mile or two. Thank heaven the 'servants', Freddie and Bessie, aren't here. Though Jane Rendel,[3] her husband Sandy, and two little children are sleeping here they are mostly out at the Hoylands' opposite, leaving Margaret, Lionel and me. And all isn't well, oh dear me, no. When (after a morning's work in the telly room) I went in to the drawing-room at one-fifteen (lunch was announced to be one) Margaret was in tears and a row in progress. She got up and rushed out, banging the door. Oh, *how* she bangs, shouts and stamps. I can't help finding it infuriating at times. Her shouting makes Lionel and me talk softer in the hope of inducing her to do likewise, but that only makes her shout louder. She cooked us some 'fillets of sole', about which there had been much talk. They were burnt to slivers of hard coconut matting; spinach was slopped into a dish, while she wiped her nose on the roller-towel. The banging down of dishes and crashing about and slopping makes one feel one is in an orphanage. Then she contrived to drop her spectacles on a walk so that they were crushed by a car. It is infinitely distressing – I felt her pathos, her goodness and kindness, her insensitivity – all of it acutely. Lionel is in a way much more sensitive but also more selfish. Going a walk with the two of them is agony – Lionel takes well-known (to me) angina walks, slow (especially at the start) and with pauses. Margaret pays no attention, plods ahead, and then suddenly drops

[1] One of Janetta's telling locutions.
[2] Husband of one of my godmothers, a member of Henry James's circle at Rye.
[3] My great-niece.

behind and stares about her, but is never with us. As I remember *intimately* how aware I was of keeping in time with Ralph, and never hurrying him, making excuses to stop and pick a flower when I sensed he wanted to dally, I simply can't understand it. I feel *great* sympathy for poor Lionel in his plight, walking down his one-way corridor, and also great affection. Margaret must be dreadfully unhappy, but it makes her behave almost insanely at times. For instance, after lunch she was eager to go for a walk (I would rather have gone alone with her and had her troubles out, but she asked Lionel). I went upstairs to change my shoes and when I got down she was lying on the sofa, fast asleep. She goes often to the cupboard and pours herself out a nip of whisky which (far from having a calming effect) makes her noisier and angrier.

August 15th

Yesterday afternoon Margaret announced that Lionel was putting a call through to Warsaw, and took me off to look at her seakale, which was hopeless, about six months too old to eat. I asked her what had upset her so much before lunch. 'We were having the worst row we've ever had in our lives.' It started by Lionel asking Margaret about her possibly going abroad with the Sissons, while he pays a six-week visit to Dunyusha. 'I don't want to keep travelling about with the Sissons,' she said. But with awful detachment I saw that Lionel had tried to show an interest in her life, some solicitude; had he *not*, she would have had cause for indignation. Then out flew various bottled charges: 'How could Lionel blame her for this and that, when he was all the time committing adultery? Did he want her to divorce him?' 'That couldn't be nice for *you*,' he said (clumsily, but it's certainly what he feels).

I asked Margaret if she would really rather divorce him, and she said anything was better than the present state of things. Dunyusha has made Lionel promise to 'be faithful to her', so Margaret has moved into another room. Of course she is the greater sufferer. He's having the fun; and when he talked to me (he's invariably charming to me) he seemed quite sanguine about his health. So perhaps Margaret's view that he will die soon is (as he thinks or says) partly wish-fulfilment.

Though two good human beings are involved, it's a sordid situation, just as the unkempt house, greasy wash basins, tin spoons and forks, Woolworth glasses and packet non-foods are sordid. No feeling at all for quality.

August 20th: the Slade

The peace here is greater than anywhere except Bunny's Verger. Concentration on reading and thought is easy. Talked about this to Eardley at lunch, describing the torturous situation at Thorington. He admitted that love was always, if truly love, possessive, but thought that that side shouldn't be indulged in, and was strenuously in favour of independence. What gave independence? Well, it seemed to boil down to living in separate houses, as he and Mattei do. If there was marriage for homosexuals, I asked, would many go in for it? He thought only a few; I'm not so sure. I asked if he had shared a habitation with Frank Coombs? In theory no, but in practice yes, for months at a time. Whatever Eardley's practical philosophy, it works, and he has been happily spending hours painting in a sandpit near Bedales. But he admits that unless he looks at television he can't endure the evening solitude.

August 20th

Polished off my stint of translation and took a lonely, drizzling walk but enjoyed it. Mattei was expected for dinner, for which I cooked a chicken in cider and tarragon and Eardley made peaches in orange juice. The advent of the loved one produced a rather giggly state in him, and I'm sure this waiting happens every weekend. Mattei refused to be met at the station and finally arrived in Robert Wellington's car about nine-thirty, looking bronzed from a Greek holiday, thinner and very handsome.

August 24th

I returned to a glorious batch of letters, fine long ones from Robert, Bunny, Heywood, and poor Margaret's curly script like a row of midget cauliflowers, oblivious as ever (I could hear the tramp and bang of her progress) but deeply cast down because Marjorie Sisson has had a stroke and is lying possibly at death's door.

August 28th: San Stefano, Corfu

My bus to the air terminal was so empty that I thought the aeroplane would be empty too. But not a bit of it. Arrived at Heathrow, we were hurried straight to our exit gate, no time to buy whisky or have a drink, and in the intestine leading to the creature our bags were searched and our persons frisked by a posse of police in shirt sleeves, looking disarmingly defenceless because they had deposited their helmets on the floor. A female bobby searched us women, investigating even the tall boots one girl was wearing. Was it a spot check or had they cause for suspicion? A nice Greek girl sitting beside me in the aeroplane thought the latter. Horrified to find a whole busload had already taken their seats before us, so I had to take the middle seat between my Greek companion and a soporific businessman. Soon after take-off, 'turbulence' was announced and the huge prehistoric monster with its load of over a hundred souls began to pitch, judder and roll, not really disagreeably but it shook me into a passive state. I rang for a drink. A Greek hostess got up as a beautiful blonde but really ugly, dark and cross, said rudely, 'No, madam. Not while seat-belts are fastened.' Not till midnight by Greek time were we hastily served with whisky and food (the turbulence having stopped) and there was only just time to swallow it. Then I was walking through the darkness, sniffing hard at a resinous waft in the air. It must be what goes into the wine, I thought vaguely. I saw Janetta's dear brown face through the door – how many airports hasn't she welcomed me at!! Behind her, Jaime and Alexandra Henderson. We drove off along the countless bends of the coast for nearly an hour, flashing through Corfu town, with its noble houses shining honey-coloured, cream and pink in the headlights; afterwards indistinguishable olive-clad slopes, and the last bit of road down to this hamlet was supremely bumpy and rough.

I've now spent two nights in their rented house close to the edge of what seems more like a lake than the sea, because straight in front, extraordinarily close, is the unattainable shore of Albania, where no one is allowed to land. I am amazed and obsessed by the nearness of this unknown country.

The house is unpretentious but convenient, just built and not even quite finished. We look out on the taverna, one or two fishing boats, and the quay where the steamboat from Corfu puts in and some yachts. Across the water comes the shrill typewriter rattle of Greek voices, and calling of names ('Nico!' usually) and at nights the three-note tune of a bird, over and over, both melancholy and poetic. The morning light is brilliant, still and transparent.

Yesterday Jaime drove us to look at Jacob's[1] house, where a great many workmen were busy. Janetta, Alexandra and I descended into the next bay to bathe, near a two-storeyed farmhouse with striped rugs hanging from the windows, old women hooded in thin white cotton scarves and children on a swing. We went off the rocks into beautifully clear water and then lay in sun or shade.

I remember Julian saying in a small apologetic voice that he was 'bored' here. I'm pretty sure I shan't be and don't at all crave excursions. But I'm still dazed by the shock of transportation. An at-once noticeable change in Janetta is that she has started doing pen and ink drawings, with the same concentration she puts into everything. They are delightful and accomplished, and I feel it's an excellent sign of her settled happiness. Rose has gone to Crete. Jaime is tremendously involved in Jacob's house, and apparently happily.

And I shall read, write letters and bathe.

August 29th

When Janetta and Jaime went off together to his house I sat down on the terrace to write to Robert, but soon saw that Alexandra was needing attention. She responded at once. The Lycée had been a very bad education; she found it terribly difficult to express herself (this is quite true – it's all 'ackshally, sort-of, you know').

As for the married pair, they seem relaxed and content as never before. Janetta takes very little trouble with her appearance, but Jaime looks at her lovingly and is appreciative of what she does, particularly the new drawing phase. It's certainly the best thing that's happened to her for a long time, and I remember that when a year ago I suggested her going back to painting she said, 'Yes I want to, but I want to do it from a basis of allrightness and not as a sort of drug.' It's certainly her natural form of expression, and writing was not.

August 30th

Our plan of life: breakfast downstairs on the back terrace between nine and ten, some dressed, some not, Jaime usually straight from bed with tousled hair; he then goes off to Jacob's house, elegantly stepping up the hill in bathing shorts and espadrilles carrying a briefcase – an odd sort of businessman.

There is a new craze for austerity, for healthy foods like grapefruit and Ryvita. Jaime is anti-whisky; Alexandra won't eat fish; Janetta won't eat meat.

We've twice sallied forth in a tubby blue rubber boat with an engine to neighbouring bays to bathe, bumping over choppy seas, yesterday to a tiny beach cleft between rocks. The water is perfectly transparent and very warm, no shock at getting in.

Yesterday we started for Corfu at five-thirty. We drove off and I saw for the first time the winding route we had traversed in the dark, so winding that one was never sure if one was looking at Corfu town or Albania. Corfu is a fine Venetian town, packed with tourists. I followed Janetta through the narrow streets to fish

[1] Rothschild. Jaime was at work on his house.

and fruit shops and then sat down with a newspaper in a café, watching the promenade – girls in white Minnie Mouse shoes or with plastic Grecian thongs right up to the knee, sailors and blackamoors, noisy Americans, women in evening dress, remarkably disgusting-looking hippies with pale, bespectacled or bearded faces peering through their lank Jesus hair.

We started home in the dark and stopped to eat halfway in a wayside restaurant. Delicious chicken pie in flaky pastry.

Sunday evening. We've had a dream of a day, bathing in an idyllic place in crystalline water warm as one's own blood and sitting on smooth rocks to eat the most delicious and imaginative picnic. Janetta has been touchingly sweet and affectionate to Jaime and he to her and she's now baking an elaborate cake for Alexandra's birthday, all this interspersed with dedicated hours spent drawing the olive trees.

August 31st

My delight in what seems to be the stability and happiness of the relationship between the J.'s grows. Whether the ceremony of marriage was cause or effect I don't know, but their life seems much more of a joint life than it was, and Janetta relieved from that restlessness that has possessed her so long. In fact they appear to delight in each other, and it's joy to see it.

To celebrate Alexandra's birthday an outing was planned to the western coast, via Corfu. I had been buying a sponge as a birthday present and was heading back to the bar where we meet, when I heard a shriek and there was Susu's long brown willowy shape hurtling towards me. There, too, was Magouche, whom I was delighted to see – in her dashing way she had hired a car for her two days with us. In these two cars we reached a little taverna hung with morning glory perched above an unattractive beach with seaweed, and the sea smelling of sulphur. High up on the white face of the opposite hill workmen toiled with yellow bulldozers in clouds of dust, making the foundations of a new hotel. But the taverna produced three very fresh fish, some eggs, tomatoes and retsina, which I've grown to like.

After lunch the party disintegrated – Susu and Alexandra went off in the hired car, Jaime went indoors to snooze, Janetta was lost in her world of drawing, sitting bolt upright on a kitchen chair. Magouche and I sat talking amid clouds of wasps and newspapers, until it was time to drive off to another bay and walk, which one can only do in the cool of evening, along a stony path through the olive groves. The olives of Corfu! They are unlike any others I've ever seen; allowed to grow free, unbranched and fantastically tall, their trunks are full of large 'eyes' or loopholes. We've seen several with fig trees growing out of them. We had started too late on our walk and the monastery was still far ahead when the scarlet football sun began to sink into the sea. Magouche was all for going on, but Janetta – to my relief – said it would be madness. As it was, we got home late and she valiantly at once began cooking tender little chickens in rice, almonds and sultanas. Conversation about Saxon Sydney-Turner for some reason; Janetta and I trying to convey him to the others.

September 2nd

On Magouche and Susu's last evening (out of two) Jaime went into Corfu and returned with a bright-eyed, excited-looking Rose behind him. She had arrived from Crete unannounced and was in tremendous form, telling us all about her adventures with José and Lucy Durán.[1]

In the evening heavy rain fell suddenly, making spots as big as half-crowns and soon everything was swimming and maquis smells filled the air. Janetta, Rose and I lunched in an open-air restaurant near the Achilleion – now a casino, formerly the house of Elizabeth, Empress of Austria and then of the Kaiser – and afterwards visited it. Its sumptuous garden was full of the smell of jasmine and pines and huge statues of Achilles. One of him trying to pull the arrow from his tendon fascinated Janetta, evoking from her sympathetic groans which greatly amused a gardener. We play Scrabble in the evenings – sometimes in Spanish, very difficult.

September 3rd

After the Magouche irruption, the four of us are leading a quiet family life. Feeling of change in the air; I have let time flow over me in a very unspeculative, semiconscious way, most of my attention being focused on the life of Charlotte Brontë I'm reading. Rose, Janetta and I walked up the hill behind the village. Jaime brought a letter to us from Julian, written in the aeroplane to Australia.

Every night I swathe myself in my loose, striped sheet of Greek handwoven cotton like a soldier on the battlefield, lie down on my platform bed with its hard pillow and fall almost instantly asleep, usually to be woken by the arrival of the Corfu boat at five thirty, but fall asleep again.

September 4th

A quiet private morning with Charlotte Brontë and letter-writing on the terrace; lunch at a taverna by the sea where Lawrence Durrell once lived. Jaime said, 'It would be nice perhaps to drive to the top of our mountain, Pantocrator, where there's a monastery.' We set off just as dusk was falling and turned inland off the Corfu road and began to climb steadily till the pink sun made a second appearance above the horizon. Up and up, through villages where everyone was sitting relaxed and watchful under their vine-covered arbours. Up and up, the huge mountain suddenly towering awfully above us. Excelsior. We left the good road and bumped and rattled and wound higher still, till some sort of wireless station appeared on a col above us. 'Is that the top?' Janetta asked nervously. Jaime said, 'No, I'm afraid we're still a very long way from the top.' And he now told us that he and Ed had tried to reach the top once before and Ed had got frightened because a huge wind was blowing and they turned back.

'Is this Windy Corner?' 'No, not yet,' said Jaime smiling rather sadistically. 'But say, of course, if you find it too frightening.' Frightening it certainly was, and Janetta sometimes softly said, 'Oh, Jaime!' as we wound round lacets so sharp that the car had to take two goes on a skiddy corner with nothing between us and the abyss. Then at last we were at the top. Almost the whole island and a lot of Albania lay mapped out below us in different pale blues, and in the foreground the village and its pitiful attempts at cultivation. The ground fell away so steeply that it must have been easy for the monks to contemplate eternity from there. But was it really a monastery? A small belfry, stalls with tables and seats for pilgrims. One mad-looking monk with a squint and hair growing out in two wild tufts from under his

[1] One of the Euston Road artists.

tall black hat was hacking away with a spade beside a wall. Rose boldly pushed open the door and we entered a chapel with a lot of seats of delicious-smelling cypress wood and a barrel roof with faded frescoes glowing dimly. The guidebook says this amazing place was begun in the fourteenth century.

September 5th

The present closeness between J. and J. gives me intense pleasure, but inevitably shuts others out. I'm aware of the lack of intimate conversation between Janetta and me, and that she seems to feel no need of it. All is sweetness and light, however. Rose remains in a state of high articulacy and told me she was quite looking forward to London. Saturday is called 'Jaime's Sunday' as he takes time off from Jacob's house; this one was spent on a long excursion to Agios Gordis on the west coast involving a marvellous drive through gorges crammed with luscious vegetation – bamboos, apples, pears, cypresses – and small, unspoiled villages, with flocks of sheep, girls riding donkeys, and old women looking really pretty with their brown wrinkled faces and dark burning eyes emerging from scarves of finest white cotton which they wear variously folded, with white blouses under dark bodices and full skirts of faded dark blue. This combines in a marvellous way with the grey olives, blue sea, green cypresses and fruit trees.

September 7th

Mid-morning we set off for the Glenconners' house on the west coast. In a huge white barrel-roofed sitting-room, decorated in pale, washed-out blues, greys and greens, we found Elizabeth Glenconner and her daughter Catherine (a plump, handsome girl with alert responsive eyes and a ready smile full of excellent teeth). We were sent to a guest room to put on our bathing things and then embarked in a solid boat in merciful charge of a solid Corfiote boatman, and tossed, pitched and rolled appallingly round several headlands to a bay under a towering cliff, where we bathed in a purest peacock-blue water, while kingfishers swooped from the cliff. I knew that Janetta was dreading the return voyage as much as I was, and was equally appalled when Elizabeth Glenconner asked if we would mind going on further still before we went home to lunch. Janetta bravely said, 'Let's go back,' and back we went, in a considerably rougher sea. A young cousin, Simon Tennant, had also joined us, a member of Constable's publishing firm. I sat next him at lunch on the terrace and we talked about Ivy Compton-Burnett and her novels. Did I talk too much in general? And if so, was it because we have been going easy on talk?

September 11th

I flew from Corfu to Rome yesterday evening; a crashing thunderstorm and deluges of rain darkened the skies and came through the glass roof of the Minerva Hotel just as Dadie was due to arrive at the airport. I descended to wait for him about eight, after a peaceable day by myself, and very soon he dashed in, eager and voluble, with his friend John Cambridge, now at the Embassy, who either by nature or infection generated as much noise and excitement as Dadie. This genial fellow drove us off to his huge bachelor flat in the Doria Pamphili palace, where he had four or five grand, large sitting-rooms full of sumptuous furniture and dubious old masters, and opened a bottle of champagne in our honour. A plumpish, clever man, with neat features making spots on the cubical dice of his head. We stared out into the darkness over two of the courtyards of this vast palace, which is a town in itself. Then to a restaurant in the ghetto quarter for dinner of prosciutto and figs followed by little globe artichokes fried whole 'in the Jewish style'. Before bed, Cambridge whisked us up to look at the floodlit Campidoglio and Forum.

We woke this morning to more thunder and drenching rain. Raymond's friends Viv Wanamaker and her lover were sending a car to fetch us to their castello; but first Dadie and I splashed round to the two nearest churches, as well as the Pantheon and Piazza Navona. In teeming traffic and rain we drove out to the astonishing castle rented by Raymond's friends. I liked them both – he is a film producer with heart trouble and she a friendly, grey-haired woman, simple in manner and looking extremely elegant in her bright red stockings. After lunch these kind people sent us on in their car to Orvieto; Raymond very chatty as we sat in the back, he asked me almost nothing about Corfu.

Here at Orvieto – the Signorellis and the mystery of memory. I couldn't have described them before seeing them, for my brief and only previous visit was at least thirteen years ago (more I think) with Ralph and the Lambs. But as I studied them I knew their image had been latent somewhere in my mind. So had the façade of the cathedral, made almost hideous and shocking by its gaudy modern mosaics, but beautiful bas-reliefs. After a clear, warm evening, whisky, thunder again and a good dinner at the star restaurant belonging to our hotel. From my window I look out over roofs and a high terrace full of flowerpots where a woman is busy ironing, sewing or watering.

September 12th

There's an unexpected ding-dong going on between Raymond and Dadie. Raymond suspects Dadie of teasing him, but it's done affectionately, almost flirtatiously. Dadie keeps us up to the mark of course, but I don't mind that a bit, and love his enthusiasm and vitality. I've been appointed map-reader and Common-Purse holder.

The more we saw of Orvieto the more we loved it and its brown streets hung with flowerpots. The lack of pavements is, though dangerous, always a pleasure; as in Rome the bare right angle between wall and cobbled street gives a curious pang of delight. Back to the Signorellis, with even greater wonder and admiration. An uncompromising painter, original, modern, inventive, sometimes almost coarse in detail. A jolly dinner at our star restaurant. We're getting on well, I think. There's been talk between the others of Dadie's 'fits of hysteria or rage', but so far no sign of them! They both like to go into *what's happening* in pictures more than I do. This morning I managed to hound down the blue-and-white church of a convent of austere nuns; it was very pretty, not austere and rather feminine.

Then we took the train to Arezzo.

September 13th: Arezzo

Our hotel here is impersonal and unsympathetic but perfectly all right – each room with shower and lavatory. Raymond always finds something wrong, however – the light in the wrong place, the room too SMALL, the bed too LARGE, his towel doesn't MOP him properly. In fact he pounces on these defects so eagerly that I think it would disappoint him not to find them, and as Dadie pointed out he even found fault with his friends' luxurious castello ('bed facing the window'). Dadie and I are more adaptable and 'manage' better, I think.

After late lunch yesterday we went straight off to look at the Pieros – and my God, they are *stunning*. In the presence of such genius one's emotions well up, brim and overflow. One can now put a hundred-lire piece in a machine which lights them up for five minutes – a great improvement. So we put in more and more lire pieces and gazed and gazed. Then to Santa Maria della Pieve, and the great Duomo, with another Piero of Mary Magdalen, holding her cloak in fascinating folds. These buildings, and the streets of tall houses and the Piazza Grande with its enormous loggia are all lavish in space and proportions. So is the long, steep street for walkers only, paved with flagstones set diamond-wise and dipping in the middle to collect the rain. Alas, this had returned to us, but by the hour of the *paseo* it stopped and crowds began their parade – a lot of them young and handsome, few beards, thick curly well-cut hair, girls in sandals with thongs to the knee, all moving well.

September 14th

Raymond always goes down to breakfast, while Dadie and I delight in our bedroom trays. When I went down yesterday I found Raymond triumphant at having engaged a car to take us to Cortona, and on to Urbino tomorrow. I congratulated him, but Dadie was disapproving. 'You should have asked us first; you must never engage a car before consulting "the tourist office"!' This irritation between Raymond and Dadie puts me in a slightly awkward position, having to balance the issues without favouritism.

I begin to remember how *factual* Raymond's approach is. Apart from what's going on in pictures and his pleasure in recognition of styles and periods, I do wonder how much he *enjoys* works of art. As soon as he enters a church he halts and says quickly, 'Early Tuscan Romanesque, with sixteenth-century additions, and the dome added later of course.' What can one reply? Is it a sort of game of snap, which he always wins and in any case no one else is playing – or just a form of boasting?

Back to Arezzo, Dadie and I went late in the afternoon for another look at the stupendous Pieros, but long and hungrily as I looked, I felt my inadequacy to grasp and digest them all, and a sort of frustration before the glory emanating from those walls which I shall probably never see again.

Raymond tells me that Dadie is a puritan at heart and always prides himself on doing without what others are enjoying. This is partly based on the fact that at stations he prefers to carry Raymond's appallingly heavy suitcase as well as his own instead of getting a porter, which *is* a trifle self-immolatory, perhaps.

September 15th

We've seen no other Signorellis as masterly as those of Orvieto; he makes intricate constructions of shapes, especially with hands and feet, and this combined with all-overish Turkey-carpet colour gives me the impression of a serious and intellectual, rather sombre character who doesn't glorify the universe like Piero.

We have now reached Urbino by car, via Montecchio and San Sepolcro. The *Resurrection* just as tremendous as it can be; each time the eyes leave it and return there's the same authentic thrill. I come nearer to understanding religious emotion when I'm looking at that painting than at any other time. We are lodged in a small hotel in a narrow, cobbled alley, in monks' cells with crucifixes over the bed and a communal bathroom. An ailing, middle-aged man coughs and sneezes as he brings our breakfasts up.

September 16th

We saw Urbino very thoroughly yesterday – the splendid Palazzo Ducale, Piero's gentle, unsadistic *Flagellation, Hercules and Iole*. Raymond in capricious mood, hunting out 'amusing' oddities to enjoy, showing off his information more compulsively as we become less responsive. I find Dadie's enquiring approach much more sympathetic. But I think we're trying to stuff in too much, and wonder if what refuses to detach itself from the *mêlée* (like the Duomo at Urbino) has left behind anything worth having.

September 18th

And thence to Modena – to which Raymond was keen to come apparently because 'forty years ago I spent a miserable night here trying to go to bed with a woman and failing'.

Walked to the Duomo and its museum of sculpture, its crypt and inlaid wooden stalls. Dined in a two-star restaurant, ate too much and felt uncomfortably gorged. Conversation never centres on general subjects; the jokes are of a teasing, donnish sort; Raymond likes to talk about the book he is reading (all right if others have read it) and catalogue facts. I find this dull, and the fact that he never listens to a word one says to him, and the longest reply one gets to a remark is 'Ah', both snubbing and frustrating. *I love him, of course.* But though I tend every time to forget his defects as a travelling companion, they don't decrease with the years.

September 20th: Mantua

A 'day of rest' ending with a visit to Mantegna's tomb in the Church of St Andrea, shown us by a tiny boy with a piping voice, manipulating a wavering electric torch like a hose. I quite deliberately tried to start a subject of conversation at dinner, about different sorts of selfishness and their relation to insensitivity, and whether it was worse not to be aware what other people were feeling, or to know and still ruthlessly pursue your own ends. Raymond seemed to say 'Ah!' to all this, but in fact, after a few moments' digestion, took it up and it carried us through the meal, along with the infectious fits of laughter of a little boy of about five at another table.

September 21st: Mantua to Verona

This last an emendation of our route, which delights me, though I had no part in it. We went to see the Palazzo Ducale at Mantua first thing. It's the only place we've been herded round with other tourists and I hated that, but the Mantegna room, if nothing else, made up for it. Beside these masterpieces the halls of mirrors, and the apartment of the dwarfs, grow dim. Then to the summer palace de Te, architecturally pretty, with frescoes of giants by Giulio Romano, a coarse painter whom I don't care for.

I love Mantua; it has been in no way disappointing.

One of Dadie's rare moments of grumpiness when, arrived at Verona, neither

Raymond nor I wanted to dash out at once. I like my quiet time, even though I
don't sleep during it. When we did follow our scoutmaster leader out into the
marvellous centre of the town, he resisted Raymond's desire to sit in a café in the
Piazza d'Erbe but, backed by me, we did. Verona's richness and beauty is great
compared to Ferrara and Modena. During our whisky session Dadie and I talked
unguardedly, unaware how thin was the door between Raymond's room and mine.
What did he hear? Dadie saying firmly that he meant to divert Raymond from
adding Brescia to our itinerary? Or just the jollity that always goes on at these
times? I think Dadie was more irritated by 'Ray' at Verona than I was; I've come to
terms with the fact that he never listens to a word I say. After dinner he wanted to
walk to the Piazza again (Dadie's third visit today). He is excited by the handsome
young men with their renaissance hair and elegant clothes and figures, gets carried
away and waves and beckons at them embarrassingly, murmuring that they are
'very pretty'.

September 23rd

Set off in our hired car about ten and found our way with difficulty to the heart of
Brescia – a piazza surrounded by disparate buildings which gave Raymond plenty
of opportunity to say 'snap'. Arrived rather late at Bergamo in an unsympathetic
hotel in the lower town. On the way there Raymond suddenly said, 'I'm so sorry
our tour is coming to an end. I've been looking forward to it for months, and now
I shall have nothing to look forward to,' touchingly, like a child. I do hope he has
enjoyed it, and that we haven't been too disappointing in our lack of response to
his information. Part of his looking forward was probably to imparting it, and the
other day he said semi-comically that he hoped we 'were making notes of his
pearls of wisdom'.

But my worst moment was yet to come. Late, too late, to the picture gallery, to
find an astonishing collection: Botticellis, Bellinis, Antonello da Messina, Lorenzo
Monaco, Titian, Tintoretto, Velásquez, Guardi, Raphael, Perugino – so over-
poweringly exciting to me that I suddenly overboiled with irritation at Raymond's
constant interruptions of my all-too inadequate concentration on these masterpieces with his 'pearls of wisdom', or actually getting in between me and the
picture I was looking at in the physical sense. This last was what I brutally charged
him with, but of course it was the interruption of his whole approach to looking
at pictures that I was really protesting against. I'm ashamed and guilty, and the
pleasure of being able to go on looking undisturbed and unjogged was small
consolation.

We postponed our visit to the High Old Town till dark and dinner-time, and it
was a great success, a stupendous experience. Taking a very steep, funicular train
up into the blackness of night made it seem like going up to another world. And
so it was, a magic one. Though the town is small (and can't spread, enclosed within
its walls and on its rock) the buildings are on a gigantic, splendid scale of tallness.
It's as if several imaginative geniuses had been set loose building a town for quite
a few of Giulio Romano's giants: an octagonal baptistery, a noble, vastly tall portico,
the Colleoni tomb richly coated in white marble sculpture. All made more magical
by floodlighting. We wandered round corners and gasped at some new wonder,
trying to avoid the cars and lambrettas that use the narrow, cobbled streets as a

sort of race-track. Bergamo comes high in the exciting experiences of this trip. Mantua and Verona too.

September 24th

I'm hoping yesterday's irritability was charged to my feeling unwell. All right again now. Up to look at the High Town in morning daylight. Dadie inclined to challenge Raymond's view about 'the way'; I thought it politic to stay with Raymond. After lunch Raymond returned to rest, and Dadie and I continued with our non-stop sightseeing, walking down the gradually sloping town wall towards the Pinacoteca. Little boys were eagerly collecting bags and baskets full of shining chestnuts; several fell from the trees as we walked, and down below the wall were neat vegetable gardens sprouting as if it were spring. Why was it that with Dadie I spent two happy hours looking at the pictures in the gallery, comparing impressions, drawing attention and having it drawn, and that he didn't once irritate me? Walked on down to the hotel – a long road, and up to dinner in the Old Town again.

September 28th: West Halkin Street

I've spent three nights on my own bed and hardly feel I've come to my senses yet. Looking back on my extra-long holiday, I feel as if I must have been so relaxed in Corfu as to be semi-conscious, and in Italy almost stupefied by the packed, intensive programme of sightseeing day after day. I slept well and have come back feeling well, yet almost at once London pincers have gripped me, the noise, responsibilities (for myself and some other people), and I sleep less deeply.

Joan greeted me most sweetly with bunches of flowers and dinner on my first night. She has taken in Rose as a lodger and of course loves her.

Both Kees on Sunday looked and said they felt ill. Robert with a heavy cold; Cynthia much too thin and complaining of a pain in her chest but refusing to see a doctor. When I remarked that Rose had had a red nose and purple fingers when she was anorexic, she said, 'Oh, did you know that "cyanosed extremities" was a symptom of anorexia?' I think she has it herself; she once told me she had in the past, but I believe it's with her still.

October 5th

A second visit from the young American, Stanley Olson, who is writing about the Hogarth Press, was heralded with a nightmare – I had lost Ralph in a huge, horrible liner, and was searching desperately for him, but large pieces of Victorian furniture blocked the corridors. I could find no trace of him but toothpaste and passports. I woke in terror and horror. 'Day's residues'; pictures in the paper of pathetic passports after a fatal air crash – and of course the fact that I knew I must 'search for Ralph' among his letters. There can still, after all these years, be a ghastly shock that breaks like a wave, and this submerged me as I sat listening to a concert of superb Mozart and Haydn, which blended with my tumultuous feelings. What sort of emotions? Pity, terror and beauty.

October 6th

I'm disturbed by certain reclusive tendencies I've lately found in myself, a desire to withdraw from the world, perhaps be as unaware as possible, a dislike for whatever I'm doing, and a way of doing things as mechanically and unconsciously as I can. All of this is totally contrary to what I believe to be my philosophy of life. Almost the only thing I haven't rejected is the pleasure I get at the orchestra. I was looking forward to meeting Margaret in the pub, first, but there was something rebarbative about her. 'You're looking *absolutely exhausted'*, was her first remark. '*Are* you?'

Last night I went to a small dinner given by Ralph Jarvis – present Nancy Shuckburgh, a great friend of Joan's, Robin Fedden, and an old Etonian friend of Ralph's – euphoric, clever and semi-conventional. The Establishment premises lay like a firm skeleton beneath most of the conversation – viz. that we all subscribed to some religion (the Etonian several times mentioned proudly that he had a son who was a Roman Catholic priest), that Eton was the best school and Old Etonians were therefore better than other men; that class distinctions must be preserved and the rich allowed to remain so or get richer, if necessary by soaking the poor; that a classical education, horses and hunting and the arts were all equally valuable and made one an 'all-rounder', than which nothing was better.

One of the reasons I feel a recluse is that most of my contemporaries have moved to the right to support the Establishment, and only among my very young friends do I find those who agree about war and peace, class distinctions, or dislike of conventions. I crave more bohemian company, or maybe none at all.

The Emperor of Japan is paying us an official visit. This has led to an outburst of old war hatred, and of people on the radio loudly patting themselves on the back for maintaining their hostility. 'I for one shall never forget, and never talk to a Japanese.' This ghastly racialism is to be found now even among many civilised people, whether towards the Irish, Germans, Russians or Japanese. And how on earth can they say such things about the Japanese if they for one second remember what *we* did to them at Hiroshima? How can they talk smugly about forgiveness?

October 9th

Weekend in London, fine and still. I feel pretty low and still obsessed with a persistent desire to give up the struggle and turn my face to the wall. Human and other contacts are the only thing that keep me going and I hurl myself from one to the other rather compulsively, wishing I could simply tuck up in bed between whiles. This may be partly the effect of a long struggle to fight off a cold, ending as these always do in a sort of truce.

Stanley Olson came again yesterday. I do like him, and think his head is screwed on the right way; but one may tend to assume these young addicts of Bloomsbury get it more nearly right than they do. And what *is* right anyway? How can one balance the childishness with the maturity, the rationality with the emotionalism? A reviving 'contact' was the first night of *Aïda* with Desmond, which I greatly enjoyed, though I could always dispense with Act 2 Scene 2 and its dreadful ballet. Towards the end, when the final love duet was being touchingly sung, a couple made their way out, disturbing a Japanese man at the end of the line, who continued rustling his paper bag, to the frenzy of Desmond, who finally got up, darted across the gangway and (I think) hit him!

October 11th

This morning, Monday, I feel better. I worried rather about Rose in the night, because she wrote me a sad little note about the horror of London Sunday. She comes to tea, and Margaret (whom I had slightly on my conscience) to lunch. She said on the telephone that Julia had rung her up saying she was going to commit suicide and wanted to discuss the means. Margaret seems to have been rather tough with her and more or less said, 'Go ahead.' Result – Julia has gone to stay with Lawrence and Jenny. She has to leave her flat – maybe she'll settle in with them. But I wonder if such an arrangement can possibly survive her desire to assert herself.

A comic Julia story from Margaret. At Thorington, anxious there shouldn't be a repetition of 'the milk is cold', she put some to heat for Julia's breakfast and went to have her bath. Thundering on the door, Julia cried, 'Where is the milk-strainer?' Margaret shouted, 'On the kitchen windowsill.' The old retainers, Freddie and Bessie, later became involved, declared that Julia had been shown the milk-strainer, and said, 'That! It's too disgusting. I can't possibly use it.' Julia, when this was perhaps unwisely reported back by Margaret, flew in to Freddie and Bessie, rated them soundly and told them they were liars. Lunch-time came, when the retainers usually sit lunching at a side table. Freddie rose to his feet, slowly put on a cloth cap and said he couldn't sit down to eat with someone who called them liars. Somehow or other, Margaret can't remember how, the breach was healed; Julia and the retainers were chattering away and each thinking the other delightful. 'They're *not*!' said Margaret. 'I simply can't abide Freddie and Bessie!' The moral is that Julia is starved of drama and feels happier when she can introduce some into ordinary life, of whatever sort. Also knowing the state of Margaret's kitchen, I expect the milk-strainer *was* in a disgusting state and Julia did say so! I delight in the way small insignificant objects like milk-strainers take a prominent part in emotional situations.

October 20th

Answering a letter from Gerald attacking principles in politics (they ought, he said, to be dealt with pragmatically), I said I was all in favour of pragmatism, but that when applied to politics they become as dull as drains and plumbing. That the only aspect of politics that interests me is when principles are involved because this means drawing universals from particulars, general ideas – which are the breath of life – from facts. I realised as I wrote that it was Raymond's failure to find general ideas the breath of life that distressed me about him.

The *Sunday Times* dealt a shattering blow to those prepared to believe it by producing convincing and detailed evidence that the Ulster internees are being tortured to get information about the IRA. The details are sickening and there's been an attempt on some sides to get it enquired into. However one MP said in the House, 'I'm sure a lot of us would agree that where the safety of our soldiers depends on this information, we are not too concerned as to the methods used to get it.' (Some cheers.) I remember Ralph saying long ago à propos of ends and means, and capital punishment as a deterrent, that one must realise that there are some things one would never do *whatever* the end in view – and torture was one of them. At the time it seemed something *no one* would question, but we've descended into barbarism a long way since then. What's more, people are becoming rather pleased with their barbarism.

October 22nd

The pleasure of talking to Robert yesterday, and finding him in agreement on all current political issues – horror at our descent into racialism and torture, desire for a Maynard Keynes to state, without shame and boldly, the importance of principles in politics as in other forms of thinking! I was able (having been tongue-tied before) to thank him for saying he would write something about Ralph, and say he mustn't let it become a millstone, that he could write it after I was dead. He said he very much wanted to do it, and was merely pondering in what sort of way. I told him of Stanley Olson's interest, and he said, 'Send him to see me.' As Stanley rang me up this morning, and as he does seem to have taken a genuine interest in Ralph, I mentioned it to him, and I think he might go. Stanley is a bit of a mystery. I really like him and can't help trusting my judgement, but how much he sees things as they are I'm not sure. He's so quick and accurate that I may credit him with too much power to penetrate the mists of time, but he's sensitive and knows how to say things in a way that gives no offence, as he told me on the telephone that he wanted to say how much he liked Ralph, and how a friend he'd told about him said, 'That sounds like a very nice man.'

October 29th

Stanley Olson arrived soon after 10 a.m. and talked steadily, or I read what he had written, until twelve-thirty. I take back yesterday's remarks absolutely, and return to my view that he is the most intelligent and perceptive of the Bloomsbury hounds and I really respect his judgement. I gave him one or two small essays of Ralph's I had found, one on the equation of money and shit, which he laughed a good deal over. But he says he doesn't quite feel he's 'got' Ralph and that he sat up until three the night before pondering his character. The difficulty I suppose is that he believes me (I think), and can't fit in what I tell him with the Holroyd–Gerald image. I dropped him off at the end of Parsifal Road and went on to lunch and play trios with Margaret.

November 1st

Anne Hill broke her leg and wrist a few weeks ago slipping up on her kitchen floor. I went down last weekend, partly to see her in Ipswich Hospital and – as I hoped – to help look after Heywood. In fact Ruth Gathorne-Hardy was doing this and Anthony and Eddie were both staying. The two brothers are *extraordinary* – I felt as if I were on the stage in a play performed by Gielgud and Richardson. By the time I arrived they were both well away on the evening sozzle, sitting in two armchairs, one on either side of the fire and talking slowly and indistinctly in identical voices. Anthony's lifelong drinking was complicated by his getting cancer of the throat, so that eating was once painful and he has now given it up altogether, doesn't come in to meals but swallows a jug of milk with eggs beaten in it. After about six there are ceaseless requests: 'Since you're up, Heywood, bring me another drop of whisky, will you? Mine's the bottle *under* the table.' Heywood went to and fro like a butler. After dinner Eddie and I got into a fairly drastic argument, starting from agreement about the Colonels, going on to disparagement of almost every other nation, particularly the Germans, on Eddie's part, my accusing him of racialism, whether we believed in democracy, etc. Eddie got crosser than I did.

Heywood remained totally silent while this, to me rather enjoyable, artillery sped across the room; Ruth ditto, and Anthony once ejaculated 'BALLS' loudly – but in reference to what I don't know. Anthony apparently always takes a bottle of sherry to bed each night and finishes it. Other people's 'drinking' was talked about as if it was the business of life ('she doesn't *drink*' with evident disapproval).

Both these intelligent men are steadily killing themselves. Anthony (with his cancer) has more excuse. Eddie used to be nervous because of his 'hobnailed liver', but that's all over. He really looks pretty ghastly now, 'like a very old seagull', Heywood said to me with a slight laugh. His memory and mind remain remarkably clear except late at night. Both of them have foot trouble and hobble around like octogenarians. Eddie's selfishness is phenomenal. Twice he said, 'I wish Anne could have broken her leg just *after I went* back to Athens my dear, it's most inconvenient for me.' When I asked him if he would enjoy visiting the Bevans and Harrods, 'Oh, yes, my dear, there's plenty of booze and good food, and they bring me my breakfast in bed, my dear, so that's all right, my dear.' He spent hours planning a very expensive solitary lunch at the Savoy: 'I think I'll have a *woodcock* my dear, but it must be hung and cooked exactly right, and then, my dear, perhaps some *raspberries*, if one can still get them.' Yet on the plus side, beside his intelligence, he has a mild but genuine affection for old friends and took great trouble to be appreciative of Ruth's cooking. He does pretty well nothing all day but read *The Times*, do the crossword puzzle and read thrillers, gets up at about eleven, and goes to bed after lunch until six-thirty. The worst aspect of the old reprobate was his disagreeableness to Anthony, in whom I had begun to see the traces of a human being by Sunday evening, a nicer though less clever one than Eddie. And after Friday night's lively argument, and Saturday night when I fled to the television room with Heywood and Ruth, Eddie got up to pour himself another drink, and Anthony asked him politely to get him one 'while he was there'. 'No, I *WON'T*, my dear, I'm bloody well not going to, my dear. I'm older than you, my dear, and much iller and you must do it yourself, my dear.' He toddled slowly off into the kitchen to get a glass, while Anthony muttered, 'He's the most selfish person in the world.' Feeling, though older than either of them, incomparably more spry, I got up and poured out Anthony's drink and was told, 'Thash the sweeshesh thing you've done.' The other 'sweesh thing' was to ask to see a belt he's elaborately knotting out of fine string for his daughter Rose, and watch him deftly doing it. I was touched by this: one can't possibly imagine Eddie doing anything for anyone but himself. Patrick Kinross says rather acutely that Eddie has decided to make a sort of performance of his own selfishness, and so benefit by it.

One can just carry on the ghost of a conversation with the two old monsters and I became almost hysterically amused by the situation. I had to kiss them both at bedtime.

Ruth: a good kind person, over-emotional and a worrier, very likeable and conversable, has strong reminiscences of her son Jonny. You have only to press a button and everything pours out. She's extremely happy at Snape and feels better in health (she suffers from a painful disfiguring rash) chiefly because of the 'angelic Heywood, and my loving him and Anne so much'. She takes a lot of trouble over meals, and clearly enjoys being away from her incarceration with Anthony. I heard about the break-up of Jonny's marriage, her fears for the two children, doubts about the new girl, and the situation of her Rose. She's rather ludicrously obsessed with the Gathorne-Hardy family, and Caroline Jarvis and Juliet's husband were obviously expected to toe the Cranbrook line. I felt (but didn't really express) some revulsion to this family glorification; however, when I went to bed, in my head was ringing, 'And family pride must be denied, and set aside, and mortified.'

But oh, the goodness and lovability of Heywood. As both the brothers were in bed most of the day, Heywood and I had several marvellous walks in still, warm, brilliant autumn weather. On Sunday we drove to Ipswich and he left me with Anne for an hour, returning to eat sandwiches and drink champagne. Anne looked blooming and serene, and didn't complain at all. But she won't be back to normal for three months.

So now I'm speeding back to London, in a hot train through a summery landscape and wondering what I'll find there.

November 10th

The very last bit of my translation went off to America two days ago. The days seem to be fuller without any work on hand – but I have been beset by the Bloomsbury boys: Stanley Olson and Paul Levy, to each of whom I gave dinner last week. Stanley isn't as clever as Paul but I like him just as much, and I think he likes me. Invited to dinner on Guy Fawkes' night, he spent five hours here! So after correcting his spelling and grammar and answering his questions, I turned the tables on him and asked him some. He's the son of a rich (very rich, I suspect) businessman from Ohio, and left there two and a half years ago because 'the family situation was too dominant'. Apart from his passion for Wagner, he has a girlfriend called Tish and means to take cello lessons. Money seems to be no object with him.

November 16th

Last weekend at Crichel alone with Raymond and Desmond, and with visits from Cecils, Cecil Beaton and Kitty. Wonderfully brilliant days; without the intense usual pleasure I got from them my walks with Moses would have taken the dutiful place of needed work. As for my time, it fills up easily enough. Raymond positively courts me, and even brought up a possible new journey together, to Egypt. We were getting on so well that I considered it with interest.

It can't be said that he and Desmond get on brilliantly, in spite of what is I suppose a basic mutual affection. Raymond kept drawing my attention to 'the heavy weather Desmond makes over every little task', 'his passion for keeping people waiting', 'his appalling hair-do', while Desmond complained – and indeed it *is* extraordinary – that 'Raymond never once went out of doors and enjoyed this marvellous weather, but spent the twenty-four hours stewing, sighing and smoking over his review all morning, snoozing in the smoke-filled room all afternoon and all night.' He says the smell of stale smoke in it is appalling and no fresh air is ever let in and, 'Wouldn't it be a good thing if he sometimes took a little walk?'

November 22nd

Two Bloomsbury occasions: on Friday 'An evening with Duncan Grant' at the Institute of Contemporary Arts. I took Joan and we were squired by Stanley, who had an appalling cold but laughed appreciatively at Duncan's jokes. The contrast between Duncan's physical presence as he climbed onto the platform and the film taken of him a year or two ago was distressing – he has got a lot older all at once, but his humour and intelligence seem untarnished. A bad start to the evening, with Claude Rogers[1] making an endless rambling speech composed of sentences which contrived to branch off before they ever reached a full stop, fumbling among a lot of papers, bumbling into his beard. After which all went well, a mixture of Dunconian charm and Bloomsbury muddle. Henrietta, sitting on the platform beside Richard Shone,[2] looked beautiful – and the two of them read extracts about Duncan and his work that were amusing and pointful.

Now I'm lying on my bed trying to recover from the second occasion – the unveiling of a plaque to Lytton on the wall of 51 Gordon Square, a speech from Noel Annan, and glasses of bad champagne two doors along. This took place in the middle of the morning, and I so dreaded confronting Julia that I felt quite shaky beforehand. What a bloody bore it is – I almost feel like trying again to make it up. Especially inconvenient was that Noel Annan asked me to lunch, and suggested Christopher Strachey and Julia as co-guests, so that I *had* to say that Julia wouldn't speak to me. I took greatly however to Christopher who, with his intelligent face and bright brown eyes, looks more Strachey than anyone, and our three-cornered conversation at lunch was extremely lively. Most of the company were unknown to me – except for the Holroyds, Pansy Lamb, Paul Levy, Raymond and Lionel (who had done his best but without success to keep Margaret from accompanying him). A female dwarf asked me if I'd ever met Lytton. I replied that 'I had known him intimately' but she was deaf and didn't hear. 'I believe there are some very old people here who actually *knew* him,' she said.

The inevitable keying-up before such social occasions and the rich Greek food and resinated wine we had at the White Tower have quite floored me. What with an extremely social weekend at Stowell (dinner party for eight, trailing skirts and dinner-jacketed, on Saturday, and sumptuous lunch with Ian MacCallum at the American Museum, Bath, on Sunday), I feel it's high time I swam back into the quieter waters to which I'm accustomed.

November 29th

Stanley gave a party on Friday night, to which I was bidden, and asked me to pick up William Gerhardi on the way – a writer Ralph and I both greatly admired years ago. He lives in a block of flats called Rossetti House; it lived up to its name. I ascended in a shining tin lift to the fifth floor and pressed the bell outside the dead-looking pre-Raphaelite front door. No response. Press again. Silence. I gave a good bang with the knocker and a shape loomed within. The face was somehow familiar: old but spry, tilted slightly forwards, pink, with pale, wide-awake eyes set like headlamps. 'Oh no, the bell doesn't work – it saves me from unwanted callers.' He sent us down in the lift with a stylish swaggering push on the button, climbed into my Mini and off we went. 'Are you a safe driver?' 'Yes, very.' 'Because I want to finish the book I'm writing.' Stanley had warned me that his return to popularity had given him *folie de grandeur*. We talked easily – about the MacCarthys (Desmond had 'given him a rave review' and 'the girl, what was her name?'). I told him what I could about Rachel, remembering that years ago she had fallen for him rather

---

[1] One of the Euston Road artists.
[2] Art historian and critic.

and come the nearest ever to an infidelity to David. Gerhardi tried to get me straight. 'Then there was a lot about you in Holroyd's book?' Later at dinner I heard him talking about that 'extraordinary woman in Holroyd's book who committed suicide'. I enjoyed the party – beside Stanley (whose girl, Tish, had measles) there were Paul Levy, a nice young paintress called Lyn and her man. And a little girl from Gerhardi's publisher who looked stupider than she was. The food was splendid: 'a failed *pâté*', Hungarian chicken with rice in a creamy sauce. I sat between Stanley and Paul, and conversation throve and even sparkled. Stanley veered between compulsive greed and going off into back-leaning swoons at the thought of some '*exquisite* performance' by Leontine Price or some other singer. It was a jolly evening; I left and drove the publishing girl home before midnight.

Early next morning I drove down to Cambridge with Nadine, who had come up for the funeral of her mother – delightful old Mrs Hambourg. I got to the house of her sister Michal at nine-thirty, and found Michal in a purple nightdress, paunchy Ian her husband and two repulsive dogs like Woolworth brooches, oblong, hairy and hysterical. Nadine was in her compulsively delaying mood. 'I must just write a letter to sack my mother's gardener.' At last we got off to the deceased's house in Maida Vale and collected 'Mother Mary', as Nadine's eldest sister Sonia is now called. Once married to a needy Prince de Bessarabie, she's now an Orthodox Greek nun in France, and dresses in rusty black from top to toe, a black woollen skullcap on her head from which descends a sort of Arabian black cape which meets the voluminous skirts. From this a pale, bespectacled face juts out, ending in a noticeable fringe of beard – and from this singular apparition emerges a charming, cultivated and humorous voice. She's a manic depressive but was obviously in one of her euphoric spells, ecstatically admiring the flat grey landscape through which we drove to Cambridge.

Back to walk into the town for shopping and listen to Monteverdi *Poppea* till bed-time.

December 13th

Returned in Eardley's car last night from a gentle, grey weekend at the Slade, and went straight round to dinner with Janetta and Robert. It was her last evening and I wanted to see her, yet I think perhaps I ought to have left them alone together. Robert looked knotted and desperate and I had the feeling that his unhappiness had created a false callousness, a shell of indifference impossible to penetrate, on which all efforts at contact rebounded.

December 15th

Reading through this year's diary, I'm amazed at its sadness. Whether this is just the effusion of what I had tried to repress, or the naked truth, I don't know. How sad *is* my present life? Sometimes I trudge out, impelled by some inner urge, and find myself stumping, blind and unconscious, down Sloane Street; sometimes I get involved – against my will – in social antics. On Monday I was invited by Andrew Murray-Thripland to a party at the Reform Club. Julian was to have come, but after one or two telephone calls I realised he was in dire distress, and drove round to see him. I think he was suffering from sheer understandable exhaustion after his Australian tour. But he had the desperate person's desire to press to extremes, to tell me he was 'ill', feeling suicidal. His use of 'ill' I've long ago noticed is an emergency exit whether for himself or others; but I was saddened by his haunted expression, and large tragic eyes, and tried to give sensible advice while dreading being too much of a hospital nurse or schoolmistress: rest, give up all commitments, take Valium, postpone going back to work by means of a medical certificate till after Christmas. Off I drove again to the Reform Club, and arrived late in its dignified hall. When I asked for Andrew, 'He seems to be a very popular young gentleman,' said the porter. In a room off the hall thirty or forty mostly young people were sitting at small tables round the walls, eating compulsively (as if engaged on writing theses) curried chicken or steak and kidney pie. The popular young gentleman rushed up, offered me a drink, cried, 'The drink has given out,' and rushed away again. I was left standing until I spied Raymond sitting by an unctuous Jew and joined them. Later came Pat and Freda Berkeley, pretty far gone in drink.

We drank red wine; I talked to Freda, who was hardly present; Andrew, looking very charming, was telling everyone how the party had taken shape around his attempt to bring his two mistresses together. He asked Raymond, 'Would you have liked to be married?' Raymond, in a very soft but meaning voice: 'No.' Andrew admitted he would, and indicated a likely wife, a short, plump girl whose thick brown hair covered her face entirely.

I waver whether to accept this playgirl's life, which doesn't really suit me; I rest and read more but there's too much time and opportunity to be aware of other people. Yesterday Joan very touchingly declared that were I to fall ill, she would come and look after me, and if it was my 'terminal illness' she would see that I didn't suffer. (We had been talking of horrible deaths.) This she said with transparent sincerity, and indeed I believe her, and it's a real comfort to me to know it. She's perhaps the only one of my friends who has no one she's more committed to than me, and this, unexpectedly, turns out to be enormously valuable. I thought I could help her. I see now *she* greatly helps *me*. I was grateful to her for making this comforting promise, and got her to agree that the arrangement would be mutual. I'm only three years older than her, and who knows? But it is a *good* pact to have made. She accepted it as such, but I could see didn't for a moment consider it possible that she might die first. I hope she doesn't.[1]

December 21st

Mary took me to *Figaro* last night – a splendid performance, perhaps the best I've ever been to. Her other guest, a slender, elegant woman dressed tightly in well-cut black, with a profile reminiscent of Cocteau (whose life I've been reading); her name, Lady Daphne Straight.

My hackles always rise, I hope and believe invisibly, when confronted by consciousness of superiority which isn't *real* superiority – i.e. not such as Shakespeare displays in the Sonnets. And I noticed that, though I was the oldest by ten years, they both tended to walk out of the doors first, leave me the back seat in the car and generally treat me rather like an old governess. They prattled away: 'Oh, do you know, Robert wrote to Bobo apologising for being so drunk the other night.' 'Oh, NO! DID he really? How SWEET!' Gossip galore about the rich or noble, Mrs Heinz of Beans, or Lord Lansdowne. Complaints about how booked up the best

---

[1] Joan died in 1995.

chiropodist in London was, so that you 'simply have to devote a whole morning to having your hair and feet done.' Or 'Rosie *will* complain of my drinking habits. She says if I didn't drink red wine at lunch I wouldn't have to have my afternoon kip, but I told her that in that case I'd have to go to bed at seven-thirty because I *must* have my ten hours.'

In our box at the opera my companions took care to break the rules and smoke without going into the passage. 'And they won't let one leave one's glass on the edge of the box!' 'Perhaps they're afraid it might fall into the stalls,' I suggested. 'The class war more likely,' said Lady D. The stalls, I see, are the lower classes! I observed Mary's touchingly old-fashioned belief that the waiters were relishing her glamorous superiority, whereas I could see the cold look of calculation in their eyes as to what tip she was good for, and their annoyance that her bringing her own drink made it less. The same with the market lorry drivers as we wound our way out. They, the aristos, fondly believe these men love seeing expensive cars and women with diamonds among them. What fatuous folly!

Last week's opera was *Poppea* with Duncan, Magouche and Joan. Duncan is incredible! The Christmas traffic is appalling at present, so I tried all day to get him on the telephone to say I would fetch him in my Mini. At five I got him; he had only just come in, having been at the Tate since about eleven looking at the Hogarths. 'There were such a lot of them that it took me some time.' He declared he could easily get to the Coliseum by tube. I did fetch him, and he sat through the opera without nodding, came back to supper and was still going strong at one-thirty when everyone else decided it was bed-time and we put him in a taxi. It was glorious music, well sung and moving. I don't think I'll ask Joan to the opera again though, as she keeps her eyes shut ('Because I'm so visual and it was awful to look at') and only liked 'some of the music'.

Sophie has given me a photo of her own sweet face blown up to ten times lifesize. I have pinned it on my bedroom door, and it gives me enormous pleasure.

Dadie has been to lunch here – as splendidly life-enhancing as I knew he would be. I got Mary to come and have a drink first, a great success.

December 22nd

Suddenly heavy-hearted, I sat down on my typewriter and began free-associating in the shape of an unsent, unsendable letter to Julian. Amongst a lot of trivial rubbish, there suddenly popped out straight from the unconscious. 'Will ye no come back again?' from the Scotch song. No – that's just the trouble. He never will. At the moment the wooden determination of those who would rather be dead lies heavily on my mind. Yesterday I went to a curious function in memory of Dolly Hambourg. The proceedings began with old Mark Hambourg playing Dolly's favourite bit of Beethoven *outre-tombe* on a scratchy record. Then eulogies – quite good – from Tom and Gerald Moore (who included some funny stories). A final piece of Schumann by Michal, who was obviously moved herself. Yet the whole thing, with its evocation of a personality and its obliteration, was strangely affecting, even to me, who liked and admired her.

December 23rd

What I think terrifies a lonely person out of his or her wits is the awareness of a thin steel barrier between every individual and the next. It sometimes seems impossible, and not even desirable, to penetrate it, except in the relationship of love. But which sorts of love? Sexual, and that between parent and child at its best. In friendship permeability is subject to unexpected variations, and when it is lost, panic follows. Then again the barrier is sometimes breached without effort – sometimes through conviviality, food and drink.

December 24th

Or, as yesterday, when I was 'taken out of myself' as it is ludicrously called, by talking to Stanley. Our conversation was about metaphysical speculation, and whether the taste for it increased with age or not. He – at twenty-four – thought it did. I assured him he would find it wouldn't go on much longer, also that most people stop altogether in middle age, and also move further and further to the political right. He says even his contemporaries are rapidly doing so. His failure to act on his socialistic beliefs appears to worry him. I said I thought the sin against the holy ghost was not to stand up for one's beliefs in *speech*. I enjoy talking to him much as if he was someone of my own age. He has had his long bob shortened, which makes him look thinner, and less like my private nickname for him – the Wombat. A nice friendly creature with an independent will of its own.

Christmas is upon us, oh Lord preserve us.

Christmas Day at the Cecils'

Can one have too much even of good talk? Yes. For me at any rate, though apparently not for any of this family – they talk and talk and talk torrentially, all at the same time, hardly able to wait while others hold the floor. It's as if some current was flowing out of them all the time. Don't they long, as I do, sometimes for a pause to put something back into what must be an empty receptacle? Music, a book, or silence. But a lot of it is stimulating, interesting, amusing, *if only* there were time to digest it. Naturally stories get repeated, by David anyway. He remembered our conversation about Hamlet and revenge last Christmas, as I do. I called it an 'argument'. D.: 'Not an argument, a discussion.' F.: 'But that's what I mean by an argument – I *love* arguing.' D.: 'Ah, you use it in a purist sense.'

Well, I do believe thinking and talking to be two of the highest activities, but as with a meal, digestion is a necessity. I've been reading the Reith lectures on communication – mild, well-meaning and honest explorations, which insist that communication must be founded on a common ground of feeling and judgement, and must be more than an Ancient Mariner's 'desire to get something off one's chest', and that as such it is possible – a desire most people feel and that can be gratified.

December 26th

And what a lot of each day here is spent in communication. When and how do they curdle within them the thoughts that they want to communicate? People often say how 'solitaries' become so garrulous when they meet others. But the batteries of great talkers who live with others are always flashing their lights and never recharging. I heard David say ruefully to Jonathan, 'I'm beginning to repeat myself. It's awful. You must stop me.' Indeed his loquacity sometimes quite worries me – I feel he'll collapse, pale and drained, after such marathon talk. All that so far happens is that the quality gets somehow thinner. With six of us in the house there are often three conversations going on at once, full lick and *fortissimo*. I am getting used to it, but I think I miss my normal silence. A record is the only thing to stop talk, or retirement to one's room. On a walk it goes on in a sustained duet.

Yesterday, we went over to Crichel before lunch for a drink with six bachelors, and for another before dinner to the Trees, Andrew Devonshire's handsome sister and her flashy husband (who appeared in a bright cherry-coloured velvet evening suit, bulky and genial). Elizabeth Cavendish, Betjeman's 'Feeble', was also there. David has twigged that there were difficulties in Australia.[1] I was interested that the forceful Feeble said she had been knocked out for three weeks by the thirty-four-hour flight home.

It's delightful to witness the happy relations within this family. Hugh (with Mirabel Walker) and Laura (with Angelo Hornak) have their extra-family supports; hour-long telephone calls go on; each starts up when the telephone rings. As for Jonathan with his broken marriage, I think it has matured him, but I wonder how painful it is. Vivien rang him last night and he came back, leant on the mantelpiece and poured himself out a whisky. The lack of irritation, friction or non-comprehension between them all astonished me. I came in yesterday upon a talk about religion – Hugh holding forth in his deliberate way, punctured by very encouraging grunts, but few words, from Jonathan. I was interested and wanted to find out where Hugh stood. He seemed to want to justify his position somehow, but his approach to ideas is like a potter with a lump of clay on a wheel, often reversing so that the lip of the pot vanishes and he begins again.

Paper games in the evening; wild, childish and salutary laughter; Rachel striking her unexpected note of inspiration.

December 27th

After absurd near-panic on Christmas Eve (how was I to last out for five whole days of constant contact with five other people?) I have settled down to feel I could enjoy it for ever. It was only a momentary queasiness.

Each day I have walked out into the monochrome grey-brown countryside with Rachel, and each has its social occasion, when all six of us squash into the car and drive off for miles through the darkness to some large house with lit windows, holly and Christmas cards, butlers and – last night – an immense throng standing up and shouting face to face. We went into a room to arm ourselves with drinks and there was Cecil Beaton, who now has a habitual tease about my being 'the most popular guest in England, who has to be booked weeks ahead', looking at me sideways with little snake's eyes and smile, and wondering what on earth makes people ask me. Then I was adrift, no known face in sight. I had something approaching a conversation with deaf 'Duchess' Ashley-Cooper about Carrington's Letters, Holroyd and the Johns, in which I sensed but couldn't analyse some strongish emotion. Back after not too long a session in the social lists to cold supper and a quiet evening. David read a chapter on Queen Elizabeth to Rachel, Jonathan and me. I thought it good. Poor Rachel, tired out with household responsibilities, kept nodding her brown head over her sewing. As for David, I really feel he will need a long convalescence after all this non-stop talking. Does he keep it up always? *Is* the spider left with no more web material?

[1] Where Betjeman had been with Julian Jebb.

December 28th

We have gently slipped into the last day here. Yesterday afternoon, David and I went out and paced gently through the gardens of Cranborne Manor, where there was much to delight the eye, even if David's was turned inwards onto the landscape of his thought: neatly trimmed plants in clean dark earth, some precocious poly-anthus in flower, rooks swinging in the branches of the magnificent beeches, the beautiful grey face of the Manor theatrically lit by the pale sinking sun. 'A little sleep now, I think,' he said as we got in after a flurry of rain. But not a bit of it. From my room above the drawing-room, where I retired to read and be alone, I heard animated non-stop talk between David and his children below. It's like a myth; it's also beyond anyone's capacity, as David proved later on.

People came to have a drink, the Goldings and a young brother and sister, musicians. I talked to William Golding about Russia; he's a short, squarish, bearded man, smelling rather like an old labourer, doesn't drink at all because he can't in moderation, and has a twinkling blue eye. I dare say both David and Jonathan had drunk too much, but at dinner they got into a *row* – a one-sided row, if such a thing is possible, because I've never heard Jonathan lose his temper. But the difference between his tempo and David's was increased until Jonathan's words drifted off and slowed almost to a standstill. David's face became red and contorted, and he almost screamed: 'Well, *DO* let me finish! ...' Rachel got involved on Jonathan's behalf and clamoured for him to be heard. David sprang up and said, 'I'll go away if I mayn't speak!' What *was* it all about? It veered towards the existence of poverty and whether the gap between rich and poor was widening or not. David was passionately optimistic and thought two years' unemployment would lead inevitably to happiness for all. Everything, too, was related to Hatfield in the days of his youth, just as all schools are to his own Eton days, America only to the nice time *he* had there. On the whole I think all the young and I were on one side. Hugh said little; I interposed once or twice about the damaging psychological effect of unemployment. 'But it's going to get BETTER! It's going to be all RIGHT!' David shrieked and I said gloomily that I hoped so, but saw no signs of it at present. The argument continued in one way or another till bedtime. David, full of compunction as he always touchingly is, went and sat by Jonathan, who revealed interesting things about the wild waste of public money by the BBC – a woman designer sent twice by air to Rome, and put up in a grand hotel, to buy lace for a cardinal's robe which wasn't even used. The cardinal made himself some out of two paper doilies and anyway it didn't show. Jonathan, as far as one could gather from his slowly developed thoughts, felt that it was wicked for this waste to be allowed when so much poverty and unemployment existed. There's no doubt the speed and non-stop quality of David's talk has inhibited and slowed up that of both his sons, which doesn't mean they don't think.

December 30th: London

Winter has struck. Big flakes are falling between me and the stucco façade opposite. I came up from Dorset yesterday with Jonathan and Laura and sank into a semi-coma most of the afternoon. Joan came to supper in the evening. As usual I'm inclined to feel guilty about the part I took in the 'rich-poor' argument. On Tuesday night we all went to eat mashed-up turkey on our knees with Frank and Billy. The other guests, Billy and Jenny Hughes. Billy made his contribution to the current theme by saying as he came into the room that he had just been made a judge and therefore was very much richer than ever before 'but it goes absolutely nowhere'. I liked him. He reminded me of my visit with Ralph to his flat, and how he had pointed to the Greville diaries and said, 'That's the best-indexed book in existence,' and Ralph said, 'I indexed it.'

Index

Page references in **bold** show the fullest account of that person or place.